Chemistry

Chris Conoley
Phil Hills

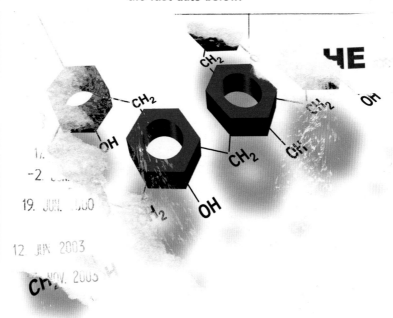

Collins Educational

An imprint of HarperCollinsPublishers

Published by Collins Educational
An imprint of HarperCollins*Publishers* Ltd
77–85 Fulham Palace Road
London W6 8JB

© Chris Conoley and Phil Hills 1998

First published 1998
ISBN 000 322 3299

British Library Cataloguing in Publication Data:
A catalogue record for this book is available from the British Library.

Publishing Coordinator Pat Winter
Editor John Day
Designers Ken Vail Graphic Design and Glynis Edwards
Cover design by Michael Faulkner
Illustrations by Illustrated Arts
Commissioned photographs by Andrew Lambert
Picture research by Caroline Thompson
Index by Julie Rimington
Printed and bound by Scotprint

Acknowledgements
To my wife Anne Conoley and my children Simon, Elizabeth and Victoria whose support, encouragement, understanding and forbearance enabled me to complete this book. Also to my parents Pat and Vera Conoley who always understood and supported me when participation in my wider family life proved difficult. *Chris Conoley*
To my mother and my two sons David and Peter for their patience and understanding throughout this project. *Phil Hills*

Examination questions
The publisher thanks examination boards for their permission to reproduce examination questions. Questions are acknowledged as follows:
AEB   The Associated Examining Board (AQA)
NEAB   Northern Examinations and Assessment Board (AQA)
OCSEB Oxford and Cambridge Schools Examination Board
UCLES   University of Cambridge Local Examinations Syndicate
ULEAC London Examinations, a division of Edexcel Foundation

CONTENTS

About this book

To the student

THIS BOOK GIVES you a clear and thorough coverage of the chemistry you will study at advanced level - this may be A level, GNVQ, Scottish Higher or International Baccalaureate – and it covers all the material in the Advanced Chemistry Core.

At the same time as making continual links with pre-A-level chemistry, the book will also be very supportive to students in the first year of undergraduate courses.

Whether or not you choose to continue your study of chemistry at a higher level, Chemistry will give you an insight into this essential science. Through its pages the authors hope you will find the chemistry you are studying relevant, enjoyable, exciting and accessible.

Everything is made up of chemicals

Chemistry is about understanding chemicals. Everything we see, touch, smell or taste is made up of chemicals. All our body parts are composed of chemicals, from the DNA of cell nuclei to the protein enzymes which catalyse almost all of the reactions which support our very existence.

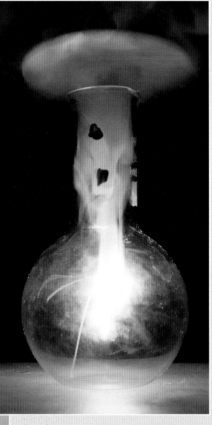

Two dangerous, highly reactive elements, sodium and chlorine, combine to form a compound, salt, that is essential to life

Many of us live longer and in more comfort than a century ago because of the chemicals we manufacture, such as fertilisers which enable us to grow more food, drugs which combat disease, polymers which clothe us and fuels which keep us warm and transport us.

All chemicals are made up of the atoms of about 100 different elements, and how these atoms join together and interact determines the properties of every substance in the universe.

For example, sodium is a very reactive, silvery, metallic element which rapidly tarnishes in air. It is a solid which reacts violently with water. Chlorine is a green gas. It is a very reactive non-metallic element used to destroy bacteria in water supplies. If either of these chemicals entered your body it could prove fatal. Yet when they react together they produce the compound sodium chloride (table salt) with an entirely different set of properties from either of the elements which make it up.

Sodium chloride is an essential chemical within our bodies. About 1 per cent of the mass of your blood and body cells is sodium chloride. Sodium chloride has been prized throughout history for its seasoning and preservative properties. The word salary comes from the Latin *salarium* because salt made up part of the wages of Roman soldiers. The chlor-alkali industry is one of the largest in the world producing sodium hydroxide and chlorine from concentrated solutions of sodium chloride.

Chemists have changed our world and transformed almost every aspect of our daily lives by understanding the properties of chemicals and in so doing they are making millions of new ones. It is the way chemicals react together that lies at the heart of any study of chemistry.

Computers, telephones and televisions are at the centre of a communications and information revolution. Without chemists, none of these would have existed because most of the materials in them have been developed and manufactured by chemists.

But the word 'chemical' can have negative connotations in the mind of the general public. It is a word associated with pollution, such as photochemical smog, the contamination of water supplies, or with environmental disasters such as the destruction of the ozone layer by CFCs. Yet it is chemists who have the task of understanding these problems, explaining the dangers and finding the solutions, and this book includes discussions of the environmental, technological, social and economic aspects of chemistry in practice.

Understanding chemistry helps us to put these aspects of chemistry in an informed perspective, and the authors hope that through the pages of this book you will capture something of the extraordinariness of chemistry, the excitement of its advances and an understanding of how it is developing.

Using this book

This book is filled with colourful diagrams and photographs. The illustrations are to clarify the concepts described and to show the relevance of chemistry to everyday life. This should help you to learn by reinforcing what you read in the text.

The Opener

Each chapter begins with some interesting information which is relevant to the subject matter of the chapter. Openers range from how atoms were first created in the Big Bang, to how drugs are designed through the use of computer modelling. You will find out why denim jeans are usually dyed blue and why the cloth is called denim in the first place. Controversial issues are included, such as the banning of chlorine and its compounds and our use of the car. You will also discover chemistry that is at the very frontier of our understanding.

1 Reactions, equations and energy

THE HUMBER BRIDGE is the largest single span suspension bridge in the world. It contains 27 000 tonnes of steel, all supplied by British Steel: 16 500 tonnes make up the deck section and 11 500 tonnes are in the cables which support it.

Each part of such a large construction needs a different type steel with different properties to meet particular needs, which may include rigidity, flexibility, strength in tension and ease of being welded. The properties of steel depend on its composition. Steels contain a little carbon in the iron, and can include very small amounts of manganese, niobium, vanadium and titanium. Phosphorus and sulphur are impurities from iron ore that can make steel brittle. The number of times the steel sheet is rolled will also affect its final properties. It is the job of the metallurgist to get the balance of composition and treatment of the steel that suits a specific need.

For a gas or oil pipeline, a low carbon content and some niobium and vanadium in the steel will make a clean, strong weld that won't crack or leak, while for reinforcing structures in buildings, more carbon gives steel greater rigidity and strength.

Laser welding is one of the developing areas in working with sheet steel. In conventional 'oxyacetylene' welding, the parts to be joined are heated extensively to melt and join the surfaces. Then, when the steel cools and shrinks, there is inevitably distortion at the join. In a construction such as a ship's hull, large patchworks of 20 mm thick sheets have to be trimmed to the right size before they can be joined. This costs a great deal of money. With laser welding, the beam is focused to a small spot that moves along the joint. Only the surfaces of the sheets are heated, very intensely and for a very short time, so the process avoids distortion and the expense of trimming.

The Humber bridge - the largest of its kind in the world

In the manufacture of steel, enormous amounts of water are used to cool the rolling mills. The water is recycled many times and can pick up contaminants including cyanide, nitrite and chloride from the steel. So chemists regularly check that the water that is eventually discharged meets environmental requirements

Introduction

Nearly all the materials you touch, the polymers and dyes in

The text

The main text introduces ideas from scratch. Key words are high-lighted in bold and explained. Throughout each chapter the text is supported by full colour photos and diagrams with explanatory labels and captions.

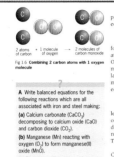

In the blast furnace, coke, which is carbon, reacts with air to produce carbon monoxide. This can be represented by a word equation:

carbon + oxygen → carbon monoxide

However, it is more convenient and much more informative to use formulas in an equation. A **molecular formula** tells you how many atoms of each element there are in a molecule of the compound. Oxygen has two atoms per molecule: O_2. But not all substances are made up of molecules. For example, sodium chloride is a giant lattice made up of sodium and chloride ions. For these it is more correct just to use the term **formula** or **formula unit**. So the equation can be written:

$$C + O_2 \rightarrow CO$$

> A Write balanced equations for the following reactions which are all associated with iron and steel making:
>
> **(a)** Calcium carbonate ($CaCO_3$) decomposing to calcium oxide (CaO) and carbon dioxide (CO_2).
>
> **(b)** Manganese (Mn) reacting with oxygen (O_2) to form manganese(II) oxide (MnO).
>
> **(c)** Phosphorus (P) reacting with oxygen to form phosphorus(V) oxide (P_4O_{10}).
>
> See questions 1 and 2

This equation is unbalanced. There are more oxygen atoms on the left side of the equation than there are on the right where one atom of oxygen has 'disappeared'. Because atoms are not made or destroyed in chemical reactions, in any chemical equation, the number of atoms of each element must be the same on both sides. This makes for a *balanced* equation.

It would be simple to balance the equation above by making CO into CO_2. But this changes the chemical carbon monoxide into carbon dioxide, a different gas with completely different properties. Instead, as shown in Fig 1.6, the balanced equation for the reaction is:

$$2C + O_2 \rightarrow 2CO$$

Marginal reminders

Marginal reminders are small boxes headed by a tick. Some sum-marise or amplify essential points in the main text, while others give you an instant reminder of information contained in other chapters. Some are useful exam hints.

> ✔ This is an easy way to remember what exothermic and endothermic mean:
> Energy **ex**its in **ex**othermic reactions. Look for the minus sign (ΔH is negative).
> Energy **en**ters in **en**dothermic reactions. Look for the plus sign (ΔH is positive).

carbon dioxide. Stored energy is know is not possible to measure enthalpy, b easily be found by measuring temperature at constant pressure. Enthalpy change is a Greek letter pronounced 'delta' and 'change of'.

In the coke and oxygen reaction, the joules (kJ) for every mole of carbon re

$$C + O_2 \rightarrow CO_2 \quad \Delta H = -$$

Notice that ΔH has a negative sign. Th proceeds, *energy is lost from the reactan*

Self-test questions

You will find these a valuable and instant way to check that you understand the text alongside them. Work through the questions as you read: they test your progress and make you think. Thankfully, you will find the the answers to many of them at the back of the book - but no cheating: try the question first.

6 YIELD AND PERCE

> ?
>
> **G** What is the percentage yield of iron produced if 10.0 tonnes of iron(III) oxide yields 0.67 tonnes of iron?
>
> **H** Another ore of iron has the formula Fe_3O_4. In a blast furnace, 1 tonne of this ore makes 6.50 tonnes of iron.
>
> **(a)** Write down the balanced equation for the reaction of Fe_3O_4 with carbon monoxide making iron and carbon dioxide.
>
> **(b)** How many tonnes of iron can be made from 10.0 tonnes of Fe_3O_4? Note: This will be the theoretical yield.
>
> **(c)** Calculate the percentage yield.
>
> See question 6

You should now be able to use balance masses of substances involved in reac 10 tonnes of iron(III) oxide can give 7. iron produced is known as the **yield**. achieve this yield in a real blast furna calculation from the balanced equation which is the maximum amount if all to products. There are many reasons w achieved: reactions may not be finish some of the product may be lost durin

The **actual yield** from a reaction ca reaction. From 10.0 tonnes of iron(III) o 7.00 tonnes. Percentage yield is a co how close the actual yield is to the theo

$$\text{Percentage yield} = \frac{\text{actua}}{\text{theoret}}$$

Industrial processes aim for 100 per get. the less is the waste of raw materia

Feature boxes

The feature boxes contain information of special interest. They fill out the relevance of the chemistry you are studying – it may be a new development in modern chemistry, or a look back of the life of one of the great chemists of history. The information may not be essential to the syllabus you are studying but they are included because they are likely to interest you.

BRITISH STEEL LINKS WITH HONG KONG

AMID A WORLDWIDE DECLINE in steel production, British Steel won a huge contract to supply steel for building the Tsing Ma Bridge linking Kowloon and Hong Kong Island to Hong Kong's new island airport, which was opened in 1997.

The 54 000 tonnes of steel ordered was twice the amount used in the Humber bridge (which still has the widest span between towers in the world). This amount was needed since the Tsing Ma Bridge has two three-lane carriageways above two railway lines and two emergency roads.

The lower deck is fully enclosed, protected by stain-less steel sheet to deflect the gusts of up to 83 metres a second that can occur during typhoons that hit Hong Kong. The cables suspending the bridge from its towers could circle the Earth four and a half times.

Fig 1.17 **The Tsing Ma Bridge linking Hong Kong to its airport**

A worker on the project at the time described it as 'one of those unique engineering and construction projects that manages to combine practicality, romance and adventure in one package'.

Extension boxes

These cover ideas which go beyond the basic requirements of most chemistry syllabuses at advanced level. But they will help you towards a better grade and aid your understanding of topics.

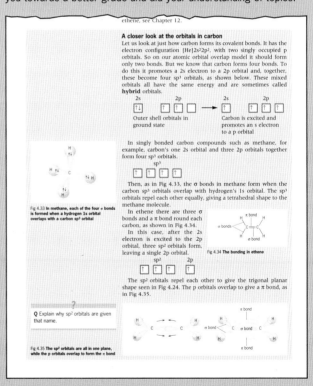

ethene, see Chapter 12.

A closer look at the orbitals in carbon
Let us look at just how carbon forms its covalent bonds. It has the electron configuration $[He]2s^2 2p^2$, with two singly occupied p orbitals. So on our atomic orbital overlap model it should form only two bonds. But we know that carbon forms four bonds. To do this it promotes a 2s electron to a 2p orbital and, together, these become four sp^3 orbitals, as shown below. These mixed orbitals all have the same energy and are sometimes called **hybrid** orbitals.

Outer shell orbitals in ground state

Carbon is excited and promotes an s electron to a p orbital

In singly bonded carbon compounds such as methane, for example, carbon's one 2s orbital and three 2p orbitals together form four sp^3 orbitals.

Then, as in Fig 4.33, the σ bonds in methane form when the carbon sp^3 orbitals overlap with hydrogen's 1s orbital. The sp^3 orbitals repel each other equally, giving a tetrahedral shape to the methane molecule.

In ethene there are three σ bonds and a π bond round each carbon, as shown in Fig 4.34.

In this case, after the 2s electron is excited to the 2p orbital, three sp^2 orbitals form, leaving a single 2p orbital.

Fig 4.33 **in methane, each of the four σ bonds is formed when a hydrogen 1s orbital overlaps with a carbon sp^3 orbital**

Fig 4.34 **The bonding in ethene**

The sp^2 orbitals repel each other to give the trigonal planar shape seen in Fig 4.24. The p orbitals overlap to give a π bond, as in Fig 4.35.

> Q Explain why sp^2 orbitals are given that name.

Fig 4.35 **The sp^2 orbitals are all in one plane, while the p orbitals overlap to form the π bond**

Examples

Most chapters contain worked examples. They should help you to see that the calculations in chemistry are not as difficult as you thought.

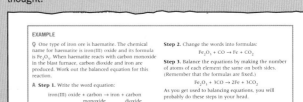

EXAMPLE

Q One type of iron ore is haematite. The chemical name for haematite is iron(III) oxide and its formula is Fe_2O_3. When haematite reacts with carbon monoxide in the blast furnace, carbon dioxide and iron are produced. Work out the balanced equation for this reaction.

A **Step 1.** Write the word equation:

iron(III) oxide + carbon → iron + carbon
monoxide   dioxide

Step 2. Change the words into formulas:

$$Fe_2O_3 + CO \rightarrow Fe + CO_2$$

Step 3. Balance the equations by making the number of atoms of each element the same on both sides. (Remember that the formulas are fixed.)

$$Fe_2O_3 + 3CO \rightarrow 2Fe + 3CO_2$$

As you get used to balancing equations, you will probably do these steps in your head.

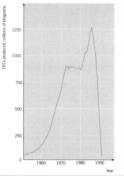

10 Halogenoalkanes ■ 223

Assignment
THE RISE AND FALL OF CFCS

The first CFC to be discovered was CFC12 in 1892, but it was not until 1928 that Thomas Midgley was able to develop a simple one-step process for making CFCs. He used the reaction of tetrachloromethane with anhydrous hydrogen fluoride with an antimony(V) chloride catalyst:

$$CCl_4 + xHF \rightarrow CCl_{4-x}F_x + xHCl$$

1 Write down an equation to show how CFC11 ($CFCl_3$) can be prepared from tetrachloromethane.

2
a) Write down an equation to show how CFC12 (CF_2Cl_2) can be prepared from tetrachloromethane

b) Use the equation to calculate the minimum mass of tetrachloromethane that is needed to make 1 tonne of CFC12.
Hint: You may need to look at page 7.

By 9.55 p.m. on 29 June 1990, the death warrant for CFCs had been signed in London, some 70 years after their first commercial production. By this time, CFCs had been used world-wide in industrial and domestic applications in the belief that they were inert and harmless to both life and the environment.

The detection of ozone depletion in the stratosphere and the rapid increase in the concentration of CFCs became unquestionably linked. Table 10.A1 shows how the concentrations of CFC have increased up to the first international protocol on the use of CFCs in Montreal in 1987, when the first restrictions on their use came into force.

Table 10.A1 **Atmospheric concentrations of CFCs**

Year	CFC11 (CCl₃F)	CFC12 (CCl₂F₂)
1976	133	217
1978	159	266
1980	179	307
1982	193	330
1984	213	366

3 Draw a graph of the data in Table 10.A1 and estimate the atmospheric CFC concentration of each CFC in 1994. Assume that there had been no significant changes in production, use and government legislation.

It is not just the concentrations of CFCs that are a cause for concern. It is also the estimated lifetime of these compounds in the atmosphere and their ozone-depleting potential (ODP). The latter compares the ability of different CFCs to destroy the ozone layer in the stratosphere.

Table 10.A2 **Lifetime and ODP values for some CFCs and related compounds**

Compound	Lifetime in atmosphere/years	ODP	% contribution to ozone depletion
CFC 11	74	1	26
CFC12	111	1	45
CFC113	90	0.8	12
CCl₄	67	1.1	8
CH₃CCl₃	8	0.1	5
Halon 1301	110	10	4

By 1994 the production of CFCs had dropped dramatically, as shown in Fig 10.A1.

Fig 10.A1 **Change in production of CFCs since 1950** (source: DuPont, Worldwatch estimates)

4 Governments agreed by the mid-90s to cut down and eventually stop the production and use of CFCs within the following few years. Use the data in Fig 10.A1 and Table 10.A3 to estimate the possible changes in atmospheric CFC concentration and ozone depletion.

5 Halon 1301 (CBrF₃) has the highest ODP value.
a) Which halogen free radical is most likely to be produced in the stratosphere? Write an equation for this reaction.

b) Use your answer in part a) to suggest why it has the highest ODP of all the values quoted.

Assignments
Most chapters have an assignment. Typically, this is a self contained extended exercise with information about an application of chemistry or an in-depth treatment of an aspect of chemical theory. It can include real data to analyse. Questions range from simple comprehension to more challenging ones where you manipulate information in the Assignment.

Summaries and Chapter maps
These are both at the end of each chapter. The Summary tells you the main points that are covered by the chapter – really useful when it comes to revision. It also helps if you want to know what the chapter as a whole is about. The Chapter Maps too will assist you in understanding the range of concepts that are covered in the chapter, and how these relate to other chapters. For example, the concept of reaction rates is first introduced in Chapter 1 and is developed in Chapter 27.

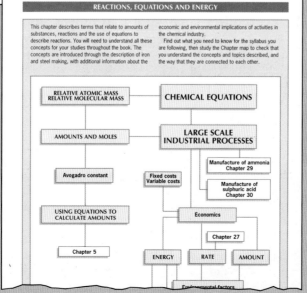

SUMMARY

After studying this chapter, you should know and understand the following.

■ A **molecular formula** tells you how many atoms of each element there are in a molecule of the compound.

■ The term **formula** applies to ionic compounds as well as molecules. It is the number of atoms of the different elements making up the smallest complete unit of a substance.

■ In the **relative atomic mass**, A_r, scale, the masses of atoms are measured relative to one atom of carbon-12 which is given an A_r of exactly 12. For a more complete definition, see page 29.

■ The **Avogadro constant** is the number of atoms or molecules in one mole which is 6.02×10^{23}.

■ The **theoretical yield** is the maximum amount obtainable if all the reactants are converted to products. This is calculated from the balanced equation:

$$\text{percentage yield} = \frac{\text{actual yield}}{\text{theoretical yield}} \times 100\%$$

■ The **rate of reaction** is affected by temperature, pressure, concentration, surface area of reactants and catalysts.

■ The **enthalpy change**, ΔH, is a measure of the

1 Reactions, equations and energy ■ 19

REACTIONS, EQUATIONS AND ENERGY

This chapter describes terms that relate to amounts of substances, reactions and the use of equations to describe reactions. You will need to understand all these concepts for your studies throughout the book. The concepts are introduced through the description of iron and steel making, with additional information about the economic and environmental implications of activities in the chemical industry.
Find out what you need to know for the syllabus you are following, then study the Chapter map to check that you understand the concepts and topics described, and the way that they are connected to each other.

- RELATIVE ATOMIC MASS / RELATIVE MOLECULAR MASS
- CHEMICAL EQUATIONS
- AMOUNTS AND MOLES
- LARGE SCALE INDUSTRIAL PROCESSES
- Avogadro constant
- Fixed costs / Variable costs
- Manufacture of ammonia Chapter 29
- Manufacture of sulphuric acid Chapter 30
- USING EQUATIONS TO CALCULATE AMOUNTS
- Economics
- Chapter 27
- Chapter 5
- ENERGY
- RATE
- AMOUNT
- Environmental factors

What maths will I need?

The mathematical requirements of chemistry syllabuses have been considerably reduced in recent years. However, numeracy is a key skill which you will be able to practise through your study of chemistry. Whenever mathematical calculations are required, worked Examples are provided which show in a series of steps how you can successfully carry out each calculation. You will also find a section on significant figures and standard form in the appendices.

Practical work

Although chemistry is an experimental science this is not a practical manual, so you will not find procedures and detailed descriptions of laboratory experiments, but you will find out about chemical reactions and the conditions required to carry them out, with illustrations of many of them.

1 Reactions, equations and energy

THE HUMBER BRIDGE is the largest single span suspension bridge in the world. It contains 27 000 tonnes of steel, all supplied by British Steel: 16 500 tonnes make up the deck section and 11 500 tonnes are in the cables which support it.

Each part of such a large construction needs a different type steel with different properties to meet particular needs, which may include rigidity, flexibility, strength in tension and ease of being welded. The properties of steel depend on its composition. Steels contain a little carbon in the iron, and can include very small amounts of manganese, niobium, vanadium and titanium. Phosphorus and sulphur are impurities from iron ore that can make steel brittle. The number of times the steel sheet is rolled will also affect its final properties. It is the job of the metallurgist to get the balance of composition and treatment of the steel that suits a specific need.

For a gas or oil pipeline, a low carbon content and some niobium and vanadium in the steel will make a clean, strong weld that won't crack or leak, while for reinforcing structures in buildings, more carbon gives steel greater rigidity and strength.

Laser welding is one of the developing areas in working with sheet steel. In conventional 'oxyacetylene' welding, the parts to be joined are heated extensively to melt and join the surfaces. Then, when the steel cools and shrinks, there is inevitably distortion at the join. In a construction such as a ship's hull, large patchworks of 20 mm thick sheets have to be trimmed to the right size before they can be joined. This costs a great deal of money. With laser welding, the beam is focused to a small spot that moves along the joint. Only the surfaces of the sheets are heated, very intensely and for a very short time, so the process avoids distortion and the expense of trimming.

The Humber bridge - the largest of its kind in the world

In the manufacture of steel, enormous amounts of water are used to cool the rolling mills. The water is recycled many times and can pick up contaminants including cyanide, nitrite and chloride from the steel. So chemists regularly check that the water that is eventually discharged meets environmental requirements

Introduction

Nearly all the materials you touch, the polymers and dyes in clothes, the food on your plate, or the paracetamol in the bathroom cabinet, have at some stage involved industrial chemists. This chapter will give you an insight into the world of the chemical industry. You will discover that organising the economics of a large manufacturing plant depends on understanding the chemistry of industrial processes.

Also, throughout this chapter you will find out more about chemical equations, the chemical reactions that they represent, and how energy is transferred in reactions.

Fig 1.1 **Chemicals called liquid crystals are used in the liquid crystal diode (LCD) displays in clocks and watches. You may read more about them on page 102**

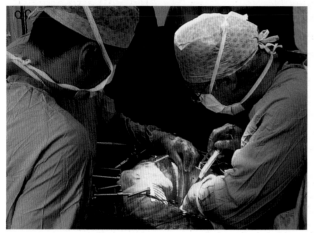

Fig 1.2 **(lower left) The artificial aorta that is fitted to the heart of this man is made of a polyester fibre called Dacron**

Fig 1.3 **Oral rehydration powders contain sodium chloride, glucose, trisodium citrate and potassium chloride. As the treatment for victims of dehydration, this mixture dissolved in water has saved the lives of millions of people, especially children**

1 CHEMICAL FORMULAS AND CHEMICAL EQUATIONS

Iron and steel have transformed the world around us in a way no other chemicals have. Think of their use in various means of travel – bridges, railways, cars, the Channel Tunnel and ships – in buildings such as skyscrapers, factories and warehouses, as well as in leisure products such as golf clubs and garden furniture.

Anyone fortunate enough to tour an iron and steel making plant comes away impressed by the large scale of it all. Yet the process is fairly simple and uses only four major raw materials: iron ore, coal (made into coke), limestone and air. The principles of iron making have not changed much since Roman times, so where does the chemist fit in today? Chemists have the best understanding of the manufacturing process, so they can, for example, calculate the exact amounts of raw materials required and advise on the best reaction conditions. In sections 7, 10 and 11 of this chapter, you can read about the role of chemists in optimising the efficiency of processes, controlling the properties of steels, and in avoiding industrial pollution.

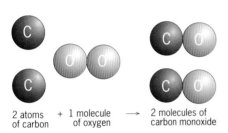

Fig 1.4 **The Queen Victoria blast furnace in British Steel's Scunthorpe iron making works**

Fig 1.5 **The base of the blast furnace: hot air at about 750 ºC is blown into it**

2 atoms + 1 molecule → 2 molecules of
of carbon of oxygen carbon monoxide

Fig 1.6 **Combining 2 carbon atoms with 1 oxygen molecule**

?

A Write balanced equations for the following reactions which are all associated with iron and steel making:

(a) Calcium carbonate ($CaCO_3$) decomposing to calcium oxide (CaO) and carbon dioxide (CO_2).

(b) Manganese (Mn) reacting with oxygen (O_2) to form manganese(II) oxide (MnO).

(c) Phosphorus (P) reacting with oxygen to form phosphorus(V) oxide (P_4O_{10}).

See questions 1 and 2. ▨

In the blast furnace, coke, which is carbon, reacts with air to produce carbon monoxide. This can be represented by a word equation:

carbon + oxygen → carbon monoxide

However, it is more convenient and much more informative to use formulas in an equation. A **molecular formula** tells you how many atoms of each element there are in a molecule of the compound. Oxygen has two atoms per molecule: O_2. But not all substances are made up of molecules. For example, sodium chloride is a giant lattice made up of sodium and chloride ions. For these it is more correct just to use the term **formula** or **formula unit**. So the equation can be written:

$$C + O_2 \rightarrow CO$$

This equation is unbalanced. There are more oxygen atoms on the left side of the equation than there are on the right where one atom of oxygen has 'disappeared'. Because atoms are not made or destroyed in chemical reactions, in any chemical equation, the number of atoms of each element must be the same on both sides. This makes for a *balanced* equation.

It would be simple to balance the equation above by making CO into CO_2. But this changes the chemical carbon monoxide into carbon dioxide, a different gas with completely different properties. Instead, as shown in Fig 1.6, the balanced equation for the reaction is:

$$2C + O_2 \rightarrow 2CO$$

EXAMPLE

Q One type of iron ore is haematite. The chemical name for haematite is iron(III) oxide and its formula is Fe_2O_3. When haematite reacts with carbon monoxide in the blast furnace, carbon dioxide and iron are produced. Work out the balanced equation for this reaction.

A **Step 1.** Write the word equation:

iron(III) oxide + carbon → iron + carbon
monoxide dioxide

Step 2. Change the words into formulas:

$$Fe_2O_3 + CO \rightarrow Fe + CO_2$$

Step 3. Balance the equations by making the number of atoms of each element the same on both sides. (Remember that the formulas are fixed.)

$$Fe_2O_3 + 3CO \rightarrow 2Fe + 3CO_2$$

As you get used to balancing equations, you will probably do these steps in your head.

2 RELATIVE ATOMIC MASSES

The masses of different atoms can be compared using the **relative atomic mass scale**, also called the A_r **scale** (r stands for 'relative'). On this scale, the isotope carbon-12 is given an A_r of exactly 12. The isotope carbon-12 is the standard and the A_r values of all other atoms are measured relative to this standard.

Historically, the standard for the A_r scale was hydrogen. As the lightest element, it was given an A_r of 1. Carbon-12 is now used because it is easier to handle than gaseous hydrogen and is an abundant isotope. Table 1.1 shows some approximate relative atomic masses.

Notice in Table 1.1 that the relative atomic masses have no units. The relative atomic mass just tells you *how many times heavier* one atom is compared to another. So one atom of silicon is 28 times heavier than one atom of hydrogen, and calcium atoms are twice as heavy as neon atoms.

Table 1.1 **The approximate relative atomic masses of some elements**

Element	Symbol	Relative atomic mass, A_r
Hydrogen	H	1
Carbon	C	12
Oxygen	O	16
Neon	Ne	20
Silicon	Si	28
Sulphur	S	32
Calcium	Ca	40
Iron	Fe	56
Copper	Cu	64

You can find out more about isotopes in Chapter 2.

A full list of relative atomic masses is given in Appendix 2.

3 AMOUNTS AND THE MOLE

When chemists use the word *amount*, they are talking about the number of particles in a substance. The particles can be atoms, molecules, ions, electrons etc. Amount may also mean other things, for instance the mass of a substance, which has units of grams or kilograms. To describe the amount of something such as eggs, you would probably use the unit dozens. When chemists talk about the amount of substance they use the unit **moles**.

The A_r of copper is 64, and so each copper atom is twice as heavy as a sulphur atom. Imagine that 64 grams of copper and 64 grams of sulphur, whose A_r is 32, are weighed out. The mass of each substance is the same, but to a chemist the amount of each substance is very different. 64 grams contains twice as many sulphur *atoms* as copper atoms: there are double the *amount* of sulphur atoms.

Using relative atomic masses, you can work out amounts of atoms or molecules in different masses of substances. Weigh out 32 grams of sulphur, and you have the same number of atoms as there are in 64 grams of copper. Also, weigh out the relative atomic mass in grams of different elements, and you are weighing the same *amount* of atoms each time. This amount is called the mole:

The relative atomic mass in grams of any element contains one mole of atoms.

The mole is a unit in the same way that the gram is a unit. The shortened form of the mole unit is **mol**. (Care: This is not short for molecule!) This is its definition:

One mole is the amount of substance which contains as many particles as there are atoms in exactly 12 g of carbon-12.

These are some examples:

The amount of atoms in 32 g sulphur is 1 mol.

In 32 g of copper there is 0.5 mol of copper atoms.

32 g of oxygen atoms is 2 mol of oxygen atoms.

?

B Work out how many times heavier the following are:

(a) Fe atoms than H atoms;

(b) S atoms than O atoms;

(c) Fe atoms than O atoms.

To work out how many moles of atoms are in a particular mass of substance, use this equation:

$$\text{amount in moles} = \frac{\text{mass in grams}}{\text{mass of one mole (in grams)}}$$

EXAMPLES

Q How many moles are there in 56 g silicon?

A Amount in moles = $\dfrac{\text{mass in grams}}{\text{mass of one mole (in grams)}}$

  moles of silicon = $\dfrac{56\ g}{28\ g}$

        = 2 moles

Q What is the mass of 0.25 mol of iron?

A Mass in grams = amount in moles × mass of 1 mole

  mass of iron = 0.25 mol × 56 g

        = 14 g

C (a) Work out how many moles of atoms there are in:
56 g of iron; 20 g of calcium;
128 g of copper; 4 g of sulphur.

(b) Give the mass of: 3.0 mol of calcium atoms; 0.3 mol of neon atoms.

One mole of substance is 6.02×10^{23} particles. This is a very large amount of atoms or molecules to try and imagine. It is so large that there is not even a mole of sand grains around the whole coastline of the British Isles. The number of atoms or molecules in one mole is called the **Avogadro constant.**

4 RELATIVE MOLECULAR MASS

See questions 3 and 4 ■

Fig 1.7 **Working out the relative molecular mass of carbon dioxide**

We saw on page 4 that carbon dioxide is made up of molecules each with the molecular formula CO_2. Fe_2O_3 is the formula unit of iron(III) oxide. It is not a molecular formula because this compound is not made up of separate molecules. Most equations that chemists deal with involve either molecules or formula units.

The **relative molecular mass**, M_r, is calculated using the relative atomic mass scale. Again, we use the standard carbon-12 as a comparison for the masses of molecules or formula units. Suppose we want to find the M_r of carbon dioxide (see Fig 1.7).

$$\text{The } M_r \text{ of } CO_2 = A_r \text{ of C} + (A_r \text{ of O} \times 2)$$
$$= \quad 12 \quad + \quad (16 \times 2) \quad = 44$$

D Give the relative formula mass (M_r) of: **(a)** P_4O_{10}; **(b)** O_2; **(c)** $CaSiO_3$.

$$\text{The } M_r \text{ of } Fe_2O_3 = (A_r \text{ of Fe} \times 2) + (A_r \text{ of O} \times 3)$$
$$= \quad (56 \times 2) \quad + \quad (16 \times 3) \quad = 160$$

In this case, the M_r refers to the formula Fe_2O_3 and is called the **relative formula mass**.

During your Advanced course, you will come across many formulas with brackets, for example, $Ca(OH)_2$. Fig 1.8 shows what this means.

E Give the M_r of: **(a)** $Fe(OH)_2$; **(b)** $Al_2(SO_4)_3$; **(c)** $(CH_3CO)_2O$.

Notice that the particles in $Ca(OH)_2$ are ions and have positive and negative charges. The charges on ions do not affects their A_r values. So:

$$M_r \text{ of } Ca(OH)_2 = A_r \text{ of Ca} + 2 \times (A_r \text{ of O} + A_r \text{ of H})$$
$$= \quad 40 \quad + \quad 2(16 + 1)$$
$$= \quad 40 \quad + \quad 2 \times 17 = 74$$

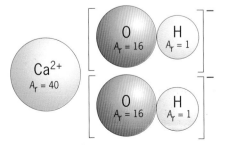

Fig 1.8 **Diagram to explain the parts of the formula $Ca(OH)_2$**

5 USING EQUATIONS IN INDUSTRY

We have seen that the chemical formula CO means that 1 molecule contains 1 atom of carbon combined with 1 atom of oxygen. It also means that 1 mole of carbon atoms is combined with 1 mole of oxygen atoms. This is sometimes called the **stoichiometric ratio**. In the equation for the reaction of coke in the blast furnace:

$$2C \quad + \quad O_2 \quad \rightarrow \quad 2CO$$

This means: 2 atoms C   +   1 molecule O_2 $\rightarrow$ 2 molecules CO

If instead of 2 atoms of carbon we had 2 million atoms, then:

2 million		1 million O_2		2 million CO
C atoms	+	molecules	$\rightarrow$	molecules

We now use moles:

2 mol carbon		1 mol oxygen		2 mol carbon
atoms	+	molecules	$\rightarrow$	monoxide molecules

The carbon monoxide formed in the blast furnace **reduces** (removes oxygen from) the iron(III) oxide to iron:

$$Fe_2O_3 \quad + \quad 3CO \quad \rightarrow \quad 2Fe \quad + \quad 3CO_2$$

So: 1 mol Fe_2O_3 + 3 mol CO → 2 mol Fe + 3 mol CO_2

Now that we know the amounts of the chemical substances in this equation, we can work out the masses of the substances involved using the A_r scale.

The mass of 1 mol of Fe_2O_3 is $(56 \times 2)g + (16 \times 3)g = 160$ g
The mass of 1 mol of CO   is 12 g + 16 g   = 28 g
The mass of 1 mol of Fe   is 56 g   = 56 g
The mass of 1 mol of CO_2 is 12 g + $(16 \times 2)g$ = 44 g

To work out the masses of substances involved in converting 160 g of iron(III) oxide to iron, we can use the following steps:

Step 1. Write the balanced equation:

$$Fe_2O_3 \quad + \quad 3CO \quad \rightarrow \quad 2Fe \quad + \quad 3CO_2$$

Step 2. Convert the equation to amounts:

1 mol Fe_2O_3 + 3 mol CO → 2 mol Fe + 3 mol CO_2

Step 3. Work out the amount being used:

Moles of Fe_2O_3 in 160 g = $\dfrac{\text{mass in grams}}{\text{mass of one mole (in grams)}} = \dfrac{160}{160} = 1$ mol

Step 4. Scale the amounts in the equation:
In this case, only 1 mol Fe_2O_3 is used, so the amounts do not need to be scaled.

1 mol Fe_2O_3 +   3 mol CO   →   2 mol Fe   +   3 mol CO_2

Step 5. Convert amounts (moles) to masses:
160 g Fe_2O_3 + 3 × 28 g = 84 g CO
→ 2 × 56 g = 112 g Fe + 3 × 44 g = 132 g CO_2

So, from 160 g of Fe_2O_3, in theory 112 g of iron could be produced and 132 g carbon dioxide given off. In the iron and steel industry, amounts this size are ridiculously small. A typical blast furnace can produce up to 10 000 tonnes a day of molten iron.

✓ Extraction of a metal from its ore always includes a reduction reaction. Many metal ores contain oxygen, but for those that don't, a suitable definition of reduction is to be found in Chapter 21.

■ See question 8.

■ See questions 2 and 5.

Suppose we now want to find out how much iron can be produced from 10 tonnes of iron(III) oxide. We can still use the same method. The first step is identical, so we can start at Step 2.

Step 2. Convert the equation to amounts:

$$1 \text{ mol } Fe_2O_3 \text{ gives } 2 \text{ mol } Fe$$

Note: In this example we do not need to know the moles of CO or CO_2.

Step 3. Work out the amount being used (1 tonne = 1 000 000 g):

$$\text{Moles of } Fe_2O_3 \text{ in 10 tonnes} = \frac{\text{mass in grams}}{\text{mass of one mole (in grams)}}$$

$$= \frac{10\ 000\ 000 \text{ g}}{160 \text{ g}}$$

$$= 62\ 500 \text{ mol}$$

Step 4. Scale the amounts in the equation:

$$1 \text{ mol } Fe_2O_3 \text{ produces } 2 \text{ mol } Fe$$
$$62\ 500 \text{ mol } Fe_2O_3 \text{ produces } 125\ 000 \text{ mol } Fe$$

Step 5. Convert amount (moles) of Fe to a mass:

$$125\ 000 \text{ mol} \times 56 \text{ g} = 7\ 000\ 000 \text{ g} = 7.0 \text{ tonnes of Fe (to 2 sig figs)}$$

6 YIELD AND PERCENTAGE YIELD

You should now be able to use balanced equations to calculate the masses of substances involved in reactions. We have found that 10 tonnes of iron(III) oxide can give 7.0 tonnes of iron. The mass of iron produced is known as the **yield**. But British Steel could never achieve this yield in a real blast furnace. Therefore we say that the calculation from the balanced equation gives the **theoretical yield**, which is the maximum amount if all the reactants were converted to products. There are many reasons why the theoretical yield is not achieved: reactions may not be finished in the time available, or some of the product may be lost during the purification procedure.

The **actual yield** from a reaction can be found only by doing the reaction. From 10.0 tonnes of iron(III) oxide, it is going to be less than 7.00 tonnes. Percentage yield is a convenient way of expressing how close the actual yield is to the theoretical yield.

$$\textbf{Percentage yield} = \frac{\text{actual yield}}{\text{theoretical yield}} \times 100\%$$

Industrial processes aim for 100 per cent yield. The closer they get, the less is the waste of raw material.

F Coke also reacts directly with iron ore in the hotter part of the blast furnace to give iron and carbon monoxide.

(a) Work out the balanced equation for this reaction.

(b) How many tonnes of carbon monoxide are produced in this part of the furnace for every tonne of iron produced?

For a note about significant figures, refer to Appendix 2.

G What is the percentage yield of iron produced if 10.0 tonnes of iron(III) oxide yields 0.67 tonnes of iron?

H Another ore of iron has the formula Fe_3O_4. In a blast furnace, 1 tonne of this ore makes 6.50 tonnes of iron.

(a) Write down the balanced equation for the reaction of Fe_3O_4 with carbon monoxide making iron and carbon dioxide.

(b) How many tonnes of iron can be made from 10.0 tonnes of Fe_3O_4? Note: This will be the theoretical yield.

(c) Calculate the percentage yield.

See question 6. ■

7 RATE OF REACTION

The aim of chemical industry is to get as close as possible to a 100 per cent yield. However, in producing any chemical economically, the yield from a reaction is just one of the factors involved. Another very important factor is the *rate* of reaction. It is no use having a high yield of iron in a process that is extremely slow. As a simple definition:

The rate of a reaction is the amount of substance formed per unit of time.

The rate could be in moles per second. For industry, it is more convenient to give the rate as the mass of substance, such as kilograms or tonnes, formed per unit of time. Reactions can be very fast and uncontrolled, such as a gas explosion (Fig 1.9). Reactions can also be very slow, as in the rusting of iron (Fig 1.10).

You can find out more about rates of reaction in Chapter 27.

Fig 1.9 **An explosion is just a reaction with a very rapid rate**

Fig 1.10 **The owner of this fishing trawler knows that it will be a long time before his boat starts leaking because of rust**

An industrial chemist needs to control the rate of a reaction. This could either mean speeding it up or slowing it down. In industry, the rate often needs to be increased so that the amount of product formed in, say, a day is enough to make a profit.

Factors that affect rate of reaction

Chemists control the rate of a reaction by changing the conditions of the reaction. These are some of the conditions.

- **Temperature**: an increase in temperature makes a reaction go faster (except for those involving enzymes).
- **Pressure**: increasing pressure can increase the rate of reactions involving gases.
- **Concentration**: increasing the concentration normally increases the rate of reaction.
- **Surface area of reactant**: an increase in surface area increases the rate of reaction.
- **Catalyst**: the addition of a catalyst usually increases the rate of a reaction.

Reactions involve the rearrangement of atoms when bonds are broken and others are made. This rearrangement seldom takes place spontaneously; the particles normally need to be colliding with each other. All the conditions listed above will change the collision rate between particles. And if the collision rate is increased then the rate of reaction will increase.

The rate of reaction can be controlled by changing temperature, pressure, concentration and surface area. However, these factors can also reduce the yield of an industrial process, so there is often a compromise between rates of reaction and yield. Remember, the first concern is the economics of the process, that is, making product quickly enough to give the maximum profit. We will look at this compromise in more detail in section 11.

See question 7.

You can read about the manufacture of ammonia in Chapter 29 and sulphuric acid in Chapter 30.

8 CHEMICAL REACTIONS AND ENERGY CHANGES

All chemical reactions involve a change of energy, meaning *the transfer of energy to or from chemicals*. This is crucial not only to industry, but to the reactions of life itself. In many chemical reactions, *energy is given out by the reactants as they form products*, causing the temperature of the surroundings to rise. Such reactions are known as **exothermic reactions**.

In the blast furnace (Fig 1.14), blasts of hot air at 750 °C are blown in at the base and start a reaction between coke and oxygen:

$$C + O_2 \rightarrow CO_2$$

This reaction is highly exothermic, raising the temperature at the base of the furnace to about 2000 °C. This is because the stored energy in carbon and oxygen is greater than the stored energy of carbon dioxide. Stored energy is known as **enthalpy**, symbol H. It is not possible to measure enthalpy, but **enthalpy changes** can easily be found by measuring temperature changes during reactions at constant pressure. Enthalpy changes are given the symbols ΔH. Δ is a Greek letter pronounced 'delta' and is used by chemists to mean 'change of'.

In the coke and oxygen reaction, the energy released is 394 kilojoules (kJ) for every mole of carbon reacting. So we write:

$$C + O_2 \rightarrow CO_2 \quad \Delta H = -394 \text{ kJ mol}^{-1}$$

Notice that ΔH has a negative sign. This is because as the reaction proceeds, *energy is lost from the reactants*. This energy heats up the surroundings, in this case the contents of the blast furnace. We show the reaction and its enthalpy changes in an **energy level diagram**, see Fig 1.11.

Not all reactions are exothermic. **Endothermic** reactions are the opposite of exothermic reactions. In endothermic reactions *energy is taken in by the reactants to form products*. The energy comes from the surroundings which lose energy and cool down, so there is a drop in temperature.

The carbon dioxide produced at the base of the blast furnace reacts with more coke to produce carbon monoxide. This is an endothermic reaction.

$$CO_2 + C \rightarrow 2CO \quad \Delta H = +173 \text{ kJ mol}^{-1}$$

The plus sign shows that carbon monoxide *takes in energy when it is formed* (Fig 1.12). This is one of the reasons why the blast furnace gets cooler towards the top. (See also Fig 1.14.)

You can read more about enthalpy changes in Chapter 6, starting on page 116.

✔ This is an easy way to remember what exothermic and endothermic mean:
Energy **ex**its in **ex**othermic reactions. Look for the minus sign (ΔH is negative).
Energy **en**ters in **en**dothermic reactions. Look for the plus sign (ΔH is positive).

? **I** The following reactions are all associated with iron and steel manufacture. For each reaction, draw its energy level diagram and say whether the reaction is exothermic or endothermic.

(a) $S + O_2 \rightarrow SO_2$
   $\Delta H = -297 \text{ kJ mol}^{-1}$

(b) $CaCO_3 \rightarrow CaO + CO_2$
   $\Delta H = +178 \text{ kJ mol}^{-1}$

(c) $Fe_2O_3 + 3CO \rightarrow 2Fe + 3CO_2$
   $\Delta H = -27 \text{ kJ mol}^{-1}$

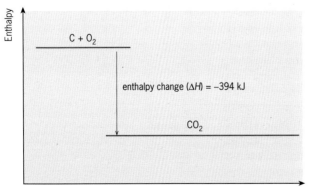

Fig 1.11 **Energy level diagram for the exothermic reaction** $C + O_2 \rightarrow CO_2$

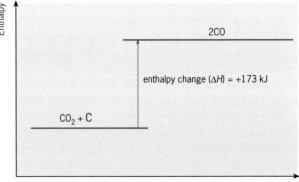

Fig 1.12 **Energy level diagram for the endothermic reaction** $CO_2 + C \rightarrow 2CO$

9 THE BLAST FURNACE

The blast furnace smelts the iron ore. Smelting means that the ore is melted, mixed with the other reactants, and reduced to the metal. The reaction of iron ore with coke, limestone and hot air, produces the iron (Fig 1.13).

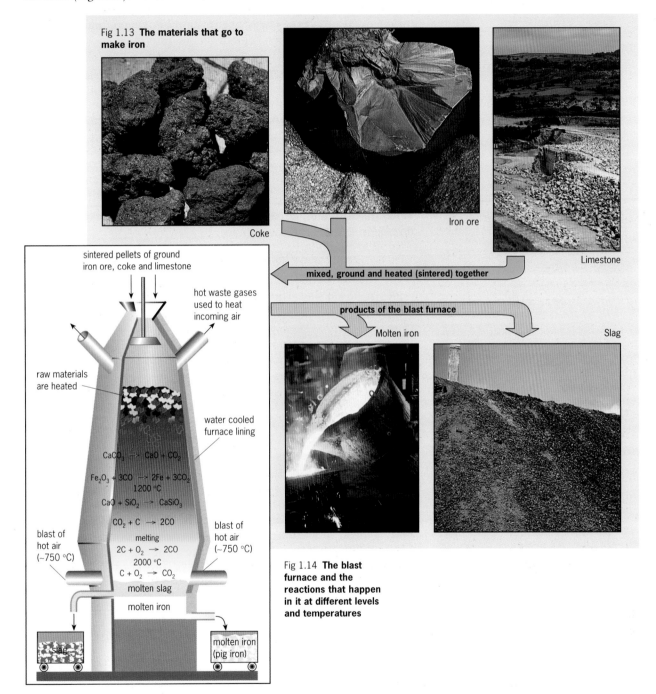

Fig 1.13 **The materials that go to make iron**

Coke

Iron ore

Limestone

mixed, ground and heated (sintered) together

products of the blast furnace

Molten iron

Slag

sintered pellets of ground iron ore, coke and limestone

hot waste gases used to heat incoming air

raw materials are heated

water cooled furnace lining

$CaCO_3 \rightarrow CaO + CO_2$

$Fe_2O_3 + 3CO \rightarrow 2Fe + 3CO_2$
1200 °C

$CaO + SiO_2 \rightarrow CaSiO_3$

$CO_2 + C \rightarrow 2CO$

melting
$2C + O_2 \rightarrow 2CO$
2000 °C
$C + O_2 \rightarrow CO_2$

molten slag

molten iron

blast of hot air (~750 °C)

blast of hot air (~750 °C)

slag

molten iron (pig iron)

Fig 1.14 **The blast furnace and the reactions that happen in it at different levels and temperatures**

The iron making process needs high quality iron ore that contains at least 60 per cent iron. Most iron ores contain impurities such as sand (SiO_2), sulphur compounds and phosphorus compounds so, if not pure enough, the ore has to be pre-refined to increase the percentage of iron.

The blast furnace lining has to last for many years to save the cost of replacing it and to minimise shutdown time for replacement work, since the loss of production may cost millions of pounds.

Conditions in the blast furnace

Some of the blast furnace reactions require high temperatures, so a great input of energy is needed. Fortunately, the reaction of carbon with oxygen that gives carbon dioxide provides the energy, since it is an extremely exothermic reaction.

The blasts of hot air which give the blast furnace its name are enriched with oxygen. The concentration of oxygen, higher than in air, speeds up the reaction. The faster the rate of reaction, the more the energy produced by the exothermic reactions. In this way, the high temperatures are easier to maintain.

The carbon dioxide formed near the base travels upwards through the melt and solids, and is converted into carbon monoxide. See Fig 1.14. It is the carbon monoxide rather than the solid carbon which does most of the reducing of iron ore, since gases react faster than solids. The use of pelletised reactants ensures that carbon monoxide comes into very close contact with the iron(III) oxide. This helps to speed up the reaction.

Finally, there are the reactions involving limestone. Limestone (calcium carbonate) decomposes to calcium oxide (lime) and carbon dioxide in the heat of the furnace:

$$CaCO_3 \rightarrow CaO + CO_2$$

The calcium oxide removes impurities such as sand (silicon(IV) oxide) as liquid slag. The reaction for sand is:

$$CaO + SiO_2 \rightarrow CaSiO_3$$

Fortunately, the reaction products slag and iron can be removed easily. Since they are both liquids in the high temperatures of the furnace, they can be run off. Conveniently, the less dense slag floats on top of the more dense iron, so they are tapped off separately at different levels.

The production of iron is a **continuous process**. In continuous processes, raw materials are constantly added and the products are continually removed. A continuous process is a very efficient and cost-saving way of producing materials in large quantities. By comparison, in **batch processes**, the reactor vessel must be closed down and reset to make another batch. This is expensive because there is 'dead time' when no product is being produced. However, a range of products can be made in the same vessel, although care is exercised to ensure no contamination occurs. For small quantities, the batch process is more cost effective.

J The temperature of the furnace may reach 2000 ºC, especially near the base. Most materials melt at this temperature. What properties does the lining material of the blast furnace need to have?

K Explain why companies prefer to use continuous processes instead of batch processes whenever possible.

L (a) Coke, iron ore and limestone are mixed and ground together. Suggest why this is done.

(b) The powder produced is heated (sintered) to make loosely packed pellets. What is the advantage of having pellets rather than powder in a blast furnace?

Disposal of waste

The waste gases and slag could cause pollution problems, but ways have been found to minimise them. Much of the slag goes to build roads and make cement. Some of it is even used to insulate houses: Rockwool, used for non-flammable loft insulation, is produced by blowing air into the molten slag to make it light and fluffy.

10 MAKING STEEL FROM IRON

Steel – a very versatile material

Iron from a blast furnace is impure, brittle and not very strong, so most iron produced is changed immediately into steel. Steel is the name given to countless **alloys** containing iron, carbon and usually small amounts of other elements.

> **An alloy is a mixture of two or more elements, at least one being a metal, which are mixed when they are molten and allowed to cool down to form a uniform solid.**

Alloys have different properties from the elements that make them up. It is the addition of different elements to iron that changes the properties of the alloy, making steels such versatile materials.

Below: **fractured bones are held together by permanent steel pins**

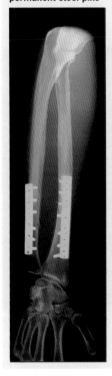

Above: **the Thames Barrier is mainly steel and concrete**

Right: **well over half the components of a typical car are made of steel, including the body shell, clutch plates and engine**

Left: **Fruit Drop at Blackpool is made of steel to meet high safety levels**

Right: **many utensils are made of stainless steel**

Fig 1.15 **Different types of steel have properties that iron lacks, giving steel a very wide range of uses**

Carbon steels

As the name suggests, carbon steels are alloys of mainly iron with some carbon. The sheet steel used in car bodies contains just 0.2 per cent of carbon, and this amount makes it easy to bend and shape.

As the carbon content of steel is increased, the steel becomes stronger and more rigid. Most of the steel used to construct a bridge, which needs some flexibility, contains between 0.3 and 0.6 per cent carbon. The steel used in drill bits has to be very hard and contains up to 1.5 per cent carbon. It is tempting to think that by increasing the carbon content the steel would carry on getting stronger. Unfortunately this is not the case, and at just 4 per cent carbon, steel becomes very brittle.

Alloy steels

Alloy steels are steels which contain one or more other metals. These metals include manganese, tungsten, chromium and vanadium. Stainless steels are probably the best known alloy steels, containing at least 12 per cent chromium. The chromium increases steel's rust resistance. A common stainless steel is called 18–8 and contains 18 per cent chromium and 8 per cent nickel. Steels containing tungsten are very hard wearing. Adding molybdenum (with certain other elements), enables drill bits to retain their cutting edge, even when hot.

Steel making

The main process for converting iron to steel is the **basic oxygen process**. Impure iron from a blast furnace is known as pig iron and contains about 4 per cent carbon, together with other elements such as silicon, manganese and phosphorus. To convert the iron into steel, the carbon content is lowered and other elements are removed by reacting them with oxygen. An oxygen lance is lowered into the basic oxygen furnace (Fig 1.17) and oxygen is blown into the molten iron at twice the speed of sound.

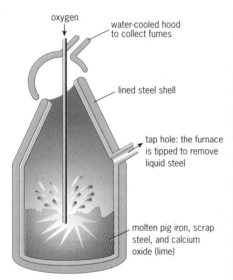

Fig 1.16 **The arrangement for the basic oxygen process**

Fig 1.17 **The oxygen furnace for making steel being charged with iron**

The impurity elements form oxides. These are some of the reactions:

$$2C + O_2 \rightarrow 2CO$$
$$2Mn + O_2 \rightarrow 2MnO$$
$$4P + 5O_2 \rightarrow P_4O_{10}$$
$$Si + O_2 \rightarrow SiO_2$$

Being a gas, carbon monoxide bubbles out of the liquid mixture. SiO_2 and P_4O_{10} are acidic oxides and are removed by adding lime (calcium oxide) which is a basic oxide – hence the name 'basic' in the basic oxygen process. They react to form a slag that floats on the top of the molten steel.

These chemical reactions with oxygen are highly exothermic and generate great heat, so the reactions inside the furnace keep the contents molten. In fact, the temperature has to be stopped from getting too high. Scrap iron and steel are added to prevent the mixture from overheating because as it melts it takes in energy – melting is an endothermic process.

If the temperature rose unchecked, then the rate of the exothermic reactions would increase, causing yet more energy to be released and making the reaction faster still. Eventually, the process would get out of control and the furnace lining would be damaged.

It is the job of industrial chemists known as metallurgists to ensure that the reaction conditions of the steel making process are optimised. They also establish and monitor the best mix of elements for a particular type of steel to match customer demand.

> **?**
> **M** Adding scrap to the oxygen furnace is a way of regulating temperature.
>
> Suggest another reason why using scrap iron and steel is a good idea.

Steel – matching supply and demand

Steel manufacture is a business, and so the production of steels must be tied closely with long-term planning to sell it. An industrial plant the size of an iron and steel works cannot run economically if you have to start and stop manufacture to match short-term demands. A blast furnace works efficiently only if it is running all the time. But if furnace production is stopped, the furnace has to cool down and then be cleaned out. Starting it up again is a costly and difficult process that requires a lot of energy. But if production of steel outstrips demand, the only economic solution may be to close down the whole steel works.

So to keep steel works operating, the staff in charge of sales are constantly searching for new markets. See the Feature box.

Saving on energy

We have seen that steel making has very expensive energy requirements. About 15 per cent of the cost of making steel is spent on the energy that the process consumes, so that companies are continually on the look-out for ways to make savings.

Building the steel works next to the blast furnace allows molten iron to be used as soon as it is made. Since the iron doesn't cool much between processes, its energy is not wasted. Also, the energy from hot waste gases and slag can be transferred to other parts of the operation. The waste gases can even be burnt to release energy.

BRITISH STEEL LINKS WITH HONG KONG

AMID A WORLDWIDE DECLINE in steel production, British Steel won a huge contract to supply steel for building the Tsing Ma Bridge linking Kowloon and Hong Kong Island to Hong Kong's new island airport, which was opened in 1997.

The 54 000 tonnes of steel ordered was twice the amount used in the Humber bridge (which still has the widest span between towers in the world). This amount was needed since the Tsing Ma Bridge has two three-lane carriageways above two railway lines and two emergency roads.

The lower deck is fully enclosed, protected by stainless steel sheet to deflect the gusts of up to 83 metres a second that can occur during typhoons that hit Hong Kong. The cables suspending the bridge from its towers could circle the Earth four and a half times.

Fig 1.17 **The Tsing Ma Bridge linking Hong Kong to its airport**

A worker on the project at the time described it as 'one of those unique engineering and construction projects that manages to combine practicality, romance and adventure in one package'.

11 ECONOMICS AND THE UK CHEMICAL INDUSTRY

With exports worth £12 billion, the chemical industry as a whole is the largest export earner in the UK. So it is not surprising that some of Britain's largest companies are in the chemical industry. They contribute towards our quality of life by supplying the products we buy and the raw materials used to make them, and by providing jobs and earning income for the nation.

The chemical principles of energy changes, yield and rate of reactions have been described for iron and steel making. For any industrially produced chemical, the same factors influence manufacturing costs. Other economic decisions that have to be made include which raw materials to start from, and which chemical reactions to use. These are some of the economic principles applied:

- **Raw materials**. These must be as cheap as possible.

- **Location of the plant**. This should be as near as possible to its raw materials. It should have good rail and road links. Iron and steel plants are often close to ports for easy export and import. It should be near an appropriately skilled workforce.

- **Type of process**. Research chemists are constantly seeking processes that minimise costs.

- **Energy costs**. The enormous amount of energy that iron and steel making requires is a significant part of the total cost of a finished product. In all chemical production processes, energy transfer is carefully controlled to optimise its use.

- **Safety.** Before any new plant is built or any existing plant modified, the safety of the workers on the site and the people who live in the area are given top priority. All potential risks are assessed and minimised in the design, from the possibility of a pipe leaking to the threat of an explosion.

- **Pollution control.** A growing public awareness of the problems of the emission of gases and other pollutants means that industry must take steps to reduce pollution. However, this increases process costs.

The costs of a process are either **fixed** or **variable costs**. The fixed costs are incurred whether one tonne or one million tonnes are manufactured. These include the capital costs of setting up the plant, the rent, rates and payment of any loans, and depreciation in value of the plant. Variable costs change with output. If there is no production, then these will not be incurred. Examples of variable costs include the costs of raw materials, fuel, labour and transport.

Do the benefits of a chemical plant outweigh disadvantages?

This a question which has no right answer. We are ready to enjoy the tremendous benefits that manufactured chemicals have brought us – giving us the polymers in our clothing, the paint on our buildings, the materials which make these buildings, the fertilisers that help us to grow more food for more people, the medicinal drugs which combat so many potentially fatal diseases – and so the list goes on.

The chemical industry is part of our society and we have come to need many of its products. However, for every chemical process there are costs as well as benefits. But any *cost/benefit analysis* depends on the viewpoint of the person doing the analysis.

We can easily recognise the costs of damage to the environment through chemical pollution. There is no doubt that nowadays we are more aware than we used to be of pollution and its consequences and that chemists have improved detection methods. We have seen that pressure to take action has led to more effective laws to control emissions of toxic and other waste products.

Now that we understand much more about the consequences of pollution, in designing new chemical plants a main concern is the possible effect on the environment. Also, as a society, we need to decide which chemicals are essential to maintain a healthy and comfortable lifestyle, and which are not.

Minimising environmental damage

Returning to iron and steel making, we said at the outset of this chapter that no other process had so transformed the world around us. Yet mining the iron ore can devastate large areas of land with its quarries and large spoil heaps. Likewise, slag from the blast furnace and steel making used to be piled high. Now it is used to make cement. So not only is the Humber bridge made of British steel, the concrete in it is also made of British steel slag!

The chemist is at the forefront of pollution control, both in its detection and in the development of control procedures. The waste gases from the blast furnace are harmful, so it is chemists who have developed ways to reduce these emissions. Carbon monoxide is a waste gas from iron and steel manufacture and is toxic to all vertebrates. Any trace of sulphur, particularly in iron sulphide ores, leads to the production of sulphur dioxide which causes acid rain (see more about atmospheric pollutants on pages 167 and 170).

The chemical industry still suffers from a negative public image, despite the essential nature of many of its products. But a world without manufactured chemicals would now be unimaginable.

■ See question 2.

SUMMARY

After studying this chapter, you should know and understand the following.

■ A **molecular formula** tells you how many atoms of each element there are in a molecule of the compound.

■ The term **formula** applies to ionic compounds as well as molecules. It is the number of atoms of the different elements making up the smallest complete unit of a substance.

■ In the **relative atomic mass**, A_r, scale, the masses of atoms are measured relative to one atom of carbon-12 which is given an A_r of exactly 12. For a more complete definition, see page 29.

■ The **relative molecular mass**, M_r, is calculated using the relative atomic mass scale using the same standard, carbon-12. The A_r value of each atom in the molecule are added together to give the M_r. When dealing with ionic compounds we use the term **relative formula mass**.

■ The **amount** is the number of particles (atoms, molecules, ions, electrons etc) in a substance. The unit of amount is the mole (mol).

■ The **mole** is defined as the amount of substance which contains as many particles as there are atoms in exactly 12 g of carbon-12.

■ The relative atomic mass in grams of any element contains one mole of atoms.

$$\text{amount in moles} = \frac{\text{mass in grams}}{\text{mass of one mole (in grams)}}$$

■ The **Avogadro constant** is the number of atoms or molecules in one mole which is 6.02×10^{23}.

■ The **theoretical yield** is the maximum amount obtainable if all the reactants are converted to products. This is calculated from the balanced equation:

$$\text{percentage yield} = \frac{\text{actual yield}}{\text{theoretical yield}} \times 100\%$$

■ The **rate of reaction** is affected by temperature, pressure, concentration, surface area of reactants and catalysts.

■ The **enthalpy change**, ΔH, is a measure of the transfer of energy into or out of a reacting system at constant pressure.

■ **Exothermic reactions** give out energy and cause the temperature of the surroundings to rise. ΔH is negative.

■ **Endothermic reactions** take in energy and causes the temperature of the surroundings to fall. ΔH is positive.

■ Iron ore, coke, limestone and air are the raw materials used in a blast furnace. The iron ore is reduced to iron by carbon monoxide. A high carbon content makes the iron very brittle.

■ Steels are alloys of iron with carbon and other elements such as manganese and vanadium. The percentage of the elements alloyed with iron gives a particular steel its unique properties.

1

a) The following hydrocarbon is a constituent of the fuel used in road vehicles. Give its molecular formula.

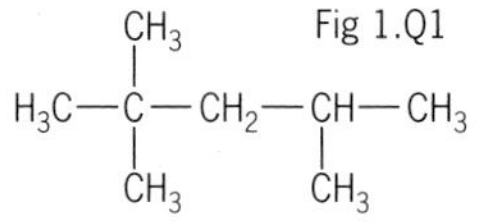

Fig 1.Q1

$$H_3C—\underset{\underset{CH_3}{|}}{\overset{\overset{CH_3}{|}}{C}}—CH_2—\underset{\underset{CH_3}{|}}{CH}—CH_3$$

b) Using the molecular formula, write an equation for the complete combustion of the hydrocarbon **X** to form carbon dioxide and water.

2 The principal source of zinc is the sulphide, ZnS, major deposits of which are found in Australia, Canada and the USA. After concentration, the ore is roasted in air to produce zinc oxide, which may then be thermally reduced using coke.

a) Write an equation for the reactions that occur when:
   (i) zinc sulphide is roasted in air to produce zinc oxide and sulphur dioxide,
   (ii) zinc oxide is reduced by coke.

b) Approximately 200 000 tonnes of zinc are produced annually in the UK. What mass of zinc sulphide is required to obtain this?

c) Give the name of an environmental problem that can arise from roasting zinc sulphide ores.

d) Discuss the major factors which would influence the location of a zinc producing plant

e) Give **two** variable costs in the production of zinc.

[AEB Summer 1996 Paper 3 0654/3, q.7]

3 The table below gives the accurate masses of two atoms.

	^1H	^{12}C
Mass/g	1.6734×10^{-24}	1.9925×10^{-23}

a) Calculate accurate values for the mass of one mole of each atom.
(The Avogadro constant, L = 6.0225×10^{23}.)

b) Why is ^{12}C referred to when defining the relative atomic mass of an element?

4 In the human body, oxygen, carbon and hydrogen are the three most abundant elements by mass.

Element	Per cent by mass
oxygen	65.0
carbon	18.0
hydrogen	10.0

If a person weighs 50.0 kg calculate the moles of atoms of each element and state which one is the most abundant in terms of its atoms.

5 A coal-fired power station is fitted with a Flue Gas Desulphurisation (FGD) plant, which removes some of the sulphur dioxide from the waste gases.

In the FGD plant, the waste gases are treated with powdered limestone, producing calcium sulphite, $CaSO_3$.

This is then oxidised by air to form calcium sulphate, $CaSO_4$.

$$CaCO_3(s) + SO_2(g) \rightarrow CaSO_3(s) + CO_2(g)$$
$$\tfrac{1}{2}O_2(g) + CaSO_3(s) \rightarrow CaSO_4(s)$$

a) Calculate the maximum mass of sulphur dioxide which could be removed by 3.0×10^5 t of limestone in the FGD plant. (t = tonne = 1000 kg)

b) Calculate the maximum mass of calcium sulphate which would be produced from 3.0×10^5 t of limestone.

c) The FGD plant removes 90% of the sulphur dioxide from the waste gases.

Calculate the mass of sulphur dioxide which is released into the atmosphere each year by this power station when 5.0×10^6 t of coal are burned, assuming that this coal contains 2.0% by mass of sulphur.

[UCLES March 1996 Sciences: Trends and Patterns, q.6]

6 In 1979 the Nobel prize for Chemistry was shared by Herbert Brown (American) and George Wittig (German) for their work on the development of boron and phosphorus compounds. Brown used the gas diborane, B_2H_6, to prepare new organic compounds. One of the methods of preparing diborane involves this reaction:

$$3NaBH_4 + 4BF_3 \rightarrow 3NaBF_4 + 2B_2H_6$$

If 56.7g of $NaBH_4$ reacts with an excess of BF_3 to produce 20.7g of B_2H_6, what is the percentage yield of diborane?

7 One of the ways of providing hot food in war torn or starvation areas is by the reaction of magnesium and water.

$$Mg + 2H_2O \rightarrow Mg(OH)_2 + H_2 \quad \Delta H = -352.9 \text{ kJ mol}^{-1}$$

The food to be heated is stored in a pouch made of aluminium and plastic. When required it is placed inside a bag which contains magnesium powder and a small amount of water is added. The reaction releases enough energy to make the food hot.

a) Explain why, at a given temperature, magnesium powder reacts faster than strips of magnesium ribbon.

b) Sketch an energy level diagram for this reaction.

8

a) **(i)** What type of chemical reaction is always involved in the extraction of a metal from its ore?
   (ii) Which element is most likely to be combined with a metal in its ore?

b) **(i)** Give an overall equation to show the industrial extraction of iron from its ore.
   (ii) What environmental problem may arise during this extraction even if pure iron ore is used as the starting material?
   (iii) Explain what further environmental problem might occur if the ore was contaminated with sulphide ores.

[NEAB February 1996 Further Inorganic Chemistry Module test CH05, q.1]

REACTIONS, EQUATIONS AND ENERGY

This chapter describes terms that relate to amounts of substances, reactions and the use of equations to describe reactions. You will need to understand all these concepts for your studies throughout the book. The concepts are introduced through the description of iron and steel making, with additional information about the economic and environmental implications of activities in the chemical industry.

Find out what you need to know for the syllabus you are following, then study the Chapter map to check that you understand the concepts and topics described, and the way that they are connected to each other.

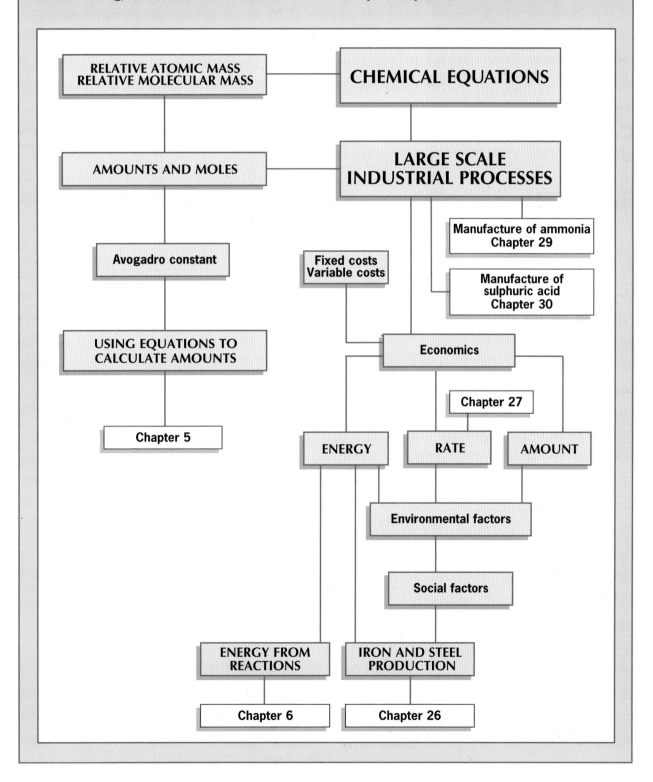

2 The nucleus and radioactivity

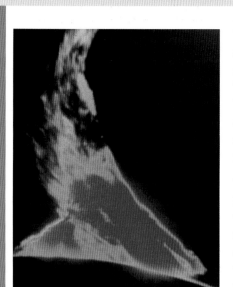

Jet of glowing gas on the surface of the Sun
– evidence of nuclear fusion at its core

THE EIGHT MOST abundant elements of the Earth's crust are oxygen, silicon, aluminium, iron, calcium, sodium, potassium and magnesium. Hydrogen is the ninth, at less than 1 per cent. Yet 92 per cent of all atoms in the Universe are hydrogen, 7 per cent are helium, and only 1 per cent are all the other elements. So the Earth is very rich in its range of elements, much richer than some other parts of the Universe, and we may ask: Why are the elements so unevenly distributed?

The reason lies in the way the Universe, and later the Earth, first began. It is generally thought that the Universe started with tremendous fury in the Big Bang, about 15 thousand million years ago, when a super-hot, super-dense 'soup' of sub-atomic particles exploded with unimaginable force. It was then that hydrogen atoms were first created. Some of these fused to give helium, and so a second element was born.

Then, after about a thousand million years, stars began to form. Gaseous hydrogen with a little helium came together in local areas, contracting and becoming denser. The temperature rose to levels at which other light elements could form, and even more heat was produced. Stars continue to be born in this way from the dispersed material of the Universe.

The heavier elements appeared only in the relatively few very massive stars. Those with a much larger mass than the Sun became unstable after a few million years and exploded, propelling atoms out into the cosmos, to become the raw material of a second generation of stars with the heavier elements already formed.

It is thought that the Solar System was formed from such recycled material about 4500 million years ago. The Sun itself is a gigantic fusion reactor, its heat and light helping to sustain life on Earth. The Earth itself contains some ninety light and heavy elements from the remains of earlier stars. In its intensely hot core, it retains some of the heat from when it was formed. More heat is produced by radioactive elements which decay and release energy. In fact, as well as the heat of the core and from the Sun, this decay process is significant in maintaining the Earth's present-day heat balance.

A history of ideas about the elements

In 580 BC, the Ancient Greek philosopher Thales suggested that water was the fundamental 'element' from which all matter in the Universe was composed. Two hundred years later, Aristotle added earth, air and fire, proposing that four elements made up the world, with a fifth 'aether', making up the heavens. This idea persisted for

Fig 2.1 **Robert Boyle (1627–1691)**

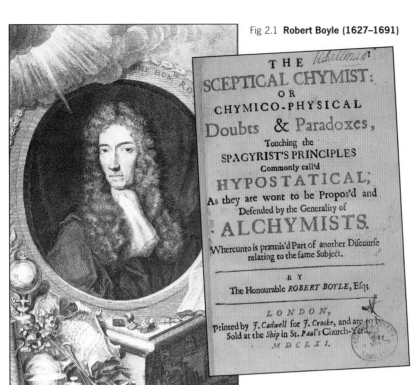

Fig 2.2 **The title page of Boyle's book,** *The Sceptical Chymist*. **In it he first introduced the idea of the 'chemist'. He also proposed the idea that elements cannot be changed into anything simpler and that they could be discovered by experimentation**

Fig 2.3 **John Dalton (1766–1844) and the symbols he used to represent the elements which were known at the time**

almost 2000 years until Robert Boyle published a book called *The Sceptical Chymist* in 1661.

Boyle's book was a turning point in chemistry. It put forward the first modern concept of an **element** as something that cannot be changed into anything simpler. The book also marked the beginning of chemistry as an experimental science, since Boyle was urging chemists to carry out practical investigations rather than merely observe, think and make deductions, as the Greeks had done.

His advice was heeded. In 1803, the English chemist, John Dalton, summed up a hundred and fifty years of progress through experiment with his **atomic theory**. He used the Greek word 'atomos', which means 'cannot be cut', to describe the particles which make up elements. The idea that all matter was made up of tiny, indivisible particles had been proposed in 450 BC, again by an Ancient Greek, Democritus. But now, Dalton could back it up with experimental results. These are the main points of his theory:

- Atoms are indivisible and indestructible.

- All atoms of the same element have identical mass and identical chemical properties.

- When atoms react, they join together to form 'compound atoms' (now called molecules).

Today, we still hold Dalton's view of an element as a substance composed of only one type of atom. So the element iron is made up of only iron atoms, and they are different from copper atoms which make up the element copper.

We now know that an atom can be subdivided into smaller parts called **sub-atomic particles**, discovered since Dalton's time. But the atom is still the smallest particle with all the *chemical* properties of an element, and Dalton's atomic theory provided the foundation on which other scientists have built.

1 STRUCTURE AND PROPERTIES OF THE ATOM – DISCOVERIES

The electron

The first sub-atomic particle to be identified was the electron. In the 1870s, scientists doing electrical experiments passed an electric current through a gas at very low pressure (Fig 2.4), and discovered that a ray was emitted from the cathode (the conducting material connected to the negative pole of a battery). The experimenters suggested that this **cathode ray** (which produces the picture on our television screens) was made up of negatively charged particles.

In 1897, J. J. Thomson was working at the Cavendish Laboratories in Cambridge, when he found evidence that cathode rays were indeed made up of particles which he called **electrons**. He calculated the mass of an electron to be two thousand times lighter than the hydrogen atom. In 1906, this work gained him a Nobel Prize.

Fig 2.4 **A simplified diagram of a cathode ray tube**

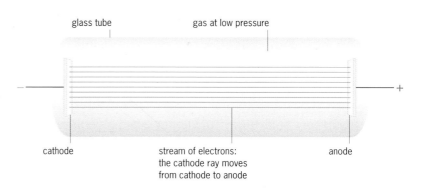

glass tube   gas at low pressure

cathode   stream of electrons: the cathode ray moves from cathode to anode   anode

Radioactivity

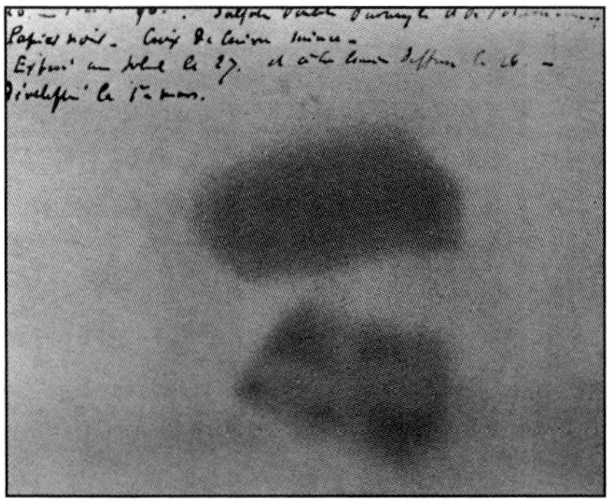

While Thomson was experimenting on cathode rays, another momentous discovery was being made. The Frenchman Henri Becquerel was investigating crystals which phosphoresce – that is, chemicals that glow in the dark after being exposed to sunlight. Becquerel assumed that sunlight was causing the crystals to give out X-rays, which had just been discovered (see page 27). X-rays were not understood then, which is why they were called 'X'. But they were known to make a dark blurred image, called 'fogging', on photographic film, even when it was sealed in opaque black paper.

Becquerel decided to test his assumption. He put crystals of a uranium salt on top of a photographic film which was sealed in black paper that kept out all light. He let the Sun shine on the crystals and, as he expected, when the film was developed, it had become fogged.

On 26 February 1896, clouds shut out the Sun, so Becquerel just put the crystals, unexposed to sunlight, in a drawer on top of some sealed photographic film. Three days later, he decided to develop the film anyway, just to check that there was no image. To his amazement, he found a clear area of darkening on the film below the crystals (Fig 2.5). He concluded that some unknown kind of radiation not dependent on the Sun must have come from the crystals that could pass through the black paper. It took the work of others to discover more about this radiation.

Fig 2.5 **Becquerel's photographic film on which he had put crystals unexposed to sunlight: the first recorded evidence of radioactivity**

?

A What was the control experiment in Becquerel's work with phosphorescent crystals?

With her husband Pierre, Marie Curie began to study this phenomenon. She investigated other uranium compounds and found that they too gave off this new radiation. She called it **radioactivity**. (Radioactivity is the spontaneous breakup of atomic nuclei, giving off rays called radiation.)

The Curies observed that pitchblende, an ore known to contain uranium, was much more radioactive than they expected from the uranium in the ore alone. The Curies later discovered two new radioactive elements, radium and polonium. It was radium that gave pitchblende its high radioactivity. The radiation of radium had so much energy that it burned the skin and, while uranium fogged film after a few hours, radium did so instantly. Marie Curie also discovered another radioactive element, thorium.

Ernest Rutherford, a New Zealander working under Thomson at Cambridge, also investigated radioactivity. Over several years of work, he found that the radioactivity which Becquerel had first observed was composed of three main types of radiation. Rutherford named the first two **alpha (α)** and **beta (β)** radiation. When the third was eventually discovered this was called **gamma (γ)**. (See Fig 2.7.)

Fig 2.6 **Marie Curie (1867–1934) was the first person to receive two Nobel Prizes. The first was for physics (1903) which she shared with her husband and Becquerel for work on radioactivity. The second was for chemistry (1911) for her discovery of radium and polonium (named after her homeland, Poland)**

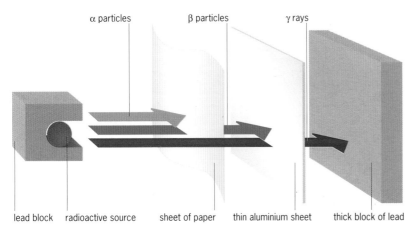

Fig 2.7 **The different penetrating properties of the three radiations. A lead block has to be about 10 cm thick to halt gamma rays**

Rutherford showed that alpha radiation was composed of particles which were four times heavier than hydrogen. In fact, they are the same as positively charged helium atoms. (We refer to them as helium nuclei.) The beta particles were soon found to be very high energy electrons, which of course are negatively charged. Gamma rays were identified later as electromagnetic rays similar to X-rays, but of much higher energy. Being electromagnetic rays, gamma rays were found to have no particle properties, and therefore no mass. You can find out more about radioactivity on pages 33–40.

B Fig 2.8 shows how the three different types of radiation are affected by an electric field. **(a)** What do you deduce about the charge on the different types of radiation? **(b)** Why do you think the beta particle is deflected so much more than the alpha particle?

Fig 2.8 **Deflection of the three types of radiations by charged plates**

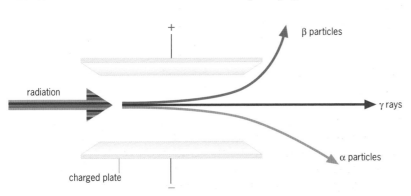

Rutherford's model of the atom

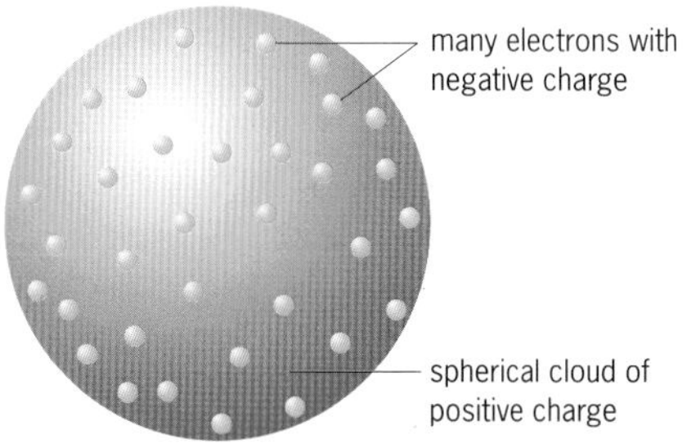

When J. J. Thomson identified the first sub-atomic particle as the electron, he put forward his **model of the atom**. (A scientist suggests a model to explain observations, and so long as this model explains all the known observations, the scientific community accepts the model.) In Thomson's model of the atom, negatively charged electrons with mass were embedded in a sphere of positive charge which had no mass. It was known that atoms had no net charge, that they were neutral, so the positive charge was needed to balance the charge of the electrons. To account for the mass of atoms, Thomson assumed that they must all have thousands of electrons. His model was known as the 'plum pudding' model because the electrons were pictured like raisins in a pudding.

Fig 2.9 **Thomson's plum pudding model of the atom. Negative and positive charge cancels out**

Rutherford's scattering experiment

At Manchester University, Rutherford set up his own research group, which included Hans Geiger and Ernest Marsden. In their

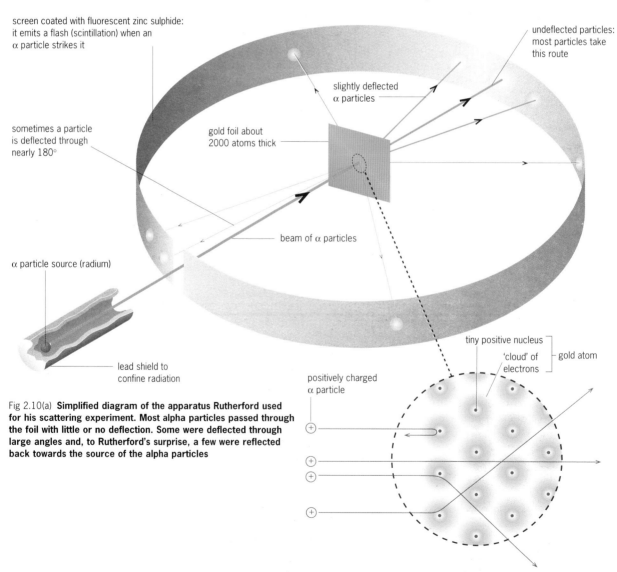

Fig 2.10(a) **Simplified diagram of the apparatus Rutherford used for his scattering experiment. Most alpha particles passed through the foil with little or no deflection. Some were deflected through large angles and, to Rutherford's surprise, a few were reflected back towards the source of the alpha particles**

Fig 2.10(b) **What happened, not what Rutherford expected: The alpha particles which passed through undeflected were travelling through the empty space between the nuclei of gold atoms. The closer the particle came to the nucleus, the larger the deflection. Those which came straight back had been in head-on collision with a gold nucleus**

investigations into the structure of the atom, they fired alpha particles at gold foil, using the equipment shown in Fig 2.10(a). From Thomson's model of the atom, it was expected that a few alpha particles would be deflected slightly from a straight route when they passed through foils. Even the thinnest foils were about 2000 atoms thick, and some of the alpha particles were sure to collide with electrons. Marsden was asked to see if any alpha particles were scattered through large angles.

Rutherford said, 'I may tell you that I did not believe they would be, since we knew that the alpha particle was a very fast, massive particle, with a great deal of energy.'

But then a few days later Geiger announced that some alpha particles had been recorded which bounced back from gold foil. Rutherford recalled, 'It was quite the most incredible event that has happened to me in my life. It was almost as incredible as if you fired a fifteen inch [artillery] shell at a piece of tissue paper, and it came back and hit you.'

It was now clear to Rutherford that Thomson's model of the atom could not be correct. If it were, then the alpha particles should have shot through the foil with hardly any deflection. But one in 8000 had apparently been halted in its tracks and deflected back. Most particles passed through without any deflection, and Rutherford concluded that they were travelling through empty space. The positively charged alpha particles deflected through larger angles must have encountered (and been repelled by) another positive charge of considerable mass, and this he called the **nucleus.**

From the angles of deflection and other data, Rutherford calculated that the radius of the gold nucleus was 10^{-14} metre. (We now know that the radius is closer to 10^{-15} metre.) He calculated, too, that the radius of the atom was approximately 10^{-10} metre. This means that the nucleus was 100 000 times smaller in diameter than the atom – an astonishing difference. If a full stop on this page represented the nucleus, then the outer limit of the atom would be about 25 metres away. No wonder that only a very few alpha particles were seen to come back.

C A tennis ball has a radius of 3.1 cm. Assume it represents a nucleus. What is the radius of the atom on this scale to the nearest kilometre?

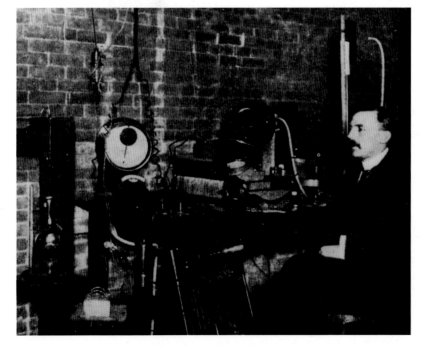

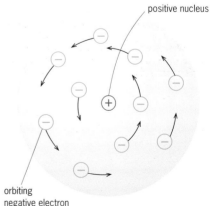

Fig 2.11(a) **Ernest Rutherford (1871–1937) in his laboratory**

positive nucleus

orbiting negative electron

Fig 2.11(b) **Rutherford's model of the atom proposed after the scattering rexperiment shown in Fig 2.10(a)**

Rutherford now proposed his model of the atom – a minute, central nucleus containing all the positive charge of the atom and almost all of the mass, surrounded by empty space in which electrons orbited the nucleus, rather like planets round the Sun.

This model of the atom raised some difficult questions. In particular, since opposite charges attract, why didn't the electrons just fall into the nucleus? The Danish scientist, Niels Bohr, came up with the answer to this question, and you can read more about this in Chapter 3. The idea of the minute, central, positive nucleus is fundamental to all models of the atom accepted today.

Protons and neutrons

The proton was the next sub-atomic particle to be discovered, and again the alpha particle was the tool used in research. When alpha particles were fired through hydrogen gas, positive particles emerged which were about the same mass as the hydrogen atom. In 1919, Rutherford said that these same particles could be knocked out of other atoms, suggesting that they must be present in the other atoms. He gave the name **protons** to these positive particles. The model of a nucleus made up of protons was now taking shape.

A year later, Rutherford suggested that protons were not the only type of particle in the nucleus, and that there must be particles of equal mass but neutral charge in the nucleus as well. In suggesting this, Rutherford was almost a lone voice in the scientific community. Then, in 1932, James Chadwick, another of his research team, was able to show that this neutral particle did exist.

Chadwick fired alpha particles at beryllium atoms. Instruments which detected charged particles were unable to detect any radiation, as in Fig 2.12(a). Yet when paraffin wax was put between the beryllium and the detector, a shower of protons was detected, as in Fig 2.12(b). Rutherford guessed that the protons were coming from the paraffin because some sort of radiation was hitting it. He said this radiation was like the effect of an invisible man who cannot be seen directly, but who is known to be there because he collides with other people in a crowd.

The invisible particle in the radiation of Chadwick's experiment – with no charge and with mass equal to the proton – was named the **neutron**. In this way, protons and neutrons became known to scientists.

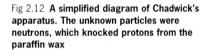

Fig 2.12 **A simplified diagram of Chadwick's apparatus. The unknown particles were neutrons, which knocked protons from the paraffin wax**

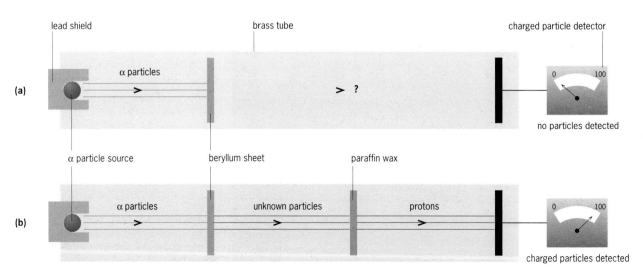

2 DESCRIBING THE ATOM

Atomic number (proton number)

Five years before Rutherford announced the discovery of the proton, Henry Moseley, another of his research team, had been working with X-rays. These were discovered in 1895 by Wilhelm Röntgen in Germany. Röntgen had been trying to make substances fluoresce by bombarding them with cathode rays (streams of high energy electrons). Fluorescing substances absorb energy of one wavelength, usually outside the visible spectrum, and give out energy at another wavelength which is visible. (For more information about the spectrum, refer to Chapter 3.) Some substances emitted what Röntgen called an X-ray. The X-ray could penetrate some matter, and blackened photographic film, as Röntgen was able to show by making an image of his wife's hand.

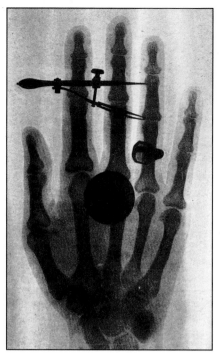

Fig 2.13 **The first X-ray image of a human taken by Röntgen of his wife's hand, showing her wedding ring, a coin and a compass**

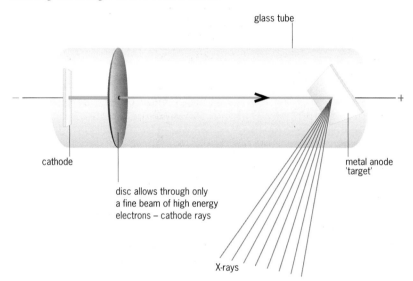

Fig 2.14 **Moseley's experiment, in which he bombarded different metal targets with a beam of high energy electrons – cathode rays – and measured the frequency of X-rays produced**

Moseley bombarded different metal targets with cathode rays (Fig 2.14), and measured the frequency of the X-rays which emerged from the anode. Frequency increased with the increase in mass of the metal atom. From Moseley's results, Rutherford calculated the positive charge on the nucleus, which he called the **atomic number**.

The atomic number is the number of protons in the atom.

It has the symbol **Z**. It is also known as the **proton number.**

The atomic number tells us:

- what the element is: only atoms of the same element have the same atomic number
- the element's numbered position in the Periodic Table: the Periodic Table is arranged in atomic number order (see Chapter 19)
- the number of electrons in a neutral atom: the charge on an electron is equal, but opposite, to the charge on a proton

Information we now know about the three fundamental particles in an atom is summarised in Table 2.1.

D Sodium is the eleventh element in the Periodic Table. Work out its atomic number, the number of protons in its nucleus and the number of electrons which orbit outside the nucleus.

Particle	Symbol	Relative mass	Relative charge	Location
Proton	^1_1p	1	+1	in nucleus
Neutron	^1_0n	1	0	in nucleus
Electron	$^0_{-1}e$	0.00055	−1	orbiting nucleus

Table 2.1 **Some properties of the three main sub-atomic particles**

Mass numbers (nucleon numbers) and isotopes

The mass of the atom is almost entirely the mass of the protons and neutrons in its nucleus. Even the 92 electrons in an atom of uranium will have hardly any effect on its mass. Since protons and neutrons contribute to an atom's mass, we call the total of both in an atom the **mass number.**

The mass number is the total number of protons and neutrons in the atom.

It has the symbol A.

Because protons and neutrons are constituents of the nucleus, they are referred to as **nucleons.** So A is also known as the **nucleon number.** (Note that the mass number is not the *mass* of a nucleus.)

Mass number = number of protons + number of neutrons

$$A \quad = \quad Z \quad + \quad N$$

Chemists summarise information about an atom in this way:

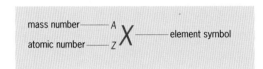

mass number —— A
atomic number —— Z X —— element symbol

The atomic number Z is always the same for a particular element, and it indicates the position of the element in the Periodic Table. But it is often left out of symbol notation, since the element symbol itself identifies the atom.

EXAMPLES

Q An atom of phosphorus has 16 neutrons. Write the full symbol notation for this atom.

A First you need to find out the atomic number of phosphorus. The atomic number, Z, for phosphorus is 15, and its symbol is P.

$A = Z + N$, so $A = 15 + 16 = 31$

The full symbol notation is $^{31}_{15}\text{P}$.

It specifies a particular atomic number and mass number, and hence represents an atom with a particular number of protons and number of neutrons. It is called a **nuclide.**

Q How many protons, neutrons and electrons does the following atom have?

Fluorine, $^{19}_{9}\text{F}$

A $Z = 9$, so the number of protons = 9.
The atom is neutral, so the number of electrons = 9.

$A = 19$, so $Z + N = 19$.

Since $Z = 9$, $N = 10$.

The number of neutrons (N) = 10.

Now try question E in the margin.

?

E Work out the name, mass number, atomic number, number of protons, electrons and neutrons in these nuclides:

$$^{56}_{26}\text{Fe} \text{ and } ^{200}_{80}\text{Hg}$$

The **mass spectrometer** made it possible to determine the masses of atoms very accurately (see Chapter 9), and it became clear that not all atoms of the same element had the same mass. This meant that there had to be a change to Dalton's atomic theory which said that all atoms of an element had an identical mass.

The accurate masses gave rise to the idea of the **isotope.** In Greek, isotope means 'same place', but it is more helpful to think of it as meaning 'alternative'. So we cannot say that an element has only one isotope. An element has to have more than one nuclear arrangement (more than one nuclide) before its atoms can be described as isotopes. A good example is chlorine which has two isotopes.

Table 2.2 shows that isotopes are atoms of the same element and so have the same atomic number. The only difference between the isotopes is their mass number, indicating that the nucleus of one isotope has more neutrons than another. Thus:

Isotopes have the same atomic number, but different mass numbers.

Table 2.2 **The two naturally occurring isotopes of chlorine**

Isotope	$^{35}_{17}$Cl	$^{37}_{17}$Cl
Mass number, A	35	37
Atomic number, Z	17	17
Number of protons	17	17
Number of neutrons, N	18	20
Number of electrons	17	17

Relative atomic mass

Chapter 1 explains that the relative atomic mass, A_r, compares the masses of atoms to the mass of one atom of carbon-12, an isotope of carbon whose relative atomic mass is taken as exactly 12. Its symbol is $^{12}_6$C, or ^{12}C because, as we have seen, once the element is known, the atomic number is fixed. In nature, most elements are composed of isotopes.

The relative mass of an isotope (its relative isotopic mass) is the mass of one atom of that isotope compared to one atom of carbon-12.

Some elements have only one nuclide and, as most of the mass of an atom is made up of protons and neutrons, the mass number is very nearly the same as the relative atomic mass. For example, naturally occurring fluorine has just one nuclide, ^{19}F, and the A_r of fluorine is 18.998 40. But for all except the most accurate work, 19 is used.

?

F Most of the carbon in nature is the isotope $^{12}_6$C. But two other isotopes exist, $^{13}_6$C and $^{14}_6$C. $^{14}_6$C is radioactive and is used to estimate the age of very old objects (see page 37).

Draw out and complete a table similar to Table 2.2 for the isotopes of carbon.

Isotopic abundance

The two isotopes of chlorine are ^{35}Cl and ^{37}Cl. If these two isotopes had the same abundance, then the A_r of chlorine would be 36. But ^{35}Cl has a 75 per cent abundance and ^{37}Cl has a 25 per cent abundance.

This means that for every 100 atoms, 75 have a relative isotopic mass of 35, and 25 have a relative isotopic mass of 37.

The A_r is calculated as follows.

$$A_r \text{ chlorine} = \frac{(75 \times 35)}{100} + \frac{(25 \times 37)}{100} = \frac{3550}{100} = 35.5$$

This leads to the statement:

The relative atomic mass of an element is the average mass of the atom (taking into account all of its isotopes and their abundance) compared to one atom of carbon-12.

Table 2.3 **Isotopes of bromine and magnesium**

Element	Isotope	Abundance
Bromine	^{79}Br	50%
	^{81}Br	50%
Magnesium	^{24}Mg	78.6%
	^{25}Mg	10.1%
	^{26}Mg	11.3%

?

G Study Table 2.3 and work out the A_r of bromine and magnesium.

3 NUCLEAR FUSION

Fig 2.15 **The Sun can be thought of as an immense fusion reactor that provides energy which reaches all parts of the Solar System**

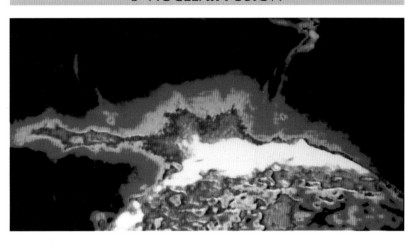

This chapter began by describing the immense energy which powers the Sun and builds up heavier elements starting from hydrogen. This energy comes from the nucleus, or rather countless billions of nuclei. When atoms could be weighed very accurately, their mass was found to be less than the sum of the masses of their sub-atomic particles. Some of the mass appeared to be 'missing', and the missing amount is called the **mass defect**. Einstein explained this in perhaps the most famous equation of all time,

$$E = mc^2$$

E is the energy in joules, m is the missing mass in kilograms, and c is the speed of light in metres per second (3×10^8 m s^{-1}). The missing mass is released as energy when nucleons (the protons and neutrons) fuse to form a nucleus. This energy is called the **binding energy**, and the resulting nucleus is in a lower, more stable energy state than the separate protons and neutrons. The speed of light is an extremely large number squared, and it can be seen that just a small mass produces a very large amount of energy.

EXAMPLE

Q Deuterium is an isotope of hydrogen ($^2_1$H) which is made up of one proton and one neutron. What is the missing mass of deuterium, and what energy is released in its formation?
The actual mass of a deuterium nucleus
= $3.343\ 586 \times 10^{-27}$ kg
Mass of one proton = $1.672\ 623 \times 10^{-27}$ kg
Mass of one neutron = $1.674\ 928 \times 10^{-27}$ kg
Speed of light = 3.00×10^8 ms^{-1}

A The combined mass of the proton and neutron
= $3.347\ 551 \times 10^{-27}$ kg

'Missing' mass = $0.003\ 965 \times 10^{-27}$ kg

Energy released when the proton and neutron fuse = mc^2.

= $0.003\ 965 \times 10^{-27} \times (3.00 \times 10^8)^2$
= 3.5685×10^{-13} J
= 3.57×10^{-13} J (to 3 sig. fig.)

The result in the Example looks a small amount of energy, but it is only for one nucleus. Consider a mole (6.02×10^{23}) of protons and neutrons which fuse; the energy released is 2.15×10^{11} J (215 million kJ). Compare this to burning one mole of carbon in oxygen, which gives a mere 394 kJ. The energy released in chemical reactions is clearly tiny compared to the awesome amount released from nuclear reactions. In the intense heat and pressure at the core of the Sun, for example, when nuclei fuse they release the tremendous amounts of energy we see and feel on Earth.

NUCLEAR FUSION AS AN ENERGY SOURCE?

IT IS THE DREAM of scientists to provide a cheap, unlimited source of power which has harmless by-products, by fusing nuclei and harnessing the vast amounts of energy released. Scientists see deuterium as the most likely candidate since, for every 20 000 hydrogen atoms in water molecules, three are deuterium atoms, so the supply from the oceans of the world is limitless. The reaction proposed is:

$$^2_1H + {}^2_1H \rightarrow {}^3_2He + {}^1_0n + energy$$

The energy released in this reaction is 290 million kilojoules per mole.

In the process, deuterium nuclei stripped of their electrons would have to be brought together. A temperature of 40 million K is needed to overcome the repulsion forces of their positive charges, and sustaining such a high temperature on Earth is the challenge. Scientists are using very powerful lasers and heating with an electric current, but making the dream a reality is likely to be some years off.

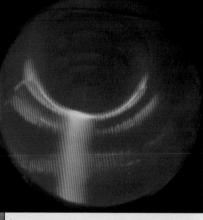

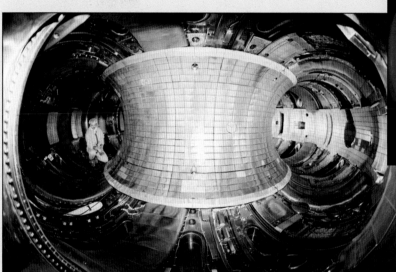

Fig 2.16 **The Tokamak fusion test reactor and deuterium plasma inside it. At the temperatures that exist inside stars, the electrons and nuclei of atoms separate to give a new state of matter called a plasma, and nuclei can fuse. For a fusion reactor to work on Earth, it needs to keep a plasma at a high enough temperature and density long enough for the nuclei to fuse**

4 DESCRIBING NUCLEAR REACTIONS

Representing sub-atomic particles

We have used the standard notation for mass number, symbol A, and atomic number, symbol Z, to represent atoms of elements and their isotopes. Soon we will be looking at nuclear reactions using this notation. These reactions involve atoms, and some also include sub-atomic particles. So that we can balance nuclear equations, we use the system of notation for the sub-atomic particles which matches the one we use for the atoms, shown in Table 2.4.

The diagram in the margin explains what the numbers mean for the sub-atomic particles in Table 2.4.

We know that protons and neutrons determine the mass numbers and atomic numbers of atoms. The information above shows us that the numbers given to the sub-atomic particles are connected with these mass numbers and atomic numbers, and we will find this is useful in writing nuclear equations.

Table 2.4 **Properties of sub-atomic particles**

Particle	Symbol	Relative mass	Relative charge	Location
Proton	^1_1p	1	+1	in nucleus
Neutron	^1_0n	1	0	in nucleus
Electron	$^0_{-1}e$	0.00055	−1	orbiting nucleus

contributes to the mass number of an element
↓
^1_1p
↑
contributes to the atomic number of an element

contributes to the mass number of an element
↓
^1_0n
↑
does not contribute to an element's atomic number

the negligible mass of an electron: nearly zero
↓
$^0_{-1}e$
↑
the charge on an electron

Balancing nuclear equations

The following is an example of a **nuclear equation:**

$$_1^1H \; + \; _1^2H \; \rightarrow \; _2^3He + energy$$

hydrogen   deuterium   helium
isotope

Notice that the mass numbers and the atomic numbers balance. In any nuclear equation, atomic numbers and mass numbers must balance in this way. The major fusion reaction of the Sun is thought to be between nuclei of deuterium and nuclei of another hydrogen isotope, tritium, to give helium and a neutron.

$$_1^2H + _1^3H \rightarrow _2^4He + _1^0n + energy$$

?

H Our Sun is a relatively small star. In stars that are about thirty times bigger than the Sun, much higher temperatures allow helium to fuse to form other elements. Complete this nuclear equation and work out the identity of element X.

$$_?^4He + _?^4He \rightarrow _?^?X + energy$$

ELEMENTS FORMED IN STARS

THE NUCLEAR FUSION reaction in question H is just one of many reactions of large stars, in which the nuclei of light elements fuse to make heavier elements. All these reactions give out energy. But when iron nuclei fuse, they *take in* energy rather than releasing it, and this fusion marks the end for a star. Iron builds up right at its centre and, when fusing, iron nuclei take up too much of the star's energy, the core collapses with incredible speed and force, and its density increases hundreds of millions of times.

Then, the collapsing matter rebounds. In a stupendous explosion, the outer layers of the dying star are blown off into the cosmos and, for a short time, we see the star as a supernova, shining as brightly as an entire galaxy. Look at Fig 2.17 to see Supernova 1987A as its matter was blasted into space, to become part of a new generation of stars.

Our own Sun is a second generation star containing recycled remnants from past supernovae, and the many elements found on Earth come from giant stars that exploded as supernovae billions of years ago.

Fig 2.17 **On 23 February 1987, a brilliant star-like object about 170 000 light years away was first seen from the Earth. A supergiant star had collapsed in on itself and then exploded. It became known as Supernova 1987A. The photo shows the Tarantula nebula, an enormous cloud of ionised gas, and below it, the exploding star**

5 TYPES OF RADIATION, AND INSTABILITY

Three radiations

Radioactivity is the spontaneous breakdown (disintegration) of a nucleus and the emission of radiation. 'Spontaneous' means something that happens without anything seeming to cause it.

Some naturally occurring isotopes are unstable and will break down. As a result, they release at least one of the three principal types of radiation mentioned earlier in the chapter – alpha (α), beta (β), and gamma (γ) radiation. All three can knock electrons off atoms they collide with, and so they are called **ionising radiations**.

Type	Nature	Speed	Charge	Relative mass	Distance travelled in air	Stopped by
α	helium nucleus, He^{2+} or ^4_2He, ie 2 protons + 2 neutrons	10% light speed	+2	4	a few centimetres	paper, skin or clothing
β	high-speed electron speed	90% light speed	−1	0.000 55	a few metres	thin aluminium sheet
γ	electromagnetic wave of high energy	light speed	0	0	a few kilometres	10 cm sheet of lead or several metres of concrete

Table 2.5 **Some properties of the three main types of radiation. See also Fig 2.7, page 23**

What makes some isotopes unstable?

Some nuclei are stable (non-radioactive), while others decay until they achieve stability. For example, a helium nucleus is very stable, and many other proton:neutron combinations are also stable. If we plot the number of protons against the number of neutrons for stable isotopes, as in Fig 2.18, a zone of stability emerges. Radioactive isotopes are usually outside this zone, and get nearer to it as they decay.

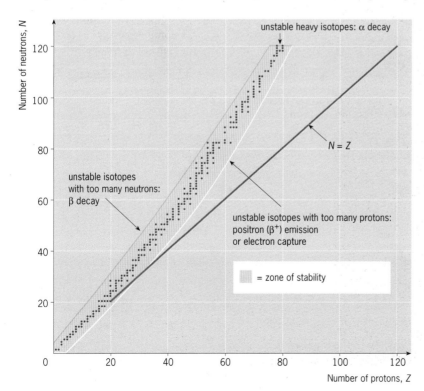

Fig 2.18 **For stable nuclei, the number of neutrons plotted against the number of protons. The stable nuclei lie in the zone of stability. Most radioactive nuclei fall outside this zone and, when they decay, the resulting nuclei move nearer to it.**

A positron has the same mass as an electron but opposite charge.

Electron capture is when a proton captures an orbiting electron and changes into a neutron

Heavy isotopes and alpha radiation

At the upper limit of the stability zone is lead, $^{206}_{82}$Pb. The next element, bismuth, $^{209}_{83}$Bi, is unstable. Any atom with an atomic number greater than 82 will be radioactive, and most of these elements decay by emitting alpha radiation.

Americium, with an atomic number of 95, is the radioactive isotope used in smoke detectors. The nuclear equation for its **alpha decay** is:

$$^{241}_{95}\text{Am} \rightarrow {}^{237}_{93}\text{Np} + {}^{4}_{2}\text{He}$$

americium   neptunium   alpha particle

Study this equation carefully. We have already seen that mass numbers and atomic numbers need to balance on each side of the equation. There are two other points to note.

1 In alpha decay equations, we do not write He^{2+}. This is because the alpha particle comes from the nucleus of a larger atom – it is not a helium atom which has lost electrons. However, alpha particles do eventually gain electrons and become helium atoms.

2 In nuclear equations, we always write the atomic number, even though we know the name of the element.

Now look closely at what happens to americium. It becomes a new element because its atomic number decreases by 2. The event of one element changing into another in this way is called a **transmutation.**

?

I Ernest Rutherford and Frederick Soddy were the first people ever to observe a transmutation. They discovered that radium (^{226}Ra) decayed by releasing an alpha particle to give an element never before known. Use the Periodic Table in Appendix 1 to help you decide what this element is called, and write a nuclear equation to describe this decay.

SMOKE DETECTORS USE RADIOACTIVITY

SMOKE CAN BE the first sign that a house is on fire, and detecting smoke before the fire has a chance to take hold can be a real life saver.

This device makes use of the radioactivity of americium-241 to detect smoke. A small sample of americium-241 in the chamber of the detector gives off alpha radiation which keeps the air in the chamber permanently ionised. This allows a small current to keep flowing between two electrodes, as shown in Fig 2.19.

Smoke entering the sensing chamber interferes with the ionised particles and allows them to recombine with electrons. This reduces the current, and when the current falls, the smoke alarm is set off.

A smoke detector, well sited inside a house, will often respond to a level of smoke concentration that the people in it are not aware of. Smoke detectors save hundreds of lives every year, and also people's homes.

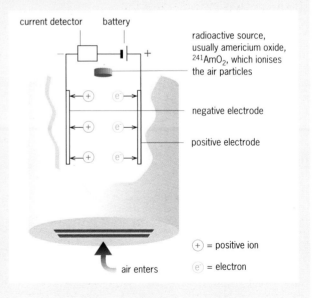

Fig 2.19 **The smoke sensing chamber of a smoke detector**

?

J Read the Feature box on smoke detectors.

(a) Why is α radiation used in smoke detectors rather than β or γ radiation? Hint: Look at Table 2.5, page 33.

(b) The useful life of a smoke detector is about 10 years. Why should it not then be thrown away with household waste?

Isotopes with too many neutrons

Refer back to Fig 2.18, page 33. Lighter elements with isotopes that have too many neutrons lie to the left of the zone of stability. Such an isotope decays by emitting a beta particle (a high-speed electron). When a nucleus releases a beta particle, a neutron changes to a proton, and this brings the atom of the new element nearer to the stability zone.

The next nuclear equation is the equation for **beta decay**. Note that in this equation, the electron is given values of zero and −1. Look back to page 31 to remind you of this numbering.

$$_0^1n \rightarrow _1^1p + _{-1}^0e \quad (_{-1}^0e \text{ is a beta particle})$$

The nuclear reaction of carbon-14 is a good example of beta decay, and beta particles are detected in radiocarbon dating (see page 37).

$$_6^{14}C \rightarrow _7^{14}N + _{-1}^0e$$

Since a neutron changes into a proton, the atomic number of the new element is increased by one, but the mass number stays the same.

Gamma rays

Gamma rays arise when the nucleus has excess energy – when it is in an **excited state**. The nucleus is usually excited after a nuclear decay, for instance, after releasing alpha or beta particles. It loses its excess energy by emitting **gamma rays**, which are very high energy electromagnetic radiation. Gamma radiation on its own does not result in the formation of a new element.

Radioactive decay series

When a radioactive isotope decays, the new isotope formed may still be unstable and radioactive. Then, a whole series of decays may occur before the nucleus is finally stable. One such decay series starts with uranium-238 and ends with lead-206. Here are just the first three nuclear reactions in the series.

$$_{92}^{238}U \rightarrow _{90}^{234}Th + _2^4He \quad (\alpha \text{ decay})$$

$$_{90}^{234}Th \rightarrow _{91}^{234}Pa + _{-1}^0e \quad (\beta \text{ decay})$$

$$_{91}^{234}Pa \rightarrow _{92}^{234}U + _{-1}^0e \quad (\beta \text{ decay})$$

?

K Strontium-90 used to be produced in nuclear explosions. It decays by beta radiation. Write the nuclear equation for this decay, and state what new element has formed.

?

L Study Fig 2.18 on page 33 and decide where the following three isotopes are placed on the graph. Then predict which type of radioactive decay is most likely to occur in each, and write the balanced nuclear equation. Hint: work out the number of protons and neutrons to find the isotope's position in relation to the zone of stability.

(a) Uranium-235: $_{92}^{235}U$

(b) Iodine-131: $_{53}^{131}I$

(c) Silicon-32: $_{14}^{32}Si$

M The next three decays in the uranium-238 series are all alpha emissions. Write down the three nuclear equations.

See question 4.

7 HALF-LIFE AND THE RATE OF RADIOACTIVE DECAY

Radioactive isotopes never stop decaying and, unlike chemical reactions, their rate of decay is not affected by pressure and temperature. The rate of decay of a radioisotope is measured as the **half-life**, $t_{1/2}$, which is the time it takes for half of the isotope to decay, and is unique to every isotope. The most stable are those with the longest half-lives, and the least stable have the shortest half-lives. For this reason, many of the very unstable isotopes which can be artificially synthesised do not exist in nature.

Iodine-131 is a very unstable isotope. Half of it will decay in 8.1 days ($t_{1/2} = 8.1$ days). It is useful in medical diagnosis, to detect liver and brain tumours and to investigate the human thyroid gland.

Cobalt-60 is a much more stable isotope. It takes more than five years for cobalt to decay to half its original mass. Its beta and gamma rays are used to sterilise medical equipment and to attack cancer cells in the human body.

At the other end of the scale, uranium-238 was formed before the Solar System existed, and takes 4.5×10^9 years for half of it to decay.

When atomic weapons were tested in the 1950s and 1960s, the isotope strontium-90 was released into the Earth's atmosphere for the first time, to be deposited throughout the world. It entered the human food chain through water supplies and, in particular, through milk from cows grazing on contaminated pastures. Since strontium is chemically very similar to calcium, it became incorporated into people's teeth and bones, and was thought to increase the risk of developing leukaemia and bone cancer.

Strontium-90 has a half-life of 28 years so, starting with 20 mg, 28 years later half will have decayed, leaving 10 mg of strontium-90. In a further 28 years there will be only 5 mg. After 84 years, which is three half-lives, only 2.5 mg would remain, and so on. No matter how much strontium-90 there is to begin with, half disintegrates every 28 years. Fig 2.20 is a graph of this decay, known as an **exponential decay**, and its shape is typical of all radioactive isotopes.

Table 2.6 **The half-life of some radioactive isotopes**

Isotope	Nuclear equation	Half-life ($t_{1/2}$)
polonium-212	$^{212}_{84}Po \rightarrow {}^{208}_{82}Np + {}^{4}_{2}He$	3×10^{-7} seconds
sodium-24	$^{24}_{11}Na \rightarrow {}^{24}_{12}Mg + {}^{0}_{-1}e$	15.0 hours
iodine-131	$^{131}_{53}I \rightarrow {}^{131}_{54}Xe + {}^{0}_{-1}e$	8.1 days
cobalt-60	$^{60}_{27}Co \rightarrow {}^{60}_{28}Ni + {}^{0}_{-1}e$	5.3 years
uranium-238	$^{238}_{92}U \rightarrow {}^{234}_{90}Th + {}^{4}_{2}He$	4.5×10^9 years

?

N (a) Why is it important that radio-isotopes for use in the body have a short half-life?

(b) Xenon-133 is a gas which is used to form a picture of the ventilation pathways of the lungs. It has a half-life of 5.3 days. How much of a 100 g sample of xenon-133 will remain after 53 days?

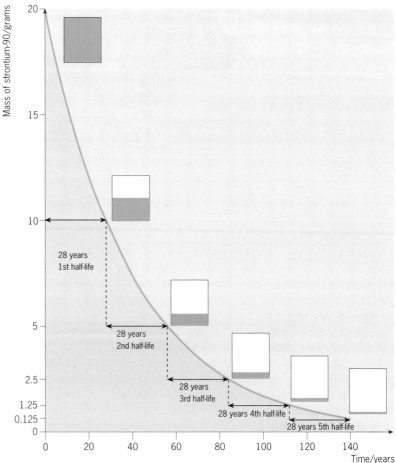

Fig 2.20 **Graph of the decay of 20 mg of $^{90}_{38}Sr$, a beta particle emitter**

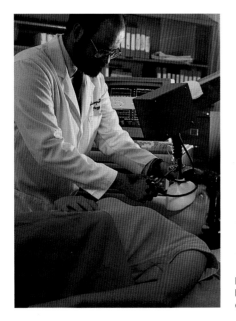

Fig 2.21 **The patient is breathing a gas containing xenon-133 which becomes concentrated in the blood vessels of the brain. Gamma rays enable an image of the blood flow in the brain to be made on screen**

EXAMPLES

Q In experiments, cobalt-60 has been used to irradiate strawberries to prevent them developing mould. (At the time of publication, irradiation of food was not permitted in the UK.) As Table 2.6 shows, the half-life of cobalt-60 is 5.3 years. If a food company were to start with 2.00 g of the isotope, how much would be left after 21.2 years?

A Find out how many half-lives 21.2 years is:

$$21.2 \div 5.3 = 4 \text{ half-lives}$$

2 g: $t_{1/2} = 5.3$ years → **1 g:** $t_{1/2} = 5.3$ years → **0.5 g:** $t_{1/2} = 5.3$ years → **0.25 g:** $t_{1/2} = 5.3$ years → **0.125 g**

You can see that the starting amount of the sample has been reduced four times by a half:

$$2 \times \tfrac{1}{2} \times \tfrac{1}{2} \times \tfrac{1}{2} \times \tfrac{1}{2} = 2 \times (\tfrac{1}{2})^4 \doteq 0.125 \text{ g}$$

Q All the isotopes of technetium are radioactive, they do not occur naturally on Earth and all are artificially made. Technetium-99 has a half-life of 6 hours. It is used in medicine to assess the damage to heart muscles after a heart attack. A sample has an initial count rate of 3000 counts per minute (c.p.m.). How long will it take for the count rate to fall to 94 c.p.m?

A   **3000:** $t_{1/2} = 6$ h → **1500:** $t_{1/2} = 6$ h → **750:**
$t_{1/2} = 6$ h → **375:** $t_{1/2} = 6$ h → **187.5:**
$t_{1/2} = 6$ h → **93.75** ≈ **94 c.p.m.**

As shown, it takes 5 half-lives for activity to reduce to 94 c.p.m. Therefore, 6 × 5 = 30 hours.

When the count rate does not correspond to an exact number of half-lives, a graph can be drawn, similar to the curve of Fig 2.20, and the time corresponding to the count rate can be read off from it.

See questions 1 and 2.

8 DATING USING RADIOACTIVITY

It is because radioactive isotopes have fixed half-lives, which temperature or pressure cannot alter, that we can use half-lives to date objects, and even age the Earth itself.

Carbon-14 dating

The best-known radioactive dating technique uses carbon-14, which has a half-life of 5730 years. The Earth is continually bombarded by particles from the cosmos. These 'cosmic rays' crash into atoms in the upper atmosphere and cause them to release high-energy neutrons. They, in turn, smash into the nuclei of nitrogen-14 atoms in the upper atmosphere, and produce carbon-14 which is radioactive.

$$^{14}_{7}\text{N} + ^{1}_{0}\text{n} \rightarrow ^{14}_{6}\text{C} + ^{1}_{1}\text{H}$$

Carbon-14 reacts with oxygen to form $^{14}\text{CO}_2$, and this is used by plants in photosynthesis to make carbohydrates (see Fig 2.22). Through food chains, the isotope becomes incorporated into all living things, including ourselves. As soon as the carbon-14 is produced it starts to decay by emitting beta particles:

$$^{14}_{6}\text{C} \rightarrow ^{14}_{7}\text{N} + ^{0}_{-1}\text{e}$$

The amount of carbon-14 in the atmosphere stays roughly constant because, over time, the rate of decay of carbon-14, and its rate of production by cosmic rays, have become balanced. It is important to realise that the amount of carbon-14 produced each year is very small indeed – only about 7.5 kg in total – and that the ratio of carbon-14 to carbon-12 all around us and inside us is also very small. There are twelve million million carbon-12 atoms for every one carbon-14 atom. This ratio of carbon-12 to carbon-14 in any organism stays constant while it is alive, because any carbon-14 that decays is replaced in the turnover of food and nutrients from its environment. When the organism dies, it takes in no more carbon-14, so the amount of carbon-14 starts to decrease.

?

O The amount of carbon-14 becomes too small to measure accurately when it falls below 1 per cent of the amount originally present when the organism was alive. How many half-lives are involved in the amount of carbon-14 falling to below 1 per cent? About how many years will this go back in time? Hint: The carbon-14 present when the organism was alive is 100 per cent.

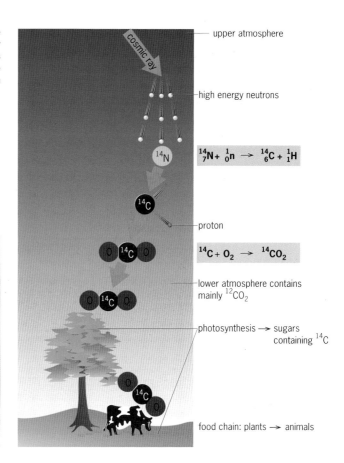

Fig 2.22 **The path taken by carbon-14 as it enters the food chain**

upper atmosphere

cosmic ray

high energy neutrons

$^{14}_{7}N + ^{1}_{0}n \rightarrow ^{14}_{6}C + ^{1}_{1}H$

proton

$^{14}C + O_2 \rightarrow ^{14}CO_2$

lower atmosphere contains mainly $^{12}CO_2$

photosynthesis → sugars containing ^{14}C

food chain: plants → animals

Fig 2.23 **To radiocarbon date a bone, it is cut into pieces and the collagen is extracted chemically. It is this material that is analysed for its carbon-14 content in a counting chamber that operates like a Geiger counter. Depending on age, the count rate may vary from several disintegrations per hour to a few per day. For very old material, counting may last several months**

Imagine that archaeologists find a wooden carving they think is thousands of years old. They find that its carbon-12 to carbon-14 ratio is 24 million million to 1, that is, the carving has half the amount of carbon-14 that is found in wood cut down today. The carving is therefore one half-life old, or about 5730 years.

DATING THE TURIN SHROUD

THIS HAS BEEN one of the most famous uses of radiocarbon dating. The Shroud of Turin is a linen cloth, over 4 metres long, bearing two images of a man – one of the front and the other of the back of someone who appears to have been crucified. For centuries many people have believed that the cloth wrapped the body of Jesus after his death. According to the first reliable records, the cloth appeared in France in 1350, and was later taken to the Italian city of Turin.

In recent years, chemical tests were done on small samples of the cloth. They revealed that the image was not painted on to the cloth by any known method, and that the blood stains are definitely human.

In 1988, laboratories in Oxford, Zurich and Arizona were each given pieces 2 centimetres square to date independently. The linen was found to have come from flax grown somewhere between 1260 and 1390. For the cloth to have been the burial shroud of Jesus, the flax would have had to have grown some time before his death. But some people still claim that a burst of energy during the resurrection could have made the flax seem younger than it is. Many questions remain unanswered, including the way that the image was formed.

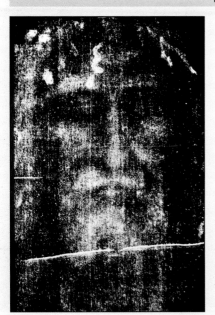

Fig 2.24 **The face on the Shroud of Turin which is thought by many people to have been the burial shroud of Jesus**

RADIOACTIVITY – SAFE OR UNSAFE?

RADIOACTIVE MATERIALS have proved themselves useful to society, especially in medicine. Yet we often hear that exposure to radiation is dangerous. Is there a contradiction?

We have looked at three types of radiation – alpha, beta and gamma – which come from the breakdown of unstable nuclei. These are called **ionising radiations** because when they pass through molecules they can knock off electrons and form ions. This disrupts molecules. In living matter, many of the molecules – biomolecules – are complex and contain weak bonds. DNA, the carrier of genetic information is an example. So exposure to ionising radiation can alter or destroy important biomolecules, and can result in illness and even death.

Whether ionising radiation causes damage depends on two properties, the *penetrating power* of the radiation and its *ability to ionise* (and so disrupt) molecules. Alpha particles are relatively massive, so can be very damaging, but their penetrating power is very low, so they do not progress far in living tissue. Beta particles penetrate further, but they are lighter and so cause less ionisation of molecules. Gamma radiation is the most penetrating of the three, but because it has no mass or charge, it is the least ionising.

In using radioisotopes, particularly in medicine, we balance the risk of the damage that a form of radiation may do to biomolecules with the benefits that using it can bring. We are exposed to natural radiation all the time (see the Assignment to this chapter), and our own molecules contain radioisotopes, but we also have mechanisms to repair radiation damage. We cannot eliminate exposure altogether, but we can minimise and control it.

?

P 15 million potassium-40 atoms decay inside each person's body every hour. How many grams is this? Hint: How many atoms in a mole?

11 RADIOACTIVITY MADE USEFUL

Radioactive materials are being used in an increasing number of ways. You have already learned about some of them in this chapter, and here are brief descriptions of others.

Treating cancer

Cancerous cells are abnormal cells which divide at a rapid rate, producing tumours that invade surrounding tissues. Some radiations can cause a cancer. At the same time, cancerous cells are easily destroyed by carefully controlled doses of radiations which do not affect other surrounding cells. Over a period of weeks, a tumour in a patient can be made inactive by exposure to doses of gamma rays. The radioisotope generally used for this treatment is cobalt-60.

Tracers for diagnosis and treatment

A radioisotope has the same chemical properties as any other atom of the same element, and molecules of a substance 'labelled' with a radioisotope can therefore be traced because their radiation can be detected. For example, iron-59 can be introduced into haemoglobin to follow the production of red blood cells in bone marrow. Iodine-131 as a label in sodium iodide ($Na^{131}I$) is used to investigate the activity of the thyroid gland and to diagnose and treat diseases of this gland. Labelled iodine also helps to detect liver and brain tumours. Sodium-24 as sodium chloride ($^{24}NaCl$) solution is put into the bloodstream to follow blood flow and locate clots and obstructions in vessels.

Tracers in industry and agriculture

Labelled sodium iodide in boreholes indicates the route taken by water underground. Barium sulphate, which is insoluble in water, can be labelled with barium-140, and the labelled compound $^{140}BaSO_4$ is used to monitor how silt is deposited in rivers. Phosphorus-32 in phosphate compounds helps to trace the uptake of fertilisers by plants. Radioactive isotopes are also used to measure and check thicknesses, as shown in Fig 2.26.

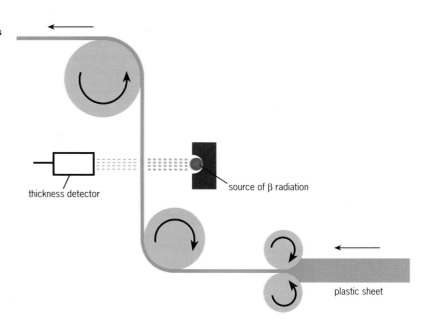

Fig 2.26 **A thickness detector. An increase in the thickness of the plastic sheet is recorded as a reduction in the amount of radiation reaching the detector. For thick, dense materials, gamma rays are used**

thickness detector

source of β radiation

plastic sheet

GLOWING FIBRES

A METHOD BEING developed by scientists in the United States to detect soil contamination round nuclear sites uses plastic fibres impregnated with compounds which fluoresce when struck by beta particles. The compounds emit radiation in the visible spectrum, and this glow is detected by photosensors which translate the signal into an electrical current.

An operator, using the sensor connected to a portable computer, can analyse soil on site in minutes, rather than having to wait weeks for results of soil analyses from a laboratory.

This equipment is expected to dramatically cut time and costs of monitoring the levels of contamination in the soil round nuclear sites.

?

Q How might radiation detection be used to measure the level of liquid in a sealed container?

Geothermal energy

At the start of this chapter, you read that radioactive decay gives out thermal energy and helps to keep the planet warm. This is because each decay involves a conversion of mass to energy. Without such an energy release, the Earth would have cooled much faster. Much of the thermal energy of the Earth's crust arises from the decay of very long-lived isotopes of the three elements potassium, uranium and thorium.

More than twenty countries now harness geothermal energy. In the Philippines, it provides about 15 per cent of electricity needs. Water is pumped down deep holes bored into the Earth's crust. It passes through hot rocks and returns to the surface as steam which drives a generator. Pilot schemes are being run in the United Kingdom, but investment and development in the technology are needed before we see geothermal energy stations here.

Table 2.7 **Isotopes which contribute most to keeping the planet warm**

Isotope	Half-life, $t_{1/2}$/years
potassium-40	1.3×10^9
thorium-232	1.4×10^{10}
uranium-235	7.13×10^8
uranium-238	4.51×10^9

SUMMARY

Having studied this chapter, you should be able to know and understand the following.

▪ An atom has a minute central nucleus of protons and neutrons which is surrounded by electrons. Proton: relative mass 1, relative charge +1. Neutron: relative mass 1, no relative charge.

▪ Atomic (proton) number = number of protons in the atom.

▪ Mass (nucleon) number = number of protons and neutrons in the atom.

▪ Isotopes have the same atomic number but different mass numbers.

▪ The relative atomic mass of an element is the average mass of the atom (taking into account all the naturally occurring isotopes and their abundance) compared to one atom of carbon-12.

▪ Radioactivity is the spontaneous disintegration of the nucleus of an atom. Three kinds of radiation emitted from the nucleus are: alpha particles (helium nuclei), beta particles (electrons) and gamma rays (electromagnetic radiation).

▪ The stability of a nucleus depends on the number of protons and neutrons in it. A plot of number of protons against number of neutrons shows a zone of stability.

▪ The half-life of a radioisotope is the time it takes for half of the isotope to decay. The smaller the half-life, the more unstable the nucleus.

▪ Radioisotopes are used to date objects.

QUESTIONS

1 In recent years, the age of volcanic rocks has been calculated by the analysis of helium isotopes. A typical sample of helium exists as its helium-4 isotope and extremely small proportions of helium-3. Analysis has shown that volcanic rocks have a higher proportion of helium-3 than a typical sample of helium has.

A sample of helium from a volcanic rock was found to have the following percentage composition, by mass:

^{3}He, 0.992%;
^{4}He, 99.008%.

a) Explain the term *isotope*.

b) State the difference between the atomic structures of helium-3 and helium-4.

c) Relative atomic masses, A_r, can be used to compare the masses of atoms of different elements.
    (i) What isotope is used as the standard for relative atomic mass measurements?
    (ii) Calculate the relative atomic mass of the volcanic helium sample above.

[UCLES: A/AS Sciences, 1995, Chemistry Foundation paper.]

2

a) Identify, and give the main characteristics of the particles contained in atomic nuclei.

b) Chlorine is essentially a mixture of two isotopes, ^{35}Cl and ^{37}Cl. Explain what is meant by the term *isotopes*.

c) Complete the following equations for nuclear reactions:

    (i) $^9_4\text{Be} + ^4_2\text{He} \rightarrow ^{12}_6\text{C} +$

    (ii) $^{238}_{92}\text{U} \rightarrow ^{234}_{90}\text{Th} +$

    (iii) $^{14}_6\text{C} \rightarrow ^{14}_7\text{N} +$

    In **(i)**, how many grams of $^{12}_6\text{C}$ would be produced from 1 g of ^4_2He?

d) State what is meant by the term *half-life* of a radioactive isotope.

[ULEAC: A/AS Chemistry, 1996, Module Test 1, part question]

3 Airport security devices often include a thermal neutron analyser to detect explosives. This device bombards luggage with low-energy neutrons. Nitrogen atoms often make up a high proportion of explosives and the neutrons convert nitrogen-14 into nitrogen-15 and gamma rays. The gamma rays are then detected and indicate the possible location of a bomb.

a) What are gamma rays?

b) Write a nuclear equation for the formation of nitrogen-15 from nitrogen-14.

4 Smoking cigarettes can damage your health through the radioactivity which may be present in the tobacco.

Tobacco is grown using phosphate fertilisers which are relatively rich in uranium and its decay products.

a) One of the decay products of the uranium-238 series is radon-222. This is produced from radium-226. Write a nuclear equation for this reaction.

b) Radon-222 gas is present in the soil and in the air surrounding the tobacco leaves. It decays in four steps to lead-210. The first step involves alpha decay. Write the nuclear equation for this reaction and identify the element produced.

c) Isotopes from the decay of radon are present on and in the tobacco leaves. When cigarettes are smoked, the isotopes are inhaled with the smoke particles. These pass through the lining of the lungs and concentrate in the liver, spleen and bone marrow. Lead-210 decays to bismuth-210 and this decays to polonium-210. Write nuclear equations for these reactions and identify the type of radiation involved.

5 One of the many uses of the radioactive isotope technetium-99 in medicine is to detect brain tumours. If it is injected into the bloodstream, cancerous cells in a tumour will absorb it while healthy brain cells will not. The tumour can then be detected by a brain scan. The half-life of ^{99m}Tc is 6 hours. The raised 'm' indicates an excited state.

a) What is meant by: **(i)** radioactive, **(ii)** isotope, **(iii)** half life?

b) The atomic number of technetium is 43. How many protons, neutrons and electrons are found in one atom of this isotope?

c) What percentage of the isotope will remain 24 hours after an injection?

d) ^{99m}Tc decays to ^{99}Tc. What type of radiation is released during this process?

e) In a laboratory, Tc is prepared by the following nuclear reactions:

$$^{98}_{42}\text{Mo} + \underline{\quad} \rightarrow ^{99}_{42}\text{Mo}$$

$$^{99}_{42}\text{Mo} \rightarrow ^{99m}_{43}\text{Tc} + \underline{\quad}$$

Complete these nuclear equations and identify the type of radiation emitted from the second reaction.

Assignment

RADON IN THE HOME

In December 1985, Stanley Watras, an engineer at a nuclear power plant in Pennsylvania, set off radiation alarms as he went in to work. His home proved to be to blame, or rather, the radioactive radon gas that had seeped into it. The Watras home had radon levels of about 100 000 becquerels in every cubic metre of air. This is written 100 000 Bq m^{-3}. A becquerel is one atomic disintegration per second. This was a staggering amount compared with the average concentration in UK homes of 20 Bq m^{-3}, and dramatically illustrates that some houses are at a high risk of accumulating radioactive radon gas.

Uranium-bearing rocks such as granite are responsible for the release of radon gas. Uranium-238 decays through a sequence to a stable isotope of lead, and radon-222 is one member of the sequence. As a gas, radon can escape through the ground and out into the air. In the air, it rapidly disperses to very low, harmless levels. However, when it emerges from the ground, it can be drawn into homes and public buildings because the heat in them slightly lowers the air pressure, and a building which is particularly well insulated will trap radon more effectively than a draughty one.

1

a) The half-life of radon-222 (^{222}Rn) is 3.8 days. What does this mean?

b) Assume that no more radon entered Stanley Watras's home, and that it was completely insulated. Calculate how many days would it take for the radiation from radon to reduce from 100 000 Bq m^{-3} to below 200 Bq m^{-3} – the level which is considered dangerous in the UK.

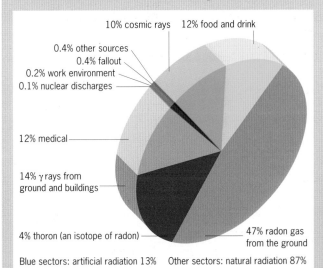

Fig 2.A1 **Radon makes up nearly half of all the radiation reaching the average person in the United Kingdom**

10% cosmic rays
12% food and drink
0.4% other sources
0.4% fallout
0.2% work environment
0.1% nuclear discharges
12% medical
14% γ rays from ground and buildings
4% thoron (an isotope of radon)
47% radon gas from the ground

Blue sectors: artificial radiation 13% Other sectors: natural radiation 87%

The radon risk

Studies of uranium miners have shown that radon causes lung cancer. The level of radon in a small proportion of UK homes approaches that found in the mines, so there is probably a tiny risk of contracting lung cancer in these houses. However, we are all exposed to radiation every day of our lives, and almost half of this comes from radon.

As one of the noble gases, radon is very unreactive, so the radon we breathe in does not combine with chemicals in the lining of the lungs or enter the blood. However, radon-222 decays to polonium-218. This in turn decays to produce three more radioactive isotopes before reaching lead-210 which has a half-life of 20.4 years. The four nuclides produced in this sequence are known as radon daughters. They each have a half-life of under 30 minutes and are present as particles in the air of a radon-contaminated home.

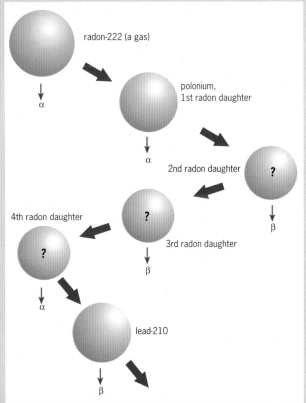

radon-222 (a gas)
α
polonium, 1st radon daughter
α
2nd radon daughter ?
β
3rd radon daughter
4th radon daughter ?
β
?
α
lead-210
β

Fig 2.A2 **The radioactive decay sequence of radon**

When radon-222 and two of its daughter isotopes decay, they produce alpha particles. The alpha particle travels only a short distance before being stopped, but is relatively massive and highly charged. If alpha-emitting radon daughters lodge inside the lungs, the alpha particles can disrupt the chemical bonds within the cells. As some of the weakest bonds are in vital molecules such as DNA, this is how cancer can start.

It has been calculated that the risk of dying of cancer after a lifetime exposed to a concentration of 20 Bq m^{-3} every year is about 1 in 300. The lifetime risk increases to 1 in 30 at a level of 200 Bq m^{-3}. This is also the UK

Government's Action Level, at which steps should be taken to reduce the concentration of radon in a home. For smokers, the risk of dying of cancer is much greater – it is 1 in 10.

Fig 2.A3 **In the red areas, 1 per cent or more of homes are above the level at which action is recommended to reduce radon concentrations**

Detecting radon in the home and removing it

The level of radon can be detected by a small plastic sheet. As radon decays, the alpha particles leave tracks on the surface of the plastic, and these build up over time. The plastic sheet is then sent for analysis.

Fig 2.A4 **A small yellow detector is used by the National Radiological Protection Board in buildings where the concentration of radon may be high. Inside is a plastic detector sheet which is 'developed' to show the exposure level**

Once the level of radon is found to be above the action level, radon concentration must be reduced. Often this requires only a fan underneath the floorboards, preventing radon from accumulating in the air inside the house.

2

a) What is the atomic number, mass number, number of protons, number of electrons and number of neutrons in radon-222?

b) What is an alpha particle and why does it move to a negative electrode?

c) In the pie chart of Fig 2.A1, 4 per cent of the radiation is due to thoron. Thoron is the name for another isotope of radon. How will it differ from radon-222?

d) From the text below the heading The radon risk, work out the nuclear equation which produces the first radon daughter.

e) Polonium decays by alpha decay to give the second radon daughter. This in turn decays, again by releasing a beta particle, to give the third radon daughter. The fourth radon daughter results from another beta decay. What are the names and mass numbers of these three nuclides?

3

a) At what period of the year would you expect radon levels in homes to be greatest? Explain your reasoning.

b) Radon continues to be a problem in many homes. Write a leaflet to go to householders explaining the dangers of radon without causing unnecessary panic. Explain the scientific terms you are using so that people will have all the facts without being blinded by the science.

THE NUCLEUS AND RADIOACTIVITY

This chapter map brings together the central ideas that you have read about in the chapter. It shows how they are interlinked with each other and with the subjects of other chapters in the book. You can use the map to review aspects of the chapter and to help you plan your revision.

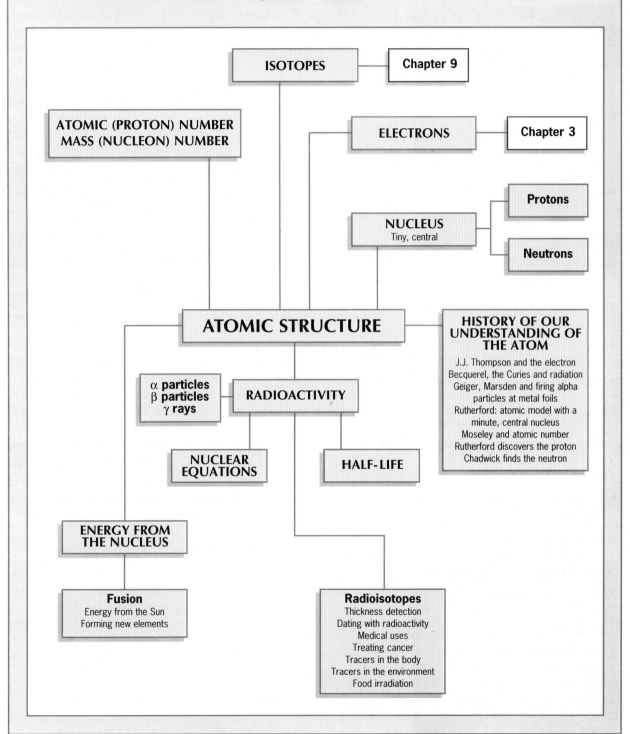

A close look at electrons

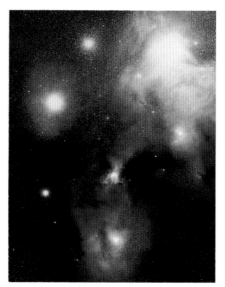

Interstellar clouds contain some very interesting molecules which are identified by their spectra. Some may represent the forerunners of the molecules of life itself

THE GIANT GAS CLOUDS in interstellar space – the space between stars – contain vast amounts of very thinly dispersed atoms, ions and molecules. We know what this material consists of because each type of atom, ion or molecule absorbs and emits energy of particular wavelengths across the electromagnetic spectrum, depending on the arrangement of its electrons. From Earth, we can detect and record the patterns of these absorbed and emitted wavelengths: each type of particle has its own pattern which reveals its presence, rather like a fingerprint. Hydrogen, for example, emits radio waves at a wavelength of 21 cm.

Chemists are very interested in the molecules of interstellar space. So far, they have identified over eighty. Some are also common on Earth, such as hydrogen chloride, carbon monoxide, water and ethanol. Others are unusual, and several were discovered in space before they were even identified in the laboratory. An example is a three-membered carbon ring, C_3H_2, an interstellar molecule widespread in our Galaxy and common in others.

It is thought that many small molecules and ions are formed in space when atoms are bombarded by cosmic radiation. They include the diatomic molecule carbon monoxide, CO, the ion HCS^+ and the 3-carbon ring of C_3H_2. At the same time, there seems to be a size limit to these molecules, probably because the intense radiation also disrupts larger molecules. However, the very existence of the smaller molecules in interstellar space may point the way to understanding the chemistry that led to life on Earth, and may perhaps reveal it elsewhere in the Universe.

Introduction

The glorious colours of fireworks, the discovery of helium in the Sun before it was discovered on Earth (page 55), our knowledge of the atoms and molecules in distant stars – all these are connected with electrons. To a chemist, the most interesting part of an atom is its electrons because it is the electrons, not the protons or neutrons, that account for every chemical reaction.

Scientists in the nineteenth century investigated the light that materials absorb and emit, and went on to discover new elements. In the twentieth century, our understanding of the nature of light has led scientists to release the energy of lasers (see page 55).

Fig 3.1 **The spectacular colours of fireworks are due to the electrons in the atom releasing energy at different wavelengths in the visible spectrum**

1 ALL THE COLOURS OF THE RAINBOW

In 1666, Sir Isaac Newton first recorded the fact that, when visible light was passed through a prism, it was split to produce a **continuous spectrum** of rainbow colours containing all the wavelengths of light.

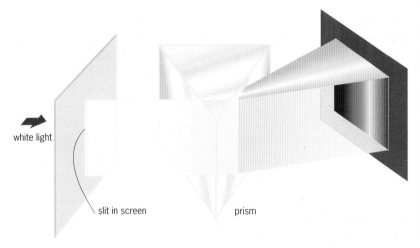

white light

slit in screen   prism

Fig 3.2(a) **Light from a white light source passes through a slit and then through a prism. It is split into its different wavelengths, producing a continuous spectrum – a rainbow effect**

Fig 3.2(b) **Isaac Newton, who used a prism to split visible light and produce a continuous spectrum**

Robert Bunsen is best known for inventing the Bunsen burner. But, with Wilhelm Kirchhoff, he invented a far more important instrument in the progress of chemistry – the spectroscope. When put in a flame, compounds containing sodium were known to colour the flame yellow; potassium compounds coloured it lilac. The spectroscope took these observations and Newton's visible spectrum a step further.

In the spectroscope, light passes through a narrow slit and a prism, and forms a spectrum. When Bunsen and Kirchhoff viewed the sodium flame with this light, they saw bright lines (images of the slit) in the yellow part of the spectrum and some less bright lines in other parts. They viewed light from compounds of other metals in the same way, and soon realised that each element had its own characteristic *fingerprint* of lines in different parts of the spectrum.

With this technique, they discovered the elements rubidium and caesium while examining the spectrum of a lithium ore. They found strong red and blue lines (Fig 3.4) which could not be accounted for by the elements known to be in the ore. Rubidium is from the Latin for 'red' and caesium is named after the Latin for 'blue'.

Fig 3.3 **Robert Bunsen (centre) and Wilhelm Kirchhoff (left)**

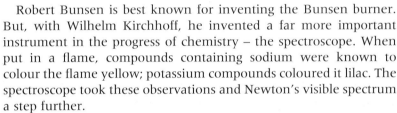

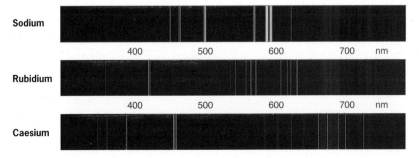

Sodium

400   500   600   700   nm

Rubidium

400   500   600   700   nm

Caesium

Fig 3.4 **The line emission spectra of sodium, and of rubidium and caesium which Bunsen and Kirchhoff discovered**

As elements were being discovered and identified by their spectral fingerprints, astronomers were soon pointing spectroscopes at the stars to look for characteristic lines of elements and finding that the cosmos was made up of the same elements as the Earth.

2 THE ELECTROMAGNETIC SPECTRUM

The 'light' our eyes detect is just a small part of a very much wider **electromagnetic spectrum**. This spectrum is made up of all the **electromagnetic radiations**, and includes X-rays used by dentists, the infrared radiation of microwaves used to heat food, and radio waves which bring us radio and television signals. Fig 3.5 is the **continuous spectrum** of electromagnetic radiation, called continuous because all the wavelengths are represented. We shall now look more closely at electromagnetic radiation to help us understand electrons and how they are arranged in atoms.

As its name suggests, electromagnetic radiation is made up of two components: an electrical and a magnetic one. Electromagnetic radiation is one of the ways energy is transmitted through space. It is why we feel the warmth of the Sun on Earth, and why we get sunburned if we have too much ultraviolet radiation.

Fig 3.5 **The electromagnetic spectrum. Notice that visible light – the radiation our eyes can detect – is only a very small part of the spectrum**

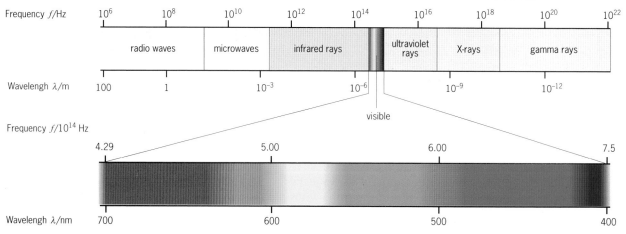

3 LIGHT AS WAVES

Electromagnetic radiation is usually thought of as **waves** and, like all waves, they can be described by their **wavelength**, **frequency** and **speed**. Wavelength is measured in metres (m), and its symbol is the Greek letter λ (lambda). Frequency, f, is measured in hertz (Hz), which means cycles per second, and which can also be written as s^{-1}. The speed of electromagnetic waves is the speed of light, with the symbol c, which is in metres per second ($m\,s^{-1}$).

In Fig 3.6, you can see what these terms mean, and that when the frequency is higher, the wavelength is smaller. The terms are related in a simple equation:

$$\begin{array}{ccc} c & = & \lambda \times f \\ (m\,s^{-1}) & & (m) \quad (s^{-1}) \end{array}$$

Fig 3.6 **Two electromagnetic waves, showing their wavelength λ and frequency f. The wavelength is the distance between two identical points on the waves. Here, it is between the crests. The speed of these waves is identical because all electromagnetic radiation travels at the speed of light, c, so the shorter the wavelength, the higher the frequency**

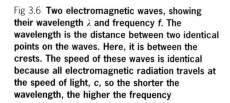

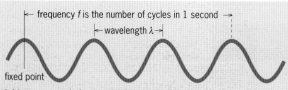

(a) In one second, three waves have passed a particular point. So the frequency is three cycles per second, or 3 hertz (this is far lower than the frequency of actual electromagnetic radiation)

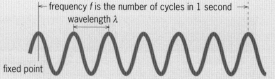

(b) In one second, six cycles have passed the same fixed point. So the frequency is 6 cycles per second, or 6 hertz (again, far lower than real frequencies)

EXAMPLE

Q The wavelength of a red traffic light is centred on 700 nm. What is the frequency of this radiation?

A First, you need to convert the wavelength to metres: 700 nm is 700×10^{-9} m, and the speed of light c is 3.00×10^8 m s^{-1}. Inserting these values into the equation:

$$3.00 \times 10^8 = \lambda \times 700 \times 10^{-9}$$

Rearranging: $\lambda = \dfrac{3.00 \times 10^8}{700 \times 10^{-9}} = 4.29 \times 10^{14}$

So the frequency of the red light is 4.29×10^{14} Hz.

?

A Barium nitrate is added to fireworks to colour them. When heated, this compound emits light of frequencies around 5.45×10^{14} Hz. Calculate the wavelength, and use Fig 3.5 to work out what colour the fireworks will be.

4 LIGHT AS PARTICLES

Up to the beginning of the twentieth century, scientists agreed on a model of electromagnetic energy in which it was radiated and absorbed by matter in the form of waves. The model did not explain all the observations, notably the fact that heated objects emit radiation that has particular spectra.

In 1900, Max Planck proposed that particles such as atoms and molecules absorb and emit energy in discrete (separate) amounts or packets called 'quanta'. Planck's equation is:

$$E = hf$$

where E is the energy in joules (J), h is Planck's constant, with a value of 6.626×10^{-34} J s, and f is the frequency in hertz (Hz or s^{-1}).

A **quantum of energy** is a precise packet of energy. These packets can have different energy values, depending on their source, but you cannot have parts of packets, only whole ones.

The photoelectric effect

In 1905, Albert Einstein used Max Planck's equation to explain another phenomenon that baffled scientists, the **photoelectric effect**. This is the release of electrons by some metals when light is shone on them. It was found that the light had to be above a minimum frequency (and so a minimum energy) before electrons were emitted. It did not matter how intense (bright) the electromagnetic radiation was below this *threshold frequency*; only with a high enough frequency were electrons released. Then, the more intense the light, the greater the number of electrons released.

Fig 3.7 **Albert Einstein. By the age of 26, while an assistant in a Swiss patent office, he had written three papers in his spare time that were to change twentieth-century science**

According to the old *wave-only* model, the electrons would absorb even low-energy radiation and eventually release it. Einstein developed Planck's idea of quanta, saying that some of the properties of electromagnetic radiation could be explained only if light were thought of as consisting of *particles* that we now call **photons**. He also said that each photon is associated with a particular quantum (amount) of energy, linked to its frequency by Planck's equation: $E = hf$.

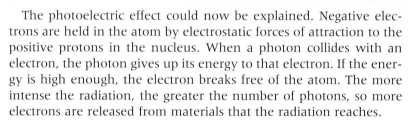

B The microwave radiation used in ovens has a frequency of 1.0×10^{10} Hz.

(a) What is the wavelength of this radiation?

(b) What is the energy of one photon?

(c) What is the energy of one mole of these photons?

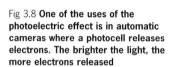
Fig 3.8 **One of the uses of the photoelectric effect is in automatic cameras where a photocell releases electrons. The brighter the light, the more electrons released**

C Exposure to both gamma radiation and ultraviolet light can cause cancer. Use Fig 3.5 and Planck's equation to suggest why gamma radiation is much more harmful than ultraviolet light.

The photoelectric effect could now be explained. Negative electrons are held in the atom by electrostatic forces of attraction to the positive protons in the nucleus. When a photon collides with an electron, the photon gives up its energy to that electron. If the energy is high enough, the electron breaks free of the atom. The more intense the radiation, the greater the number of photons, so more electrons are released from materials that the radiation reaches.

The wave–particle nature of light

In 1905, Einstein wrote three papers. One was on his famous theory of special relativity, another an explanation of Brownian motion. His third, an explanation of the photoelectric effect, gained him a Nobel prize in 1921, three years after his great friend Max Planck. All three papers had a profound effect on twentieth-century science and Einstein was seen by many as one of the two greatest scientists that ever lived, the other being Isaac Newton.

We have noted some observations suggesting that light is made up of particles and others suggesting it is made up of waves. So we now think of light as having a *dual* nature, of both particles and waves. This **wave–particle duality** is not just confined to light; matter too can sometimes behave as if it were made up of waves, as you will see on page 56.

5 THE ATOMIC EMISSION SPECTRUM OF HYDROGEN

When hydrogen is placed in a discharge tube at low pressure and with a high voltage between the two plates, some of the bonds in the hydrogen molecules (H_2) are broken to give separate hydrogen atoms. See Fig 3.9(a). When the radiation coming from the discharge tube is passed through a spectroscope, a series of characteristic lines shows up in the visible spectrum.

Fig 3.9(a) **A hydrogen discharge tube showing the colour emitted by hydrogen atoms**

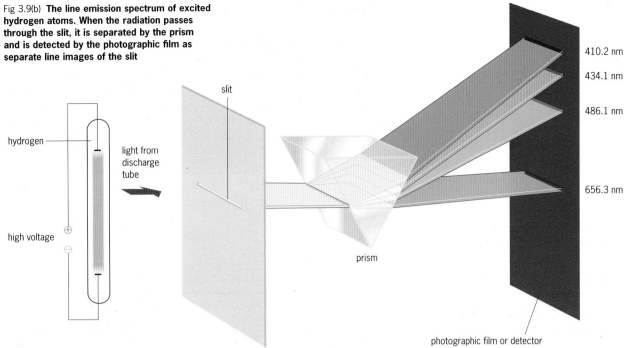

Fig 3.9(b) **The line emission spectrum of excited hydrogen atoms. When the radiation passes through the slit, it is separated by the prism and is detected by the photographic film as separate line images of the slit**

slit

hydrogen

light from discharge tube

high voltage

prism

410.2 nm

434.1 nm

486.1 nm

656.3 nm

photographic film or detector

The Balmer series

You read earlier about Bunsen and Kirchhoff's work in identifying elements by their characteristic spectral lines. These spectra are called **line emission spectra** for the following reason. When an element's atoms are given energy, they emit radiation as discrete (separate) lines, at specific frequencies (and hence energies) for that element. For example, hydrogen, which has just one electron, has several prominent lines in the visible part of its emission spectrum (Fig 3.10, page 52). These are known as the **Balmer series** after a Swiss music teacher who worked out a mathematical relationship between the lines.

Other series

Other series of lines for hydrogen are found in different parts of the electromagnetic spectrum. The **Lyman series** is found in the ultraviolet section and the **Paschen series** in the infrared. Both these series are named after their discoverers.

Like the photoelectric effect, the different series of lines (characteristic for an element) was another nineteenth-century mystery that could not be explained by theories at that time. An explanation had to wait for the ideas of Planck and Einstein to be developed.

6 NIELS BOHR'S MODEL OF THE HYDROGEN ATOM

In Chapter 2 we were left with the Rutherford model of the atom. However, there are problems with this model. Rutherford proposed that electrons orbited the nucleus rather like planets round the Sun. Planetary motion was well understood by this time – the Sun's gravity tends to pull planets towards it, while their acceleration due to being in a circular orbit creates a balancing force. (In order for an object to travel at constant speed and travel in circular motion, constantly changing direction, it has to accelerate constantly.)

Negative electrons in circular motion are attracted to the positive protons in the nucleus by electrostatic forces. If they orbited the nucleus like planets, their acceleration would keep them from falling into the nucleus. But electrons are charged particles, and *accelerating* charged particles were known to emit electromagnetic radiation and lose energy. If Rutherford's model was correct, instead of a few separate lines, a continuous spectrum should have been observed, with the atom emitting light all the time and the electron losing its energy and falling into the nucleus, causing the hydrogen atom to collapse. Clearly, this does not happen!

Another model of the atom was needed to explain the observations. As we saw in Chapter 2, a model is intended to explain all observations at the time. If it does so, then it becomes accepted by the scientific community. Niels Bohr used the quantum ideas developed by Planck and Einstein to propose his model for the hydrogen atom.

Fig 3.10 **The Balmer series for the hydrogen atom, and its line emission spectrum. The lines in the visible spectrum are produced when the excited electron falls back to the** $n = 2$ **energy level. The higher the energy level from which it falls, the higher the frequency of the photon emitted. Note that the energy levels eventually merge at** $n = \infty$**. This is when the electron has escaped from the attraction of the nucleus so that the atom has become ionised**

Fig 3.11(a) **Niels Bohr**

Fig 3.11(b) **A staircase model for the energy levels of a hydrogen atom**

far from the nucleus

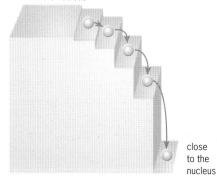

close to the nucleus

Bohr's model still had the hydrogen electron orbiting the nucleus. But the orbits, or **energy levels** the hydrogen electron could occupy, were *quantised*, that is, they had fixed energy values. With this model, hydrogen's line emission spectrum could be explained.

In Bohr's model, the electron normally occupies the lowest possible energy level, called the **ground state**. This is the energy level of the electron when it is not excited. Raising the electron to an **excited state** (giving it energy), say, by an electron discharge, causes it to move up to a higher energy level by absorbing a quantum of energy (Fig 3.10). When it returns to the lower, ground state energy level, it releases this quantum of energy as a photon of light, of a specific frequency, so giving a line in the emission spectrum.

Imagine that the hydrogen electron is like a ball on a staircase, as in Fig 3.11(b). The ball can rest on any step, but it cannot stop in between. This is the case with the electron. The ball needs energy to go up the step, and when it falls back down it releases this energy. The lines in an emission spectrum get closer together at one end because the higher energy levels that the electron can occupy also get closer together. This happens as the electron moves away from the nucleus. We can see this in Fig 3.11(b).

When the electron is closest to the nucleus, it is at its lowest energy level. Moving the electron away from the nucleus requires energy, and the further away it is moved, the more energy it requires. So the more energy an electron receives, the higher it can rise through the energy levels, and the more energy it will release as it falls back down again.

Each energy level is given a number, called the **principal quantum number, n.** The term 'principal quantum number' is still used to describe the main energy levels of electrons in an atom. When the hydrogen's electron is in the $n = 1$ level, it is not excited, so this is the ground state.

The Balmer series of lines is for the energy transitions when the excited hydrogen electron falls back from higher energy levels to $n = 2$, see Fig 3.10. We see the lines because they are in the visible spectrum. The higher the energy level the electron falls from, the higher the frequency of the emitted photon. Note that the energy levels eventually merge at $n = \infty$ (infinity). This is when the atom has become ionised.

USING THE LIGHT OF ELECTRON TRANSITIONS

Neon is used extensively in advertising signs. An electric current is passed through the gas at low pressure. The fast-moving electrons of the electric current excite electrons in the neon atoms into higher energy levels and, when they return to lower energy levels, orange-red light is emitted. The colour can be varied by adding other atoms such as argon or mercury, or by colouring the glass tube the neon is in.

Street lights usually contain sodium or mercury and they work on the same principle as neon lights. When excited mercury atoms return to their ground state, the radiation they emit has frequencies in the ultraviolet, yellow, green and blue parts of the spectrum.

Sodium street lights are tending to replace mercury ones because the radiation emitted by excited electrons in sodium atoms when they return to their lower levels is centred upon yellow. This has longer wavelengths than the light from mercury and is not as readily scattered by fog, so it can illuminate further. Also sodium atoms require less energy to excite their electrons, and sodium is not as toxic as mercury.

Fluorescent lights in the home or office also contain low-pressure mercury vapour. The inside of the lighting tube is coated with zinc sulphide, which absorbs the energy of ultraviolet light when its electrons are excited and, on returning to the ground state, produces many frequencies of light in the visible range. These combine to give white light.

The advantage of fluorescent lights over filament lamps is that they use less energy, since nearly all the energy is radiated in the visible spectrum. They feel cool to touch, while ordinary light bulbs with tungsten filaments waste energy by getting very hot.

Fig 3.12 **Excited electrons in atoms of neon produce the colours for these advertising signs at Piccadilly Circus**

D Look back to Fig 3.9(b). It shows the lines getting closer together towards one end of the spectrum for hydrogen. Are they closer together at the higher energy end of the spectrum or the lower energy end?

A substance fluoresces when it takes in light of one wavelength, usually outside the visible spectrum, and gives out light of another, often in the visible spectrum. This is described on page 27.

E The Paschen series is one of the series of spectral lines for hydrogen, this time in the infrared part of the spectrum and for movement of the electron to the $n = 3$ level.

(a) Draw a diagram similar to the Lyman series diagram in Fig 3.13 to show the first three electron transitions of the Paschen series.

(b) Which transition in this series will result in the lowest energy line in the infrared spectrum?

The Lyman series of lines is found in the ultraviolet part of the spectrum. It is due to the excited hydrogen electron returning from higher levels to the $n = 1$ ground-state energy level. As this is the lowest level nearest to the nucleus, far more energy is released when an electron excited to a particular energy level returns to $n = 1$ than when it returns to $n = 2$, and so the lines show up in the more energetic ultraviolet part of the spectrum.

Each line of hydrogen's emission spectrum represents one electron **transition**, a movement from a higher to a lower level. Because there are large numbers of hydrogen atoms involved, all the possible transitions are represented, giving the full spectrum of lines.

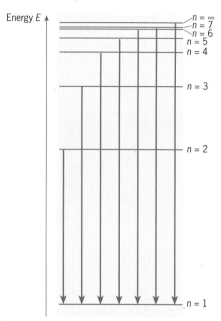

Fig 3.13 **The Lyman series for a hydrogen atom. In this series, the transitions of the electron are to $n = 1$**

Ionisation energy

From the Lyman series we can work out the energy needed to remove an electron completely from a hydrogen atom. This is the ionisation energy for hydrogen. It is the energy required to take the electron from the ground state, at $n = 1$, to where the energy levels converge, at $n = \infty$ (infinity), when the electron is free of the attraction of the nucleus.

See question 1. ■

Summary of the Bohr model of the atom

- Electrons exist only in certain permitted energy levels and in these levels they do not emit energy.

- Electrons move to higher energy levels by absorbing quanta of energy. They return to lower energy levels by emitting these quanta as photons of light, which show up as lines in different parts of the electromagnetic spectrum.

The Bohr model of the atom successfully explained the lines in the emission spectrum of the hydrogen atom. It worked for hydrogen, the simplest atom with just one electron, but it did not predict accurately the spectral lines of atoms with several electrons.

The Bohr model is important because it used the idea of *quantised* energy levels to explain atomic structure and provided a foundation on which others could build. The Nobel prize went to Bohr in 1922, one year after Einstein had received the prize for his explanation of the photoelectric effect.

F Read the box on the absorption spectrum of the Sun on the next page. In the spectrum, what is the colour of the helium line that Janssen observed?

THE ABSORPTION SPECTRUM OF THE SUN REVEALS ITS ELEMENTS

Discovering sodium

ALMOST FIFTY YEARS before Kirchhoff and Bunsen used emission spectra to identify elements (see page 47), the German scientist Josef von Fraunhofer was experimenting with light. When he passed sunlight through a very fine slit and a high quality prism, some wavelengths were missing from sunlight's absorption spectrum. They showed up as black lines in the otherwise continuous spectrum. These lines represented energies that were being absorbed by some unknown material.

Fraunhofer recorded the wavelengths of several hundred black lines, which are now named after him. Two were close together in the yellow part of the spectrum at almost 600 nm. At exactly the same wavelengths, Bunsen and Kirchhoff found two characteristic yellow lines in the emission spectrum of sodium (look back to Fig 3.4, on page 47). They concluded that sodium must be in the Sun's atmosphere. Using this hypothesis, they soon discovered other elements in the Sun.

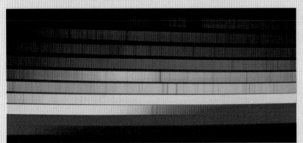

Fig 3.14 **Fraunhofer found over 600 dark lines in the visible spectrum of the Sun. These represent wavelengths missing from a continuous spectrum of light from the Sun. Some of the lines have been matched with the elements responsible for them**

To explain the Fraunhofer lines more fully, we need to look at the Bohr model of the atom again. When excited, electrons fall from higher energy levels to lower levels: they *emit* energy to give a line *emission* spectrum. In reverse, they reach the higher (excited) energy levels by *absorbing* quanta of energy (photons).

So, in an *absorption* spectrum, the quanta of energy the electrons absorb in going to these higher energy levels will be represented as black lines for the wavelengths missing from the spectrum.

Looking at Fraunhofer's spectrum for sunlight, the light from the interior of the Sun passes through the Sun's atmosphere. Assuming that there is sodium vapour in the Sun's atmosphere and that its electrons are being excited to higher energy levels, then the corresponding points in the spectrum for the light reaching Earth will be missing – hence the dark lines for sodium.

Discovering helium

In 1868, the French astronomer Pierre Jules Janssen took his spectroscope to India to view a total eclipse of the Sun. In the spectrum of light from the Sun's corona, he saw a bright line very close to the two sodium lines. This line could not be accounted for by the line spectra of any known element. In the same year the English scientist, Norman Lockyer, also observed this line and suggested that it was due to a new element. It was given the name helium, after the Greek word *helios* for the Sun.

At the time, Lockyer was ridiculed for his suggestion that he had identified a new element. Yet this discovery later helped helium to be discovered on Earth. In 1895, a quarter of a century after helium was found on the Sun, it was isolated by the Scottish chemist William Ramsey. He found the gas trapped in a uranium ore where it had been formed as a product of radioactive decay. (See Chapter 2 on how uranium atoms decay to give helium.)

LASERS – AMPLIFYING THE ENERGY FROM ELECTRON TRANSITIONS

THE LETTERS in the word laser stand for **l**ight **a**mplification by **s**timulated **e**mission of **r**adiation. Lasers, invented in 1960, have revolutionised medicine, technology and science. The ruby laser was the first and works by using a burst of ultraviolet light to excite electrons in atoms of a ruby rod. In the same instant, a few electrons fall back to lower energy levels and produce photons. These photons are bounced back and forth by mirrors at the ends of the rod and stimulate other excited electrons to fall back to lower levels, emitting a simultaneous burst of photons of the same frequency. This laser pulse is very intense and, provided one of the mirrors is partially transparent, it can pass through. The ruby laser produces a wavelength in the red part of the spectrum. Other lasers use other materials and produce wavelengths from infrared to X-ray.

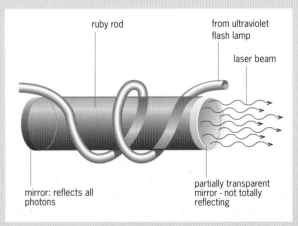

Fig 3.15 **A ruby laser emitting laser light**

Electrons as waves

In 1923, Louis de Broglie proposed that, just as light could behave as a particle or a wave, so too could matter. He suggested that electrons, regarded as particles, also had wave-like properties. Four years later, a beam of electrons was diffracted (bent and scattered) by a metal crystal to form a pattern. This diffraction could only be explained by assuming that the electrons were behaving as waves.

IMAGES OF SMALLER AND SMALLER OBJECTS

THE ELECTRON MICROSCOPE uses the wave-like behaviour of electrons. It allows us to see images of very small objects in much greater detail than we can see with ordinary microscopes which rely on visible light. Light is visible to us between wavelengths of about 400 to 700 nm. To form an image of an object, the object cannot be smaller than half the shortest wavelength, that is, 200 nm (or a twenty thousandth of a millimetre).

Electrons travelling at high speed have very short wavelengths, and they allow images of objects measuring 2×10^{-3} nm to be made and magnified. The electron microscope, then, is a very helpful tool in biological and chemical research.

aid of a computer to process the data and enhance the image, scientists used the charge on the electrons round atoms to make images of separate atoms and molecules. This technique, and the newer technique using the scanning probe microscope (SPM), hold out the prospect of producing new materials and structures by controlling and rearranging atoms and molecules.

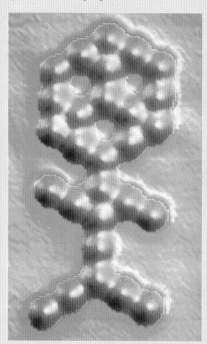

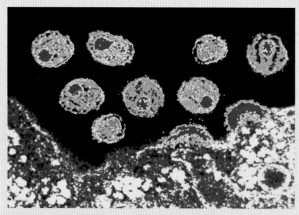

Fig 3.16(a) **An electron micrograph of AIDS viruses budding off from the surface of a human T-lymphocyte white blood cell. The detail in images of organisms that cause disease help scientists to seek a way to combat infection**

In 1986, the scanning tunnelling microscope (STM) took electron microscopy one stage further. With the

Fig 3.16(b) **A scanning tunnelling microscope was used to produce this piece of 'atomic art'. Twenty-eight carbon monoxide (CO) molecules were positioned on a piece of platinum by using a charged probe wire to make this molecular person**

7 A MODERN MODEL OF HOW ELECTRONS ARE ARRANGED

Once it was realised that electrons could behave like waves, a new model of the atom was possible. This model is based on some very complicated mathematics to describe the wave properties of electrons. Erwin Schrödinger takes the credit for devising an equation that describes the energy levels for electrons in hydrogen and other atoms. (The mathematics is beyond the scope of this book.) His model is known as the **quantum mechanical model**.

Electron shells

Electron shells correspond to the energy levels that Bohr first identified in his model of the atom. The first shell has a **principal quantum number** $n = 1$, the second shell's principal quantum number is $n = 2$, and so on, as in Table 3.1. The first shell is closest to the nucleus and has the lowest energy. As the principal quantum number (or shell number) increases, so does the energy associated with it.

Each shell can hold a maximum number of electrons. You first met shells in your GCSE course, and you may remember that the arrangement of electrons is known as its **electron configuration,** also referred to as **electronic structure**.

EXAMPLE

Q Magnesium has an atomic (proton) number (Z) of 12. Work out the arrangement of electrons in the shells of a magnesium atom.

A The atomic number tells you there are 12 electrons. (The atomic number is the number of protons in an atom, and as the atom has no net charge, it has the same number of electrons. If you need to remind yourself about this, look back to page 27.)
The shells of lowest energy are filled first, so:
   shell 1 will take 2 electrons, which is all it can hold;
   shell 2 will take the next 8 electrons, the maximum it can hold;
   shell 3 will take the remaining two.

So the electron configuration of magnesium is 2,8,2. You can use a *dot and cross* diagram to represent this, as shown in Fig 3.17.

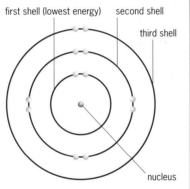

first shell (lowest energy) second shell
third shell
nucleus

Fig 3.17 **The arrangement of the electrons in the shells of a magnesium atom. This is known as a dot and cross diagram because the electrons are represented by dots (as here), or crosses, or both. The first shell is at the lowest energy. The second and third shells are at increasingly higher energies. It requires little additional energy to remove electrons from the third shell**

Evidence for shells

Earlier in this chapter, we met the term ionisation energy which is the energy that an electron must be given to remove it from an atom (or ion). Now let's look at this term more closely. In order to measure ionisation energy, the atoms have to be separated, and this means they must be in the gaseous state. For convenience, the value for ionisation energies is given for one mole of atoms (or ions).

All atoms except hydrogen have more than one electron. The energy required to remove one mole of electrons from one mole of gaseous atoms to give one mole of ions with a single positive charge, is called the **first ionisation energy.** So the first ionisation energy is the energy required to do this:

$$X(g) \rightarrow X^+(g) + e^- \quad \Delta H = \text{ionisation energy in kJ mol}^{-1}$$

where X is any element, (g) tells you that it is gaseous, and e^- is the symbol for an electron.

✓ The energy level of an electron is given a principal quantum number, and this number is also given to the shell it is in.

Table 3.1 **Principal quantum numbers for electrons, and the maximum number of electrons each shell can contain**

Principal quantum number, n	Shell	Max. no. of electrons in shell
1	first	2
2	second	8
3	third	18
4	fourth	36

?

G If you think like a mathematician, you may be able to work out a simple formula containing the principal quantum number, n, which can be used to predict the maximum number of electrons in the nth shell. Hence, calculate the number of electrons in the fifth shell.

Hint: the same formula can be used to predict the maximum number in the first four shells.

?

H Make drawings like that in Fig 3.17 of the following atoms:

(a) aluminium ($Z = 13$),

(b) carbon ($Z = 6$),

(c) chlorine ($Z = 17$).
Hint: refer also to Table 3.1.

The second ionisation energy is the energy required to remove a second mole of electrons:

$$X^+(g) \rightarrow X^{2+}(g) + e^-$$

Let's look again at magnesium with its electron configuration of 2,8,2.

First ionisation energy: $Mg(g) \rightarrow Mg^+(g) + e^-$
$\Delta H = +738 \text{ kJ mol}^{-1}$

Second ionisation energy: $Mg^+(g) \rightarrow Mg^{2+}(g) + e^-$
$\Delta H = +1451 \text{ kJ mol}^{-1}$

Third ionisation energy: $Mg^{2+}(g) \rightarrow Mg^{3+}(g) + e^-$
$\Delta H = +7733 \text{ kJ mol}^{-1}$

The ionisation energy increases as each successive electron is removed. This is the reason: the positive nuclear charge stays the same, because there are still twelve protons in the nucleus, and each time an electron is removed, the remaining ones are attracted more strongly by the nucleus. Notice that there is a large jump in the energy required to remove the third electron. This is because we are breaking into the second shell which is closer to the nucleus.

From these values, you can see that there is a large range in the ionisation energies of magnesium. It would be difficult to choose a scale to plot them. But if we convert the ionisation energies into logarithms to the base 10, $\log_{10}$, we condense the scale and make it more manageable, as in Fig 3.18. Don't worry if you are not familiar with logarithms. Using them here is just a way of making the pattern of the graph easier to see.

?

I (a) Write an equation for the eleventh ionisation energy of magnesium (omitting the energy value).

(b) The energy required to remove the eleventh electron is almost 170 000 kJ mol^{-1} but the tenth ionisation energy is 'only' 35 500 kJ mol^{-1}. Explain this huge jump in energy to remove the eleventh electron.

?

J Sketch a graph like Fig 3.18 for $\log_{10}$ of the successive ionisation energies of sodium, and explain its shape.
Hint: sodium has an electron configuration of 2,8,1.

See question 2. ▪

Fig 3.18 **Graph of the successive ionisation energies (as logarithms to base 10) of the magnesium atom against the number of electrons removed. The values for electrons closest to the nucleus are on the right**

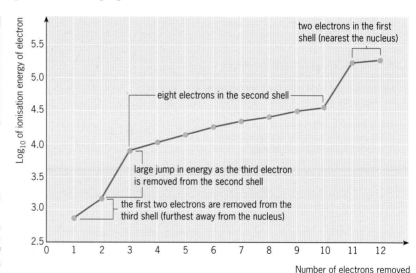

Arranging electrons in subshells

Let us now return to the atomic emission spectra of elements. When looked at in finer detail, the lines on these spectra are seen to be divided into more lines. Each finer line represents the energy level of a subshell. So electrons arranged in shells are also subdivided into subshells or sub-levels. The fine lines result from electron transitions (movement of electrons) between the subshells. The subshells are known by letters.

- **s** subshell contains 2 electrons
- **p** subshell contains 6 electrons
- **d** subshell contains 10 electrons
- **f** subshell contains 14 electrons

The letters go back to the early twentieth century and refer to spectral lines. Some of the lines were **s**harp, hence **s**, some were more spread out or **d**iffuse, and some of the lines were brighter and called **p**rincipal lines.(Note: In this book we do not go into detail about the f subshell.)

We can now see in Table 3.2 how the shells are split into subshells.

Table 3.2 **The system for arranging electrons in shells**

Principal quantum number, n	Shell number	Subshells	Maximum number of electrons	
1	1	1s	2	Total = 2
2	2	2s	2	Total = 8
		2p	6	
3	3	3s	2	Total = 18
		3p	6	
		3d	10	
4	4	4s	2	Total = 32
		4p	6	
		4d	10	
		4f	14	

Notice that the subshell (sub-level) takes the number of the principal quantum number or shell.

The energies of the subshells are shown in Fig 3.19. Notice that the 3d subshell has a higher energy than the 4s subshell. This has important consequences for the chemistry of the transition elements, which you can read more about in Chapter 25.

Evidence for subshells

This too comes from ionisation energies. If we plot the first ionisation energy of different elements against their atomic numbers, a regular pattern emerges. The repeating pattern of a property is called **periodicity.** It forms the basis of the Periodic Table, and you can find out more about it in Chapter 19.

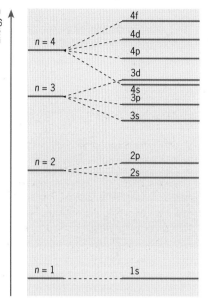

Fig 3.19 **The energies of the various subshells in an atom with many electrons**

Fig 3.20 **Graph showing the periodicity of first ionisation energies as they vary with atomic number (proton number)**

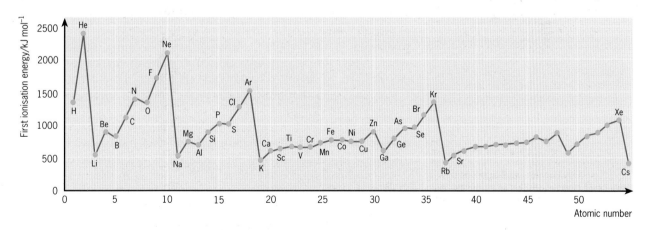

Several features of this graph point to the existence of subshells. Let's look at the eight elements lithium to neon, which have electrons in shell 2. We would expect an increase in first ionisation energy as the atomic number increases. This is because the number of protons in the nucleus is increasing, which increases the nuclear charge. If the electrons were all in the same energy level we would expect the graph to be a straight line, showing a steady increase in first ionisation energy as the protons in the nucleus increase.

The 2,3,3 pattern of first ionisation energies tells us that the electrons removed from this second electron shell are not all arranged to be in the same energy level.

■ See questions 1 and 5.

?

K (a) What is meant by the first ionisation energy of an element?

(b) Explain why the first ionisation energy of neon is higher than that of lithium.

See question 2. ■

L Read about the 2,3,3 pattern for first ionisation energies of the elements lithium to neon and look at Fig 3.20. Then answer the following questions:

(a) Why is there an increase in first ionisation energy from sodium to magnesium?

(b) Explain why there is a drop at **(i)** aluminium and **(ii)** sulphur.

M The first ionisation energy of beryllium (Be) is 900 kJ mol^{-1}, while that of boron (B) is 801 kJ mol^{-1}. Explain this, using information about subshells in the text.

From reading this section on subshells, you may be able to explain the 2,3,3 pattern. Refer back to Fig 3.20 as you read on.

The first part of the 2,3,3 pattern is due to electrons being taken from the 2s subshell. There is an increase in first ionisation energy from Li to Be because Be has an extra proton attracting the outer electrons. Then, instead of a further increase from Be to B, there is a decrease in first ionisation energy as the electron in B is taken from the 2p subshell: this electron is at a higher energy level than the 2s subshell and further from the nucleus.

In moving from B to N, there is the expected increase in first ionisation energy, but another dip occurs at O. After N, the electrons in the 2p subshell start to pair up. (This pairing of electrons in subshells is covered in the next section.) There is more electrostatic repulsion between paired electrons which means that the fourth electron in the 2p subshell is easier to remove, explaining the dip at O.

You can see the same pattern repeated for elements starting with Na when the next shell is being filled. After Mg, there is a drop at Al, and another drop at S. The 3p subshell is complete at Ar.

After this, there is an interruption to the 2,3,3 pattern. There is the expected increase from K to Ca as electrons are taken from the same 4s subshell. Then we have electrons removed from the slightly higher energy 3d subshell (refer back to Fig 3.19) before the 3,3 pattern returns, beginning with Ga, as the 4p subshell electrons are removed.

8 ATOMIC ORBITALS

Another great scientist of the twentieth century was Werner Heisenberg, whose work has clarified our current model of the way electrons are arranged in atoms. In 1927, he said that you could determine either the speed of an electron or its position, but not both at the same time. This he summed up in the **Heisenberg uncertainty principle**. While it applies to any particle, it becomes important only when the particle is very tiny. Heisenberg's mathematics has enabled electron arrangements to be worked out in even more detail.

We have seen that lines appear in the emission spectra of excited atoms, representing the wavelengths (energies) of photons emitted by excited electrons returning to lower energy levels. When this light is passed through a magnetic field, even more lines show up, and these are evidence of what we can now call **atomic orbitals**.

An atomic orbital is a region around the atom where there is a high probability of finding an electron at any moment in time.

The existence of electrons in orbitals helps the chemistry of atoms and molecules to fall into place, and so is tremendously useful.

In the s subshell there is only one orbital, the s orbital. If we draw around the region of the atom where the electron spends most of its time, then we find the s orbital is spherical, see Fig 3.21(a).

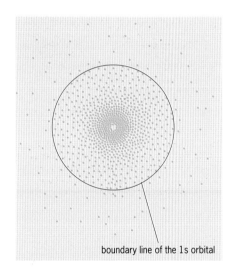

boundary line of the 1s orbital

Fig 3.21(a) **A section through the 1s orbital. If we could map the position of an electron as a dot at regular intervals, then over a period of time, 90 per cent of the dots could be enclosed by drawing a boundary that is spherical. This drawing represents a slice through the sphere. Notice that the electron charge is concentrated close to the nucleus and tails off further out**

Fig 3.21(b) **The boundary surface of 1s, 2s and 3s orbitals. In each case, the imaginary 'surface' is the limit of the space in which the 1s, 2s and 3s electrons are likely to be found. Also in each case, the orbital is centred on the nucleus, and the boundary represents a 90 per cent probability of finding an electron within it**

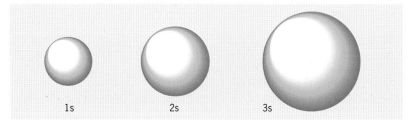

1s   2s   3s

There are three p orbitals in the p subshell. They are dumb-bell shaped and arranged at right angles to each other with the nucleus in the centre of each dumb-bell.

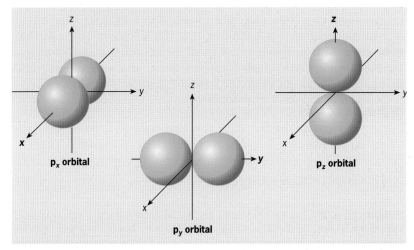

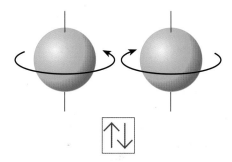

p$_x$ orbital

p$_y$ orbital

p$_z$ orbital

Fig 3.22 **The three p orbitals found in the p subshell**

The d subshell contains five d orbitals. We shall look at d orbitals in more detail in Chapter 25.

Spinning electrons

Each atomic orbital can hold a maximum of two electrons. As the electrons move in their orbitals they are also spinning on their own axes. If there are two electrons, one spins clockwise while the other spins anticlockwise. This keeps the repulsion of the electrons to a minimum. Electron spin is often represented by box diagrams, where each box is an atomic orbital, and arrows represent the electrons spinning in opposite directions, as in Fig 3.23.

Addressing electrons

So we are now in a position to give *addresses* to electrons. In the same way that a letter can be addressed with the country, the town, the street and house number, to arrive at only one unique destination, so we can give a unique 'address' to represent the state of an electron in an atom. The idea of a unique state for every electron is known as the **Pauli exclusion principle**. According to this principle, an electron is precisely defined by:

- its shell – the main energy level,
- its subshell – the sub-energy level division of the shell,
- its atomic orbital – each subshell possesses at least one atomic orbital, and all orbitals in a subshell possess the same energy,
- and its direction of spin – a maximum of two electrons of opposite spin can occupy one atomic orbital: orbitals in the same subshell are singly filled first, with electrons of parallel spin.

Fig 3.24 shows the electron configuration of the magnesium atom in its ground state. Remember, this is the lowest energy state of the atom, so the electrons occupy orbitals in subshells of the lowest possible energy.

Notice that:

- the s subshells contain one s atomic orbital,
- the p subshells contain three p orbitals,
- each orbital contains a maximum of two electrons with opposite spin.

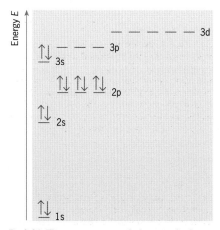

Fig 3.23 **Two electrons in the same atomic orbital spin in opposite directions and this is represented by a box diagram with arrows showing the opposite spin of each electron. The box is the atomic orbital**

Fig 3.24 **The arrangement of electrons in the atomic orbitals of a magnesium atom. The atom is in its ground state, so no electrons have been excited into higher energy orbitals**

9 THE ELECTRON CONFIGURATIONS OF THE FIRST TWENTY ELEMENTS

Let us now look at how electrons fill orbitals in an atom. The orbitals of lowest energy are occupied first, and this is known as the **aufbau principle.** Aufbau is a German word for building up. So when you are building up the electron configuration of an element, remember that each electron goes into the lowest energy orbital available.

Hydrogen ($Z = 1$)
The lowest energy orbital is in the first shell that has a principal quantum number $n = 1$ and is an s orbital, so it is written 1s.

1s

| ↑ | electron configuration $1s^1$

Helium ($Z = 2$)

1s

| ↑↓ | electron configuration $1s^2$

Note: When you say $1s^2$, it is 'one s two', not 'one s squared'!

The next atom has three electrons, and the aufbau principle tells us that this electron will occupy the next orbital of lowest energy, which is in the $n = 2$ shell, so it will start with 2 and be an s orbital, therefore it is 2s.

Lithium ($Z = 3$)

1s   2s

| ↑↓ | | ↑ | electron configuration $1s^2 2s^1$

Beryllium ($Z = 4$)

1s   2s

| ↑↓ | | ↑↓ | electron configuration $1s^2 2s^2$

Next, we come to filling the p subshell. Notice that each orbital is occupied singly at first. This is because two electrons in the same orbital exert a repulsion that raises the energy of a doubly filled orbital higher than a singly filled one. Notice that the spins are all in the same direction. The repulsion that results helps to keep the electrons apart.

Boron ($Z = 5$)

1s   2s   2p

| ↑↓ | | ↑↓ | | ↑ | | | | | electron configuration $1s^2 2s^2 2p^1$

Carbon ($Z = 6$)

1s   2s   2p

| ↑↓ | | ↑↓ | | ↑ | | ↑ | | | electron configuration $1s^2 2s^2 2p^2$

Nitrogen ($Z = 7$)

1s   2s   2p

| ↑↓ | | ↑↓ | | ↑ | | ↑ | | ↑ | electron configuration $1s^2 2s^2 2p^3$

Oxygen ($Z = 8$)

1s   2s   2p

| ↑↓ | | ↑↓ | | ↑↓ | ↑ | | ↑ | electron configuration $1s^2 2s^2 2p^4$

Fluorine (Z = 9)

1s   2s   2p

[↑↓] [↑↓] [↑↓][↑↓][↑]   electron configuration $1s^2 2s^2 2p^5$

Neon (Z = 10)

1s   2s   2p

[↑↓] [↑↓] [↑↓][↑↓][↑↓]   electron configuration $1s^2 2s^2 2p^6$

The next eight elements follow the same pattern, filling up the s and p orbitals of the third shell.

Potassium and calcium come next. The 3d subshell is available, but remember (Fig 3.19, page 59) that the 4s subshell has a lower energy, so it is filled first.

Potassium (Z = 19)

1s   2s   2p   3s   3p   3d   4s

[↑↓] [↑↓] [↑↓][↑↓][↑↓] [↑↓] [↑↓][↑↓][↑↓] [ ][ ][ ][ ][ ] [↑]

electron configuration $1s^2 2s^2 2p^6 3s^2 3p^6 4s^1$

Notice that we do not write $3d^0$ in the electron configuration. We leave it out. Similarly we can draw the box diagram for calcium like this:

Calcium (Z = 20)

1s   2s   2p   3s   3p   4s

[↑↓] [↑↓] [↑↓][↑↓][↑↓] [↑↓] [↑↓][↑↓][↑↓] [↑↓]

EXAMPLE

Q What is the electron configuration of sulphur (Z = 16)?

A The atomic number is 16, so there are sixteen electrons. We already know that the arrangement in the first two shells is:

$$1s^2 \ 2s^2 \ 2p^6$$

This takes ten electrons, leaving six electrons to place. Remember to start with the lowest energy orbital available, the 3s. This orbital takes two electrons:

$$1s^2 \ 2s^2 \ 2p^6 \ 3s^2$$

leaving another four to make the electron configuration for sulphur:

$$1s^2 \ 2s^2 \ 2p^6 \ 3s^2 \ 3p^4$$

■ See question 4.

?

N Write down the electron configuration of sodium (Z = 11), chlorine (Z = 17) and aluminium (Z = 13).

10 ELECTRON CONFIGURATIONS AND THE PERIODIC TABLE

When we know the electron configurations of the elements, we can organise and explain the chemical properties of the elements, because it is the electrons that determine these properties. Long before electrons were even known to exist, Mendeleev grouped together elements with similar properties in his Periodic Table. You can read much more about this in Chapter 19. However, from your GCSE course you will know about the Periodic Table, so let's see how electron configurations fit in.

Group	1	2											3	4	5	6	7	0
Period 1							H $1s^1$											He $1s^2$
2	Li $2s^1$	Be $2s^2$											B $2p^1$	C $2p^2$	N $2p^3$	O $2p^4$	F $2p^5$	Ne $2p^6$
3	Na $3s^1$	Mg $3s^2$											Al $3p^1$	Si $3p^2$	P $3p^3$	S $3p^4$	Cl $3p^5$	Ar $3p^6$
4	K $4s^1$	Ca $4s^2$	Sc $3d^14s^2$	Ti $3d^24s^2$	V $3d^34s^2$	Cr $3d^54s^1$	Mn $3d^54s^2$	Fe $3d^64s^2$	Co $3d^74s^2$	Ni $3d^84s^2$	Cu $3d^{10}4s^1$	Zn $3d^{10}4s^2$	Ga $4p^1$	Ge $4p^2$	As $4p^3$	Se $4p^4$	Br $4p^5$	Kr $4p^6$

Fig 3.25 **The Periodic Table, showing the first 36 elements and their outer orbital electron configurations. For the transition elements, we include the 3d orbital as well as the 4s orbital. Although the outermost subshell for the transition elements is d, it is written with the rest of its quantum shell number 3**

Fig 3.25 shows the electron configuration for the outermost sub-shell of the first 36 elements. In Period 4, containing the transition elements, electron configurations show the two outermost sub-shells, because it is the d subshell that is being filled. Notice that the elements in each of the eight main groups end with the same number of electrons in their outer subshell. So Group 7 always has a p^5 subshell and Group 2 always has a filled s^2 orbital. The Periodic Table is often divided into blocks, as in Fig 3.26, according to the subshell being filled.

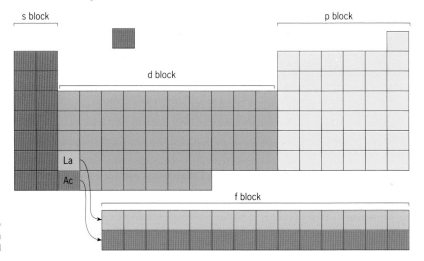

See question 4.

Fig 3.26 **The Periodic Table, showing the different blocks labelled according to which outer orbital is being filled**

So when we know how electrons are arranged in atoms, we have a better understanding of how the Periodic Table is arranged. It groups elements together with similar properties, and we can now see that it is the electron configuration that determines this similarity in properties.

SUMMARY

When you have studied this chapter, you should be able to understand the following ideas.

■ Evidence for the arrangement of electrons in energy levels comes from the line emission spectra of atoms.

■ Energy levels are quantised, which means that each level has a fixed amount of energy.

■ An electron can move from a lower to a higher energy level by absorbing a quantum (packet) of energy. It releases the same quantum of energy when it falls back, as a photon of light of a particular frequency (which gives a line in the emission spectrum).

■ The arrangement of electrons in an atom is called its electron configuration.

■ Energy levels are also known as shells and subshells.

■ Shells are numbered 1, 2, 3 and so on. The shell number is also known as the principal quantum number.

■ The higher the shell number, the higher is its energy and the further the shell is from the nucleus.

■ Successive ionisation energies of atoms provide evidence of shells.

■ Within each shell there are subshells s, p, d and f, of different energies. Shell 1 only contains an s subshell. Shell 2 contains two subshells, s and p, while shell 3 contains three subshells s, p and d.

■ A plot of first ionisation energy against atomic number provides evidence of subshells. In each subshell the electrons are arranged in atomic orbitals.

■ Atomic orbitals are regions in the atom where there is a high probability of finding the electron.

■ There is one s atomic orbital in the s subshell, three p orbitals in the p subshell and five d orbitals in the d subshell.

■ Each atomic orbital can accommodate two electrons of opposite spins.

■ The Periodic Table is arranged in blocks, s, p, d and f, according to the subshell that is being filled.

QUESTIONS

1

a) Describe the main features of the atomic spectrum of hydrogen, and show how their interpretation provides strong evidence for quantised energy levels in the atom.
b) The ionisation energy of a hydrogen atom is 2.178×10^{-18} J. Discuss briefly the meaning of this statement, and calculate the minimum frequency of radiation required to ionise a hydrogen atom in its ground state ($n = 1$).
(Planck's constant $h = 6.626 \times 10^{-34}$ J s.)
c) Comment, with appropriate explanation, on how you would expect the ionisation energy of hydrogen to compare with the first ionisation energy of
(i) helium and (ii) lithium.
[JMB Advanced Chemistry Syllabus B, Paper II, Section B, June 1986]

2

a) The table gives the standard molar first ionisation energies (IE) of a series of consecutive elements in the Periodic Table:

Element	Na	Mg	Al	Si	P	S	Cl	Ar	K	Ca
IE/kJ mol⁻¹	496	738	578	789	1012	1000	1251	1521	419	590

Define the term molar first ionisation energy.
b) Explain in terms of electron configurations why:
(i) K has a lower standard molar first ionisation energy than Ar;
(ii) K has a lower standard molar first ionisation energy than Na;

(iii) Mg has a higher standard molar first ionisation energy than Na;
(iv) Al has a lower standard molar first ionisation energy than Mg;
c) For the element Al, sketch a graph showing the variations of its first 12 ionisation energies and explain its shape.
[AEB Advanced Chemistry Specimen Terminal Paper 1, 1993] Note: Molar first ionisation energy is another term for first ionisation energy.

3

a) What is meant by the phrase 'the ground state of an atom'?
b) Identify the following elements from their electron configurations. One of them is in an excited state. State which one and give its ground state electron configuration.
A $1s^2\ 2s^2\ 2p^2$ C $1s^2\ 2s^2\ 2p^6\ 3s^1$
B $1s^2\ 2s^2\ 2p^4\ 3s^1$ D $1s^2\ 2s^2\ 2p^6\ 3s^2\ 3p^2$

4

a) Write the electron configuration of the element with atomic number 19 using atomic orbital box diagrams.
b) Why is the 4s orbital occupied before the 3d orbitals?
c) To which block of the Periodic Table does this element belong? Give a reason for your answer.

5

Sketch a graph of the first ionisation energies of the elements lithium to neon. Explain as fully as you can the reasons for the shape of this graph.

Assignment

THE COLOURS OF FIREWORKS

We think fireworks were invented by the Chinese over a thousand years ago. They used black powder (we call it gunpowder) to produce loud bangs. But the brilliant colours we see today only found their way into fireworks in the nineteenth century. Before this time a firework would have produced one colour – gold – due to the burning of charcoal in gun powder. It is the movement between energy levels of electrons in compounds that causes the colours we see. A yellow colour is obtained with sodium compounds. The electrons in a sodium ion are excited to higher energy levels by absorbing energy. This energy is supplied when the fuel used in a firework is oxidised in an exothermic reaction. When the electrons return to lower energy levels they release some of this energy at a wavelength of 589 nm, which is yellow in the visible spectrum.

Fig 3.A1 **The spectacular colours of fireworks are due to excited electrons**

1

a) What is the frequency of the yellow light emitted by the sodium ion?
b) What is the energy of **(i)** one photon of this yellow light, **(ii)** one mole of these photons?
c) Explain what is meant by the following terms used in this Assignment: **(i)** excited electron, **(ii)** exothermic, **(iii)** energy level.

2

Before the firework is let off, the electrons in the sodium ion are in their ground state.
a) What is meant by ground state?
b) What is the ground state electron configuration using s,p,d notation of **(i)** the sodium atom, **(ii)** the sodium ion?

Different colours are produced using other metal salts. Strontium in strontium carbonate produces colours at 606 nm and 636 nm, while barium nitrate produces a green colour due to the green lines in its emission spectrum between 505 and 535 nm. Blue is a difficult colour to produce well, but it is done using copper salts.

The colour of a firework is intensified using compounds that donate chlorine. While the firework is alight they cause the very unstable compounds $BaCl$, $SrCl$ and $CuCl$ to be produced in the flame. One of the chlorine donors is the polymer PVC.

3

a) What colour is produced by strontium? Hint: Look back at Fig 3.5.
b) Strontium and barium are both in Group 2 of the Periodic Table. What is their outer shell configuration in s,p,d notation?
c) Copper is a transition metal. To which block of the Periodic Table does it belong?

4

a) You may have carried out a flame test. Research and write down the procedure you would follow to do a flame test on a potassium compound.
b) Explain the result you would expect to observe in terms of energy levels and electrons.

5

a) Mercury chloride was once used to intensify the colours of fireworks. Why is it no longer used?
b) Should we be concerned about any of the metal salts that colour fireworks and so are dispersing into the atmosphere? Explain your answer.

A CLOSE LOOK AT ELECTRONS

This Chapter Map draws together the main ideas covered in this chapter. It will help you remember the coverage of the chapter and how the ideas are interlinked. You can use the map to make connections with your studies of other chapters, in particular Chapters 19 to 21 covering the Periodic Table. The map will also help in planning your revision.

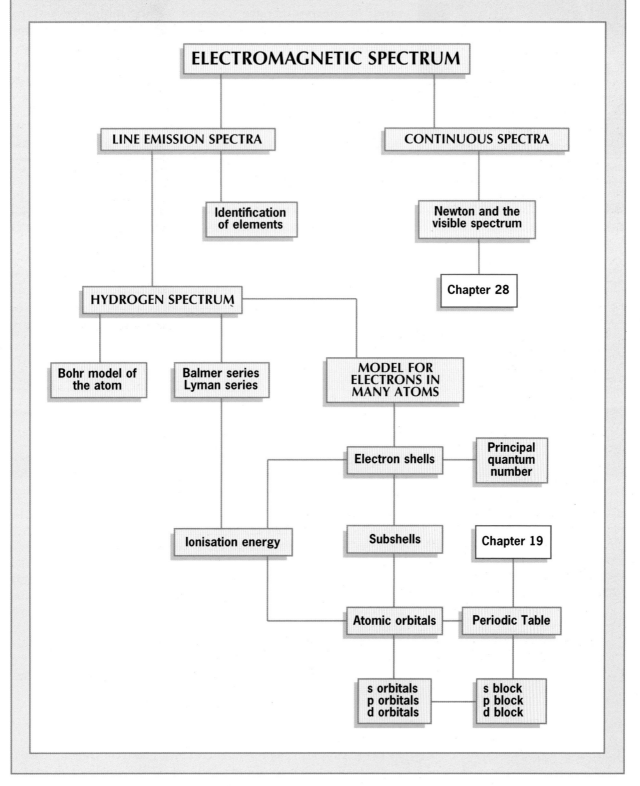

4 Chemical bonding and molecular structure

MOST OF THE DRUGS used to treat illnesses today have been discovered after a process of search and trial. Many thousands of compounds are screened for any biological activity before a promising compound is found. Now, this time-consuming and enormously expensive process is being dramatically speeded up by computer-aided drug design, based on knowing the three-dimensional shape of chemicals and how shape affects biological activity.

Drugs work on complex chemical receptor sites around the body, rather like keys fitting into locks. Researchers first use X-ray crystallography to work out the shape and structure of a receptor site they are interested in. Then they can start to design a drug that fits into the site and may turn out to be useful. It is here that computers help, since molecular shapes are easily visualised using computer graphics.

During on-screen design, different groups of atoms are made to probe the surface of the site, and gradually the shape of the active part of a drug, the pharmacophore, can be built up. Investigators then see if the designed compound is known or if it can be synthesised. Databases of known compounds are searched for compounds with the right pharmacophore.

While computers will not replace laboratory chemistry, they greatly reduce the cost and time of finding suitable compounds to investigate further.

Computers aid drug design: the geometry of biological molecules is studied on screen, and this helps to design drugs that are likely to fit receptor sites and alter biological activity

1 NOBLE GASES AND STABILITY

Until 1962, chemists thought that the elements in Group 0 were inert (totally unreactive and so unable to form compounds). The group was even called the inert gases. Then in 1962, the British chemist Neil Bartlett synthesised the first Group 0 compound containing xenon, xenon hexafluoroplatinate. This caused a sensation, and chemists rushed to make more. Three years later there were textbooks devoted to noble gas chemistry. Only helium and neon deserve the title 'inert' as they still seem not to form any compounds, so Group 0 now bears the name of 'noble'.

The noble gases were discovered more than 50 years before chemists made compounds of them. Why did it take so long? It is largely because chemists learnt about elements through their reactions, so unreactive elements remained unknown longer.

Outer shell stability of noble gases

In 1916, American chemists Gilbert Lewis and Irvin Langmuir separately realised that the outer shells of all the noble gases except helium contained eight electrons, and they suggested that it was this electron configuration that made the noble gases unreactive. They put forward the idea that when atoms of other elements formed compounds they gained, lost or shared electrons to make a noble gas outer shell of eight – or two for the lighter elements close to helium.

The ionisation energy of the noble gases also confirms this stability (see Fig 3.20, page 59); as you go across a period, the first ionisation energy rises to a maximum at Group 0. Because the configuration is so stable it takes a great deal of energy to remove an electron.

A What is the outer shell electron configuration (using s and p orbital notation) of the noble gases? Hint: look back at Chapter 3, page 64. Electron configuration means the number of electrons and their arrangement in orbitals within an atom or a molecule.

2 IONIC BONDING

A **chemical bond** is an electrostatic force of attraction between two atoms or ions. **Ions** are formed when atoms lose or gain electrons and become charged.

An ionic bond is the electrostatic attraction that forms between oppositely charged ions.

Sometimes ionic bonds are called **electrovalent bonds**.

A common ionic compound is sodium chloride, an industrially important raw material (see Chapter 24). The dot and cross diagram of Fig 4.1 shows how the atoms of sodium and chlorine achieve noble gas configurations. Usually only the outer electrons are shown, as the inner shells stay the same.

The sodium atom loses one electron, leaving a noble gas core of 2,8. But because it still has 11 protons it now has a +1 positive charge. It has formed a positive ion: positive ions are called **cations**.

The chlorine atom gains one electron to make the noble gas configuration of 2,8,8: it has one more electron than protons in the nucleus, giving it a charge of –1. Negative ions are called **anions**. Opposite charges attract by electrostatic attraction and this holds the sodium ions and chloride ions together.

Sodium ions and chloride ions are roughly spherical, and the negative charge is distributed evenly all over the spheres. Each sodium ion attracts several chloride ions and vice versa, so the ionic bonding is not just between one sodium ion and one chloride ion. The ions form an ordered three-dimensional structure known as a **lattice**, shown in Fig 4.2(a). The formula unit of this lattice is NaCl (see Chapter 1, page 4). Because the ionic bonds in the lattice are strong, it takes a lot of energy to separate the ions, and so sodium chloride has a high melting point.

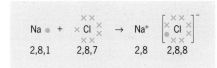

Fig 4.1 **Dot and cross diagram for the outer electrons of sodium chloride. The transfer of an outer shell electron from sodium to chlorine gives two oppositely charged ions. Both ions have a noble gas configuration**

B When sodium and chlorine form ions, which noble gas configuration does each have?

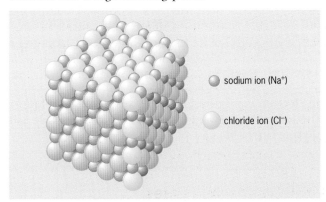

Fig 4.2(a) **Part of a sodium chloride lattice. Each ion is surrounded by six oppositely charged ions (find out more about ionic lattices and their properties in Chapters 21 and 22)**

Fig 4.2(b) **Crystals of sodium chloride**

Note that, although we draw dots and crosses, one electron is the same as any other, and you may well see diagrams with all dots. We use dots and crosses purely for the convenience of showing which atom they come from. Note also that the dots and crosses do not represent the positions of electrons in an atom (see Chapter 3, page 60).

C Work out dot and cross diagrams for:

(a) potassium fluoride,

(b) magnesium oxide,

(c) calcium chloride,

(d) sodium oxide.

State the formula of each compound.

D (a) Fluorine, chlorine, bromine and iodine are all in Group 7. How many electrons are there in the outer shell of each?

(b) How many electrons are in the outer shell of:

(i) Group 1 elements,

(ii) Group 2 elements?

E Sodium ions and chloride ions are isoelectronic with which noble gases?

EXAMPLE

Q Work out the dot and cross diagrams for calcium fluoride and aluminium oxide.

A

Calcium fluoride

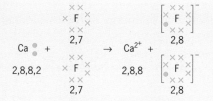

Fig 4.3

Calcium must lose two electrons to achieve noble gas configuration, and fluorine needs only one. So there are two fluoride ions for each calcium ion, giving a formula of CaF_2.

Aluminium oxide

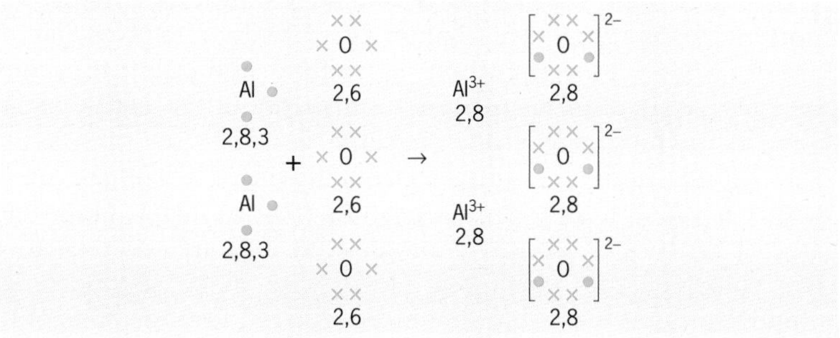

Fig 4.4

From Fig 4.4, the formula is Al_2O_3.

Ionic bonding and atomic orbitals

So far we have seen the formation of ions in terms of dot and cross diagrams. This is a good model to explain how ions are formed. But how does this fit in with the atomic orbital model of the atom on pages 60–63? Let's look at some examples.

In sodium chloride:

$$Na \quad + \quad Cl \quad \rightarrow \quad Na^+ \quad + \quad Cl^-$$

$$1s^22s^22p^63s^1 \quad 1s^22s^22p^63s^23p^5 \quad 1s^22s^22p^6 \quad 1s^22s^22p^63s^23p^6$$

$$\hookrightarrow 1 \text{ electron moves} \rfloor$$

We can write electron configurations using a simplified notation; we represent the inner shells (sometimes known as the **noble gas core**) by the appropriate noble gas:

$$[Ne]3s^1 \quad + \quad [Ne]3s^23p^5 \quad \rightarrow \quad [He]2s^22p^6 \quad + \quad [Ne]3s^23p^6$$

Both ions have attained noble gas configurations on the right: they are **isoelectronic** with the noble gases, meaning that they have the same electron configuration.

The 3s electron is removed from the sodium atom because the 3s orbital is the highest energy orbital in the outer shell, and so needs the least amount of energy to transfer it. Electrons in the inner shells are not removed during a normal chemical reaction: their orbitals are at a much lower energy because they are part of a stable full shell closer to the nucleus, so their removal would require very high energies.

For calcium fluoride:

$$Ca + F \rightarrow Ca^{2+} + F^-$$
$$1s^22s^22p^63s^23p^64s^2 \quad 1s^22s^22p^5 \quad 1s^22s^22p^63s^23p^6 \quad 1s^22s^22p^6$$
$$[Ar]4s^2 \quad [He]2s^22p^5 \quad [Ne]3s^23p^6 \quad [He]2s^22p^6$$

$$F \quad\quad\quad F^-$$
$$1s^22s^22p^5 \quad\quad 1s^22s^22p^6$$
$$[He]2s^22p^5 \quad\quad [He]2s^22p^6$$

F Write out the full and simplified electron configurations (using s, p, d notation) to show how ionic bonding arises in:

(a) potassium fluoride,

(b) magnesium chloride,

(c) aluminium oxide.

▥ See question 5.

The energy considerations of ionic bonding

Notice that ionic bonds are formed between metal atoms which lose electrons and non-metal atoms which gain electrons. Look back at Fig 3.20, page 59, to see that metals have low first ionisation energies. So the energy required to remove electrons from metals to attain a noble gas structure is relatively low. Non-metals, particularly oxygen and those in Group 7, have a strong affinity (attraction) for electrons. **Electron affinity** can be measured and is the energy change when *gaseous atoms* attract electrons. Fluorine has a very large electron affinity:

$$F(g) + e^- \rightarrow F^-(g) \quad \Delta H = -328\,kJ\,mol^{-1}$$

To be strictly correct, this is the first electron affinity of fluorine and this is its definition:

> **The first electron affinity is the energy change when one mole of gaseous atoms accepts one mole of electrons to form one mole of singly charged anions.**

Looking at the first ionisation energy of sodium:

$$Na(g) \rightarrow Na^+(g) + e^- \quad \Delta H = +496\,kJ\,mol^{-1}$$

We can see that the energy released by fluorine gaining an electron is not enough to remove an electron from sodium. So why do sodium and fluoride ions form in the compound sodium fluoride? It is because of the very large amount of energy released when solid sodium fluoride forms from these gaseous ions:

$$Na^+(g) + F^-(g) \rightarrow Na^+F^-(s) \quad \Delta H = -918\,kJ\,mol^{-1}$$

> **The energy released when one mole of solid sodium fluoride is formed from its gaseous ions is called the lattice energy.**

It is this highly exothermic **lattice energy**, caused by the strong electrostatic attraction of oppositely charged ions, which makes sodium fluoride much more stable than the elements sodium and fluorine. This shows that, while ions that are being formed need to achieve full noble gas shells, we have to look at all the energy changes to get the full picture.

Energy is released when gaseous atoms each attract an electron. Since the atoms *lose* energy, the value for electron affinity is *negative*.

G What does the minus sign tell you about the electron affinity of fluorine?

You can read more about lattice energy, electron affinity and first ionisation energy in the formation of ionic compounds on page 467.

3 COVALENT BONDING AND THE FORMATION OF MOLECULES

Many of the compounds we come across in everyday life are covalent compounds. The wood or plastic of a table top, the clothes we wear, nearly all the food we eat and most of the body's chemicals have atoms which are joined together by **covalent bonds.**

So what is a covalent bond? The answer again lies in the stability of noble gas electron configurations: with the exception of helium, there are eight electrons in an outer shell. For elements in Groups 4 to 7 in the Periodic Table, the loss of four or more electrons to achieve a noble gas configuration requires a great deal of energy which could not be paid back by the formation of a stable lattice. So ions with a charge of 4+ or more do not occur under the usual conditions of a chemical reaction. Instead, the atoms of these elements achieve noble gas configurations by *sharing* electrons.

Let us look at the example of methane, CH_4 (Fig 4.5), found in natural gas. Its molecule contains one carbon atom and four hydrogen atoms.

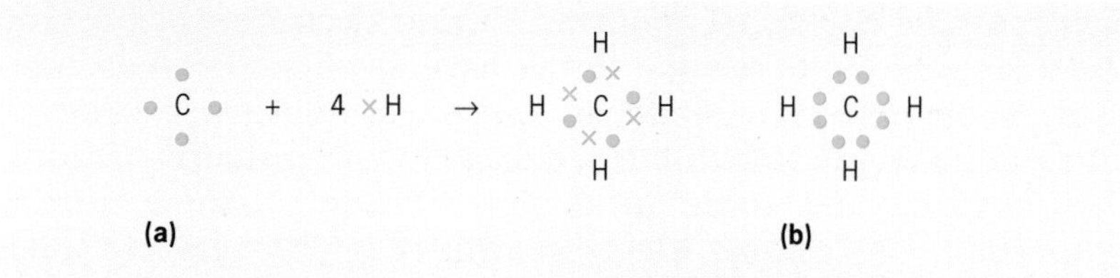

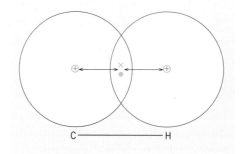

(a)   **(b)**

Fig 4.5(a) **Dot and cross diagram for methane. Remember that electrons can be represented by dots or crosses, and this dot and cross diagram could be written just using dots, as in** (b), **or just using crosses**

By sharing outer shell electrons, hydrogen has the noble gas configuration of helium (ie 2) and carbon has the neon configuration (2,8).

Now we can answer the question: What is a covalent bond?

A covalent bond is a pair of electrons shared between two atoms.

The force holding the carbon and hydrogen atoms together in this bond is electrostatic attraction between their positive nuclei and the shared pair of negative electrons.

We represent the shared pair of electrons as a line, as shown for the C–H bond in Fig 4.6 and the methane molecule in Fig 4.7.

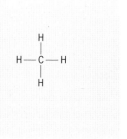

Fig 4.6 **The C–H bond: electrostatic forces between the shared pair of electrons and the nuclei hold the carbon and hydrogen atoms together in the covalent bond**

Fig 4.7 **The methane molecule**

The bonding in a fluorine molecule (Fig 4.8) is also covalent. Fluorine is in Group 7, so has 7 electrons in its outer shell.

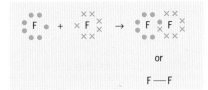

Fig 4.8 **The fluorine molecule**

Each fluorine atom has achieved an **octet** (8 electrons) through sharing a pair of electrons. In this molecule there is one **bonding pair** of electrons and three **non-bonding pairs** or **lone pairs.** While lone pairs play no part in the bond, they are important in determining the shape of a molecule. We will look at this more closely on page 79.

EXAMPLE

Q Use dot and cross diagrams to show the covalent bonding in water, H_2O.

A The oxygen atom has 6 electrons (it is in Group 6). Draw out the separate atoms first, and then combine them in the molecule.

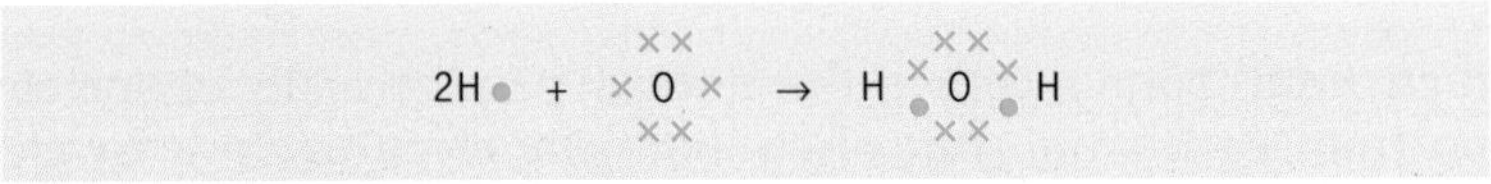

$$2H \bullet \ + \ \times O \times \ \rightarrow \ H \ O \ H$$

Fig 4.9

H Draw electron dot and cross diagrams for the following molecules:

(a) ammonia, NH_3,

(b) hydrogen, H_2,

(c) chlorine, Cl_2.

Multiple bonds

Sometimes sharing one pair of electrons is not enough to make up a noble gas configuration. Carbon dioxide is a very common molecule held together by **double bonds** (Fig 4.10).

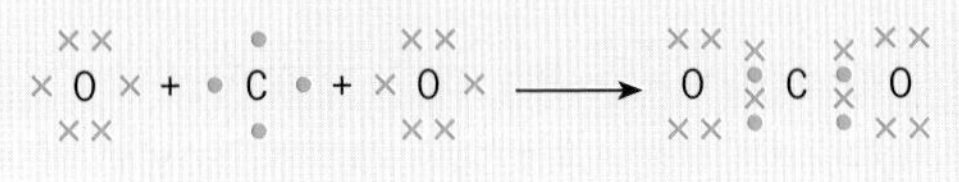

$$\times O \times + \bullet C \bullet + \times O \times \longrightarrow O \ C \ O \qquad O{=}C{=}O$$

Fig 4.10 **The carbon dioxide molecule** 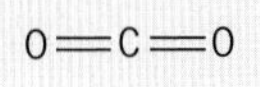   Fig 4.11 **Bonds in carbon dioxide**

Carbon shares two pairs of electrons with each oxygen, so all three atoms achieve the noble gas octet. Count the electrons round each atom to be convinced of this. As in Fig 4.11, double bonds are shown by two lines.

Seventy-nine per cent of our atmosphere is nitrogen, N_2. It is a very unreactive molecule because its very strong **triple bond** needs to be broken before it can react.

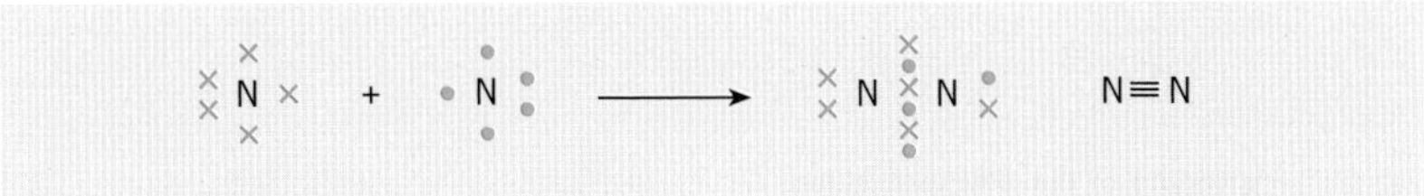

$$\times N \times \ + \ \bullet N \bullet \longrightarrow \ \times N \ N \bullet \qquad N{\equiv}N$$

Fig 4.12 **The nitrogen molecule**

EXAMPLE

Q Methanal, HCHO, reacts with phenol to make the glue which holds plywood together. Draw out the dot and cross diagram for methanal and hence show the covalent bonds.

A **Step 1.** Draw dot and cross diagrams for the separate atoms of the molecule:

Step 2. Arrange the atoms in the order they are in the molecule (if you know this) and put in shared pairs of electrons for those atoms which can only form a single bond – in this case, the hydrogen atoms:

Step 3. Now make up noble gas configurations for the other atoms using one, two or three shared pairs:

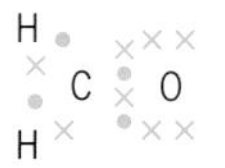

Now you can draw the bonds for each of the shared pairs:

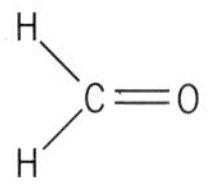

?

I Draw dot and cross diagrams for the following molecules and draw separate diagrams to show the covalent bonds.

(a) oxygen

(b) ethene, C_2H_4

(c) hydrogen cyanide, HCN

See questions 2, 3 and 6.

4 COORDINATE (DATIVE COVALENT) BONDS

When atoms bond together, the electron pair is usually of one electron from each atom. But often, both the electrons in a covalent bond come from just one of the atoms. This bond is called a **dative covalent bond**, or a **coordinate bond**.

The poisonous gas carbon monoxide is a good example, see Fig 4.14(a). As in (b), an arrow is sometimes used to show which atom has donated the pair of electrons. But since the bond, once formed, is exactly the same as any other covalent bond, we usually draw it as in (c).

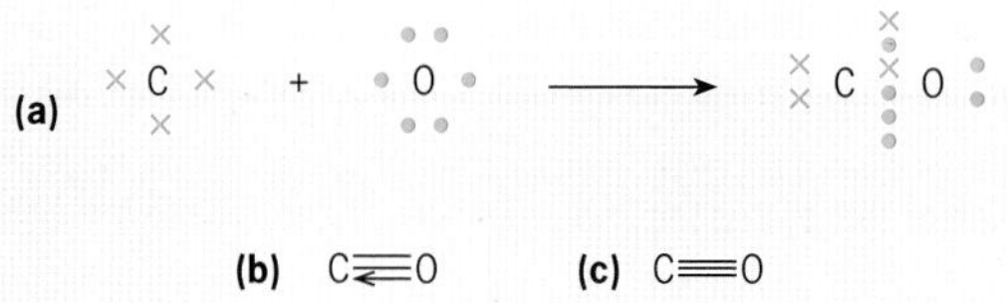

(a)

(b)   C≷O   (c)   C≡O

Fig 4.14 **The carbon monoxide molecule**

?

J Draw the dot and cross diagram for the oxonium ion, H_3O^+. Hint: This is made up of water and a proton.

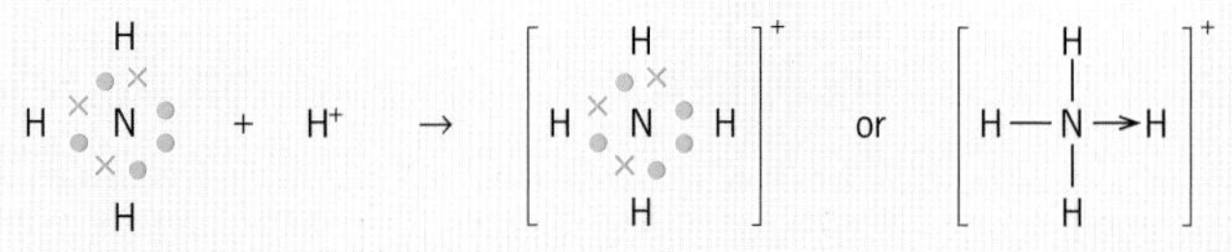

Another example is the ammonium ion, formed when an ammonia molecule bonds with a proton (H^+). Note that when a hydrogen atom loses its electron we are left with a nucleus consisting of one proton.

Fig 4.15 **Formation of the ammonium ion**

The whole species has a charge of +1 because there is still one more proton than there are electrons.

5 EXCEPTIONS TO THE OCTET RULE

We work out how a molecule is bonded using noble gas configurations. Since the atoms of the noble gases (apart from helium) contain eight outer shell electrons, this is sometimes called the **octet rule**. However, some atoms can expand their octets.

More electrons than an octet

At the start of this chapter we saw that the first noble gas compound was made in 1962, more than fifty years after noble gases were discovered. Chemists had not tried earlier since they were convinced that an atom with eight outer shell electrons would be inert (unreactive). One of the first compounds to be synthesised was xenon tetrafluoride. Fig 4.16(b) shows the dot and cross diagram for this molecule.

Before chemists found that noble gases could expand their octets, many other compounds were known that broke the octet rule, for example phosphorus(V) chloride, PCl_5, see Fig 4.17.

Fewer electrons than an octet

Some compounds have less than an octet of electrons. Aluminium chloride as a gas exists as $AlCl_3$, as Fig 4.18(a).

(Aluminium chloride has another surprise: it has covalent bonds between metal and non-metal atoms. We shall return to this on page 85.)

Though there are only six electrons round the aluminium, we can produce an imaginary dot and cross diagram with a stable octet, see Fig 4.18(b). But this does not agree with the experimental evidence obtained using X-rays which shows three single covalent bonds round the aluminium.

When aluminium chloride gas is cooled, the formula of the molecule is found to be Al_2Cl_6, as in Fig 4.18(c). There are two dative covalent bonds, shown with arrows: you can see that every atom now has its noble gas octet.

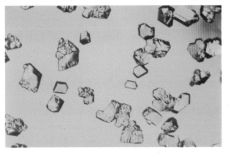

Fig 4.16(a) **Xenon tetrafluoride crystals. One of the first noble gas compounds to be made**

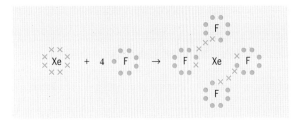

Fig 4.16(b) **The xenon tetrafluoride molecule**

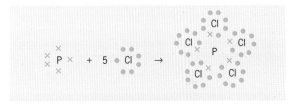

Fig 4.17 **The phosphorus(V) chloride molecule**

K Draw dot and cross diagrams for sulphur(VI) fluoride, SF_6.

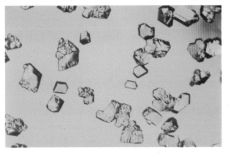

Fig 4.18 **The aluminium chloride gas molecule** (a) **as a gas with six electrons round the aluminium atom,** (b) **with an octet round Al –** *this form does not exist*, (c) **in the cooled gas**

See question 1.

L BF$_3$ reacts with NH$_3$ to form the molecule BF$_3$NH$_3$. In this molecule, boron has eight electrons in its outer shell. Draw the dot and cross diagram for this molecule and a diagram of the molecule showing the bonds as lines.

Many compounds of boron are called electron deficient because the boron has just 6 electrons round its atom, as in boron trifluoride, BF$_3$, shown in Fig 4.19.

Fig 4.19 **The boron trifluoride molecule**

DISCOVERING CRYSTAL STRUCTURES WITH X-RAY CRYSTALLOGRAPHY

X-RAY CRYSTALLOGRAPHY is one of the most effective techniques used to find out the structure of compounds. It has its origins back in 1912, when the German scientist Max von Laue first suggested that atoms in crystals might diffract (bend and scatter) X-rays. Crystals diffract X-rays because the wavelength of X-rays is about the same as the distance between the nuclei in a crystal. As the X-rays scatter, some of the waves constructively interfere – they follow parallel wave paths, see Fig 4.20(a) – and this leads to spots on a photographic film, as shown in the diffraction pattern of Fig 4.20(c).

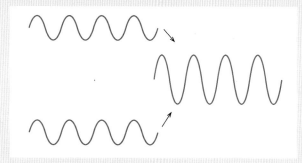

Fig 4.20(a) **X-rays that follow parallel wave paths (are in phase) constructively interfere to reinforce each other**

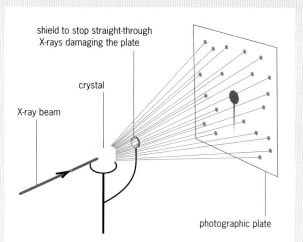

shield to stop straight-through X-rays damaging the plate

crystal

X-ray beam

photographic plate

Fig 4.20(c) **Arrangement for obtaining the X-ray diffraction pattern of a crystal**

The pattern of spots must now be matched to the positions of atoms or ions. The English scientists William and Lawrence Bragg, a father-and-son team, worked out the mathematical calculations to match patterns to three-dimensional positions, and received the Nobel Prize for Physics in 1915.

Nowadays, the X-ray diffraction pattern is usually detected electronically, and the calculations are done by computer. X-ray crystallography is a very important tool for the chemist. It has been used recently to confirm the structure of the new form of carbon, buckminsterfullerene (see page 410), and has determined the structure of well over 1000 proteins.

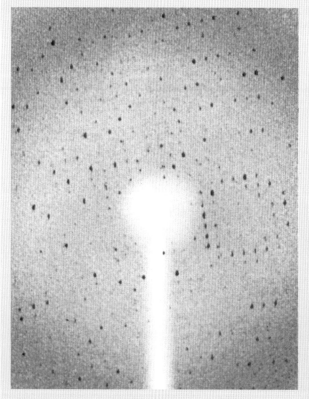

Fig 4.20(b) **X-ray diffraction pattern for lysozyme. This is an enzyme found in body fluids (such as tears and saliva) which destroys bacteria. The X-ray image helped researchers to work out the structure of lysozyme and the part of the molecule that acts against bacteria**

6 THE SHAPES OF MOLECULES

We now have a way of working out the *bonds* in a molecule; and the model we have used will also tell us about a molecule's *shape*, which is often important in determining the properties of the molecule. For example, the taste of substances is thought to depend on the shape of molecules and how they fit into taste receptor molecules on the tongue. In the same way, the shape of drug molecules can determine just how effective they are in treating illness (see the Opener to this chapter).

Dorothy Hodgkin, pioneer in X-ray crystallography

At the age of 11, Dorothy Hodgkin started at secondary school in Beccles, Suffolk. The school allowed pupils to follow physics and chemistry for one period each a week. But because she was female she could not do physics as it clashed with domestic science. Fortunately, this was the only time that Hodgkin's gender affected her scientific career.

At Oxford University she joined a newly formed X-ray crystallography group, and by 1945 she had used the technique to work out the structure of penicillin. She pioneered the use of the computer in helping to interpret the X-ray

Dorothy Mary Crowfoot Hodgkin (born 1910)

images, and by 1956, after eight years of work, she had unravelled the complex structure of vitamin B12, a molecule of more than 90 atoms. Once its structure was known, chemists could synthesise the vitamin and use it to combat pernicious anaemia. It was for this that she received her Nobel Prize for Chemistry in 1964.

By 1969 she had achieved a lifetime ambition: twenty-five years earlier she had been given a tiny sample of insulin, and she was able to work out the structure of this complex molecule containing more than 800 atoms.

Electron pair repulsion and shapes of molecules

There are two types of electron pairs represented by the dot and cross diagrams. A pair of electrons involved in bonding is called a **bonding pair**, while a pair of electrons not involved in bonding is known as a **non-bonding pair** or **lone pair**. We now look at a model of molecular shape. In this model, pairs of electrons repel each other and move as far apart from each other as possible.

Beryllium chloride (Fig 4.21(a)) has two bonding pairs and no lone pairs round its central atom – the only pairs we are interested in here since the three lone pairs round each chlorine atom do not affect the molecule's shape. As Fig 4.21(b) shows, the position of minimum repulsion has a **bond angle** of 180°. We describe the shape as **linear** because the atoms lie in a straight line.

In this model of molecular shape, we group together the bonding pairs of electrons in double and triple bonds, so that one group is the

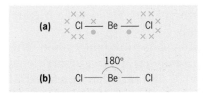

Fig 4.21(a) and (b) **Beryllium chloride is a linear molecule**

Fig 4.21(c) **Ball and stick model of beryllium chloride**

?

M Explain why hydrogen cyanide, HCN, is a linear molecule. You may have already drawn the dot and cross diagram in answer to question **I(c)**.

equivalent of one electron pair. Carbon dioxide, with two double bonds (Fig 4.22(b)), then has a linear shape.

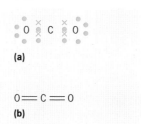

(a)

$$O = C = O$$

(b)

Fig 4.22(a) and (b) **Carbon dioxide is a linear molecule**

Fig 4.22(c) **Ball and stick model of carbon dioxide**

Boron trichloride has three bonding pairs and no lone pairs round the central boron (Fig 4.23).

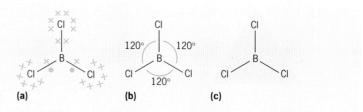

(a)   **(b)**   **(c)**

Fig 4.23(d) **Ball-and-stick model of boron trichloride**

Fig 4.23(a)–(c) **Boron trichloride is a trigonal planar molecule**

The furthest apart these bonding pairs can get is 120°, which gives a **trigonal planar** shape. Trigonal tells us that the atoms are where the points of a triangle would be, and planar means that the molecule would lie flat on a plane.

Ethene, C_2H_4, is used in industry to make a wide range of important chemicals including polythene and antifreeze.

You can find out more about ethene in Chapter 12.

(a)   **(b)**

Fig 4.24 **Ethene is a trigonal planar molecule**

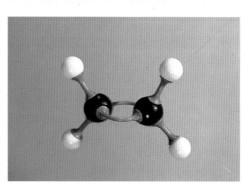

Fig 4.24(c) **Ball and stick model of ethene**

The double bond is one group of electrons and counts as one bonding pair (Fig 4.24), so there are the equivalent of three bonding pairs of electrons round each carbon atom. This gives a trigonal planar shape round each carbon atom.

Methane (Fig 4.25) has four bonding pairs round the carbon. This molecule does not lie in one plane but has a three-dimensional structure with all bond angles 109.5°. The shape is **tetrahedral** because the hydrogen atoms are at the points of a tetrahedron. All carbon atoms with four bonding pairs have a tetrahedral structure.

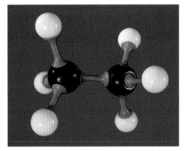

Dot and cross diagram

The arrangement of bonds round the central carbon. All bond angles are 109.5°

Hydrogens are at the four corners of a tetrahedron

Fig 4.25(a) Three ways of representing the structure of methane, a tetrahedral molecule.

The bond comes out of the plane of the paper

The bond goes into the plane of the paper

The bond lies on the plane of the paper

Fig 4.25(b) Ways of representing the directions of bonds

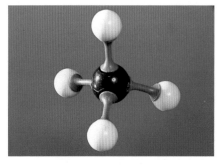

Fig 4.25(c) Ball and stick model of methane

Fig 4.26(a) The ethane molecule: the hydrogen atoms are arranged tetrahedrally round the carbon atoms. The carbon atom can rotate about its single bond, so the hydrogens at one end could be in any position relative to those at the other end. But they remain in the position shown in (b): there is the least repulsion of bonding pairs of electrons, and it is the most stable arrangement. However, the energy difference between this and other positions is very small, and there is free rotation about the carbon–carbon single bond at room temperature

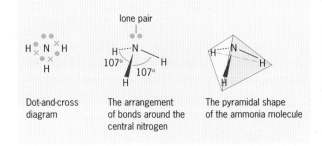

Fig 4.26(b) Ball and stick model of ethane

? **N** Draw the shape of the butane molecule, C_4H_{10}.
Hint: It is a chain of four carbon atoms: look at the shape of the ethane molecule to help you.

O Draw the dot and cross diagram for the ion AlF_4^-. Predict its shape.
Hint: Although this is a negative ion, the extra electron it has is used to form an Al–F bond.

So far, we have looked at compounds with no lone (non-bonding) pairs of electrons round the central atom. Ammonia has three bonding pairs of electrons and one lone pair (Fig 4.27). According to the electron pair repulsion theory, we could expect the shape to be based on a tetrahedron. But if we look at the arrangement of the atoms, the actual shape of the ammonia molecule is described as pyramidal.

lone pair

Dot-and-cross diagram

The arrangement of bonds around the central nitrogen

The pyramidal shape of the ammonia molecule

Fig 4.27(a) Three ways of representing the ammonia molecule

Fig 4.27(b) Ball and stick model of ammonia

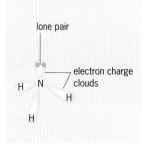

lone pair

electron charge clouds

Fig 4.27(c) The ammonia molecule showing the bonding pairs and the lone pair as electron charge clouds

Repulsion by lone pairs

We have seen that, when we name the shape of a molecule, we are looking at the position of just the atoms. We do not include the lone pairs, yet they are critical in determining that shape.

Ammonia

Notice in ammonia that, although the shape is based on a tetrahedron, the bond angles are not the expected 109.5°. The three bonds have been squeezed closer together because the lone electron pair exerts a greater repulsion than the bonding pairs.

Think of the pairs of electrons as electron clouds and the reason for the greater repulsion becomes clear. The bonding pair clouds are not as spread out as the lone pair cloud because the bonding electrons are held between the nuclei of two atoms and attracted to both, so the bonding pair cloud is relatively thin. Only one nucleus holds the lone pair cloud, its electrons are pulled closer to the nucleus, it spreads out more and is therefore fatter, as in Fig 4.27(c). This is why lone pairs have greater repulsion.

Water

Now let us examine the shape of the water molecule (Fig 4.28). The bond angle is even more squeezed by two lone pairs. In this molecule there are three different sorts of repulsion:

- bonding pair:bonding pair repulsion
- lone pair:bonding pair repulsion
- lone pair:lone pair repulsion

increasing repulsion

P Draw the shape of:

(a) CCl_4,

(b) NH_4^+ (see page 74 if you are unsure of the dot and cross diagram),

(c) PCl_3.

In each case, state the number of bonding pairs and lone pairs and use this information to make an estimate of the bond angles.

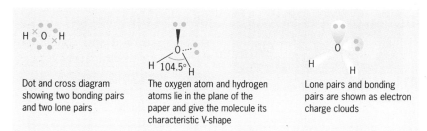

Dot and cross diagram showing two bonding pairs and two lone pairs

The oxygen atom and hydrogen atoms lie in the plane of the paper and give the molecule its characteristic V-shape

Lone pairs and bonding pairs are shown as electron charge clouds

Fig 4.28(a) **Three ways of representing the water molecule**

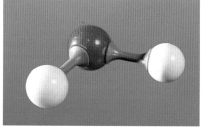

Fig 4.28(b) **Ball and stick model of water**

Phosphorus(V) fluoride, PF_5 (Fig 4.29), has five bonding pairs and no lone pairs, so the shape that puts the bonding pairs furthest apart is trigonal bipyramidal (two triangular pyramids base to base).

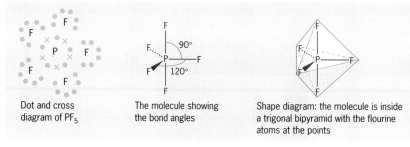

Dot and cross diagram of PF_5

The molecule showing the bond angles

Shape diagram: the molecule is inside a trigonal bipyramid with the flourine atoms at the points

Fig 4.29(a) **Three ways of representing the phosphorus(V) fluoride molecule**

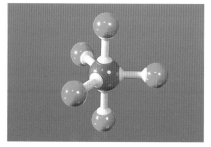

Fig 4.29(b) **Ball and stick model**

Sulphur hexafluoride, SF_6 (Fig 4.30), has an octahedral shape where all bond angles are 90° because it has six bonding pairs and no lone pairs.

See questions 1–4 and 6–8. ■

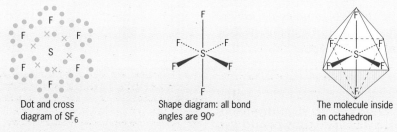

Dot and cross diagram of SF_6

Shape diagram: all bond angles are 90°

The molecule inside an octahedron

Fig 4.30(a) **Three ways of representing the sulphur hexafluoride molecule**

Fig 4.30(b) **Ball and stick model**

SULPHUR HEXAFLUORIDE GAS REPLACES PCBS

SULPHUR HEXAFLUORIDE (also known as sulphur(VI) fluoride) is an interesting gas finding increasing uses since it is non-toxic, odourless, colourless and very unreactive. Because of its insulating properties it is now used in high voltage transformers and circuit breakers, replacing PCBs (polychlorinated biphenyls).

PCBs are manufactured chemicals which are very widespread pollutants in the environment today and break down extremely slowly. They are thought to cause cancer, accumulating in the fatty tissues of humans and other animals at the top of the food chain. They even appear in breast milk. Although most production ended by the late 1970s, about 30 per cent of the 1.2 million tonnes made is still around today. Disposing of PCBs in old transformers is going to remain a problem for many years to come.

Sulphur hexafluoride is also used to trace air flow in the ventilation systems of buildings, and is used to dilute oxygen breathed in during lung X-rays. It is an FFC (fully fluorinated compound) and its use in replacing ozone-depleting CFCs (chlorofluorocarbons) is increasing.

However, its very stability could cause future problems in the atmosphere. Molecule for molecule, it is the most 'warming' greenhouse gas ever evaluated. Its concentration in the atmosphere is very small, yet increases by 8 per cent each year, and it is reckoned to persist in the atmosphere for thousands of years. At the moment there is no restriction on its use, but perhaps there should be.

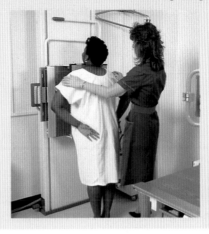

Sulphur hexafluoride can be used to dilute the oxygen breathed in by a person having a lung X-ray

7 COVALENT BONDING AND THE OVERLAP OF ATOMIC ORBITALS

The simple dot and cross model agrees with much of the experimental evidence. But how does our atomic orbital model of atoms in Chapter 3 treat covalent bonding? A covalent bond is formed by the overlap of two atomic orbitals (one from each atom). Each orbital must be occupied by a single electron so that when they overlap the bond formed contains two electrons.

σ and π bonds

In hydrogen chloride, a covalent bond forms when an s orbital overlaps with a p orbital, as in Fig 4.31. Note that the s orbital is spherical and the p orbital has two lobes.

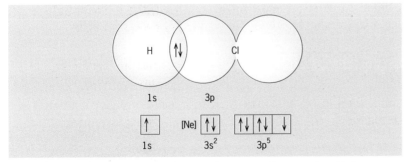

Fig 4.31 **Hydrogen chloride: a σ bond forms by the overlap of two atomic orbitals**

This kind of covalent bond is known as a **σ bond (sigma bond)**. A σ bond is formed when two atomic orbitals overlap at one point: there is always a σ bond between two atoms if they are covalently bonded. A σ bond gives the greatest possible electron density between the two nuclei.

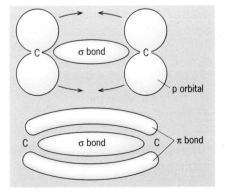

Fig 4.32 **A carbon–carbon double bond: a π bond forms by the sideways overlap of two p orbitals. This arrangement is found in molecules such as ethene, C_2H_4, but for clarity the following have been omitted: the two σ bonds on each carbon atom, and the other atoms which would be joined to double-bonded carbon atoms**

In double and triple bonds there is a sideways overlap between two p orbitals, and a **π bond** (**pi bond**) forms (Fig 4.32). Ethene has a carbon–carbon double bond made up of a σ bond and a π bond.

The π bond is what makes ethene such a versatile industrial chemical. Being above and below the plane of the nuclei, the π bond is more loosely held by the carbon nuclei than the σ bond and therefore allows ethene to be very reactive. To find out more about ethene, see Chapter 12.

A closer look at the orbitals in carbon

Let us look at just how carbon forms its covalent bonds. It has the electron configuration $[He]2s^22p^2$, with two singly occupied p orbitals. So on our atomic orbital overlap model it should form only two bonds. But we know that carbon forms four bonds. To do this it promotes a 2s electron to a 2p orbital and, together, these become four sp^3 orbitals, as shown below. These mixed orbitals all have the same energy and are sometimes called **hybrid** orbitals.

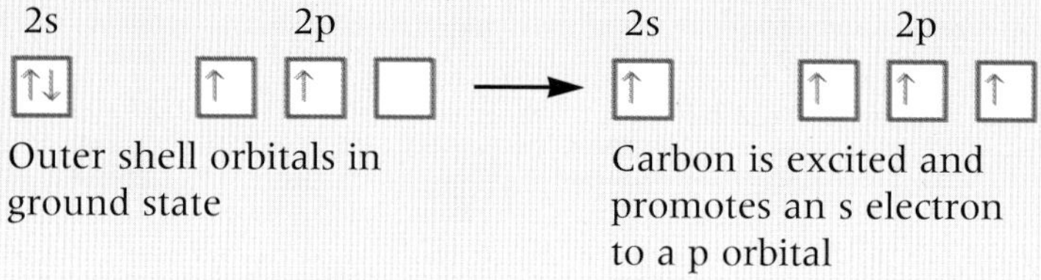

2s	2p			2s	2p		
↑↓	↑	↑	☐	↑	↑	↑	↑

Outer shell orbitals in ground state

Carbon is excited and promotes an s electron to a p orbital

In singly bonded carbon compounds such as methane, for example, carbon's one 2s orbital and three 2p orbitals together form four sp^3 orbitals.

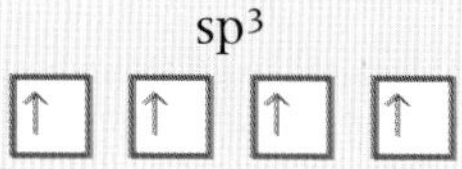

sp^3

↑	↑	↑	↑

Then, as in Fig 4.33, the σ bonds in methane form when the carbon sp^3 orbitals overlap with hydrogen's 1s orbital. The sp^3 orbitals repel each other equally, giving a tetrahedral shape to the methane molecule.

In ethene there are three σ bonds and a π bond round each carbon, as shown in Fig 4.34.

In this case, after the 2s electron is excited to the 2p orbital, three sp^2 orbitals form, leaving a single 2p orbital.

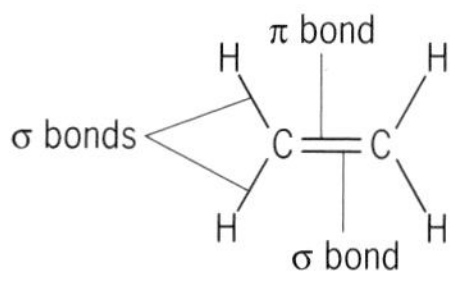

sp^2 2p

↑	↑	↑		↑

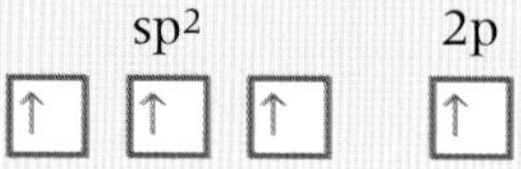

The sp^2 orbitals repel each other to give the trigonal planar shape seen in Fig 4.24. The p orbitals overlap to give a π bond, as in Fig 4.35.

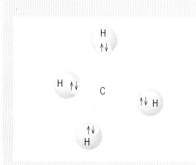

Fig 4.33 **In methane, each of the four σ bonds is formed when a hydrogen 1s orbital overlaps with a carbon sp^3 orbital**

Fig 4.34 **The bonding in ethene**

Q Explain why sp^2 orbitals are given that name.

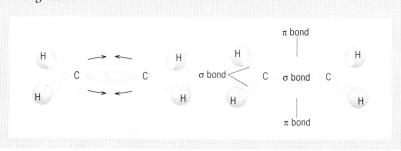

Fig 4.35 **The sp^2 orbitals are all in one plane, while the p orbitals overlap to form the π bond**

Polar covalent bonds and electronegativity

So far, we have looked at compounds with covalent bonds. We know that a covalent bond is a shared pair of electrons. But is the pair of electrons shared equally? If we look at the hydrogen molecule, H_2 the electrons are shared equally between the two atoms.

The force of attraction between the two nuclei and the electrons in the covalent bond is what holds the hydrogen molecule together: being the same, both atoms exert the same force, so the electrons are shared equally.

H ─×─ H

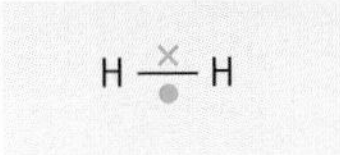

Fig 4.36 **In a hydrogen molecule the electrons in a pair are equally shared**

However, in hydrogen chloride the electrons are not shared equally. The shared pair is attracted more by the chlorine atom. This means that chlorine has a slight excess of negative charge which is not balanced out by the protons in the nucleus. We say that the chlorine has a partial negative charge and this is shown by the symbol $\delta-$. Hydrogen has a $\delta+$ charge because the electrons in the covalent bond are nearer the chlorine atom giving hydrogen a partial positive charge. This bond is called a **polar covalent bond**, or just a **polar bond**.

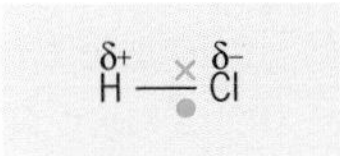

$\overset{\delta+}{H}$ ─×─ $\overset{\delta-}{Cl}$

Fig 4.37 **Electrons in this covalent bond spend more time nearer the chlorine atom, giving it a slightly negative charge and the hydrogen a slightly positive charge**

In any covalent bond between two different atoms there is likely to be unequal sharing of electrons, because different atoms have different powers to attract bonding pairs of electrons. The power of an atom in a molecule to attract electrons to itself is called its **electronegativity**. The most electronegative element is fluorine. It is given a value of 4.0 on a scale devised by one of this century's most famous scientists, Linus Pauling. Next comes oxygen at 3.5 and the third most electronegative elements are chlorine and nitrogen, both having a value of 3.0.

PAULING AND HIS WORK ON CHEMICAL BONDS

IN A LIFE THAT spanned much of the twentieth century, the American Linus Pauling was one of its most influential chemists. He worked briefly with Niels Bohr (see Chapter 3) and in 1954 he received the Nobel Prize for Chemistry for his work on the nature of the chemical bond. His book *The Nature of the Chemical Bond* has deeply influenced scientists. It explains how atoms combine and helped predict the way compounds react. He put forward the ideas of hybrid orbitals and the partial ionic character of covalent bonds.

Shortly after the Second World War, helped by his wife, he spearheaded a campaign for nuclear disarmament. This led in 1963 to a limited test ban treaty. For this he received the Nobel Peace Prize in 1963 and became the first person (and to date the only person) to be the sole recipient of two Nobel prizes.

Linus Carl Pauling, 1901–1995

In the Periodic Table, we see that electronegativity increases up a group and across a period.

Fig 4.38 The Periodic Table showing electronegativity values

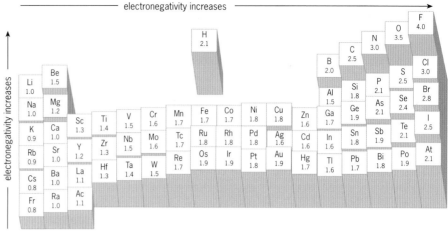

$\delta+$ $\delta-$
H $\underset{\times}{—}$ Cl
2.1 3.0

Fig 4.39 The difference in electronegativities causes hydrogen chloride to be polar

See questions 4 and 8. ▮

?

R Use Fig 4.38 to decide whether the following bonds are polar. Where appropriate show the negative and positive poles using $\delta-$ and $\delta+$. Rank the polarity of these bonds putting the most polar first.
C–Cl, P–H, H–F, O–H, F–F, N–H, C–I.

?

S Work out the core charge of oxygen and sulphur in Group 6 of the Periodic Table. What will the core charge of the other elements in this group be? Explain why the electronegativity of these atoms increases as you go up the group.

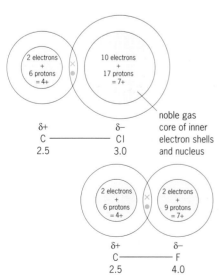

Fig 4.40 Inner shell electrons and protons in carbon–chlorine and carbon–fluorine

Fig 4.39 shows the difference in electronegativity between hydrogen and chlorine in a hydrogen chloride molecule.

Chlorine is the more electronegative element, so it attracts electrons more and has a partial negative charge, $\delta-$. In this molecule the difference in electronegativities is 1.9. The larger the difference in electronegativities, the more polar is the covalent bond, and a value of 1.9 means that the hydrogen chloride molecule is very polar.

Core charge

Why do different atoms have different powers to attract electrons in a covalent bond? To answer this question we must look at the **core charge** of atoms and at their size.

> **The core charge is the negative charge of the inner electron shells plus the positive charge due to the protons in the nucleus.**

On page 70 we saw that the inner shells of an atom can be called the noble gas core. As seen in Fig 4.40, chlorine has a noble gas core of 10 electrons in its two inner shells. There are 17 positive protons in the nucleus, so the outer bonding electrons experience a core charge of 7+. Fluorine also has a core charge of 7+ because it has two electrons in its inner shell and nine protons in the nucleus. It is more electronegative than chlorine because fluorine is a smaller atom, so the outer bonding electrons are closer to its nucleus. With a core charge of 7+ and being a small atom, fluorine is strongest of all atoms in attracting electrons to itself.

A carbon–chlorine bond is polar because the shared pair is attracted more to the larger core charge. However, a bond with even greater polarity is the carbon–fluorine bond because the fluorine atom is so small. See Fig 4.40.

To summarise, the two factors which help to determine electronegativity are the core charge of an atom and its size. Small atoms with high core charges are the most electronegative atoms.

The ionic character of many covalent bonds

The more polar a covalent bond, the greater the electron shift towards the more electronegative element. In some compounds this shift is so great that, instead of covalent bonds, ions are formed.

In fact, very few covalent bonds have exactly equal sharing of electrons. Most have some ionic character. The greater the difference in electronegativity between two atoms in a bond, the more ionic is its character. When the electronegativity difference is more than about 2.0, the bond is more ionic than covalent, and we call it ionic. Thus there are pure covalent bonds and pure ionic bonds, but most compounds lie between these two extremes.

The covalent character of ionic bonds

In the same way that covalent bonds have some ionic character, so all ionic bonds have some degree of covalent character. We think of ions as spheres of negative charge surrounding the nucleus, but negative ions (anions) can be polarised by positive ions (cations). Negative ions have more electrons than protons, so the electron cloud is held more loosely than in an atom. A positive ion may cause some distortion of this electron cloud and this is called **polarising** the negative ion.

To work out how much covalent character there is likely to be in an ionic bond, we need to start by knowing the sort of cation that has the most polarising power over an anion, and the sort of anion that is most easily polarised.

A cation has high polarising power if:
– it has a **high positive charge**
 (to attract the electrons in the anion)
– it is a **small cation**
 (the nucleus has more attraction for the electrons in the anion)

An anion is easily polarised if:
– it has a **high negative charge**
 (is loosely held by the nucleus)
– it is a **large anion**
 (the nucleus is further away from the outer electrons, so has less of an attraction for them)

These ideas were first proposed by the Polish chemist Kasimir Fajans in 1923 and are often known as Fajans' rules.

T Using the electronegativity trends in Fig 4.38, decide which of the following bonds are ionic, polar covalent or covalent:

(a) the C–C bond in diamond,

(b) the bond in caesium fluoride, CsF,

(c) the bond in hydrogen fluoride, HF.

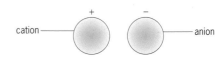

Fig 4.41(a) **There is no polarisation of the anion by the cation, so there is no covalent character**

Fig 4.41(b) **The cation is polarising the anion, so there is some covalent character in the ionic bond**

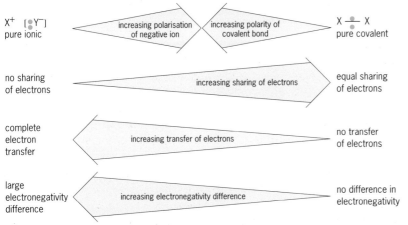

Fig 4.42 **The change from ionic to covalent bonding is gradual**

■ See question 8.

U Which of the following compounds show the most covalent character? Sodium chloride, magnesium chloride or aluminium chloride.

EXAMPLE

Q Explain why the covalent character of the chlorides in Group 1 of the Periodic Table increases on going up the group.

A All Group 1 ions have a 1+ charge. As you go down the group, an extra electron shell is added, so the cations get larger and this means they become less polarising.

The anion is the chloride ion in each compound. It is going to be most readily polarised by the smallest positive ion, which in this case is lithium, and least distorted by the largest ion, which is the francium ion. Thus, covalent character increases as you go up Group 1.

You can read more about the ionic and covalent character of compounds in Chapter 21.

SUMMARY

When you have finished studying this chapter, you should understand and be able to use the following ideas.

■ Usually when atoms bond together in a compound they lose, gain or share electrons to make stable noble gas configurations of outer shell electrons.

■ Ionic bonding involves the complete transfer of electrons between atoms to create oppositely charged ions, which are held together by strong electrostatic forces of attraction. Lattice energy is the energy released when one mole of lattice is formed from its gaseous ions.

■ A covalent bond is a shared pair of electrons between two atoms. It is an electrostatic attraction between the pair of negative electrons and the positively charged nuclei. Double and triple bonds can also form between atoms. When the pair of electrons in a covalent bond comes from one atom it is called a dative covalent (coordinate) bond. Sometimes atoms in a covalent compound have more or less than the usual noble gas octet.

■ The shape of molecules can be determined by counting up the number of electron pairs round the central atom. Bonding pairs exert the least repulsion on each other; lone pair:bonding pair repulsion is greater; while two lone pairs give the most repulsion.

■ A single covalent bond is formed by the overlap of two atomic orbitals to form a σ bond. π bonds occur in double or triple bonds (together with σ bonds). π bonds are formed by the sideways overlap of p orbitals.

■ Ionic and covalent bonds are two extreme forms of bonding. Most bonds are neither purely ionic nor purely covalent. Pure covalent bonds are formed between atoms with the same electronegativities. Polar covalent bonds arise when there is a difference in electronegativities between the atoms in the bond and the pair of electrons is not equally shared. Electronegativity is the power of an atom within a molecule to attract bonding pairs of electrons to itself.

■ All ionic compounds have some degree of covalent character. Small highly charged cations are best at distorting the electron cloud around anions. Large highly charged anions are the most easily distorted.

1 In the gaseous state, phosphorus(V) chloride exists as a molecule with the formula PCl_5. However, when it is a solid it is ionic with the formula $PCl_4^+ PCl_6^-$.

Draw dot and cross diagrams for the PCl_5 molecule and the ions PCl_4^+ and PCl_6^-. Then work out, draw and label the shapes of these three species.

2 Describe and explain the shape of the following species:

NH_3, NH_4^+, NH_2^-.

Your answer should include reference to the bond angles involved.

3 Ethanoic acid (CH_3CO_2H) is found in vinegar.

a) Draw a dot and cross diagram for this molecule.

b) Draw another diagram to show the covalent bonds and bond angles.

4 The following are hydrides of Group 6 elements going from the top to the bottom of the group:

H_2O, H_2S, H_2Te, H_2Se.

a) Draw the shape of the water molecule and give its bond angle.

b) What is meant by the term electronegativity?

c) Explain the trend in electronegativity you would expect on going down the Group 6 elements.

d) Name the H–X bond (where X is a Group 6 element) which would be the most polar, and explain why.

5 Write the full electron configurations, in terms of s and p electrons, of the following ions:

K^+, Ca^{2+}, Cl^-, S^{2-}.

With which noble gas are these ions isoelectronic?

6 Sulphur dioxide is an important atmospheric pollutant.

a) Draw the dot and cross diagram for sulphur dioxide.

Hint: sulphur is bonded to each oxygen by a double bond.

b) Draw the shape of sulphur dioxide and estimate the bond angle.

c) Organic nitrates are pollutants found in photochemical smog. One compound is particularly unpleasant, causing breathing difficulties and making the eyes water. It has the following structure.

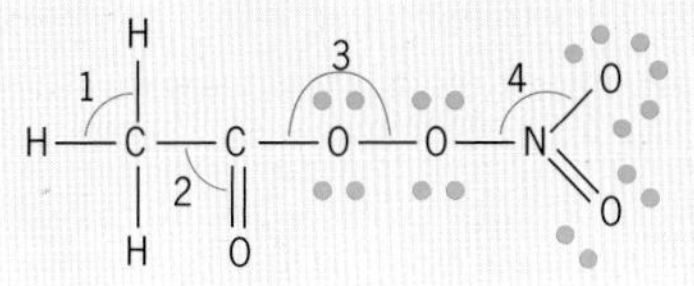

Estimate the bond angles labelled 1 to 4.

7 Many of the symptoms of hay fever are caused by the production of histamine in the body when pollen grains enter the nose.

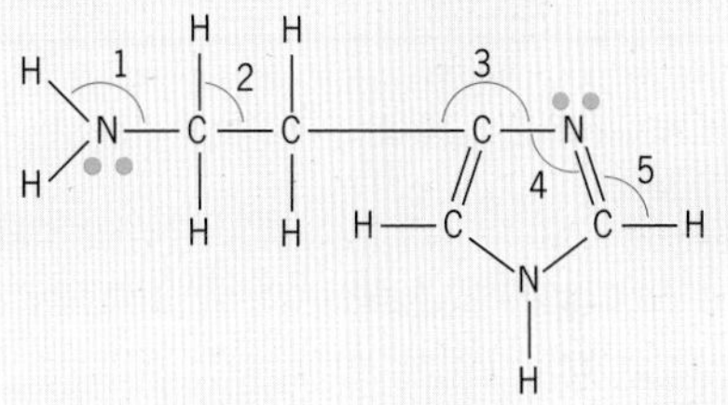

a) Estimate the five bond angles shown in this molecule.

b) How many σ (sigma) bonds and how many π (pi) bonds are there in a molecule of histamine?

8

a) What is meant by the terms ionic bond and covalent bond?

b) Most covalent bonds are polar. Put the following bonds in order of their polarity with the most polar first. Use Fig 4.38, page 84, to help you.

C—I, C—Cl, C—Br, C—H, C—F, C—O

c) Lithium iodide and caesium iodide are both ionic compounds. Explain which has the greater degree of covalent character.

d) Draw the shapes of the following molecules and give reasons for their bond angles:
CH_4, NH_3, H_2O.

Assignment

INSECT PHEROMONES

A pheromone is a chemical secreted by an animal that affects the behaviour of other individuals of the same species – we can say that the pheromone communicates an instruction. It may be ants laying a trail to tell other ants the way to a good source of food, or female moths sending out a sex attractant to attract mates, or the queen bee of a hive producing a chemical to tell the workers that she is in the hive and not to start producing new queens.

Fig 4.A1 **The female silkworm moth. Female moths use pheromones to attract males**

Our understanding of insect pheromones has increased rapidly since the first pheromone – from a female silkworm moth – was isolated in 1959.

Fig 4.A2 **The structure of the female silkworm moth sex pheromone**

A pheromone has its effect because of the shape of its molecules. They fit into receptor sites in receiving creatures and trigger complex chemical reactions that produce the desired response.

1

a) The atoms in the silkworm sex attractant are joined together by chemical bonds. Name these bonds and explain how they hold the atoms together.
b) Work out the likely bond angles labelled 1, 2 and 3. Give reasons for your answers.
c) Explain why the C–C bonds in this compound are non-polar, while the O–H bond is polar.
d) There are two π bonds in this pheromone, together with 46 σ bonds. Describe the difference between these two types of bond.

The sex pheromones of moths are among the simplest known. They have linear carbon chains of C_{10} to C_{20} atoms. They differ in their terminal groups of atoms which are called **functional groups**. Two of the functional groups found at the ends of moth sex pheromones are:

—O—H   alcohol functional group: look for this on the end of the silkworm pheromone, Fig 4.A2

aldehyde functional group

2

a) Copy the two functional groups shown above and mark on the polarity of any polar bonds using δ+ and δ–.
b) Predict, giving your reasons, the bond angles in the aldehyde functional group.

The other way moth sex pheromones can differ is in the position of the double bonds and the shape they give to the molecule. Notice that the double bonds in the silkworm pheromone are slightly different: one double bond has the hydrogens on the same side, while the other has the hydrogen atoms on opposite sides. Double bonds do not allow the carbon atoms to spin round, so the hydrogen atoms are fixed in position and this affects the shape of the pheromone.

We can draw a **skeletal formula** which shows the carbon skeleton shape clearly. The single lines in Fig 4.A3 represent single bonds and the carbon atoms are at the corners of the zigzags. You can see that the two different arrangements of the hydrogen atoms round the double bond do affect its shape. (You can read more about skeletal formulas on page 144.)

Fig 4.A3 **The skeletal formula of the silkworm moth sex pheromone**

3 Using information in Fig 4.A4, suggest why the carbon skeleton is reckoned to be a zigzag shape.

Fig 4.A4 **There is free rotation about the C–C bond at room temperature, but this is the position of least repulsion of bonding pairs**

In moths, a mixture of two, three or four different chemicals, similar to the ones described, make a species-specific pheromone cocktail to attract the males of the same species.

4 Research into insect pheromones has already proved very important in agriculture. Why do you think this is? Look through scientific journals such as *New Scientist*, to find one important use for insect pheromones in agriculture and describe it briefly in your own words.

CHEMICAL BONDING AND MOLECULAR STRUCTURE

In this chapter map you will find the ideas you have studied in the chapter. The map will help you remember these ideas, and the way that they connect and progress in explaining how atoms react and build up molecular structures.

Use the map to remind you of these concepts and to satisfy yourself that you have understood them. The map should also help you to plan your revision.

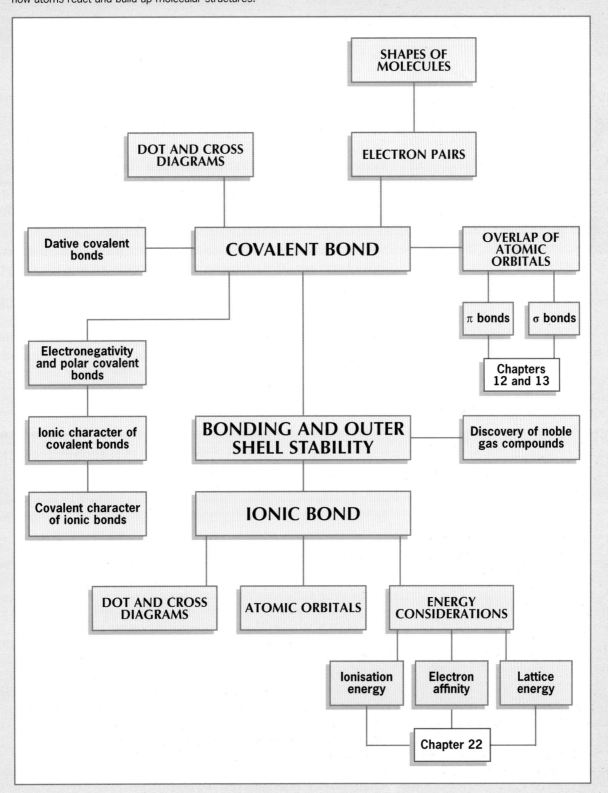

5 States of matter

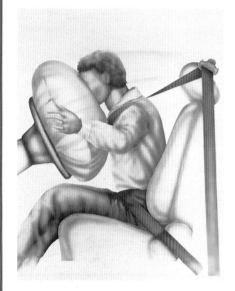

AIRBAGS ARE A FAMILIAR addition to car safety these days. But a crash happens very fast, so how does the airbag inflate in time to protect the driver from injury? One type of airbag uses a very fast gas-producing chemical reaction to blow up the bag.

First, the rapid deceleration of the car triggers an electric current, and the energy from this current explodes a detonator cap. The explosion makes the solid substance sodium azide (NaN_3) decompose and release nitrogen gas extremely rapidly. The nitrogen inflates the airbag, cushioning the driver and reducing the likelihood of injury.

This is the equation for the decomposition of sodium azide:

$$2NaN_3(s) \rightarrow 2Na(s) + 3N_2(g)$$

Sodium azide is a solid, so its particles are arranged very close together. The nitrogen it produces is a gas with widely spaced particles. For a relatively small amount of solid, the volume of gas that inflates the airbag is very large. At the same time, because the particles are now widely spaced, they can be compressed and cushion the driver. The whole process takes about 40 milliseconds. Then the specially designed bag deflates rapidly, so that the driver has vision and movement after the crash. This also applies where airbags are fitted for other passengers.

Airbags work, then, because of the different arrangements of particles in the different states of matter, an application of chemistry that regularly saves lives.

1 GASES

The Greeks thought that air was one of four elements making up the Earth (see start of Chapter 2). Later, alchemists produced what they called 'airs' or 'vapours' in their efforts to change common metals such as iron and lead into gold. It was a Dutch scientist, Jan van Helmont, who realised that not all these 'airs' were the same, though they would fill any container they were put into.

The Greeks had a name for the substance that they thought the gods had changed into the four elements of Earth – chaos. In 1624, van Helmont used this word for 'airs'. When pronounced in Dutch the word became 'gas'. It is now recognised as a **state of matter**, together with the other two states, solid and liquid.

Volumes of gases

Towards the end of the eighteenth century, chemists were experimenting with reactions that involved gases. The French chemist

Joseph Gay-Lussac studied a large number of these reactions and realised that when gases reacted their volumes were in a simple whole-number ratio, provided he measured the volumes at the same temperature and pressure. If the product was a gas this volume too was in a simple ratio to the reactants.

When Gay-Lussac reacted 5 dm³ of hydrogen gas with 5 dm³ of chlorine gas, he produced 10 dm³ of hydrogen chloride. The simple whole-number ratio for this reaction is:

| 1 volume of hydrogen | : | 1 volume of chlorine | : | 2 volumes of hydrogen chloride |

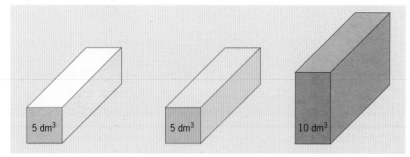

Fig 5.1

In 1808, Gay-Lussac summed up his experimental observations in his law of combining volumes:

When gases react, they do so in volumes that bear a simple whole-number ratio to each other and to the volumes of any gaseous products, provided the temperature and pressure are the same when the volumes are measured.

Fig 5.2 **Joseph Gay-Lussac (1778–1850) is most famous for his experiments with gases. He also made the highest balloon flight of his day. At over 7 kilometres, the record stood for a very long time**

> **A** What is the simple whole-number ratio of gas volumes for the reaction of 5 dm³ of hydrogen with 2.5 dm³ of oxygen producing 5 dm³ of steam?

> A cubic decimetre (dm³) contains 1000 cm³. It is the same as a litre.

Avogadro's law

In 1811, an Italian named Amedeo Avogadro put forward a theory to explain the experimental findings of Gay-Lussac:

Equal volumes of different gases contain equal numbers of molecules at the same temperature and pressure.

It took about fifty years of confusion before Avogadro's theory was accepted. One of the stumbling blocks was John Dalton, who in 1803 had produced his atomic theory (see page 21). He thought that all gaseous elements were made up of separate atoms. He did not understand, for instance, that hydrogen and chlorine were made up of H_2 molecules and Cl_2 molecules. If Dalton had been right, and hydrogen and chlorine were made up of atoms, then Avogadro's theory would have suggested that these atoms were split.

Fig 5.3 **Amedeo Avogadro (1776–1856), lawyer and later a professor of physics. It wasn't until four years after his death that another distinguished Italian, Stanislao Cannizzaro, rediscovered Avogadro's hypothesis and used it to explain Gay-Lussac's observations**

Let's try to follow Dalton's argument to see if it is logical:

1 volume	+	1 volume	→	2 volumes of
of hydrogen		of chlorine		hydrogen chloride

Since, according to Avogadro's theory, each volume must contain the same number of particles if they are measured at the same temperature and pressure, then:

1 million atoms	+	1 million atoms	→	2 million molecules
of hydrogen		of chlorine		of hydrogen chloride

So: 1 atom H   +   1 atom Cl   →   2 molecules HCl

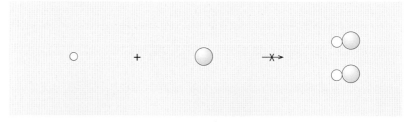

Fig 5.4

This is wrong. If it were correct then there would have to be two hydrogen atoms created from one. This confusion held up progress in chemistry for half a century.

But if we accept that hydrogen and chlorine are made up of diatomic molecules then the observations of Gay-Lussac are easily explained by Avogadro:

1 million	+	1 million	→	2 million
molecules H_2		molecules Cl_2		molecules HCl

So: 1 molecule H_2 +   1 molecule Cl_2 → 2 molecules HCl

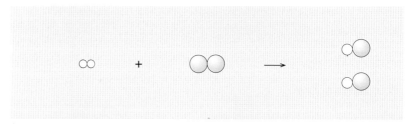

Fig 5.5

Avogadro's theory is also called Avogadro's law because it is obeyed by gases at low pressures.

Molar gas volume

We first introduced the **mole** in Chapter 1. It is the unit chemists use for the **amount** of a substance and is 6.02×10^{23} particles. It follows from Avogadro's law that the volume of one mole of any gas – the **molar gas volume** V_m – must be the same under identical conditions of temperature and pressure, because we are dealing with the same number of particles.

At 273 K (0 °C) and a pressure of 101 kilopascals, kPa (1 atmosphere), 1 mole of gas occupies 22.4 dm³. These conditions of temperature and pressure are called **standard temperature and pressure (s.t.p.)**. So:

The molar gas volume at s.t.p. is 22.4 dm³.
At 298 K and 101 kPa, the molar gas volume is 24 dm³.

These conditions are sometimes referred to as **room conditions**.

B Dalton thought that the formula of water was HO. It was known that 2 volumes of hydrogen reacted with 1 volume of oxygen to give two volumes of steam. Explain how this observation suggests that the formula of water is H_2O.

One mole is the amount of substance that contains as many particles as there are atoms in exactly 12 g of carbon-12. The number of particles in a mole is 6.02×10^{23} and is called the **Avogadro constant**. You can find out more about the mole on page 5.

C What is 298 K in degrees Celsius?

Calculations from chemical equations

An understanding of the laws of Gay-Lussac and Avogadro is very useful to chemists. It allows them to use equations to work out the volumes of gases required for a particular reaction, or to predict the volumes of gases that are produced.

2 THE GAS LAWS

Gas is in some ways the simplest of the three states of matter. Through doing countless experiments, scientists have investigated the physical properties of different gases. They have found that, with minor variations, all gases behave in a similar way under room conditions and that there are definite relationships between pressure, volume, temperature and amount. These relationships have been defined in what we call the gas laws.

The relationship between pressure and volume: Boyle's law

If you have read the beginning of Chapter 2 (page 21) you will know that Robert Boyle had a deep influence on modern chemistry in urging chemists to do experiments to find elements. He also conducted his own experiments on gases.

In 1662 he did a series of experiments using a glass tube 5 metres high, shaped like a letter J and closed at the short end. He trapped an amount of air in the short end of the J tube by pouring mercury into the other end. He found that the more mercury he added, the smaller the volume of air became. He had thus discovered that the volume of air depended on the pressure of the mercury upon it and he summarised this finding in what we now know as Boyle's law:

The volume of a fixed amount of gas is inversely proportional to its pressure at constant temperature.

We can express this mathematically as:

$$p \propto \frac{1}{V} \quad \text{or} \quad pV = \text{a constant}$$

G What temperature and pressure are considered to be room conditions? (See page 92.)

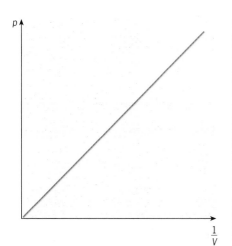

Fig 5.6 **Graph showing the effect of pressure on the volume of a fixed amount of gas at constant temperature**

H A balloon containing 1 dm³ of helium gas at 100 kPa is allowed to float up 6 kilometres into the air. At this height, the pressure is 50 kPa. What is the volume of the balloon?

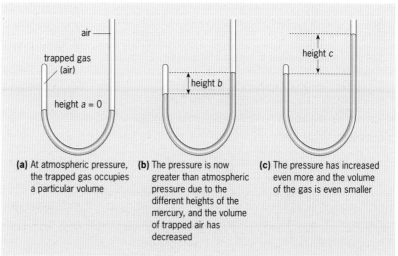

(a) At atmospheric pressure, the trapped gas occupies a particular volume

(b) The pressure is now greater than atmospheric pressure due to the different heights of the mercury, and the volume of trapped air has decreased

(c) The pressure has increased even more and the volume of the gas is even smaller

Fig 5.7 **Robert Boyle's J tube experiment. Boyle was the first to carry out quantitative experiments on gases. He measured the volume of gas and the difference in heights of the mercury columns to work out the pressure.**
Note that the temperature is kept constant throughout the experiment

We can show this graphically by plotting pressure against 1/volume as in Fig 5.6.

So if we double the pressure on a gas the volume will halve, and if the volume increases four times then the pressure on the gas must have decreased to a quarter, provided the temperature stays constant.

BREATHING AND BOYLE'S LAW

WHEN WE ARE at rest we breathe in and out about twelve times a minute. As we breathe in, the volume of our chest cavity expands, increasing the volume of our lungs. This causes the pressure of air inside the lungs to decrease. Since the pressure of the air outside our bodies is now greater than that inside, air flows in. The reverse happens when we breathe out: the chest volume reduces, increasing the pressure of air in the lungs. The air is now at a higher pressure than that outside, so air flows out.

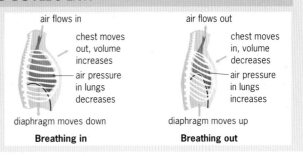

Breathing in

Breathing out

Pressure p times volume V is always equal to the same constant for a fixed amount of gas at the same temperature. So we can write:

$$p_1V_1 = k = p_2V_2 \quad \text{or} \quad p_1V_1 = p_2V_2$$

where p_1 and V_1 are one set of conditions, and p_2 and V_2 are another set.

We can use this equation, which comes from Boyle's law, to work out the effect of changing the pressure on a particular volume of gas. It can also be used to find the effect on the pressure exerted by a gas of changing the volume of that gas.

EXAMPLE

Q A 400 cm³ mixture of petrol vapour and air is taken into the cylinder of a car engine at 200 °C and a pressure of 100 kPa. The piston compresses this gaseous mixture to 50 cm³. What is the pressure of the compressed gas if the temperature does not change?

A

Initial conditions   **Final conditions**

$p_1 = 100$ kPa $p_2 = ?$
$V_1 = 400$ cm³ $V_2 = 50$ cm³

Since: $p_1V_1 = p_2V_2$:

$100 \times 400 = p_2 \times 50$

$p_2 = 800$ kPa

The relationship between volume and temperature: Charles' law

During the eighteenth century, several experimenters, including Boyle, noticed that temperature had an effect on the volume of a gas. In about 1800, two French scientists carried out experiments on the relationship between volume and temperature, as a spin-off to their ballooning activities. Jacques Charles was the first and Gay-Lussac, working independently, was the second.

Both workers discovered that, when a fixed amount of gas was kept at constant pressure, the volume varied in proportion to the temperature. Gay-Lussac also noticed that if the volume of gas at 0 °C was taken, then for every 1 °C drop in temperature the volume decreased by 1/273 under the same conditions of pressure and amount. This suggested that at –273 °C there would be a zero volume of gas.

?

I A 5 cm³ bubble of gas rises up from ocean floor where it is at a pressure of 2000 kPa. The pressure just below the surface is 100 kPa. What is the volume of the bubble when it reaches this point?

Fig 5.8 **During 1783, hot-air balloon flights became possible thanks to the enterprising Montgolfier brothers. In the same year, Jacques Charles filled a balloon with hydrogen, as seen here, for the first ascent in a hydrogen balloon and the second ever manned balloon flight**

?

J What is the value of the following temperatures on the absolute temperature scale:

(a) 25 °C,

(b) 100 °C,

(c) –50 °C?

Hint: Temperature in K = 273 + temperature in °C.

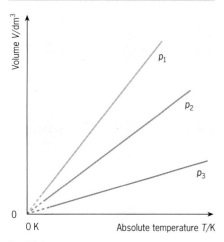

Fig 5.9 **Three graphs plotted at three different pressures (p_1, p_2, p_3) demonstrate Charles' law. All gases condense before absolute zero and the dashed portion of the graph shows the extrapolation assuming that gases do not condense**

?

K A sample of carbon dioxide in a syringe occupies 50.0 cm³ at 20.0 °C. What will the volume of CO_2 be at 100.0 °C if the pressure is constant?

It was Lord Kelvin, a British scientist, who realised the significance of this fifty years later. He called –273 °C the **absolute zero** temperature below which it was impossible to go. This gave rise to a new temperature scale – the absolute temperature scale. Absolute zero has a value of 0 K (zero kelvin), and a 1 K rise in temperature is the same as a 1 °C rise in temperature. This means that at 0 °C the temperature on the Kelvin scale is 273 K.

The relationship between volume and temperature is called Charles' law:

The volume of a fixed amount of gas is directly proportional to its absolute temperature at constant pressure.

This can be expressed mathematically:

$$V \propto T \quad \text{or} \quad V = kT$$

where k is a constant and T is absolute temperature. Note that k is not the same as the constant in Boyle's law.

For a fixed amount of gas at the same pressure, the same constant will apply, so we can write:

$$\frac{V_1}{T_1} = k = \frac{V_2}{T_2} \quad \text{so} \quad \frac{V_1}{T_1} = \frac{V_2}{T_2}$$

EXAMPLE

Q A balloon is filled 1250 cm³ of helium gas at 25.0 °C. Overnight the temperature cools to 10.0 °C. What is the new volume of the balloon, assuming the pressure is constant?

A The temperatures must first be converted to absolute temperatures. To do this, 273 is added to the temperature in Celsius so:

$$25 \,°C = 273 + 25 = 298 \,K \quad \text{and} \quad 10 \,°C = 273 + 10 = 283 \,K$$

Initial conditions   **Final conditions**

$V_1 = 1250 \,cm^3$ $V_2 = ? \,cm^3$

$T_1 = 298 \,K$ $T_2 = 283 \,K$

Since:

$$\frac{V_1}{T_1} = \frac{V_2}{T_2}$$

$$\frac{1250}{298} = \frac{V_2}{283}$$

$$V_2 = \frac{1250 \times 283}{298}$$

$$V_2 = 1190 \,cm^3 \text{ (to 3 sig. figs)}$$

The ideal gas equation

Another way of expressing Avogadro's law on page 91 is:

The volume of a gas is directly proportional to its amount at constant temperature and pressure.

Mathematically: $V \propto n$ where n = amount in moles

So the volume of a gas is related to three other properties: amount, temperature and pressure.

Avogadro's law $V \propto n$ (constant p and T)
Boyle's law $V \propto 1/p$ (constant n and T)
Charles' law $V \propto T$ (constant n and p)

Combining these:

$$V \propto \frac{nT}{p} \quad \text{or} \quad V = \frac{RnT}{p}$$

where R is a constant called the **gas constant**. Rearranging them, we have the **ideal gas equation**:

$$pV = nRT$$

When p is measured in pascals (Pa), V in cubic metres (m³), n in moles (mol) and T in kelvins (K), **R is 8.31 J K⁻¹ mol⁻¹**. These units are internationally agreed and are called **SI units** after the French words *Système Internationale*.

Gases that obey the ideal gas equation exactly are called **ideal gases.** In reality, no gas is an ideal gas, but the variations from ideal behaviour are quite small over wide temperature and pressure ranges. This enables us to use the ideal gas equation as a very useful tool to relate the four properties of volume, temperature pressure and amount.

EXAMPLE

Q At 90.0 °C how many moles of nitrogen are present in a flask of volume 750.0 cm³ at 100 kPa pressure?

A First convert the units to SI units.
The volume in cm³ must be converted to m³. There are 100³ cm³ in a m³ (ie 10⁶ cm³), so:

$$V = 750.0 \times 10^{-6} = 7.50 \times 10^{-4}\,\text{m}^3$$

$$p = 100 \times 10^3\,\text{Pa}$$

$$T = 273 + 90.0 = 363\,\text{K}$$

Then substitute into the ideal gas equation:

$$pV = nRT \text{ so } n = \frac{pV}{RT}$$

$$n = \frac{100 \times 10^3 \times 7.50 \times 10^{-4}}{8.31 \times 363}$$

$$n = 0.0249\,\text{mol}$$

?

L (a) What is the volume in cm³ of 2 mol fluorine gas at 27 °C and 100 kPa?

(b) The balloon used by Jacques Charles for his historic flight contained 1300 moles of hydrogen. What was its volume at 17 °C and 100 kPa?

Using the ideal gas equation to calculate relative molecular mass

Nowadays mass spectrometers are used to measure relative molecular mass M_r accurately. However, when this instrument is not available the M_r of gases and volatile liquids can be calculated using the ideal gas equation:

$$pV = \frac{mRT}{M_r}$$

One way of doing this is to use a gas syringe (Fig 5.10). If the substance is a gas, it can be passed into a syringe of known mass and the syringe reweighed to give the mass of gas. The volume of gas is read from the syringe and the temperature and pressure are measured. Then these values are simply inserted into the ideal gas equation.

✔

Amount in moles:

$$n = \frac{\text{mass in grams}}{\text{mass of one mole (in grams)}}$$

and M_r is numerically equal to the mass of one mole: see pages 6 and 7.

Also, see Chapter 9, page 182, for information about the mass spectrometer.

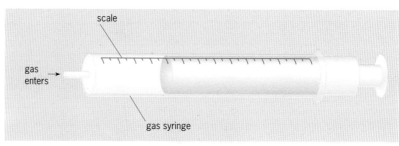

Fig 5.10 **Using a gas syringe to measure the M_r of a gas**

EXAMPLE

Q The gas propane contains hydrogen and carbon only. When 100.0 cm³ of it is passed into a syringe, the mass is found to be 0.178 g. The pressure and temperature are 298 K and 100 kPa respectively. Calculate the M_r.

A The measurements are converted to SI units with the exception of the mass, which is left as grams. (The SI unit for mass is the kilogram.)
$p = 100 \times 10^3$ kPa, $V = 100 \times 10^{-6}$ m³, $m = 0.178$ g, $M_r = ?$, $R = 8.31$ J K⁻¹ mol⁻¹ and $T = 298$ K.

Insert these values into the ideal gas equation:

$$pV = \frac{mRT}{M_r}$$

$$100 \times 10^3 \times 100 \times 10^{-6} = \frac{0.178}{M_r} \times 8.31 \times 298$$

Rearranging:
$$M_r = \frac{0.178 \times 8.31 \times 298}{100 \times 10^3 \times 100 \times 10^{-6}}$$

$$M_r = 44.1$$

?

M A gaseous compound containing sulphur and fluorine is used to trace leaks in air conditioning systems. If 100.0 cm³ has a mass of 0.586 g at 27.0 °C and 100.0 kPa pressure, what is the M_r of the compound?

The same method is used to determine the M_r of a volatile liquid, only this time the end of the syringe is sealed with a self-sealing rubber cap through which a known mass of the liquid under investigation is injected. Since the liquid is volatile it has a low boiling point, and if the syringe is heated to above the boiling point the volume of the gas produced can be measured on the syringe. In practice, there is usually a small volume of air in the syringe. So long as this volume is known at the temperature of the experiment, it can be subtracted from the volume of the vaporised sample.

?

N Often there is a small volume of air in the syringe. Why is it important to know the exact volume of this air?

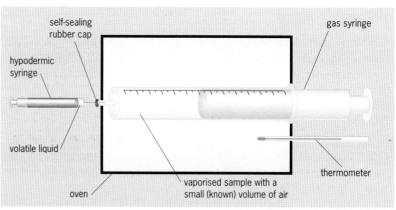

Fig 5.11 **The apparatus used to measure the M_r of a volatile liquid**

EXAMPLE

Q The following results were obtained from a sample of volatile liquid injected into a syringe:

Mass of liquid sample   0.180 g
Volume of air   10 cm³
Volume of vapour + air   100 cm³
Temperature   80°C
Pressure   100 600 Pa

Calculate the M_r of the sample.

A Volume of vapour = 100 cm³ − 10 cm³ = 90 cm³.
Once again, the measurements are converted to SI units with the exception of the mass which is left as grams.
p = 100 600 Pa, V = 90 × 10⁻⁶ m³, m = 0.180g,
M_r = ?, R = 8.31 J K⁻¹ mol⁻¹ and T = 273 + 80 = 353 K.

Insert these values into the ideal gas equation:

$$pV = \frac{mRT}{M_r}$$

$$100\,600 \times 90 \times 10^{-6} = \frac{0.180}{M_r} \times 8.31 \times 353$$

Rearranging: $$M_r = \frac{0.180 \times 8.31 \times 353}{100\,600 \times 90 \times 10^{-6}}$$

$$M_r = 58$$

---

3 A KINETIC-MOLECULAR MODEL FOR HOW GASES BEHAVE

So far, we have considered the experimental observations of the behaviour of gases that relate pressure, volume, temperature and amount through the ideal gas equation. The concise statements of these observations we have called **laws** because they are true for all gases under a range of conditions.

However, scientists soon began to produce **models** to explain gas behaviour. The simple model that we accept today for the behaviour of ideal gases is called the **kinetic-molecular model** or the **kinetic theory**, after the Greek work *kinein*, to move. The model was developed by several notable scientists in the nineteenth century, in particular Ludwig Boltzmann, an Austrian, and James Maxwell, a Scot.

In the kinetic-molecular model, ideal gases are assumed to be made up of particles (atoms, molecules or ions) that:

- are very widely separated,
- have negligible (zero) volume,
- exert no force of attraction on each other,
- move continuously and randomly,
- have perfectly **elastic collisions** with each other and the container walls (this means that there is no net gain or loss of energy in collisions),
- have an average kinetic energy that is directly proportional to the absolute temperature of the sample.

?

O In a gas syringe, 0.121 g of an alcohol is vaporised to produce 80 cm³ of gas at 370 K at 101 kPa pressure. Calculate the M_r of the alcohol.

A scientist puts forward a model to explain observations and, so long as this model explains all the known observations, it is accepted by the scientific community. See Chapter 2 page 24.

Ideal gases obey the ideal gas equation exactly under all conditions.

Kinetic energy is the energy due to the motion of the particles. Not all molecules move at the same speed, or velocity, at any particular temperature above 0 K, so molecules possess a range of kinetic energies at a particular temperature.
For example, in any sample of gas, some molecules will be moving very fast, while others will be moving fairly slowly. This range of speeds leads to a range of energies. You can read more about this in Chapter 27, where we discuss the Maxwell–Boltzmann distribution of molecular energies.

Now that we have a model we can see how well it fits the experimental observations – the true test of any model.

Gases can be compressed – the kinetic–molecular model explains this because the particles are widely spaced.

Boyle's law – the collisions of particles with the container walls cause pressure. Two factors determine the pressure: the number of collisions in a certain time on a specific area, and the force of these collisions. If we keep the temperature and amount of gas particles constant and decrease the volume of the container that the gas is in, more particles will collide with a specific area of container wall, so the pressure will increase.

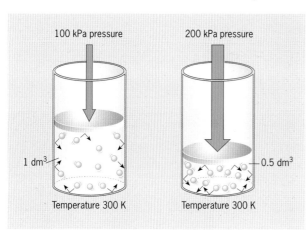

Fig 5.12 **Boyle's law explained by the kinetic theory. There is a fixed amount of gas at constant temperature. The pressure is doubled and the volume is decreased by half**

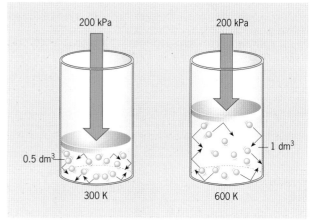

Fig 5.13 **Charles' law explained by the kinetic theory. The amount of gas and pressure remain the same but as the temperature doubles the average kinetic energy of the molecules also doubles causing a doubling of the volume**

Charles' law – According to the kinetic-molecular model, the average kinetic energy of the particles is proportional to the absolute temperature. As the temperature of a gas increases, so does the average kinetic energy of its particles. This means that the particles will collide with the container walls more often and with greater force. So doubling the absolute temperature doubles the average kinetic energy of particles in a gas, and this leads to a doubling of volume provided the pressure stays constant.

Real gases

So far, we have looked at ideal gases that obey the ideal gas equation exactly under any conditions. In the calculations, you have assumed that gases behave ideally, and at room conditions this assumption is a good one. However, the kinetic-molecular model assumes that particles in a gas have negligible (zero) volume. This is reasonable at room temperature and pressure, when the particles are very widely spaced. But as the particles in a gas get closer together their volume becomes significant. The kinetic-molecular model also assumes that there are no attractive forces between molecules. This again is reasonable provided that the particles are far apart, but, as they get closer together, forces of attraction are increasingly important. The higher the temperature, the faster the particles are moving, and this too tends to make the forces of attraction between particles negligible.

Thus the conditions that allow a gas to approach ideal gas behaviour are high temperatures and low pressures.

?

P (a) Use the kinetic-molecular model to explain why the pressure of a gas decreases when the volume increases provided amount and temperature stay constant.

(b) How many particles of gas are there in the container in Fig 5.12?

Hint: You will need to use the ideal gas equation.

(c) On page 96 we said that one way of stating Avogadro's law is: The volume of a gas is directly proportional to the amount of gas at constant temperature and pressure. Explain this, using the kinetic theory.

✔

If there were no attractive forces between particles, gases would never liquefy and liquids would never solidify.

Conditions where real gases do not show ideal behaviour will be those where the particles are close together.

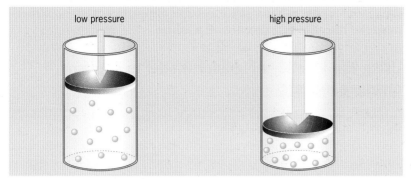

Fig 5.14(a) **At low pressures the particles are far apart, so their volume is negligible compared with the volume of the gas**

Fig 5.14(b) **At high pressures the gas particles take up a larger proportion of the volume, so the volume of the particles becomes significant. Also, because the particles are closer together, attractive forces can operate**

At low temperatures the speed of the particles is slower, so forces of attraction between them can operate. At the boiling point of a substance the forces of attraction are great enough to allow the gas to condense to a liquid. So the closer the temperature of a gas is to its boiling point, the more it will deviate from ideal behaviour. This can be seen for nitrogen gas in Fig 5.15. If nitrogen were an ideal gas it would obey the ideal gas equation $pV = nRT$. So if we had one mole of nitrogen:

$$\frac{pV}{RT} = 1$$

We can plot pV/RT against pressure, and at any pressure the value should be 1. However, at a low temperature of 200 K the graph shows wide deviation from this value, while at higher temperatures the deviation from ideal behaviour is much less.

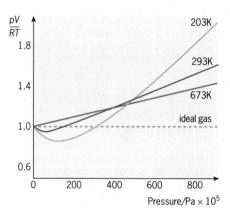

Fig 5.15 **Graphs of pV/RT against p for nitrogen gas at three different temperatures. Notice that as the temperature increases, the gas begins to approach ideal behaviour**

How particles are arranged in liquids and solids

The kinetic-molecular model can be extended to include the liquid and solid states of matter. The particles in a liquid are much closer together than they are in a gas and because of this they exert considerable attractive forces on each other. The particles are also free to move, but are much slower than in the gas.

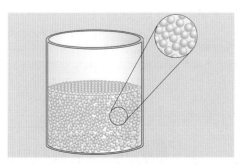

Fig 15.16 **Left: The particles in a liquid are close together and in constant motion**

Fig 15.16 **Right: The particles in a solid are very close together and fixed into position, so they can vibrate but not move out of position**

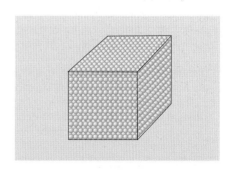

In the solid state, particles are even closer than liquids, so while it is possible to compress liquids slightly, solids are almost incompressible. The particles are also fixed into position, held by attractive forces, vibrating but not free to move out of position. This three-dimensional arrangement of particles gives solids a definite shape and is called a **lattice**. Most solids are crystalline, which means that the particles are

X-ray diffraction is used to investigate crystalline lattices – the regular arrangement of particles. You can read more about this on page 76.

Q Explain the following in terms of the kinetic-molecular model:

(a) 1300 dm³ of steam condenses to only 1 dm³ of water.

(b) Gases are easily compressed but liquids are only slightly compressible.

(c) The density of a liquid is much higher than a gas.

(d) A liquid will take the shape of the container it is in.

(e) Solids do not flow whereas gases and liquids do.

arranged in an orderly way. You can read more about some of the different attractive forces in crystalline lattices in Chapters 20 and 21.

However, not all solids are crystalline. Glass may have a fixed shape and so we call it a solid, but the arrangement of its particles have the disorder associated with a liquid.

Using the kinetic–molecular model to explain changes in state

It takes energy to change a substance from a solid to a liquid and then to a gas, as shown in Fig 5.18. As energy is transferred to a solid, the particles vibrate more until they break out of their fixed lattice positions. This is when the solid melts. There is no change in temperature during this time because all the energy transferred to the substance goes to breaking the forces holding the particles in the lattice. The energy needed to change one mole of substance from a

---

LIQUID CRYSTALS: A NEW STATE OF MATTER

YOU OFTEN COME ACROSS liquid crystal displays (LCDs): the numbers displayed on a digital watch use liquid crystals, you may have seen liquid crystal thermometers that change colour depending on the temperature, and laptop computer screens also use liquid crystals. LCDs are commonplace now, but they have only been around for about thirty years.

Fig 5.17(b) **A digital watch showing its LCD**

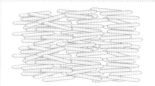

Fig 5.17(c) **The nematic arrangement of molecules in a liquid crystal state. Much of the order of the crystalline state has disappeared but the molecules are still, on average parallel to each other**

Fig 5.17(a) **A laptop computer with a liquid crystal display**

When crystals melt, the ordered crystalline arrangement of their particles breaks down into the disordered liquid state. However, some crystals melt to give particles in an ordered state. This effect was first noticed over 100 years ago by an Austrian botanist, Friedrich Reinitzer. He was heating cholesteryl benzoate to try to determine its molecular structure, and noticed that at 145 °C a cloudy liquid was produced. The liquid went completely clear at 179 °C. This process was reversible on cooling. Reinitzer had discovered a new state of matter that was intermediate between the liquid and solid states.

The liquid crystal state was an interesting curiosity, but thought to be of no practical use since there were no stable compounds that showed the liquid crystal state at room temperature. In the late 1960s, the search was on to replace the heavy cathode ray tubes in aircraft. (Your television screen is part of a cathode ray tube.) There was renewed interest in trying to produce chemicals that showed liquid crystal properties at room temperature. In 1972 at Hull University, the world's first stable, room-temperature liquid crystal was made.

Liquid crystals all contain long, thin, rigid organic molecules. There are three different arrangements of molecules in the liquid crystal state. The one that is used in digital watches is called nematic: an electric field alters the orientation of some of the liquid crystal molecules in a thin film; this causes parts of the display to go dark and so gives the shapes of different numbers. Another arrangement of liquid crystals gives different colours at different temperatures and these are used in thermometers.

Liquid crystals are now very big business and there is a lot of research to produce new molecules that show this interesting state of matter.

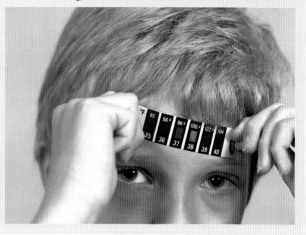

Fig 5.17(d) **Using a liquid crystal thermometer**

solid to a liquid at the melting point is called the **enthalpy change of fusion** (ΔH_m). When all the solid has melted, the temperature begins to rise and the particles have more energy and move faster.

At the boiling point, the liquid begins changing to a gas and the temperature again stays constant since all the energy taken in by the liquid is used to overcome the forces holding particles close together in the liquid state. The **enthalpy change of vaporisation** (ΔH_b) is the energy that must be supplied to change one mole of liquid to a gas at a particular temperature. When all the liquid has boiled to form a gas, the temperature rises again as the particles move faster. The process of changing state is a physical process because no chemical bonds are broken.

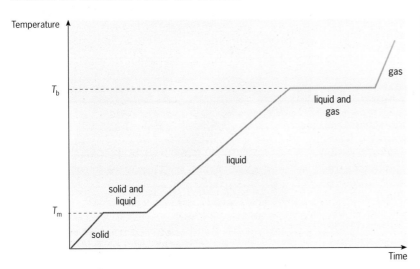

Fig 5.18 **A plot of temperature against time as energy is supplied at a constant rate to a substance that starts in the solid state**

R In Fig 5.18, notice that the flat portion of the heating curve is much less at the melting point (T_m) than at the boiling point (T_b). What does this tell you about the relative magnitudes of ΔH_m and ΔH_b?

Vapour pressure

Although a liquid changes to a gas at its boiling point, we know that a liquid can change to a gas at temperatures below the boiling point. If a glass of water is left on a window sill for a week, some of it changes to a gas and the volume of water decreases. The process is **evaporation**. At any temperature, the particles in a liquid have a range of kinetic energies. Some particles have enough energy to break free of the forces holding them in the liquid state and they evaporate. Since it is the particles with most kinetic energy that evaporate, this leaves the particles with lower kinetic energies in the liquid, so the average kinetic energy of the liquid drops and the liquid temperature falls. On a windy day in winter, weather forecasters talk about the wind chill factor. This is because air moving over the skin causes water to evaporate from the skin faster so the apparent temperature we feel is much colder than the air temperature.

If the liquid is in a closed vessel, then the rate at which the particles escape from the liquid surface equals the rate at which the particles rejoin the liquid. When the rate of evaporation is the same as the rate of condensation we say that the liquid is in **equilibrium** with its vapour (or gas). The pressure due to the vapour above the liquid at equilibrium is called its **vapour pressure**. As the temperature increases, so does the average kinetic energy of the particles in the liquid. This means that more particles have sufficient energy to escape into the gas and so the vapour pressure increases. When the vapour pressure of a liquid is the same as the external pressure above its surface, then the liquid boils. For example, water boils when its vapour pressure equals atmospheric pressure. This is why water boils at 70 °C on the top of Mount Everest where the atmospheric pressure is very much less than it is at sea level.

SUBLIMATION AND FREEZE-DRIED COFFEE

WHEN A SOLID changes straight to a gas without passing through the liquid state, the change of state is known as **sublimation**. The reason that some solids  can do this is that they possess relatively high vapour pressures. Iodine and carbon dioxide are two examples of solids with high vapour pressures so at atmospheric pressure their solid forms sublime.

Fig 5.19 **A flask containing solid iodine in equilibrium with its purple vapour**

While we expect ice to melt rather than sublime, it can change straight to water vapour: you may have noticed that frozen puddles gradually shrink in freezing weather. This phenomenon is used in the production of instant coffee. The coffee is brewed and then frozen in a container from which air is removed by a vacuum pump. Lowering the pressure causes the ice in the frozen brewed coffee to sublime. When nearly all the ice has been removed, the coffee is said to be freeze-dried and is ready for packaging. This method of removing water leaves the flavour molecules intact, and so freeze-dried instant coffee has a much better flavour than coffee that is dried by slow heating.

Fig 5.20 **In the freeze-dry process, the sample is put in a chamber and frozen very fast. Then the chamber is evacuated and the sample is slowly heated, when any ice turns straight to vapour**

4 PHASE DIAGRAMS

Solid, liquid and gas are the three states of matter, but these states can be called by a different name – **phases.** A phase is defined as a homogeneous (uniform) portion of matter separated from other portions of matter by a boundary surface. A mixture of gases is one phase because there is no boundary surface between the different gases. However, oil and water have a boundary layer so there are two phases. A solid completely dissolved in a liquid is one phase because the solution is homogeneous. A mixture of solids has as many phases as there are solids in the mixture, because each solid is separated from the other solids by a definite boundary surface.

We have seen that both temperature and pressure affect which phase of matter a particular substance exists in. A phase diagram shows whether solid, liquid or gas exists at a particular temperature and pressure for a closed system. (A closed system means that no matter can escape or enter.)

?

S How many phases are there in:

(a) a saturated solution if there is excess solute?

(b) solder which is a homogenous mixture of lead and tin?

Hint: Are there any boundary surfaces in the system you are considering?

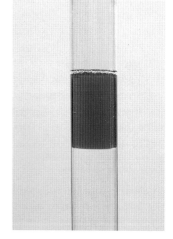

Fig 5.21 **Oil floating on water gives two liquid phases, because there is a definite boundary surface**

Water

There are three areas on the phase diagram of Fig 5.22 representing ice, water and water vapour. The lines that separate these areas indicate the temperatures and pressures at which two phases can exist in equilibrium.

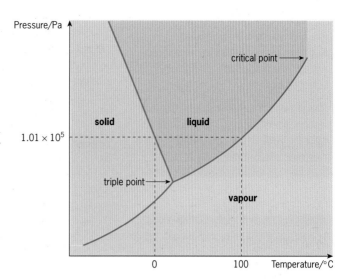

Fig 5.22 **Phase diagram for water**

The line between the water and water vapour gives the variation of vapour pressure of water with temperature. At a pressure of 1.01×10^5 Pa (normal atmospheric pressure at sea level), water boils at 100 °C. The line between the liquid and solid shows how the melting point varies with pressure.

For most substances the melting point increases with an increase in pressure, but water is unusual because its melting point decreases as pressure increases.

The line between solid and vapour gives the conditions needed for ice to sublime and explains why it sublimes in the freeze-drying process in instant coffee production described in the Feature box opposite.

There is one point on the phase diagram where it is possible for all three phases to coexist in equilibrium. This is called the **triple point**. Notice also that the line between liquid and vapour ends at the **critical point**. Beyond this particular temperature it is not possible to liquefy water vapour. We will return to the critical point later.

Carbon dioxide

The phase diagram for carbon dioxide is similar to that for water except that the solid–liquid line has a positive slope. This is because when liquid carbon dioxide freezes the volume decreases as the particles come closer together to form a solid lattice. This happens with most solids.

Fig 5.23 **Phase diagram for carbon dioxide**

However, as water approaches 0 °C, the particles move slightly apart, so the water expands on freezing and becomes less dense. If pressure is increased, the equilibrium of ice and liquid shifts to produce more liquid, hence the melting point decreases and we get a negative slope.

?

T Ice is less dense than liquid water, so ice floats. Most solids sink in their liquids. Imagine what would happen if ice sank in the oceans. For one thing, it would probably never melt as it would be away from the warming of the Sun's rays. Describe the effects you think this would have on our weather systems and on life on Earth.

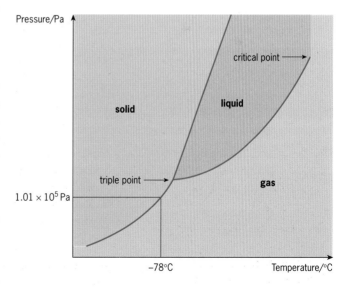

You can find more about what happens when conditions are altered for a system in equilibrium by reading Chapter 16.

The lattice structure of ice is due to a special form of intermolecular bonding called hydrogen bonding, which you can read more about in Chapter 21.

?

U (a) What is the critical temperature of hydrogen on the Celsius scale?
(b) A gaseous element discovered on Earth in 1895 was finally condensed in 1908. It has a critical temperature of 5 K. What is the name of this gas?
See page 55 to check your answer.

A point to note is that at atmospheric pressure (1.01×10^5 Pa) solid carbon dioxide sublimes at $-78\,°C$ instead of melting. This is why it is called dry ice. It is used to keep objects cold and can be packed round them because it does not turn into a liquid when it warms up. Solid carbon dioxide also produces the mist you see at pop concerts: as it sublimes, the cold CO_2 gas makes water vapour in the air condense to water droplets, forming clouds of mist.

The critical point

We have already seen that the liquid–vapour line finishes at the critical point. The temperature at this point is known as the **critical temperature**. At this temperature, no pressure, however high, can force the particles in a gas to condense to a liquid: they have too much kinetic energy to liquefy.

During the early part of the nineteenth century, experimenters managed to liquefy many of the gases that had resisted liquefaction. However, nitrogen, oxygen and hydrogen appeared to be 'permanent gases' – it did not seem possible to liquefy them. But this was because scientists could not reach temperatures below their critical temperatures. For hydrogen it is 33 K. Hydrogen was eventually liquefied in 1898 by the Scotsman James Dewar who a year later managed to solidify it at 14 K.

5 MIXTURES OF TWO COMPLETELY MISCIBLE LIQUIDS

When we considered the phase diagram for water we were dealing with a **one-component** system because in all the phases the chemical substance was water. The carbon dioxide phase system is also a one-component system.

However, two liquids that are completely **miscible** in each other form a two-component system. **Miscible liquids** dissolve completely in each other in all proportions to form a homogeneous mixture. Because the mixture is homogeneous it is one phase, but contains two components. A good example of a mixture of two miscible liquids is ethanol and water.

Chemists express the proportions of the two liquid components in a mixture in terms of **mole fractions**.

> **The mole fraction is the ratio of the number of moles of a particular component to the *total* number of moles present in the system.**

So for a mixture of two miscible liquids A and B:

$$\text{Total number of moles} = n_A + n_B$$

$$\text{The mole fraction of liquid A, } x_A = \frac{n_A}{n_A + n_B}$$

$$\text{The mole fraction of liquid B, } x_B = \frac{n_A}{n_A + n_B}$$

?

V A mixture of ethanol and water contains 20 moles of ethanol and 5 moles of water. What are the mole fractions of ethanol and water in this mixture?

Note that symbol x is used for the mole fraction, and in a two-component system:

$$x_A + x_B = 1$$

Raoult's law

Suppose we start with pure liquid A which is volatile. It will have a vapour above its liquid surface and this will exert a vapour pressure. If we now start mixing in another volatile liquid, B, then the vapour above the mixture will contain some molecules of B. When only A is present, the vapour pressure will be that of pure A: p^0_A. As it is diluted with liquid B, the mole fraction of A falls, and so also does the *number of molecules* of A in the vapour. This then reduces the vapour pressure of A to p_A. Meanwhile, as the mole fraction of B is increased, so will the number of molecules of B in the vapour, therefore increasing the contribution to the total vapour pressure made by B: p_B. You can see the effect of changing the proportions (mole fractions) of A and B in Fig 5.24.

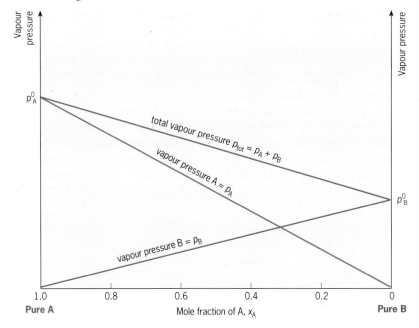

Fig 5.24 **Vapour pressure–composition diagram for two volatile miscible liquids at constant temperature**

> **?**
>
> **W** When the mole fraction of A in Fig 5.24 is 0.8, what is the mole fraction of B?

Notice that in Fig 5.24 the total vapour pressure above the mixture (p_{tot}) is the sum of the vapour pressures due to liquid A (p_A) and due to liquid B (p_B):

$$p_{tot} = p_A + p_B$$

Raoult's law states that:

The vapour pressure due to liquid A (p_A) equals the vapour pressure of pure A (p^0_A) multiplied by the mole fraction of A (x_A) present in the mixture:

$$p_A = p^0_A \times x_A$$

Raoult's law applies to **ideal mixtures** in which there is:

- no enthalpy change when the liquids are mixed,
- no change in volume on mixing,
- no change in intermolecular forces between molecules of the pure substances and between the different molecules in the mixture.

Any ideal mixture obeys Raoult's law.

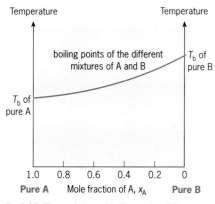

Fig 5.25 **The variation of boiling point with composition for ideal mixture of liquids A and B at constant pressure. Notice that in Fig 5.24 liquid A has the higher vapour pressure when pure, so it boils at a lower temperature than liquid B**

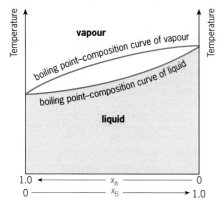

Fig 5.26 **Phase diagram for liquid mixtures of A and B. The two curves are boiling point–composition curves – one for the liquid and one of the vapour. At any given temperature when the liquid is boiling (lower curve), it produces a vapour which contains a greater proportion of A, because A is more volatile than B**

How boiling point varies with composition for an ideal mixture of two miscible liquids

The vapour pressure of a liquid increases with an increase in temperature. At the temperature at which the vapour pressure equals atmospheric pressure, the liquid boils. At a particular temperature, if the vapour pressure of a liquid is already high, the boiling point will be at a temperature that is not much higher. For a liquid with a low vapour pressure, the temperature will need to be raised much more before it can boil. In Fig 5.24, the total vapour pressure above the liquid mixture varies according to its composition, so the boiling point too will change, and we have shown this in Fig 5.25.

The boiling point line is a curve, not a straight line. This is because vapour pressure increases at a faster rate than the rate of increase of temperature.

Fractional distillation

Fig 5.26 is a phase diagram for mixtures of liquids A and B. On this diagram there are two boiling point–composition curves. The one for the liquid phase is identical to Fig 5.25, but as the liquid mixture boils it turns into a vapour phase, which is richer in the more volatile component – in this case, A. So the composition of the vapour is different from the boiling liquid, and this is why fractional distillation works. The gap between the two curves does not represent any phase and should be regarded as a 'no go area'.

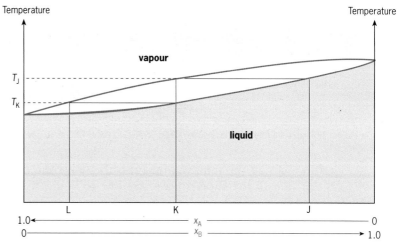

Fig 5.27 **Phase diagram for mixtures of liquids A and B, showing what happens when a mixture of composition J is boiled and its vapour condensed to give a liquid of a different composition K. The boiling and condensing process is repeated to give a liquid mixture of composition L. Each time, the condensed vapour is richer in the more volatile liquid A**

Study Fig 5.27: imagine that you have a liquid mixture of A and B with a composition J. This mixture boils at a boiling point T_J. Compared with the mixture, the vapour formed on boiling is richer in A: the composition of the vapour at T_J can be found by drawing a horizontal line to the vapour composition curve. If the vapour is now separated and condensed, the liquid has a composition K. This process is a simple distillation where the liquids are boiled and the vapour condensed. When the liquid mixture is boiled again it will boil at temperature T_K. It will be even richer in component A and will have a composition of L. This process of separating and condensing the vapour can continue until pure A is obtained.

In practice, boiling the liquid mixture and condensing its vapour in a separate piece of apparatus would involve many separate distillations and so would be too time-consuming. A fractionating column does this in one piece of apparatus, vaporising and condensing the mixture many times. Apparatus for fractional distillation in a laboratory is shown in Fig 5.28. As vapour enters the fractionating column it begins to cool and condense. The condensed liquid falls back but is reheated by vapour coming from the flask, so it re-boils. As the vapour rises up the tower it becomes richer in the more volatile component A through a series of redistillations. The longer the column, the closer to pure A the composition of the vapour becomes. The glass beads are there to provide a large surface area for the liquid and vapour to boil and condense. The liquid in the flask becomes richer in component B as A boils off.

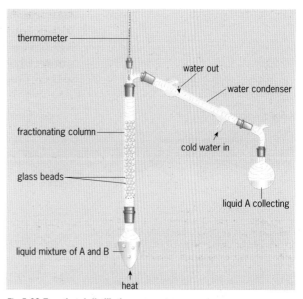

Fig 5.28 **Fractional distillation apparatus**

Fractional distillation is used to separate liquid mixtures with components of different boiling points. Nitrogen, oxygen and the noble gases are obtained industrially from liquid air by fractional distillation. Crude oil is separated in oil refineries into fractions containing mixtures of hydrocarbons with closely similar boiling points.

(For fractional distillation of crude oil see page 148.)

?

X As the composition of the liquid in the flask becomes richer in B, what happens to its boiling point?

Non-ideal liquid mixtures

For a liquid mixture to be ideal it must obey Raoult's law. Very few mixtures do this exactly. Some have a positive deviation from the law, showing higher than predicted vapour pressures when mixed (see Fig 5.29), and some mixtures of liquids have a negative deviation, producing a lower than expected vapour pressure (see Fig 5.30).

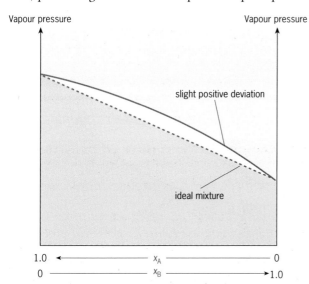

Fig 5.29 **Vapour pressure–composition curve showing a slight positive deviation**

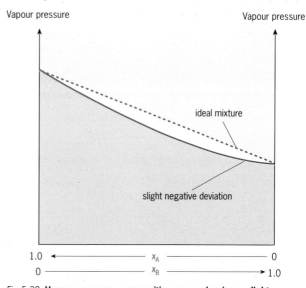

Fig 5.30 **Vapour pressure–composition curve showing a slight negative deviation**

Figs 5.29 and 5.30 show relatively minor deviations from the ideal mixture and have no maximum or minimum vapour pressures. Consequently they have no maximum or minimum boiling points. These mixtures can be separated by fractional distillation.

Azeotropic mixtures

When liquid mixtures have a large deviation from the ideal they will have maximum or minimum vapour pressures in their composition curves, as shown in Figs 5.31 and 5.32. Those with maximum vapour pressures will have minimum boiling points and vice versa.

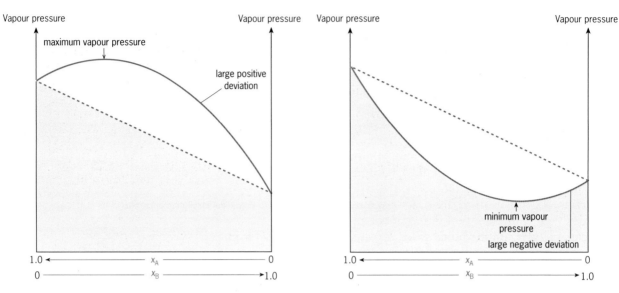

Fig 5.31 **Vapour pressure–composition curve showing a large positive deviation. Note that there is a maximum vapour pressure**

Fig 5.32 **Vapour pressure–composition curve showing a large negative deviation. Note that there is a minimum vapour pressure**

This is shown in Figs 5.33 and 5.34. In each case, we can see what happens if we start with a mixture of composition z and fractionally distil it. Notice that only one pure component separates, leaving a constant boiling mixture called an **azeotrope**. Azeotropes boil to give a vapour of the same composition. Nitric acid and water form a maximum boiling point azeotrope, while mixtures of benzene and ethanol give a minimum boiling point azeotrope.

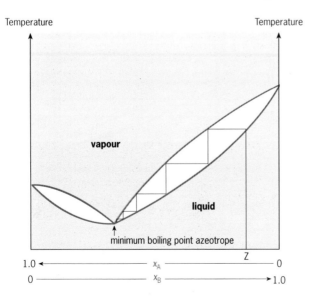

Fig 5.33 **Phase diagram for mixtures of liquids A and B with a large positive deviation, showing what happens when a mixture of composition z is fractionally distilled. Note that the azeotrope produced has a minimum boiling point, and this will boil off first, leaving, in this case, pure liquid B in the distillation flask**

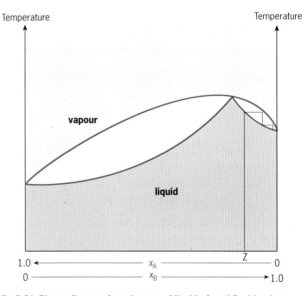

Fig 5.34 **Phase diagram for mixtures of liquids A and B with a large negative deviation, showing what happens when a mixture of composition z is fractionally distilled. Note that the azeotrope produced has a maximum boiling point, and this will be left in the distillation flask, while pure liquid B is distilled first from the top of the column**

6 AQUEOUS SOLUTIONS

Aqueous solutions have water as the solvent. When we write equations and we want to show that a reactant is dissolved in water, we write the state symbol (aq). So a dilute solution of sulphuric acid is written: $H_2SO_4(aq)$.

Water covers most of the surface of our planet, and many reactions take place in aqueous solution. Nearly all the chemical reactions of our bodies occur in the aqueous environment of our cells.

One mole is the amount of substance that contains as many particles as there are atoms in exactly 12 g of carbon-12. The number of particles in a mole is 6.02×10^{23} and is called the **Avogadro constant.** You can find out more about the mole on page 5 of Chapter 1. Now work through the Examples.

Concentration

Chemists are interested in the *amount* of a substance present. When we considered gases at the beginning of this chapter, it was not long before we came across the mole. It is the same with solutions. We need to know how many moles of solute are present in a particular volume of solution.

The concentration of a solute in a solution is measured in **moles per cubic decimetre – mol dm⁻³**.

EXAMPLES

Q Work out how many moles of solute are dissolved in these solutions:
(a) 250 cm³ of 1.0 mol dm⁻³ NaOH(aq)
(b) 20 cm³ 0.50 mol dm⁻³ HCl(aq)

A

(a) 1 dm³ = 1000 cm³
Number of moles NaOH in 1000 cm³ = 1 mol

So number of moles NaOH in 250 cm³ = $1 \times \dfrac{250}{1000}$
= 0.25 mol

(b)
Number of moles of HCl in 1000 cm³ = 0.50 mol

So number of moles HCl in 20 cm³ = $0.50 \times \dfrac{20}{1000}$
= 0.010 mol

Q What is the concentration (in mol dm⁻³) of the following aqueous solutions?
(a) 0.25 mol HCl dissolved in 50 cm³
(b) 5.85 g of NaCl dissolved in 250 cm³

A

(a) There are 0.25 mol HCl in 50 cm³
So in 1000 cm³, the number of moles = $0.25 \times \dfrac{1000}{50}$
= 5.0 mol
Concentration of HCl in solution = 5.0 mol dm⁻³

(b) Moles of NaCl in 5.85 g
$= \dfrac{\text{mass in grams}}{\text{mass of one mole (in grams)}} = \dfrac{5.85g}{58.5g} = 0.100\, mol$
There are 0.100 mol NaCl in 250 cm³
So in 1000 cm³, the number of moles
$= 0.100 \times \dfrac{1000}{250} = 0.400\, mol$

Concentration of NaCl solution = 0.400 mol dm⁻³

---

7 ENTROPY

Entropy is a measure of the disorder of a system. Think of your bedroom – when it is tidy everything has a place and there is a high degree of order. We could say that the entropy of your room is low. But it is all too easy for the entropy to rise as things get out of place and it becomes untidy.

When particles are in a solid they cannot move out of position, they can only vibrate. In the solid state there is usually a high degree of order and a limited number of ways of arranging the particles, so the entropy of a solid is usually low. The liquid state tends to have a higher entropy than the solid state because the particles can move about, so there are many more arrangements possible. A gas has widely spaced particles moving very rapidly in all directions. All gases have high entropies.

?

Y **(a)** Calculate how many moles of solute are present in these solutions:
(i) 100 cm³ of 2 mol dm⁻³ H_2SO_4.
(ii) 25.0 cm³ of 5.00 mol dm⁻³ HNO_3.
(iii) 5 dm³ of 0.2 mol dm⁻³ KCl.
(iv) 10 cm³ of 0.5 mol dm⁻³ Na_2CO_3.
(v) 50 cm³ of 0.050 mol dm⁻³ $NaNO_3$.
(b) Calculate the concentration of the following solutions:
(i) 0.40 mol $CaCl_2$ dissolved in 250 cm³.
(ii) 16 g $CuSO_4$ dissolved in 100 cm³.
A_r: Cu = 64, S = 32, O = 16.

Table 5.1

Substance	Entropy (S)/J K^{-1} mol^{-1}
He(g)	126.0
Ne(g)	146.2
H$_2$O(l)	69.9
H$_2$O(g)	188.7
C$_{(graphite)}$	5.7
C$_{(diamond)}$	2.4

?

Z Predict whether each of the following leads to an increase or decrease in the entropy of the substances involved:

(a) Ice melting.

(b) Water vapour condensing.

(c) Cooling oxygen from 60 °C to 20 °C.

(d) Dissolving sugar in water.

(e) Subliming solid iodine.

(f) Freezing liquid bromine.

The entropies of different substances can be determined for a particular temperature. Entropy is given the symbol S and is measured in joules per kelvin per mole (J K^{-1} mol^{-1}). Table 5.1 gives the entropy values for some substances at 298 K and 101 kPa.

You can see from the table that water vapour has a much higher entropy than water liquid. This is to be expected, since water molecules are more spread out in the vapour and more arrangements are possible. Diamond has a lower entropy than graphite and this means that diamond has a more ordered structure. Neon and helium are both gases and so have relatively high entropies. However, neon has heavier atoms. This tends to bring its energy levels closer together, which in fact provides more possibilities of arranging quanta of energy.

Entropy, then, is not just about the number of possible ways of arranging particles. It is also about how the energy of the particles are arranged in the energy levels. This is an aspect of entropy that we shall continue in Chapter 6.

SUMMARY

After studying this chapter, you should know and understand the following points and be able to use the equations.

■ Equal volumes of gases contain equal numbers of molecules at the same temperature and pressure (Avogadro's law).

■ 1 mole of any gas at standard temperature and pressure occupies 22.4 dm³. Under room conditions the molar gas volume is 24 dm³.

■ Boyle's law relates pressure and volume of a fixed amount of gas and is expressed mathematically as:

$p \propto 1/V$, where p = pressure and V = volume.

■ Charles' law relates volume and temperature of a gas and is expressed mathematically as:

$V \propto T$, where T = absolute temperature in kelvin.

■ The ideal gas equation relates pressure, volume and temperature for a fixed amount of gas:

$$pV = nRT.$$

■ The kinetic-molecular model explains the behaviour of ideal gases by making a number of assumptions, such as zero intermolecular forces and assuming that the volume of particles is negligible.

■ Real gases approach ideal behaviour when at a high temperature or low pressure.

■ The kinetic-molecular model can be extended to include solids and liquids.

■ Vapour pressure is the pressure above a liquid when it is in equilibrium with its vapour.

■ A phase is a homogeneous portion of matter separated from other portions by a definite boundary surface.

■ An ideal liquid mixture obeys Raoult's law. Raoult's law states that:

$$p_A = p^0_A \times x_A.$$

■ Fractional distillation separates two liquids of different boiling points in a homogeneous mixture.

■ Non-ideal mixtures show either positive or negative deviations from Raoult's law.

■ An azeotrope is a constant boiling mixture. Azeotropes occur when there is a maximum or minimum vapour pressure.

■ The concentration of a solute in a solution is measured in mol dm^{-3}.

■ Entropy is a measure of the disorder of a system. Solids usually have a low entropy whereas gases have high entropies.

QUESTIONS

1

a) Explain why the vapour pressure of a liquid increases with increasing temperature.

b) **A** and **B** are two identical closed evacuates vessels each with a volume of $0.001\,m^3$ (1 litre). **X** is a volatile liquid which behaves as an ideal gas in the vapour phase.

2.1 g and 4.2 g of liquid **X** are placed in vessels **A** and **b**, respectively. The two vessels are immersed in a water bath and heated. When the temperature reaches 40 °C, the last trace of liquid **X** evaporates from vessel **A** in which the pressure is then 44.0 kPa (0.434 atm). Once the temperature reaches 87 °C, the last trace of liquid **X** just evaporates from vessel **B**.

   (i) State the relationship between pressure and temperature of a fixed mass of an ideal gas at constant volume.

   (ii) Calculate the pressure in **A** at 87 °C.

  (iii) Using your answer to **(ii)** above, calculate the pressure in **B** at 87 °C.

  (iv) State the relationship between pressure, volume and temperature for n moles of an ideal gas.

   (v) Determine the relative molecular mass of **X**.

[NEAB June 1995 Chemistry Syllabus B: Paper 1 Section B, q.2]

2

The gaseous behaviour of helium closely approximates to that of an *ideal* gas, whereas ammonia is better described as a *real* gas.

a) Fig 5.Q2 shows a plot of pV against p at constant temperature for helium and ammonia. (V is the volume occupied by the gas and p is the pressure.)

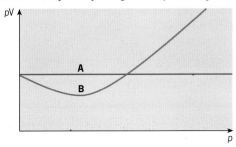

Fig 5.Q2

   (i) Which of these lines, **A** or **B**, represents helium?

  (ii) Suggest **two** reasons for any difference between the shapes of these two lines.

  (iii) Explain how an increase in pressure may cause a gas to liquefy.

b) On vaporisation, 0.135 g of a liquid fuel gave 90.0 cm^3 of vapour, measured at 373 K and 101 kPa. Calculate the relative molecular mass of this fuel.

c) Suggest why propane, C_3H_8, is a better bottled gas fuel than butane, C_4H_{10}, in cold climates.

[UCLES March 1996 Sciences: Trends and Patterns paper, q.3]

3

a) With reference, where appropriate, to the kinetic theory of matter:

   (i) explain why a gas exerts a pressure;

  (ii) describe what happens as an ionic substance such as sodium chloride, melting point 801 °C, is steadily heated from room temperature until it melts;

  (iii) account for the relatively high melting points of ionic substances.

b) A volatile liquid, of mass 0.148 g, when vaporised occupies a volume of $63.0\,cm^3$ at a pressure of $1.01 \times 10^5\,Pa$ at a temperature of 100 °C. State the ideal gas equation and use it to calculate the relative molecular mass of the liquid.

[AEB June 1996 Chemistry: Paper 1, q.2]

4

In an experiment to determine the relative molecular mass of chloroethane, 0.18 g of chloroethane was vaporised at 100 °C and was found to occupy $82\,cm^3$ at exactly 1 atmosphere pressure.

   (i) Sketch the apparatus you could have used to carry out this experiment.

  (ii) Calculate the relative molecular mass of chloroethane.

(1 atmosphere = 101.3 kPa; $R = 8.31\ J\ K^{-1}\ mol^{-1}$)

[AEB Jan 1995 Chemistry: Paper 6, q.2]

5

a) State Raoult's law for an ideal binary liquid mixture.

b) Liquid oxygen and liquid nitrogen form an ideal liquid mixture. At 70 K the vapour pressures are 38.3 kPa for N_2 and 6.40 kPa for O_2. Find the composition of the vapour in equilibrium with a liquid mixture which at equilibrium is an **equimolar** mixture of the two elements.

c) Show by means of sketches of boiling point/composition diagrams and a brief comment why ideal mixtures of liquids of similar boiling temperature are more difficult to separate by fractional distillation than those with boiling temperatures ore widely separated.

d) The vapour pressure/composition diagram at constant temperature for a mixture of two liquids **A** and **B** shows a strong deviation from Raoult's law is shown in Fig 5.Q5. ($x(\mathbf{A})$ = mole fraction of **A**.)

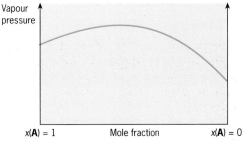

Fig 5.Q5

[ULEAC Jan 1996 Chemistry: Module Test 4, q.3]

Assignment

SUPERCRITICAL FLUIDS

Above a certain temperature it is not possible to condense a gas, no matter how much pressure is applied. This phenomenon was discovered in 1821 when Baron Charles Cagniard de la Tour sealed an amount of a liquid and its vapour in a cannon. He heated the cannon, tilted it backwards and forwards, and measured the temperature at which the sloshing sound of the liquid disappeared. This temperature is called the critical temperature. The pressure at which this happens is the critical pressure and both combine to define the critical point. At this critical point, the two phases of gas and liquid become indistinguishable from each other and have the properties of both.

As the liquid was heated up inside the cannon it expanded and this reduced its density. Also, more molecules escaped into the vapour phase, so the density of the gas increased, until at the critical temperature the densities of gas and liquid become the same and we say that the substance is a **fluid**.

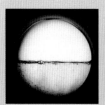  

Fig A1(left) **A fluorinated hydrocarbon close to the critical point. The phase boundary between the liquid and gas phases**

Fig A1(centre) **The critical temperature has almost been reached and the phase boundary is disappearing**

Fig A1(right) **A supercritical fluid is present as the temperature rises above the critical point**

1

a) What assumptions are made in the kinetic-molecular model about the particles in an ideal gas?

b) Explain in terms of intermolecular forces why cooling a gas below its critical temperature causes it to condense.

c) In the sealed cannon experiment, explain why the pressure increased as the liquid and vapour were heated

d) Draw a phase diagram for carbon dioxide and mark the critical point on it.

2

Some gases, such as nitrogen and hydrogen, were known as 'permanent gases' in the nineteenth century because they could not be liquefied by using even very high pressures. Why was this?

Supercritical fluids SCF's will fill the volume of any container just like a gas, but, like liquids, they have solvent properties. For more than a century the phenomenon of SCFs was regarded as a scientific curiosity of little practical value. However, in the early 1960s, the German chemist Kurt Zosel used supercritical carbon dioxide to remove caffeine from wet coffee beans and opened a treasure chest of important industrial applications that we are still discovering to this day.

3

Before supercritical CO_2 was used to decaffeinate coffee, liquid organic solvents were used and some of these contained chlorine.

a) Find out and describe the environmental problems of using chlorine containing organic solvents.

b) Because carbon dioxide is removed as a by-product during the fractional distillation of liquid air, it does not have any significant impact on the greenhouse effect. It has several advantages. One of these is that it is non-toxic. What are some of its other advantages?

4

Supercritical CO_2 is used as a solvent to remove cholesterol from egg yolk. Why are food manufactures very interested in this process?

Carbon dioxide becomes supercritical at just 31 °C and so can be used to dissolve complex molecules that would be destroyed by higher temperatures. This is opening up possibilities of extracting drugs from plants and micro-organisms. Already the chemicals responsible for some odours and flavours can be extracted from foodstuffs. The possibility of removing the cooking oil from potato chips is also under investigation to produce healthier, oil-free chips.

Water, too, exhibits unusual properties when it becomes supercritical above 374 °C and 218×10^5 Pa. In particular, non-polar organic compounds that would not normally dissolve in polar water are able to dissolve. Supercritical water can be used to carry out reactions with molecular oxygen that convert hazardous organic compounds into small harmless species such as CO_2, H_2O and Cl^-. The notorious polychlorinated biphenyls (PCBs) can be destroyed using this technique, and much research is being carried out to destroy military stockpiles of chemical weapons safely using supercritical water. (You can read more about PCBs on page 81 of Chapter 4.)

5

a) Draw a dot and cross diagram for the chloride ion.

b) What properties of compounds containing chloride ions make these a safer alternatives to compounds made up of molecules containing chlorine?

6

Why are processes involving supercritical water expensive?

Fig A2 **A flame is produced spontaneously in a mixture of supercritical water and methane at 1000×10^5 Pa and 500 °C when oxygen is injected**

STATES OF MATTER

This chapter contains a number of difficult ideas about gases in particular, but also about solids and liquids, and changes between states of matter. Study the map to see how the ideas and laws connect with each other, and with related information in other chapters. Use the map to check the material you feel confident about, and to identify what you need to study further.

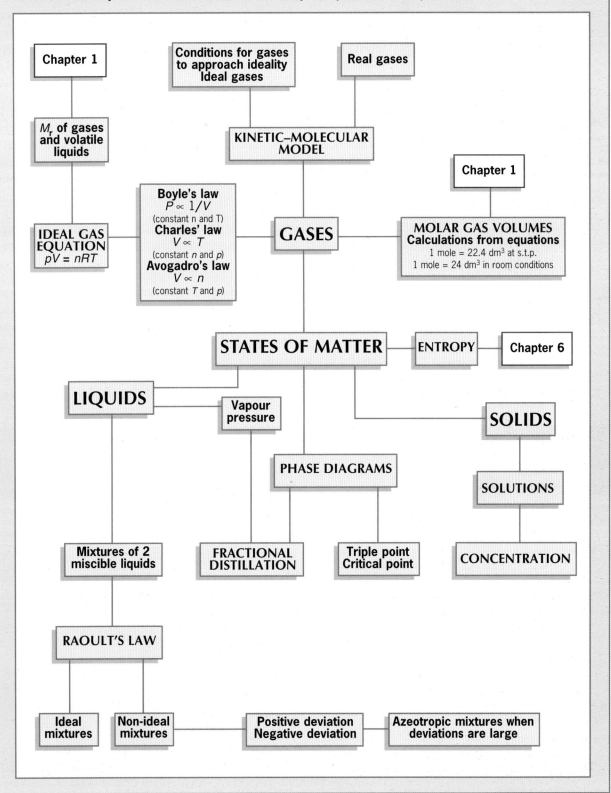

6 Fuels

Hydrogen is dangerous to transport, as the Hindenburg disaster of 1937 showed. The Hindenburg was a hydrogen-filled airship which blew up, killing 35 people

Hydrogen has become a fuel in space exploration: the US space shuttle piggy-backs a lift on giant tanks containing 1.74 million litres of liquid hydrogen and 0.65 million litres of liquid oxygen

A car with an experimental engine that runs on hydrogen

You can read more about greenhouse gases and some of the other harmful by-products of using petrol as a fuel on page 164.

?

A Magnesium produces energy on burning. Why don't we class magnesium as a fuel?

✓

kJ mol⁻¹ is the energy released per mole of equation. This means the mole quantities given in the equation release so many kilojoules.

WORLD SUPPLIES OF OIL are likely to run out before the end of the twenty-first century, but by then, other energy sources will have been developed. A possibility is hydrogen, derived from water. Hydrogen has several advantages: when it burns it produces no harmful products, it gives out more energy per gram than natural gas or petrol, and existing car engines need only minor modifications to use it as a fuel.

The reason we don't start splitting water now to get hydrogen is that the process requires energy. In the UK, this would have to come from burning fossil fuels, cancelling out any environmental advantages. Alternatively, more efficient solar cells might provide the energy to split water by electrolysis. The possibility of producing hydrogen from the photosynthetic reactions of plants has been investigated, but so far with little success.

The problem is how to carry hydrogen around, since to stay liquid and occupy a convenient volume it would have to be stored below –253 °C. One promising area of research is the use of metal hydrides, solid compounds of a metal and hydrogen: the hydrogen could be produced from them as needed by heating.

What is a fuel?

A fuel is a substance which releases energy that can do work. Most fuels release this energy during combustion reactions. So what properties make an ideal fuel? Petrol is a popular fuel, but is it ideal?

For its mass, petrol produces a lot of energy, which makes the expense of transporting and storing it worthwhile. It doesn't produce solid waste that needs to be dumped. But an ideal fuel produces no harmful by-products when it burns, and petrol does. Even if they were just carbon dioxide and water, we now know that carbon dioxide is a major greenhouse gas and its continued output at today's levels will lead to global warming.

1 HOW A FUEL RELEASES ITS ENERGY: EXOTHERMIC REACTIONS AND ENTHALPY CHANGES

When natural gas burns it releases its energy to the surroundings, which could be the water in a central heating system. This is an **exothermic reaction** between methane (in natural gas) and oxygen.

$$CH_4(g) + 2O_2(g) \rightarrow CO_2(g) + 2H_2O(l) \quad \Delta H^\ominus_{298} = -890 \, kJ \, mol^{-1}$$

ΔH (pronounced 'delta H') is the **enthalpy change** of the reaction. The stored energy of the reactants, methane and oxygen, is higher than the stored energy of the products of the reaction, carbon dioxide and water, and the difference in energy is released to the surroundings when methane and oxygen react. We can see this in Fig 6.1.

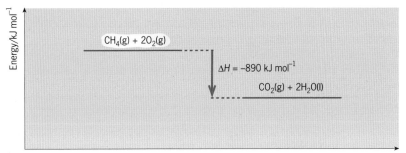

Fig 6.1 **Energy level diagram for methane burning**

Standard conditions

The symbol $^\ominus$ tells us that the conditions for this enthalpy change are **standard conditions** at a particular temperature. Standard conditions are 1 atmosphere (101 kPa) pressure and, for solutions, a concentration of 1 mol dm^{-3}. The particular temperature for these standard conditions is usually 298 K (25 °C). A small 298 following $\Delta H^\ominus$ (pronounced 'delta H standard') tells us that this is the temperature. The substances in the chemical reaction (the reactants and products) are known as the **system**, and all substances in the system are in their **standard states**. The standard state is the most stable physical state at 1 atmosphere pressure and the particular temperature, usually 298 K (25 °C). So the standard state of methane is a gas and the standard state of water is a liquid.

> **The enthalpy change of a reaction under standard conditions at 298 K, with all substances in their standard states, is called the standard enthalpy change of reaction.**

It refers to the mole quantities given in the balanced equation for the reaction.

The **surroundings** are everything which is not the system. It could be the reaction vessel, the air around the reaction vessel, the mercury in a thermometer and anything else which is not a reactant or product. But the surroundings must be what is associated thermally with the system, which means that heat can transfer between system and surroundings.

In exothermic reactions, ΔH is negative. In endothermic reactions, ΔH is positive.

Enthalpy, H, is the stored energy in a compound. Enthalpy *changes*, ΔH, are transfers of energy into or out of the system at constant pressure. We first met these terms on page 10.

State symbols should always be shown in chemical equations when dealing with energy from chemical reactions. The enthalpy change which produces gaseous water (steam) is not the same as one which ends up with liquid water. Remember (s) = solid, (l) = liquid, (g) = gas.

You will sometimes see the standard enthalpy change of reaction written as the **standard molar enthalpy change of reaction.**

2 STANDARD ENTHALPY CHANGE OF COMBUSTION

Methane burning in oxygen is called a combustion reaction. The enthalpy change is an enthalpy change of reaction, but if we burn one mole of methane completely in oxygen it can also be referred to as an **enthalpy change of combustion**.

> **When one mole of a substance burns completely in oxygen under standard conditions at 298 K, the enthalpy change is called the standard enthalpy change of combustion, $\Delta H^\ominus_{c,298}$.**

So the standard enthalpy change of combustion of methane is written:

$$\Delta H^\ominus_{c,298}(CH_4) = -890 \, \text{kJ mol}^{-1}$$

and because the standard temperature is 298 K, we often write:

$$\Delta H^\ominus_c = -890 \, \text{kJ mol}^{-1}$$

You will sometimes see standard enthalpy change of combustion called **standard molar enthalpy change of combustion.**

We say *burns completely* to show clearly that only carbon dioxide and water are formed. With not enough oxygen, there may be incomplete combustion, producing carbon monoxide or even carbon (soot). The enthalpy changes for both these reactions will affect any measurement of enthalpy change of combustion.

In practice, when methane burns in oxygen, the temperature is a lot higher than 25 °C, so adjustments must be made to calculate the value under standard conditions.

EXAMPLE

Q Explain fully what is meant by:
$\Delta H^{\ominus}_{c,298}(H_2) = -286\,kJ\,mol^{-1}$.

A This is the standard enthalpy change of combustion of hydrogen. It is the enthalpy change when one mole of hydrogen is completely burnt in oxygen under standard conditions of 101 kPa pressure and 298 K, with reactants and products in their standard states at this temperature.

$$H_2(g) + \tfrac{1}{2}O_2(g) \rightarrow H_2O(l) \quad \Delta H^{\ominus}_c = -286\,kJ\,mol^{-1}$$

Notice that this includes the state symbols. Also, $\tfrac{1}{2}O_2$ does not mean half a molecule of oxygen, but half a mole.

We could have written:

$$2H_2(g) + O_2(g) \rightarrow 2H_2O(l) \quad \Delta H^{\ominus}_r = -572\,kJ\,mol^{-1}$$

The standard enthalpy change of this reaction, $\Delta H^{\ominus}_r$ (small r for reaction; or just $\Delta H^{\ominus}$) is twice that for the standard enthalpy change of combustion of hydrogen. This is because $\Delta H^{\ominus}_r$ applies to the mole quantities in the equation – 2 moles of hydrogen – whereas the standard enthalpy change of combustion is for burning *one* mole of hydrogen.

?

B Why do we need to include the state symbols in the equation in the Example? Hint: The answer is on page 123.

Alternative fuels to petrol

Table 6.1 gives the standard enthalpy changes of combustion of some fuel alternatives to petrol. There is no standard enthalpy change for petrol because it is a complex mixture of about 100 compounds, mainly hydrocarbons, of which most are alkanes.

BIOFUELS

BIOFUELS ARE FUELS produced from vegetable matter, and biofuels account for 15 per cent of the total world energy production. A significant proportion is used in developing countries for cooking and heating.

Fig 6.2(b) **Brazilians use Alcool as vehicle fuel. It is made from the fermented and distilled juice of sugar cane**

Fig 6.2(a) **The oil from this field of oilseed rape can be converted into biodiesel fuel**

But scientists are also very interested in biofuels for transport. Italy produces some of its diesel from rapeseed oil, and 5 per cent of Austria's diesel is biodiesel. Sugar cane and wheat can be fermented to produce ethanol, and this is blended with petrol or used on its own (see this chapter's Assignment and Fig 6.2(b)).

Growing crops for fuel is the subject of heated debate. Some say biofuels are the answer to increasing levels of carbon dioxide in the atmosphere: the crops remove carbon dioxide from the atmosphere to make sugars and oil, and the gas goes back into the atmosphere when fuels made from them are burnt, so there is no net carbon dioxide increase. But others point out that this ignores the fossil fuels which must be burnt to provide the fuel for planting the crop, making the fertiliser, harvesting the crop, and transporting and processing it.

This debate will run for years, but as oil extraction gets more costly, it is likely that by 2025 a significant amount of Europe's fuel will be biofuel.

The standard enthalpy change of combustion of octane, one of the constituents of petrol, is $-5470\,\mathrm{kJ\,mol^{-1}}$, which is a good indication of why petrol is used in cars.

Table 6.1 **The standard enthalpy changes of combustion of fuels alternatives to petrol**

Fuel	Main constituent	Formula and standard state	$\Delta H_c^{\ominus}$ of main constituent (kJ mol⁻¹)
hydrogen	hydrogen	$H_2(g)$	−286
compressed natural gas (CNG)	90% methane	$CH_4(g)$	−890
liquid petroleum gas (LPG)	95% propane	$C_3H_8(g)$	−2219
methanol	methanol	$CH_3OH(l)$	−726
ethanol	ethanol	$C_2H_5OH(l)$	−1367

3 MEASURING THE ENTHALPY CHANGE OF COMBUSTION

See Table 6.1 for some enthalpy changes of combustion. Being combustion reactions, they are all exothermic. We can find them by measuring the increase in temperature of a certain mass of water to which energy from the combustion reaction is transferred, making its temperature rise. One gram of water requires 4.2 joules of energy to raise its temperature by $1\,^{\circ}\mathrm{C}$.

The energy required to raise the temperature of 1 gram of substance by 1 K is called the specific heat capacity (c) of that substance.

So the specific heat capacity of water is $4.2\,\mathrm{J\,g^{-1}\,K^{-1}}$ (joules per gram per kelvin).

We can use a simple equation to work out the energy transferred to the water:

$$\text{Energy transferred} = \underset{\substack{\text{mass of} \\ \text{water} \\ \text{g}}}{m} \times \underset{\substack{\text{specific heat} \\ \text{capacity of water} \\ \mathrm{J\,g^{-1}\,K^{-1}}}}{c} \times \underset{\substack{\text{temperature} \\ \text{change} \\ \mathrm{K}}}{\Delta T}$$

Simple determination of the enthalpy change of combustion of a liquid fuel

A simple experimental set-up to measure the enthalpy change of combustion of ethanol is shown in Fig 6.4. The experiment is as follows:

Step 1. Weigh the spirit burner with ethanol in it at the beginning of the experiment and take the water temperature.

Step 2. Allow the spirit burner to heat up the water by about $20\,^{\circ}\mathrm{C}$. Stop heating and take the temperature of the water. This gives the temperature rise in Kelvin.

Step 3. Weigh the spirit burner again. This gives the mass of the ethanol used.

The next Example explains how this experiment may be used to calculate the enthalpy change of combustion for ethanol.

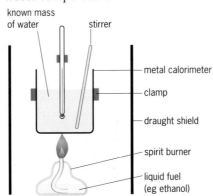

known mass of water · stirrer · metal calorimeter · clamp · draught shield · spirit burner · liquid fuel (eg ethanol)

Fig 6.4 **Measuring the enthalpy change of combustion of a liquid fuel**

See page 162 to find out more about the composition of petrol.

C Draw energy level diagrams for the standard enthalpy changes of combustion of hydrogen and propane.
$$\Delta H_c^{\ominus}(H_2) = -286\,\mathrm{kJ\,mol^{-1}}$$
$$\Delta H_c^{\ominus}(C_3H_8) = -2219\,\mathrm{kJ\,mol^{-1}}$$

Fig 6.3 **This car runs on CNG which is 90 per cent methane**

A temperature rise of 1 K is the same as a temperature rise of $1\,^{\circ}\mathrm{C}$.

D How many kilojoules of energy will be required to raise the temperature of 1 kg of water by **(a)** $1\,^{\circ}\mathrm{C}$, **(b)** $20\,^{\circ}\mathrm{C}$?

Sometimes you will see enthalpy change of combustion referred to as just **enthalpy of combustion**. The fact that enthalpy is changing in the reaction is understood.

E Read the method for measuring enthalpy change of combustion and look at Fig 6.4.

(a) Why is the calorimeter made of metal and not glass?

(b) Why does a temperature rise in °C give you the temperature rise in Kelvin?

(c) The draught shield is used to reduce loss of energy to the surroundings. What other things could be done to minimise energy losses in this experiment?

EXAMPLE

Q 0.40 g ethanol raises the temperature of 100.00 g water in the metal calorimeter by 21.0 °C. Calculate the enthalpy change of combustion of ethanol.

A

Step 1. Work out the energy transferred to the water:

Energy transferred to the water = $mc\Delta T$

$= 100.00 \times 4.2 \times 21.0 = 8820\,J = 8.82\,kJ$ (ignoring sig. figs)

Step 2. Calculate the amount of fuel used in moles:

Mass of 1 mole of ethanol (C_2H_5OH)

$= (12 \times 2) + (1 \times 5) + 16 + 1 = 46\,g$

Moles of ethanol in 0.40 g $= \dfrac{\text{mass in grams}}{\text{mass of one mole (in grams)}}$

$= \dfrac{0.40}{46} = 0.0087\,mol$ (correct to 2 sig. figs)

Step 3. Work out the enthalpy change of combustion, that is, the energy transferred when 1 mole of ethanol burns:

0.0087 mol ethanol releases 8.82 kJ

1 mole of ethanol releases $8.82 \times \dfrac{1}{0.0087} = 1014\,kJ$

So enthalpy change of combustion of ethanol $= -1000\,kJ\,mol^{-1}$ (correct to 2 sig. figs)

F The experiment in the Example gives an inaccurate result. Compare the value of the enthalpy change of combustion of ethanol in the Example with the value given in Table 6.1, on page 119. What aspects of the experiment lead to such a low calculated value?

The bomb calorimeter

The bomb calorimeter (see Fig 6.5) measures enthalpy changes of combustion. The weighed sample is inside a stainless steel container – the bomb – filled with oxygen under pressure, and the fuel is ignited electrically.

The principle is the same as for the simplified experiment on page 119. Energy is transferred from the combusted fuel to the surrounding water, and the temperature rise is measured. However, this apparatus gives a much more accurate value, provided the readings are taken quickly, because energy losses to the surroundings are reduced to almost zero. In our simplified experiment on page 119, another potential error arises when the spirit burner is weighed, as some of the ethanol may evaporate between weighings.

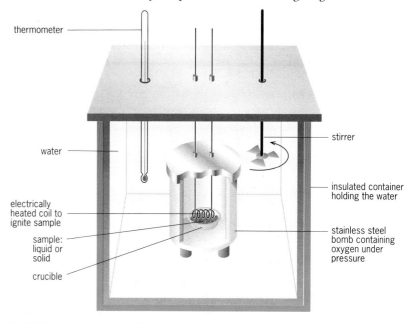

thermometer

water

stirrer

insulated container holding the water

electrically heated coil to ignite sample

sample: liquid or solid

crucible

stainless steel bomb containing oxygen under pressure

Fig 6.5 **The bomb calorimeter. The sample is ignited electrically and as it burns the energy is transferred to the water with minimal loss. The thermometer measures the rise in temperature**

Enthalpy change is transfer of energy into or out of the system *at constant pressure*. Because the bomb has a constant *volume*, it does not exactly measure enthalpy change. However, because the difference is small, we need not be concerned with the mathematical correction used to adjust the value to constant pressure.

THE ENERGY VALUES OF FOOD

THE BOMB CALORIMETER is used to measure the enthalpy changes of combustion of different foods. Although our bodies don't burn foods in quite the same way as we burn natural gas on a cooker, the outcome is the same. Oxygen is still required and the energy we obtain from compounds in foodstuffs is the same as if they were burnt in a bomb calorimeter. The crucial difference is that when we burn fuels in cooking or in the combustion engine of a car, most of the released energy is wasted and goes to heat up the surroundings.

When we 'burn' glucose in our bodies, there is not just one high-temperature reaction, but several small steps with small transfers of energy, each step catalysed by complex molecules called enzymes. The human machine is nowhere near 100 per cent efficient, and we do lose energy to our surroundings (hence, our body warmth), but much of the energy of the step-wise reactions is either used to maintain electrical and chemical body functions, or is stored, and so does not emerge as heat. Of course, when we store energy it is usually as fat, so taking in more energy than we require will make us obese.

We call the enthalpy change of combustion of a food its **energy value**. For ease of comparison, values are usually given for 100 g of food. Most foods contain a lot of water, so, after weighing the food, the water is removed before placing the food in the bomb. Some typical energy values of foods are given in Table 6.2.

Food	Energy content (kJ/100 g)
Apple	200
Milk	270
Potatoes	370
White bread	900
Bacon	1470
Cheddar cheese	1700
Butter	3040

Table 6.2 **The energy values of some common foods**

G Look back to page 119 and the enthalpy of combustion experiment.

(a) (i) If some of the ethanol evaporates between weighings, and so is not burnt, would this lead to a higher or a lower value for the calculated enthalpy change of combustion?
(ii) How could the weighings be carried out in the bomb calorimeter experiment to avoid any losses due to evaporation?

(b) (i) Study Fig 6.5 showing the bomb calorimeter and explain the features of the apparatus that minimise energy loss to the surroundings.
(ii) What is the purpose of the stirrer?

H The recommended daily intake of energy for a woman aged 18 is approximately 9000 kJ, while for a man of the same age it is 12 000 kJ. This assumes that both are moderately active. How much energy will be contributed to the daily intake if two slices of bread and cheese and a packet of crisps are eaten? Assume one slice of bread weighs 25 g and 50 g of cheese is used in each slice, together with 10 g butter. You will need to look at a packet of crisps to obtain its energy value.

4 RELEASING ENERGY FROM FUEL MOLECULES

We know that fuel molecules need oxygen to combust and so release energy. Where does this energy come from? To answer this question we need to look at the energies of the bonds that hold atoms together, and what happens when these bonds are broken and made.

Breaking bonds: bond energy

Bond energy or **bond enthalpy** is the energy required to break a bond between two atoms in a gaseous molecule. But because the energy required to break one bond is so small, we define bond energy (bond enthalpy) as the energy required to break *one mole* of bonds.

Consider hydrogen which has an H–H bond.

$$H–H(g) \rightarrow H(g) + H(g) \qquad \Delta H^\ominus = +436 \text{ kJ mol}^{-1}$$

The process is at standard conditions at 298 K.

Remember: A covalent bond is the electrostatic attraction between the shared pair of electrons and the positive nuclei.

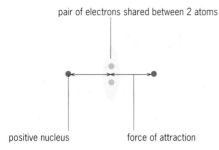

pair of electrons shared between 2 atoms

positive nucleus   force of attraction

Fig 6.6 **The force of attraction between the shared pair of electrons and the positive nuclei keep these two hydrogen atoms together. Breaking this covalent bond will require energy**

I The nitrogen molecule is very unreactive. Why is this so?
Hint: if you are not sure, look at Fig 4.12, page 73.

Table 6.3 **Average bond energies of some common bonds**

Bond	$E(X-Y)/kJ\,mol^{-1}$
C–C	+347
C=C	+612
C≡C	+838
C–H	+413
C–O	+358
C=O (in CO_2)	+805
H–H	+436
O–H	+464
O=O	+498

J (a) Two bond energies in Table 6.3 are not average bond energies. Identify these and explain your reasoning.

(b) Use Table 6.3 to calculate the amount of energy to atomise one mole of gaseous methanol (convert the molecule to its separate, gaseous atoms).

$CH_3OH(g) \rightarrow C(g) + 4H(g) + O(g)$

(c) Methanol is normally a liquid at 298 K. Explain why it must be a gas in this calculation.

Hint: What other energy is involved if methanol is not gaseous?

Bond energy, E, is often written as:

$$E(H–H) = +436\,kJ\,mol^{-1}$$

Notice that **bond breaking is an endothermic process**. This is because we are *putting in* energy to overcome the force of electrostatic attraction in the bond.

The bond energy in oxygen molecules is for breaking a *double* bond:

$$O=O(g) \rightarrow O(g) + O(g) \qquad \Delta H^{\ominus} = +498\,kJ\,mol^{-1}$$

So:
$$E(O=O) = +498\,kJ\,mol^{-1}$$

This is larger than for the H–H bond because double bonds are stronger than single bonds and so take more energy to break.

Up to now, we have considered bond energies only in *diatomic* molecules (molecules containing two atoms). There are two O–H bonds in the triatomic water molecule. The energy required to break the first O–H bond is not the same as the energy required to break the second:

$$H–O–H(g) \rightarrow H(g) + O–H(g) \qquad \Delta H^{\ominus} = +502\,kJ\,mol^{-1}$$

$$O–H(g) \rightarrow O(g) + H(g) \qquad \Delta H^{\ominus} = +427\,kJ\,mol^{-1}$$

The first bond is in a molecular environment where two O–H bonds exist, and more energy is required to break this bond. The second O–H bond is in a changed environment, and clearly this has an effect on its bond energy. A total of $929\,kJ\,mol^{-1}$ is required to break both the O–H bonds in water, so we say the *average* bond energy for the O–H bond in this molecule is $+464\,kJ\,mol^{-1}$.

We also find differences in the bond energy of the O–H bond in other molecules due to the different molecular environments of the bond. For example, the bond energy of the O–H bond in methanol is $+437\,kJ\,mol^{-1}$. Usually the differences in bond energies are not very great and we average them to give a good approximation which we can use.

Making bonds

So far, we have only considered *breaking* bonds and this requires energy, but we still have not answered the question: Where does the energy come from which is released when fuels burn in oxygen?

If it takes energy to break bonds, the same amount of energy must be released when bonds are formed. This reflects the law of **conservation of energy – energy can neither be created nor destroyed** – and it certainly applies to chemical reactions. Take hydrogen:

$$H–H(g) \rightarrow H(g) + H(g) \qquad \Delta H^{\ominus} = +436\,kJ\,mol^{-1}$$

$$H(g) + H(g) \rightarrow H–H(g) \qquad \Delta H^{\ominus} = -436\,kJ\,mol^{-1}$$

Bond making is exothermic

We are now in a position to look at energy changes from bond breaking and bond making. For example, when hydrogen burns in oxygen:

$$H–H(g) + \tfrac{1}{2}O=O(g) \quad \rightarrow \quad H–O–H(g)$$

$$E(H–H) + \tfrac{1}{2}E(O=O) \quad \rightarrow \quad 2\times \; -E(O–H)$$

$$+436 \; + \; \tfrac{1}{2}(498) \qquad\qquad 2(-464)$$

The enthalpy change for this reaction is:

$$\Delta H^{\ominus} = +436 + 249 + (-928) = -243\,kJ\,mol^{-1}$$

On page 121 we looked at the energy values of certain foods per 100 g. With transport fuels it is more convenient to know the amount of energy released by 1 kg of fuel. We call this the **energy density** of the fuel. To calculate the energy density we need to know the standard enthalpy change of combustion ($\Delta H_c^{\ominus}$) and the mass of one mole of the fuel.

Table 6.4 **The energy density values of four fuels $\Delta H_c^{\ominus}$**

Fuel	Formula	$\Delta H_c^{\ominus}$/kJ mol^{-1}	Mass of 1 mole/g	Energy density/kJ kg^{-1}
hydrogen	$H_2(g)$	−286	2	143 000
methane	$CH_4(g)$	−890	16	27 800
methanol	$CH_3OH(l)$	−726	32	22 700
ethanol	$C_2H_5OH(l)$	−1367	46	30 000

Petrol has an energy density of approximately 46 000 kJ kg^{-1}, which makes it a very concentrated energy source. It is a mixture of many hydrocarbons and you can read about it in Chapter 8.

From Table 6.4, hydrogen would appear to have excellent prospects as a fuel of the future. But there is still the problem of how to store it on board a vehicle. If you try Self-test question **O(b)**, you will see why.

$$\text{Energy density} = \Delta H_c^{\ominus} \times \frac{1000}{\text{mass of 1 mole}}$$

O (a) What is the energy density of propane which makes up 95 per cent of liquid petroleum gas (LPG)? You will need information from Table 6.1 on page 119 to answer this question.

(b) (i) What is the volume of 1 kg of hydrogen at 25 °C and 101 kPa? 1 mole of any gas at this temperature occupies 24 dm^3 (see page 92).

(ii) 1 litre of petrol has a mass of 740 g. How many litres of petrol are there in 1 kg?

■ See question 1.

METAL HYDRIDES: THE KEY TO ON-BOARD HYDROGEN STORAGE?

ONE MAJOR disadvantage of hydrogen as a fuel is how to store it. Liquefying it means cooling it to −253 °C, which costs four times more than making an equivalent amount of petrol. Then it has to be kept cold. The expense is worth it for the Space Shuttle, page 116, but it is no surprise that alternative storage methods are being sought for the more general use of hydrogen as a fuel.

One possible method is storing hydrogen as a solid. This doesn't mean freezing it, which takes too much energy, but combining it as a **metal hydride**. Magnesium hydride, MgH_2, is 7.7 per cent hydrogen by mass.

A litre of magnesium hydride contains almost as much hydrogen as a litre of liquefied hydrogen, though it is a great deal heavier.

The hydrogen is released by this reaction:

$$MgH_2(s) + H_2O(l) \rightarrow Mg(OH)_2(s) + H_2(g)$$

In magnesium hydride, magnesium is ionically bonded to hydrogen in a small whole-number ratio. But another type of metal hydride – an **interstitial hydride** – can soak up hydrogen rather like a sponge. The metal is *bathed* in hydrogen. At the metal surface, the hydrogen molecule splits into its atoms and the atoms occupy *holes* in the metal lattice. Very large quantities of hydrogen can be absorbed and released on heating. There remains the problem of the weight of the hydride, but chemists are actively searching for new alloy hydrides which don't weigh as much.

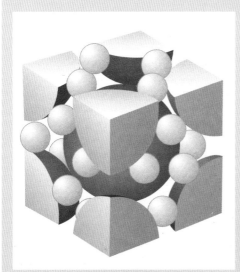

Fig 6.9 **An interstitial metal hydride (metal = niobium). The smaller hydrogen atoms get trapped between the larger metal atoms in the lattice**

Fig 6.10 **A prototype coach run on hydrogen in Augusta, Georgia, USA. A petrol engine requires only slight modification and the hydrogen is stored as an interstitial metal hyride**

5 ACTIVATION ENERGY AND ENERGY PROFILES

How a reaction gets started

Octane, one of the components of petrol, has an enthalpy change of combustion of $-5470\,kJ\,mol^{-1}$. So why doesn't it burst into flames as soon as it is exposed to oxygen in the air? The reason is that it takes energy to break bonds. This must happen before oxygen molecules and octane molecules can react together.

To break all the bonds in oxygen and octane vapour would require $+7437\,kJ\,mol^{-1}$ of energy – a very large amount. So in fact it is difficult to get octane to start reacting at all. Yet we know that a match thrown on to petrol causes it to react spectacularly. Clearly, not *all* the bonds need to be broken before other bonds start forming, and once bonds start to form, energy is released to break other bonds. This keeps the reaction going. (Look back at page 123 and do the calculation for the energy required to break all the bonds in octane and oxygen.)

The minimum energy required for a reaction to start is called the **activation energy**, E_a. When this energy is supplied to molecules in the system, the bonds begin to stretch and break. Reactions usually occur because the molecules collide with enough energy to make this happen. Sometimes there is sufficient energy in the system for a reaction to occur at room temperature, but for petrol in an engine, energy needs to be supplied to reach the activation energy level, and this comes from a spark.

Chemists draw **energy profiles** for reactions such as those in Fig 6.11. They show how the energy changes as the reactions proceed.

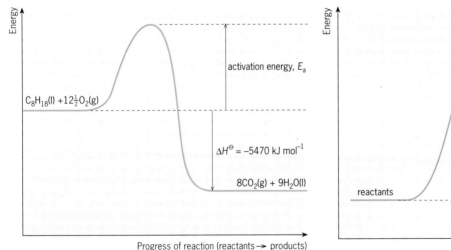

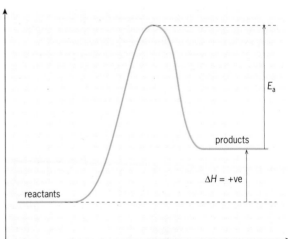

Fig 6.11 **Energy profile for (a) the exothermic reaction of octane with oxygen, and (b) an endothermic reaction. Notice that activation energy E_a is always endothermic**

See Chapter 27 to learn more about activation energy and energy profiles.

?

P Draw an energy profile for:

(a) methanol burning in oxygen (see Table 6.1, page 119);

(b) nitrogen reacting with oxygen to give nitrogen monoxide:

$$\tfrac{1}{2}N_2(g) + \tfrac{1}{2}O_2(g) \rightarrow NO(g) \quad \Delta H^{\ominus} = +90\,kJ\,mol^{-1}$$

This occurs in the high temperatures of car engines and leads to pollution. See page 169.

(c) Why is the reaction in **(b)** not an enthalpy change of combustion?

Activation energy and stability

The higher the activation energy for a reaction, the less likely it is to occur. Even though octane looks very unstable compared with carbon dioxide and water, the high energy of activation acts like an **energy barrier** to the reaction. In petrol, this prevents the reaction from occurring when the tank is filled at the garage, and is the reason why there are 'No smoking' signs!

Reaction kinetics is the study of *rates* of reactions. We say petrol is **kinetically stable**, even though it is **energetically unstable**.

Lowering the energy barrier: catalysis

In your previous chemistry course you probably learnt that catalysts usually increase the rate of chemical reactions. We also mentioned this in Chapter 1. **Catalysts** are substances which alter the rate of a chemical reaction without becoming permanently involved in it.

But they do become involved temporarily, because a catalyst works by providing an alternative reaction pathway with a lower energy of activation. While we don't use a catalyst in the combustion of petrol, catalysts are now used in catalytic converters to speed up reactions which control emissions from the exhausts of cars.

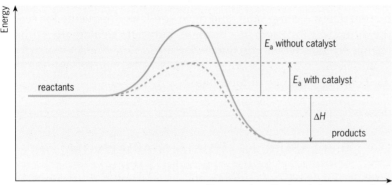

Sometimes catalysts slow down the rate of a reaction. When they do, they are called negative catalysts or **inhibitors**. They do not work by raising the activation energy, but usually react with molecules produced in the intermediate stages of a reaction, removing them from the reaction pathway.

Octane is energetically unstable because it is at a higher energy level than carbon dioxide and water. Sometimes we use the term **thermodynamically unstable** instead of energetically unstable.

The rate of a reaction can be simply defined as the amount of substance formed per unit of time (eg moles per second).
See page 9 for a simple treatment. Chapter 27 takes reaction kinetics further.

Catalysts are not put into the overall chemical equation for reactions because they are not permanently involved in them.

For more information on catalytic converters in car exhausts see pages 167 to 169.

Fig 6.12 **Energy profile of a catalysed and uncatalysed reaction. Notice that the enthalpy change is the same, whichever route is followed. Otherwise, it would break the law of conservation of energy**

■ See questions 6 and 7.

6 ANOTHER ENTHALPY CHANGE: THE ENTHALPY CHANGE OF FORMATION

Like the enthalpy change of combustion on page 117, the **enthalpy change of formation** is just one more enthalpy change of reaction. But this time, instead of burning one mole of compound completely in oxygen, we *form one mole of compound from its elements.*

The standard enthalpy change of formation $\Delta H_{f,298}^{\ominus}$ is the enthalpy change when one mole of a compound is formed from its elements under standard conditions, that is, 298 K and 101 kPa (1 atmosphere) pressure.

The standard enthalpy change of formation of water:

$$\Delta H_f^{\ominus}(H_2O(l)) = -286 \text{ kJ mol}^{-1}$$

applies to this reaction:

$$H_2(g) + \tfrac{1}{2}O_2(g) \rightarrow H_2O(l)$$

Notice that the value above is also the standard enthalpy change of combustion of hydrogen.

The equation for the standard enthalpy change of formation of methanol is:

$$C(s) + 2H_2(g) + \tfrac{1}{2}O_2(g) \rightarrow CH_3OH(l) \qquad \Delta H_f^{\ominus} = -239 \text{ kJ mol}^{-1}$$

$\Delta H_f^{\ominus}$ can be used instead of $\Delta H_{f,298}^{\ominus}$, because we assume that the temperature is 298 K unless another temperature is quoted.

Standard molar enthalpy change of formation is another name for standard enthalpy change of formation.

Carbon exists in two forms, **diamond** and **graphite**. The most stable of these forms is graphite and this is the standard state used for standard enthalpy changes of formation. Sometimes you will see $C_{graphite}$ written in the equation. To find out about a third form of carbon, buckminsterfullerene, read Chapter 20.

■ See questions 2, 4 and 8.

You will find **standard enthalpy changes of formation** for compounds in almost any chemistry data book.

Why standard enthalpy changes of formation are important

Q Write equations for:

(a) $\Delta H_f^\ominus$ (CO_2(g)) = −393 kJ mol^{-1}

(b) $\Delta H_f^\ominus$ (CH_4(g)) = −75 kJ mol^{-1}

(c) When these compounds are formed from their elements, in which direction is energy transferred – to the compound or to its surroundings? Are they more or less stable than the elements which make them up?

You can see the value of knowing enthalpy changes of combustion – because, for example, they allow us to work out the energy we can get from a fuel. But why bother with the standard enthalpy changes of formation?

The enthalpy of a substance is its energy content. We cannot measure this and give it an absolute value. It is all the energy associated with the molecules in the substance, and that includes the nuclei, the electrons and the movements of whole molecules.

We can only measure enthalpy *changes*, and to do this we must have a reference point. The one that scientists have chosen is the **standard enthalpy change of formation**. It applies to any compound, *while for elements it is zero*. It is a very important piece of information about a compound, and once you know the value for each of the different substances in a reaction, you can calculate the enthalpy change for that whole reaction.

But, before we consider this, how do we obtain values for the standard enthalpy change of formation?

6 MEASURING THE STANDARD ENTHALPY CHANGE OF FORMATION

R To measure $\Delta H_f^\ominus$ (CO_2(g)), graphite is burnt in the bomb calorimeter rather than diamond. Both are forms of carbon. Why is graphite chosen? (Hint: If you are not sure, look back to page 127.)

Some standard enthalpy changes of formation can be measured experimentally. For example, we can measure $\Delta H_f^\ominus$ of carbon dioxide by using a bomb calorimeter and combusting graphite. The $\Delta H_f^\ominus$ of magnesium oxide can be measured in the same way.

When a compound is easily synthesised from its elements under normal conditions, we can usually measure $\Delta H_f^\ominus$ directly. However, many standard enthalpy changes of formation cannot be measured directly, and this is where we need an indirect approach using **energy cycles**.

The indirect method for calculating enthalpy changes of formation using energy cycles

This method relies on **Hess's law** which states:

> **If a change can be brought about by more than one route, then the overall enthalpy change for each route must be the same – provided that the starting and finishing conditions are the same for each route.**

This is conservation of energy again – energy cannot be created or destroyed in chemical reactions – so the energy changes for a reaction must be the same, whether it takes place in one step or in a whole series of steps. We can show this by constructing an energy cycle like the one in Fig 6.13.

Methane cannot be prepared directly from its elements, but we can use Hess's law to calculate its standard enthalpy change of formation. By burning carbon, hydrogen and methane, we can measure their standard enthalpy changes of combustion directly. We can therefore devise an energy cycle with two routes in it, as shown in Fig 6.14.

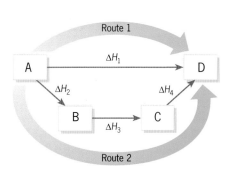

Fig 6.13 **An energy cycle illustrating Hess's law. It does not matter whether the reaction takes place by the one-step route or goes through several intermediates. The overall enthalpy change for route 2 must be the same as for route 1, so:**
$\Delta H_1 = \Delta H_2 + \Delta H_3 + \Delta H_4$

See Chapter 22 for information about another energy cycle, the Born–Haber cycle, used for ionic compounds.

Fig 6.14 **A Hess's law energy cycle being used to calculate $\Delta H_f^{\ominus}$ (CH₄(g)) indirectly**

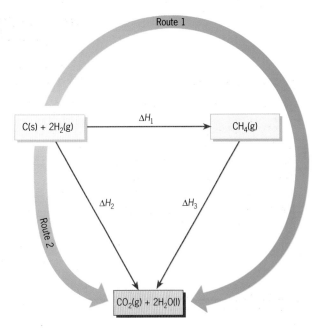

By Hess's law:

the overall enthalpy change = the enthalpy change
        for route 1   for route 2

So: $\Delta H_1 + \Delta H_3$ = ΔH_2

ΔH_1 is what we are trying to find, in this case the standard enthalpy change of combustion of methane, $\Delta H_f^{\ominus}$ (CH₄(g)). For route 1:

ΔH_2 is $\Delta H_c^{\ominus}$ for carbon (graphite) = $-393 \, \text{kJ mol}^{-1}$

plus $2 \times \Delta H_c^{\ominus}$ for hydrogen = $2 \times -286 \, \text{kJ mol}^{-1}$

Remember: $\Delta H_c^{\ominus}$ for hydrogen is for burning one mole of hydrogen. In this energy cycle there are two moles of hydrogen.

ΔH_3 = standard enthalpy change of combustion of methane, $\Delta H_c^{\ominus}$ (CH₄(g)) = $-890 \, \text{kJ mol}^{-1}$.

So: $\Delta H_1 = \Delta H_2 - \Delta H_3 = -393 + 2(-286) - (-890)$
        $\Delta H_f^{\ominus}$ (CH₄(g)) = $-75 \, \text{kJ mol}^{-1}$

EXAMPLE

Q Calculate the standard enthalpy change of formation of methanol, given that: $\Delta H_c^{\ominus}$(CH₃OH(l)) = $-726 \, \text{kJ mol}^{-1}$, $\Delta H_c^{\ominus}$(C(s)) = $-393 \, \text{kJ mol}^{-1}$, $\Delta H_c^{\ominus}$(H₂(g)) $-286 \, \text{kJ mol}^{-1}$.

A

Step 1. Write out the enthalpy change you have been asked to calculate – in this case $\Delta H_f^{\ominus}$(CH₃OH(l)):

$$C(s) + 2H_2(g) + \tfrac{1}{2}O_2(g) \rightarrow CH_3OH(l)$$

Step 2. Construct an energy cycle with two alternative routes. It helps if you always put the enthalpy change you want to calculate along the top of the cycle and call it ΔH_1.

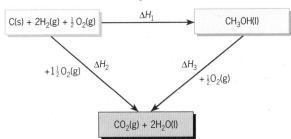

Fig 6.15 **A Hess's law energy cycle to calculate $\Delta H_f^{\ominus}$ (CH₃OH(l))**

Step 3. Write out the enthalpy changes for the two routes:

$$\Delta H_1 + \Delta H_3 = \Delta H_2$$

Step 4. Decide what enthalpy changes are represented by ΔH_1, ΔH_2 and ΔH_3. It is a good idea to do this on the energy cycle diagram first.

$$\Delta H_1 = \Delta H_f^{\ominus}(CH_3OH(l))$$

that is, the enthalpy change we wish to calculate.

$$\Delta H_2 = \Delta H_c^{\ominus}(C(s)) + 2\Delta H_c^{\ominus}(H_2(g))$$
$$\Delta H_3 = \Delta H_c^{\ominus}(CH_3OH(l))$$

Step 5. Rearrange the equation in step 3 and insert the values of the enthalpy changes which are known:

$$\Delta H_1 = \Delta H_2 - \Delta H_3$$
$$\Delta H_f^{\ominus}(CH_3OH(l)) = \Delta H_c^{\ominus}(C(s)) + 2\Delta H_c^{\ominus}(H_2(g)) - \Delta H_c^{\ominus}(CH_3OH(l))$$
$$\Delta H_f^{\ominus}(CH_3OH(l)) = -393 + 2(-286) - (-726)$$
$$= -239 \, \text{kJ mol}^{-1}$$

Thus the standard enthalpy change of formation of methanol is $-239 \, \text{kJ mol}^{-1}$.

S Work out the standard enthalpy change of formation of:

(a) propane – see Table 6.1 and the Example above for the values you need.

(b) carbon monoxide ($\Delta H_c^{\ominus}$(CO(g)) = $-283 \, \text{kJ mol}^{-1}$).

(c) Why is it impossible to obtain $\Delta H_f^{\ominus}$ (CO(g)) directly?

7 USING STANDARD ENTHALPY CHANGES OF FORMATION TO CALCULATE ENTHALPY CHANGES OF REACTION

See questions 2, 3, 5 and 7. ■

With standard enthalpy changes of formation we can calculate enthalpy changes of reaction, and again we can apply Hess's law.

EXAMPLE

Q The Space Shuttle Orbiter uses methylhydrazine as fuel, and this is oxidised by dinitrogen tetroxide to provide the energy for propulsion. Calculate the standard enthalpy change $\Delta H_r^{\ominus}$ for this reaction:

$$4CH_3NHNH_2(l) + 5N_2O_4(l) \rightarrow 4CO_2(g) + 12H_2O(l) + 9N_2(g)$$

These are the standard enthalpy changes of formation:

$$\Delta H_f^{\ominus}(CH_3NHNH_2(l)) = +54\,kJ\,mol^{-1} \quad \Delta H_f^{\ominus}(N_2O_4(l)) = -20\,kJ\,mol^{-1}$$
$$\Delta H_f^{\ominus}(CO_2(g)) = -393\,kJ\,mol^{-1} \quad \Delta H_f^{\ominus}(H_2O(l)) = -286\,kJ\,mol^{-1}$$

A We can follow a similar procedure to the previous Example.

Step 1. Write out the enthalpy change you have been asked to calculate. This has already been given in the question, so this step is not required.

Step 2. Construct an energy cycle with two alternative routes. Remember that it helps if you always put the enthalpy change you want to calculate along the top and call it $\Delta H_1^{\ominus}$.

Step 3. Write out the enthalpy changes for the two routes:

$$\Delta H_2^{\ominus} + \Delta H_1^{\ominus} = \Delta H_3^{\ominus}$$

Notice that this is different from the previous Example.

Step 4. Decide what enthalpy changes are represented by $\Delta H_1^{\ominus}$, $\Delta H_2^{\ominus}$ and $\Delta H_3^{\ominus}$. Remember that it is a good idea to do this on the energy cycle diagram first.

$\Delta H_1 = \Delta H_r^{\ominus}$, that is, the enthalpy change we wish to calculate:

$$\Delta H_2 = 4\Delta H_f^{\ominus}(CH_3NHNH_2(l)) + 5\Delta H_f^{\ominus}(N_2O_4(l))$$
$$\Delta H_3 = 4\Delta H_f^{\ominus}(CO_2(g)) + 12\Delta H_f^{\ominus}(H_2O(l))$$

Step 5. Rearrange the equation in step 3 and insert the values of the enthalpy changes which are known:

$$\Delta H_1 = \Delta H_3 - \Delta H_2$$
$$\Delta H_r^{\ominus} = 4\Delta H_f^{\ominus}(CO_2(g)) + 12\Delta H_f^{\ominus}(H_2O(l))$$
$$- [4\Delta H_f^{\ominus}(CH_3NHNH_2(l)) + 5\Delta H_f^{\ominus}(N_2O_4(l))]$$
$$\Delta H_r^{\ominus} = 4(-393) + 12(-286) - [4(+54) + 5(-20)]$$
$$= -5004 - [+116] = -5020\,kJ\,mol^{-1}$$

So:

$$4CH_3NHNH_2(l) + 5N_2O_4(l) \rightarrow 4CO_2(g) + 12H_2O(l) + 9N_2(g)$$
$$\Delta H_r^{\ominus} = -5020\,kJ\,mol^{-1}$$

Fig 6.16 **The Space Shuttle Orbiter is powered by methylhydrazine and dinitrogen tetroxide**

```
4CH3NHNH2(l) + 5N2O4(l)  --ΔH1-->  4CO2(g) + 12H2O(l) + 9N2(g)

        ΔH2              ΔH3
4ΔHf⊖(CH3NHNH2(l))            4ΔHf⊖(CO2(g))
        +                          +
5ΔHf⊖(N2O4(l))              12ΔHf⊖(H2O(l))

            4C(s) + 9N2(g) + 10 O2(g)
```

Fig 6.17 **A Hess's law energy cycle to calculate $\Delta H_r^{\ominus}$**

The standard state of dinitrogen tetroxide is a gas at 298 K. But in this case we have used the standard enthalpy change of formation of the liquid dinitrogen tetroxide, because this is how it is carried in the Orbiter. This is the standard enthalpy change of formation in its non-standard state.

Look closely at step 5 in the Example on the page opposite, and you will notice that:

$$\Delta H_r^\ominus = \Sigma \Delta H_f^\ominus \text{ (products)} - \Sigma \Delta H_f^\ominus \text{ (reactants)}$$

The symbol Σ means 'the sum of', and remember that the standard enthalpy changes of formation must be multiplied by the number of moles given in the equation.

The equation above in bold can be used to calculate the enthalpy change for any chemical reaction, which makes it very useful. You do not need to draw an energy cycle, but as you can see, it is still an application of Hess's law.

8 ENTROPY AND ENTHALPY CHANGES

Spontaneous reactions

When a spark ignites petrol, there is a **spontaneous reaction** with oxygen which produces carbon dioxide and water. It does not matter that energy was needed to start this reaction – once started, it is spontaneous (takes place of its own accord).

Let's consider the spontaneous combustion of octane, which is one of the compounds in petrol:

$$C_8H_{18}(g) + 12\tfrac{1}{2}O_2(g) \rightarrow 8CO_2(g) + 9H_2O(g)$$

We know that this is an exothermic reaction and that energy is released to the surroundings because the energies of octane and oxygen are higher than the energies of carbon dioxide and water – see page 126. So we could say that for a reaction to occur it must be exothermic.

But this does not explain spontaneous reactions which are endothermic, such as the reaction between nitrogen and oxygen to produce nitrogen monoxide:

$$N_2(g) + O_2(g) \rightarrow 2NO(g) \qquad \Delta H^\ominus = +180 \text{ kJ mol}^{-1}$$

As this reaction is a major cause of pollution from vehicle exhausts, we know that it happens spontaneously in the high temperature of a petrol engine. To understand why spontaneous reactions occur we must seek another explanation which involves **entropy**.

Entropy changes and spontaneous reactions

We first met entropy on page 111. Entropy is a measure of the disorder of a system. The entropy of a gas is higher than the entropy of a solid: because there are more ways of arranging molecules in a gas, so there is more disorder.

> **For a reaction to occur spontaneously there must be an overall increase in entropy.**

This is the **second law of thermodynamics**. Thermodynamics is the study of energy transfer.

We have already encountered the first **law of thermodynamics**:

> **Energy can neither be created nor destroyed in physical and chemical processes.**

This is the basis of Hess's law.

T (a) Work through the Example on page 130. Why don't we need to look up the standard enthalpy change of formation of nitrogen?

(b) Methanol can be produced from coal and the final stage of this process is:

$$CO(g) + 2H_2(g) \rightarrow CH_3OH(l)$$

Calculate the standard enthalpy change for this reaction using the following information:

$\Delta H_f^\ominus$ (CO(g)) = -110 kJ mol^{-1}

$\Delta H_f^\ominus$ (CH$_3$OH(l)) = -239 kJ mol^{-1}

U Why is energy needed to start the reaction between the compounds in petrol and oxygen?

V You may already have drawn the energy profile for this reaction (see Self-test question **P(b)**, page 126). Why is the enthalpy change for this reaction different from the one given in question **P**.

W State, with reasons, whether there is an entropy increase, decrease or no significant change in the systems:

(a) $2H_2(g) + O_2(g) \rightarrow 2H_2O(g)$

(b) $H_2O(g) \rightarrow H_2O(l)$

(c) $CH_3OH(g) + 1\frac{1}{2}O_2(g) \rightarrow CO_2(g) + 2H_2O(g)$

(d) $\frac{1}{2}N_2(g) + \frac{1}{2}O_2(g) \rightarrow NO(g)$

Think of quanta as packets of energy. Electrons at a particular energy level have a definite amount of energy. The electrons move between levels by absorbing or emitting energy quanta.

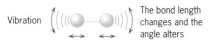

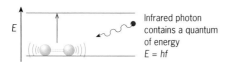

Fig 6.18 **The three forms of kinetic energy that molecules possess**

Fig 6.19 **The vibrating molecule is excited into a higher energy level by receiving a photon of infrared radiation and vibrates faster. Energy $E = hf$ (Planck constant × frequency)**

Microwaves at a precise frequency make water molecules rotate more. The rise in rotational energy of water molecules in food leads to an overall increase in energy. The colliding water molecules make the food hot.

Let's examine the combustion of octane (eg in petrol vapour, see Chapter 8) and see if the entropy of the system increases.

$$C_8H_{18}(g) + 12\frac{1}{2}O_2(g) \rightarrow 8CO_2(g) + 9H_2O(g)$$

$13\frac{1}{2}$ moles of reactant molecules → 17 moles of product molecules

In this reaction the entropy increases as there are more ways of arranging 17 moles of product molecules than $13\frac{1}{2}$ moles of reactant. But it is not quite that simple. We have only considered the system. Entropy also increases because this reaction is exothermic and energy too can be arranged in different ways.

Arranging energy in molecules

In Chapter 4 we saw that electrons in atoms are arranged in quantised energy levels. So the energy of electrons is one of the ways that energy exists in particles (atoms, molecules and ions). Looking now at the molecular level, we find that molecules also possess other energy. This is energy due to the movements of atoms in the molecule. It includes energy of **translation**, energy of **rotation** and energy of **vibration**. These energies associated with the different aspects of a diatomic molecule's behaviour are shown in Fig 6.18. But any molecule shows the same behaviour, with the energies also quantised.

When infrared radiation shines on molecules, they vibrate more because they absorb quanta of energy and move to a higher energy level. Similarly, a hot object makes us feel warm because the molecules in our skin 'pick up' quanta of energy emitted by the object's molecules, making them vibrate more.

We make use of this energy transfer in infrared spectroscopy; you can read about it on page 187. The microwave region of the electromagnetic spectrum increases *rotational* energy in particular – which is the reason why microwave cookers work!

Now let's see how 3 quanta of energy can be shared by 2 molecules.

Molecule 1	Molecule 2	
0	3	all 3 quanta are gained by molecule 2
1	2	
2	1	
3	0	all 3 quanta are with molecule 1

So there are 4 ways of arranging 3 quanta. Try this for yourself: Arrange 6 quanta among 2 molecules. You will find that there are 7 ways. But if you increase the number of molecules to 3 and arrange 3 quanta, there are 10 ways of doing it. With just 10 quanta and 10 molecules, the number of arrangements is 92 378. The ways of arranging a mole of quanta amongst a mole of molecules is mind-boggling!

When we consider entropy changes, we don't just consider the arrangements of the molecules, but the way the energy in the system is arranged as well. Remember that if a reaction is to be spontaneous, it must bring about an overall increase in entropy – which means not only in the system, but the surroundings as well.

Condensing water vapour

The process by which water vapour in the air condenses on the cold surface of a window pane is a spontaneous process. At first sight, there appears to be a *decrease* in entropy (an increase in order):

because water molecules are less spread out in the liquid, they would be arranged in fewer ways than molecules in the vapour. So because the water undergoes a negative entropy change on condensation, you might not expect the change of state to occur spontaneously.

But the condensation of water vapour is an *exothermic* process, so the surroundings heat up. If we also consider the ways that energy is arranged in the molecules of the surroundings, when we calculate the overall *entropy* for the system of the condensing molecules and the surroundings, it turns out that there is a positive entropy change – and this is why condensation is spontaneous.

X Which has the greater energy – infrared radiation or microwave radiation?
If you are not sure, use $E = hf$ and see Fig 3.5 on page 48.

9 USING ENTROPY CHANGES TO DECIDE IF A REACTION WILL OCCUR

It is entropy changes, ΔS (of the system together with the surroundings), not enthalpy changes, ΔH, which determine whether a reaction will occur. We need to know the total entropy change, and if this is positive then the reaction will be spontaneous. We can calculate the entropy change in the surroundings by a simple equation:

$$\Delta S_{surr} = \frac{-\Delta H}{T}$$

ΔS_{surr} = entropy change of the surroundings. T = temperature of the system and the surroundings – we assume both are at the same temperature.

The entropy change of the surroundings is inversely proportional to the temperature of the surroundings. So the higher the temperature, the lower the change in entropy of the surroundings will be when the system changes.

Let us consider water condensing again at 298 K:

$$H_2O(g) \rightarrow H_2O(l) \qquad \Delta H^{\ominus} = -44.0\,kJ\,mol^{-1}$$
$$\Delta S^{\ominus}_{system} = -118.8\,J\,mol^{-1}\,K^{-1}$$

As already discussed, the entropy change of the system is negative. But let's consider the entropy of the surroundings using:

$$\Delta S_{surr} = \frac{-\Delta H}{T} = \frac{-(-44\,000)}{298}$$

$$\Delta S_{surr} = 148\,J\,mol^{-1}\,K^{-1} \text{ (to 3 sig. figs)}$$

Note: kilojoules is converted to joules.

Taking the total entropy change:

$$\Delta S_{total} = \Delta S_{system} + \Delta S_{surr}$$
$$\Delta S_{total} = -118.8 + 148 = 30\,J\,mol^{-1}\,K^{-1}$$

So the overall entropy change for the condensation of water is positive and the change of state will occur spontaneously.

Remember: $^{\ominus}$ means standard conditions, so $\Delta S^{\ominus}_{system}$ means the change of entropy under standard conditions.

Y Calculate the total entropy change for the reaction of octane burning in oxygen at 298 K.
$C_8H_{18}(l) + 12\tfrac{1}{2}O_2(g)$
$\rightarrow 8CO_2(g) + 9H_2O(l)$
$\Delta H^{\ominus} = -5470.2\,kJ\,mol^{-1}$
$\Delta S^{\ominus}_{system} = 663.6\,J\,mol^{-1}\,K^{-1}$

A note of caution

The total entropy change in self-test question **Y** is positive at 298 K. So, at 25 °C (298 K), octane reacting in oxygen is spontaneous. But we know that the rate of reaction is very slow because of the high activation energy. So, even though we now have a way of predicting whether a reaction is energetically feasible, kinetic stability may still mean it is very, very slow.

You can learn more about entropy in Chapters 16, 26 and 27.

■ See question 9.

SUMMARY

When you have studied this chapter, you should be able to understand the following ideas.

■ The enthalpy, H, of a compound is the energy stored in it.

■ Enthalpy changes, ΔH, are transfers of energy into or out of a system at constant pressure.

■ The standard enthalpy change of reaction ($\Delta H_{298}^{\ominus}$) is the enthalpy change when the mole quantities expressed in a balanced equation react under standard conditions (298 K, 1 atmosphere or 101 KPa) with all substances in their standard states.

■ The standard enthalpy change of combustion, $\Delta H_{c,298}^{\ominus}$, and the standard enthalpy change of formation, $\Delta H_{f,298}^{\ominus}$, are both standard enthalpy changes of reaction.

■ Some enthalpy changes can be measured directly, using a bomb calorimeter.

■ Other enthalpy changes are measured indirectly by using Hess's law.

■ Average bond energies can give a good estimate of the enthalpy change of a reaction.

■ Activation energy is the minimum energy required for a reaction to occur.

■ High activation energies make reactants kinetically stable, even if they are energetically unstable.

■ Catalysts lower the activation energy by providing an alternative reaction pathway.

■ For a reaction to be spontaneous, the overall entropy increase must be positive.

■ Entropy is a measure of the number of arrangements of both molecules and energy.

QUESTIONS

1

a) Both methane and butane can be used as fuels. Their respective enthalpies of combustion are –890 kJ mol⁻¹ and –3000 kJ mol⁻¹.
(Relative atomic masses: H = 1.00, C = 12.0)
   (i) Calculate the energy liberated on combustion of 1 g of butane.
   (ii) The energy liberated on combustion of 1 g of methane is 56 kJ. Why is butane, rather than methane, used in cylinders of bottled gas?

b) Write a balanced equation for the complete combustion of butane.
[ULEAC 1996 AS Synoptic Specimen Paper CH5, q.2]

Notes on question **2**: The equation for reaction in a) is:

$$CH_3CH_2CH_2CH_2CH=CH_2(l) + H_2(g) \rightarrow$$
$$CH_3CH_2CH_2CH_2CH_2CH_3(l)$$

Standard molar enthalpy change means the same as standard enthalpy change.

2

a) This question is concerned with the reaction of hex-1-ene and hydrogen giving hexane. The standard molar enthalpy changes of formation of hex-1-ene and hexane are –72.4 and –198.6 kJ mol⁻¹ respectively. Define the term standard molar enthalpy change of formation.

b) By drawing a suitable cycle, calculate the value of ΔH for the reaction:

hex-1-ene + hydrogen → hexane.

c) Using the following average bond enthalpy terms: C–C 347, C–H 413, C=C 612 and H–H 436 kJ mol⁻¹, calculate a second value for ΔH for the reaction:

hex-1-ene + hydrogen → hexane.

d) Which of your two answers do you think is more accurate, and why?

e) The molar enthalpy change of formation of hexane cannot be measured directly, but its enthalpy change of combustion can. What other quantities would you need to measure to be able to calculate the enthalpy change of formation of hexane once you had measured its enthalpy change of combustion?
[AEB 1993 Chemistry Module Paper 6 Specimen Paper, q.4]

3

Sulphur dioxide is present in the atmosphere from natural and industrial sources.
When hydrogen sulphide in gases emitted from volcanoes mixes with the air, it reacts with oxygen:

$$2H_2S(g) + 3O_2(g) \rightarrow 2H_2O(l) + 2SO_2(g)$$

Use the following data to calculate the enthalpy change for this reaction (data at 298 K).

$$\Delta H_f^{\ominus} [H_2S(g)] = -20.6 \text{ kJ mol}^{-1} \text{K}^{-1}$$
$$\Delta H_f^{\ominus} [H_2O(l)] = -285.8 \text{ kJ mol}^{-1} \text{K}^{-1}$$
$$\Delta H_f^{\ominus} [SO_2(g)] = -296.8 \text{ kJ mol}^{-1} \text{K}^{-1}$$

[ULEAC 1996 Nuffield Chemistry Paper 3, Module Test 3 (CN3) Specimen Paper, q.2]

4 The standard enthalpy change of formation of ozone, O_3, is $+143\,kJ\,mol^{-1}$. As it is made up of the element oxygen, why is $\Delta H^{\ominus}_{f,298}$ not 0?

5 Oxyacetylene welding relies on the high energy released from this reaction:

$$C_2H_2(g) + 2\tfrac{1}{2}O_2(g) \rightarrow 2CO_2(g) + H_2O(l)$$
$$\Delta H^{\ominus} = -1301\,kJ\,mol^{-1}$$

Fig 6.Q8 **Oxyacetylene welding or ethyne–oxygen welding**

a) State Hess's law.

b) Construct an energy cycle to calculate
$\Delta H^{\ominus}_{f,298}(C_2H_2(g))$, given:
$\Delta H^{\ominus}_{f,298}(CO_2) = -393\,kJ\,mol^{-1}$
$\Delta H^{\ominus}_{f,298}(H_2O) = -286\,kJ\,mol^{-1}$

c) The standard enthalpy change of combustion of hydrogen $\Delta H^{\ominus}_{c,298}(H_2) = -286\,kJ\,mol^{-1}$. Explain why this is the same value as the standard enthalpy change of formation of water.

6 The standard enthalpy change of combustion of sucrose, $C_{12}H_{22}O_{11}$ (table sugar) is $-5640\,kJ\,mol^{-1}$.

a) Write down the balanced equation for this reaction.

b) Draw an energy level diagram for this combustion

c) Why doesn't a packet of sugar react violently in the air? Hint: Your answer should make reference to activation energy – see page 126.

7 The bombardier beetle defends itself from attack by mixing together solutions of hydrogen peroxide and hydroquinone which react, producing enough energy to bring the mixture to its boiling point. An audible explosion occurs as the beetle fires a hot spray at its attacker.

$$C_6H_4(OH)_2(aq) + H_2O_2(aq) \rightarrow C_6H_4O_2(aq) + 2H_2O(l)$$

hydro-   hydrogen   quinone
quinone   peroxide

Fig 6.Q10 **When under attack, the bombardier beetle uses chemical warfare**

a) State Hess's law.

b) Construct an energy cycle based on Hess's law, using data from the following reactions:

$$C_6H_4(OH)_2(aq) \rightarrow C_6H_4O_2(aq) + H_2(g)$$
$$\Delta H^{\ominus}\ +177\,kJ\,mol^{-1}$$
$$H_2O_2(aq) \rightarrow H_2O(l) + \tfrac{1}{2}O_2(g) \quad \Delta H^{\ominus} = -95\,kJ\,mol^{-1}$$
$$H_2(g) + \tfrac{1}{2}O_2(g) \rightarrow H_2O(l) \qquad \Delta H^{\ominus} = -286\,kJ\,mol^{-1}$$

c) Calculate the enthalpy change of the reaction inside the beetle.

d) Enzymes catalyse the hydroquinone/hydrogen peroxide reaction. Define the term catalyst, and explain how a catalyst functions in this reaction.

8 Heat packs are used by skiers trapped by snowstorms. Placed in gloves and boots, they will keep hands and feet warm for about 6 hours. They work on the following reaction:

$$4Fe(s) + 3O_2(g) \rightarrow 2Fe_2O_3(s) \quad \Delta H^{\ominus} = -1648\,kJ\,mol^{-1}$$

The heat pack is sealed in an airtight plastic film. Inside this is a paper packet containing finely powdered iron. When the plastic seal is broken, oxygen penetrates the paper and there follows a series of reactions, represented by the overall equation above.

a) Why is the iron ground into a fine powder?

b) What is the standard enthalpy change of formation of $Fe_2O_3(s)$?

c) A pack contains $448\,g$ of iron. How much energy is released from the reaction?

9 Ozone is a pollutant from car exhausts. A hypothetical reaction with rainwater has been proposed which produces hydrogen peroxide. Hydrogen peroxide is a bleach. So, will ozone react with rainwater spontaneously and bleach clothes under standard conditions?

$$O_3(g) + H_2O(l) \rightarrow H_2O_2(l) + O_2(g) \quad \Delta H^{\ominus} = -44.7\,kJ\,mol^{-1}$$
$$\Delta S^{\ominus} = -96.6\,J\,mol^{-1}\,K^{-1}$$

Assignment

ETHANOL: A GREEN FUEL OF THE FUTURE?

Brazil is the world's largest user of ethanol as a transport fuel. It is made from the juice of sugar cane which is fermented and distilled to give a hydrated mixture of 95 per cent ethanol and 5 per cent water. Four million cars, trucks and vans have engines that run on it. Another five million use gasohol, a blend of 22 per cent ethanol and 78 per cent petrol (gasoline).

1

a) Explain what is meant by $\Delta H^{\ominus}_{c,298}(C_2H_5OH)$ = $-1367\,kJ\,mol^{-1}$. Draw an energy level diagram to represent this enthalpy change.

b) Using average bond energies from Table 6.A1, calculate a value for the enthalpy change of combustion of ethanol. Why does this differ from the value given in **a)**?

Table 6.A1 **Some average bond energies**

Bond (X–Y)	Av. bond energy /kJ mol^{-1}	Bond (X–Y)	Av. bond energy /kJ mol^{-1}
C–C	+347	O–H	+464
C–H	+413	O=O	+498
C–O	+336	C=O	+805

c) Although fermentation takes place in aqueous solution, we can estimate the enthalpy change of reaction using:

$$C_6H_{12}O_6(s) \rightarrow 2C_2H_5OH(l) + 2CO_2(g)$$

Calculate the standard enthalpy change of this reaction from the following data:

$\Delta H^{\ominus}_{f,298}(C_6H_{12}O_6(s)) = -1273\,kJ\,mol^{-1}$,
$\Delta H^{\ominus}_{f,298}(C_2H_5OH(l)) = -277\,kJ\,mol^{-1}$,
$\Delta H^{\ominus}_{f,298}(CO_2) = -393\,kJ\,mol^{-1}$.

During the first world oil crisis in 1973, the price of a barrel of oil rose from $2.5 to $10.5. Until then, Brazil was earning a little more in world trade than it was spending. But with few oil reserves, the country depended entirely on imported oil, which it could no longer afford. In 1975, the Brazilian Pro-Alcool programme was born, aimed at reducing the country's dependence on imported oil. All cars made after 1979 had to run on either gasohol or ethanol fuel.

Economics were the issue, and not the environment, when it was decided to use ethanol as the main transport fuel. Yet, when the fuel is burnt, it releases into the atmosphere just the amount of carbon dioxide that the sugar cane plant took in to make the sugar in the first place. But what of the energy needed to produce ethanol from sugar?

All the energy used to crush the cane, ferment the juice

and distil it, comes from burning the crushed cane stems and not from fossil fuels, so the carbon dioxide intake and output remain in balance. Also, though artificial fertilisers are used to increase sugar cane production, a variety of cane has been bred that requires only a low nitrogen input.

Fig 6.A1 **Much of Brazil's sugar cane is cut by hand**

2

a) In terms of the carbon dioxide balance in the atmosphere, how do you think producing sugar for fuel compares with **(i)** producing oil for fuel, **(ii)** producing sugar for food?

b) In Brazil, most of the sugar cane is harvested by hand. Explain why this reduces extra carbon dioxide emissions significantly.

c) How many tonnes of carbon dioxide are produced by one tonne of ethanol?

(Values for A_r: C = 12, H = 1, O = 16.)
Hint: See pages 7 and 8.

d) Suggest why the production of artificial fertilisers releases carbon dioxide into the atmosphere.

Ethanol is an excellent motor fuel. Because it is an oxygenate, it burns very efficiently in the car engine, producing almost 60 per cent less carbon monoxide from the exhaust than petrol. Emissions of nitrogen dioxide are reduced as well. Ethanol has a high octane number, so avoiding 'knocking' in the engine and the need for lead or other compounds to be added to increase its octane rating. (Knocking is covered on page 162.)

3

a) What is meant by the term 'oxygenate'?

b) Why is carbon monoxide produced from car exhausts?

c) How do you think that ethanol in petrol, or on its own, reduces carbon monoxide emissions? Hint: See page 124.

d) Why does it matter if carbon monoxide is produced?

The European Union over-produces many of the foods it grows, and using land to grow crops to produce fuels is becoming an attractive alternative. It will reduce dependence on fossil fuels and may contribute to the EU's commitment to stabilise and reduce carbon dioxide emissions.

4

a) Will carbon dioxide emissions be reduced by growing fuel crops? Explain your answer.

b) What are the advantages and disadvantages of embarking on a Brazilian-type organically derived alcohol programme?

FUELS

This chapter concentrates on the concepts related to energy transfer during chemical reactions. They are important ideas and can also be quite difficult: you could get confused over energy, enthalpies and entropy, for example. So it is worth giving time to make sure you understand the terms, how they are used correctly and how to calculate values from equations and data. Use the Chapter Map to help you see how the ideas are linked and where you can find more information about them.

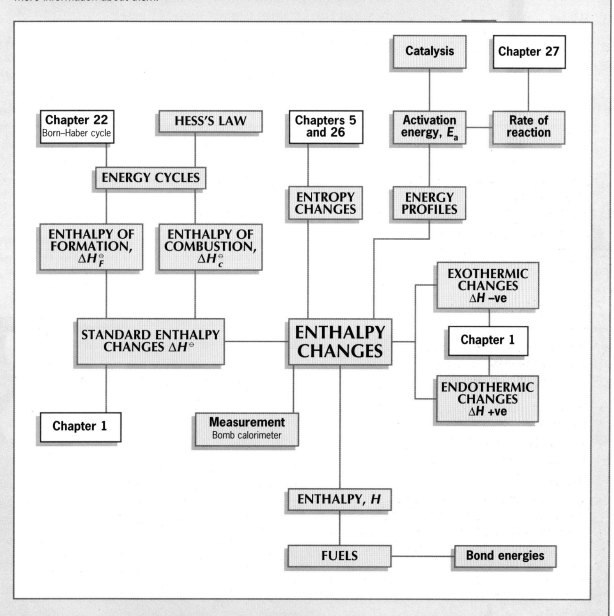

Oil and the petrochemical industry

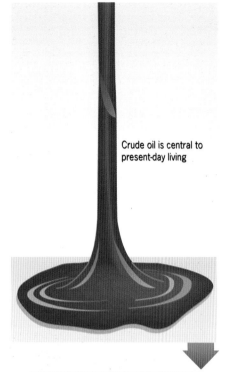

Crude oil is central to present-day living

THE STONE AGE, the Iron Age and the Bronze Age are periods of history when humans began to exploit particular substances and so made massive improvements to their lives over a short period of time. In our own time, it is oil which has had the greatest impact on our lives.

From 1859, when the first oil well was sunk by Edwin Drake in the United States, societies have relied increasingly on the production of oil, especially for fuel: 90 per cent of oil is burnt, very much of it used to provide energy for cheap transport. But if the present were to become known as the Age of the Car, this would ignore what we now do with the remaining 10 per cent of oil. This is transformed through chemical reactions into medicines, paints, insecticides, dyes, detergents, plastics and other chemicals on which we now depend.

Oil is suitably named when called 'black gold', indicating how precious it is. Maybe future historians will look back and call the age we live in the Oil Age, but it will probably have lasted a brief 200 years from the drilling of the first well to the exhaustion of supplies. In fact, we may well see the end of the Oil Age in our own lifetimes.

1 CRUDE OIL

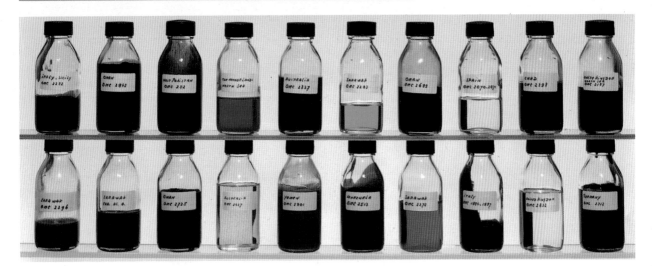

Fig 7.1 **Crude oil is a complex mixture of hydrocarbons. As with all mixtures, the composition varies.**

The oil that comes out of the ground is known as crude oil, or petroleum (from the Latin *petra* for rock and *oleum* for oil). It is a thick, dark, smelly liquid. Two thousand years ago, the Chinese occasionally came across it when they dug for brine; then, they used it as a fuel. Inhabitants of the Middle East found it lying on the ground, and because the **volatile (**easily evaporated**)** components had evaporated, a sticky tar called pitch remained. This they used to waterproof their wooden boats. The ancient Mexicans even used it as chewing gum!

Crude oil is a very complex mixture of hundreds of different compounds. Most are **hydrocarbons**, compounds of carbon and hydrogen only. There are also compounds containing nitrogen, oxygen and sulphur and even some molecules that have metals in them.

Because crude oil is a mixture, its composition varies. Oil from some wells may contain up to 98 per cent hydrocarbons, while others may have as little as 50 per cent. It is the hydrocarbons which are most sought after, for energy and for making the thousands of compounds from plastics to drugs, which are essential to modern society. Hydrocarbon composition also varies. But more about this on page 146.

How oil was formed

The process of oil formation began up to 400 million years ago when tiny marine animals and plants died, sank to the bottom of the oceans and became trapped in mud. Here, there was no oxygen, and bacteria decomposed them anaerobically. An **anaerobic reaction** is one which occurs without oxygen. The decay products stayed in the mud and were acted on by pressure, radioactivity and high temperatures, until finally the mixture we know as oil was created. This took millions of years. As evidence that crude oil came from living organisms, some of the hydrocarbon molecules resemble those found in rubber, cholesterol and vitamin A.

Under pressure, the mud eventually turned into rock, squeezing out the oil into porous rock above. In some areas, the oil seeped to the surface. But fortunately in others it became trapped in the porous rock, which became a reservoir because there was an impervious layer of rock above it.

?

A Natural gas is associated with oil deposits. What is the principal component of natural gas?

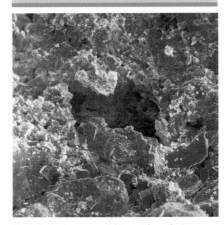

Fig. 7.2 **A microscope picture of sandstone grains. The spaces in between the grains are known as pores. In an oil reservoir, these pores contain crude oil and water**

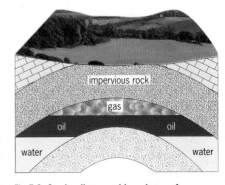

Fig 7.3 **Crude oil trapped by a layer of impervious rock to form an oil reservoir**

RECOVERING OIL FROM THE GROUND

THERE ARE WIDELY differing estimates of how much oil is left on Earth, and of how much can actually be extracted. So estimates of how long oil supplies will last vary even more widely.

When a new oil reservoir is discovered and wells are sunk, the oil often flows quite freely to the surface, squeezed out by the pressure of rock above it. This is called **primary recovery**. It recovers only 10 to 30 per cent of the oil in the reservoir. **Secondary recovery** methods may involve flooding the reservoir with steam. The energy from the steam makes heavier components of the oil less viscous and drives the oil to the well. Even so, much of the oil still stays in the ground. Whether secondary methods are employed depends on economics. When the price of oil is low, it may cost more to retrieve the extra oil from the ground than it is worth.

Tertiary methods are being developed for the twenty-first century, and these require new chemistry and new techniques. Detergents allow oil and water to mix, and may be used to help to extract some of the deposits of heavier oil. The use of polymer solutions and alkalis may also help wrest the oil from the pores of the rock. If these methods succeed, thousands of millions more barrels of oil could be extracted. But the price of oil will have to rise considerably before tertiary extraction becomes cost-effective. Clearly, decisions made in the next few years will decide how long we can enjoy the benefits of crude oil.

Drilling on the Brent Charlie oil rig in the North Sea

2 WHY ARE THERE SO MANY CARBON COMPOUNDS?

It was once thought that the chemicals produced in living organisms were different from those found in non-living materials. They were thought to have an associated 'life force' and were therefore known as organic chemicals. The rocks and minerals of the Earth, and the chemicals made from them, were called inorganic chemicals. But in 1828, a German chemist, Fredrich Wöhler, managed to produce an organic compound, urea (found in urine), from an inorganic compound, ammonium cyanate, just by heating it in his laboratory:

$$\underset{\text{ammonium cyanate}}{NH_4OCN} \xrightarrow{\text{heat}} \underset{\text{urea}}{NH_2CONH_2}$$

This simple experiment helped to dispel the myth of a life force, but we still refer to the chemistry of carbon compounds as **organic chemistry,** and all other compounds as inorganic chemicals. During the nineteenth century, many organic chemicals were synthesised (made) and this has continued at an increasing rate, particularly during the last few decades. There are now over eight million recorded organic chemicals, and most of these do not occur in nature. Some are completely new compounds, while others are variations of those found in nature, designed to enhance the properties of particular groups of atoms. The search for new compounds and new ways of synthesising known compounds is a very exciting aspect of chemistry. (You can read about how computers are helping to design drug molecules on page 68.)

Metal carbonates, carbon dioxide and carbon monoxide are considered to be inorganic chemicals.

Synthesis is the production of one compound from two or more other substances.

3 THE SPECIAL NATURE OF CARBON

There are about 100 000 known inorganic substances, which is tiny compared with the vast array of carbon compounds. To explain this, we need to consider just what is so special about carbon.

Carbon cannot expand its octet

Carbon forms covalent bonds. It is in Group 4, so it has four electrons in its outer shell, which means that it can form four covalent bonds. In common with all the elements in Period 2, it cannot expand its outer shell of eight electrons. This means that its compounds are resistant to chemical attack. We know that methane, CH_4, in natural gas does not react with water at normal temperatures and pressures. Silicon is also in Group 4, but it can expand its octet. Because of this ability, the silane SiH_4 reacts vigorously with water. The **mechanism** for this reaction involves a water molecule donating a lone pair of electrons to the silicon atom.

See page 75 to remind yourself about atoms which can expand their octets.

Fig 7.4 **SiH_4 reacting with a water molecule. Notice that when the water molecules form their covalent bonds with this silane, there are 12 outer-shell electrons around the silicon atom**

Carbon can form strong bonds with itself

The ability to form bonds between atoms of the same element in a compound is called **catenation**. While this is not unique to carbon, the C–C bond energy is very high, as you can see from Table 7.1. This means that carbon can form chains of carbon atoms. On page 124 we described octane, a component of petrol, which has a chain of eight carbon atoms:

Bond	Bond energy/kJ mol^{-1}
C–C	347
Si–Si	226
N–N	158
P–P	198
C–H	413
Si–H	318
Si–O	466

Table 7.1 **Some average bond energies between atoms of the same elements near carbon in the Periodic Table. Also included are the bond energies of C–H, Si–H and Si–O**

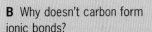

Bond energy is the energy required to break a bond between two atoms in a gaseous molecule, leaving two separate atoms. See page 121 for more information.

```
    H   H   H   H   H   H   H   H
    |   |   |   |   |   |   |   |
H — C — C — C — C — C — C — C — C — H
    |   |   |   |   |   |   |   |
    H   H   H   H   H   H   H   H
```

But in poly(ethene), commonly called polythene, there are thousands of carbon atoms in a chain:

```
     H   H   H   H   H   H   H   H   H   H   H   H
     |   |   |   |   |   |   |   |   |   |   |   |
ᾬᾬ C — C — C — C — C — C — C — C — C — C — C — C ᾬᾬ
     |   |   |   |   |   |   |   |   |   |   |   |
     H   H   H   H   H   H   H   H   H   H   H   H
```

Both octane and poly(ethene) are energetically unstable in air under normal conditions because their products, carbon dioxide and water, are at a much lower energy level. The reaction with oxygen is spontaneous at room temperature, but poly(ethene) bags and petrol don't suddenly catch fire. This is because of the large activation energy which makes them kinetically stable. This activation energy is due to the energy required to break the C–C and C–H bonds.

Although silicon atoms form short chains with each other, they are not stable under normal conditions. Take, for example, the silane:

```
      H   H   H   H
      |   |   |   |
 H — Si— Si— Si— Si— H
      |   |   |   |
      H   H   H   H
```

This compound is unstable and decomposes to silicon and hydrogen at room temperature without oxygen. In air, it bursts into flame for two reasons. First, the reaction with oxygen has a low energy of activation; and second, the Si–O bond is very strong.

B Why doesn't carbon form ionic bonds?

C Draw the dot and cross diagrams for methane and water. You can check your diagrams by looking back to pages 72 and 73.

D When water donates a lone pair of electrons to silicon, what is the name of the bond formed? See page 74 if you are not sure.

See pages 259 and 375 for more information on poly(ethene).

A reaction may be spontaneous at a particular temperature, but the rate may be so very slow that it cannot really be monitored. You can find out more by looking back at page 131 and also by reading Chapter 27.

See Chapter 20 for more information about the structure of silicon dioxide.

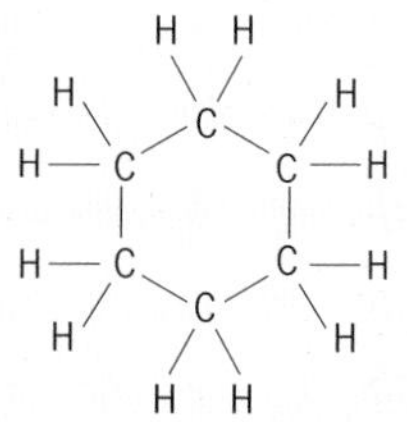

Fig 7.5 **Cyclohexane: an example of a ring structure**

See pages 78 and 82 to remind yourself about the bonding in ethene. There is much more about its chemistry in Chapter 12.

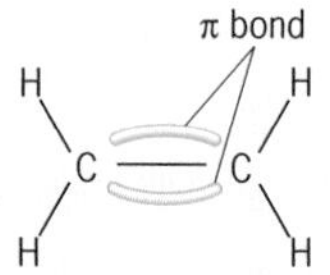

Fig 7.6 **A molecule of ethene showing the π-bonds**

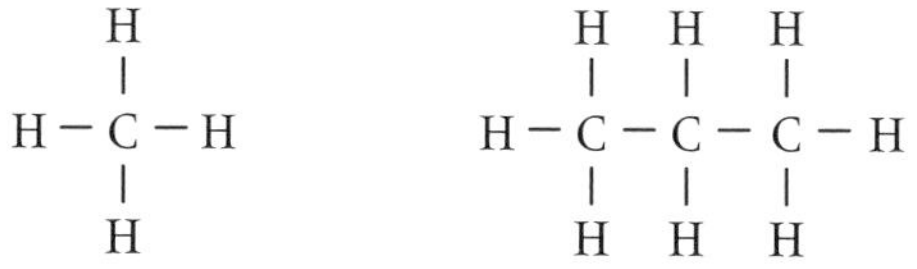

A **molecular formula** tells you how many atoms of each element there are in a molecule of the compound (see page 4).

E What is the molecular formula of octane? You can see its structural formula on page 140.

Fig 7.7 **Ball-and-stick models of methane and propane**

Fig 7.8 **Shape diagram of methane and propane**

F Draw the displayed formulas (showing all atoms and bonds) of ethane, CH_3CH_3 and pentane, $CH_3CH_2CH_2CH_2CH_3$.

This means that silicon dioxide, which is sand, is energetically very stable. The stability of the Si–O bond is the reason why so much of the Earth's rocks and soils are made up of silicon dioxide and silicates.

No other element forms chains with itself like carbon. But its uniqueness does not stop at chains – it can form rings as well, such as the example in Fig 7.5.

Carbon can form double and triple bonds

Because of the strength of the C–H and C–C bonds, compounds such as octane are fairly unreactive with other chemicals, the reaction with oxygen being a notable exception. But the inclusion of double and triple carbon–carbon bonds changes all this. Ethene, for example, is the backbone of the organic chemical industry and it is the π-bond which makes it so reactive (see Fig 7.6).

4 REPRESENTING HYDROCARBON MOLECULES

Molecular and structural formulas

We first met molecular formulas on page 4. Structural formulas show more information about the arrangement of atoms in a molecule. The molecular formula of methane is CH_4 and that of propane is C_3H_8. These can be drawn out to show how the atoms are bonded together:

These representations of molecules are often referred to as **displayed formulas, graphical formulas** or even **full structural formulas.** We shall use the term *displayed formula* when we draw out all the atoms and bonds. Structural formulas can also be written in an abbreviated form. For example, the abbreviated structural formula of propane can be shown as:

$$CH_3–CH_2–CH_3 \quad \text{or even} \quad CH_3CH_2CH_3$$

None of these accurately represents the three-dimensional shape of the molecule. The ball-and-stick models are shown in Fig 7.7. Notice the tetrahedral arrangement of the hydrogen atoms around the carbon atoms. This can be represented as in Fig 7.8.

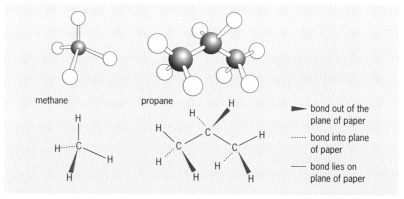

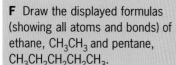

To keep drawing three-dimensional representations of the shapes of molecules would be very inconvenient, which is why we use displayed or structural formulas instead.

Compounds with carbon–carbon double bonds

Ethene and propene have carbon–carbon double bonds in their compounds. They are known as **unsaturated hydrocarbons,** because the double bond can allow them to bond with more atoms. Any hydrocarbon with double or triple carbon–carbon bonds in it is called **unsaturated**. Hydrocarbons with no double bonds are called **saturated hydrocarbons.**

The structural formulas of ethene and propene are:

$$CH_2{=}CH_2 \quad \text{and} \quad CH_3CH{=}CH_2$$

Their displayed formulas are shown in Fig 7.9. Notice that we show the bonds around a double-bonded carbon at about 120°.

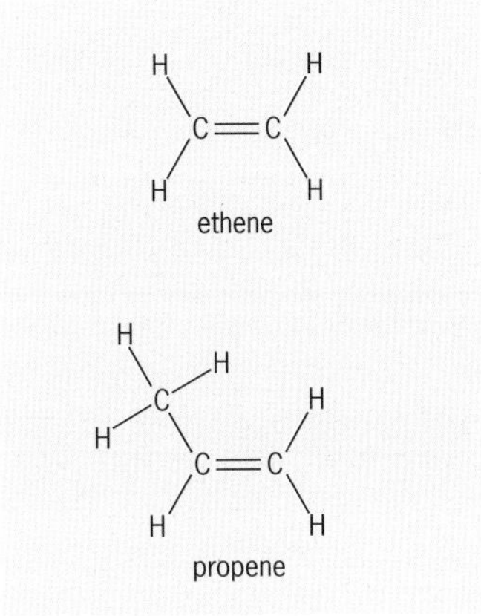

Fig. 7.9 **The displayed formulas of ethene and propene**

Ring compounds

As we noted earlier in the chapter, carbon can form rings as well as chains, and this adds enormously to the variety of possible organic compounds. Three examples are given in Fig. 7.10.

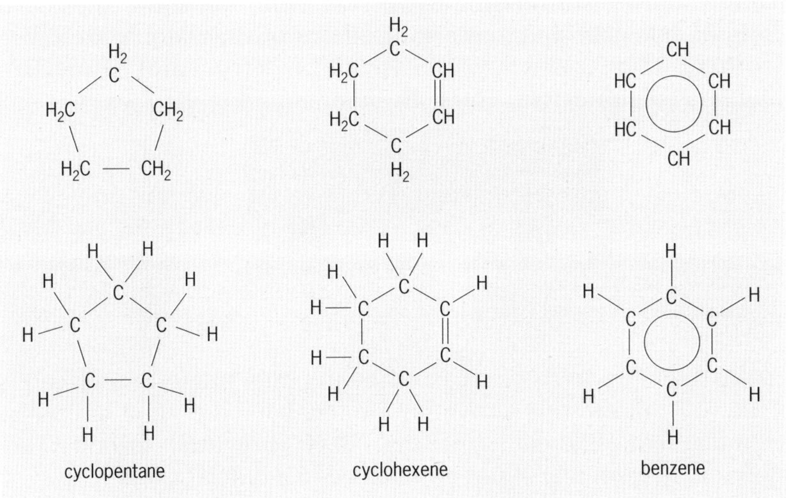

Fig 7.10 **The structural and displayed formulas of cyclopentane, cyclohexene and benzene**

Benzene has a ring inside its carbon skeleton and from the above formula it does not seem to have four bonds around each carbon. The ring represents a **delocalised** π cloud of electrons and this gives benzene a different set of properties from other ring compounds. **Delocalised electrons** are electrons that do not belong to any one carbon atom.

G (a) Work out which of the following compounds will be unsaturated from the molecular formulas: C_4H_{10}, C_7H_{14} and C_9H_{18}.
Hint: Remember that carbon always has four bonds.

(b) Draw the displayed formulas of the following compounds:

$CH_3CH_2CH{=}CH_2$ $CH_3CH{=}CHCH_3$

What do you notice about the molecular formulas of these two compounds?

See page 78 to remind yourself about the shape of ethene.

■ See questions 1 and 2.

H (a) Draw the displayed formula of cyclobutane, C_4H_8.

(b) Compare this molecular formula with the molecular formulas in part **(b)** of question **G**. What do you notice?

See Chapter 13 for more information on benzene and its structure.

I Draw the skeletal formulas of:

(a) octane

(b) $CH_3CH_2CH=CH_2$

(c) $CH_3CH=CHCH_3$

Note: there are two ways of drawing this skeletal formula. The Assignment on page 88 tells you why.

See the Assignment on page 88, which shows how skeletal formulas can be useful in representing larger hydrocarbon chains.

Fig 7.12 **The skeletal formula of oct-3-ene**

cyclopentane   cyclohexene   benzene

Fig 7.13 **The skeletal formulas of cyclopentane, cyclohexene and benzene**

J Draw the structural formulas and displayed formulas of the following compounds:

(i)   **(ii)**

(iii)   **(iv)**

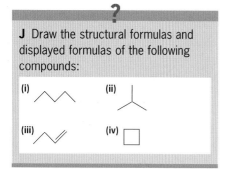

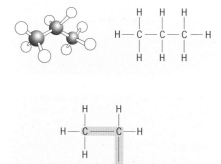

Fig 7.16 **The tinted area shows that the carbons are still part of the same unbranched chain**

Skeletal formulas

Formulas which show only how the carbon atoms are bonded are called **skeletal formulas.** These depict the carbon skeleton of the molecule without any hydrogen atoms. However, when there are other atoms (such as oxygen or nitrogen) in the molecule, these are shown. Hexane is a hydrocarbon found in crude oil and used in petrol. Its skeletal formula, shown in Fig 7.11, is the typical zigzag shape of a hydrocarbon chain.

Fig. 7.11 **Ball and stick model of hexane and its skeletal formula**

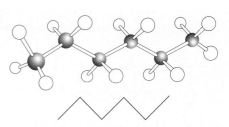

Oct-3-ene has the structural formula:

$$CH_3CH_2CH_2CH_2CH=CHCH_2CH_3$$

Its skeletal formula is shown in Fig 7.12.

The skeletal formulas you will encounter most are those of ring compounds. Fig 7.13 illustrates the skeletal formulas of the compounds in Fig 7.10.

5 ISOMERISM

If you have done the margin questions in the previous section, you may have noticed that sometimes compounds with the same molecular formula can have different arrangements of their atoms. This is called **isomerism**. Molecules with the same molecular formula but with different arrangements of their atoms are called **isomers**. There are two types of isomerism: **structural isomerism** and **stereoisomerism.** These are summarised in Fig 7.14.

Fig 7.14

Isomerism
Molecules with the same molecular formula but different arrangement of their atoms

Structural isomerism
Atoms are bonded in a different order

Stereoisomerism
Atoms are bonded in the same order but are arranged differently in space. See Chapters 12 and 17

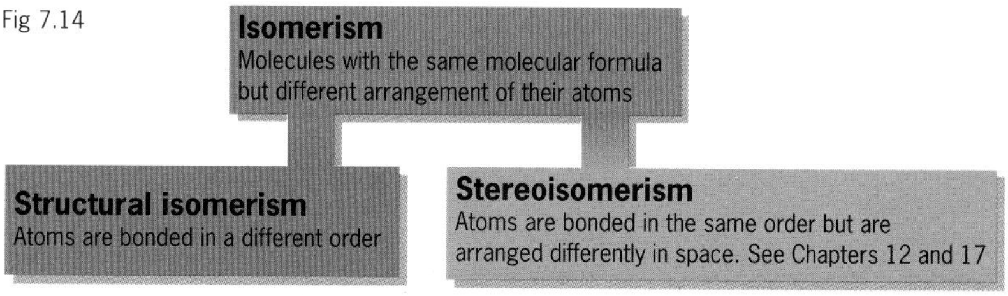

We shall deal in this chapter with structural isomerism. From Fig 7.14 you can see that structural isomers have the same molecular formula, but different structures. Their structural formulas are different because the atoms are bonded in a different order.

Fig 7.15 **Ball and stick model of propane and its displayed formula**

Consider propane, found in liquefied petroleum gas fuel. It has the molecular formula C_3H_8 but only *one* arrangement is possible for its molecule. Even though the carbon atoms can rotate about a single bond, there is still only one structure, which is shown in Fig 7.15.

The displayed formula used to show the rotation of the carbon atom looks exaggerated, so it is tempting to think that it is not the same structure. In Fig 7.16, the carbon atom chain has been shaded so that you see immediately that the three carbons are still in one unbranched chain.

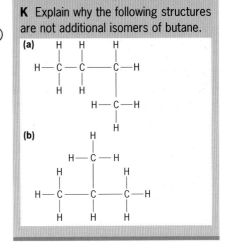

Fig 7.17 **Ball and stick models of butane and methylpropane and their structural formulas**

butane

methylpropane

Now we consider the molecular formula C_4H_{10}. It is possible to have the two different structures shown in Fig 7.17. These two isomers have different properties, even though they have the same molecular formula. For example, butane boils at a higher temperature than methylpropane.

As the number of carbons in the molecular formula goes up, the number of isomers increases dramatically. For the molecular formula $C_{10}H_{22}$, there are 75 isomers, but when the formula is $C_{30}H_{62}$, the number of possible isomers is more than 400 million! However, hardly any of these have been synthesised and very few occur in nature. But these figures do illustrate how carbon forms so many different compounds.

?

K Explain why the following structures are not additional isomers of butane.

(a)

(b)

■ See questions 1 and 3.

EXAMPLE

Q Draw the structural formulas of the possible isomers of C_5H_{12}.

A You are unlikely to be asked to find the number of isomers of hydrocarbons with molecular formulas of more than seven carbon atoms. The only way you can approach this problem is by making attempts and then improving them, but try to be systematic.

Always start with the longest hydrocarbon chain you can make from the given formula:

pentane

Now look for possible branches. But remember, the carbon atoms can rotate about a single bond. In this case, there are only two more possible structures which have branches from the longest chain:

2–methylbutane

2,2–dimethylpropane

A common mistake is to draw a third structure, as shown on the right. But this is, in fact, the structure of 2-methylbutane, and all that has happened is that the molecule has been turned round.

2-methylbutane

So far, we have not explained how we name the different hydrocarbons. Don't worry – it is easier than it looks. We deal with naming some of these on pages 156 to 158.

?

L Draw the structural formulas of isomers with the molecular formula C_6H_{14}.

Hint: If you draw more than five, they will not all be different isomers.

6 MORE STRUCTURAL ISOMERS

So far, we have only looked at saturated hydrocarbon chains. But structural isomers occur whenever there are different ways of bonding the atoms together. Two examples are given in Fig 7.18.

Fig 7.18 **Structural isomers**

but-1-ene   but-2-ene

Earlier in this chapter, we said that carbon could bond to atoms other than hydrogen. When this happens, the properties of the molecule change. When we substitute an atom, or a group of atoms, into a hydrocarbon molecule, we call the atom or group a **functional group.**

A functional group largely determines the set of properties a molecule will possess. The C=C double bond in a molecule is a functional group, because it gives a characteristic set of properties to the molecule. Cl is a halogen functional group and the molecular formula C_3H_7Cl has two isomers, which are shown in Fig 7.19.

1-chloropropane   2-chloropropane

7 THE HYDROCARBONS IN CRUDE OIL

Crude oil is a mixture, and because of this its composition varies. Most of crude oil is composed of hydrocarbons, and we have already seen that there can be several hundreds of these because of carbon's ability to form stable chains, branched chains and rings. No two deposits of oil contain exactly the same hydrocarbons in the same proportions. However, we can divide the hydrocarbons found in oil into three major classes of compound: **alkanes**, **cycloalkanes** and **arenes** (also known as **aromatic hydrocarbons**). We have met representatives of all three classes earlier in this chapter.

Alkanes

Alkanes are saturated hydrocarbons. They can either be branched chains or straight chains. Table 7.2 on the next page summarises some of the alkanes featured in this chapter.

Look at the molecular formulas of the alkanes in Table 7.2 and you should spot a mathematical relationship. For every carbon atom in each formula, their are twice that number of hydrogen atoms, plus another two. This can be represented by the **general formula** C_nH_{2n+2} where n is the number of carbon atoms. Let's try out this general formula with methane:

$$n = 1 \quad \text{because there is one carbon atom.}$$

So the molecular formula for methane is:

$$C_1H_{(2\times1)+2} = CH_4$$

M (a) What is the molecular formula of the two isomers in Fig 7.18?

(b) Why is this structure not another isomer?

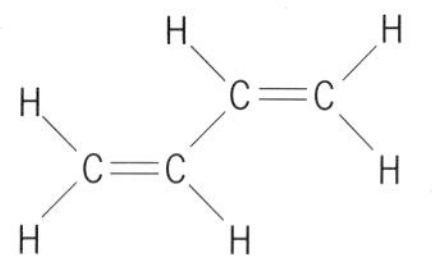

See question 2. ■

There is more about functional groups on page 151

Fig 7.19 **The two isomers of C_3H_7Cl**

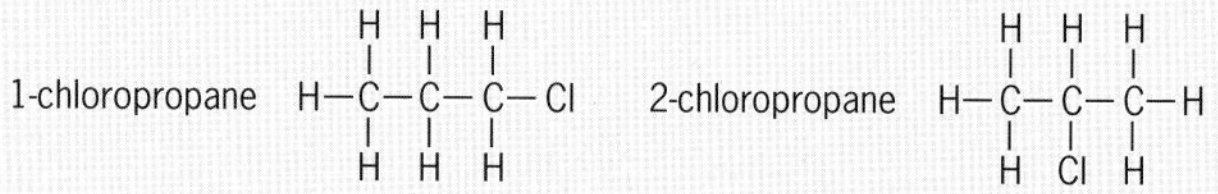

N There are two possible isomers with the formula C_2H_6O. One is an ether with a functional group C–O–C. Ethers do not feature much in your advanced course, but the other isomer has a different functional group and has already appeared in Table 6.1 on page 119.

(a) Draw the displayed formula of both isomers. You can check one of the displayed formulas by looking at page 233.

(b) Identify the functional group of the isomer of ether. You can check your answer by looking at Table 7.4 on page 151.

Remember: saturated hydrocarbons have no double bonds. The carbon atoms are bonded to the maximum possible number of hydrogen atoms.

See questions 2 and 4.

Table 7.2

Alkane	Molecular formula	Structural formula	Displayed formula
methane	CH_4	CH_4	$\begin{array}{c} H \\ | \\ H-C-H \\ | \\ H \end{array}$
ethane	C_2H_6	CH_3CH_3	$\begin{array}{cc} H & H \\ | & | \\ H-C-C-H \\ | & | \\ H & H \end{array}$
propane	C_3H_8	$CH_3CH_2CH_3$	$\begin{array}{ccc} H & H & H \\ | & | & | \\ H-C-C-C-H \\ | & | & | \\ H & H & H \end{array}$
butane	C_4H_{10}	$CH_3CH_2CH_2CH_3$	$\begin{array}{cccc} H & H & H & H \\ | & | & | & | \\ H-C-C-C-C-H \\ | & | & | & | \\ H & H & H & H \end{array}$
methylpropane	C_4H_{10}	$\begin{array}{c} CH_3CHCH_3 \\ | \\ CH_3 \end{array}$	$\begin{array}{ccc} H & H & H \\ | & | & | \\ H-C-\!\!-\!\!-C-\!\!-\!\!-C-H \\ | & | & | \\ H & H-C-H & H \\ & | \\ & H \end{array}$

O What is the name given to molecules such as butane and methylpropane which have the same molecular formula?

P What is the molecular formula of alkanes with nine carbon atoms?

Cycloalkanes

Most of the cycloalkanes found in crude oil are based on five- or six-membered carbon rings, as shown in Fig 7.20.

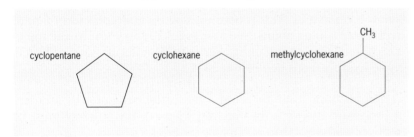

cyclopentane   cyclohexane   methylcyclohexane CH_3

Fig 7.20 **Three examples of cycloakanes**

Arenes

Arenes or **aromatic hydrocarbons** contain at least one benzene ring (see Fig 7.21). The name 'aromatic' originally came from the characteristic smell of some naturally occurring compounds which contained a benzene ring.

See Chapter 13 for more information on arenes.

■ See questions 2 and 4.

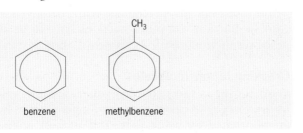

benzene   methylbenzene CH_3

Fig 7.21 **Two examples of arenes**

THE THIRST OF THE INDUSTRIALISED WORLD FOR CRUDE OIL

ALTHOUGH CRUDE oil deposits are found throughout the world, over half known oil reserves are concentrated in the Middle East. So, on 2 August 1990, when Iraq invaded Kuwait, a major exporter of crude oil, worldwide supplies were threatened. The invasion highlighted modern society's dependence on oil for energy, and sent shock waves through countries, including the United States and member states of the European Union, which depend on importing this vital energy supply. The politics of the Middle East is an essential concern to most of the world and will remain so as supplies of crude oil dwindle in the twenty-first century.

Fig 7.22 **A Kuwaiti oil field on fire after the retreat by Iraq in the Gulf War**

8 MAKING CRUDE OIL USEFUL

Crude oil as it comes out of the ground is of little practical use. To make it useful, it must first be separated into its components and this is done by **fractional distillation**.

Fractional distillation

Fractional distillation is the separation of a mixture of compounds by their different boiling points. When crude oil is separated there are five major fractions, which are shown in Table 7.3.

When crude oil reaches a refinery it is heated to about 400 °C and much of it vaporises. As vapour and liquid, it is fed into a fractionating column, which is about 60 metres high (see Fig 7.23). The liquid collects at the bottom of the column and this is called the residue. The vapour passes on up the column and as it cools it turns back to liquid, collecting in trays at various heights. The smaller the vapour molecules, the further the vapour can travel up the column before it condenses. This is because smaller molecules form liquids with lower boiling points (see also pages 158 to 160). At the top of the column, gases containing very small molecules are collected. These hydrocarbons boil below 20 °C.

This is the first distillation – the **primary distillation** – and the fractions coming from the column are further separated by a variety of processes. Before a fraction can be used, the sulphur must be removed and this forms a valuable by-product.

Meeting the demand: using all the fractions

The gasoline fraction is the main source of petrol for car and other vehicle engines, but the amount of gasoline fraction produced is never enough to meet the demand for petrol. Typically, about 40 per cent of the output from a distillation column may be required as petrol. Compare this percentage with that given in Table 7.3 for the gasoline fraction. So, other fractions have to be altered by chemical processes to produce the extra petrol needed.

Cracking larger molecules

Petrol for use in cars and other vehicles requires alkanes in the range from C_5 to C_{10}. To meet demand, longer alkanes from other fractions are shortened by being split. This process is known as **cracking**.

Q Some sulphur remains after refining.

(a) What compound is formed when sulphur is burnt?

(b) What environmental consequences are there when this compound is released into the atmosphere?

See page 171 to check your answer.

The composition of petrol is discussed in greater detail in Chapter 8.

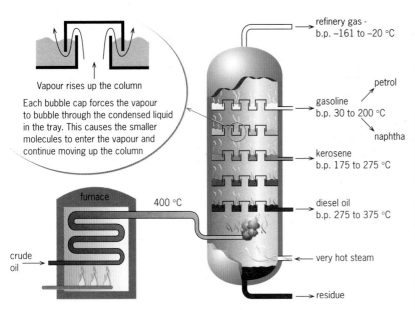

Vapour rises up the column

Each bubble cap forces the vapour to bubble through the condensed liquid in the tray. This causes the smaller molecules to enter the vapour and continue moving up the column

furnace

400 °C

crude oil

refinery gas - b.p. −161 to −20 °C

petrol

gasoline b.p. 30 to 200 °C

naphtha

kerosene b.p. 175 to 275 °C

diesel oil b.p. 275 to 375 °C

very hot steam

residue

Fig 7.23 **The primary fractional distillation of crude oil takes place in a fractionating column. The column is cut away to show some of the trays. Each tray contains many bubble caps, although only three are shown here**

Fig 7.24 **A fractionating column in a refinery**

Table 7.3 **The major fractions of crude oil and their uses**

Fraction	Boiling point range/°C	Number of carbon atoms	Percentage of crude oil	Uses
refinery gas	−161 to +20	C_1 to C_4	1 to 2	fuel and as a feedstock for petrochemicals
gasoline /naphtha	30 to 200	C_5 to C_{10}	15 to 30	petrol for transport and as a feedstock for petrochemicals; the part of the fraction so used is called naphtha
kerosene	175 to 275	C_{10} to C_{16}	10 to 15	fuel for jets, paraffin for heating
diesel oil	275 to 375	C_{12} to C_{25}	15 to 25	fuel for transport, power plants and heating
residue	375	$>C_{25}$	40 to 50	oil-fired power stations, polishing waxes, lubricating oils, bitumen on roads

There are two basic processes for splitting alkane chains: using heat, which is called **thermal cracking**; and using catalysts, which is called **catalytic cracking** (or 'cat cracking' for short). Whichever process is employed, sufficient energy must be supplied to split the very strong C–C and C–H bonds. Look back at Table 7.1, page 141. The advantage of thermal cracking is that molecules in the **residue** can be cracked. Catalytic cracking only works on the **distillate** (the liquid which has been distilled) such as that from the diesel oil fraction. But catalytic cracking tends to produce more branched chain alkanes, which are better for use in petrol.

Take, for example, the molecule of dodecane, $C_{12}H_{26}$:

$$CH_3CH_2CH_2CH_2CH_2CH_2CH_2CH_2CH_2CH_2CH_2CH_3$$

$$\xrightarrow[\text{catalyst}]{\text{zeolite}} CH_3\overset{\overset{\displaystyle CH_3}{|}}{C}HCH_2CH_2\overset{\overset{\displaystyle CH_3}{|}}{C}HCH_3 + CH_3CH_2CH=CH_2$$

Notice that in this case the molecule has been split and a branched chain alkane has been produced. Branched chains are useful in petrol blending because they have higher octane numbers (see page 162). Of course, the molecule can split in almost any way, so a huge variety of hydrocarbons, both straight chains and branched, are produced. These are separated by fractional distillation.

■ See questions 4, 6 and 8.

?

R (a) In which fraction will dodecane be found?
Hint: See Table 7.3.

(b) Write equations to show the cracking reactions of dodecane to form:

(i) ethene and a straight chain alkane;
(ii) propene and a branched chain alkane.

If you cannot remember the formulas for ethene and propene, look at page 143.

ZEOLITES

ZEOLITE MEANS BOILING STONE (from the Greek *zeein* for boiling and *lithos* for stone). The name was coined by a Swedish scientist, Baron Cronstedt, in 1756, when he discovered a mineral which released steam and appeared to boil when heated. This name now applies to about 40 naturally occurring minerals which display the same property when heated. Many more zeolites are made synthetically. The steam comes from water trapped in tiny pores and channels in the zeolite. These channels are the key to understanding how this remarkable substance is such an effective catalyst. It took some 200 years from Cronstedt's discovery until synthetic zeolites were first used commercially in 1959 to crack hydrocarbons.

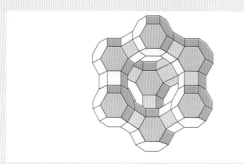

Fig 7.25 **Zeolite Y is used in cracking hydrocarbon molecules**

Zeolites are a family of aluminium silicates. Their silicon, oxygen and aluminium atoms provide a regular network of pores and interconnecting channels, rather like a sponge (see Fig 7.25). The size of the pores is critical to the use of zeolites as catalysts for the host chemicals. Pore sizes (in picometres, 10^{-12} m) range from 300 pm to 1000 pm, which is why the pores trap water molecules (which have an effective diameter of about 270 pm). If the pore size is large enough, the zeolite can accommodate hydrocarbon molecules, which are cracked inside the structure.

Synthetic rather than natural zeolites are now used for catalytic cracking, and there is much research into ways of altering the sizes of pores and channels by inserting different atoms into the structure. Zeolites have saved the oil industry billions of pounds because they are so efficient and produce more commercially desirable products than the previous clay catalysts.

The uses for zeolites don't stop with cracking. In New Zealand, which has vast reserves of natural gas, but hardly any oil, a synthetic zeolite, ZSM-5, converts methanol into petrol. Methane is first converted to methanol, then ZSM-5 removes water from the molecules, leaving hydrocarbon chains trapped inside the zeolite. These are then driven out of the zeolite as petrol.

Zeolites in washing powder

Almost certainly you have zeolites in your house. Look at a packet of washing powder and you will probably find more than a quarter of the powder is made from zeolites. The function of zeolites here is to remove calcium ions, which cause water hardness, and replace them with sodium ions, which soften the water. About three-quarters of the world's production of zeolites ends up in detergents.

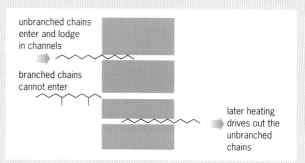

Fig 7.27 **Zeolite acting as a molecular sieve. Unbranched chains can enter channels whereas branched chains cannot. The zeolite is removed and the unbranched chains are driven from the zeolite by heating**

Zeolites also function as molecular sieves. For example, detergents need to be biodegradable. The largest part of the detergent molecule is a hydrocarbon chain. If this chain is branched, microorganisms at the sewage works cannot break down the detergent.

At the refinery, unbranched hydrocarbons for detergent manufacture are separated from those with branched chains by passing them into the channels of a zeolite. The branched chains are too large to enter the zeolite, so just the unbranched hydrocarbons pass through it.

There is speculation that zeolites may have provided the organising influence that produced the biologically active molecules which form the basis of life on Earth.

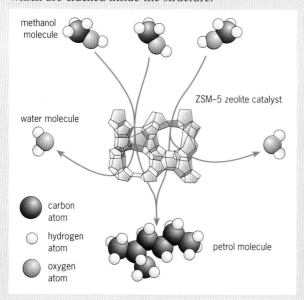

Fig 7.26 **Zeolite ZSM-5 converts methanol produced from natural gas into petrol**

Reforming

Catalytic **reforming** is used to modify molecules to suit demand. We have already mentioned the need to produce branched chain alkanes to increase the octane number of petrol. This can be done by taking a straight chain alkane, heating it to break one of the C–C bonds, and allowing the molecule to reform, which often produces a branched chain. Catalysts such as platinum are used:

$$CH_3CH_2CH_2CH_2CH_3 \xrightarrow{\text{platinum catalyst; heat}} CH_3CH_2CHCH_3$$
$$\underset{\displaystyle CH_3}{|}$$

Another reforming reaction can convert straight-chain alkanes to cycloalkanes and arenes. Again, different catalysts can be used. An example is given in Fig 7.28. Notice that during reforming, whatever happens to the molecule, the number of carbon atoms remains the same.

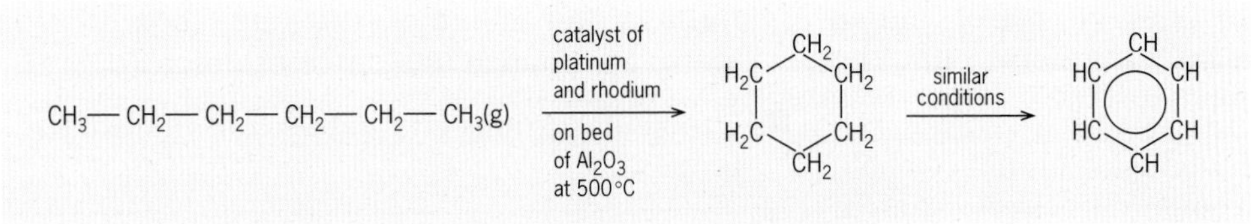

Fig 7.28 **Catalytic reforming to produce cycloalkanes and aromatic compounds**

9 PETROCHEMICALS

More than 90 per cent of crude oil is burnt. But the rest forms the basis of the petrochemical industry, which produces almost all of our organic chemicals. We have already said that alkanes are rather unreactive. However, the cracking process produces small chain alkenes, of which ethene is the most important. Ethene provides a synthetic route to many organic chemicals. The reactivity of its double bond provides a way to insert many different functional groups into hydrocarbon molecules and thereby allow the full potential of hydrocarbons to be realised.

Functional groups

A functional group is an atom or group of atoms which determines the properties of a molecule. It is usually the functional group that provides the reaction site of the molecule. Table 7.4 summarises some of the functional groups you will meet in subsequent chapters.

■ See question 2 and 7.

S (a) The first example of a reforming process is sometimes called isomerisation. Explain why. Hint: look back to page 144.

(b) Read the Feature Box on zeolites. Explain how zeolites can be used to separate branched chain alkanes from unbranched ones.

T (a) Name the molecules shown in Figs 7.28.

(b) What valuable by-product is produced in the catalytic-reforming reaction?

■ See questions 2 and 5.

Table 7.4

Functional group	Name of class of compound	A typical example	Use of example
–C–X X = F, Cl, Br, I	halogenoalkanes	chloroethane C_2H_5Cl	starting material for the production of time-release capsules for medicines
–O–H	alcohols	ethanol C_2H_5OH	industrial solvent
$-C\underset{O}{\overset{H}{<}}$	aldehydes	ethanal CH_3CHO	making synthetic rubber
$>C=O$	ketones	propanone CH_3COCH_3	industrial and domestic solvents, eg nail polish remover
$-C\underset{O}{\overset{OH}{<}}$	carboxylic acids	ethanoic acid CH_3CO_2H	production of pharmaceuticals and in vinegar
$-N\underset{H}{\overset{H}{<}}$	amines	ethylamine $C_2H_5NH_2$	important intermediate for many industrial compounds

SUMMARY

After studying this chapter, you should know that:

■ Carbon is unique in its formation of stable chains, branched chains and rings, giving rise to millions of different chemicals.

■ Crude oil is a hydrocarbon mixture of alkanes, cycloalkanes and arenes.

■ Components of crude oil can be separated by fractional distillation in a fractionating column. The five major fractions separated in a fractionating column are: refinery gases, gasoline (includes petrol and naphtha), kerosene, diesel oil and residue.

■ Larger hydrocarbon molecules are broken down (cracked) into smaller ones for petrol and to produce alkenes, such as ethene, for the petrochemical industry.

■ Reforming is a way of producing branched chain alkanes and cyclic compounds from straight chain alkanes.

■ Crude oil is a finite resource. Its use as a feedstock for most organic chemicals has changed the world, yet most of it is burnt as fuel.

■ Saturated hydrocarbons have no double or triple carbon–carbon bonds in their molecules.

■ Unsaturated hydrocarbons possess double or triple carbon–carbon bonds.

■ Isomerism occurs when molecules have the same molecular formula but different ways of arranging their atoms. There are two types of isomerism: structural isomerism and stereoisomerism.

■ Structural isomers have the same molecular formula but different structures because the atoms are bonded in a different order.

■ Functional groups give a molecule characteristic properties.

QUESTIONS

1 Silicon forms compounds with hydrogen called 'silanes', similar in structure to the saturated hydrocarbons, the alkanes.

Silanes form a homologous series of which the first member has the formula SiH_4.

a) Explain the term *saturated hydrocarbon*.

b) Suggest the general formula for a silane.

c) Explain the term *structural isomer*.

d) Draw the displayed formula of each of two possible isomers of the silane containing four silicon atoms.

e) For a molecule of the silane SiH_4,
   (i) draw a dot-and-cross diagram showing outer electrons only,
   (ii) draw a diagram showing the shape and bond angles.

[UCLES March 1995 Sciences: Chemistry Foundation, q.2]
Note: Part **e)** requires information which is in Chapter 4.

2 Explain the meaning of the following terms, giving an example:

a) functional group,

b) general formula,

c) unsaturated hydrocarbon,

d) arene,

e) cracking,

f) reforming.

3 Draw displayed formulas for five structural isomers of C_7H_{16}.

4 The formulas of five hydrocarbons associated with the oil industry are:

   A C_8H_{16} **B** C_2H_4 **C** $C_{15}H_{32}$ **D** C_3H_6 **E** C_6H_6

a) Which of these is an alkane?

b) Draw the displayed formulas of molecules **B** and **C**.

c) What is the name given to the arene molecule **E**? Draw its displayed formula.

d) Molecule **C** is a straight chain hydrocarbon which can be cracked to produce molecules **A**, **B** and **D**. Write balanced equations to represent three possible cracking reactions which produce these three hydrocarbons.

e) Explain why molecules **B** and **D** are such important molecules in petrochemical manufacture.

5 Name the functional groups in the following molecules:

a) C_3H_7OH **b)** CH_3NH_2 **c)** C_2H_4

d) $C_2H_5CO_2H$ **e)** CH_3CHO

6 A gas oil fraction from the distillation of crude oil contains hydrocarbons in the C_{15} to C_{19} range. These hydrocarbons can be cracked by strong heating.

a) Explain why molecules of this size are chosen for cracking.

b) Name **two** types of compound produced by cracking and give a different use for each.

c) Write the molecular formula for the alkane with 19 carbon atoms.

d) Write an equation for one possible cracking reaction of the alkane $C_{16}H_{34}$ when the products include ethene and propene in the molar ratio 2:1 and only one other compound.

[NEAB February 1995 Chemistry: Kinetics and Organic Chemistry Module Test, q.2]

7 Cracking and reforming are essential processes in producing useful substances from oil.

a) Why is cracking a useful process?

b) Suggest an equation for the cracking of decane, $C_{10}H_{22}$.

c) Although heat alone can be used to crack hydrocarbons, it is far more common for oil companies also to use catalysts. A catalyst will speed up the rate of a chemical reaction. Suggest another reason why oil companies use catalysts.

d) State **two** ways in which *reforming* changes the structure of the oil fractions.

For question **8**, refer to Chapter 1, and for part **d)**, refer to Chapter 8.

8

a) In considering the economics of the *refining* of crude petroleum (**not** its production), explain what is meant by the following terms: **(i)** fixed costs, **(ii)** variable costs.

b) What are the *major* factors which influence the choice of a site for an oil refinery?

c) The two *major* processes used in the initial refining of crude petroleum are: **(i)** fractional distillation, **(ii)** cracking.
Briefly describe the principles of each process, and explain why each process is necessary.

d) Some of the compounds found in crude petroleum contain sulphur. Petrol is obtained by refining crude petroleum. State and explain **two** reasons why sulphur compounds are removed from petrol during its manufacture.

e) Outline the major disadvantages of the world's dependence on refined crude petroleum as a source of energy.

[AEB 1993 Chemistry Specimen, General Paper 3, q.7]

Assignment

A CRACKING WAY TO PRODUCE ETHENE

One of the fundamental components of a petrochemical plant is the steam cracker. The process of steam cracking involves heating a hydrocarbon feedstock to temperatures of 800–850 °C in the presence of steam. The chief product is ethene, but other alkenes, such as propene, butenes and buta-1,3-diene, are produced as well.

Steam cracking is thermal cracking and it is used in preference to catalytic cracking, even though the temperatures required when using catalysts are much lower. Catalytic cracking produces high-quality petrol with many branched chain alkanes, but the yield of ethene tends to be low.

a) What is meant by the terms hydrocarbon and cracking?

b) Explain, using the bond energy data in Table 7.1, page 141, which bonds in the hydrocarbon feedstock are most easily broken.

Approximately 0.6 tonnes of steam are used for every tonne of feedstock. The purpose of using steam is to dilute the feedstock and this produces a high yield of ethene.

However, an added benefit of steam is that it reduces carbon deposits, which would clog up the cracker, and allows more even heating of the reactants.

The steam–hydrocarbon mixture passes into the furnace where it is heated to the high temperatures required for cracking. However, it stays in the furnace only a short time and this **residence time** is critical in producing good yields of alkenes. A typical residence time is between 0.1 and 0.5 seconds, depending on the feedstock used.

Fig 7.A1 **A steam cracker furnace in the Joint Venture Olefine 6 complex at Wilton. The complex was commissioned in 1979 and is jointly owned by ICI and BP. It is the largest unit in Europe, with the capacity to produce almost 800 000 tonnes of ethene per year**

Table 7.A1 gives the product yields for different feedstocks. Once the cracked mixture has left the furnace, it must be cooled rapidly, which is done with cold water. This prevents recombination of product molecules. The different compounds are then separated mainly by fractional distillation.

Table 7.A1 **Different feedstocks and the percentage by mass of the different products obtained after cracking**

Product	Feedstock				
	Ethane	Propane	Butane	Naphtha	Diesel oil
ethene	78	43	39	30	23
propene	3	16	15	16	14
C_4s (ie butenes and buta-1,3-diene)	3	5	7	10	11
light gases (hydrogen, methane, other)	14	31	27	17	10
petrol (rich in aromatics)	2	4	10	23	20
fuel oil	0	1	2	4	22

2

a) Which feedstock gives the highest yield of ethene?

b) What other factors must be taken into account when deciding on which feedstock to use?

3

a) Butenes have the molecular formula C_4H_8. Draw the two straight chain structural isomers.

b) What is meant by the term aromatics?

c) Naphtha is part of which main fraction?

d) How many carbon atoms are in the diesel oil hydrocarbons?

4

a) Write a balanced equation using displayed formula for the production of ethene and hydrogen from ethane.

b) Work out the percentage yield of ethene from ethane. Hint: Look back at page 8 for details of percentage yield calculations.

c) Steam cracking is a continuous process. What is meant by this statement? (See page 12 if you are not sure.)

The economics of this continuous industrial process are complex. In some years, over-production of ethene in the world has led to dramatic falls in its price, while in other years there has been a worldwide shortage, making ethene a valuable commodity.

C_4 compounds are also very useful by-products of ethene production. For example, buta-1,3-diene (CH_2=CHCH=CH_2) is widely used in the manufacture of synthetic rubber for tyres. However, Europe produces a surplus of buta-1,3-diene while the US is a net importer, and this is related to the feedstock that goes into the cracker. In order to maintain the price of buta-1,3-diene, much of it must be converted into butane and its isomer by hydrogenation (reaction with hydrogen). Some of this butane is recycled back into the cracker, while the rest is sold on the LPG (liquefied petroleum gas) market.

5

a) In Europe, much of the ethene produced comes from naphtha. Why might this lead to a surplus of buta-1,3-diene?

b) Which feedstock might the USA be using?

c) Draw the displayed formula of buta-1,3-diene.

d) Write a balanced equation for the hydrogenation of buta-1,3-diene to produce butane.

e) What advantage is there to the petrochemical manufacturer in recycling butane made from buta-1,3-diene into the cracker?

6 Find out the main uses of ethene and benzene. While there is plenty of information in this book, also investigate other source material.

OIL AND THE PETROCHEMICAL INDUSTRY

The Chapter Map below brings together the main groups of compounds found in crude oil, its treatment to separate them, their important reactions and uses, and the underlying concepts relating to their chemistry. Study the map to make sure you clearly understand these ideas and the connections between them.

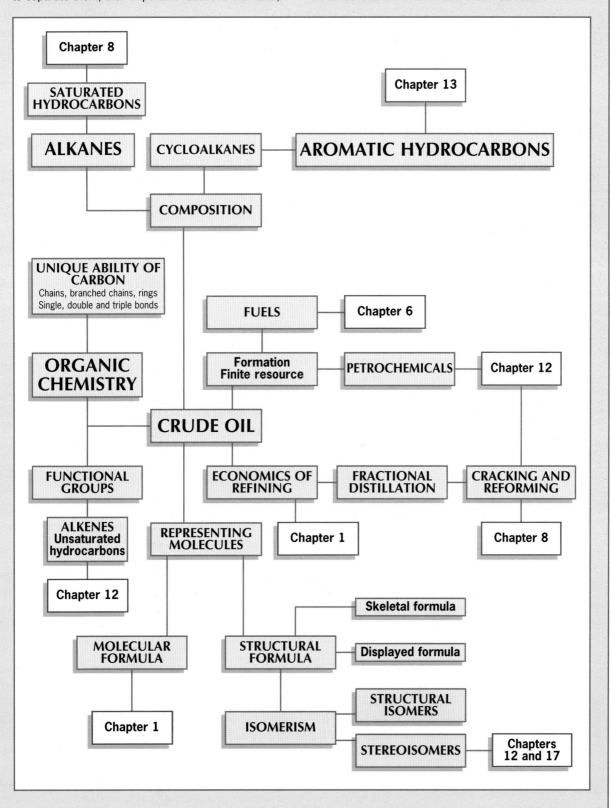

8   Alkanes and the car engine

Smog in the 90s. Canary Wharf in London's Docklands

PEOPLE HAVE BECOME too reliant on the car. In the UK, for example, seven out of ten journeys of a mile or more are now made by car, accounting for 86 per cent of the total distance travelled by any means – and this is likely to increase. Travel by bus and coach, once much more important than travel by car, has been declining steadily for the past 40 years and now accounts for only 6 per cent.

Over four days in December 1991, nitrogen dioxide built up in the London atmosphere to unusually high concentrations and 160 more deaths than expected were recorded. The culprit was almost certainly the car. In August 1994, hot weather led to an increase of ozone in the lower atmosphere across Europe, and in the UK, the Department of the Environment urged drivers to leave their cars at home. On 1 October 1997, the atmosphere in Paris was so polluted that half the cars were banned from entering the city and free public transport was offered.

The amount of carbon dioxide in the atmosphere is increasing and the burning of petrol in cars is a major contributor to this increase. Chemists and engineers can do only so much to reduce car emissions. So people must somehow be weaned from their addiction to the car if the present trend towards serious global warming, with its alarming consequences, is to be stopped.

1 ALKANES

Petrol and diesel, the most common fuels for road transportation, are both mixtures consisting mainly of alkane hydrocarbons. Chapter 6 explains where the energy comes from when these fuels are burnt in air, and shows that petrol and diesel are both concentrated energy sources. Chapter 7 shows that both fuels are the products of the fractional distillation of crude oil. In this chapter, we look more closely at these two fuels and the properties of the alkanes which they contain. We also look at the environmental consequences of using petrol and diesel.

Naming alkanes

Alkanes are saturated hydrocarbons. Around each carbon atom are four σ bonds (sigma bonds) to hydrogen atoms or other carbon atoms. In Chapter 7, page 146, we found that alkanes could be represented by a general formula C_nH_{2n+2}. Table 8.1 lists the first six straight chain alkanes.

Past four, the number of carbon atoms in a molecule is given by a prefix derived from either the Latin or Greek word for the number.

Remember that **saturated** hydrocarbons have no double bonds. The carbon atoms are bonded to the maximum possible number of hydrogen atoms (see page 143). The term refers to a time when chemists added hydrogen to various organic compounds and those which would not take up extra hydrogen were called saturated.

Table 8.1 **The molecular formulas, structural formulas and names of the first six straight chain alkanes**

Molecular formula	Structural formula	Name
CH_4	CH_4	methane
C_2H_6	CH_3CH_3	ethane
C_3H_8	$CH_3CH_2CH_3$	propane
C_4H_{10}	$CH_3CH_2CH_2CH_3$	butane
C_5H_{12}	$CH_3CH_2CH_2CH_2CH_3$	pentane
C_6H_{14}	$CH_3CH_2CH_2CH_2CH_2CH_3$	hexane

For example, in pentane, *pent* tells you that there are five carbon atoms, and *ane* tells you that the compound is saturated. (The suffix ane was coined by August Hofmann, an eminent German chemist.)

Try this with nonane.

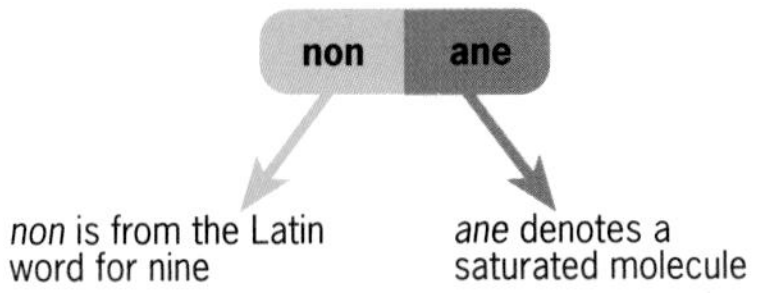

non	ane

non is from the Latin word for nine

ane denotes a saturated molecule

So the molecular formula is C_9H_{20}.

Naming straight chain alkanes is thus straightforward. But what about branched chains? Look at Table 8.2, which shows some **alkyl groups**. Alkyl groups are alkanes with one hydrogen removed so that they can bond with other atoms.

Name	Structural formula
Methyl	CH_3-
Ethyl	CH_3CH_2-
Propyl	$CH_3CH_2CH_2-$
Butyl	$CH_3CH_2CH_2CH_2-$

Table 8.2 **The names and structural formulas of some alkyl groups**

The name of this branched chain alkane is methylpropane:

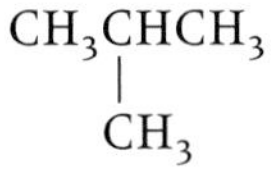

$$CH_3CHCH_3$$
$$|$$
$$CH_3$$

The longer carbon chain has three carbons (hence propane) and it has a methyl side group. Sometimes, the molecule is called 2-methylpropane to show that the methyl group is attached to the second carbon in the propane chain. But in the case of this molecule, the 2- is usually left out, as this is the only place the methyl group can go.

Fig 8.1 shows the structural formula of 2-methylbutane. Note that the carbon atoms in the longer chain are numbered so that the position of attachment of the alkyl group is the lowest number possible, 2.

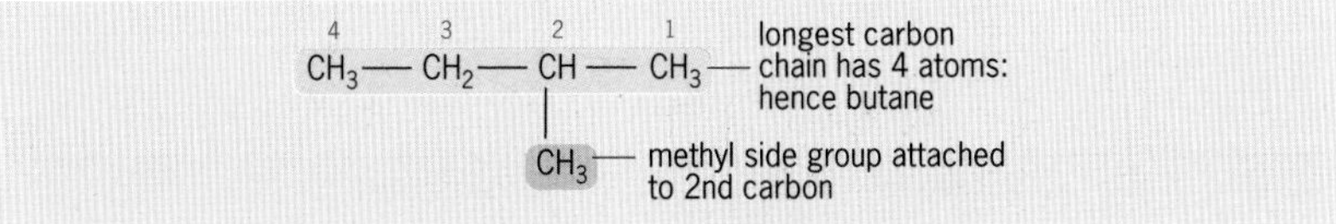

Fig 8.1

The molecule in Fig 8.2 is **not** called 2-ethylbutane, because the longest continuous carbon chain has five carbon atoms, hence its name is 3-methylpentane.

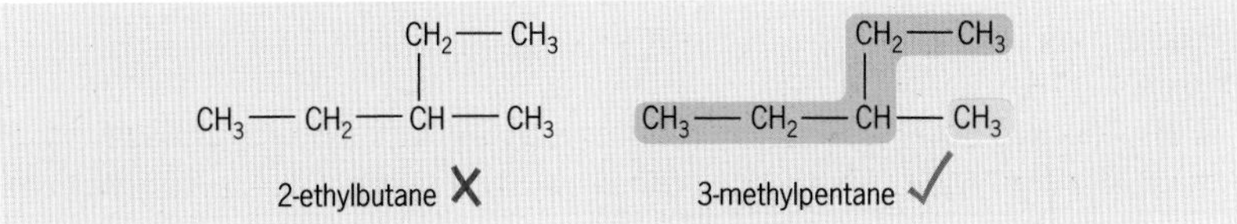

Fig 8.2

You will need to remember the prefixes of the first eight alkanes.

?

A Look at Table 8.1. The next two straight chain alkanes in this series are heptane with seven carbon atoms per molecule and octane with eight. What are their molecular formulas and structural formulas?

B (a) Draw the structural formula and the displayed formula of nonane.

Hint: Look back at page 142 if you need to remind yourself about displayed formulas.

(b) What is the name of the straight chain alkane with a molecular formula $C_{10}H_{22}$? Look at Table 8.3 on page 158 to check your answer.

Sometimes it is convenient to refer to an alkyl group as R.

?

C (a) What is the name of the alkyl group with five carbon atoms?

(b) Work out the general formula for the alkyl group.

D Draw the straight chain isomer of methylpropane.
Hint: If you are not sure how to do this, look back at page 145.

E (a) Why is the following not a structural isomer of 2-methylbutane? To check your answer, see page 145.

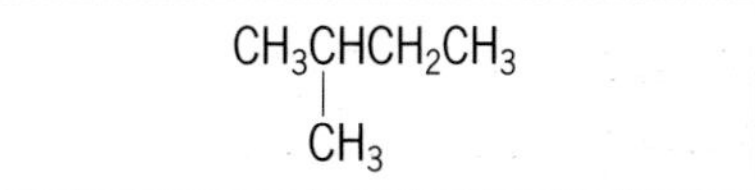

$$CH_3CHCH_2CH_3$$
$$|$$
$$CH_3$$

(b) Sometimes this molecule is just called methylbutane. Why?

F Draw the structural formula of 3-ethyl-2,2-dimethylhexane and 4-propylheptane.
Note that in the first compound, *ethyl* comes before *methyl*: by convention, side groups are put in alphabetical order. See example, page 158.

EXAMPLE

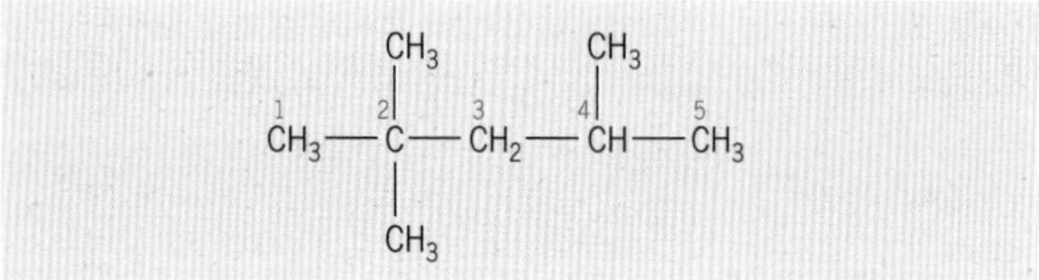

$$CH_3 - \underset{\underset{CH_3}{|}}{\overset{\overset{CH_3}{|}}{\underset{2}{C}}} - CH_2 - \underset{4}{CH} - \underset{5}{CH_3}$$

Fig 8.3

Q The compound shown in Fig 8.3 used to be called iso-octane. It is important in working out the octane numbers of fuels (see page 162). What is its systematic name?

A **Step 1.** Look for the longest carbon chain (called the **parent alkane**) and name it. In this case, the chain has five carbon atoms, so it will be called pentane.

Step 2. Name every side group. The methyl group is the only side group, but there are three of them. We must ensure the name includes all the side groups, so we use *tri* hence trimethylpentane. If there were two groups, we would use *di,* and if four, *tetra.*

Step 3. Indicate the position of all of the side groups on the longest carbon chain by numbering the carbon atoms. Remember to use the lowest numbers possible. When there are two or more different alkyl groups, they are placed in alphabetical order irrespective of their numbered position on the chain. (See the compound named in Self-test question **F**).

We have numbered the carbon atoms on the molecule so that two of the methyl groups have the lowest possible number, 2. You will notice that the numbers in a name are separated by commas, that the numbers and letters are separated by hyphens, and that every side group has a number.

So the **systematic name** of iso-octane is 2,2,4-trimethylpentane.

The system we have used to name this compound is recommended by the International Union of Pure and Applied Chemistry (IUPAC) and is accepted by chemists throughout the world. However, if you enter the chemical industry, you may still hear non-systematic names such as iso-octane.

See questions 1 and 2.

?

G Look at Table 8.3. As the number of carbon atoms in each molecule increases, what is the increase in the number of hydrogen atoms?

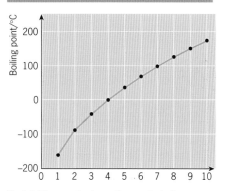

Fig 8.4 **The graph shows the gradual change of boiling points of straight chain alkanes as the number of carbon atoms per molecule increases**

Table 8.3 **Three physical properties of the first ten straight chain alkanes. Note the gradual change in these physical properties**

For the separation of the components of crude oil, see page 148.

Alkanes form a homologous series

We have already seen that alkanes can be represented by a general formula, C_nH_{2n+2}. This makes them a **homologous series**. The compounds in a homologous series have similar chemical properties, and gradually changing physical properties as the number of carbon atoms increases.

As you go through this book you will encounter other homologous series. Chemists find it useful to classify organic compounds into homologous series because of the similar chemical properties of the members. This means they can be studied as a group, rather than studying each individual compound.

Physical properties of alkanes

The term **physical properties** refers to those properties of a substance which can be measured or observed without changing the composition or identity of the substance. Physical properties include melting point, boiling point, colour and density.

As already stated, the physical properties in a homologous series change gradually as the number of carbon atoms increases. The steady change in the boiling points of the alkanes is used to separate them when crude oil is passed into a fractionating column.

Alkane	Structural formula	Melting point/°C	Boiling point/°C	Density/g cm⁻³
methane	CH_4	−182	−164	0.466
ethane	CH_3CH_3	−183	−89	0.572
propane	$CH_3CH_2CH_3$	−190	−42	0.585
butane	$CH_3(CH_2)_2CH_3$	−138	−1	0.601
pentane	$CH_3(CH_2)_3CH_3$	−130	36	0.626
hexane	$CH_3(CH_2)_4CH_3$	−95	69	0.660
heptane	$CH_3(CH_2)_5CH_3$	−91	98	0.684
octane	$CH_3(CH_2)_6CH_3$	−57	126	0.703
nonane	$CH_3(CH_2)_7CH_3$	−54	151	0.718
decane	$CH_3(CH_2)_8CH_3$	−30	174	0.730

The effect of branched chains on the boiling point

The occurrence of branching on a carbon chain reduces the boiling point. The more branching there is in an alkane, the lower its boiling point is compared with its straight chain structural isomer. Pentane and its isomers (Fig 8.5) clearly demonstrate this.

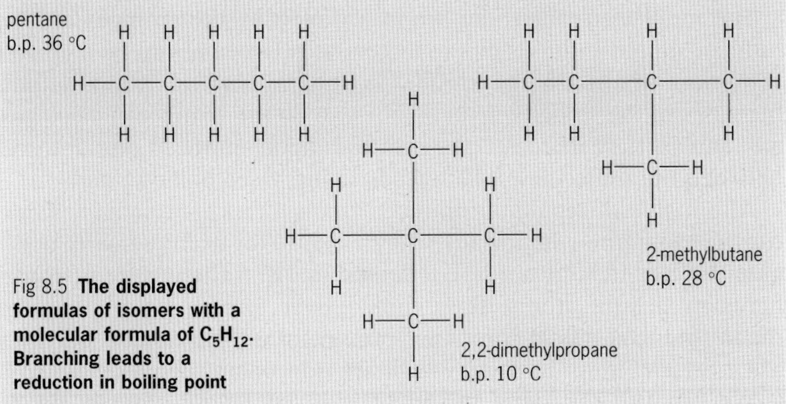

Fig 8.5 The displayed formulas of isomers with a molecular formula of C_5H_{12}. Branching leads to a reduction in boiling point

pentane
b.p. 36 °C

2-methylbutane
b.p. 28 °C

2,2-dimethylpropane
b.p. 10 °C

Branching also affects the **volatility** of an alkane. Volatility describes the tendency of a liquid to evaporate. Branched chain alkanes are very important in blending petrol because of their volatility, as you can see on page 160.

H (a) In Table 8.3, the density measurements for each alkane were taken at 298 K, except for those which are gases at this temperature. For these compounds, measurements were taken at just below their boiling points. Which density measurements were not taken at 298 K? (See page 96 if you are not sure how to convert Kelvin to degrees Celsius.)

(b) (i) Dodecane has 12 carbon atoms in its molecule. Predict its boiling point and density by drawing graphs similar to the one in Fig 8.4. **(ii)** By drawing a graph of melting point against the number of carbon atoms in a molecule, predict how many carbon atoms the first alkane to be a solid at 298 K will have.

2 INTERMOLECULAR FORCES IN ALKANES: INDUCED DIPOLE–INDUCED DIPOLE

We have seen two trends in the boiling points of alkanes. Straight chain alkanes show an increase in boiling point as the number of carbon atoms increases, and branching reduces the boiling point when the number of carbon atoms remains the same.

The particles in a liquid are held close together by forces. The stronger the forces, the higher is the boiling point of the liquid. The forces holding alkane molecules in a liquid are weak **intermolecular forces,** which is why alkanes have relatively low boiling points.

Fig 4.39, page 84, shows that a molecule of hydrogen chloride is polar because the centres of negative and positive charge do not coincide. In a polar molecule, there is a **permanent dipole**: one part of the molecule always has a slightly positive charge and another part always has a slightly negative charge. Highly polar molecules can often attract each other quite strongly. Alkanes are sometimes referred to as **non-polar** molecules because they have no permanent dipole. So how do intermolecular forces arise and cause the molecules to attract each other? And how is the increase in carbon atoms related to the trend of increasing boiling point?

The electrons in atoms and molecules are in constant motion. Although alkanes have no permanent dipole, the electron charge cloud around their molecules is not always evenly distributed. At any one instant, there may be a temporary dipole where the centres of positive and negative charge do not coincide. This **instantaneous dipole** induces dipoles in neighbouring molecules. A positive charge at one end of a molecule induces a negative charge in a molecule close to it.

These opposite charges can now attract. The force between them is known as an **induced dipole-induced dipole force,** or a **van der Waals force** after the Dutch physicist Johannes van der Waals

To remind yourself about particles in solids, liquids and gases see pages 99 to 101.

Intermolecular means between molecules.
Remember that δ+ and δ– show the positive and negative poles in a molecule. The symbol δ tells you that it is a partial charge.

I Why do you think highly polar molecules can often attract each other quite strongly? To check your answer, look at page 204.

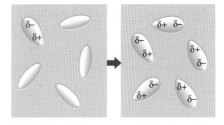

Fig. 8.6 **Left: An instantaneous diploe forms due to the uneven distribution of the electron cloud. Right: This induces dipoles in neighbouring molecules, which then attract each other**

(1837–1923). In the next instant, the movement of electrons in the molecules leads to a collapse of these temporary dipoles and elsewhere in the substance other instantaneous dipoles form. Averaged over time, alkane molecules do not have a permanent dipole, but billions of instantaneous dipoles are continuously occurring, providing a weak intermolecular force.

The more electrons there are in a molecule, the stronger are the induced dipole–induced dipole forces, because there can be a greater distortion of the charge cloud. As the number of carbon atoms increases in the straight chain alkanes, so do the number of electrons, and this in turn increases the induced dipole–induced dipole forces between the molecules, which leads to increased boiling points.

Although induced dipole–induced dipole forces are relatively weak, they are extremely important. They explain, for example, why noble gases such as helium can be condensed at 4 K. If there were no forces between helium atoms, they could never form a liquid. Induced dipole–induced dipole forces are present in all substances, but they are most important in those which are non-polar, such as alkanes.

We can use the same model of induced dipole–induced dipole forces to explain why branching in alkanes reduces the boiling point. Look back at Fig 8.5. You will see that pentane is a straight chain, which allows the molecules to line up beside each other, thereby giving a greater surface area over which these weak forces can act. Branching reduces this surface area and so the intermolecular forces are correspondingly weaker, leading to lower boiling points.

> ✔
>
> Because the first dipole that is formed at any one instant is called an instantaneous dipole, induced dipole–induced dipole forces are sometimes referred to as **instantaneous dipole–induced dipole forces**.

> ?
>
> **J** Explain why the boiling points of the noble gases increase as you descend Group 8.

Read more about induced dipole–induced dipole forces in noble gases and other elements on page 422

GETTING THE VOLATILITY RIGHT

FOR PETROL to burn in an engine, it must vaporise and be mixed with air. So a crucial property of petrol is high volatility. On extremely cold winter mornings, the petrol must be volatile enough to vaporise and mix with air. If it isn't, the engine won't start. However, on hot summer days, if the petrol is too volatile, it may vaporise in the fuel feed-pipe, causing a vapour lock which prevents the petrol mixing with air and getting to the engine. Again, the engine won't start. Another drawback of high volatility is that if the petrol vaporises too readily, too much of it enters the engine and there won't be enough oxygen for it to burn efficiently.

In the UK, the composition or blend of petrol is changed four times a year, according to the season. So, during the winter, petrol has more low boiling point alkanes in it, such as butane and pentane, while in the summer, the proportion of volatile components is reduced and more compounds of low volatility are incorporated.

3 REACTIONS OF THE ALKANES

> ?
>
> **K (a)** Explain why the volatility of petrol in Spain is different from that of petrol in the UK.
>
> **(b)** Increasing the volatility of petrol can be done by using short straight chain alkanes. What other alkanes can be used to increase volatility?

Alkanes are quite unreactive due to the nature of the C–C and C–H bonds. First, both are very strong bonds which are difficult to break. Second, both these bonds are non-polar due to the similar electronegativities of carbon and hydrogen. The non-polar nature of the molecules makes them unreactive to polar reagents and ions, and they do not react with acids, bases, metals or oxidising agents such as potassium manganate(VII). It is their very unreactivity that makes them so useful as lubricants and plastics.

The few reactions which alkanes can undergo are of fundamental importance. Two of these reactions – cracking and reforming – are used to produce petrol with desirable properties (see pages 148 to 151). Another involves halogens (for more about the reaction of halogens with alkanes, see pages 206 to 211). Cracking also produces alkenes, which are the bedrock of the petrochemical industry. For more about the petrochemical industry, see pages 151 and 246.

4 COMBUSTION OF ALKANES

We know that a spark produces a spontaneous reaction between petrol vapour and oxygen. The spark provides the activation energy for this reaction. Alkanes burn in oxygen, releasing a great deal of energy, which is one of the reasons why they are such popular fuels. They all produce carbon dioxide and water when there is enough oxygen for them to burn completely.

Butane is used to increase the volatility of petrol. Its reaction with oxygen is:

$$C_4H_{10}(g) + 6\tfrac{1}{2}O_2(g) \rightarrow 4CO_2(g) + 5H_2O(l) \quad \Delta H_c^{\ominus} = -2877\,kJ\,mol^{-1}$$

Heptane is another component of petrol. Its reaction with oxygen is:

$$C_7H_{16}(g) + 11O_2(g) \rightarrow 7CO_2(g) + 8H_2O(l) \quad \Delta H_c^{\ominus} = -4817\,kJ\,mol^{-1}$$

If there is insufficient oxygen, alkanes are not completely oxidised. They produce carbon monoxide, which is very poisonous, and even carbon (soot). This is a real problem when burning petrol in vehicle engines.

L (a) What is the name given to reactions which release energy to the surroundings?

(b) What are the meanings of the terms *spontaneous reaction* and *activation energy*?

(c) Alkanes and oxygen need a spark before they react. So chemists say that they are kinetically stable but energetically unstable. Explain what they mean by this statement.

(d) What are the desirable properties of a fuel?
The answers can be found in Chapter 6.

To check what is meant by $\Delta H_c^{\ominus}$ see page 117.

THE PETROL ENGINE

THE PETROL ENGINE is classed as an internal combustion engine because the fuel burns inside the engine and the products of this combustion drive the engine directly. Fig 8.7 illustrates the four-stroke cycle on which vehicle engines work.

The drive to make petrol engines more fuel efficient centres upon how much the petrol–air mixture can be compressed. In engines of the 1920s, each piston compressed the mixture to a quarter of its original volume. But in today's engines the petrol–air mixture in each cylinder is compressed to one-tenth of its original volume, thereby extracting much more energy from the combustion of the hydrocarbons.

Fig 8.7 **How a four-stroke petrol engine works**

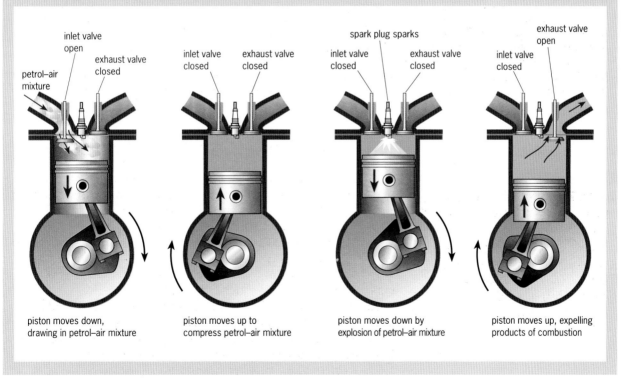

piston moves down, drawing in petrol–air mixture

piston moves up to compress petrol–air mixture

piston moves down by explosion of petrol–air mixture

piston moves up, expelling products of combustion

Octane number of a petrol blend

As the petrol–air mixture is compressed in a cylinder (see Fig 8.7), it becomes hot and sometimes ignites without the aid of a spark from the spark plug (**auto-ignition).** When this happens, the fuel does not burn smoothly, but explodes in different parts of the cylinder, generating a rapid knocking noise. **Knocking** can damage the cylinder and piston head and, because the petrol–air mixture does not ignite at the right time, it leads to a loss of power and inefficient use of fuel.

It is the job of the petrol blender to produce a knock-free fuel. So the blender needs a measure of a blended petrol's resistance to knocking. Branched chain alkanes burn more smoothly in an engine than straight chain alkanes. 2,2,4-trimethylpentane has a low tendency to auto-ignite when compressed and is given an octane number of 100. The unbranched chain alkane heptane knocks readily, even under mild compression. It is given an octane number of 0. Mixtures of these two alkanes are used to assign octane numbers to petrol blends. So if, under test conditions, a petrol blend knocks at the same compression as a mixture of 90 per cent 2,2,4-trimethylpentane and 10 per cent heptane, the octane number of the petrol will be 90.

> ✔ 2,2,4-trimethylpentane used to be known as iso-octane, which is why the scale is called **octane number** or **octane rating**.

Adding lead compounds to petrol

The advantage of high octane fuels is that they can be highly compressed, which gives more power per piston stroke and more efficient use of fuel. In the 1920s, it was discovered that adding small amounts of a certain lead compound to petrol significantly increased the octane number, a practice which was adopted by all the major petrol suppliers.

However, the use of lead in petrol to raise the octane number is now being phased out for two reasons, both of them connected to the pollution of the environment by lead discharged through exhausts. The first is that lead is a poison which accumulates in the bodies of humans and other animals. Evidence suggests that when children breathe in airborne lead, their IQ level is liable to be lowered, and for adults, their ability to concentrate is reduced. Lead in petrol remains a major source of airborne lead in the environment, but since the advent of unleaded petrol in the UK in 1986, its concentration has been reduced by 80 per cent. The second reason why leaded petrol is being phased out is that it inhibits the action of catalysts in catalytic converters, which are essential to reducing pollution from vehicle exhausts.

For more information on the volatility of petrol, see page 160.

BLENDING UNLEADED PETROL

IF LEAD IS NOT USED to improve octane number, an alternative way must be found. One solution is to dissolve into the blended petrol small straight-chain alkanes such as butane. The shorter the chain, the less likely is the mixture to auto-ignite. As the chain gets longer, so the tendency to auto-ignite increases and the octane number decreases. However, too many short chain alkanes with low boiling points increase the volatility of the petrol too much. This could lead to vapour lock (page 160), and it also increases the evaporation of hydrocarbons from the fuel tank and engine – yet another source of atmospheric pollution.

[Fig 8.8 **This child is at exhaust fume level**

Using branched chain alkanes is another way to raise the octane number of petrol. The more branched the chain, the higher its octane number. Branched chain alkanes are produced at the refinery by cracking and reforming reactions; more about this on page 151.

A third way is to add aromatic hydrocarbons. Some 40 per cent of the petrol used in the UK contains such additives. One of them is benzene, a known carcinogen (cancer-causing agent), which can make up to 5 per cent by volume of a petrol. Benzene is now being linked to childhood leukaemia, thought to be the major cause in some cases, and the level of benzene inside a car can be up to ten times higher than outside.

The octane number can also be improved by adding **oxygenates.** We first came across oxygenates on page 124. Oxygenates are partly oxidised fuels, which already contain oxygen in their molecules. Methanol (CH_3OH) has an octane number of 114 and ethanol (C_2H_5OH) 111, so they burn smoothly under high compression. Also, because they have an oxygen atom already in the molecule, when they are combusted they require less oxygen in the petrol–air mixture. So petrols containing oxygenates produce less carbon monoxide when burnt.

5 POLLUTION FROM VEHICLES

At the outset of this chapter, we pointed to the problem of vehicle emissions. Now we are going to look in more detail at the chemistry behind the pollution associated with the burning of hydrocarbon fuels, such as petrol in vehicle engines.

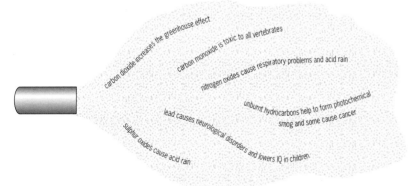

Fig 8.9 **Uncontrolled exhaust emissions cause increasing concern**

Carbon dioxide and the greenhouse effect

When a hydrocarbon completely combusts, it produces just two products: carbon dioxide and water. Both of these are referred to as **greenhouse gases**. But what are greenhouse gases and how did they get their name?

M Methanol and ethanol are members of the homologous series the alcohols.

(a) What is the general formula of this homologous series?

You can check your answer by looking at page 229.

(b) How would you expect the physical and chemical properties to change in this homologous series?

■ See question 5.

N Decane is one of the components of petrol. Write the equation for its complete combustion in air.

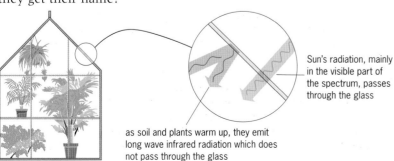

Sun's radiation, mainly in the visible part of the spectrum, passes through the glass

as soil and plants warm up, they emit long wave infrared radiation which does not pass through the glass

Fig 8.10 **Visible light from the Sun enters the greenhouse through the glass. Plants and soil absorb this energy and emit mainly long-wave infrared radiation. The long-wave infrared radiation cannot pass out through the glass, so the greenhouse warms up inside**

The Earth's surface is also warmed by radioactive decay from inside its crust. You can read more about this on page 40.

O (a) Which radiation transfers the most energy: infrared or visible light?

(b) Explain why the Earth does not radiate light in the visible region of the electromagnetic spectrum.
Hint: If you are not sure, look back at pages 48 to 49.

A **quantum** is the indivisible unit or packet of radiation energy (also called a photon). A molecule can exist only in certain fixed **vibrational energy levels**. When it absorbs a quantum of energy, it becomes excited and jumps to a higher energy level. In this level, it vibrates more. This is similar to electrons absorbing quanta of energy and moving to higher electron energy levels. See pages 132 and 152.

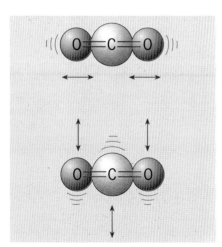

Fig 8.12 **Molecules of carbon dioxide absorb infrared radiation, increasing their vibrations**

The atmosphere of the Earth acts like glass in a greenhouse. For a start, the atmosphere reflects 30 per cent of the Sun's energy back into space. The remaining 70 per cent, which is mainly visible spectrum light, passes through the atmosphere to strike the Earth. While some of this energy is used by plants for photosynthesis, and some is used to evaporate water from the oceans, lakes and vegetation, most of it warms the surface of the planet. The warm Earth's surface in turn emits its own radiation, and this is where certain gases in the atmosphere act like greenhouse glass. The energy radiated by the Earth's surface is in the long-wave infrared (IR) region of the spectrum. The greenhouse gases absorb this IR radiation, and their molecules become excited.

Two of the most important greenhouse gases are water and carbon dioxide. Their molecules absorb quanta of infrared radiation, which increases their vibration and thus promotes them to higher vibrational energy levels. When they fall back to a lower vibrational energy level, they radiate these quanta of energy in all directions. Some of this energy warms the atmosphere, but the rest is transmitted back to the Earth's surface. This is the greenhouse effect.

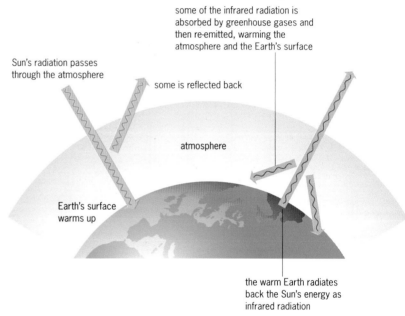

Fig 8.11 **The Sun's visible radiation passes through the atmosphere to strike the Earth. The Earth warms up and emits infrared radiation. Some of this is trapped by the greenhouse gases, as shown**

Why we need the greenhouse effect in moderation

If carbon dioxide and water were not present in the atmosphere, the Earth would be many degrees cooler. We only have to look at our two closest planetary neighbours to see the effect of greenhouse gases. Venus has an extremely dense atmosphere. It is 96 per cent carbon dioxide and keeps the temperature on Venus to a scorching 450 °C. The atmosphere of Mars has about the same proportion of carbon dioxide as the atmosphere on Venus, but is only 1 per cent as dense as the Earth's atmosphere. Though Mars is further from the Sun than Venus and you would expect Mars to be cooler, it has greater temperature fluctuations and cools during its night to −80 °C because there are not enough carbon dioxide molecules to trap the infrared radiation.

Fig 8.13 **The extremely dense atmosphere seen here round Venus is mostly carbon dioxide, which keeps its surface roasting hot**

Fig 8.14 **Earth enjoys moderate temperatures due to the presence of greenhouse gases in its atmosphere**

Fig 8.15 **Mars has little atmosphere to prevent infrared radiation from escaping. The temperature of its surface is never greater than 40 °C and can plunge to −80 °C**

The greenhouse effect and global warming

There are about 2750 gigatonnes of carbon dioxide in the Earth's atmosphere, but its concentration in air is small at 0.0355 per cent, or 355 parts per million (p.p.m.) by volume. We know from analysing the air trapped in polar-ice cores that 250 years ago, at the beginning of the Industrial Revolution, there were about 280 ppm of carbon dioxide. Most of the increase has occurred in the last 40 years. This is clearly shown by Fig 8.16, which is a graph of readings taken by the Mauna Loa Observatory in Hawaii.

P The Earth is in an orbit between those of Mars and Venus, and it has a similar origin. When the atmosphere of Mars and Venus have such a high percentage of CO_2, suggest why the Earth has as little as 0.0355 per cent?

A gigatonne (Gt) is 10^9 tonnes.

Q Each year there is a seasonal variation in carbon dioxide concentration.

(a) What causes the troughs and during which season of the year does a trough occur?

(b) What causes the peaks and in what season?

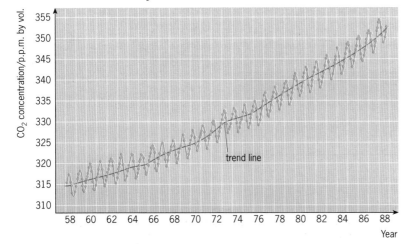

Fig 8.16 **The readings taken by the Mauna Loa Observatory, Hawaii, show clearly the trend of increasing carbon dioxide concentration in the atmosphere**

At the present time, the rate of increase in carbon dioxide is about 1 ppm per year, which means that 8 Gt of the gas is added to the atmosphere. However, more than 25 Gt of carbon dioxide is produced each year, much of it due to the burning of fossil fuels for electricity generation or transport. So, where is all the carbon dioxide going? Of course, some is removed by plants during photosynthesis, and a lot more dissolves in the oceans, lakes and waterways, but there is still much uncertainty as to where the remainder ends up.

Many geoscientists firmly believe that adding such large quantities of carbon dioxide to the atmosphere must contribute to the warming of the Earth. If this happens, sea levels will rise and weather patterns throughout the world will be altered. In 1992, an Earth Summit was held in Rio de Janeiro in Brazil, and the world's

Something which removes carbon in the form of carbon dioxide is known as a **sink**. So plants and open waters are sinks for carbon. Crude oil is another sink for carbon, and so are the bodies of animals. The amount of time carbon spends in a sink is known as the **residence time**.

?

R (a) What carbon dioxide emission targets is the UK currently working towards?

(b) There are more than 400 million cars in the world today. Assume that petrol consists only of octane, which has a density of $0.7\,g/cm^3$.
(i) What is the mass of $1\,dm^3$ of petrol?
(ii) Write the equation for the complete combustion of octane. Check your answer on page 132.
(iii) What mass of CO_2 is produced by burning $1\,dm^3$ of petrol?
(iv) How many tonnes of carbon dioxide are produced daily if 400 million cars use $1\,dm^3$ of fuel a day?

Hint: You may need to look at pages 4 to 8 to remind yourself of work on moles and equations.

first climate treaty was hammered out by more than 150 nations. This treaty committed the industrialised countries to reduce their greenhouse-gas emissions to 1990 levels by the year 2000.

In 1994, the nations met again to review progress and it was agreed that in order to stabilise the atmosphere, more ambitious targets would have to be set in the years after 2000. So far, there is no agreement as to what these targets should be, or by when they should be achieved. At the same time, carbon dioxide emissions are increasing yearly as the developing countries start to industrialise on a large scale, generate more electricity and use more hydrocarbon-driven transport.

The 1992 Earth Summit treaty and the consensus of the 1994 meeting suffered a severe setback in October 1997 when the USA announced that its aim would be to stabilise its emissions at 1990 levels by 2013, with reductions of 5 per cent per year thereafter. The USA is the biggest emitter of greenhouse gases, accounting for some 22 per cent of the world's total emissions, so a further delay of 13 years is of considerable significance.

Other greenhouse gases

Carbon dioxide is not the most potent greenhouse gas. If its concentration in the Earth's atmosphere were to double, the effect would probably be an increase in temperature of 1.5–4.5 °C. However, the concentration in the atmosphere of hydrocarbons such as methane, chlorofluorocarbons (CFCs), dinitrogen oxide (N_2O) and ozone (O_3) are also increasing due to human activity, and these strongly absorb infrared radiation. Clearly, the build-up of all greenhouse gases needs careful monitoring and evaluation.

✔

Even a 1°C rise in global temperature would produce unpredictable and possibly devastating climate changes.

Table 8.4 **Global warming potentials of some atmospheric gases. (Data taken from the Intergovernmental Panel on Climate Change: 1992 Supplement)**

Gas	Global warming potential
CO_2	1
CH_4	11
N_2O	270
CFC12	7100

METHANE GALORE

METHANE-PRODUCING BACTERIA decompose carbohydrates, such as glucose and cellulose, into CH_4 and CO_2, which are discharged into the atmosphere. We know from analysing the air in polar ice cores that atmospheric methane is increasing. The process is **anaerobic**: it does not require oxygen, so it happens in bodies of stagnent water. From glucose:

$$C_6H_{12}O_6 \rightarrow 3CO_2(g) + 3CH_4(g)$$

For example, paddy fields produce large amounts of methane because the water and mud covering the rotting vegetation provides the right conditions for anaerobic bacteria to work. Cattle, too, produce enormous amounts of methane (each cow discharges about $500\,dm^3$ a day in belches from partly digested food in its gut). Even when methane reacts in the atmosphere, it produces mostly ozone, another greenhouse gas.

Fig 8.17(a) **The growing of rice contributes significantly to atmospheric methane**

MODELLING THE GLOBAL CLIMATE

Geoscientists do not agree on the contribution made by carbon dioxide to global warming. Some dispute that global warming has occurred at all. This makes it difficult for governments to act and it leaves the public confused. All predictions are based on models of how the climate will react to the increasing quantities of greenhouse gases.

As the Earth warms up, more water vapour will be released into the atmosphere. Because water is a potent greenhouse gas, will this warm the Earth? Or will increased cloud formation lead to global cooling? As carbon dioxide concentration increases, plants will probably photosynthesise more, thus removing extra carbon dioxide from the atmosphere. Tiny particles in the air, in particular sulphate particles, reflect solar radiation back into space, which leads to global cooling. (Sulphate particles arise mainly from the burning of sulphur in fuels.) The oil fires during the war in Kuwait,

and recent volcanic eruptions produced particles which caused global cooling. Any climate model must take account of such factors. Small wonder, then, that there is a heated debate over global warming.

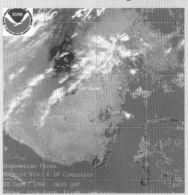

8.17(b) **Forests burning in Indonesia in 1997 set up dust clouds that covered the whole region. In this satellite image, the dust is pink and the fires are red.**

Carbon monoxide emissions and catalytic converters

In the UK, transport is responsible for 90 per cent of all emissions of carbon monoxide. When petrol does not have enough oxygen for complete combustion, carbon monoxide is produced. It is toxic to all vertebrates (and some invertebrates) and reacts quickly with haemoglobin in red blood cells to produce carboxyhaemoglobin. Once carbon monoxide has reacted with haemoglobin molecules, they will not carry oxygen. Mild symptoms of carbon monoxide poisoning include headaches, dizziness and tiredness. Severe symptoms are fainting and a possibly fatal coma.

The World Health Organisation guidelines for carbon monoxide are often exceeded in urban areas all over the world. For example, in New York when carbon monoxide concentrations exceed recommended levels, the incidence of heart attacks increases.

Catalysts can be used to reduce exhaust emissions. Platinum, for example, catalyses the oxidation of carbon monoxide:

> Remember: Catalysts are substances which alter the rate of a chemical reaction without becoming permanently involved in it. A catalyst works by providing an alternative reaction pathway with a lower activation energy. See page 127 and Chapter 17 for more information.

$$2CO(g) + O_2(g) \xrightarrow{\text{Pt catalyst}} 2CO_2(g)$$

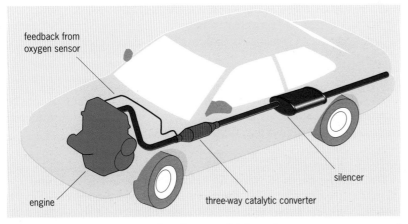

Fig 8.18 **The three-way catalytic converter is sited near the engine so that it warms up quickly. An oxygen sensor monitors the oxygen flowing through the exhaust system, and this feeds back to control the fuel–air mixture entering the engine. Too little oxygen flowing over the catalyst slows down oxidation of carbon monoxide and unburnt hydrocarbons**

A catalytic converter is fitted to a vehicle exhaust system to speed up this reaction (see Fig 8.18). It is sited near the engine so that it heats up quickly, because platinum does not start catalysing until its

S Why is a very large surface area required in a catalytic converter?

temperature is 240 °C. This temperature is reduced to about 150 °C when platinum is mixed with rhodium. The mixture of platinum and rhodium is known as a three-way catalyst, because, in addition to catalysing the oxidation of carbon dioxide, it catalyses two other reactions involving emission pollutants. Only 1–2 g of each element is used, but because they are coated onto a honeycomb filter of aluminium oxide, the surface area of the catalyst is equivalent to that of two football pitches.

Fig 8.19(a) **The catalytic converter unit**

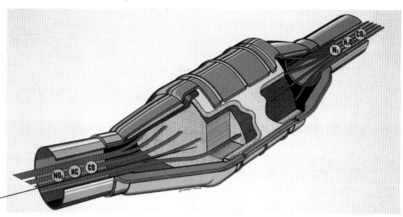

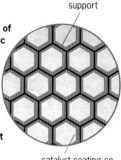

Fig 8.19(b) **Cutaway of a three-way catalytic converter showing the honeycomb filter. The gases enter the filter where a mixture of platinum and rhodium catalyses reactions of exhaust gases to remove pollutants**

support

catalyst coating on honeycomb support

Unburnt hydrocarbons C_xH_y and catalytic converters

When there is too little oxygen in a petrol engine, unburnt hydrocarbons are present in the exhaust emissions together with carbon monoxide. Also, volatile hydrocarbons, such as butane, evaporate from the petrol tank on a warm day when a vehicle is stationary. There is increasing concern about volatile organic compounds (VOCs), especially those in the environment. In the UK, almost 40 per cent are due to fuel evaporation and exhaust emissions. Long-term exposure to hydrocarbon emissions can impair lung function, while even-short term exposure can irritate the lung lining. Also, some VOCs such as benzene are known carcinogens.

T On a car journey, when are exhaust emissions of carbon monoxide and C_xH_y likely to be greatest?

MINIMISING HYDROCARBON EVAPORATION

Evaporation of hydrocarbons can occur at any time from the blending of petrol at the refinery to the refuelling of a vehicle at a petrol pump. The UK is now well on the way to introducing a closed system for the loading and transport of petrol, so that all hydrocarbon vapours are trapped and recycled before they escape. Hydrocarbon vapours still escape at the petrol pump, almost always because of a poor seal between the tank and the nozzle.

One way to reduce refuelling emissions and evaporation from the petrol tank is to use activated charcoal. The charcoal is contained in a large canister fitted to the air vent of the fuel tank, where it absorbs 90 per cent of hydrocarbon emissions while the vehicle is standing. When the vehicle is moving, air flow over the charcoal returns the hydrocarbons to the tank and reactivates the charcoal.

The platinum in a converter catalyses the oxidation of C_xH_y in the exhaust emissions. This is the second way in which pollutants are removed in a three-way catalytic converter:

$$C_xH_y \xrightarrow{\text{O}_2,\ \text{Pt catalyst}} CO_2 + H_2O$$

The catalyst needs to warm up before it becomes effective, and it is during cold starts that most emissions of exhaust hydrocarbons occur. Enough oxygen is also required through the exhaust to oxidise C_xH_y and carbon monoxide. For this reason, an oxygen sensor is fitted just before the catalytic converter to feed back information about oxygen concentration to the vehicle's fuel injection system.

U (a) Write a balanced equation for the oxidation of benzene (C_6H_6).

(b) What environmental problem is worsened by the oxidation of carbon monoxide and C_xH_y?

Oxides of nitrogen and catalytic converters

Air contains mostly nitrogen. Under normal conditions, nitrogen is very unreactive. However, a petrol engine reaches temperatures of 1000 °C, and this supplies enough energy to split the very strong triple bond in nitrogen. Nitrogen then reacts with oxygen to form nitrogen oxides (NO_x) – mainly nitrogen monoxide (NO).

NO can be further oxidised in the air to give nitrogen dioxide (NO_2). While NO is colourless, NO_2 is brown, and when the atmospheric conditions allow, this can build up as a brown haze in large cities. NO_2 contributes to acid rain, reacting with water to form nitrous and nitric acids:

$$2NO_2(g) + H_2O(l) \longrightarrow HNO_2(aq) + HNO_3(aq)$$

NO_2 also catalyses the oxidation of sulphur dioxide in the atmosphere (see page 170) and cause respiratory diseases such as bronchitis. The Opener to this chapter mentions the unusual build-up of nitrogen dioxide in London in December 1991. This far exceeded World Health Organisation guidelines and was linked to 160 more deaths than were expected at that time of the year.

The third way in which a three-way catalytic converter works is to reduce NO_x back to nitrogen and oxygen, this time using a rhodium (Rh) catalyst:

$$2NO_x(g) \xrightarrow{\text{Rh catalyst}} N_2(g) + xO_2(g)$$

Too much oxygen passing from the engine into the catalytic converter reduces the efficiency of this reaction. So, getting the correct fuel–air mixture is critical to the functioning of a catalytic converter. Hence the need for an oxygen sensor in the exhaust system.

Heterogeneous catalysis and catalyst poisoning

Just two tanks of leaded petrol are enough to render a catalytic converter useless. This is called **catalyst poisoning**.

The catalysts in converters are always solids, and the reactants are always gases. So the catalysts are said to be **heterogeneous**, because they are in a different physical state to the reactants. The reactants are **adsorbed** onto the catalyst surface, which means they weakly bond to it. So lead poisons the catalyst because it is adsorbed more strongly than the reactant molecules. (It was for this reason that the US government made it illegal to use leaded petrol in cars fitted with catalytic converters, and required that the opening to the petrol tank in these cars was made too small to take a leaded-petrol nozzle.)

> **V** Write a balanced equation for the formation of NO.

> The chemical reactions that lead to the production of acid rain are complicated and beyond the scope of this book. This account is a much simplified one.

> **W** Dinitrogen oxide (N_2O) is also formed in vehicle engines. This is non-toxic to humans and is used as an anaesthetic; one of its names is laughing gas. Seven per cent of N_2O in the atmosphere comes from vehicle exhausts. What major environmental problem is linked to a build-up of N_2O? To check your answer, look at Table 8.4, page 166.

■ See question 5.

> The optimum ratio of air to petrol in most car engines is 15:1. Less air gives a *rich* mixture, which happens when the choke is operated. Some engines are called *lean burn* because the ratio of air to petrol is about 18:1. Lean-burn engines produce less CO and NO_x and give better fuel economy because less petrol is used for each cylinder firing. However, they often produce more C_xH_y.

> **Adsorb** is the word used when reactants are weakly bonded to a surface. Do not confuse this with **absorb**, used for substances which enter the material like a sponge soaking up water.

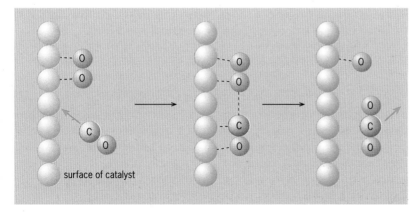

Fig 8.20 **The catalytic oxidation of carbon monoxide. CO molecules and O_2 molecules form weak bonds on the catalyst surface. The adsorbed molecules are held close together and their internal covalent bonds weaken, allowing a reaction with a lower activation energy**

✔

H$_2$SO$_3$ is sulphurous acid. It is a weak acid and only exists in dilute solution.

?

X Explain why NO$_2$ is acting as a catalyst in these two reactions.

SO$_2$(g) + NO$_2$(g) $\longrightarrow$ SO$_3$(g) + NO(g)

NO(g) + $\frac{1}{2}$O$_2$(g) $\longrightarrow$ NO$_2$(g)

Fig 8.21 **These statues on the outside of Exeter Cathedral show the effects of acid rain**

✔

NO$_2$ is really a secondary pollutant, as NO is the principal gas coming from the exhaust. It is oxidised to NO$_2$ in the atmosphere.

$$X \overset{\bullet}{\underset{\bullet}{\text{—}}} Y \longrightarrow X^+ + {}^{\bullet\bullet}Y^-$$

Fig 8.22 **Heterolytic fission**

Sulphur oxides and acid rain

Most emissions of the sulphur oxides are due to the burning of sulphur in fossil fuels. Sulphur dioxide is produced in large quantities by the reaction:

$$S \text{ (in fuel)} + O_2(g) \longrightarrow SO_2(g)$$

and can be further oxidised to sulphur trioxide in the atmosphere:

$$2SO_2(g) + O_2(g) \longrightarrow 2SO_3$$

Nitrogen dioxide can act as a catalyst in this reaction, which is another reason why nitrogen dioxide emissions should be reduced where possible.

Both SO$_2$ and SO$_3$ react with water in the atmosphere to form acidic solutions:

$$SO_2(g) + H_2O(l) \longrightarrow H_2SO_3(aq)$$
$$SO_3(g) + H_2O(l) \longrightarrow H_2SO_4(aq)$$

Dilute solutions of sulphuric acid in rainwater are the main cause of acid rain. (NO$_x$ in the atmosphere also contributes to acid rain by forming nitrous and nitric acid solutions – see page 169.)

Acid rain has had serious and far-reaching consequences, killing trees in forests and lowering the pH in lakes so that fish die. Burning petrol and diesel in vehicle engines is not the main contributor to sulphur dioxide in the atmosphere, accounting for only 2 per cent of emissions in the UK. By far the worst culprit is the burning of coal in power stations (see Chapter 22.)

Photochemical smog

The word 'smog' was first used to describe the combination of smoke, fog and sulphur dioxide which used to build up in London and cause hundreds of extra deaths. The Clean Air Act of 1956 made this type of smog a thing of the past in the UK. However, photochemical smog caused by exhaust emissions from vehicles is a problem in many urban areas. Los Angeles and Athens are two infamous examples. The atmosphere around a large city forms a vast mixing bowl for chemical reactions, and sorting out just what causes photochemical smog has not been easy. Even now, it is not fully understood.

Light and the formation of secondary pollutants

Any pollutant in an exhaust emission is called a **primary pollutant**. A **secondary pollutant** is formed in air as a result of the chemical reactions of a primary pollutant. Sunlight supplies the energy to initiate the reactions which form the secondary pollutants ozone (O$_3$) and organic nitrates. Reactions in which the energy is supplied by light are called **photochemical reactions**.

NO$_2$ absorbs photons of ultraviolet light which supply the energy (*hf*) to split one of the covalent bonds holding N and O together:

$$NO_2(g) \xrightarrow{hf} NO(g) + O(g)$$

The splitting of the covalent bond is sometimes called **bond fission**. There are two ways in which a covalent bond can split: heterolytic fission and homolytic fission. In **heterolytic fission** (Fig 8.22), both electrons from the bond go to one atom. The atom which gains an electron becomes negatively charged, while the atom which loses an electron becomes positively charged.

In **homolytic** fission (Fig 8.23), when the bond breaks the bonding pair of electrons are equally shared, so that each atom in the bond gets one electron. The atoms are not charged because the number of protons is balanced by the number of electrons.

Free radicals result from homolytic fission. Free radicals are species with an unpaired electron which often makes them highly reactive. So, in our example, X and Y are both free radicals. The unpaired electron on a free radical can be shown by a raised dot, X•.

Take the homolytic fission of NO_2 by light:

Both NO and O are free radicals. In fact, atomic oxygen has two unpaired electrons and is called a **diradical**:

Oxygen atoms are very reactive and one of their reactions involves the production of ozone (O_3):

$$O(g) + O_2(g) \longrightarrow O_3(g)$$

The presence of ozone in the stratosphere is essential to prevent too much ultraviolet light penetrating to the lower atmosphere (troposphere). But its build-up close to the Earth is dangerous as it causes respiratory problems and in high concentrations produces coughing and nausea. It is also involved in a series of other reactions with unburnt hydrocarbons, producing yet more ozone and a group of very unpleasant molecules called organic nitrates (Fig 8.24).

Solutions to vehicle pollution

Particularly through the development of catalytic converters, chemists have reduced exhaust emissions of some pollutants. Catalysts need to heat up before they can start to operate, so emissions on short journeys or in cold weather are particularly high. Because of the tremendous problems with vehicle pollution in Los Angeles, Californian legislation ruled that from 1998, 2 per cent of cars sold had to be zero emission vehicles (ZEVs), rising to 10 per cent by 2003. The USA has led the way in reducing emissions and up to now US manufacturers have responded. ZEV really means an electric car, but is this truly zero emission when fossil fuels are burnt to provide the electricity to charge up the batteries?

People need to change their attitude to the car. Unless personal car use is reduced, we shall have to continue to accept growing deterioration of the environment.

Fig 8.23 **Homolytic fission**

✔ 'Hetero' comes from the Greek word for 'different'. 'Homo' is from the Greek for 'same'.

■ See question 8.

?

Y Use s,p,d notation to write the full electron configuration of an oxygen atom.
If you are not sure how to do this, look back at page 62.
Why do you think it has two unpaired electrons?

For more information about ozone in the stratosphere, see page 219.

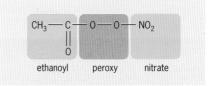

ethanoyl   peroxy   nitrate

Fig 8.24 **The organic nitrate peroxyethanoyl nitrate (often called PAN after its traditional name peroxyacetyl nitrate). PAN causes breathing difficulties and makes eyes water. It also damages plants**

Fig 8.25 **The cycle path and tramway in Amsterdam, encourage people to leave their cars at home**

Fig 8.26 **The Supertram is one way in which Sheffield is making public transport more attractive**

SUMMARY

After studying this chapter, you should know the following.

■ Alkanes are named systematically using IUPAC conventions.

■ A homologous series is a group of compounds which have similar chemical properties, and gradually changing physical properties. They can be represented by a general formula.

■ Trends in melting point, boiling point and volatility can be explained by the weak intermolecular forces called induced dipole–induced dipole forces (a van der Waals force).

■ As the chain length of alkanes increases, so does the number of electrons, which increases the strength of the induced dipole–induced dipole forces.

■ Branching reduces the surface area over which induced dipole–induced dipole forces can act.

■ Alkanes are non-polar molecules, so do not react with polar reagents.

■ Complete combustion of alkanes produces CO_2 and H_2O.

■ Branched chain alkanes combust smoothly under pressure in a petrol engine and have high octane numbers.

■ Lead compounds can be added to petrol to increase its octane number, but emissions of airborne lead are toxic and also poison the catalysts in a catalytic converter.

■ CO_2 in the atmosphere is an important greenhouse gas. Increasing its concentration could lead to global warming.

■ Exhaust emissions include CO, unburnt hydrocarbons and NO_x. Three-way catalytic converters reduce the concentrations of these pollutants but need to heat up before they can start operating.

■ Heterogeneous catalysts are in a different physical state to the reactants.

■ SO_2 and SO_3, produced when sulphur-containing fossil fuels are burnt, are the main cause of acid rain.

■ Free radicals are produced by the homolytic fission of covalent bonds, for which light can provide the energy.

■ Ozone is a secondary pollutant.

■ Photochemical smog is produced by the interaction of sunlight with vehicle exhaust emissions.

QUESTIONS

1 Name the following compounds:

(a)
$$CH_3-CH_2-\underset{\underset{CH_3}{|}}{CH}-CH_3$$

(b)
$$CH_3-CH_2-\underset{\underset{CH_3}{|}}{CH_2}$$

(c)
$$CH_3-CH_2-\underset{\underset{CH_3}{|}}{\overset{\overset{CH_3}{|}}{C}}-CH_3$$

(d)
$$CH_3-CH_2-\underset{\underset{CH_2-CH_3}{|}}{CH}-CH_2-CH_3$$

(e)
$$CH_3-CH_2-CH_2-\underset{\underset{CH_3}{|}}{\overset{\overset{CH_2-CH_3}{|}}{C}}-CH_2-CH_3$$

2 Draw the structural formulas of

a) 3-methylhexane,

b) 2,2-dimethylpentane,

c) 3-ethylheptane,

d) 3-ethyl-2-methylpentane,

e) 2,2,3-trimethylpentane.

3 Alkanes are members of a homologous series. Give three characteristics of members of a homologous series.

4

a) Explain how intermolecular forces arise between alkanes.

b) Explain why boiling points increase as carbon chain length increases in straight chain alkanes.

c) Draw the displayed formula of three isomers with the molecular formula C_5H_{12}, and name them.

d) Explain the effect of branching on the boiling point of the three isomers you have drawn.

5 MTBE is an oxygenate which is added to petrol. It has the following structural formula:

$$CH_3-\overset{\overset{\displaystyle CH_3}{|}}{\underset{\underset{\displaystyle CH_3}{|}}{C}}-O-CH_3$$

a) What is the molecular formula of MTBE?

MTBE belongs to the homologous series ethers and has a functional group C–O–C.

b) Explain the meaning of the terms *homologous series* and *functional group*.

Oxygenates are fuels with oxygen atoms in their molecules, which means they require less oxygen to combust completely.

c) Write an equation for the complete combustion of MTBE.

MTBE has a high octane rating.

d) What is the advantage of a high-octane component in petrol?

e) Name three major pollutants from petrol-engine exhaust and explain, using balanced equations, how three-way catalytic converters remove these pollutants.

Ozone is a secondary pollutant from exhaust emissions.

f) Explain what is meant by the term *secondary pollutant*.

g) Show, using equations, how ozone arises in the lower atmosphere.

h) Name one other secondary pollutant present in photochemical smog.

Lead compounds in petrol are still used in some petrol blends to increase octane rating.

i) What are the two main reasons for phasing out lead in petrol?

6

a) Explain **briefly** the 'greenhouse effect' and how carbon dioxide contributes to it. Suggest **two** major ways in which humankind could act to reduce the build-up of carbon dioxide in the atmosphere.

b) Give the names of **two** other gases that might be implicated in causing the 'greenhouse effect'.

c) What are the **two** main chemical causes of 'acid rain'? How do the substances involved get into the atmosphere?

[AEB 1996 Chemistry General Paper 3, Specimen Paper, q.8]

7 The graph in Fig 8.Q7 shows a plot of the monthly average concentration $[CO_2]_m$, of carbon dioxide in the atmosphere for a number of years at an observatory in the Northern Hemisphere.

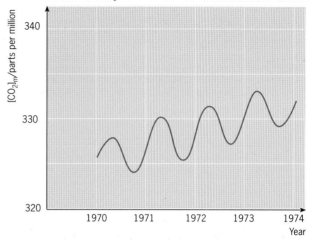

Fig 8.Q7

a)　(i) Identify the variation shown each year in the monthly average concentration of carbon dioxide.
　　(ii) Explain this variation.

b) Suggest **two** regions of the Earth where you would expect the magnitude of the annual variation in $[CO_2]_m$ to be smaller than that shown in the graph.

In each case, state why you would expect a smaller annual variation.

c)　(i) State the longer term trend of $[CO_2]_m$ shown by the graph, and suggest **two** reasons for the trend.
　　(ii) Explain why many scientists are concerned about this longer term trend.

[UCLES 1994 Modular Sciences: Environmental Chemistry Specimen Paper, Section A, q.1]

8

a) Draw dot-and-cross diagrams for the following species and state which of them are free radicals:
　(i) Cl
　(ii) OH
　(iii) H_2O
　(iv) NO_2
　(v) O_3
　(vi) CH_3

b) Explain what is meant by
　(i) homolytic fission,
　(ii) photochemical reaction.

THE DIESEL ENGINE – HOW IS IT DIFFERENT?

The diesel engine was invented by Rudolph Diesel, a German engineer, who patented his idea in 1892. Diesel engines were used first as generators and marine engines, and it was not until 1922 that they appeared in cars.

Diesel fuel is produced from a higher boiling point fraction of crude oil than that used for petrol. It normally contains C_{16} to C_{20} hydrocarbon molecules, but slow-speed diesel engines of the type fitted in large ships burn hydrocarbons up to C_{25}. As with petrol, diesel fuel is composed mostly of alkanes.

1

a) What is the molecular formula of hexadecane, an alkane molecule which contains 16 carbon atoms?

b) What is meant by *higher boiling point fraction*?

c) In what crude oil fraction would you find the molecule $C_{20}H_{42}$? (See Table 7.3, page 149)

d) Explain, using the concept of intermolecular forces and instantaneous dipoles, why straight chain alkanes in petrol have a lower boiling point than straight chain alkanes in diesel fuel.

While everything is done to eliminate auto-ignition in the petrol engine, it is fundamental to the operation of the diesel engine, which has no spark plugs. The energy for the combustion of the fuel–air mixture is supplied by compressing air in each cylinder by 20:1 (ie 1 dm^3 of air is compressed to 50 cm^3). At the top of the compression stroke, diesel fuel is injected into the cylinder and the high temperature of the compressed-air charge provides the activation energy to detonate the fuel.

2

a) In a petrol engine, what provides the activation energy to detonate the petrol–air mixture?

b) Why must diesel engines be built more strongly than petrol engines?

c) Why is auto-ignition a big disadvantage in petrol engines?

d) What name is given to the scale which measures petrol's ability to auto-ignite?

e) Why are lead compounds added to some petrol blends?

f) What are the environmental consequences of leaded fuels?

Diesel engines are more efficient than petrol engines because at least 90 per cent of the fuel is burnt, compared with about 70 per cent in petrol engines. This reduces carbon monoxide emission to less than that of a petrol engine fitted with a catalytic converter, although hydrocarbon emissions tend to be about the same. Because combustion is more efficient, the fuel consumption of a diesel engine is lower than that of a comparable petrol engine.

3

a) Why is it important to burn fuel efficiently?

b) Explain how emissions of CO occur.

c) How does a catalytic converter reduce CO emissions?

The sulphur content of diesel fuel is still a problem, although refineries are gradually reducing it. Also, more nitrogen oxides are produced from diesel-driven vehicles than from petrol-driven vehicles with catalytic converters. The other emissions from diesel-engine exhausts are carbon particles and aromatic compounds. The technology to reduce carbon particles is already far advanced, so if the presence of aromatic compounds could be reduced substantially, the diesel engine would have much more to recommend it.

4

a) What environmental problem is caused by sulphur in fuels? Include balanced chemical equations in your answer.

b) Explain how nitrogen oxides are produced in diesel exhaust emissions.

c) What are the environmental consequences of NO_x?

d) How do catalytic converters reduce emissions of NO_x?

e) What health hazards are associated with aromatic compounds in exhaust emissions?

Whatever fuel is used, some people are beginning to question whether the disadvantages of the car outweigh the advantages.

5

a) What are the advantages of car use?

b) Car exhaust emissions are a major problem in urban areas. How might car use in these areas be discouraged?

Hint: Positive as well as negative measures should be considered.

c) Comment on the statement: Cars produce less emissions per mile on long journeys than on short journeys, so they should not be used for very short journeys.

ALKANES AND THE CAR ENGINE

Use the map below to understand the connection between the concepts, chemicals and processes associated with the alkanes, and to see how they are linked to information in other chapters. Review those that are on the syllabus you are following or any that you are unsure of.

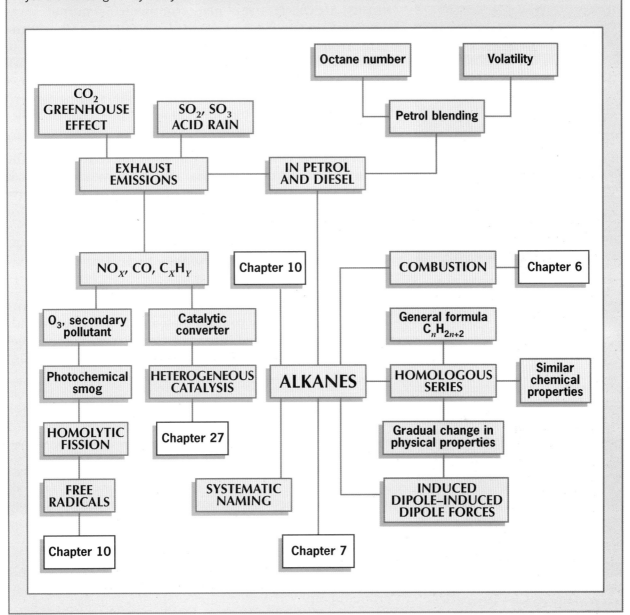

Separating and identifying substances

Herbal medicine has always been the norm in China and is gaining greater acceptance in the West

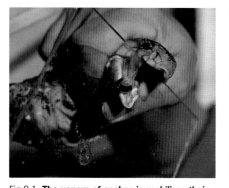

Fig 9.1 **The venom of snakes immobilises their prey by dramatically reducing blood pressure. This discovery has already led to greater understanding of how to treat high blood pressure, a potentially fatal condition**

THE FIRST RECORDED USE of plants for medicinal purposes was found on Egyptian papyrus dated about 1500 BC. All over the world, from tribal medicine in Africa to folk remedies in Britain, many thousands of plants have been used to cure all sorts of ailments. Often, this knowledge has been handed down by word of mouth, and there is now increasing concern that much of it will be lost for ever as cultures change, tribes disperse and Western medicines dominate.

The bark of the cinchona tree was used for centuries by the people of Peru to treat malaria, and we now know that it contains the anti-malarial drug quinine. The Chinese use herbal medicines extensively: one of their herbal cures for asthma has been shown to contain ephedrine, which is used in Western medicine to enlarge the air passages of the lungs. Even aspirin has its origins in willow bark.

Interest in tribal and folk remedies has been reawakened since the 1960s. Chemists investigate thousands of plants each year to see if they contain biologically active chemicals that might be developed into medicinal drugs. There is real hope that newly documented remedies will lead to drugs which treat cancer, heart disease and AIDS.

Introduction

Many organic chemicals come from crude oil; many come from plants and animals; and others are made synthetically. Chemists use separation techniques to isolate these substances followed by analytical techniques to find out their chemical structure. The methods chemists use to identify the formulas of these organic compounds and determine their structures are the subject of this chapter.

1 CHROMATOGRAPHY

Chromatography is a method of separating and identifying the components of a mixture. (The name is derived from two Greek words, *chroma* for colour and *graphe* for writing.) The technique was discovered and developed by a Russian botanist, Mikhail Tswett, who first reported it in 1903. He was using powdered calcium carbonate packed into a tube to separate coloured plant pigments called chlorophylls. Before this, chemists mainly used crystallisation techniques to separate and purify substances. Today, chromatography in one form or another is used in nearly all chemical laboratories, not just to separate and purify, but also to analyse substances, most of which are colourless.

All forms of chromatography operate on the same principle. The mixture is introduced into two different phases, one remaining stationary while the other flows over it. The phases are known respectively as the **stationary phase** and the **mobile phase**. The components of the mixture distribute themselves differently between the two phases, according to their affinity for each phase.

There are two main types of chromatography: **partition chromatography** and **adsorption chromatography**.

Partition chromatography

In partition chromatography, the stationary phase is a non-volatile liquid film held on an inert solid surface. The mobile phase is a liquid or gas. The components to be separated distribute themselves between the two phases according to how soluble they are in each.

Adsorption chromatography

In adsorption chromatography, the stationary phase is a solid and the mobile phase is a liquid or gas. The components to be separated are **adsorbed** on (bonded to) the solid surface of the stationary phase. Those that are only weakly adsorbed travel faster in the mobile phase than those that are strongly adsorbed.

Paper chromatography

Chromatography using paper is the one you are probably most familiar with. It is an example of partition chromatography (Fig 9.2). The stationary phase is water adsorbed on the cellulose fibres of the paper. The mobile phase is another liquid solvent.

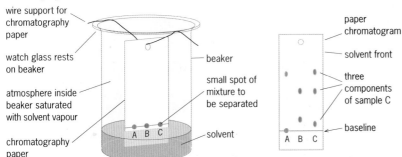

wire support for chromatography paper

watch glass rests on beaker

atmosphere inside beaker saturated with solvent vapour

chromatography paper

beaker

small spot of mixture to be separated

solvent

A B C

paper chromatogram

solvent front

three components of sample C

baseline

A B C

Fig 9.2 **The principle of paper chromatography**

The sample is spotted along a base-line drawn in pencil on the paper (Fig 9.2). When the spots are dry, the paper is placed in the solvent, which rises up the paper, taking the components of the sample with it. As they travel up the paper, the components separate according to their different solubilities in the mobile and stationary phases. When the **solvent front** (the leading edge of the solvent) is almost at the top of the paper, the **chromatogram** is taken out and dried (Fig 9.2). If the components are colourless, the chromatogram needs to be **developed** to make them visible. Sometimes, just heating the chromatogram does this. If not, some other method, such as exposure to ultraviolet light, is used.

Components can be identified by the distances they have travelled up the paper compared with the distance travelled by the solvent front. This is known as the **retention ratio R_f**:

$$R_f = \frac{\text{distance moved by component from base-line}}{\text{distance moved by solvent front from base-line}}$$

To obtain the separated components as samples, their spots are cut out and they are dissolved off in solvents.

A **phase** is a homogeneous part of a system that is physically distinct. It is separated from the other parts by a boundary surface. Petrol is a mixture but it is in one phase, as is a solution of sodium chloride in water. But petrol and water form two physically distinct phases because they do not mix. You can read more about phases on page 104.

Adsorption of reactants by heterogeneous catalysts is a mechanism by which reactions are speeded up. You can read about this on page 169.

A Compound **Y** is very soluble in the mobile phase and almost insoluble in the stationary phase. Compound **X** has greater solubility in the stationary phase than in the mobile phase. Which will travel further during chromatography?

A **chromatogram** is the record of a separation of components achieved through chromatography.

B Look at Fig 9.2.
(a) Why is the base-line drawn in pencil?

(b) Why is the air inside the beaker saturated with solvent vapour before the chromatography paper is put in?

(c) Calculate the R_f values for the two components in sample **B**.

(d) Explain why one of the components in sample **A** has not risen off the base-line.

COLUMN CHROMATOGRAPHY

THIS WAS THE FIRST WAY in which chromatography was carried out, and it is still the simplest. When Tswett was separating plant pigments, he used a column of calcium carbonate powder as the stationary phase, and a hydrocarbon liquid mixture as the mobile phase. He placed the sample on top of the column, where it made contact with the hydrocarbon mixture, which dissolved the pigments in the sample.

Tswett's arrangement is still used today. The column is kept topped up with fresh solvent which washes the pigment down through the inert solid stationary phase (usually aluminium oxide powder or silica gel). The components which are adsorbed most strongly by the stationary phase take the longest time to flow through the column.

Fig 9.3 **Modern column chromatography in operation**

When the components are coloured, they can be identified by eye. But, if colourless, other techniques are used: for example, some components fluoresce in ultraviolet light. Once separation is finished, the solvent is removed by evaporating it off.

Column chromatography in laboratories is usually used to separate minute quantities of mixtures, while in industry it is used in large-scale separation processes requiring columns several metres high.

High-performance liquid chromatography (HPLC)

The performance of column chromatography can be improved by using very fine powder as the stationary phase. In this case, gravity alone is not enough to force the mobile liquid phase through the column, and therefore high pressure must be applied. This is a very efficient process requiring short columns of between 10 and 30 cm in length. Many of the components separated by HPLC absorb ultraviolet light, so it is generally used to identify them.

HPLC has many applications, particularly for the separation and identification of non-volatile substances. Foodstuffs, for example can be checked for additives and contaminants. The detection of steroids in athletes' body fluids is another example.

Some chemist prefer to call this technique high-*pressure* liquid chromatography, but the abbreviation is the same: HPLC.

The solvent of the mobile phase is called the **eluant.** As each compound in the sample passes out of the bottom of the column we say it is **eluted.**

C Is column chromatography adsorption or partition chromatography?

Fig 9.4 **The main features of a gas–liquid chromatography apparatus**

D (a) Why does the liquid used in GLC need to have a high boiling point?

(b) Explain why GLC is an example of partition chromatography.

Gas–liquid chromatography (GLC)

An unreactive gas, such as nitrogen or helium, is used as the **carrier gas** (the mobile phase). The stationary phase consists of a liquid coating adsorbed on the particles of a finely powdered inert solid. The powder fills a coiled narrow-bore tube called a column. The temperature of the column is controlled by an oven. The arrangement is shown in Fig 9.4. Typically, the tube forming the column can be 5 to 10 m long, with a bore of 2 to 10 mm.

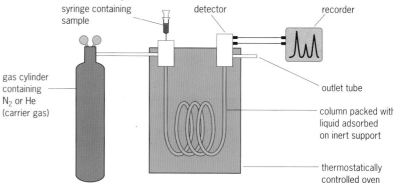

The vaporised sample is injected into the carrier gas as it streams into the column at an even rate. As the components of the sample are carried through the column, those which are more soluble in the stationary phase move at a slower rate. Volatile components are carried more quickly than non-volatile ones, which therefore have a greater opportunity to dissolve in the liquid stationary phase. So the volatile components emerge first from the column.

The time each component remains in the column is known as its **retention time**. This depends on such factors as the flow-rate of the carrier gas, the temperature of the oven, and the length and diameter of the column. Each retention time is characteristic of a particular component, allowing it to be separated and identified. The area under each peak displayed on the recorder is the measure of the amount of that component present. The relative amounts of components in a mixture can therefore be calculated, an operation now done by computer.

Gas–liquid chromatography is very sensitive and is capable of detecting and measuring minute amounts of substances. It has therefore become a standard method for detecting banned substances in sport, and for determining the amount of alcohol in a motorist's blood when it is close to the legal limit. When connected to a mass spectrometer, it is used to identify substances in foods and medicinal plants.

E A database of retention times is compiled for each GLC machine using known compounds. Why is it essential to keep the conditions constant after forming this database?

In GLC, a chromatogram is the record of the analysis displayed on a screen. In paper chromatography, it is the components themselves separated on the paper.

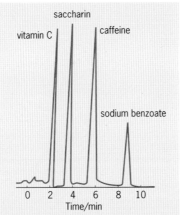

Fig 9.5 **A gas–liquid chromatogram of additives in a soft drink**

REVEALING THE SECRETS OF OLD MASTERS

WHEN YOU NEXT GO round an art gallery and look at the work of a great artist who perhaps lived four or five centuries ago, give some thought to its chemistry. Paint pigments provide the colour, but they don't stick to the canvas or wooden panel on their own. They need to be bound together and to the supporting surface. For some 5000 years before the Renaissance, artists mainly used egg yolk (called tempera) as the binding medium. Then, in the 1400s, Italian and Flemish artists started to switch to oils that dried, such as linseed, poppy or walnut oil, and this is where GLC comes in.

When a gallery wants to restore a painting, it is essential to know what binding medium the artist used. In the oils used, long chain fatty acids are present as esters (see pages 342 and 351) and these have characteristic retention times in a gas chromatograph. By performing GLC, the different oils used can be identified and then the same oils are mixed with pigments for restoring the picture.

Fig 9.6 **The Virgin and Child Embracing by Sassoferrato (1609–1685), during restoration of the painting**

Fig 9.7 **Chromatograms of known oils can be compared with the chromatogram of a tiny sample of paint removed from the picture to be restored to determine which drying oil the artist used. Shown here is the chromatograph of a paint sample from a picture painted about the year 1500**

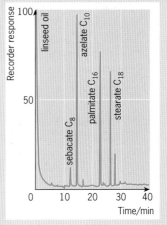

Thin-layer chromatography (TLC)

This is similar to paper chromatography, except that the stationary phase is a fine, inert powder, such as silica gel, which is made into a paste and spread in a thin, even layer over a plastic or glass plate. The layer of paste is then baked on to the plate. Spots of the mixture are applied near the bottom of the plate. As the solvent

Fig 9.8 **Thin layer chromatography of felt tip pen inks**

?

F Is TLC adsorption or partition chromatography?

See question 1. ■

rises by capillary action up through the spaces between the inert powder particles, the components of the mixture are carried up and separated. When the solvent is almost at the top of the plate, the plate is taken out and dried. R_f values can be obtained in the same way as for paper chromatography.

TLC has three advantages over paper chromatography: it is quicker, the results are more easily reproduced, and the separations are more efficient. The technique is used in industry to follow the course of a reaction by studying which components are present. The separated components can be retrieved by scraping off the spots on the stationary phase and dissolving them in a suitable solvent.

2 WORKING OUT THE FORMULA OF A COMPOUND

We have seen that chromatography provides a way of separating and purifying a mixture of compounds. The technique can even be used to identify compounds where the compounds have been analysed previously, so that characteristic properties, such as retention times, are known.

Although chromatography is a powerful tool in analysing compounds, it needs to be combined with other techniques to determine the formula of an unknown substance. We are now going to see how you can work out the formulas of completely unknown compounds, such as those that might be present in a medicinal herb.

Percentage compositions and empirical formulas

One very useful piece of information about any compound is its **percentage composition**. This means the percentage by mass of each element in the compound.

If you have just discovered what you think is a new compound, finding the percentage composition would be one of the first investigations you would carry out. You can either decompose a known mass of the compound into its constituent elements, or burn it in oxygen and weigh the products formed, such as carbon dioxide and water (called **combustion analysis**). The masses of any other elements present in the compound such as nitrogen and chlorine, are found by other means.

?

G Why is combustion analysis done mostly on organic compounds?
Hint: Think about the products formed.

H What are the empirical formulas of ethane C_2H_6 and ethanoic acid CH_3CO_2H?

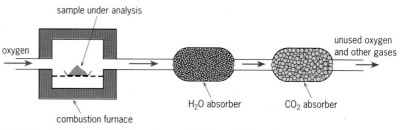

sample under analysis

oxygen

unused oxygen and other gases

H_2O absorber CO_2 absorber

combustion furnace

Fig 9.9 **Combustion analysis for carbon and hydrogen. A few milligrams of the compound being analysed are completely combusted. The carbon and hydrogen in the compound form respectively CO_2 and H_2O. The increased masses of the two absorbent materials are measured to give the masses of CO_2 and H_2O produced. Given that the mass of the original sample is known, the percentage composition can be calculated**

✔

Remember that the molecular formula tells you the number of atoms of each element in a molecule of a compound. See page 4.

Once the percentage composition is known, the **empirical formula** of a compound can be calculated. The empirical formula is the simplest whole-number ratio of the number of atoms of each element in a compound. For example, benzene has a molecular formula of C_6H_6, but its empirical formula is CH.

EXAMPLE

Q Combustion analysis shows that the compound which gives cinnamon its characteristic aroma has a percentage composition of 81.8 per cent carbon, 6.1 per cent hydrogen and 12.1 per cent oxygen. Calculate its empirical formula. (A_r: C = 12.0, H = 1.0, O = 16.0)

A The simplest way to deal with this problem is to imagine that you have 100.0 g of the compound so that the masses of the elements are easy to work out as shown below.

	Carbon	Hydrogen	Oxygen
Mass in grams:	81.8	6.1	12.1
Amount in moles:	$\frac{81.8}{12.0} = 6.8$	$\frac{6.1}{1.0} = 6.1$	$\frac{12.1}{16.0} = 0.756$
Simplest ratio: (Divide by the smallest number)	$\frac{6.82}{0.756} = 9.02$	$\frac{6.1}{0.756} = 8.1$	$\frac{0.756}{0.756} = 1.00$
Simplest whole-number ratio:	9	8	1

So its empirical formula is C_9H_8O

Another way of calculating the empirical formula from combustion analysis data is to use the actual masses of the different compounds produced, as shown in the next Example.

EXAMPLE

Q 0.100 g of a sugar, known to contain only carbon, hydrogen and oxygen, is completely combusted to give 0.147 g CO_2 and 0.0600 g H_2O. Calculate its empirical formula.

A First, we need to calculate the masses of C, H and O in the compound.

There are 12.0 g of C in 44.0 g CO_2
(Remember: 1 mol CO_2 = 12.0 + (16.0×2) g)

Therefore, mass of C in 0.147 g = $0.147 \times \frac{12.0}{44.0} = 0.0401$ g

There are 2.0 g H in 18.0 g H_2O (1 mol H_2O = (1.0×2) + 16.0 g)

Therefore, mass of H in 0.060 g = $0.060 \times \frac{2.0}{18.0} = 0.0067$ g

Since we now know the masses of C and H in 0.100 g of sugar, the rest of the mass must be due to O:

0.0401 + 0.0067 = 0.0468 g

Therefore, mass of O in 0.100 g = 0.100 − 0.0468 = 0.053 g

We can proceed now as we did in the previous Example:

	Carbon	Hydrogen	Oxygen
Mass in grams	0.040 1	0.006 7	0.053
Amount in moles	$\frac{0.040\,1}{12.0} = 0.003\,34$	$\frac{0.006\,7}{1.0} = 0.006\,7$	$\frac{0.053}{16.0} = 0.003\,3$
Simplest ratio (Divide by the smallest number)	$\frac{0.003\,34}{0.003\,3} = 1.0$	$\frac{0.006\,7}{0.003\,3} = 2.0$	$\frac{0.003\,3}{0.003\,3} = 1.0$
Simplest whole-number ratio:	1	2	1

So its empirical formula is CH_2O

Remember:

amount in moles = $\dfrac{\text{mass in grams}}{\text{mass of one mole in grams}}$

?

I (a) A hydrocarbon is found to contain 84.5 per cent carbon. What is its empirical formula?

(b) An amino acid contained 0.601 g carbon, 0.799 g oxygen, 0.125 g hydrogen and 0.349 g nitrogen. Calculate its empirical formula. (The answer is $C_2H_5O_2N$.)

■ See questions 2, 3 and 4.

?

J 0.200 g of a compound found in vinegar on complete combustion gave 0.293 g CO_2 and 0.120 g H_2O. The compound contained C, H, and O only.
Work out its empirical formula.

Finding the molecular formula

The empirical formula tells you the simplest ratio of different atoms in a compound. It does not tell you the actual number of atoms of each element in a molecule. To find the molecular formula, you need to know the **relative molecular mass, M_r,** of a compound, which is:

$$M_r = \frac{\text{mass of 1 molecule of the compound}}{\frac{1}{12}\text{ mass of one atom of carbon-12}}$$

The molecular formula may be the same as the empirical formula, or it may be a multiple of it. In Self-test question **J**, the empirical formula of the substance found in the vinegar is CH_2O. So we have:

$$\text{Relative mass of } CH_2O = 12 + (2\times1) + 16$$
$$= 30$$

But $M_r\,(CH_2O) = 60$, so because $30\times2 = 60$, the empirical formula must be multiplied by 2 to find the molecular formula:

$$(CH_2O)\times2 = C_2H_4O_2$$

In the second Example, the empirical formula of the sugar is also CH_2O, but in this case, $M_r = 180$. This is 30×6, so the molecular formula is:

$$(CH_2O)\times6 = C_6H_{12}O_6$$

So, when we analyse a compound, we need to know its relative molecular mass. This is where the mass spectrometer comes in.

?

K What are the molecular formulas of the following compounds?

(a) An arene hydrocarbon with empirical formula CH and $M_r = 78$.

(b) An acid in ant sting with empirical formula CH_2O_2 and $M_r = 46$.

(c) Caffeine with empirical formula $C_4H_5N_2O$ and $M_r = 194$.

3 MASS SPECTROMETRY

This is the most accurate method of determining relative atomic and molecular masses. But mass spectrometry has many other applications. The mass spectrometer is used by geologists to date rocks, by anaesthetists to analyse compounds in a patient's breath, by pharmaceutical companies to determine the structure of novel compounds, and by the oil industry to work out where samples of crude oil have originated. A mass spectrometer has even been taken to Mars to analyse rocks and dust on the planet's surface and gases in its atmosphere. Clearly, the potential of mass spectrometry is enormous.

The mass spectrometer was developed in 1919 by the eminent English physicist Francis Aston, from apparatus used by J.J. Thomson (the discoverer of the electron, see page 22). Aston used his mass spectrometer to show that neon gas was composed of **isotopes**.

Neon atoms were ionised, separated, and then made to hit a photographic plate. Two lines were produced, one much darker than the other, corresponding to relative isotopic masses of 20 and 22. By measuring the relative darkness of the two lines, Aston found that neon-20 atoms were ten times more abundant than neon-22.

From this information, he worked out the average atomic mass of neon to be 20.2. As mass spectrometers became more accurate, a third isotope of neon, neon-21, was discovered. It did not show up in Aston's instrument because only 0.26 per cent of naturally occurring neon is ^{21}Ne (only 26 atoms in 10 000).

✔

In 1922, Aston received the Nobel prize for his work in developing the mass spectrometer.

Remember: The **relative atomic mass** of an element is the average mass of the atom compared to one atom of carbon-12, taking into account all of its isotopes and their abundance. See page 29.

Isotopes are atoms of the same element with the same atomic number, but different mass numbers. See page 28. Relative isotopic mass is defined on page 29.

How a mass spectrometer works

All mass spectrometers have five basic operations:

■ A vaporised sample is injected into the instrument.

■ The sample is ionised to form positive ions.

■ The positive ions are accelerated by an electric field.

■ The accelerated positive ions are deflected by a magnetic field.

■ Positive ions of a particular mass/charge ratio are detected.

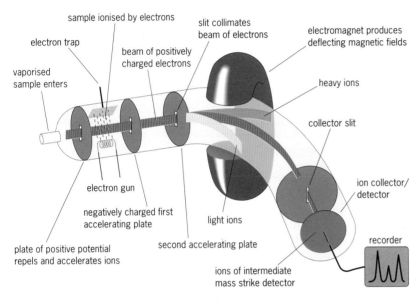

Fig 9.10 **A simplified diagram of the workings of a mass spectrometer**

When the sample is not a gas or a volatile liquid, it has to be heated to produce a vapour before it can be introduced into the mass spectrometer. Because of the exceptional sensitivity of the instrument, only nanograms (10^{-9} g) of a sample are required. Once inside, the vaporised sample is ionised by bombardment with high-energy electrons. The bombarding electrons knock electrons from the atoms or molecules in the sample, creating positively charged ions.

$$M(g) \quad + \quad e^- \quad \longrightarrow \quad M^+(g) \quad + \quad e^- \quad + \quad e^-$$
sample · · high-energy · · · · ion
· · · · · · electron

The positive ions formed are accelerated by an electric field of several thousand volts between negatively charged plates. They then enter a strong magnetic field which deflects them into a series of separate circular paths according to their mass/charge ratio.

Positive ions with higher mass/charge ratios are deflected less than those with lower ratios. So, by varying precisely the strength of the magnetic field, ions of a particular mass/charge ratio can be deflected to the collector and recorded. In this way, each separated positive ion beam can be focused on the collector in sequential order of mass/charge ratio, to build up a spectrum.

?

L Why is a very low pressure maintained inside the mass spectrometer?

Fig 9.11 **A modern mass spectrometer with digital readout and screen monitor**

In the double-focusing mass spectrometer, there is a second electric field whose strength can be varied. This focuses the ions according to their energy before they are deflected by the magnetic field. The resolution of the instrument is therefore improved, allowing a more accurate determination of molecular masses. See page 185.

On the mass spectra in this book, the *x*-axis is labelled: Mass/charge ratio (*m/e*). Although 2+ ions do occur (when two electrons are removed), 1+ ions are far more abundant. This means that the charge *e* = +1, which makes the mass/charge ratios of the peaks equal to the relative masses of the ions. This is why you will sometimes see the *x*-axis labelled simply: Mass.

Finding relative atomic masses

Relative atomic masses can be worked out very accurately using a mass spectrometer. (This was one of the first uses for the instrument.) Take neon, for example, whose mass spectrum is shown in Fig 9.13.

To calculate its A_r, we follow the same procedure as that on page 29:

$$A_r(\text{neon}) = \frac{(90.92 \times 20) + (0.26 \times 21) + (8.82 \times 22)}{100} = \frac{2018}{100}$$

$$= 20.18$$

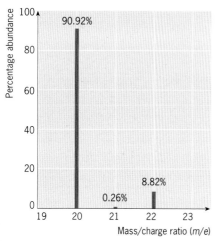

Fig 9.12 **The mass spectrum of naturally occurring neon, showing the percentage abundance of each isotope. It is easy to see why Aston's crude instrument failed to reveal the third isotope**

The molecular ion is sometimes called the **parent ion**.

M Calculate germanium's A_r from its mass spectrum, shown in Fig 9.13.

Finding relative molecular masses and molecular formulas

The mass spectrometer is more commonly used to find relative molecular masses. When a compound such as butane, C_4H_{10}, is analysed, its mass spectrum shows a whole series of peaks (Fig 9.14). The peak with the highest mass is the **molecular ion, M⁺**. It is the molecule with one electron removed.

A simple calculation of M_r tells you to expect the molecular ion to have its peak at 58, but Fig 9.14 also shows a peak at 59. This peak is due to those molecules of butane which contain an atom of carbon-13 (^{13}C). Known as the **M+1 peak**, it is always smaller than the molecular-ion peak because there are far fewer naturally occurring carbon-13 atoms. However, as shown later, the M+1 peak can help you to work out the number of carbon atoms in the molecule.

The other peaks in the mass spectrum are due to butane molecular ions which have broken into fragments. This **fragmentation** is important in working out the identity of molecules.

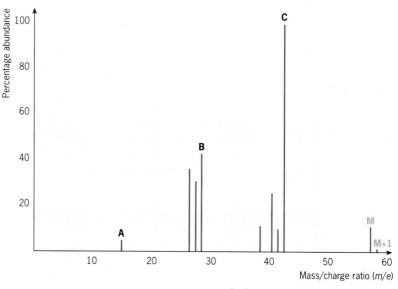

Fig 9.14 **The mass spectrum of butane**

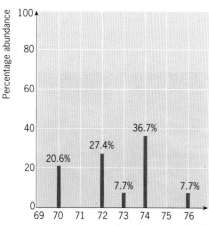

Fig 9.13 **The mass spectrum of germanium**

The mass spectrum in Fig 9.14 is from a spectrometer set for low resolution. At higher resolutions, it may be possible to deduce the molecular formula. We know that butane has an approximate M_r of 58, but C_4H_{10} is not the only possible molecular formula for this value of M_r: all the molecules shown in Table 9.1 have an approximate M_r of 58. But very accurate values for M_r can be obtained using high-resolution mass spectrometry. So it is possible to determine which compound is present if accurate values for relative isotopic masses are used.

Formulas	Accurate M_r (m/e values for M+ ion)
C_4H_{10}	58.0780
C_3H_6O	58.0417
$C_2H_2O_2$	58.0054
$C_2H_6N_2$	58.0530

Table 9.1 **Relative isotopic masses:**
$^{12}C = 12.0000$ $^{1}H = 1.0078$
$^{14}N = 14.0031$ $^{16}O = 15.9949$

Using fragmentation to determine structure

The mass spectrum of butane in Fig 9.14 has several peaks due to the way in which the butane molecular ion fragmented in the mass spectrometer. These fragments can be used to identify parts of the molecule and, in many cases, build up a picture of the structure of the whole molecule. This is illustrated in Fig 9.15, which we can use to identify some of the peaks in Fig 9.14, opposite.

A is due to CH_3^+, **B** to $C_2H_5^+$ and **C** to $C_3H_7^+$. The other peaks in the spectrum result from the loss of hydrogen atoms from these fragments. Typical ion fragments produced in the mass spectrometer are shown in Table 9.2.

Table 9.2 **The masses of some typical positive ion fragments**

Ion	Mass/charge ratio (m/e)	Ion	Mass/charge ratio (m/e)
CH_3^+	15	CH_3CO^+	43
CO^+	28	$C_3H_7^+$	43
$C_2H_4^+$	28	$C_2H_5O^+$	45
CHO^+	29	$C_4H_9^+$	57
$C_2H_5^+$	29	$C_6H_5^+$	77

Apart from deciding the identity of the peaks, the other important thing to look for is the differences in masses between the peaks. A difference of 15 is almost certainly due to the loss of a methyl fragment, and so it is highly likely that the original molecule contains a CH_3 group.

When a molecular ion fragments, the chemistry becomes rather complicated, and so we discuss only a small part of it here. In Fig 9.14, the molecular ion peak (M) is 58. The loss of a methyl fragment produces the peak at 43. The butane molecular ion has fragmented to give $C_3H_7^+$ and a free radical $CH_3\bullet$, which is neutral and so is not affected by the electric and magnetic fields of the mass spectrometer.

$$C_4H_{10}^+ \longrightarrow C_3H_7^+ + CH_3\bullet$$

There are other characteristic differences in the masses between peaks that give clues to which other groups have been lost as free radicals. For example, a loss of 17 suggests that an OH group may have been removed, and a loss of 29 suggests a C_2H_5 group.

N An acidic substance found in the sting of an ant is analysed using high-resolution mass spectrometry, giving $M_r = 46.0054$. A database of compounds is searched and the following molecules are revealed to have values of M_r in this region: C_2H_6O, CH_2O_2 and NO_2. Using accurate values of A_r, work out which molecule is present in an ant sting.

■ See questions 5 to 9.

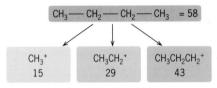

Fig 9.15 **Fragmentation of butane**

O **(a)** Why are the m/e values of the ions in Table 9.2 also their masses?

(b) Which fragment is responsible for the peak at m/e = 28 of the butane mass spectrum?

The most abundant ion gives the strongest signal at the detector. This is called the **base peak** and is given a relative abundance of 100 per cent. All other abundances are percentages of the base peak.

(c) What is the mass of the base peak in butane?

P Free radicals are highly reactive species with unpaired electrons.

(a) Why is $C_4H_{10}^+$ sometimes written $C_4H_{10}^{+\bullet}$?

(b) Why is the particle $CH_3\bullet$ not detected by the mass spectrometer?

Q What groups may have been removed when there is a mass difference of **(a)** 28, **(b)** 45, **(c)** 77?

?

R The compound responsible for the sting of an ant has the mass spectrum shown in Fig 9.17. It has a molecular formula CH_2O_2.

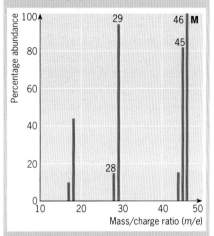

Fig 9.17

(a) What group of atoms could be lost from the molecular ion to form a peak at m/e 29?

(b) Which ions are probably responsible for the peaks at $m/e = 28$, 29 and 45?

(c) Suggest a displayed formula for this compound.

S (a) A component of petrol gives an M+1 peak that is 11.1 per cent of the M peak. How many carbon atoms does the molecule contain?

(b) In Fig 9.18, the peaks at $m/e = 49$ and 51 are in the ratio 3:1.
(i) Which ions are responsible for these peaks?
(ii) Both peaks at 64 and 66 are due to molecular ions. Identify these ions.
(iii) Which group has been lost from the M peak to give a peak at 49?

(c) Bromine has two isotopes, ^{79}Br and ^{81}Br, which are present in equal amounts, that is, 50:50. Sketch the mass spectrum you would expect for bromoethane.

(d) When analysed, chlorine gas gives peaks at $m/e = 74$, 72 and 70.
(i) Explain which ions are responsible for these peaks.
(ii) Why is the peak at $m/e = 74$ the smallest?

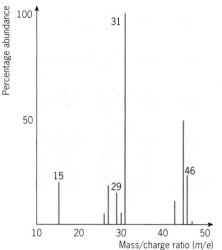

Fig 9.16 **The mass spectrum of ethanol**

Let's now look at the spectrum of ethanol, CH_3CH_2OH (Fig 9.16). The molecular ion peak is 46, which corresponds to $CH_3CH_2OH^+$. The base peak is at 31. The difference between 46 and 31 is 15, so it is probable that a CH_3 group has been lost. Therefore, the ion responsible for the base peak is CH_2OH^+. The peak at 29 is due to $CH_3CH_2^+$, and that at 15 is CH_3^+.

Notice that there is an M+1 peak at 47 due to the isotope carbon-13. In the next section, we see how this peak can be used to determine the number of carbon atoms present in the molecule.

Isotope peaks

The presence of isotopes in a compound will give characteristic peaks. We met one of these peaks when we examined butane and ethanol (see Figs 9.14 and 9.16). The M+1 peak was due to the isotope carbon-13. Carbon-13 is present naturally as 1.1 per cent of all carbon atoms, and this information allows us to work out the number of carbon atoms in a molecule. If there were one carbon atom in a molecule, the M+1 peak height would be 1.1 per cent of the molecular ion peak, because 1.1 per cent of molecules would contain carbon-13. So, in a molecule containing five carbon atoms, about 5.5 per cent will be carbon-13. That is, the M+1 peak height will be about 5.5 per cent of the M peak height.

Chlorine and bromine atoms also give characteristic peaks due to their isotopic compositions. In the case of chlorine, 75 per cent is ^{35}Cl and 25 per cent is ^{37}Cl. This means that when a molecule contains a chlorine atom, there are two peaks at M and M+2 in the ratio of 75:25, namely 3:1 (see Fig 9.18). Although we refer to these peaks as M and M+2, they both are molecular ions.

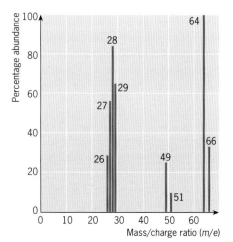

Fig 9.18 **The mass spectrum of chloroethane**

4 INFRARED SPECTROSCOPY

Atoms in molecules vibrate about their bonds. These vibrations have definite (quantised) energy levels, in the same way that electrons have quantised energy levels in atoms (see page 52). To increase the vibration in a molecule from one level to the next, a definite amount of energy must be absorbed. These amounts of energy correspond to radiation in the infrared part of the electromagnetic spectrum.

For infrared radiation to be absorbed, the vibrations must cause a change in the dipole moment of the molecule. Therefore, the symmetrical bonds in N_2 and O_2 do not absorb infrared radiation. This is why N_2 and O_2 are not greenhouse gases – they cannot absorb the infrared radiation emitted by the Earth. However, we know from Chapter 8 that carbon dioxide is an important greenhouse gas because it can absorb infrared radiation, due to the ways in which it can vibrate.

(a) Asymmetric stretch

(b) Symmetric stretch: causes no change in dipole moment

(c) Bending: occurs in two ways (in the plane of the paper) and also at right angles to this, so there are two modes due to bending

Fig 9.19 **Ways in which the carbon dioxide molecule vibrates**

Fig 9.19 shows four vibrational modes of carbon dioxide. There is no change in the dipole moment in Fig 9.19(b), and so there is no absorption of infrared radiation in this mode. However, the infrared spectrum of carbon dioxide (Fig 9.20) shows that the modes shown in (a) and (c) absorb in this region.

Notice that in Fig 9.20 the x-axis represents **wavenumber**. This is the reciprocal of wavelength ($1/\lambda$) and is usually measured in cm^{-1}. Using it makes the numbers more manageable, since the wavelength of the infrared region lies between 2.5×10^{-5} m and 2.5×10^{-6} m.

Remember: A **dipole** occurs in a molecule when one part of the molecule has a slightly positive charge and another part has a slightly negative charge. Dipole moment measures the size of the charges and the distance separating them. HCl is a polar molecule whose vibrations cause fluctuations in the dipole moment as the distance separating the charges varies, so it absorbs infrared radiation.

The infrared spectrum in Fig 9.20 appears to be upside down. But notice that the y-axis represents transmittance, so the sample is at maximum transmittance (allowing the passage of all infrared radiation) when it is not absorbing radiation.

Equation for the velocity of light:
$$c = \lambda f$$
where c = velocity of light, λ = wavelength, f = frequency. So, $1/\lambda$ is directly proportional to f. Since energy $E = hf$, the higher the wavenumber (and the higher the frequency), the higher the energy. h = Planck's constant.

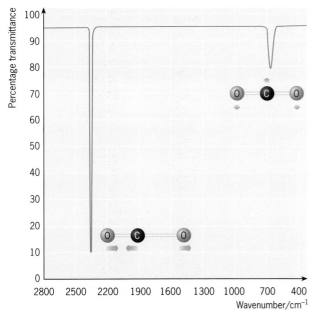

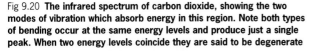

Fig 9.20 **The infrared spectrum of carbon dioxide, showing the two modes of vibration which absorb energy in this region. Note both types of bending occur at the same energy levels and produce just a single peak. When two energy levels coincide they are said to be degenerate**

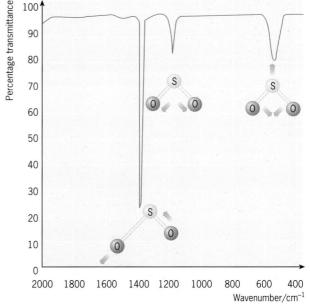

Fig 9.21 **The infrared spectrum of sulphur dioxide, showing the vibrations responsible for the peaks**

?

T (a) Why is there no absorption peak in the infrared spectrum of hydrogen molecules?

(b) Why is there only one absorption peak in the infrared spectrum of HCl?

(c) The absorption peaks of HCl and HI are 2886 cm⁻¹ and 2230 cm⁻¹ respectively. What does this tell you about the bond energies of H–Cl and H–I?

In the case of sulphur dioxide, all three vibrational modes lead to infrared absorption, as shown in Fig 9.21. This is because the V-shaped SO_2 molecule has a different shape from the linear CO_2 molecule, so all three modes lead to a change in the dipole moment. Notice that the absorptions do not occur at the same wavenumbers. This is because the energy required to excite vibration depends on the strength of the bond. As the C=O bond is stronger than the S=O bond, the corresponding vibrations occur at a higher wavenumber in CO_2.

As molecules get more complex, so do their vibrational modes. You may meet terms such as scissoring or rocking. Don't worry about these. When you have to interpret an infrared spectrum, you look for one or two peaks which are characteristic of particular bonds.

The infrared spectrometer

The spectrometer shown in Fig 9.22 is a double-beamed instrument, in which one infrared beam passes through the sample and the other passes through the reference cell. The reference cell may contain air, or the solvent of a solid being analysed as a solution. The purpose of the reference is to eliminate absorptions due to CO_2 and water vapour in the air or due to the solvent. The difference in the intensities of the two beams is measured by the detector at each wavenumber and fed to the recorder, which produces a spectrum. When the sample does not absorb, there is no peak at that wavenumber. But when it does absorb radiation, the difference in intensities of the two beams produces a peak at that wavenumber.

Notice that when a prism is fitted instead of a diffracting grating, it is made from sodium chloride rather than glass. This is because sodium chloride is transparent to most infrared radiations, whereas glass absorbs it strongly.

A more sophisticated instrument is the Fourier transform infrared spectrometer, in which a single beam containing all the required infrared frequencies is passed through the sample. The emerging beam is fed into a computer which produces an infrared spectrum by a mathematical technique known as Fourier transformation. This instrument has enabled us to understand how photochemical smog develops by analysing samples taken from a 1.6 km long path of air over Los Angeles and determining concentrations of pollutants down to parts per billion (per 10^9).

Preparing samples for analysis

Gases are passed into the sample cell about 10 cm long, which has sodium chloride windows at each end. (Why can't glass windows be used?)

Liquids are smeared into a thin film between two potassium bromide or sodium chloride discs. (Sodium chloride is not transparent to all infrared, so potassium bromide can be used.)

Solids are made either into a solution, or into a disc or a **mull**. To make a disc, the solid is finely ground with KBr and pressed into a mould under very high pressure. The advantage of a disc is that it produces the spectrum of the pure compound. A mull is made by grinding up the sample with a drop of nujol, a long chain hydrocarbon. The mull is then smeared between discs, as for a liquid sample. The disadvantage of using a mull is that nujol absorbs infrared radiation, which shows up on the spectrum.

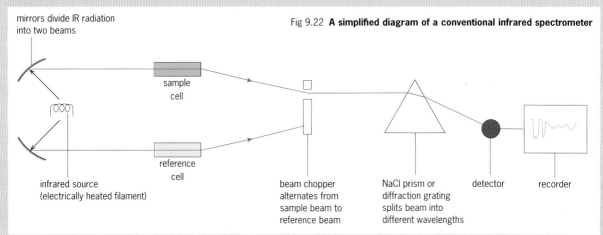

mirrors divide IR radiation into two beams

Fig 9.22 **A simplified diagram of a conventional infrared spectrometer**

sample cell

reference cell

infrared source (electrically heated filament)

beam chopper alternates from sample beam to reference beam

NaCl prism or diffraction grating splits beam into different wavelengths

detector

recorder

Interpreting infrared spectra

The spectrum of each and every compound acts like a unique finger-print and thus makes it possible to identify any compound, often through a computer database. When a totally new compound is discovered, perhaps isolated from a medicinal herb, it will not match any spectrum in the database. But we can still infer a great deal about the compound from the peaks in its spectrum. For example, the functional group C=O absorbs in the range 1680–1750 cm^{-1}, so a peak in this region is a strong indication that C=O is present.

Table 9.3 contains some examples of bonds and their characteristic infrared absorption bands. Notice that some bonds give strong absorptions while others are weaker. The explanation lies with bond polarity. Very polar bonds, such as C=O and O–H, are subject to a greater change in their dipole moments when they vibrate than non-polar bonds, such as C–H. So polar bonds absorb more energy, thereby giving a stronger peak.

> The *fingerprint* of a complex molecule arises through the vibrations of the whole molecule and this can be used to check batches of drugs for purity. The identifying peaks of the fingerprint are usually below 1600 cm^{-1}.

For more information on hydrogen bonding, see page 230

Table 9.3 **Bonds and their characteristic infrared absorption bands.**
Intensity classification: s = strong, m = medium

Bond	Location	Wavenumber range/cm^{-1}	Intensity
O–H	alcohols and phenols, free (not hydrogen bonded)	3580–3670	s
N–H	primary amines	3350–3500	m
O–H	alcohols and phenols, hydrogen bonded	3230–3550	s (broad)
C–H	alkanes, alkenes, arenes	2840–3030	m–s
O–H	carboxylic acids, hydrogen bonded	2500–3300	m (broad)
C≡N	nitriles	2200–2280	m
C=O	aldehydes, ketones, carboxylic acids, esters	1680–1750	s
C=C	alkenes	1610–1680	m
C–O	alcohols, ethers, esters	1000–1300	s
C–Cl		700–800	s

> Arenes are aromatic compounds and have a benzene ring. For more information on arenes, see Chapter 13.

Fig 9.23 **Preparing a mull**

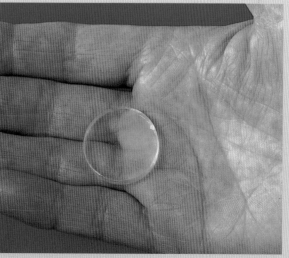

Fig 9.24 **A potassium bromide disc**

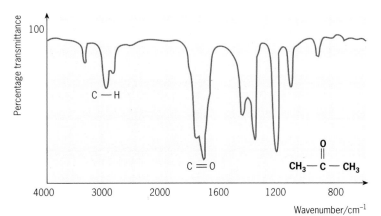

Fig 9.25 **The infrared spectrum of propanone**

Let's now look at the infrared spectra in Figs 9.25, 9.26 and 9.27. Notice that we have not attempted to identify all the peaks in these three spectra. The more atoms and bonds there are in a molecule, the more complex its spectra becomes.

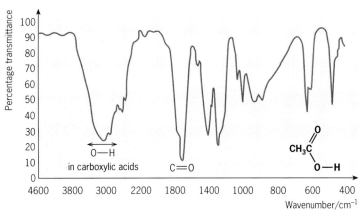

Fig 9.26 **The infrared spectrum of ethanoic acid**

Infrared spectroscopy is rarely used on its own to identify unknown compounds. But, coupled with data from mass spectrometry, gas–liquid chromatography or combustion analysis, it gives important information about the presence of functional groups.

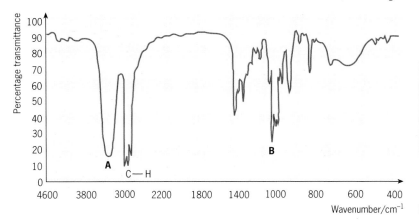

Fig 9.27 **The infrared spectrum of butan-1-ol**

?

U Fig 9.27 shows the infrared spectrum of butan-1-ol, $CH_3CH_2CH_2CH_2OH$. Using Table 9.3, identify the peaks marked **A** and **B**.

INFRARED ABSORPTION AT THE POLICE STATION

ALL ALCOHOLIC DRINKS slow down the body's response times. So drinking and driving can be a fatal combination and anyone driving over the legal limit of 35 micrograms per $100\,cm^3$ of breath is likely to be prosecuted.

The roadside breathalyser gives the first indication that a driver may be over the limit. When a breathalyser test proves positive, the next step is to take the driver to the police station for a more accurate analysis, which is now often done using infrared absorption. Until a few years ago, a urine or blood sample would be taken and the samples sent away for GLC analysis. This is still an option when the breath alcohol concentration is between 40 and $50\,\mu g$ per $100\,cm^3$. Above this range, infrared absorption alone is accurate enough to secure a conviction.

Fig 9.28 **The Intoximeter 3000 shown here has been widely adopted by the British police to analyse breath. It checks the C–H absorption at about $3000\,cm^{-1}$**

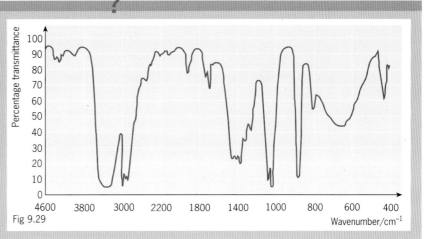

V Look at the infrared spectrum for ethanol in Fig 9.29.

(a) Identify the bond responsible for the broad peak at about 3400 cm^{-1}.

(b) Breath contains water vapour. Why can't the peak at 3400 cm^{-1} be used to check for alcohol concentration?

(c) Diabetics may have propanone on their breath. Look at Fig 9.25 and suggest why this could be a problem for the Intoximeter 3000.

Fig 9.29

5 NUCLEAR MAGNETIC RESONANCE SPECTROSCOPY

In nuclear magnetic resonance (NMR) spectroscopy, organic chemists have a very powerful technique for determining the detailed structures of compounds. Like infrared spectroscopy, it uses absorption – but in NMR it is the absorption of radio waves by certain nuclei when they are in a strong magnetic field. When a new organic compound is discovered, its NMR spectrum is often the first to be looked at because it gives detailed information about the hydrogen nuclei (protons) in the molecule. It can also be used to investigate other nuclei, such as ^{13}C.

A hydrogen nucleus acts like a tiny bar magnet because it spins, generating a minute magnetic field. When a strong external magnetic field is applied to a compound containing hydrogen atoms, many of their spinning nuclei (protons) line up so that their magnetic fields are all in the same direction as that of the external field (like a group of compass needles, every one pointing north). However, some of the nuclei directly oppose the external magnetic field. (Imagine a compass needle pointing south!) This requires more energy, so these nuclei are at a higher energy level than the rest.

If the compound is now irradiated with a pulse of radio waves of a particular frequency, the lower-energy nuclei absorb these waves and thereby flip to the higher level. This causes a peak in the NMR spectrum.

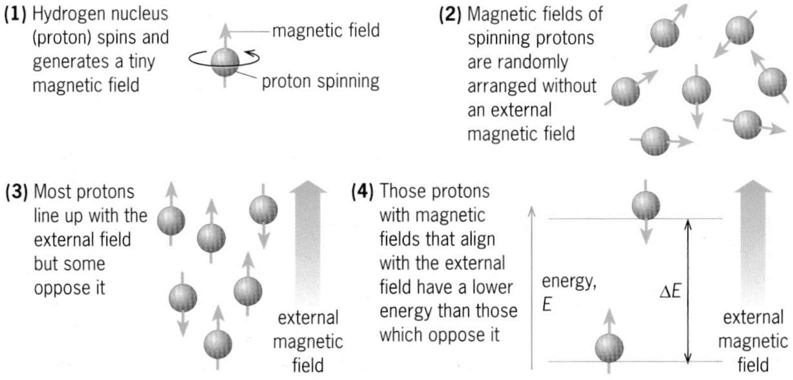

Nuclear magnetic resonance spectroscopy is also called magnetic resonance imaging (MRI), especially when its use in medicine is described.

Remember that hydrogen $^1_1$H has a nucleus consisting of only one proton.

W As well as ^{13}C and ^{1}H, the following nuclei also exhibit the property known as spin and generate a magnetic field: ^{19}F, ^{31}P, ^{15}N. Look at the mass numbers and identify a pattern.

X An NMR spectrum is often referred to as a PMR spectrum when the nucleus involved is hydrogen. What does PMR mean?

(1) Hydrogen nucleus (proton) spins and generates a tiny magnetic field

magnetic field

proton spinning

(2) Magnetic fields of spinning protons are randomly arranged without an external magnetic field

(3) Most protons line up with the external field but some oppose it

external magnetic field

(4) Those protons with magnetic fields that align with the external field have a lower energy than those which oppose it

energy, E

ΔE

external magnetic field

Fig 9.30 **How hydrogen nuclei behave when an external magnetic field is applied to their molecular environment**

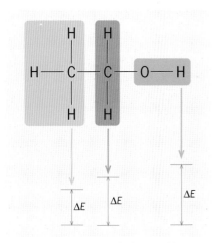

Fig 9.31 **The hydrogen nuclei (protons) in ethanol are in three different chemical environments. Each gives different proton NMR energy levels**

The energy needed to promote a hydrogen nucleus (proton) to a higher energy level, and the strength of the applied magnetic field experienced by the nucleus, both depend on the chemical environment of the nucleus. So, hydrogen atoms in different environments in a molecule absorb radio waves in slightly different parts of the spectrum. Take, for example, the ethanol molecule (CH_3CH_2OH) shown in Fig 9.31.

The hydrogen nuclei are in three different chemical environments. This means that the energy gap between the higher and lower energy levels is different for each of these environments. So, when a pulse of radio waves is applied, more of the lower energy nuclei jump to the higher energy level, absorbing radio waves of a particular frequency. In the case of ethanol, there are three peaks corresponding to the three different frequencies absorbed by the detector.

A compound called tetramethylsilane, $Si(CH_3)_4$, or TMS for short, has all 12 protons (hydrogen nuclei) in the same chemical environment. It therefore gives a very sharp signal. This is used as the standard against which all signals due to other proton chemical environments are measured, because its protons absorb at a frequency well away from the frequencies of most interest to chemists. TMS is given a value of zero, and the difference between the protons in TMS and the protons in other chemical environments is known as the **chemical shift**, symbol δ.

Fig 9.32 **The low-resolution NMR spectrum of ethanol**

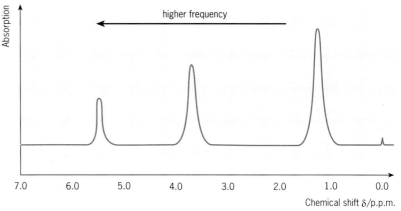

✔ Notice that δ is in p.p.m. (parts per million). This relates to the difference in frequency and applied fields, but a full explanation is beyond the scope of this book.

The NMR spectrum of ethanol is shown in Fig 9.32. The area under each peak is proportional to the number of protons in the particular environment. Many NMR spectrometers give these areas as an **integration trace** which is superimposed on the NMR spectrum. By measuring the height of each step on the integration trace, the ratio of the protons in each environment can be worked out. This is shown in Fig 9.33, with the ratio of protons given in parentheses.

Fig 9.33 **The low-resolution NMR spectrum of ethanol, showing the integration trace**

? **Y** Give the number of peaks the following molecules show in their NMR spectra:
(a) benzene (C_6H_6), **(b)** propanone (CH_3COCH_3), **(c)** methanol (CH_3OH).

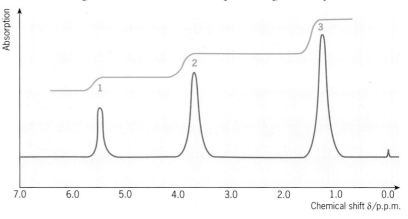

Table 9.4 **Some typical chemical shift values for different types of proton**

Type of proton	Chemical shift (ppm)	Type of proton	Chemical shift (p.p.m.)
R–CH₃	0.9	R–CH₂–Hal	
R–CH₂–R	1.3		3.2–3.7
R₃CH	2.0	R–O–CH₃	3.8
		R–O–H	4.5*
		RHC=CH₂	4.9
CH₃–C(R)(OR)	2.0	RHC=CH₂	5.9
R–C(CH₃)=O	2.1	⬡–OH	7*
⬡–CH₃	2.3	⬡–H	7.3
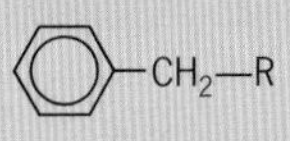 ⬡–CH₂–R	2.3–2.7	R–C(=O)H	9.7*
R–C≡C–H	2.6	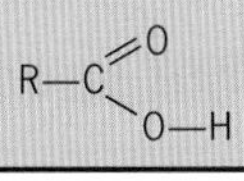 R–C(=O)O–H	11.5*

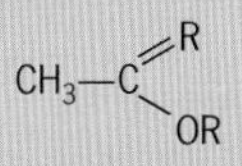

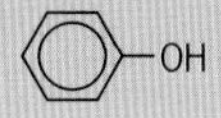

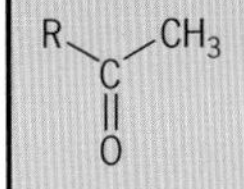

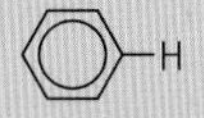

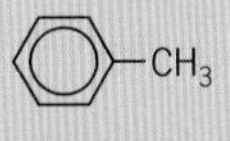

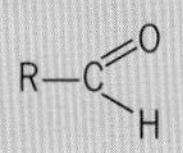

*The value varies according to the solvent, the nature of R and concentration.

> Chemical shifts give an indication of the types of proton to be found in a molecule. Some typical values are shown in Table 9.4. Chemists use these values when they are trying to identify molecules and work out structures.

Using Table 9.4, let's work through another NMR spectrum and determine the structure of the compound.

EXAMPLE

Q A hydrocarbon has a molecular formula C_8H_{10}. Work out its displayed formula from the low-resolution NMR spectrum in Fig 9.34.

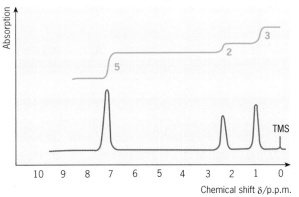

Fig 9.34

A As there are three peaks, there must be three types of proton (three different chemical environments).

The peak at 7.2 is probably due to a benzene ring. The integration trace gives a ratio of 5:2:3. This adds up to ten, which in this case is the actual number of

hydrogens in the molecule. So there are five hydrogens on the benzene ring. In other words, it is **monosubstituted**. (Monosubstituted means that only one hydrogen in the benzene ring has been substituted by another atom or group.)

Since there are two more peaks, the peak at 2.4 corresponds to $C_6H_5–CH_2–R$, not $C_6H_5–CH_3$. From the integration trace, we can see that it does indeed have two hydrogen atoms.

The integration trace shows that three hydrogen atoms are responsible for the peak at 1.0. Even though the value of the peak does not correspond precisely to the value in Table 9.4, it is certainly CH_3.

These data give the structural formula in Fig 9.35. The compound is ethylbenzene.

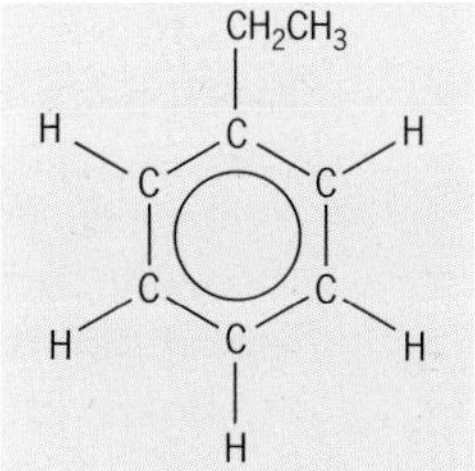

CH₂CH₃

Fig 9.35

?

Z Using Table 9.4, draw the NMR spectrum you might expect for ethanal (Fig 9.36).

Fig 9.36

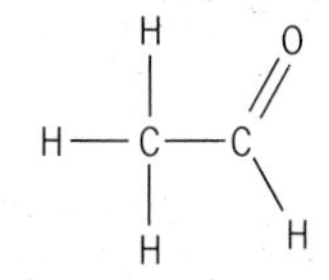

Using the NMR spectrometer

The sample is dissolved in a solvent which does not contain hydrogen atoms, such as CCl_4, or a solvent in which hydrogen has been replaced by its isotope deuterium. The solution is then placed in a strong magnetic field and a pulse of radio waves passes through it, exciting hydrogen nuclei into their higher spin energy levels. The absorption of radio waves at particular frequencies is detected and recorded.

Either the radio frequency or the magnetic field can be varied to give characteristic peaks.

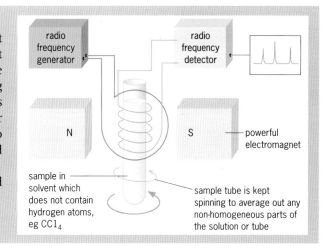

Fig 9.37 **A schematic diagram of an NMR spectrometer**

radio frequency generator

radio frequency detector

N   S

powerful electromagnet

sample in solvent which does not contain hydrogen atoms, eg CCl_4

sample tube is kept spinning to average out any non-homogeneous parts of the solution or tube

✔

Deuterated solvents contain deuterium instead of hydrogen. The deuterium nucleus contains a proton and a neutron and does not respond to NMR at the same radio frequencies.

CD_3COCD_3 is propanone, CH_3COCH_3, with the hydrogen atoms exchanged for deuterium.

High-resolution NMR spectroscopy

The NMR spectra of ethanol and ethylbenzene (Figs 9.32 and 9.34) are at low resolution. High-resolution instruments give more peaks, as shown in Fig 9.38. These extra peaks yield more information about the structure of molecules.

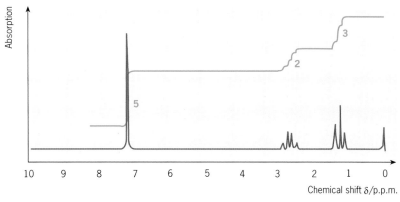

Fig 9.38 **The high-resolution NMR spectrum of ethylbenzene**

Absorption

Chemical shift δ/p.p.m.

When different types of proton are next to each other in a molecule, they exert an effect on their respective magnetic fields known as **spin–spin splitting** or **spin–spin coupling**. Look closely at the displayed formula of ethylbenzene in Fig 9.35. The CH_3 protons are next to the CH_2 protons, so they have a direct effect on each other. However, the protons in the benzene ring are not next to any other type of proton.

The CH_3 protons experience three different magnetic fields due to the way the CH_2 protons spin, while the CH_2 protons experience four different magnetic fields due to the way the CH_3 protons spin, as shown in Fig 9.39.

Fig 9.39 **Spin–spin splitting in ethylbenzene**

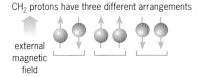

CH_2 protons have three different arrangements

external magnetic field

So CH_3 protons are affected in three ways, giving a **triplet** of peaks

1.5   1

?

A' There are two types of proton in CH_3CHO. How many arrangements are there of the magnetic field for the CHO proton? How many peaks will there be in the CH_3 part of the spectrum?

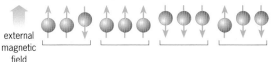

CH_3 protons have four different arrangements

external magnetic field

So CH_2 protons are affected in four ways, giving a **quartet** of peaks

2.8   2.4

So, with high-resolution NMR, we can work out the number of nearest neighbour hydrogen atoms there are in different groups in a molecule. This helps us to gain greater insight into the structure of unknown molecules.

Using D₂O to identify labile protons

Certain functional groups, such as OH and NH_2, rapidly exchange protons with neighbouring molecules. These protons are said to be **labile**. They usually appear in high-resolution NMR spectra as single peaks, because they do not interact with neighbouring protons.

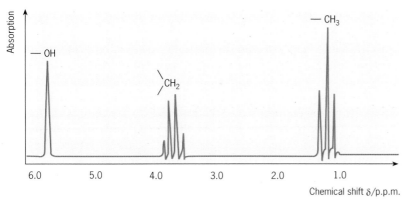

Fig 9.40 **The high-resolution NMR spectrum of ethanol**

To identify functional groups with labile protons, heavy water, deuterium oxide (D₂O), is used. In the case of ethanol, there is an exchange which produces CH_3CH_2OD, and the peak corresponding to the proton in the OH group disappears.

IMAGING THE HUMAN BODY WITH NMR

NUCLEAR MAGNETIC RESONANCE is becoming increasingly important in medicine, where it is more usually known as magnetic resonance imaging. The most common nucleus in the body is that of hydrogen, and whole-body scanners investigate tissues by producing images based on the fact that protons in different tissues have different **relaxation times**. When protons are excited and flipped into higher energy levels, they return to the lower energy stage, emitting energy. The time they take to do this is called the relaxation time. This is detected and the data transformed by computer into an image. With NMR, doctors can see an image of the soft tissues in the body which X-rays cannot distinguish. An added advantage is that, unlike X-rays, there are no known side-effects and therefore scans can be safely taken of a patient at regular intervals.

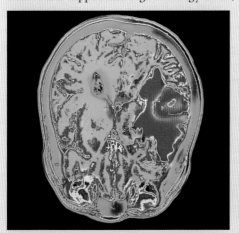

Fig 9.41 **A brain tumour is shown by magnetic resonance imaging as a magenta coloured area surrounded by damaged brain tissue in scarlet. Protons in tumours have longer relaxation times than protons in normal tissue, and this provides a way of locating them**

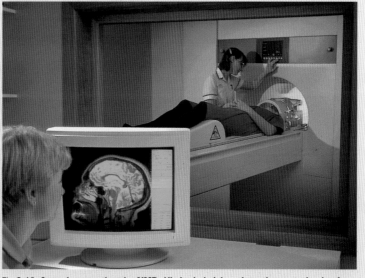

Fig 9.42 **Scanning a patient by NMR. His body is lying along the central axis of a superconducting electromagnet**

6 COMBINING TECHNIQUES

As you have seen, the chemist has many techniques to call upon when determining the structure of an unknown molecule, and they are hardly ever used in isolation.

Gas chromatography is an excellent way to separate large numbers of components, whereas mass spectrometry is not the instrument to use if you want to identify substances in complex mixtures because the spectra are too complicated. By combining the two techniques, the separation is first carried out by gas chromatography, and then the separated components are analysed by the mass spectrometer.

In the same way, infrared spectrometry gives good evidence of the presence of functional groups, but its information needs to be pooled with that from other techniques to gain the complete picture.

Combustion analysis gives information about the percentage composition of elements in a compound by burning a sample in oxygen. Gases produced such as CO_2, H_2O and SO_2 can be fed directly into gas–liquid chromatography apparatus where they are separated and analysed, and their amounts determined.

Another example is the combination of NMR, which determines the different environments of hydrogen nuclei; and mass spectroscopy, which gives fragmentation patterns and an accurate M_r. The use of a combination of analytical techniques makes the determination of structural formulas more likely.

SUMMARY

After studying this chapter, you should know and understand the following.

■ Chromatography involves the distribution of the components of a mixture between a stationary phase and a mobile phase, and provides a way of separating compounds.

■ There are several types of chromatography. They include paper chromatography, thin-layer chromatography (TLC), column chromatography and gas–liquid chromatography (GLC).

■ Percentage composition by mass of different elements in a compound may be obtained by combustion analysis.

■ Empirical formulas can be determined from percentage composition data.

■ A mass spectrometer separates streams of positive ions according to their masses and charges.

■ Mass spectra of elements can be used to work out accurate values of A_r.

■ When molecules are ionised in the mass spectrometer, they often break up into fragments which can give information about the structure of a molecule.

■ High-resolution mass spectrometry gives highly accurate values of M_r which may lead to the molecular formula of a compound.

■ Infrared spectroscopy can be used to identify functional groups which absorb infrared radiation due to their vibrations.

■ Nuclear magnetic resonance (NMR) spectroscopy gives information on the location and number of hydrogen atoms in a molecule because spinning protons create a magnetic field.

■ Chemical shift in an NMR spectrum occurs due to protons in different chemical environments experiencing slight variations in the externally applied magnetic field.

QUESTIONS

1 Chromatography is a versatile technique that may be used to separate and identify compounds.

a)   **(i)** Name a type of chromatography that could be used to separate and identify dissolved solids.

   (ii) Draw a labelled sketch to illustrate the resulting chromatogram.

   (iii) State what quantitative value may be determined from the chromatogram to identify the solids present in the solution.

   (iv) On your diagram in **a)(ii)**, show how this quantity may be found.

b)   **(i)** Name a type of chromatography that could be used to separate and identify gases and vapours.

   (ii) Draw a labelled sketch to illustrate the resulting chromatogram.

   (iii) State what quantitative value may be determined from the chromatogram to identify the gases and vapours present.

   (iv) On your diagram in **b)(ii)**, show how this quantity may be determined.

[UCLES 1994 Sciences, Methods of Analysis and Detection, Specimen Paper q.1]

2 A compound **L** has the following composition by mass:

C 35.0% **H** 6.6% **Br** 58.4%

Calculate the empirical formula of **L**.

[AEB 1996 Chemistry, Specimen Terminal Paper 1, q.1]

3 When an aqueous solution of magnesium chloride was evaporated to dryness, a product of composition Mg 35.5%, Cl 52.6%, O 11.9% by mass, was obtained. Calculate the empirical formula of the product.

[ULEAC 1996, A Chemistry, Specimen Module Test 1, part-q.2]

4 Fig 9.Q4 shows the mass spectrum of chlorine, Cl_2.

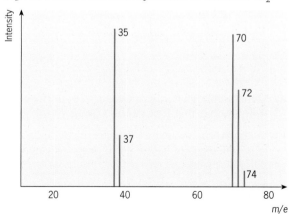

Fig 9.Q4

Identify the species responsible for each peak in the spectrum.

[ULEAC 1996, Chemistry, Specimen Module Test 1, q.2]

5

a) The mass spectrum of an organic compound which can be obtained by the oxidation of an alcohol, is shown in Fig 9.Q5.

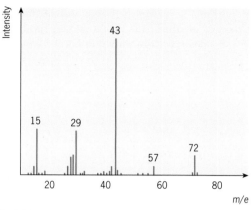

Fig 9.Q5

The compound has the following composition by mass:

C = 66.7%   H = 11.1%   O = 22.2%

Calculate the empirical formula of the compound and, by interpreting the labelled peaks on the mass spectrum, determine the structural formula of the compound.

b) Explain the occurrence of a small peak at a mass of 73 in the mass spectrum in **a)**.

c) Give the name of the compound identified in **a)**.

[ULEAC 1996 AS Chemistry Specimen Synoptic Paper, part-q.5]

6 The diagram of Fig 9.Q6 represents part of the mass spectrum of ethanol, C_2H_5OH.

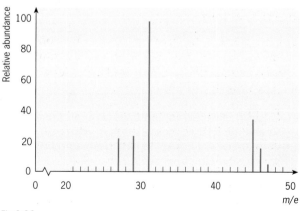

Fig 9.Q6

a) Identify on the diagram **(i)** the M^+ (molecular ion) peak, **(ii)** the (M+1) peak.

b) Explain why this (M+1) peak occurs.

c) Explain the presence of the other peaks in the diagram.

[UCLES 1994 Sciences, Methods of Analysis and Detection Specimen Paper, q.4]

7 A sample of oxygen consisting mainly of the isotope oxygen-16 was enriched with oxygen-18.
The composition of the mixture was 75.0% oxygen-16 and 25.0% oxygen-18, by volume.

a) Calculate the relative atomic mass of oxygen in the sample.

b) Some carbon-12 was burned in another sample of the oxygen mixture. The carbon dioxide produced gave the mass spectrum shown in Fig 9.Q7.

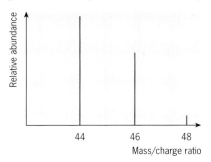

Fig 9.Q7

Identify the peaks shown.

[UCLES 1994 Sciences, Chemistry Foundation Specimen Paper, part-q.2]

8 Look at Fig 9.Q8 which shows the mass spectrum of a simple molecule **A**.

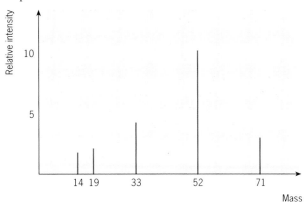

Fig 9.Q8

a) What is the relative molecular mass of **A**?

b) Calculate the difference in mass between the peak at 52 and the relative molecular mass. Hence suggest what atom or atoms could have been detached from **A** to produce the peak at 52.

c) Calculate the difference in mass between the peak at 33 and the relative molecular mass, and similarly suggest what atom or atoms could have been detached from **A** to produce the peak at 33.

d) Calculate the difference in mass between the peak at 14 and the relative molecular mass, and similarly suggest what atom or atoms could have been detached from **A** to produce the peak at 14.

e) Suggest what the peak of mass 14 might represent, bearing in mind the absence of peaks of lower mass. Include the charge of the ion producing the peak.

f) From your answers to the questions above, suggest what **A** might be.

[AEB 1996 Chemistry Specimen Module Paper 9, q.2]

9

a) Mass spectrometry and infrared spectroscopy are complementary techniques in chemical analysis. Explain:
   (i) the chemical principles involved in these techniques,
   (ii) what information may be obtained from the spectra,
   (iii) the importance of high resolution in mass spectrometry.

b) Analysis of an organic compound **Z** containing carbon, hydrogen and oxygen gave the following data:

composition by mass: C 66.7%, H 11.1%

infrared spectrum: strong absorption band at $1715\,cm^{-1}$

mass spectrum: lines of m/e values 72, 57, 43.

Use these data to suggest the identity and molecular structure of **Z**, showing your reasoning.

[UCLES 1994 Modular Sciences, Methods of Analysis and Detection Specimen Paper, section B, q.7]

10 The mass spectrum of an element is shown in Fig 9.Q10.

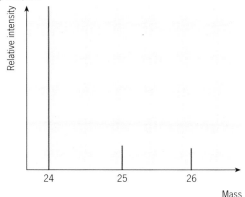

Fig 9.Q10

a) State briefly what you can deduce about the element from the fact that it produces 3 peaks.

b) State two changes which must be made to a sample of a solid element before it can be investigated in a mass spectrometer.

c) The relative intensities of the three peaks in Fig 9.Q10 are in the ratio 8:1:1. Calculate the accurate relative atomic mass of this sample of the element.

[NEAB 1996 Chemistry Specimen End-of-course Assessment, Section B, part-q.B1]

11 This question concerns compounds derived from ethane, C_2H_6.

a) Parts of the infrared spectrum of ethanol, C_2H_5OH, and ethane are shown in Fig 9.Q11.

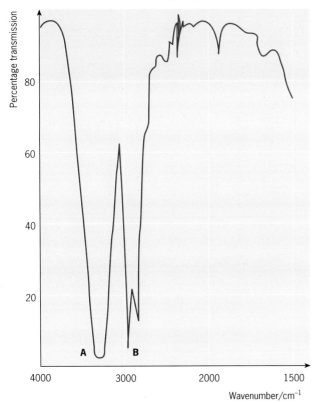

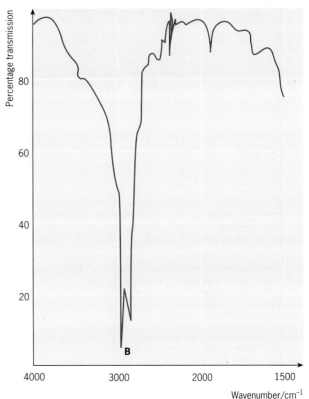

Fig 9.Q11

What chemical bonds do you think are responsible for the absorption of radiation at 3200–3400 cm^{-1} (Peak **B**)?

b) The infrared spectrum of ethylamine [$C_2H_5NH_2$] is very similar to that of ethanol, including a peak of similar shape to that of peak **A** at almost the same wavenumber.

Suggest what group in ethylamine is responsible for this peak, and justify your answer.

[ULEAC 1996 Nuffield Chemistry Module Test 3 Specimen Paper, q.4]

12 Which one of the following compounds gives a proton NMR spectrum showing only one peak?

    A propan-1-ol [$CH_3CH_2CH_2OH$]
    B propan-2-ol [$CH_3CH(OH)CH_3$]
    C propanal [CH_3CH_2CHO]
    D propanone [CH_3COCH_3]

[NEAB 1996 Chemistry Specimen End-of-course Assessment, q.5]

13

a) Outline the principles of each of the following, and their scope in determining the molecular structures of organic compounds.
    (i) Infrared spectroscopy.
    (ii) Nuclear magnetic resonance spectroscopy.

b) A compound **L**, isolated from tobacco, contains carbon, hydrogen and one other element. When 1.106 g of **L** is burnt in pure dry oxygen, 3.001 g of carbon dioxide and 0.860 g of water are formed. The relative molecular mass of **L** is known to be in the range 150–165. Calculate the carbon:hydrogen ratio, and the number of carbon atoms in the molecule. Hence suggest what the third element is, and find the molecular formula.

How could the relative molecular mass be found experimentally with greater accuracy?

[AEB 1996 Chemistry Specimen S Paper, q.2]

Assignment

WONDER CURE FROM WILLOW

In 1763, Edmund Stone sent a letter to the Royal Society (see Fig 9.A1). He had been investigating willow bark to see whether its properties were similar to those of the bark of the Peruvian cinchona tree, which was used to treat malaria. Stone found that, while willow bark did not cure malaria, it did relieve some of the painful symptoms. This was not the first time willow had been used to relieve pain: in 400 BC, Hippocrates, the famous Greek physician, recommended willow leaves to ease the pain of childbirth.

[195]

XXXII. *An Account of the Success of the Bark of the Willow in the Cure of Agues. In a Letter to the Right Honourable George Earl of* Macclesfield, *President of R. S. from the Rev. Mr.* Edmund Stone, *of* Chipping-Norton *in* Oxfordshire.

My Lord,

Read June 2d, 1763.

A Mong the many useful discoveries, which this age hath made, there are very few which, better deserve the attention of the public than what I am going to lay before your Lordship.

There is a bark of an English tree, which I have

Fig 9.A1 **Part of the letter sent by Edmund Stone to the Royal Society in 1763**

1 The active chemical in willow bark was isolated in 1829 and called salicin.

a) It has the molecular formula $C_{13}H_{18}O_7$. Calculate its percentage composition.

b) What technique is used in an analytical laboratory to work out percentage composition?

2 The pharmacologically active part of salicin is salicylic acid. When this is analysed, it has the following percentage composition: C = 60.86 per cent, H = 4.35 per cent, O = 34.78 per cent. Calculate its empirical formula.

3 The six most prominent peaks for salcylic acid are shown in a simplified, low resolution mass spectrum in Fig 9.A2.

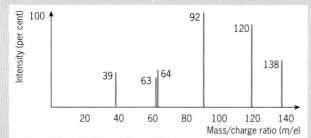

Fig 9.A2 **The mass spectrum of salicylic acid**

a) Which is the molecular ion peak?

b) Which is the base peak?

c) What is the approximate molecular mass of salicylic acid?

4 The infrared spectrum for salicylic acid is shown in Fig 9.A3. Use Table 9.3, page 189, to identify the groups responsible for some of the major peaks.

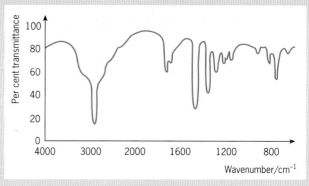

Fig 9.A3 **The infrared spectrum of salicylic acid**

5 What information does NMR spectroscopy give to further determine the structure of salicylic acid?

Fig 9.A4 **The structural formula of 2-hydroxybenzoic acid (salicylic acid)**

The structure of salicylic acid is shown in Fig 9.A4. While it was regarded in its day to be a wonder drug, salicylic acid systematic name 2-hydroxybenzoic acid was unpleasant to take and irritated the mouth and stomach. By modifying the structure of salicylic acid, a German chemist, Felix Hofman, succeeded in producing a new molecule which we now know as aspirin. It is still used in many medicines, and is thought to help combat heart disease by suppressing the formation of blood clots.

Fig 9.A5 **The structural formula of aspirin**

6 Aspirin is an ester of salicylic acid. Research the following:

a) The functional group of an ester.

b) How aspirin might be synthesised in the laboratory from salicylic acid.

c) The use of esters as food flavourings.

SEPARATING AND IDENTIFYING SUBSTANCES

This chapter covers a range of analytical techniques used to separate the components from mixtures and to identify compounds. The Chapter Map summarises these topics and the way they are connected to chemical concepts. Check against the map that you understand the use of each, and refer back to the chapter for any aspects that you do not feel confident about.

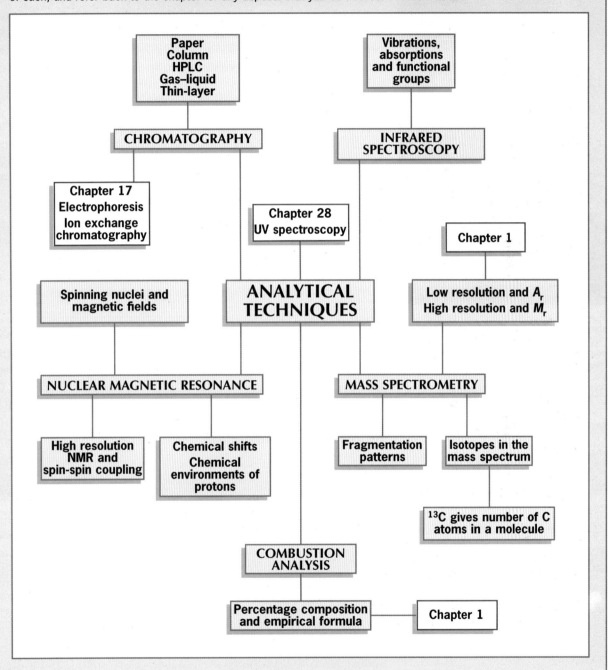

10 Halogenoalkanes

A polyfluorohydrocarbon may well prove to be the right compound for a synthetic blood substitute. It would enable emergency medical workers at accident and injury sites to give life-saving transfusions immediately

See page 83 for information on polar covalent bonds.

AFTER A SERIOUS ACCIDENT, such as a plane crash in a remote area, blood transfusions may have to be carried out under difficult conditions, but there may not be time to identify and match a victim's blood group beforehand. Ideally, the rescue team needs a synthetic blood substitute that will suit all victims and do the vital job of carrying large amounts of oxygen efficiently around the body.

The blood substitute must also be inert and non-toxic. It needs to be chemically stable so that it has a long shelf-life. Some polyfluorohydrocarbons have these properties, and so the search is now on for the best polyfluoro compound to be a synthetic blood substitute.

For over 50 years, it was because of these properties – of being inert, non-toxic and chemically stable – that the related chemicals chlorofluorocarbons (CFCs) were thought to be the best choice for industrial and domestic applications – as refrigerants, electrical insulators and aerosol propellants.

Then, in the 1980s, the same properties were found to make CFCs an environmental hazard: geoscientists confirmed that CFCs released into the air were breaking down the ozone in the stratosphere. They warned that, even if CFCs were banned, because they are so stable, it would be a long time before the ozone could build up to its original level. Since then, CFCs are being replaced in their previous applications by alternative compounds.

1 HALOGENO HYDROCARBONS

A **halogeno hydrocarbon** (also called halogenated hydrocarbon) is a compound that contains carbon, hydrogen and at least one of the halogens. This means that the molecule contains at least one polar covalent bond, namely, the carbon–halogen bond.

A **halogenoalkane** is an alkane in which one or more of the hydrogen atoms have been substituted by halogen atoms.

Uses of halogeno hydrocarbons

Halogenated hydrocarbons are synthesised as useful chemicals in their own right, as well as being intermediates in the synthesis of other chemicals.

As chemicals in their own right

Chloroalkanes have been used as solvents and anaesthetics for at least a century, but they are poisonous and damage vital organs in the body, including the liver. Then came synthetic methods that successfully introduced several different halogen atoms into a carbon skeleton.

This changed the situation immediately. The new chlorofluorocarbons were non-toxic, low-boiling liquids or gases at room temperature and chemically inert. They seemed just the answer for many applications, for example as the fluids for air conditioning systems, refrigerators, aerosols and blowing plastic foams.

Later, other halogen atoms were introduced and the **halons** were developed for fire extinguishers. Unfortunately, as the Opener points out, the very properties that make halogeno hydrocarbons so useful have caused a global environmental problem – ozone depletion in the upper atmosphere.

Some chlorinated hydrocarbons have been synthesised as insecticides and pesticides. But again, their chemical stability leads to environmental problems.

Fig 10.1 **The sales of aerosol cans that contain CFCs have been phased out since the damage that CFCs do to the atmosphere has been understood**

You can read more about pesticides and insecticides in Chapter 29.

As synthetic intermediates

The manufacture of many pharmaceutical products and polymers requires halogenated hydrocarbons as intermediates in their organic synthesis. A chlorine or bromine atom in an organic molecule often increases its reactivity and allows a change of functional groups or an extension of the carbon skeleton. The polymer poly(chloroethene), PVC, is manufactured from chloroethene; and tetraethyl lead(IV), which is the 'lead' in petrol, is synthesised from chloroethane.

Fig 10.2 **Clothes made of PVC can be fashionable and practical**

Naming the halogeno hydrocarbons

Although many halogeno hydrocarbons have traditional names, such as chloroform ($CHCl_3$) or vinyl chloride (CH_2CHCl), it is important that you can systematically name halogeno hydrocarbons.

The names of all organic compounds are based on the carbon skeleton and the functional groups present. In halogeno hydrocarbons, the hetero-atoms are the halogens. The presence of a halogen is indicated by the use of a prefix, namely *fluoro*, *chloro*, *bromo* or *iodo*. The number and location of the halogen atoms must also be specified. The number of each halogen atom is specified by the use of *mono*, *di*, *tri*, *tetra*, *penta*, *hexa*, and so on, before the prefix. For example, the trichloromethane molecule contains three chlorine atoms, and the dibromo-dichloroethane molecule contains two chlorine atoms and two bromine atoms.

Isomers are substances that have the same molecular formula but have different arrangements of their atoms. They may have different structural or displayed formulae, or different arrangements about a double bond. This means that, for example, dibromo-dichloroethane is not sufficient to fully describe one particular compound.

See page 156 to find out how to name the carbon skeleton.

?

A How many halogen atoms are there in one molecule of 1,2,2,3-tetrachloro-5-iodoheptane?

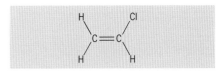

Fig 10.3 **The displayed formula for vinyl chloride shows it has the hydrocarbon skeleton of ethene, so its systematic name is chloroethene**

See page 144 for more information on isomerism.

Fig. 10.4 **The displayed formulas for all the isomers of dichloro-dibromoethane**

?

B (a) What is the systematic name for compounds with structures labelled **C** and **D** in Fig 10.4?

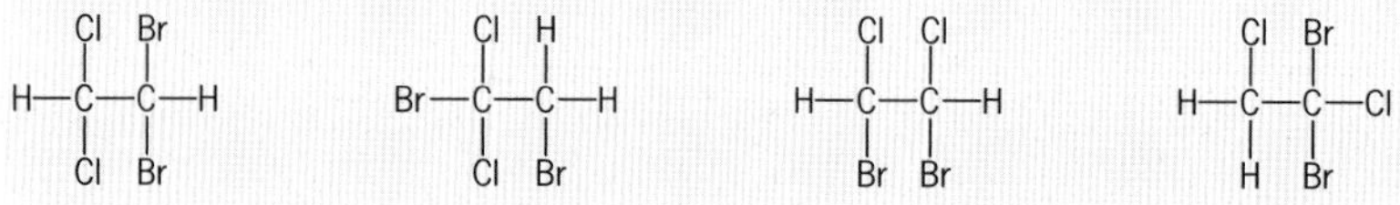

(b) Draw the displayed formulas for the following halogeno hydrocarbons:
(i) 2,2-dichloropropane,
(ii) 1,2,3,4-tetrachlorocyclohexane,
(iii) 1,2-dichloro-3,3,4-triiodoheptane,
(iv) 1,2-difluoroethene,
(v) tetrafluoroethene.

✓

Sometimes, all the hydrogen atoms in an alkane are replaced by halogen atoms. If the halogen atoms are all identical, the prefix 'per' is often used. So that, for example, C_2F_6 is often referred to as perfluoroethane rather than hexafluoroethane.

?

C (a) What is the name of C_4F_{10}?

(b) What is the name of $CH_3CH_2CHClCH_3$?

(c) What is the name of C_6Cl_{14}?

Fig 10.4 shows the four different structural isomers that could all be called dichloro-dibromoethane.

A   **B**   **C**   **D**

This means that the *position* of the halogen atom must also be specified in the name. We use the system of numbering each carbon atom which we started to use on page 157. In Fig 10.4, structure **A** is called 2,2-dibromo-1,1-dichloroethane, and structure **B** is called 1,2-dibromo-1,1-dichloroethane. Notice that the order of the halogens in the name is alphabetical.

2 PHYSICAL PROPERTIES OF HALOGENOALKANES

The uses of halogenoalkanes generally depend on their physical properties. One notable property is their low boiling point, which accounts for many of their applications (see the Feature box opposite).

The boiling point of a substance depends on the nature and strength of the *inter*molecular forces in the liquid.

Intermolecular forces in halogenoalkanes

Halogenoalkanes are all covalently bonded and form simple molecules. The presence of simple molecules in the liquid phase makes them solvents that are electrically non-conducting.

Halogen atoms tend to withdraw electrons from a carbon–halogen bond. In a monohalogenoalkane, the halogen atom will be slightly negative (δ–) and the carbon atom it is bonded to will be slightly positive(δ+). We say that the molecule has a **permanent dipole** and that it possesses a **dipole moment**, a measurable degree of polarity.

chloromethane   trichloromethane

Fig 10.5 **The high electronegativity of chlorine gives both chloromethane and trichloromethane a dipole moment**

Chloromethane and trichloromethane are both molecules with a dipole moment, so they have permanent dipoles. The positive part of one molecule can attract the negative part of another molecule. This intermolecular force is referred to as a **permanent dipole–permanent dipole interaction**.

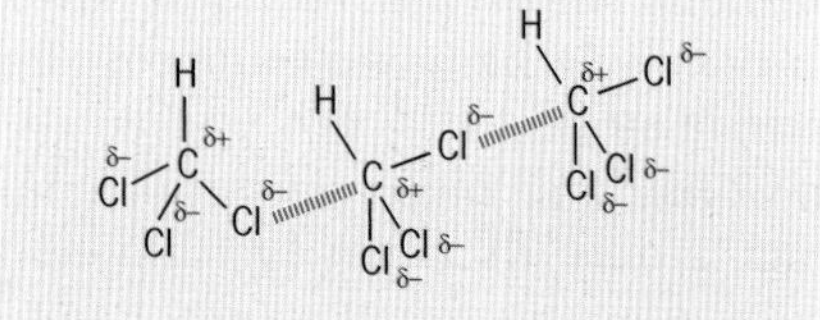

Fig 10.6 **The permanent dipole causes a weak electrostatic attraction between the negative chlorine atom and the positive carbon atom in a neighbouring trichloromethane molecule**

CHLOROFLUOROCARBONS AND HALONS

THE MOST WELL-KNOWN AND INFAMOUS of the halogenoalkanes are the chlorofluorocarbons, known as CFCs. As their name suggests, these are halogenoalkanes in which every hydrogen atom has been replaced with either a chlorine or a fluorine atom. Table 10.1 shows some CFCs.

Table 10.1 **Some typical CFCs and their uses**

Molecular formula	Name	CFC designation	Uses
$CFCl_3$	trichloro-fluoromethane	CFC11	blowing foam plastics, refrigeration, air conditioning
CF_2Cl_2	dichloro-difluoromethane	CFC12	blowing foam plastics, refrigeration, air conditioning, aerosol propellant, sterilisation and food freezing
$C_2F_3Cl_3$	trichloro-trifluoroethane	CFC113	solvent
$C_2F_4Cl_2$	dichloro-tetrafluoroethane	CFC114	blowing foam plastics, refrigeration, air conditioning
C_2F_5Cl	chloro-pentafluoroethane	CFC115	refrigeration, air conditioning

Fig10.7 **The CFC refrigerant circulates through pipes at the back of the fridge**

Fig 10.8 **Halon fire extinguishers, once used on fires near electrical equipment, are now being replaced by carbon dioxide gas extinguishers**

When a hydrogen atom is included in a CFC, the compound is called HCFC (hydrogen-chlorofluorocarbon). Another variety of fully halogenated alkanes is called the **halons**. These contain bromine atoms as well as fluorine and chlorine atoms. Halons are used extensively in fire extinguishers because they are chemically unreactive and non-toxic. Being much denser than air, they effectively blanket a fire and keep out the air and so extinguish the fire.

Typical halons include trifluoro-bromomethane (Halon 1301), and bromo-chloro-difluoromethane (Halon 1211). Unfortunately, these halons also cause the same environmental problems as CFCs, and research is under way to find substitutes.

When a large alkyl group is present as well, part of the intermolecular attraction consists of induced dipole–induced dipole van der Waals attractions.

See page 159 for information on induced dipole–induced dipole forces.

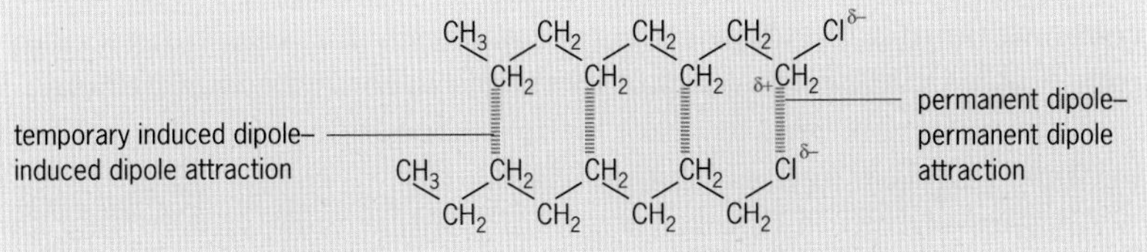

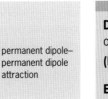

temporary induced dipole–induced dipole attraction

permanent dipole–permanent dipole attraction

Fig 10.9 **The intermolecular forces in 1-chlorooctane are both due to induced dipole–induced dipole and permanent dipole–permanent dipole interactions**

D (a) Suggest the molecular formula of (i) CFC13, (ii) CFC112.

(b) Suggest the name for CFC112.

E Why is it important for a halon to be more dense than air?

Table 10.2 **Boiling points of some halogenated alkanes**

Compound	Boiling point / °C
1-fluorobutane	(see **F** below)
1-chlorobutane	77
1-bromobutane	100
1-iodobutane	130

See question 1. ■

F (a) Predict the boiling point of 1-fluorobutane.

(b) What does the difference in boiling points of the compounds in Table 10.2 suggest about the strength of intermolecular attraction in 1-chlorobutane and 1-iodobutane?

(c) The boiling point of 2-chloro-2-methylpropane is 51 °C, and that of 1-chlorobutane is 77 °C, even though they have the same molecular mass. Explain why there is this difference. Hint: read page 160 for some ideas.

G Draw in the bond polarities for trichlorofluoromethane, and hence draw in the dipole moment of the molecule

Fig 10.11 **A summary of the preparation routes for halogenoalkanes. Electrophilic addition is described in Chapter 12, and the conversion of alcohols to halogenoalkanes is described later in this chapter and in Chapter 11**

Boiling points of CFCs

Boiling occurs when intermolecular forces are overcome. So, the stronger the intermolecular attraction, the higher the boiling point. The type of intermolecular forces in CFCs will be similar to those in other halogenoalkanes but the dipole moment of the molecules is likely to be much smaller since very often the individual bond polarities will tend to cancel out. This means that the attraction due to permanent dipole–permanent dipole interactions is liable to be quite weak. As a result, even though the relative molecular masses of CFCs are quite large compared with, say, the mono-halogenoalkanes, they will have low boiling points.

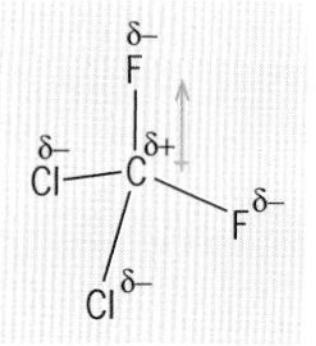

Fig 10.10 **The bond polarities nearly cancel out one another, so that dichloro-difluoromethane has a small dipole moment**

Because CFCs have weak intermolecular attraction, they vaporise easily at low temperatures. Many CFCs have two properties which make them efficient refrigerants: they absorb heat energy readily when vaporising, and they can be easily compressed back into liquids, releasing this energy. Provided the heat released during liquefaction is removed efficiently by the heat exchanger then net cooling of the refrigerant will occur. If the intermolecular forces were larger, it would be difficult to vaporise the CFC and so little heat would be absorbed.

3 PREPARATION OF HALOGENOALKANES BY FREE RADICAL SUBSTITUTION

Even before the wide-scale use of halons and CFCs, the preparation of halogenoalkanes had become an important synthetic reaction because halogenoalkanes are extremely useful in making other chemicals.

The main methods of preparation of halogenoalkanes is described in Fig 10.11. One route involves a direct substitution of a hydrogen atom by a halogen atom. It is called **free radical substitution**.

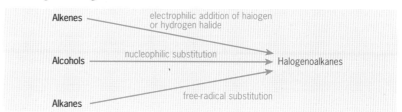

Free radicals

Alkanes are very unreactive compounds with the exception of their reaction with oxygen. Their lack of polar covalent bonds is the reason for this behaviour. Nucleophiles are particles that seek out electron-deficient centres and donate pairs of electrons to form a covalent bond and electrophiles are particles that seek out electron-rich centres and accept pairs of electrons to form a covalent bond. It is difficult for alkanes to react with nucleophiles and electrophiles because they are non-polar molecules.

Alkanes require a different type of particle with which they can react, that is, one which is highly reactive and does not need to seek out a polar covalent bond before it can react. The particle in question is called a **free radical**. This is an atom or group of atoms that possesses at least one unpaired electron in its outer shell.

Most free radicals are extremely reactive because they pair up the unpaired electron with an electron removed from a covalent bond.

A free radical is usually indicated by a dot on the right-hand side of the formula of the particle. For example, a chlorine atom Cl is a free radical, which is made clear by writing Cl•.

Homolytic fission

Because they are so reactive, free radicals cannot be stored in reagent bottles. They must be made in the reaction vessel ready to react immediately. To make a free radical, a covalent bond is broken in such a way that the electrons in the shared pair of the covalent bond become two single electrons, one electron per atom. This is known as **homolytic fission** of a covalent bond.

In Fig 10.13, you can see a representation of this process to make a chlorine free radical from a chlorine atom. The movement of one electron is shown by a curly half-headed arrow.

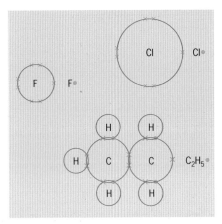

Fig 10. 12 **Dot and cross diagrams of three important free radicals**

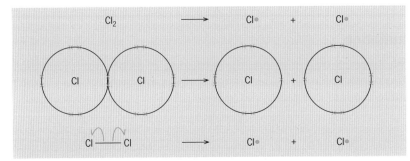

Fig 10.13 **Chlorine free radicals are formed by the homolytic fission of a single bond in a chlorine molecule**

The homolytic fission of a covalent bond requires energy (it is an endothermic process). For example, the production of the chlorine free radical requires half of the bond energy of a chlorine molecule:

$$\tfrac{1}{2}Cl_2(g) \rightarrow Cl•(g)$$

Free radical substitution of ethane

Ethane is a typical alkane, which reacts with chlorine in the presence of ultraviolet light to give a large variety of products.

From Fig 10.14 you can get an idea of the variety of **substitution** products resulting from the free-radical chlorination of ethane. This is where a hydrogen atom has been swapped for a chlorine atom.

?

H Draw a dot and cross diagram of each of the following and use this to decide which particle is a free radical: Cl^-, Cl^+, I, BF_3, CH_3.

✔

The electron shells are shown here as circles, but in Chapter 4 they are not. Either way is acceptable

?

I **(a)** What is the energy required to make 1 mole of fluorine free radicals from fluorine molecules under standard conditions? (Refer to data tables.)

(b) Predict whether bromine, chlorine or fluorine will be the most reactive towards ethane.

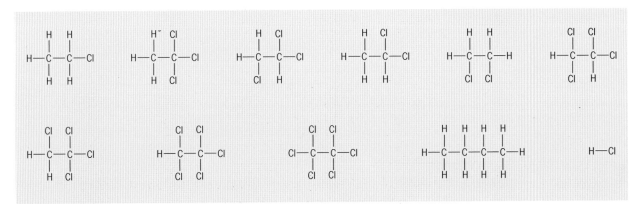

Fig 10.14 **The displayed formulas of eleven products of the free-radical chlorination of ethane**

But there are also other products whose origin is less obvious. The only way to explain this large collection of products is to examine the **mechanism** of the reaction.

Reaction mechanisms

The **mechanism** of a reaction details the smaller steps in the process which happens between the starting materials and the end products. In particular, a mechanism seeks to explain which bonds are broken and formed, and when and how they are broken and formed.

Free-radical substitution is split into three, clearly defined steps:

- **Initiation** This is the formation of the free radical.

- **Propagation** This involves reactions which maintain the presence of the free radicals.

- **Termination** This involves reactions which remove the free radicals.

Initiation

We have already described the formation of a chlorine free radical. Ultraviolet radiation is used to supply the energy to break the chlorine molecule into free radicals as follows:

$$Cl_2(g) \xrightarrow{\text{ultraviolet light}} 2Cl\bullet(g)$$

The equation tends to mislead, since it suggests that all the chlorine molecules are changed into free radicals. In fact, only an extremely small percentage of chlorine molecules are dissociated, most remaining as chlorine molecules.

Propagation

Reactions take place when the appropriate particles collide. Since free radicals are so reactive, they almost invariably react with any particle they collide with. Continuing with the chlorine free-radical substitution of ethane, once the very first free radical is produced, it is most likely to collide with either a chlorine molecule or an ethane molecule. The collision with the chlorine molecule does not lead to any change.

$$Cl\bullet(g) + Cl_2(g) \rightarrow Cl_2(g) + Cl\bullet(g)$$

When the highly reactive free radical collides with an ethane molecule, it gains an electron from one of the bonds in the molecule. In this case it is the C–H bond. This gives:

$$C_2H_6(g) + Cl\bullet(g) \rightarrow C_2H_5\bullet(g) + HCl(g)$$

This reaction produces a new free radical, $C_2H_5\bullet$, which is the ethyl free radical. The ethyl free radical is also very reactive and as soon as it collides with a particle, it reacts. Which particle it collides with is just a question of chance or probability. The most likely will be the particles which are in the greatest concentration. Certainly, at the start of the reaction, these will be either ethane or chlorine molecules:

$$C_2H_5\bullet(g) + Cl_2(g) \rightarrow C_2H_5Cl(g) + Cl\bullet(g)$$

Notice that two of the steps just described regenerate the chlorine free radical, which explains why they are called propagation steps.

J Explain why the collision of an ethyl free radical with an ethane molecule does not lead to a reaction.

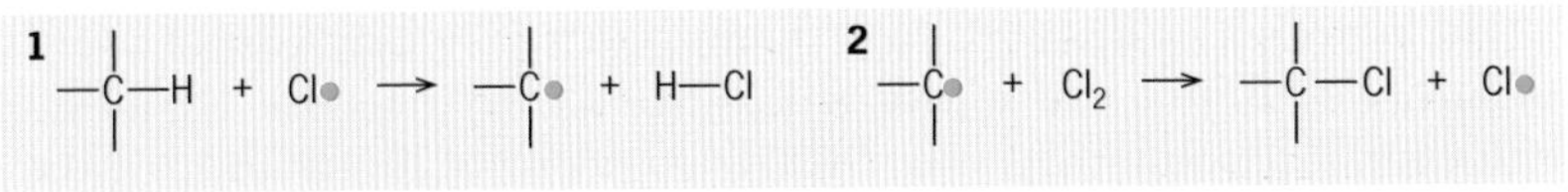

$$1 \quad -\overset{|}{\underset{|}{C}}-H + Cl\bullet \;\rightarrow\; -\overset{|}{\underset{|}{C}}\bullet + H—Cl \qquad 2 \quad -\overset{|}{\underset{|}{C}}\bullet + Cl_2 \;\rightarrow\; -\overset{|}{\underset{|}{C}}-Cl + Cl\bullet$$

Fig 10.15 **The propagation steps in the free-radical substitution of a C–H bond. Notice that the chlorine free radical is regenerated at the end of the second step**

Fig 10.15 generalises these two steps, explaining the process as a characteristic reaction of a C–H bond associated with a carbon atom with four single bonds.

The product chloroethane still has five hydrogen atoms all bonded to carbon atoms. So, when a chlorine free radical collides with a chloroethane molecule, a reaction will take place:

$$C_2H_5Cl(g) + Cl\bullet(g) \rightarrow C_2H_4Cl\bullet(g) + HCl(g)$$
$$C_2H_4Cl\bullet(g) + Cl_2(g) \rightarrow C_2H_4Cl_2(g) + Cl\bullet(g)$$

Provided there is sufficient chlorine present, this reaction can continue until all the hydrogen atoms have been substituted. The composition of the reaction mixture varies with the time allowed for the reaction and the mole ratio of ethane and chlorine.

Termination

The propagation steps cannot go on forever because eventually chance takes a hand and a free radical collides with another free radical. Although this is not very likely, it is not impossible – particularly when there are millions of collisions per second.

When two free radicals collide, they react and form a covalent bond. As any two free radicals may collide, note that all of the following are possible termination steps.

$$Cl\bullet(g) + Cl\bullet(g) \rightarrow Cl_2(g)$$
$$Cl\bullet(g) + C_2H_4Cl\bullet(g) \rightarrow C_2H_4Cl_2(g)$$
$$C_2H_5\bullet(g) + C_2H_5\bullet(g) \rightarrow C_4H_{10}(g)$$

Also note that one of the products is butane, a molecule which does not even contain chlorine.

Fluorination of alkanes

Fluorine is a much more reactive halogen than chlorine, and so it should react much more readily with alkanes. The bond energy for a fluorine molecule is $158\,kJ\,mol^{-1}$, considerably smaller than that for a chlorine molecule at $244\,kJ\,mol^{-1}$. The reason for this low bond energy is the repulsion experienced by each atom due to the very small bond length of 254 pm in a fluorine molecule. This makes the initiation step for fluorine much easier than that for chlorine.

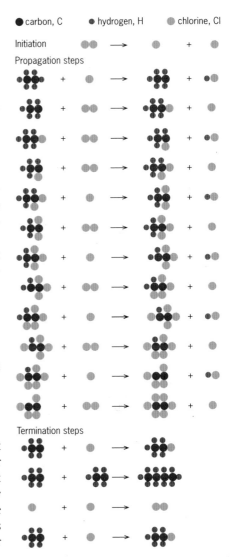

Fig 10.16 **The complete mechanism of the free-radical substitution of ethane**

See questions 2, 3 and 4. ■

See questions 2, 3 and 4. ■

?

K (a) How could you ensure that you get a large proportion of chloroethane during the free-radical substitution of ethane with chlorine?

(b) How could you ensure that you get a large proportion of hexachloroethane during the free-radical substitution of ethane with chlorine?

?

L Write down two more possible termination steps during the free-radical chlorination of ethane.

M Methane reacts with chlorine in the presence of ultraviolet light to form a mixture of products, including chloromethane, dichloromethane, trichloromethane, tetrachloromethane, hydrogen chloride and ethane. Account for the formation of each of these products by writing down the detailed mechanism for the reaction.

?

N Write down the mechanism of the reaction of methane with excess fluorine by a free-radical substitution.

The reaction of fluorine with alkanes does not need the presence of ultraviolet light and it proceeds much faster than the reaction of chlorine. Consequently, it is difficult to produce monofluoro derivatives of alkanes. The reaction is often explosive and produces the perfluoro derivative (all H atoms are substituted by F atoms). The reaction of fluorine with alkanes is slowed down by diluting fluorine with nitrogen.

USES OF ORGANOFLUORINES

ORGANOFLUORINE COMPOUNDS occur rarely in nature but because of the wide range of their applications – from inert solvents in the electronics industry to highly active pharmaceuticals – their development and production are increasingly important.

The three-dimensional shape of an organoflourine molecule determines its biological activity. Substitution of a fluorine atom for a hydrogen atom rarely changes the shape since the change in bond length is minimal, being from 120 pm in a C–H bond to 147 pm in a C–F bond. The C–F bond is also very strong and resistant to reaction with water (hydrolysis), which is why pharmaceuticals are liable to remain active in the aqueous medium of a living cell for a long time.

Perfluoro compounds are very unreactive, which has led to yet further applications where being chemically inert is vital. Perfluorodecalin, for example, dissolves oxygen very efficiently and has been successfully transfused into human volunteers as a blood substitute.

Other perfluorohydrocarbons are being developed to provide a fluid that will preserve donor organs before transplantation. There are still problems with these perfluoro compounds, since to be of use they must remain as an emulsion in water. Unfortunately, they tend to separate during storage.

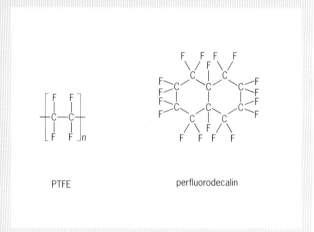

PTFE   perfluorodecalin

Fig 10.17 **The displayed structures of PTFE and perfluorodecalin**

Polytetrafluoroethene (PTFE) is a perfluorinated polymer that is used to make non-stick surfaces, such as in saucepans and frying pans.

Coatings are being developed from polymers that include fluoro-substituted alkanes, since these side chains make the surface much easier to clean by their ability to shrug off stains and dirt. Recently, clothes have been developed with such a coating, and it may be possible to make a surface that could remain graffiti free.

Fig 10.18 **Will organofluorines provide surfaces to building materials that will make them easy to wipe free of graffiti?**

Bromination of alkanes

Bromine is less reactive than chlorine, and the free-radical reaction with alkanes is much slower than with chlorine. This is surprising since the bond energy for a bromine molecule is only $151\,\mathrm{kJ\,mol^{-1}}$. The reason for this is related to the strength of the carbon–halogen bond that is formed, since a carbon–chlorine bond is much stronger than a carbon–bromine bond, and hence more stable.

When a few drops of liquid bromine are added to hexane, a liquid alkane, and the mixture is left in direct sunlight, there is a very slow reaction (Fig 10.19). Eventually, the orange colour of the bromine disappears, leaving a mixture of all the structural isomers of monobromoalkane as the main products:

$$C_6H_{14}(l) + Br_2(l) \rightarrow C_6H_{13}Br(l) + HBr(g)$$

Fig 10.19(a) **The colour of hexane to which a few drops of bromine have been added is orange**

Free-radical substitution as a synthetic reaction

Substitution in alkanes

Although free-radical substitution is a very successful way of introducing halogen atoms into an alkane molecule, it suffers from the major drawback: often a large variety of products is formed.

The aim of synthesis is to make a compound in high yield and purity, using few reactions and involving cheap starting materials. The large number of products formed during free-radical substitution makes it a poor tool in organic synthesis.

The only way to make the reaction useful is to minimise the number of possible products, so that you get a relatively high yield of the required product. Simply, this means involving reactants with very few hydrogen atoms that can be substituted.

Fig 10.19(b) **Exposure to ultraviolet light from the lamp causes a slow reaction: after the time shown, the mixture becomes colourless**

?

O Draw the displayed formulas of all the structural isomers of monobromohexane.

Substitution in benzene

Look at the reaction in Fig 10.20. Methylbenzene only has three C–H bonds not attached to the benzene ring and these hydrogen atoms are chemically identical. Therefore, it is quite easy to synthesise chloromethylbenzene by passing chlorine into boiling methylbenzene in the presence of ultraviolet light. By keeping the available chlorine

Synthesis of the amino acid glycine

Amino acids are the building blocks of proteins. Glycine (aminoethanoic acid) is the simplest amino acid. It has a two-carbon skeleton, so an ideal candidate for its synthesis is ethanoic acid. Fig 10.21 shows a synthetic route that could be used to make glycine, employing the free-radical halogenation reaction.

Fig 10.20 **The reaction of methylbenzene with chlorine**

Fig 10.21 **The synthesis of the amino acid glycine from ethanoic acid**

CH_3CO_2H $\xrightarrow{Cl_2/hf}$ $ClCH_2CO_2H$ $\xrightarrow[\text{(ii) } H^+(aq)]{\text{(i) } NH_3}$ $NH_2-CH_2-CO_2H$

ethanoic acid   free-radical substitution   chloroethanoic acid   nucleophilic substitution   glycine

concentration low, the monosubstituted product chloromethylbenzene acid is the major product.

In the same way, ethanoic acid is chlorinated to give chloroethanoic acid:

$$CH_3COOH(l) + Cl_2(g) \rightarrow CH_2ClCOOH(l) + HCl(g)$$

?

P How might you modify the reaction conditions to make trichloromethylbenzene? Write an equation for this reaction.

4 PREPARATION OF HALOGENOALKANES BY THE HALOGENATION OF ALCOHOLS

You can read much more about the mechanism of the halogenation of alcohols on pages 234.

Monohalogenoalkanes are best prepared by replacing the hydroxyl group in an alcohol by a halogen atom. A variety of reagents can be used for this conversion and some of these are shown in Table 10.3. Note that R stands for an alkyl group such as methyl, ethyl and propyl.

Table 10.3 **Reagents and conditions that can be used to make halogenaoalkanes from alcohols. Concentrated hydrochloric acid and concentrated hydrobromic acid are often generated in situ by the reaction of the corresponding sodium halide with concentrated sulphuric acid:**

$$NaBr + H_2SO_4 \rightarrow NaHSO_4 + HBr$$

Halogenoalkane	Reagent	Conditions	Equation
chloroalkane	concentrated hydrochloric acid		$ROH + HCl \rightarrow RCl + H_2O$
	phosphorus(V) chloride		$ROH + PCl_5 \rightarrow RCl + HCl + POCl_3$
	sulphuryl(IV) chloride	heating under reflux	$ROH + SOCl_2 \rightarrow RCl + SO_2 + HCl$
bromoalkane	concentrated hydrobromic acid		$ROH + HBr \rightarrow RBr + H_2O$
	phosphorus(III) bromide		$3ROH + PBr_3 \rightarrow 3RBr + H_3PO_3$
iodo-alkanes	concentrated hydroiodic acid		$ROH + HI \rightarrow RI + H_2O$
	red phosphorus and iodine		$3ROH + PI_3 \rightarrow 3RI + H_3PO_3$

Fig 10.22 **The laboratory preparation of 1-bromobutane**

5 REACTIONS OF HALOGENOALKANES

Halogenoalkanes are saturated compounds, which means that they have no double or triple bonds in their molecules. This limits the reactions available, since saturated compounds cannot undergo addition reactions. Halogenoalkanes undergo two major types of reaction, **substitution** and **elimination**. During substitution, the halogen atom is swapped for one atom or a group of atoms. The elimination reaction involves the loss of a molecule of hydrogen halide to produce an alkene.

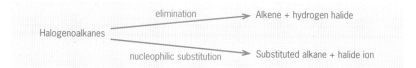

Fig 10.23 **The two different reactions of halogenoalkanes**

Q (a) What is the major product when 3-methylhexan-2-ol is refluxed with concentrated hydroiodic acid?

(b) Which reagents do you need to make (i) iodoethane, (ii) 3-iodohexane?

R State which one of the following compounds has the most electron-deficient carbon atom: bromomethane, chloromethane, fluoromethane or iodomethane.

Substitution reactions

Polar covalent bond

The carbon–halogen bond is a polar covalent bond. The carbon atom is electron deficient, because the pair of electrons within the covalent bond is drawn closer to the highly electronegative halogen atom. A polar covalent bond, such as a carbon–chlorine bond, is open to attack by a species (an ion or a molecule) that seeks out electron-deficient centres.

Fig 10.24 **The electron clouds in the carbon–halogen bonds**

Nucleophiles

A **nucleophile** is a chemical species (ion or molecule) which donates an electron *pair* in order to make a covalent bond with an electron-deficient centre. A nucleophile has a complete outer shell of electrons and at least one lone pair. It is this lone pair of electrons that is donated to form the covalent bond.

S Draw a dot-and-cross diagram for each of the following and use it to decide whether the particle is a nucleophile: **(a)** NH_2^-, **(b)** CN^-, **(c)** BCl_3.

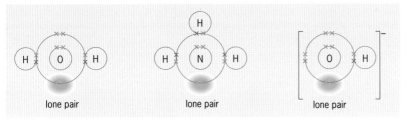

Fig 10.25 **Dot and cross diagrams of nucleophiles H_2O, NH_3, OH^-**

When we describe a species as a good nucleophile, the term 'good' refers to the ability of the species to donate an electron pair to form a covalent bond. The halide ions, for example, do not very easily donate the lone pair of electrons in their outer shells, and are therefore classed as poor nucleophiles.

Nucleophilic substitution

The δ+ carbon atom of the polar carbon–halogen bond is attacked by a nucleophile which donates a pair of electrons to make a covalent bond. Since a carbon atom is normally surrounded by no more than four covalent bonds (four bonding pairs of electrons), this donation must result in the breaking of another bond.

In Fig 10.26 you can see that when a nucleophile reacts with a halogenoalkane, a substitution reaction takes place. This reaction is called **nucleophilic substitution,** since the species that starts the substitution is a nucleophile.

Fig 10.26 **Nucleophilic substitution of a halogenoalkane by a nucleophile**

During the reaction, a carbon–nucleophile bond is made and a carbon-halogen bond is broken. The halogen is sometimes called the **leaving group,** because it is the species that is lost. In this case, the leaving group must be able to gain the pair of bonding electrons. This is not a problem for a halogen atom, since it forms a halide ion which easily supports a negative charge.

During nucleophilic substitution, there is **heterolytic fission** of a covalent bond. In heterolytic fission, one of the two atoms joined by the covalent bond that breaks receives both electrons from the bond, so after the fission one atom carries a positive charge and the other a negative charge.

Energy considerations during nucleophilic substitution

It is possible to estimate the enthalpy change of reaction by considering the bond energies of the carbon–nucleophile bond and carbon–halogen bond. Although this ignores the energy changes due to the formation of the nucleophile and the enthalpy changes due to interactions with the solvent, it is nevertheless a good way to make some predictions.

On page 121, we describe bond breaking as an endothermic process, requiring the transfer of energy *from* the surroundings; and bond formation as an exothermic process, involving energy transfer *to* the surroundings.

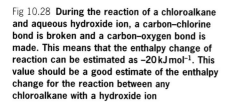

Bonds broken C—Hal (endothermic)
Bonds made C—Nu (exothermic)

So enthalpy change of reaction = bond energy – bond energy
C—Hal   C—Nu

Fig 10.27 Bond breaking and bond forming for enthalpy calculations

An estimate for the enthalpy change for the nucleophilic substitution can be calculated using:

$$\Delta H = \begin{pmatrix} \text{bond energy of} \\ \text{carbon–halogen} \end{pmatrix} - \begin{pmatrix} \text{bond energy of} \\ \text{carbon–nucleophile} \end{pmatrix}$$

Fig 10.28 During the reaction of a chloroalkane and aqueous hydroxide ion, a carbon–chlorine bond is broken and a carbon–oxygen bond is made. This means that the enthalpy change of reaction can be estimated as –20 kJ mol^{-1}. This value should be a good estimate of the enthalpy change for the reaction between any chloroalkane with a hydroxide ion

You can read more about the feasibility of reactions on page 131 and Chapter 26.

A useful guide to the feasibility of a reaction can be obtained by looking at the enthalpy change of reaction. An exothermic reaction is often more feasible than an endothermic reaction that has a positive ΔH. In the same way, a reaction that is highly exothermic is often more feasible than one which is less exothermic.

This discussion ignores entropy considerations, which are difficult to predict in the example we are looking at.

This analysis of the energy changes during reactions leads to some simple ideas. Consider the reaction of hydroxide ion with fluoroalkanes, chloroalkanes, bromoalkanes and iodoalkanes. The same bond is made each time, namely the carbon–oxygen bond. But the bond that is broken, the carbon–halogen bond, gets weaker and weaker, and so the overall enthalpy change gets more negative. So, nucleophilic substitution will be easier with iodoalkanes than with fluoroalkanes. The strength of the bond to be broken in the reaction, the carbon–halogen bond, plays an important part in determining whether nucleophilic substitution will take place.

?

T Estimate the enthalpy change of reaction for:

(a) reaction of hydroxide ion with fluoroethane,

(b) reaction of hydroxide ion with bromoethane.
You will need to look up the appropriate bond energies.

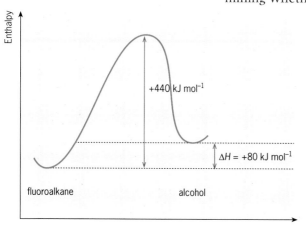

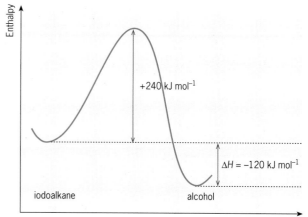

Fig 10.29 Energy profile diagrams for the reaction of a fluoroalkane and an iodoalkane with a hydroxide ion

See question 5. ◼

This also means the nucleophile must make a strong bond with the carbon atom rather than a weak bond which releases little energy into the surroundings. Because the C–Hal bonds are quite weak, the halide ions do not act as nucleophiles in this reaction.

Mechanism of nucleophilic substitution

So far, we have only discussed which bonds have been broken and which ones have been formed. The next question to ask is: What is the sequence of bond making or bond breaking? One mechanism assumes that the two processes take place together, so that as one bond is forming the other bond is breaking. This mechanism is called S_N2, since it involves two particles colliding in the slowest step of the mechanism. This mechanism is shown in Fig 10.30. The curly arrow shows the movement of an electron pair.

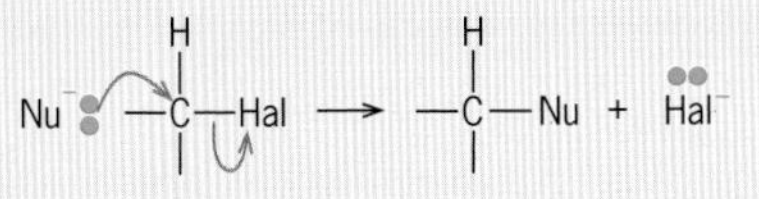

Fig 10.30 **This mechanism is known as S_N2, since two species, the nucleophile and the halogenoalkane, are involved in the only step. In this mechanism, there is only one step involved. Primary and many secondary halogenoalkanes show this mechanism during nucleophilic substitution**

An alternative mechanism involves the breaking of the carbon–halogen bond first, with the formation of a positive species called a **carbonium ion** or **carbocation**. This mechanism, shown in Fig 10.31, is called S_N1, with just one particle in the slowest step. A carbocation is a cation in which the positive charge resides on a carbon atom surrounded by only six outer electrons.

carbocation

Hydrolysis

Halogenoalkanes react extremely slowly, if at all, with water. However, as we have already seen, they undergo a nucleophilic substitution reaction with aqueous hydroxide ions. This reaction is known as **hydrolysis** and involves boiling aqueous sodium hydroxide, for example, with the halogenoalkane. A hydroxyl group is substituted for the halogen atom and so an alcohol is produced. So, 1-bromobutane would be hydrolysed to form butan-1-ol:

$$CH_3CH_2CH_2CH_2Br + NaOH \rightarrow CH_3CH_2CH_2CH_2OH + NaBr$$

In these reactions, the hydroxide ion is behaving as a nucleophile.

Fluoroalkanes are not hydrolysed since the carbon–fluorine bond is too strong. The ease with which halogenoalkanes can be hydrolysed increases as the atomic number of the halogen increases and the carbon–halogen bond gets weaker.

Reaction with ammonia

Ammonia is another nucleophile (Fig 10.25), since the lone pair on nitrogen can be donated to an electron-deficient centre to make a covalent bond. Ammonia reacts with halogenoalkanes to form an amine. For example, 1-bromobutane will produce butylamine:

$$CH_3CH_2CH_2CH_2Br + NH_3 \rightarrow CH_3CH_2CH_2CH_2NH_2 + HBr$$

There are two serious drawbacks with this reaction: ammonia reacts with one of the products (HBr), and the amine produced is also a nucleophile that can further react with the halogenoalkane, see page 217.

In section 2 of this chapter, we met a similar problem: a reaction that gives a poor yield and many products is of little use as a synthetic method.

✔ S_N2 stands for substitution, nucleophilic and second order. Second order reactions have two particles colliding in the slowest step of the mechanism. S_N1 stands for substitution, nucleophilic and first order. First order reactions have only one particle in the slowest step of the mechanism. You can read more about orders of reaction and mechanisms in Chapter 27.

■ See question 6.

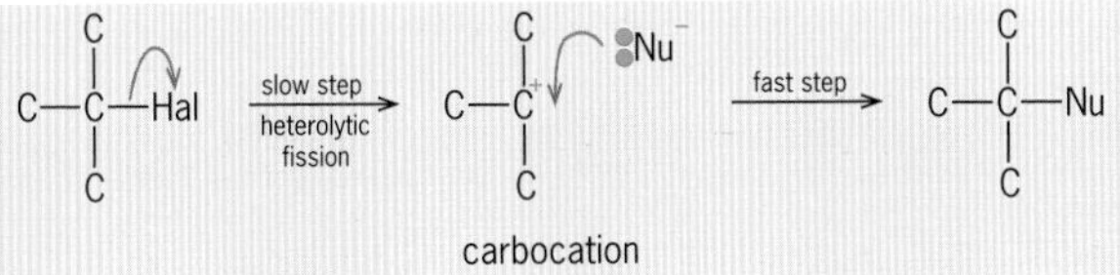

Fig 10.31 **This mechanism is known as S_N1, since only one species, the halogenoalkane, is involved in the slowest step. The nucleophilic substitution of tertiary halogenoalkanes have this mechanism. The carbocation formed is stabilised by having three alkyl groups attached which all push electron density towards the positive carbon**

✔ A primary halogenoalkane has one alkyl or aryl groups attached to the carbon of the C–Hal bond, a secondary halogenoalkane has two alkyl or aryl groups, and a tertiary halogenoalkane has three alkyl or aryl groups

? **U** What is the product of the reaction of 2-iodopentane with aqueous potassium hydroxide?

■ See questions 6, 7, 8, 9 and 10.

Luckily, the reaction conditions can be manipulated to produce good yields. By using excess concentrated ammonia, the acidic hydrogen halide product reacts with the excess ammonia to produce an ammonium salt. So, in our example, ammonium bromide would be produced:

$$HBr + NH_3 \rightarrow NH_4Br$$

The excess ammonia also means that there is always a vast excess of ammonia nucleophile compared with the product. This ensures the maximum yield of amine. The best reaction conditions involve heating the halogenoalkane and the excess concentrated aqueous ammonia in a sealed tube.

See questions 4, 6, 7 and 9.

Analysis of halogenoalkanes

Aqueous silver nitrate can be used to detect the presence of aqueous halide ions, but it will not detect the halogen in a halogenoalkane since the halogen is present in a covalent bond. To detect the halogen, the halogenoalkane must first be hydrolysed to produce aqueous halide ions.

The halogenoalkane is heated with aqueous sodium hydroxide. During hydrolysis, aqueous halide ions are produced. The hydrolysis mixture is acidified with dilute nitric acid, then aqueous silver nitrate is added. The halide ion present in the mixture is precipitated as the silver halide:

$$Ag^+(aq) + X^-(aq) \rightarrow AgX(s) \quad \text{where } X = Cl, Br \text{ or } I$$

The colours of the precipitate are given in Table 10.3 and shown in Fig 10.32.

Table 10.3 **Test for halide ion in the hydrolysis mixture**

Halide ion in hydrolysis mixture	Add excess nitric acid followed by aqueous silver nitrate
Chloride	white precipitate
Bromide	pale cream precipitate
Iodide	pale yellow precipitate

Fig 10.32 **The resulting precipitates in halide ion test**

PREPARATION OF AMPHETAMINE

THE DRUG AMPHETAMINE is a stimulant that gives a sense of well-being and speeds up the metabolism, so that someone taking it before doing a sport would feel less fatigued. It is prepared using a halogeno compound as an intermediate. Fig 10.33 shows the synthetic route employed.

An alcohol 2-phenylpropan-2-ol is halogenated to give 2-bromo-2-phenylpropane, which then allows a nucleophilic substitution to take place using excess ammonia. The bromo compound is a synthetic intermediate that allows the conversion of an alcohol into an amine while keeping the same carbon skeleton.

Fig 10.33 **The synthesis of amphetamine**

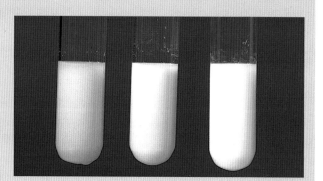

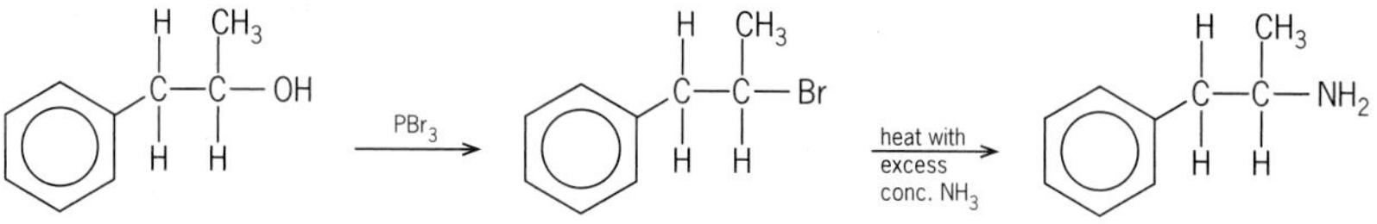

You can read more about amines in Chapter 29.

Reaction with amines

Amines are nucleophiles because of the lone pair on the nitrogen atom, so they can react with halogenoalkanes to give secondary, tertiary or quaternary ammonium salts.

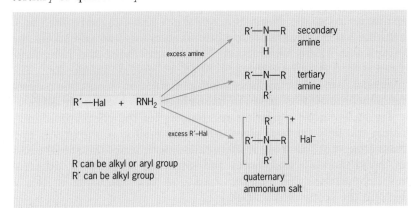

Fig 10.34 **The reactions of amines with halogenoalkanes**

?

V Draw the displayed formulae of the products of the following reactions:

(a) excess ammonia with 2-chlorobutane,

(b) excess ammonia with 3-iodopentane,

(c) ethylamine with excess 2-iodopropane.

Reaction with the cyanide ion

Whenever possible, the starting material chosen for a synthesis already has the correct carbon skeleton. The synthesis of amphetamine in Fig 10.33 illustrates this point, where the nine-carbon skeleton is in place in the starting material. There are times, however, when the chosen starting material does not have the correct carbon skeleton and part of the synthesis is the construction of the correct skeleton. An important synthetic reaction is the *extension* of the carbon skeleton by one carbon.

One convenient way involves the nucleophilic substitution of a halogen atom with a cyanide ion. Fig 10.35 shows the dot-and-cross diagram for the cyanide ion. The negative charge resides on the carbon atom, and it is the non-bonding pair on carbon that is donated to an electron-deficient carbon.

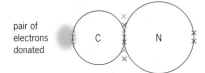

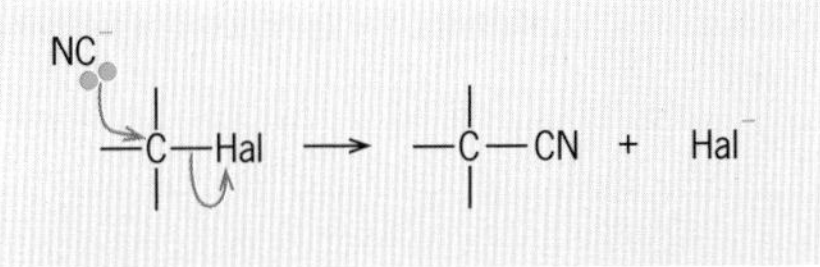

Fig 10.35 **The dot-and-cross diagram for the cyanide ion**

A nucleophilic substitution reaction with the cyanide ion leads to the formation of a carbon–carbon bond rather than a carbon–nitrogen bond. The mechanism of this is clearly shown in Fig 10.36. The net effect is to increase the carbon skeleton by one carbon. The resulting functional group is called a **nitrile**.

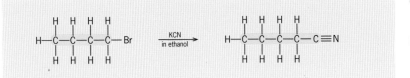

Fig 10.36 **The mechanism of the reaction of the cyanide ion with a halogenoalkane**

The normal reaction conditions are potassium cyanide or sodium cyanide in ethanol or propanone as a solvent. An organic solvent is chosen so that the halogenoalkane dissolves and thus allows more intimate contact with the ionic sodium cyanide. 1-bromobutane reacts with potassium cyanide in ethanol to form pentanenitrile, changing a four-carbon skeleton into a five-carbon skeleton.

?

W Draw the displayed formula for the organic product of the reaction between 3-iodo-2-methylhexane with potassium cyanide in ethanolic solution.

Fig 10.37 **Changing a four-carbon skeleton into a five-carbon skeleton**

■ See questions 6, 7 and 9.

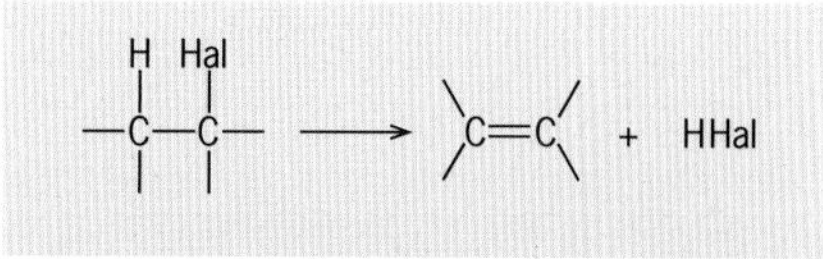

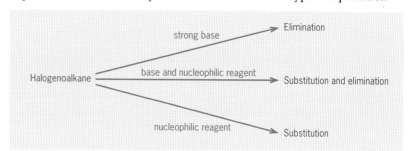

Fig 10.38 **A general example of elimination from a halogenoalkane**

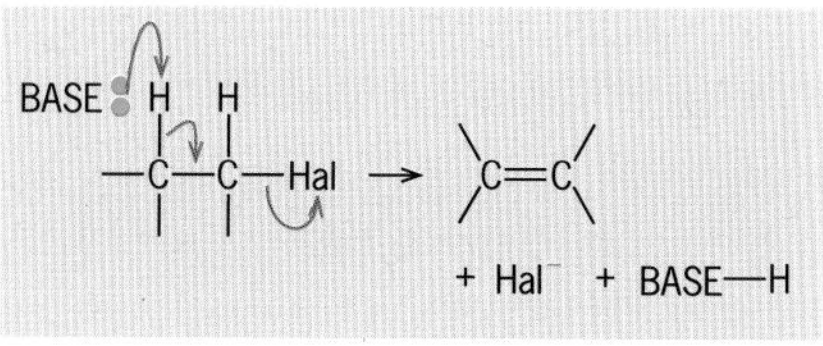

Fig 10.39 **The mechanism for the elimination of a hydrogen halide from a halogenoalkane**

✔

In heterolytic fission, a covalent bond is broken so that both electrons in the bond move to one of the atoms (see page 253)

See question 11. ■

See pages Chapter 29 for information on bases.

Fig 10.40 **A summary of the elimination and substitution reactions**

See questions 6 and 10. ■

?

X (a) 1-iodopropane reacts with hot aqueous sodium hydroxide to give both elimination and substitution products. Draw the displayed formulae of both sets of products, and explain with the aid of equations how they arise.

(b) 1-iodopentane is refluxed under heating with ethanolic sodium hydroxide. Predict the major product of the reaction.

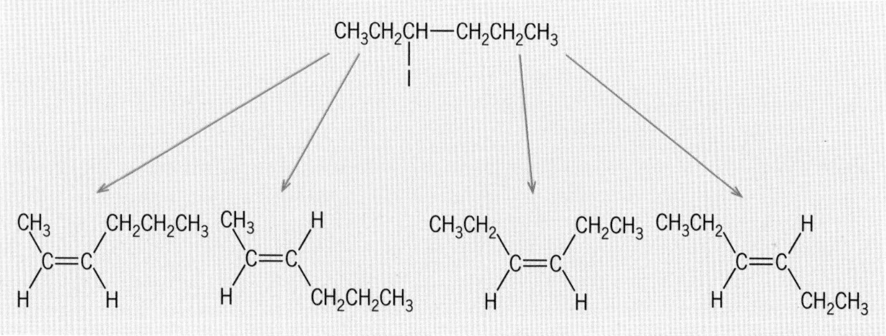

Fig 10.41 **Elimination products of 3-iodohexane**

Elimination reactions

When halogenoalkanes are heated strongly in the absence of air, an elimination reaction takes place with the formation of an alkene and the hydrogen halide. This reaction is quite impractical to use for manufacture, so the elimination reaction is encouraged by the use of a strong base. Strong bases are proton acceptors and will accept the proton lost during elimination. This in turn helps the heterolytic fission of the carbon–halogen bond to give a halide ion. The hydroxide ion is a strong base in ethanol solution. A suitable reagent for the elimination reaction in halogenoalkanes is ethanolic KOH.

Fig 10.39 shows a possible mechanism for the elimination, indicating the help the base gives in the elimination of the proton and the halide ion. Just as in nucleophilic substitution, the actual order of bond making and bond breaking can vary with different halogenoalkanes and different bases. (A full discussion of this is beyond the scope of this book.)

Elimination versus substitution

Perhaps you may have already thought of this problem: the hydroxide ion is a nucleophile as well as a strong base, which means that in reaction with a halogenoalkane there is always the possibility of substitution *and* elimination products. It would be more accurate to say that there will always be a mixture of both types of product.

The proportion of elimination and substitution products can be varied by changing both the temperature and the solvent used for the reaction. Table 10.4 summarises how the proportions can be changed.

	Elimination	Substitution
nucleophile	poor nucleophile	good nucleophile
basicity	strong base	weak base
solvent	ethanol	water
temperature	high	low

Table 10.4 **A summary of changing conditions for competing reactions**

There is a further complication: there can often be more than one elimination product because there may be several hydrogen atoms that can be lost.

6 REACTIONS OF CHLOROFLUOROCARBONS (CFCS)

The most remarkable thing about CFCs is their complete lack of reactivity towards reagents that react with monohalogenoalkanes. CFCs do not undergo nucleophilic substitution or elimination reactions. This lack of reactivity can be explained by the inability of carbon to expand its octet and by the strength of the C–F bond.

Once CFCs are released into the environment there are no natural ways in which the compounds can be broken down. The normal decomposition processes involving hydrolysis with water, reaction with oxygen, or bacterial or microbial decay do not take place. This naturally leads to a build-up of CFCs in the environment, and there is a risk that they will build up inside the cells of living organisms. In the stratosphere, there is a way in which CFCs react, but only because of the presence of ultraviolet light.

You can read more about the lack of reactivity of tetrachloromethane in Chapter 21.

Free-radical reactions of CFCs

CFCs contain two types of carbon–halogen bonds: the C–F and the C–Cl bonds. The C–F bond is very strong, as shown by its bond energy of $439\,\text{kJ}\,\text{mol}^{-1}$ whereas the C–Cl bond is weaker with a bond energy of $330\,\text{kJ}\,\text{mol}^{-1}$. This means that in the presence of ultraviolet light the C–Cl bond will undergo homolytic fission to form a chlorine free radical rather than a C–F bond. The equation shows the homolytic fission of a CFC:

$$CF_3Cl(g) \rightarrow CF_3{\cdot}(g) + Cl{\cdot}(g)$$

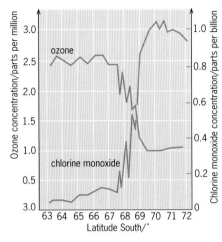

Fig 10.42 **Chlorine monoxide concentration and ozone concentration at different latitudes**

■ See question 12.

Ozone depletion

We have seen that the chlorine free radical is very reactive and will react with many other particles. In the stratosphere, it collides with ozone molecules to form chlorine monoxide and oxygen:

$$Cl{\cdot}(g) + O_3(g) \rightarrow ClO{\cdot}(g) + O_2$$

Chlorine monoxide is a free radical itself and this reaction is one of the propagation steps. The concentrations of ozone and chlorine monoxide in the stratosphere seem to confirm this reaction. The graphs in Fig 10.42 show that where there is a high chlorine monoxide concentration, there is a low ozone concentration, and vice versa.

Chlorine monoxide reacts with oxygen atoms present in the stratosphere to regenerate the chlorine free radical. The regeneration of the chlorine free radical completes the propagation step. The chlorine free radical can then react with more ozone:

$$ClO{\cdot}(g) + O(g) \rightarrow Cl{\cdot}(g) + O_2(g)$$

The net result of these two reactions is the conversion of an oxygen atom and an ozone molecule into two oxygen molecules:

$$O(g) + O_3(g) \rightarrow 2O_2(g)$$

It is estimated that on average one chlorine free radical (hence one CFC molecule) can destroy over 100 000 ozone molecules before the chain reaction stops. It stops when the chlorine free radical collides with other molecules, such as hydrocarbons, to form hydrogen chloride that can leave the stratosphere dissolved in water. The rate of ozone depletion by the presence of chlorine free radicals now exceeds its rate of formation in parts of the stratosphere, especially over the Antarctic.

?

Y Draw the dot-and-cross diagram for chlorine monoxide to show it has one unpaired electron.

Z State a function of the chlorine free radical in the process described in the text.

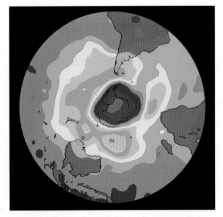

Fig 10.43 **The 'ozone hole' (purple and grey) over the Antarctic. It will get larger unless the use of chlorofluorocarbons declines. The consequences include damage by excess ultraviolet radiation to skin and the DNA of plant and animal cells which could lead to mutations**

THE NATURE OF OZONE

THERE ARE TWO FORMS of oxygen, O_2 and O_3. They are called **allotropes**. Ozone, O_3, is thermodynamically unstable with respect to oxygen, O_2:

$$2O_3(g) \rightarrow 3O_2(g)$$

Ozone is pale blue as a gas and deep blue as a liquid. It has a sharp, irritating odour and produces headaches in humans. In less than one part per million in air, it is poisonous. But the presence of ozone in the stratosphere (a layer 12 to 50 km above the Earth's surface) acts as a protective barrier which prevents much of the high energy UV-B radiation from the Sun reaching the Earth and destroying organisms. It is a strange paradox that we are worried both about an increase in ozone concentration in the lower atmosphere and about a decrease in concentration in the stratosphere.

Ozone is present in the lower atmosphere, formed there by the reaction between nitrogen oxides and volatile organic compounds in the presence of sunlight. It is produced along with photochemical smogs. In this century, the levels of ozone concentration have doubled over much of Europe and North America.

The effects of ozone in the lower atmosphere include an estimated 5 to 10 per cent loss in potential crop yield. It damages textiles and makes their colours fade faster. Rubber (such as car tyres) deteriorate faster, and human lungs function less well, as the airways are irritated and cause coughing.

Ozone in the stratosphere is produced by the reaction of oxygen atoms and oxygen molecules:

$$O(g) + O_2(g) \rightarrow O_3(g)$$

Stratospheric ozone absorbs UV-B radiation by undergoing homolytic fission to form an oxygen atom and an oxygen molecule. If the ozone layer were absent or depleted much more UV-B would reach the Earth's surface and severely damage plant, marine and human organisms. For example, there would be an increased incidence of skin cancers and cataracts, crop yield would decrease and fish stocks would plummet.

Fig 10.44 **Photochemical smog. In Paris for a period from 1 October 1997, cars were restricted from entering the city, in order to cut down on pollution. A policeman stops a car whose licence plate ends with an even number and is travelling on an odd numbered date**

You can read more about photochemical smogs on page 170.

SUMMARY

After studying this chapter, you should know that:

▧ Bromoalkanes, chloroalkanes and iodoalkanes can be prepared by the reaction of alcohols with concentrated hydrobromic acid, concentrated hydrochloric acid and concentrated hydroiodic acid respectively, or by the reaction of the appropriate phosphorus halides with an alcohol.

▧ Alkanes react with chlorine, fluorine and bromine by free-radical substitution to give a mixture of halogeno and polyhalogenoalkanes.

▧ Free-radical substitution involves three steps: initiation by ultraviolet light, propagation and termination.

▧ Fluoroalkanes are very unreactive because of the strength of the C–F bond.

▧ Bromoalkanes, chloroalkanes and iodoalkanes react by nucleophilic substitution with cyanide ion to form nitriles, with ammonia to give amines and with aqueous hydroxide ion to give alcohols.

▧ Bromoalkanes, chloroalkanes and iodoalkanes can eliminate hydrogen halides to form alkenes when treated with hot ethanolic alkali.

▧ CFCs and halogenoalkanes have weak permanent dipole–permanent dipole interactions in the liquids state, so often have low boiling points.

▧ CFCs are non-toxic and inert, and have a low boiling point.

▧ CFCs are responsible for ozone depletion in the upper atmosphere by providing chlorine free radicals

QUESTIONS

1 Chlorofluorocarbons, CFCs, are small alkane molecules in which some of the hydrogen atoms have been replaced by chlorine atoms and fluorine atoms. One such compound is a chlorotrifluoroethane, **A**.

$$CHClF–CHF_2$$
A (b.p. 17°C)

a) What are CFCs used for, what environmental hazard to they pose and how, chemically, does this hazard arise?

b) One of the properties that determine which CFC to use in a particular application is the size of the forces between the molecules.

Illustrate the factors that determine intermolecular forces by suggesting how, and explaining why, the boiling points of the following CFCs might differ from that of **A** and from each other.

$$CHClF_2 \qquad CHClF–CCl_3$$
B \qquad **C**

c) Another CFC, compound **D**, contains the following elements with the given percentages by mass.

C 17.8%; H 1.5%; Cl 52.6%; F 28.1%

The peak with the highest m/e value in the mass spectrum of **D** was at m/e 138. Use these data to deduce the empirical and the molecular formula of **D**.
[UCLES November 1994 Chemistry, 9250/1, Paper 1 Section A, q.1]
For mass spectra, part **c)**, refer to Chapter 9

2 In the presence of ultraviolet light, methane reacts with chlorine in a free-radical reaction to form chloromethane:

$$CH_4 + Cl_2 \rightarrow CH_3Cl + HCl$$

a) The reaction is initiated by the production of chlorine free radicals:

$$Cl_2 \rightarrow 2Cl\bullet$$

Use dot-and-cross diagrams to show the outer electron arrangement in
 (i) a chlorine molecule,
 (ii) a chlorine free radical.

b) Propagation proceeds following the initiation stage of the reaction. Complete the two equations below to illustrate what is meant by *propagation*.
 (i) $CH_4 + Cl\bullet \rightarrow$
 (ii) $CH_3\bullet + Cl_2 \rightarrow$

c) The reaction stops by means of termination reactions. Give the equation for a possible termination reaction in the chlorination of methane.
[UCLES Modular Chemistry June 1994, 1020/2, q.2]

3
a) Polychlorinated methanes are useful solvents. Describe the reagent and conditions used to produce these substances from methane and the mechanism of the reaction.

This process also produces small quantities of chlorinated *ethanes*. How might these arise?

b) Suggest a route by which ethane could be converted into chloroethene, $CH_2=CHCl$.
[UCLES Chemistry November 1994, 9250/1, q.9]

4 When chlorine is bubbled through boiling ethanoic acid in the presence of ultraviolet light, a chain reaction similar to that between methane and chlorine occurs. A product of this reaction is chloroethanoic acid, $ClCH_2CO_2H$.

a) By referring to bond energy data, state and explain which bond in the reactants is broken in the initiation step.

b) Write a balanced equation for one of the propagation steps in the chain reaction.

c) Write an equation for a reaction by which chloroethanoic acid might be converted into aminoethanoic acid ($NH_2CH_2CO_2H$)
[UCLES Modular Chemistry March 1993, 1021/2, q.4]

5 Using the appropriate bond enthalpies (energies) suggest why:

a) hydroxide ions will react with 1-iodobutane but iodide ions will not react with butan-1-ol,

b) fluorocarbons are less susceptible to nucleophilic substitution than iodoalkanes,

6
a) A sample of 1-bromopropane is divided into two portions. The first portion is heated with aqueous sodium hydroxide and the second portion is heated with ethanolic sodium hydroxide.
 (i) Identify the major organic product for each reaction.
 (ii) Explain the mechanism that leads to each product.
 (iii) Write a balanced equation for each reaction.

b) Starting with 1-bromopropane, outline how you would prepare a sample of
 (i) propylamine (1-aminopropane),
 (ii) butanenitrile

7 Predict the major organic product for the following reactions of 2-bromopentane with:

a) warm aqueous potassium hydroxide,

b) potassium cyanide in ethanol,

c) with excess heated ammonia in a sealed tube.

d) potassium methoxide, $K^+\ ^-OCH_3$, in methanol.

8 Aqueous silver nitrate can be used to monitor the hydrolysis of halogenated compounds. The procedure used is to heat the halogenated compound with aqueous sodium hydroxide and then to test a small sample of the reaction mixture with excess nitric acid, followed by aqueous silver nitrate.

a) Describe and explain the results of testing the following substances in this way
  (i) 1-iodobutane
  (ii) 2-bromopentane,
  (iii) 3-chlorohexane.

b) Rank the following halogenated compounds in order of increasing ease of hydrolysis. Explain how you choose the order.

1-bromopentane, 1-chloropentane, 1-fluoropentane, 1-iodopentane.

9 The reactions described below refer to compounds with the molecular formula C_4H_9Br.

a) Write down a general equation to show the hydrolysis of C_4H_9Br using aqueous potassium hydroxide.

b) Write down a general equation to show the elimination of C_4H_9Br using ethanolic sodium hydroxide.

c) **(i)** Draw the displayed formula and name all the isomers of C_4H_9Br.
  (ii) Which isomer on hydrolysis gives an alcohol with three methyl groups?
  (iii) Which isomer reacts with concentrated ethanolic sodium hydroxide to give a single hydrocarbon?
  (iv) Which isomer reacts with excess ammonia to make butylamine?
  (v) Which isomer reacts with sodium cyanide in ethanol to give 2-methylbutanenitrile?

10 The reaction scheme shows some of the reactions of methylbenzene and some of its derivatives.

a) Give the reagents and essential conditions for each of the three steps.

b) Conversion of B to C is nucleophilic substitution.

  (i) What is the name of the competing reaction that often takes place along with nucleophilic substitution?
  (ii) Explain why this competing reaction cannot take place with compound B.

c) Suggest a reason why methylbenzene is not directly converted into structure D.

d) Describe how compound D can be changed into a compound with eight carbons in its carbon skeleton.

11
a) A compound **L** has the following composition by mass:
  C 35.0%; H 6.6%; Br 58.4%

Calculate the empirical formula of **L**. (For help, see page 180.)

b) When **L** is treated with dilute aqueous KOH solution, the alcohol 2-methylpropan-1-ol is formed. Draw the structural or displayed formula of this alcohol and hence the displayed formula of **L**.

c) When **L** is heated with alcoholic KOH, an alkene **M** is formed. Give the name and displayed formula of **M**.

12 Fluoroalkanes and chlorofluoroalkanes are two classes of important industrial chemicals.

a) Explain in terms of bond energies why these compounds are relatively inert compared with the corresponding iodo- and bromo-compounds.

b) Fluoroalkanes and fluorohalogenoalkanes have many important uses. Give three uses and explain how the chemical and physical properties of these compounds make them suitable for the use given.

Assignment

THE RISE AND FALL OF CFCS

The first CFC to be discovered was CFC12 in 1892, but it was not until 1928 that Thomas Midgley was able to develop a simple one-step process for making CFCs. He used the reaction of tetrachloromethane with anhydrous hydrogen fluoride with an antimony(V) chloride catalyst:

$$CCl_4 + xHF \rightarrow CCl_{4-x}F_x + xHCl$$

1 Write down an equation to show how CFC11 ($CFCl_3$) can be prepared from tetrachloromethane.

2
a) Write down an equation to show how CFC12 (CF_2Cl_2) can be prepared from tetrachloromethane

b) Use the equation to calculate the minimum mass of tetrachloromethane that is needed to make 1 tonne of CFC12.

Hint: You may need to look at page 7.

By 9.55 p.m. on 29 June 1990, the death warrant for CFCs had been signed in London, some 70 years after their first commercial production. During this time, CFCs had been used world-wide in industrial and domestic applications in the belief that they were inert and harmless to both life and the environment.

The detection of ozone depletion in the stratosphere and the rapid increase in the concentration of CFCs became unquestionably linked. Table 10.A1 shows how the concentrations of CFC have increased up to the first international protocol on the use of CFCs in Montreal in 1987, when the first restrictions on their use came into force.

Table 10.A1 **Atmospheric concentrations of CFCs**

Year	CFC11 (CCl_3F)	CFC12 (CCl_2F_2)
1976	133	217
1978	159	266
1980	179	307
1982	193	330
1984	213	366

3 Draw a graph of the data in Table 10.A1 and estimate the atmospheric concentration of each CFC in 1994. Assume that there had been no significant changes in production, use and government legislation.

It is not just the concentrations of CFCs that are a cause for concern. It is also the estimated lifetime of these compounds in the atmosphere and their ozone-depleting potential (ODP). The latter compares the ability of different CFCs to destroy the ozone layer in the stratosphere.

Table 10.A2 **Lifetime and ODP values for some CFCs and related compounds**

Compound	Lifetime in atmosphere/years	ODP	% contribution to ozone depletion
CFC 11	74	1	26
CFC12	111	1	45
CFC113	90	0.8	12
CCl_4	67	1.1	8
CH_3CCl_3	8	0.1	5
Halon 1301	110	10	4

By 1994 the production of CFCs had dropped dramatically, as shown in Fig 10.A1.

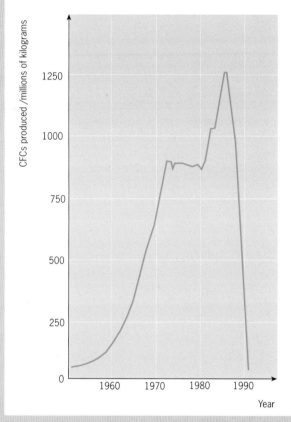

Fig 10.A1 **Change in production of CFCs since 1950 (source: DuPont, Worldwatch estimates)**

4 Governments agreed by the mid-90s to cut down and eventually stop the production and use of CFCs within the following few years. Use the data in Fig 10.A1 and Table 10.A3 to estimate the possible changes in atmospheric CFC concentration and ozone depletion.

5 Halon 1301 ($CBrF_3$) has the highest ODP value.

a) Which halogen free radical is most likely to be produced in the stratosphere? Write an equation for this reaction.

b) Use your answer in part **a)** to suggest why it has the highest ODP of all the values quoted.

Now that the dangers of CFCs are apparent, there is a need to ensure that no more are allowed to escape into the environment. The disposal of CFCs is a problem since they cannot be dumped at sea or in a land-fill site. One way is to incinerate the waste CFCs with other organic waste materials. This is very difficult because it needs very high temperatures and leads to other dangerous acidic gases polluting the atmosphere. There is also the risk that a CFC will not burn and so will still escape into the atmosphere. Research is underway to find a way of combusting CFCs that does not produce poisonous gases and is 100% efficient.

6 One way of disposing of CFC is incineration. CFCs burn very poorly except at extremely high temperatures. Suggest why it is very difficult to burn CFCs.

Now that CFCs are being phased out, the chemical industry faces the problem of finding alternatives to CFCs. The obvious replacement is to incorporate hydrogen molecules into CFCs to get HCFCs. HCFCs have the same physical properties as CFCs and so offer the same opportunities for use as refrigerants and solvents. But these compounds pose much less of a threat to the ozone layer since the hydrogen atom gives more reactivity to the molecule. However, these products will inevitably still have an effect on the ozone layer, although they have a much reduced ODP value, typically between 0.02 and 0.1.

Unfortunately, there are still several important environmental issues to sort out since HCFCs react in the atmosphere to produce a cocktail of highly dangerous acidic compounds, such as hydrogen fluoride, hydrogen chloride and trifluoroethanoic acid. One suggestion is that HCFCs should only be used if there is a recycling programme, so that only minute amounts of HCFCs actually escape into the atmosphere.

7 Describe some of the advantages and disadvantages of using HCFCs rather than CFCs.

8 Many scientific advances seem to offer a greater quality of life but, often, not many years pass before drawbacks appear. Discuss this statement with respect to CFCs.

9 The full environmental impact of HCFCs is not yet known and it may take tens of years before it is fully established. Should this stop the introduction of HCFCs now?

The Assignment in Chapter 27 is also concerned with CFCs and ozone depletion.

HALOGENOALKANES

This chapter covers the formation, properties, reactions and importance of halogenoalkanes. The Chapter Map will help you to see the connection between ideas related to these chemicals, and to check the aspects you need to know for the syllabus you are following.

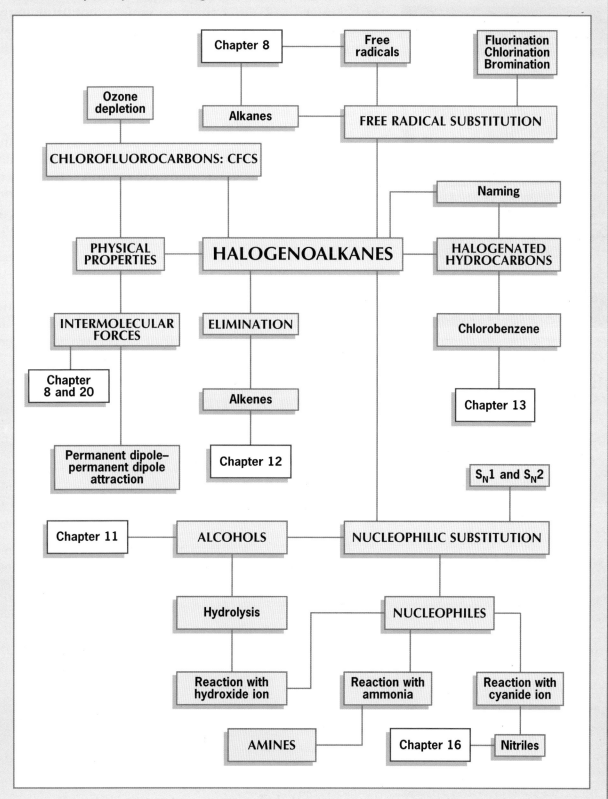

11 Alcohols and phenols

Tea leaves contain water-soluble phenols that contribute to the taste and colour of a cup of tea

TEA IS ALMOST CERTAINLY the most popular hot drink in the world. In the United Kingdom alone, each person drinks on average 3½ cups every day. There are several reasons why this simple infusion of dry plant leaves is so popular. It has a characteristic taste and attractive colour derived from the compounds in the leaves.

Every cup of tea contains about 40 mg of caffeine, which is a stimulant to the central nervous system. There are also amino acids, carbohydrates and mineral ions. Complex molecules called phenols, that have hydroxyl groups attached to aromatic rings, are water soluble and give the tea the astringent taste and refreshing effect we find appealing. As tea leaves are processed, some compounds are oxidised, and this gives the brown colour characteristic of tea.

Many people add sugar to their tea to sweeten it. This involves the addition of an organic compound that is highly soluble in water because it has a molecule that contains many hydroxyl (OH) functional groups characteristic of alcohols. So, the taste of a cup of sweet tea is a direct consequence of its containing both phenols and alcohols.

1 THE HYDROXYL GROUP

Alcohols and phenols are organic compounds that contain carbon, hydrogen and oxygen. Both contain the hydroxyl group, OH, which is an oxygen atom bonded to a hydrogen atom. The hydroxyl group is bonded directly to an alkyl or cycloalkyl group in an *alcohol*, and to a benzene ring in a *phenol* (see Fig 11.1). However, it is best to treat alcohols and phenols as different classes of compounds, even though they both contain the hydroxyl group.

There is sometimes confusion in the use of the names alcohol and phenol, because they are the names of classes of compounds as well as the names of particular compounds. Alcohol is the popular term for ethanol, and phenol is also the name of one compound in the class of compounds called phenols. But in this book, you can safely assume that when we refer to alcohols or to phenols, these are the class of compounds – not the single compound.

Make sure that you can recognise an alcohol or a phenol when it is part of a very complicated molecule.

R = alkyl group
eg CH₃CH₂–

R = cycloalkyl group

eg

R—O—H

R = aryl group

eg

a phenol

Fig 11.1 **The generalised structure of alcohols and phenols**

ALCOHOLS AND PHENOLS IN NATURE

MANY NATURALLY occurring products are alcohols or phenols, including sugars and other carbohydrates, some fragrances, vitamins, pheromones, amino acids and steroids.

Tyrosine and serine are amino acids used by organisms in the construction of proteins. Tyrosine is a phenol and serine is an alcohol. Their structures are shown in Fig 11.2.

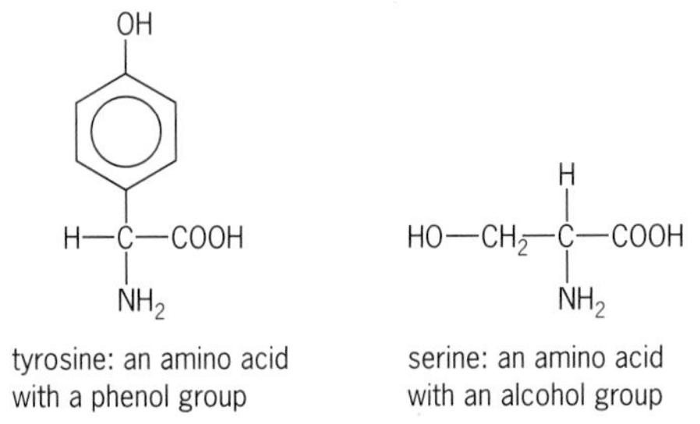

tyrosine: an amino acid with a phenol group

serine: an amino acid with an alcohol group

Fig 11.2 **The structures of tyrosine and serine**

A lack of the alcohol vitamin A in a person's diet causes night blindness and dry skin. And without sufficient vitamin C – another compound containing alcohol functional groups – a person would suffer from scurvy. The structures of these two vitamins are shown in Fig 11.4.

Fig 11.3 **Citrus fruit, such as the oranges shown here, are rich in vitamin C, which contains the alcohol functional group**

Vitamin A is a polyene and also a primary alcohol

Vitamin C is a cyclic molecule with more than one alcohol group

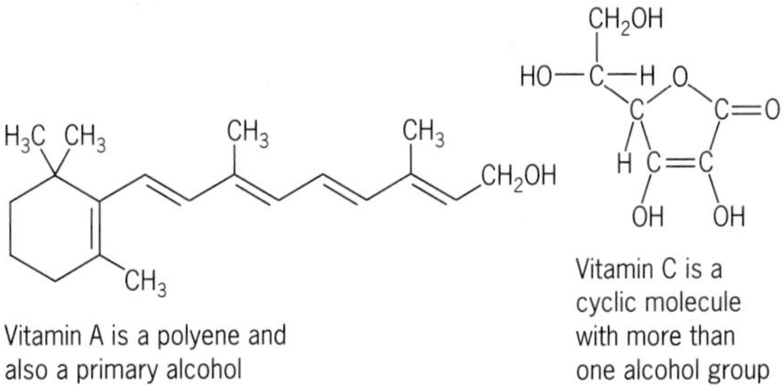

Fig 11.4 **The structures of vitamin A and vitamin C**

The fragrance of scented flowers is due to a complex mixture of compounds, many of which are alcohols. The structures of three of them are shown in Fig 11.5.

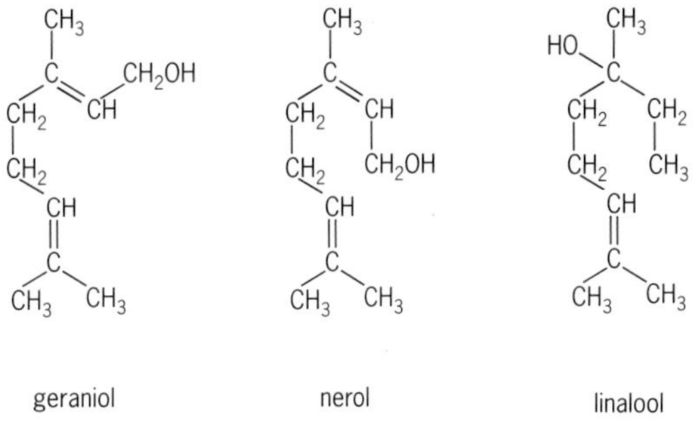

geraniol

nerol

linalool

Fig 11.5 **The structures of three of the many compounds responsible for the fragrance of flowers. Geraniol, for example, is a constituent of rose fragrance**

Propane-1,2,3-triol is used to make fats and oils that the human body uses as energy stores, as insulation and in the construction of membranes surrounding living cells.

Fig 11.6 shows one of the phenolic components of tea. You can see that it is a much more complicated molecule than the compound phenol itself, with several benzene rings incorporated in the structure.

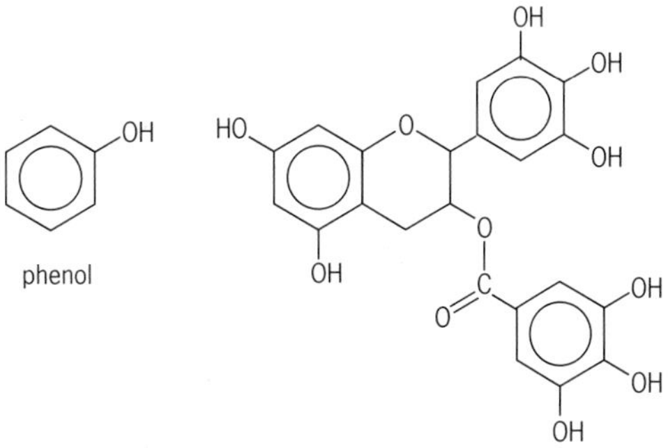

phenol

Fig 11.6 **The structure of phenol and one of the phenolic constituents of tea, epigallocatechin gallate**

Polysaccharides contain many hydroxyl groups, as shown by the structure of the sugar maltose in Fig 11.7.

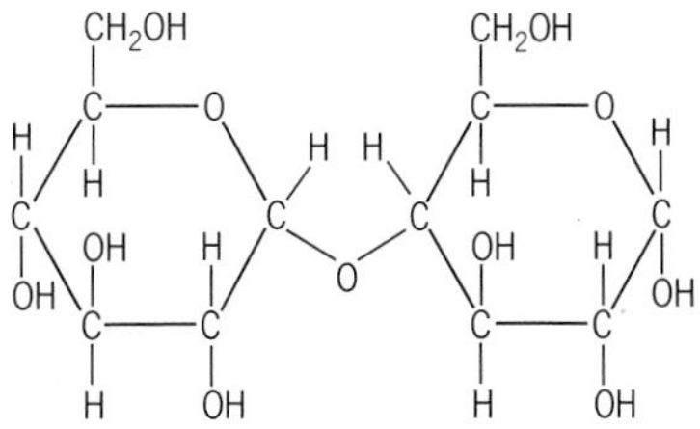

Fig 11.7 **The structure of maltose, a polyhydric alcohol containing six hydroxyl groups**

Alcohols and phenols in use

Alcohols with low relative molecular mass, such as methanol, ethanol, the propanols and the butanols, are liquids used extensively as solvents both for chemical reactions and in the production of paints and cosmetics. Many alcohols have the ability to dissolve both polar and non-polar compounds. This property is explained later (see page 230) in terms of the different types of intermolecular attraction between alcohol molecules and other molecules.

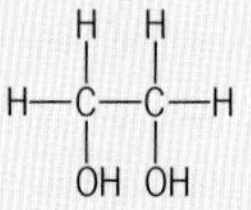

ethane 1,2-diol: a component of antifreeze

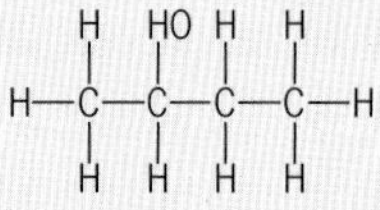

butan-2-ol: used extensively as a solvent and to make butanone, another solvent

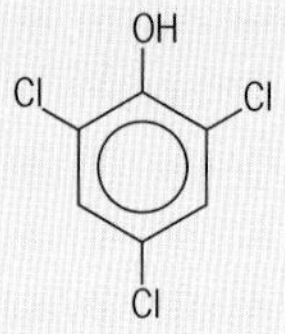

2,4,6-trichlorophenol: the active component in TCP

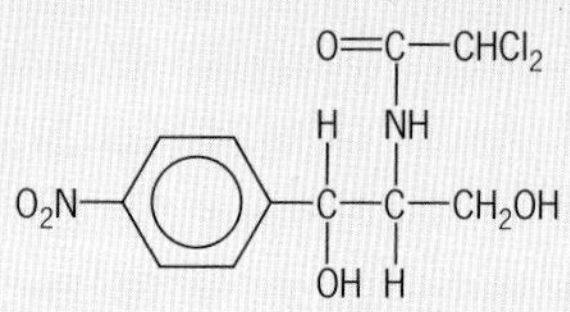

chloramphenicol: a selective bactericide

Fig 11.8 **The displayed formulas of four typical alcohols with their main uses. Chloramphenicol is not a phenol because the OH groups are not attached to the benzene ring**

Alcohols are also very useful intermediates for synthesising compounds, since they have a functional group that can undergo different types of reaction.

Naming alcohols and phenols

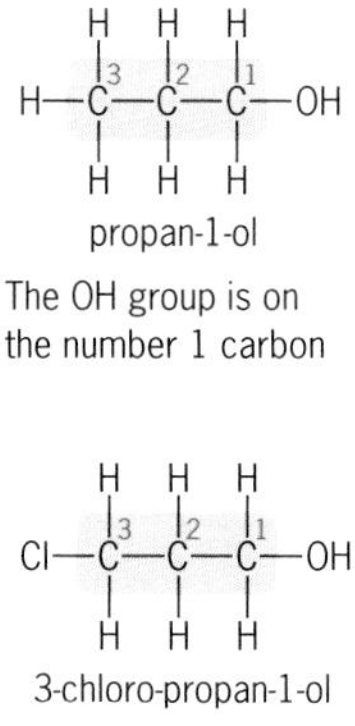

propan-1-ol

The OH group is on the number 1 carbon

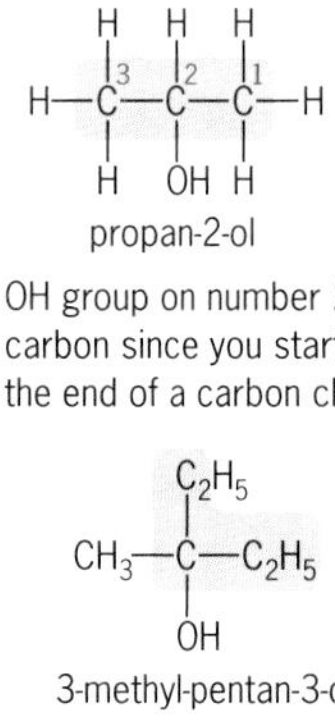

propan-2-ol

OH group on number 2 carbon since you start at the end of a carbon chain

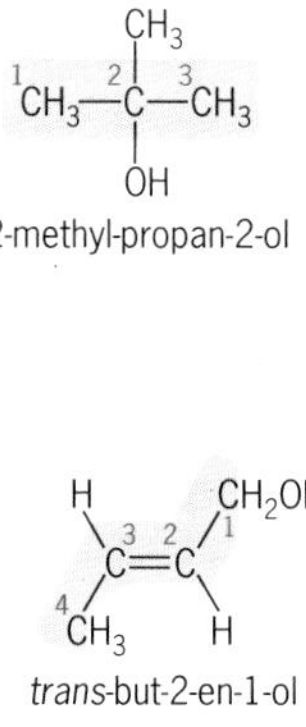

2-methyl-propan-2-ol

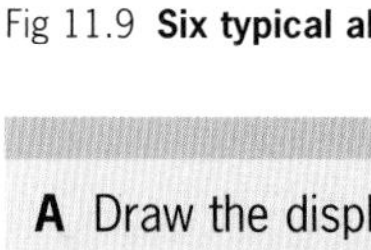

3-chloro-propan-1-ol

The OH group is more important than the Cl for naming purposes, so it is on the number 1 carbon

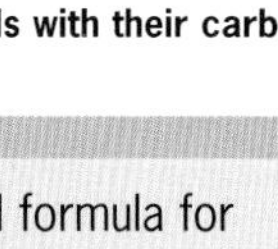

3-methyl-pentan-3-ol

You must choose the longest carbon chain containing the OH group as the skeleton

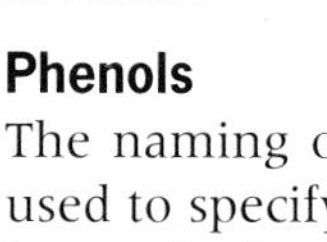

trans-but-2-en-1-ol

Fig 11.9 **Six typical alcohols with their carbon position-numbers**

Alcohols

The name of an alcohol is derived from the name of its carbon chain, using the suffix *ol*. The position-number for the hydroxyl group must also be specified in the name. The rule is that the carbon atom attached to the hydroxyl group is given the lowest number possible. When there is more than one functional group present, the position-numbers are determined by the most important group for naming purposes. (For example, the position of the hydroxyl group is more important than the position of a double bond or of a halogen atom, but less important than the position of a carbonyl group.) The presence of two or more hydroxyl groups is designated by *di*, *tri*, and so on, placed immediately before the suffix *ol*.

Phenols

The naming of a phenol is rather easier, since the term phenol is used to specify the benzene ring with one OH group already directly attached. All that needs to be done is to specify the other groups attached to the benzene ring. The carbon atom attached to the OH group is given position-number 1.

Notice that when there are two hydroxyl groups on the benzene ring, it is more convenient to use the prefix *hydroxy* than the suffix *ol*.

?

A Draw the displayed formula for

(a) 2-methylpropan-1-ol,

(b) 2-chloroethan-1-ol,

(c) 3-hydroxypropanoic acid.

B Draw the structural or displayed formula for

(a) 2-methylphenol,

(b) 2,4-dibromophenol,

(c) 1,2,4-tetrahydroxybenzene.

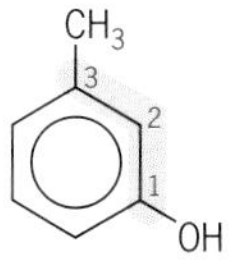

3-methylphenol

The number 1 carbon has the OH attached and the numbers go round the ring to put the methyl group on the lowest possible carbon

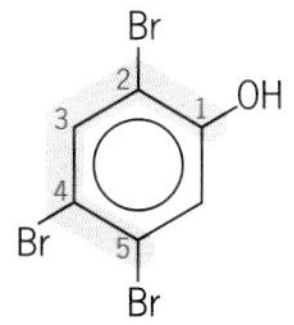

2,4,5-tribromophenol

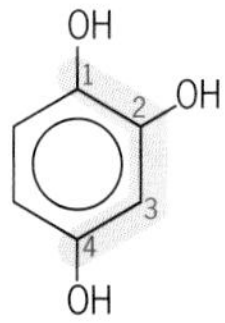

1,2,4-trihydroxybenzene

The numbering of the carbon atoms goes clockwise, so the OH groups are on the lowest set of numbers possible

Fig 11.10 **Three phenols with their position-numbers**

2 TYPES OF ALCOHOL

There are three major categories of alcohols: **primary**, **secondary** and **tertiary** alcohols. This classification is based on the number of carbon atoms attached to the carbon to which the OH group is bonded. A primary alcohol has one carbon atom attached, a secondary alcohol has two carbon atoms attached and a tertiary alcohol has three carbon atoms attached. The significance of this classification is that, although all alcohols have some reactions in common, their other reactions are different and depend on whether they are primary, secondary or tertiary alcohols.

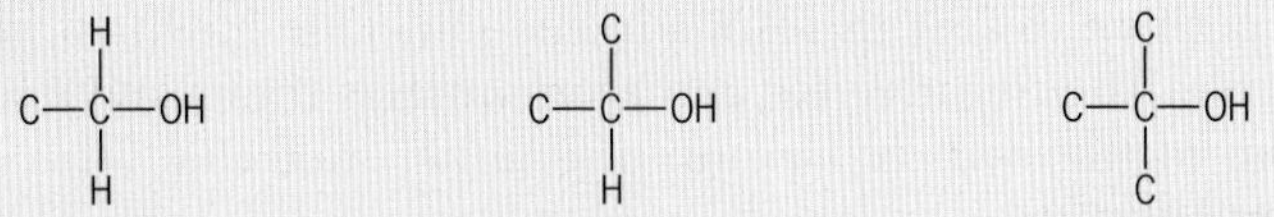

Fig 11.11 **The basic structure of primary, secondary and tertiary alcohols**

For convenience, methanol is classified as a primary alcohol, even though it does not have a carbon atom attached to the carbon to which the OH group is bonded.

C (a) Draw the displayed formula for each of the following alcohols and state whether they are primary, secondary or tertiary alcohols:
(i) propan-1-ol
(ii) 2-methylpentan-3-ol
(iii) propane-1,2,3-triol
(iv) cyclohexanol

(b) Look at the displayed formulas for geraniol, nerol and linalool in Fig 11.5. Classify each as a primary, secondary or tertiary alcohol.

■ See questions 2, 6 and 8.

Monohydric, dihydric, trihydric and polyhydric alcohols

Another classification of alcohols is based on the number of hydroxyl groups present per molecule. A **monohydric** alcohol has one hydroxyl group, a **dihydric alcohol** has two, a **trihydric alcohol** has three, and a **polyhydric** alcohol has many hydroxyl groups per molecule.

Ethane-1,2-diol is a dihydric alcohol that is used in car antifreeze. Propane-1,2,3-triol (otherwise known as glycerol) is a trihydric alcohol that is an important component of fats. Glucose, the major source of energy in animals, is a polyhydric alcohol, having five hydroxyl groups per molecule.

Alcohols as a homologous series

Methanol, ethanol, propan-1-ol, butan-1-ol, pentan-1-ol are alcohols which are members of a homologous series (see pages 158). They are all primary alcohols with similar chemical properties, and can be represented by the general formula $C_nH_{2n+1}OH$.

As in all homologous series, the physical properties of each member show observable trends as the number of carbon atoms per molecule increases. Table 11.1 summarises this.

Table 11.1 **Physical properties of the homologous series of primary alcohols**

Alcohol	Formula	Melting point/°C	Boiling point/°C
methanol	CH_3OH	–98	65
ethanol	CH_3CH_2OH	–117	78.5
propan-1-ol	$CH_3CH_2CH_2OH$	–127	(see **E**)
butan-1-ol	$CH_3CH_2CH_2CH_2OH$	–90	116
decan-1-ol	$CH_3(CH_2)_8CH_2OH$	6	228

D (a) What type of alcohol is propane-1,3-diol?

(b) Draw the displayed formula of a dihydric alcohol whose molecular formula is $C_4H_{10}O_2$.

(c) Look back to the structures in Figs 11.5 and 11.7. Classify each compound as a monohydric, dihydric or polyhydric alcohol.

E Using data from Table 11.1, estimate the melting point of propan-1-ol.

For more information on induced dipole–induced dipole forces, see pages 159 and 421.

See question 2. ■

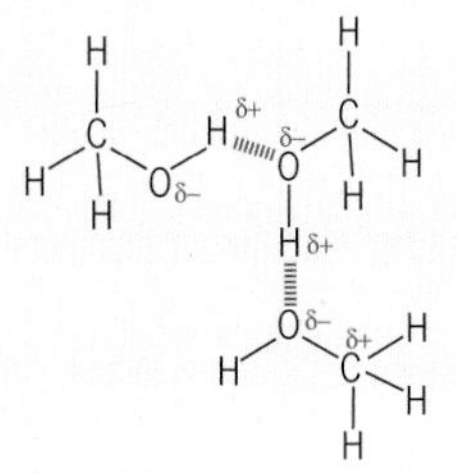

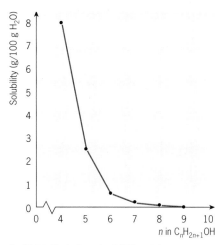

Fig 11.12 **Hydrogen bonding in methanol**

F (a) Explain why the boiling point of butan-1-ol is higher than that of methanol.

(b) Explain why the boiling points of decane and decan-1-ol are quite similar but those of methane and methanol are very different.

Fig 11.14 **Variation of solubility of the homologous series of primary alcohols in water**

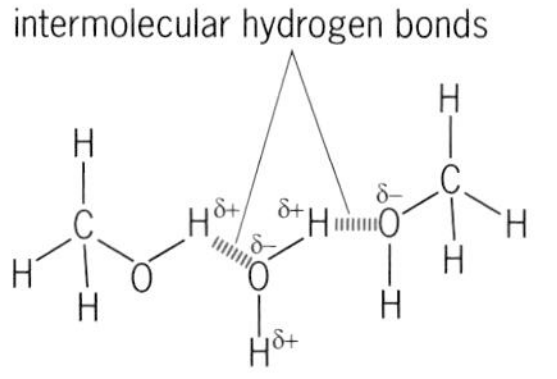

There is more about dissolving in Chapter 21 and 22.

Boiling points

Table 11.1 shows that the boiling points of the primary alcohols $C_nH_{2n+1}OH$ increase with chain length, n. For an alcohol to boil, its molecules must overcome the two types of intermolecular force keeping them together. One is the weak induced dipole–induced dipole force that operates between all molecules as a result of the temporary dipoles within the molecules. This force becomes stronger as the molecule becomes bigger and contains more electrons. The induced dipole–induced dipole force in alcohols is the attraction between the alkyl part of one molecule and the alkyl part of another molecule.

The other intermolecular force is the much stronger **hydrogen bond**. The hydroxyl group has a polar covalent bond in which the oxygen atom is slightly negative ($\delta-$) and the hydrogen atom is slightly positive ($\delta+$). This results in the molecule having a permanent dipole. The negative oxygen atom attracts the positive hydrogen atom of the hydroxyl group of another molecule. This is the hydrogen bond.

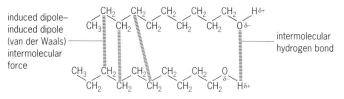

Fig 11.13 **Hydrogen bonding and induced dipole–induced dipole forces in decan-1-ol. The intermolecular forces of attraction in decan-1-ol are induced dipole–induced dipole forces between alkyl groups and hydrogen bonds between hydroxyl groups. With a long chain alkyl group, the strength of the induced dipole–induced dipole force is nearly the same as that in the corresponding alkane**

Solubility in water

The solubility of these primary alcohols decreases as the number of carbon atoms per molecule increases. Methanol and ethanol mix completely with water in all proportions, whereas nonan-1-ol is virtually insoluble in water. For a molecule to dissolve in water, it must be able to interact with water molecules. Water is a polar solvent and the two hydroxyl groups in a water molecule can form intermolecular hydrogen bonds with methanol or ethanol molecules.

Fig 11.15 **Intermolecular hydrogen bonds between methanol and water**

In the case of nonan-1-ol, its hydroxyl groups form hydrogen bonds with the water molecules, but its long carbon chains form induced dipole–induced dipole interactions only with other nonanol molecules. Therefore, the predominant intermolecular attractions are between nonanol's own molecules rather than with water's.

G Is methanol or nonan-1-ol more soluble in an alkane solvent such as nonane than in water? Explain your answer, using ideas about intermolecular forces.

Sugars

Sugars are a group of naturally occurring polyhydric alcohols that normally have a carbon chain or ring of six or five carbon atoms. They also contain one ketone group or one aldehyde group.

The glucose molecule has five hydroxyl groups. It readily dissolves in water because its hydroxyl groups can form hydrogen bonds with water molecules. It is this solubility that enables us to taste sugar in food or drink. There is more information on sugars and other carbohydrates on pages 302 and 305.

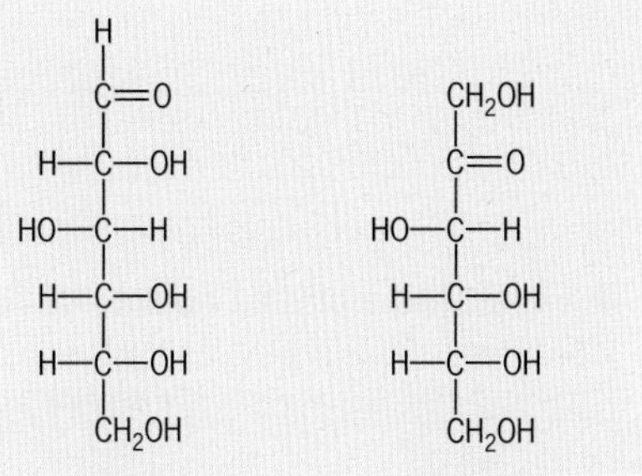

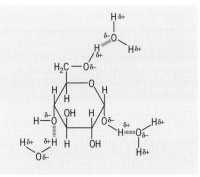

glucose   fructose

Fig 11.16 **Structures of two simple sugars**

ARTIFICIAL SWEETENERS

DIABETICS DO NOT produce sufficient insulin to change the excess glucose in their blood into glycogen, a storage carbohydrate. So they must carefully regulate their intake of glucose to stop the blood sugar level from getting too high. But diabetics like sweet-tasting foods. The solution is to use artificial sweeteners, such as **sorbitol** which is used to sweeten diabetic chocolate and other confectionery.

The 3-D shape of the sorbitol molecule is very like that of the glucose molecule. The receptors in the tongue respond to sorbitol in the same way that they respond to glucose, and so sorbitol tastes sweet. But, despite sorbitol's similar taste to glucose, it isn't metabolised by the body, and a diet too rich in sorbitol can cause diarrhoea.

Sorbitol is also used to sweeten dry wines. Adding extra sugar would sweeten the wine, but would also promote unwanted additional fermentation with the production of carbon dioxide, and the pressure could burst the bottle. Since sorbitol is not metabolised by yeast, further fermentation is not a problem.

Fig 11.17 **Intermolecular forces between a glucose molecule and water molecules. (For the sake of clarity, an interaction is not shown at every hydroxyl group)**

Fig 11.18 **The structure of sorbitol**

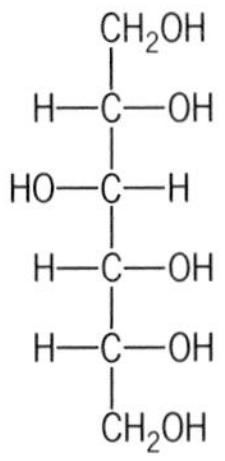

Fig 11.19 **The structure of aspartame. Notice that it is completely different from the structure of glucose**

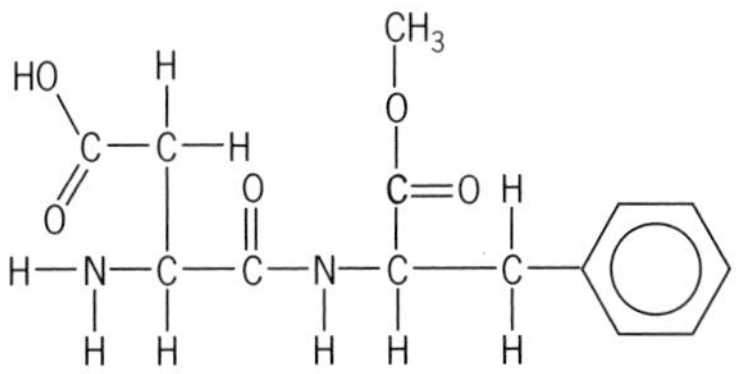

?

H Describe the structural differences between the ring form of glucose in Fig 11.17 and the chain form in Fig 11.16.

?

I (a) Describe the structural differences between sorbitol and glucose.

(b) Why does sorbitol dissolve in water?

The market for artificial sweeteners goes beyond helping diabetics and wine-making. There are now many low-calorie products which have replaced sugar as an ingredient. Many artificial sweeteners chemically decompose with heating, so they cannot be used to sweeten products, such as cake mixtures, which are cooked.

Most artificial sweeteners are much sweeter than sugar, and that means that a much smaller mass of the substance will give the same taste. **Saccharin**, for example, is about 300 times sweeter than sugar, though it has a bitter aftertaste. Another sweetener is **aspartame**, which is 200 times sweeter than sugar, but some people are seriously affected by it.

These molecules have a different shape from those of the simple sugars, so chemists are not yet sure which molecular shapes are responsible for the sweetness. Recent research has attempted to make sugar-like molecules by substituting some OH groups with chlorine atoms. But there must be extensive testing before such products can be put into foods, in order to ensure that they are completely free of side effects.

Solubility of phenols

The compound phenol is sparingly soluble in cold water. Although it contains the polar hydroxyl group which forms hydrogen bonds with water molecules, it also contains the benzene ring which cannot form intermolecular bonds with water. Therefore, the solubility of phenols in water increases as the number of hydroxyl groups in their molecules increases. For example, the soluble phenols in tea (see the Opener) contain several hydroxyl groups. Even though the molecule is very large, the number of hydroxyl groups present ensures that it dissolves in water.

J Phenol has a melting point of 42°C. What does this suggest about the nature of the intermolecular forces in solid phenol?

3 PREPARATION OF ALCOHOLS

There are five ways of making alcohols, which are summarised in Fig 11.20. It follows that alcohols feature in a large number of reactions, which makes them good synthetic intermediates.

There is further information on the processes given in Fig 11.20 as follows:
hydrolysis of halogenoalkanes, page 215;
reduction of aldehydes and ketones, page 300;
reduction of carboxylic acids, page 328;
hydrolysis of esters, page 342.

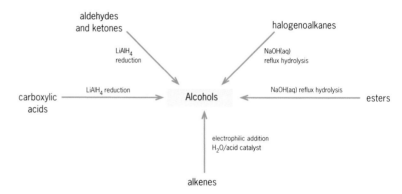

Fig 11.20 **Preparative routes to alcohols**

Fig 11.21 **Yeast floating on the liquid of a brewing fermentation vat**

There is more information on the use of fermentation in producing an alternative fuel on page 136.

Manufacture of ethanol

Ethanol is a compound in great demand as a solvent, a fuel, and as a synthetic intermediate in the production of other chemicals. It is, of course, present in alcoholic drinks, for which it is produced by the fermentation of glucose contained in grapes, for example.

Fermentation of sugars

Ethanol is one of the oldest manufactured chemicals, going back to the time when someone is thought to have first accidentally discovered the fermentation process – possibly 5000 years ago.

During fermentation (anaerobic respiration), aqueous glucose is converted to carbon dioxide and aqueous ethanol. The reaction is catalysed by the enzymes present in yeast:

$$C_6H_{12}O_6(aq) \rightarrow 2CH_3CH_2OH(aq) + 2CO_2(g)$$

This reaction does not produce pure ethanol but aqueous ethanol. To get higher concentrations of ethanol, the aqueous ethanol has to be fractionally distilled.

Hydration of ethene

Ethene is readily available from the cracking of larger hydrocarbon molecules. It can be hydrated to form ethanol. Industrially this is achieved by reacting ethene and steam together at 300°C and 6000 kPa pressure in the presence of a phosphoric(V) acid catalyst:

$$C_2H_4(g) + H_2O(g) \rightarrow CH_3CH_2OH(g)$$

In the laboratory, ethene is bubbled through concentrated sulphuric acid. The ethene undergoes an addition reaction to form ethyl hydrogensulphate, which is hydrolysed to give ethanol:

$$C_2H_4 + H_2SO_4 \longrightarrow CH_3CH_2OSO_3H$$

$$CH_3CH_2OSO_3H + H_2O \xrightarrow{60\,°C} H_2SO_4 + CH_3CH_2OH$$

Further information on the addition reactions of ethene is in Chapter 12.

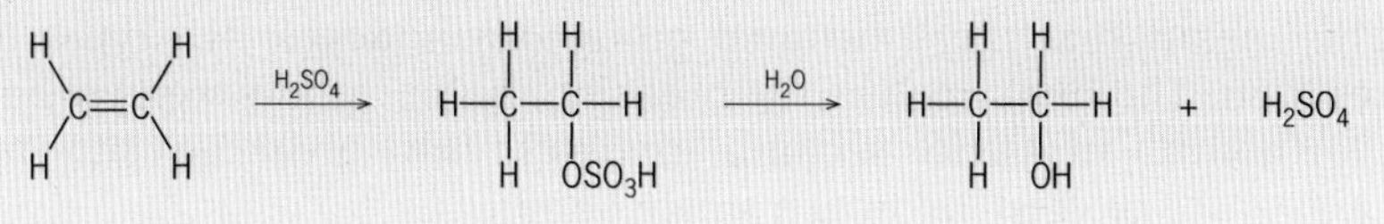

Fig 11.22 **Flow diagram showing hydration of ethene**

THE MANUFACTURE OF METHANOL

METHANOL IS USED in industry and in the laboratory as a solvent and reagent; also as car antifreeze and as an engine fuel. Though an alcohol, methanol is poisonous and can cause blindness if inhaled or drunk.

Until about 1925, methanol was made by heating wood in the absence of air, and collecting and condensing the volatile substances given off. This is why methanol is sometimes called wood spirit. It is now manufactured by the reaction of carbon monoxide or carbon dioxide with hydrogen. Both reactions are carried out at about 400 °C and under a pressure of some 1500 kPa, using heterogeneous catalysts (for more about heterogeneous catalysts, see Chapter 27):

$$CO(g) + 2H_2(g) \rightarrow CH_3OH(g)$$

K **(a)** Write down the equation for the addition reaction between concentrated sulphuric acid and ethene.

(b) Write down the equation for the hydrolysis of ethyl hydrogensulphate to give ethanol.

(c) What is the name of the alcohol produced when cyclopentene is hydrated?

L Write down the equation for the reaction of carbon dioxide with hydrogen to make methanol.

ALTERNATIVE ROUTES TO HYDROCARBON FUELS

THE CATALYSED CONVERSION of either carbon monoxide or carbon dioxide to methanol provides a route (at least in theory) for converting the products of combustion of a fuel to a practical liquid fuel. The methanol itself can be further converted into other useful products.

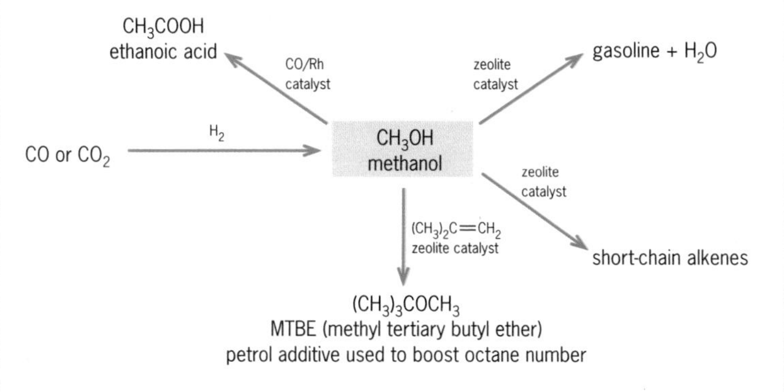

Fig 11.23 **The catalytic conversion of methanol**

These synthetic routes provide a way for alkanes and alkenes to be synthesised without the need of a raw material such as crude oil. Perhaps more research will have to be directed this way if people are going to continue to rely on hydrocarbons as an energy source and as a raw material for the petrochemical industry.

The nature of the hydroxyl functional group

The hydroxyl functional group in an alcohol contains one covalent bond and is attached to a carbon atom by another covalent bond. This means that the functional group can undergo two types of reaction. The first involves the breaking of the carbon–oxygen single bond, and the second involves the breaking of the oxygen–hydrogen single bond.

The C–O bond can be broken either by a substitution reaction or by an elimination reaction.

When the O–H bond is broken, an alcohol behaves as an acid. This is because the breaking of the bond results in the transfer of a hydrogen ion. Since the oxygen atom of the hydroxyl group has lone pairs of electrons, an alcohol can also behave as a nucleophile, reacting with a molecule with an electron-deficient centre. Finally, an alcohol can take part in redox reactions.

The large range of reactions available to this functional group helps to explain why alcohols are very good synthetic intermediates.

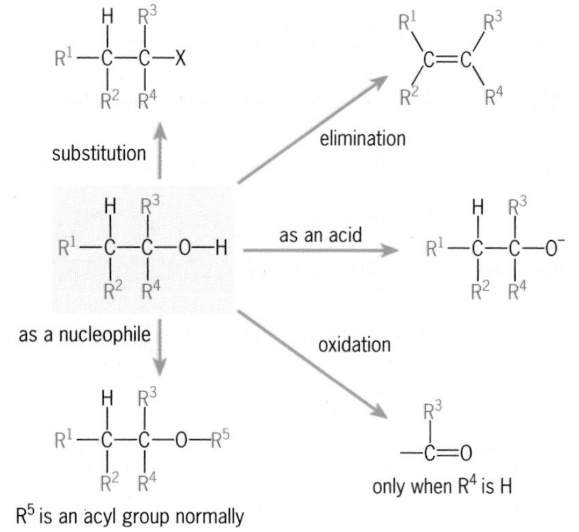

R^5 is an acyl group normally

Fig 11.24 **General summary of the reactions of alcohols. R^1, R^2, R^3 and R^4 are either alkyl groups or hydrogen atoms**

Substitution reactions: halogenation of alcohols

The conversion of an alcohol to a halogenoalkane is a substitution reaction which involves the swapping of a halogen atom for a hydroxyl group. However, a halide ion is not a good enough nucleophile to directly substitute a hydroxyl group. The strength of the C–O bond is a great barrier to the substitution reaction.

The competition between substitution and elimination in halogenoalkanes is discussed on page 218.

The role of bond energy in nucleophilic substitution is covered on page 214.

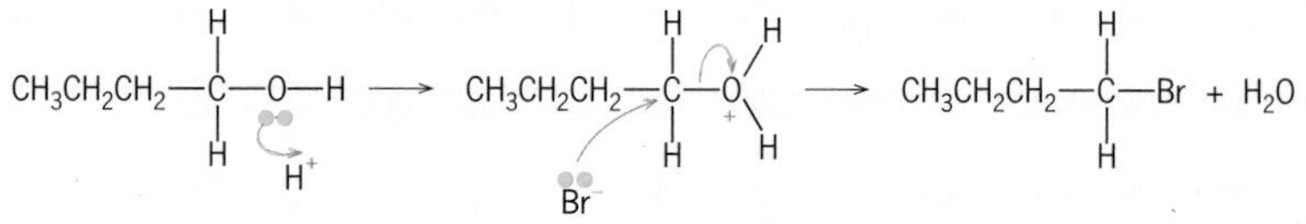

Fig 11.25 **The mechanism of the substitution of an alcohol using concentrated hydrobromic acid**

The only way that the substitution reaction can succeed is if the C–O bond is substantially weakened. This can be done by using an acidic catalyst.

A lone pair of electrons on the oxygen atom is donated to a proton in an acid–base type interaction. The intermediate formed has a very weak C–O bond since the oxygen has developed a positive charge. Nucleophilic substitution by a bromide ion is now very easy, with the water molecule being the leaving group. Normally, the reaction is carried out by refluxing together a mixture of alcohol, sodium bromide and concentrated sulphuric acid. The concentrated sulphuric acid and the sodium bromide together generate concentrated hydrobromic acid:

$$H_2SO_4 + NaBr \rightarrow HBr + NaHSO_4$$

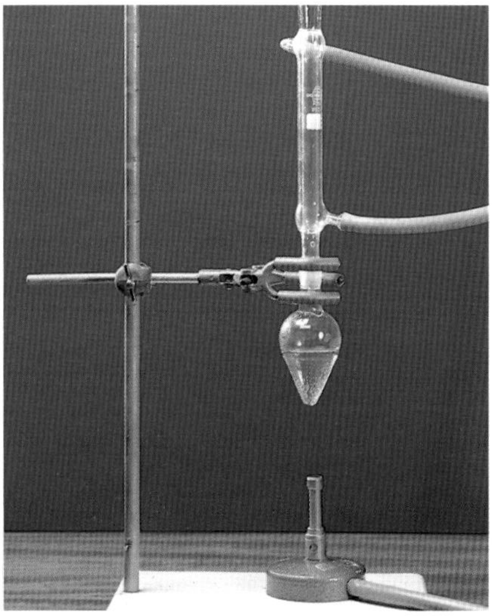

Fig 11.26 **The preparation of bromobutane**

For the substitution of the hydroxyl group by a halogen atom, the corresponding acid can be used. Iodo compounds are prepared by refluxing the alcohol with concentrated hydroiodic acid, bromo compounds by refluxing with concentrated hydrobromic acid and a trace of concentrated sulphuric acid as a catalyst, and chloro compounds by refluxing with concentrated hydrochloric acid using zinc chloride as a catalyst.

There are alternative ways of making this substitution. All of them involve weakening the C–O bond by a reaction with a phosphorus or sulphur atom. Typically, phosphorus(V) chloride, sulphuryl(IV) chloride, phosphorus(III) bromide, or a mixture of phosphorus and iodine (as phosphorus(III) iodide) is refluxed with the alcohol to get the corresponding halogenoalkane. Representing an alcohol by the formula ROH, where R is an alkyl group, the equations for these four reactions are:

$$PCl_5 + ROH \rightarrow RCl + POCl_3 + HCl$$

$$SOCl_2 + ROH \rightarrow RCl + SO_2 + HCl$$

$$PBr_3 + 3ROH \rightarrow 3RBr + H_3PO_3$$

$$PI_3 + 3ROH \rightarrow 3RI + H_3PO_3$$

Fig 11.27 **Summary of the preparation of halogenoalkanes from alcohols**

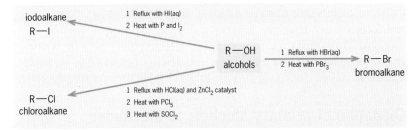

PHOSPHORUS(V) CHLORIDE FOR WORKING OUT STRUCTURES

PHOSPHORUS(V) CHLORIDE reacts with hydroxyl groups in alcohols and carboxylic acids (but not those in phenols) to produce fumes of hydrogen chloride which are easily detected. So this reaction is used in analysing compounds to identify hydroxyl groups and establish whether they are alcohols or carboxylic acids.

M Predict the products of the following reactions:

(a) pentan-2-ol refluxed with concentrated hydrobromic acid with a trace of concentrated sulphuric acid;

(b) cyclohexanol refluxed with concentrated hydroiodic acid;

(c) propan-1-ol refluxed with concentrated hydrochloric acid and zinc chloride catalyst.

■ See questions 4, 5 and 9.

N How would you prepare:

(a) iodoethane,

(b) 2-chloropentane,

(c) 2-iodo-3-methylhexane?

O A compound has the formula C_2H_6O. It does not give fumes of hydrogen chloride when reacted with phosphorus(V) chloride. Suggest an identity for the compound.

Elimination reactions: dehydration to form alkenes

As already mentioned, in alcohols there is a competition between elimination and substitution. The elimination reaction is more frequently referred to as dehydration, since it involves the loss of a molecule of water as well as the formation of an alkene (Fig 11.28).

For dehydration, an alcohol is heated with a suitable catalyst. The catalysts are often dehydrating agents, such as concentrated sulphuric acid or concentrated phosphoric(V) acid.

Laboratory dehydration

In the laboratory, it is convenient to take an alcohol and reflux it with a dehydrating agent. Concentrated sulphuric acid can be used, but concentrated phosphoric(V) acid is usually preferred, because it minimises the number of side products formed. Fig 11.29 shows the dehydration of cyclohexanol to give cyclohexene.

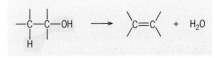

Fig 11.28 **The dehydration of an alcohol to form an alkene**

There is more on the dehydration of alcohols on page 252.

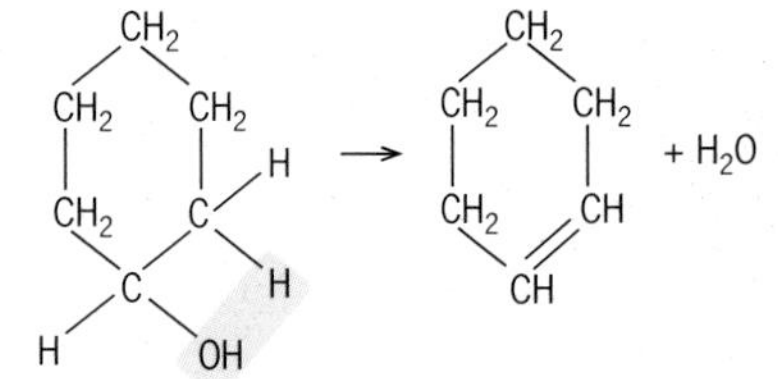

Fig 11.29 **The dehydration of cyclohexanol to give cyclohexene**

P (a) Draw the dehydration product of cyclohexanol.

(b) Draw all the alkenes that can be made by the dehydration of butan-2-ol.

(c) Which of these alkenes is likely to be formed in greatest amount?

With some alcohols, several alkenes may be produced. But normally the most substituted alkene is the major product.

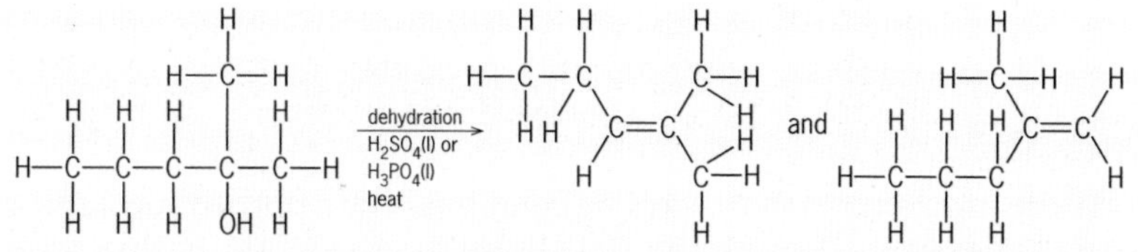

Fig 11.30 **The dehydration products of 2-methylpentan-2-ol**

5 OXIDATION OF ALCOHOLS

To read about redox reactions in more detail, look at Chapter 21.

See questions 1, 4 and 5. ■

As a working definition in organic chemistry, *oxidation* can be considered as either the gain of an oxygen atom by a substance, or the loss of two hydrogen atoms from it. (To memorise this, think of water, H_2O: one oxygen and two hydrogen atoms.)

Since reduction is the chemical opposite of oxidation, *reduction* can be considered as either the gain of two hydrogen atoms or the loss of one oxygen atom.

These atoms are always denoted by [O] and 2[H]. The square brackets signify that we are not referring to atomic hydrogen or oxygen. The substance that supplies the oxygen, [O], or removes the hydrogen, 2[H], is called the **oxidising agent**. The **reducing agent** removes the oxygen, [O], and supplies the hydrogen, 2[H].

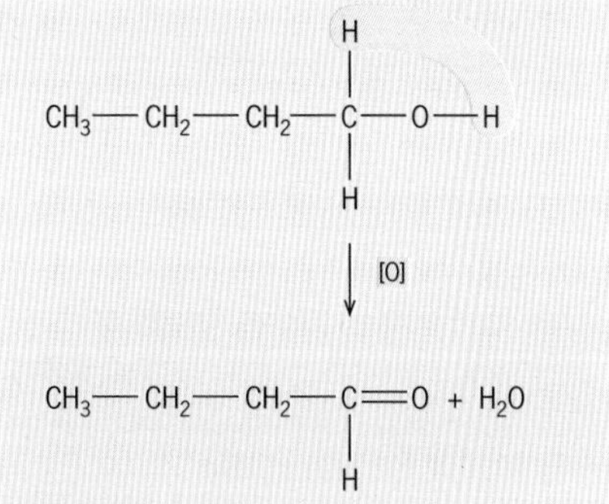

Oxidation of primary alcohols to aldehydes

Consider butanol (Fig 11.31). The removal of two hydrogen atoms produces a new functional group – the aldehyde group, CHO.

In the oxidation of a primary alcohol, the reagent is acidified aqueous potassium dichromate(VI), a mixture of aqueous potassium dichromate(VI) and dilute sulphuric acid.

The conditions must be chosen to prevent subsequent oxidation of the aldehyde to form a carboxylic acid. Either the reaction is carried out at room temperature, or the reagents are heated and the aldehyde product is allowed to distil out from the reaction vessel before it can be oxidised further.

During the oxidation, orange dichromate(VI) ions are reduced to form blue-green chromium(III) ions. The equation can be written as:

$$RCH_2OH + [O] \rightarrow RCHO + H_2O$$

In this equation, the oxidising agent is not given in full but is represented by the oxygen [O] that it supplies to remove the two hydrogen atoms. This is a much simpler expression of the reaction than the full stoichiometric and ionic equations for the reaction.

The oxidation of ethanol to ethanal by acidified potassium dichromate(VI) can be written as:

$$CH_3CH_2OH + [O] \rightarrow CH_3CHO + H_2O$$

The primary alcohols found in rose oil can be oxidised in the same way to give the corresponding aldehydes. It is interesting to note that this change of functional group alters their rose scent to that of a citrus fruit.

Fig 11.31 **The formation of butanal from butan-1-ol**

Q Write an equation to show that pentan-1-ol is oxidised to the aldehyde pentanal by the loss of 2[H].

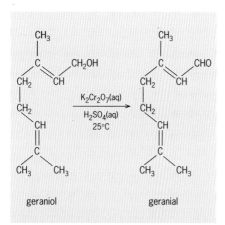

geraniol   geranial

Fig 11.32 **The oxidation of geraniol to geranial completely changes the odour of the molecule**

Stoichiometric and half equations

The stoichiometric equation for the oxidation of a primary alcohol is very complicated and tends to hide the processes taking place. For example:

$$3RCH_2OH + K_2Cr_2O_7 + 4H_2SO_4 \rightarrow$$
$$3RCHO + K_2SO_4 + Cr_2(SO_4)_3 + 7H_2O$$

Even the slightly simpler ionic equation is still complicated:

$$3RCH_2OH + Cr_2O_7{}^{2-} + 8H^+ \rightarrow 3RCHO + 2Cr^{3+} + 7H_2O$$

It is easier to look at the oxidation half equation for the reaction (see Chapter 21). During the reaction, the alcohol loses two electrons, giving the half equation:

$$RCH_2OH \rightarrow RCHO + 2H^+ + 2e^-$$

The electrons supplied by the oxidation of the alcohol reduce the dichromate(VI) ion.

R Draw the structure of the products obtained when the two primary alcohols in Fig 11.5 are oxidised by acidified potassium dichromate(VI) at room temperature.

■ See questions 5, 6 and 8.

S Draw the displayed formula of the product of the reaction of acidified potassium dichromate(VI) with 2-methylhexan-1-ol, at room temperature.

Oxidation of primary alcohols to carboxylic acids

By changing the conditions of oxidation, it is possible to remove two hydrogen atoms and gain one oxygen atom to produce a carboxylic acid. The oxidation is represented by:

$$RCH_2OH + 2[O] \rightarrow RCO_2H + H_2O$$

Two reagents can be used for this oxidation. The alcohol is refluxed with either acidified potassium dichromate(VI) or acidified potassium manganate(VII). In both cases, the acid is dilute sulphuric acid. When potassium manganate(VII) is used, the purple manganate(VII) ions are reduced to the almost colourless manganese(II) ions.

Ethanol is oxidised to ethanoic acid by refluxing with either acidified potassium dichromate(VI) or acidified potassium manganate(VII). In both cases, the reaction can be represented as:

$$CH_3CH_2OH + 2[O] \rightarrow CH_3COOH + H_2O$$

The half equation for the oxidation of ethanol to the carboxylic acid involves ethanol losing four electrons. This corresponds to the gain of [O] and the loss of 2[H]:

$$H_2O + CH_3CH_2OH \rightarrow CH_3COOH + 4H^+ + 4e^-$$

Ethanol can sometimes be oxidised by atmospheric oxygen. This can happen during fermentation, giving the ethanol a vinegary taste.

Fig 11.33 **The ethanoic acid in wine vinegars is obtained by the aerial oxidation of ethanol**

T **(a)** Write an equation to show the oxidation of butan-1-ol by refluxing with acidified potassium dichromate(VI).

(b) Draw the displayed formula of the reaction of 2-methylhexan-1-ol with acidified potassium manganate(VII).

Oxidation of secondary alcohols to ketones

Secondary alcohols can be oxidised only to ketones, whether acidified potassium dichromate(VI) or acidified potassium manganate(VII) is used. In both cases, the alcohol is refluxed with the acidified reagent. Potassium dichromate(VI) is often chosen because potassium manganate(VII) often oxidises other functional groups present in the alcohol.

The reaction involves the removal of two hydrogen atoms. So, for example, propan-2-ol is oxidised to propanone as follows:

$$3CH_3CHOHCH_3 + Cr_2O_7{}^{2-} + 8H^+ \rightarrow 3CH_3COCH_3 + 2Cr^{3+} + 7H_2O$$
$$5CH_3CHOHCH_3 + 2MnO_4{}^- + 6H^+ \rightarrow 5CH_3COCH_3 + 2Mn^{2+} + 8H_2O$$

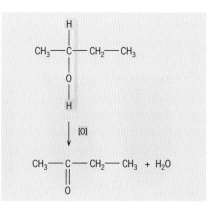

Fig 11.34 **Equation describing the oxidation of butan-2-ol**

U (a) What is the name of the organic product when cyclohexanol reacts with acidified potassium dichromate(VI)?

(b) Write an equation for the oxidation of butan-2-ol by acidified dichromate(VI) ions.
Hint: Use the given equation and substitute butan-2-ol for propan-2-ol.

V Write down a possible product from the reaction of vitamin C (Fig 11.4) with acidified potassium dichromate(VI).

W Name the product, if any, when

(a) butan-1-ol,

(b) butan-2-ol,

(c) 2-methylpropan-2-ol, are mixed with acidified potassium dichromate(VI) at room temperature.

See questions 1, 3, 4, 5 and 7. ▪

Notice that we have used the ionic formulas and left out the potassium ions, which remain unchanged during the reaction. The half equation for the oxidation of a secondary alcohol involves two electrons and is similar to the half equation for ethanol being oxidised to ethanal. Another, simpler way of representing the oxidation of a propan-2-ol is:

$$CH_3CHOHCH_3 + [O] \rightarrow CH_3COCH_3 + H_2O$$

CUTTING COSTS TO MAKE PROPANONE

PROPANONE IS an important industrial and domestic solvent. It is manufactured from propan-2-ol, but acidified potassium dichromate(VI) is not used because the reagents are expensive and the special conditions required are difficult to maintain in a large industrial plant. Instead, propan-2-ol vapour is passed over a copper catalyst at 300 °C, which removes hydrogen molecules in a reaction called **dehydrogenation** (Fig 11.35).

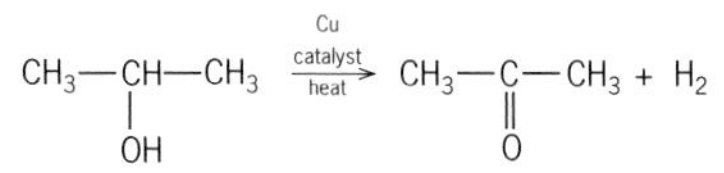

Fig 11.35 **The dehydrogenation of propan-2-ol**

Oxidation of tertiary alcohols

It is impossible to oxidise a tertiary alcohol without breaking a carbon–carbon bond. The two reagents used with primary and secondary alcohols, acidified potassium dichromate(VI) and acidified potassium manganate(VII), have no effect on tertiary alcohols. (Look back to Fig 11.11 for the structure of a tertiary alcohol.)

Distinguishing primary, secondary and tertiary alcohols

Since the three classes of alcohols give different reactions with the common laboratory oxidising agents, they can be distinguished from one another by the products and colour changes in these reactions, as Table 11.2 shows.

Table 11.2 **Distinguishing alcohols**

Alcohol	Acidified potassium dichromate(VI) at room temperature		Refluxing under heating with acidified potassium dichromate(VI)		Refluxing under heating with acidified potassium manganate(VII)	
	Product	Observation	Product	Observation	Product	Observation
primary	aldehyde	orange to green	carboxylic acid	orange to green	carboxylic acid	purple to colourless
secondary	ketone	orange to green	ketone	orange to green	ketone	purple to colourless
tertiary	no reaction	stays orange	no reaction	stays orange	no reaction	stays purple

Fig 11.36 **During the oxidation of primary and secondary alcohols using acidified potassium dichromate(VI), the colour changes from orange to green, but tertiary alcohols do not change**

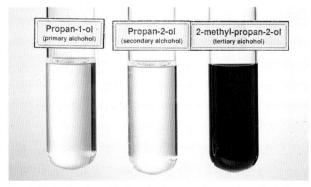

Fig 11.37 **During the oxidation of primary and secondary alcohols using acidified potassium manganate(VII), the colour changes from purple to colourless, but tertiary alcohols do not change**

Tri-iodomethane test for CH₃CHOH group

Alkaline aqueous iodine reacts with ethanol and secondary alcohols containing the CH$_3$CHOH group to give a yellow precipitate of tri-iodomethane. This reaction is used as a chemical test in analysis and identification (see also page 302).

6 ALCOHOLS AND PHENOLS AS ACIDS

Relative acidity of alcohols

An acid is a proton donor. An alcohol is an acid because it can donate a proton if the O–H bond is broken. So, the weaker the O–H bond, the stronger the acidity of the alcohol. The strength of the O–H bond can be changed by changing the atoms attached to it. For example, electron-releasing groups strengthen the O–H bond and thereby make the alcohol a weaker acid.

Alkyl groups are electron releasing compared with the hydrogen atom, so it follows that the order of increasing acid strength in alcohols is tertiary, secondary, primary. Water, which also contains the O–H bond, is a stronger acid than primary alcohols.

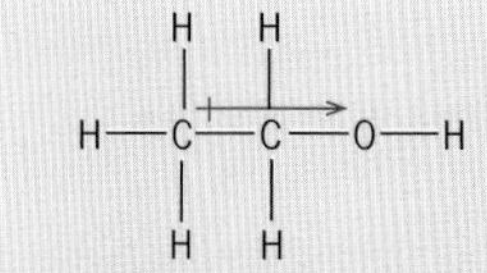

Reaction of sodium with alcohols

Sodium reacts violently with water to form hydrogen and aqueous sodium hydroxide. During the reaction, an O–H bond is broken:

$$2H_2O(l) + 2Na(s) \rightarrow 2NaOH(aq) + H_2(g)$$

Ethanol reacts in the same way with sodium, producing hydrogen and a compound called sodium ethoxide. During the reaction, the sodium fizzes and produces a colourless solution. The reaction is slower than that of sodium with water because the O–H bond in ethanol is harder to break than the O–H bond in water:

$$2C_2H_5OH + 2Na \rightarrow 2C_2H_5O^-Na^+ + H_2$$

Notice that the two equations show the same pattern.

Sodium reacts with other alcohols, producing hydrogen and what is known as an **alkoxide**. The name of the alkoxide is derived from the alkyl chain of the alcohol:

$$2ROH + 2Na \rightarrow 2RO^-Na^+ + H_2$$

The alcohol in this example is acting as a very weak acid, since it loses a proton. RO$^-$Na$^+$ is known as a sodium alkoxide.

Reaction of sodium with phenols

Phenols react with sodium to produce phenoxides. As in the case of alcohols, the reaction involves the heterolytic fission of the O–H bond. The reaction must be carried out in an inert solvent to ensure that the sodium and the phenol, both solids, do make contact.

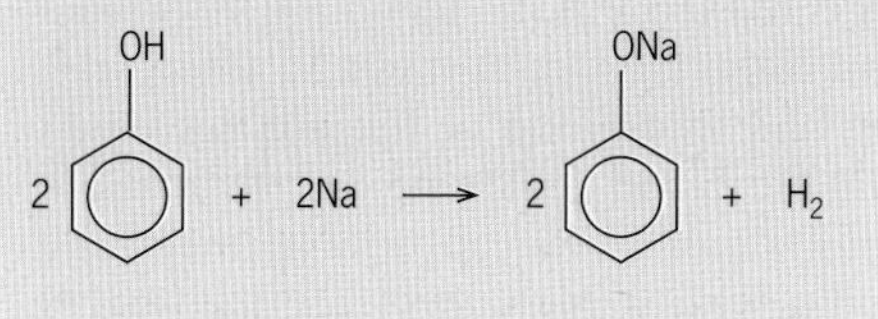

Fig 11.39 **The formation of sodium phenoxide**

X One of the straight chain alcohols with the formula C$_5$H$_{11}$OH reacts with acidified potassium dichromate(VI) to give a ketone and in a separate test also gives a yellow precipitate with alkaline aqueous iodine. Suggest an identity for the alcohol that is consistent with this data.

See questions 4 and 6.

The methyl group is electron releasing compared with a hydrogen atom, so it strengthens the O–H bond

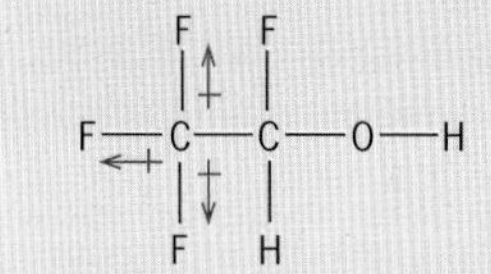

$$pK_a = 15.5$$

Fluorine atoms are highly electronegative and withdraw electrons from the O–H bond which weakens it

$$pK_a = 12.4$$

Fig 11.38 **Structures and pK$_a$ values for two alcohols: the larger the value of pK$_a$ the weaker the acid. (Read about pK$_a$ on page 312)**

Y Explain why 2-chloroethanol is a stronger acid than ethanol.
Hint: What is the effect of the very electronegative chlorine atom on the strength of the O–H bond?

Z Write down the equation for the reaction of methanol with sodium. What is the name of the alkoxide produced?

For further information on weak acids, turn to page 311.

Heterolytic fission involves breaking a covalent bond so that one atom receives both of the shared pair of electrons from the covalent bond.

Other reactions of phenols as acids

Phenoxides are also produced by the reaction of sodium hydroxide with phenols. The reason for this is that the O–H bond in phenols is much weaker than it is in alcohols, and so a proton can be lost more easily:

$$C_6H_5OH(s) + OH^-(aq) \rightarrow C_6H_5O^-(aq) + H_2O(l)$$

The lone pairs of electrons on the oxygen atom allow the π-system of the benzene ring to extend to the oxygen atom, thus making the phenoxide anion more stable than the alkoxide anion.

There are strong electrostatic interactions between the phenoxide ion and water molecules. These interactions are much stronger than the intermolecular hydrogen bonds due to the partial negative charge, δ–, on the hydroxyl group of a neutral phenol molecule. This means that a phenol dissolves much more readily in aqueous alkali than in water. (Strictly speaking, a phenol reacts with aqueous alkali rather than physically dissolving in it.)

The π-system of electrons in benzene rings is covered on page 272.

There is more about the strength of acids in Chapter 15.

See questions 6 and 9. ■

7 ALCOHOLS AS NUCLEOPHILES

The oxygen atom of the OH group can donate a pair of electrons to make a covalent bond, which allows the group to act as a nucleophile.

Alcohols are poor nucleophiles, but they can react with electron-deficient centres provided the deficiency is sufficiently high. Typically, alcohols behave as nucleophiles in their reaction with carboxylic acids or their derivatives. Probably the most important reaction is that with a carboxylic acid to form an **ester**. Esters are sweet-smelling substances which are used in perfumes and in food flavourings.

The reactions of alcohols with carboxylic acids and their derivatives are described in more detail in Chapter 16.

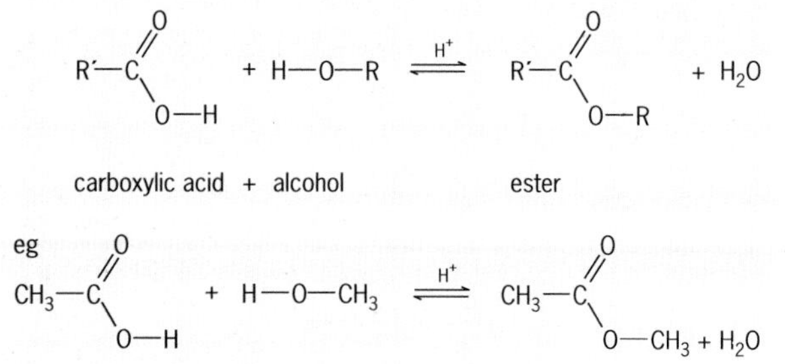

Fig 11.40 **The esterification reaction**

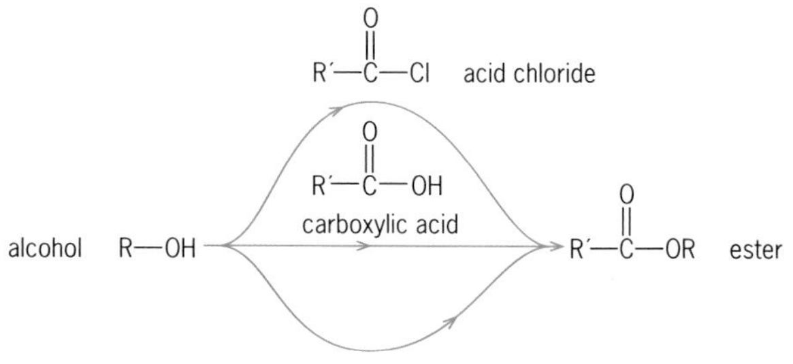

Fig 11.41 **Reaction network showing an alcohol behaving as a nucleophile**

CHOLESTEROL

CHOLESTEROL IS a member of the class of naturally-occurring and synthetic chemicals called steroids. The most abundant steroid is cholesterol which, as its name suggests, contains an alcohol group. It is found in practically all animal tissues, and forms an important part of cell membranes. Cholesterol is particularly abundant in the brain and spinal cord. It is estimated that the total amount of cholesterol in a 75 kg person is about 250 g.

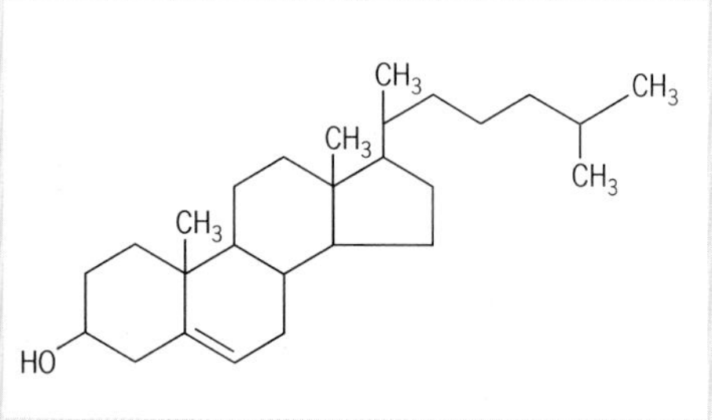

High levels of cholesterol in the blood are associated with two medical conditions, gallstones and atherosclerosis (hardening and thickening of the arteries when cholesterol from the blood builds up on their inside walls). Blood cholesterol levels can now be measured easily, and people with a high level are advised to reduce their intake of cholesterol-rich foods and saturated fats.

Fig 11.42
Cholesterol

Cholesterol was first isolated in 1770, but it took almost another two centuries before the full structure was established. As Fig 11.42 shows, cholesterol has a complicated structure, containing four rings and two functional groups.

Other steroids (Fig 11.44) include the female and male sex hormones, dealt with on page 294. Notice that steroids do not have to contain the alcohol functional group, but they all have the same ring system.

Fig 11.43 An artery of the heart (coronary artery). The wall is orange. The build-up of cholesterol is yellow. The pink between is tissue that the artery wall produces as a reaction to the cholesterol. Blood is confined to the blue area

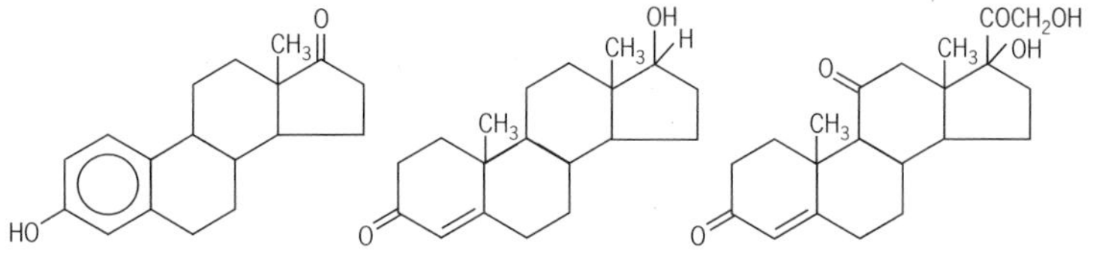

Fig 11.44
Structure of three other steroids

estrone: human hormone

testosterone: male sex hormone

cortisone: hormone of the adrenal cortex used for treatment of arthritis

?

A' (a) What type of alcohol is cholesterol?

(b) Draw the product of the reaction of cholesterol with acidified potassium dichromate(VI).

SUMMARY

After studying this chapter, you should know:

■ Alcohols contain the hydroxyl, OH, functional group attached directly to a carbon atom.

■ Short chain alcohols are soluble in water but long chain alcohols are insoluble. Polyhydroxyphenols are soluble in water.

■ Primary alcohols can be oxidised by mild oxidising agents, such as acidified potassium dichromate(VI), at room temperature to give aldehydes, and by more powerful oxidising agents, such as hot acidified potassium dichromate(VI) or hot acidified potassium manganate(VII), to give carboxylic acids.

■ Secondary alcohols can be oxidised to ketones but tertiary alcohols cannot be oxidised.

■ Alcohols can be converted by substitution into halogenoalkanes, using phosphorus halides and the appropriate hydrohalic acid, HBr(aq), HCl(aq) or HI(aq).

■ Alcohols can be dehydrated to give alkenes.

■ Alcohols can behave as nucleophiles and react with carboxylic acids and acyl chlorides to form esters.

■ Many alcohols are used as solvents.

■ Ethanol in drinks is produced by the anaerobic fermentation of aqueous glucose, catalysed by yeast.

■ Phenols are weak acids and can react with aqueous sodium hydroxide to give sodium phenoxides. Alcohols are much weaker acids than phenols and cannot react with aqueous sodium hydroxide.

■ Phenols and alcohols react with sodium to give sodium phenoxides or sodium alkoxides.

QUESTIONS

1 There are several alcohols with the molecular formula $C_5H_{12}O$, including pentan-1-ol, which has the structural formula: $CH_3CH_2CH_2CH_2CH_2OH$.

a) Write down the names and displayed formulas for the two other alcohols having the same molecular formula as pentan-1-ol.

b) In an experiment, 8.8 g of pentan-1-ol was heated with excess concentrated phosphoric(V) acid. A yield of 4.2 g of the organic product of the reaction was obtained after purification.

(i) Name the organic product.
(ii) Write an equation for the reaction using a displayed formula.
(iii) Calculate the percentage yield of the product.
[ULEAC 1996 Chemistry Specimen Papers, CN1, q.7]

2
a) Draw the displayed formula and name all the alcohols with the molecular formula $C_4H_{10}O$. Classify each alcohol as primary, secondary or tertiary.

b) Explain how you would distinguish experimentally between the primary, secondary and tertiary alcohols of $C_4H_{10}O$.

3 Cyclohexene can be converted to cyclohexanol.

a) Draw the displayed formula for cyclohexene and cyclohexanol.

b)   **(i)** Describe briefly how cyclohexene can be converted into cyclohexanol.
  (ii) Write an equation for this reaction
  (iii) What type of reaction is this?

c) Cyclohexene has a boiling point of $83\,°C$ but cyclohexanol has a boiling point of $161\,°C$. Explain why cyclohexanol has a much higher boiling point than cyclohexene.

4

a) State the type of reaction undergone and give the structural formula of each of the organic products obtained when propan-2-ol reacts with the following reagents:
  (i) HBr;
  (ii) sodium metal;
  (iii) alkaline aqueous iodine.

b) Alcohol **A** has esters which are responsible for the flavours of various fruits and has the molecular formula $C_5H_{12}O$. Reaction of **A** with acidified potassium dichromate(VI) produces a compound **B**, $C_5H_{10}O_2$. Heating **A** over Al_2O_3 produces **C**, C_5H_{10}. Vigorous oxidation of **C** forms 2-methylpropanoic acid as one of the products.
Suggest structures for **A**, **B** and **C**, and explain the reactions involved.

5 Predict the products for each of the following reactions. For each reaction give a detailed explanation for your choice of product.

a) $CH_3CH_2CH_2CH_2CH_2CH_2OH \xrightarrow{\text{HBr(aq), reflux}}$

b) $CH_3CH_2CH_2CH_2CH_2CH_2OH \xrightarrow[\text{H}_2\text{SO}_4\text{(aq) 0–5 °C}]{\text{K}_2\text{Cr}_2\text{O}_7\text{(aq)}}$

c) $CH_3CH_2CH_2CH_2CH_2CH_2OH \xrightarrow{\text{conc H}_2\text{SO}_4\text{, 130 °C}}$

d) $CH_3CH_2CH_2CH_2CH_2CH_2OH \xrightarrow[\text{heat 50 °C}]{\text{KMnO}_4\text{(aq)/H}_2\text{SO}_4\text{(aq)}}$

6 Salbutamol, with structure shown below, is used in Ventolin inhalers to help asthma sufferers breathe more easily.

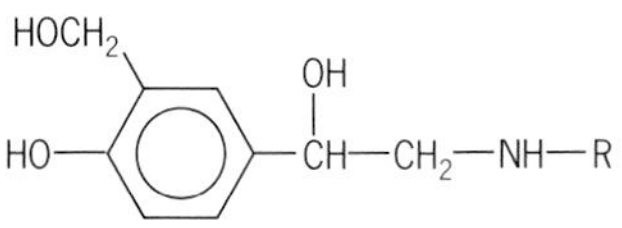

R is an alkyl group, which for the purpose of this question does not affect the rest of the molecule.

a) Name **four** reactive organic groups in salbutamol.

b) State **two** of these groups which are affected by mild oxidation, and what groups are produced.

c) Would you expect the salbutamol molecule to be acidic, neutral or alkaline? Explain your answer.
[UCLES June 1995 Chemistry 9250/3, q.6]

7 Samples of butan-1-ol, butan-2-ol and 2-methylpropan-2-ol were reacted under reflux with aqueous acidified potassium dichromate(VI).

a) Copy and complete the table below for each of the three alcohols. State what you would observe and identify the organic product of each reaction.

Alcohol	Observation	Organic product (if any)
butan-1-ol		
butan-2-ol		
2-methylpropan-2-ol		

b) Describe a simple chemical test by which you could distinguish between the organic products you have given in **a)** for butan-1-ol and for butan-2-ol.

8 Draw the structures of **one** example each of a primary, a secondary and a tertiary alcohol. Describe, and explain, the reactions (if any) of your chosen alcohols with acidified potassium dichromate(VI). Where appropriate, include names and structural formulae of the organic products.
[UCLES Spring 1994 Modular: Chains and Rings 1021/2, Section B, q.6]

9 Menthol, a cyclohexane derivative, is used in skin lotions since it counteracts itching; the structural formula of menthol is shown in Fig 11.Q11.

a) Write down the molecular formula of menthol.

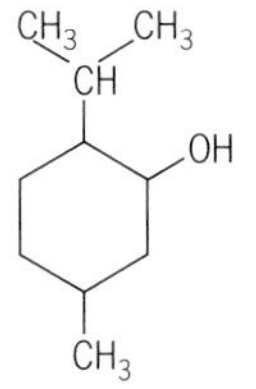

b) Circle any chiral centres in the molecule of menthol.

c) Draw the structural formula of the organic product formed by the action of acidified dichromate(VI) ions on menthol.

d) Draw the structural formula of the organic product formed by the reaction of menthol with refluxing concentrated hydrobromic acid.
Explain the mechanism of this reaction.
[UCLES June 1992 Chemistry, 9250/3, q.4

Assignment

FERMENTATION AND LOW-ALCOHOL BEERS

The fermentation processes involved in bread-making, wine-making and brewing are among the oldest applications of chemistry. But chemists did not begin to understand what happens during fermentation until the 1800s. In 1810, Gay-Lussac published the equation for the conversion of sugar to ethanol and carbon dioxide, but almost 90 years elapsed before Buchner demonstrated that yeast extract without yeast cells would ferment aqueous glucose. We now realise that the reaction is catalysed by many enzymes, collectively called zymase.

1 Explain the importance of fermentation in bread-making.

Glucose can exist as a chain form and a ring form, shown in Fig 11.A1. In aqueous solution, it is almost entirely in the ring form.

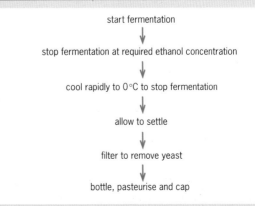

Fig 11.A1 **Displayed formulas of the ring and chain forms of glucose**

2

a) The number 1 carbon in the chain structure is part of the aldehyde functional group. Give the systematic name for the chain structure of glucose.
Hint: Read the Assignment on page 305.

b) Compare the structures of the two forms of glucose. You may want to consider the shape of each molecule, isomerism and the functional groups present.

The fermentation of aqueous glucose requires anaerobic conditions to make ethanol. Also, the temperature must not rise significantly above 32 °C, otherwise the rate of fermentation slows down and the reaction eventually stops.

3

a) Write down an equation to represent the fermentation of glucose to form ethanol and carbon dioxide.

b) Suggest the names of the products when the fermentation is carried out in the presence of oxygen.

c) Explain why the fermentation of aqueous glucose slows down and eventually stops when the temperature is raised significantly above 32 °C.
Hint: You may want to read about enzymes in Chapter 17.

d) The fermentation of aqueous glucose is an exothermic process. What precautions must brewers take to ensure efficient fermentation?

The manufacture of alcoholic drinks accounts for much of the ethanol produced by fermentation. Once fermentation is finished, beer, lager and wine need only to be bottled, canned or casked. Spirits such as whisky require a higher concentration of ethanol. This is achieved by distilling the fermentation mixture.

Since the mid-1980s, there has been a significant increase in the consumption of low-alcohol and alcohol-free beers (Table 11.A1). Low-alcohol beer is manufactured in two ways. One way is to ferment partially and then stop the process (Fig 11.A2). The second way is to ferment fully and then remove the alcohol (Fig 11.A3).

Partial fermentation produces low-alcohol beer rather than alcohol-free beer. The method has two drawbacks: the beer tastes sugary, and it is susceptible to microbial contamination. On the other hand, full fermentation followed by removal of the ethanol allows both low-alcohol and alcohol-free beer to be brewed. The ethanol is removed by distillation, which is carried out at reduced pressure in order also to remove and store the esters responsible for taste and aroma. An additional benefit of low-pressure distillation is that other flavour components are not subjected to high temperatures that may degrade them.

Further distillation completely removes the ethanol, which is stored for other uses. The beer can be reconstituted by adding the esters extracted during distillation, carbon dioxide and as much ethanol as is required.

Table 11.A1 **Categories of beer**

Category	Percentage by volume of ethanol
alcohol-free	no more than 0.05
de-alcoholised	0.05–0.5
low-alcohol	0.5–1.2
typical beer	4–5

start fermentation

↓

stop fermentation at required ethanol concentration

↓

cool rapidly to 0 °C to stop fermentation

↓

allow to settle

↓

filter to remove yeast

↓

bottle, pasteurise and cap

Fig 11.A2 **Making low-alcohol beer by partial fermentation**

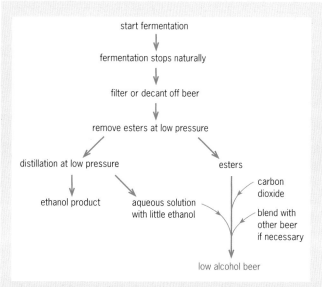

Fig 11.A3 **Making low-alcohol beer by distillation at reduced pressure**

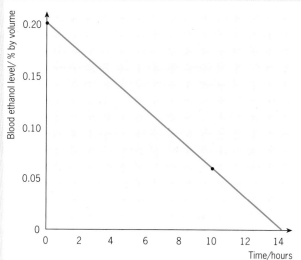

Fig 11.A4 **The rate of removal of ethanol from the blood after drinking has stopped**

a) What is fractional distillation, and what property does its success depend on?

b) Compare the advantages and disadvantages of the two methods for making low alcohol and alcohol-free drinks.

c) One of the reasons for the increase in the consumption of alcohol-free beer is that it enables people to drink beer without breaking religious observance. Suggest some more reasons for this change of habit.

Most people still prefer to drink normal beer rather than alcohol-free beer, but they should be aware of the dangers of ethanol. Ethanol is a mild depressant which slows down both physical and mental activity. In sufficient quantities it can kill.

Table 11.A2 **The relationship between the non-stop consumption of beer and the effect of ethanol for a man weighing 70 kg**

Volume of typical beer/dm³	Blood ethanol level/ % by volume	Effect
0.72	0.05	mild sedation and tranquillity
1.44	0.1	lack of coordination
2.16	0.15	obvious intoxication
3.60	0.3	unconscious
7.70	0.5	possible death

a) Suggest from the information in Table 11.A2 why it is difficult to keep drinking ethanol until you die.

b) What do you notice about the rate of removal of ethanol from the blood?

c) Explain why it can still be dangerous for you to drive some hours after you have finished drinking.

d) A 70 kg moderate drinker has 2 dm³ of beer.
  (i) Estimate the time it takes for ethanol to be absent from the blood.
  (ii) Give reasons why this can only be an approximate answer.

e) A person, who weighs 70 kg, drinks 2 dm³ of beer per hour for 4 hours. Estimate the blood ethanol level after 4 hours.
Hint: Use a graph.

ALCOHOLS AND PHENOLS

This chapter is an introduction to the properties of alcohols and phenols, their reactions and uses. Use the Chapter Map below to check that you have covered the aspects of alcohols and phenols that are required by the syllabus you are following, and to see where additional information can be found in other chapters.

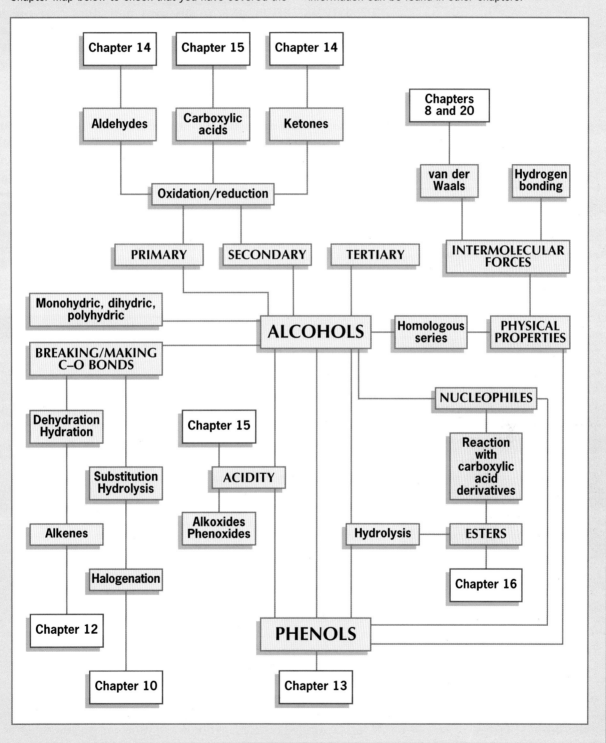

12 Alkenes

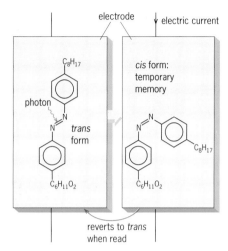

A memory molecule changes shape to its *cis* form when it absorbs a photon of ultraviolet light. This form could correspond to the binary digit 1 or 'on'. The *trans* form of the molecule would then correspond to the binary digit 0 or 'off'

Fig 12.1 **Introducing alternative energy sources, such as this wind farm, may reduce the demand for crude oil. But alternative energy sources will have to be better developed and more freely available before they supply a sizeable fraction of the energy we consume**

The fractional distillation of crude oil is decribed on page 148.

CHEMISTS ARE BEGINNING to discover molecules that can be made to act like the memory of a computer which stores binary information by switching between two states – 'on' or 'off'. The molecular shape of certain molecules containing double bonds alters when they undergo a reversible photochemical change, and this is the 'switch' that chemists are exploiting.

For when such a molecule is changed from a *trans*-isomer into a *cis*-isomer, the distinct change in shape of the molecule offers a way of storing information. For example, the *trans* form could be designated 'off' (corresponding to binary digit 0) and the *cis* form designated 'on' (corresponding to binary digit 1). Given that the change easily reverses, information storage, retrieval and erasure become feasible. The hope is that, by depositing such memory molecules on an electrode, a hundred million bits of information could be stored on an area the size of a fingernail.

1 THE PETROCHEMICAL INDUSTRY

The petrochemical industry produces very many organic substances from crude oil and natural gas. About 90 per cent of the world's output of basic organic chemicals is now derived from these two fossil fuels. Petrochemicals include substances as diverse as solvents, detergents, pesticides, insecticides, polymers, plastics, drugs, paints and textiles. Without doubt, improvements in the quality of life since the early 1900s are a direct consequence of the development of the petrochemical industry.

Dmitri Mendeleev, who originated the Periodic Table, wrote that crude oil was too valuable to be burnt as a fuel but should be used as a source for organic chemicals. That was in 1872, and many people would argue that it is still the case.

Cracking and the production of alkenes

Crude oil is a complex mixture of organic compounds. Even after the fractional distillation of crude oil, the fractions obtained are still complex mixtures (although the components of a fraction do have similar boiling points). Therefore, particular components have to be extracted from the fractions as starting materials for the manufacture of petrochemicals.

Most of the hydrocarbons present in crude oil fractions are alkanes, which normally are unreactive. However, alkanes can undergo the process called cracking to produce a variety of organic molecules that can be used to synthesise other, more generally useful organic compounds. Cracking converts saturated hydrocarbons into unsaturated hydrocarbons. In particular, a group of versatile and important unsaturated hydrocarbons called **alkenes** are made.

Importance of alkenes

Why are alkenes so important to the petrochemical industry? The main reason is that the carbon–carbon double bond of an alkene molecule makes its carbon chain reactive. So, compounds with different carbon chains or with different functional groups can readily be synthesised from alkenes.

The chemistry of the alkene functional group is described in this chapter, illustrating the wide range of substances that can be made from quite simple alkenes.

The second reason for their importance is that alkenes are readily available in large amount from the cracking of crude oil. Despite the widespread use of petrochemicals as raw materials, an ever-present problem is that an economic downturn can leave the petrochemical industry producing enormous surpluses of its diverse range of materials (including alkenes) and facing a low demand for its end-product chemicals.

ALKENES AND ALKYNES AS FUELS

SURPLUS ALKENES can be used as fuels as well as starting materials for petrochemical processes. Being hydrocarbons, alkenes can burn, transferring energy to their surroundings.

Similarly, the alkyne ethyne (C_2H_2), which has a triple bond, is mixed with oxygen and burnt to produce an extremely high temperature flame, which is used to cut iron and steel. The equipment is commonly known as the oxyacetylene torch (acetylene is the traditional name for ethyne).

$$C_2H_2(g) + 2\tfrac{1}{2}O_2(g) \rightarrow 2CO_2(g) + H_2O(g)$$

Fig 12.2 **The temperature an oxyacetylene flame is high enough to cut easily through steel**

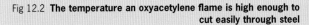

?

A Write down the equation for the complete combustion of ethene (C_2H_4) and of propene (C_3H_6).

?

B (a) Write down the equation for the complete combustion of methane in air.

(b) Suggest how the risk of explosion during the oxidative coupling reaction can be reduced (see below).

NATURAL GAS AS A SOURCE OF PETROCHEMICALS

NATURAL GAS IS an abundant resource. Even if no new gas fields are discovered, present known sources should last until about 2050. So, could natural gas be used as a source of petrochemicals as well as a fuel?

Unfortunately, natural gas is mainly methane, which does not contain any carbon–carbon double bonds. However, much research is in progress to find ways of using methane to make alkenes to provide an alternative supply of raw materials for the petrochemical industry. For example, in a process known as an *oxidative coupling*, methane is reacted with oxygen at high temperatures in the presence of an oxide catalyst. In one such reaction, methane is converted to ethene – a precursor of a large number of petrochemicals:

$$2CH_4 + O_2 \rightarrow C_2H_4 + 2H_2O$$

The coupling reaction is believed to have a free-radical mechanism. Because of this, the selectivity is low, so many other products are formed. Oxidative coupling has to be closely controlled since, with the wrong proportions of methane and oxygen, there could be an explosion as combustion takes place.

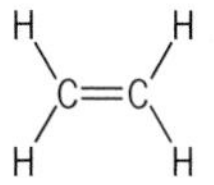

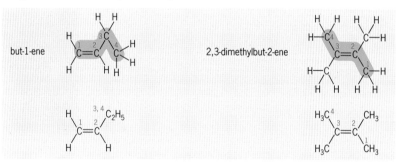

Fig 12.3 **The displayed formula of ethene**

?

C Using the number of electron pairs around a carbon atom, explain why the bond angles in ethene are about 120°. Hint: If you have difficulty doing this, read page 78.

Naming a carbon skeleton and numbering its carbon atoms are covered on pages 156 to 158.

See question 1. ■

?

D (a) Draw the displayed formula for **(i)** pent-1-ene, **(ii)** cyclopentene and **(iii)** penta-1,3-diene.

(b) Name each of the following.

(i)

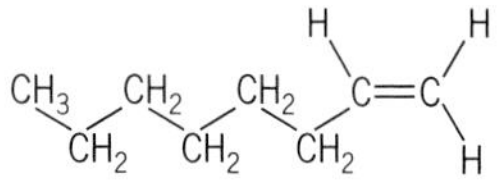

(ii)

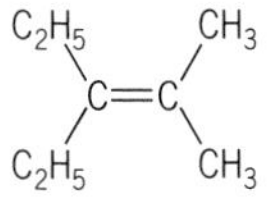

(iii)

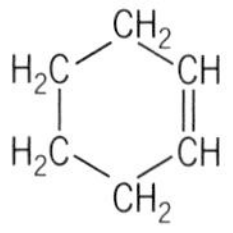

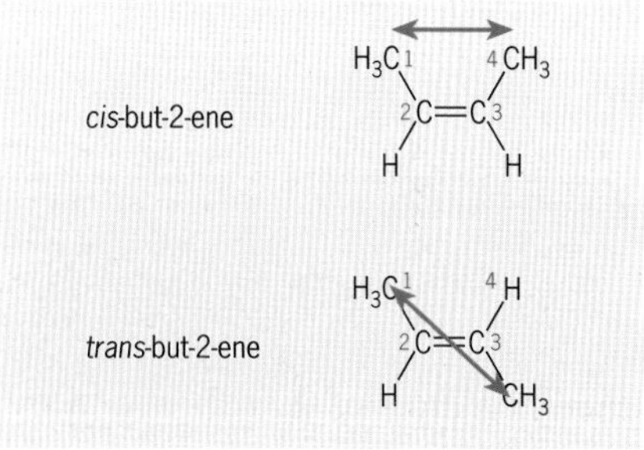

cis-but-2-ene

trans-but-2-ene

2 ALKENES AND ISOMERISM

Alkenes are unsaturated hydrocarbons which have a single carbon–carbon double bond. This means that their carbon chain has two fewer hydrogen atoms than the same carbon chain in alkanes, giving the general formula C_nH_{2n}. It is the presence of the double bond that gives alkenes much greater reactivity than alkanes.

Naming alkenes

The presence of the carbon–carbon double bond (C=C) is identified by the suffix *ene*. So, for example, ethene (Fig 12.3) has a two-carbon chain with one C=C bond, and propene has a three-carbon chain with one C=C bond. Notice that the displayed formula of ethene has been drawn with angles of about 120° between the bonds, which is their actual value. It is not essential to draw these bond angles accurately, but it is good practice, and will help you to remember them.

The name of an alkene must also specify the position of the C=C bond and the number of carbon atoms in the longest chain containing the C=C bond. The use of *eth*, *prop*, *but*, and so on, to indicate the length of the carbon chain is described on page 157.

We therefore proceed as follows:

• First, locate the longest chain containing the double bond.

• Then, number the carbon atoms in the chain from the end that gives the lowest possible position-number to the C=C bond.

but-1-ene

2,3-dimethylbut-2-ene

Fig 12.4 **The displayed formulas of but-1-ene and 2,3-dimethyl but-2-ene. The formulas underneath are easier to write and give practically as much information, as the formulas above. The coloured patches show the longest carbon chain containing the C=C bond**

Stereoisomerism

The C=C bond is stronger than the C–C bond, but is locked in position and cannot rotate in the way that the C–C rotates. This gives rise to **stereoisomerism** in compounds with double bonds. Compounds which are stereoisomers of one another have the same make-up of atoms, and their atoms are bonded in the same order, but the arrangements of the atoms in space are different.

Fig 12.5 shows two compounds which have the same name, but-2-ene. But are they really the same? Each molecule has its own molecular shape, defined by the bond length and the bond angles within the molecule. Simple geometry shows that the length from carbon 1 to carbon 4 is not the same in both compounds. So they cannot be identical – they are **isomers**.

Fig 12.5 **The displayed formula of geometric isomers of but-2-ene. The distance between carbon 1 and carbon 4 is different in these two forms. This is because the shape of the *cis* molecule is different from that of the *trans* molecule**

These two isomers have different physical properties. For example, the melting point of *cis*-but-2-ene is −139 °C but that of the *trans*-but-2-ene is −106 °C. But the chemical properties are very similar since both molecules contain the same type and number of bonds.

This type of isomerism is known as **geometric isomerism** or ***cis–trans* isomerism**, since the bond angles are all identical but the geometries and shapes of the molecules are different. The prefix *cis* (Latin) means 'on the same side', and so the *cis* isomer has the two methyl groups on the same side of the double bond. The prefix *trans* (also Latin) means 'on the other side', and so the *trans* isomer has the methyl groups on opposite sides of the double bond. The *trans* isomer has the greater distance between carbon 1 and carbon 4.

The diagram below summarises the different types of isomerism.

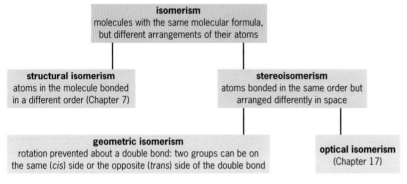

The diagram shows:

isomerism — molecules with the same molecular formula, but different arrangements of their atoms

branching into:

structural isomerism — atoms in the molecule bonded in a different order (Chapter 7)

stereoisomerism — atoms bonded in the same order but arranged differently in space

with stereoisomerism branching into:

geometric isomerism — rotation prevented about a double bond: two groups can be on the same (*cis*) side or the opposite (*trans*) side of the double bond

optical isomerism (Chapter 17)

■ See questions 1, 2, 3 and 4.

Nature of the double bond

Cis–trans isomers exist because the C=C bond is not free to rotate. This is unlike the behaviour of the C–C carbon bond, where there is free rotation about the bond, and therefore (see Fig 12.6) the positions of the two methyl groups in butane are not fixed. In but-2-ene, the carbon–carbon double bond hinders rotation, and so the two methyl groups are locked in their positions.

butane   but-2-ene

Fig 12.6 **Butane has free rotation at the C–C bond, while in but-2-ene the C=C bond prevents rotation. When the single C–C bond between carbon 2 and carbon 3 rotates, the methyl groups also rotate. Although the conformations look like *cis* and *trans*, rotation of the C–C bond changes one conformation into the other, and back again. The double bond cannot rotate, so the *cis* form cannot become the *trans* form**

The inability of the double bond to rotate is explained by the nature of the bond itself. Any double bond is composed of two different types of bond, the σ bond and the π bond (Fig 12.7).

The σ bond is formed by the overlap of two atomic orbitals, one on each carbon atom. The bond lies mainly in the region directly *between* the two nuclei. The π bond is formed by the side-to-side overlap of two 2p atomic orbitals, one on each carbon atom. As a result, the π bond lies *above and below* the σ bond. The two carbon atoms are thus bonded together in two different ways, with the π bond preventing rotation about the carbon–carbon bond.

Note that the overlap of the orbitals is less for the π bond, so the energy needed to break the π bond is less than that needed to break the σ bond.

E (a) Draw the displayed formula for **(i)** *cis*-pent-2-ene and **(ii)** *trans*-hex-3-ene.

(b) What is the full name of each of the following?

(i) CH_3CH_2 ... H ... C=C ... H ... $CH_2CH_2CH_3$

(ii) Cl ... Cl ... C=C ... C_2H_5 ... CH_3

(c) State which of the following molecules can have *cis* and *trans* isomers: prop-1-ene, cyclopentene, hex-1-ene, hex-2-ene, hex-3-ene and 2,3-dimethylbut-2-ene.

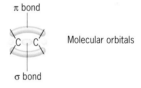

π bond

σ bond

Molecular orbitals

Sideways overlap of 2p atomic orbitals (gives π bond)

Overlap of atomic orbitals

Overlap of sp² orbitals (gives σ bond)

Fig 12.7 **The orbital model of the double bond showing the two types of bond**

The nature of the double bond is also covered on page 8.

F Use the bond energies given in Table 6.3, page 122, to estimate the strength of the σ bond and that of the π bond in the carbon–carbon double bond.

INTERCHANGE OF *CIS* AND *TRANS* ISOMERS AND THE PHOTOCHEMISTRY OF VISION

THE ONLY WAY to change a *cis* isomer to a *trans* isomer is first to break the π bond, thereby allowing free rotation about the σ bond, and then to re-form the π bond. This can be done by a **photochemical reaction** using ultraviolet light.

When ultraviolet light of the correct frequency is absorbed by the molecule, the π bond is broken, forming a **diradical**. A diradical is a particle that contains two atoms each with an unpaired electron.

During the time that the diradical exists, there is free rotation about the σ bond. Because free radicals are highly reactive, the diradical very quickly re-forms the double bond to pair up the electrons. The result is a mixture of the *cis* and the *trans* isomer.

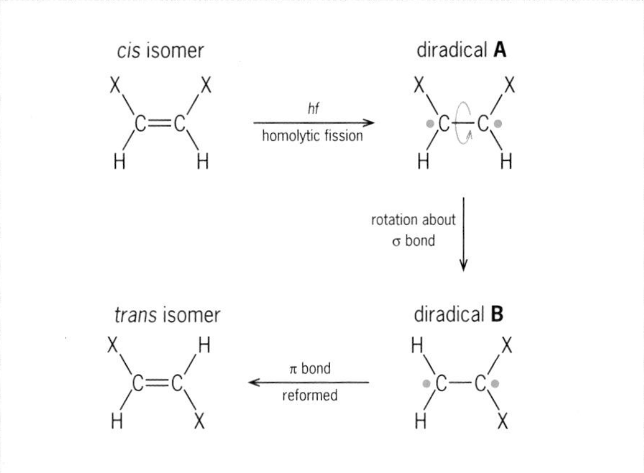

Fig 12.8 Photochemical *cis–trans* transformations. The π bond can re-form in either structure A or B, producing both *cis* and *trans* isomers

The property of *cis–trans* isomerism is not limited to compounds with carbon–carbon double bonds. Compounds with carbon–nitrogen and nitrogen–nitrogen double bonds also form geometric isomers. For example, Fig 12.9 shows a candidate for the kind of memory molecule mentioned in the chapter Opener. The completely different shapes of the two isomers are obvious.

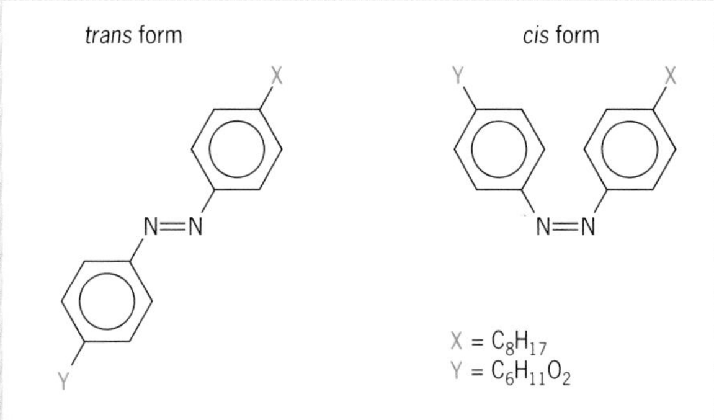

$X = C_8H_{17}$
$Y = C_6H_{11}O_2$

Fig 12.9 A possible memory molecule. The distance between X and Y is much shorter in the *cis* isomer than in the *trans* isomer. The *trans* isomer can be changed into the *cis* isomer by a photochemical reaction

Photochemistry of vision

Light is detected on the inner wall of the eye known as the retina. The retina consists of two types of cell that can respond to light: rods and cones. Rods respond to differences in intensity of light, but not to colour. Cones respond to colour. But both types of cell function in a similar way.

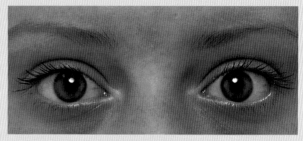

Fig 12.10 Detection of light by the retina is a direct result of the photochemical transformation of a *cis* isomer to a *trans* isomer

Light is detected because retinal, a molecule inside the cells of the retina, undergoes a photochemical reaction. When a photon of light reaches a *cis*-retinal molecule, it is changed to the *trans*-retinal form, as in Figs 12.11 and 12.12, and so its shape changes.

Retinal interacts with a protein responsible for producing the nerve impulses which are sent along the optic nerve to the brain, and when the form changes from *cis* to *trans*, a nerve impulse is generated. It is not yet fully understood how the change of shape within the protein molecule produces a nerve impulse, but the energy from the light is in some way transferred, and an electrical signal results.

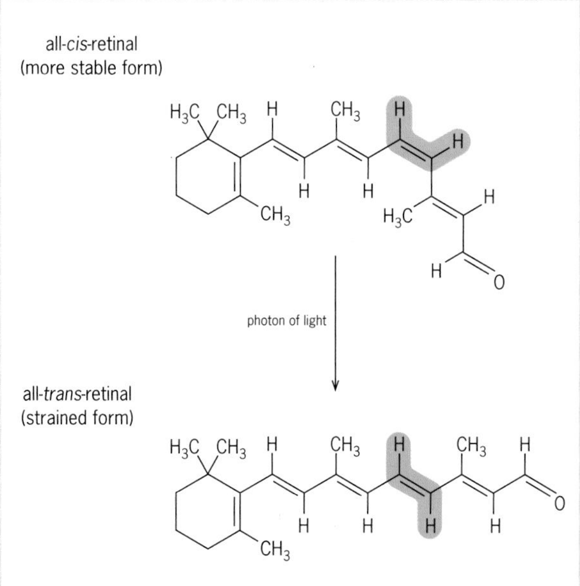

all-*cis*-retinal
(more stable form)

photon of light

all-*trans*-retinal
(strained form)

Fig 12.11 *Cis*- and *trans*-retinal. The two isomers have completely different overall shapes. The coloured patches highlight the *cis* and *trans* double bonds at which the difference arises

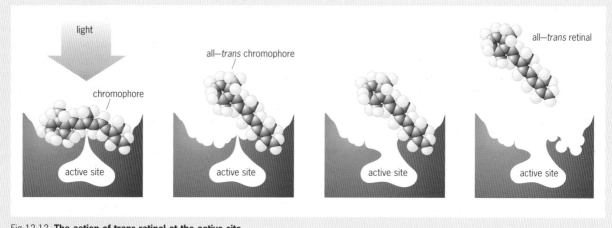

Fig 12.12 **The action of trans-retinal at the active site**

Physical properties of alkenes

The alkenes form a homologous series. The first three members are gases, but all the higher members are liquids or solids. The increase in the boiling point of compounds as the number of carbon atoms per molecule increases is typical for all homologous series, not just the alkenes.

Table 12.1 **Melting and boiling points of four alkenes**

Alkene	Structural formula	Melting point/°C	Boiling point/°C
ethene	$CH_2=CH_2$	−169	−105
propene	$CH_3CH=CH_2$	−185	−48
but-1-ene	$CH_3CH_2CH=CH_2$	−185	−6
pent-1-ene	$CH_3CH_2CH_2CH=CH_3$	−165	30

3 PREPARATION OF ALKENES

■ See question 5.

Cracking alkanes

Saturated hydrocarbons can be cracked to give alkenes (see page 148). Though cracking can be done in the laboratory, this method is unsuitable because it produces a mixture that is difficult to separate into individual alkenes.

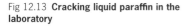

Fig 12.13 **Cracking liquid paraffin in the laboratory**

?

G (a) Explain why the boiling points of the alkenes increases as the number of carbon atoms per molecule increases.
Hint: Read pages 158 and 159 about the boiling points of the alkanes.

(b) Predict the boiling point of hex-1-ene.

Free-radical mechanism of cracking

Thermal cracking involves heating long chain alkanes at a very high temperature so that the molecules break down to give hydrocarbons with shorter carbon chains. Since the C–C bond in alkanes is non-polar, the breaking of this bond is believed to involve homolytic fission with the formation of alkyl free radicals. Homolytic fission is normally initiated by ultraviolet light, but a very high temperature provides sufficient thermal energy for the process.

Cracking lacks selectivity since its progress is determined by which carbon–carbon bond is first broken, and then by the type of collision that the free radical is involved in. Typically, the cracking of a hydrocarbon such as decane leads to a collection of short chain alkanes, alkenes and hydrogen. (Free radicals and homolytic fission are described on pages 206 and 207.)

There is more about the dehydration of alcohols on page 235.

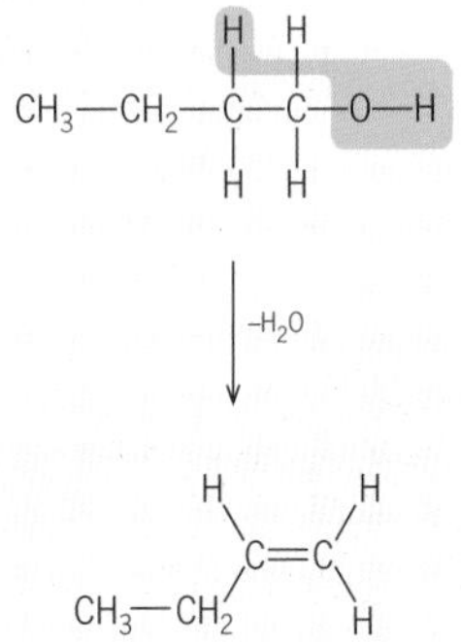

Fig 12.14 **Butan-1-ol loses a water molecule in an elimination reaction to form but-1-ene**

See question 1. ■

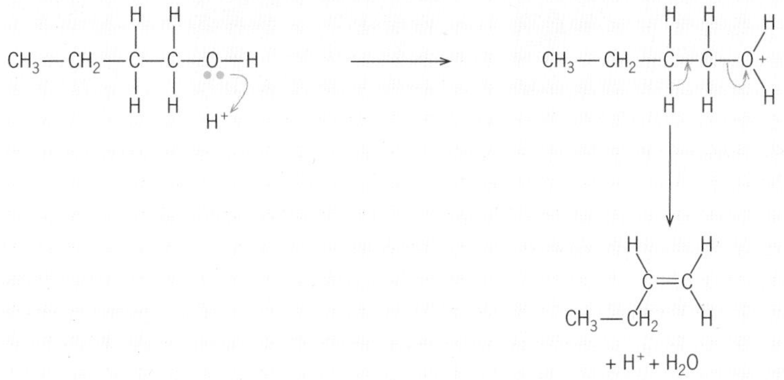

Fig 12.15 **Dehydration of an alcohol (butan-1-ol) is catalysed by an acid. So the reaction starts with the protonation of the alcohol. After elimination of the water molecule, the proton is regenerated**

?

H (a) State which alcohol you would need to make **(i)** ethene, **(ii)** propene, and **(iii)** cycloheptene.

(b) (i) Write down all the possible isomers that can be formed by the dehydration of pentan-2-ol.
(ii) Which of these is likely to be produced in the greatest amount?

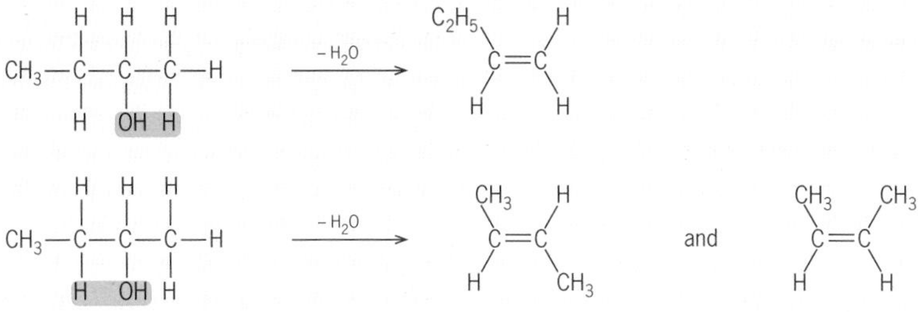

For more information about the elimination of hydrogen halides from halogenoalkanes, see page 218.

See questions 1 and 2. ■

?

I Draw all the alkenes that can be produced when 2-iodohexane is heated with ethanolic sodium hydroxide.

Dehydration of alcohols

A suitable way to prepare alkenes is to dehydrate an alcohol. This reaction is an example of elimination and involves the loss of a molecule of water (Fig 12.14). Normally, an acidic catalyst, such as concentrated phosphoric(V) acid or concentrated sulphuric acid, is used to aid elimination of the water (Fig 12.15). Industrially, the dehydration is usually catalysed by passing the alcohol vapour over heated aluminium oxide.

Sometimes, the dehydration of an alcohol leads to the formation of two or more alkenes, which can be either structural or geometric isomers (Fig 12.16). Normally, the most stable alkene is produced. This is the alkene with most alkyl groups attached to the carbon atoms that form the double bond.

Fig 12.16 **Dehydration of butan-2-ol. Three isomeric butenes can be made by the removal of different hydrogen atoms**

Elimination of hydrogen halides from halogenoalkanes

When a halogenoalkane is heated with a strong base, such as ethanolic sodium hydroxide, the corresponding alkene is produced. Again, the reaction may give more than one alkene and may be complicated by substitution products as well (Fig 12.17).

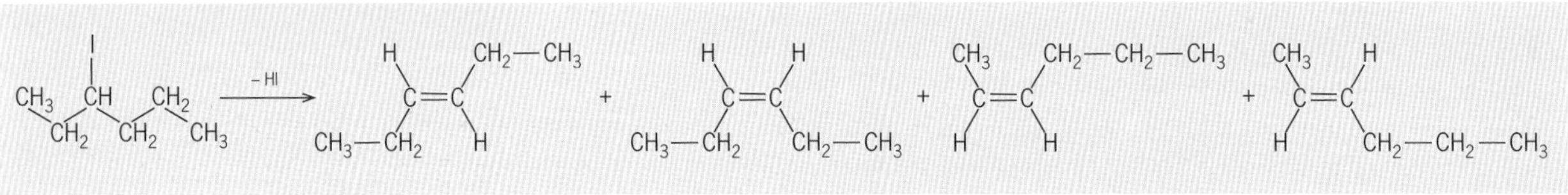

Fig 12.17 **Elimination of hydrogen iodide from 3-iodohexane**

4 REACTIONS OF ALKENES

The double bond in an alkene is non-polar but it is electron rich because of the π bond. When the π bond is broken, the carbon atoms remain joined together by the σ bond.

?

J Explain why the π bond can be broken more easily than the σ bond.

Electrophiles

An **electrophile** is a particle which can accept a pair of electrons to make a covalent bond. Often, an electrophile has only six electrons in its outer shell, so that by accepting two others it gets a stable octet. A typical electrophile is Cl^+, with only six electrons in its outer shell. Metal ions are not electrophiles because, although they are positive, they cannot gain a pair of electrons to make a covalent bond. In fact, a metal ion is positive to preserve a stable octet of electrons.

Electrophiles are generated by **heterolytic fission** of a covalent bond. In heterolytic fission, the bond is broken by both electrons migrating to the atom that is the more electronegative, leaving the less electronegative atom positive. Fig 12.18 shows the heterolytic fission of a covalent bond. Again, we follow the convention of using a curly arrow to show the migration of a pair of electrons.

?

K State which of the following particles are electrophiles: Br^+, $CH_3•$, CH_3^+, H_2O and Na^+.

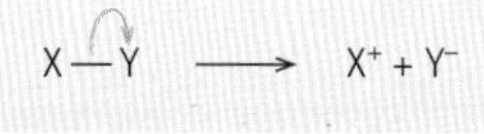

Fig 12.18 **Heterolytic fission of a covalent bond. Atom Y is normally more electronegative than atom X. It therefore accepts the bonding pair of electrons during heterolytic fission**

Electrophilic addition

Almost all double bonds will undergo a reaction known as **addition**. During addition, two substances react together to give one product and the original double bond becomes a single bond. In the case of the C=C bond, an electrophile is often needed to break the bond. Because the initial step in the mechanism involves an electrophile, it is called **electrophilic addition**.

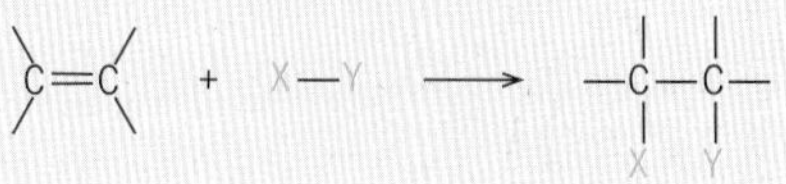

Fig 12.19 **A generalised addition reaction. During addition, two reactants form one product and the double bond becomes saturated**

Mechanism of electrophilic addition

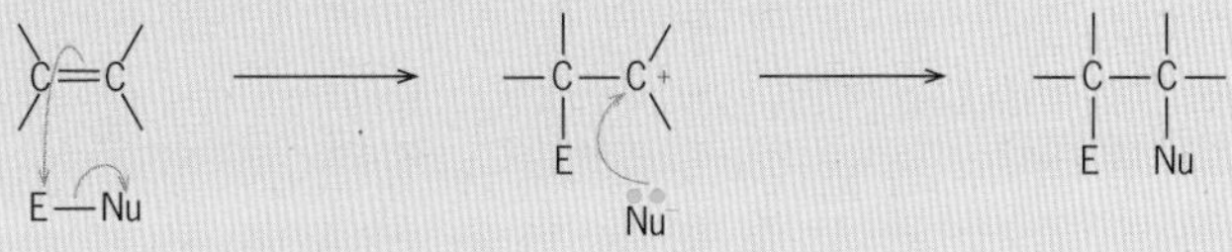

Fig 12.20 **A generalised mechanism for electrophilic addition to an alkene. E = electrophile, Nu = nucleophile**

The first stage in electrophilic addition is the formation of the electrophile. (We will return later to discuss this stage in more detail, because it is not always as simple as is shown in Fig 12.20.) The electrophile 'attacks' the double bond. At the same time, a pair of electrons migrates from the double bond towards the electrophile. As seen in Fig 12.20, the effect of this is to break the carbon–carbon double bond and to make a single bond to the electrophile. In the last stage, the nucleophile reacts with the carbocation that has been formed, completing the addition.

The net effect is to add at the double bond to form a saturated compound. It is this ability to react by addition that accounts for the difference in reactivity between an alkane and an alkene.

The absence of reactivity in alkanes is covered on page 160.

?

L Hydrogen bromide will add to ethene to form bromoethane. Describe the mechanism of this reaction.
Hint: The hydrogen atom in HBr is electron deficient.

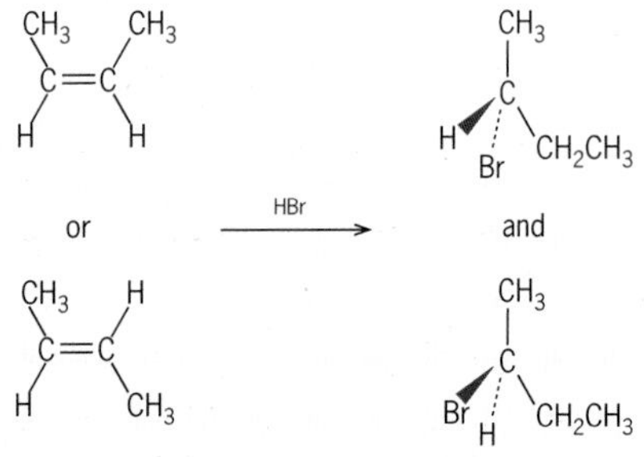

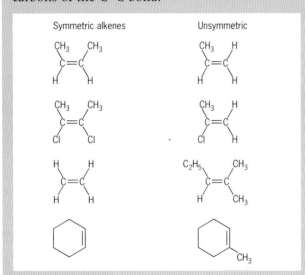

Fig 12.21 **The addition of hydrogen bromide to either *cis-* or *trans-*but-2-ene gives the two optical isomers of 2-bromobutane**

Optical isomerism is another form of steroisomerism: see page 355.
The reactions of halogenoalkanes are covered in detail in Chapter 10.

Addition of hydrogen halides

Hydrogen bromide reacts with alkenes to produce bromoalkanes. The other hydrogen halides react with alkenes in a similar way. The reaction with hydrogen iodide is particularly favoured because of the relatively low bond energy of the H–I bond. Ethene reacts with hydrogen chloride to give chloroethene. Likewise, both *cis-* and *trans-*but-2-ene yield 2-bromobutane. It does not matter what the starting isomer is, because after the addition the saturated product has acquired a single bond that can freely rotate, with the loss of the *cis–trans* isomerism. In fact, as Fig 12.21 shows, two products are formed, which in this case are **optical isomers**.

The production of many petrochemicals starts with this type of electrophilic addition to give a halogenoalkane. The introduction of the carbon–halogen bond offers further possibilities for organic synthesis.

Addition of hydrogen halides to unsymmetric alkenes: Markovnikov's rule

An unsymmetric alkene, such as propene, is an alkene which has different groups attached to the carbons of the C=C bond.

Fig 12.22 **The displayed formulas of four symmetric and four unsymmetric alkenes**

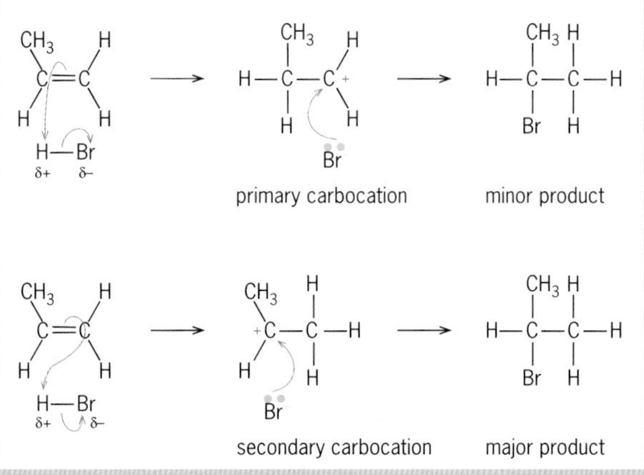

Fig 12.23 **The mechanism of the electrophilic addition of hydrogen bromide to propene**

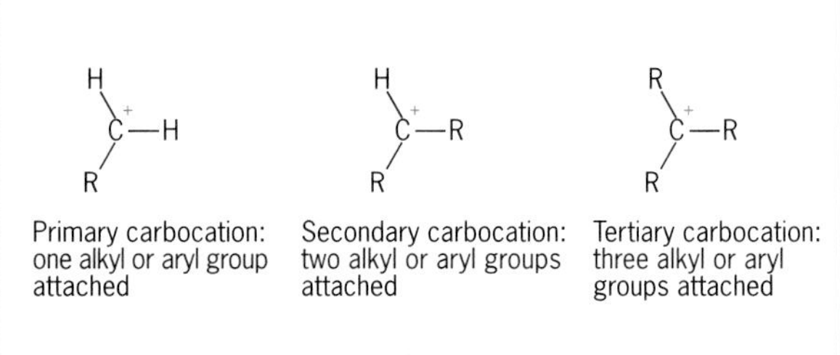

Fig 12.24 **The three types of carbocation**

Primary carbocation: one alkyl or aryl group attached

Secondary carbocation: two alkyl or aryl groups attached

Tertiary carbocation: three alkyl or aryl groups attached

The electrophilic addition of a hydrogen halide to an unsymmetric alkene can give more than one addition product, because it depends on which end of the double bond is attacked by the electrophile. For example, the electrophilic addition of hydrogen bromide to propene can yield two products, 1-bromopropane and 2-bromopropane, depending on which end of the double bond is attacked by the electrophile (the proton). As Fig 12.23 shows, the two products arise from different carbocations, which have different stabilities.

A **primary carbocation** (Fig 12.24) is a species in which a positive carbon atom is attached to just one other carbon atom (of the alkyl or aryl R group). It is much less stable than a **secondary carbocation**, which is much less stable than a **tertiary carbocation**. The source of this stability is the alkyl or aryl group, which tends to donate electron density to the positive carbon atom and thereby stabilises the positive charge. It follows that two alkyl (or aryl) groups give more stability than one, and three give more stability than two. This action of pushing the electron density is called the **inductive effect**. The major product is formed from the most stable carbocation. Therefore, in the present example it is 2-bromopropane.

Markovnikov's rule predicts the way that hydrogen halides are added to unsymmetric alkenes:

> **An electrophile adds to an unsymmetric C=C bond so that the most stable carbocation is formed as an intermediate.**

The term 'electrophile' is used to express the general concept, although the electrophile is often an electron deficient hydrogen atom.

Hydration of alkenes

The hydration of an alkene is the electrophilic addition of water to give an alcohol. This reaction needs an acidic catalyst, since water itself is not a good electrophile. In the laboratory, sulphuric acid is used as the catalyst. With reactive double bonds, dilute acid is sufficient, but with alkenes such as propene and ethene, concentrated acid is required.

Fig 12.26 details the use of concentrated sulphuric acid as a catalyst. The proton transferred by the acid is needed to start the reaction by facilitating the breaking of the double bond. At the end of the reaction, the acid is regenerated.

In the petrochemical industry, alkenes are hydrated to give several important solvents. Hydration is achieved either by the catalytic addition of water as steam to the alkene at 70 atmospheres pressure at 300 °C using H_3PO_4 as a catalyst, or by using the concentrated sulphuric acid route just described. Ethene is converted to ethanol, propene to propan-2-ol, and but-2-ene to butan-2-ol (Fig 12.27). All three alcohols are extremely useful industrial solvents.

M Which of the carbocations in Fig 12.25 is the most stable?

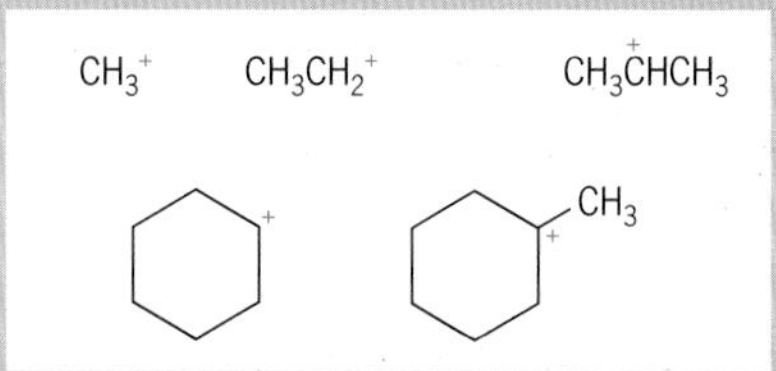

$$CH_3^+ \qquad CH_3CH_2^+ \qquad CH_3\overset{+}{C}HCH_3$$

Fig 12.25 **Five different carbocations**

N Predict the major product in the reaction of hydrogen bromide with

(a) *cis*-but-2-ene,

(b) cyclohexene,

(c) pent-1-ene.

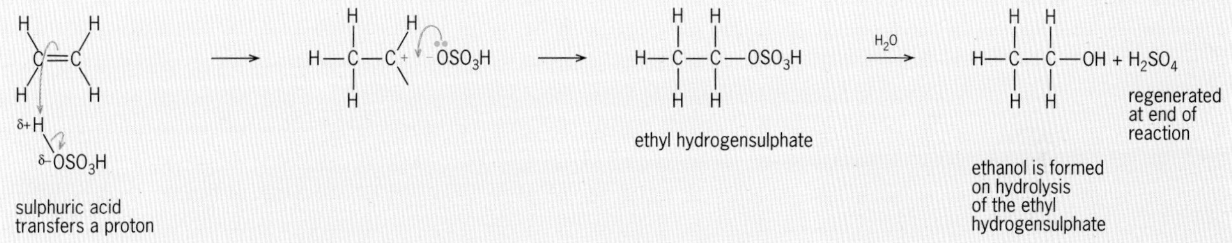

Fig 12.26 **The mechanism of the electrophilic addition of water, as shown by the hydration of ethene using concentrated sulphuric acid and subsequent hydrolysis of the intermediate**

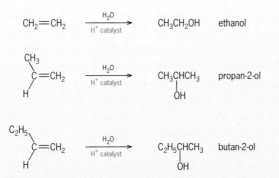

Fig 12.27 **The hydration of ethene, propene and butene. Because of Markovnikov's rule, the hydration of propene and but-1-ene does not produce a large proportion of the primary alcohols propan-1-ol and butan-1-ol. Instead, the secondary alcohols propan-2-ol and butan-2-ol are formed**

Fig 12.28 **In a paint factory, large quantities of solvents are used to mix with the pigments**

Because the addition at double bonds follows Markovnikov's rule, the number of alcohols that can be made is limited. In particular, it is difficult to make primary alcohols.

O Why is it difficult to make primary alcohols by the hydration of an alkene? Hint: consider the acid-catalysed addition of water to propene.

?

P Draw the displayed formula of the product of the reaction between

(a) bromine and ethene,

(b) chlorine and cyclohexene,

(c) chlorine and ethene.

See questions 3, 4, 6 and 7. ■

intermediate positive ion

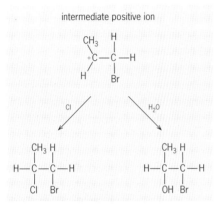

Fig 12.30 **The intermediate positive ion can react with other nucleophiles, such as a chloride ion or water, if they are present**

See questions 6 and 8. ■

?

Q Chlorine will react with ethene to give 1,2-dichloroethane. The mechanism is identical to the bromination of ethene. Write down the mechanism for this reaction.

See questions 2 and 9. ■

?

R Explain the formation of two products during the reaction between aqueous bromine and but-2-ene. Hint: Read about the interception of a carbocation by other nucleophiles.

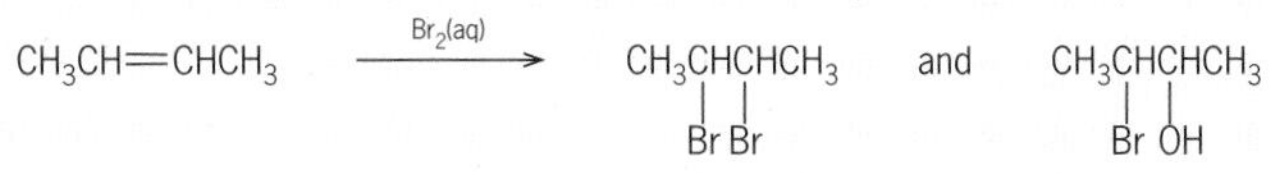

Reaction with halogens

Halogens can add to double bonds to give dihalogenoalkanes. For example, bromine reacts with propene to give 1,2-dibromopropane:

$$CH_3CH=CH_2 + Br_2 \rightarrow CH_3CHBrCH_2Br$$

Mechanism of the reaction

Compared with a hydrogen halide, it is much more difficult to visualise a bromine *molecule* as an electrophile, since it is not a polar molecule and both of its atoms have a stable octet of electrons. Nevertheless, a bromine molecule is capable of accepting an electron pair, provided that, at the same time, the bromine–bromine single bond is broken by *heterolytic* fission.

intermediate positive ion

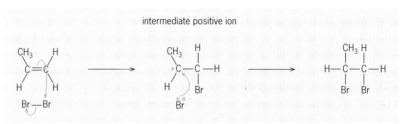

Fig 12.29 **The mechanism of the electrophilic addition of bromine to propene**

As the bromine molecule approaches the double bond, the pair of electrons in the Br–Br bond moves to one of the bromine atoms (Fig 12.29). Why should this happen? After all, there is no positive or negative end to the bromine molecule, as there is in the addition of hydrogen bromide. The reason is that a temporary dipole is created in the bromine molecule as it approaches the π electrons of the double bond. It is as though the electrons in the bromine–bromine single bond are repelled by the π electrons. This temporary dipole produces an electron deficiency at the end of the molecule nearer the double bond, thereby allowing the electrophilic attack.

The intermediate carbocation then reacts with a bromide ion to complete the electrophilic addition. However, it is possible to intercept the carbocation with other nucleophilic reagents (Fig 12.30). So, if a chloride ion is also present in the reaction mixture, it can react as a nucleophile; and if the reaction is carried out in the presence of water, a water molecule can react with the carbocation. This means that the choice of solvent used for the bromination is important. If it were aqueous bromine, for example, it would be impossible to stop the interception of the carbocation by a water molecule acting as a nucleophile.

Test for unsaturation

Aqueous bromine may be used to test for the presence of a double bond, since the reagent changes colour during electrophilic addition. Aqueous bromine is orange, but after reaction with an alkene it forms colourless products. Alternatively, bromine in an inert solvent, such as tetrachloromethane or hexane, can be used.

$$CH_3CH=CHCH_3 \xrightarrow{Br_2(aq)} CH_3CHCHCH_3 \text{ and } CH_3CHCHCH_3$$
$$\quad\quad\quad\quad\quad\quad\quad\quad\quad\quad\quad\quad\quad\; |\; |\quad\quad\quad\quad\quad\quad |\; |$$
$$\quad\quad\quad\quad\quad\quad\quad\quad\quad\quad\quad\quad\; Br\, Br\quad\quad\quad\quad Br\, OH$$

Fig 12.31 **Aqueous bromine reacts with but-2-ene to give two products**

Hydrogenation

Alkenes can also undergo other sorts of addition reactions, such as catalytic hydrogenation. In this case, hydrogen is added to the double bond to make a saturated compound (Fig 12.32). The reaction mechanism is not electrophilic addition but often involves heterogeneous catalysis (catalyst and reactant in different phases) using a nickel catalyst and high pressure (Fig 12.33).

Fig 12.32 **Hydrogenation converts an alkene to an alkane**

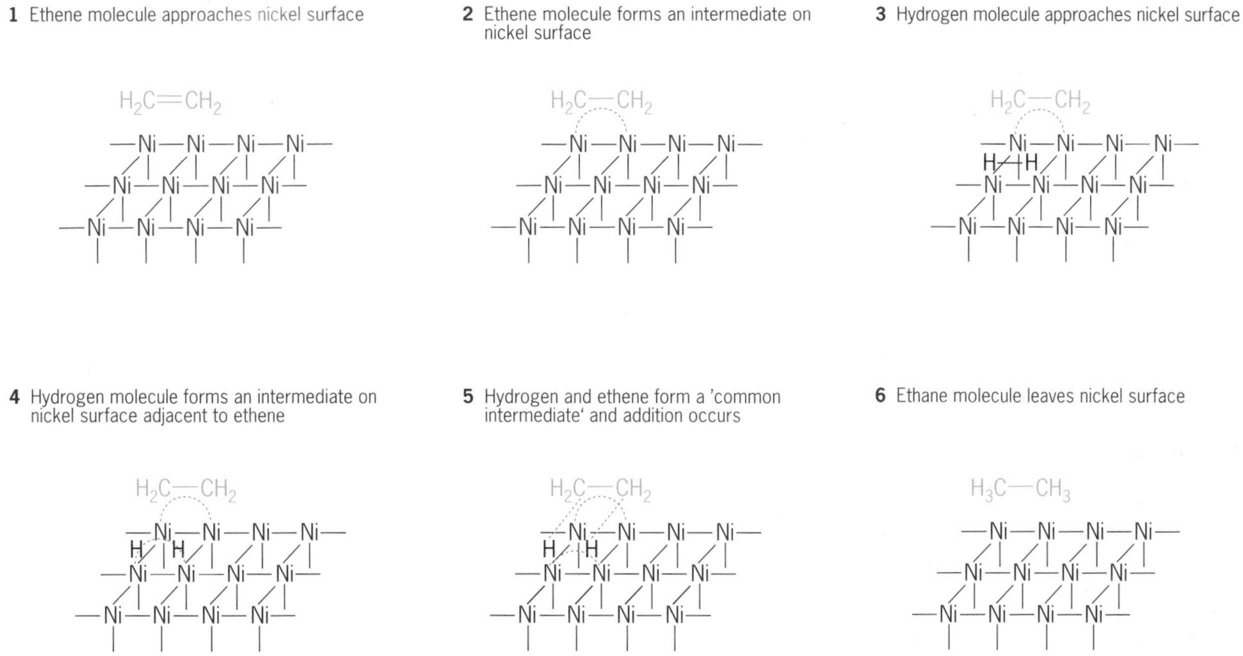

1 Ethene molecule approaches nickel surface

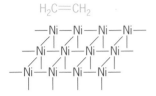

2 Ethene molecule forms an intermediate on nickel surface

3 Hydrogen molecule approaches nickel surface

4 Hydrogen molecule forms an intermediate on nickel surface adjacent to ethene

5 Hydrogen and ethene form a 'common intermediate' and addition occurs

6 Ethane molecule leaves nickel surface

Fig 12.33 **Heterogeneous catalysis in the hydrogenation of ethene**

Hydrogenation is not an important reaction in the petrochemical industry because it leads to the formation of saturated (unreactive) compounds, and petrochemical feedstocks are often already saturated. As a synthetic reaction, it is used when the raw material is derived from a natural source. For example, margarines are produced by the hydrogenation of polyunsaturated compounds derived from plant oils.

Fig 12.34 **The unsaturated compounds in sunflower oil have some of their double bonds hydrogenated to change the oil into a solid**

Polyunsaturated fats are the subject of the Assignment on pages 265 and 266.

 See questions 7 and 9.

Working out structures

Hydrogenation is used to determine the number of carbon–carbon double bonds in a compound. One mole of carbon–carbon double bond requires one mole of hydrogen to fully hydrogenate it. Therefore the number of double bonds in the compound can be estimated by comparing the number of moles of hydrogen that have reacted with a fixed amount of compound.

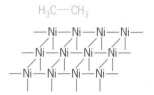

?

S A sample of a natural product, 0.0100 moles, with molecular formula $C_{22}H_{26}$ needs 0.0502 mole of hydrogen for complete hydrogenation. How many C=C bonds are present in one molecule of the natural product?

Oxidative addition

Alkenes react with cold acidified dilute potassium manganate(VII) to give a **diol** product (with two OH groups). The reaction involves both oxidation and addition to the double bond, so it is sometimes called an **oxidative addition**. During the reaction, the colour of the manganate(VII) ion changes from purple to colourless. When ethene is bubbled into cold acidified dilute potassium manganate(VII), ethane-1,2-diol (a component of antifreeze) is produced:

$$CH_2{=}CH_2 + H_2O + [O] \rightarrow CH_2OHCH_2OH$$

Fig 12.35 **The oxidative addition of alkenes to give diols. When the alkene is ethene, the product is ethane-1,2-diol**

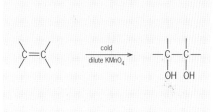

Notice that the oxidation is represented in the equation in its simplified form using [O] (see page 236).

This reaction is not used to prepare diols, since an excess of potassium manganate(VII) will oxidise the diols further.

When the alkene is treated with acidified hot concentrated potassium manganate(VII), the double bond in the alkene is broken to give two carbonyl compounds. So, for example, hex-2-ene is oxidised to give ethanoic acid and butanoic acid (Fig 12.36).

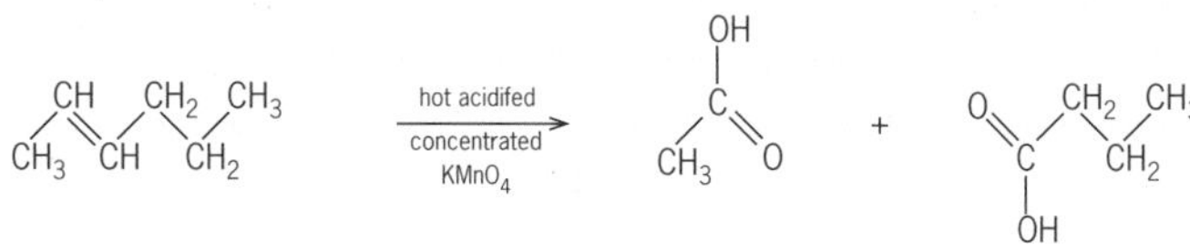

Fig 12.36 **Cleavage of the carbon–carbon double bond of hex-2-ene gives two carboxylic acids**

This cleavage of the double bond can be useful during synthesis, particularly when the alkene is a cyclohexene, since it changes the carbon skeleton without changing the number of carbon atoms (Fig 12.37). The dioic acid obtained is an important intermediate in the manufacture of nylon 6,6.

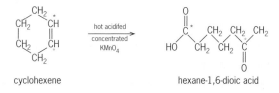

cyclohexene   hexane-1,6-dioic acid

Fig 12.37 **Cleavage of the double bond in a ring compound such as cyclohexene produces a chain compound. The cleavage is shown by the changed positions of the asterisked carbon atoms**

Ozonolysis

Ozone can cleave a double bond to give two carbonyl compounds (Fig 12.38).

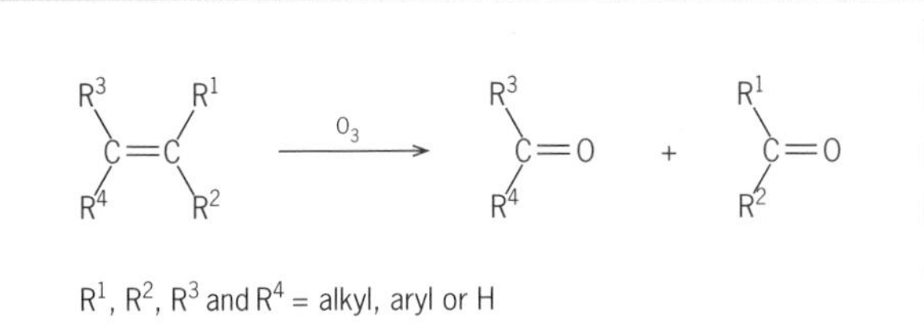

R^1, R^2, R^3 and R^4 = alkyl, aryl or H

Fig 12.38 **Ozone cleaves carbon–carbon double bonds to give aldehydes and ketones**

The reaction proceeds through two cyclic intermediates containing oxygen (Fig 12.39). At least to start with, the first intermediate can be thought of as an addition product.

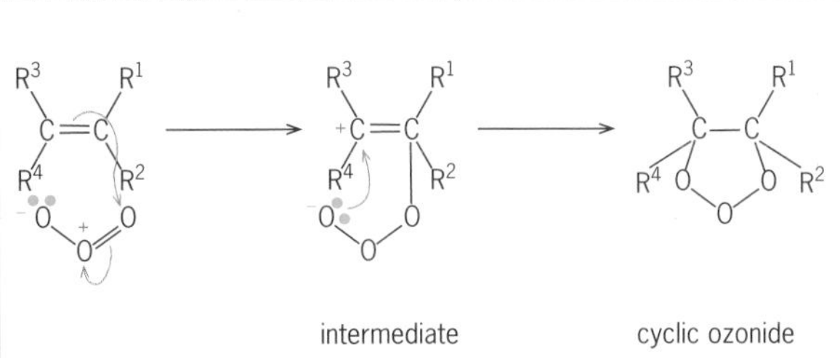

intermediate   cyclic ozonide

Fig 12.39 **The mechanism of ozonolysis involves the addition of ozone to form a cyclic intermediate. Further complex changes take place to cleave the carbon–carbon single bond to form carbonyl compounds**

Ozonolysis is particularly useful in working out the structure of unsaturated compounds with C=C bonds. By analysing the carbonyl compounds formed in ozonolysis, the position of the double bond in the original molecule can be found.

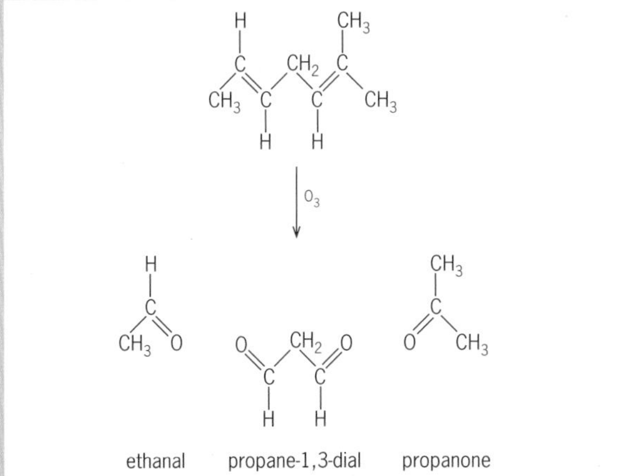

ethanal   propane-1,3-dial   propanone

Fig 12.40 **Ozonolysis shows clearly the positions of the double bonds in C_8H_{14}**

The compound C_8H_{14} contains two double bonds. On ozonolysis, it makes three compounds: ethanal, propanone and propane-1,3-dial. Fig 12.40 shows that there is only one way in which each of these carbonyl compounds can be formed, so it is possible to suggest both the structure of the carbon chain and the position of the double bonds.

One of the defence chemicals secreted by the termite is a polyunsaturated alkene (Fig 12.41).

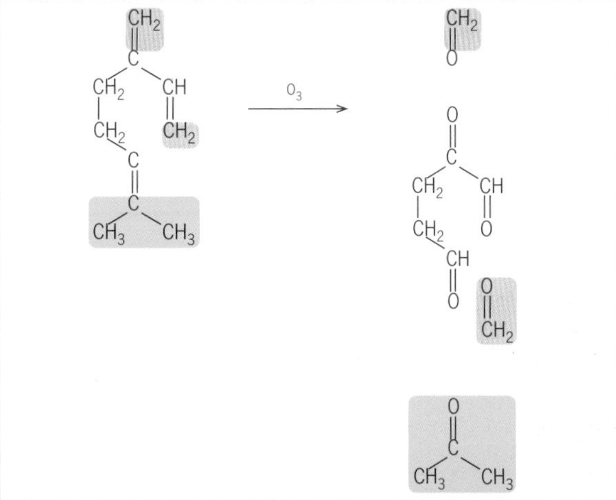

Fig 12.41 **The structure of the chemical defence secretion from the termite _Nasutitermes_ can be established by ozonolysis**

Ozonolysis of this secretion gives methanal, propanone and pentan-2-one-1,5-dial in the mole ratio 2:1:1, respectively. This demonstrates clearly that cleaving the carbon chain at particular carbon atoms is a powerful way of finding out its length and whether the chain is branched or not.

Fig 12.42 **One of the chemical defence secretions from _Nasutitermes_ is a polyunsaturated alkene – a polyene**

The analysis and identification of carbonyl compounds, such as aldehydes and ketones, are described on page 298.

Addition polymerisation

Alkene molecules can be joined to give very long chain molecules known as **polymers**. The constituent alkene molecules of polymers are called **monomers**. In polymerisation, thousands of monomers are combined to form a single polymer chain. An alkene forms an addition polymer when a double bond is converted to a single bond and two extra single bonds are created. The resulting polymer consists of repeating units called **monomer units**.

For example, ethene is converted to poly(ethene) or polythene by the action of a catalyst, high pressure and a moderate temperature (Fig 12.43). Table 12.2 lists five addition polymers and their uses.

There is more information on addition polymers and polymerisation in Chapter 18.

Fig 12.43 **Poly(ethene) is formed by the repeated catalysed addition of ethene monomers to give a saturated polymer**

Table 12.2 **Five common addition polymers and their uses**

Alkene monomer		Polymer	Structure of polymer (monomer unit)	Uses
ethene	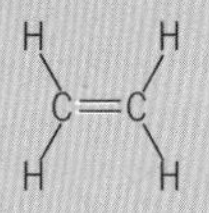	poly(ethene)	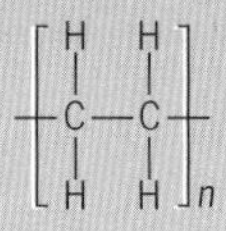	bags, insulation for wires, squeezy bottles
propene	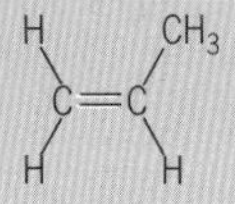	poly(propene)	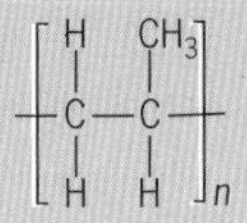	bottles, plastic plates, clothing, carpets, crates, ropes and twine
phenylethene	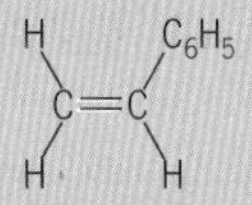	poly(phenylethene)	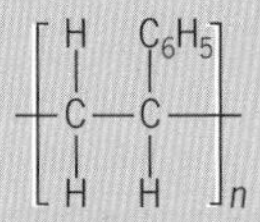	insulation, food containers, model kits, flowerpots, housewares
chloroethene	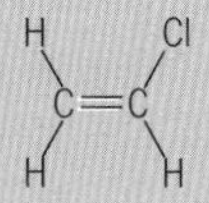	poly(chloroethene)	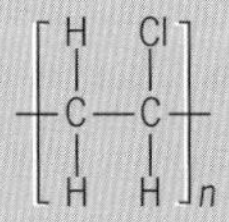	synthetic leather, water pipes, floor covering, guttering, window frames, curtain rails, wall cladding
methyl-2-methylpropenoate	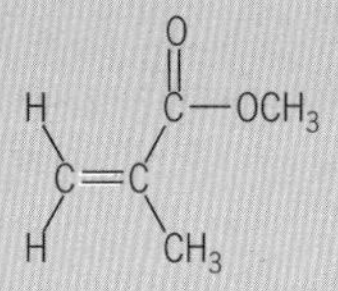	poly(methyl-2-methylpropenoate)	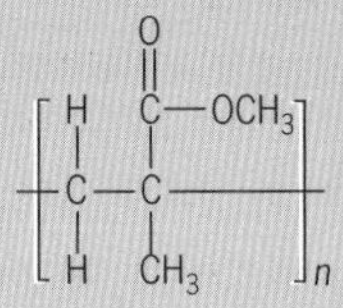	light fittings, car rear lights, record player lids, tap tops, simple lenses

See question 4. ■

Fig 12.44 **Poly(methyl-2-methylpropenoate) is a transparent polymer used for car lights and record player lids**

MANUFACTURE OF POLY(CHLOROETHENE) FROM ETHENE

POLY(CHLOROETHENE) is an important polymer, as seen from those uses listed in Table 12.2. It is manufactured from chlorine and ethene in a series of simple chemical reactions. First, ethene is reacted with chlorine to form 1,2-dichloroethane in a typical electrophilic addition:

$$Cl_2 + CH_2=CH_2 \rightarrow CH_2ClCH_2Cl$$

Next, the 1,2-dichloroethane from this reaction is heated very strongly to eliminate hydrogen chloride to form the monomer chloroethene. This involves a typical reaction of halogenoalkanes:

$$CH_2ClCH_2Cl \rightarrow CH_2=CHCl + HCl$$

Hydrogen chloride is a hazardous chemical which must not be allowed to reach the atmosphere. But it is also a source of valuable chlorine. Therefore, the hydrogen chloride generated in the second reaction is recycled to make more 1,2-dichloroethane:

$$CH_2=CH_2 + \tfrac{1}{2}O_2 + 2HCl \xrightarrow{\underset{catalyst}{Cu^{2+}}} CH_2ClCH_2Cl + H_2O$$

Chloroethene from the second reaction is a known carcinogen, and so it too is not allowed to escape from the reaction vessel into the atmosphere. Instead, this monomer is kept in a liquid state by increasing the pressure, and is polymerised in the presence of a free-radical initiator to form poly(chloroethene):

$$nCH_2=CHCl \rightarrow \text{+}CH_2\text{–}CHCl\text{+}_n$$

The polymerisation is highly exothermic and has a free-radical chain mechanism. The rate of reaction is carefully controlled to avoid explosions by adding 'scavenger' chemicals to remove any free radicals.

Fig 12.45 **Houses with uPVC wall fittings, window frames and doors**

5 ALKENES AS PETROCHEMICAL STARTING MATERIALS

With their double bonds, alkenes can take part in many useful synthetic reactions. Almost all involve electrophilic additions and the introduction of functional groups to the carbon chain. It is these functional groups that allow further synthetic reactions and provide a route to a large number of organic substances.

?

V (a) Identify the reactions on Fig 12.47 that are examples of electrophilic addition.
(b) Identify the reactions on Fig 12.46 that are examples of polymerisation.

Ethene, propene and butene

Fig 12.46 features seven substances that can be synthesised directly from ethene. Most of the reactions involve electrophilic addition to the double bond and demonstrate why alkenes are of much more use than alkanes in the manufacture of petrochemicals. Alkanes have such a limited range of reactions that ethane could only easily be converted to one of the substances in Fig 12.46, chloroethane.

Fig 12.46 **Addition and polymerisation reactions of ethene lead to a variety of useful petrochemicals**

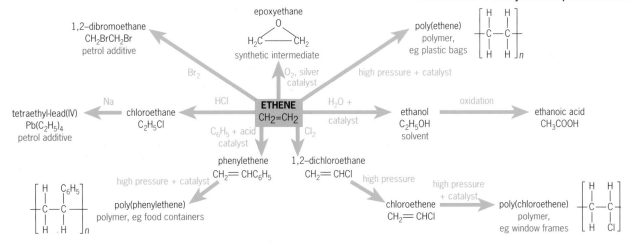

Some uses of propene and butene

Fig 12.47 **Propene is converted to many useful petrochemicals and synthetic intermediates**

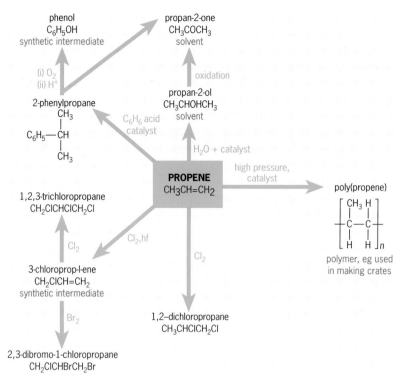

phenol
C_6H_5OH
synthetic intermediate

propan-2-one
CH_3COCH_3
solvent

(i) O_2
(ii) H^+

oxidation

2-phenylpropane
CH_3
C_6H_5—CH
CH_3

propan-2-ol
$CH_3CHOHCH_3$
solvent

C_6H_6 acid
catalyst

H_2O + catalyst

high pressure,
catalyst

PROPENE
$CH_3CH=CH_2$

1,2,3-trichloropropane
$CH_2ClCHClCH_2Cl$

Cl_2

Cl_2,hf

Cl_2

poly(propene)

$\left[\begin{array}{cc} CH_3 & H \\ | & | \\ C & C \\ | & | \\ H & H \end{array}\right]_n$

polymer, eg used
in making crates

3-chloroprop-l-ene
$CH_2ClCH=CH_2$
synthetic intermediate

1,2–dichloropropane
$CH_3CHClCH_2Cl$

Br_2

2,3-dibromo-1-chloropropane
$CH_2ClCHBrCH_2Br$

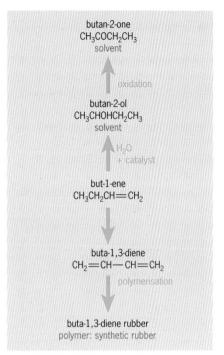

butan-2-one
$CH_3COCH_2CH_3$
solvent

oxidation

butan-2-ol
$CH_3CHOHCH_2CH_3$
solvent

H_2O
+ catalyst

but-1-ene
$CH_3CH_2CH=CH_2$

buta-1,3-diene
$CH_2=CH—CH=CH_2$

polymerisation

buta-1,3-diene rubber
polymer: synthetic rubber

Fig 12.48 **But-1-ene is converted to solvents and synthetic rubber**

Fig 12.49 **Poly(propene) is used to make marine rope**

SUMMARY

After studying this chapter, you should know the following.

■ Alkenes are more reactive than alkanes because of the presence of an electron-rich π bond.

■ Alkenes are manufactured from long chain alkanes by thermal or catalytic cracking.

■ Alkenes are a major source of petrochemicals, such as polymers and plastics, solvents, detergents and pharmaceuticals.

■ Alkenes burn in excess air to give carbon dioxide and water. Gaseous alkenes are sometimes used as fuels.

■ Alkenes react by electrophilic addition with halogens to give dihalogenoalkanes, hydrogen to give alkanes, hydrogen halides to give halogenoalkanes and water (catalysed by acid) to give alcohols.

■ The addition of an electrophile to an unsymmetric alkene forms the most stable carbocation.

■ Alkenes can be oxidised by cold dilute potassium manganate(VII) to give diols.

■ Alkenes can be oxidised by hot acidified concentrated potassium manganate(VII) to give carbonyl compounds, the reaction cleaving the carbon–carbon double bond.

■ Alkenes are monomers which form addition polymers.

■ The double bond involves the overlap of two different types of atomic orbital to form a σ bond and a π bond.

■ Unsymmetric alkenes show geometric (cis–trans) isomerism because of the absence of free rotation about the carbon–carbon double bond.

QUESTIONS

1 The diagrams in Fig 12.Q1 show the structure of four isomers of molecular formula C_4H_8.

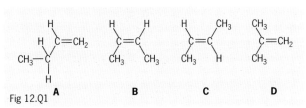

Fig 12.Q1   **A**   **B**   **C**   **D**

a)   **(i)** To which class of compounds do the four isomers belong?

    (ii) Which two diagrams show compounds which are *cis–trans* isomers?

    (iii) Compound **A** reacts with steam to form a pair of optical isomers. Draw the structure of one of these isomers. Draw a circle around the chiral carbon atom.

b)   **(i)** Which of the above compounds could be formed from 2-methylpropanol by the elimination of water?

    (ii) State the reagents and conditions by which this reaction could be carried out in the laboratory.

[UCLES Autumn 1993 Modular Chemistry Section A, q.1]

2

a) Give a reagent which could be used to test for the presence of unsaturation in an organic molecule. What would be the observable result of this test?

b)   **(i)** Write down the structural formulae of the two isomers of but-2-ene (C_4H_8).

    (ii) What type of isomerism is shown by these structures? Indicate briefly the reason it occurs.

    (iii) Give the structural formulae of two further structural isomers having the molecular formula C_4H_8. Name each isomer.

c)   **(i)** Describe how 2-chlorobutane could be converted to one of the isomers in **b)**. Give reagents, conditions and equation.

    (ii) What type of reaction is this?

    (iii) Which one of the isomers in **b)** could not be formed by this reaction? Briefly explain your answer.

[ULEAC 1996 Chemistry Specimen Paper CH2, q.4]

3 Citronellol is an organic compound used in the manufacture of some perfumes. Fig 12.Q3(a) shows its molecular structure.

Fig 12.Q3(a)

a) Copy the diagram of the structure of citronellol and draw a circle around any chiral carbon atom.

b) Name **two** functional groups present in the molecule.

c)   **(i)** State what you would expect to see happen if the molecule was reacted with bromine dissolved in an organic solvent.

    (ii) Draw the structure of a possible product.

d) Citronellol shows no *cis–trans* isomerism, but the related compound geraniol, shown in Fig 12.Q3(b), exists as a pair of *cis–trans* isomers.

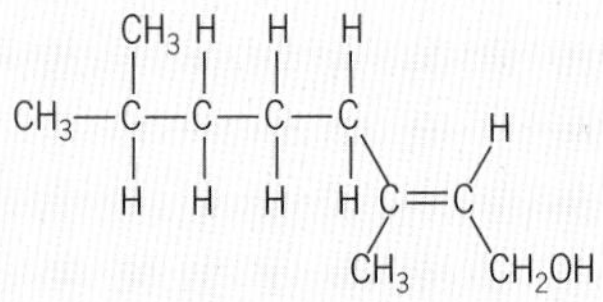

Fig 12.Q3(b)

> **(i)** Draw another geometric (*cis–trans*) isomer of geraniol.
> **(ii)** Explain why citronellol has no geometric (*cis–trans*) isomers.

e) From the structure given, explain why geraniol does not possess optical isomers.

[UCLES Spring 1995 Modular: Chains and Rings, q.3]

4 But-2-ene, $CH_3CH=CHCH_3$, is one of the isomers of compounds of molecular formula C_4H_8.

a) Explain the term *isomer*.

b) Draw the displayed (full structural) formulae of two other isomers of C_4H_8.

c) But-2-ene was reacted according to the reaction scheme shown in Fig 12.Q4.

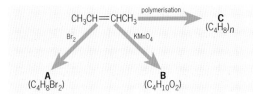

Fig 12.Q4

> **(i)** Draw displayed formulae for compounds **A** and **B**.
> **(ii)** Draw a section of polymer **C** containing 2 repeating units.

[UCLES Spring 1995 Modular: Chains and Rings, q.3]

5 The following table gives data about the homologous series of alkenes.

Alkene	Molecular formula	M_r	Boiling point/°C	Melting point/°C	Density/ g cm^{-3}
ethene	C_2H_4	28	–105	–169	
propene	C_3H_6	42	–48	–185	
but-1-ene	C_4H_8	56	–6	–185	
pent-1-ene	C_5H_{10}	70	30	–165	0.641
hex-1-ene	C_6H_{12}	84	64	–140	0.674

a) Hept-1-ene is the next member of this homologous series. Predict a value for each of the following for hept-1-ene: **(i)** molecular formula, **(ii)** M_r, **(iii)** boiling point, **(iv)** melting point, **(v)** density.

b) Explain the increasing boiling points with increasing relative molecular mass.

c) Which members of this series are gases at room temperature and atmospheric pressure?

6 Explain each of the following observations.

a) When hot acidified concentrated potassium manganate(VII) reacts with either *cis-* or *trans*-but-2-ene, only one product is formed. But when it reacts with *cis-* or *trans*-pent-2-ene, two products are formed.

b) Bromine in hexane reacts with ethene to give one product, but aqueous bromine reacts to give two products.

c) Chlorine in the dark reacts with but-1-ene to give one product, but in the presence of sunlight it gives several products.

7 Predict the major organic products for the reaction of 2,3-dimethylbut-2-ene with the following reagents. (Look at Fig 12.4 if you need to remind yourself of the displayed formula for 2,3-dimethylbut-2-ene.)

a) cold acidified potassium manganate(VII),

b) aqueous bromine,

c) chlorine in the dark,

d) hydrogen in the presence of a nickel catalyst,

e) hydrogen bromide.

8 Ethene is bubbled through aqueous bromine.

a) Two products containing bromine are formed.

> **(i)** Draw displayed formulae for the two products.
> **(ii)** Describe the mechanism for the formation of one of these two products.

b) If the aqueous bromine contains aqueous sodium chloride, a third product is formed, 2-bromo-1-chloroethane. Explain how this product is formed.

9 Fig 12.Q9 shows a polyunsaturated alkene, **Y**, found in the secretion of a termite.

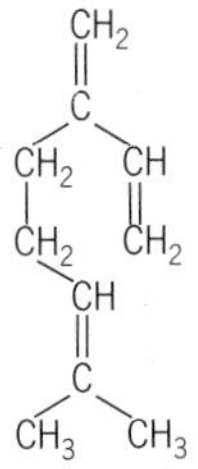

Fig 12.Q9

a) Write down the molecular formula for **Y**.

b) Does **Y** possess geometric (*cis–trans*) isomers? Explain your answer.

c) 0.012 mole of **Y** was hydrogenated. How many moles of hydrogen were needed to completely hydrogenate **Y**?

d) **Y** is shaken with aqueous bromine water. Describe and explain the observations you would make.

Assignment

UNSATURATED AND SATURATED FATTY ACIDS

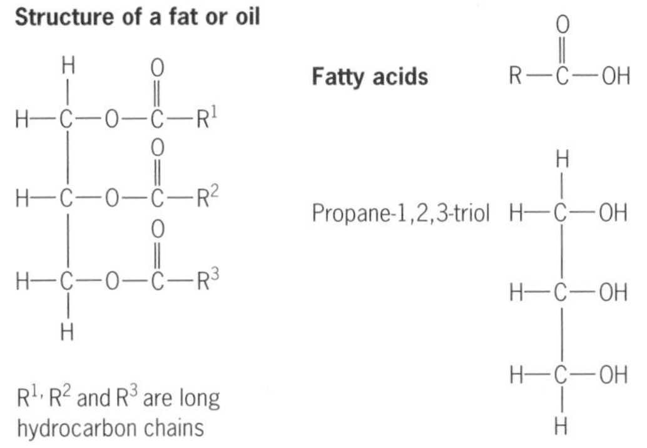

Between a quarter and a half of the normal energy content of a person's diet comes from fats and oils. (This figure is beginning to decline as people become more aware of the dangers of eating too much fatty food.)

Fats and oils are members of a group of organic compounds called esters. There is no structural difference between a fat and an oil. The two terms merely distinguish between the state of the substances: a fat is a solid and an oil is a liquid at room temperature.

Esters are the result of the reaction between a carboxylic acid and an alcohol called propane-1,2,3-triol. The carboxylic acids in nature are often referred to as fatty acids and normally consist of even-numbered carbon chains (Table 12.A1). The fatty acids were given trivial names after their sources, so palmitic acid was derived from palm oil, lauric acid from the laurel tree, myristic acid from *Myristica fragrans* (the biological name for nutmeg) and stearic acid from *stear* (the Greek word for tallow or fat).

Structure of a fat or oil

R^1, R^2 and R^3 are long hydrocarbon chains

Fig 12.A1 **Structures of fats and oils and of the alcohol and acids that react to make them**

Table 12.A1 **Eight fatty acids**

Number of C atoms	Systematic name	Trivial name	Structural formula
12	dodecanoic acid	lauric	$CH_3(CH_2)_{10}COOH$
14	tetradecanoic acid	myristic	$CH_3(CH_2)_{12}COOH$
16	hexadecanoic acid	palmitic	$CH_3(CH_2)_{14}COOH$
	cis-hexadec-9-enoic acid	palmitoleic	$CH_3(CH_2)_5CH=CHCH_2(CH_2)_6COOH$
18	octadecanoic acid	stearic	$CH_3(CH_2)_{16}COOH$
	cis-octadec-9-enoic acid	oleic	$CH_3(CH_2)_7CH=CHCH_2(CH_2)_6COOH$
	cis,cis-octadec-9,12-dienoic acid	linoleic	$CH_3(CH_2)_4(CH=CHCH_2)_2(CH_2)_6COOH$
	cis,cis,cis-octadec-9,12,15-trienoic acid	linolenic	$CH_3CH_2(CH=CHCH_2)_3(CH_2)_6COOH$

1

a) Octadecanoic acid is a solid, and *cis*-octadec-9-enoic acid is a liquid. In simple terms, how can you explain this difference, since they both have almost the same relative molecular mass? Hints see page 159.

b) What is the molecular formula for hexadecanoic acid?

c) Suggest a chemical test that could be used to distinguish between octadecanoic acid and *cis*-octadec-9-enoic acid.

d) *cis,cis,cis*-octadec-9,12,15-trienoic acid is a polyunsaturated fatty acid. Explain the meaning of the term polyunsaturated.

e) Fatty acids can be synthesised by animals and plants. What evidence is there in Table 12.A1 that the synthesis involves a derivative of ethanoic acid, CH_3COOH?

Vegetable oils tend to have a greater proportion of unsaturated fatty acids than animal fats, as in shown in Table 12.A2 Saturated fats are thought to be part of the cause of atherosclerosis, a thickening of the arteries. It is now recognised that unsaturated and, in particular, polyunsaturated fats (those containing the polyunsaturated fatty acid residues) are much better for health.

Table 12.A2 **The composition of eight fats and oils**

Fat or oil	Saturated fatty acids						Unsaturated (one C=C double bond)		Polyunsaturated	Unsaturated
	C_4, C_6, C_8, C_{10}	C_{12}	C_{14}	C_{16}	C_{18}		C_{16}	C_{18}	C_{18}	C_{20}, C_{22}, C_{24}
tallow (cow)			2–3	24–32	14–32		1–3	35–48	2–4	
lard (pork)			1–2	28–30	12–18		1–3	41–48	6–7	2
butter	7–10	2–3	7–9	23–26	10–13		5	30–40	4–5	2
whale			4–5	11–18	2–4		13–18	33–38		17–31
olive			0–1	5–15	1–4		0–1	69–84	4–12	
coconut	10–22	45–51	17–20	4–10	1–5			2–10	0–2	
soya bean			0–1	6–10	2–6			21–29	54–67	
linseed				4–7	2–5			9–38	28–91	

2

a) Why is whale oil a healthier source of fat than tallow or lard?

b) Suggest why whale oil is no longer considered to be an acceptable alternative to tallow or lard in a human diet.

c) What is unusual about the composition of coconut oil?

d) Linseed oil is not used as an edible oil. One of its uses is to harden the surface of wood (such as the willow in a cricket bat). On exposure to air, the oil solidifies and hardens. Suggest a reason, in terms of its composition, why this happens to linseed oil, whereas olive oil remains a liquid.

The consumption of low-fat spreads and margarines has greatly increased. These products contain vegetable oils that have been solidified. The only way to solidify polyunsaturated fats is to hydrogenate some of their double bonds. To do this, the vegetable oil is mixed with a nickel catalyst in the presence of hydrogen under pressure.

3

a) Write down an equation to show the hydrogenation of cis-hexadec-9-enoic acid.

b) What is the name of the product formed?

c) Explain how hydrogenation could be used to find out the number of double bonds present in a pure sample of an unknown fatty acid of known relative molecular mass.

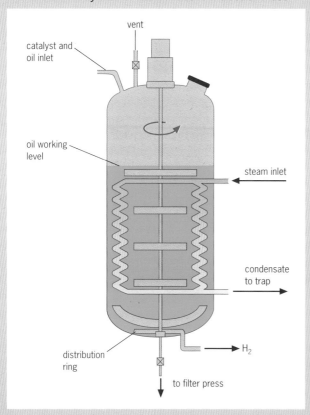

Fig 12.A2 **The apparatus used to hydrogenate unsaturated oils**

Not all the double bonds in the polyunsaturated fatty acid are hydrogenated – just those needed to produce the correct physical properties required of a margarine or low-fat spread. However, there is one problem with the hydrogenation: it can change the geometric isomerism present in the fatty acid.

Most naturally occurring fatty acids are of the cis variety, but after hydrogenation up to 25 per cent of the cis double bonds may be changed into trans double bonds. The presence of the trans double bond completely alters the three-dimensional shape of a fatty acid. Such trans fatty acids are no longer 'essential', and there is unconfirmed evidence that they may be responsible for certain heart diseases. It seems that the promotion of polyunsaturated fats as healthier food may have inadvertently introduced a further health risk from trans fatty acids.

4

a) During hydrogenation, some trans double bonds are produced. What must happen to the double bond during the hydrogenation for a cis-isomer to be changed into a trans-isomer?

b) Draw the displayed formula of cis-octadec-9-enoic acid, showing clearly the arrangements of the atoms around the carbon–carbon double bond.

c) Draw the displayed formula of trans-octadec-9-enoic acid, showing clearly the arrangements of the atoms around the carbon–carbon double bond.

d) Suggest why the trans-isomer cannot be metabolised in the same way as the cis fatty acids.

Fats such as butter turn rancid when left at room temperature for some time. During this change, a complex oxidation reaction occurs that involves the cleavage of double bonds in the fatty acids, with the formation of much shorter chain carboxylic acids. It is these carboxylic acids that have such an unpleasant odour.

5

a) Butter contains some cis,cis-octadec-9,12-dienoic acid. Suggest the identity of some of the short chain carboxylic acids that can be formed from the oxidation of this unsaturated fatty acid.

b) Suggest what can be done to prevent butter from going rancid.

ALKENES

The alkenes are a very important group of compounds used in many industrial reactions to make a wide range of useful compounds and materials. This chapter covers these uses, the reactions of alkenes and the mechanisms of reaction. Use the Chapter Map to check that you have understood the concepts and reactions, and to identify those that you may need to study further.

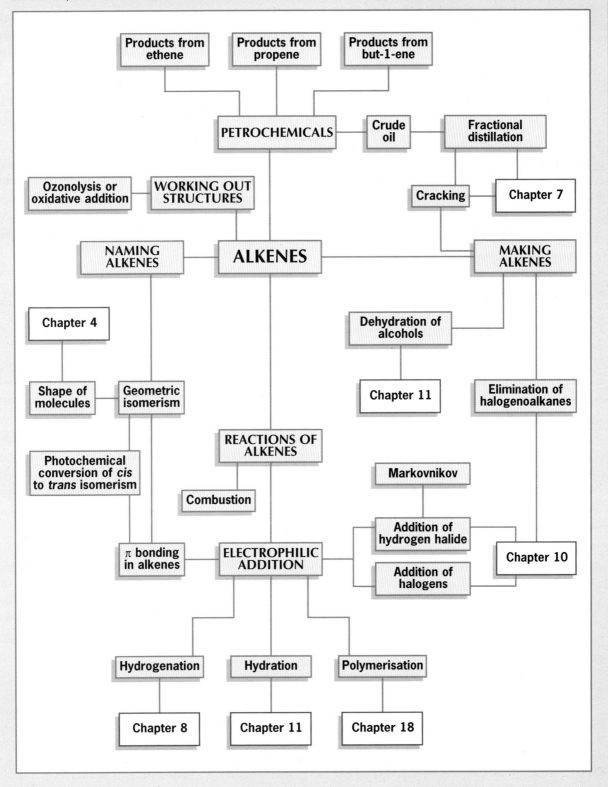

13 Aromatic compounds and arenes

The use of envirocats will greatly reduce the pollution of waterways by effluents

BENZENE IS ONE of the most industrially important organic molecules. It features in the manufacture of petrochemicals which are solvents, detergents, insecticides, dyes and polymers. The benzene molecule is normally unreactive, so to make these compounds requires special conditions such as high pressures and high temperatures. Almost all the reactions of benzene require catalysts, many of them hazardous environmental pollutants which can pollute water supplies and poison the organisms in them.

So there is an urgent need to develop environmentally friendly catalysts – *envirocats* – that can easily be separated by filtration from mixtures after they have reacted. Envirocats are based upon clay materials which are made acidic by adding metal salts. Since they can be filtered from any aqueous effluent, envirocats do not get to harm water supplies and aquatic life. In addition, since envirocats are solid, their controlled disposal is easy. They have the economic benefit of conventional catalysts, too – envirocats can be used again and again until they lose their catalytic activity.

1 AROMATIC COMPOUNDS AND THEIR USES

In Chapter 24, you can read about some of Faraday's other chemical discoveries.

In 1825, a young scientist at the Royal Institution of London was asked to remove the oily residue collecting in the gas cylinders of gas lamps and analyse it. He found that the residue contained a previously unknown hydrocarbon, whose molecular formula was later shown to be C_6H_6. The scientist was Michael Faraday, one of the greatest scientists of the nineteenth century, though his name is seldom linked with organic chemistry.

The molecule of every aromatic compound contains at least one benzene ring. The name 'aromatic', meaning 'with an odour or smell', was given to these compounds because the first few to be discovered and used do indeed have odours. But now we know that this was just a coincidence. Many aromatic compounds have no odour; others have a particularly nasty smell. Also, there are fragrant compounds which do not contain a benzene ring (see page 227). Many aromatic compounds contain other functional groups as well as alkyl groups.

The benzene ring is based upon a hexagonal arrangement of six carbon atoms and six delocalised π electrons, which give the ring unique stability. Fig 13.1 shows benzene itself. The hydrogen atoms in the benzene molecule can be replaced by alkyl, aryl or other functional groups, as Fig 13.2 shows. Note the way in which the benzene ring is represented in compounds: the atomic symbols are not included, so remember that the benzene ring consists of six hydrogen atoms and six carbon atoms. The significance of the circle drawn inside the hexagon is explained on pages 269 and 270.

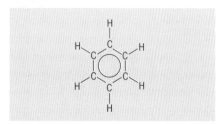

Fig 13.1 **The displayed formula of benzene**

?

A Draw the structure of each of these aromatic compounds: **(a)** C_7H_8, **(b)** C_6H_5Cl and **(c)** C_8H_{10}.

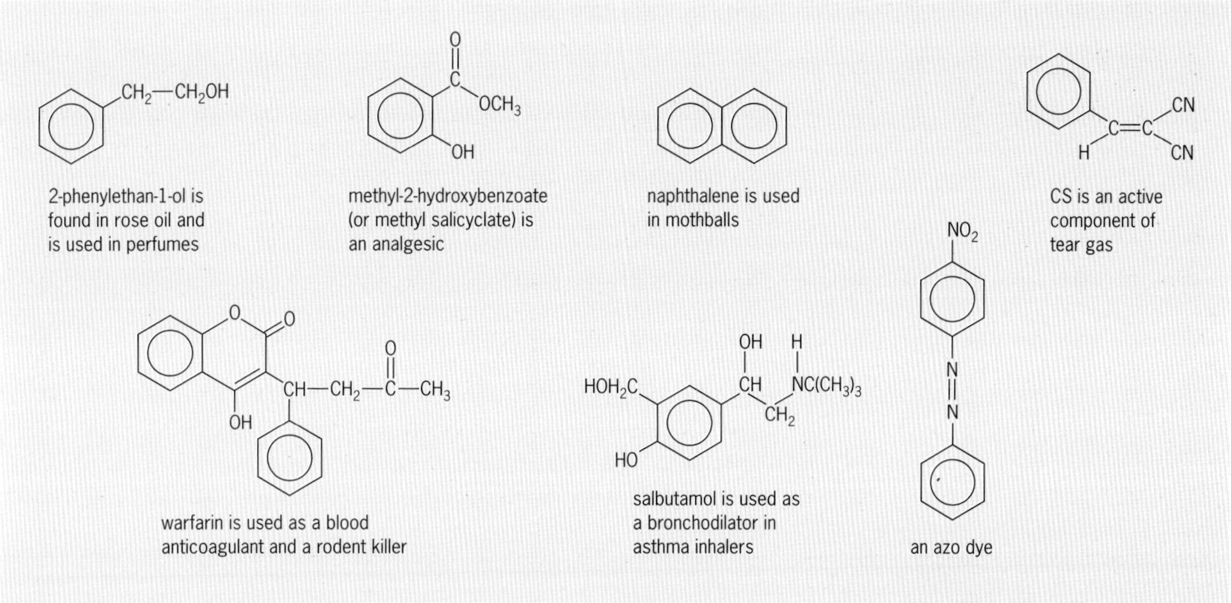

Fig 13.2 **Seven aromatic compounds and their uses. Note that each compound has at least one benzene ring**

2-phenylethan-1-ol is found in rose oil and is used in perfumes

methyl-2-hydroxybenzoate (or methyl salicyclate) is an analgesic

naphthalene is used in mothballs

CS is an active component of tear gas

warfarin is used as a blood anticoagulant and a rodent killer

salbutamol is used as a bronchodilator in asthma inhalers

an azo dye

Some uses of aromatic compounds

Fig 13.2 features seven compounds that have one thing in common: the benzene ring. They are therefore all called aromatic compounds. All but two (2-phenylethan-1-ol and naphthalene) have to be synthesised industrially. The starting point for some of these compounds is benzene, C_6H_6, so the benzene part of their carbon skeleton is in place. Chemical changes are then needed to substitute one or more of the hydrogen atoms for one or more of the alkyl or aryl groups.

Fig 13.3 **Salbutamol, an aromatic compound containing alcohol and amine functional groups, is the world's most widely used bronchodilator: a bronchodilator relaxes the airways of people with breathing problems**

2 STRUCTURE OF BENZENE

Benzene is one of the class of hydrocarbons known as **arenes**. Arenes are unsaturated hydrocarbons, characterised by great stability and non-reactivity, which distinguishes them from alkenes. All arenes contain a delocalised π system of electrons in their benzene rings.

Kekulé and the first structure of benzene

Following the discovery of benzene, chemists had the challenge of trying to determine its structure. Benzene's molecular formula, C_6H_6, didn't fit the way that chemists thought carbon atoms bonded in organic molecules.

Forty years later, August Kekulé proposed the ring structure of benzene, the first time a chemist realised that carbon atoms could form rings as well as chains. His brilliantly original idea was attributed to a dream he had about a snake biting its tail. Kekulé drew the structure of benzene as cyclohexa-1,3,5-triene (Fig 13.5).

Kekulé's structure suggests that benzene has three single bonds and three double bonds, so that it should react in the same way as cyclohexene and be able to undergo electrophilic addition. It further suggests that the single bonds are long bonds, and the double bonds are short bonds.

Arenes are strictly hydrocarbons. **Aromatic compounds** can contain other functional groups.

Fig 13.4 **A snake biting its tail featured in Kekulé's inspirational dream**

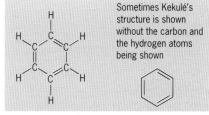

Sometimes Kekulé's structure is shown without the carbon and the hydrogen atoms being shown

Fig 13.5 **Kekulé's structure of benzene**

The abbreviation pm stands for picometre, a unit of length equal to 10^{-12} m.

Faults in Kekulé's model

Structural investigations show that the benzene molecule is a regular hexagon of carbon atoms, with the lengths of all six carbon–carbon bonds equal to 140 pm. This value lies between the average bond length for a single bond, 154 pm, and the average bond length for a double bond, 134 pm.

A further complication is that benzene does not behave like an alkene. It reacts by electrophilic *substitution* rather than by electrophilic addition (see page 253). Table 13.1 shows some of the differences between cyclohexene, an alkene with a six-carbon ring and benzene. The reactions of the two compounds are very different. This suggests that benzene cannot be an alkene and therefore cannot have Kekulé's structure of cyclohexa-1,3,5-triene.

See questions 1 and 2. ■

Such observations and measurements suggested in the early 1920s that Kekulé's model of benzene was incorrect. Since then, other models have been used to describe the structure of benzene.

Table 13.1 **Comparison of the reactions of benzene and cyclohexene**

Reagent	Cyclohexene (alkene)		Benzene (arene)	
bromine	electrophilic addition to give 1,2-dibromocyclohexane		electrophilic substitution to give bromobenzene if catalyst used	
chlorine	electrophilic addition to give 1,2-dichlorocyclohexane		electrophilic substitution to give chlorobenzene if catalyst used	
hydrogen	addition to give cyclohexane		addition to give cyclohexane	
cold aqueous acidified potassium manganate(VII)	oxidative addition to give cyclohexane-1,2-diol		no reaction	
hydrogen bromide	electrophilic addition to give bromocyclohexane		no reaction	
oxygen (combustion)	carbon dioxide and water		carbon dioxide and water	
iodomethane	no reaction		electrophilic substitution to give methylbenzene if catalyst is used	

Enthalpy change of hydrogenation

Unsaturated compounds such as alkenes react with hydrogen under pressure in the presence of a nickel catalyst to form alkanes (Fig 13.6 and 13.7). This reaction is known as hydrogenation (see page 257).

Bonds broken during hydrogenation of 1 mole of alkene:

1 mole of C=C
1 mole of H—H

Bonds made during hydrogenation of 1 mole of alkene:

1 mole of C—C
2 mole of C—H

Fig 13.6 **Bond breaking and bond making during hydrogenation. Whatever groups are attached to the double bond, the bonds made and broken during hydrogenation are the same. When a molecule has a C=C bond, 1 mole of molecules will involve the breaking of 1 mole of C=C and 1 mole of H–H to make 1 mole of C–C and 2 moles of C–H**

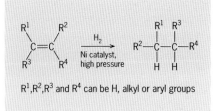

R^1, R^2, R^3 and R^4 can be H, alkyl or aryl groups

Fig 13.7 **Hydrogenation of alkenes to form saturated compounds called alkanes**

In the reaction of one mole of an alkene with hydrogen to form an alkane, the enthalpy change is called the **enthalpy change of hydrogenation**. Studies of the hydrogenation of different alkenes show that for a molecule with one C=C bond, the enthalpy change of hydrogenation is about $-120\,\text{kJ mol}^{-1}$. For a molecule with two double bonds, the enthalpy change of hydrogenation is about $-240\,\text{kJ mol}^{-1}$.

Kekulé's structure for benzene has three C=C bonds, so we might expect the enthalpy change of hydrogenation for his benzene to be about $-360\,\text{kJ mol}^{-1}$. But experimental data shows that its value is $-208\,\text{kJ mol}^{-1}$, which is considerably smaller than the theoretical value. The only conclusions that can be drawn from the experimental data is that the benzene ring does not contain C=C bonds, and it is more stable than expected.

B (a) Write down equations to show the hydrogenation of: **(i)** cyclohexene, **(ii)** cyclohexa-1,3-diene and **(iii)** cyclohexa-1,3,5-triene (Kekulé's structure).

(b) Predict the enthalpy change of hydrogenation for **(i)** cyclohexene, **(ii)** cyclohexa-1,3-diene and **(iii)** cyclohexa-1,3,5-triene.

Fig 13.8(a) **Benzene molecules as seen by a scanning tunnelling electron microscope, which shows the electron distributions in the molecules**

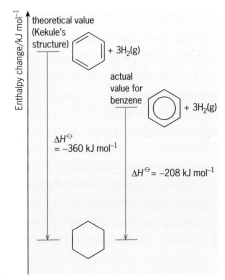

theoretical value (Kekule's structure)

$+ 3H_2(g)$

actual value for benzene

$+ 3H_2(g)$

$\Delta H^\ominus = -360\ \text{kJ mol}^{-1}$

$\Delta H^\ominus = -208\ \text{kJ mol}^{-1}$

Fig 13.8(b) **Enthalpy change of hydrogenation for benzene**

Modern theories of the benzene molecule

The value of the enthalpy change of hydrogenation of benzene is conclusive evidence that the benzene ring does not have the C=C bonds that Kekulé predicted. In addition, the enthalpy change transfers much less energy to the surroundings than his model predicts, which indicates that the bonding of the carbon atoms in the benzene ring is much stronger than Kekulé's model predicted, and so benzene is more stable.

Resonance structure

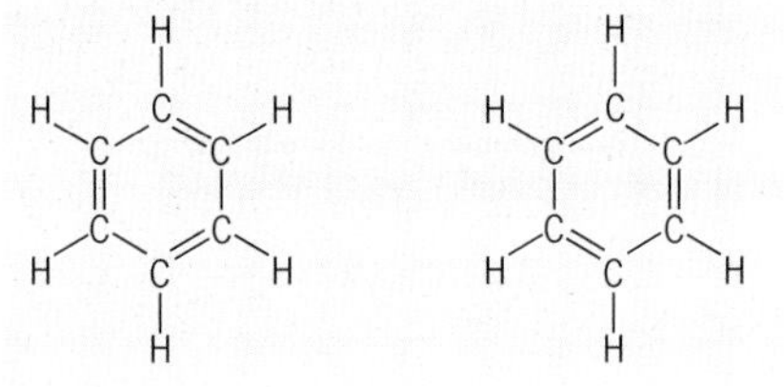

Kekulé's model of benzene is inaccurate in the ways we have seen, and does not match the known physical dimensions of the benzene molecule. Now let's look at Fig 13.9, showing the actual structure represented as a hybrid of two Kekulé structures. Despite the name 'resonance structure', this model does not imply that the hybrid structure is continually changing from one to the other, but rather that it is a cross between the two structures, possessing some of the characteristics of each. This means that each carbon–carbon bond has some single-bond and some double-bond character.

Fig 13.9 **Two Kekulé structures of benzene that contribute to the resonance hybrid model of benzene**

Orbital overlap model

Covalent bonds are formed when atomic orbitals overlap (Fig 13.10). The C–H bond is a σ bond formed by the overlap of the hydrogen 1s atomic orbital with an atomic orbital on carbon. The C–C bond is a σ bond formed by the overlap of two atomic orbitals, one from each carbon atom.

In benzene, there is a third type of bond, which is formed by the side-to-side overlap of six 2p atomic orbitals on carbon. This forms an orbital that spreads, rather like a ring doughnut, above and below the plane of the carbon atoms that possess the six electrons. These electrons are not found between any particular atoms and so are known as **delocalised** π electrons.

See question 3. ■

Orbital overlap is covered on page 81, and bonding in ethene on page 249.

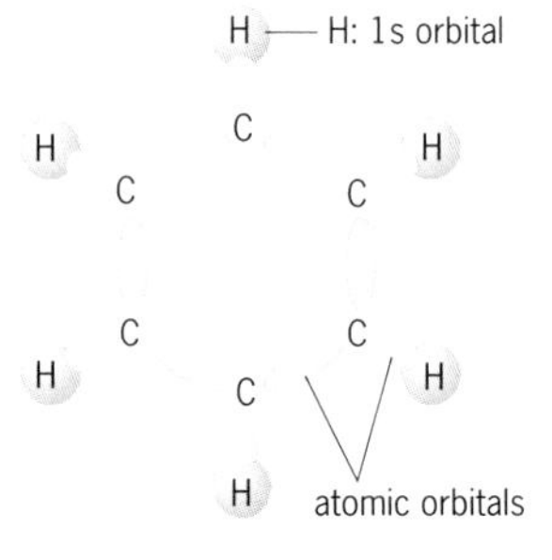

C–H σ bonds are made by the overlap of a hydrogen atomic orbital with a carbon atomic orbital
C–C σ bonds are made by the overlap of two carbon atomic orbitals

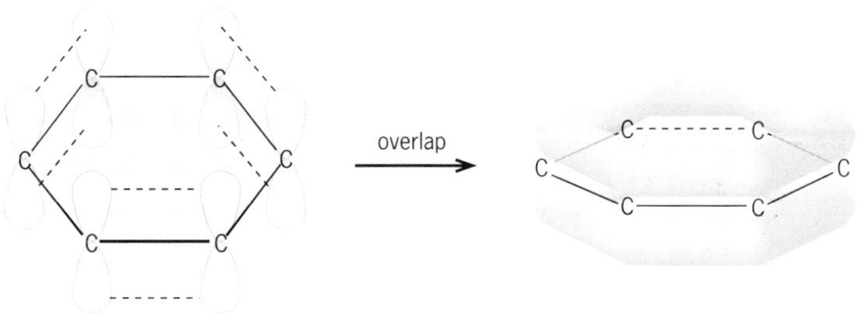

π bonds are formed by side-by-side overlap of all six 2p atomic orbitals

Fig 13.10 **Molecular orbital description of benzene**

?

C (a) Write down the balanced equation for the complete combustion of benzene in air.

(b) Would you expect the enthalpy change of combustion predicted from the bond energies of the Kekulé's model to be the same as the experimentally measured value? Explain your answer. Hint: You many need to read page 123 about the enthalpy changes during bond breaking and bond making.

Stabilisation energy

Earlier in the chapter, we saw that the enthalpy change of hydrogenation of benzene is about 150 kJ mol^{-1} less than expected from the Kekulé model. This suggests that benzene is about 150 kJ mol^{-1} more stable than cyclohexa-1,3,5-triene (Kekulé's structure). This energy difference is sometimes referred to as the **stabilisation energy** of benzene and is associated with the delocalised π electrons.

The idea of stabilisation energy means that to break the benzene ring you need *more* energy than is predicted from Kekulé's model.

Displayed formula for benzene

Fig 13.13 shows three ways of representing the displayed formula for benzene. Note that neither the hydrogen atoms nor the carbon atoms are shown. Every time you see one of these representations of the benzene ring, remember that there are six hydrogen atoms attached to the ring. The circle inside the third hexagon represents the delocalised electrons. A problem with this representation is that the ring does not specify how many electrons are delocalised.

Fig 13.12 **The displayed structure of benzene, in which the six delocalised π electrons are represented by a circle**

Fig 13.13 **Three other representations of the benzene ring. These are all skeletal formulas**

Fig 13.11 **In combustion, benzene transfers less energy to its surroundings than would be expected from the Kekulé structure. This is because of the stability due to the delocalised electrons in the benzene ring**

3 NAMING AROMATIC COMPOUNDS

Arenes is the group name we give to benzene and the hydrocarbons that are just benzene rings joined together (fused). Arenes have similar chemical properties because their benzene rings have delocalised electrons. Fig 13.14 shows three arenes and their traditional names.

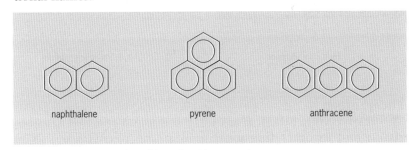

naphthalene   pyrene   anthracene

Fig 13.14 **Three arenes: they all have fused benzene rings**

We have already described aromatic compounds in general as those that contain at least one benzene ring. Aromatic compounds are not necessarily hydrocarbons but can contain a wide variety of other functional groups.

Substituted arenes

To name aromatic compounds, we use the name of the parent arene together with a prefix or suffix to indicate the groups of atoms attached to the benzene ring. So, for example, the prefix 'methyl' in the name methylbenzene indicates that the methyl group has replaced one of the hydrogen atoms in the benzene ring. When more than one hydrogen atom is replaced by methyl groups, as in dimethylbenzene, we specify the positions of the methyl groups by numbering the carbon atoms.

✔

Remember: In a displayed formula, a shared pair of electrons is shown by a straight line between atoms.

?

D What is the molecular formula for **(a)** naphthalene and **(b)** pyrene?

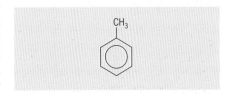

Fig 13.15 **Methylbenzene**

E Draw the structure of:

(a) ethylbenzene,

(b) 1,2-dimethylbenzene,

(c) 1,3-dimethylbenzene.

F (a) Draw the structure of
(i) 1-chloro-3-iodobenzene and
(ii) 1-chloro-4-iodobenzene.

(b) A student names a compound 4,5-dichlorobenzene. Explain why this name must be incorrect.

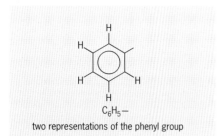

Fig 13.18 **An active ingredient of TCP is 2,4,6-trichlorophenol**

G Draw the structure of

(a) 2,4,6-trichlorophenol and

(b) 2,4,6-trimethylphenol.

1,3-dichlorobenzene has a benzene ring with two chlorine atoms in place of hydrogen atoms. The first chlorine is attached to the carbon we number as carbon 1, and the second to carbon 3. A benzene ring is numbered clockwise or anticlockwise, depending on which direction gives the lower position-numbers. Fig 13.16 shows an example of the procedure.

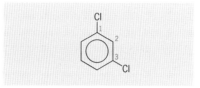

Fig 13.16 **Naming 1,3-dichlorobenzene Note:** this is 1,3-dichlorobenzene and not 1,5-dichlorobenzene, in order to keep the position-numbers as low as possible. The structure could equally well have been drawn as its mirror image, in which case the numbering would have been anticlockwise

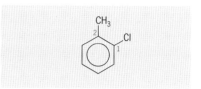

Fig 13.17 **1-chloro-2-methylbenzene**

As Fig 13.17 shows, 1-chloro-2-methylbenzene has two different groups attached to the benzene ring. Notice that we number the carbon attached to the chloro group as carbon 1, rather than the carbon attached to the alkyl group. (Halogens are named before alkyl groups.)

Some substituents (groups) on the benzene ring retain their traditional names. We refer to phenol instead of hydroxybenzene. In phenol, the carbon attached to the OH group is called carbon 1.

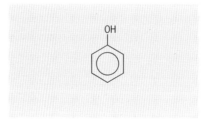

Fig 13.19 **Phenol**

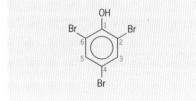

Fig 13.20 **2,4,6-tribromophenol**

Phenyl group

The phenyl group is C_6H_5 (Fig 13.21). It is found attached to carbon chains and to other functional groups. The phenyl group is an example of an **aryl group**. An aryl group is the aromatic equivalent of an alkyl group (see page 157) and always contains at least one benzene ring. In phenylamine, for example, the phenyl group is attached to the amine functional group. Phenylamine has the formula $C_6H_5NH_2$.

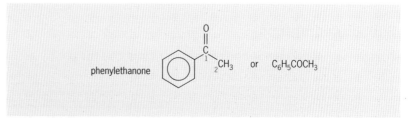

Fig 13.22 **Phenylethanone. The position number of the phenyl group is not given, because the phenyl group has to be on carbon 1 in order to be a ketone**

two representations of the phenyl group

Fig 13.21 **The phenyl group**

H (a) Write down the displayed formula for
(i) 2-phenylethan-1-ol and
(ii) phenylethene.

(b) What is the name of each of the four compounds in Fig 13.23?

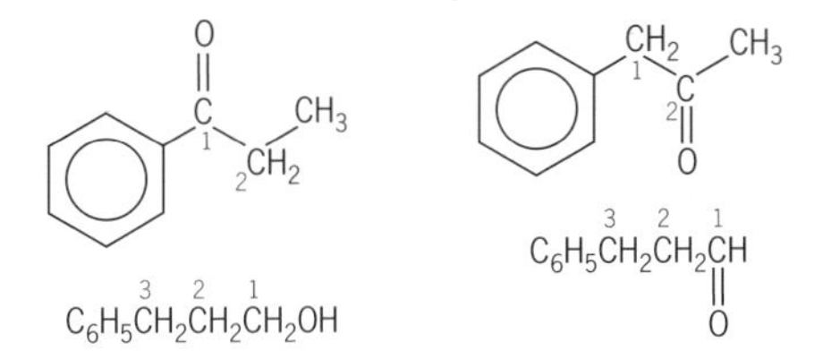

Fig 13.23

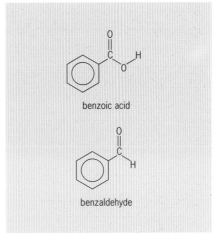

benzoic acid

benzaldehyde

Fig 13.24 **Benzoic acid and benzaldehyde**

Benzoic acid and benzaldehyde

Chemists have retained the traditional names for many aromatic compounds, including benzoic acid and benzaldehyde (Fig 13.24). Note carefully that both of these compounds contain seven carbon atoms rather than six because the functional groups contain a carbon atom.

ARENES IN EXHAUST FUMES

Fig 13.25 **Gas–liquid chromatography and spectroscopic analysis of the volatile components of the soot from diesel-engine exhaust reveal many different arenes (structurally represented here as hexagons)**

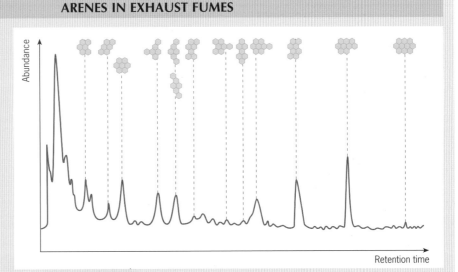

Fig 13.26 **There is much concern about the amount of arenes emitted in vehicle exhaust fumes, since many arenes are known carcinogens**

PETROL CONTAINS aromatic hydrocarbons which help to improve its octane rating. (See an account of octane rating on page 162).

In an internal combustion engine, you rarely get complete combustion of the fuel (petrol or diesel). There is always some carbon monoxide, soot and smoke produced. Analysing the soot by gas–liquid chromatography and spectroscopy shows that it contains the arenes benzene, naphthalene, phenanthrene, pyrene, coronene and ovalene (Fig 13.25). The presence of benzene is of particular concern, since it is a known carcinogen.

Fig 13.27 **There is evidence that aromatic hydrocarbons exist in space. Meteorites with carbon in them contain many different aromatic compounds, and spectra of nebulae, such as the Crab Nebula seen here, look remarkably similar to those found in the exhaust fumes of automobiles**

I Deduce the molecular formula for each of the arenes shown in Fig 13.14.

The synthesis of aromatic compounds often starts with one of the arenes. Aromatic compounds are needed for new technologies and new synthetic methods, and so the demand for arenes continues to expand, coupled with new ways found to make the arenes. Until the 1940s, the main source of commercially produced benzene was coal but, today, the principal source is crude oil.

Aromatic compounds from coal

When coal is heated to a high temperature in the absence of air, coke and a complex mixture of compounds are produced. Fig 13.28 shows the variety of aromatic compounds that can be formed. Notice that not only are arenes produced, but also substituted benzenes such as phenols.

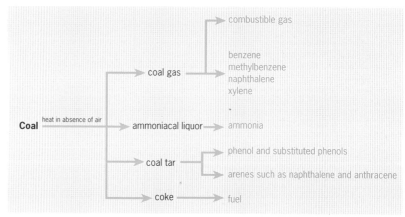

Fig 13.28 **Destructive distillation of coal to produce arenes and substituted arenes. The importance of coal in this application is declining**

Aromatic compounds from crude oil

Benzene and other aromatic compounds form only a small proportion of crude oil, and fractional distillation does not produce sufficient benzene or other aromatic compounds to match demand. So, as in the case of alkenes, cracking and reforming are processes used to increase the supply of arenes.

Catalytic reforming

In **catalytic reforming**, C_6 to C_{10} hydrocarbon vapours are heated in the presence of hydrogen at high pressure and high temperature, typically $900\,^{\circ}C$, using a transition element catalyst.

During the reforming process, the number of carbon atoms per molecule remains the same, but there is a change in the carbon skeleton and/or the number of hydrogen atoms per molecule. For example, cyclohexane can be reformed to give benzene (Fig 13.29), and heptane can be reformed to give methylbenzene (Fig 13.30). Note that in the second example, as well as hydrogen atoms being lost, the carbon skeleton is also rearranged.

Manufacture of benzene

Naphtha is a light fraction of crude oil containing liquid alkanes of low relative molecular mass (see page 149). To make benzene, its vapour is passed over a catalyst such as platinum or molybdenum(VI)

Cracking and reforming are covered on pages 148 to 151.

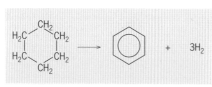

Fig 13.29 **Reforming of cyclohexane to give benzene. Note that the carbon skeleton (the six-membered ring) remains intact**

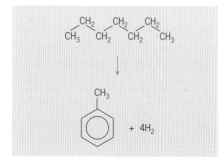

Fig 13.30 **Reforming of heptane**

oxide on aluminium oxide at 500 °C at 10–20 atmospheres of pressure. Cyclisation takes place:

$$CH_3CH_2CH_2CH_2CH_2CH_3 \rightarrow C_6H_{12} \rightarrow C_6H_6$$

hexane   cyclohexane benzene

5 ELECTROPHILIC SUBSTITUTION REACTIONS OF BENZENE

In almost all synthetic schemes which start with an aromatic hydrocarbon (such as benzene), there is the substitution of one or more of the hydrogen atoms. This substitution is normally electrophilic, and so only those groups that can behave as electrophiles are able to replace hydrogen atoms attached to the benzene ring.

Mechanism of electrophilic substitution

The presence of the delocalised electrons means that benzene is electron rich. Therefore, an electrophile which is able to accept an electron pair donated by the ring is the most likely type of reagent to react with the benzene. This is very similar to the first step in the electrophilic addition of an alkene (see page 253). The resulting positive species is much more stable than a normal carbocation, since it is possible to delocalise the positive charge around the ring (Fig 13.31).

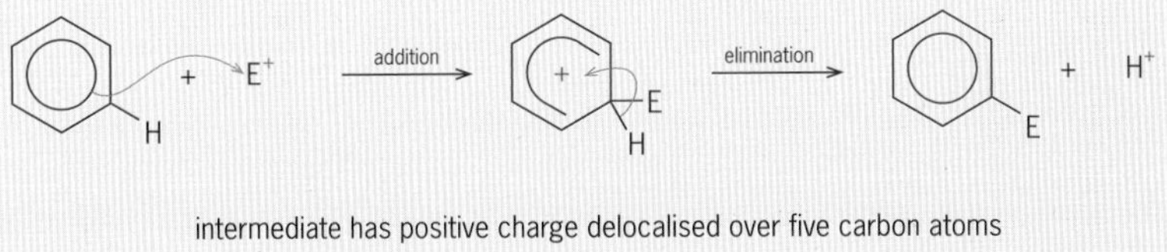

intermediate has positive charge delocalised over five carbon atoms

Fig 13.31 **The mechanism of electrophilic substitution of benzene using structures with delocalised electrons**

We saw the unique stability of the benzene ring when looking at the bonding in benzene. This stability is also apparent in the mechanism of electrophilic substitution. Here, a proton is eliminated and the benzene ring is reformed with the substituted electrophile group attached.

The electrophile must be fully positive

Electrophilic substitution clearly needs an electrophile, but what is not obvious is that the electrophile must be an exceptionally good electrophile. This is because it has to react with a molecule made extremely stable by the presence of the π system of delocalised electrons. Benzene has a delocalised π system of electrons over all six atoms of the ring. But Fig 13.31 shows that in the positive intermediate, the π system involves only five of the carbon atoms. In practice, this means that the electrophile normally needs to be a fully positive species that is formed as a result of the heterolytic fission of a covalent bond (Fig 13.33). An induced dipole in a molecule is not normally enough to achieve electrophilic attack in benzene.

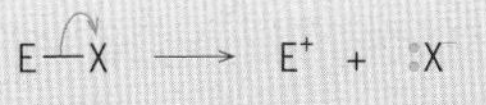

It takes a catalyst in the reaction mixture to generate the electrophile. Typical electrophiles that can be generated in this way include Br^+, Cl^+, R^+, RCO^+ and NO_2^+. (R is an aryl or alkyl group.)

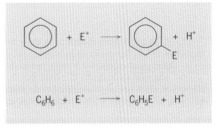

$$C_6H_6 + E^+ \longrightarrow C_6H_5E + H^+$$

Fig 13.32 **The overall reaction of electrophilic substitution**

$$E\!-\!X \longrightarrow E^+ + {:}X$$

Fig 13.33 **The electrophile is formed by the heterolytic fission of a covalent bond, so that both electrons in the bond go to atom X**

Chlorination of benzene

When chlorine is bubbled through a mixture of refluxing benzene in the presence of a catalyst (such as aluminium chloride or iron(III) chloride), electrophilic substitution takes place to produce chlorobenzene:

$$C_6H_6 + Cl_2 \xrightarrow{\text{FeCl}_3,\ \text{reflux}} CH_5Cl + HCl$$

Notice that the equation is written with molecular formulas rather than structural or displayed formulas. This is acceptable provided that when you use the molecular formulas there is only one structure possible.

We already know the mechanism of this reaction: Cl^+ is represented by E^+ in Fig 13.31. The major question is: How does aluminium chloride help to generate the electrophile?

We might expect aluminium chloride to be ionic since it is a metal compound. But in the anhydrous state it has a high degree of covalent character, so it is better when drawing a dot and cross diagram to show the electrons as shared (Fig 13.34). This structure has the molecular formula $AlCl_3$, though there is strong evidence to suggest that the formula is actually Al_2Cl_6.

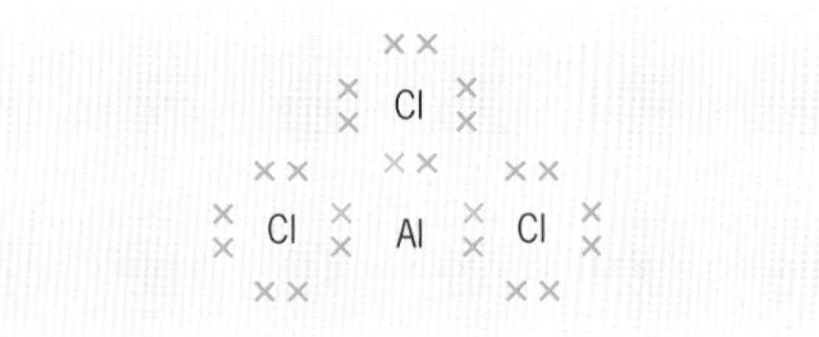

The dot and cross diagram of Fig 13.34 shows that $AlCl_3$ is an electron-deficient molecule, since the outer shell of the aluminium atom has only six electrons.

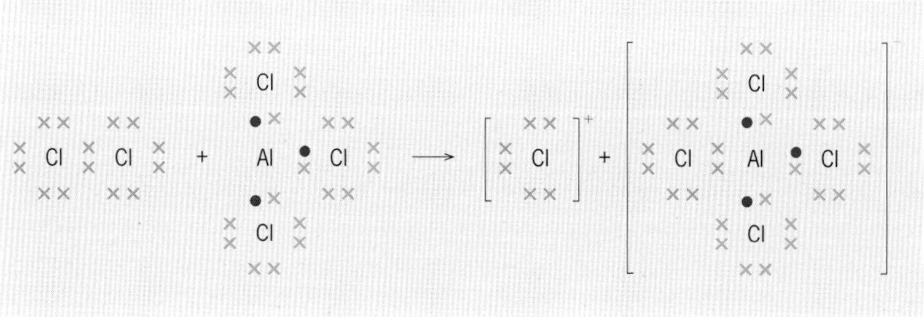

For more information on anhydrous aluminium chloride, see Chapter 21.

Fig 13.34 **Dot and cross diagram for aluminium chloride**

Fig 13.35 **Dot and cross diagrams to show the formation of Cl^+. The electron deficiency of the aluminium chloride is transferred to the chlorine electrophile Cl^+. Note that the aluminium atom has eight electrons in its outer shell after the reaction, while the Cl^+ ion has six**

Anhydrous aluminium chloride transfers its electron deficiency to a chlorine atom, to form the electrophile Cl^+ (Fig 13.35) and a tetrachloroaluminate ion, $AlCl_4^-$. The catalyst is often referred to as a halogen carrier. Once the electrophile is generated, the reaction proceeds to give the substitution product. The proton eliminated by the benzene ring at the end of the reaction can then react with the $AlCl_4^-$ ion to give hydrogen chloride.

Anhydrous iron(III) chloride acts as a catalyst in the same way. In fact, iron filings could be used as a catalyst, because iron(III) chloride would be formed in the reaction vessel by the reaction between iron and chlorine.

See question 4. ■

?

L Write down the equation for the reaction between a proton (hydrogen ion) and a tetrachloroaluminate ion.

Bromination of benzene

When a solution of bromine in benzene and aluminium chloride are refluxed together, electrophilic substitution takes place to form bromobenzene:

$$C_6H_6 + Br_2 \rightarrow C_6H_5Br + HBr$$

See questions 5 and 6. ■

?

M Explain, using dot and cross diagrams, how the electrophile, Br^+, can be produced from bromine and anhydrous aluminium chloride.

Notice that the catalyst is not included in the overall chemical equation, even though it is intimately involved in the production of the electrophile. We don't have to use aluminium bromide as the catalyst: aluminium chloride will do instead, when bromo-trichloroaluminate ion, $AlBrCl_3^-$, is formed.

Alkylation of benzene

This reaction is known as the Friedel–Crafts reaction. In it, a hydrogen atom is substituted for an alkyl group (Fig 13.36). The importance of this reaction is that a carbon–carbon bond is made. This time the problem is to make a carbocation that can act as an electrophile.

There are two main ways in which the electrophile (the carbocation) can be generated. One involves the heterogeneous fission of a halogenoalkane, and the other the electrophilic addition of a proton to an alkene (Fig 13.37).

There is more information about carbocations on pages 215 and 254.

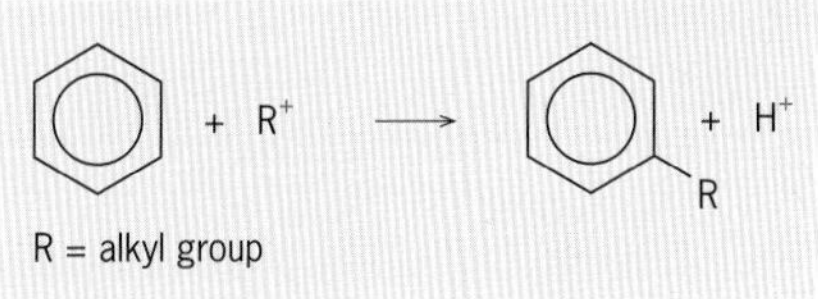

R = alkyl group

Fig 13.36 **The alkylation of benzene: the Friedel–Crafts reaction**

■ See questions 5 and 6.

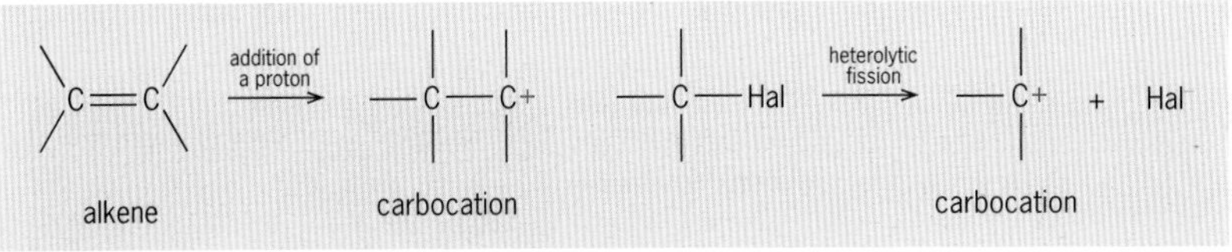

alkene   carbocation   carbocation

Fig 13.37 **Generation of carbocations by two routes**

Carbocations from halogenoalkanes

Typically, benzene, a halogenoalkane and anhydrous aluminium chloride are refluxed together to give an alkylbenzene. For example, iodomethane gives methylbenzene.

$$C_6H_6 + CH_3I \xrightarrow{\text{AlCl}_3, \text{ reflux}} C_6H_5CH_3 + HI$$

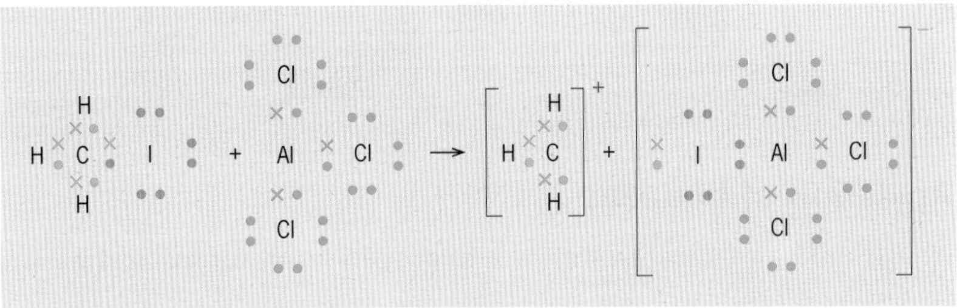

Fig 13.38 **Dot and cross diagram to show the formation of a methyl carbocation from iodomethane**

Let's look at the formation of the carbocation that permits this reaction. Fig 13.38 shows that it is similar to the way in which the electrophile Cl^+ is formed in Fig 13.35. Again, the aluminium chloride can transfer its electron deficiency, this time to an alkyl group to form the carbocation.

This reaction is discussed further in the Assignment (page 291), because it is rather more complex than Fig 13.38 would suggest: namely, the product will react again to give more than one substitution product.

Carbocations from alkenes

Alkenes typically react by electrophilic addition (Fig 13.39). When the electrophile is a proton, a carbocation is formed as an intermediate. When this is formed in the presence of benzene, the carbocation can react with benzene rather than completing the addition reaction.

Many different types of acid catalyst can be used in this reaction, including concentrated sulphuric acid, concentrated phosphoric(V) acid and aluminium chloride.

N Draw the structure of the main organic product formed during the reaction between iodomethane and benzene in the presence of aluminium chloride.

Electrophilic addition to alkenes is covered on pages 253 to 256.

■ See question 8.

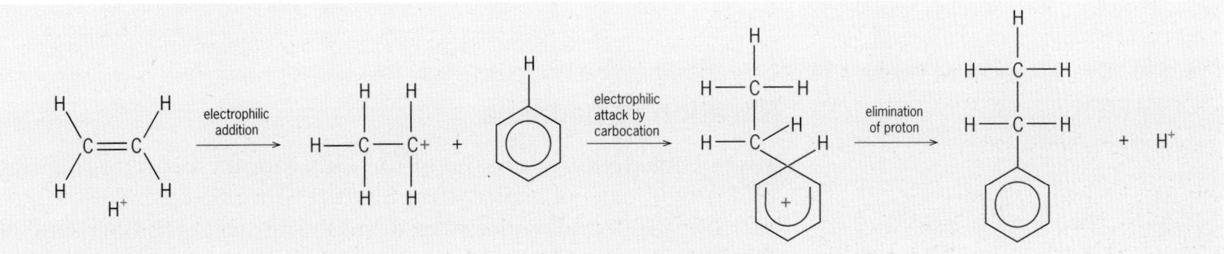

Fig 13.39 **The mechanism of the acid-catalysed reaction of an alkene (in this case, ethene) with benzene. Note that the proton H+ reacts to generate the carbocation, but is later regenerated, hence it is a catalyst**

Manufacture of poly(phenylethene)

Poly(phenylethene), common name polystyrene, is familiar to us as the material of hot drinks cups, ceiling tiles and packaging for fragile objects. It is

Fig 13.40 **The manufacture of poly(phenylethene)**

in which two hydrogen atoms are lost to form phenylethene. Finally, the phenylethene is polymerised normally under the influence of a free-radical initiator.

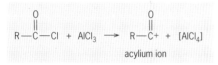

manufactured from two readily available hydrocarbons, ethene and benzene (Fig 13.40).

Ethene reacts with benzene in the presence of aluminium chloride, with hydrochloric acid as an acid catalyst, to form ethylbenzene. This is an example of electrophilic substitution. The purpose of the acid catalyst is to generate an ethyl carbocation which acts as the electrophile.

The ethylbenzene from the first reaction provides the correct carbon skeleton for the next stage. This involves a dehydrogenation reaction,

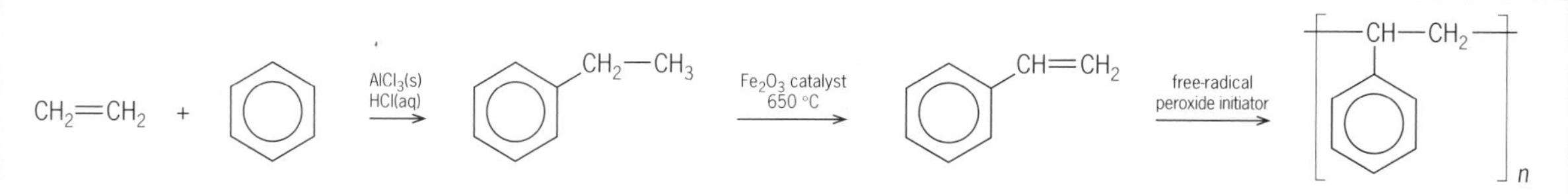

Fig 31,41(a) **Telephones are made from poly(phenylethene)**

Fig 31.41(b) **Expanded poly(phenylethene), also known as polystyrene, is used for packaging material**

Acylation of benzene

Acylation is the substitution of a hydrogen atom for an acyl group, RCO (Fig 13.42).

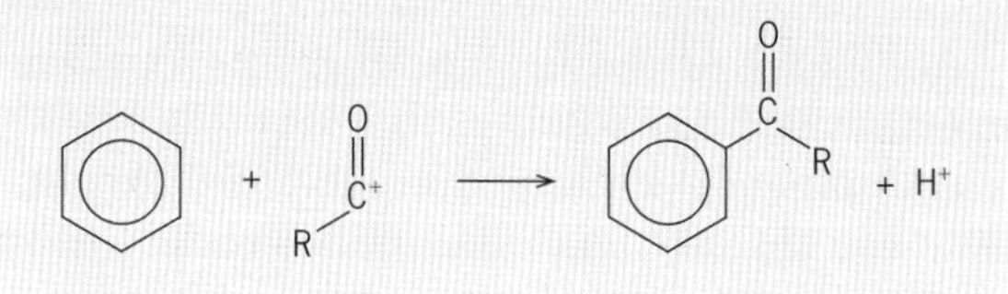

Fig 13.42 **Acylation of the benzene ring. A hydrogen atom is substituted by the acyl group RCO**

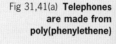

This reaction requires the formation of an acylium ion, RCO^+, to act as an electrophile. The acylium ion is produced by the heterolytic fission of a carbon–chlorine bond in an acyl chloride catalysed by anhydrous aluminium chloride (Fig 13.43). For example, ethanoyl chloride, aluminium chloride and benzene react together to give phenylethanone (Fig 13.44).

$$R-\overset{\overset{O}{\|}}{C}-Cl + AlCl_3 \longrightarrow R-\overset{\overset{O}{\|}}{C}+ + [AlCl_4]$$
acylium ion

Fig 13.43 **Generation of an acylium ion**

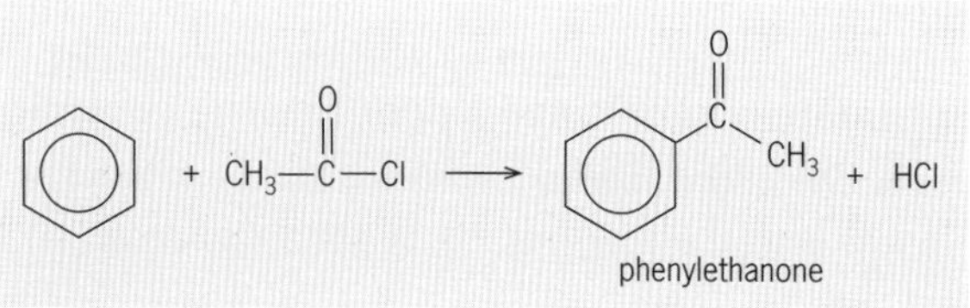

There is more information on this reaction in the Assignment, page 291.

?

O (a) Write down the structure of the product formed in the reaction between propanoyl bromide, CH_3CH_2COBr and benzene.

(b) Draw the structure of the reagent used to make 1-phenylbutan-1-one from benzene.

Fig 13.44 **Reaction of ethanoyl chloride with benzene**

phenylethanone

Nitration of benzene

It is possible to introduce the nitro group into the benzene ring (Fig 13.45) by means of a **nitrating** mixture – in this case, concentrated nitric acid and concentrated sulphuric acid. Nitrobenzene is formed when benzene is heated at less than 60 °C with a nitrating mixture. Keeping the temperature below 60 °C stops the formation of di- or trinitrobenzene.

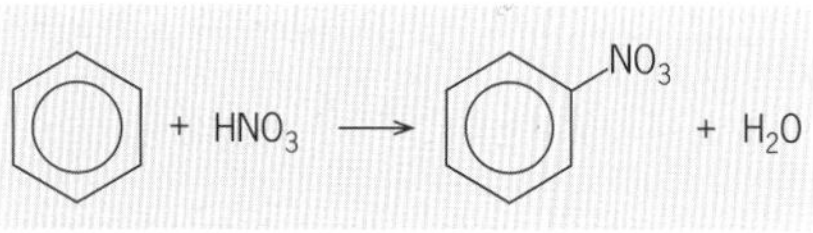

Fig 13.45 **Nitration of benzene**

The electrophile in the reaction (Fig 13.46) is the nitryl or nitronium ion, NO_2^+ which is generated by a reaction between the two acids:

$$2H_2SO_4 + HNO_3 \rightarrow NO_2^+ + 2HSO_4^- + H_3O^+$$

This equation represents the overall process that starts with an acid–base reaction using two acids. The concentrated sulphuric acid donates a proton to the nitric acid, and then the protonated nitric acid loses a molecule of water:

$$H_2SO_4 + HNO_3 \rightarrow HSO_4^- + H_2NO_3^+$$
$$H_2NO_3^+ \rightarrow H_2O + NO_2^+$$

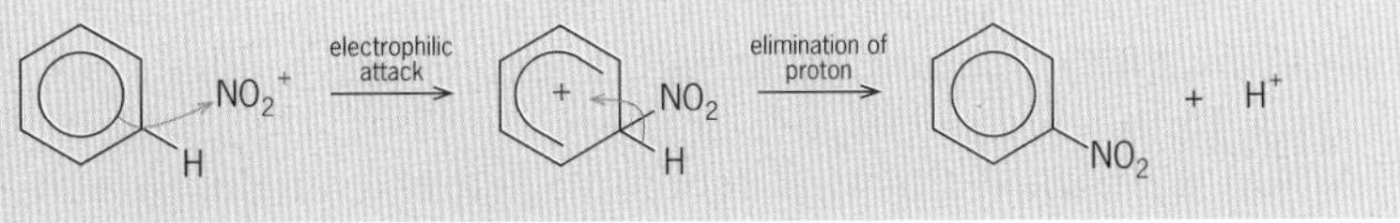

Fig 13.46 **Mechanism of the nitration of benzene. The nitryl ion, NO_2^+ electrophile and accepts an electron pair from the delocalised π system of the benzene ring. The positively charged intermediate is stabilised because it has a delocalised π system, but only over five carbon atoms. In this way, the positive charge is spread around the five atoms. Finally, a proton is eliminated from the intermediate to form a benzene ring. The proton reacts with HSO_4^- to regenerate the sulphuric acid**

The nitration of benzene allows other nitrogen-containing functional groups to be introduced, since, for example, it is easy to reduce the nitro group to an amine, giving phenylamine. It is otherwise impossible to introduce the NH_2 group into a benzene ring: NH_2 is nucleophilic in nature and not electrophilic, so it cannot react with a benzene ring.

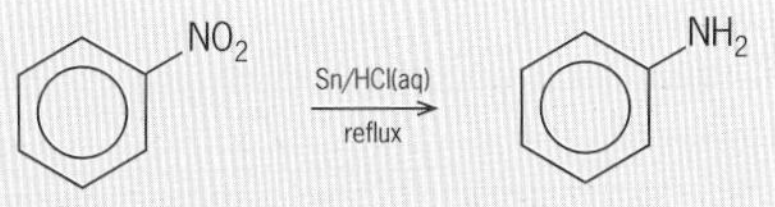

Sulphonation of benzene

Sulphonation involves the reaction of concentrated sulphuric acid on its own with benzene (Fig 13.48). It is believed that sulphur trioxide, SO_3, is the electrophile. In the reaction, a hydrogen atom in the benzene ring is replaced by the sulphonic acid functional group to produce benzenesulphonic acid. Aromatic sulphonic acids are important components of detergents.

In the presence of cold, dilute, aqueous sodium hydroxide, the sodium salt of benzenesulphonic acid is produced:

$$C_6H_5SO_3H + NaOH \rightarrow C_6H_5SO_3^-Na^+ + H_2O$$

Benzenesulphonic acid is hydrolysed by boiling with aqueous sodium hydroxide to form sodium phenoxide (Fig 13.49). In this way, the OH group can be introduced into a benzene ring. So, in two easy steps, phenols can be produced from benzene or substituted benzenes.

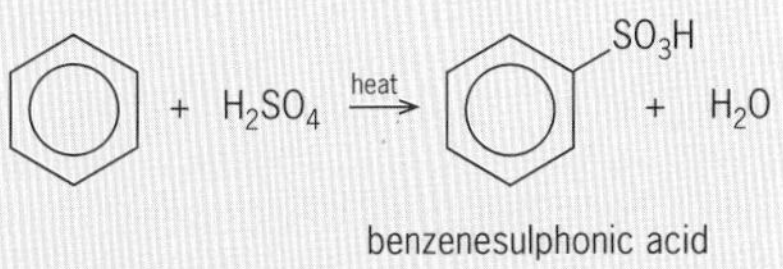

Fig 13.47 **The reduction of nitrobenzene to form phenylamine. This provides a route to a reactive intermediate in the manufacture of dyes (see Chapter 28)**

Fig 13.48 **The sulphonation of benzene**

benzenesulphonic acid

?

P Write down the equation to show the hydrolysis of benzenesulphonic acid to form sodium phenoxide.

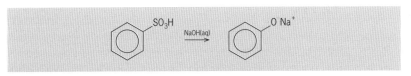

Fig 13.49 **The hydrolysis of benzenesulphonic acid to form phenol**

6 ADDITION REACTIONS OF BENZENE

Although it doesn't contain carbon–carbon double bonds, benzene is clearly an unsaturated compound, and under certain conditions will undergo an addition reaction to give a cyclohexane ring. The reaction is difficult, because the exceptional stability of the benzene ring has to be overcome.

Hydrogenation of benzene

Benzene is converted into cyclohexane when it is reacted with hydrogen under pressure in the presence of a nickel catalyst:

$$C_6H_6 + 3H_2 \rightarrow C_6H_{12}$$

It is impossible to stop the reaction to give either cyclohexene or cyclohexadiene, which is further evidence that benzene has a delocalised system of electrons rather than individual C=C bonds.

Addition of chlorine to benzene

In the presence of chlorine and a catalyst, such as aluminium chloride or iron(III) chloride, benzene undergoes electrophilic substitution to form chlorobenzene. If the conditions are changed, and chlorine is bubbled through refluxing benzene in the presence of ultraviolet light without a catalyst, an addition reaction occurs with chlorine to give isomers of 1,2,3,4,5,6-hexachlorobenzne.

7 REACTIONS OF SUBSTITUTED BENZENES

Electrophilic substitutions are characteristic of all compound with a benzene ring, not just arenes and other aromatic hydrocarbons. This raises the question: What happens to a molecule that has two functional groups – for example, in phenol, the benzene ring and the hydroxyl group? The answer is simple: the compound, in this case phenol, has two sets of reactions, one due the benzene ring and the other due to the hydroxyl group.

Consider a substituted benzene C_6H_5X where X is an atom or a group of atoms such as a methyl group. Because the compound contains the benzene ring, it will undergo electrophilic substitution. It may also undergo another set of reactions because of the presence of X.

Limiting the discussion to reactions of the benzene ring in the substituted benzene, C_6H_5X, two questions arise. The first is: Will the reaction be faster or slower than that with benzene? The second is: Which hydrogen atom will be substituted? When the reaction is faster, X is said to **activate** the benzene ring. When the reaction is slower, X is said to **deactivate** the benzene ring.

Now look at Fig 13.50, which shows a substituted benzene. There are three sets of hydrogen atoms that can be substituted.

Electrophilic reactions of phenol

Phenol consists of the benzene ring and the attached hydroxyl group. What effect does the hydroxyl group have on electrophilic substitution? The answer is easy to find out experimentally: aqueous bromine reacts with a solution of phenol in aqueous sodium hydroxide at room temperature to give 2,4,6-tribromophenol, which is a white precipitate. The reaction proceeds without a catalyst – the substitution does not require a catalyst to generate the electrophile. Also, more than one hydrogen atom is substituted.

Therefore the hydroxyl group is *highly activating*, since the reaction takes place much faster and more easily than with benzene. The hydroxyl group also *directs* the substitution to positions 2,4 and 6 in the benzene ring (Fig 13.52).

Q What is the molecular formula of the hydrocarbon obtained by the hydrogenation of naphthalene?

R Write down the equation to show the addition of chlorine to benzene.

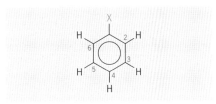

Fig 13.50 **In a substituted benzene, there are three sets of hydrogen atoms: on carbon atoms 2 and 6, on carbon atoms 3 and 5, and on carbon atom 4**

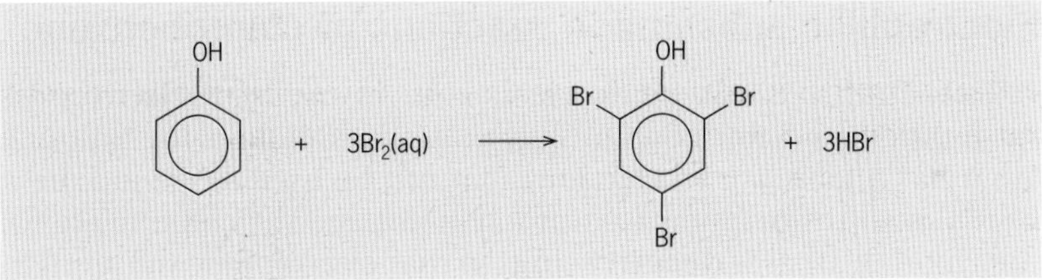

Fig 13.51 **Reaction of aqueous bromine with phenol**

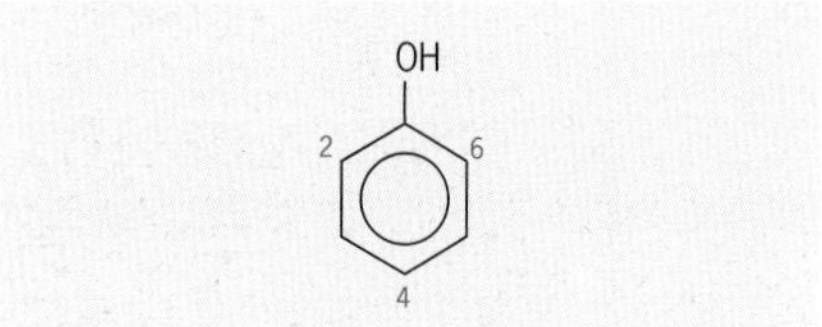

Fig 13.52 **The positions to which the hydroxyl group in phenol directs substitution**

The reason why phenol reacts much faster than benzene is that the lone pair of electrons on the oxygen atom becomes part of the delocalised π system. The π system is therefore extended over *seven* atoms rather than six. This has the effect of *increasing the electron density* in the π system, thereby making the benzene ring much more susceptible to electrophilic attack.

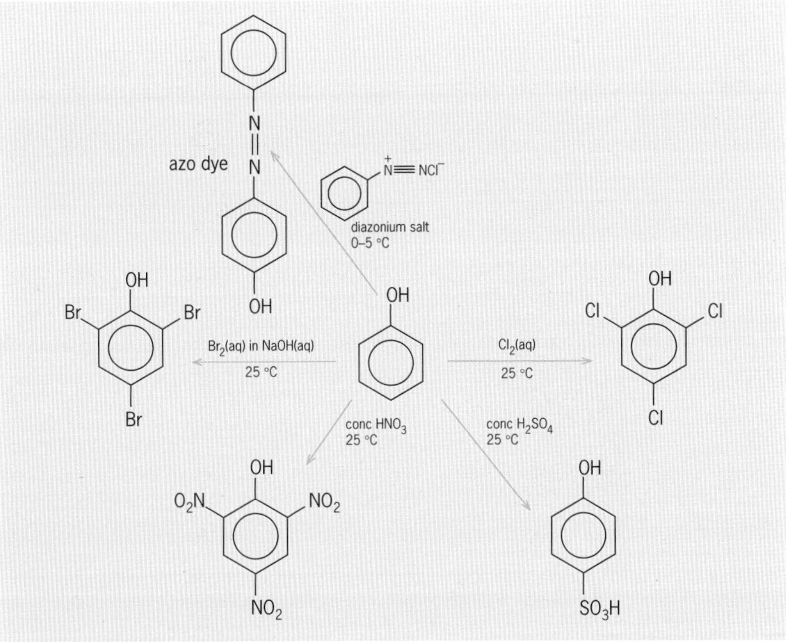

Fig 13.53 **Five important electrophilic substitution reactions of phenol. Note that because phenol has an activated benzene ring, the conditions are less extreme than conditions required for substitution in benzene**

Electrophilic substitution reactions of phenylamine

Phenylamine ($C_6H_5NH_2$) behaves towards electrophilic reagents in the same way as phenol, because the NH_2 functional group is very similar to the OH group in terms of its effect on π system of the benzene ring. Both the group and the OH group have lone pairs.

The π system is again extended over seven atoms, this time to include the nitrogen atom of the amine group. As for the OH group, the net effect is to increase the electron density of the π system, so making electrophilic substitution much easier than in benzene. Phenylamine reacts with aqueous chlorine to give 2,4,6-trichlorophenylamine, and with aqueous bromine to give the tribromo derivative.

Table 13.2 **Summary of the effects of substituents on electrophilic substitution of the benzene ring**

Substituent	Reactivity compared with benzene	Direction of substitution
CH$_3$ and other alkyl groups	activating	2, 4 and/or 6
Cl, Br and I	deactivating	2, 4 or 6
NO$_2$	deactivating	3 or 5
NH$_2$	highly activating	2, 4 or 6
OH and OCH$_3$	highly activating	2, 4 and 6

S (a) Write equations to show the reaction of phenylamine with
(i) aqueous chlorine and
(ii) aqueous bromine.

(b) Use the information in Table 13.2 to predict the product of the nitration of
(i) chlorobenzene,
(ii) 1,3-dichlorobenzene and
(iii) nitrobenzene.

Electrophilic substitution reactions of chlorobenzene

Chlorobenzene is very unreactive, both in terms of electrophilic substitution and nucleophilic substitution. Although the chlorine atom has a lone pair of electrons that can be used to extend the π system over seven atoms (six carbon atoms and the chlorine atom), the chlorine atom is **deactivating**, so that electrophilic substitution is very slow compared with that of benzene itself.

The chlorine atom directs substitution at positions 2, 4 and 6, but in practice only one hydrogen atom is normally substituted by an electrophile. When electrophilic substitution occurs in chlorobenzene, it gives a mixture of products (Fig 13.54).

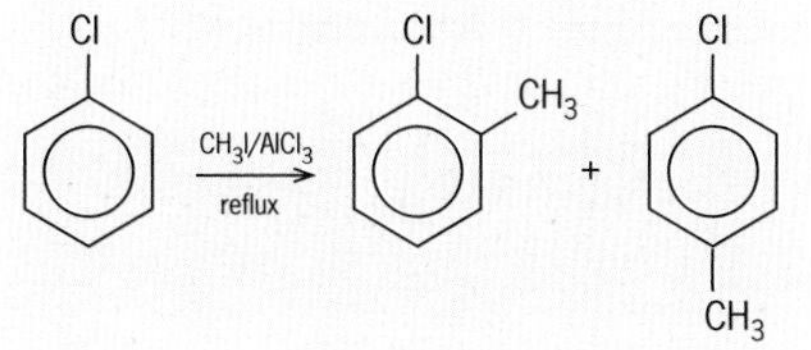

Fig 13.54 **Alkylation of chlorobenzene**

Also, the carbon–chlorine bond in chlorobenzene is much stronger than the carbon–chlorine bond in chloroalkanes, so that *nucleophilic* substitution does not take place.

DDT AND DIOXINS

DDT, AN ORGANOCHLORINE compound, was developed as an insecticide, originally to eradicate the malaria-carrying mosquito. At first, it was highly effective, but then DDT-resistant insects evolved.

The structure of DDT shows that it is related to chlorobenzene. So it is not surprising that DDT is virtually unreactive.

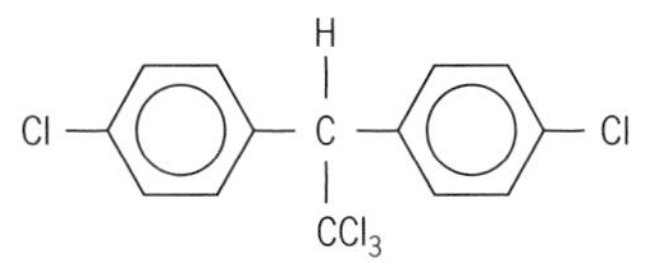

Fig 13.55 **Displayed structure of DDT**

Being unreactive, DDT began to build up in the environment and in its wildlife. So, severe restrictions on the use of DDT were introduced world-wide. In the United Kingdom, it was totally banned. But the restrictions have had little effect on the amount of DDT still in the environment.

Dioxins are a family of compounds which are also related to chlorobenzene. They are therefore exceptionally stable and so persist in the environment for a very long time. They cause birth defects and chloracne, a severe skin complaint.

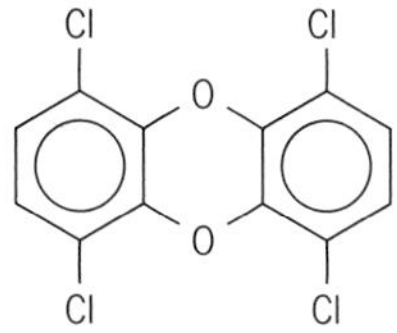

Fig 13.56 **Displayed structure of a typical dioxin**

Dioxins are by-products formed during the manufacture and disposal of chlorinated phenols. They enter the environment in a variety of ways – from incineration of chlorinated phenols to the emission of vehicle exhausts from leaded fuels. (See also Chapter 24.)

Reactions of methylbenzene

The traditional name for methylbenzene is toluene. As Table 13.2 indicates, the methyl substituent activates the benzene ring and directs the electrophilic substitution to positions 2, 4 and 6. In practice, the electrophilic substitution of methylbenzene always leads to a mixture of products.

The reactions of alkylbenzenes also appear in the Assignment to this chapter.

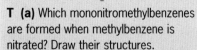

T (a) Which mononitromethylbenzenes are formed when methylbenzene is nitrated? Draw their structures.

(b) Which dinitromethylbenzenes are formed when methylbenzene is nitrated? Draw their structures.

Nitration of methylbenzene

The explosive compound TNT, trinitrotoluene, or more correctly 2,4,6-trinitromethylbenzene, is made by the nitration of methylbenzene (Fig 13.57). The reaction has three stages: first, one nitro group is substituted for a hydrogen atom, then a second group, and finally a third group.

The mononitro compound is produced by heating concentrated nitric acid and concentrated sulphuric acid at 60 °C. Above this temperature, dinitro compounds are produced, and the trinitro compound is only produced above 120 °C.

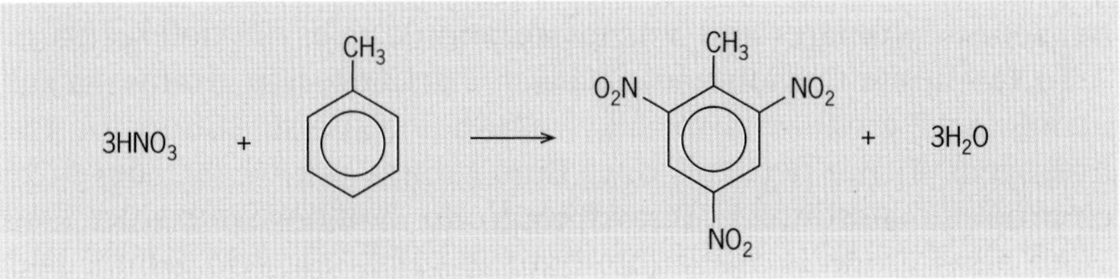

Fig 13.57 **Making TNT by nitrating methylbenzene**

Nitromethylbenzenes have an odour that resembles musk (Fig 13.59). They are therefore used in fragrances (perfumes).

Side-chain oxidation of methylbenzene
Methylbenzene is oxidised by acidified potassium manganate(VII) to form benzoic acid:

$$C_6H_5CH_3 + 3[O] \rightarrow C_6H_5COOH + H_2O$$

This is called **side-chain oxidation**, since it is the side chain rather than the ring that is oxidised.

Fig 13.60 **Side-chain oxidation of ethylbenzene to form benzoic acid**

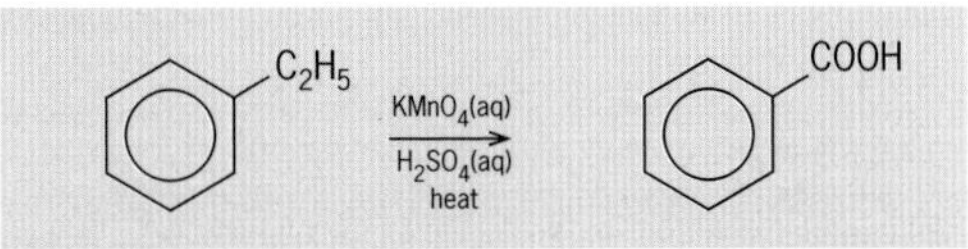

Side-chain oxidation occurs with any alkyl group, but always forms benzoic acid, regardless of the chain length of the alkyl group (Fig 13.60). When the benzene ring contains more than one alkyl group, each one is oxidised in the same way. This reaction can be used to determine the substitution pattern within an aromatic hydrocarbon. For example, if the side-chain oxidation of a hydrocarbon of molecular formula C_8H_{10} gives benzoic acid, then the hydrocarbon must be ethylbenzene.

Chlorination of methylbenzene
Methylbenzene is chlorinated by substituting a hydrogen atom with a chlorine atom. Methylbenzene has two kinds of hydrogen atom because of its two distinct types of C–H bond. One kind of hydrogen is bonded to carbon atoms in the benzene ring, and the other to the carbon atom of the methyl group. The hydrogen that is substituted, and hence the products formed, will depend on the choice of reagent.

When chlorine is bubbled through hot methylbenzene in the presence of aluminium chloride or iron(III) chloride, there is electrophilic substitution of one of the hydrogen atoms bonded to the carbon atoms in the benzene ring, with the formation of a mixture of 1-chloro-2-methylbenzene and 1-chloro-4-methylbenzene.

Alternatively, when chlorine is bubbled through methylbenzene in the presence of ultraviolet light, free radical substitution takes place and the methyl C–H bonds react. Again, a mixture of products is formed, including chloromethylbenzene, dichloromethylbenzene, and trichloromethylbenzene:

$$C_6H_5CH_3 + Cl_2 \xrightarrow{hf} C_6H_5CH_2Cl + HCl$$

$$C_6H_5CH_2Cl + Cl_2 \xrightarrow{hf} C_6H_5CHCl_2 + HCl$$

$$C_6H_5CHCl_2 + Cl_2 \xrightarrow{hf} C_6H_5CCl_3 + HCl$$

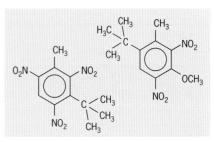

Fig 13.58 **TNT used in a limestone quarry**

Fig 13.59 **Two artificial musks, used in making fragrances**

?

U (a) The side-chain oxidation of an aromatic hydrocarbon C_8H_{10} gives benzene-1,2-dicarboxylic acid. What is the name of the hydrocarbon?

(b) Draw the structural formulas of the product of the side-chain oxidation of **(i)** butylbenzene, **(ii)** octylbenzene and **(iii)** 1,2,4-trimethylbenzene.

Free-radical chlorination is covered on page 206.

?

V (a) Draw the structures of the products of the reaction between chlorine and methylbenzene in the presence of aluminium chloride.

(b) Draw the structures of the products of the reaction between chlorine and methylbenzene in the presence of ultraviolet light.

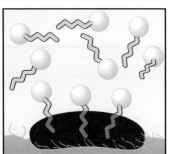

4–methylbenzenesulphonic acid

Fig 13.61 4-methylbenzenesulphonic acid (above) and a long chain alkylbenzenesulphonic acid

?

W (a) You want to make 4-nitromethylbenzene. Construct a flow chart to show how you would do the transformation.

(b) You want to make 3-nitromethylbenzene. Construct a flow chart to show how you would do the transformation.

Hint: You will need to refer to Table 13.2 on page 283.

8 BENZENE AND THE PETROCHEMICAL INDUSTRY

Production of detergents

Benzenesulphonates and benzenesulphonic acids are detergents.

To synthesise the sulphonic acids in Fig 13.61, two groups – a sulphonic acid group and an alkyl group – must substitute for two hydrogens in the benzene ring. Both groups can be introduced by electrophilic substitution. But which group should we introduce first?

An alkyl group is activating, but the sulphonic acid group, with similar properties to a nitro group, is deactivating. Therefore, the electrophilic substitutions need to be alkylation first and sulphonation second.

Long-chain alkenes, readily available from crude oil, are used for the alkylation. The particular alkene required is mixed with the benzene in the reaction, and becomes an electrophile in the presence of an acid catalyst.

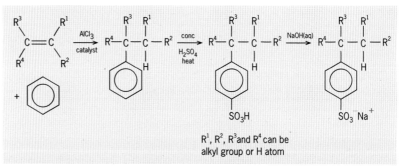

R^1, R^2, R^3 and R^4 can be alkyl group or H atom

Fig 13.62 Making alkylbenzenesulphonates by the alkylation of benzene, followed by sulphonation. This order of reaction gives the substitution pattern 1,4

DETERGENTS

1 The hydrophobic end of each detergent molecule forms induced dipole–induced dipole forces with the hydrocarbon molecules in the oil drop. The hydrophilic end is polar and forms intermolecular hydrogen bonds with water molecules

2 The oil is slowly lifted off the surface being cleaned and more detergent molecules surround it. Eventually they completely surround the oil drop

3 The oil drop is completely surrounded by detergent molecules with the hydrophilic sulphonate group on the outside. With the oil drop shielded by the detergent molecules, the polar water molecules cannot be in contact with the non-polar oil molecules

DETERGENTS ARE extremely versatile cleaning agents. They can remove dirt and grease from articles as varied as hair, crockery, clothes, household and industrial surfaces, machinery and vehicle engines.

Soaps are detergents, too, but they have the disadvantage of forming scum when used with hard water. This hastened the development of detergents, such as

Fig 13.63 How a detergent works

the alkylbenzenesulphonates: they don't form scum with hard water and can be made from readily available raw materials.

A detergent molecule has two distinct regions, one water loving (the **hydrophilic** region) and the other water hating (the **hydrophobic** region).

There are intermolecular forces of attraction between the hydrophilic region and water molecules because the detergent and water molecules are both polar. The hydrophobic region of the detergent, normally an alkyl group, is non-polar and so cannot form intermolecular forces with water molecules. However, it is able to form induced dipole–induced dipole attractions with other non-polar molecules (see page 160). Figs 13.63 and 13.64 explain the way in which a detergent works.

At first, alkylbenzenesulphonate detergents were made with branched chain alkyl groups (Fig 13.65) but when discharged into rivers, they formed polluting foams that bacteria could only degrade slowly. A change to straight chain alkyl groups solved this problem, because bacteria were able to degrade the new structures more quickly.

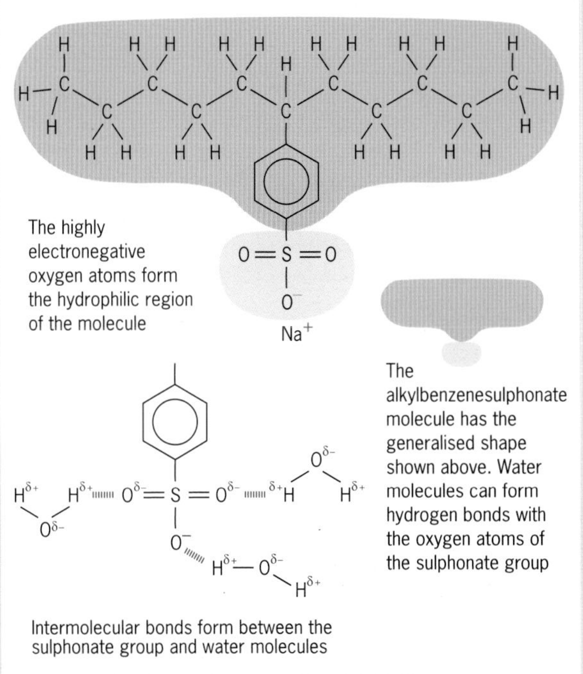

Fig 13.64 Alkylbenzenesulphonate, showing hydrophilic and hydrophobic regions

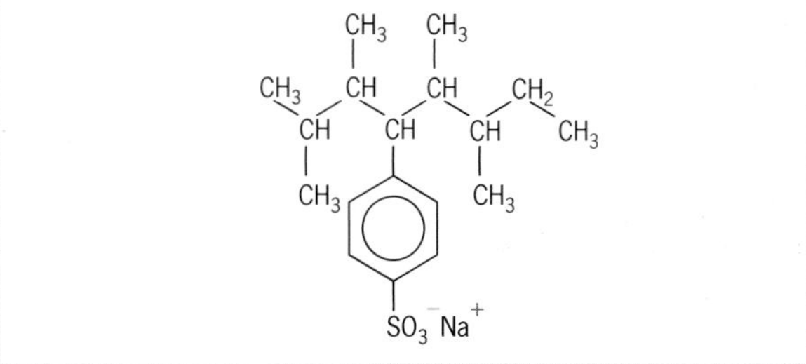

The highly electronegative oxygen atoms form the hydrophilic region of the molecule

The alkylbenzenesulphonate molecule has the generalised shape shown above. Water molecules can form hydrogen bonds with the oxygen atoms of the sulphonate group

Intermolecular bonds form between the sulphonate group and water molecules

Fig 13.65 **A branched chain alkylbenzenesulphonate**

Fig 13.66 **A typical case of foaming caused by detergents made from branched chain alkylbenzenesulphonates**

The cumene process

Phenol and propanone are two extremely useful chemicals made by the petrochemical industry. Phenol is used in the manufacture of dyes and (less important nowadays) as an antiseptic, and propanone is used as a solvent.

As we have already seen, the one-step conversion of benzene to phenol is difficult, since OH^+ is not available as an electrophile. So the conversion, known as the cumene process after the intermediate that is formed (Fig 13.67), must be in two stages. The process has the attraction of using common, cheap starting materials – benzene and propene – to give two useful products, not just one.

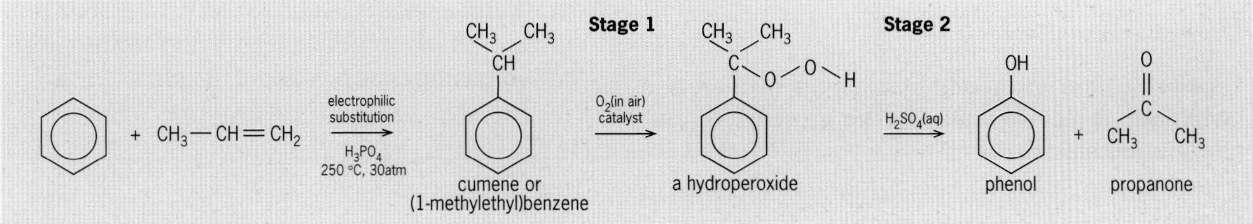

Fig 13.67 **The cumene process**

X Suggest why air rather than oxygen is the preferred reactant in the cumene process.

The intermediate cumene reacts with oxygen to form a hydroperoxide in a free-radical reaction. Next, the hydroperoxide is converted into phenol and propanone by reaction with dilute sulphuric acid.

Benzene and petrochemicals

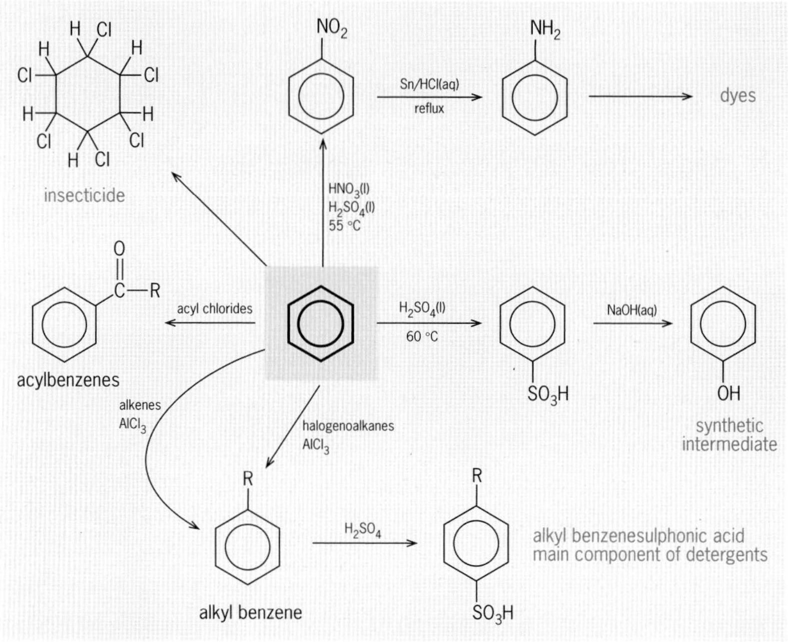

Fig 13.68 **A summary of the reactions of benzene**

SUMMARY

After studying this chapter, you should know the following.

■ The benzene ring is a regular hexagon of carbon atoms joined by six π bonds. Six π electrons are delocalised in an orbital above and below the ring.

■ Benzene can be obtained by cracking the naphtha fraction and by reforming C_6 alkanes or cycloalkanes.

■ Arenes react by electrophilic substitution rather than electrophilic addition, where an electrophile is substituted for a hydrogen atom, which is lost as a proton.

■ An arene is alkylated by reaction with a halogenoalkane in the presence of aluminium chloride, and is acylated by reaction with an acyl chloride or acyl bromide in the presence of aluminium chloride.

■ An arene is alkylated by reaction with alkenes in the presence of an acidic catalyst.

■ An arene is chlorinated or brominated by the reaction between chlorine or bromine and the arene in the presence of iron(III) chloride or aluminium chloride.

■ A nitrating mixture consists of concentrated sulphuric acid and concentrated nitric acid, and produces NO_2^+ that can react with arenes to form nitroarenes.

■ Phenol and phenylamine have highly activated benzene rings and form trisubstituted substitution products at positions 2, 4 and 6 with electrophiles.

■ Methylbenzene reacts faster than benzene towards electrophilic reagents and forms substitution products at position 2, 4 or 6.

QUESTIONS

1 Outline three pieces of experimental evidence for the delocalised model of benzene compared with a structure corresponding to the molecule cyclohexatriene.
[UCLES Spring 1995 Paper 1021/2, q.7]

2 By the use of a suitable example of each mechanism, describe the similarities and differences between those reactions classified as electrophilic substitutions and those classified as electrophilic additions. You should include in your answer:

a) the reagents used and their function;

b) the reaction conditions used;

c) the products formed;

d) the mechanism of each reaction;

e) how the structure of a molecule determines the mechanism.
[UCLES Summer 1994 Paper 9250/1, q.11]

3
a) Describe the bonding present in benzene.

b) Explain how the shape of the benzene molecule can be explained in terms of its bonding.

4 This question is about the sequence of reactions shown in Fig 13.Q4.

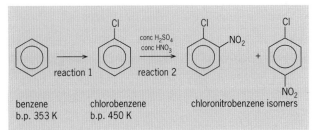

Fig 13.Q4

a) **(i)** State the reagents and conditions for **reaction 1** to take place.
(ii) State the type of reaction.

b) By what process could any excess of benzene in the product mixture formed by reaction 1 be removed?

c) **(i)** Give the name and formula of the electrophile responsible for **reaction 2**.
(ii) Show by means of an equation how this electrophile is formed.

d) **(i)** Draw the displayed formula of a third isomer of chloronitrobenzene.
(ii) Suggest a systematic name for this isomer.
[UCLES Winter 1994 Paper 1021/2, q.2]

5 Benzene reacts by electrophilic substitution. This reaction takes place in two stages. The first is electrophilic addition and the second the elimination of a hydrogen ion, H^+. The formation of an electrophile is quite difficult and often involves the use of a catalyst.

a) Explain with the aid of equations how the NO_2^+ electrophile is generated in a mixture of concentrated sulphuric acid and concentrated nitric acid.

b) **(i)** Draw the electron arrangement of aluminium chloride assuming that it has a molecular formula of $AlCl_3$.
(ii) What do you notice about the electron arrangement of $AlCl_3$?
(iii) Draw the electron arrangement in a molecule of bromine.
(iv) Explain how aluminium chloride can aid the heterolytic fission of a bromine molecule to form the electrophile Br^+.
(v) Explain how aluminium chloride can aid the heterolytic fission of a carbon–chlorine bond in 1-chlorobutane to form the electrophile $C_4H_9^+$.
(vi) Anhydrous aluminium chloride will act as a catalyst for many electrophilic substitution reactions of benzene, but hydrated aluminium chloride will not. Account for this fact.

6 Explain how you can carry out the following conversions. In each case, give the reagents and essential conditions used for each reaction described.

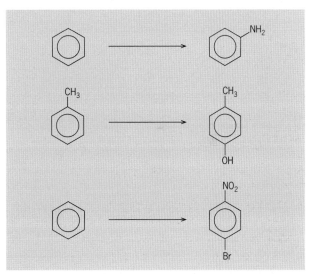

Fig 13.Q6

7
a) Phenylethanone ($C_6H_5COCH_3$) can be prepared from benzene.
(i) Give the reagents necessary to bring about this reaction.
(ii) Give the conditions necessary to bring about this reaction.
(iii) Write an equation for this reaction.
(iv) The reaction is an electrophilic substitution. What is the electrophile?

b) Phenylethanone can be reduced to ethylbenzene by using zinc amalgam and hydrochloric acid.
(i) By using [H] to represent the reducing agent, write an equation for this reduction.

(ii) Ethylbenzene can also be prepared from benzene. Give the reagents and the conditions needed to bring about this reaction.

[ULEAC 1996 Specimen paper 9081 CH4, q.1]

8 If ethylbenzene is treated with bromine in the presence of strong light, $C_6H_5CHBrCH_3$ is formed. If ethylbenzene is treated with bromine and iron(III) bromide, the product is a mixture of these two compounds:

Fig 13.Q8

a) Classify each reaction as nucleophilic, electrophilic or free-radical substitution, and identify what species attacks the ethylbenzene molecule.
   (i) with light;
   (ii) with FeBr$_3$.

b) What other product is formed in each case?

c) Predict the products obtained when ethylbenzene reacts with
   (i) a mixture of concentrated nitric acid and concentrated sulphuric acid at 50 °C;
   (ii) ethanoyl chloride in the presence of aluminium chloride;
   (iii) concentrated sulphuric acid at 60 °C.

d) Ethylbenzene is used to manufacture phenylethene.
   (i) Give the conditions for this conversion.
   (ii) Give the equation for the reaction taking place.

[AEB 1996 Specimen paper 654/8, q.2]

9 When benzene is nitrated, the main product is nitrobenzene. Further nitration is more difficult and produces mainly 1,3-dinitrobenzene (Fig 13.Q9).

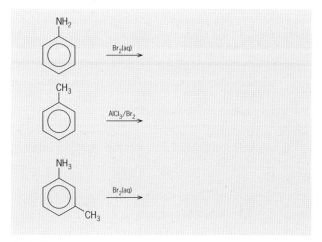

Fig 13.Q9

In an experiment to produce 1,3-dinitrobenzene, nitrobenzene was refluxed at 100 °C with an excess of a mixture of concentrated sulphuric acid and fuming nitric acid. The mixture was then cooled and poured into cold water, with stirring. The dinitrobenzene solidified in the mixture and was filtered off, washed with water and dried.

   The crude dinitrobenezene was purified by recrystallisation using a minimum of hot ethanol as solvent. The pure solid was filtered off, washed with cold ethanol and dried.

a) **(i)** What type of reaction takes place during the nitration of benzene?
   (ii) Give the name, and write the formula of the ion responsible for nitration.

(ii) Write the equation for the reaction between concentrated sulphuric acid and concentrated nitric acid which produces this ion.

b) What conditions for the further nitration suggest that the introduction of the second nitro group is more difficult than introducing the first?

c) Benzene reacts with chlorine forming two different products. The product of one of these reactions is hexachlorocyclohexane.
   (i) What conditions are necessary for this product to be formed?
   (ii) Draw a displayed formula for hexachlorocyclohexane.
In the presence of a catalyst, the major product is chlorobenzene.
   (iii) Name a suitable catalyst for this reaction.
   (iv) Write a balanced equation for the formation of chlorobenzene in this reaction.

[UCLES Spring 1994 Paper 1021/2, q.4]

10

a) Explain why it is impossible to make phenol from benzene in a one step reaction.

b) Describe a two step process that can convert benzene into phenol.

c) In the presence of a suitable catalyst it is possible to hydrogenate phenol. Draw the displayed structure of the product of this hydrogenation.

d) The OH group in phenol is said to highly activate the benzene ring. Explain what this means.

11

a) Predict the main organic products formed in each of the following reactions.

Fig 13.Q11

b) Explain why a catalyst is needed in reaction **(ii)** but not reaction **(i)** and **(iii)**.

Assignment

THE FRIEDEL–CRAFTS REACTIONS OF ARENES

In 1877, the French chemist Charles Friedel and his American co-worker James Crafts discovered an important type of reaction for arenes. Known as the Friedel–Crafts alkylation and acylation, it enables alkyl groups and acyl groups to be substituted into the benzene ring (Fig 13.A1 and 13.A2). The importance of the Friedel–Crafts reactions is that they make carbon–carbon bonds by linking straight or branched chains to arene rings.

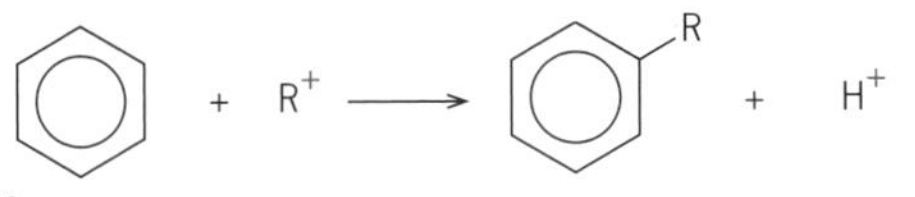

R = alkyl group

Fig 13.A1 **The alkylation of benzene**

R = alkyl group

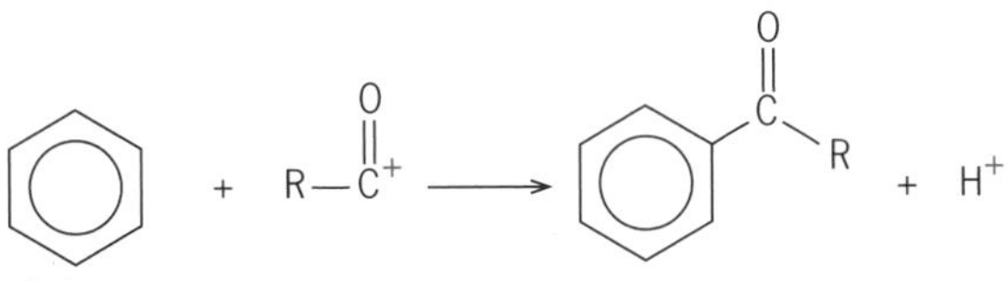

Fig 13.A2 **The acylation of benzene**

1

a) Draw the structure of the main organic product of the Friedel–Crafts reaction of butanoyl chloride, $CH_3CH_2CH_2COCl$, with benzene.

b) Suggest the structure of one of the main organic products of the Friedel–Crafts reaction of
(i) naphthalene with ethanoyl chloride, CH_3COCl, and
(ii) anthracene with iodoethane.

The alkylation and acylation reactions were found to be catalysed by Lewis acids (electron pair acceptors), such as anhydrous aluminium chloride, anhydrous iron(III) chloride, and anhydrous zinc chloride. Later on, the reaction was developed to include the alkylation of arenes using alkenes (Fig 13.A3). In this Friedel–Crafts reaction, acidic catalysts such as phosphoric(V) acid can be used.

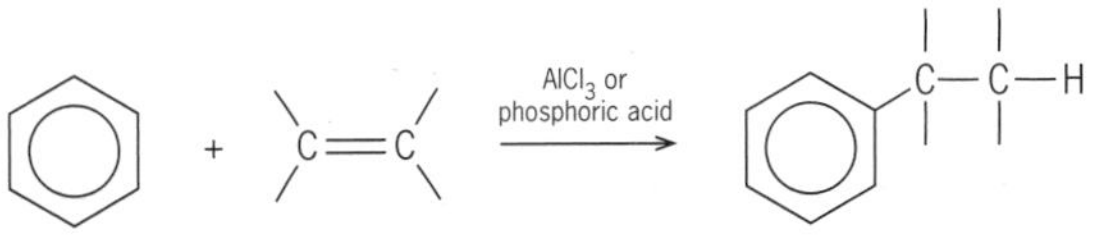

Fig 13.A3 **The alkylation of benzene using an alkene**

2

Suggest the structure of one of the main organic products of the Friedel–Crafts reaction between pyrene and ethene.

A Friedel–Crafts reaction is normally carried out by mixing the liquid arene with the catalyst and then adding the alkylating or acylating agent. (When the arene is a solid, a solvent such as nitrobenzene or carbon disulphide has to be used.) All reactants and apparatus must be kept absolutely dry during the reaction.

The temperature of the reaction varies, depending on the reactivity of the particular benzene ring in the arene. So, some Friedel–Crafts reactions need heat, while others take place at room temperature. Once the reaction is finished, the reaction mixture is added to water, this effectively destroys the catalytic properties of aluminium chloride.

On an industrial scale, these reactions produce a large volume of effluent that may contain carcinogenic arenes and a high concentration of metal ions, such as aluminium.

3

a) Suggest why the reaction itself must be carried out in dry conditions.

b) What problems do you foresee in carrying out a Friedel–Crafts reaction on an industrial scale?

c) Suggest one possible problem in the use of nitrobenzene as a solvent for a Friedel–Crafts reaction of a solid arene.

Envirocats (see page 268) are being developed for Friedel–Crafts reactions. The right clays are made porous and have metal ions inserted to produce insoluble solids with Lewis acid properties. Added to the reaction mixture, they catalyse Friedel–Crafts reactions. The envirocats developed so far cost about the same as the standard Friedel–Crafts catalysts, but the yield and the rate of reaction is lower. At the end of the reaction, the envirocats are filtered off, dried and reused many times. When they finally lose their catalytic activity, they can be safely buried in land-fill sites.

4

Discuss critically the advantages of using envirocats in an industrial process over the usual Friedel–Crafts catalysts. The mechanism of the Friedel–Crafts reaction is electrophilic substitution. The purpose of the catalyst is to generate the electrophile (Figs 13.A4 and 13.A5).

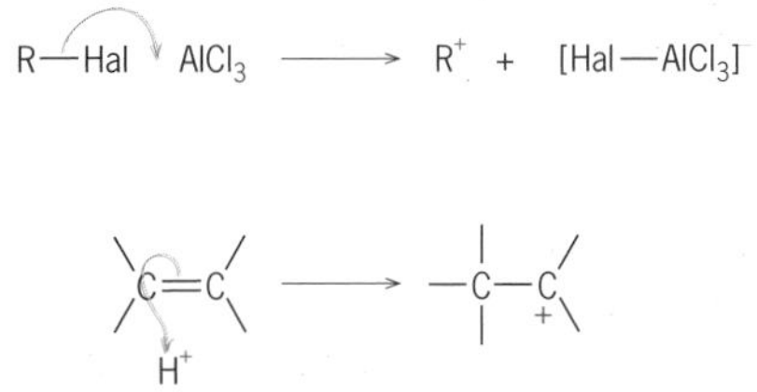

Fig 13.A4 **The generation of a carbocation electrophile from a halogenoalkane and from an alkene**

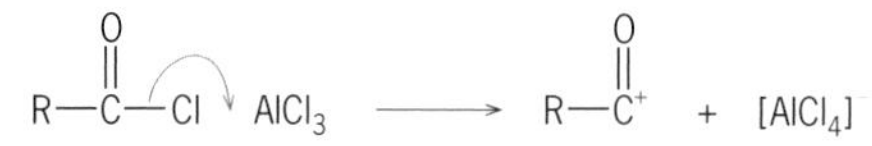

Fig 13.A5 **The generation of an acylium ion electrophile from an acyl chloride**

Fig 13.A6 **Two ways of representing the structure of an acylium ion**

5

a) What feature of anhydrous aluminium chloride allows it to facilitate the heterolytic fission of a carbon–halogen bond?

b) Using bond energies, suggest a reason why iodoalkanes are preferred over chloroalkanes in the Friedel–Crafts reaction.

c) Complete the mechanism for the reaction of the carbocation and for the acylium ion (Fig 13.A6) with benzene.

Fig 13.A4 does not fully detail the generation of the electrophile. Very often, the carbocation rearranges its carbon skeleton to make a more stable carbocation. Tertiary carbocations are more stable than secondary carbocations, which are more stable than primary carbocations. This means that there is a limited access to alkylbenzenes because the final electrophilic substitution product comes from the rearranged carbocation (Fig 13.A7). So, reactions of 1-iodobutane, 2-iodobutane and 2-iodo-2-methylpropane with benzene all form the same alkylbenzene via a tertiary carbocation. See page 254 for more information on carbocations.

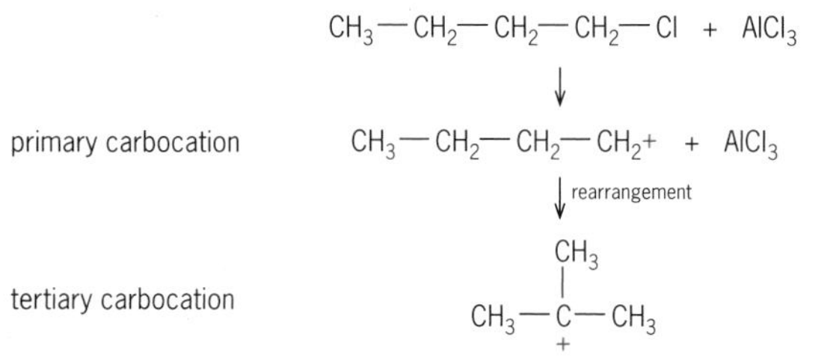

$$CH_3-CH_2-CH_2-CH_2-Cl \ + \ AlCl_3$$
$$\downarrow$$
primary carbocation $\quad CH_3-CH_2-CH_2-CH_2{+} \ + \ AlCl_3$
$$\downarrow \text{rearrangement}$$

tertiary carbocation
$$CH_3-\underset{\underset{+}{|}}{\overset{\overset{CH_3}{|}}{C}}-CH_3$$

Fig 13.A7 **Rearrangement of the carbon skeleton to form the most stable carbocation, which then reacts with the benzene ring**

6

a) Explain the order of stability of carbocations, from tertiary (most stable) to primary (least stable).

b) Draw the tertiary carbocation that 1-iodobutane, 2-iodobutane and 2-iodo-2-methylpropane form in Friedel–Crafts reactions. Hence draw the product of the reaction of any of these three isomers with benzene.

There is a further complication with alkylation. Once one alkyl group has been substituted, it activates the benzene ring, and so sometimes more than one alkylation per benzene ring takes place.

There is an alternative two-stage route to alkylbenzenes that does not suffer from either a second electrophilic substitution or the rearrangement of the electrophile. It involves an acylation to give a ketone, followed by reduction to give an alkylbenzene (Fig 13.A8). But there is one drawback with this method: it requires much more aluminium chloride catalyst, since the ketone produced after the acylation forms a complex with the catalyst.

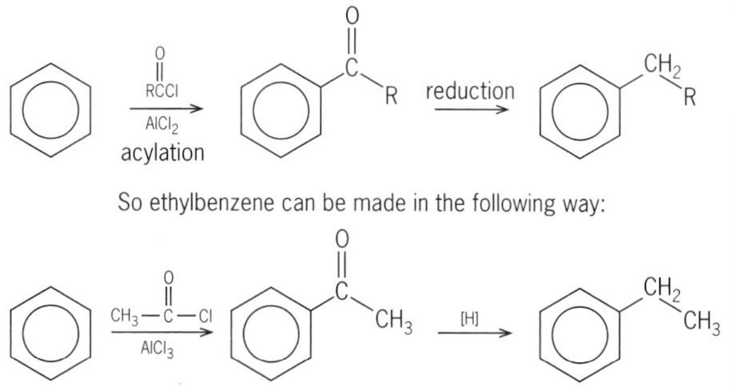

So ethylbenzene can be made in the following way:

Fig 13.A8 **The indirect alkylation of benzene**

7

a) Calculate the overall percentage yield for the missing entry marked ? in Table 13.A1 (see page 274).

b) Explain why you cannot make 2-phenylpropane from Route 2.

c) Discuss the advantages and disadvantages of making alkylbenzenes by **(i)** the one-step alkylation method, and **(ii)** the two-step alkylation–reduction method.

Table 13.A1 **The comparative percentage yields when some alkylbenzenes are made in a one- or two-step process**

Alkylbenzene to be made	Route 1: direct alkylation using and iodoalkane and aluminium chloride	Route 2: acylation using acyl chloride aluminium chloride followed by reduction		
	% yield	% yield acylation	% yield reduction	overall % yield from benzene to alkylbenzene
ethylbenzene	76	87	91	79
propylbenzene	5	85	90	?
2-phenylpropane	78	cannot be made this way		

AROMATIC COMPOUNDS AND ARENES

This chapter deals with the reactions that are possible in benzene and in compounds based on benzene. These reactions are affected by the ring structure of benzene and the resulting distribution of electrons in the ring. The Chapter Map below will help you find your way through the range of properties and reactions that are characteristic of aromatic compounds and arenes, and also to pinpoint the main industrial processes that these compounds are involved in. Refer to the additional chapters for more information about some of the topics.

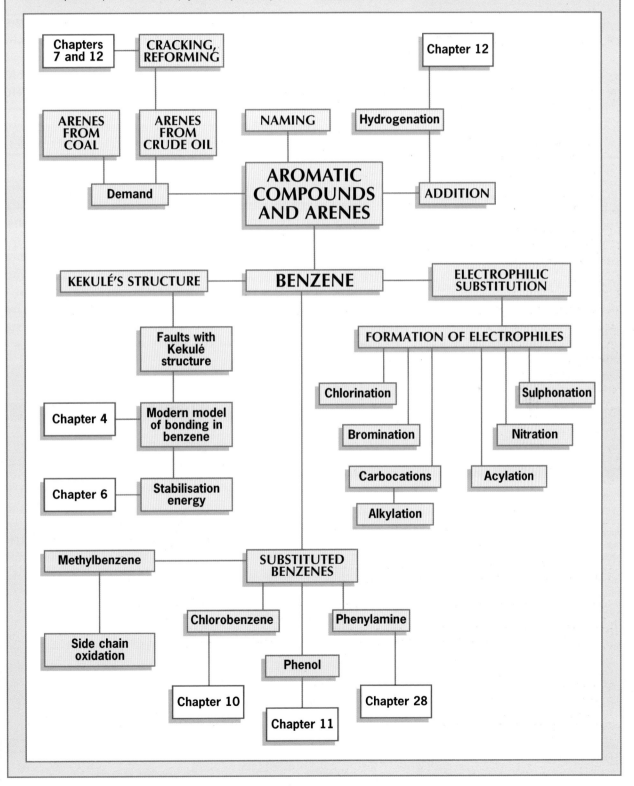

14 Aldehydes and ketones

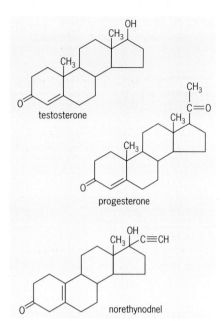

testosterone

progesterone

norethynodrel

Notice the four-ring structure which all steroids possess. You can read about cholesterol, another steroid on page 240.

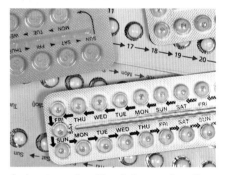

Oral contraceptives liberated women from the fear of unwanted pregnancies and thereby revolutionised sexual behaviour. At the same time, these chemicals in recycled drinking water have been partly blamed for reducing the sperm count of males

See question 1. ■

A **functional group** is an atom or group of atoms which gives a molecule a characteristic set of properties. See page 151.
A **pheromone** is a chemical which communicates information between members of the same species. See pages 88.
An **aryl** group contains a benzene ring.

THE MOST PUBLICISED hormones must be progesterone and testosterone. The reason is sex.

Progesterone is the female sex hormone which prepares the uterus for pregnancy after an egg has been fertilised, and which prevents the ovaries from releasing any more eggs. Testosterone is the male sex hormone responsible for sexual development and drive in males, and for muscle growth. Although having very different functions, these hormones are structurally very similar (they are steroids with a carbonyl functional group), and it takes only a simple chemical reaction in the laboratory to convert progesterone to testosterone.

Once their structures became known in the 1940s, chemists set about synthesising them, and soon synthetic sex hormones featured in a number of medical applications. However, few people would have predicted the social revolution that was to follow when synthetic progestins, a group of chemicals which mimic the action of progesterone were developed. The synthetic progestin norethynodrel was the basis of the first oral contraceptive, known simply as 'the pill', introduced in 1960. There is perhaps no more striking example of the influence of chemistry on our lives.

1 RECOGNISING AND NAMING ALDEHYDES AND KETONES

Aldehydes and ketones contain perhaps the most important functional group in organic chemistry – the carbonyl group, C=O (Fig 14.1). Hence, they are known as carbonyl compounds. The **carbonyl functional group** is found in many important biological molecules, from insect pheromones to human sex hormones. It occurs in the molecules in our eyes which are responsible for vision, and gives lemons their characteristic flavour. It is also involved in the manufacture of many important industrial chemicals, from plastics to solvents.

Fig 14.1 **The carbonyl functional group**

In aldehydes (Fig 14.2), the carbon atom of the carbonyl group (the carbonyl carbon) is bonded to at least one hydrogen atom, while in ketones (Fig 14.3) it is bonded to two carbon atoms from either an alkyl or an aryl group.

Fig 14.2 **An aldehyde. R can be hydrogen, an alkyl group or an aryl group**

Fig 14.3 **A ketone. The R¹ group may be different from the R group. R cannot be hydrogen, otherwise the compound is an aldehyde**

Four naturally occurring carbonyl compounds are shown in Fig 14.4.

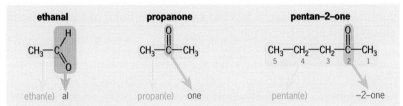

Menthone: found in mint leaves; gives a peppermint flavour

Citral: an oily liquid contributing to the flavour and aroma of oranges and lemons

CH₃(CH₂)₉CHO
A moth sex phermone

Oestrone: a female sex hormone

Fig 14.4 **Four naturally occurring carbonyl compounds**

Naming aldehydes and ketones

The systematic naming of aldehydes and ketones is simple. The names of aldehydes end in *al*, and those of ketones end in *one*. The number of carbon atoms in the chain (including the carbon of the functional group) provides the rest of the name and this is based on the alkane name with the end *e* removed.

ethanal

$CH_3-C \begin{smallmatrix} H \\ \\ O \end{smallmatrix}$

ethan(e) al

propanone

$CH_3-\overset{O}{\underset{\|}{C}}-CH_3$

propan(e) one

pentan–2–one

$\underset{5}{CH_3}-\underset{4}{CH_2}-\underset{3}{CH_2}-\underset{2}{\overset{O}{\underset{\|}{C}}}-\underset{1}{CH_3}$

pentan(e) –2–one

Eight of the more important aldehydes and ketones are listed in Table 14.1.

Table 14.1 **Some important aldehydes and ketones**

Structural formula	Systematic name
HCHO	methanal
CH₃CHO	ethanal
CH₃CH₂CHO	propanal
⬡—CHO	benzaldehyde
CH₃COCH₃	propanone
CH₃CH₂COCH₃	butanone
⬡—COCH₃	phenylethanone
CH₃CH₂CH₂COCH₃	pentan-2-one

METHANAL

FORMALDEHYDE, the traditional name for methanal, is still used by most industrial chemists. In fact, it is the most used industrial aldehyde. Methanal is produced by the air oxidation of methanol, using an iron or silver catalyst:

$$CH_3OH(l) + \tfrac{1}{2}O_2(g) \xrightarrow{\text{Fe or Ag catalyst, 500 °C}} HCHO(g) + H_2O(l)$$

Methanal is used to make plastics such as Bakelite (one of the first plastics) and other phenolic resins (where it is reacted with phenol),

A (a) Which of the carbonyl compounds in Fig 14.4 are aldehydes and which are ketones?

(b) Oestrone contains another functional group. What is its name?

It is important to remember that the carbon of the functional group counts towards the number in the carbon chain. The naming of alkanes is covered on page 156.

Fig 14.5 **Deriving the names of aldehydes and ketones**

Non-systematic or *traditional* names are still very common. Thus, you may see methanal referred to as formaldehyde, ethanal as acetaldehyde, and propanone as acetone.

B (a) Work out the molecular formulas of propanone and propanal.
(i) What do you notice?
(ii) What is the name given to compounds with this feature?

(b) The unpleasant odour of rancid butter is caused by butanal. Write down its structural formula.

(c) Write down the structural formula of pentan-3-one.

■ See questions 2, 3 and 4.

?

C Apart from the aromatic compounds, all the other aldehydes and ketones in Table 14.1 are very soluble in water.

(a) What type of intermolecular bonding explains this solubility? Hint: If you are not sure of your answer, look back at page 230.

(b) Draw a diagram to show the intermolecular bonding between an ethanal molecule and a water molecule.

(c) Why do you think aromatic carbonyl compounds are not very soluble in water?

alkene functional group   carbonyl functional group

Fig 14.7

Remember: An **electrophile** is a species which can accept a lone pair of electrons to form a covalent bond. A π bond is formed by the sideways overlap of two p orbitals.

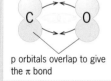

p orbitals overlap to give the π bond

Fig 14.9 **The sideways overlap of two orbitals**

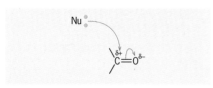

Fig 14.10 **Nucleophile Nu: attacks the carbonyl carbon and the π bond breaks**

See question 5. ■

A nucleophile has a lone pair of electrons with which it can form a covalent bond. It is attracted to a centre of positive charge.

urea–formaldehyde resins (where it is reacted with urea), melamine resins and Formica.

Your kitchen almost certainly contains surfaces and equipment which are products of reactions with methanal – kitchen work tops and pan handles are just two examples. So will your bathroom, because methanal is used as a preservative in some shampoos and bath foams.

A 40 per cent aqueous solution of methanal – better known as formalin – is used to preserve biological specimens (Fig 14.6) and as a disinfectant and fungicide.

Fig 14.6 **The head end of a dogfish, preserved in formalin, showing blood vessels of the gills**

2 THE CARBONYL GROUP AND NUCLEOPHILIC ADDITION

Because the carbonyl functional group has a double bond, it undergoes *addition* reactions – just like the double bond of the functional group in alkenes (see page 253).

Alkenes undergo **electrophilic addition** reactions because the loose electron cloud of the π bond (see page 81) is attractive to electrophiles. There is a π bond in the carbonyl group as well, but it is between two atoms of different electronegativities, C and O. So the density of the electron cloud is greater at the more electronegative oxygen end, thereby making the bond polar.

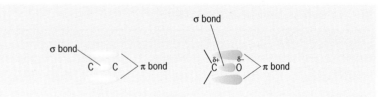

Fig 14.8 **The difference between the π bonds in the alkene and carbonyl functional groups**

Because C=O is polar, the electron-deficient carbonyl carbon is susceptible to attack by nucleophiles. We have already come across nucleophilic reactions with the polar carbon–halogen bond of halogenoalkanes (page 212), and with the polar C–O bond of alcohols (page 234). In both these cases, substitution reactions occur. But the carbonyl group has a *double* bond, and therefore as the nucleophile attacks and forms a covalent bond with the carbonyl carbon, the π bond splits and forms another single covalent bond, resulting in an addition reaction.

Nucleophilic addition by hydrogen cyanide

The reaction of hydrogen cyanide (HCN) with the carbonyl group is a very important *synthesis* reaction because it adds another carbon atom to the molecule.

Fig 14.11 shows two nucleophilic addition reactions. The reaction with propanone is used in the production of poly(methyl-2-methyl-propenoate), better known by its ICI trade name of Perspex. The first reaction in the synthesis of Perspex is the production of a hydroxynitrile (cyanohydrin).

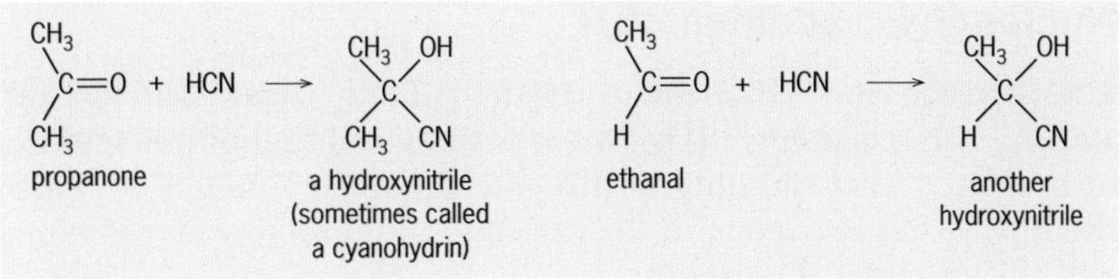

The structures at the top show two nucleophilic addition reactions:

$$\underset{\substack{\text{propanone}}}{\underset{CH_3}{\overset{CH_3}{>}}C=O} + HCN \longrightarrow \underset{\substack{\text{a hydroxynitrile}\\\text{(sometimes called}\\\text{a cyanohydrin)}}}{\underset{CH_3}{\overset{CH_3}{>}}C\overset{OH}{\underset{CN}{<}}}$$

$$\underset{\substack{\text{ethanal}}}{\underset{H}{\overset{CH_3}{>}}C=O} + HCN \longrightarrow \underset{\substack{\text{another}\\\text{hydroxynitrile}}}{\underset{H}{\overset{CH_3}{>}}C\overset{OH}{\underset{CN}{<}}}$$

Fig 14.11 **Two nucleophilic addition reactions**

The nucleophilic addition reaction of hydrogen cyanide was one of the first reaction mechanisms ever to be investigated, and it was done by a British chemist, Arthur Lapworth, in 1903. A **reaction mechanism** shows the steps by which a reaction takes place. The nucleophile is the cyanide ion (CN^-) rather than the HCN molecule. HCN is a poor nucleophile, and if CN^- ions are not present, the reaction is very slow. Either the addition of potassium cyanide (KCN) can provide the CN^- ions, or they can be generated from HCN by adding an alkali:

$$HCN + OH^- \rightarrow H_2O + CN^-$$

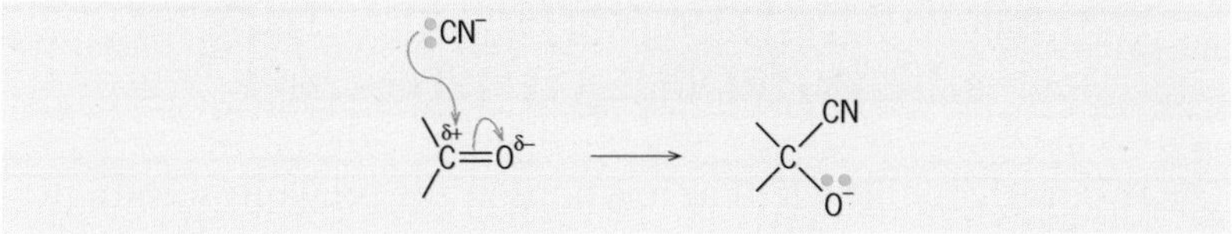

D Write the equation for the reaction of benzaldehyde with HCN.

A proton then bonds to the oxygen atom. Often this proton is transferred from HCN or H_2O:

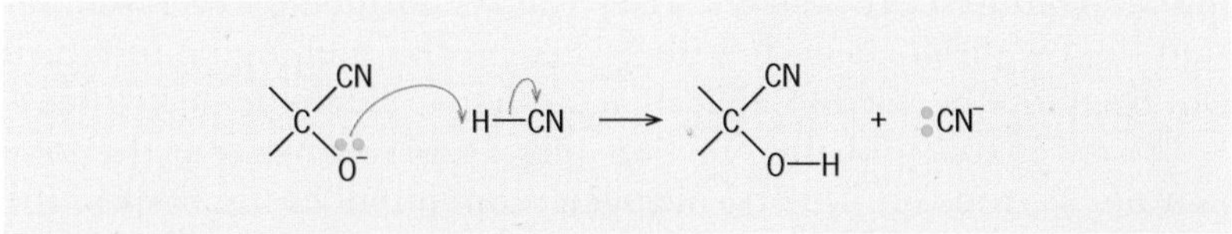

The net result is the addition of HCN to the molecule. Notice that in this case the proton was transferred from HCN, and a CN^- ion is regenerated.

■ See questions 3, 6 and 7.

HYDROXYNITRILE: THE MILLIPEDE'S DEFENCE

TO DETER PREDATORS, if not finish them off for good, one species of millipede uses the deadly gas HCN – hydrogen cyanide – yet manages not to harm itself. This is because inside the millipede are separate stores of a hydroxynitrile derivative of benzaldehyde, which is harmless, and an enzyme which catalyses the compound's reaction to benzaldehyde and HCN, and the two are not mixed until they leave the animal's body.

When the millipede is attacked, it discharges both compounds, the enzyme becomes mixed with the hydroxynitrile, and the the hapless attacker is enveloped in hydrogen cyanide.

Fig 14.12 *Apheloria corrigata.* Curled up, this giant millipede looks harmless, but it has a lethal spray for any attacker

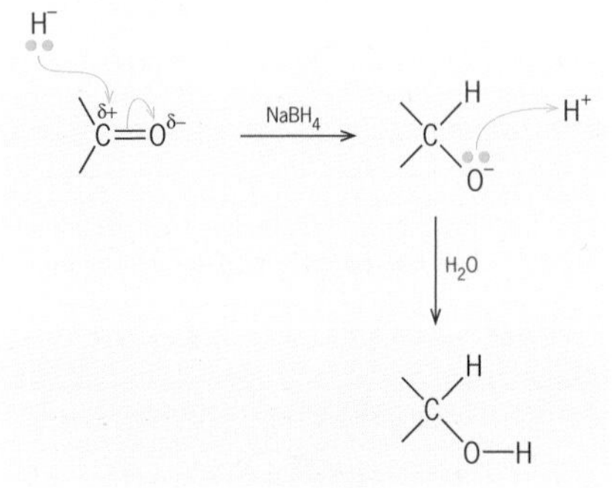

Fig 14.13 **Nucleophilic addition takes place in the first step, and water then transfers the proton to make an alcohol functional group**

See questions 6 and 8. ■

?

E Ethanal and propanone both react with NaBH₄ to produce alcohols.

(a) Identify the alcohols formed, and draw their structural formulas.

(b) Which of the alcohols is a primary alcohol and which is a secondary alcohol?

(c) Write a balanced equation for the reaction of propanone with NaBH₄. You should use [H] in this equation. Hint: If you need to be reminded about these alcohols, look at page 229.

Nucleophilic addition of H^-

The hydride ion (H^-) comes from sodium tetrahydridoborate, $NaBH_4$. The mechanism (Fig 14.13) is similar to that of the addition of hydrogen cyanide, only in this case the nucleophile is H^-. Once the $NaBH_4$ has reacted with the carbonyl compound, water is added and this provides the protons.

Notice that an alcohol functional group is produced. This reaction is also called a *reduction*. The equation for the reduction of aldehydes in general is written:

$$RCHO + 2[H] \rightarrow RCH_2OH$$

H is put in brackets to signify that *it comes from a reducing agent*, which in this case is $NaBH_4$. This reaction occurs again on page 300 when we look at the reduction of aldehydes and ketones. In the meantime, try Self-assessment question **E**, then find the answer at the end of the book to check that you got it right.

3 ADDITION–ELIMINATION REACTION OF 2,4-DINITROPHENYLHYDRAZINE

The two nucleophilic addition reactions in the previous section produce stable products. The next reaction gives an unstable product which spontaneously reacts, eliminating a water molecule.

2,4-dinitrophenylhydrazine reacts with carbonyl groups to give orange-coloured precipitates. They can be purified by recrystallisation to give products each with a very precise melting point which can therefore be used to identify a particular aldehyde or ketone.

The mechanism of the reaction (Fig 14.14) shows that the lone pair of electrons on the first nitrogen atom provides the basis of the nucleophilic addition, and the intermediate compound is then formed by an internal rearrangement. The final product, a 2,4-dinitrophenylhydrazone (Figs 14.15 and 14.16), is formed from the unstable intermediate by the elimination of a water molecule. So this reaction involves both an addition reaction and an elimination reaction – hence addition–elimination.

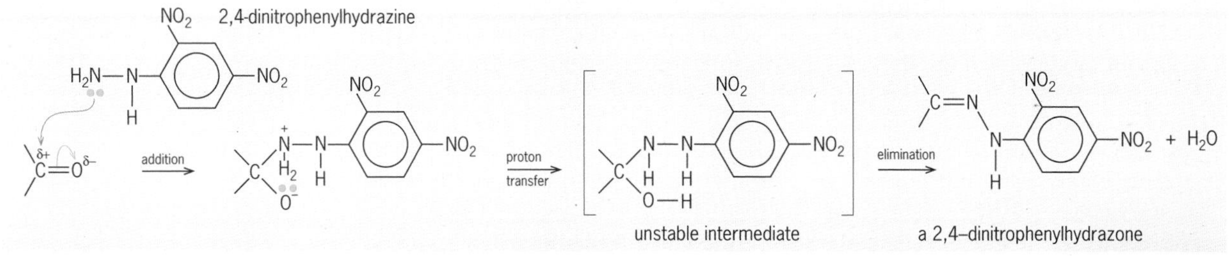

See questions 2, 6 and 8. ■

Fig 14.14 **Addition–elimination reaction of 2,4-dinitrophenylhydrazine**

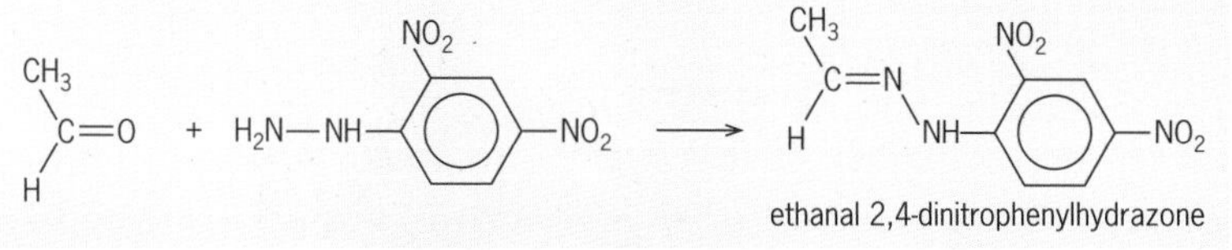

Fig 14.15 **Production of ethanal 2,4-dinitrophenylhydrazone**

?

F Write balanced equations for the reaction of 2,4-dinitrophenylhydrazine with phenylethanone and benzaldehyde. Hint: See Table 14.1 for the formulas of these carbonyl compounds.

Fig 14.16 **2,4-dinitrophenylhydrazone is brightly coloured**

The *ethanal derivative* ethanal 2,4-dinitrophenylhydrazone melts at exactly 168 °C, so its melting point can be used to identify ethanal, a method that used to be important before different types of spectrometers became widely available for identifying substances (see Chapter 9). Before this, the best way of recognising unknown carbonyl compounds was to produce from the liquid a solid derivative with a sharp melting point. The melting point is also a good means of checking the purity of a sample, since any impurity lowers melting point.

The production of 2,4-dinitrophenylhydrazone derivatives is still important for X-ray crystallography, which requires solid compounds.

For information on X-ray crystallography, see page 76.

A mixture of carbonyl compounds can be separated by reacting the mixture with 2,4-dinitrophenylhydrazine and then using thin-layer chromatography. The various 2,4-dinitrophenylhydrazones separate when a suitable solvent is used.

For information on thin-layer chromatography, see page 179.

SUN TAN FROM A BOTTLE

OVER-EXPOSURE to sunlight is known to cause skin cancer, yet millions of people still work hard to get a suntan because they think it makes them look healthier and more attractive.

But suntans haven't always been fashionable. Until about two hundred years ago, upper-class women going on leisurely walks would protect their pale complexions with bonnets and parasols. This distinguished them from the bronzed working men and women labouring outdoors in the sunshine.

Attitudes gradually began to change with the industrial revolution. While factory and office workers toiled in buildings which shut out the sunshine all day, better off people began to think of a suntan as a sign of wealth and position in society. This trend grew when it was the fashion in the early 1900s to go on touring holidays of continental Europe – the forerunners of today's package holidays.

A natural tan is caused by the dark pigment melanin which is produced in the skin to absorb harmful ultraviolet rays. A similar tan-like effect can be produced after a few hours using DHA, a colourless ketone which reacts with the protein in the outer skin to produce a brown pigment. DHA, traditionally called dihydroxy-acetone, is dihydroxypropanone:

Fig 14.17 **Despite grim warnings about the consequences, sunbathing still has millions of devotees**

$$HOCH_2-\overset{\displaystyle O}{\overset{\displaystyle \|}{C}}-CH_2-OH$$

There are problems with a 'chemical' tan. Cells of the outer layer of skin are dead and so within a few weeks these have rubbed off – and so has the tan! Also, because only dead cells react with DHA, where these are in a thicker layer, such as at the elbows and knees, the tan is darker than elsewhere. It is also worth noting that a chemical tan does nothing to protect the skin from harmful ultraviolet rays.

4 DIFFERENCES BETWEEN ALDEHYDES AND KETONES

So far, we have treated carbonyl compounds together and looked at the reactions of the C=O functional group in both aldehydes and ketones. They do, however, differ in their reactions to oxidising and reducing agents. Therefore, we'll now look at reactions of the aldehyde functional group separately from the ketone functional group.

G In Fig 14.18, what do R and R' stand for?
Hint: If you are not sure, see the beginning of this chapter.

aldehyde functional group

ketone functional group

Fig 14.18 **The aldehyde and ketone functional groups**

✔

Remember: Primary alcohols have an R–CH$_2$OH group. Secondary alcohols have an R–CHOH-R' group. For further information about alcohols, see Chapter 11.

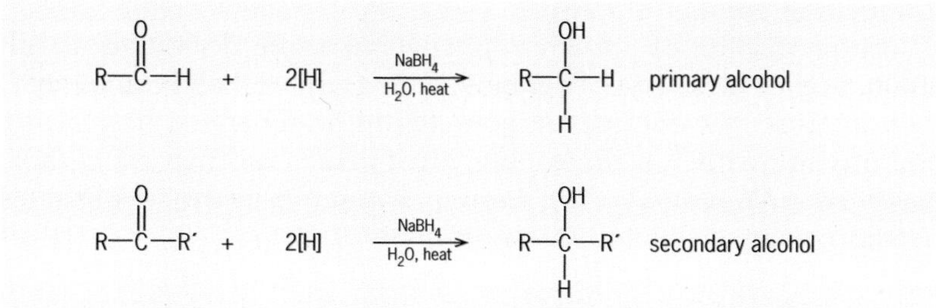

Reduction of aldehydes and ketones

With a reducing agent, such as NaBH$_4$ or LiAlH$_4$, aldehydes give **primary alcohols** and ketones give **secondary alcohols**, as shown in Fig 14.19. Notice that the reducing H in the equation is in brackets. This is a simplified way of balancing the equation and doesn't represent atomic hydrogen. The reaction is not that simple, as you can see from its mechanism on pages 297 and 298.

Fig 14.19 **Reduction of aldehydes and ketones**

As an example, benzaldehyde gives the balanced equation shown in Fig 14.20.

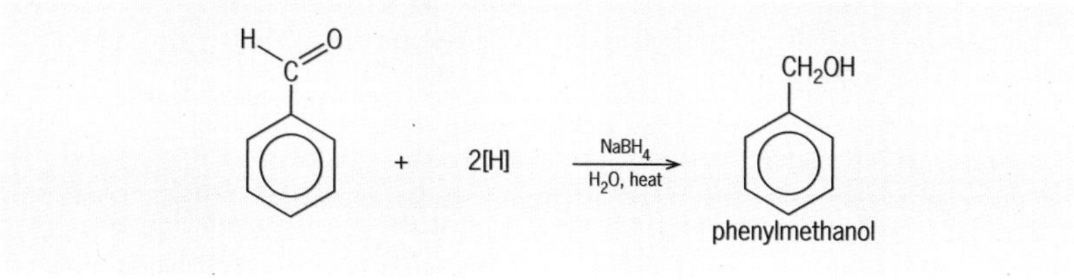

Fig 14.20 **Reduction of benzaldehyde**

The reduction reactions of aldehydes and ketones are essentially the reverse of the oxidation reactions of primary and secondary alcohols (see page 236).

Reduction with hydrogen

In the presence of a catalyst, such as platinum or nickel, hydrogen under pressure will add across the double bond to produce a primary or secondary alcohol. This is shown in Fig 14.21.

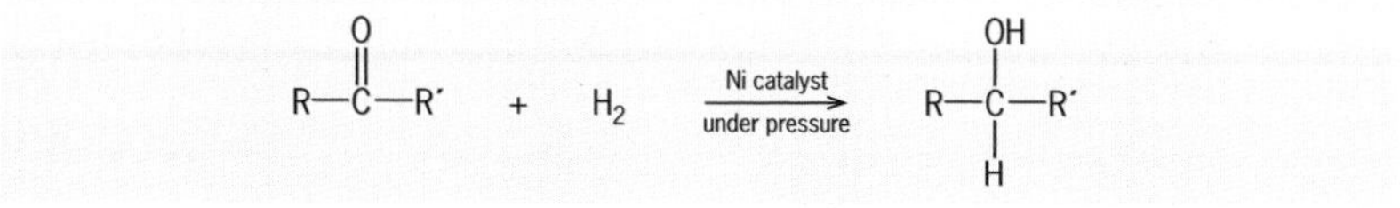

Fig 14.21 **Reduction of a ketone with hydrogen**

?

H (a) What species does the reducing when NaBH$_4$ is used? Hint: See page 297.

(b) Using [H], write balanced equations for the reduction of CH$_3$CHO and CH$_3$COCH$_3$.

See questions 4 and 7. ▉

✔

The addition of hydrogen across the double bond also occurs with the C=C double bond in alkenes. See page 257.

?

I (a) Using the general formula for an aldehyde (RCHO), write the equation for the reduction with hydrogen.

(b) Write a balanced equation for the reaction of hydrogen with phenylethanone.

See question 2. ▉

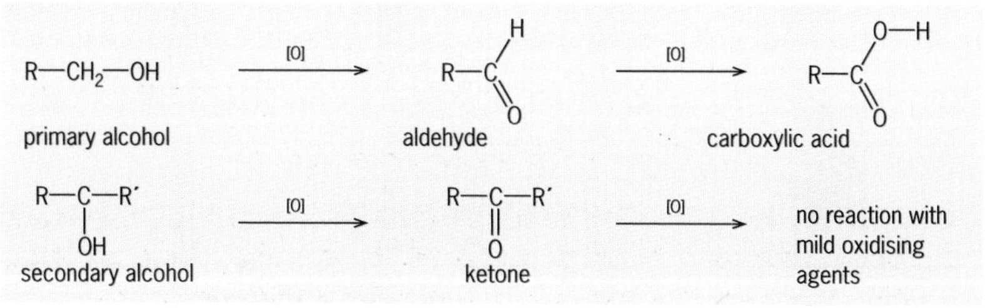

Oxidation of aldehydes

Aldehydes are prepared by oxidising primary alcohols, and ketones by oxidising secondary alcohols. In the case of primary alcohols, if the aldehyde is not removed from the oxidising agent immediately it is formed, it is further oxidised to give the carboxylic acid. The aldehyde is removed from the reacting mixture by distillation (Fig 14.22).

Fig 14.22 **Oxidation of primary and secondary alcohols to form aldehydes and ketones respectively**

Ketones resist further oxidation because they have no oxidisable hydrogen bonded to the carbonyl group. But they can be oxidised by strong oxidising agents with prolonged heating.

By contrast, the oxidation of aldehydes occurs even in air, so that bottles of opened aldehydes soon contain amounts of carboxylic acids. This difference in the reactivities of aldehydes and ketones to oxidation is one of the main reasons they are considered as separate classes of compounds. It also provides an ideal way of distinguishing between them.

Oxidation of aldehydes by acidified potassium dichromate(VI)

When an acidified solution of the orange dichromate(VI) ion is warmed with an aldehyde, it is reduced to the green chromium(III) ion. This reaction is shown in Fig 14.23, in which the aldehyde is ethanal.

The equation for the reaction with ethanal is given in Fig 14.24.

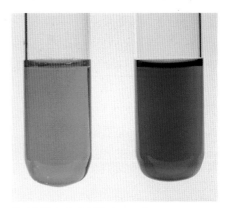

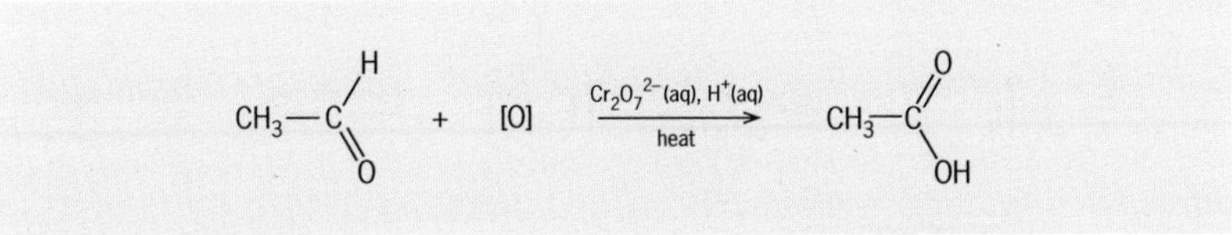

Fig 14.23 **Left: Acidified potassium dichromate(VI) before ethanal is added and the mixture heated. Right: After the oxidation of ethanal, the green Cr^{3+} is clearly visible**

Fig 14.24

■ See questions 8 and 9.

Using half equations

The half equations for this reaction are:

$$Cr_2O_7^{2-}(aq) + 14H^+(aq) + 6e^- \rightarrow 2Cr^{3+}(aq) + 7H_2O(l)$$
$$CH_3CHO(aq) + H_2O(l) \rightarrow CH_3CO_2H(aq) + 2H^+(aq) + 2e^-$$

Combining these to cancel out the electrons gives the redox equation:

$$3CH_3CHO(aq) + Cr_2O_7^{2-}(aq) + 8H^+(aq) \rightarrow$$
$$3CH_3CO_2H(aq) + 2Cr^{3+}(aq) + 4H_2O(l)$$

The use of half equations in redox reactions is covered in Chapters 21 and 26.

Oxidation of aldehydes by Fehling's and Benedict's solutions

Either or both of these reagents may be used in your chemistry course. They are alkaline solutions which contain copper(II) as **complex ions** (see Chapter 25), so the colour of both is blue (Fig 14.25). The copper(II) ions act as a mild oxidising agent. When the reagent is mixed with an aldehyde and heated, the aldehyde is oxidised to a carboxylic acid, while the copper(II) ions are reduced to a brick-red precipitate of copper(I) oxide, Cu_2O.

A balanced equation for this reaction is:

$$RCHO + 2Cu^{2+} + 2H_2O \rightarrow RCO_2H + Cu_2O(s) + 4H^+$$

The reaction for ethanal is shown in Fig 14.26.

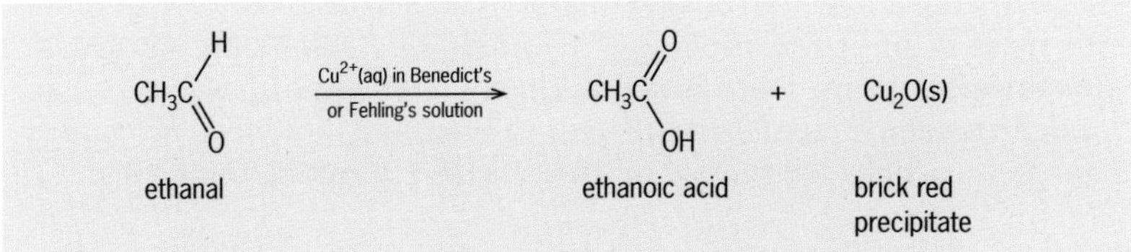

CH₃C (ethanal) → [Cu²⁺(aq) in Benedict's or Fehling's solution] → CH₃C—OH (ethanoic acid) + Cu₂O(s) (brick red precipitate)

Fig 14.26 **The oxidation of ethanal by Fehling's and Benedict's solutions**

This reaction can be used to distinguish between an aldehyde and a ketone. While this reaction is less used, now that we have spectrometers, it is still an important test in some situations. For example,

Fig 14.25 **Left: The copper(II) complex ion is responsible for the blue colour of Fehling's solution. Right: After oxidation of the aldehyde, the copper(II) ion is reduced to Cu_2O, in the form of a brick-red precipitate**

Fig 14.27 **Left: Ammoniacal silver nitrate before the addition of the aldehyde. Right: The aldehyde reduces the [Ag(NH$_3$)$_2$]$^+$ to Ag to give the silver mirror effect**

diabetes is easily diagnosed using Benedict's or Fehling's reagent which detects glucose in urine samples, and Benedict's reagent in tablet form is used by diabetics to monitor their blood sugar levels.

Tollen's reagent and the oxidation of aldehydes

Tollen's reagent provides yet another way of testing for aldehydes. This time, the oxidising agent is a complex of silver(I) ions, which are reduced to silver in the test. Fig 14.27 shows silver coating the inside of a test tube, making a 'silver mirror'.

The complex, whose formula is [Ag(NH$_3$)$_2$]$^+$, is made by mixing together aqueous solutions of ammonia and silver nitrate. The resulting solution is called Tollen's reagent, or ammoniacal silver nitrate. When warmed with an aldehyde, it produces the 'silver mirror'.

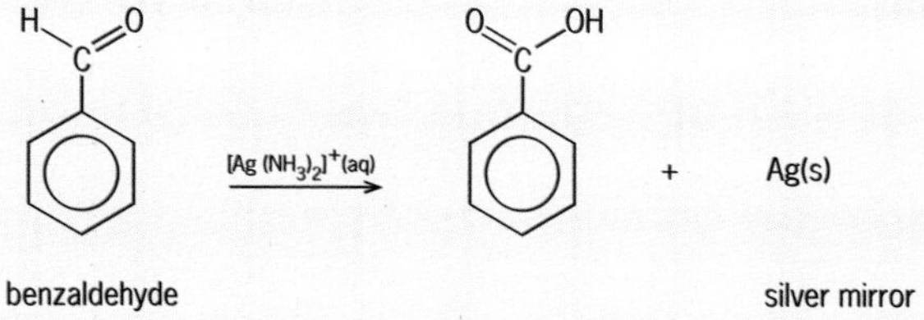

benzaldehyde [Ag (NH$_3$)$_2$]$^+$(aq) →   + Ag(s) silver mirror

Fig 14.28 **Producing a silver mirror by reacting benzaldehyde with Tollen's reagent**

This is a simplified balanced equation for the reaction:

$$RCHO + 2Ag^+ + H_2O \rightarrow RCO_2H + 2Ag(s) + 2H^+$$

See questions 6, 8 and 9. ■

The reaction provides one of the ways in which mirrors are silvered.

Sugars

More information on glucose and another sugar, fructose, can be found in the Assignment on pages 305.

See question 10. ■

As mentioned above, glucose gives a positive test with both Fehling's and Benedict's solutions. Because of this reducing property, glucose is known as a **reducing sugar**. In one of its forms, glucose contains an aldehyde group which accounts for this property.

ALCOHOLIC DRINKS AND THE FORMATION OF ALDEHYDES

WHEN YOU HAVE an alcoholic drink, ethanol passes into your bloodstream. It is the liver which has the job of breaking down ethanol. In the first stage, it is oxidised to ethanal:

$$CH_3CH_2OH + [O] \xrightarrow{\text{enzyme in liver}} CH_3CHO + H_2O$$

Ethanal is then oxidised to other products. But if you drink a lot of ethanol in a short space of time, ethanal entering the bloodstream is distributed throughout the body. Your face goes red, you may get unpleasant tingling in the limbs, feel nausea and your blood pressure may drop.

Methanol is added to ethanol that is intended for other uses, in order to make it unfit for drinking. This mixture is commonly known as methylated spirits. Once inside the body, methanol is oxidised to an aldehyde which rapidly causes liver damage and blindness. So, unfortunately, people determined to drink meths are risking their lives.

?

J What is the name of the aldehyde formed in the bodies of meths drinkers?

Triiodomethane test

There is a little more about the triiodomethane test with the CH$_3$CO group on page 239.

This is a useful test for the CH$_3$CO group in carbonyl compounds. An alkaline solution of aqueous iodine is warmed with the substance suspected of containing this group (Fig 14.29). (Iodine has a very low solubility in water. Therefore, the aqueous solution is made up by dissolving it in KI solution.) If a yellow precipitate of triiodomethane is produced, it is highly likely that CH$_3$CO is present.

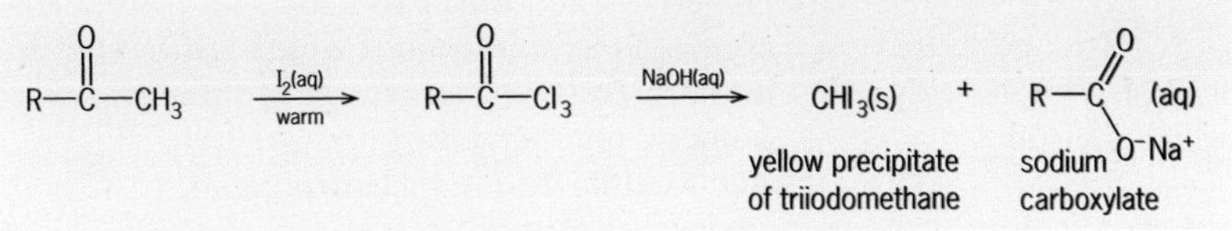

Fig 14.29 **Triiodomethane test. Note: R could also be hydrogen in this case**

Because I$_2$(aq)/NaOH(aq) is an oxidising agent, the triiodomethane test also gives a positive result with alcohols containing the CH$_3$CH(OH) group (Fig 14.30).

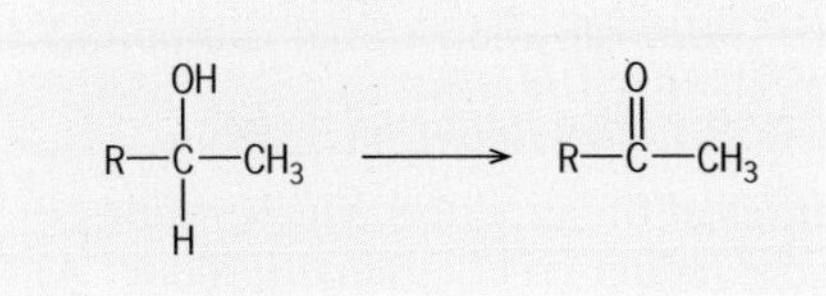

Fig 14.30 **Note that R could also be hydrogen in this case**

K State which of the following compounds will give a positive result with the triiodomethane test.

(a) CH$_3$CHO

(b) the compound in Fig 14.31

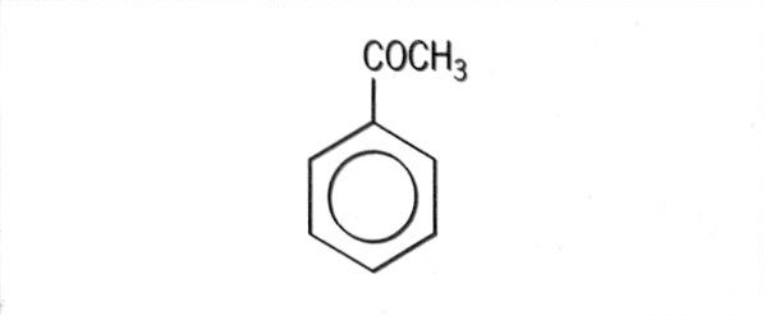

Fig 14.31

(c) C$_2$H$_5$COCH$_3$

(d) C$_2$H$_5$CHO

(e) C$_2$H$_5$OH
Hint: Draw the structures out more fully before you decide. Only one of the five compounds does not give a positive test.

■ See questions 8 and 9.

SUMMARY

After studying this chapter, you should know the following.

■ The carbonyl group C=O is found in both aldehydes (RCHO) and ketones (RCOR′), so they are called carbonyl compounds.

■ The polar nature of the carbon–oxygen double bond in the carbonyl group makes it susceptible to nucleophilic addition reactions. This contrasts with the electrophilic addition reactions of the alkene carbon–carbon double bond.

■ 2,4-dinitrophenylhydrazine undergoes an addition elimination reaction with carbonyl compounds. The resulting 2,4-dinitrophenylhydrazone derivatives can be used to identify specific aldehydes and ketones using their precise melting points.

■ Both aldehydes and ketones undergo nucleophilic addition reactions with HCN and with H$^-$ ions (from, for example, NaBH$_4$).

■ Aldehydes (but not ketones) are oxidised to carboxylic acids by mild oxidising agents, such as Cr$_2$O$_7^{2-}$/H$^+$, alkaline solutions of Cu^{2+} (Fehling's solution) and Ag$^+$ (Tollen's solution). These reactions can be used to distinguish between aldehydes and ketones.

■ Monosaccharide sugars, such as glucose, are called reducing sugars because they all give positive tests with the reagents Tollen's solution and Fehling's solution.

■ Alkaline aqueous iodine gives triiodomethane (CHI$_3$) with CH$_3$CO compounds, and also with alcohols containing CH$_3$CH(OH).

QUESTIONS

1

a) Explain fully what is meant by the terms *aldehyde* and *ketone*. For each term give, as an example, the structure of a compound containing three carbon atoms.

b) **(i)** Outline the mechanism of the reaction between ethanal, CH_3CHO, and HCN (KCN + a trace of H_2SO_4).
  (ii) This type of reaction is characteristic of aldehydes and ketones. To which mechanistic type does this reaction belong?
  (iii) Why are aldehydes susceptible to this type of reaction?
  (iv) Why does this reaction not proceed if the pH is very low?

c) Give an equation for the reaction between hydroxylamine, NH_2OH, and ethanal.

d) Explain briefly how the reaction of an aldehyde with hydroxylamine differs in mechanism from its reaction with HCN.
[OCSEB June 1997 Further Organic Chemistry 126/26, q.1]
Note: The reaction in **c)** above is similar to that of 2,4-dinitrophenylhydrazine on page 298.

2

The following reactions were observed for a compound **G** of formula C_3H_6O.
  I The compound did not react with alkaline aqueous copper(II) ions, even when heated.
  II On adding 2,4-dinitrophenylhydrazine, a yellow-orange precipitate formed.
  III Reaction with hydrogen in the presence of a catalyst produced a colourless liquid **H**. Liquid **H** reacted with sodium to give hydrogen.

a) Draw the displayed (full structural) formulae of two compounds of formula C_3H_6O.

b) What does the result of reaction **I** show?

c) The formation of a yellow-orange precipitate in reaction **II** is a positive test for a particular organic group. Identify this group.

d) Using the formula of the compound and the results of reactions **I** and **II**, identify **G**.

e) Write balanced equations for:
  (i) the reduction of **G** to give **H**;
  (ii) the reaction of **H** with sodium.

f) Draw the displayed (full structural) formula of **H**, and give its systematic name.

g) Under suitable conditions, **G** will react with hydrogen cyanide to form a compound of formula C_4H_7ON. What type of reaction is this?
[UCLES 1994 Modular Sciences Chains and Rings Specimen Paper 4821, q.6]
For question **2**, you may need to consult page 239 to answer part **e)(ii)**.

3

a) **(i)** Write an equation for the reaction between phenylethanone and hydrogen cyanide.
  (ii) Give a mechanism for this reaction.

b) **(i)** Draw the structure of pentan-2-one.
  (ii) Pentan-2-one forms two 2,4-dinitrophenylhydrazones which are geometric isomers. Draw the structures of these two isomeric phenylhydrazones.
[ULEAC 1996 Module Test 4 Specimen paper, CH4, q.1]

4

a) **(i)** Give the full structural formula of the aldehyde ethanal, and the full structural formula of the ketone propanone.
  (ii) Show clearly the functional group of each of the above [aldehyde and ketone] compounds.

b) What is meant by the term *functional group*?

c) Give the structures of the products which would be obtained from the reduction of ethanal (product **A**) and propanone (product **B**).

d) To what class of organic compounds do both compounds **A** and **B** belong?

e) **A** and **B** may be further classified by use of the terms *primary*, *secondary* or *tertiary*. Which of these terms applies to **A** and which to **B**?

f) Ethanal reacts with water, reversibly, as follows:
$$C_2H_4O + H_2O \rightleftharpoons CH_3CH(OH)_2$$
  (i) What type of reaction is this? Is it *addition, elimination, substitution, oxidation*?
  (ii) This reaction is sometimes described as a hydration reaction. Give, as an equation, another example of a hydration reaction of an organic compound which is neither an aldehyde nor a ketone.
  (iii) What structural feature has this organic compound, in common with ethanal, which enables the hydration to take place?
[OCSEB 1995 Unit 3 Essential Organic Chemistry 123/23, q.1]
Note: You may need to look at page 255 to answer parts of **f)**.

5

A carbonyl group C=O contains a double covalent bond between the carbon and oxygen atoms. This is made up of one σ bond and one π bond.
Explain, using words or diagrams, what is meant by

(a) a σ bond and

(b) a π bond.

6

a) Give a chemical test by which you could distinguish between ethanal and propanone. State the reagent(s) and conditions for the test, describe what you would observe, and give the name or formula of the organic product.

b) Consider the series of reactions involving ethanal that is shown in Fig 14.Q6, then answer the questions which follow.

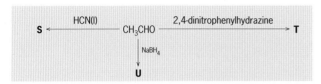

Fig 14.Q6

    (i) Draw graphical formulae to show the structures of compounds **S**, **T** and **U**.
    (ii) Give the name of compound **T** and describe its appearance.

c) Give the name and an outline of the mechanism for the reaction of ethanal with HCN(l) to produce compound **S**.
[AEB June 1996 Paper 2 0654/2, q.4]
Note: Graphical formulae are also known as displayed formulas.

7

Both alkenes and carbonyl compounds undergo addition reactions.

a) Write an equation for the reaction of **(i)** propene with bromine; **(ii)** propanal with hydrogen cyanide.

b) What type of addition reaction is occurring in **a)(ii)**?

c) Using a diagram, outline the mechanism of the reaction described in **b)**.

d) Draw a reaction scheme, indicating reagents and essential conditions, showing how you could convert propanal to propene.
[UCLES June 1996 Sciences: Chains and Rings, q.5]
Note: You will also need information from pages 253 and 256 to answer parts of this question.

8

The oxidation of an alkene with trioxygen (ozone), O_3, followed by hydrolysis (a process known as 'ozonolysis') gives two carbonyl compounds, as in Fig 14.Q8.

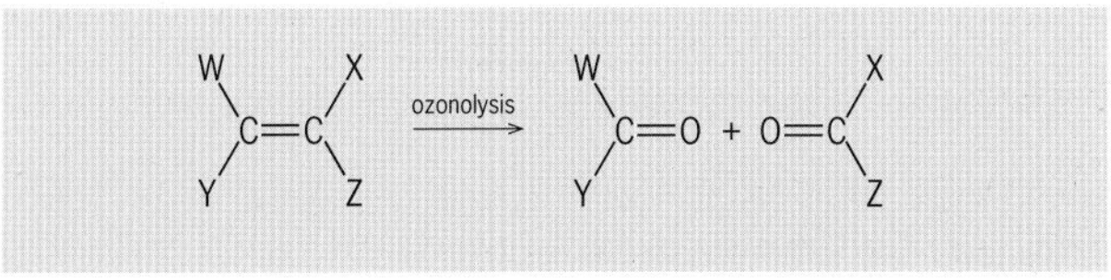

Fig 14.Q8

In such an experiment an alkene C_6H_{12} gave an aldehyde **K** and a ketone **L**, both of molecular formula C_3H_6O.

a) Describe a test, giving the result in each case, which would:
    (i) show that both **K** and **L** contain a carbonyl group;
    (ii) distinguish **K** from **L**;
    (iii) show that **L** contains the CH_3–CO unit.
    (iv) Draw the structures of the products formed when **K** and **L** are reduced with sodium tetrahydridoborate(III) ($NaBH_4$).

b) Aldehydes can be prepared by the controlled oxidation of alcohols according to the general scheme, where **R** is an alkyl group:

$$R–CH_2OH \quad \rightarrow \quad R–CHO \quad \rightarrow \quad R–CO_2H$$
    alcohol   aldehyde   carboxylic acid

    (i) State the reagents and conditions required to bring about this oxidation.
    (ii) How might you carry out the oxidation in the laboratory to maximise the yield of aldehyde?
[ULEAC 1996 Module Test 4 Specimen Paper CH4, q.4]

9

2-oxopropanal, **B**, is one of a number of compounds responsible for the characteristic smell of burnt sugar.

$$\overset{\displaystyle O}{\overset{\displaystyle \|}{\textbf{B} \quad CH_3–C–CH=O}}$$

a) Describe what you might **observe** when this compound is:
    (i) heated gently with acidified potassium dichromate(VI),
    (ii) added to alkaline aqueous iodine,
    (iii) warmed gently with Fehling's solution.
In each case, suggest the structural formula of each organic product.
[UCLES November 1997 Paper 1, q.7]

10

Glucose is an optically active reducing sugar.

a) Describe a simple experiment which would demonstrate that glucose is a *reducing* sugar.

b) Explain what feature of its molecular structure makes it reducing.

Assignment

SUGARS

Sugars are important and well-known biological molecules. They contain a carbonyl group, so they are either aldehydes or ketones. Two examples, glucose and fructose, exist in both open-chain and ring forms, as Figs 14.A1 and 14.A2 show.

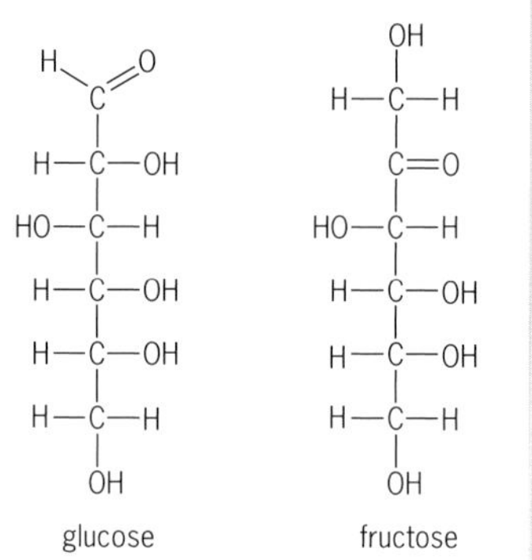

Fig 14.A1 Open-chain forms of glucose and fructose

glucose   fructose

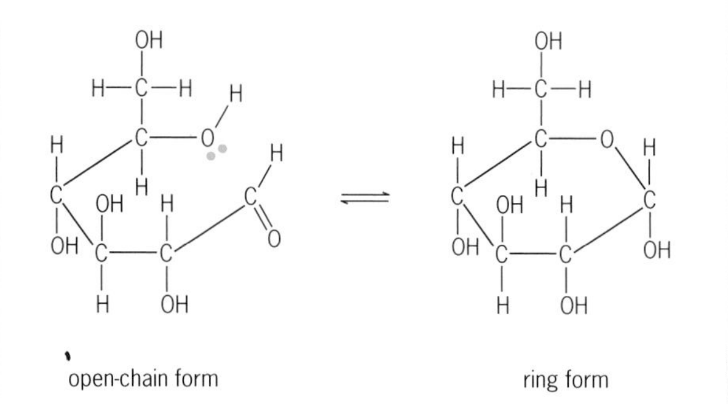

Fig 14.A2 Open-chain and ring forms of glucose

open-chain form   ring form

1

a) What are the molecular formulas of glucose and fructose?

b) What is meant by the term carbonyl group?

c) Draw the functional group in an aldehyde and a ketone.

d) Is fructose an aldehyde or a ketone?

e) Name the other functional group present in both molecules.

In aqueous solution, the ring and open-chain forms of glucose are in equilibrium. But since the ring form is at the highest concentration, this is the structure that is usually drawn. Nevertheless, there is enough of the open-chain aldehyde to show characteristic reactions of this group.

2

a) What name is given to the mechanism of the reaction which produces the ring form from the open-chain form of glucose?
Hint: Look at the carbonyl functional group.

b) Draw the carbonyl group to show the π and σ bonds.

c) The alkene C=C also has π and σ bonds, yet its addition reactions occur by a different mechanism. Explain why there is this difference.

d) Using the open-chain form of glucose, write the equation for its reaction with HCN.

3

2,4-dinitrophenylhydrazine gives a coloured crystalline precipitate with fructose. Using the open-chain form of fructose, write the equation.

As mentioned on page 302, glucose gives a positive result with the Fehling's test because it has an aldehyde group. However, fructose also gives a brick-red precipitate with Fehling's solution – which is a surprising result. In fact, all monosaccharides, whether ketones or aldehydes, are called reducing sugars because of their ability to act as reducing agents. So, both fructose and glucose give a positive test with Tollen's reagent.

4

a) Why is it a 'surprise' that fructose gives a positive Fehling's test?

b) How do we know that fructose is reacting as a reducing reagent in this reaction?

c) What would you observe in a positive Tollen's test?

Glucose is metabolised in the body in a series of steps. In one step, pyruvic acid is converted to lactic acid (Fig 14.A3).

Fig 14.A3

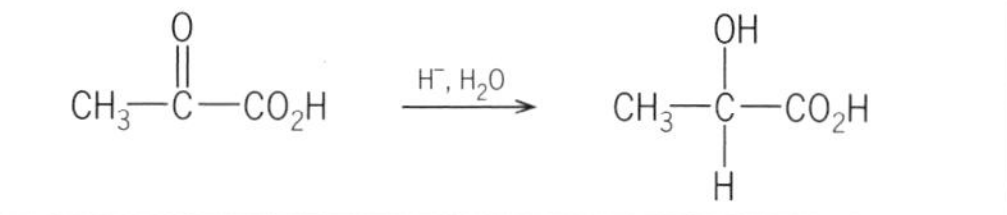

5

a) What functional group appears in both lactic acid and pyruvic acid?

b) What type of alcohol is lactic acid?

c) This reaction could be carried out in the laboratory by the addition of H$^-$ ions. Draw this mechanism.

Glucose can be reduced industrially to give sorbitol ($C_6H_{14}O_6$) which is used by diabetics as a sugar substitute.

6

a) Write a balanced equation for the production of sorbitol from glucose (open-chain form), using [H] to denote the reducing agent.

b) What reagents might be used to make sorbitol from glucose in: **(i)** the laboratory and **(ii)** industry?

Sucrose is a disaccharide formed from glucose and fructose. It is the sweetening agent we are probably all most familiar with – the white sugar of the supermarket shelves. It is a **non-reducing sugar** and so does not give a positive test with Tollen's and Fehling's reagents.

7

Find out about the reaction which forms sucrose.

ALDEHYDES AND KETONES

This chapter covers the aldehydes and ketones, their similarities and differences, and in particular the reactions of their important carbonyl functional group. See the Chapter Map below for a review of the topics in the chapter and shows how they interlink.

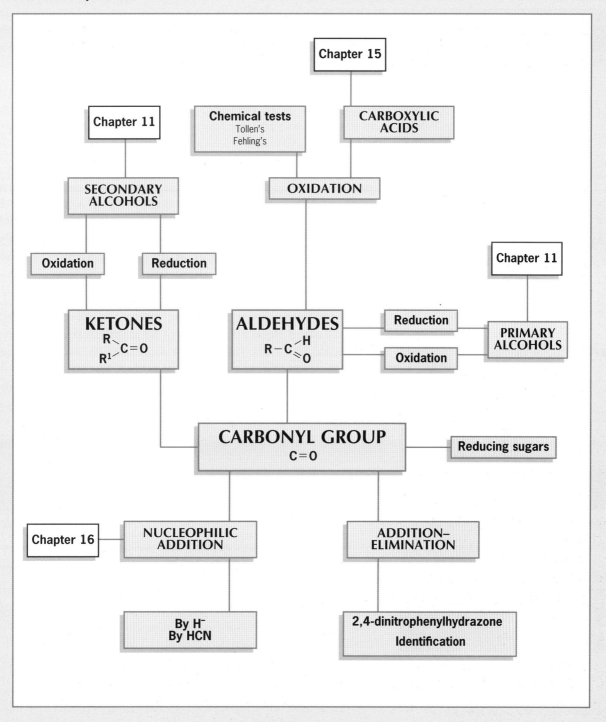

15 Carboxylic acids and pH

It is essential for the chemistry of blood that the pH value of the plasma remains fairly constant. Blood contains complex proteins and simple inorganic ions that act as buffers and together control the plasma's acidity

Fig 15.1 **Vinegar is a 5 per cent solution of ethanoic acid in water. It is acidic because ethanoic acid donates a proton – a hydrogen ion – to a water molecule. The sour taste is due to the presence of aqueous hydrogen ions**

CH_3COONa is an ionic salt and is sometimes written as $CH_3COO^-Na^+$.

BLOOD IS VERY intimately connected with the biochemistry of all our tissues, and they only function correctly while the blood is maintained at pH 7.4. In fact, death is likely to follow if the blood pH departs from this value for any length of time.

Chemical reactions in the blood itself are continually producing acids and alkalis, and these would seriously upset the pH level but for the fact that blood also contains *buffers*. These chemicals resist changes in blood pH and keep its fluctuations within safe limits.

Just as our bodies need a steady pH, so we take steps to control the pH of a wide range of foods and drinks we consume, for their stability as well as for our taste preferences and health. Wines, beers and lagers contain acids such as ethanoic acid and tartaric acid. On the one hand, acidity helps to preserve them, yet too much acid makes them sour and vinegary, so food chemists ensure that the pH strikes the right balance.

When designing new chemical processes, too, industrial chemists often need to find ways to stabilise the pH values of solutions so that they won't significantly change when small amounts of acid or alkali are added. For this they again require buffers: often these are carboxylic acids and their soluble salts, the carboxylates, the subjects of this chapter.

1 WHAT IS AN ACID?

Carboxylic acids are organic chemicals that contain a group of atoms known as the carboxyl group, COOH. Many common chemicals, such as citric acid in lemon juice and ethanoic acid in vinegar, are carboxylic acids and are described as weak acids. So before we go into the chemistry of carboxylic acids, we need to be clear what is meant by the term 'acid' and why chemists talk of 'weak acids' and 'strong acids'.

Chemists knew about the properties of acids long before they understood what makes an acid. In the late 1700s, they believed that oxygen was the essential element in acids. Then in 1810, Humphry Davy disproved this hypothesis when he discovered that hydrochloric acid consists of only hydrogen and chlorine. So, hydrogen was established as the element common to all acids.

One early definition says that an acid is a compound whose molecule has at least one hydrogen atom that can be replaced by a metal atom. For example, hydrochloric acid, HCl(aq), forms sodium chloride, NaCl, when hydrogen is replaced by sodium. In the same way, ethanoic acid, $CH_3COOH(aq)$, is an acid because it forms sodium ethanoate, CH_3COONa. But as theoretical chemistry developed, more sophisticated and generalised definitions of an acid – and a base – were introduced.

Brønsted–Lowry theory

In 1923, the Swedish chemist Johannes Brønsted and the English chemist Thomas Lowry defined acids and bases:

An acid is a proton donor and a base is a proton acceptor.

According to this definition, when an acid reacts with a base, a proton is transferred from the acid to the base.

Lewis acids and bases

Also in 1923, the American chemist Gilbert Lewis advanced an even more generalised theory of acids and bases which involved not protons but electron pairs:

A Lewis acid is any molecule or ion that can accept a pair of electrons, and a Lewis base is any molecule or ion that can donate a pair of electrons.

With this definition, hydrogen is no longer an essential element for an acid.

But in the rest of this chapter, we concentrate on the Brønsted–Lowry theory of acids and bases, and ignore Lewis acids and bases.

2 ACID–BASE REACTIONS

Put simply, an acid–base reaction is one in which an acid is neutralised by a base, or vice versa. During an acid–base reaction, a proton is transferred from the acid to the base. The Brønsted–Lowry theory of acids and bases really focuses on the behaviour of acids and bases in water. The water molecule is **amphoteric**, meaning that it can behave as either an acid or a base (see page 310).

Behaviour of Brønsted–Lowry acids in water

When an acid, HA(aq), is added to water, a proton is transferred to a water molecule:

$$HA(aq) + H_2O(l) \rightleftharpoons H_3O^+(aq) + A^-(aq)$$

In $H_3O^+(aq)$, a single water molecule has formed a dative covalent bond with a hydrogen ion (see page 74). It is called an **aqueous hydrogen ion** or an **oxonium ion**. (The term **hydronium ion** is sometimes used.)

So when, for example, pure nitric acid is added to water, there is an immediate reaction in which a proton is donated from the acid to a water molecule:

$$HNO_3(aq) + H_2O \rightarrow H_3O^+(aq) + NO_3^-(aq)$$

Be careful with the use of the formula HCl. The formula HCl(g) is hydrogen chloride, a colourless gas, and HCl(aq) is hydrochloric acid. HCl without (g) or (aq) does not, strictly speaking, refer to either of the two substances.

Fig 15.3 **The colourless gas hydrogen chloride, HCl(g), is made up of covalent molecules. It dissolves in water to form hydrochloric acid, HCl(aq), which consists of ions. When hydrogen chloride dissolves in water it donates a proton to a water molecule**

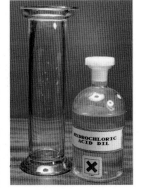

■ See question 1.

> ✔ Remember: A proton remains when a hydrogen atom loses an electron. So a proton is the same as a hydrogen ion, H^+.

> ✔ Note: an **alkali** is just a base which dissolves in water.

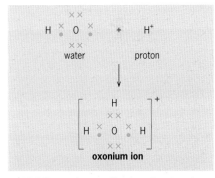

Fig 15.2 **Dot and cross diagram of an oxonium ion, also known as an aqueous hydrogen ion or a hydronium ion**

> ? **A** Write equations to show what happens when:
>
> **(a)** hydrogen chloride dissolves in water,
>
> **(b)** hydrogen iodide dissolves in water.

Behaviour of Brønsted–Lowry bases in water

When a base is added to water, it accepts a proton from the water to form a hydroxide ion. For example, when sodium oxide Na_2O is added to water, it is ionised and the oxide ion O^{2-} accepts a proton from a water molecule to form a hydroxide ion:

$$O^{2-}(s) + H_2O(l) \rightarrow OH^-(aq) + OH^-(aq)$$

The equation has been written with two separate hydroxide ions to emphasise the fact that the oxide ion becomes part of a hydroxide ion when it accepts a proton from a water molecule.

As another example, ammonia, a colourless gas, dissolves in water to form an alkaline solution:

$$NH_3(g) + H_2O(l) \rightleftharpoons NH_4^+(aq) + OH^-(aq)$$

This time, the whole ammonia molecule accepts a proton from a water molecule to form the ammonium ion.

> ✔ Notice that the equation with NH_3 does not have an arrow, but has the symbol for a reversible reaction. There is more about the significance of this symbol in relation to bases in Chapter 29.

Amphoteric nature of water

In water, there is always a very small proportion of $OH^-(aq)$ and of $H^+(aq)$. This is the result of an acid–base reaction between two water molecules:

$$H_2O(l) + H_2O(l) \rightleftharpoons H_3O^+(aq) + OH^-(aq)$$

One water molecule donates a proton and the other accepts a proton. This demonstrates that water can behave both as an acid and as a base, so it is an *amphoteric* compound.

This acid–base reaction can be written in a simpler form as the dissociation of water:

$$H_2O(l) \rightleftharpoons H^+(aq) + OH^-(aq)$$

> ✔ For the rest of the chapter, the symbol $H^+(aq)$ is used to represent an aqueous hydrogen ion rather than $H_3O^+(aq)$.

Dissociation in Brønsted–Lowry acids

When a Brønsted–Lowry acid is put into water, a chemical reaction called **dissociation** or **ionisation** takes place. A covalent bond between an electronegative atom and a hydrogen atom is broken by heterolytic fission, leaving a proton and a negative ion. So, when the gas hydrogen chloride dissolves in water, it dissociates to form a proton or hydrogen ion, and a chloride ion:

$$HCl(g) \rightarrow H^+(aq) + Cl^-(aq)$$

During this reaction, *all* the hydrogen chloride molecules dissociate to aqueous hydrogen ions and chloride ions. The chloride ion is known as the **conjugate base** of hydrochloric acid. This does not mean that the chloride ion *is* a base, but that in theory it could accept a proton. That is, it could *behave* as a base. The conjugate base of any acid is the anion formed after dissociation.

> **?** **B** Write down the equations which show the dissociation of hydrogen bromide and of hydrogen iodide in water.

$$A—H + H_2O \longrightarrow A^- + H_3O^+$$

Fig 15.4 **Dissociation of an acid**

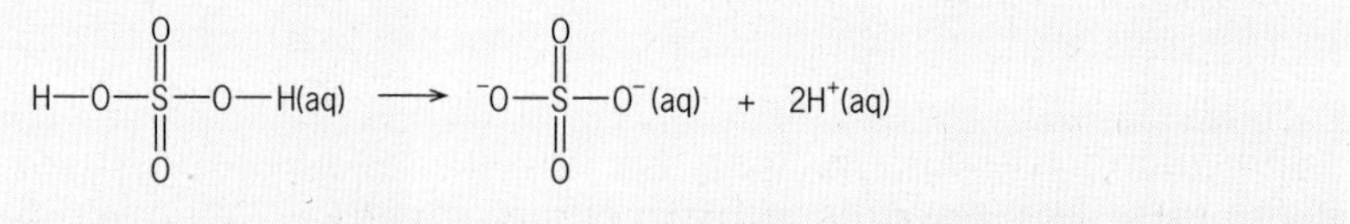

Fig 15.5 **Dissociation of sulphuric acid represented by structural formulas**

In water, sulphuric acid dissociates to form two hydrogen ions per sulphuric acid molecule:

$$H_2SO_4(aq) \rightarrow 2H^+(aq) + SO_4^{2-}(aq)$$

The arrow in the equation indicates that, in water, every sulphuric acid molecule dissociates. Note that the conjugate base of sulphuric acid is the hydrogensulphate ion, HSO_4^-, rather than the sulphate ion, SO_4^{2-} (see Table 15.1).

Conjugate acids

Just as a Brønsted–Lowry acid has a conjugate base, so a Brønsted–Lowry base has a conjugate acid, which is the particle formed once the base has accepted a proton. For example, the conjugate acid of ammonia NH_3 is the ammonium ion NH_4^+, and the conjugate acid of the hydroxide ion OH^- is the water molecule H_2O.

Strong acids

Table 15.1 shows how five common covalently bonded acids dissociate when in water. In each case, almost all the molecules of the acid dissociate to form ions. In fact, we assume that all of the molecules dissociate, and represent the dissociation by an arrow in the equation. Such acids are called **strong acids**, a term meaning that almost all of the acid's molecules dissociate when it is dissolved in water. *Do not confuse a strong acid with a concentrated acid.*

Weak acids

Other acids, such as ethanoic acid, dissolve in water but do not fully dissociate. Only a very small percentage of their molecules may be dissociated at any one time. They are known as **weak acids**. For example, in a solution containing 0.1 mol dm^{-3} of ethanoic acid, only 1.3 per cent of the molecules dissociate. Ethanoic acid is therefore a weak acid. *Do not confuse a weak acid with a dilute acid.* The term weak acid means that only a small proportion of molecules dissociate when the acid is dissolved in water:

$$CH_3COOH(aq) \rightleftharpoons CH_3COO^-(aq) + H^+(aq)$$

Note that the dissociation equation includes the symbol for a reversible reaction instead of an arrow. This indicates that the dissociation of ethanoic acid and the association of the ethanoate ion and the hydrogen ion occur at the same time.

Table 15.1 **Five acids and their dissociations**

Acid		Conjugate base
$HCl(aq)$	$\rightarrow$	$H^+(aq)$ + $Cl^-(aq)$
$HNO_3(aq)$	$\rightarrow$	$H^+(aq)$ + $NO_3^-(aq)$
$H_2SO_4(aq)$	$\rightarrow$	$H^+(aq)$ + $HSO_4^-(aq)$
$HBr(aq)$	$\rightarrow$	$H^+(aq)$ + $Br^-(aq)$
$HI(aq)$	$\rightarrow$	$H^+(aq)$ + $I^-(aq)$

?

C (a) What is the conjugate base of hydrofluoric acid, HF?

(b) What is the conjugate base of water?

(c) What is the conjugate base of the hydrogensulphate ion?

?

D (a) What is the conjugate acid of water?

(b) What is the conjugate acid of the oxide ion, O^{2-}?

(c) What is the conjugate acid of the hydrogensulphate ion?

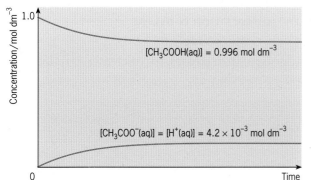

Fig 15.6 **A short time after the ethanoic acid is mixed with water, the concentration of each species remains constant. The concentrations are called equilibrium concentrations. The reaction is in equilibrium because the concentration of each species is constant.**

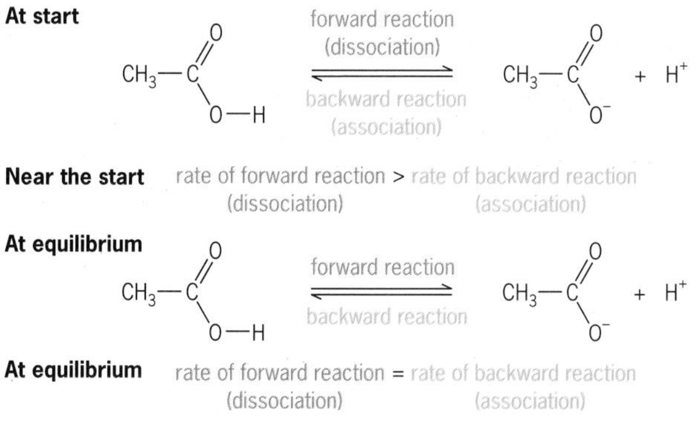

Fig 15.7 **Dissociation and association reactions of ethanoic acid in water**

This is not the whole story, however. Chemical reactions are still taking place and particles are colliding and reacting, but the rate of the forward reaction is matched by the rate of the backward reaction. Note the y (concentration) axis has no scale between 0 and 1.0. This is because on a uniform y-axis scale, the (equal) concentrations of the aqueous hydrogen ion and the ethanoate ion are so small compared with the concentration of the undissociated ethanoic acid, that they would not show as a curve above the x-axis

As in Figs 15.6 and 15.7, once ethanoic acid has dissolved in water, the rate of the dissociation reaction soon reaches that of the association reaction, so that there is no net change in the concentrations of the undissociated ethanoic acid, the ethanoate ion and the hydrogen ion. We say that the reaction reaches a state of **dynamic equilibrium**, where the concentration of each species remains the same.

Acid dissociation constant

> The acid dissociation constant is a modified equilibrium constant. Equilibrium constants are covered on page 336.

Once a weak acid has dissolved in water, it quickly reaches the state of dynamic equilibrium. It is possible to gauge just how weak an acid is by determining the **acid dissociation constant**, K_a. The $_a$ in K_a stands for 'acid'.

A weak acid HA dissociates in water and reaches a state of dynamic equilibrium:

$$HA(aq) \rightleftharpoons H^+(aq) + A^-(aq)$$

The acid dissociation constant is given by:

$$K_a = \frac{[H^+(aq)][A^-(aq)]}{[HA(aq)]}$$

The square brackets represent the concentrations of the various particles measured in mol dm^{-3}. For example, $[H^+(aq)]$ is the concentration of aqueous hydrogen ions in mol dm^{-3}. Note that the concentrations are those at the state of dynamic equilibrium.

The acid dissociation constant for ethanoic acid is:

$$K_a = \frac{[H^+(aq)][CH_3COO^-(aq)]}{[CH_3COOH(aq)]} \qquad \text{Units} = \frac{(\text{mol dm}^{-3})(\text{mol dm}^{-3})}{(\text{mol dm}^{-3})}$$

The smaller the value of the acid dissociation constant, the weaker the acid. Ethanoic acid, CH_3COOH, has a K_a of 1.8×10^{-5} mol dm^{-3}, whereas nitrous acid, HNO_2, has a K_a of 4.5×10^{-4} mol dm^{-3}. Notice that the acid dissociation constant includes a unit. It is not just a numerical value.

See question 2. ■

E (a) Write down the equation to show the dissociation of nitrous acid in water.

(b) Write down an expression for the acid dissociation constant for nitrous acid.

(c) Which is the weaker acid, ethanoic or nitrous?

pK$_a$

The numerical values of K_a for strong acids normally lie in the range from 10^{-1} to 10^2, but for weak acids they are below 10^{-4}. To avoid dealing with the small numbers associated with weak acids, we use pK$_a$. This is its definition:

> All scientific calculators have a key labelled **lg** or **log**. Do not use the key labelled **ln**, which is the natural logarithm.

pK$_a$ is the negative logarithm to base 10 of the acid dissociation constant:

$$pK_a = -\log_{10} K_a$$

Note that as the acid strength decreases, pK$_a$ increases. So a high pK$_a$ value means a very weak acid.

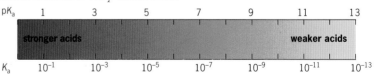

Fig 15.8 **The connection between pK$_a$ and K$_a$**

EXAMPLE

Q The acid dissociation constant for nitrous acid is 4.5×10^{-4} mol dm^{-3}. What is the pK$_a$ value for nitrous acid?

A
$$pK_a = -\log_{10} K_a$$

Substituting the value for K_a gives:

$$pK_a = -\log_{10}(4.5 \times 10^{-4})$$

$$pK_a = 3.3$$

F (a) What is the pK$_a$ value for each of these acids?
(i) Phenol, $K_a = 1.3 \times 10^{-10}$ mol dm^{-3}.
(ii) Butanoic acid. $K_a = 1.5 \times 10^{-5}$ mol dm^{-3}.

(b) Suggest why ethanedioic acid, $(COOH)_2$, has two pK$_a$ values.

Propanedioic acid has two pK_a values, because one molecule can donate two hydrogen ions. The first is donated more easily than the second:

$$HOOCCH_2COOH(aq) \rightleftharpoons HOOCCH_2COO^-(aq) + H^+(aq) \quad pK_a = 2.77$$
$$HOOCCH_2COO^-(aq) \rightleftharpoons {}^-OOCCH_2COO^-(aq) + H^+(aq) \quad pK_a = 5.66$$

Why is sulphuric acid strong and ethanoic acid weak?

The ability of a carboxylic acid, such as ethanoic acid, to donate a hydrogen ion depends on the strength of the O–H bond in the carboxyl group. Likewise, the ability of sulphuric acid to donate a hydrogen ion depends on the strength of its O–H bonds. In simple terms, the stronger the O–H bond(s), that is, the greater the bond energy, the weaker the acid. This is not the whole story, since the stability of the conjugate bases formed is also important.

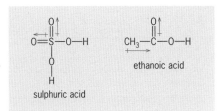

Fig 15.9 The displayed formulas of sulphuric acid and ethanoic acid. The O–H bond in sulphuric acid is very weak compared with the O–H bond in ethanoic acid. The electronegative oxygen atoms in sulphuric acid draw the electron cloud away from the O–H bonds, but this effect is less marked in ethanoic acid. So sulphuric acid is a strong acid and ethanoic acid is a weak acid

Acid		Conjugate base	
chloric(VII) acid	$HClO_4$	ClO_4^-	chlorate(VII) ion
sulphuric acid	H_2SO_4	HSO_4^-	hydrogensulphate ion
hydrogen iodide	HI	I^-	iodide ion
hydrogen bromide	HBr	Br^-	bromide ion
hydrogen chloride	HCl	Cl^-	chloride ion
nitric acid	HNO_3	NO_3^-	nitrate ion
oxonium ion	H_3O^+	H_2O	water
hydrogensulphate ion	HSO_4^-	SO_4^{2-}	sulphate ion
phosphoric(V) acid	H_3PO_4	$H_2PO_4^-$	dihydrogenphosphate(V) ion
hydrogen fluoride	HF	F^-	fluoride ion
nitrous acid	HNO_2	NO_2^-	nitrous ion
ethanoic acid	CH_3COOH	CH_3COO^-	ethanoate ion
carbonic acid	H_2CO_3	HCO_3^-	hydrogencarbonate ion
ammonium ion	NH_4^+	NH_3	ammonia
water	H_2O	OH^-	hydroxide ion
ethanol	C_2H_5OH	$C_2H_5O^-$	ethoxide ion
ammonia	NH_3	NH_2^-	amide ion

increasing acid strength →

increasing base strength →

Table 15.2 The relative strengths of some acids. Chloric(VII) acid is the strongest acid of all. It fully dissociates in water. All acids stronger than H_3O^+ fully dissociate in water. Notice that they include most of the common laboratory acids. Acids that are weaker than water are not usually considered to be acids. Ammonia, for example, is normally classified as a base

?

G (a) What is the connection between the strength of an acid and the strength of its conjugate base?

(b) Explain the difference in acid strength of the hydrogen halides HBr, HCl, HF and HI.
Hint: Think about the bond energy of the bond that must break in order for dissociation to take place.

3 pH

An acid is a proton donor and when it dissolves in water the $H^+(aq)$ concentration increases. That is, the higher the $H^+(aq)$ concentration, the more acidic a solution becomes.

But the problem in measuring hydrogen ion concentration is that for many solutions it is extremely small. For example, the hydrogen ion concentration in wine is only about 5×10^{-4} mol dm^{-3}. In blood, it is even smaller, being about 4×10^{-8} mol dm^{-3}.

In 1909, the Danish chemist Sören Sörensen, working for the brewers Carlsberg, suggested an alternative way to measure the acidity of a solution – the **pH** scale.

The pH scale is constructed from the negative logarithms to base 10 of the [H+(aq)]. Thus, aqueous hydrogen ion concentrations that may differ by, say, a hundred million million, are converted into numbers on a scale which runs from just below 0 to just above 14. Accordingly, the pH of a solution is described by the equation:

$$\mathbf{pH = -log_{10}\,[H^+(aq)]}$$

where the aqueous hydrogen ion concentration is in mol dm^{-3}.

Table 15.3 The relationship between [H+(aq)] and pH

[H+(aq)]/ mol dm^{-3}	pH	Sample solution
10^1	–1	← 1 mol dm^{-3} H_2SO_4
10^0 or 1	0	
10^{-1}	1	
10^{-2}	2	← vinegar
10^{-3}	3	← stomach acid ← wine
10^{-4}	4	
10^{-5}	5	← black coffee
10^{-6}	6	
10^{-7}	7	← pure water
10^{-8}	8	← blood
10^{-9}	9	
10^{-10}	10	
10^{-11}	11	← milk of magnesia
10^{-12}	12	← household ammonia
10^{-13}	13	
10^{-14}	14	← 1 mol dm^{-3} NaOH

■ See questions 3 and 5.

MEASURING THE pH OF A SOLUTION

OUR SENSE OF TASTE is very sensitive to pH, and it provided one of the earliest ways of distinguishing between acids and alkalis. We can detect a sour acidic taste in solutions whose pH values are as high as 5, which corresponds to $H^+(aq)$ concentrations as low as 10^{-5} mol dm^{-3}. The familiar acidic taste of most fruit juices and soft drinks is due to the presence of weak acids which give these drinks a pH value of about 3.

When the pH is below 2, we find the taste distinctly unpleasant and the liquid sufficiently acid to burn the lining of the mouth. In the same way, we can detect alkalis with a pH value of 9 to 10 as they taste bitter. Liquids with higher pH values than this are dangerous to taste and burn the lining of the mouth.

The pH of a solution is measured accurately using a pH meter (Fig 15.10), which converts the difference in electrical potential between two electrodes into a pH reading. (Electrode potentials and electrochemistry are covered in Chapter 26.)

An indicator, such as universal indicator, which gives a range of colour in solutions of different pH values (Fig 15.11), can be used to estimate the pH value of a solution.

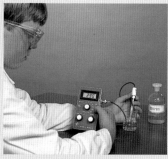

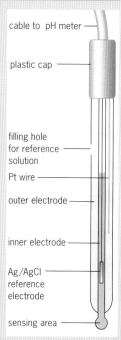

Fig 15.10 **The pH meter. When the probe is dipped into the solution, an electrical potential difference is established between the two electrodes. This potential difference is amplified and converted into a digital pH reading**

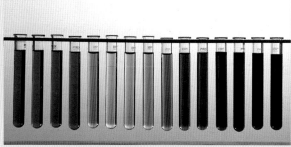

Fig 15.11 **Universal indicator gives a colour that depends on pH**

Fig 15.12 **A commercial kit that gardeners use to test the pH of soil**

See question 3. ■

✔

A negative pH value means that the concentration of aqueous hydrogen ions, [H$^+$(aq)], in mol dm^{-3}, is very high.

Calculating the pH of strong acids

To calculate the pH of a strong acid, substitute the appropriate $H^+(aq)$ concentration in the equation for pH.

> **EXAMPLE**
>
> Q What is the pH of a solution of 1.00 mol dm^{-3} sulphuric acid?
>
> A In water, sulphuric acid is assumed to be fully dissociated because it is a strong acid:
>
> $$H_2SO_4(aq) \rightarrow 2H^+(aq) + SO_4^{2-}(aq)$$
>
> From the equation, every mole of H_2SO_4 gives 2 moles of $H^+(aq)$. The concentration of 1.00 mol dm^{-3} refers to moles of the undissociated H_2SO_4, so the concentration of $H^+(aq)$ must be twice this. Therefore,
>
> $$[H^+(aq)] = 2 \times 1.00 \, \text{mol dm}^{-3} = 2.00 \, \text{mol dm}^{-3}$$
>
> Substituting this value in the equation for pH gives:
>
> $$pH = -\log_{10}[2.00] = -0.693$$

Calculating the pH of weak acids

Ethanoic acid has already been described as a weak acid which reaches a state of dynamic equilibrium when dissolved in water. When this state is reached, the concentration of aqueous hydrogen ions is very low compared with the concentration of the undissociated ethanoic acid. We can calculate the pH of aqueous ethanoic acid provided that we know the numerical value of the acid dissociation constant or the percentage of ethanoic acid molecules that have dissociated.

?

H (a) Calculate the pH of **(i)** $1.00 \, mol \, dm^{-3}$ hydrochloric acid, **(ii)** $1.00 \times 10^{-4} \, mol \, dm^{-3}$ hydrochloric acid and **(iii)** $0.0520 \, mol \, dm^{-3}$ sulphuric acid.

(b) Assuming that in $0.100 \, mol \, dm^{-3}$ nitrous acid, 6.5 per cent of the nitrous acid molecules have dissociated, calculate the pH of $0.100 \, mol \, dm^{-3}$ nitrous acid.

EXAMPLES

Q What is the pH of $0.10 \, mol \, dm^{-3}$ ethanoic acid, given that 1.3 per cent of the ethanoic acid molecules have dissociated?

A In water, ethanoic acid forms an equilibrium mixture very quickly:

$$CH_3COOH(aq) \rightleftharpoons H^+(aq) + CH_3COO^-(aq)$$

The $0.100 \, mol \, dm^{-3}$ is the concentration of CH_3COOH before any has dissociated.

Given that only 1.3 per cent of ethanoic acid molecules dissociate, then the concentration of ethanoic acid that has dissociated must be 1.3 per cent of $0.100 \, mol \, dm^{-3}$, which is $1.3 \times 10^{-3} \, mol \, dm^{-3}$. From the equation, every mole of $CH_3COOH(aq)$ that dissociates gives 1 mole of $H^+(aq)$. So, $[H^+(aq)]$ must be $1.3 \times 10^{-3} \, mol \, dm^{-3}$.

Substituting this value into the equation for pH gives:

$$pH = -\log_{10}(1.3 \times 10^{-3}) = 2.9$$

Q What is the pH of $0.10 \, mol \, dm^{-3}$ ethanoic acid given that the acid dissociation constant, K_a, for ethanoic acid is $1.8 \times 10^{-5} \, mol \, dm^{-3}$?

A Since ethanoic acid is a weak acid, it forms an equilibrium mixture in water:

$$CH_3COOH(aq) \rightleftharpoons CH_3COO^-(aq) + H^+(aq)$$

Therefore, the expression for the acid dissociation constant is:

$$K_a = \frac{[CH_3COO^-(aq)][H^+(aq)]}{[CH_3COOH(aq)]}$$

From the equation, every mole of CH_3COOH that dissociates gives 1 mole of CH_3COO^- and 1 mole of $H^+(aq)$.

So, if $[H^+(aq)]$ at equilibrium is x, then it follows that $[CH_3COO^-(aq)]$ must also be x.

It also follows that $[CH_3COOH(aq)]$ must be $0.10-x$, since some of the ethanoic acid has dissociated.

This can be summarised as follows:

$$CH_3COOH(aq) \rightleftharpoons CH_3COO^-(aq) + H^+(aq)$$
undissociated
ethanoic acid

At start, ie before equilibrium/mol dm^{-3}	0.10	0	0
At equilibrium/mol dm^{-3}	0.10 – x	x	x

These values can be substituted in the equation for the acid dissociation constant. Therefore,

$$1.8 \times 10^{-5} = \frac{x^2}{0.10-x}$$

(The dissociation of water to form $H^+(aq)$ is ignored since its concentration is so small.)

The equation may be simplified by reference to Fig 15.6 on page 311. The concentration of the $H^+(aq)$ is very small compared with that of the undissociated acid, therefore the concentration of the undissociated acid is very nearly 0.10. So we can assume that $(0.10-x)$ is approximately 0.10. Using this assumption, we can write the equation as:

$$1.8 \times 10^{-5} = \frac{x^2}{0.10}$$

which can be rearranged to give:

$$x^2 = 1.8 \times 10^{-6}$$

Therefore:

$$x = \sqrt{(1.8 \times 10^{-6})} = 1.34 \times 10^{-3} \text{ (ignoring sig. figs)}$$

Since x is the $H^+(aq)$ concentration, we can substitute this value of x into the equation for pH:

$$pH = -\log[H^+(aq)]$$
$$= -\log(1.34 \times 10^{-3}) = 2.9$$

Notice that even with the assumption made in the second calculation, the value obtained for the pH is the same as that obtained in the Example before this.

The pH of boiling water

At 298 K, the pH of pure water is 7.00, which is designated neutral on the pH scale. So the concentration of $H^+(aq)$ in pure water is 1.00×10^{-7} mol dm^{-3}. An acid has a pH below 7. That is, the concentration of $H^+(aq)$ is greater than 1.00×10^{-7} mol dm^{-3}.

When a pH meter is placed in boiling pure water, the reading is pH 6.12. So, apparently, boiling water is acidic. But how can it be? In boiling water, the concentration of $H^+(aq)$ has increased, but so has the concentration of the aqueous hydroxide ion. So, there should be no surplus of either type of ion:

$$H_2O(l) \rightleftharpoons H^+(aq) + OH^-(aq)$$

Now, this is the same situation as that in water at 298 K, which is considered to be neutral. The paradox is easy to explain. In boiling water, a greater proportion of water molecules dissociate at any one time, but there is no surplus of hydrogen ions.

?

I What is the $[H^+(aq)]$ and the $[OH^-(aq)]$ in boiling water?

J What is the pH of 0.10 mol dm^{-3} methanoic acid, HCOOH, whose K_a is 1.8×10^{-4} mol dm^{-3}?

4 CARBOXYLIC ACIDS

Carboxylic acids are weak acids. Therefore, they do not fully dissociate when dissolved in water. Many of them will not dissolve in water at all.

Carboxylic acids in nature

Many naturally occurring organic compounds are carboxylic acids. Familiar examples already mentioned are citric acid in citrus fruits and ethanoic acid in vinegar. Three more examples are given in Figs 15.13 to 15.15.

Methanoic acid is the simplest carboxylic acid. Discovered in 1670, it was originally called formic acid, after the Latin word *formicus* for ant, since it is one of the substances responsible for the sting of an ant bite (Fig 15.13).

Fig 15.13 **Two naturally occurring carboxylic acids are ethanedioic acid and lactic acid.** Ethanedioic acid is a poisonous white crystalline solid. As a metal salt, ethanedioic acid is found in rhubarb and sorrel, giving them a sour taste. Lactic acid is formed when lactose found in milk ferments. It gives the sour taste of soured milk products such as yoghurt. It is a preservative, deterring the growth of microorganisms, and is added to many foods, such as confectionery and salad dressings

Fig 15.14 **Methanoic acid, the simplest carboxylic acid, is one of the substances responsible for the irritation caused by an ant bite.** It was once prepared by distilling red ants

Fig 15.15 **Benzoic acid is an aromatic carboxylic acid which is found in raspberries and in some tree barks. It is used as a preservative and an antioxidant in numerous foods, including soft drinks, pickles, salad dressings and fruit products**

The carboxyl group

A carboxylic acid contains the carboxyl group, COOH, which you may see written as CO_2H. The carboxyl group contains a carbonyl bond C=O, and a hydroxyl bond O–H. Each bond is attached to the same carbon atom. This arrangement modifies the characteristic behaviour of both the carbonyl bond and the hydroxyl bond, which is why the carboxyl group is considered a functional group in its own right.

Naming carboxylic acids

Carboxylic acids are named by adding the suffix *oic acid* to the carbon chain (Fig 15.17). Unlike many functional groups, the carboxyl group contains one of the carbon atoms of the chain. The oic acid group is almost always on the number 1 carbon atom, so this carbon atom rarely has to be given any other position number.

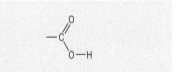

Fig 15.16 **The carboxyl group**

■ See question 6.

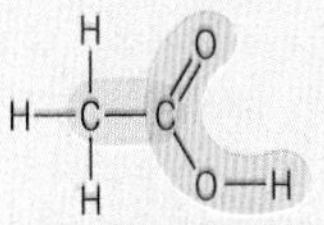

Fig 15.17 **The derivation of the name ethanoic acid**

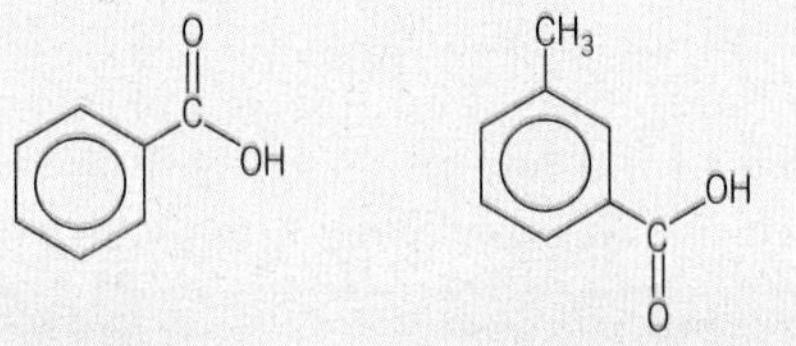

ethanoic acid

benzoic acid

3–methylbenzoic acid

CH_3CH_2COOH
propanoic acid

$CH_3CHOHCOOH$
2-hydroxypropanoic acid

$HOOCCH_2COOH$
propane-1,3-dioic acid

$ClCH_2COOH$
chloroethanoic acid

Fig 15.18 **Six carboxylic acids and their systematic names**

K (a) What is the systematic name of each of the following carboxylic acids?
(i) $CH_3CH_2CH_2CH_2COOH$
(ii) $CH_3CH_2CH_2COOH$
(iii) $HOOCCH_2CH_2CH_2COOH$

(b) Draw the structural formula of each of the following carboxylic acids.
(i) 3-chloropropanoic acid
(ii) 3-chlorobenzoic acid
(iii) 4-methylbenzoic acid
(iv) benzene-1,4-dicarboxylic acid

Physical properties of carboxylic acids

Carboxylic acids are either solids or liquids at room temperature (Table 15.4).

Table 15.4 **Melting and boiling points of six carboxylic acids**

Acid	Formula	Melting point/°C	Boiling point/°C
methanoic acid	HCOOH	8.4	110.5
ethanoic acid	CH_3COOH	16.6	118
propanoic acid	CH_3CH_2COOH	−22	141
butanoic acid	$CH_3CH_2CH_2COOH$	−5	163
ethanedioic acid	$(COOH)_2$	187	decomposes
benzoic acid	C_6H_5COOH	122	249

The melting points of methanoic acid and ethanoic acid are quite high, and so it is not unusual in cold weather for a bottle of concentrated ethanoic acid to be solid. In methanoic acid and ethanoic acid, the intermolecular forces are predominantly hydrogen bonds. But as the carbon chain gets longer, there is also a considerable contribution from induced dipole–induced dipole attractions.

L (a) Methanoic acid, ethanoic acid and propanoic acid are members of a homologous series. What is the general formula for this homologous series?

(b) (i) Predict the boiling point of pentanoic acid.
(ii) Explain why it is difficult to predict the melting point of pentanoic acid.

5 ACIDIC NATURE OF THE CARBOXYL GROUP

As mentioned already, carboxylic acids are weak acids, a property due to the heterolytic fission of the hydroxyl bond in the COOH group (Fig 15.19).

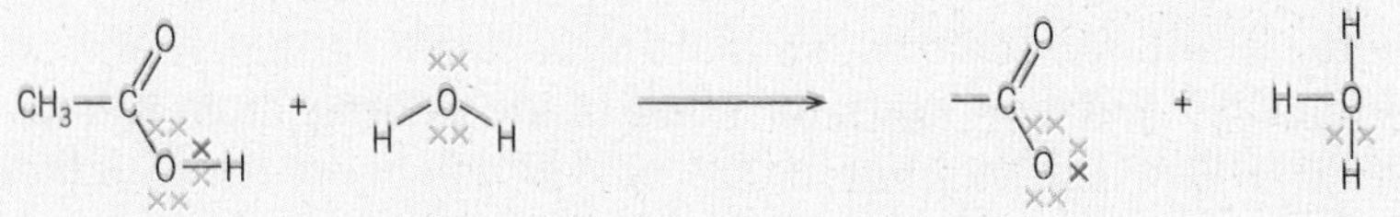

Fig 15.19 **Dissociation of the carboxyl group involves the heterolytic fission of the O–H bond and the subsequent transfer of a hydrogen ion (a proton) to a water molecule**

A carboxylic acid that can dissolve in water forms a weakly acidic solution in water. Where a carboxylic acid cannot dissolve in water, it is impossible for any of its molecules to donate a hydrogen ion to a water molecule, and so the water remains neutral. Nevertheless, insoluble carboxylic acids *are* acids, because they will react with bases, such as aqueous sodium hydroxide.

Acidity of substituted acids

On page 312, we described how the acid dissociation constant can be used to measure the strength of an acid. An acid whose K_a is small is a weak acid. So, it hardly dissociates when it is put in water and forms an equilibrium mixture. Ethanoic acid has a K_a of 1.8×10^{-5} mol dm^{-3}, but the K_a of other carboxylic acids varies according to the nature of the carbon chain and to any functional groups in the carboxylic acid molecule.

The acidic behaviour of amino acids, which contain the carboxyl group, is covered on page 360.

Table 15.5 **K_a values of seven carboxylic acids**

Carboxylic acid	Formula	Acid dissociation constant, K_a/mol dm^{-3}	pK$_a$
methanoic acid	HCOOH	1.77×10^{-4}	3.75
ethanoic acid	CH$_3$COOH	1.74×10^{-5}	4.76
propanoic acid	CH$_3$CH$_2$COOH	1.35×10^{-5}	4.87
chloroethanoic acid	ClCH$_2$COOH	1.41×10^{-3}	2.85
dichloroethanoic acid	Cl$_2$CHCOOH	5.62×10^{-2}	1.25
trichloroethanoic	CCl$_3$COOH	2.19×10^{-1}	0.66
benzoic acid	C$_6$H$_5$COOH	5.37×10^{-7}	6.27

✔ pK$_a$ values are easier to compare, since they are not very small numbers expressed as negative powers of ten.

Two factors are used to explain the relative strengths of carboxylic acids. One concerns the strength of the O–H bond being broken, and the other relates to the stability of the conjugate base, the carboxylate anion, that is formed.

To compare the acids in Table 15.5, start with methanoic acid and treat it as the standard. Ethanoic acid has a higher pK$_a$, so it is a weaker acid than methanoic acid. This is because, compared with the hydrogen atom, the methyl group tends to push electron density towards the carbonyl group, in what is called the inductive effect. This effect strengthens the O–H bond and, at the same time, makes the ethanoate ion less stable than the methanoate ion (Fig 15.20).

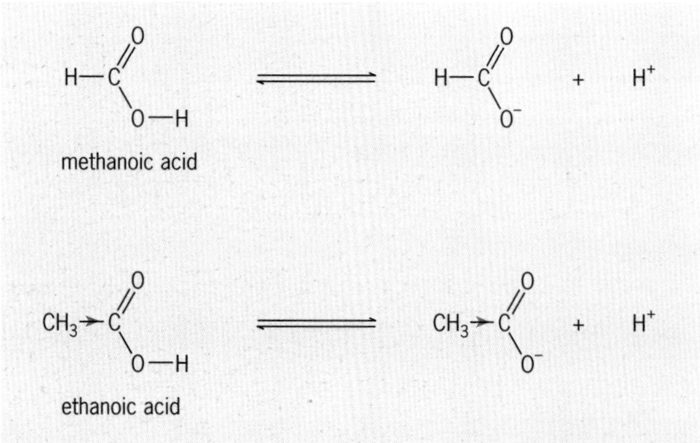

Fig 15.20 **Relative acidities of methanoic acid and ethanoic acid. The positive inductive (electron pushing) effect in ethanoic acid is represented by the arrowhead on the C–C bond. This destabilises the ethanoate ion and strengthens the O–H bond, making ethanoic acid a weaker acid than methanoic acid**

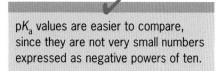

methanoic acid

ethanoic acid

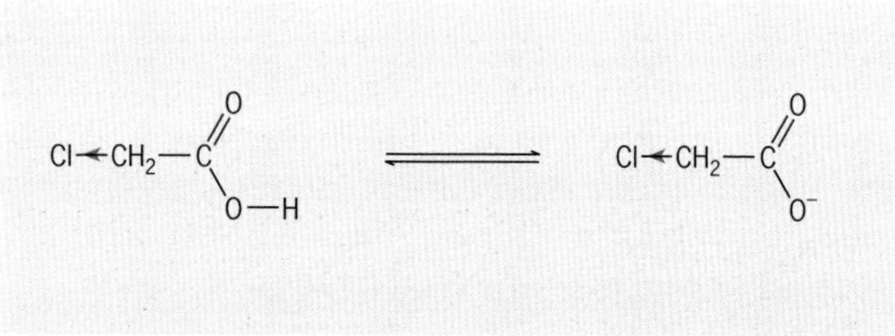

Fig 15.21 **The highly electronegative chlorine atom withdraws electrons from the carboxyl group, thereby weakening the O–H bond and making the chloroethanoate ion more stable than the ethanoate ion. So chloroethanoic acid is a stronger acid than ethanoic acid. The more chlorine atoms in the substituted ethanoic acid molecule, the greater the electron withdrawal effect and thus the stronger the acid**

Other carboxylic acids can now be compared, using ethanoic acid as the standard. Propanoic acid is a weaker acid than ethanoic acid because the ethyl group tends to push electron density just a little more towards the carboxyl group than the methyl group. In the case of the chloroethanoic acids, the effect of the chlorine atom is to pull electron density away from the carboxyl group, hence the O–H bond is weaker and the carboxylate ion more stable (Fig 15.21).

Trifluoroethanoic acid

Trifluoroethanoic acid is a very strong carboxylic acid, because it contains the most electronegative element of all. The three fluorine atoms withdraw electron density from the carboxyl group, thereby promoting the dissociation into a proton and the carboxylate ion. The carboxylate ion is stabilised by electron density withdrawal by the fluorine process.

There has been concern that trifluoroethanoic acid is an atmospheric pollutant. It forms during the breakdown of certain hydrochlorofluorocarbons, HCFCs, such as $CHCl_2CF_3$, in the upper atmosphere. The decomposition products are water soluble, so that the acid solution will be 'rained out' of the atmosphere and can only add to the problems of acid rain.

✓ Chlorine is a highly electronegative atom and so tends to attract the shared pair of electrons in a covalent bond. There is more information on electronegativity on pages 83 and 84.

?

M (a) Which of the following halogenoethanoic acids is the strongest acid: bromoethanoic acid, chloroethanoic acid, fluoroethanoic acid or iodoethanoic acid? Explain why it is.

(b) Which is the stronger acid, trifluoroethanoic acid or trichloroethanoic acid? Explain why.

6 ACID REACTIONS OF CARBOXYLIC ACIDS

The typical reactions of aqueous acids are due to the presence of the aqueous hydrogen ion. Since carboxylic acids are weak acids, such reactions are much slower than they are with strong acids, such as sulphuric acid.

The effect of concentration on reaction rate is described in Chapter 27.

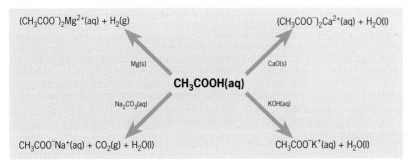

$(CH_3COO^-)_2Mg^{2+}(aq) + H_2(g)$

$(CH_3COO^-)_2Ca^{2+}(aq) + H_2O(l)$

Mg(s)

CaO(s)

CH₃COOH(aq)

Na₂CO₃(aq)

KOH(aq)

$CH_3COO^-Na^+(aq) + CO_2(g) + H_2O(l)$

$CH_3COO^-K^+(aq) + H_2O(l)$

Fig 15.22 **Acidic reactions of ethanoic acid**

As Fig 15.22 shows, the acidic reactions of ethanoic acid always form the ethanoate ion.

Reaction of carboxylic acids with alkalis

Carboxylic acids such as ethanoic acid can be neutralised by an alkali such as aqueous sodium hydroxide:

$$CH_3COOH(aq) + NaOH(aq) \rightarrow CH_3COO^-Na^+(aq) + H_2O(l)$$

This reaction is often carried out in the laboratory as a titration. An aqueous solution of the acid is added from a burette to a known volume of the alkali. At neutralisation, an indicator changes colour.

Titration curves

The changes in pH can be monitored at regular intervals as an alkali is added to an acid. The pH can then be plotted against the volume of alkali added, to obtain a graph known as a **titration curve**.

Fig 15.23 **In titration, an alkali is added dropwise from a graduated burette to an acid of known volume and concentration and which contains an indicator. The addition continues until one drop changes the colour of the indicator, signalling that the alkali has just neutralised the acid. Often, it is preferable to reverse the procedure, adding the acid to the alkali**

See question 7. ■ Fig 15.24 is such a curve for the addition of aqueous sodium hydroxide to ethanoic acid.

Note that, as the alkali is added, the pH at first changes only slightly as the buffer solution is formed (see page **323**). Then, near the point of neutralisation, it shoots up. With the addition of more alkali, it quickly levels off. The exact neutralisation point, or **equivalence point**, can be estimated as the midpoint of the near-vertical portion of the graph, that is, where there is a large change of pH for a very small addition of alkali. This is why you have add the alkali one drop at a time when you are close to the end-point in a titration.

There are four types of titration curve (Figs 15.24 to 15.27), depending on whether strong or weak acids and bases are used.

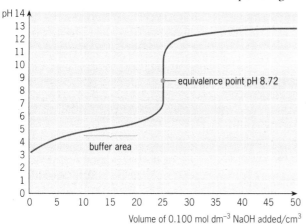

Fig 15.24 **The titration curve of a strong base, NaOH(aq), against a weak acid, CH₃COOH(aq). This titration used 0.100 mol dm⁻³ NaOH with 25.0 cm³ of 0.100 mol dm⁻³ CH₃COOH**

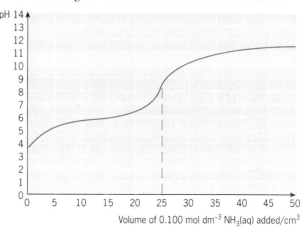

Fig 15.25 **The titration curve of a weak base, NH₃(aq), against a weak acid, CH₃COOH(aq). This titration used 0.100 mol dm⁻³ NH₃(aq) with 25.0 cm³ of 0.100 mol dm⁻³ CH₃COOH. Note that the pH changes gradually over almost the entire titration with no very sudden change in the pH at neutralisation. It is impossible to determine the exact end-point in this type of titration**

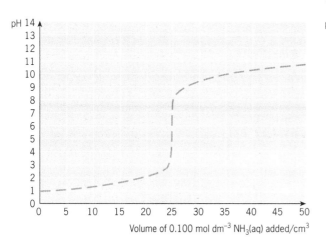

Fig 15.26 **The titration curve of a weak base, NH₃(aq), against a strong acid, HCl(aq). This titration used 0.100 mol dm⁻³ NH₃(aq) with 25.0 cm³ of 0.100 mol dm⁻³ HCl(aq). Note that as the alkali is added, the pH hardly changes until neutralisation is close, when it shoots up from pH 2 to pH 7.5. Thereafter, the pH gradually levels off**

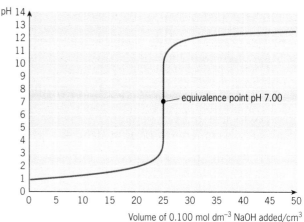

Fig 15.27 **The titration curve of a strong base, NaOH(aq), against a strong acid, HCl(aq). This titration used 0.100 mol dm⁻³ NaOH with 25.0 cm³ of 0.100 mol dm⁻³ HCl(aq). Note again that as the alkali is added, the pH hardly changes until neutralisation is close, when it shoots up**

An indicator is chosen which changes colour within the pH range of the vertical portion of the titration curve. But as the graph in Fig 15.25 shows, when a weak acid is titrated with a weak base, there is no sudden change in pH. This makes it very difficult to estimate the equivalence point, since any indicator changes colour within a range of pH values.

See questions 1, 5, 6 and 8. ■

Indicators

The approximate pH value of a solution can be determined using an indicator solution, or indicator paper, and comparing the colour obtained against a colour chart.

An **indicator** is a substance that changes colour when placed in an alkaline or acidic solution. The change of colour is because of changes in the complex organic structure of the indicator molecule which affect the absorption of visible light by the molecule (see Chapter 28).

Litmus, a common indicator, is a natural product extracted from a lichen, while methyl orange, another common indicator, is a synthetic organic molecule known as an azo dye.

Fig 15.28 **The colour of some flowers depends on the pH of the soil as shown by these hydrangeas which are pink in acid soil and blue in alkaline soil**

Indicators are often weak acids, and so in aqueous solutions they dissociate to a hydrogen ion and the conjugate base. It is convenient to use the simplified formula HIn for an indicator, where In stands for the conjugate base. In aqueous solution, the indicator dissociates:

$$HIn(aq) \rightleftharpoons H^+(aq) + In^-(aq)$$

Normally, the indicator, HIn, has one colour and the conjugate base, In^-, has another. In the case of litmus, HIn is red and In^- is blue.

In an acidic solution (one with an excess of aqueous hydrogen ions), the position of the equilibrium shifts to the left to minimise the effect of the increase of hydrogen ions. So, as the concentration of HIn increases, the solution takes on the colour of the HIn molecule, which for litmus is red. This is an example of Le Chatelier's principle (see Chapters 16 and 29).

When an indicator is added to an alkaline solution, the position of equilibrium moves to the right, because $H^+(aq)$ reacts with the alkali. Hence, there is a large concentration of In^- and the solution takes on the colour of this species.

The pH values for these colour changes vary with different indicators, as shown in Table 15.6.

Table 15.6 **The main properties of eight widely used indicators**

Indicator	pK_a	Effective pH range	Colour of acid form	Colour of base form
methyl violet	1.6	0.0–3.0	yellow	violet
methyl orange	3.2	2.1–4.4	red	yellow
bromocresol green	4.8	4.0–5.6	yellow	blue
methyl red	5.2	4.2–6.2	red	yellow
bromothymol blue	6.9	6.0–7.8	yellow	blue
thymol blue	8.7	7.9–9.4	yellow	blue
phenolphthalein	See **O**	8.3–10.0	colourless	magenta
thymolphthalein	See **O**	9.3–10.5	colourless	blue

To be useful in titration, an indicator must change colour within the almost vertical part of the titration curve. Almost all the indicators in Table 15.6 will show the end point of a titration between a strong acid and a strong alkali. However, with a weak acid and a strong base, an indicator such as phenolphthalein should be used.

?

N Write down an expression for the K_a of an indicator.

■ See questions 6 and 8.

?

O **(a)** Name an indicator suitable for the titration of a strong acid with a weak base.

(b) Estimate the pK_a of phenolphthalein and of thymolphthalein (see Table 15.6).

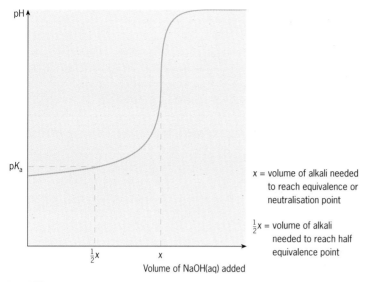

Fig 15.29 **Measuring the pK$_a$ of a weak acid from its titration curve**

x = volume of alkali needed to reach equivalence or neutralisation point

$\frac{1}{2}x$ = volume of alkali needed to reach half equivalence point

Volume of NaOH(aq) added

Determining pK$_a$ from a titration curve

The determination of the K_a of a weak acid can be difficult. However, its pK$_a$ can be easily estimated by analysis of its titration curve. The pK$_a$ is the pH value at the half-equivalence point, that is, the point at which only half of the volume of alkali needed to reach the equivalence point has been added.

The reason for this is that, at the half-equivalence point, the concentration of the conjugate base, A$^-$, and that of the undissociated acid, HA, are almost equal. Therefore, they cancel out in the expression for K_a:

$$K_a = \frac{[\text{H+(aq)}][\text{A}^-\text{(aq)}]}{[\text{HA(aq)}]}$$

So: $K_a = [\text{H}^+\text{(aq)}]$ and pK$_a$ = pH.

Titration curves for diprotic acids

See question 8. ■

In a **monoprotic acid**, such as ethanoic acid, an acid molecule can donate only one proton to water. In a **diprotic acid**, such as ethanedioic acid, an acid molecule can donate two protons to water. Thus ethanedioic acid has two K_a values, designated K_{a1} and K_{a2}. Their significance is shown in Fig 15.30, where K_{a1} refers to equilibrium 1 and K_{a2} to equilibrium 2. The titration curve for a diprotic weak acid has two equivalence points (Fig 15.31).

?

P Write expressions for K_{a1} and K_{a2} for ethanedioic acid.

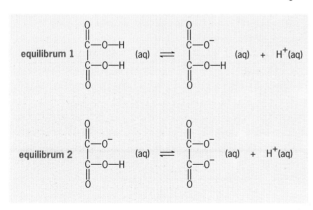

Fig 15.30 **The dissociation of ethanedioic acid**

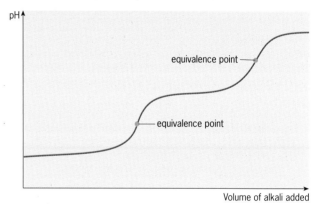

Fig 15.31 **The titration curve of a diprotic weak acid against a strong alkali. Note that there are two equivalence points**

Phosphoric(V) acid

Phosphoric acid has a similar structure to that of a carboxylic acid, but it is a **triprotic acid**, so a molecule of it can donate three protons to water. Phosphoric(V) acid is added to some soft drinks.

Phosphoric(v) acid undergoes stepwise dissociation:

$$H_3PO_4(aq) \rightleftharpoons H^+(aq) + H_2PO_4^-(aq)$$

$$H_2PO_4^-(aq) \rightleftharpoons H^+(aq) + HPO_4^{2-}(aq)$$

$$HPO_4^{2-}(aq) \rightleftharpoons H^+(aq) + PO_4^{3-}(aq)$$

Fig 15.32 **This and other soft drinks contain phosphoric(V) acid**

Each dissociation has its own K_a value. These values are markedly different and, despite the overlap in Fig 15.34, we assume that the first dissociation is complete before the second starts. Thus, at any pH value, no more than two species are present. For example, at pH 1, only $H_3PO_4(aq)$ and $H_2PO_4^-(aq)$ are present.

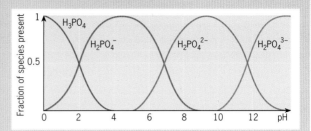

Fig 15.33 **The structure of phosphoric(V) acid. All three hydroxyl bonds can dissociate to form hydrogen ions (protons)**

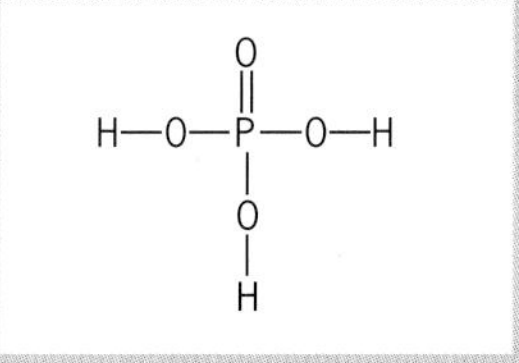

Fig 15.34 **This distribution diagram for phosphoric(V) acid shows the fraction of each species present at different pH values. Note that, at any pH value, there is always one species present and often two**

Buffer solutions

A **buffer solution** resists changes in its pH when a small amount of either acid or alkali is added to it. A buffer solution is therefore used to control the pH of another solution to which a small amount of either acid or alkali is to be added. A typical buffer solution is a mixture of either a weak acid and its conjugate base, or a weak base and its conjugate acid. For example, aqueous solutions of a carboxylic acid and its sodium or potassium salt will act as a buffer.

The chemical processes that take place in a solution containing weak acid HA and its sodium salt NaA, will produce large concentrations of A^- and HA:

$$HA(aq) \rightleftharpoons A^-(aq) + H^+(aq)$$

This equilibrium lies almost entirely on the left. So, we can assume that the concentration of HA at equilibrium is that of undissociated HA. The sodium salt completely ionises in water, forming $A^-(aq)$. Notice that this process is represented by a right-pointing arrow:

$$NaA(aq) \rightarrow A^-(aq) + Na^+(aq)$$

We can therefore assume that a solution consisting of, for example, $0.100\ \text{mol dm}^{-3}$ ethanoic acid and $0.500\ \text{mol dm}^{-3}$ sodium ethanoate contains $0.100\ \text{mol dm}^{-3}$ of undissociated acid, CH_3COOH, and $0.500\ \text{mol dm}^{-3}$ of ethanoate ion, CH_3COO^-.

What happens when an acid is added to a buffer solution

When acid is added to a buffer solution, the extra H^+ react with the conjugate base present, A^-, to produce undissociated acid, HA. This is an example of Le Chatelier's principle, since the equilibrium of the weak acid moves to the left to minimise the effect of the increase in the $H^+(aq)$ concentration. Since most of the extra $H^+(aq)$ added is converted to undissociated HA, the pH hardly decreases.

What happens when hydroxide ions are added to a buffer solution

When extra alkali is added to a buffer solution, the extra OH^- react with the H^+ present to form water:

$$H^+(aq) + OH^-(aq) \rightarrow H_2O(l)$$

Extra H^+ ions are provided by more of the weak acid dissociating to maintain the equilibrium between HA(aq), $A^-(aq)$ and $H^+(aq)$. The overall buffering action can be represented by:

$$HA(aq) + OH^-(aq) \rightarrow H_2O(l) + A^-(aq)$$

Q The pH of a soft drink containing phosphoric acid is 4.3. What species are present in the drink?

For more on the way that a weak base and its conjugate acid together act as a buffer, see Chapter 29.

R A buffer solution is $0.750\ \text{mol dm}^{-3}$ in propanoic acid and $0.350\ \text{mol dm}^{-3}$ in sodium propanoate. What is the approximate concentration in the buffer solution of undissociated propanoic acid and of propanoate ions?

There is more information on Le Chatelier's principle on page 338 and in Chapter 29.

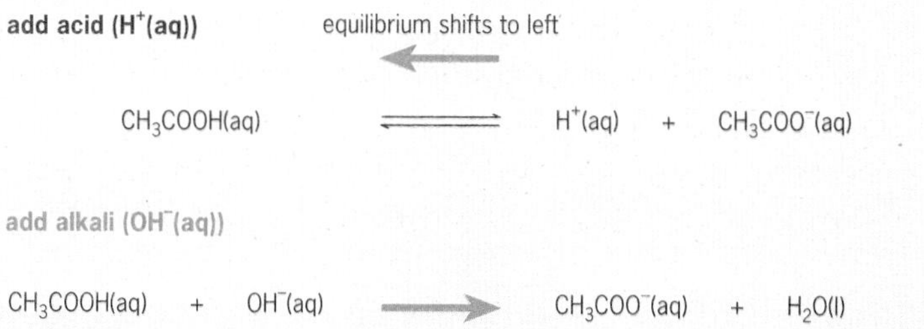

add acid (H⁺(aq))   equilibrium shifts to left

$$CH_3COOH(aq) \rightleftharpoons H^+(aq) + CH_3COO^-(aq)$$

add alkali (OH⁻(aq))

See questions 2, 5, 6 and 9. ■

$$CH_3COOH(aq) + OH^-(aq) \longrightarrow CH_3COO^-(aq) + H_2O(l)$$

Fig 15.35 **A summary of the buffering action of a mixture of sodium ethanoate and ethanoic acid**

Calculating the pH of a buffer solution

Buffer solutions with different pH values can be prepared by changing the relative proportions of HA(aq) and A⁻(aq). It is easy to calculate the pH of a buffer solution provided the K_a of the weak acid and the concentrations of the weak acid and its conjugate base are known.

See questions 4, 5 and 9. ■

EXAMPLE

Q A buffer solution is 0.10 mol dm⁻³ ethanoic acid and 0.20 mol dm⁻³ sodium ethanoate. Calculate its pH.

A Let x be the concentration of the H⁺(aq). We then have:

$$CH_3COOH(aq) \rightleftharpoons CH_3COO^-(aq) + H^+(aq)$$

At start/mol dm⁻³	0.10	0.20	0
At equilibrium/mol dm⁻³	(0.10 – x)	(0.20 + x)	x

We can assume that x is very small compared with 0.10 and 0.20, since ethanoic acid is a weak acid. Therefore, at equilibrium:

$$[CH_3COOH(aq)] = 0.10 \text{ mol dm}^{-3}$$

$$[CH_3COO^-(aq)] = 0.20 \text{ mol dm}^{-3}$$

Substituting these values into the expression for the K_a for ethanoic acid:

$$K_a = \frac{[CH_3COO^-][H^+]}{[CH_3COOH]} = \frac{0.20 \times x}{0.10} = 2x$$

Now: $K_a = 1.8 \times 10^{-5}$

So: $x = 9.0 \times 10^{-6}$ mol dm⁻³

$$pH = -\log_{10}[H^+(aq)]$$

$$= -\log_{10}(9.0 \times 10^{-6}) = 5.0$$

The pH of the buffer solution is therefore 5.0 (to 2 sig. figs).

BUFFERING IN BLOOD

TO REMAIN HEALTHY, the acid–base balance of our blood has to be maintained at a constant pH of 7.4. If, for instance, the blood were to become acidic and this value dropped (as it does in a medical condition called acidosis), we would have to breathe rapidly to expel more of the acidic gas carbon dioxide. But the main mechanism for maintaining pH at 7.4 is the buffering action of several conjugate acid/base pairs – including $H_2CO_3(aq)$ and $HCO_3^-(aq)$, and $H_2PO_4^-(aq)$ and $HPO_4^{2-}(aq)$ – together with the buffering action of plasma proteins and haemoglobin. The action of the proteins is due to the carboxyl and amino groups in the side-chains of some of the amino acids that make up proteins. The concentrations of $H_2PO_4^-(aq)$ and $HPO_4^{2-}(aq)$ are too low for this conjugate acid/base pair to have a large buffering effect.

It is the equilibrium between carbon dioxide, carbonic acid, hydrogen carbonate ion and carbonate ion that acts as the most important buffering system in blood plasma:

$$H_2CO_3(aq) \rightleftharpoons HCO_3^-(aq) + H^+(aq)$$

When the pH of blood decreases, the concentration of H⁺(aq) increases and the position of equilibrium shifts to the left to minimise this increase. The carbonic acid concentration does not rise indefinitely, since this too is in equilibrium with carbon dioxide and water, and so the concentration of dissolved carbon dioxide increases:

$$H_2CO_3(aq) \rightleftharpoons CO_2(aq) + H_2O(l)$$

Dissolved carbon dioxide is removed from blood by gas exchange in the lungs:

$$CO_2(aq) \rightleftharpoons CO_2(g)$$

When the pH of blood begins to rise, the $H_2CO_3(aq)/$HCO$_3^-$(aq) equilibrium shifts to the right to produce more $H^+(aq)$.

Strenuous exercise increases the metabolic rate, producing more carbon dioxide in tissue respiration. Representing the overall oxidation of glucose:

$$C_6H_{12}O_6(aq) + 6O_2(aq) \rightarrow 6CO_2(aq) + 6H_2O(l)$$

Therefore, the concentration of dissolved carbon dioxide in the blood starts to increase and the net effect tends to raise the blood pH. However, this effect is counteracted by an increase in breathing rate, to speed up gas exchange and thereby reduce the concentration of dissolved carbon dioxide. The blood pH therefore does not increase.

Fig 15.36 **Strenuous sport generates acidic blood which the body's buffer system counteracts**

7 CARBOXYLATES

Carboxylates are the salts of a carboxylic acid. They contain the carboxylate anion (Fig 15.37).

Measurements have established that both the carbon–oxygen bonds in the carboxyl group have the same length, which is longer than the typical C=O bond but shorter than the typical C–O bond. The reason they are not different lengths is that the negative charge on the anion is delocalised and does not reside on either of the two oxygen atoms. Fig 15.38 shows an alternative way of describing the ethanoate ion.

Fig 15.37 **The structure of the carboxylate ion**

Fig 15.38 **An alternative way of representing the carboxylate ion, which shows the delocalised nature of the ion. The curved line indicates that the electron is somewhere between the two oxygen atoms**

S What happens to the concentration of undissolved carbon dioxide if the pH of blood rises?

Delocalised electrons are covered in more detail on page 272.

T (a) Suggest why sodium benzoate has a greater solubility in cold water than benzoic acid.

(b) Suggest why it is important for food preservatives, such as sodium benzoate, to be soluble in water.

PROPERTIES AND USES OF CARBOXYLATES

MOST SODIUM AND POTASSIUM carboxylates are soluble in water. How soluble they are depends on the length of the carbon chain of the carboxylate ion and decreases as the chain gets longer.

Because they are soluble, carboxylates are widely used in the food industry, added to foods as preservatives and as acid regulators (buffers). As well as carboxylates, the food industry uses carboxylic acids, and Table 15.7 summarises these applications. You can probably identify some of them in processed foods by their E numbers.

Table 15.7 **Carboxylic acids and carboxylates as food additives**

Name	E number	Use
sorbic acid	E200	Occurs naturally in some fruits but is also made synthetically. Used as a preservative in such foods as soft drinks, cakes and frozen pizzas
sodium sorbate	E201 ⎫	
potassium sorbate	E202 ⎬	Preservatives
calcium sorbate	E203 ⎭	
benzoic acid	E210	Occurs naturally in cherry bark, raspberries and tea but normally made synthetically. Used as a preservative and as an antioxidant in fruit products, soft drinks, pickles and salad dressings
sodium benzoate	E212 ⎫	
potassium benzoate	E213 ⎬	Preservatives
calcium benzoate	E214 ⎭	
ethanoic acid	E260	Vinegar
sodium ethanoate	E281 ⎫	
calcium ethanoate	E282 ⎬	Preservatives
potassium ethanoate	E283 ⎭	
lactic acid	E270	Found naturally in soured milk and yoghurt, it acts as a preservative and a flavouring. Used in biscuits, confectionery and cakes
propanoic acid	E280	Preservative in baked foods
potassium lactate	E326	Acid regulator

8 PREPARATION OF CARBOXYLIC ACIDS

Oxidation of primary alcohols

The oxidation of primary alcohols is covered in more detail on page 237.

Carboxylic acids can be prepared by the oxidation of primary alcohols. For example, ethanol can be oxidised to give ethanoic acid, by heating under reflux either acidified potassium dichromate(VI) or acidified potassium manganate(VII):

$$CH_3CH_2OH + 2[O] \rightarrow CH_3COOH + H_2O$$

Hydrolysis of esters

When an ester is refluxed with either dilute acid or dilute alkali, the ester is hydrolysed to give the carboxylic acid or the carboxylate ion. For example, ethyl ethanoate can be hydrolysed to give ethanoic acid (with acid hydrolysis) or sodium ethanoate (with aqueous sodium hydroxide):

$$CH_3COOCH_2CH_3 + H_2O \underset{\text{acid hydrolysis}}{\rightleftharpoons} CH_3COOH + CH_3CH_2OH$$

There is more information on the hydrolysis of esters on page 342.

$$CH_3COOCH_2CH_3 + NaOH \xrightarrow{\substack{\text{alkaline} \\ \text{hydrolysis}}} CH_3COO^-Na^+ + CH_3CH_2OH$$

The sodium ethanoate can be converted to ethanoic acid by reaction with dilute hydrochloric acid.

Hydrolysis of amides

Amides can be hydrolysed in the same way as esters. Again, there is the opportunity to use either acid- or base-catalysed hydrolysis. For example, ethanamide, CH_3CONH_2, can be hydrolysed to give ethanoic acid and ammonium ion with acid hydrolysis, and ethanoate ion and ammonia with alkaline hydrolysis:

$$CH_3CONH_2 + H_2O + HCl \xrightarrow{\text{acid hydrolysis}} CH_3COOH + NH_4Cl$$

$$CH_3CONH_2 + NaOH \xrightarrow{\substack{\text{alkaline} \\ \text{hydrolysis}}} CH_3COO^-Na^+ + NH_3$$

The hydrolysis of proteins and polypeptides is covered in more detail on page 364.

Proteins and polypeptides are polymers that contain the amide linkage. They can be hydrolysed either by refluxing with concentrated hydrochloric acid, or by enzymatic action to give amino acids.

Hydrolysis of nitriles

Nitriles are hydrolysed by refluxing in either dilute acid or aqueous alkali. Acid hydrolysis gives the ammonium ion and a carboxylic acid. Alkaline hydrolysis gives ammonia and the carboxylate ion. For example, ethanenitrile can be hydrolysed by refluxing with hydrochloric acid to give ethanoic acid, but with aqueous sodium hydroxide it forms sodium ethanoate:

$$CH_3CN(l) + 2H_2O(l) + HCl(aq) \rightarrow CH_3COOH(aq) + NH_4Cl(aq)$$
$$CH_3CN(l) + H_2O(l) + NaOH(aq) \rightarrow CH_3COO^-Na^+(aq) + NH_3(g)$$

9 REACTIONS OF CARBOXYLIC ACIDS

The two most important synthetic reactions of carboxylic acids are the production of esters and the production of acyl chlorides.

Esterification

When an alcohol and a carboxylic acid are refluxed together in the presence of an acid catalyst such as concentrated sulphuric acid, an ester is produced. The reaction does not go to completion but ends up with an equilibrium mixture that must be separated to isolate the ester. For example, ethanol, ethanoic acid and a trace of concentrated sulphuric acid give the ester ethyl ethanoate:

$$CH_3CH_2OH(l) + CH_3COOH(l) \rightleftharpoons CH_3COOCH_2CH_3(l) + H_2O(l)$$

Formation of acyl chlorides

In acyl chlorides (also known as acid chlorides), the carboxyl's hydroxyl group is replaced by a chlorine atom (Fig 15.39). An acyl chloride is always named after the corresponding carboxylic acid. For example, the acyl chloride of ethanoic acid is called ethanoyl chloride and that of benzoic acid is called benzoyl chloride.

The conversion of carboxylic acids into acyl chlorides is very useful for the synthesis of esters and amides because acyl chlorides are much more susceptible to nucleophilic attack than carboxylic acids. Acyl chlorides are therefore used as synthetic intermediates.

Carboxylic acids are converted into acyl chlorides by reaction with sulphuryl(IV) chloride, $SOCl_2$, or phosphorus(V) chloride, PCl_5 (Fig 15.40). Normally, the carboxylic acid is refluxed with the $SOCl_2$ or PCl_5 and the acyl chloride product is isolated by fractional distillation. For example, ethanoic acid can easily be converted to ethanoyl chloride, and benzoic acid to benzoyl chloride:

$$CH_3COOH + SOCl_2 \rightarrow CH_3COCl + SO_2 + HCl$$
$$C_6H_5COOH + PCl_5 \rightarrow C_6H_5COCl + POCl_3 + HCl$$

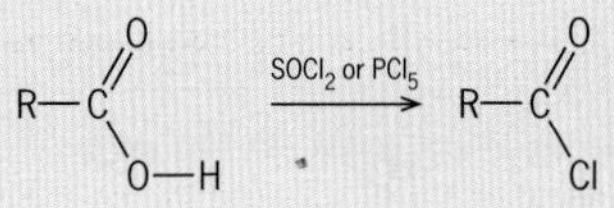

Reactions of acyl chlorides

Acyl chlorides can easily be converted to amides and esters, and readily hydrolysed back to the original carboxylic acid. The reactions involve the elimination of hydrogen chloride in a condensation reaction. Fig 15.41 shows five synthetic reactions based on acyl chlorides.

■ See question 7.

This reaction is discussed in much more detail on page 332.

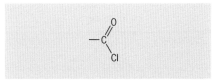

Fig 15.39 **The acyl chloride functional group, in which the highly electronegative chlorine atom is attached to the carbonyl carbon**

Fig 15.40 **The formation of acyl chlorides**

U Write down the equation for the reaction between:

(a) ethanoic acid and PCl_5, and

(b) benzoic acid and $SOCl_2$

■ See questions 7 and 10.

V Draw the structure of each product formed by the reaction of benzoyl chloride with

(a) ethanol,

(b) water,

(c) ammonia.

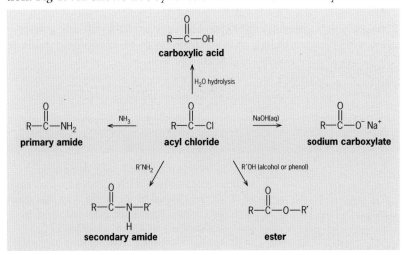

Fig 15.41 **Five reactions of acyl chlorides**

Redox reactions of carboxylic acids

With one or two exceptions, carboxylic acids cannot be oxidised by reagents such as acidified potassium dichromate(VI) and potassium manganate(VII). More powerful oxidising agents are needed to break the carbon skeleton.

> **W** Suggest why it is difficult to prepare methanoic acid by the oxidation of methanol.

Oxidation of methanoic acid

Methanoic acid is one of the exceptions. It can be oxidised by acidified potassium manganate(VII) to give carbon dioxide and water:

$$HCOOH + [O] \rightarrow H_2O + CO_2$$

Oxidation of ethanedioic acid

Ethanedioic acid, $(COOH)_2$, can be oxidised by acidified potassium manganate(VII). Again, the products are carbon dioxide and water. The two-carbon chain is broken during the reaction. This reaction occurs very slowly at room temperature but rapidly above $60\,°C$:

$$(COOH)_2 + [O] \rightarrow 2CO_2 + H_2O$$

Reduction of carboxylic acids

See question 7. ■

Powerful reducing agents, such as lithium tetrahydridoaluminate, $LiAlH_4$, reduce carboxylic acids to the corresponding alcohols (this is opposite to the preparation of carboxylic acids by oxidising primary alcohols):

$$RCOOH + 4[H] \xrightarrow{\text{(i) LiAlH}_4/\text{ether (ii) HCl(aq)}} RCH_2OH + H_2O$$

SUMMARY

After studying this chapter, you should know the following.

■ Brønsted–Lowry acids are proton donors and Brønsted–Lowry bases are proton acceptors.

■ Strong acids are assumed to dissociate fully when dissolved in water. The dissociation of weak acids is an equilibrium process, in which the position of equilibrium lies very much to the side of the undissociated weak acid.

■ K_a is the acid dissociation constant, which for the acid HA is given by the formula:

$$K_a = \frac{[H^+][A^-]}{[HA]}$$

■ pH is the negative logarithm to base 10 of the aqueous hydrogen ion concentration.

■ A buffer solution is one whose pH is not significantly changed by adding small amounts of acid or alkali.

■ Many buffer solutions are a mixture of an aqueous weak acid and its conjugate base.

■ An indicator is a compound which changes colour in a solution at a certain pH value. Many indicators are weak acids.

■ Carboxylic acids can be prepared by the oxidation of primary alcohols by heating under reflux with acidified potassium dichromate(VI), or by the acid- or base-catalysed hydrolysis of esters, amides or nitriles.

■ Carboxylic acids react with alcohols in the presence of an acid catalyst, such as concentrated sulphuric acid, to give esters.

■ Acyl chlorides are very useful synthetic intermediates in the conversion of carboxylic acids to esters and amides.

QUESTIONS

1

a) **(i)** Explain what is meant by a Brønsted–Lowry acid and state clearly the difference between two acids such as hydrochloric acid and ethanoic acid, CH_3CO_2H.

(ii) The concentration of an acid can be monitored by titration with an alkali such as aqueous sodium hydroxide. Sketch a curve in each case to show the change in pH when $0.10\ mol\ dm^{-3}$ aqueous sodium hydroxide is added, until in excess, separately to $25\ cm^3$ portions of $0.10\ mol\ dm^{-3}$ aqueous hydrochloric acid and of 0.10 mol dm^{-3} aqueous ethanoic acid. Methyl orange has a pH range of approximately 3.0 to 5.0. State and explain whether or not it would be a suitable indicator for each titration.

b) A common method for commercially peeling potatoes is to soak them for a short while in aqueous sodium hydroxide at about 75 °C and then to spray off the peel once the potatoes are removed from the solution. In order to be effective, the aqueous sodium hydroxide must have a minimum concentration of 2.0 mol dm^{-3}. A 10.0 cm^3 sample of the alkali solution is titrated at regular intervals with a 0.20 mol dm^{-3} solution of sulphuric acid. Calculate the volume of sulphuric acid that would indicate that the aqueous sodium hydroxide solution should be replaced.

c) Indicators are often weak acids and can be represented by the formula HIn such that

$$HIn(aq) \rightleftharpoons H^+(aq) + In^-(aq)$$

The indicator equilibrium constant, K_{In}, is equivalent to K_a for an acidic indicator. Calculate the pH of a 0.10 mol dm^{-3} solution of aqueous bromophenol. Bromophenol has a pK_{In} (ie pK_a) value of 4.0.
[UCLES Spring 1995 Modular Chemistry 1026/2 q.7]

2 Acidity in wine is caused by naturally occurring carboxylic acids, such as tartaric acid and ethanoic acid. Without such acids, wine would spoil easily and taste flat. Too much acid gives an unpleasant sour taste.

a) **(i)** Outline how you would estimate, in the laboratory, the total acid content of a sample of white wine. State clearly the apparatus and reagents you would use. Give step by step details of the calculation you would use.
(ii) Give an equation to show how ethanoic acid, CH_3CO_2H, reacts with water. Write an expression for the acid dissociation constant, K_a, of ethanoic acid and calculate its pK_a value. (K_a (ethanoic acid) = 1.7×10^{-5} mol dm^{-3})

b) Equal volumes of blood and water were treated separately with equal amounts of hydrochloric acid, HCl(aq). The changes in pH that occurred are shown in the table.

Sample	Initial pH	Final pH
blood	7.44	7.14
water	7.44	1.84

(i) Calculate the hydrogen ion concentration of the blood and the water before and after the addition of the hydrochloric acid. Hence deduce, in each case, the factor by which the hydrogen ion concentration has changed.
(ii) Account for the difference in the results with blood and with water.
[UCLES Summer 1994 1026/2, q7.]

3 In 1909, the Danish biochemist S.P.L. Sörensen was working for Carlsberg on problems connected with the brewing of lager. In this process, the control of acidity is

important. Continually referring to the hydrogen ion concentration of the various solution was tedious and he suggested the use of pH as a convenient measure of acidity.

a) Define pH.

b) A lager that Sörensen was investigating had a pH of 5. Calculate the hydrogen ion concentration, [H$^+$(aq)], of the solution.

c) Assuming that 10 cm^3 of the lager solution were diluted with an equal volume of water, calculate the pH of the resulting mixture.
[UCLES Summer 1994 1026/2, q.2]

4
a) Suggest a synthetic pathway for the conversion of C_2H_5OH to CH_2ClCO_2H and give reagents and conditions for each step.

b) Ethanoic acid (CH_3COOH) is described as a weak acid. It has a K_a of 1.8×10^{-5} mol dm^{-3}.
(i) What do you understand by the term 'weak acid'?
(ii) Estimate to 1 significant figure the pH of CH_3COOH of concentration 0.1 mol dm^{-3}.
(iii) What volume of NaOH of concentration 0.1 mol dm^{-3} would be required to neutralise 20 cm^3 of CH_3COOH of concentration 0.1 mol dm^{-3}.

c) If 20 cm^3 of NaOH of concentration 0.1 mol dm^{-3} is added to 20 cm^3 of HCl of concentration 0.1 mol dm^{-3} in a suitable reaction vessel, the temperature increases by 0.4 °C. Compare, qualitatively, this temperature change with that which would be observed if the same amount of NaOH of the same concentration was neutralised by 20 cm^3 of 0.100 mol dm^{-3} ethanoic acid. Explain your answer.
[ULEAC 1996 Specimen Paper CH2, q.2]

5
a) **(i)** Define pH.
(ii) Calculate the pH of 0.1 mol dm^{-3} hydrochloric acid, HCl, and 0.1 mol dm^{-3} ethanoic acid, CH_3CO_2H, given that the acid dissociation constant, K_a, for ethanoic acid is 1.7×10^{-5} mol dm^{-3}. Explain any differences in their pH values.

b) Phenolphthalein and methyl orange are common indicators and can be used to measure the end-point of an acid–base neutralisation reaction. The colour changes and the pH range of the two indicators are shown below.

Indicator	pH		
	0	7	14
methyl orange	red	yellow	
phenolphthalein		colourless	pink

Sketch the pH curves that you would expect when 0.1 mol dm^{-3} aqueous sodium hydroxide, NaOH, is added dropwise until in excess to:
(i) 25 cm^3 of 0.1 mol dm^{-3} hydrochloric acid
(ii) 25 cm^3 of 0.1 mol dm^{-3} ethanoic acid

Use the information above to determine which indicator/indicators would be suitable to measure the end-point of the neutralisation. Justify your selection of the indicator.

(c) Equal volumes of 0.1 mol dm⁻³ solutions of sodium ethanoate and ethanoic acid together can form a buffer solution. Explain how this mixture can resist a change in pH when a small amount of either acid or base is added to it.

[UCLES Spring 1993 1026/2, q.2]

6 Lactic acid and sodium lactate are both used as food additives.

a) The systematic name for lactic acid is 2-hydroxypropanoic acid. Draw a displayed formula for lactic acid.

b) A solution of 0.100 mol dm⁻³ lactic acid is titrated against 25.0 cm³ 0.100 mol dm⁻³ sodium hydroxide.

   (i) Suggest an indicator that is suitable to be used for this titration.

   (ii) Draw the pH titration curve and indicate how it can used to calculate the pK_a of lactic acid.

c) An equimolar mixture of lactic acid and sodium lactate are present in a food. They are described as acid regulators. Explain how this mixture can act as a buffer solution.

7 The compound shown in the next column is ibuprofen, a powerful painkiller.

a) Write down the molecular formula for ibuprofen.

Fig 15.Q7 **Displayed formula of ibuprofen**

b) Draw the displayed formulas for the organic products of the reaction of ibuprofen with:

   (i) aqueous sodium hydroxide

   (ii) sulphuryl(IV) chloride, $SOCl_2$

   (iii) ethanol and a trace of concentrated sulphuric acid

   (iv) lithium tetrahydridoaluminate(III)

c) Predict whether ibuprofen is a soluble or an insoluble painkiller. Explain your prediction in terms of the intermolecular forces that can exist when it is put into water.

d) When ibuprofen is heated with acidified potassium manganate(VII), a dicarboxylic acid is isolated. Suggest the structure for this dicarboxylic acid.

8 The major acidic component of soured milk is lactic acid:

$$CH_3CH(OH)CO_2H$$

When 10.0 cm³ of a solution of lactic acid was titrated against 0.050 mol dm⁻³ sodium hydroxide the following pH readings were obtained:

Volume of NaOH added/cm³	pH	Volume of NaOH added/cm³	pH
0	2.5	12	4.4
2	3.1	14	4.7
4	3.4	16	9.1
6	3.7	18	11.6
8	3.9	20	11.8
10	4.1		

a) Plot a graph of these results with pH on the y-axis and volume added on the x-axis. Comment on the shape of the curve before, at and after neutralisation.

b) Suggest an indicator, giving a reason for your choice.

c) Calculate the concentration of the lactic acid in the solution in **(i)** mol dm⁻³, **(ii)** g dm⁻³.

d) deduce the K_a value for lactic acid, giving your reasoning and the units.

[UCLES Summer 1994 Chemistry 9250/1, q.3]

9

a) Ethanoic acid, CH_3CO_2H, is a weak acid but its salt, sodium ethanoate, fully dissociates into its ions in aqueous solution. Explain this difference.

b) A buffer solution can be made from a 1.00 mol dm⁻³ aqueous solution of ethanoic acid and a 1.00 mol dm⁻³ aqueous solution of sodium ethanoate. The acid dissociation constant, K_a, for ethanoic acid may be written as

$$K_a = \frac{[H^+(aq)][CH_3CO_2^-(aq)]}{[CH_3CO_2H(aq)]} = 1.79 \times 10^{-5} \, mol \, dm^{-3}$$

   (i) The pH of 1.00 mol dm⁻³ ethanoic acid is approximately 2.38. Calculate the hydrogen ion concentration and hence deduce the ethanoate ion concentration.

   (ii) Use your answer to **b) (i)** to calculate the concentration of the undissociated ethanoic acid.

c) **(i)** Deduce the concentration of the ethanoate ions in 1.00 mol dm⁻³ $CH_3CO_2Na(aq)$.

   (ii) Explain, in terms of the dissociation equilibrium of the ethanoic acid, the effect of adding 1.00 mol dm⁻³ sodium ethanoate to 1.00 mol dm⁻³ ethanoic acid.

d) Explain how a mixture of 1.00 mol dm⁻³ ethanoic acid and 1.00 mol dm⁻³ sodium ethanoate can resist a change in pH when a small amount of acid is added.

[UCLES Summer 1994 1026/2, q.3]

Assignment

ETHANOIC ACID IN INDUSTRY

For many years, ethanoic acid was produced on a large scale just as vinegar – an aqueous solution of ethanoic acid used to preserve foods and improve their flavour. More recently, pure ethanoic acid has also been a synthetic intermediate in the production of a wide range of organic molecules.

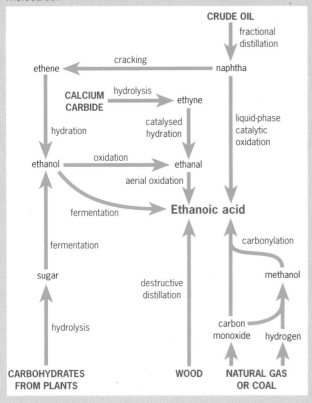

Fig 15.A1 **Five different routes to ethanoic acid**

For vinegar, ethanoic acid used to be made by the fermentation of ethanol: when dilute aqueous ethanol is oxidised, an aqueous solution of ethanoic acid is formed.

1

a) Write an equation to represent the oxidation of aqueous ethanol by atmospheric oxygen to form ethanoic acid.

b) Suggest one problem arising in the manufacture of concentrated ethanoic acid by this fermentation method.

The destructive distillation of wood is another early method for manufacturing ethanoic acid. The wood is heated in the absence of air and the volatile components produced are condensed. The condensate is a complex mixture of organic products from which ethanoic acid is extracted.

2 Suggest why the destructive distillation of wood must

be carried out in the absence of air.
Fermentation and the destructive distillation of wood have drawbacks: fermentation is slow and yields only a dilute solution of ethanoic acid; the destructive distillation of wood produces a complex mixture that needs to be separated.

So, in the early 1900s, industrial chemists began to devise new processes to make ethanoic acid, using ethanal as an intermediate. There were three principal routes to ethanal. The first involves the conversion of ethanol to ethanal, either by oxidation using atmospheric oxygen, or by dehydrogenation over a heated catalyst such as copper.

3

a) Write down the equation for the oxidation of ethanol by atmospheric oxygen to form ethanal.

b) Suggest why the industrial oxidation of ethanol is carried out using atmospheric oxygen rather than an oxidising agent such as acidified potassium dichromate(VI).

c) Dehydrogenation involves the loss of two hydrogen atoms per molecule of ethanol. Write down the equation for the dehydrogenation of ethanol.

The second route to ethanal involves the catalysed hydration of ethyne, C_2H_2 (addition of water).

4 Write down an equation for the hydration of ethyne.

The third route to ethanal involves the catalysed reaction of ethene with carbon monoxide:

$$C_2H_4 + CO \rightarrow CH_3CHO$$

5 A company wants to convert ethene into ethanal. Which of the three synthetic routes described do you think best? Give reasons for your answer.

Ethanal can be oxidised by hot acidified potassium dichromate(VI) in the laboratory to give ethanoic acid. This reagent is too expensive to use industrially and, besides, it would result in large quantities of unwanted chromium(III) salts. Instead, an efficient catalytic oxidation of ethanal is employed. The oxidation agent is atmospheric oxygen, and using a manganese–containing catalyst ensures that the reaction proceeds rapidly, even at 50 °C.

6

a) Write down the equation for the oxidation of ethanal by oxygen to give ethanoic acid.

b) What are the advantages of using atmospheric oxygen over acidified potassium dichromate(VI) in the industrial oxidation of ethanal to ethanoic acid?

Among more recent developments in the manufacture of ethanoic acid is the direct oxidation of naphtha, one of the distillation products of crude oil, to give a mixture of carboxylic acids. The catalytic oxidation can be controlled to yield much more ethanoic acid than other acids. This reaction means that crude oil can be converted by a two-stage process into ethanoic acid, avoiding the need for cracking and the use of ethene and ethanal as intermediates.

7 Give some advantages of making ethanoic acid from naphtha by the direct oxidation method rather than using routes via ethanal.

Recently, natural gas, which is mainly methane, has been developed as a source of ethanoic acid. In a series of catalytic reactions, the methane is converted into carbon monoxide and hydrogen, which in turn are converted into methanol. The methanol is then reacted with carbon monoxide to give ethanoic acid:

$$CH_4(g) + H_2O(g) \rightarrow CO(g) + 3H_2(g)$$
$$CO(g) + 2H_2(g) \rightarrow CH_3OH(g)$$
$$CH_3OH + CO(g) \rightarrow CH_3COOH$$

8 Suggest why the reaction of methanol with carbon monoxide is referred to as carbonylation.

The last series of reactions would suggest that coal might be used as a raw material in the manufacture of ethanoic acid, since the chemistry involved in converting the carbon in coal into carbon monoxide and hydrogen is well-known to industrial chemists. The advantage that coal has over crude oil is that it is not expected to run out for hundreds of years.

9 Discuss the various advantages for making ethanoic acid from each of the following raw materials:
a) crude oil,
b) natural gas,
c) carbohydrates such as sugar (fermentation),
d) wood.

Ethanoic acid has a wide variety of applications: it is used to produce esters (used in food flavourings and as industrial solvents), cellulose ethanoate (better known as cellulose acetate) and benzene-1,4-dicarboxylic acid (a precursor in the manufacture of some polyesters). Chloroethanoic acid is used to make weedkillers. Pharmaceutical products, such as aspirin, are manufactured using ethanoic acid. Ethenyl ethanoate is used in paints.

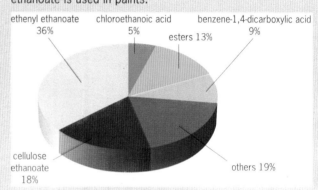

Fig 15.A2 **Applications of ethanoic acid**

10
a) Draw the displayed formula for chloroethanoic acid. Suggest how chloroethanoic acid may be prepared from ethanoic acid.

b) Pentan-2-ol reacts with ethanoic acid to give an ester used in the food flavouring industry. Draw the displayed formula of the ester produced.

c) Discuss the importance of ethanoic acid in the maintenance of today's lifestyle.

CARBYOXYLIC ACIDS AND pH

In this chapter, the properties of acids and bases are explained through carboxylic acids and carboxylates, whose reactions and derivatives are also described.

These compounds feature in several chapters and the Chapter Map gives you references to find out more about them.

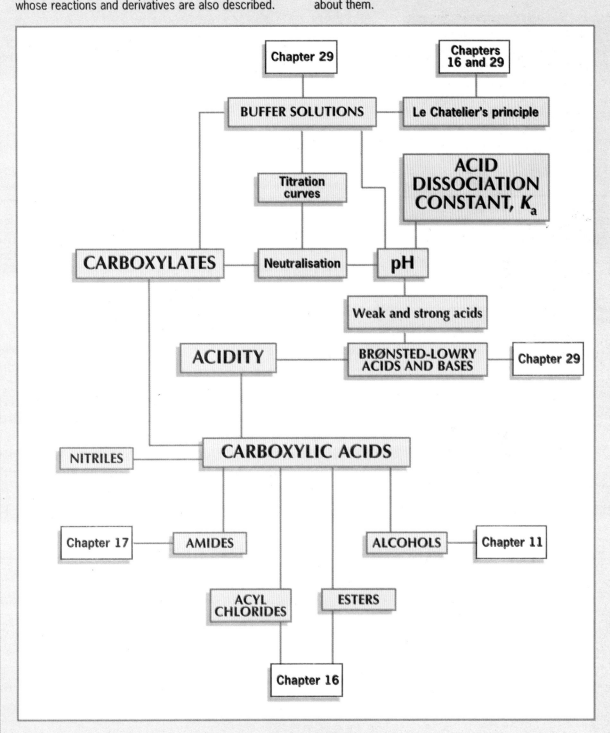

16 Esters, acyl chlorides, amides and equilibria

The characteristic flavour of pear drops is due to a cocktail of organic compounds which include carboxylic acid derivatives called esters. The organic compounds have molecules that trigger responses in sensory cells in the nose chamber and the tongue

OUR NOSES CAN DETECT hundreds of different odours at unbelievably minute concentrations amounting to perhaps just a few molecules per sniff. Some noses are so sensitive that their owners – humans and dogs included – can learn to identify scores of different substances by their smell alone! How does the nose do it?

The chamber of the nose is lined with thousands of different types of receptor cells that sense the different shapes of molecules. It is likely that a single substance may trigger several types of receptor cell, which in some way together produce the sensation of the odour of that substance. Many natural odours are not just single substances but complex cocktails of substances, and we don't understand the complicated interaction of the receptor cells involved. Also, we don't know why many substances whose structures differ widely give the same odour, so we have yet to discover the connection between molecular structure and odour.

What we do know, however, is that to have an odour a substance must be volatile enough for its vapour to diffuse into the nostrils; it must be water soluble to ensure that it makes its way into the mucus lining the nostrils; and it must be fat soluble so that it can penetrate the receptor cells. Many esters – derivatives of carboxylic acids – possess these properties, which is why they are used a lot to synthesise substances we like to smell, particularly those in food products. The subtle odours of fruits, for instance, are reproduced by blending the appropriate esters and there is an expanding market in attractive smells, such as baked bread and coffee, to distribute in supermarkets and encourage shoppers to buy more food.

1 DERIVATIVES OF CARBOXYLIC ACIDS

As explained on page 316, carboxylic acids have a carbonyl group that is directly attached to a hydroxyl group. Derivatives of carboxylic acids still have the carbonyl group but the hydroxyl group is replaced by either an electronegative element or an oxygen atom attached to a carbon chain. The main derivatives of carboxylic acids are esters, amides (sometimes called acid amides) and acyl chlorides.

Fig 16.1 **A generalised carboxylic acid and its derivatives. R′ is an alkyl group such as C_2H_5, an aryl group such as C_6H_5, or a cycloalkyl group**

Polar carbonyl groups

Look at Fig 16.1, the general structure of a carboxylic acid and its derivatives. They all possess a highly polar carbonyl group whose normal polarity is enhanced when the extra atom attached to it is highly electronegative. In carboxylic acids and esters, this atom is an oxygen atom; in amides, it is a nitrogen atom; and in acyl chlorides, it is a chlorine atom.

A What is electronegativity?

Use of carboxylic acid derivatives

Esters and amides have numerous commercial applications including perfumes, polymers and pharmaceuticals (Figs 16.3 and 16.4). Acyl chlorides are important synthetic intermediates but do not have many everyday uses in their own right.

■ See question 1.

Fig 16.2 **Oils from plants, such as olive oil, are esters of long-chain carboxylic acids and the alcohol propane-1,2,3-triol**

Fig 16.3 **Among the functional groups in vitamin C (ascorbic acid) is a lactone, which is a cyclic ester**

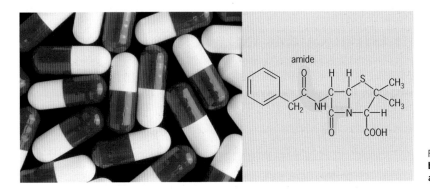

Fig 16.4 **Penicillins are powerful bactericides whose molecules contain an amide functional group**

2 ESTERS

An ester is a carboxylic acid derivative in which the hydroxyl group of the acid is replaced by an oxygen atom attached to a carbon chain. Fig 16.5 shows how esters are related to carboxylic acids and to alcohols. An ester has two carbon chains, one related to a carboxylic acid, and the other related to an alcohol or a phenol.

Naming esters

Because esters have two carbon chains, they are more difficult to name than other classes of compounds. For this reason, the main carbon chain of an ester is taken to be the one related to the carboxylic acid, so the main (second) part of the name of an ester is based on the name of this carboxylic acid (like a surname).

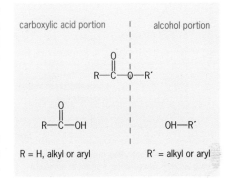

Fig 16.5 **Esters have a structure which consists of a carboxylic acid portion and an alcohol portion**

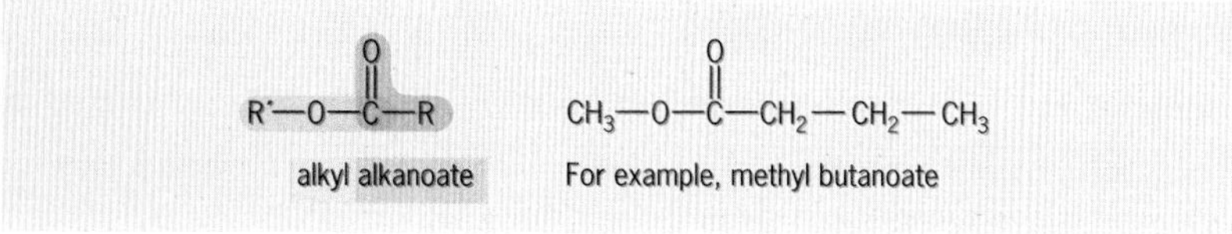

See question 1. ▪

Fig 16.6 **The name of an ester is derived from the name of its alcohol (alkyl) group and the name of its carboxylic acid (alkanoate) group. Note that the structure shown here is the reverse of that given in Fig 16.5**

Take, for example, methyl propanoate, Fig 16.7(a). The carbon chain that is related to the carboxylic acid (the one containing the carbonyl group) contains three carbon atoms, and the chain related to the alcohol contains one carbon atom. Its formula is therefore written as:

$$CH_3CH_2COOCH_3 \quad \text{or} \quad CH_3CH_2CO_2CH_3$$

Note that in these formulas and in the structures of Fig 16.7, the main (carboxylic acid) part is on the left, rather than on the right as in their names.

In the same way, phenyl ethanoate, Fig 16.7(b), consists of two portions: a two-carbon unit containing the carbonyl carbon, and the phenyl group (the benzene ring). It has the formula:

$$CH_3COOC_6H_5 \quad \text{or} \quad CH_3CO_2C_6H_5$$

Ethyl benzoate is related to benzoic acid and has the formula:

$$C_6H_5COOC_2H_5 \quad \text{or} \quad C_6H_5CO_2C_2H_5.$$

B Write down the displayed formulas for each of these esters: methyl ethanoate, propyl propanoate, pentyl butanoate and methyl benzoate.

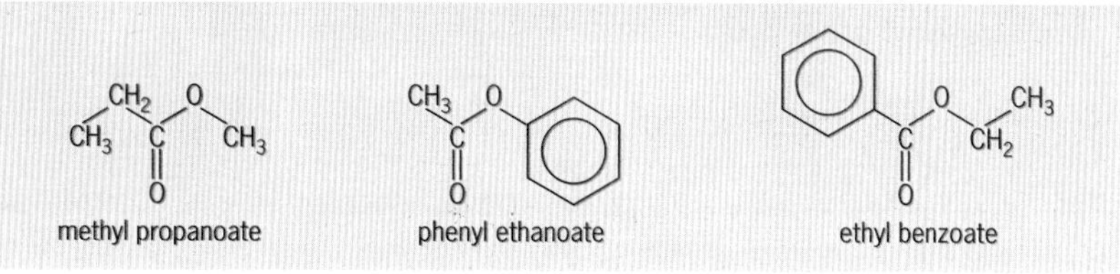

Fig 16.7 **Displayed formulas of methyl propanoate, phenyl ethanoate and ethyl benzoate**

3 ESTERIFICATION AND EQUILIBRIUM CONSTANTS

Making an ester should be simple enough, since when heated in the presence of an acid catalyst, a carboxylic acid and an alcohol react to give an ester and water. This is known as **esterification**.

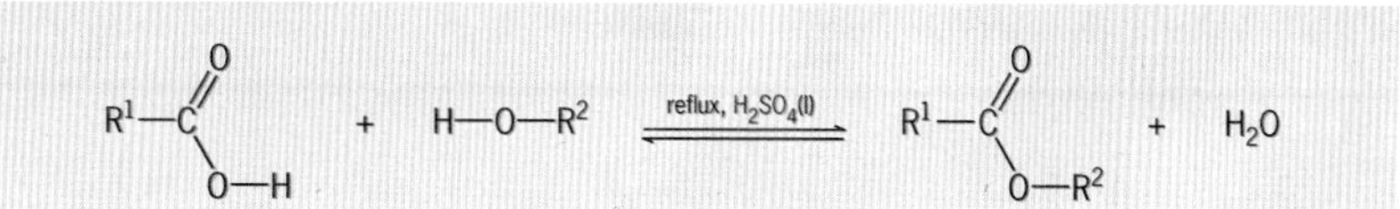

Fig 16.8 **The esterification reaction. R^1 is an alkyl, an aryl or hydrogen. R^2 is an alkyl group**

The equation (Fig 16.8) does not really indicate the problems with the reaction. To get a good yield of ester, the reaction has to be managed carefully since it is reversible. Fig 16.9 shows that when a carboxylic acid is reacted with an alcohol, the reaction is not completed. It reaches a balance point at which the concentrations of all four substances (carboxylic acid, alcohol, ester and water) remain constant. The **reaction** has not stopped but the concentrations do not change, which means that the rate of the forward reaction then equals the rate of the backward reaction. A situation known as a **dynamic equilibrium** has been reached.

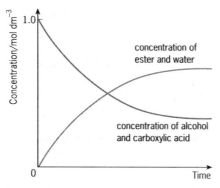

Fig 16.9 **The concentration changes occurring during esterification, when 1 mole of alcohol is refluxed with 1 mole of carboxylic acid. Note that each concentration eventually reaches a constant value known as the equilibrium concentration**

Equilibrium constants

Any dynamic equilibrium can be described in terms of its **equilibrium constant, K_c**. The equilibrium constant relates the molar concentrations at equilibrium of each species in the reaction:

The equilibrium constant is the (mathematical) product of the molar concentrations of the products each raised to the power of its coefficient in the stoichiometric equation, divided by the product of the molar concentrations of the reactants, each raised to the power of its coefficient in the stoichiometric equation.

So, for the reaction $wA + xB \rightleftharpoons yC + zD$, the equilibrium constant is given by:

$$K_c = \frac{[C]^y[D]^z}{[A]^w[B]^x}$$

where [ ] stands for the concentration of the species in $mol\,dm^{-3}$.

For esterification, the general reaction is shown by the equation:

$$RCOOH + R'OH \rightleftharpoons RCOOR' + H_2O$$

where R and R' represent carbon skeletons, such as alkyl or aryl groups.

The equilibrium constant is thus given by:

$$K_c = \frac{[RCOOR'][H_2O]}{[RCOOH][R'OH]}$$

This equilibrium constant does not have a unit, since the units for concentration cancel out.

Notice that, although esterification normally requires an acid catalyst, the catalyst is not shown in the expression for the equilibrium constant. This is because it is not shown in the stoichiometric equation. The catalyst decreases the time it takes to reach equilibrium but *does not change the concentrations* obtained at equilibrium.

A reaction whose equilibrium constant has a large numerical value is one which, at equilibrium, the concentrations of the products are much higher than the concentrations of the reactants.

Calculations involving the equilibrium constant

Despite the problem of having to extract the required product from an equilibrium mixture, esters are made via the acid-catalysed reaction of an alcohol and a carboxylic acid. The reaction is carried out in a batch process, so the ester is not made continuously but only as needed. When using this equilibrium process on an industrial scale, the chemists need to estimate the yield of ester, and the amounts of starting materials left unreacted, and for this they use the equilibrium constant.

Example

Q The K_c for the esterification reaction between ethanol and ethanoic acid is 4.0.
Calculate the yield of ester when 1.0 mole of ethanol and 1.0 mole of ethanoic acid are left to reach equilibrium.

A First, write down the stoichiometric equation. At the start of the reaction there is no product. But once equilibrium has been reached, the reaction vessel contains ethanoic acid, ethanol, ethyl ethanoate and water.

From the equation, every mole of ethanoic acid requires 1 mole of ethanol and makes 1 mole of ethyl ethanoate and 1 mole of water. This means that if the yield at equilibrium is x moles of ethyl ethanoate, then x moles of each of ethanol and ethanoic acid must have reacted. This leaves behind $(1.0 - x)$ moles of each of ethanoic acid and ethanol. This part of the calculation is summarised on the next page.

✔ The term 'stoichiometric equation' is equivalent to 'balanced equation'. That is, the mole ratios of the reactants and the products are stated.

✔ Remember: The concentrations used to calculate K_c must be those after equilibrium has been reached.

■ See question 2.

Another equilibrium constant – the acid dissociation constant, K_a – is discussed on page 312.

C (a) Write down expressions for the equilibrium constant for each of the following reactions:
(i) $(COOH)_2 + 2C_2H_5OH \rightleftharpoons (COOC_2H_5)_2 + 2H_2O$
(ii) $2NO_2 \rightleftharpoons N_2O_4$
Show that in **(i)** K_c has no unit and in **(ii)** the unit is $mol^{-1}\,dm^3$.

(b) Ethanoic acid and pentan-1-ol are refluxed together to obtain an equilibrium mixture. The concentration of each substance at equilibrium is shown in the table.

Substance	Molar concentration at equilibrium/$mol\,dm^{-3}$
ethanoic acid	2.12
pentan-1-ol	2.12
pentyl ethanoate	4.32
water	4.32

(i) Write down a balanced equation for the esterification reaction.
(ii) Write down an expression for the equilibrium constant.
(iii) Calculate the numerical value for the equilibrium constant.

$$CH_3COOH + C_2H_5OH \rightleftharpoons CH_3COOC_2H_5 + H_2O$$

At start of reaction/moles	1.0	1.0	0	0
At equilibrium/moles	$1.0 - x$	$1.0 - x$	x	x

The equilibrium constant is: $K_c = \dfrac{[CH_3COOC_2H_5][H_2O]}{[CH_3COOH][C_2H_5OH]}$

The concentration of each substance must be substituted into the above expression, so the moles at equilibrium must be converted to concentrations.

Remember (page 111) that concentration is in $mol\,dm^{-3} = \dfrac{moles}{volume\,(dm^3)}$

So be careful to substitute concentrations into the expression for K_c, *not* the number of moles.

Assuming that the volume of the esterification mixture is $V\,dm^3$, this gives:

$$K_c = 4.0 = \dfrac{\left(\dfrac{x}{V}\right)\left(\dfrac{x}{V}\right)}{\dfrac{1.0 - x}{V}\,\dfrac{1.0 - x}{V}}$$

Cancelling v gives: $4.0 = \dfrac{x^2}{(1.0 - x)^2}$

Taking the square root of both sides gives: $2.0 = \dfrac{x}{1.0 - x}$

So: $2.0 - 2.0x = x$

That is, $x = 0.67$ moles

This means that the exact composition of the equilibrium mixture can be estimated.

See questions 3, 4, 5, and 6. ▪

?

D The equilibrium constant, K_c, for the reaction between propanoic acid and ethanol is 4.3 at a particular temperature. 1.0 mole of water and 1.0 mole of ethyl propanoate are refluxed together with an acid catalyst. Calculate the number of moles at equilibrium of:

(a) water,

(b) ethyl propanoate,

(c) propanoic acid and

(d) ethanol.

The Example shows that when an equimolar mixture of ethanol and ethanoic acid are refluxed together, only about 67 per cent of the starting ethanol and ethanoic acid are converted to ethyl ehanoate. In the laboratory, the ester can be separated from the starting materials, but industrially this represents a large loss of valuable reactants, unless they can be recycled. Therefore, an industrial chemist needs to find a way for this reaction to give a maximum yield, especially when the ester is derived from an expensive starting material.

Le Chatelier's principle

Le Chatelier's principle states:

> **The position of the equilibrium of a system changes to minimise the effect of any imposed change in conditions.**

It therefore describes the effect that a change in the pressure, temperature, or concentration of a substance in an equilibrium mixture will have on the position of equilibrium. Le Chatelier's principle applies to any reaction that is in equilibrium and allows chemists to manage and manipulate equilibrium reactions.

Effect of concentration changes on equilibrium

Changing the concentration of a reactant or a product does not change the numerical value of the equilibrium constant. However, it does change the position of equilibrium. As an example, let's look at what happens to the equilibrium mixture formed by the reaction of an alcohol with a carboxylic acid when extra alcohol is added. Temporarily, the reaction is not in equilibrium, but equilibrium is quickly restored by reaction of the alcohol to form the ester. A new equilibrium mixture is produced that has the same equilibrium constant. Fig 16.10 shows what happens to the concentrations of each substance during this process.

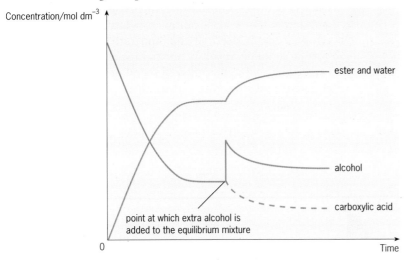

Fig 16.10 **The effect of increasing the concentration of alcohol on the esterification equilibrium. Note that an even higher equilibrium concentration can be achieved if even more alcohol is added to the mixture**

This effect is an example of how Le Chatelier's principle operates in practice. The change is the increase of alcohol concentration which disturbs the equilibrium of the mixture. But once a new state of equilibrium is established, some of the extra alcohol is changed into ester.

Generally, the position of equilibrium is shifted towards the right side of the equation by increasing the concentration of one of the reactants in the equilibrium mixture, and to the left side by increasing the concentration of one of the products.

Industrially, this means that if an ester is to be made starting from an expensive alcohol, it is more economical to use an excess of the cheaper carboxylic acid. This ensures that the equilibrium is shifted to the right side and that as much as possible of the expensive alcohol is converted to the ester.

Another way to manage the reversible reaction is to *remove* one of the products the moment it has formed. This prevents the reaction from achieving equilibrium, but it will nevertheless `keep trying' to, as long as the product continues to be removed from the reaction mixture. In esterification, water is the easier product to remove.

Effect of pressure changes on equilibrium

Changing the pressure has no effect on the esterification reaction. This is because all the reactants and products are liquids, so there is no significant change of volume during the reaction.

Effect of temperature changes on equilibrium

Changing the temperature of a reaction has two distinct effects, both of interest to industrial chemists. As the temperature rises, the rate of a reaction increases and the position of equilibrium shifts. Consequently, the numerical value of the equilibrium constant alters too.

To predict the effect of increasing temperature, it is necessary to know the enthalpy change of reaction, that is, whether the reaction is exothermic or endothermic.

E You want to make an ester starting from ethanol and an expensive carboxylic acid. Suggest conditions that will maximise the conversion of the carboxylic acid into the corresponding ester.

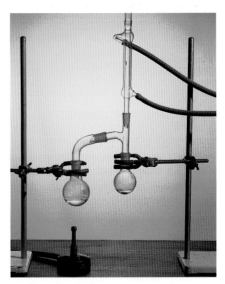

Fig 16.11 **An esterification reaction using a Dean-Stark apparatus**

The effect of pressure change on equilibrium is also discussed in Chapter 29.

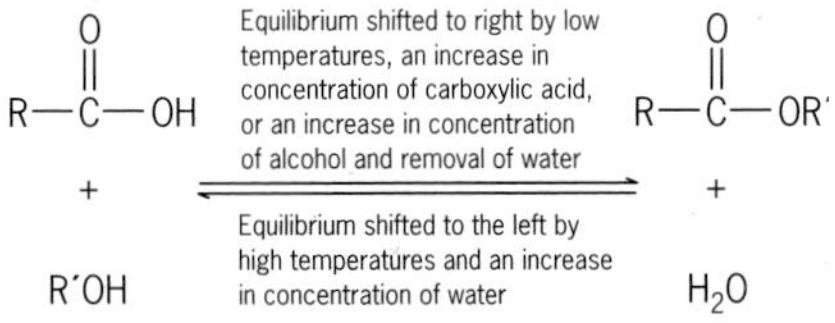

Fig 16.12 **A summary of the effect of Le Chatelier's principle on esterification**

If you want to read more about energy changes that occur during chemical reactions, see pages 10 and 116.

Esterification is an exothermic process: when a carboxylic acid and an alcohol react, energy is transferred to the surroundings. So, if the temperature of the esterification is raised, the equilibrium shifts to absorb energy, that is, in the direction of the endothermic reaction (the left side). As the temperature is increased, the yield of ester gets lower, though the rate of production of ester gets faster. For esterification in industry, a compromise temperature is used so that the rate and the yield are both acceptable and it is normal for the alcohol and the carboxylic acid to be refluxed together in the presence of concentrated sulphuric acid as a catalyst.

Fig 16.13 **In the laboratory, esterification is usually carried out by refluxing an alcohol and a carboxylic acid in the presence of an acid catalyst, such as concentrated sulphuric acid**

F Predict the effect of increasing separately the temperature, the catalyst concentration and the concentration of ammonia, NH_3, on the position of equilibrium for the following reaction.

$$4NH_3(g) + 5O_2(g) \rightleftharpoons 4NO(g) + 6H_2O(g)$$
$$\Delta H = -908 \, kJ \, mol^{-1}$$

Effect of catalysts on equilibrium

A catalyst has no effect on the position of equilibrium. But it does increase the rate of both the forward and reverse reactions, decreasing the time taken to reach equilibrium.

Applications of the esterification reaction

The importance of esters as a source of pleasant smelling substances and food flavourings has been mentioned earlier (see page 334). Almost all these esters are manufactured using the esterification reaction just described with the formation of the ester linkage.

There are several examples of the esterification reaction used to link two carbon chains to form a molecule that has a particular shape associated with biological activity. Two such molecules, benzocaine and procaine, are anaesthetics based on 4-aminobenzoic acid. Amongst other uses, there are ester solvents (including ethyl ethanoate), ester plasticisers in PVC and ester synthetic fibres (polyesters).

G Write down the names of the carboxylic acid and alcohol used to make each of the following esters:

(a) ethyl ethanoate,

(b) ethyl butanoate and

(c) propenyl ethanoate.

H Explain how an excess of ethanol drives the equilibrium reaction between ethanol and 4-aminobenzoic acid to the right hand side.

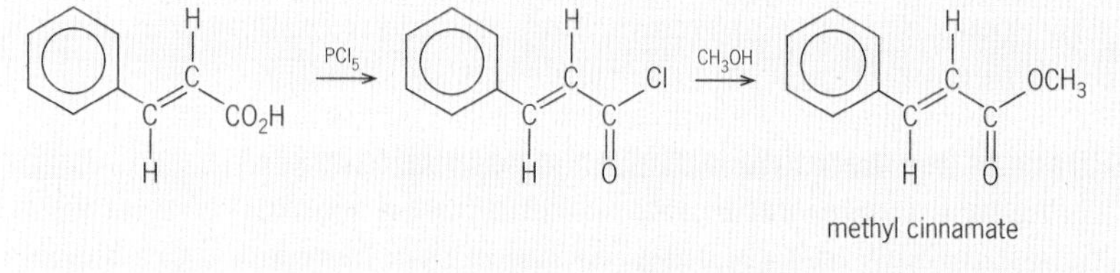

Fig 16.14 **The preparation of methyl cinnamate, an ester responsible for the spicy aroma of the matsutake mushroom. It can be prepared from cinnamic acid (3-phenylpropenoic acid), the corresponding carboxylic acid. Note that the esterification occurs via the acyl chloride**

ESTERS AND THE FOOD FLAVOURINGS INDUSTRY

THE SIMPLE ESTERS, that is, those with only a few carbon atoms per molecule) tend to have pleasant odours. The characteristic flavours of fruits and the fragrances of flowers are often due to esters – commonly a subtle blend of esters and other odoriferous compounds.

When we talk about 'flavour' we mean a combination of taste and odour by receptors on the tongue and in the nose. Almost always, it is a combination of substances which our various receptors detect that allow us to recognise a particular flavour.

Table 16.1 shows the 11 chemicals, and the amount of each, that chemists have put together to imitate the flavour of pineapple. Notice that many of the esters listed are still known by their traditional names – the result of long established use in the food industry. Almost all the esters in this formulation are made by the reaction of the appropriate alcohol and carboxylic acid.

Table 16.1 **Components of imitation pineapple flavouring**

Compound	% in formulation
allyl caproate	5
butanoic acid	12
caproic acid	8
ethanoic acid	5
ethyl butanoate	22
ethyl crotonoate	5
ethyl ethanoate	15
isoamyl acetate	3
isoamyl isovalerate	3
terpinyl propanoate	3
other essential oils	19

LOCAL ANAESTHETICS

BENZOCAINE AND PROCAINE are local anaesthetics (Fig 16.15), meaning that they make only small areas of the body insensitive to touch and pain. They were used a lot until recently, benzocaine as an ointment, drug or aerosol to relieve painful conditions of the skin, mouth and respiratory tract, and procaine for dental injections. Both compounds are usually prepared by esterification reactions.

Benzocaine has the systematic name of ethyl 4-aminobenzoate. It is synthesised from 4-aminobenzoic acid (Fig 16.16). The acid is esterified with ethanol in the presence of a little concentrated sulphuric acid to speed up the attainment of equilibrium. An excess of ethanol is used to drive the equilibrium to the right, according to Le Chatelier's principle.

In a very similar process, procaine is also synthesised from 4-aminobenzoic acid (Fig 16.17). This time the alcohol has a much more complicated structure but the chemistry behind the reaction is the same.

Fig 16.15 A **local anaesthetic, numbs just the area being treated**

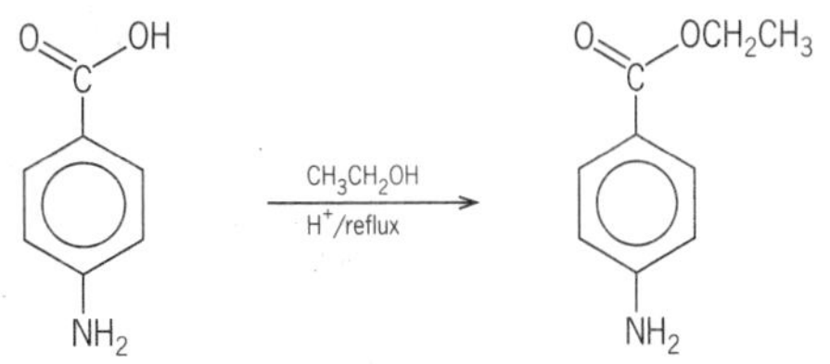

Fig 16.16 **The preparation of benzocaine by esterifying 4-amino-benzoic acid with ethanol**

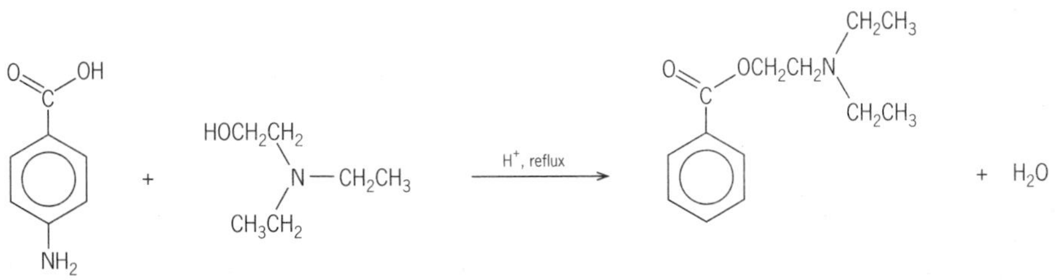

Fig 16.17 **The preparation of procaine by esterifying 4-aminobenzoic acid**

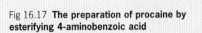

Fig 16.18 **Esters in perspiration are hydrolysed to form unpleasant-smelling carboxylic acids. These constitute the scent which a sniffer dog picks up when tracing someone**

4 REACTIONS OF ESTERS

The carbonyl carbon in the ester group is susceptible to nucleophilic attack. The principal nucleophiles which react with it are the water molecule, the hydroxide molecule, the ammonia molecule and the hydride ion.

Hydrolysis of esters

In the hydrolysis of esters, water reacts with the carbonyl carbon and an alcohol is eliminated. The reaction is very slow because the water molecule is a poor nucleophile. It is also a reversible reaction:

$$RCOOR' + H_2O \rightleftharpoons RCOOH + R'OH$$

(Note that it is the esterification reaction in reverse.)

It is this reaction with water that prevents esters from being used in some perfumes and deodorants. Pleasant smelling esters are liable to be hydrolysed by chemicals in perspiration to form carboxylic acids, many of which have an unpleasant smell. They include butanoic acid which gives the odour we detect in rancid butter. These carboxylic acids are among the components of body odour and are in the scent that dogs pick up when tracking humans (Fig 16.18).

Base-catalysed hydrolysis of esters

Also known as **saponification**, this reaction involves boiling an ester with aqueous sodium hydroxide to form the sodium salt of the acid and the corresponding alcohol. Fats and oils are natural esters and their alkaline hydrolysis is the basis of soap-making.

During saponification of a natural fat or oil, propane-1,2,3-triol (glycerol) and the sodium salt of a long-chain fatty acid are formed (Figs 16.19 to 16.21). The sodium salt is a major constituent of soaps. Its carboxylate ion is negatively charged at one (hydrophilic) end and non-polar at the other (hydrophobic) end. The action of detergents is covered on pages 286 to 287.

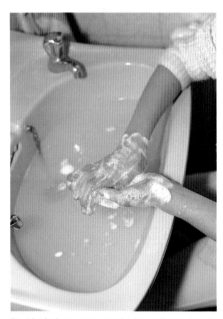

Fig 16.19 **Soaps are mainly the sodium salts of carboxylic acids known as fatty acids**

Fig 16.20 **Soaps are made by the hydrolysis of fats and oils during boiling with aqueous sodium hydroxide. The reaction is called saponification**

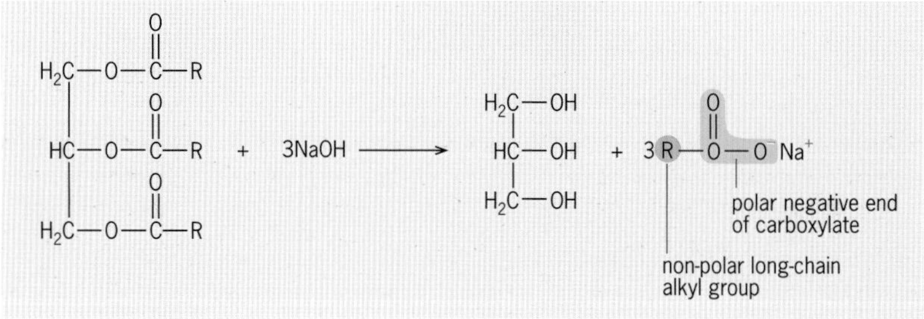

Fig 16.21 **Saponification. The fats and oils used are esters whose alcohol part is propane-1,2,3-triol and whose carboxylic acid part is a so-called fatty acid. Hydrolysis of such an ester forms a sodium carboxylate, the main constituent of soap. Note that the carboxylate ion has a polar end and a non-polar end**

An ester such as an ethyl benzoate is hydrolysed to form sodium benzoate and ethanol (Fig 16.22).

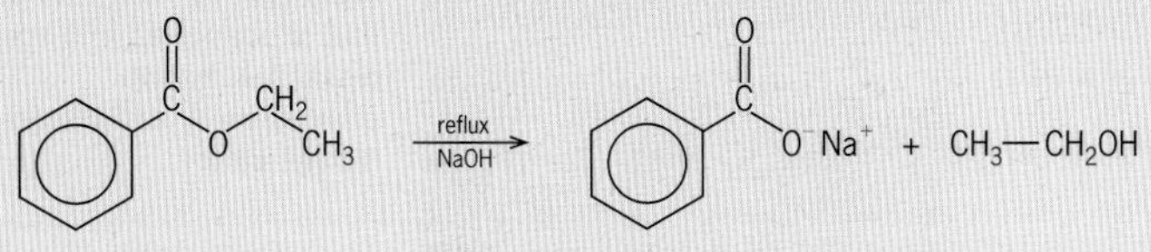

Fig 16.22 **The hydrolysis of ethyl benzoate to form sodium benzoate and ethanol**

Acid-catalysed hydrolysis of esters

It is also possible to hydrolyse an ester by refluxing with a dilute acid. Normally, dilute sulphuric acid or concentrated hydrochloric acid is used as the acid catalyst. This is really the reverse reaction of esterification and, in theory, should lead to an equilibrium mixture containing carboxylic acid, alcohol, ester and water. However, the use of excess water from the dilute acid drives the reaction to the left side of the equation and almost completely hydrolyses the ester. Notice that in acidic hydrolysis, the carboxylic acid is obtained rather than the carboxylate salt.

Ethyl methanoate is hydrolysed to give methanoic acid and ethanol:

$$HCOOC_2H_5(l) + H_2O(l) \overset{H^+(aq)}{\rightleftharpoons} HCOOH(l) + C_2H_5OH(l)$$

I Write down the names of the products of the reactions between the following esters and hot, aqueous sodium hydroxide:

(a) ethyl ethanoate,

(b) propyl propanoate and

(c) ethyl benzoate.

■ See question 7.

Reduction of esters

Powerful reducing agents, such as lithium tetrahydridoaluminate(III), $LiAlH_4$, reduce esters to two alcohols. During the reaction, the ester linkage is broken and the carbonyl group is reduced to a primary alcohol. This is not a useful reaction industrially, because water and air have to be excluded and lithium tetrahydridoaluminate(III) is very expensive.

$$RCOOR' \overset{LiAlH_4 \text{ in ether}}{\longrightarrow} RCH_2OH + R'OH$$

where R and R^1 are alkyl or aryl groups.

J Write down the structural formulas of the products of the reactions of the following esters with hot concentrated hydrochloric acid:

(a) butyl ethanoate,

(b) phenyl benzoate and

(c) diethyl ethanedioate, $(COOC_2H_5)_2$.

FUELS FROM OILS AND FATS

IT IS IMPOSSIBLE to oxidise esters without breaking their carbon–carbon bonds: they burn in excess oxygen to give carbon dioxide and water. This is the reaction that supplies energy when vegetable oils are used as alternative fuel sources.

Both fats and vegetable oils are used by living systems to transfer energy. They are converted to the corresponding carboxylic acids, which are then oxidised in a complicated series of reactions to form carbon dioxide and water.

Vegetable oils and animal fats are made up of molecules called triglycerides (Fig 16.23). These are esters of the alcohol propane-1,2,3-triol and long-chain carboxylic acids. Vegetable oils are easily extracted from the seeds of plants, and several of them are used in cooking, the most popular ones being olive oil, sunflower oil, soya oil and palm oil.

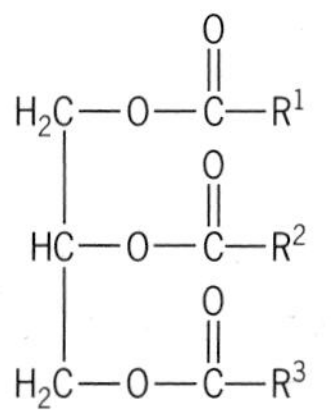

Fig 16.23 **The structure of triglycerides, the constituents of vegetable oils. When the carbon chain contains a double bond, it is an unsaturated oil or fat**

The long carbon chain of the carboxylic acid portion of the triglyceride resembles a long chain alkane, and hence it can be used to make a renewable source of fuel. But the oil as extracted can't be burnt in an engine because the propane-1,2,3-triol residues that form during combustion would soon clog it up. So the vegetable oil is hydrolysed with an alkali and then acidified, and the carboxylic acid products are isolated. They are then reacted with methanol to form methyl esters (Fig 16.24). The methyl esters are much more volatile than the original oil and it is these that are used as a substitute for diesel fuel.

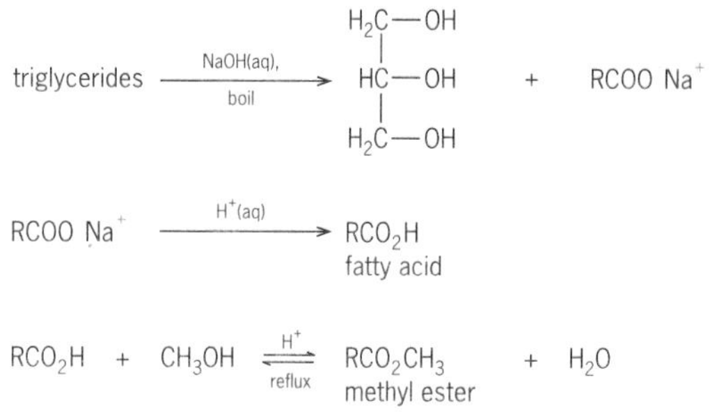

Fig 16.25(a) **Rape is easily grown in the United Kingdom. Its seed, commonly called rapeseed, contains the oil that is converted into the diesel fuel known commercially as RME (rape methyl ester)**

$$triglycerides \xrightarrow[boil]{NaOH(aq),} \begin{array}{c} H_2C-OH \\ | \\ HC-OH \\ | \\ H_2C-OH \end{array} + RCOO^- Na^+$$

$$RCOO^- Na^+ \xrightarrow{H^+(aq)} RCO_2H \\ \text{fatty acid}$$

$$RCO_2H + CH_3OH \underset{reflux}{\overset{H^+}{\rightleftharpoons}} RCO_2CH_3 + H_2O \\ \text{methyl ester}$$

Fig 16.24 **The synthesis of methyl esters of fatty acids from vegetable oils. The triglycerides in vegetable oils can be hydrolysed to form sodium salts of fatty acids. These salts can be converted into the fatty acids, and finally esterification occurs to form a methyl ester. Methyl esters of fatty acids burn easily and therefore look promising as substitutes for diesel fuel**

In the United Kingdom, over one million tonnes of rapeseed is produced each year (Fig 16.25(a)). The oil from rapeseed is easily converted to methyl esters known as rape methyl ester. Rape methyl ester can be used as a diesel substitute and offers several environmental advantages over conventional diesel fuel. It

doesn't form sulphur dioxide and emits fewer sooty particles during combustion.

Fig 16.25(b) **A Reading bus that runs on RME biodiesel**

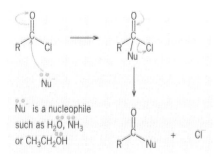

Fig 16.26 **The structure of an acyl chloride. Because of the highly electronegative chlorine atom, its carbonyl group is highly polar, too**

?

K Suggest why the esterification of the fatty acids by methanol is carried out in the presence of an excess of methanol.

L Draw the structure of:

(a) benzoyl chloride,

(b) propanoyl chloride,

(c) hexanedioyl dichloride.

5 ACYL CHLORIDES

An acyl chloride is a carboxylic acid in which the hydroxyl group has been replaced with a chlorine atom (Fig 16.26).

Acyl chlorides are highly reactive compounds which make very useful synthetic intermediates. The preparation of acyl chlorides by reacting sulphuryl(IV) chloride, $SOCl_2$, or phosphorus(V) chloride, PCl_5, with a carboxylic acid is described on page 327.

Naming acyl chlorides

Acyl chlorides are named after the corresponding carboxylic acid, using the suffix *oyl* followed by chloride. For example, CH_3COCl is ethanoyl chloride, and C_6H_5COCl is benzoyl chloride.

Addition–elimination reactions of acyl chlorides

An acyl chloride has an extremely electron-deficient carbonyl carbon because of the electron-withdrawing effect of the highly electronegative chlorine atom. This enhances the reaction of a nucleophile with the carbonyl carbon. Nucleophilic addition occurs and the carbon–oxygen double bond is broken. The addition product then eliminates the chloride as an ion to regenerate the carbonyl carbon. This mechanism is shown in Fig 16.27. The curly arrows show the movement of an electron pair.

Fig 16.27 **The mechanism of the addition–elimination reaction of an acyl chloride**

The addition–elimination reaction is an example of a **condensation reaction**, in which two molecules react together with the elimination of a *simple* molecule, such as water, hydrogen chloride or an alcohol. In an acyl chloride, hydrogen chloride is eliminated.

Hydrolysis of acyl chlorides

An acyl chloride reacts readily with water to form the corresponding carboxylic acid. Most acyl chlorides fume in air because of this reaction with water vapour: the hydrogen chloride gas formed dissolves in atmospheric moisture to form tiny droplets of hydrochloric acid.

For instance, ethanoyl chloride fumes in moist air to form ethanoic acid and hydrogen chloride:

$$CH_3COCl(l) + H_2O(g) \rightarrow CH_3COOH(l) + HCl(g)$$

In water, hydrochloric acid would be formed instead.

This reaction of the carbon–chlorine bond is much more rapid than reactions involving other carbon–chlorine bonds. The highly electron deficient carbonyl carbon encourages nucleophilic addition, to be followed later by elimination.

In particular, this situation contrasts with the inability of chlorobenzene to react with water. In chlorobenzene, the carbon atom attached to the chlorine atom cannot react with a nucleophile because the C–Cl bond is much stronger than in other C–Cl bonds, because of the delocalised π electrons in the benzene ring which extend over the chlorine atom as well.

Compare the hydrolysis of acyl chlorides with the reaction of chloroalkanes with water described on page 215.

When an acyl chloride is hydrolysed in alkaline solution, the carboxylate ion is formed instead of the acid:

$$RCOCl + 2NaOH \rightarrow RCOO^-Na^+ + H_2O + NaCl$$

Preparation of esters from acyl chlorides

As already noted on page 366, the reaction of a carboxylic acid with an alcohol is an equilibrium process, which makes it difficult to obtain good yields of esters. An alternative way of making an ester from a carboxylic acid involves the formation of an acyl chloride and the subsequent reaction of the acyl chloride with an alcohol (Fig 16.28). Acyl chlorides react completely with alcohols and do not form an equilibrium mixture. This provides, in the laboratory, a powerful synthetic route to make esters. Both steps of the process can be achieved with yields over 90 per cent.

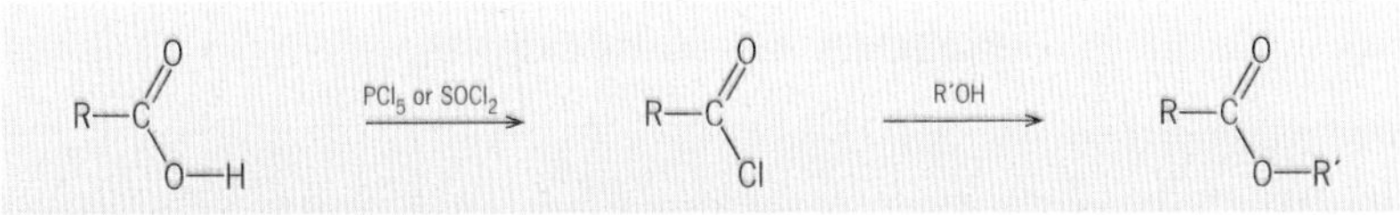

Fig 16.28 **Synthesis of an ester via an acyl chloride. An ester can be prepared from a carboxylic acid in a two-stage reaction. First, the acid is converted into an acyl chloride by reaction with either phosphorus(V) chloride or sulphuryl(IV) chloride. Then, the acyl chloride is used in a condensation reaction with an alcohol to give an ester. The advantage of this method is that there are no equilibrium reactions**

Mechanism of the reaction of acyl chlorides with alcohols

This mechanism is an example of addition–elimination. Its first stage is nucleophilic addition of the alcohol. An alcohol molecule can act as a nucleophile by donating a lone pair of electrons from the oxygen atom to the electron-deficient carbonyl carbon atom, thereby forming a covalent bond (Fig 16.29, next page).

■ See questions 8, 9, and 10.

?

M Write equations for the hydrolysis of

(a) benzoyl chloride and

(b) propanoyl chloride.

N Benzoyl chloride reacts with cold aqueous sodium hydroxide to form sodium benzoate, whereas chlorobenzene will not react with aqueous sodium hydroxide under any conditions.

(a) Write an equation to show the hydrolysis of benzoyl chloride in aqueous sodium hydroxide.

(b) Explain why benzoyl chloride is hydrolysed by aqueous sodium hydroxide but chlorobenzene is not. Hint: Read page 284.

■ See questions 8, 9 and 10.

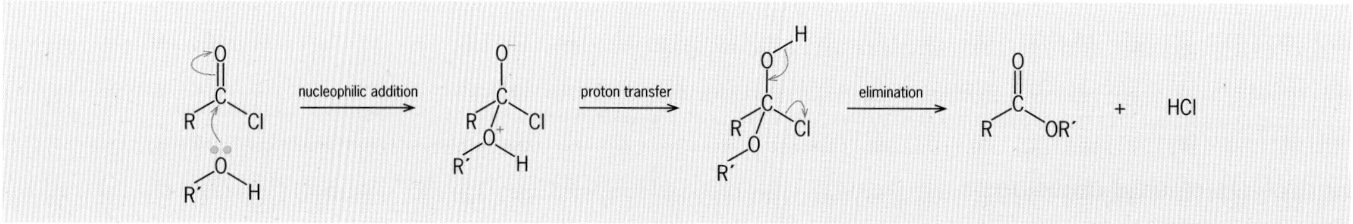

Fig 16.29 **The mechanism of the reaction of an alcohol with an acyl chloride**

The mechanism's next stage involves the transfer of a proton from one highly electronegative atom to another highly electronegative atom. Following proton transfer, hydrogen chloride is eliminated. When the reaction is carried out in the presence of an alkali, the hydrogen chloride reacts to form a chloride ion and it becomes impossible for the reaction to be reversed.

Phenol reacts with acyl chlorides in the same way, and the presence of an alkali can assist the reaction in a second way (Fig 16.30). Phenol is sufficiently acidic for a reaction with an alkali, such as aqueous sodium hydroxide, to form the phenoxide ion, $C_6H_5O^-$. This ion is a much better nucleophile than the neutral phenol molecule, and so the first stage of the reaction, nucleophilic addition, occurs easily.

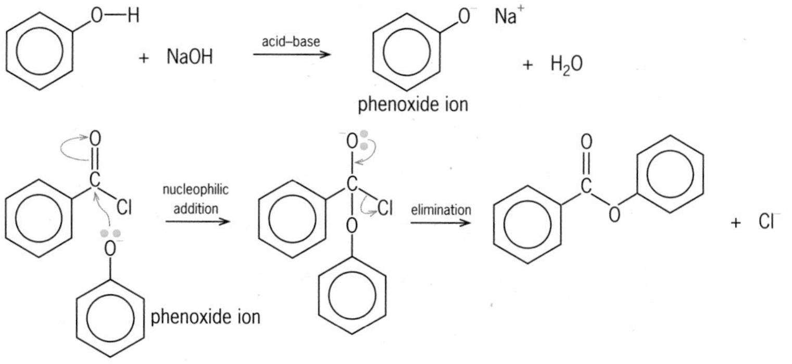

Fig 16.30 **The mechanism of the reaction of phenol with acyl chloride**

Other addition–elimination (condensation) reactions of acyl chlorides

Ammonia and other amines are nucleophiles because they have a lone pair of electrons on the nitrogen atom. They can react with acyl chlorides in the same way as alcohols. This time, the products formed are amides. Amides are difficult to make from carboxylic acids, since they react with ammonia in an acid–base reaction to form an ammonium salt:

$$RCOOH + NH_3 \rightarrow RCOO^-NH_4^+$$

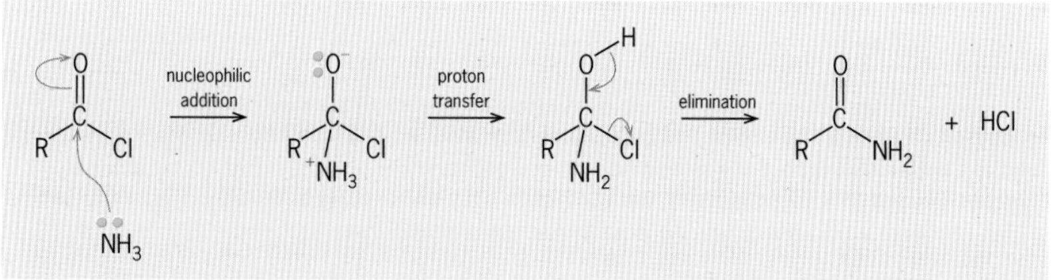

Fig 16.31 **The mechanism of the reaction of ammonia with acyl chlorides**

So the use of an acyl chloride as a synthetic intermediate solves this problem. And it is easy to produce amides by the reaction of an amine or ammonia with an acyl chloride (Fig 16.32). It is normal to use an excess of the amine or ammonia, so that the excess is available to remove the hydrogen chloride eliminated at the end of the acid–base reaction.

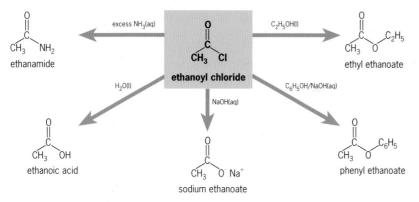

Fig 16.32 **Five useful reactions of ethanoyl chloride**

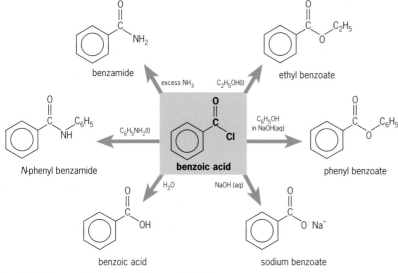

Fig 16.33 **Six useful reactions of benzoyl chloride**

O (a) Draw the mechanism of the reaction of phenylamine, $C_6H_5NH_2$, with benzoyl chloride to give *N*-phenyl benzamide, $C_6H_5CONHC_6H_5$.

(b) Predict the products of each of the following reactions: **(i)** ethanoyl chloride and aqueous sodium hydroxide, **(ii)** ethanoyl chloride and excess ammonia, **(iii)** benzoyl chloride and ammonia, **(iv)** benzoyl chloride and methanol and **(v)** benzoyl chloride and sodium benzoate.

■ See questions 8 and 10.

Fig 16.34 **This mountaineer's rope is made from nylon, which is a polyamide. This is a polymer molecule containing repeating units linked by amide bonds. It is made by the reaction of an acyl chloride (hexanedioyl dichloride) and an amine (1,6-diaminohexane)**

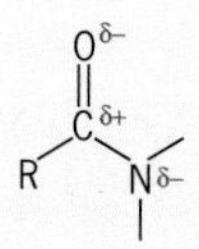

6 AMIDES

Amides have an amino group directly attached to the carbonyl carbon (Fig 16.36). Amides are named by adding the suffix *amide* to the name of the carbon skeleton. Take, for example, ethanamide, pentanamide and benzamide. Ethanamide is a two-carbon chain in which the number 1 carbon is part of the amide functional group. Its formula can be written as CH_3CONH_2. Pentanamide is a five-carbon chain in which the number 1 carbon is part of the amide group. Benzamide consists of a benzene ring attached to an amide functional group (Fig 16.37). It has the formula $C_6H_5CONH_2$.

These amides are known as **primary amides**, because they have only one carbon atom attached to the nitrogen atom of the amide. **Secondary amides** have two carbon atoms attached, and **tertiary amides** have three carbon atoms attached, as Fig 16.37 shows.

Fig 16.35 **The displayed formula of amides. Note that they contain a polar carbonyl bond attached to a nitrogen atom**

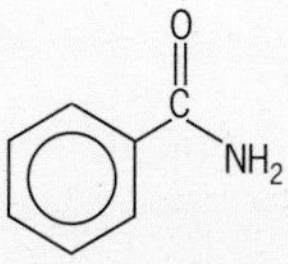

Fig 16.36 **The structure of benzamide**

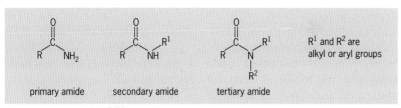

primary amide   secondary amide   tertiary amide

R^1 and R^2 are alkyl or aryl groups

Fig 16.37 **The structure of the three types of amide**

P Write down the formula for pentanamide.

Q What is the structure of N-ethyl ethanamide?

You can read more about secondary amides in proteins and polymers on pages 364 and 382.

Note that the extra carbon atoms are not part of the carbon chain containing the carbonyl group, so they are considered as substituents. Their position is indicated by *N*-, which signifies they are bonded to the nitrogen atom. For example, *N*-methyl ethanamide has the formula $CH_3CONHCH_3$. It has a two-carbon chain which includes the carbonyl carbon, and a methyl group which is attached to the nitrogen atom.

Reactions of amides

Amides show the same types of reaction as the other derivatives of carboxylic acids, but they are rather less reactive.

Hydrolysis of amides

Just as with esters, the reaction of an amide with water is extremely slow, but the reaction can be catalysed by an acid or a base (Fig 16.38). For example, when hydrolysed using boiling hydrochloric acid, ethanamide forms ethanoic acid and ammonium chloride, but when refluxed with aqueous sodium hydroxide, it forms sodium ethanoate and ammonia:

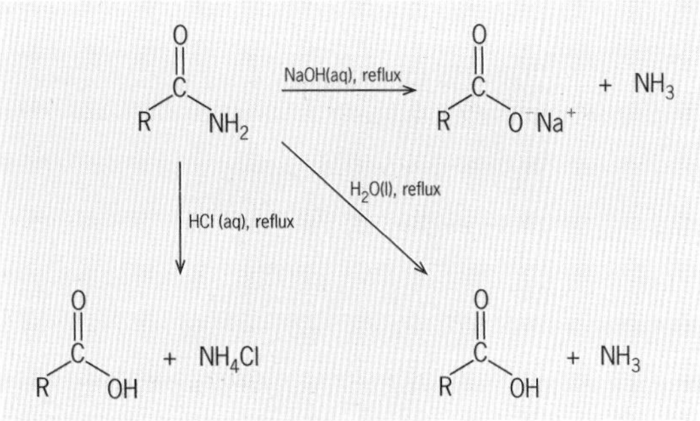

$$CH_3CONH_2 + H_2O + HCl \rightarrow CH_3COOH + NH_4Cl$$
$$CH_3CONH_2 + NaOH \rightarrow CH_3COO^-Na^+ + NH_3$$

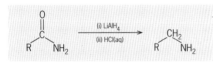

Fig 16.38 **The hydrolysis of amides. These reactions are much faster than with water alone**

See question 11. ■

The hydrolysis of secondary amides in peptides is discussed on page 364.

Reduction of amides

Amides can be reduced by lithium tetrahydridoaluminate(III) to give a primary amine (Fig 16.39).

Reaction with phosphorus(V) oxide to form nitriles

Amides can be dehydrated to form a new class of compounds called nitriles. A nitrile contains the C≡N group:

$$RCONH_2 \xrightarrow[\text{heat}]{P_4O_{10}} RCN + H_2O$$

Fig 16.39 **Reduction of an amide**

Nitriles are useful synthetic intermediates, since they can be hydrolysed in either acidic or basic conditions, and they can be reduced to form primary amines:

$$RCN + H_2O + NaOH \rightarrow RCOO^-Na^+ + NH_3$$
$$RCN + 2H_2O + HCl \rightarrow RCOOH + NH_4Cl$$

$$RCN + 4[H] \xrightarrow[\text{or } H_2]{LiAlH_4} RCH_2NH_2$$

R (a) Draw the structure of the major organic product of the reaction of ethanamide with **(i)** boiling hydrochloric acid and **(ii)** lithium tetrahydridoaluminate(III).

(b) Draw the structure of the major organic product of the reaction of propanamide with **(i)** boiling aqueous sodium hydroxide and **(ii)** lithium tetrahydridoaluminate(III).

Reaction with alkaline aqueous bromine

Primary amines react with alkaline aqueous bromine to form amines. The amine has one less carbon atom than the amide. This reaction is sometimes referred to as the Hofmann degradation, because a carbon–carbon bond is broken during the reaction. Normally, the amide is heated with concentrated aqueous sodium hydroxide and aqueous bromine:

See question 11. ■

$$RCONH_2 \xrightarrow[\text{heat}]{Br_2(aq)/KOH} RNH_2$$

SUMMARY

After studying this chapter, you should know that:

■ Esters, acyl chlorides and amides are all derivatives of carboxylic acids.

■ Esters can be prepared by refluxing a carboxylic acid and an alcohol in the presence of a small amount of concentrated sulphuric acid as a catalyst.

■ Esterification is a reversible reaction that reaches a dynamic equilibrium.

■ At equilibrium, the concentrations of all the substances involved remain constant, and the rate of the forward reaction is equal to the rate of the backward reaction.

■ Le Chatelier's principle states that the position of equilibrium changes to minimise any change imposed on the conditions at equilibrium.

■ The equilibrium constant for a reversible reaction is the product of the molar concentrations of the products, each raised to the power of its coefficient in the stoichiometric equation, divided by the product of the molar concentrations of the reactants, each raised to the power of its coefficient in the stoichiometric equation.

■ Acyl chlorides react with alcohols to form esters in reactions that go to completion.

■ All derivatives of carboxylic acids react by nucleophilic addition–elimination i.e. by condensation reactions

■ Acyl chlorides can be hydrolysed by water to give the corresponding carboxylic acid, whereas amides and esters need to be hydrolysed using an acid or a base catalyst.

■ Amides can be made by the reaction between acyl chlorides and ammonia.

QUESTIONS

1 Benzene-1,4-dicarboxylic acid and ethane-1,2-diol are two important industrial compounds.

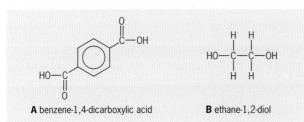

A benzene-1,4-dicarboxylic acid   **B** ethane-1,2-diol

Fig 16.1

a) Name one possible source of these two compounds.

b) **(i)** Draw a displayed formula of the organic products you would expect to obtain from the reaction of one mole of A with one mole of B.
(ii) Name the type of compound formed in **(i)**
(iii) Name a suitable catalyst and the conditions required for the formation of the compound.

c) Name an everyday product which uses ethane-1,2-diol in its manufacture.
[UCLES Autumn 1994 Modular Chemistry 1021/2, q.5]

2 A student was given the following instructions for the preparation of ethyl ethanoate.
Place 20 cm³ (15.8 g) of ethanol in a 250 cm³ round-bottomed flask and add 30 cm³ (31.5 g) of glacial ethanoic acid. Add carefully, with stirring, 2 cm³ of concentrated sulphuric acid. Attach a condenser to the flask and reflux under heating for 30 minutes. Allow to cool and then arrange the flask for fractional distillation and collect the distillate boiling up to 90 °C in a receiver. When the

fraction has been collected, carefully add 25 cm³ of aqueous sodium carbonate to it. Shake the mixture and separate the organic layer. Allow this to stand overnight in contact with a suitable drying agent. Remove the drying agent and redistill the liquid, collecting the fraction which boils at about 75 °C.

a) **(i)** Write a balanced equation for the reaction.
(ii) Draw the structural formula of the organic product.

b) Explain the function of the sulphuric acid in this preparation.

c) Calculate which of the reagents is present in excess.

d) The reaction described usually produces a yield of around 20 per cent. Suggest two reasons why the yield is so low.

3

a) Write an equation for the reaction between ethanoic acid and ethanol.

b) 0.6 mol ethanoic acid, 0.5 mol ethanol, 0.6 mol ethyl ethanoate and 0.4 mol of water containing a small amount of hydrogen ions, were mixed together at 20 °C. At equilibrium only 0.4 mol of ethanoic acid remained.
(i) How many moles of each of the following were present at equilibrium? Ethanol, ethyl ethanoate, water.
(ii) Write an expression for the equilibrium constant, K_c, for this reaction.
(iii) Calculate the value of K_c for this reaction.
[ULEAC 1996 Specimen Paper CH5 8081 q.3]

4 A mixture of 0.50 mol of ethanoic acid and 1.00 mol of ethanol was shaken for a long time to reach equilibrium. The whole mixture was titrated quickly with $1.00 \, mol \, dm^{-3}$ sodium hydroxide and $80 \, cm^3$ of alkali were required.

a)   (i) Write an equation for the reaction between ethanoic acid and ethanol.
   (ii) Explain why the reaction mixture was titrated *quickly*.

b) By making use of the titration results, and the equation in a) (i), calculate:
   (i) how many moles of ethanoic acid remained at equilibrium.
   (ii) how many moles of ethanoic acid had reacted.
   (iii) how many moles of ethanol were left in the equilibrium mixture.

c)   (i) Write the expression for the equilibrium constant, K_c, for the reaction you have given in a) (i).
   (ii) calculate a value for K_c for this reaction.
[UCLES June 1993, 9250/3 q.3]

5 Ethanoic acid, CH_3CO_2H, reacts with ethanol, C_2H_5OH, to produce ethyl ethanoate, $CH_3CO_2C_2H_5$, and water.

a) Outline, with essential detail, how you would carry out an experiment to determine the equilibrium constant, K_c, for the following reaction at 25 °C.

$$CH_3CO_2H + C_2H_5OH \rightleftharpoons CH_3CO_2C_2H_5 + H_2O$$

b) A mixture of 6.0 g of ethanoic acid and 6.0 g of ethanol was added to 4.4 g of ethyl ethanoate and the overall mixture allowed to reach equilibrium. It was found that 0.040 mol of the ethanoic acid was present in the equilibrium mixture.
Calculate the equilibrium constant for the reaction.
[UCLES Summer 1995 Modular Chemistry 1026/2,q.5]

6 For the reaction:

$$CH_3CO_2H(l) + C_2H_5OH(l) \rightleftharpoons CH_3CO_2C_2H_5(l) + H_2O(l)$$

the value of the equilibrium constant is 4.0.

a) Write an expression for the equilibrium constant, K_c, of the reverse reaction, ie the hydrolysis of ethyl ethanoate, stating its numerical value.

b) In an experiment, 2 mol of ethyl ethanoate and 2 mol of water are mixed.
Calculate the number of moles of each substance present when equilibrium is reached.
[UCLES Winter 1994 Chemistry 9250/3, q.3]

7 The displayed formula shown in Fig 16.Q7 is that of an ester found in pineapples.

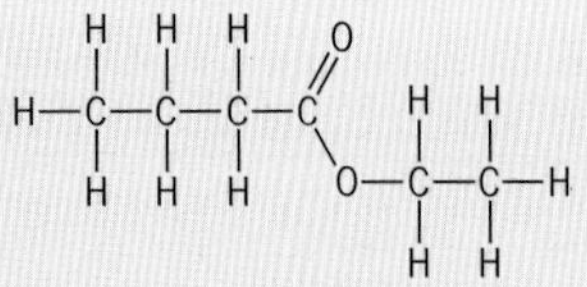

Fig 16.Q7

a)   (i) Name this ester.
   (ii) Name the two products of the acid hydrolysis of this ester.
   (iii) How, and with what reagent, would you carry out this hydrolysis in the laboratory?

b) Draw the displayed formula of an ester isomeric with the ester above.
[UCLES Spring 1994, 1021/2 q.2]

8

a) Draw a displayed structural formula of benzoyl chloride, C_6H_5COCl. How can it be made starting from benzoic acid?

b) Describe three reactions of benzoyl chloride, giving reagents and products in each case. How and why does the reactivity of benzoyl chloride differ from that of chloromethylbenzene (benzyl chloride), $C_6H_5CH_2Cl$?
[UCLES Summer 1994 9250/1, q.8]

9

a) Describe how you can make benzoyl chloride starting from benzoic acid.

b) Describe with the aid of equations how benzoyl chloride reacts with: (i) water, (ii) aqueous sodium hydroxide, (iii) phenol in aqueous sodium hydroxide.

10 Describe the reaction of ethanoyl chloride with:

a) ethanol,

b) ammonia,

c) water

Give the mechanism for one of these reactions.

11 Ethanamide is a white solid.

a) Give the full displayed formula for ethanamide and explain why it is a primary amide.

b) Draw the structure of one secondary amide.

c) Hydrolysis with hot aqueous sodium hydroxide ethanamide produces an alkaline gas, but this gas is not produced when the hydrolysis is carried out in refluxing concentrated hydrochloric acid.
Explain these results with the aid of equations.

d) When ethanamide is heated with phosphorus(V) oxide, a colourless liquid **A** can be distilled from the mixture. **A** will react with hot aqueous sodium hydroxide to give an alkaline gas **B** and a solution **C**. **A** will also react with refluxing hydrochloric acid to form a solution containing two compounds **D** and **E**. Liquid **A** can be reduced to a compound **F** with formula C_2H_7N.
Identify all the substances **A** to **F**.
Give reasons for your answers and include equations for all reactions involved.

Assignment

CARBOXYLIC ACID DERIVATIVES AND FOOD

Many foods contain fats or oils. These fats and oils are esters, and they include triglycerides. Triglycerides are formed between propan-1,2,3-triol and long carbon chain carboxylic acids.

1 Many fats and oils are triglycerides. Draw the general structure of a triglyceride. Use R to represent a long-chain alkyl group.

The annual world production of natural oils and fats such as soya bean oil, palm oil and sunflower oil is about 50 million tonnes. Natural oils vary in colour and flavour and are refined to produce oils suited for particular uses. For example, in a butter substitute, the fat needs a particular texture, flavour and melting range.

Many manufactured foods contain both an oil and water, which must remain mixed and not separate during storage. Additives control this separation and also flavour.

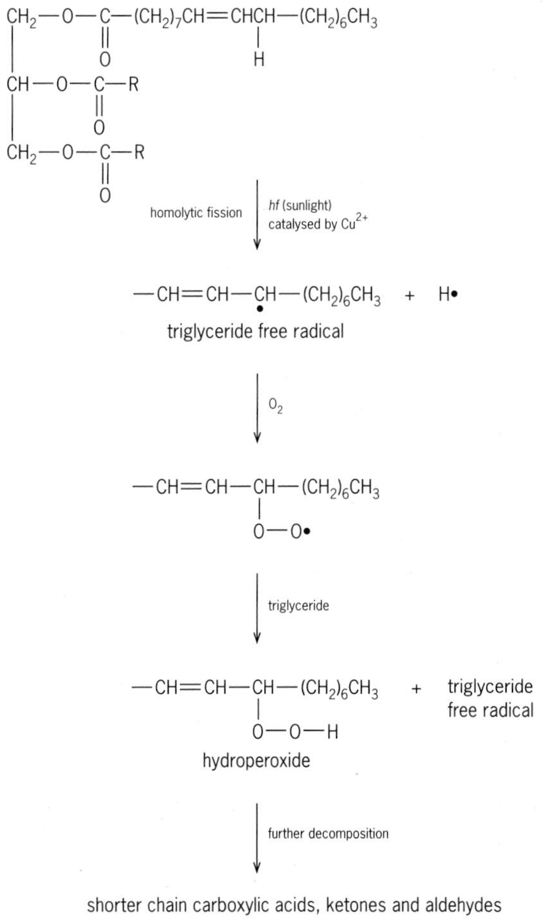

CH_2—O—C—$(CH_2)_7$CH==CHCH—$(CH_2)_6CH_3$
        ‖ |
        O   H
CH—O—C—R
      ‖
      O
CH_2—O—C—R
        ‖
        O

homolytic fission hf (sunlight)
                     catalysed by Cu^{2+}

—CH==CH—CH—$(CH_2)_6CH_3$ +   H•
           •
    triglyceride free radical

            O_2

—CH==CH—CH—$(CH_2)_6CH_3$
           |
           O—O•

            triglyceride

—CH==CH—CH—$(CH_2)_6CH_3$ +   triglyceride
           | free radical
           O—O—H
    hydroperoxide

            further decomposition

shorter chain carboxylic acids, ketones and aldehydes

2

a) Make a list of four food products that contain fats. Then list the fat content of each product and the additives present.

b) Use a data booklet to identify the different types of food additive found in the foods you listed in part **a)**.

Although the texture and melting range of fats can be controlled, their flavour poses a problem. Fats and oils can deteriorate by aerial oxidation to products that have unpleasant odours and flavours. For example, oxygen reacts with triglycerides to form hydroperoxides. They contain an oxygen–oxygen single bond, which makes them particularly reactive, because the bond can break homolytically, forming free radicals. These are then involved in a chain reaction shown in Fig 16.A1.

3

a) The initiation step (see page 208) involves the homolytic fission of a carbon–hydrogen bond. What is meant by homolytic fission?

b) Explain why the oxidation process is referred to as a chain reaction.

The hydroperoxides themselves don't have unpleasant odours or flavours, but they are tend to decompose to form short-chain aldehydes, ketones or alcohols that do smell and taste worse.

Because in aerial oxidation, a hydroperoxide is formed first, and then catalyses further oxidation, there is a time delay before the rate of this auto-oxidation becomes significant. During the delay, there is not enough hydroperoxide to maintain the free radical chain reaction. Antioxidants added to food interfere with the propagation stage in the oxidation process to slow it down.

Metal ions present in the food, such as copper(II) ions, speed up the initial formation of hydroperoxides. To stop this, antioxidant additives, such as citric acid, form a complex with the metal ions and thus slow down the initial formation of hydroperoxides. Two common antioxidants added to fatty foods are BHA (E310) and BHT (321) whose structures are shown in Fig 16.A2. These substances remove free radicals but get used up in the process.

4

a) Suggest ways of storing foods containing fats and oils that would slow down the initial formation of hydroperoxides.

b) Suggest ways of storing foods which would slow down the chain reaction leading to autoxidation.

Fig 16.A1 **The oxidation of triglycerides**

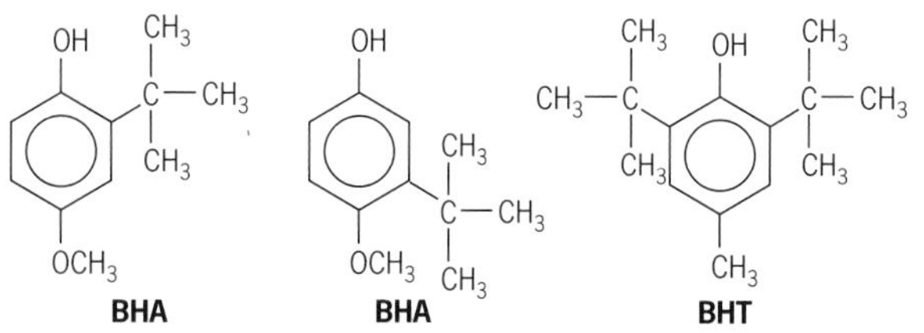

Fig 16.A2 **Antioxidants, such as BHA and BHT, prevent the oxidation of fats by reacting with free radicals, which stops the chain reaction**

5 Explain why the autoxidation of fats starts slowly and then progresses rapidly, even when antioxidants are present. The separation of the oil from the water in foods is a constant problem. Ideally, an emulsion should be formed which will not separate. Emulsifiers such as lecithin (Fig 16.A3) are added to the oil/water mix to prevent the separation process.

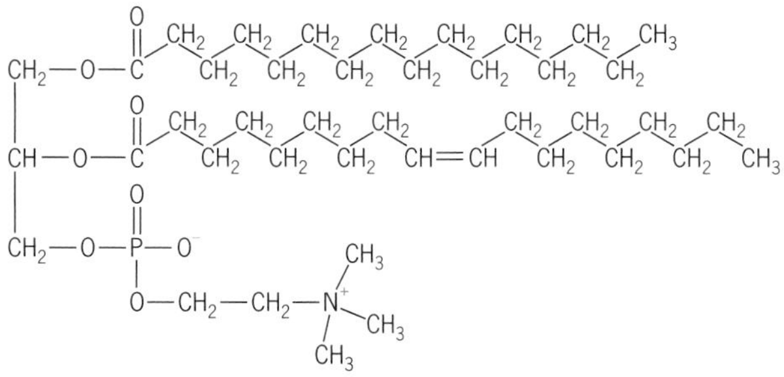

Fig 16.A3 **The structure of lecithin**

6
a) Name the functional groups found in lecithin.

b) Explain the differences between lecithin and a triglyceride.

The lecithin molecule has an extremely polar end which is capable of forming intermolecular attractions with water molecules. At the other end is a non-polar alkyl chain that can form induced dipole–induced dipole interactions with either fat or oil molecules. Lecithin behaves very similarly to household detergents.

7 Explain how the structure of lecithin enables it to function as an emulsifier.

ESTERS, ACYL CHLORIDES, AMIDES AND EQUILIBRIA

The related groups of compounds covered in this chapter form the basis of many industrial processes because of their reactivity and the usefulness of their products. Many reactions are reversible and so they demonstrate the concepts of equilibrium constant and Le Chatelier's principle. These and other ideas in the chapter are brought together in the Chapter Map.

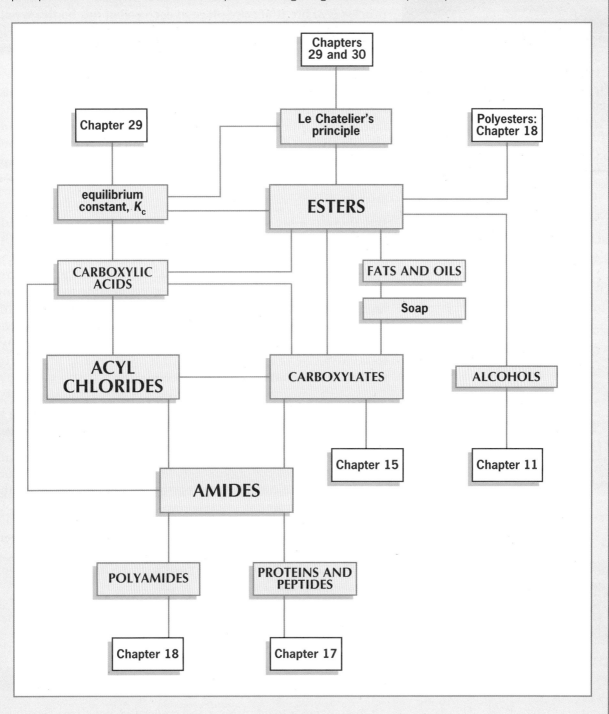

17 Amino acids and proteins

Organisms such as the algae that colour this volcanic spring in Yellowstone National Park, USA, survive because their enzymes can tolerate high temperatures

WITHOUT ENZYMES – biochemical catalysts – the chemical processes of life that take place in each cell of our bodies would be impossibly slow. When in action, each of these special proteins catalyses its specific chemical reaction with a turnover of thousands – even millions – of molecules per minute.

The suggestion is that enzymes could possibly revolutionise large-scale industrial processes. They are thousands of times faster than inorganic catalysts and most work best at body temperature. Industry uses vast amounts of energy to speed up many reactions, so enzymes could save precious energy. Moreover, they are environmentally friendly because it is easy to dispose of them safely.

But there is a big snag. Enzymes lack stability over the wide range of reaction conditions encountered in industry. So the race is on to find 'extremozymes' – enzymes which can tolerate higher temperatures and a wider range of other conditions. Because their enzymes must be able to withstand high temperatures, organisms which survive in volcanic springs are a promising starting point. By understanding the structure of these enzymes, biochemists can work out ways to synthesise extremozymes that will make industrial reactions more efficient – and greener, too.

1 WHY PROTEINS ARE IMPORTANT

Proteins make up about 15 per cent of our body weight. They are the major components of skin, muscle, nails and hair, giving structural support and holding cells together. While these may be the obvious proteins, just as essential are other proteins: the enzymes which catalyse the chemical reactions going on inside our bodies; the many protein hormones which act as chemical messengers within and between cells; the protein antibodies which protect us from disease; and the protein haemoglobin which transports oxygen through our arteries.

So, proteins are crucial biological molecules (biomolecules). Yet, despite being so diverse, they all are made up from just 20 small molecules called amino acids.

> Not all hormones are proteins. Some, including the sex hormones are steroids (see page 294).

2 NATURALLY OCCURRING AMINO ACIDS

As their name implies, amino acid molecules have two functional groups, an amine group and a carboxylic acid group (Fig 17.1). All naturally occurring amino acids have the amine group on the second carbon atom of the molecule (next to the carboxylic acid group). This is often called the **α-carbon**, see Fig 17.2.

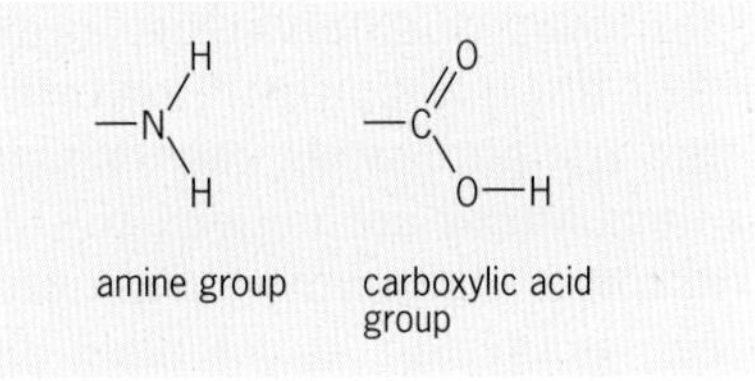

Fig 17.1

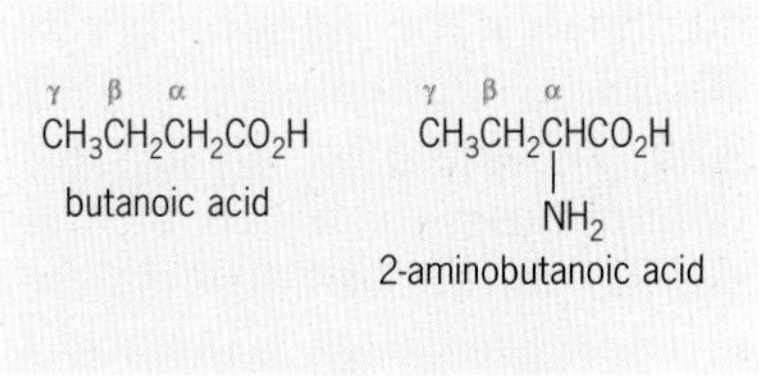

Fig. 17.2 **The Greek lettering of the carbon atoms. 2-aminobutanoic acid is an α-amino acid**

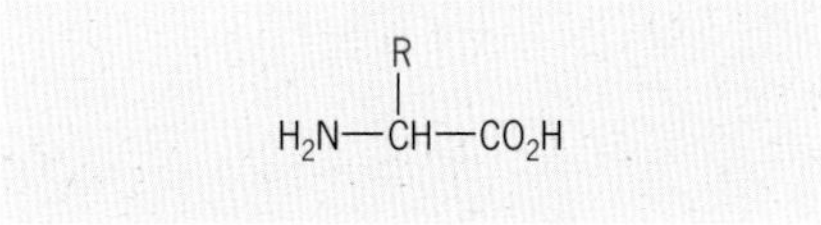

Fig 17.3 **General formula for α-amino acids**

■ See question 1.

2-aminobutanoic acid is an **α-amino acid**, or a **2-aminocarboxylic acid**. The more commonly used term is α-amino acid. In this type of acid, the amine and the carboxylic acid functional groups are both bonded to the same carbon atom. α-amino acids are represented by the *general formula* given in Fig 17.3.

The side chain R varies considerably, as Fig 17.4 shows. The composition of the R group confers an individual set of properties to each amino acid and this, of course, affects the properties of the proteins in which they are found.

A (a) Draw the ß-amino acid based on butanoic acid.

(b) 4-aminobutanoic acid is also known as gamma-aminobutanoic acid (GABA for short) and is involved in transmitting nerve impulses. Draw this amino acid.

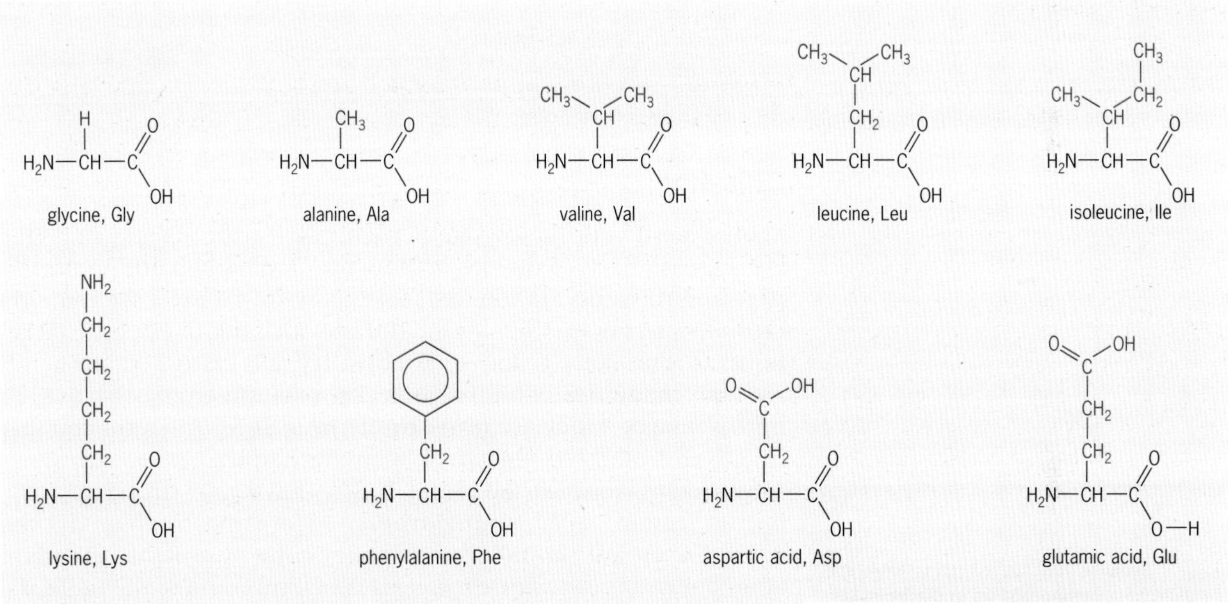

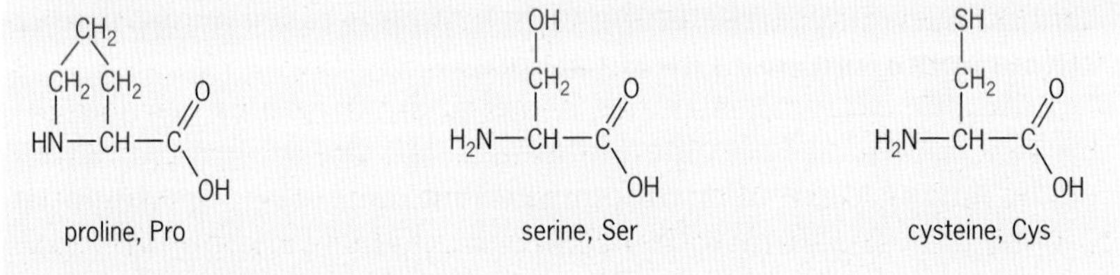

Fig 17.4 **Twelve of the 20 naturally occurring amino acids which make up most proteins. In each case, the R group is in colour**

Of the 20 amino acids needed to make up our proteins, eight cannot be synthesised in our bodies. These eight are called essential amino acids and must be part of our diet.

B (a) Which amino acids in Fig 17.4 have polar side chains?

(b) Look at leucine and isoleucine. Why is isoleucine so named?

(c) (i) The R group of threonine (Thr), another amino acid found in proteins, is $CH_3CH(OH)–$
Draw the displayed formula of this amino acid.
Hint: Remember that the displayed formula shows all the atoms and bonds (including those in OH groups).
(ii) What type of alcohol side chain is this?
(iii) How does the R group in Thr differ from that in serine?

3 OPTICAL ISOMERISM AND CHIRAL CARBONS

As discussed on page 144, there are two types of isomerism: **structural isomerism** and **stereoisomerism** (Fig 17.5). The amino acids leucine and isoleucine (see Fig 17.4) are structural isomers because they both have the same molecular formula but different structural formulas (which answers part **(b)** of Self-test question **B**). However, with the exception of glycine, all the α-amino acids can exhibit stereoisomerism, which means that their atoms are bonded in the same order but arranged differently in space. One form of stereoisomerism, known as geometric (*cis–trans*) isomerism, is described on page 248. The other form of isomerism which is shown by these α-amino acids is **optical isomerism**.

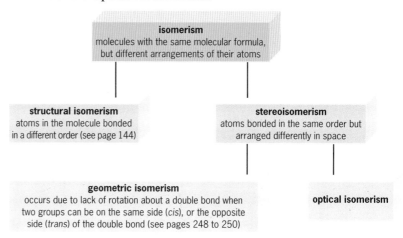

isomerism
molecules with the same molecular formula, but different arrangements of their atoms

structural isomerism
atoms in the molecule bonded in a different order (see page 144)

stereoisomerism
atoms bonded in the same order but arranged differently in space

geometric isomerism
occurs due to lack of rotation about a double bond when two groups can be on the same side (*cis*), or the opposite side (*trans*) of the double bond (see pages 248 to 250)

optical isomerism

Fig 17.5 **Different types of isomerism**

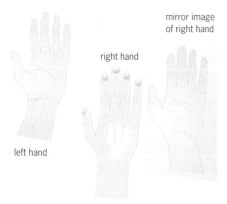

mirror image of right hand

right hand

left hand

Fig 17.6 **Because your hand is not symmetrical, it cannot be superimposed on its mirror image**

Chirality

Look at both your hands together with their palms facing you. One is a mirror image of the other. Now put one hand palm up on this page and the other on top of it, also palm up. You will see that you cannot superimpose them – the thumbs stick out in opposite directions. This property is known as **chirality** and exists because hands are not symmetrical. Chiral objects cannot be superimposed on their mirror images – they are **non-superimposable**. The term chirality is derived from *kheir*, the Greek word for hand.

Molecules, too, can be chiral and so have non-superimposable mirror images called **enantiomers**. In organic compounds, the usual reason why a molecule is chiral is because it has a carbon atom bonded to *four different groups*. When this occurs, the molecule cannot be symmetrical and the carbon atom is called an **asymmetric carbon atom** or a **chiral carbon**.

Take, for example, alanine. It has a chiral carbon because this atom is bonded to four different groups. It is therefore a chiral molecule, having a pair of enantiomers which cannot be superimposed.

Now look at glycine in Fig 17.9. Note that its carbon is no longer asymmetric because it has two identical groups attached (the

mirror

Fig 17.7 **A common way for a molecule to be chiral is when it contains a carbon atom bonded to four different groups. The mirror image of this molecule is non-superimposable and is called an enantiomer**

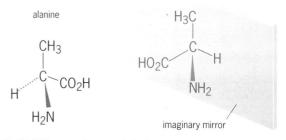

alanine

imaginary mirror

Fig 17.8 **The enantiomers of alanine are shown using an imaginary mirror. Note that although the central carbon atom is bonded to two carbon atoms, these atoms are part of two different groups**

hydrogen atoms). The glycine molecule and its mirror image can be superimposed, so they cannot be enantiomers of each other.

The enantiomers of chiral molecules have the same chemical properties in ordinary test-tube reactions, which might be expected given that their atoms are bonded in the same order. But because their atoms are arranged differently in space, we might expect differences in their physical properties such as melting point, boiling point and solubility. However, these too, are identical except in one unusual way which gives rise to optical isomerism.

What is optical isomerism?

With any pair of enantiomers, one enantiomer rotates plane-polarised light in one direction, and the other enantiomer rotates it in the opposite direction. But the angles of rotation are equal. In 1815, Jean-Baptiste Biot, a French physicist, was the first to discover that the crystals of certain substances could rotate a beam of plane-polarised light either to the right (clockwise) or to the left (anticlockwise), looking at the incoming light. At the time, the reason for this rotation was a mystery. It was later discovered that solutions of certain compounds could also exhibit this **optical activity.**

Molecules which rotate plane-polarised light to the left (anticlockwise) are said to be **laevorotatory**. Those which rotate it to the right (clockwise) are called **dextrorotatory**.

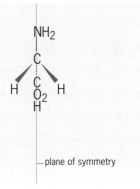

—plane of symmetry

Fig 17.9 **Glycine**

Although enantiomers have identical chemical properties, they do interact differently with the enantiomers of other chiral molecules. This is why some enantiomers do not smell and taste the same, because they interact differently with the chiral taste and smell receptors.

Light and optical activity

Normal light consists of electromagnetic waves which vibrate in all directions perpendicular to the direction of travel, as shown in Fig 17.10. (The electromagnetic nature of light is covered on page 48.) Certain crystals allow light with vibrations in one plane only to pass through them. Such crystals are known as polarisers. The light which emerges from a polariser is called plane-polarised light, or just polarised light. A good example of polarisers is provided by the lenses of Polaroid sunglasses.

When certain substances are placed between two aligned polarisers through which plane-polarised light is passing, the second polariser stops transmitting light. This is because the substance has rotated the plane of polarisation of the light. The substance is said to be **optically active**. Rotating the second polariser through a certain angle restores its transmission of light. This is the way in which the angle of rotation caused by a substance is measured, and is the principle of the polarimeter.

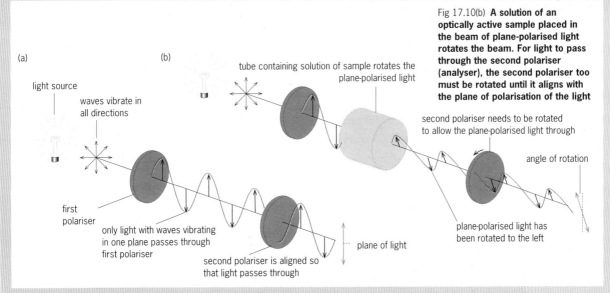

Fig 17.10(b) **A solution of an optically active sample placed in the beam of plane-polarised light rotates the beam. For light to pass through the second polariser (analyser), the second polariser too must be rotated until it aligns with the plane of polarisation of the light**

Fig 17.10(a) **Unpolarised light from a source passes through the first polariser and the light emerges from it in one plane only. This plane-polarised light passes through the second polariser (analyser) only when both polarisers are aligned**

In 1848, French scientist, Louis Pasteur, discovered the important connection between the structure of crystals and their optical activity. He was examining salts of tartaric acid when he noticed that samples of the sodium salt included two sorts of crystal which were mirror images of each other. Pasteur separated the two sorts of crystal and made a solution of each. He then examined both solutions in a polarimeter, an instrument used to measure optical activity. He found that one sort of crystal rotated plane-polarised light clockwise, while the other rotated it anticlockwise. He also found that, when the concentrations were the same, the two angles of rotation were equal, but in opposite directions.

Pasteur proposed that the molecules making up the crystals must also be mirror images of one another. This proved to be an advance of fundamental importance. Less than 20 years later, the tetrahedral model was proposed for those carbon-containing molecules in which each carbon atom has four single bonds (see the description of methane on page 78). It was then recognised that when a carbon atom is bonded to four different groups, it is asymmetric or chiral.

LOUIS PASTEUR

MOST PEOPLE HAVE HEARD of Louis Pasteur as the inventor of the so-called pasteurisation of milk, heat treatment which destroys the bacteria that are naturally in milk and which would otherwise make it 'go off'. But this process was just one aspect of his revolutionary work on microorganisms and how they cause food to spoilage and fermentation.

Fig 17.11 **Louis Pasteur (1822–1895)**

Among Pasteur's other achievements was his intense research on silkworm disease which led to his pioneering germ theory. Putting his theory into practice, he produced vaccines for anthrax and rabies.

Pasteur's achievements outside scientific medicine were just as significant. For instance, he solved the puzzle of why certain crystals and solutions are able to rotate plane-polarised light. He observed that the sodium ammonium salt of tartaric acid (crystals of tartaric acid are found on wine casks) rotated plane-polarised light to the right, while the sodium ammonium salt of racemic acid (another acid found on wine casks during fermentation) had no effect. Apart from this observation, the salts of racemic acid and tartaric acid appeared to be the same, having identical chemical composition

and properties. The shapes of the crystals apparently looked the same. However, under the microscope he noticed right- and left-handed crystals in racemic acid.

Pasteur pressed on, painstakingly sorting the two sorts of crystalswith the aid of a microscope and tweezers. He made a solution of each sort and examined both solutions in his polarimeter.

Pasteur's discovery of right- and left-handed crystals in racemic acid owed much to luck. He was doing his experiments in winter. Above 26 °C, racemic acid would not have crystallised out into two different forms. Also, the salt of racemic acid he had chosen to investigate is the only salt whose mirror-image crystals have faces clear enough to allow separation with the aid of a microscope (which would not have been a powerful as today's instruments). But, as Pasteur himself remarked, 'Chance favours the prepared mind.'

Racemic acid contains a 50:50 mixture of dextrorotatory and laevorotatory crystals of tartaric acid. Until Pasteur's separation of racemic acid, the laevorotatory form of tartaric acid was unknown. Any 50:50 mixture of left- and right-handed molecules is called a **racemic mixture** after the salt of racemic acid which Pasteur separated. In a racemic mixture, the optical activity of one isomer cancels out the optical activity of the other isomer.

Fig 17.12 **Mirror-image crystals of the sodium ammonium salt of tartaric acid**

EXAMPLE

Q Lactic acid, $CH_3CH(OH)CO_2H$, is isolated from milk. It is an optical isomer of the lactic acid present in muscles.

a) Explain what is meant by the term optical isomerism.

b) Draw the full structural formulas of the two enantiomers, showing clearly the feature which causes optical isomerism.

A a) Optical isomerism occurs when a molecule has a non-superimposable mirror image (Fig 17.13). The molecules of such a pair are called enantiomers. The two enantiomers rotate plane-polarised light in opposite directions.

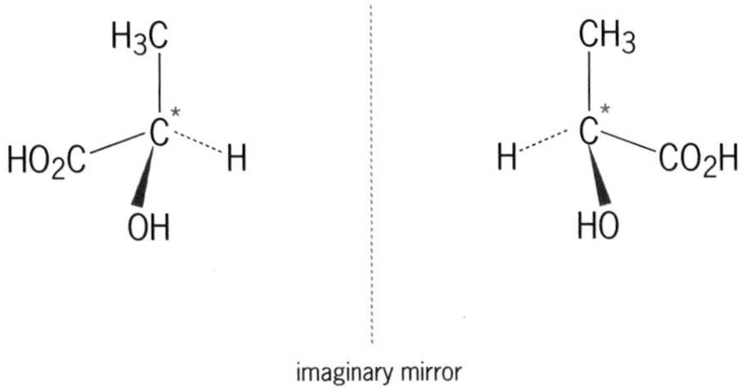

Fig 17.13
Enantiomers of the same compound, lactic acid

imaginary mirror

b) It is often helpful to include an imaginary mirror when drawing optical isomers. In Fig 17.13 the groups around the chiral carbon atom are shown as mirror images, but this is not essential. The feature which causes optical isomerism in lactic acid is a chiral carbon, which is often indicated by an asterisk (C*).

To depict a pair of optical isomers, draw the 3-D structure of one molecule and then swap the positions of two of the groups in the other molecule.

C What is the systematic name of lactic acid?

D Optical isomers of the molecule carvone produce different taste sensations. One enantiomer gives the taste of spearmint and is used in spearmint chewing gum. The other enantiomer gives the taste of caraway seeds, which are used to flavour seed cakes.

(a) Explain what is meant by the term enantiomer.

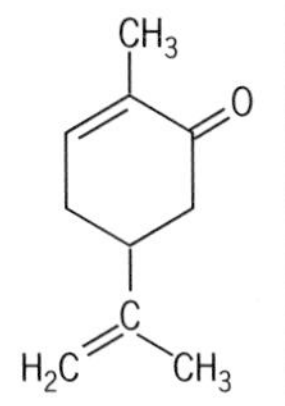

(b) Copy the displayed formula of carvone and mark the chiral carbon. If you are in doubt, look at Fig 17.16 and its caption.

Fig 17.14 **Carvone**

In many molecules, there is more than one chiral carbon. For example, the chain form of the glucose molecule has four chiral carbon atoms (Figs 17.15 and 17.16).

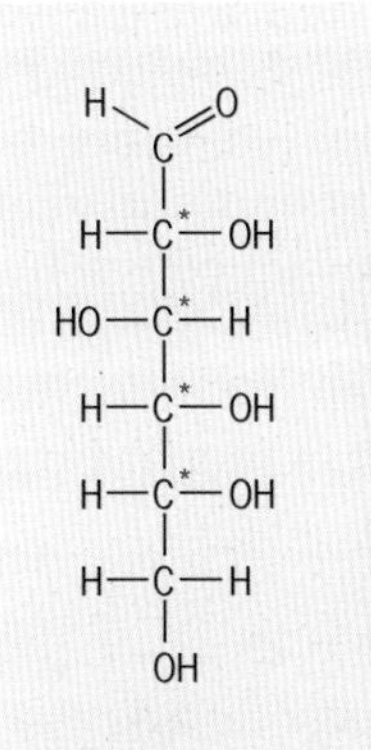

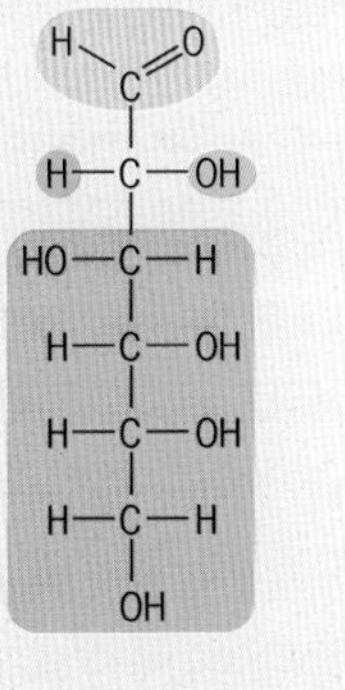

Fig 17.15 (left) **The structural formula of the chain form of glucose showing the four chiral carbon atoms, each identified by an asterisk**

Fig 17.16 (right) **Although each chiral carbon is bonded to two other carbon atoms, to decide if a carbon atom is chiral you must consider the whole of each group attached to it. This has been done for one carbon atom, showing clearly that there are four different groups around it. Can you see why the other three carbon atoms indicated in Fig 17.15 are chiral?**

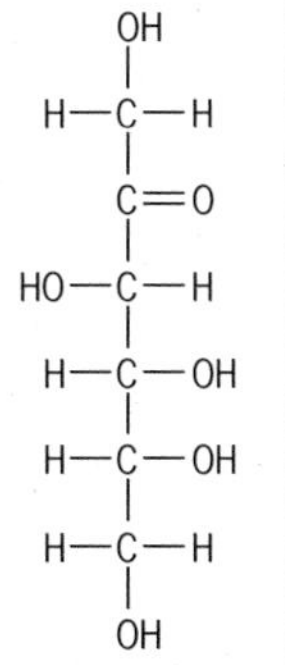

E Copy the fructose molecule shown in Fig 17.17 and identify the chiral carbons using asterisks.

Fig 17.17

L- and D- enantiomers of α-amino acids

Nearly all the amino acids in every organism are made up from one type of enantiomer, known as the L-enantiomer. In the L-enantiomer, the arrangement of the four groups spell CORN (CO_2H, **R**, NH_2) when you look directly down on the H atom and go clockwise round the molecule (Fig 17.18).

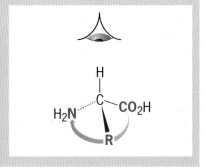

Fig 17.18 **To identify an L-amino acid, see whether the groups spell CORN in a clockwise direction when you look down on the hydrogen atom**

The proteins in the cell wall of a bacterium are made up of D-amino acids, which is unusual in organisms. The antibiotic penicillin kills bacteria because it interferes with the building of new cell walls of bacteria which are dividing. Penicillin does not destroy our cell walls when they divide because our protein is made of L-amino acids.

AGEING A SKULL BY ITS SMILE

WHEN WE ARE BORN, the dentine inside our teeth contains L-aspartic acid (see Fig 17.4). As we grow older, this starts to change to the D-form. When we die, this process continues at the same rate for hundreds of years. This means that we can accurately date a skull that has been dug up, just by knowing the proportions of D- to L-aspartic acid in its teeth – provided that the skull is not too old. This technique is reliable back to the tenth century AD.

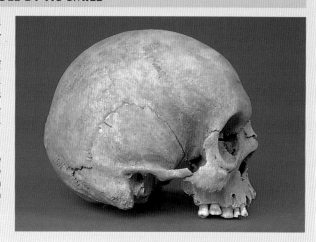

Fig 17.19 **As a skull ages, there is an increase in the ratio of the D- to L- isomers of aspartic acid in its teeth. Exhumed skulls have been dated by determining this ratio. This is the skull of a mediaeval Ilford man**

See questions 2, 3, and 4. ■

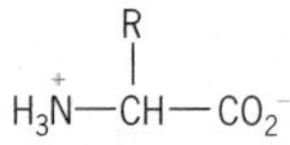

Fig 17.20 **An amino acid zwitterion**

Bases are proton acceptors and acids are proton donors (see page 309).

The reaction of CO_2H with alkalis is covered on page 319, and the reaction of NH_2 with acids on page 640.

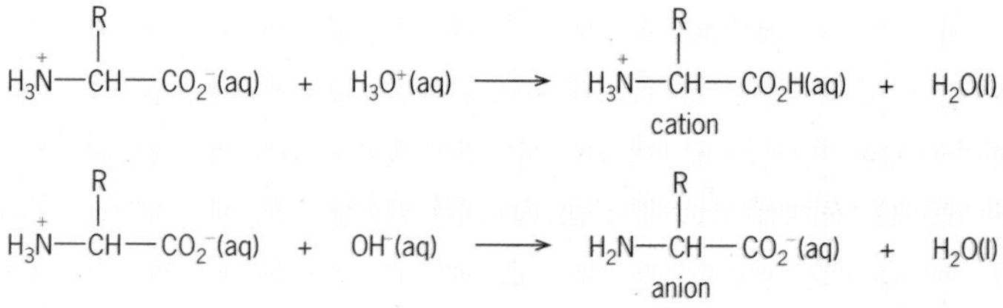

Fig 17.21 (top)

Fig 17.22 (bottom)

?

F Write balanced equations for the reactions of **(a)** glycine with sodium hydroxide solution, and **(b)** leucine with dilute hydrochloric acid. Salts are produced in both cases, so remember to show the charges on the ions.
Hint: See Fig 17.4 for the formulas of amino acids.

See questions 1, 3, 4, 5 and 8. ■

Zwitterions

Amino acids have two functional groups. The chemical properties of compounds with two functional groups are often the sum of the chemical properties of each individual group. However, with amino acids, the basic amine group and the acidic carboxylic acid group can react with each other. A proton from CO_2H can be donated to the NH_2 group of the same molecule to give a **zwitterion** (Fig 17.20), a molecule which carries both a positive and a negative charge. (*Zwitter* is the German term for hybrid.)

Their relatively high melting point and their high solubility in water indicate that amino acids exist as zwitterions, both in the solid state and in solution. When a dilute acid is added to an aqueous solution of an amino acid (Fig 17.21), the CO_2^- group accepts a proton to form CO_2H. This leaves a positive ion (a cation). When the pH of the aqueous solution is raised by adding OH^- (Fig 17.22), a proton from NH_3^+ is removed to form NH_2 and a negative ion (an anion).

The pH at which zwitterions have the highest concentration in solution in equal amounts is known as the **isoelectric point**. For those with a neutral R group, the isoelectric point is about pH 6. By contrast, lysine has a basic side chain which contains an extra NH_2 group (Fig 17.23). This means that a solution of lysine is alkaline and its isoelectric point is about 9.5. Those amino acids with an additional CO_2H in the side chain are acidic and have low isoelectric points.

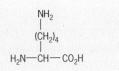

Fig 17.23 **Lysine has two NH₂ groups, making it a basic amino acid**

?

G Look at Fig 17.4, page 355. Which amino acids have an acidic side chain?

Electrophoresis

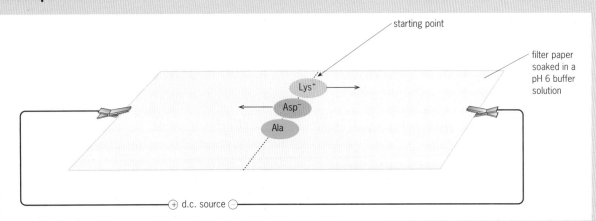

Fig 17.24 **Electrophoresis of a mixture of three amino acids. The pH used in this example is 6, so alanine exists as a zwitterion. At this pH, aspartic acid is negatively charged and lysine is positively charged**

Electrophoresis can be used to separate a mixture of amino acids according to the ionic charge at a particular pH. The mixture is placed in a gel or on filter paper (Fig 17.24) in an electric field. Positively charged ions migrate to the cathode, negatively charged ions to the anode. When the pH is at a value at which zwitterions are formed with equal positive and negative charge, the zwitterions cannot move in either direction. So, the pH value must be carefully chosen before the mixture of amino acids can successfully be separated and analysed.

Electrophoresis can also be used to separate and identify different proteins in a gel. The large number of different amino acids making up a protein give the protein an overall charge at a particular pH. This, combined with the protein's mass and shape, enables it to be separated from other proteins by electrophoresis. (The higher the mass and more irregular the shape, the slower they move.)

Genes, too, can be analysed by electrophoresis. DNA, the molecule which carries genetic information, is broken up into small fragments. These fragments are negatively charged and can be separated into bands using gel electrophoresis. The bands are made visible by tagging them with

molecules containing radioactive phosphorus, ^{32}P, and allowing them to fog a photographic film. This forms the basis of genetic fingerprinting used by forensic scientists to identify criminals.

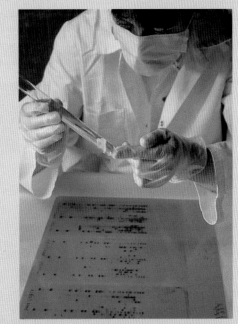

Fig 17.25 **A researcher with autoradiograms of DNA fragments separated by gel electrophoresis**

■ See question 6.

ION EXCHANGE CHROMATOGRAPHY

AS IN ELECTROPHORESIS, in ion exchange chromatography amino acids are separated using the different charges on them at particular pHs. It is rather like column chromatography (see page 178), except that the material packing the column consists of charged chemical groups bound to a resin called a cation-exchange resin.

For separating amino acids, the groups usually have a negative charge, such as SO_3^- and the resin is called cation-exchange resin. The cations in the resin are usually sodium ions, Na^+.

At pH 3, most amino acids have a net positive charge (ie they are also cations) and therefore can exchange with the sodium ions and be adsorbed on the resin. Those with the greatest positive charge at this pH (such as lysine) are attracted most strongly to the cation-exchange resin and remain in the column longest, while those least attracted to the exchange resin pass out of the column quickest, where each amino acid sample can be detected.

By gradually increasing the pH of the solvent, the positive charge on the most basic amino acids decreases, allowing them to flow out of the column and be collected.

This process is now automated in an amino acid analyser and the different amino acids are recognised by their colour reaction with a compound called ninhydrin.

4 FORMING PEPTIDES

H Which amino acid in Fig 17.4 passes quickest through the column at pH 3?

When two amino acids react together, the compound formed is known as a **dipeptide**. The reaction is between the CO_2H of one amino acid and the NH_2 of the other (Fig 17.26), giving a dipetide. By convention, the amino acid containing the free NH_2 is always placed on the left. A molecule of water is eliminated and so the reaction is called a **condensation reaction**.

A condensation reaction is an addition–elimination reaction.
The small molecule eliminated can be H_2O, NH_3 or HCl. See page 345.

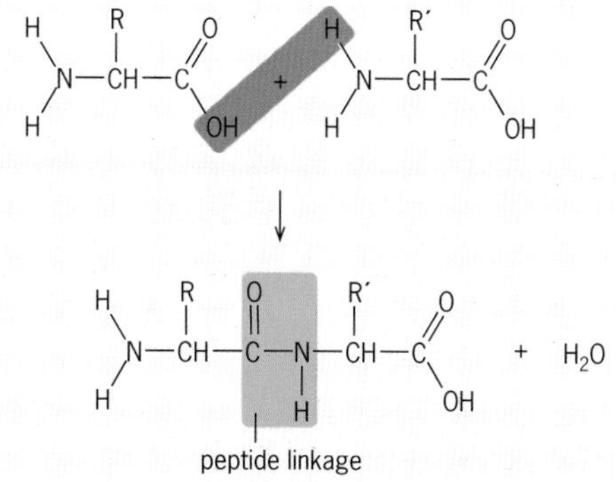

Fig 17.26 **The formation of a peptide linkage in a condensation reaction between two amino acids**

See questions 1 to 7. ■

The shorthand notation for a dipeptide made from alanine and glycine is Ala–Gly. The peptide link is shown by the dash. Three-letter codes or abbreviations are used for the names of the amino acids, as in Fig 17.4.

The CO–NH group is a **secondary amide** functional group, often referred to as just an **amide** group. The **peptide group** or **peptide link** is the amide functional group joining two amino acids. Either end of the dipeptide can react with another amino acid to form a tripeptide. Amino acids can keep reacting to form longer and longer amino acid chains known as **polypeptides**. The amino acids in peptides and polypeptides are called **amino acid residues**. **Proteins** are made up of one or more long polypeptide

I When alanine reacts with glycine, two dipeptides can be formed: Ala–Gly and Gly–Ala.
Draw the structural formulas of both dipeptides.

chains. Thus, polypeptides and proteins are condensation polymers of amino acids. In our bodies, the condensation reaction is catalysed by enzymes.

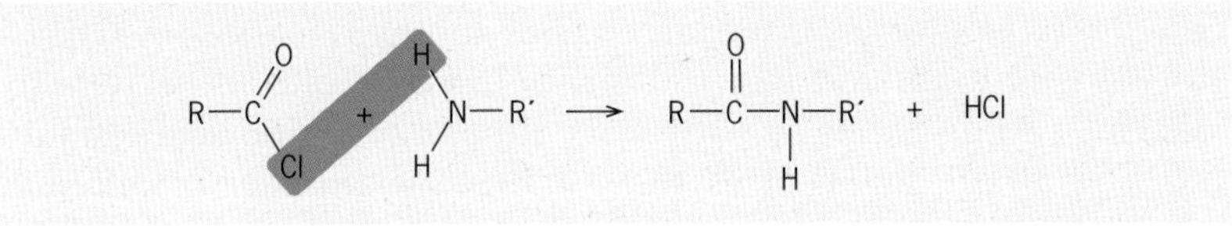

R—C(=O)—Cl + H—N—R′ (with H below) → R—C(=O)—N—R′ (with H below) + HCl

Fig 17.27

> Secondary amides are usually made in the laboratory by reacting a primary amine (RNH_2) with an acyl chloride ($R'COCl$), as in Fig 17.27. This is also called a condensation reaction because a small molecule is eliminated. (See page 345.)

PEPTIDES DON'T HAVE TO BE LARGE

MANY BIOLOGICALLY IMPORTANT peptides contain just a few amino acid residues. For example, the human brain produces a peptide called leucine enkephalin containing just five amino acid residues. This peptide was first discovered when the pain-killing action of morphine and codeine were being investigated in the 1970s. Both morphine and codeine fit into a brain receptor site, and this was found to be the start of their pain-killing action.

The mystery that scientists set out to unravel was how these two drugs, both obtained from the dried sap of poppies (called opium), could fit into brain receptor sites. They looked for compounds made in the body that might fit into these sites and discovered that the brain produces its own pain-killers called enkephalins, of which leucine enkephalin is one (Fig 17.28).

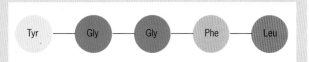

Fig 17.28 **Leucine enkephalin. By convention, the amino acid with the free NH$_2$ group is at the left end of the molecule, while the amino acid with the CO$_2$H group is at the right end**

Oxytocin, which contains eight amino acid residues, is another small peptide. It is a hormone secreted by the human pituitary gland and is responsible for inducing the uterus to contract at the end of pregnancy. It was the first natural peptide to be synthesised in a laboratory. Vincent du Vigneaud, the biochemist who made this important breakthrough in 1954, was awarded the Nobel Prize for Chemistry for his achievement.

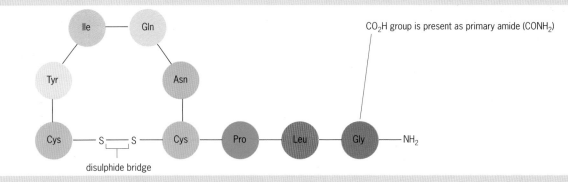

Fig 17.29 **The two sulphur atoms form a bridge holding six of the amino acids in a ring. (Disulphide bridges are covered on page 364)**

5 PROTEIN STRUCTURE

Proteins are very large molecules, having values of M_r which range from 5000 to several million. When proteins are formed inside a cell, they are too large to pass through the cell membrane and so stay trapped inside. That is, unless tissues are damaged. For example, certain enzymes (which we have seen are proteins) can be found outside cells after a heart attack. Normally, these enzymes would be confined inside the cells of the heart, but during a heart attack some of the cells rupture, allowing these enzymes to escape. The more massive the heart attack, the more cells split open and the higher the concentration of the enzymes found in the blood. In the same way, certain proteins in urine indicate that a kidney has been damaged.

> **J** Human insulin, consisting of 51 amino acid residues, is a relatively small protein. It has a molecular formula of $C_{254}H_{377}N_{65}S_6$. What is its relative molecular mass?

Primary structure of proteins

Although there are only 20 amino acids which usually make up our proteins, the number of ways in which they are combined is vast. Take, for example, lysozyme, an enzyme found in tears, saliva, nasal mucous and milk, and which destroys the cell walls of bacteria by breaking certain bonds by hydrolysis. It has 129 amino acid residues and uses all 20 amino acids (Fig 17.30). The number of different arrangements of the amino acids in the protein chain is 20^{129} (7.0×10^{167}), which is estimated to be more than twice the number of atoms in our galaxy.

The sequence of the amino acids in a protein is called its **primary structure** and this forms the backbone of the protein.

Fig 17.30 **The primary structure of the enzyme lysozyme. Notice the disulphide bridges**

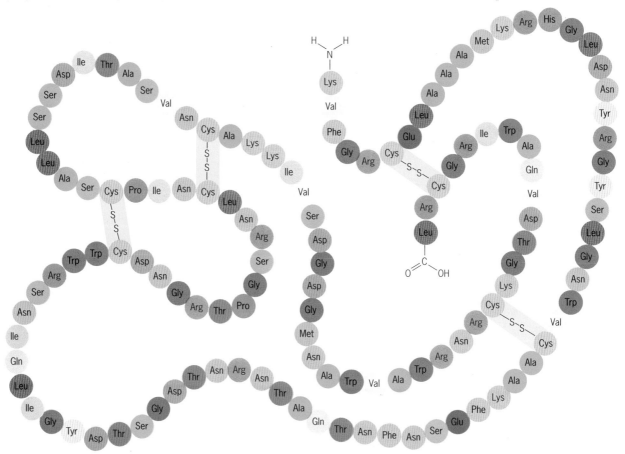

To find the sequence of amino acids in a protein, the peptide links are hydrolysed. This is done by boiling the protein with an acidic or alkaline solution (Fig 17.32), or by using certain enzymes. The protein chain may be completely hydrolysed, leaving a mixture of individual amino acids which can be separated using chromatography. This gives information as to how many different amino acids are present.

If different hydrolysing agents are used, the protein chain is split in different places. Some of the amino acid sequences overlap, allowing the overall sequence of amino acids to be worked out.

Disulphide bridges are formed between two cysteines by the oxidation of two S–H groups to S–S.

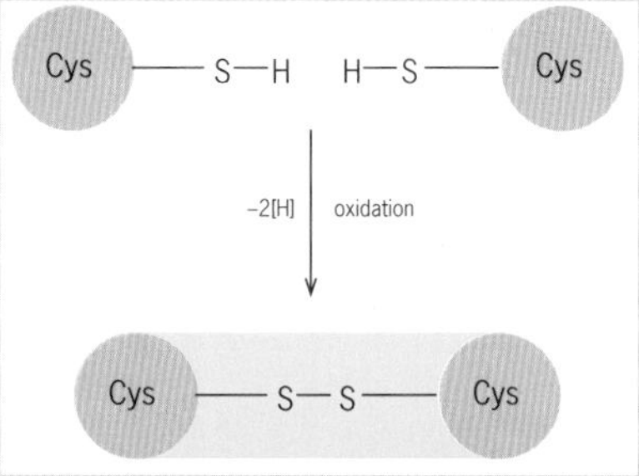

Cys ——— S–H   H–S ——— Cys

$-2[\text{H}]$ oxidation

Cys ——— S— S ——— Cys

Fig 17.31

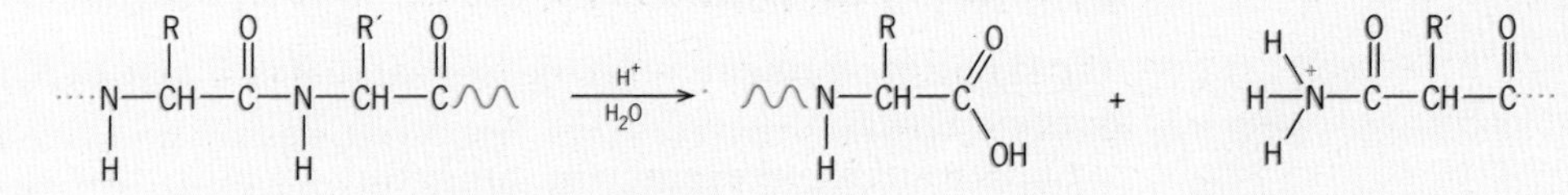

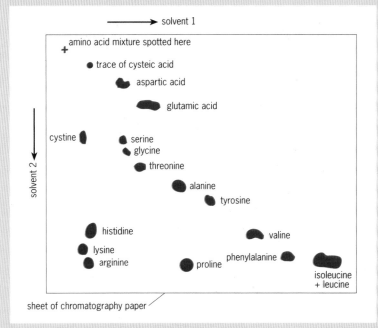

Fig 17.32 **The acid hydrolysis of one peptide link in a protein chain**

K Write an equation similar to that in Fig 17.33 for the alkaline hydrolysis of the peptide link. Hint: To remind yourself about hydrolysis, see page 348.

L Work out the sequence of this simple peptide which contains five amino acid residues. It is an enkephalin, similar to the one on page 363. The chain has been partially hydrolysed by two different reagents:

Reagent A produces Gly–Phe–Met and Tyr–Gly

Reagent B produces Tyr–Gly–Gly and Phe–Met

Hint: Remember the convention that the amino acid with a free NH_2 group is always placed on the left of the molecule, while the amino acid with the CO_2H group is at the right end.

PRIMARY STRUCTURE OF INSULIN

INSULIN WAS THE FIRST PROTEIN to have its amino acid sequence (primary structure) worked out. This was done by the English biochemist Frederick Sanger, who began in 1944 and spent ten years on the task. One of the techniques he used was to completely hydrolyse the insulin into its component amino acids by heating a mixture of $6 \, mol \, dm^{-3}$ hydrochloric acid and insulin in a sealed tube for 24 hours.

Sanger then separated the amino acids, using paper chromatography (Fig 17.33). Instead of using just one solvent to separate the amino acids, he used two, one after the other, in a technique called two-dimensional chromatography. A chromatogram is made using the first solvent. and is left to dry. Then it is turned on its side and the second solvent is applied.

Fig 17.33 **Insulin contains 17 amino acids. A spot of the amino acid mixture obtained by hydrolysing insulin was placed at the cross. The first solvent was allowed to run almost to the top of the paper, causing some of the amino acids to separate out. To complete the separation, after drying, the chromatography paper was turned through 90° and a second solvent was run up the paper. The amino acids are made visible as purple spots using ninhydrin solution**

For his painstaking research, Sanger received the Nobel Prize for Chemistry in 1958. In 1980, he was awarded a second Nobel Prize jointly with two American scientists for work on DNA, making him only the third person in history to win two Nobel prizes in scientific disciplines.

■ See questions 2, 4 and 6.

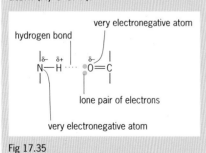

coloured patches = —C— of the different amino acids
(with R above and H below the central C)

The hydrogen bond is a weak electrostatic attraction between an H atom bonded to a highly electronegative atom (N, O or F) which gives it a partial positive charge, and a lone pair of electrons on a neighbouring highly electronegative atom (N, O or F).

hydrogen bond
very electronegative atom

$\overset{\delta-}{N}—\overset{\delta+}{H}\cdots\overset{\delta-}{O}=C$

lone pair of electrons

very electronegative atom

Fig 17.35

See questions 5, 7 and 8. ■

Secondary structure of proteins and hydrogen bonding

The shape of a protein molecule is what makes it able to perform its enzyme function.

Linus Pauling, the eminent American scientist, first turned his attention to protein structure in the 1930s (see also page 83). Fifteen years later, he and another American, Robert Corey, proposed that the primary structure of proteins could have one of two orderly arrangements, both held together by hydrogen bonds. The first arrangement is a regular coiling of part of the polypeptide chain: this is called an **α-helix**. The second arrangement is a folding of the polypeptide chain to make sheets: this is called a **β-pleated sheet**. These are known as the **secondary structures** of a protein. Both were subsequently discovered through X-ray crystallography.

The hydrogen bonding which holds a secondary structure together is between the N–H of one peptide link and the C=O of another. Since this is within the molecule, it is known as **intramolecular** hydrogen bonding. The α-helix is a right-handed spiral (Fig 17.34) and hydrogen bonds form between every fourth amino acid residue. It is found extensively in wool fibres and allows wool to stretch. When it is pulled, the α-helix elongates, breaking the hydrogen bonds. When the α-helix is released, the hydrogen bonds re-form as the α-helix returns to its usual shape.

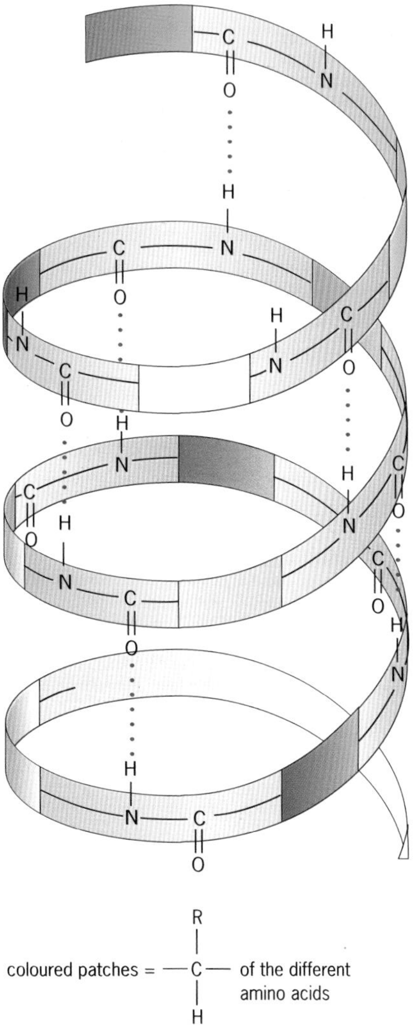

Fig 17.34 **The shape of the α-helix is maintained by hydrogen bonds**

The β-pleated sheet occurs when the amino acid backbone of the primary structure folds to give sections of parallel chains of amino acids, which again hydrogen-bond through their peptide links (Fig 17.36). Although the β-pleated sheet is fairly flexible, it cannot be stretched, as the chains of amino acids are already extended. Silk, for example, is composed of the protein silk fibroin. This is almost entirely β-pleated sheet, which is the reason why silk cannot be stretched like wool.

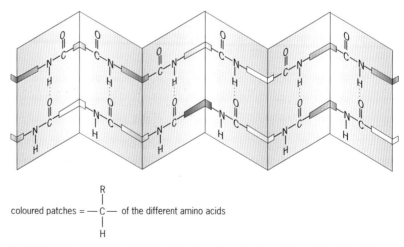

coloured patches = —C— of the different amino acids
(with R above and H below the central C)

Fig 17.36 **The β-pleated sheet is due to hydrogen bonding between parallel chains of amino acids**

Tertiary structure of proteins

The overall three-dimensional shape of a protein is the result of yet more folding and bending to give what looks like a random structure, but most definitely is not. This is the **tertiary structure** and is specific to a particular polypeptide chain. It is this shape which determines how each protein will function.

Proteins can be divided into two sorts: **globular proteins** and **fibrous proteins**.

Globular proteins, as their name implies, are roughly spherical (Fig 17.37). Our enzymes and protein hormones are globular proteins, and their polypeptide chains are extensively folded to give a very compact structure. These proteins are usually soluble because they are arranged in a way that leaves the **hydrophilic** R-groups of individual amino acid residues on the outside of their structures.

Fig 17.38 **Collagen is a triple helix of polypeptide chains**

See questions 6 and 7. ■

polypeptide chain

The tertiary structure of a protein is held together by four different types of interaction between the various R side chains of the different amino acids. These are shown in Fig 17.39.

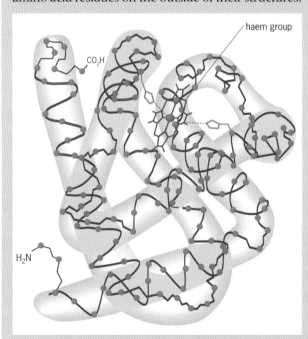

Fig 17.37 **The tertiary structure of the protein myoglobin. Note that sections of the secondary α-helix structure have been folded to give the overall three-dimensional shape. In the middle of the protein is a haem group containing an iron atom. Myoglobin is found in muscles and is responsible for binding oxygen and releasing it as needed. It was the first protein whose three-dimensional structure was worked out**

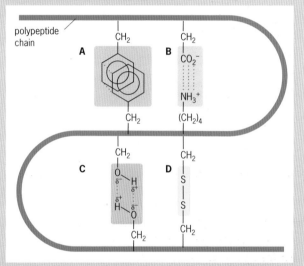

Fig 17.39 **The four types of interaction which hold the tertiary structure of a protein together:**

A Van der Waals forces (induced dipole–induced dipole bonding) exist when non-polar R groups come close together. They are usually found on the inside of globular proteins where, because they are hydrophobic, they do not interfere with solubility

B Ionic linkages occur between CO_2^- and NH_3^+

C Hydrogen bonding occurs between polar R groups such as those containing OH and NH_2

D Disulphide bridges result from two cysteine residues coming close together and the two S–H groups oxidising to S–S

Fibrous proteins have their polypeptide chains arranged in bundles to form fibres. They have a structural function. Collagen is a fibrous protein in tendons and muscles which consists of intertwining polypeptide chains (Fig 17.38). The α-keratin of hair, wool and claws is a fibrous protein in which the α-helix is twisted so that several strands can intertwine. The silk fibroin protein is also fibrous, only this time β-pleated sheets become bound together.

?

M Hydrophilic means water-loving, whereas hydrophobic means water-hating. Hydrophilic groups can interact with water through, for example, hydrogen bonding.

(a) Look at Fig 17.4 and work out which amino acids have R groups which could hydrogen bond with water.

(b) Non-polar R groups tend to be hydrophobic. Which amino acids in Fig 17.4 have hydrophobic R groups?

IT MAKES YOUR HAIR CURL!

OUR HAIR IS MADE UP of strands of the protein α-keratin. Its shape is maintained by hydrogen bonds, ionic linkages and disulphide bridges between the keratin strands. The very act of washing our hair disrupts these forces because water molecules can get in between the strands and affect all three interactions – in particular, the hydrogen bonds.

As hair dries, the water molecules leave the keratin and the original forces reassert themselves. So, if we do not immediately comb and set our hair in the shape we want, hydrogen bonds may re-form to curl our hair in a way we don't want.

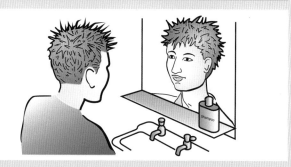

Fig 17.40 **The very act of washing hair disrupts some of the weaker forces holding the protein molecules of the hair together**

Enzymes

An enzyme is a biomolecule catalyst. Almost all enzymes are proteins, and most are found inside cells. Like all catalysts, enzymes alter the energy of activation of a reaction by providing an alternative route for reactants to interact without becoming permanently involved in the reaction. They differ from other catalysts in their amazingly high activity, being between a million and 20 million times more efficient than inorganic catalysts.

Sometimes, each enzyme molecule can catalyse the reaction of thousands of molecules per second. An example is the enzyme catalase which catalyses the decomposition of hydrogen peroxide:

$$H_2O_2(l) \xrightarrow{\text{catalase}} H_2O(l) + O_2(g)$$

One molecule of catalase catalyses about 50 000 molecules of H_2O_2 per second at 0 °C, whereas manganese(IV) oxide, an inorganic catalyst for this reaction, works very much less efficiently at 0 °C.

Enzymes can also be very specific in the reactions they catalyse. For example, out of the vast number of chemicals in the body, an enzyme may catalyse just one particular reaction of one chemical.

The three-dimensional shape of an enzyme is critical to its catalytic ability. This shape can be disrupted by changes of temperature, by altering the pH of the environment of the enzyme or by exposing it to heavy metal ions, such as mercury(II) ions (Hg^{2+}) and lead(II) ions (Pb^{2+}). Enzymes have an optimum temperature and pH at which they work best. Their catalytic activity decreases markedly outside a narrow range, which is why it is dangerous to have a very high temperature for too long during an illness. Most enzymes work efficiently in the range of 25–40 °C, and their shape is irreversibly changed at about 50–60 °C. The optimum pH for most of our body enzymes is about pH 7, but pepsin, a digestive enzyme, has an optimum pH of 2, with its maximum activity in the acid conditions of the stomach.

(You can read more about catalysis on page 597.)

IMMOBILISING ENZYMES

AT THE START of this chapter, you read about the advantages of using enzymes in industry. But if an enzyme is just mixed with the reactants to be catalysed, the enzyme is difficult to separate at the end of the reaction and is usually destroyed. However, if the enzyme is attached to an inert surface across which the reactants pass, the enzyme functions as a heterogeneous catalyst (see page 601) and can be used several times over.

Various surfaces can hold the enzyme – from polystyrene to glass beads – and immobilised enzymes are used increasingly in food and chemical manufacture. They are also important in medical diagnosis: clinical tests for glucose and cholesterol rely on immobilised enzymes reacting with these compounds.

SUMMARY

After studying this chapter, you should know the following:

■ Amino acids have two functional groups: CO_2H and NH_2.

■ Naturally occurring amino acids have the general formula:

$$H_2N—CH—CO_2H$$
with R attached to CH

■ Optical isomerism occurs when two molecules, called enantiomers, exist as non-superimposable mirror images of each other. These molecules are said to be chiral.

■ A carbon atom bonded to four different groups is called a chiral carbon. Such carbon atoms give rise to optical isomers.

■ A pair of enantiomers rotates plane-polarised light in equal but opposite directions.

■ A zwitterion is formed when a CO_2H group donates a proton to an NH_2 group on the same molecule, to give an ion which is both positively and negatively charged.

■ CO–NH is called a peptide group or peptide link when it joins two amino acids together.

■ Polypeptides are long chain molecules containing many amino acids joined by peptide links. Proteins are very large molecules which have M_r values of from 5000 to several million.

■ The primary structure of a protein (either an α-helix or a β-pleated sheet) is the sequence of its constituent amino acids. It forms the protein backbone.

■ The secondary structure of a protein (either an α-helix or a β-pleated sheet) is held together by hydrogen bonding between C=O and N–H in different peptide groups.

■ The tertiary structure is the overall three-dimensional shape of a polypeptide in a protein. It is the result of the secondary structure folding and bending.

■ Enzymes are biomolecule catalysts and nearly all are proteins. They have a very high activity and usually a high specificity. They are also very sensitive to changes in pH and temperature.

QUESTIONS

1 Fig 17.Q1 shows the structure of a typical amino acid.

Fig 17.Q1

a) (i) Name the **two** functional groups shown in this molecule.
(ii) Suggest a possible chemical formula for R.
(iii) State **two** interactions which enable R groups to stabilise the tertiary structure of proteins.
(iv) Draw a displayed formula showing the zwitterion form of the amino acid shown in Fig 17.1.

b) (i) Draw a diagram to show the peptide bond formed when two molecules of the amino acid in Fig 17.1 combine.
(ii) Name the **type** of reaction involved when amino acids combine in this way.
(iii) Name the test which can be used to show the presence of the peptide bond.

[UCLES June 1996 Sciences: Biochemistry Section A, q.1]

2
a) The graphical formulae of alanine and glycine, two important amino acids, are given in Fig 17.Q2.

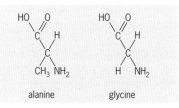

alanine   glycine   Fig 17.Q2

(i) State, with a reason which of these two amino acids can exist as optical isomers.
(ii) Show the formation of a peptide link between these two amino acids.

b) Outline the procedure for determining the primary structure of a peptide.

[UCLES Summer 1995 Chemistry Paper 9, q.4]

3 The structures in Fig 17.Q3(a) show three amino acids.

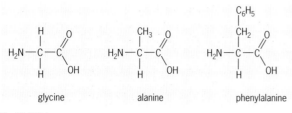

glycine   alanine   phenylalanine

Fig 17.Q3(a)

a) Explain why glycine does **not** have optical isomers but the other two amino acids do.

b) Amino acids can react both with acids and with bases and are also capable of forming zwitterions. Write equations for the reactions between:
   (i) phenylalanine and HCl,
   (ii) alanine and NaOH.

c) The pH at which an amino acid forms its zwitterion is different for each amino acid and is known as the isoelectric point.
   (i) The isoelectric point for glycine is at pH = 5.97. Draw the zwitterion formed by glycine at this pH.
   (ii) The isoelectric points of alanine and phenylalanine are at pH = 6.00 and at pH = 5.48 respectively.
   Draw the ions that would be formed at pH = 5.75 by alanine and phenylalanine.

d) Glycine ad alanine can react together to form the dipeptide shown in Fig 17.Q3(b).

Fig 17.Q3(b)

Draw the displayed formula of a different dipeptide that could be formed from the reaction between glycine and alanine.
[UCLES June 1997 Sciences: Chains and Rings, q.4]

4 A sodium salt of glutamic acid, monosodium glutamate (MSG), is a flavour enhancer that occurs naturally in tomatoes, mushrooms and some other vegetables. See Fig 17.Q4.

MSG   glutamic acid   Fig 17.Q4

a) What type of isomerism can be shown by MSG, and what part of the molecule is responsible for it?

b) MSG can act as a buffer by reacting with either acids or bases. Write balanced equations for its reactions with:
   (i) an excess of aqueous hydrochloric acid,
   (ii) an excess of aqueous sodium hydroxide.

c) The concentration at which MSG has its optimum flavour-enhancing effect is $1.0\,g\,dm^{-3}$. Calculate how many moles of MSG there are in $300\,cm^3$ of soup with this concentration.

d) Suggest a likely pH for an aqueous solution of glutamic acid.

e) Glutamic acid is a component of many proteins and peptides. Draw the structural formula of a dipeptide formed between glutamic acid and glycine, $NH_2CH_2CO_2H$.

f) What reagents and conditions are needed to hydrolyse peptides to amino acids in the laboratory?
[UCLES June 1996 Chemistry Paper 1, q.7]

5 Lysine (2,6-diaminohexanoic acid) has the formula $H_2N(CH_2)_4CH(NH_2)CO_2H$.

a) Write the formula of the ionic organic species present in:
   (i) a highly alkaline solution of lysine;
   (ii) a highly acidic solution of lysine;
   (iii) the zwitterion form of lysine.

b) Poly(lysine) is the name given to a polymer containing only lysine residues. Write a possible structure of poly(lysine) showing two repeating units.

c) A polypeptide chain may be folded and twisted into two types of secondary structure.
   (i) Name these two types of secondary structure.
   (ii) For each of these structures, indicate clearly by a diagram the shape of the structure and the means by which it is stabilised.
[UCLES June 1997 Sciences: Biochemistry, Section A, q.1]

6 Interactions occur between the R groups of amino acids in adjacent polypeptide chains: see Fig 17.Q6.

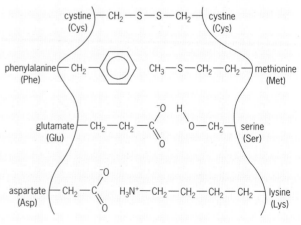

Fig 17.Q6

a) Name the main type of interaction on Fig 17.6 which occurs between:
   (i) cystine and cystine;
   (ii) phenylalanine and methionine;
   (iii) glutamate and serine;
   (iv) aspartate and lysine.

b) Draw the displayed formula showing all the atoms and bonds in one of the dipeptides formed between serine and methionine.

c) Explain why lysine moves towards the cathode during electrophoresis at pH 7.

d) **(i)** Under suitable conditions, a tripeptide is broken down into its three constituent amino acids which are Glu, Ser and Lys.
Write down all the possible sequences of the amino acids that could exist in the tripeptide.

(iii) Given that the breakdown of the tripeptide with trypsin gives lysine as the only free amino acid, which **two** sequences in **d)(i)** cannot be the tripeptide?

[UCLES November 1995 Sciences: Biochemistry, q.2]

7 The formulae of some amino acids are shown in Fig 17.Q7.

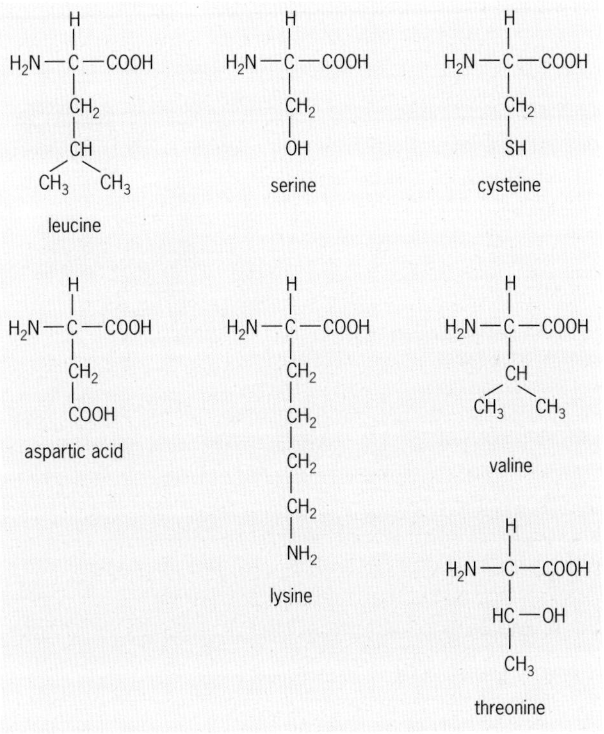

leucine
$$H_2N-\underset{\underset{\underset{CH_3\quad CH_3}{CH}}{\overset{|}{CH_2}}}{\overset{H}{\overset{|}{C}}}-COOH$$

serine
$$H_2N-\underset{\underset{OH}{\overset{|}{CH_2}}}{\overset{H}{\overset{|}{C}}}-COOH$$

cysteine
$$H_2N-\underset{\underset{SH}{\overset{|}{CH_2}}}{\overset{H}{\overset{|}{C}}}-COOH$$

aspartic acid
$$H_2N-\underset{\underset{COOH}{\overset{|}{CH_2}}}{\overset{H}{\overset{|}{C}}}-COOH$$

lysine
$$H_2N-\underset{\underset{\underset{\underset{\underset{NH_2}{\overset{|}{CH_2}}}{\overset{|}{CH_2}}}{\overset{|}{CH_2}}}{\overset{|}{CH_2}}}{\overset{H}{\overset{|}{C}}}-COOH$$

valine
$$H_2N-\underset{\underset{CH_3\quad CH_3}{CH}}{\overset{H}{\overset{|}{C}}}-COOH$$

threonine
$$H_2N-\underset{\underset{CH_3}{\overset{|}{HC-OH}}}{\overset{H}{\overset{|}{C}}}-COOH$$

Fig 17.Q7

a) **(i)** Draw a displayed formula to show the primary structure of a tripeptide formed from three of the amino acids above.

(ii) The secondary structure of a protein is stabilised by hydrogen bonding. Using the formulae of two of the amino acids in Fig 17.Q7, draw a diagram to show hydrogen bonding.

(iii) Using the formulae of the amino acids in Fig 17.Q7, draw a diagram to show **two other** interactions which stabilise the tertiary structure of a protein. State the name of each interaction shown.

[UCLES November 1996 Sciences: Biochemistry, Section A, q.1]

8

a) The amino acid 2-aminopropanoic acid (alanine) has the formula $CH_3CH(NH_2)COOH$.

(i) Write down the structural formulae of the predominant ionic species present at pH 1, pH 7 and pH 13.

(ii) Give the formula of the peptide, alanylalanylalanine (Ala–Ala–Ala).

b) Many proteins show considerable amounts of secondary structure.

(i) Name **two** types of secondary structure commonly found.

(ii) Draw a diagram to show the essential features of one of these structures.

(iii) How are these structures stabilised?

[NEAB 1996 Specimen paper Module Test: The Chemistry of Living Systems and Food, Section A, q.1]

Assignment

ASPARTAME – A MULTIMILLION POUND SWEETENER

Many of us are sweet-toothed and particularly enjoy the sweetness provided by carbohydrates – in particular, sucrose. Sadly, over-indulgence usually makes us obese. Carbohydrates, such as the sucrose of table sugar, can provide too much energy for the body's immediate use, so it is stored as fat. Hence the attraction of artificial sweeteners, such as aspartame, which provide the sweetness without the excess energy.

Aspartame was discovered in 1965 by James Schlatter while he was doing research on anti-ulcer drugs. It is a methyl ester of a dipeptide and weight for weight is about 160 times as sweet as sucrose. Aspartame is one of the biggest-selling artificial sweeteners on the market today.

Fig 17.A1 **Aspartame**

1

a) Use Fig 17.4 on page 355 to identify which two amino acids make up this dipeptide.

b) Copy the aspartame molecule in Fig 17.A1. On your diagram:
 i) circle the peptide group and the ester functional group,
 ii) identify the two chiral carbon atoms using an asterisk.

c) Draw the structural formulas of the ions which are likely to exist in **(i)** an acidic solution, **(ii)** an alkaline solution and **(iii)** a neutral solution.

2

Another dipeptide molecule is possible if the two amino acids you identified in question **1a)** react differently. Draw the structural formula of this dipeptide.

It is the shape of aspartame which gives it its sweetness. Our taste buds contain protein receptors into which aspartame can fit and form hydrogen bonds. It is the formation of the hydrogen bonds which are thought to create the sensation of sweetness.

3

a) Which groups on the aspartame molecule could form hydrogen bonds?

b) In order to form a receptor site, the protein must have a particular shape.
 (i) Explain what is meant by primary structure and secondary structure.
 (ii) State the types of force which maintain each structure.

Aspartame has a limited shelf life and its molecules decompose at room temperature at the rate of about 10 per cent per month. It is therefore used to sweeten foods with a quick turnover, such as soft drinks and yoghurts. At higher temperatures, the rate of decomposition is much faster, so aspartame cannot be used in cooking.

Fig 17.A2 **Some products that contain aspartame**

Aspartame is believed to be a safe food additive. Unfortunately, about 1 in 15 000 people have a genetic condition called phenylketonuria, which means they cannot metabolise the essential amino acid phenylalanine contained in aspartame. Most people have an enzyme called phenylalanine hydroxylase which converts phenylalanine to another amino acid, tyrosine, which is harmless. But in people who suffer from phenylketonuria, the enzyme is defective and so phenylalanine cannot be converted to tyrosine. Though it is eventually excreted, it accumulates in the blood. If not diagnosed and treated, the condition can cause mental retardation.

4

a) Draw the general formula for an α-amino acid.

b) The R group of tyrosine is shown in Fig 17.A3. Draw this amino acid.

Fig 17.A3

c) Phenylalanine is an essential amino acid. What is meant by this term?

AMINO ACIDS AND PROTEINS

The chapter describes vital groups of nitrogen-containing molecules found in all living organisms. It emphasises the reactivity of the amine and carboxyl groups, which are covered in several other chapters in this book. Refer to the Chapter Map to be reminded of the connection between concepts in the chapter, and for further sources in other chapters.

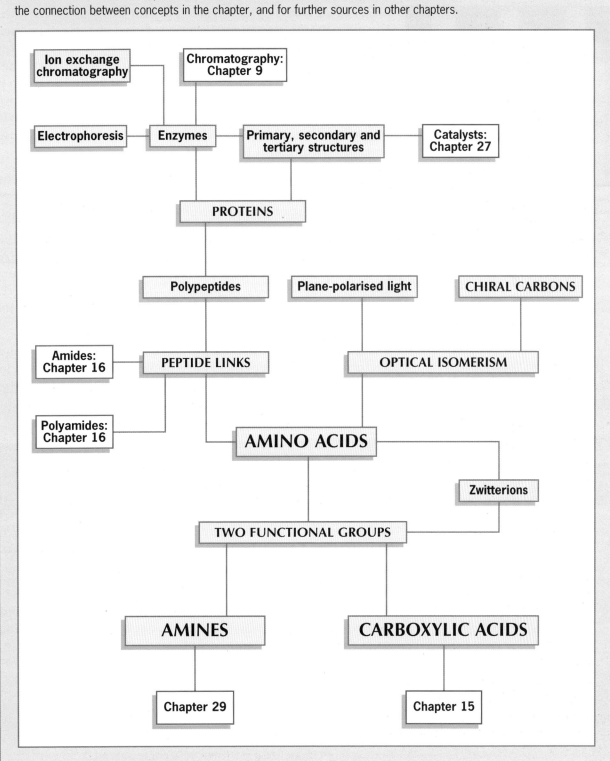

18 Polymers

Biopol bottles at stages of increasing biodegradation

MOST POLYMERS that have revolutionised twentieth-century living are manufactured from chemicals which come from non-renewable crude oil. As the reserves of this precious resource are used up, the hunt is on for other sources of polymers, and growing crops that provide them is one promising option. We are all familiar with the natural polymers starch, cellulose and protein; certain bacteria produce other polymers which are the subject of intense research throughout the world.

Biopol, a polyester, is the world's first bacterial polymer to be produced commercially. The polymer makes up 80 per cent of the dry weight of the bacterium *Alcaligenes eutrophus*, which uses it as an energy store in the same way that we use fat.

The first articles made of Biopol, bottles for hair-care products, appeared in 1990. At present, bacterial polmyers are much more costly to produce than synthetic polymers, but they have one outstanding advantage – they are totally biodegradable.

The genes that produce Biopol have been isolated from the bacterium, and bioengineers are hoping to implant them in potatoes and other crops. So, perhaps fields producing the polymers essential to modern living will be a familiar sight by the mid-twenty-first century.

1 WHAT IS A POLYMER?

More chemists work with polymers than with any other type of material. Polymers enter every aspect of our lives. The DNA that carries the genetic code is a natural polymer, as are proteins, starch and cellulose. Chemists started making synthetic polymers in the early 1900s and now we are dependent on them. They are in clothing, packaging, furniture, adhesives, inks, coatings and electrical equipment, to mention just a few of their uses.

Polymers are very large molecules with very high molecular masses. It took chemists some time to realise that they were dealing with such large molecules. The German chemist Hermann Staudinger working in the early 1900s was the first to realise that compounds such as rubber were not just collections of tiny molecules held together by intermolecular forces, but were made up of huge molecules containing many thousands of atoms covalently bonded together. It was thought at the time that a molecular mass of 5000 was the limit for any molecule, so it took some time for Staudinger's model of a polymer to become accepted.

The word polymer is derived from two Greek words: *polys* which means many and *meros* which means a part. Polymers, then, are large molecules made up of many small molecules called **monomers**.

For more information on proteins, see pages 363 to 368.

In 1953, Hermann Staudinger (1881–1963) was awarded the Nobel Prize in Chemistry for his pioneering work with polymers.

The process of forming polymers from monomers is called **polymerisation**. **Plastics** – derived from the Greek word *plastikos* which means shaped – is the general name for materials which, when heated under pressure, can be shaped or moulded or extruded (extruded means forced through a hole, for example to make rods or tubes). Not all polymer materials possess this property, so to avoid confusion the word is not used until environmental issues are considered on page 368.

2 ETHENE AND ADDITION POLYMERISATION

Poly(ethene) – or polythene as it is popularly known – was discovered by accident in 1933. Two British chemists working at ICI, Eric Fawcett and Reginald Gibson, were trying to produce a ketone using benzaldehyde and ethene under very high pressure (Fig 18.1). They decided to leave the reaction mixture at high pressure over a weekend, even adding more ethene when the reaction vessel sprang a leak.

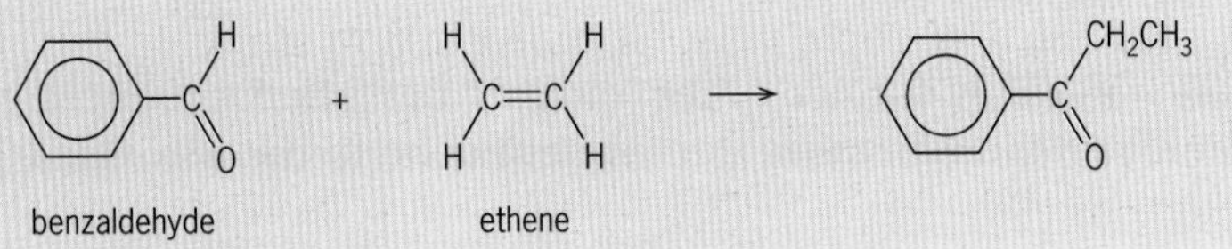

Fig 18.1 **The reaction Fawcett and Gibson were expecting**

By Monday morning, the hoped-for ketone had not been produced. Instead, there was a minute amount of a white waxy solid. They tried to repeat the experiment but the reaction mixture exploded. The unpredictability of the reaction meant that making this unusual substance was very hazardous, so they stopped.

However, it was eventually realised that this was a polymer. Interest grew, and in 1935 Fawcett and Gibson made another attempt to produce it, this time with reactor vessels which could withstand very high pressures. By December, they had made 8 grams. They continued their experiments in order to find the optimum conditions. When they added cold ethene at a controlled rate, the reaction stopped going out of control. Soon they had enough solid polymer to establish that it could be melted and moulded.

Another British chemist, Michael Perrin, who took charge of the project in 1935, realised that oxygen was essential to produce this white waxy solid, polythene. (It is probable that oxygen had got into the original reaction vessel when it sprang its leak.) Perrin also showed that polythene was produced without the benzaldehyde of the 1933 experiment.

?

A If the reaction between benzaldehyde and ethene had worked, it would have been an addition reaction. Explain what is meant by addition reaction.
Hint: To check your answer, see page 253.

POLYTHENE AND THE SECOND WORLD WAR

THE CLAIM IS OFTEN MADE that penicillin, the first antibiotic, was one of the chemicals that won the war because it prevented the terrible suffering and needless death of thousands of soldiers from wound infections. Polythene, too, had a valued role in the war. It was commercially produced in 1939, three years before penicillin. Unlike other insulators, it was impervious to rainwater and sea water, and one of its first uses was in insulating the electrical wiring of aircraft radar sets – radar being crucial to Britain's survival in the war's early years.

There is more about addition reactions and addition polymerisations on pages 254 and 260.

Poly(ethene) is called an **addition polymer** because, when the ethene monomers join together in the reaction, no small molecules are eliminated: the polymer is the only product, as Fig 18.2 shows.

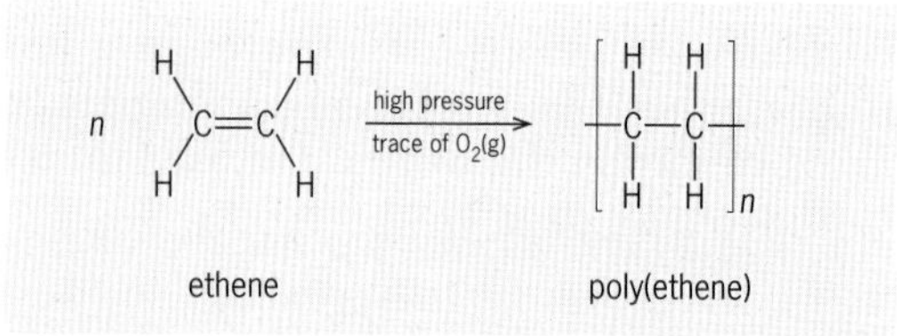

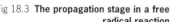

ethene   poly(ethene)

Fig 18.2 **Polymerising ethene**

In the equation of Fig 18.2, n represents a very large number. Poly(ethene) chains can be made up of thousands of ethene monomers, hence its systematic name. In the formula for the poly(ethene), the ethene unit is enclosed in brackets which cut the covalent bonds to show that we are representing the **repeating unit** of a very long chain.

Mechanism of addition polymerisation

Addition polymerisation is a free-radical chain reaction and, as for any such reaction, there must be an **initiation stage**. In this stage, a free radical is formed. Free radicals are often produced from organic peroxides because the covalent bond in the peroxide (O–O) group is weak:

$$R-O-O-R \rightarrow 2R-O\bullet$$

The R-group could be an alkyl group, but a common reagent used to produce free radicals is benzoyl peroxide, $(C_6H_5CO)-O-O-(COC_6H_5)$.

Once formed, this free radical goes on to form another free radical, starting a chain reaction. This is called the **propagation stage** (Fig 18.3).

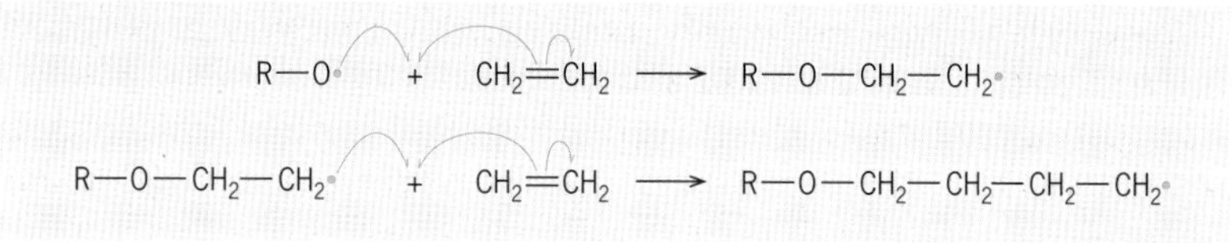

B (a) Draw the displayed formula of part of a poly(ethene) chain showing three ethene units.

(b) Explain why poly(ethene) may be classed as an alkane.
Hint: See page 156 to remind yourself about alkanes.

Free radicals are reactive species with an unpaired electron (see page 206).

C The formation of the free radical from organic peroxides involves homolytic fission. What is meant by this term?
Hint: If you are not sure, refer to page 207.

Fig 18.3 **The propagation stage in a free radical reaction**

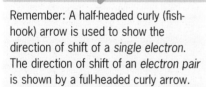

Very long chains containing thousands of ethene units are produced in less than a second, which is why the reaction can easily go out of control and explode.

Sometimes a large chain folds back on itself and shifts the position of the unpaired electron to the middle portion of the chain by removing a hydrogen atom from a CH_2 as shown in Fig 18.4. This means that branched chains can form which is what happened in Gibson and Fawcett's experiment. Branching gives polythene particular properties: in particular, it affects the density.

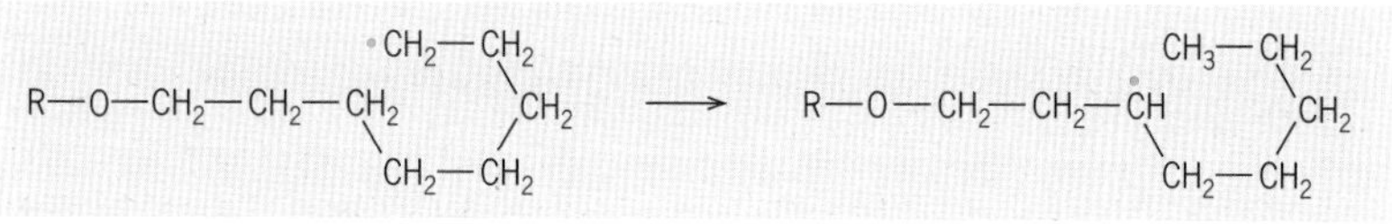

Remember: A half-headed curly (fishhook) arrow is used to show the direction of shift of a *single electron*. The direction of shift of an *electron pair* is shown by a full-headed curly arrow.

Fig 18.4 **Sometimes a chain folds back on itself and shifts the position of the unpaired electron. This allows branching to occur**

See question 5. ■

The **termination stage** of this chain reaction occurs when two free radicals combine without producing new free radicals (Fig 18.5).

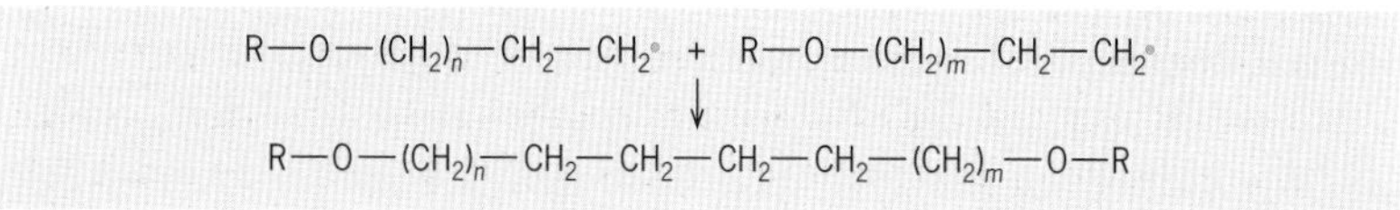

Fig 18.5 **Letters _m_ and _n_ refer to the number of CH₂ groups in the chain which may be very large**

Oxygen molecules are also free radicals

Oxygen might have initated the poly(ethene) chain reaction in Gibson and Fawcett's original experiments because it can also exist as a free radical. On page **4xx**, the model used for bonding in O_2 is based on the production of octets of electrons. In the case of oxygen, this gives a double bond:

The bonding in O_2 is known to be more complicated than this. Each O atom in the molecule has an unpaired electron making oxygen a free radical, sometimes known as a diradical:

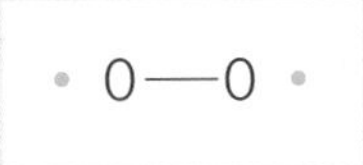

The bond between the O atoms is more complicated than just a single covalent bond.

Low-density poly(ethene)

We have seen that the process invented at ICI to manufacture polythene produces branched chains. This means that the polymer chains do not all lie in parallel as unbranched molecules could. Instead, they form a tangled mass (Fig 18.6). Because the chains cannot lie close together, the density of this polythene is low. It is therefore called **low-density poly(ethene)** or **LDPE.**

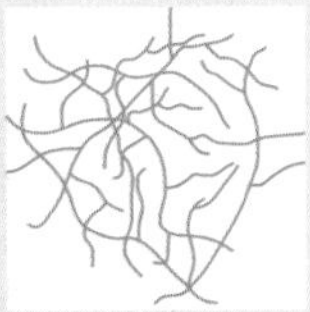

Fig 18.6

The intermolecular forces holding the poly(ethene) chains together are induced dipole–induced dipole forces (see 159). As the chains get longer, these weak forces act over a larger surface area. And as they become tangled, the tensile strength increases because when one chain is pulled it drags other chains along with it. However, because the branching keeps the chains further apart, LDPE has a lower tensile strength than polymers with no branched chains. Branching also keeps the melting point fairly low, at about 130°C.

Some 6 million tonnes of LDPE are manufactured world-wide each year under very high pressures and with a trace of oxygen or an organic peroxide. Among the uses of LDPE are electrical insulation, tough transparent film in packaging, dustbin liners and carrier bags (Fig 18.7).

High-density poly(ethene)

Linear chains of poly(ethene) – chains with no branching – can lie closer together than branched chains. This increases the density. **High-density poly(ethene), HDPE**, was first produced in 1953 in Germany by Karl Ziegler as he was experimenting with an organometallic catalyst. This catalyst consisted of ethyl groups covalently bonded to aluminium atoms (Fig 18.8).

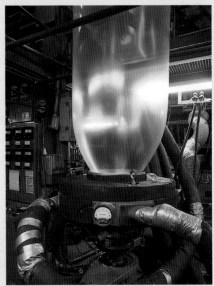
Fig 18.7 **Hot low-density poly(ethene) being blown to form a bag**

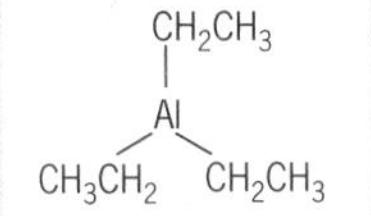

Fig 18.8 **Triethylaluminium is an organometallic catalyst**

Ziegler found that a little titanium(IV) chloride, $TiCl_4$, mixed with triethylaluminium in an alkane solvent caused ethene to polymerise at room temperature and atmospheric pressure. Long linear chains of about 100 000 ethene units were formed. Today, the world production of HDPE is 7.5 million tonnes. The conditions for its production have changed little.

$$nC_2H_4 \xrightarrow[50°C,\ 1.5\ atm]{(C_2H_5)_3Al/TiCl_4} \left[CH_2-CH_2 \right]_n$$

The mechanism for the addition polymerisation of HDPE is ionic, not free radical.

Being linear, HDPE chains can form ordered structures by aligning themselves. This leads to large regions of **crystallinity** within HDPE (Fig 18.9), which give it a higher density than LDPE. The melting point and tensile strength are also higher, and HDPE is harder than LDPE. The molecular regions which are not ordered are known as **amorphous regions**.

Almost half of the HDPE produced is blow-moulded to make bottles and other containers for a range of chemicals from shampoos to bleaches. Another quarter is injected into moulds (injection moulding) to make food storage containers, car petrol tanks, buckets and crates. Medical appliances

areas of crystallinity

Fig 18.9 **The crystalline regions in HDPE are the result of linear chains becoming aligned**

such as bed pans are made from HDPE because its higher melting point allows high-temperature sterilisation without loss of shape.

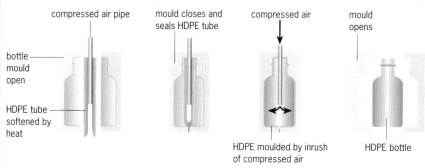

Fig 18.10(a) **Blow-moulding a bottle**

Fig 18.10(b) **Two bottles made from poly-(ethene). The one on the right was made from LDPE, the other from HDPE**

Poly(propene): another addition polymer

The equation for the addition polymerisation of propene is given in Fig 18.11.

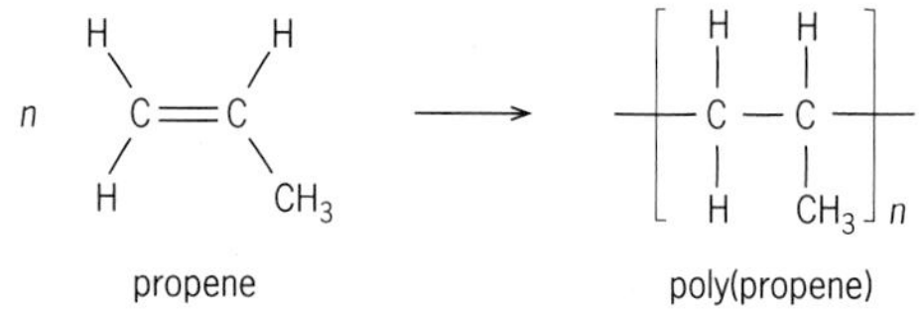

Fig 18.11 **The polymerisation of propene**

If all the methyl groups are oriented in the same direction, the polymer chains can get very close together and be crystalline. A year after Ziegler had used $(C_2H_5)_3Al/TiCl_4$ to catalyse the low-pressure polymerisation of ethene, the Italian chemist Giulio Natta used the same catalyst to produce crystalline poly(propene) in which all the methyl groups pointed in the same direction (Fig 18.12).

At the suggestion of his wife, he called this **iso-tactic** propene, after the Greek words *isos*, which means equal, and *taktos*, which means ordered. This was the first time catalysts had been used to produce a **stereoregular polymer**. Catalysts which are used to produce stereoregular polymers are called **Ziegler–Natta catalysts.** In 1963, Natta and Ziegler jointly received the Nobel Prize for Chemistry for their contributions to polymer chemistry.

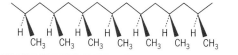

Fig 18.12 **Isotactic poly(propene). Notice that the methyl groups are all pointing in the same direction**

Atactic poly(propene) has no ordered orientation of its CH_3 groups, which means that the polymer chains cannot lie very close together. As would be expected, atactic poly(propene) has a lower melting point and is softer than the isotactic form. Isotactic poly(propene) is moulded into objects such as car bumpers and battery cases, and drawn into fibres for carpets and clothing. It is also made in sheet form for packaging. Isotactic poly(propene) is particularly useful for athletics wear because it does not absorb perspiration but allows it to evaporate, unlike cotton clothing which absorbs and holds moisture. The atactic form is used in weather-proofing materials and sealants.

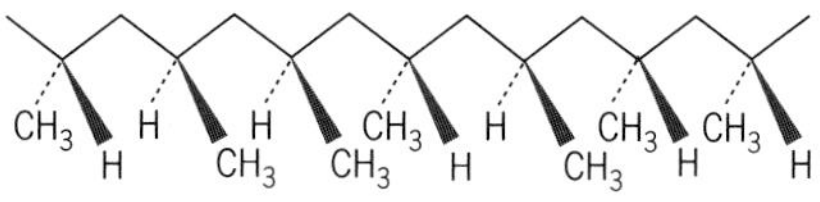

Fig 18.13 **Atactic poly(propene): the random orientation of the methyl groups prevents the polymer chains lying close together**

■ See question 5.

D After reading the Extension box above, explain why linear polymer chains have higher melting points than branched chains containing similar numbers of carbon atoms.

E There is another stereoregular form of poly(propene) called syndiotactic poly(propene). In this form the CH_3 groups are on alternating sides.

(a) Draw a portion of its chain structure using similar diagrams to Figs 18.12 and 18.13.

(b) Predict which properties might be different from atactic poly(propene).

PVC and additives

Look at Table 12.2 (page 260) where examples are given of other addition polymers whose monomers are based on the ethene structure and add together in a similar way. PVC or poly(chloroethene) is made from chloroethene monomers, as shown in Fig 18.14.

The non-systematic name for chloroethene is vinyl chloride, hence the name by which the polymer was first known: polyvinyl chloride or PVC. When first made in 1912 in Germany, PVC was hard and brittle. These properties come from the chlorine atom.

Being highly electronegative, the chlorine atom forms a dipole with the carbon atom and the partial negative charge on the chlorine atom attracts a slightly positive hydrogen atom, which also forms a dipole with the carbon atom. This gives rise to permanent dipole–permanent dipole forces which are stronger than induced dipole–induced dipole forces, making PVC stronger than poly(ethene).

The brittleness arises because the larger chlorine atoms tend to catch on each other when the polymer chains are pulled apart. Add to this the fact that PVC often decomposed before it could be moulded, and it is small wonder that the German company allowed its patent to lapse in 1926.

However, in the same year it was discovered that certain additives change the properties of PVC, making it more flexible and easier to mould. As a result, PVC is now the world's most versatile polymer and second only to poly(ethene) in the amount produced.

The additives which make PVC more flexible and softer are called **plasticisers**. Plasticisers are molecules which get in between the chains, allowing them to slide over one another more easily. But there is concern that plasticisers in PVC food wrapping film may migrate into fatty foods and be harmful.

Another additive prevents the decomposition of PVC by ultraviolet light. Hence the polymer that is used in door and window frames has this additive and is called uPVC.

The use of additives to alter its properties means that PVC is found everywhere. Credit cards are made from it, as are precision engineering items, flooring and footwear. If your house has polymer gutters, down-pipes and plumbing, the material is almost certainly PVC.

Glass transition temperature

Most polymers contain some crystalline regions and some amorphous regions. Below a certain temperature called the **glass transition temperature**, T_g, the long polymer chains are fixed in position and cannot move over one another. As the polymer warms up, the chains in the amorphous regions are able to slide over one another and so the polymer softens and becomes more flexible. But the crystalline regions stay rigid and do not start to move until the polymer melts.

Poly(propene) bumpers on cars become brittle in very cold winters when the temperature falls below its T_g of –10 °C. Even a slight knock can cause a bumper to shatter. Another example is poly(propene) food containers kept in a refrigerator. They too can become brittle and then they crack when someone tries to open them.

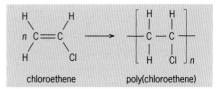

Fig 18.14 **The polymerisation of chloroethene**

■ See question 6.

Fig 18.15 **The non-glass surfaces of these flats are made of uPVC**

?

F Poly(phenylethene) is the systematic name of polystyrene. Part of the polymer chain is shown in Fig 18.16. Draw the structural formula of the monomer.
Hint: Check your answer by looking at page 260. There is also more information about this important polymer on page 280.

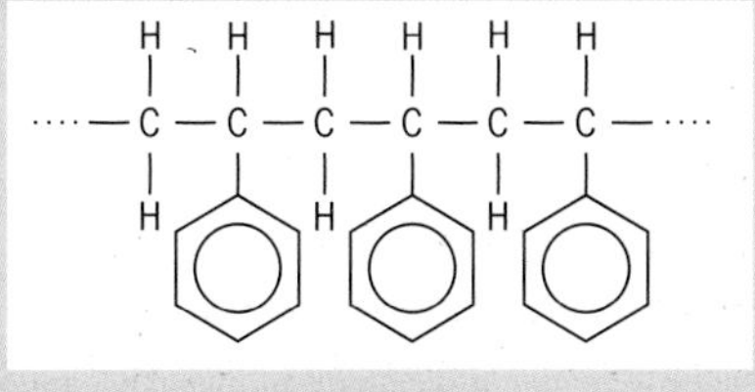

Fig 18.16 **Poly(phenylethene)**

TEFLON: THE NON-STICK POLYMER

TEFLON WAS DISCOVERED by accident in 1938 when Roy Plunkett, a chemist working for the Du Pont company on tetrafluoroethene gas, could not get any of the gas from one of the steel storage cylinders he wanted to use. Instead of jumping to the conclusion that the gas must have escaped, he weighed the cylinder and found that it weighed the same as if it were full. He sawed it open and found a white powder, which turned out to be poly(tetrafluoroethene) or PTFE – better known as Teflon. Ten years later it was in commercial production.

Teflon has a virtually friction-free surface, it is very resistant to heat and chemicals, and is an excellent electrical insulator. Apart from its use in coating non-stick frying pans (Fig 18.17), Teflon is used to coat bearings (even those supporting loads as heavy as bridges) and in human joint replacements. Unlike other polymers, its properties remain constant over a wide temperature range (–70 to 350 °C).

Fig 18.17 **Teflon makes this frying pan non-stick**

See questions 1, 2 and 3. ■

G The displayed formula of tetrafluoroethene is shown in Fig 18.18. Write an equation for the production of this polymer.

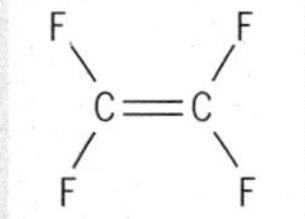

Fig 18.18 **Tetrafluoroethene**

3 CONDENSATION POLYMERISATION

In 1928 a brilliant young American chemist, Wallace Carothers, was invited to join the Du Pont company to head a team researching into polymers. Here he made an immense contribution to our understanding of polymer science, which was probably his most valuable work. But, this is not what posterity remembers him for, because in 1935 he produced the first nylon – a wholly synthetic fibre which mimics the protein silk.

WALLACE CAROTHERS

WORKING AT the Du Pont company in Delaware, Wallace Carothers led the research team which produced the world's first nylon. He was an internationally renowned expert on polymers whose theoretical ideas are the foundation of today's polymer science. He was the first industrial chemist to become a member of the prestigious National Academy of Sciences in the USA.

However, his success masked the depression which had plagued him since childhood and in 1937, feeling that his life's work had been a failure, he committed suicide by drinking a solution of cyanide. Yet, only three years later, nylon was proclaimed an outstanding commercial success.

Fig 18.19 **Wallace Carothers (1896–1937)**

Within three years of Carothers joining Du Pont, his group produced the first commercial synthetic rubber, Neoprene, an addition polymer (*neo* means new). Then they switched their attention to **condensation polymerisation**. (When monomers form condensation polymers, small molecules, such as water, are eliminated.) Two different types of polymer were investigated by Carothers' group: **polyesters** and **polyamides**. Their first success was the production of a polyester fibre – the world's first wholly synthetic fibre.

See question 3. ■

Polypesters

Before reading about polyesters you will find it helpful to turn to page 340 and revise how esters are made.

Polyesters

Carothers realised that for condensation polymers to be formed, the monomers which make them up need two reactive ends. So monomer A (Fig 18.20) could contain two OH groups while monomer B could contain two CO_2H groups, to give polyesters whose monomer units are joined by ester functional groups.

The polyesters which the Du Pont team produced were thought to be of theoretical interest, but of little practical use. The water eliminated in the condensation reaction appeared to prevent the formation of very long chains.

H Write an equation for the formation of ethyl ethanoate from ethanoic acid and ethanol.

Fig 18.20 **Forming ester links between monomers in a polyester**

Remember:

carboxylic acid	+	alcohol	⇌	ester	+	water

$$RC\text{-}OH + R'\text{-}OH \rightleftharpoons RC\text{-}O\text{-}R' + H_2O$$

The M_r of polymers is an average value, since not all the polymer chains have the same M_r.

This problem was solved by Carothers, who invented a 'molecular still' which evaporated the water molecules as they were produced. This enabled very long polymer chains to be produced with M_r values of about 10 000. However, the polyesters made of them were just sticky masses when hot, and tough, opaque solids when cold. Then, in a happy accident, one of the team, Julian Hill, pulled a stirring rod out of a hot, sticky ball of polyester. The result was a long, thin fibre of the polymer which, when it cooled, could be stretched considerably and was very strong.

X-ray analysis revealed what had occurred. Pulling the polymer into a long filament had aligned the polymer chains, which increased the tensile strength of the material (Fig18.21(b)). The pulling process is known as cold drawing.

The polyester fibres that the Du Pont group led by Carothers produced were never destined for commercial success. Although the fibres were strong and pliable, they melted at too low a temperature to be of practical use in clothing which would have to be ironed. They were also slightly water soluble, another considerable disadvantage!

The polyester story now switches to the laboratories of the Calico Printers' Association in England, where in 1941 J Whinfield and J Dickson invented Terylene, building on the foundations laid by Wallace Carothers. This polyester is produced from benzene-1,4-dicarboxylic acid and the alcohol ethane-1,2-diol (Fig 18.22).

Fig 18.21(a) **Julian Hill demonstrating the birth of the first completely synthetic fibre**

Examples of happy accidents occur throughout the development of science. Another name for this is serendipity. However, it is recognising of the implications of serendipity which marks out great scientists. It was Louis Pasteur who said, 'Chance favours the prepared mind.' Pasteur's serendipitous discovery is featured on page 358.

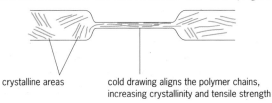

crystalline areas

cold drawing aligns the polymer chains, increasing crystallinity and tensile strength

Fig 18.21(b) **Cold drawing of a polymer aligns its chains in the fibre produced**

I (a) The dimethyl ester of benzene-1,4-dicarboxylic acid also produces Terylene.

(i) Draw the structural formula of this molecule.

(ii) Predict the small molecule which is lost during the condensation polymerisation reaction with ethane-1,2-diol.

(iii) Predict the products of the hydrolysis of this type of Terylene by referring to page 34.

(b) Another polyester can be produced using benzene-1,4-dicarboxylic acid and propane-1,3-diol. Draw the structural formula of the repeating unit of this polymer.

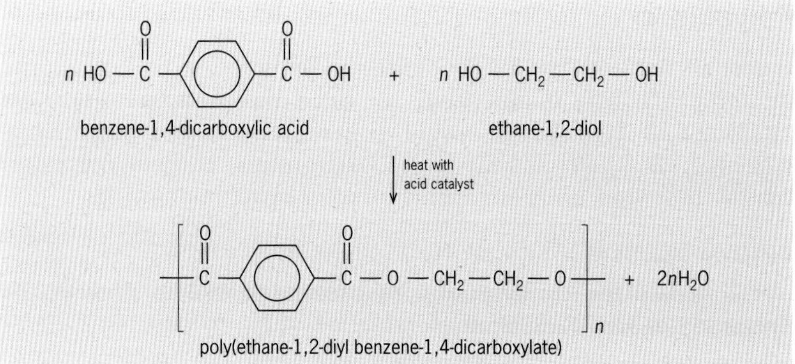

Fig 18.22 **Condensation reaction for the polyester Terylene**

The systematic name for this polyester need not concern us. In industry, it is usually referred to simply as polyester or PET.

Terylene and PET are derived from the traditional names for the two monomers and the polymer respectively. Benzene-1,4-dicarboxylic acid is also called **tere**phthalic acid and ethane-1,2-diol is also called ethyl**ene** glycol – hence Terylene. The traditional name for the polymer is **p**oly(**e**thylene **t**erephthalate), which gives the acronym PET.

Polyester is the leading synthetic fibre with world-wide production of about 10 million tonnes. Its principal use is in clothing, because it is crease-resistant. Often, it is mixed with other synthetic or natural fibres. For example, a mixture of cotton and polyester is very popular because the cotton absorbs moisture. Since polyester is a good thermal insulator, duvets and anoraks are filled with its fibres. Apart from fibres, it can be produced as an extremely tough yet very thin film, which provides the backing for video tapes and computer discs. It is also becoming the dominant material in packaging and is used in some carbonated drinks bottles.

18.23 **PET is an ideal material for carbonated drinks bottles because it is light, tough and won't shatter when dropped**

See questions 4, 7 and 8. ■

J Terylene and similar polyesters are water repellent. Why is it an advantage that, when blended with cotton fibres, the resulting fabric should absorb moisture?

K Polyesters also find many uses in medicine. For example, as mesh tubes they can replace blood vessels with human tissue growing into and around the mesh. While sometimes a permanent mesh is required, it is an advantage at other times to insert a mesh that can be degraded by enzymes in the body. A polymer made from 2-hydroxypropanoic acid (lactic acid, Fig 18.24) will form a degradable mesh.

Fig 18.24 **2-hydroxypropanoic acid**

$$CH_3$$
$$|$$
$$HO—CH—CO_2H$$

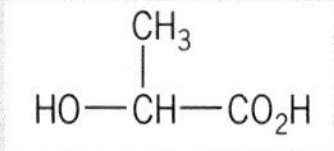

Write an equation for the production of this polyester.

For secondary amide links – called peptide linkages in proteins – see page 362.

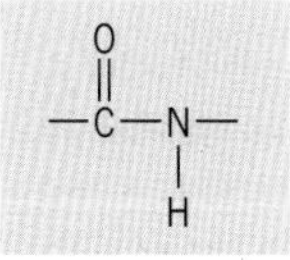

Fig 18.25 **The secondary amide linkage**

Nylon: a polyamide

After working on polyesters, Carothers and his team focused their efforts on another type of polymer, in which the monomer units are joined through secondary amide linkages (Fig 18.25), instead of ester linkages. These secondary amide linkages are the same linkages found in proteins such as silk.

In 1935, the team produced a polymer, now called nylon 6,6, from a diamine and a dicarboxylic acid (Fig 18.26). Notice the similarity of this condensation reaction to that which produces a polyester. Both use a dicarboxylic acid monomer, but the alcohol groups at each end of the other monomer are replaced with primary amine functional groups (NH_2).

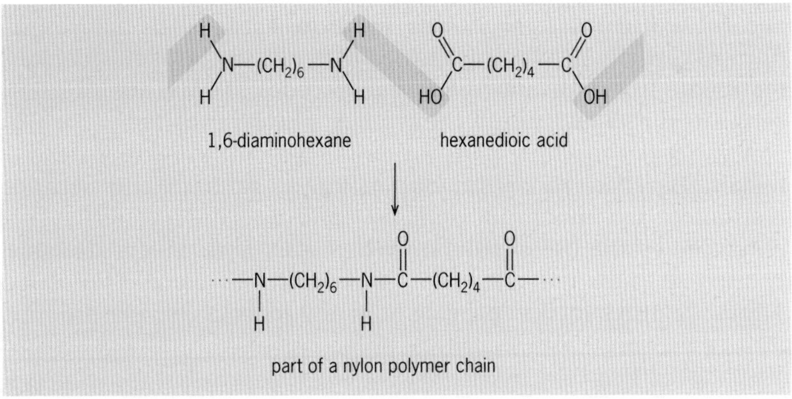

1,6-diaminohexane   hexanedioic acid

part of a nylon polymer chain

Fig 18.26 **The reaction of Carothers and his team that gave rise to nylon 6,6**

?

L Nylon 5,10 is another polyamide produced by Carothers and his team. He favoured this as the nylon to be developed commercially. But he was overruled and nylon 6,6 became the first nylon to be manufactured. Write the structural formulas of the monomers used for nylon 5,10.

Nylon 6,6 is not the only polyamide which Carothers' team produced, and so each is distinguished by a pair of numbers unique to that nylon. The first number after the word nylon is the number of carbon atoms in the diamine. The second number is the number of carbon atoms in the dicarboxylic acid.

When nylon 6,6 is cold drawn, it is stretched to four times its original length, giving the fibres produced a high tensile strength and elasticity. As a fibre is drawn, the polymer chains align parallel to one another and the tensile strength comes from the hydrogen bonding between the CO and NH groups of adjacent chains (Fig 18.27). The cold drawing also increases the lustre (shininess) of nylon. In a commercial nylon plant, molten nylon is forced through tiny holes to produce the fibres which are then cold drawn (Fig 18.28).

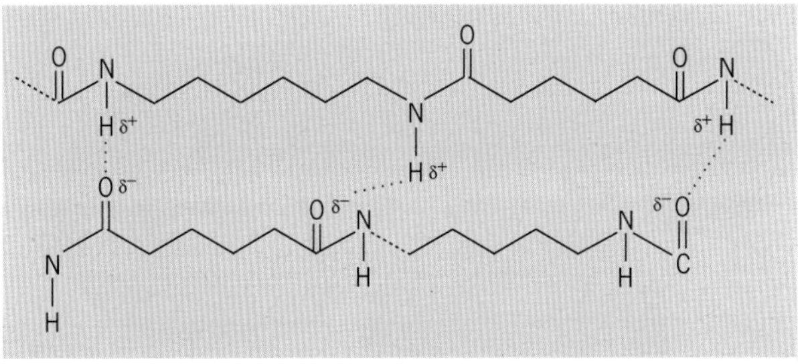

Fig 18.27 **Part of two linear chains of nylon, showing intermolecular hydrogen bonding**

granules of monomer

molten monomer undergoes condensation

tiny holes in spinneret

molten polymer forced through spinneret forms fine fibres

Fig 18.28 **The spinneret through which molten nylon is forced before being cold drawn**

Du Pont went from the laboratory preparation of nylon 6,6 to its manufacture in the remarkably short time of under five years. By 1937 a pilot plant was operational, and by the end of 1939 a full-scale plant had been built and was in production – all this when the techniques of large-scale condensation polymerisation were unknown and there were no bulk supplies of either monomer. Add to this the different technologies required to spin nylon fibres, and we have a remarkable achievement.

The first article to contain nylon was Dr West's Miracle Toothbrush, in which nylon bristles replaced animal bristles. Meanwhile, Du Pont had test marketed women's nylon stockings and recognised their enormous sales potential. Skirt lengths had become shorter and silk stockings were highly fashionable, but were very expensive. When nylon stockings became widely available in 1940, the commercial success of nylon was assured. However, there was not enough production capacity to supply the consumer market and the United States war requirements, for nylon was in great demand for ropes and, in particular, for parachutes, which had previously been made from silk.

Nylon stockings were rationed in the US until the end of the Second World War, and it took until the early 1950s before production capacity in Western Europe matched the insatiable demand for nylon stockings and other nylon goods. Today, nylon goods accounts for 95 per cent of the women's hosiery market.

A variety of machine parts are now made from nylon instead of metals. Here, its properties of toughness, strength and abrasion resistance are much in demand, and specific properties are enhanced by the use of **fillers**, such as glass fibre. Fillers are widely used to tailor the properties of polymers to specific functions. Fillers are also added to provide bulk and make a cheaper product.

> **?**
>
> **M** With reference to page 364, what are the products of the complete hydrolysis of nylon 6,6? What reagents and conditions could be used to carry out this reaction in the laboratory?

See questions 3 and 9. ▪

Thermoplastic and thermosetting polymers

All the polymers so far discussed have one property in common – they are **thermoplastics**. Thermoplastic polymers soften when heated and can be moulded. The process of heating and moulding can be repeated many times. At a molecular level, the forces between the polymer chains are weak, such as induced dipole–induced dipole forces or hydrogen bonds (Fig 18.29(a)). They are sometimes referred to as **secondary bonds**. On warming a thermoplastic polymer, these forces are broken and the polymer chains can slide over one another, allowing the polymer to be shaped. When the polymer cools, the forces reform with the chains in their new positions.

This ability to be remoulded makes these polymers very versatile and therefore in much demand. Consequently, the annual world production of thermoplastic polymers is seven times that of thermosetting polymers.

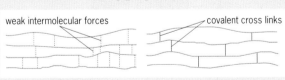

Fig 18.29(a) **Diagrammatic representation of a thermoplastic showing the weak intermolecular forces between the polymer chains which can be overcome on heating to allow the chains to slide over one another. On cooling, the intermolecular forces reform**

Fig 18.29(b) **Diagrammatic representation of a thermosetting polymer. The covalent bonds form a three-dimensional network which, once formed, cannot be melted again**

Thermosetting polymers can be moulded only when they are first produced. With strong heating, they decompose and cannot be softened and remoulded. A thermosetting polymer has covalent cross links between its chains, so the polymer is a three-dimensional network of strong covalent bonds (Fig 18.29(b)). On heating, these break, causing the polymer to decompose before melting can occur.

Bakelite: the first synthetic polymer

Leo Baekeland, a Belgian who had emigrated to the United States, invented the first wholly synthetic polymer, which he called Bakelite. He made it from the reaction of phenol with methanal. Bakelite was first manufactured in 1910.

Fig 18.30 **78 r.p.m. records were made from Bakelite**

The initial reaction involves a substitution in the benzene ring of phenol, which can be at either position 2 or position 4 (Fig 18.31(a)). Once formed, the product can react with another molecule of phenol with the elimination of a water molecule (Fig 18.31(b)). The three-dimensional network is then built up through a series of similar reactions (Fig 18.31(c)).

Because of its high number of cross-links, Bakelite forms a hard, rigid structure. Like most polymers, it is a good electrical and heat insulator. It was widely used in all types of articles, among them electric sockets and plugs, pan handles, and even music records before PVC superseded it. But phenol–methanal resins are still important.

N (a) Is Bakelite:
(i) a condensation polymer or an addition polymer?
(ii) a thermoplastic or a thermosetting polymer?

(b) What properties of Bakelite would make it a suitable material for pan handles?

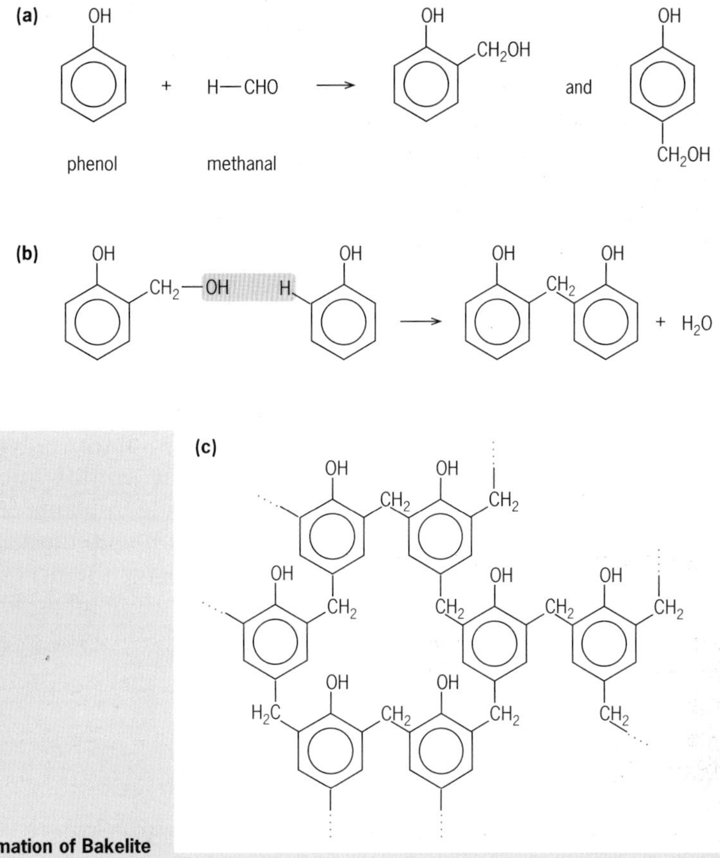

Fig 18.31 **Reactions in the formation of Bakelite**

4 TWO NATURAL POLYMERS: STARCH AND CELLULOSE

Natural polymers are mentioned in the chapter opener, and proteins, which are polymers of amino acids, are discussed in some detail on pages 363 to 368. Two other important polymers are the polysaccharides, starch and cellulose, both made from glucose monomers. Glucose can exist in two distinct forms, as Fig 18.32 shows.

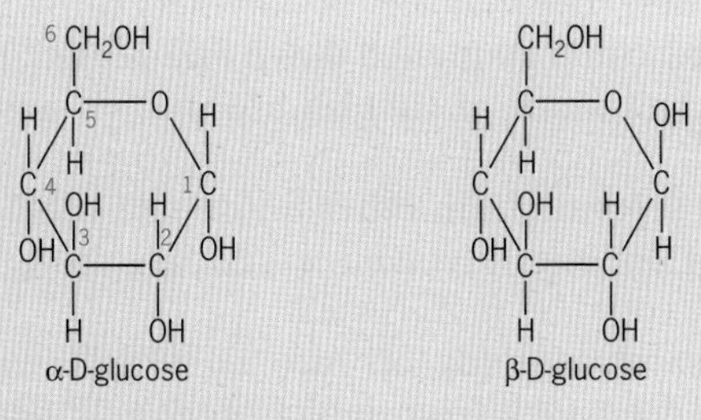

Fig 18.32 **The two ring forms of glucose**

You can learn more about glucose by reading the Chapter 14 Assignment, pages 306.

Note the difference between these two glucose molecules by looking at carbon 1. This seemingly minor difference has a marked effect on the properties of starch and cellulose.

Starch is a polymer of alpha-glucose monomers. It is linked by α-1,4 linkages (Fig 18.33), also called glycosidic linkages. This form of starch is called amylose and is a straight chain polymer.

O Another form of starch, called amylopectin, has branches formed by reaction between the OH groups of carbon 1 and carbon 6. Draw part of this polymer, showing the carbon 1,6 linkage.

Fig 18.33 **Starch**

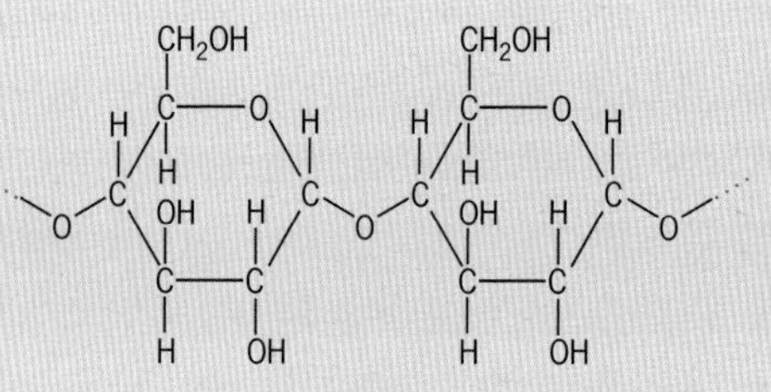

We digest starch by hydrolysing it with enzymes to give glucose. Starch is therefore an energy-storage compound, since once we have broken it down to glucose, it can be metabolised in the body to give energy. Starch can also be hydrolysed by acids in the laboratory to give α-glucose:

$$(C_6H_{10}O_5)_n + nH_2O \xrightarrow{H^+(aq)} nC_6H_{12}O_6$$

Cellulose, a linear polymer formed from β-glucose (Fig 18.34), is probably the world's most abundant organic chemical. It has a structural role in plants and is the source of cotton fibre.

In common with most animals, we cannot digest cellulose because we do not have the necessary enzymes to hydrolyse the β-1,4 linkage. However, cellulose forms the fibre we require in our diet.

Fig 18.34 **Cellulose**

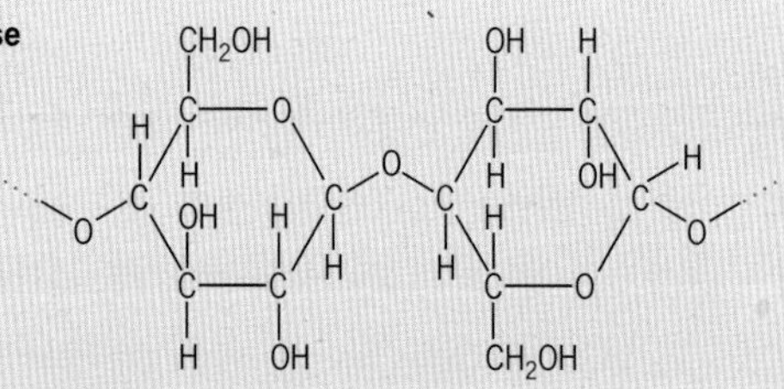

> **?**
>
> **P** Cellulose has considerable strength because its linear chains are able to pack closely together.
> What intermolecular forces give cellulose its strength?

> **?**
>
> **Q** Explain why the molecular structure of thermoplastics allows them to be melted and remoulded.
>
> **R** Epoxy resin is a common component of household waste, but it is a major obstacle to plastics recycling because it is a thermosetting polymer. Why is this a problem?
>
> **S** What processes cost energy in recycling a PET coke bottle?

5 WHAT DO WE DO ABOUT PLASTIC WASTE?

This problem won't go away, mainly because the polymers we throw away do not degrade (break down). In the UK, most plastic waste goes into landfill (Fig 18.35) and that is where it will stay. So, what are the options?

Most polymers come from non-renewable crude oil, and it takes energy to produce them. In fact, of the energy that goes into making a plastic article, most is used in producing the polymer. So, why not recycle the polymer? The majority of polymers thrown out are thermoplastics, so they could be melted down and reused. However, with some exceptions, all kinds of rubbish are thrown away together. It would take much energy and be fairly costly to sort it. Even if plastic waste were kept separate from other household rubbish, the several different types of polymer involved would have to be further separated before they could be reprocessed.

However, research is going on into melting down polymers to form a chemical feedstock from which new polymers can be produced. A project in Japan holds out the prospect of producing petrol from the waste. But to be economically viable and environmentally friendly, any recycling scheme must not use up more energy than it takes to make the polymer in the first place.

Some articles themselves can be reused, and this is done successfully for PET (polyester) bottles in some countries in Europe. But in this case, the energy consumption of recycling must also be taken into account.

Fig 18.35 **Most of the plastic waste in the UK goes into landfill sites**

Biodegradable plastics

The world's first totally biodegradable polymer in commercial production was Biopol (see page 374). Biopol is made by living organisms, so it is called a **biopolymer.** Starch is a biopolymer which is being developed as a biodegradable packaging material. However, it is brittle and requires the addition of plasticisers. Though water and alcohols can fulfil this function through hydrogen bonding with the polymer chains, they are too volatile. Propane-1,2,3-triol (glycerol) could provide a promising, non-toxic alternative plasticiser.

Apart from biopolymers, there are other ways of making synthetic polymers degradable. For example, cellulose, starch or protein can be impregnated into plastic articles such as poly(ethene) bags. When such an article is buried in a landfill site, microorganisms break down the cellulose, starch or protein. The article then disintegrates. The synthetic polymer chains which remain have an increased surface area, which speeds up their decomposition.

Another way with some polymers is to impregnate them with chemical activators so that on exposure to ultraviolet light the polymer chains break down into much shorter chains, which can then be biodegraded. Such polymers are called photodegradable.

There are environmental issues even with degradable plastics. If polymers degrade, then the articles made of them may not be recyclable. Also, there is some concern over the unknown nature of the decomposition products, which may cause more long-term damage to the environment than the original plastics.

?

T If plastics biodegrade, the energy of their bonds is not reused. An alternative is to burn plastic waste to give steam which is used to generate electricity. What are the environmental and energy issues of incinerating the plastics in household rubbish?

See question 4.

SUMMARY

After studying this chapter, you should know:

■ Polymers are very large molecules made up of many small molecules called monomers.

■ Addition polymers form when monomers react together without the elimination of small molecules.

■ Many addition polymers form through a free-radical mechanism.

■ Condensation polymers are formed from monomers with the elimination of small molecules such as water.

■ Polyesters such as Terylene (PET) and polyamides such as nylon 6,6 are synthetic condensation polymers.

■ Starch, cellulose and proteins are natural polymers.

■ Many synthetic polymers are not biodegradable and so there are environmental issues surrounding the disposal or recycling of plastic waste.

■ Poly(ethene), PTFE, PVC (poly(chloroethene)) and poly(phenylethene) are all synthetic addition polymers.

QUESTIONS

1 The Perspex monomer is shown below.

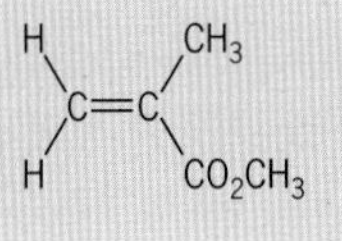

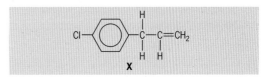

Fig 18.Q1 **The Perspex monomer**

It undergoes addition polymerisation to form Perspex.

a) What is meant by the term addition polymerisation?

b) Draw the polymer repeat unit for Perspex.

2

a) Phenylethene (styrene) can undergo polymerisation to form poly(phenylethene). This polymer is also known as polystyrene.

    (i) State the name of this type of polymerisation and draw a small section of the polymer.

    (ii) Outline the difficulties in the disposal of waste containing this polymer.

Fig 18.Q2

b) Compound **X** in Fig 18.Q2 can be polymerised. Draw a section of its polymer, showing two repeat units. Suggest a possible problem in its disposal which is additional to the problems of disposing poly(phenylethene).

3

a) Describe, using suitable examples, the difference between *addition* polymerisation and *condensation* polymerisation. Name an example of a commercially important polymer produced by **each** method.

b) Proteins and nylon are polymers which have the same type of bond linking the monomer molecules. Outline the similarities and differences between these two types of polymer.

[UCLES June 1996 Sciences: Chains and Rings, q.7]

4

a) Terylene is a polymer derived from benzene-1,4-dicarboxylic acid and ethane-1,2-diol.

   (i) Draw graphical formulae to represent benzene-1,4-dicarboxylic acid and ethane-1,2-diol.
   (ii) What type of polymer is Terylene?
   (iii) Draw the structure of the repeat unit of this polymer.

b) **(i)** Explain the term *biodegradable*.
   (ii) State **one** environmental benefit of using biodegradable plastics.

[AEB Summer 1996 Chemistry Module Paper 9, q.4]

5 Polypropene can be made from propene either by using a Ziegler-Natta catalyst, or by a free radical mechanism.

a) Draw a diagram to show the structure of poly(propene).

b) Explain the differences in the properties of the products from the two ways of polymerising propene.

6 Chloroethene is the feedstock for the manufacture of the polymer poly(chloroethene).

a) Draw the displayed formula of chloroethene

b) Draw the displayed structure of the polymer poly(chloroethene) showing three repeating units.

c) What type of polymer is poly(chloroethene)?

7 Propane-1,2-diol, $CH_3CH(OH)CH_2OH$, can be used to manufacture a polymer.

a) Give the structure of a suitable compound which could react with propane-1,2-diol to form a polymer.

b) Give the repeat unit of the polymer formed and name the type of linkage formed between the molecules.

c) This polymer is not considered to be particularly hazardous to the environment. Comment on possible reasons for this.

[ULEAC June 1996 Chemistry Module Test 4, q.2]

8

a) Terylene is polyester made from the two monomers:

$HOCH_2CH_2OH$ and HO_2C—⟨◯⟩—CO_2H

Fig 18.Q9

   (i) Draw the structural formula of one repeat unit of Terylene.
   (ii) Describe the type of polymerisation occurring during the production of Terylene.

b) Compound **A**, $C_4H_{10}O_2$, reacts with sodium metal but is insoluble in aqueous sodium hydroxide. On treatment with hot acidified sodium dichromate(VI), **A** gives **B**, which is soluble in aqueous sodium hydroxide. **B** can also be formed from fumaric acid, HOOCCH=CHCOOH, by treatment with hydrogen over a nickel catalyst. Compounds **A** and **B** can be co-polymerised to produce a polyester.

   (i) Identify **A** and **B** and explain the above reactions.
   (ii) Draw the structural formula of one repeat unit of the polymer formed from **A** and **B**.
   (iii) Assuming the same chain length in each case, suggest, with a reason, how the melting point of 'poly(**A**-**B**)' might differ from that of Terylene.

[UCLES June 1995 Chemsitry Paper 1, 9520, q.11]
Information in Chapter 11 may be helpful in answering part **b)(i)**.

9

a) **(i)** In order that a polymer may be used as a fibre, it is necessary for it to have strong attractive forces between adjacent chains.
   For nylon 66, identify the groups responsible for the attraction and name the type of interaction involved.
   (ii) By means of simple diagrams, indicate how the structure of freshly prepared nylon 66 is modified to improve its use as a fibre. How is this improvement brought about?
   (iii) Suggest a reason why poly(ethene) does not have fibre properties.

b) One of the main advantages of a natural fibre, such as wool, over a synthetic nylon is the greater ability of wool to absorb moisture. This makes garments made from wool more comfortable to wear but more difficult to dry.
   Suggest a reason why wool has a greater moisture absorbency than nylon, even though both polymers contain similar condensation linkages.

c) In the UK, the principal form of nylon is nylon 66; in France and Germany, it is nylon 6 which is derived from a single monomer caprolactam.

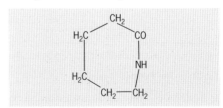

Fig 18.Q10

Suggest how caprolactam could polymerise to form nylon 6 and draw a section of the polymer chain containing two repeat units.

[UCLES June 1995 Paper 2 Option Topics, 9520, q.18]

Assignment

MORE ABOUT POLYAMIDES

Following their invention of nylon 6,6, the Du Pont team led by Wallace Carothers found that the material had two important properties. One was the high tensile strength of its cold-drawn fibres. The other was its high melting point of about 263 °C.

Shortly after the invention of nylon-6,6, another nylon with similar properties was invented by Paul Schlack, working for IG Farbenindustrie in Germany called nylon 6. For nearly 60 years, these two nylons dominated the polyamide market, in both fibre and sheet form. However, this dominance is now being challenged by another nylon, bearing the tradename Stanyl. Stanyl has greater tensile strength than nylon 6,6 and nylon 6, and softens and melts at a higher temperature.

Stanyl is made from 1,4-diaminobutane and hexanedioic acid. It was first prepared by Carothers but was rejected for further development because it had a low M_r and its properties did not seem at all promising. However, a Dutch company has devised a process whereby Stanyl's M_r is 30 000.

1 The repeating unit of nylon 6 is shown in Fig 18.A1. Predict the structural formula of its monomer.

Fig 18.A1 **The nylon 6 repeating unit**

2

a) Write the equation for the production of Stanyl from its monomers.

b) Stanyl is a type of nylon. Use the nylon naming system to identify it.

c) The M_r of Stanyl is 30 000. Approximately how many monomer units are in the chain.

d) Why is the M_r of a polymer an average value?

3 What is meant by the term cold drawing? Why does this process increase the tensile strength of nylon fibres?

Even though nylons have such high softening and melting points, the temperatures at which articles made of them can be in continuous use is much lower. The maximum working temperature of nylon 6,6 is 120 °C, while that of Stanyl is 150 °C. These temperatures can be increased by using a glass filler. However, the higher the working temperature, the quicker nylons deteriorate and lose the properties on which their industrial and domestic use depends.

Du Pont have been in the forefront of research on aromatic polyamides, now called aramids, for a number of years. Their first commercial success came with an aramid fibre they called Nomex. It is made using the reaction in Fig 18.A2.

Fig 18.A2 **The reaction for making Nomex**

Nomex has a melting point above 400 °C. It can be made into fibres but cannot be moulded like nylon. Its main application is as a fire-resistant material, particulary in lining racing-drivers' suits and firefighters' tunics. Also, it is used in hot-gas filters and is made into a honeycomb paper which, when bonded to other materials, forms flame-resistant building materials.

Fig 18.A3 **Being fire resistant, Nomex is used to line the suits of racing drivers**

4

a) Name these functional groups: **(i)** COCl and **(ii)** NH_2.

b) What is the name given to the functional group which links the benzene rings in Nomex?

c) Explain why Nomex is a condensation polymer.

5 Another monomer which Du Pont has investigated is given in Fig 18.A4. Draw the repeating unit of this polymer.

Fig 18.A4 **3-aminobenzoic acid**

The tensile strength of Nomex is an improvement on that of nylon. However, another aramid, called Kevlar, has been developed from monomers with functional groups in the 1,4 position on the benzene ring (Fig 18.A5).

Fig 18.A5 **Kevlar**

Unlike Nomex, Kevlar polymer chains can be aligned to make very strong fibres. A 7 cm diameter steel cable has a breaking strain of about 40 tonnes. An identical Kevlar cable has the same breaking strain, but is five times lighter than the steel cable. Kevlar is embedded in tyres in place of steel reinforcement, reducing the weight of a typical truck tyre by 9 kg. However, the market for Kevlar-reinforced tyres has been slow to take off because tyre manufacturers have invested in equipment to produce steel reinforcement, believing that customers would prefer the strength which the word steel implies.

Kevlar is renowned as the padding in bullet-resistant vests (Fig 18.A7). It is also incorporated into aircraft wings, where strength combined with lightness is essential.

7

a) Draw the repeating unit for Kevlar and predict its monomers.

b) What is the intermolecular force which holds Kevlar fibres together?

c) Why is Kevlar so much stronger than Nomex?

d) Why is Kevlar less dense than steel? Hint: Think about what density means.

8 Getting the chemistry right to produce fibres with the remarkable properties of Kevlar is only one aspect of its commercial development. After the laboratory stage, what other aspects did Du Pont have to consider to ensure the commercial success of their product?

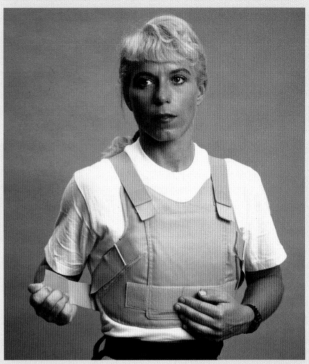

Fig 18.A7 **A bullet-proof vest made from Kevlar**

Fig 18.A8 **The yacht sails are made from Kevlar**

Fig 18.A6 **Kevlar fibre being twisted into cord for radial tyres at a Goodyear plant**

POLYMERS

This chapter covers the ways that small molecules can be polymerised and describes the characteristic properties of polymers that give rise to the enoromous range of applications. The Chapter Map links the processes and mechanisms of synthesis of the polymers and helps you to check on the relationships between the ideas in the chapter.

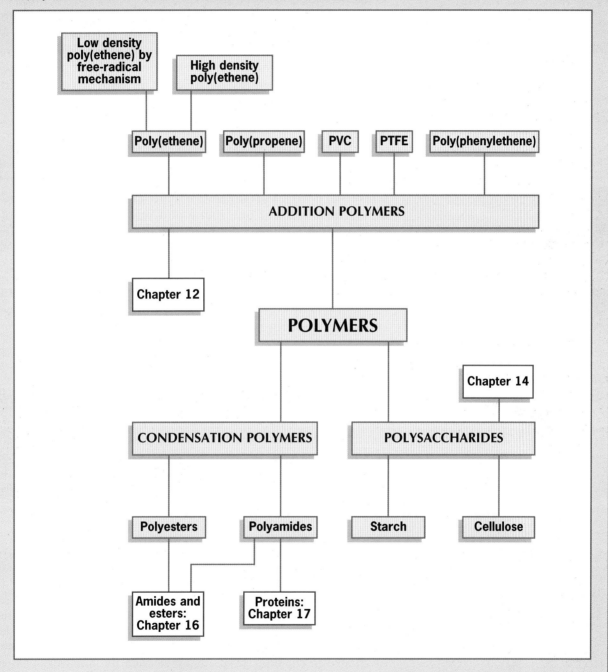

19 The search for the elements

Research is done at CERN, the European centre for Particle Physics, into the nature of the elements and their subatomic particles

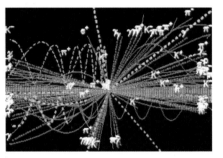

EVER SINCE MENDELEEV proposed his theory of the periodic classification of elements, scientists have set themselves the task of discovering yet more elements. During the last 30 years or so, the search has been on to discover elements that are not normally found on Earth. Scientists have bombarded atoms with high energy particles in an effort to achieve the alchemist's dream of transmutation, the changing of one element into another.

Once an element has been made and conclusively identified, the next step is to find it a name. This seemingly simple task has led to disputes between different groups of research scientists. Each group suggests a name and a symbol. Suddenly an element has not one name and one symbol but possibly three names and three symbols, and it can take more than ten years before there is any agreement between scientists.

In 1994 element number 111 was discovered. Could it be another ten years before it is given a name? Until then, this element will be known as the uninspiring 'unununium', symbol Uuu. Let's hope the scientists make their minds up soon.

Introduction

For thousands of years, people have been curious about the nature of materials in the world around them, and have had theories on the simplest forms of matter, or 'elements', that make up these materials. But it has been only in the last two hundred years, since modern experimental work began, that chemists were sure of having identified elements – substances which could not chemically be changed to anything simpler. Only then could they start to devise useful theories on how elements related to each other, theories that would help scientists progress in their knowledge and understanding of materials.

The greatest breakthrough in this recent endeavour was presented to the world of chemistry on 17 February 1869, when the Russian chemist, Dmitri Mendeleev, published his work on the properties of elements. Assembling the observations and discoveries of earlier workers, he had noted down the symbols of the chemical elements in the order of their atomic masses. Mendeleev's particular arrangement became the first modern Periodic Table, and was to prove invaluable to chemists. It greatly accelerated the discovery of new elements and understanding of their properties, and enabled scientists to predict the full range of elements that were eventually found or artificially made.

This chapter describes how the Periodic Table developed. We explore its importance, both in explaining chemical trends in the elements, long before the structure of the atom was understood, and in predicting the discovery of unknown elements.

Fig. 19.1 **Dmitri Mendeleev – father of the Periodic Table. By bringing together all the facts known then about the elements, Mendeleev made a system of classification that led to many predictions and the discovery of new elements**

1 EARLY IDEAS ABOUT THE ELEMENTS

More than two thousand years ago the Ancient Greeks pictured all the material in the world as being composed of four 'elements' – earth, water, air and fire. The idea may seem far fetched now, but the Ancient Greeks were thinkers and not experimenters. It is interesting, however, that their model reflected the three states of matter – solid, liquid and gas – and fire, which has the capacity to transform materials.

A Why were metals such as gold, silver, copper and mercury the first elements discovered?

Fig 19.2 **A caricature of about 1800 showing alchemists trying to discover the Philosopher's Stone, a process they believed would transform metals into gold**

Civilisations, some of them older than the Ancient Greeks, were able to produce metallic elements such as copper and mercury by mixing their ores with charcoal and heating them in a simple furnace. Other elements, including gold and silver, were found naturally in their elemental state. The drive to produce metals and their alloys arose not because people were interested in chemistry for its own sake, but because of the need to make tools and weapons which were hard-wearing and shatterproof.

The early Arab civilisation was noted for its practical interest in chemicals, and has given us words used in chemistry such as alchemy and alkali. In the Middle Ages, particularly, alchemists in Europe tried hard to find a way to make gold from lead and other metals, not knowing that this was chemically impossible.

The pace of discovery of the elements is shown in Fig 19.4. Notice that where the plot is nearly vertical, several elements were discovered at the same time. Typically, this happened when a new theory or idea was proposed, or new apparatus was developed.

Fig 19.3 **Fire, charcoal and copper ore were used in the process of smelting copper shown in this engraving from 1574**

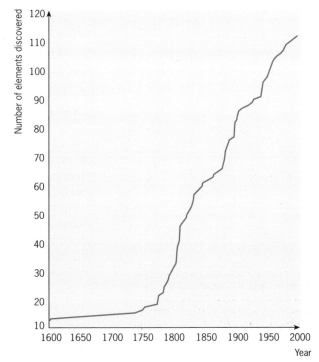

Fig 19.4 **Graph to show the number of elements known from 1600 to the present. Notice how the graph steepens as the rate of new discoveries increases, especially at the time of Mendeleev's work**

B What development happened in 1898 which allowed five elements to be discovered?
Hint: look back to page 22.

C Look at the following triads. The relative atomic mass is written underneath.

Lithium	Sodium	Potassium
7	23	39
Sulphur	Selenium	Tellurium
32	79	128
Chlorine	Bromine	Iodine
35.5	80	127
Calcium	Strontium	Barium
40	88	137

What is the mathematical connection between the atomic masses in these triads?
Give an explanation for this connection. (Hint: Consider the electronic structures described in Chapter 3 in the section Newland's Laws of Octaves.)

For example, towards the end of the eighteenth century, glassware designed for gas preparation led to the discovery of oxygen, chlorine and hydrogen, and air was shown to be a mixture of gases and not a single substance. Later, the new technique of electrolysis enabled Humphry Davy to discover another group of elements – sodium, potassium, magnesium, barium and strontium. For more information about electrolysis, see Chapter 24.

Dalton's atomic theory

Chapter 2 tells you about Dalton's atomic theory. In his theory, he proposed that an atom was the smallest part of an element and could not be split, and that atoms of a particular element had a characteristic mass. We call this the element's **relative atomic mass**, but in Dalton's time, it was known as the atomic weight.

Chemists continued their search for new elements, gradually improving their techniques, but working in an unsystematic way, as they lacked a basis for predicting the existence of unknown elements.

Döbereiner and his triads

Johann Döbereiner was amongst the scientists who were looking for ways to classify the elements. In 1829, he reported on patterns he had found amongst the elements known at the time. He noticed that elements with similar properties could be grouped into threes, or triads, and that there was a mathematical pattern in the values for their relative atomic masses. One of his triads was lithium, sodium and potassium, elements which Davy had discovered using electrolysis.

Newlands' Octaves

Döbereiner had begun to bring order to the elements, showing patterns that existed in their relative atomic masses. Then, in 1864, John Newlands arranged the elements in the order of their relative atomic mass. He, too, found a pattern, noticing that elements with similar chemical properties were eight positions away from each other, rather like the notes in a musical octave. (At this time, the noble gases, which would have added another position, had not been discovered.)

Table 19.1 **Newlands' octaves**

Hydrogen	Lithium	Beryllium	Boron	Carbon	Nitrogen	Oxygen
Fluorine	Sodium	Magnesium	Aluminium	Silicon	Phosphorus	Sulphur
Chlorine	Potassium	Calcium	Chromium	Titanium	Manganese	Iron

Look at Table 19.1. If you start with lithium as '1' and count eight elements, you come to sodium. The two elements are very similar physically and chemically. Count another eight elements and you reach potassium, also very similar to lithium and sodium.

Though the rule of octaves works for some elements, there are exceptions. Look at sulphur and iron which are, again, eight elements apart, yet have very different properties. It needed another system of grouping to make sense of these differences, but Newlands was too preoccupied with the idea of an octave to devise an explanation.

2 MENDELEEV AND THE PERIODIC TABLE

The Russian chemist Mendeleev was fascinated by the elements. He wrote down each known element and its properties on a separate card, and began to put them in a logical order. (Follow Table 19.2.) He ignored hydrogen for it did not seem to fit anywhere and started with lithium. Guided by relative atomic masses, he put beryllium, boron, carbon, nitrogen, oxygen and fluorine in a column. The next element was sodium. He put it next to lithium as both were reactive soft metals. Then the elements magnesium, aluminum, silicon, phosphorus, sulphur and chlorine duly took their place.

Mendeleev continued his list with potassium and calcium. The obvious place for the next card, for titanium, seemed to be below calcium. Then Mendeleev made a brilliant decision. He recognised that a gap had to be left between calcium and titanium for an element yet to be discovered. The chemical properties of titanium were more like those of carbon and silicon than of boron and aluminium, and so Mendeleev placed titanium next to silicon.

Mendeleev concluded, 'The elements, if arranged according to their atomic weights [relative atomic masses], exhibit an evident periodicity of properties.' Mendeleev's original Periodic Table is shown in Fig 19.5.

Table 19.2 **Mendeleev's early lists of elements**

Lithium	Sodium	Potassium
Beryllium	Magnesium	Calcium
Boron	Aluminium	?
Carbon	Silicon	Titanium
Nitrogen	Phosphorus	Vanadium
Oxygen	Sulphur	
Fluorine	Chlorine	

```
                                        Ti = 50    Zr = 90     ? = 180.
                                        V = 51     Nb = 94     Ta = 182.
                                        Cr = 52    Mo = 96     W = 186.
                                        Mn = 55    Rh = 104,4  Pt = 197,4
                                        Fe = 56    Ru = 104,4  Ir = 198.
                                  Ni = Co = 59     Pl = 106,6  Os = 199.
H = 1                                   Cu = 63,4  Ag = 108    Hg = 200.
          Be = 9,4   Mg = 24   Zn = 65,2           Cd = 112
          B = 11     Al = 27,4  ? = 68             Ur = 116    Au = 197?
          C = 12     Si = 28    ? = 70             Sn = 118
          N = 14     P = 31    As = 75             Sb = 122    Bi = 210
          O = 16     S = 32    Se = 79,4           Te = 128?
          F = 19     Cl = 35,5 Br = 80             I = 127
Li = 7  Na = 23      K = 39    Rb = 85,4           Cs = 133    Tl = 204
                     Ca = 40   Sr = 87,6           Ba = 137    Pb = 207.
                     ? = 45    Ce = 92
                    ?Er = 56   La = 94
                    ?Yt = 60   Di = 95
                    ?In = 75,6 Th = 118?
```

Fig 19.5 **Mendeleev's Periodic Table, published in his book** *Principles of Chemistry* **in 1869. In it he first set out his periodic law which earned him international fame. The question marks are for unknown elements. Mendeleev published his version of the Periodic Table with horizontal periods and vertical groups in 1870**

Notice that Mendeleev first placed the elements in columns. Soon afterwards, he decided on the arrangement of the Periodic Table that is familiar to us. Each element had its own number and fixed position in the table, and Mendeleev left several gaps for element which were then unknown but which he believed existed.

Mendeleev's table made a considerable impact amongst chemists of his time because it was so useful to them. It revealed clear patterns and trends in the properties of elements both known and unknown. For the first time, chemists could guess at the total number of elements that might exist and, in noting the gaps, they were spurred on to make discoveries of new elements.

Fig 19.6 **Mendeleev predicted germanium before it was discovered by using the properties of silicon and tin.** Right: **Silicon, used in microchips.** Centre: **Germanium, used in transistors.** Left: **Tin, used as the coating on 'tin' cans to prevent the iron from rusting**

Mendeleev used his table to predict the properties of scandium and gallium, and also germanium which he first named 'eka-silicon'. Within 20 years, all three elements had been discovered. Table 19.3 shows the properties he expected germanium to have, and how close his predictions proved to be. Altogether, Mendeleev predicted properties for 10 unknown elements, and was later proved correct in eight cases.

D Look at a modern Periodic Table.

(a) Cobalt and nickel are not in the order of their atomic masses. Explain why this is so.

(b) Write down the names of two more pairs of elements that are not arranged in order of relative atomic mass in the Periodic Table.

Table 19.3 **Properties of 'eka-silicon', germanium and tin**

	Silicon	Predicted properties for eka-silicon	Germanium	Tin
Atomic mass	28	72	72.59	118
Density/g cm^{-3}	2.3	5.5	5.3	7.3
Appearance	grey non-metal	grey metal	grey metal	white metal
Formula of oxide	SiO_2	EkO_2	GeO_2	SnO_2
Formula of chloride	$SiCl_4$	$EkCl_4$	$GeCl_4$	$SnCl_4$
Reaction with acid	none	very slow	slow with conc. acid	slow

Mendeleev positioned elements on the basis of their properties. Where elements did not fit in order of their relative atomic masses, he assumed that these had been determined incorrectly. So, for example, he placed cobalt before nickel, though cobalt has a greater mass.

Fig 19.7 **By 1905, Mendeleev's Periodic Table had a few new elements, but still looked similar to his earlier version**

Group Series	0	I	II	III	IV	V	VI	VII	VIII			
1		Hydrogen H 1.008	—	—	—	—	—	—				
2	Helium He 4.0	Lithium Li 7.03	Beryllium Be 9.1	Boron B 11.0	Carbon C 12.0	Nitrogen N 14.04	Oxygen O 16.00	Fluorine F 19.0				
3	Neon Ne 19.9	Sodium Na 23.05	Magnesium Mg 24.3	Aluminium Al 27.0	Silicon Si 28.4	Phosphorus P 31.0	Sulphur S 32.06	Chlorine Cl 35.45				
4	Argon Ar 38	Potassium K 39.1	Calcium Ca 40.1	Scandium Sc 44.1	Titanium Ti 48.1	Vanadium V 51.4	Chromium Cr 52.1	Manganese Mn 55.0	Iron Fe 55.9	Cobalt Co 59	Nickel N 59	(Cu)
5		Copper Cu 63.6	Zinc Zn 65.4	Gallium Ga 70.0	Germanium Ge 72.3	Arsenic As 75	Selenium Se 79	Bromine Br 79.95				
6	Krypton Kr 81.8	Rubidium Rb 85.4	Strontium Sr 87.6	Yttrium Y 89.0	Zirconium Zr 90.6	Niobium Nb 94.0	Molybdenum Mo 96.0	—	Ruthenium Ru 101.7	Rhodium Rh 103.0	Palladium Pd 106.5	(Ag)
7		Silver Ag 107.9	Cadmium Cd 112.4	Indium In 114.0	Tin Sn 119.0	Antimony Sb 120.0	Tellurium Te 127	Iodine I 127				
8	Xenon Xe 128	Caesium Cs 132.9	Barium Ba 137.4	Lanthanum La 139	Cerium Ce 140	—	—	—	—	—	—	
9		—	—	—	—	—						
10	—	—	—	Ytterbium Yb 173	—	Tantalum Ta 183	Tungsten W 184	—	Osmium Os 191	Indium Ir 193	Platinum Pt 194.9	(Au)
11		Gold Au 197.2	Mercury Hg 200.0	Thallium Tl 204.1	Lead Pb 206.9	Bismuth Bi 208						
12	—	—	Radium Rd 224	—	Thorium Th 232	—	Uranium U 239					

Atomic (proton) number

We have seen that, on the basis of their properties, a few elements in the Periodic Table had to be placed out of order of their relative atomic masses. We now know that relative atomic mass depends on the overall structure of the nucleus, and that it is the order of *atomic number* of elements which determines the trends in their properties.

The atomic number of an element is the number of protons found in one atom of that element.

Periods and groups in the Periodic Table

The table Mendeleev devised in 1905 (Fig 19.7) has much in common with a modern version of the Periodic Table (see Fig 19.8). *Horizontal rows* of elements represent **periods**, numbered 1 to 7. Note how the seven modern periods compare to Mendeleev's series, and how they differ.

The *vertical columns* 1 to 7 and 0 in Fig 19.8 represent the **groups** of elements. Elements in a group have very similar chemical properties. Notice in Fig 19.7 that each group has two columns. These correspond to a group in the s and p block and another group taken from the d-block elements (Fig 19.9, see later). We just refer to Group 1 as being all the elements in the vertical column headed by lithium, and similarly, Group 7 is all the elements headed by fluorine.

> In older versions of the Periodic Table, the group numbers are roman numerals – Group 7 is Group VII, for example.

Group	1	2											3	4	5	6	7	0
1	1 **H** hydrogen 1.0																	2 **He** helium 4.0
2	3 **Li** lithium 6.9	4 **Be** beryllium 9.0											5 **B** Boron 10.8	6 **C** carbon 12.0	7 **N** nitrogen 14.0	8 **O** oxygen 16.0	9 **F** fluorine 19.0	10 **Ne** neon 20.2
3	11 **Na** sodium 23.0	12 **Mg** magnesium 24.3											13 **Al** aluminium 6.9	14 **Si** silicon 28.1	15 **P** phosphorus 31.0	16 **S** sulphur 32.1	17 **Cl** chlorine 35.5	18 **Ar** argon 39.9
4	19 **K** potassium 39.1	20 **Ca** calcium 40.1	21 **Sc** scandium 45.0	22 **Ti** titanium 47.8	23 **V** vanadium 50.9	24 **Cr** chromium 52.0	25 **Mn** magganese 54.9	26 **Fe** iron 55.9	27 **Co** colbalt 58.9	28 **Ni** nickel 58.7	29 **Cu** copper 63.5	30 **Zn** zinc 65.4	31 **Ga** gallium 69.7	32 **Ge** germanium 72.6	33 **As** arsenic 74.9	34 **Se** selenium 79.0	35 **Br** bromine 79.9	36 **Kr** krypton 83.8
5	37 **Rb** rubidium 85.5	38 **Sr** strontium 87.6	39 **Y** yttrium 88.9	40 **Zr** zirconium 91.2	41 **Nb** niobium 92.9	42 **Mo** molybdenum 95.9	43 **Tc** technetium (98)	44 **Ru** ruthenium 101.1	45 **Rh** rhodium 102.9	46 **Pd** palladium 106.4	47 **Ag** silver 107.9	48 **Cd** cadmium 112.4	49 **In** indium 114.8	50 **Sn** tin 118.7	51 **Sb** antimony 121.8	52 **Te** tellurium 127.6	53 **I** iodine 126.9	54 **Xe** xenon 131.3
6	55 **Cs** caesium 132.9	56 **Ba** barium 137.3	57 **La** lanthanium 138.9	72 **Hf** hafnium 178.5	73 **Ta** tantalum 181.0	74 **W** tungsten 183.9	75 **Re** rhenium 186.2	76 **Os** osmium 190.2	77 **Ir** iridium 192.2	78 **Pt** platinium 195.1	79 **Au** gold 197.0	80 **Hg** mercury 200.6	81 **TL** thallium 204.4	82 **Pb** lead 207.2	83 **Bi** bismuth 209.0	84 **Po** polonium (209)	85 **At** astatine (210)	86 **Rn** radon (222)
7	87 **Fr** francium (223)	88 **Ra** radium (226)	89 **Ac** actinium (227)	104 **Unq** unnilquadium (261)	105 **Unp** unnilpentium (262)	106 **Unh** unnilhexium (263)	107 **Uns** unnilseptium (262)	108 **Uno** unniloctium (265)	109 **Une** unnilennium (266)									

atomic no **symbol** **name** relative atomic mass   metal   non–metal

Lanthanides	58 **Ce** cerium 140.1	59 **Pr** praseodymium 140.9	60 **Nd** neodymium 144.2	61 **Pm** promethium (145)	62 **Sm** samarium 150.4	63 **Eu** europium 152.0	64 **Gd** gadolinium 157.3	65 **Tb** terbium 158.9	66 **Dy** dysprosium 162.5	67 **Ho** holmium 164.9	68 **Er** erbium 167.3	69 **Tm** thulium 168.9	70 **Yb** ytterbium 173.0	71 **Lu** lutetium 175.5
Actinides	90 **Th** thorium 232.0	91 **Pa** protactinium (231)	92 **U** uranium 238.1	93 **Np** neptunium (237)	94 **Pu** plutonium (244)	95 **Am** americium (243)	96 **Cm** curium (247)	97 **Bk** berkelium (247)	98 **Cf** californium (251)	99 **Es** einsteinium (254)	100 **Fm** fermium (253)	101 **Md** mendelevum (256)	102 **No** nobelium (254)	103 **Lr** lawrencium (257)

Fig 19.8 A modern version of the Periodic Table with 109 elements (relative atomic mass in brackets = mass number of most stable isotope)

Electron configuration

As you may have read in Chapter 3, the electron configuration of an atom describes the arrangement of its electrons. Electrons occupy a series of shells round the nucleus, numbered 1, 2, 3, 4, and so on. Each shell has particular subshells labelled s, p, d, f etc. Each subshell has its own energy level, and these energy levels increase in the order s, p, d, f, etc. The chart on the right sums up this information:

> **E** Which element is found in Period 4 and Group 6?

Shell	Subshells			
1	1s			
2	2s,	2p		
3	3s,	3p,	3d	
4	4s,	4p,	4d,	4f

increasing energy level of subshell →

A maximum number of electrons can occupy each subshell:

Subshell	s	p	d	f
Maximum number of electrons	2	6	10	14

In each shell, electrons fill the subshells in the same order. Usually, a subshell has to be fully occupied before further electrons start to fill the next level. We indicate the number of electrons in a subshell by a raised number and describe the electrons in an atom as:

$$1s^2 \ 2s^2 \ 2p^6 \ 3s^2 \ 3p^6 \ 3d^{10} \ 4s^2 \ 4p^6 \ 4d^{10} \text{ etc.}$$

Go back to page 62 if you wish to find out more about electron configurations.

?

F Write down the electron configurations for each of the following elements: nitrogen, chlorine, calcium and titanium.

G For each of these electron configurations, state the group to which the element belongs:

(a) $1s^2\ 2s^2\ 2p^6\ 3s^2\ 3p^6\ 3d^{10}\ 4s^2\ 4p^5$

(b) $1s^2\ 2s^2\ 2p^6\ 3s^2\ 3p^6\ 3d^{10}\ 4s^2\ 4p^1$

(c) $1s^2\ 2s^2\ 2p^6\ 3s^2\ 3p^6\ 3d^{10}\ 4s^2\ 4p^6$ $4d^{10}\ 5s^2\ 5p^2$

H In which block of the Periodic Table would you place the elements with the following electron configurations?

(a) $1s^2\ 2s^2\ 2p^6\ 3s^2\ 3p^3$

(b) $1s^2\ 2s^2\ 2p^6\ 3s^2\ 3p^6\ 3d^{10}\ 4s^2\ 4p^5$

(c) $1s^2\ 2s^2\ 2p^6\ 3s^2\ 3p^6\ 3d^{10}\ 4s^2\ 4p^6$ $4d^6\ 5s^2$

(d) $1s^2\ 2s^2\ 2p^6\ 3s^2\ 3p^6\ 3d^{10}\ 4s^2\ 4p^6$ $4d^{10}\ 5s^2$

See question 8. ■

The chemical properties of an element depend on its electron configuration. Since elements are arranged in the Periodic Table in order of their atomic number and chemical properties, it is no surprise to see that elements are also ordered according to their electron configurations. It is another strength of Mendeleev's Periodic Table that it reflected electron configurations before electrons were even discovered.

We can see that electron configurations of the outer shells of elements in the Periodic Table show regular trends or periodicity. (We look again at periodicity in section 3.) The elements of any particular group have the same number of electrons in the same type of outer shell. For example, the Group 6 elements oxygen, sulphur, selenium, tellurium and polonium all have six electrons in their outer shell, namely $ns^2\ np^4$, where n is the period number.

If an element is in Period 4, then its outer electrons occupy either 4s or 4p orbitals; if an element is in Period 6, then its outer electrons occupy either 6s or 6p orbitals.

The Periodic Table is arranged in blocks

Refer to fig 19.9 as you read this section. The **s block** contains the elements with an electron configuration that ends with electrons in an s subshell, meaning that the outermost electrons are in s subshells. A typical s-block element is strontium, with an electron configuration of $1s^2\ 2s^2\ 2p^6\ 3s^2\ 3p^6\ 3d^{10}\ 4s^2\ 4p^6\ 5s^2$, so its outer electrons are in an s subshell.

The **p block** contains elements that have an electron configuration that ends with electrons in a p subshell, so the outermost electrons are in a p subshell. A typical p-block element is chlorine, with an electron configuration of $1s^2\ 2s^2\ 2p^6\ 3s^2\ 3p^5$, so the outer electrons are in p subshells.

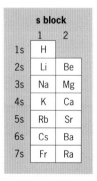

s block

	1	2
1s	H	
2s	Li	Be
3s	Na	Mg
4s	K	Ca
5s	Rb	Sr
6s	Cs	Ba
7s	Fr	Ra

d block

3d	Sc	Ti	V	Cr	Mn	Fe	Co	Ni	Cu	Zn
4d	Y	Zr	Nb	Mo	Tc	Ru	Rh	Pd	Ag	Cd
5d	La	Hf	Ta	W	Re	Os	Ir	Pt	Au	Hg
6d	Ac	(4f, see below)								
		(5f, see below)								

p block

	3	4	5	6	7	0
						He
2p	B	C	N	O	F	Ne
3p	Al	Si	P	S	Cl	Ar
4p	Ga	Ge	As	Se	Br	Kr
5p	In	Sn	Sb	Te	I	Xe
6p	Ti	Pb	Bi	Po	At	Rn

f block

Lanthanides 4f	Ce	Pr	Nd	Pm	Sm	Eu	Gd	Tb	Dy	Ho	Er	Tm	Yb	lu
Actinides 5f	Th	Pa	U	Np	Pu	Am	Cm	Bk	Cf	Es	Fm	Md	No	Lr

Fig 19.9 **The blocks of the Periodic Table**

The **d block** contains elements in Periods 4, 5 and 6. They are often called the **transition elements** or **transition metals**. Most of the d-block elements have an incomplete set of d electrons in their second-to-outermost subshell, and either one or two electrons in the outermost s-subshell. A typical element of the d block is iron, with the electron configuration $1s^2\ 2s^2\ 2p^6\ 3s^2\ 3p^6\ 3d^6\ 4s^2$, where $3d^6$ is an incomplete subshell of shell 3.

Ten electrons can fill a d subshell, and the d block is also 10 elements wide. In Period 4, for example, scandium on the far left has one electron in the d subshell and on the right, zinc has 10. Electrons are added one at a time to the 3d subshell as you go across the d-block part of the Period.

The **f block** contains elements with an incomplete set of electrons in an f subshell. These elements are often called the **lanthanides** and **actinides**, named after the elements lanthanum and actinium just before them in Periods 6 and 7.

3 PATTERNS IN THE PERIODIC TABLE

Examining the Periodic Table, we have seen that both the physical and the chemical properties of elements are repeated at regular intervals. This characteristic is called **periodicity**. Now we have seen that the fundamental structure of atoms, represented by their electron configurations, also shows the same patterns.

1 H 30																	2 He
3 Li 152	4 Be 111											5 B 88	6 C 77	7 N 70	8 O 66	9 F 64	10 Ne
11 Na 186	12 Mg 160											13 Al 143	14 Si 117	15 P 110	16 S 104	17 Cl 99	18 Ar
19 K 231	20 Ca 197	21 Sc 160	22 Ti 146	23 V 131	24 Cr 125	25 Mn 129	26 Fe 126	27 Co 126	28 Ni 124	29 Cu 128	30 Zn 133	31 Ga 122	32 Ge 122	33 As 121	34 Se 117	35 Br 114	36 Kr
37 Rb 244	38 Sr 215	39 Y 180	40 Zr 157	41 Nb 143	42 Mo 136	43 Tc 136	44 Ru 133	45 Rh 134	46 Pd 138	47 Ag 144	48 Cd 149	49 In 168	50 Sn 140	51 Sb 141	52 Te 137	53 I 133	54 Xe
55 Cs 262	56 Ba 217	57 La 188	72 Hf 157	73 Ta 143	74 W 137	75 Re 137	76 Os 134	77 Ir 135	78 Pt 138	79 Au 144	80 Hg 155	81 Tl 171	82 Pb 175	83 Bi 146	84 Po 140	85 At 140	86 Rn
(87) Fr 270	88 Ra 220	89 Ac 200															

Fig. 19.10 Atomic (covalent) radii of the elements measured as picometres (10^{-12} m)

Atomic radii

Look at Fig 19.10, which shows the atomic radii of the elements.

The atomic radius of an isolated atom cannot be measured as it is not possible to know where its outer boundary is exactly. There are several definitions for the atomic radius of an atom, but we shall use the following one.

> **The atomic radius of an element X is half of the distance between the nuclei of two atoms joined by a single covalent bond X–X.**

This is also referred to as the covalent radius of an element. The force between the negative electrons and the positive nucleus is what holds the electrons in the atom. The larger the force, the stronger is the attraction between the electrons and the nucleus and so the smaller is the covalent radius.

Look at any group in the Periodic Table. Going down the group, the number of (positively charged) protons increases, hence the nuclear charge increases. At the same time, the number of electrons increases. You might expect that, with this increase in charge, the electrons would be held more tightly, making the atomic radius smaller. But as

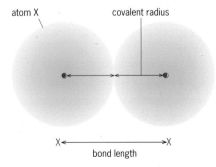

Fig 19.11 **The bond length X–X in X_2 is twice the covalent radius of X**

?

I Study the information below which is for elements in Group 5.

Nitrogen   a.r. 70   n.c. +7
  e.c. $1s^2 2s^2 2p^3$

Phosphorus   a.r. 110   n.c. +15
  e.c. $1s^2 2s^2 2p^6 3s^2 3p^3$

Arsenic   a.r. 121   n.c. +33
  e.c. $1s^2 2s^2 2p^6 3s^2 3p^6 3d^{10}$
    $4s^2 4p^3$

Antimony   a.r.141   n.c. +51
  e.c. $1s^2 2s^2 2p^6 3s^2 3p^6 3d^{10} 4s^2$
    $4p^6 4d^{10} 5s^2 5p^3$

a.r. = atomic radius in picometres $(1 \times 10^{-12}$ m), n.c. = nuclear charge due to protons, and e.c. = electron configuration.

Use this information to explain the change in atomic radius in Group 5.

See questions 3, 4 and 9.

?

J You can estimate the bond length of a covalent bond by adding together the two atomic radii of the atoms concerned. For example, the bond length of H–Cl can be estimated by adding the atomic radius of chlorine to that of hydrogen.

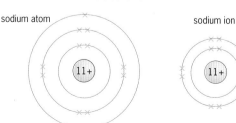

bond length = $r_H + r_{Cl}$

(a) Use the information in the Periodic Table of Fig 19.10 to calculate the following bond lengths: **(i)** the O–H bond in a water molecule, **(ii)** the bond length of the N–H bond in ammonia, NH_3.

(b) Explain why you cannot use the data in the Periodic Table to estimate the bond length of the carbon-carbon double bond in ethene, C_2H_4.

(c) The Periodic Table does not have a value for the atomic radius of helium. Why not?

See question 3.

the atomic number gets larger, and there are more electron shells, the inner electron shells shield the outermost electrons from the full positive charge, and so the outermost electrons move further away from the nucleus. Sometimes we talk about an 'effective' nuclear charge, which takes this shielding into consideration.

To summarise: as the atomic number of an element in a group increases,

- the shielding effect increases,
- the effective nuclear charge is reduced,
- the attraction of the nucleus for the outermost electrons reduces,
- and the atomic radius increases.

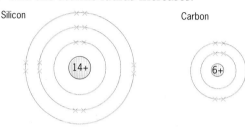

Fig 19.12 **Silicon is bigger than carbon because although it has more protons it also has an extra layer of shielding electrons**

Look at one of the short periods and notice that, as you go across the Periodic Table, the atomic radius tends to get smaller as the atomic number increases. The nuclear charge is only effectively shielded by the electrons in the inner shells, and not by the electrons in the outer shell. Going across the period, the effective nuclear charge increases, but the same outer electron shell is filling up, so there is no increase in effective shielding by inner electron shells. This means that the electrons in the filling shell are more strongly attracted towards the nucleus, and so the atomic radius decreases.

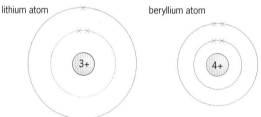

Fig 19.13 **Lithium is bigger than beryllium because of the increased nuclear charge with no extra electron shells**

Ionic radii

The ionic radii of ions have been determined experimentally from studies on ionic crystals.

A sodium ion, Na^+, is formed when a sodium atom loses one electron. Its ionic radius is 95 picometres, which is smaller than the atomic radius of a sodium atom. This is because the ion has one proton more than its number of electrons, so the electrons are held with a greater attraction and are drawn towards the nucleus.

A chloride ion, Cl^-, is formed when a chlorine atom gains one electron. A chloride ion is larger than a chlorine atom since it has one electron more than its number of protons, so the electrons are held with less attraction.

sodium atom   sodium ion

Fig 19.14 **A sodium ion is smaller than a sodium atom as the ion has one more proton than electrons and so the excess positive charge pulls the remaining electrons closer to the nucleus**

First ionisation energy

The Periodic Table features trends in the energy required to remove electrons from an atom.

> **The first ionisation energy is the energy required for one mole of gaseous atoms to lose one mole of electrons, to form one mole of gaseous ions with a single positive charge.**

The process can be represented by the equation below. It is important to include the state symbols for this process because ionisation energy only refers to gaseous atoms becoming gaseous ions.

$$X(g) \rightarrow X^+(g) + e^- \qquad \Delta H_{IE} = \text{positive (first ionisation energy measured in kJ mol}^{-1})$$

Determining first ionisation energy of an element using atomic spectroscopy

One way to find the first ionisation energy of an element uses atomic emission spectroscopy. Simply, gaseous atoms at very low pressure are supplied with electrical energy. The electrons absorb energy and move from one energy level to higher levels. Then they move back, releasing the same amount of energy as photons of electromagnetic radiation.

The wavelengths or frequencies of the electromagnetic radiation emitted are identified. It is an easy task to convert the frequency of electromagnetic radiation to the amount of energy associated with a photon by using Planck's equation:

$$\Delta E = hf$$

The largest energy gap corresponds to an electron falling back from a very high energy level to the ground state, nearly equal to the energy required to remove the first electron completely from the atom, and this is approximately equal to the ionisation energy for one atom. Then, the first ionisation energy – the energy required for one mole of atoms to lose the mole of electrons – can be worked out.

The process of one mole of gaseous atoms losing one mole of electrons is endothermic because an input of energy is needed to remove an electron from an atom being held by the force of attraction of the nuclear charge. The smaller the effective nuclear charge, then the easier it is for the electron to be removed, and so the process becomes less endothermic. Similarly, the higher the effective nuclear charge, the more endothermic the reaction.

> ✔ Sometimes gaseous atoms have to be produced by dissociation of the diatomic molecule X_2.

K (a) A sodium cation and a magnesium cation have the same number of electrons. Explain why the radius of Mg^{2+} is much smaller than Na^+.

(b) Look at the table on the right, which shows the radius of some ions and atoms.

Species						
P^{3-}	S^{2-}	Cl^-	Ar	K^+	Ca^{2+}	Sc^{3+}
Radius/pm						
212	184	181	154	133	99	81

(i) Explain why a chloride ion has a larger radius than a chlorine atom.
(ii) The species in the table are isoelectronic, meaning that they all have the same electron configuration. Explain the trend shown by the radii of these species.

Look at Fig 19.15. The line joining the values for the first ionisation energies of the elements shows a regular up-and-down pattern with peaks and troughs. It is particularly difficult to remove an electron from the gaseous atom of the elements at the peaks, and we say that the electron configuration of these elements is very stable. It is also particularly easy to remove electrons from elements in the troughs.

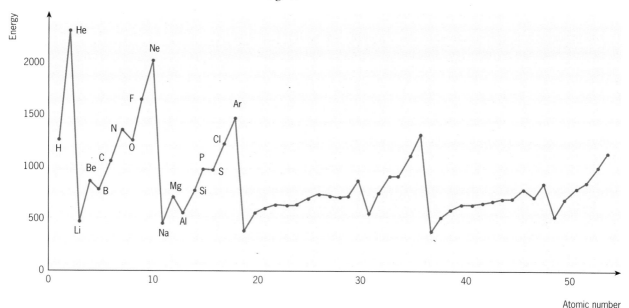

Fig 19.15 **Graph of first ionisation energy against atomic number**

All the elements of Group 0, the noble gases, are at peaks. This means their first ionisation energies are particularly high. These elements occupy the last position in a period, so their electrons are attracted by the highest effective nuclear charge for that period. Across the period, the electrons have been filling the same outer orbital, and so there has been no increase in the shielding effect. The electron configurations of the noble gases are very stable. They are shown in Table 19.4.

Table 19.4 **Electron configuration of the noble gases**

Atom	Atomic number	electron configuration
He	2	$1s^2$
Ne	10	$1s^2\ 2s^2\ 2p^6$
Ar	18	$1s^2\ 2s^2\ 2p^6\ 3s^2\ 3p^6$
Kr	36	$1s^2\ 2s^2\ 2p^6\ 3s^2\ 3p^6\ 3d^{10}\ 4s^2\ 4p^6$
Xe	54	$1s^2\ 2s^2\ 2p^6\ 3s^2\ 3p^6\ 3d^{10}\ 4s^2\ 4p^6\ 4d^{10}\ 5s^2\ 5p^6$

L Why does helium have a higher first ionisation energy than any other element?

M Give an explanation for the general increase in the first ionisation energies as you go across the elements in the second period.

N Look at the first ionisation energies for the elements scandium to zinc in the first series of the transition block. The element with the highest first ionisation energy is zinc. Account for this in terms of its electron configuration.

Look at the graph in Fig 19.15. You can see that first ionisation energies decrease down a group. The reason for this is again connected with how effectively the nuclear charge attracts the outermost electrons. The more electron shells there are, the lower is the effective nuclear charge, so that the outer electrons become less strongly held and are easier to remove. The effective nuclear charge decreases down a group as the atomic number increases, due to the increasing number of shielding inner electron shells.

There are also patterns relating first ionisation energy with atomic number. As we have seen, the peaks in ionisation energy occur when there is a particularly stable electron configuration. This also applies to elements with a full subshell. For example, beryllium with $1s^2\ 2s^2$, has a full 2s orbital. In addition, a relatively stable electron configuration occurs when a subshell is half-filled with electrons. An example is nitrogen (Fig 19.16) with an electron configuration $1s^2 2s^2 2p^3$. The three electrons in the subshell each occupy one of the 2p orbitals. The repulsion of electrons is less when an orbital contains one electron than when there are two, and so it takes more energy to remove a solitary electron.

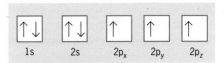

Fig 19.16 **In nitrogen, the three 2p electrons occupy different orbitals to minimise electron–electron repulsion**

■ See questions 2, 4 and 5.

Here, you might want to read Chapter 3 about how electrons fill orbitals and shells.

4 METALS, NON-METALS AND METALLOIDS

The 90 or so naturally occurring elements can go into three main groups: the metals, the non-metals and the metalloids or semi-metals.

Physical properties

Metals make up about 80 per cent of all the elements, and have many physical properties in common. A metal is generally a good conductor of heat and electricity and it often has a lustre – a shine. It is likely to be malleable, that is, it can be shaped by hammering, and ductile, meaning that it can be drawn into a wire.

Non-metal solids are normally poor conductors of heat and electricity, rarely have a lustre and are normally brittle and non-ductile. Many non-metals are gases at room temperature and pressure.

If an element cannot be classified as a metal or a non-metal it is called a **metalloid** or semi-metal and it will possess some of the properties of metals and some of the properties of non-metals. A good example of a metalloid is silicon, which is shiny but is brittle and is a poor conductor of heat and electricity.

Fig 19.17 **Metals. Clockwise from top left: zinc, silver foil, lead shot, copper crystals**

Fig 19.18 **Non-metals. Clockwise from top left: sulphur, bromine, phosphorus, carbon, iodine**

Chemical properties

The most striking property of a metal atom is its ability to lose electrons. Commonly, metals lose one, two or three electrons to form cations. They will *lose* electrons so as to obtain a stable electron configuration like that found in one of the noble gases. (You will have met this idea in Chapter 3, page XX.) Non-metals, on the other hand, tend to *gain* electrons to become anions or to make covalent bonds. It is clear, then, that metals will tend to react with non-metals, and a metal atom 'gives away' electrons to a non-metal atom.

Take, for example, the reaction of sodium with chlorine. Sodium is a typical metal, and chlorine is a typical non-metal. When they react, one electron is transferred from a sodium atom to a chlorine atom to form a sodium ion and a chloride ion. This transfer of electrons results in both the sodium ion and the chloride ion obtaining a stable electron configuration like that of a noble gas.

O Calcium reacts with chlorine to give calcium chloride. Write two equations to show the electron transfer that occurs.

The reaction may be written as follows.

$$Na \rightarrow Na^+ + e^-$$
$$\tfrac{1}{2}Cl_2 + e^- \rightarrow Cl^-$$

Taken together, the equation becomes:

$$Na + \tfrac{1}{2}Cl_2 + e^- \rightarrow Na^+ + Cl^- + e^-$$

You can see that the electron can be cancelled out on both sides of the equation, so that this reaction can be written as:

$$Na + \tfrac{1}{2}Cl_2 \rightarrow Na^+ + Cl^-$$

The equation becomes more familiar if the product is given its normal formula which ignores the charges on the ions:

$$Na + \tfrac{1}{2}Cl_2 \rightarrow NaCl$$

The final equation hides the fact that during the reaction an electron is transferred from the sodium to the chlorine. This type of reaction is called a **redox reaction**. Redox is a shorthand word for reduction–oxidation.

In a redox reaction, one particle loses electrons
and another particle gains them.

In the process of reduction, a particle loses electrons – it is an electron donor. In oxidation, a particle gains electrons – it is an electron acceptor. A particle can be an atom or a molecule or an ion.

Looking at the reaction between sodium and chlorine, you can say that sodium is reduced and chlorine is oxidised. Redox is best remembered by using OIL RIG:

Oxidation Is Loss and Reduction Is Gain of electrons.

Metals occupy the centre and left-hand side of the Periodic Table. Since the main reaction of metal atoms is to lose electrons, and since 'oxidation is loss', metals reduce other substances when they react. The most reactive of the metals will have atoms that lose electrons easily, while the noble metals, such as gold, have atoms that lose electrons with difficulty.

Non-metals occupy the right-hand side of the Periodic Table. There are two ways a non-metal can attain a stable electron configuration. One is by gaining an electron or electrons and forming an anion. The other is by sharing electrons and forming a covalent bond.

An *ionic* substance is formed when a non-metal reacts with a metal because the metal is a strong electron donor. A non-metal can form *covalent* bonds only with other non-metals because non-metals do not normally lose electrons.

A semi-metal substance has some of the properties of a metal and some of a non-metal. It is quite likely to be able to gain electrons or to lose electrons.

P Sodium reacts with hydrogen to give a substance called sodium hydride, NaH.
Explain in terms of electron transfer why this is a redox reaction.

Q The most reactive metal in Group 1 is francium, Fr. Suggest why this might be so, in terms of the ease of loss of electrons from a francium atom.

See question 5. ■

5 PREDICTIONS USING THE PERIODIC TABLE

One of the uses of the Periodic Table is that it allows you to make informed guesses about the chemical properties of an element. The Periodic Table allows you to:

- predict whether an element is a metal or non-metal,
- predict the charge of any ion that may be formed,
- predict the relative reactivity of the element compared to other elements in its group.

Take as an example the element radium. Radium is highly radio-active, so it would be impossible to study its chemistry in a school laboratory. But with the aid of the Periodic Table, we can make some sensible predictions about this element. Firstly, it is in Group 2. Its atomic number is 88 and its electron configuration is:

$1s^2\ 2s^2\ 2p^6\ 3s^2\ 3p^6\ 3d^{10}\ 4s^2\ 4p^6\ 4d^{10}\ 4f^{14}\ 5s^2\ 5p^6\ 5d^{10}\ 6s^2\ 6p^6\ 7s^2$.

(It would have been easier to state that all its inner shells were full and that the outer electrons were $7s^2$!) This means that, to get a stable electron configuration, a radium atom loses two electrons. In a reaction, the radium atom will always form a radium ion:

$$Ra \rightarrow Ra^{2+} + 2e^-$$

This property of forming an ion establishes that radium is a metal, which reacts with non-metals to form ionic compounds. Now let us make some predictions about radium.

It would be reasonable to suggest that radium could react with chlorine to give $RaCl_2$, and that its oxide would have the formula RaO. The effective nuclear charge for radium is quite small compared to other elements in Group 2 because the large number of electrons in its six inner shells shield the outer electrons from the nuclear charge. So we can reasonably guess that radium will be the most reactive metal in Group 2. As a metal, radium will probably be a good conductor of heat and electricity and is likely to be ductile and malleable.

Table 19.5 **The main properties of metals and non-metals**

Metals

Readily form cations by loss of electrons
Normally have 1, 2, or 3 electrons in their outer shell of electrons
Normally form acidic oxide
React with non-metals to form ionic compounds
Do not react with other metals
Are normally reducing agents

Non-metals

Readily form anions by gain of electrons
Normally have 4, 5, 6, 7, or 8 electrons in their outer shell
Normally form acidic oxides
React with other non-metals to form molecular compounds
React with metals to form ionic compounds
Are normally oxidising agents

■ See questions 1, 3, 6 and 7.

?

R Use the Periodic Table to make some predictions about selenium, Se.

SUMMARY

As a result of studying this chapter you should understand that:

■ In the Periodic Table, elements are arranged in order of increasing atomic number.

■ Columns of elements in the Periodic Table are in the same group.

■ Rows of elements in the Periodic Table are called periods.

■ Elements in a group have atoms with the same number of electrons in their outer shell.

■ Elements in the same period have atoms with the same number of electron shells.

■ The first ionisation energy decreases and the covalent radius increases down a group because of the increased shielding effect by the inner electron shells.

■ The first ionisation energy tends to increase and the covalent radius decreases across a period because of the increasing nuclear charge.

■ Metal atoms lose electrons and are oxidised and non-metal atoms gain electrons and are reduced during a reaction between a metal and a non-metal. Such reactions are redox reactions.

■ A positive ion is smaller than the atom from which it is formed and a negative ion is larger than the atom from which it is formed.

■ Properties of elements such as ionisation energy and covalent radius show a periodic variation (periodicity) with increasing atomic number.

■ The Periodic Table can be used to predict the properties of elements.

QUESTIONS

1 The Periodic Table can be used to make predictions. Consider the undiscovered element atomic number 119. Suppose it has a symbol of Y.

a) In which group would it be placed?

b) How many electrons would it have in its outer electron shell?

c) Which element would it most likely resemble in properties?

d) The element forms a chloride.
   (i) What is the most likely formula for this chloride?
   (ii) What type of bonding is most likely in the chloride?

e) The element forms an oxide.
   (i) What is the most likely formula for this oxide?
   (ii) What type of bonding is most likely in the oxide?

2 This question is concerned with the first ionisation energies of elements in the second period of the Periodic Table.

a) Define the term first ionisation energy.

b) Explain the difference between the first ionisation energies of the elements with atomic numbers:
    (i) 3 and 4,
    (ii) 7 and 8.

c) State the electron configuration of the element with atomic number 9.

d) Give reasons why the first ionisation energy of the element with atomic number 11 is so much lower than that of the element with atomic number 10.
[UCLES Modular Chemistry Spring 1993]

3 Astatine, At, follows iodine in the group whose properties are given below. Astatine remained undiscovered until 1940. Use the Periodic Table in Fig 19.8 to predict the listed properties for this element.

	Fluorine	Chlorine	Bromine	Iodine
Relative atomic mass	19	35.5	79.9	127
Density/g cm^{-3}	1.11 at its boiling point	1.56 at its boiling point	2.93 at its boiling point	4.93 at its boiling point
Melting point/°C	−220	−101	−7.2	113.5
Boiling point/°C	−188	−35	59	184
Appearance at room temperature	colourless gas	green gas	orange liquid	purple solid
Formula of hydrogen halide	HF	HCl	HBr	HI
Formula of sodium halide	NaF	NaCl	NaBr	NaI
Electrode potential/V	2.87	1.36	1.09	0.54
First ionisation energy/ kJ mol^{-1}	1680	1260	1140	1010

a) How many electrons does an atom of astatine have in its outer shell?

b) Use your knowledge of trends within a group to predict a numerical value for astatine for each of the following quantities:
    (i) density at its boiling point,
    (ii) melting point,
    (iii) boiling point,
    (iv) electrode potential,
    (v) first ionisation energy.

c) Suggest the appearance of astatine at room temperature and pressure.

d) What is the formula of sodium astatide and hydrogen astatide?

e) What type of bonding will be found in sodium astatide?

f) Explain why the covalent radius of the halogens increases with increasing atomic number.

g) Explain why the radius of an astatide ion is larger than the radius of an astatine atom.

4 Nitrogen and phosphorus are the first two members of Group 5.

a) Explain why both of these elements have a higher first ionisation energy than either the element with one less atomic number or one more atomic number.

b) Which of these elements has the higher first ionisation energy? Explain your answer.

c) The covalent radius of phosphorus is larger than the covalent radius of nitrogen. Explain why.

5 Sodium street lamps contain neon gas at a very low pressure. When an electric current is passed through the street lamp, neon gas is ionised. Later, sodium ions are ionised.

a) Write down an equation including state symbols to show the process associated with the first ionisation energy of: **(i)** neon, **(ii)** sodium.

b) Which of the two elements neon or sodium has the higher ionisation energy?
Explain your answer.

c) Why is the ionisation of sodium referred to as oxidation?

6 Francium, atomic number 87, is a highly radioactive metal.

a) Write down the electron configuration of francium.

b) What is the formula of a francium ion? Hence write down the electron configuration of a francium ion.

7 By using its position in the Periodic Table predict some of the physical and chemical properties of francium.

8 An element has the electron configuration $1s^2\ 2s^2\ 2p^6\ 3s^2\ 3p^6\ 3d^{10}\ 4s^2\ 4p^1$.

a) To which period does the element belong?

b) To which block does the element belong?

c) To which group does the element belong?

d) How many electrons does it have in its outer shell?

e) The element forms a chloride and an oxide. Write down the formula of both compounds and state the type of bonding present in these compounds.

9 Covalent radii can be used to estimate bond lengths.

a) What is the meaning of the term covalent radii?

b) Estimate the bond length of each of the bonds in the following molecules.
    (i) CI_4, **(ii)** HI, **(iii)** C_2H_6, **(iv)** H_3BO_3.

Assignment

FINDING OUT ABOUT NEW ELEMENTS

The Periodic Table in the 1930s (below) looked different from the version we use today. To start with, it contained only 88 elements. It finished at element 92 and had four gaps – at atomic numbers 43, 61, 85 and 87.

1

a) Briefly explain how knowledge of the Periodic Table helped scientists to discover new elements.

b) The four elements for which chemists in the 1930s left gaps are **(i)** technetium, **(ii)** promethium, **(iii)** astatine and **(iv)** francium. For each, note their position in a modern Periodic Table, and predict two physical and two chemical properties. Explain the reason for each prediction.

At that time, the elements beyond uranium (atomic number 92) were unknown. But scientists were convinced that they did exist and that, sooner or later, they would be discovered. The elements of atomic number 93 and beyond are now known as the **transuranium elements**, meaning the elements across the period from uranium. From the positions of these elements in the Periodic Table, scientists could quite confidently predict their properties.

2

a) Note down the block of a modern Periodic Table in which uranium is present.

b) Explain why scientists supposed that elements beyond 92 were radioactive.

To start with, the scientists made the mistake of looking for another set of d-block elements. This was because they had placed uranium in the Periodic Table under tungsten (symbol W, atomic number 74).

They assumed that the next element, number 93, would resemble rhenium which is next to tungsten. They did realise, though, that the element would be highly radioactive and expected it to pose experimental and safety problems.

The investigators believed that it would be possible to produce element 93 by carrying out a **transmutation**. This is a process of changing one element into another, achieved by bombarding target atoms with a beam of subatomic particles. A transmutation to produce element 93 had to wait until 1940, when Edwin McMillan and Philip Abelson succeeded in making and identifying it.

$$^{238}_{92}U + ^{1}_{0}n \rightarrow ^{239}_{92}U$$

uranium-238 + neutron → uranium-23a

This decays with a half-life of 23 minutes to give:

$$^{239}_{92}U \rightarrow ^{239}_{93}Np + ^{0}_{1}e^{-}$$

The new element was named neptunium and it was found to have properties just like those of uranium. But it was a surprise to find that its properties differed markedly from those of rhenium.

Soon afterwards, element number 94, plutonium, was discovered by Glenn Seaborg, and it too had properties similar to uranium, but not like those of osmium (number 76), as had been predicted. Its half-life was 2.3 days.

$$^{239}_{93}Np \rightarrow ^{239}_{94}Pu + ^{0}_{-1}e$$

Researchers at that time realised that their Periodic Table was incorrect and needed refining. They concluded that the elements after actinium were in fact f-block elements rather than d-block elements, and formed a series (atomic numbers 89–104 inclusive) called the **actinides** because they have similar properties to actinium.

In 1944, elements 95 and 96 were discovered. These were found to resemble the corresponding f-block elements europium and gadolinium, and provided further proof that

1																	2
H																	He
3	4											5	6	7	8	9	10
Li	Be											B	C	N	O	F	Ne
11	12											13	14	15	16	17	18
Na	Mg											Al	Si	P	S	Cl	Ar
19	20	21	22	23	24	25	26	27	28	29	30	31	32	33	34	35	36
K	Ca	Sc	Ti	V	Cr	Mn	Fe	Co	Ni	Cu	Zn	Ga	Ge	As	Se	Br	Kr
37	38	39	40	41	42	(43)	44	45	46	47	48	49	50	51	52	53	54
Rb	Sr	Y	Zr	Nb	Mo		Ru	Rh	Pd	Ag	Cd	In	Sn	Sb	Te	I	Xe
55	56	57	72	73	74	75	76	77	78	79	80	81	82	83	84	(85)	86
Cs	Ba	La	Hf	Ta	W	Re	Os	Ir	Pt	Au	Hg	Tl	Pb	Bi	Po		Rn
(87)	88	89	90	91	92	93	94	95									
	Ra	Ac	Th	Pa	U												

58	59	60	(61)	62	63	64	65	66	67	68	69	70	71
Ce	Pr	Nd		Sm	Eu	Gd	Tb	Dy	Ho	Er	Tm	Yb	Lu

Fig 19.A1 **The Periodic Table in the 1930s. Notice that four elements were undiscovered and that the activities (atomic numbers 90 and 92) are in the wrong place**

the transuranium elements were f-block elements.

Extensive studies of the chemistry of plutonium show it to have typical chemical properties of a metal. It is a very reactive metal which will reduce most non-metals such as oxygen, nitrogen, the halogens and hydrogen. It has several common oxidation states.

In terms of its physical properties, plutonium is rather a poor metal, having a low thermal and electrical conductivity, and being quite brittle. As it is highly radioactive, it is self heating and this damages the metal.

Those f-block elements which have only a small number of 5f electrons have high electrical conductivity, since these electrons are delocalised (see Chapter 20). The f-block elements with a large number of 5f electrons have a low electrical conductivity since their 5f electrons are localised.

3 Why did investigators think that neptunium would resemble the element rhenium?

4

a) Suggest why there has been a lot of research work on the chemistry of uranium and plutonium since the 1940s.

b) Write down the electron configuration for a plutonium atom.

c) Suggest possible oxidation states for plutonium.

d) Predict the level of electrical conductivity (high, low or intermediate) of plutonium.

Since the 1940s, many other elements have been made, as shown in the following table.

Table 19.A1 **Some of the transuranium elements which have been artificially synthesised**

Name	Symbol	Atomic Number	Nuclear Reaction
Neptunium	Np	93	$^{238}_{92}U + ^{1}_{0}n \rightarrow ^{239}_{93}Np + ^{0}_{-1}e$
Plutonium	Pu	94	$^{238}_{92}U + ^{2}_{1}H \rightarrow ^{238}_{93}Np + 2^{1}_{0}n$
			$^{238}_{93}Np \rightarrow ^{238}_{94}Pu + ^{0}_{-1}e$
Americium	Am	95	$^{239}_{94}Pu + ^{1}_{0}n \rightarrow ^{240}_{95}Am + ^{0}_{-1}e$
Berkelium	Bk	97	$^{241}_{95}Am + ^{4}_{2}He \rightarrow ^{243}_{97}Bk + 2^{1}_{0}n$
Californium	Cf	98	$^{242}_{96}Cm + ^{4}_{2}He \rightarrow ^{245}_{98}Cf + ^{1}_{0}n$
Einsteinium	Es	99	$^{238}_{92}U + 15^{1}_{0}n \rightarrow ^{253}_{99}Es + 7^{0}_{-1}e$
Unniquadium	Unq	104	$^{249}_{98}Cf + ^{12}_{6}C \rightarrow ^{257}_{104}Unq + 4^{1}_{0}n$
Unipentium	Unp	105	$^{249}_{98}Cf + ^{15}_{7}N \rightarrow ^{260}_{105}Unp + 4^{1}_{0}n$

Sometimes, only minute quantities of these new elements have been made. It seems extraordinary, but the scientists who first made element 109 produced only *one atom* of it, and within 5×10^{-3} seconds, it had decayed!

As soon as a new element is made, its name and symbol have to be decided on. To start with, this caused no difficulty. Like uranium, the two elements 93 and 94 were named after planets, neptunium and plutonium. The next two were named in a similar way to the elements above them in the Periodic Table.

5

a) Find out the names of elements 95 and 96 and those above them in the Periodic Table, and explain how their names relate to each other.

b) Describe, with reasons, the level of electrical conductivity (high, low or intermediate) you would expect for element 101.

Soon, other laboratories were synthesising elements and there were quarrels between scientists. Some elements were given two names. Several elements have been given a name and symbol that corresponds to the atomic number until the naming could be sorted out. For example, element 106 has a symbol of Unh and is given the name unnilhexium, which is based on the Greek and Latin for 106.

6 Scientist need to calculate the amount of radioactive isotope that remains after a period of time. It is proposed to leave a sample of 1.00 g of neptunium-239 in a storage tank for 23 days. How much of the neptunium will remain?

7 What is the atomic number of the second element in the fourth transition series?

8

a) Describe some of the problems involved in studying the chemistry of the transuranium elements.

b) The transuranium elements have been synthesised by bombarding target atoms with particles. Study the information given for the synthesis of the transuranium elements. Using that information, copy and complete the following table.

Bombarding particle	Element bombarded	New element	Other product
$^{1}_{0}n$	?	$^{240}_{?}Am$	?
$^{4}_{2}He$	?	$^{?}_{97}Bk$	?
?	$^{238}_{92}U$	?	$^{0}_{-1}e$
$^{12}_{6}C$	$^{249}_{98}Cf$	?	?
?	?	$^{260}_{105}Unp$	$^{1}_{0}n$

9 Find out about how fermium was synthesised, and write a short explanation.

10 The early work on the transmutation of elements was connected with the Manhattan Project, which was concerned with the development of an atomic bomb during the Second World War.

Working in a small group, find out about the reasons why the scientists thought this project was so important. Discuss whether you think it was right or wrong for scientists to work in this type of research.

THE SEARCH FOR THE ELEMENTS

The chapter covers aspects of the Periodic Table including its development and structure, and trends in the physical and chemical properties of elements across periods and down groups. The Chapter Map which links these ideas will help you to identify the main aspects to study and to locate further references.

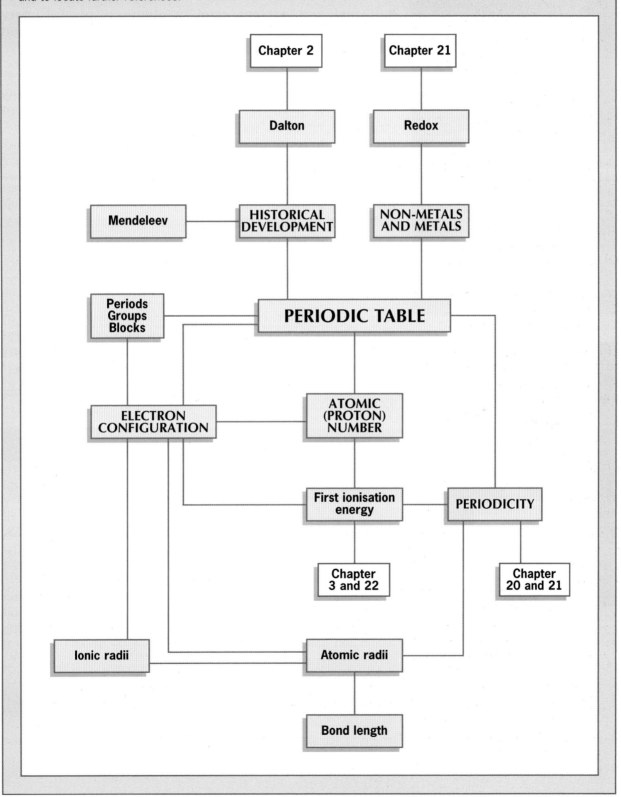

20 Structure and bonding of the elements

Buckminster Fuller's geodesic dome at Expo 67

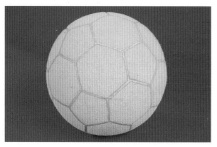

A football is a model of a fullerene

Sir Harry Kroto holding buckminsterfullerene, C_{60}, in his left hand, with other fullerenes he discovered

See question 1. ■

THE UNITED STATES PAVILION at the 1967 World Fair Expo in Montreal was a giant geodesic dome, a revolutionary structure designed by the pioneering American engineer and architect Robert Buckminster Fuller.

Little did he know that eighteen years later his design was to be repeated at atomic level in the Nobel prize-winning discovery of forms of carbon that made up the class of structures named after him – the buckminsterfullerenes – net-like spheres (and tubes), each of many atoms, possibly opening up new areas of organic chemistry.

Until Harry Kroto and his team at Sussex University discovered the chemical class of fullerenes in 1985, chemists believed that carbon had only two crystalline forms: graphite and diamond. Now there were three. Scientists were astonished, because – so they thought – carbon had been exhaustively researched over many decades. Equally astonishing was the discovery that fullerenes are present in soot.

Like Buckminster Fuller's dome whose design is held in place by natural forces, the structure of a crystalline form such as a fullerene is constrained by the forces that hold its component particles in place. It is this definite internal arrangement that determines the physical properties of all elements in the crystalline state.

1 STRUCTURE AND THE PERIODIC TABLE

On pages 397 to 398, you can read how elements in the same group of the Periodic Table have similar chemical properties because they have a similar arrangement of their outer electrons. For example, all the elements in Group 7 have an outer electron configuration that ends in p^5. The periodicity of properties, such as ionisation energy, is explained in terms of the regular recurring pattern of electron configurations from one period to another.

This chapter takes certain physical properties of elements and relates them to the structure and bonding of elements in the solid state. We look particularly at the electrical conductivity, melting points and boiling points of the elements in the second and third periods of the Periodic Table.

2 KINETIC-MOLECULAR MODEL FOR SOLIDS

For more information on the kinetic-molecular model of matter, see page 99.

In any discussion of solid-state structures we need to look at the kinetic-molecular model of matter as it applies to solids.

Fig 20.1 shows a typical arrangement of the particles in a solid.

These are their common characteristics:

- The particles may be ions, atoms or molecules.
- They are closely packed in an ordered pattern, occupying relatively fixed positions.
- This ordered arrangement of particles is called a **lattice**.
- The particles in a solid are fixed in position but are able to vibrate.
- The particles in a solid are attracted to one another.

We will look at the nature of some of the attractive forces later in the chapter.

Types of solid

When a liquid substance is cooled sufficiently, it freezes and forms a solid. Normally, the particles of the substance take up ordered positions and form a crystalline solid. Even elements that are gases at room temperature and pressure will solidify when the temperature is low enough. For helium, the temperature has to be lowered to within 3 degrees of absolute zero before it becomes a solid.

Crystalline solids

In a **crystalline** solid, the particles are arranged in a definite repeating pattern throughout the solid. Such a solid is said to be homogenous. This three-dimensional repeating pattern of particles in crystals is usually referred to as a **crystal lattice**.

Many elements form crystalline solids and have a crystal lattice that can be described geometrically. An example is diamond, one of the allotropes of carbon.

A crystalline solid has a definite melting point because all the attractive forces holding the particles in the lattice have the same strength. So the same amount of energy is required to overcome the forces between every pair of neighbouring particles.

Amorphous solids

Some elements do not always form crystalline structures. They form **amorphous** solids. Carbon black or soot is an example. In an amorphous solid, the particles do not take up a definite regular pattern during freezing. This is usually the case when the freezing process is so fast that the particles have no time to become arranged in an orderly way.

Metallic glasses are amorphous solids, formed when liquid metal cools at a rate of a million degrees per second. The particles occupy completely random positions within the amorphous solid and so do

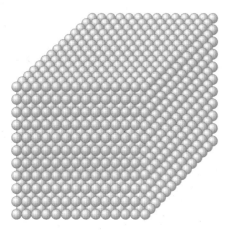

Fig 20.1 **The arrangement of particles in a solid**

■ See question 2.

?

A Describe the arrangement of particles in a liquid and in a gas.

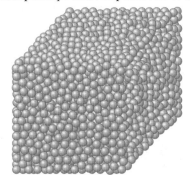

Fig 20.2 **The arrangement of particles in an amorphous solid. It is very much like the arrangement in a liquid. But particles are free to move in a liquid and not in a solid**

Fig 20.3 **Diamond has a highly ordered crystal lattice, which gives it a geometric shape. Diamond is seen here on graphite, another structured form of carbon. (Soot is an amorphous form of carbon)**

not form a crystal lattice. Nevertheless, the positions of the particles are relatively fixed.

Usually amorphous solids don't have a definite melting point but soften gradually on heating. This is because the forces holding their particles together have different strengths, and so different amounts of energy are needed to break them.

An element with an amorphous form always has at least one crystalline structure that is more stable than the amorphous form. Hence, an amorphous solid will slowly change into a crystalline solid. In this change of form, the particles are rearranged from a disordered state into an ordered pattern. Therefore, if the forces between the particles in the amorphous form of a solid are strong, it could take a very long time to change from its amorphous form to its crystalline form.

You can read about the crystals of compounds in Chapter 21.

3 PATTERNS ACROSS THE PERIODIC TABLE

In a period of elements, you won't get a match between the periodicity of their chemical properties and their physical properties, even though you can see clear patterns of properties in the period. The reason is that the chemical properties of elements are related to their *electronic* configuration, whereas their physical properties depend on the structure and bonding.

Melting and boiling points

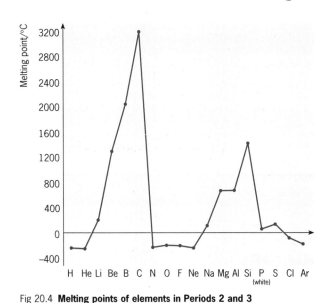

Fig 20.4 **Melting points of elements in Periods 2 and 3**

Fig 20.5 **Boiling points of elements in Periods 2 and 3**

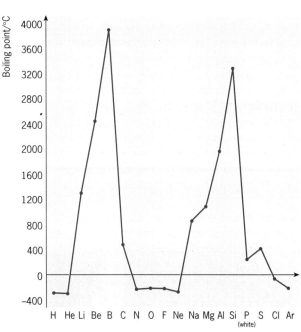

Fig 20.4 and 20.5 show how the melting points and boiling points of the elements vary with atomic number (proton number). Although we can see a pattern – the melting point tends to rise to a maximum around Group 4 and then falls to the noble gases – it cannot really be described as a periodic function. In fact, if the melting point graph extended to elements with higher atomic numbers, we would see even less of a pattern.

Put simply, it is the strength of the attraction between the particles in an element's crystal lattice that determines the value of the melting point, rather than the electron configuration of the element. The greater the force between the particles, the higher the melting point. Much the same can be said of the boiling point, but in this case it is the magnitude of the attraction between the particles in the liquid phase.

Figs 20.4 and 20.5 show that, in terms of the melting and boiling points, there are broadly three types of element. These are:

- metals that have reasonably high melting points;
- non-metals that have very high melting points (such as carbon and silicon);
- non-metals that have very low melting points.

The difference in the melting points of elements depends on their crystal structure and the strength of the bonding between atoms of the elements.

Electrical conductivity

Metals are good electrical conductors and non-metals are poor electrical conductors. For electrical conduction to take place, there must be charged particles which are free to move. In the case of an element, the charged particles are its electrons. Provided electrons in an element are free to move when subjected to a potential difference (ie when a voltage is applied), the element is a good electrical conductor. There is a complication: the electrical conductivity of elements can change under varying conditions of temperature and pressure, but this will be dealt with on page 416.

Metallic and non-metallic elements

We can understand the differences in the melting points, boiling points and electrical conductivities of the elements by looking at the types of particle which make up the crystal lattices.

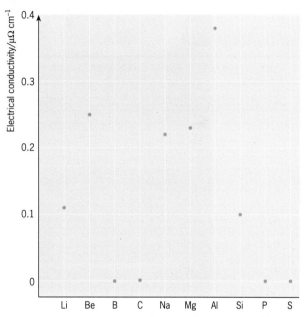

Fig 20.6 **The electrical conductivity of non-gaseous elements in Periods 2 and 3 at 298 °C**

A metal crystallises into a giant structure of closely packed metal *ions*. No molecules are present. By contrast, a typical non-metal is very different: its structure normally contains *covalent bonds*, so it consists of individual molecules. Hence, the arrangement of particles in a non-metal is described as a **molecular lattice**.

The molecules may be **giant** and we can consider the whole crystal as being one molecule, as in diamond and graphite. Alternatively, the lattice may be made up of repeating units of **simple** molecules, as in the case of solid iodine whose lattice consists of a repeating pattern of iodine molecules, I_2. The noble gases are monatomic, therefore the crystal lattice of a solid noble gas is based on a repeating pattern of atoms.

Across the whole range of crystalline elements, there is a wide variation in the strengths of the attractive forces between the particles which form their different crystal structures. Evidence for this is the wide variation in the melting points of these elements shown in the graphs of Figs 20.4 and 20.5. Small molecules, such as hydrogen, nitrogen and oxygen, have low melting points because the forces between them in the crystalline state are very weak. Graphite and diamond have very strong forces of attraction – covalent bonds – between their atoms, giving them extremely high melting points.

4 METALLIC BONDING

?

B Write down the ionic equation for the displacement reaction between

(a) zinc and aqueous silver ions,

(b) zinc and aqueous lead(II) ions.

Look at a lump of any pure metallic element. It is not obvious that it is crystalline. It does not have the regular faces that a crystal of diamond has. Nevertheless, a powerful microscope reveals its crystalline structure.

We can see crystals forming in the displacement reaction between zinc and aqueous silver nitrate or lead(II) nitrate:

$$Zn(s) + 2Ag(NO_3)_2(aq) \rightarrow Zn(NO_3)_2(aq) + 2Ag(s)$$
$$Zn(s) + Pb(NO_3)_2(aq) \rightarrow Zn(NO_3)_2(aq) + Pb(s)$$

You can watch the silver (or lead) crystals form and grow under a microscope.

Fig 20.7 **Metal crystals growing on zinc in lead nitrate solution**

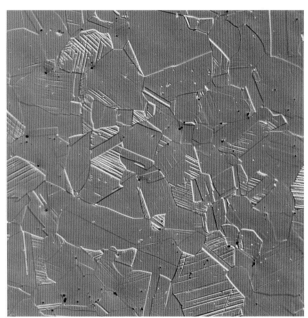

Fig 20.8 **The surface of stainless steel showing its crystalline nature**

Close packing

The existence of crystals in a piece of metal means that there must be a regular arrangement of particles in the metal. These particles are, in fact, positive ions and not metal atoms. All of these ions are the same size, so they can close pack. It is similar to the most space-saving way of packing spheres: each sphere is surrounded by six others (Fig 20.9).

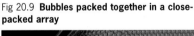

Fig 20.9 **Bubbles packed together in a close-packed array**

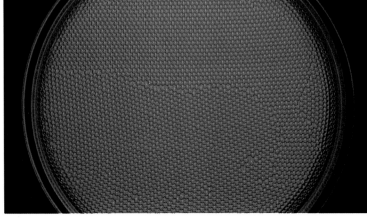

In some metals, close packing is achieved through a repeating pattern in which each positive ion is in contact with six others in the same layer. Such a crystal will have not just one but many layers of positive ions. Each additional layer is arranged to maximise the number of ions that can be packed.

However, there is more than one way of close-packing positive ions in a three-dimensional metallic crystal lattice, as Figs 20.10 to 20.14 show.

There are three different particle arrangements for metals. Each one is an example of close packing

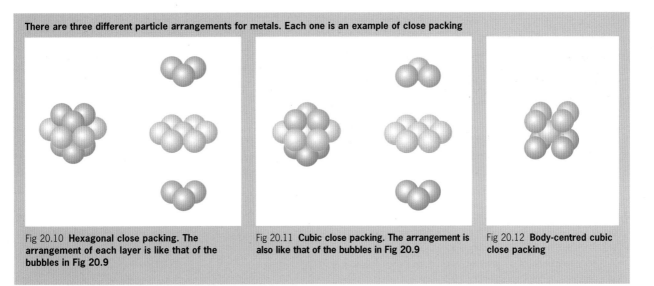

Fig 20.10 **Hexagonal close packing. The arrangement of each layer is like that of the bubbles in Fig 20.9**

Fig 20.11 **Cubic close packing. The arrangement is also like that of the bubbles in Fig 20.9**

Fig 20.12 **Body-centred cubic close packing**

The **coordination number** is the number of nearest neighbours that a particle has when it is in a crystal lattice. A **unit cell** is the simplest pattern of particles whose repetition in three dimensions produces a crystal lattice.

Since metal ions are closely packed, it is not surprising that most metals have high densities.

Positive ions in a sea of delocalised electrons

Since they all have the same charge, why don't the metal ions repel one another? Clearly, they don't, otherwise metals would not be strong and mostly hard. The answer lies in the electrons that have been removed in order to form the positive ions. These electrons are free to move throughout the metal crystal. The electrons are said to be **delocalised**, a concept used on page 273 to describe the bonding in the benzene molecule. The delocalised electrons are often referred to as a 'sea of electrons' because they occupy the whole space between the closely packed metal ions (Fig 20.13). The positive metal ions are not repelled from one another because each is attracted towards the sea of delocalised electrons.

electron cloud

Fig 20.13 **The sea of electrons model**

Electrical conductivity of metals

All metals are good electrical conductors because of the presence of delocalised electrons throughout the metal lattice. It is only the electrons in the outer shell that can be delocalised. The inner electrons are still localised around the nucleus of the metal atom. This means that, for example, 1 mole of sodium has 1 mole of delocalised electrons since it forms Na^+, whereas 1 mole of magnesium has 2 moles of delocalised electrons since it forms Mg^{2+}.

✔ Density depends on ionic radius, atomic mass and the type of close packing.

? **C** Give the coordination number (number of nearest neighbours) of a metal ion in:

(a) hexagonal close packing,

(b) cubic close packing,

(c) body centred cubic packing.

✔ Metallic bonding is often described as closely packed metal ions in a sea of electrons.

■ See question 3.

? **D** The melting point of magnesium, which has two outer electrons, is much greater than that of sodium, which has just one outer electron. Why do you think this is so?

✔ In transition elements, d electrons can also be delocalised throughout the metal lattice. See Chapter 25.

■ See questions 4 and 5.

E Which of the following metals is likely to have the greatest electrical conductivity: aluminium, magnesium or sodium? Explain your answer.

When an electrical potential is placed across a strip of metal, electrons move from the negative to the positive area of the metal, and as a result a current flows. Normally, there is a resistance to the flow of electrons in a metal. This results in some of the electrical energy being lost as heat.

SUPERCONDUCTORS

SUPERCONDUCTORS ARE MATERIALS which conduct electricity with little or no resistance. So, when a current flows through a superconductor, there should be little or no heating effect. The superconducting materials presently available work only at extremely low temperatures. Many superconductors have metal oxide structures. A few metals, such as aluminium and mercury, can be superconducting, but unfortunately at temperature just above absolute zero (1.2 K for aluminium and 4.2 K for mercury).

Superconductors offer the promise of loss-free power transmission, super-fast electronic circuits, powerful electromagnets and ultra-sensitive magnetic detectors. This will be fulfilled only if superconducting materials can be developed that work at around 20 °C.

Fig 20.14 **Levitating magnets, an example of superconductivity. This is a disc of yttrium-barium-copper oxide floating above a nitrogen-cooled cylinder of superconducting ceramic**

F Hydrogen has one electron in its outer shell. How might this help to explain why, under extremely high pressure, hydrogen can behave as a metal?

Typical non-metals, such as hydrogen and oxygen, can be made to conduct electricity when subjected to extremely high pressures in the region of 3 million atmospheres. Under these conditions, hydrogen is an opaque solid.

Other physical properties of metals

All the other typical physical properties of metals can be explained by reference to the model of bonding in which the positive ions are immersed in a sea of delocalised electrons.

● A metal is strong because when its structure is deformed by applied stress and the positive ions move, the delocalised electrons move as well, maintaining their attraction to the positive ions.
● Kinetic energy is transferred easily from one delocalised electron to another, which explains why metals are such good thermal conductors.
● The presence of delocalised electrons also explains why metals are shiny and have a lustre. These electrons are easily promoted to higher energy levels, from which they fall to lower levels, emitting the light which makes the metal shine.

Electrons and energy levels are covered in Chapter 3.

ALLOYS

PURE METALS may not have the properties needed for certain applications. This has led to the development of mixtures of metals – **alloys** – designed to have properties for specific purposes. An alloy is a *solid solution* of two or more metals, the *solvent* being the metal in greater or greatest proportion. Iron, for instance, is used as the solvent in numerous alloys whose general name is 'steel'. An example is manganese steel, which con-

tains between 10 and 18 per cent manganese. It is particularly resistant to wear and shock, and hence is used to make such items as railway lines and components in crushing machinery.

Alloys take three main forms. In one, the two metal ions are roughly the same size, so that the close-packing arrangement is only slightly disturbed. The solute metal ion merely substitutes for the solvent metal ion as shown in Fig 20.15. Hence, the alloy is called a **substitutional solid solution.** In the second type, the ions of one of the metals are sufficiently small to fit into the spaces or holes between the closely packed larger metal ions (Fig 20.16). This is called an **interstitial alloy**. In both cases, the features that define metallic bonding are present, hence the alloy retains all the physical properties typical of a metal.

The third form of alloy is called an **intermetallic** (Fig 20.17). Here, the positive ions of each metal are arranged in a regular pattern, and so an intermetallic alloy is sometimes referred to as a compound. It is possible to quote formulas for the intermetallics. For example, FeCo is an intermetallic compound used for making the magnetic core in transformers. Another such compound is Ni_3Al, which has the corrosion resistance of aluminium coupled with great tensile strength at high temperatures. It therefore has applications in the aerospace industry.

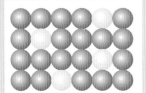
Fig 20.15 **Particle arrangement of a substitutional solid solution. The two different positive ions are about the same size**

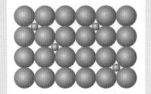
Fig 20.16 **Particle arrangement of an interstitial solid solution. The smaller positive ions fit into the holes between the larger ions**

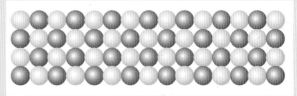
Fig 20.17 **Particle arrangement in an intermetallic. The positive ions of each metal are arranged in a regular pattern**

5 GIANT MOLECULES

Some elements have extremely high melting points. This is because the particles – atoms – in the crystal lattice are strongly attracted to one another. In a giant molecule the atoms are held together by strong covalent bonds. The whole crystal of a giant molecule should be considered as one molecule. For such a structure to melt, each atom must be able to move freely. For this to happen, every covalent bond must be broken. Covalent bonds are very strong, so need a large amount of energy to break. This means the melting point is very high. Carbon and silicon, which have very high melting points, exist as giant molecules. Elements having a giant molecular structure are also said to have a macromolecular or giant covalent structure.

■ See question 1.

Allotropy of carbon

Diamond and graphite are crystalline forms of carbon that both have a giant molecular structure known as **allotropes**. An element is said to have allotropes (show allotropy) when it exists in the same state in more than one structural form. Oxygen, for example, can exist in two forms in the gaseous state: dioxygen (O_2) and ozone (O_3).

The allotropes of an element have the same or similar chemical properties, but their physical properties are different, because each allotrope has its own crystal structure. In the case of diamond and graphite, the physical properties are markedly different. For example, graphite is a good conductor of electricity but diamond is an extremely poor conductor. These differences in properties are associated with the different internal crystal structures.

G Diamond and graphite both burn in oxygen to give a gaseous product. What is the name of this gaseous product?

■ See questions 1 and 6.

Diamond

Diamond is the hardest substance known and is the least compressible. It is a better conductor of heat at room temperature than any other material, and when completely pure it is transparent. These extreme properties make diamond technologically very useful. Its hardness makes it useful as an industrial abrasive and as a cutting tool in industry and surgery, and because of its excellent heat con-

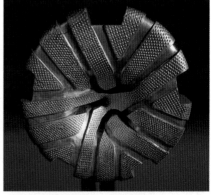
20.18 **A diamond-tipped oil drill part**

Fig 20.19 **The internal structure of diamond**

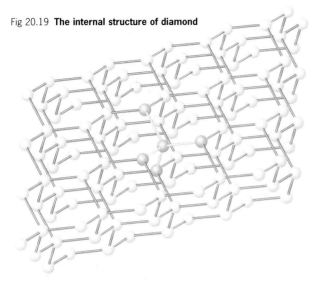

ductivity it is used as a heat sink for cooling electronic components rapidly. Certain impurities implanted in diamond can make it a semiconductor (see the Assignment, page 425). These applications are a direct result of the internal structure of a diamond crystal (Fig 20.19), coupled with the fact that the carbon atoms in diamond are more closely packed than the atoms in any other material.

Fig 20.20 **Diamonds are highly valued as jewels**

The atoms in a crystal of diamond are bonded into one giant molecule. Each carbon atom is covalently bonded to four other carbon atoms, and so each carbon atom has four nearest neighbours. That is, its coordination number is 4. When just four bonding pairs of electrons surround an atom, they are arranged tetrahedrally (see page 78). This is the case with diamond. All outer electron of the carbon atoms are involved in the formation of covalent bonds. There is no possibility of delocalised or mobile electrons. As a consequence, diamond cannot conduct electricity.

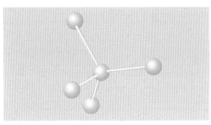

Fig 20.21 **A unit cell for diamond**

See questions 5, 6 and 7. ■

Top view of one layer of graphite – like a honeycomb

Graphite

Figs 20.22(a) and (b) show that the arrangement of carbon atoms in graphite is considerably different from that in diamond. In graphite, each carbon atom is covalently bonded to three other carbon atoms. All the bond angle are 120°, which is what would be expected if there were only three bonding electron pairs surrounding the carbon atom.

However, a check on the number of electrons reveals that there is one electron per carbon atom left over. These electrons are delocalised and explain the electrical conductivity of graphite. Although graphite is composed of giant molecules, its atoms are arranged in layers that can slide past one another. Weak van der Waals forces hold the layers together (see page 421).

The internal structure of graphite accounts for its extremely high melting point, its electrical conductivity and its brittleness. Graphite is used to make electrodes (particularly for high temperature work since they will not melt), electrical contacts and brushes for electrical motors. It is also used in lubricants and in pencil leads. Composite materials containing graphite are used to make rackets, fishing rods and golf clubs.

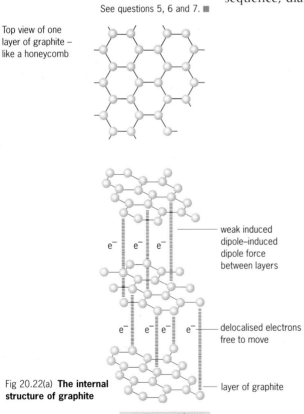

weak induced dipole–induced dipole force between layers

delocalised electrons free to move

layer of graphite

Fig 20.22(a) **The internal structure of graphite**

See questions 5, 6 and 7. ■

Fig 20.22(b) **A unit cell for graphite**

Fig 20.23 **Graphite is used in composite materials for sports equipment**

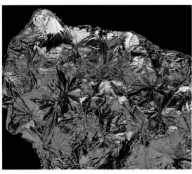

?

H (a) Which feature of the structure of graphite makes it useful as a lubricant?

(b) Explain why graphite is a suitable material to make high-temperature crucibles.

(c) Which allotrope of carbon would you expect to have the higher melting point? Explain your answer.

Fig 20.24 **When graphite is ground and compressed, it forms the 'lead' in pencils**

Stability of graphite and diamond

Given its structure, it is surprising that graphite is the most stable form of carbon. The logical conclusion from this would be that diamond should change into graphite at room temperature. Fortunately, this does not happen, because to change the structure of the diamond lattice, all of its covalent bonds would have to be broken. This would need an enormous amount of energy, which is not available at room temperature. Chemists refer to this process having a huge **activation energy**. That is, to convert graphite to diamond requires an extremely high temperature and pressure. In fact, a pressure of approximately 60 000 atmospheres and a temperature of 1500 °C are needed before diamond becomes more stable than graphite.

The conversion of graphite to diamond is endothermic:

$$C_{(graphite)} \rightarrow C_{(diamond)} \quad \Delta H = +1.9 \, \text{kJ} \, \text{mol}^{-1}$$

Natural diamonds are produced by this combined action of heat and pressure deep under the Earth's surface. Artificially, graphite and carbon-containing compounds such as coal, or even peanut butter, are processed at about 100 000 atmospheres and 2000 °C to make industrial diamonds. Despite the commercial importance of industrial diamonds, only about 100 tonnes per year are needed world-wide. Most of these industrial diamonds are used in abrasive coatings and in cutting tools. They are quite small and dull, unlike the clear, sparkling diamonds used in jewellery.

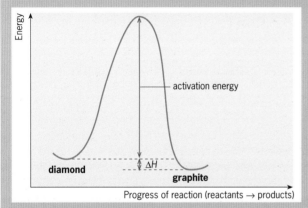

Fig 20.25 **Reaction profile for the conversion of diamond to graphite. The profile is not drawn to scale because of the magnitude of the activation energy. To convert diamond to graphite requires extremely high temperatures to provide sufficient energy to overcome the activation energy**

Fullerenes

Since the mid-1980s, a new class of allotropes of carbon has been identified. They were given the name 'fullerenes' (see the Opener). The most widely studied fullerene is C_{60}, which is a self-contained molecule that exists in both crystalline and amorphous forms. An interesting aspect of the C_{60} molecule, apart from its sheer size, is its shape, which resembles a football with hexagonal and pentagonal panels. So, originally called buckminsterfullerene, C_{60} is now almost always known as 'buckyball'. Since the discovery of C_{60}, many other arrangements have been identified: for example, C_{70}, C_{72} and C_{84}.

Silicon

Silicon is in Group 4 of the Periodic Table. From this we can reasonably predict that silicon atom forms four covalent bonds. Silicon forms a giant molecular structure in which every silicon atom is surrounded by four covalent bonds, similar to the structure of diamond.

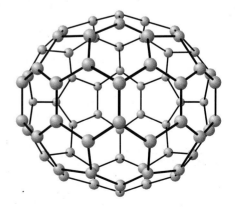

Fig 20.26 **Fullerene C_{72}**

You can read more on fullerenes in this chapter's Assignment on page 425.

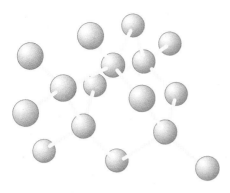

Fig 20.27 **The internal structure of silicon. Note the similarity to diamond, the only difference being the longer covalent bond**

See questions 4 and 5. ■

?

J The electrical conductivity of silicon increases as the temperature increases. Explain this property in terms of the ease with which electrons can be excited.

K (a) What is the number of electrons in the outer shell of a silicon atom and of an arsenic atom?

(b) Explain how arsenic can provide extra electrons when added in trace amounts to silicon.

L (a) Write down the electron configuration for boron.

(b) Explain how adding trace amounts of boron to silicon can produce electron holes.

Since silicon and diamond have the same internal structures, their physical properties should be similar – and they are. Silicon has a very high melting point, is very hard and in its pure state it is a very poor conductor of electricity.

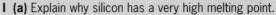

I (a) Explain why silicon has a very high melting point.

(b) Silicon carbide, SiC, is used as an abrasive on grinding wheels. It has a high melting point and does not conduct electricity.
(i) What type of structure do you think silicon carbide has?
(ii) Draw the unit cell for silicon carbide.

Semiconductors

The biggest use for silicon is in semiconductor components for electronic circuits. You may wonder how it is that a non-metallic element with a diamond-like structure can be made to conduct electricity. **Semiconductors** are materials which, to put it simply, have been altered to allow electrons to pass through them, but not as easily as through metals. We know that metals conduct because they have a sea of delocalised electrons and that an insulator such as diamond does not conduct because all its electrons are locked into covalent bonds.

In silicon, it is possible to excite electrons into vacant higher orbitals. When this happens, these electrons become free to move. But at room temperature there is not sufficient energy to promote more than a small fraction of electrons and therefore the electrical conductivity stays exceedingly low.

A way to improve the electrical conductivity of silicon is to provide *extra electrons* which are easier to excite. This improvement is made by adding trace amounts of an element such as arsenic. This process is called **doping**. The added element is called a **dopant**. As described in the Assignment (page 426), doping is a powerful way of increasing the electrical conductivity of certain materials in the solid state.

Boron is also used to dope silicon, but the mechanism is not the same as for arsenic. With boron, the number of electrons are *reduced*, which causes the formation of electron vacancies known as **holes**. This encourages electrons to move to fill the holes, thereby generating new holes. These holes are filled by other electrons moving in, and so on. There is a flow of charge through the silicon and so it conducts electricity.

THE SOLAR CELL

MOST OF THE WORLD'S electrical energy requirement is met by burning fossil fuels, using the heat of nuclear reactors and harnessing water power, all of which have environmental consequences.

Fossil fuels produce lots of carbon dioxide when they are burnt, which is assumed to contribute to the greenhouse effect. In addition, many fossil fuels have a large sulphur content, which results in sulphur dioxide emissions leading to acid rain. Sulphur dioxide emissions can be reduced but carbon dioxide cannot. Furthermore, fossil fuels are a finite resource which will eventually run out.

With nuclear fuels the main problems are how to safely dispose of nuclear waste and decommissioning nuclear power stations when they reach the end of their useful life.

Although hydroelectric power stations operate cleanly, building and running them do have ecological and hydrological consequences.

The Earth receives more energy in sunlight in two days than is stored in all the known energy resources.

So, if just a fraction of this energy could be harnessed it would provide a major alternative supply of electricity. Many solar energy plants already exist around the world, but many more are needed if they are to become a real alternative to the other sources.

Solar cells are used to convert radiant energy into electrical energy. One form of solar cell consists of two joined layers of silicon. One layer is doped with arsenic or phosphorus and is called n-type silicon (arsenic and phosphorus each have five electrons in their outer shells). This layer has *extra* electrons available for conduction, generated by the small number of dopant atoms. The other layer is doped with boron and is called p-type silicon. This layer has a *shortage* of electrons (a surplus of holes) because boron has only three outer electrons. The cell is connected into an external circuit.

Fig 20.28 **Sunraycer, which won the 1987 race in Australia for solar powered cars**

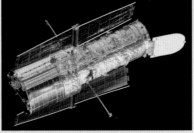

Fig 20.29 **Solar cells on the Hubble Telescope**

Fig 20.30 **Solar cells on a roof**

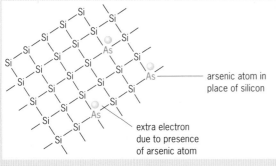

Fig 20.31 **n-type silicon**

arsenic atom in place of silicon

extra electron due to presence of arsenic atom

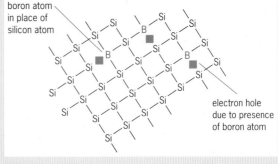

boron atom in place of silicon atom

electron hole due to presence of boron atom

Fig 20.32 **p-type silicon**

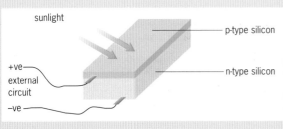

sunlight

p-type silicon

n-type silicon

+ve external circuit −ve

Fig 20.33 **A solar cell**

Electrons flow from the n-type to the p-type layer. Eventually, an equilibrium is established with a potential difference between the two layers. When sunlight falls on the cell, the equilibrium is disturbed and electrons move from the p-type to the n-type layer. The electrons return to the p-type layer via the external circuit, thereby generating an electric current.

6 SIMPLE-MOLECULE LATTICES

Some non-metals, such as solid nitrogen, oxygen, chlorine and iodine, form crystal lattices which consist of the simple molecules (N_2, O_2, Cl_2, I_2) held in place by the attractive forces between them. These **intermolecular forces** are weak between simple molecules, therefore the non-metals mentioned have relatively low melting points and boiling points. This explains why many non-metals are gases at room temperature and atmospheric pressure. It is easy to separate the molecules but difficult to atomise them, because the covalent bonds within each molecule (the intramolecular bonds) are so much stronger.

As mentioned before, many gases, including chlorine, oxygen, nitrogen and hydrogen, form diatomic molecules. They cannot have a permanent dipole as both atoms must have equal electronegativity. So it may be difficult to imagine forces of attraction between these neutral molecules.

Weak intermolecular forces are often called **van der Waals forces**.
A molecule with a permanent dipole has one end negatively charged and the other end positively charged. Polar covalent bonds are covered on page 83.

Elements with a simple molecular structure do not conduct electricity, since they do not have electrons or ions that are free to move.

The noble gases

All the noble gases have low melting points. Helium has the lowest melting point of any element, therefore it must have the weakest intermolecular forces.

The electrons in an atom are in constant motion and do not occupy set positions or set orbits (see page 56). Therefore, it is possible for both of the electrons in a helium atom to arrive simultaneously on the same side of the atom, as in Fig 20.34. This side of the helium atom thus becomes very slightly negatively charged, while the other side becomes very slightly positively charged.

The electron cloud around the helium nucleus becomes distorted (it is no longer spherical), and it causes a similar distortion in neighbouring helium atoms. In other words, a temporary or instantaneous dipole is induced in neighbouring atoms.

A very weak attraction then exists between the slightly positive side of one helium atom and the slightly negative side of a neighbouring helium atom. This is a very weak intermolecular force because it relies on an asymmetric distribution of electrons, which has a low probability since both electrons are close to the nucleus, so are firmly attracted to the nucleus. At the same time, they repel each other.

Once this force between helium atoms in the solid phase has been broken, the attraction between helium atoms in the liquid phase is negligible, and so helium boils only 4 degrees higher than the temperature at which it melts.

The larger the noble gas atom (hence the greater the number of electrons), the greater the likelihood of this asymmetric distribution of electrons. This is because the outer electrons are further away from the nucleus and are shielded from the nuclear charge. This means that the outer electrons can occupy a larger region and so undergo less electron–electron repulsion, even when asymmetrically distributed. Therefore, the melting and boiling points of the noble gases increase with increasing atomic (proton) number.

Diatomic molecules

The same type of temporary dipole can be induced in a *molecule* when its electrons are free to move, since they might move more to one end of the molecule than the other. Fig 20.35 shows the way an intermolecular force may be set up in a hydrogen molecule.

In this case, the two molecules attract each other. The intermolecular attraction is known as an **induced dipole–induced dipole interaction**. When the temperature is sufficiently low, this force may be strong enough to hold the hydrogen molecules in a solid crystalline lattice.

The melting point of hydrogen is very low, since the two electrons in a hydrogen molecule are firmly attracted to the nuclei of their atoms. The larger the molecule, the greater the intermolecular force, because there are more electrons and the outer electrons are under a weaker attractive force from the nuclei. So, more electrons are available to move to the same end of the molecule. In the case of iodine, I_2, the size of the intermolecular force is sufficient to make iodine a solid at room temperature.

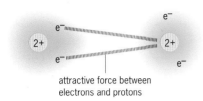

attractive force between
electrons and protons

An instantaneous dipole froms on the left atom, causing an attractive force on the nucleus of the right atom, producing a temporary induced dipole

The distortion greatly exaggerated in the figure results in only extremely weak forces of attraction

Fig 20.34 **The formation of induced dipoles in helium**

See questions 3 and 5. ■

?

M Which of the noble gases has the highest melting point?

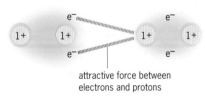

attractive force between
electrons and protons

Once an instantaneous dipole forms, attractive forces distort the electron cloud on a neighbouring molecule, producing a temporary induced dipole

The distortion (greatly exaggerated in the drawing) results in only extremely weak forces of attraction

Fig 20.35 **The formation of induced dipoles in hydrogen**

It is important to understand that in these types of simple molecular crystal lattice it is attraction *between molecules* that holds the lattice together. The atoms within the molecule are covalently bonded to one another, but the strength of this covalent bonding does not determine the magnitude of the melting point.

■ See questions 2 and 5.

?

N Which halogen is likely to have the highest melting point? Explain your answer.

Phosphorus and sulphur

Phosphorus and sulphur both form simple molecular lattices, but a discussion of the structures is complicated since both elements exhibit allotropy. Suffice it to say that phosphorus forms a lattice in which P_4 molecules are arranged in a fixed pattern, whereas sulphur has the molecule with a formula S_8. The P_4 and S_8 molecules are held in position in their respective lattices by induced dipole–induced dipole interactions, which are weak intermolecular forces.

Phosphorus and sulphur are both solids at room temperature and atmospheric pressure because the induced dipole–induced dipole interactions are much stronger than those in the diatomic molecules of nitrogen and oxygen since there are more electrons in molecules of phosphorus and sulphur.

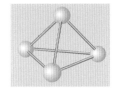

Fig 20.36 **The P_4 molecule is a regular tetrahedron**

?

O Suggest why phosphorus and sulphur are solids at room temperature and atmospheric pressure, but nitrogen and oxygen are gases.

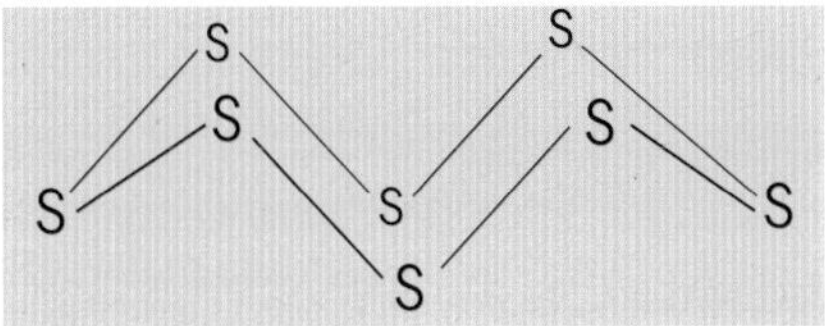

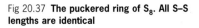

Fig 20.37 **The puckered ring of S_8. All S–S lengths are identical**

SUMMARY

After studying this chapter, you should know the following.

■ A crystalline solid has a regular arrangement of particles called a lattice that can be produced by the repetition in three dimensions of a unit cell. Crystalline solids have definite melting points.

■ An amorphous solid has a closely packed structure that is disordered, and therefore does not have a unit cell. Amorphous solids melt over a range of temperatures, and many soften on heating.

■ The structure and bonding within a crystal lattice determine the physical properties of an element.

■ The melting point of a solid is determined by the strength of the force of attraction between particles in a lattice.

■ A metal consists of closely packed positive ions in a sea of delocalised electrons.

■ Metals conduct electricity because of the movement of the delocalised electrons in the presence of a potential difference.

■ Metals are typically hard, strong, shiny and good thermal conductors. Many have high melting points. These properties can be explained by the bonding whereby the attraction of the positive ions towards the sea of delocalised electrons counterbalances the ion–ion repulsion.

■ Non-metals form molecular lattices.

■ A non-metal that forms a molecular lattice which has a regular arrangement of simple molecules held together by weak intermolecular forces called van der Waals forces (induced dipole–induced dipole interactions). Such non-metals have low melting points and low boiling points and do not conduct electricity.

■ The strength of the induced dipole–induced dipole interaction in a diatomic element depends on the molecular size (indicated by the number of electrons in the molecule).

■ A non-metal that forms a giant molecular or macromolecular lattice has a regular arrangement of atoms held together by strong covalent bonds. The whole crystal is assumed to be the molecule. Such non-metals have high melting points.

■ Non-metals are generally poor electrical conductors because they have no free electrons.

■ Different forms of the same element in the same state are known as allotropes. Allotropes have different physical properties but similar chemical properties.

■ Diamond, graphite and fullerene (C_{60}) are three allotropes of carbon. Carbon and diamond have a giant molecular structure. Graphite has mobile delocalised electrons, so it conducts electricity. Diamond does not conduct electricity.

QUESTIONS

1 Pure boron is a transparent crystalline solid. It has a melting point that is above 2000 °C. Boron crystals are made up of boron icosahedra linked together by forces of attraction.

Look at the Fig 20.Q1, which shows one of the boron icosahedra.

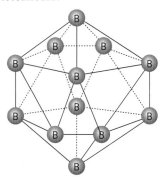

Fig 20.Q1

a) What is the formula of a boron icosahedron?

b) What is the coordination number of each boron atom in the icosahedron?

c) What deduction can you make from the fact that boron forms a crystalline solid rather than an amorphous one?

d) Would you expect boron to be a good electrical conductor? Explain your answer.

e) What deduction about the forces of attraction between boron icosahedra can you make from the magnitude of the melting point of boron?

2 Fig 20.Q2 shows the structure of crystalline iodine.

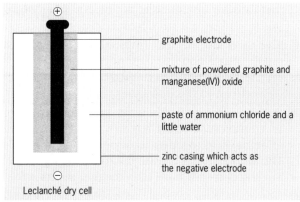

graphite electrode

mixture of powdered graphite and manganese(IV) oxide

paste of ammonium chloride and a little water

zinc casing which acts as the negative electrode

Leclanché dry cell

Fig 20.Q2

a) What type of lattice is this?

b) Describe the nature of the forces of attraction that exists between:
   (i) two iodine atoms in the iodine molecule,
   (ii) the iodine molecules.

c) When heated, iodine sublimes.
   (i) What is sublimation?
   (ii) Describe the changes in the arrangement of iodine molecules and the forces between them when iodine is heated until it sublimes.

3 Look at the following table of melting points.

Element	Formula	Relative formula mass (M_r)	Melting point/°C	Boiling point/°C
hydrogen	H_2	2	−259	−253
helium	He	4	−271	−269
sodium	Na	23	98	883
magnesium	Mg	24	651	1107
fluorine	F_2	38	−223	−188
argon	Ar	40	−189	−186
potassium	K	39	64	758
chlorine	Cl_2	71	−101	−34

a) Explain why helium has the lowest melting point of all elements.

b) Helium and argon are both noble gases. Explain why argon has a much higher melting point than helium.

c) Magnesium and sodium have very similar relative atomic masses but have different melting points. Explain why.

d) Fluorine, argon, and potassium have similar relative formula masses. Explain the differences observed in their respective melting points.

e) Describe the nature of the intermolecular force in solid chlorine.

4
a) Describe the change in electrical conductivity of the solid elements across the Period 3.

b) How do you account for these changes in terms of the structure and bonding of these solid elements?

c) Suggest why it is difficult to measure the electrical conductivity of an element such as argon or chlorine.

5 Give an explanation for each of the following observations in terms of structure and bonding.

a) Diamond has a higher melting point than graphite.

b) Aluminium is a better electrical conductor than silicon.

c) Magnesium has a higher melting point than sodium.

d) Sulphur has a higher boiling point than oxygen.

e) The range of temperature over which helium is a liquid is much less than the range of temperature in which sodium is a liquid.

f) The melting points of the elements in Group 7 increase with increasing atomic (proton) number.

6 Many elements exist in several allotropic forms.
a) What does the term allotropy mean?

b) Give the name of an element that has two allotropes in the gas phase. What are the names of these two allotropes?

c)   **(i)** Give the name of an element which shows allotropy in the solid state.
  (ii) Give the names of two of these allotropes.
  (iii) Would you expect these allotropes to give the same product when burnt in excess air? Explain your answer.

7 A number of compounds containing boron-nitrogen bonds have been prepared. One of these is boron nitride, BN.

a) Boron nitride is prepared by the direct combination of nitrogen and boron at high temperature. Construct an equation for this reaction.

b) Boron nitride can exist as a giant molecule which has a layered structure.

Look at Fig 20.Q7, which shows a part of this layered structure.

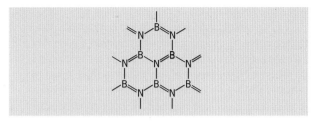

Fig 20.Q7

  (i) An allotrope of carbon has a similar structure. Which allotrope?
  (ii) Predict some of the physical properties you would expect boron nitride to possess.

c) When the layered structure of boron nitride is subjected to very high temperature and very high pressure it is changed into a very hard material.
  (i) Suggest which allotrope of carbon this form of boron nitride resembles.
  (ii) Suggest a structure for the unit cell of this very hard form of boron nitride.

Assignment

BUCKMINSTERFULLERENES

Fullerenes are a newly discovered class of carbon molecules that consist of spherical caged structures, and also tubes. The carbon atoms in a fullerene are held together by covalent bonds. C_{60} was the first fullerene to be discovered, but now many more are known. The molecules are called fullerenes after the American architect Robert Buckminster Fuller whose geodesic domes have the same structural features.

1 Predict the type of intermolecular forces that exist in a crystal of fullerene C_{60}.

Evidence for the C_{60} molecule was first found in 1985 by Sir Harry Kroto. He vaporised graphite in a helium atmosphere and then analysed the resulting carbon species using mass spectroscopy, finding a positive ion that had a mass corresponding to 60 carbon atoms. In 1996, Sir Harry and the two American chemists Richard Smalley and Robert Curl were awarded the Nobel Prize for Chemistry for their pioneering work on fullerenes.

2 Look at Fig 20.A1 and refer back to mass spectrometry covered on page 182.
a) Explain how the value of *m/e* would suggest a carbon species with the formula C_{60}.

b) About 1 per cent of all carbon atoms contain the isotope carbon-13. Look carefully at the peaks in the mass spectrum of fullerene, and see that the 720 peak is quite broad. Use the presence of the isotope carbon-13 to suggest why this may be so.

c) Suggest an identity for the peak at *m/e* = 840.

Sir Harry Kroto's deduced that he had found a new form of carbon. In 1990 Wolfgang Kratschmer announced that he had prepared and analysed this new allotrope of carbon.

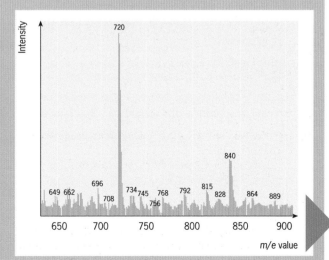

Fig 20.A1 **The mass spectrum of laser-vaporised graphite showing an *m/e* value of 720**

He vaporised graphite in an inert atmosphere by passing a very high current through it, and obtained a fluffy black soot.

X-ray crystallography showed that it contained a spherical C_{60} molecule. C_{60} gives a red-wine coloured solution with benzene, whereas other forms of carbon are insoluble in this solvent. When benzene was added to the back soot, followed by filtering and evaporation of the solvent under reduced pressure, pure mustard-coloured crystals of the buckminsterfullerene were formed.

3 Buckminsterfullerene C_{60} is made by vaporising graphite using an extremely high electric current.

a) Explain why a very high electric current is needed to vaporise graphite.

b) Suggest a reason why buckminsterfullerenes are not made by vaporising diamond using an extremely high electric current.

c) Buckminsterfullerenes must be made in an absence of air. Suggest why.

d) In an experiment, a sample of 1.204 grams of graphite was subjected to vaporisation in an inert atmosphere. The yield of purified buckminsterfullerene was only 0.0320 milligrams. Calculate the percentage yield of the buckminsterfullerene.

4 Buckminsterfullerene C_{60} is stable in the dark but fragments in ultraviolet light. Suggest what type of carbon–carbon bond fission must take place.

Interest in these molecules has been intense and chemists have tried to introduce different atoms and functional groups into fullerenes in an effort to stabilise the spherical molecule and to give it different properties. Fullerene C_{60} has been fully hydrogenated (reacted with hydrogen) to form $C_{60}H_{60}$.

5 Under certain conditions it is possible to fully hydrogenate C_{60} to form $C_{60}H_{60}$.

a) **(i)** Explain how this suggests the presence of double bonds in fullerene.

    (ii) Suggest how many double bonds are present in fullerene.

b) Suggest another chemical test that could be used to determine whether C_{60} contains a double bond.

c) Suggest a spectroscopic technique that could be used to establish the presence of a carbon–carbon double bond.

Hint: The hydrogenation of alkenes is covered in Chapter 12.

Fully fluorinated fullerene $C_{60}F_{60}$ has been prepared. By analogy with poly(tetrafluoroethene), Teflon, chemists argued that it should be highly water repellent and resistant to other chemicals. $C_{60}F_{60}$ is believed also to have excellent lubricating properties, so could we perhaps think of $C_{60}F_{60}$ as a future miniature ball bearing of diameter 0.7 nm? Unfortunately no, since $C_{60}F_{60}$ has been found to react with water to form hydrogen fluoride.

6 What type of reaction takes place between fluorinated fullerene $C_{60}F_{60}$ and water to make hydrogen fluoride?

Fullerene C_{60} does not conduct electricity since it has no delocalised electrons. However, it can be made to conduct by introducing metal atoms into the spaces between the spherical molecules. This is a doping process and potassium atoms have been successfully introduced to form K_3C_{60}. When cooled below 18 K, K_3C_{60} becomes a superconductor. The superconductivity is a result of potassium atoms donating electrons to the C_{60} molecule.

Other dopant metals have been tried with C_{60} in an effort to extend the temperature range of this type of superconductor. Success in this endeavour would revolutionise electrical engineering.

7

a) Explain why electrical engineers are excited at the prospect of making superconducting fullerenes.

b) Why are research scientists trying to develop materials that are superconductive at room temperature?

c) Calculate the percentage by mass of potassium in crystals of the doped fullerene K_3C_{60}.

8 List as many differences as you can in the structure and properties of the three allotropes of carbon (graphite, diamond and fullerene C_{60}).

9 Write a report for a scientific magazine in which you explore the possible applications of fullerenes and their derivatives. You will need to do background research using the Internet and the contemporary scientific literature.

STRUCTURE AND BONDING OF THE ELEMENTS

This chapter focuses on elements in the solid state in particular and on their structure and properties including melting and boiling points and electrical conductivity. It covers the way that these properties can be understood in terms of the internal molecular structure of the elements. Study the Chapter Map to see how the ideas are interrelated and to identify the concepts that you may wish to review.

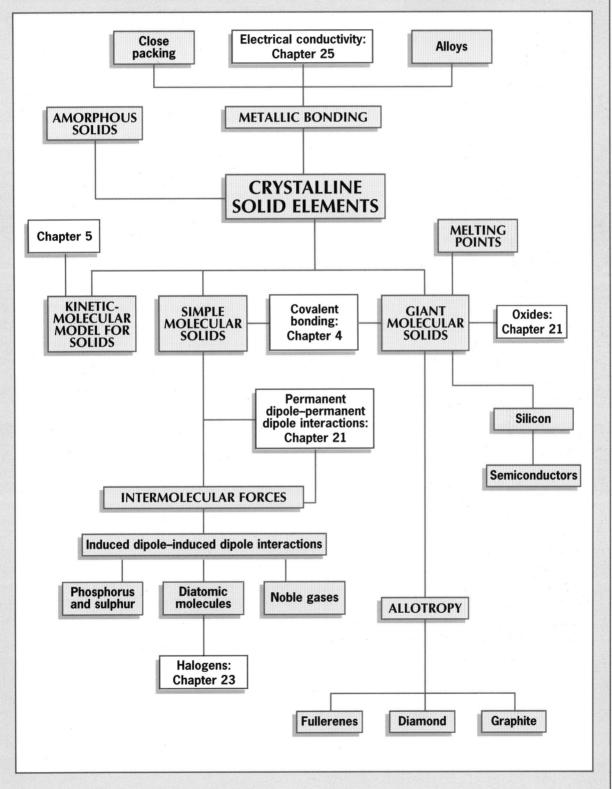

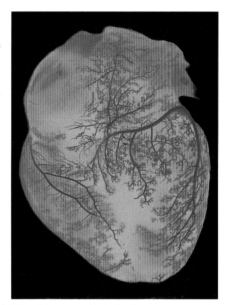

GLYCERYL TRINITRATE TABLETS have been used for many years to relieve the gripping pain of angina, a heart disease caused by the narrowing of the coronary arteries in the heart.

How glyceryl trinitrate works has been unclear. Now chemists believe they have the answer.

The muscles in the walls of arteries are partly responsible for controlling blood pressure. When the muscles are relaxed, the arteries enlarge and blood pressure drops. Instructions to the artery muscles to relax are carried from the brain by a number of messenger molecules.

One messenger, only recently discovered, is a gaseous oxide of nitrogen called nitrogen monoxide. This is a very small molecule and so is able to diffuse quickly into muscle cells, where it binds with an iron atom in the enzyme responsible for muscle relaxation. The enzyme is activated by the binding, and so the muscle relaxes.

Research evidence suggests that when someone takes glyceryl trinitrate, it is converted into nitrogen monoxide which is carried to the muscles in the coronary artery and relaxes them. Blood pressure is reduced, thereby relieving the pain of angina.

When the coronary arteries become narrowed, glyceryl trinitrate can relax them, avoiding the pain of angina

1 PERIODICITY OF PROPERTIES OF THE ELEMENTS

Oxides and chlorides are two of the most common classes of inorganic compounds. Within a single period in the Periodic Table, there is a bewildering variety of oxides and chlorides – with crystalline solids, materials that look solid but are really supercooled liquids, and colourless gases. Behind this variety, however, is a pattern that we can explain in terms of the structure and bonding of the oxides and chlorides themselves.

This chapter describes and explains the change in the properties of oxides and chlorides of the elements in Period 3 as the atomic (proton) number of the element increases. It relates these properties to both structure and bonding, and to some technological and environmental aspects of chemistry.

On pages 397 to 399, the periodic classification of the elements is described in relation to some of the properties of the atoms of elements. The similarities between the elements within a group is explained in terms of the number of electrons in the outer electron shell. This leads to a look at the periodicity of the properties of elements.

The idea of periodicity is extended in this chapter to include properties of the *compounds* of elements rather than the elements themselves.

2 REACTIONS OF ELEMENTS

Almost all the known elements, even some of the noble gases, react to form compounds. When an element reacts, it forms one of the following types of bond: ionic, covalent or dative covalent. This means that there must be a redistribution of electrons around the atom of the element. This redistribution often leads to a particle which is isoelectronic with a noble gas. Some atoms lose electrons to form cations, others gain electrons to form anions, and others share electrons.

When an element reacts, a type of reaction called **redox** occurs. Redox is short for reduction–oxidation. A redox reaction often involves electron transfer between atoms.

Oxidation

The term oxidation was originally used exclusively to describe the reaction of a substance with oxygen to form an oxide. This definition has been extended to take account of recent knowledge about the redistribution of electrons during a reaction. So this is now the definition:

Oxidation is the loss of electrons from an atom, molecule or ion.

Nevertheless, in organic chemistry, it is still useful to consider oxidation as the addition of oxygen to an atom or molecule or the removal of hydrogen from an atom or molecule.

In an equation or reaction scheme, oxidation is often shown by the symbol [O]. For example, the oxidation of ethanol, CH_3CH_2OH, to make ethanal, CH_3CHO, can be represented as:

$$C_2H_5OH + [O] \longrightarrow CH_3CHO + H_2O$$

Reduction

Reduction is the chemical opposite to oxidation:

Reduction is the gain of electrons by an atom, molecule or ion.

In organic chemistry, it is often easier to consider reduction as the addition of hydrogen to an atom or molecule, or the removal of hydrogen.

In an equation, reduction is often shown by the symbol [H]. For example, the reduction of nitrobenzene, $C_6H_5NO_2$, to form phenylamine, $C_6H_5NH_2$, can be represented as:

$$C_6H_5NO_2 + 6[H] \rightarrow C_6H_5NH_2 + 2H_2O$$

OIL RIG

Use OIL RIG to remember what happens in oxidation and reduction:

Oxidation Is Loss and Reduction Is Gain of electrons.

Two particles are **isoelectronic** when they have the same electron configuration.

Read Chapter 4 to remind yourself of the way atoms form covalent and ionic bonds.

Fig 21.1 **In an oxidation reaction, magnesium gives fireworks and flares a brilliant white colour**

Fig 21.2 **In the thermite process, a very vigorous reaction, aluminium reduces iron oxide to iron**

A For each of the following processes decide whether it is oxidation, reduction or neither oxidation nor reduction:

(a) $Na \rightarrow Na^+ + e^-$

(b) $Ca \rightarrow Ca^{2+} + 2e^-$

(c) $Cl_2 + 2e^- \rightarrow 2Cl^-$

(d) $H_2O(l) \rightarrow H_2O(g)$

(e) $Fe^{2+} \rightarrow Fe^{3+} + e^-$

(f) $2I^- \rightarrow I_2 + 2e^-$

(g) $O_2 + 4e^- \rightarrow 2O^{2-}$

■ See question 1.

Redox reactions

It is impossible to have a reaction in which only reduction or only oxidation takes place. Either both reactions take place, when the reaction is called a redox reaction, or there is no oxidation and therefore no reduction. Where there are two reactants, when an atom, molecule or ion loses an electron, it follows that the other reactant must gain an electron. This is fundamental to a redox reaction: the number of electrons lost is always equal to the number of electrons gained. Knowing this can help in constructing balanced equations for redox reactions.

Oxidising agent or oxidant

The **oxidising agent** or **oxidant** is the species (atom, molecule or ion) that gains electrons. That is, it is the substance that does the oxidising. To be an oxidising agent, a species must be able to accept electrons easily. Many non-metals have electron configurations that are only one, two or three electrons short of the electron configurations of a noble gas. This means that the atoms of these non-metals can gain electrons to make a stable octet of electrons. Consequently, such non-metals are oxidising agents.

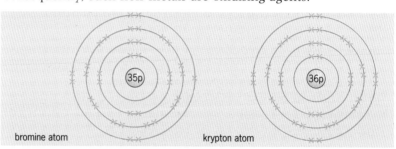

bromine atom   krypton atom

Fig 21.3 **The electron configuration of the bromine atom and of the krypton atom**

Reducing agent or reductant

The **reducing agent** or **reductant** is the species (atom, molecule or ion) that loses electrons. That is, it is the substance that does the reducing (and is itself oxidised). To be a good reducing agent, a species must be able to lose electrons easily. Many metals have electron configurations whose outer shell contains only one, two or three electrons. This means that the atoms of these metals can easily lose electrons to make a stable octet of electrons. Consequently, such metals are reducing agents.

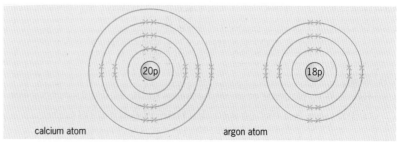

calcium atom   argon atom

Fig 21.4 **The electron configuration of the calcium atom and of the argon atom**

Redox reaction between metals and non-metals

Having established the important fact that metals are reducing agents and non-metals are oxidising agents, the immediate conclusion is that metals will react with non-metals. Furthermore, such reactions are redox. This leads to the idea that metals are oxidised during the reaction and non-metals are reduced.

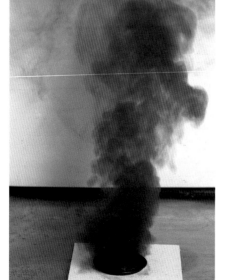

Fig 21.5 **Aluminium powder reacting with iodine powder. The purple gas is iodine vaporised during the reaction**

Half equations

It is often convenient to write the equation for a redox reaction as two half equations, one for the oxidation and the other for the reduction. A **half equation** is a balanced equation for an oxidation or a reduction that shows the atom, ion or molecule gaining or losing electrons. A half equation always includes electrons, which are designated by the symbol e^-.

Consider the reaction of magnesium with chlorine to form magnesium chloride. This is the reaction of a metal with a non-metal, so it is a redox reaction. Magnesium is the reducing agent and chlorine the oxidising agent. First, think of the oxidation process. It involves the loss of electrons. Magnesium atoms can lose electrons to form magnesium ions. Since each atom has two electrons in its outer shell, it will lose two electrons to get a stable octet. The half equation for this process is:

$$Mg \rightarrow Mg^{2+} + 2e^-$$

Fig 21.7 represents this half equation with the full electron configurations of a magnesium atom and a magnesium ion.

Fig 21.6 **Magnesium burning in chlorine**

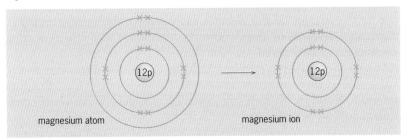

magnesium atom   magnesium ion

Fig 21.7 **Electron configurations to show the half equation** $Mg \rightarrow Mg^{2+} + 2e^-$

Now consider the reduction process. This must involve chlorine because, being a non-metal, it can gain electrons. A chlorine atom has seven electrons in its outer shell, so it needs to gain one electron

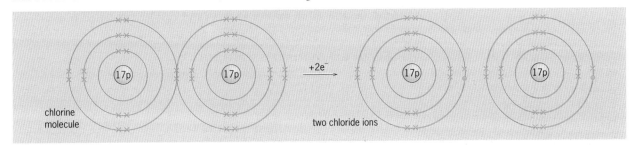

chlorine molecule   two chloride ions

Fig 21.8 **Electron configurations to show the half equation** $Cl_2 + 2e^- \rightarrow 2Cl^-$

to get a stable octet and form a chloride ion. Cl is not written in the half equation, since chlorine exists as molecules, Cl_2, at room temperature. The half equation therefore is:

$$Cl_2 + 2e^- \rightarrow 2Cl^-$$

Notice that this is a balanced equation. The atoms balance and the charges balance (each side of the equation has two negative charges).

Do not try to balance the symbol e^-, just its charge. Remember e^- is an electron, not an atomic symbol. Only atoms and charges are balanced in an equation.

There is a second point to note: the number of electrons in this half equation is the same as in the magnesium equation. That is, it states exactly how the redox reaction is taking place. Two electrons are being transferred from a magnesium atom to a chlorine molecule. When the two half equations are added together, the electrons cancel out.

B Write down the two half equations for each of the following redox reactions.

(a) Calcium reacting with chlorine to form calcium chloride.

(b) Magnesium reacting with fluorine to form magnesium fluoride.

(c) Magnesium reacting with oxygen to form magnesium oxide.

(d) Sodium reacting with nitrogen to form sodium nitride.

The two half equations added together give:

$$Mg + Cl_2 + 2e^- \rightarrow Mg^{2+} + 2Cl^- + 2e^-$$

So, the full equation is:

$$Mg + Cl_2 \rightarrow Mg^{2+} + 2Cl^-$$

Even the full equation is often simplified still further to show the two ions formed as the formula unit $MgCl_2$:

$$Mg + Cl_2 \rightarrow MgCl_2$$

Balancing redox reactions using half equations

You will have noticed that in two of the half equations in question **B**, the number of electrons lost are not equal to those gained. This apparent imbalance can be very useful in constructing a balanced equation. For example, the half equations associated with the reaction of magnesium with nitrogen to form magnesium nitride are:

Oxidation $Mg \rightarrow Mg^{2+} + 2e^-$
Reduction $N_2 + 6e^- \rightarrow 2N^{3-}$

The oxidation half equation involves two electrons, but the reduction half equation involves six. It is important to realise that the half equations do not need to each involve the same number of electrons. They need only show the oxidation and the reduction each as a self-contained reaction. Since the electrons gained by the nitrogen molecule have to be lost from the magnesium, this would suggest that three magnesium atoms are involved, which together would lose the six electrons required by nitrogen. So, the half equations could be written as:

Oxidation $3Mg \rightarrow 3Mg^{2+} + 6e^-$
Reduction $N_2 + 6e^- \rightarrow 2N^{3-}$

Now each half equation has the same number of electrons. Therefore, when the two half equations are added together the electrons are the same on both sides (and can be cancelled out):

$$3Mg + N_2 + 6e^- \rightarrow 3Mg^{2+} + 2N^{3-} + 6e^-$$

So the full equation is written as:

$$3Mg + N_2 \rightarrow Mg_3N_2$$

with the formula unit being used for magnesium nitride instead of the separate ions.

The equations for these types of redox reaction are quite easy to work out without this analysis of the half equations. But for more complicated redox reactions, this method of balancing equations is invaluable.

There is more about covalent bonding on page 72.

C (a) Write down the half equations for the reaction of aluminium with oxygen. Use the half equations to write the full equation for this redox reaction.

(b) Use the following half equations to write the full equation for the following redox reactions.

(i) Reaction between zinc and iron(III) ion:
$Zn \rightarrow Zn^{2+} + 2e^-$
$Fe^{3+} + e^- \rightarrow Fe^{2+}$

(ii) Reaction of iron(II) ion with acidified manganate(VII) ion:
$Fe^{2+} \rightarrow Fe^{3+} + e^-$
$MnO_4^- + 8H^+ + 5e^- \rightarrow Mn^{2+} + 4H_2O$

(iii) Reaction of iron(II) ion with acidified dichromate(VI) ion:
$Fe^{2+} + e^- \rightarrow Fe^{3+}$
$Cr_2O_7^{2-} + 14H^+ + 6e^- \rightarrow 2Cr^{3+} + 7H_2O$

3 OXIDATION NUMBER

So far, we have looked at only the reactions of metals and non-metals to form ionic compounds. In these, it is easy to see the transfer of electrons in terms of electrons being gained and lost (which is precisely what happens during the formation of an ionic bond). However, non-metals can react with one another, and these too are redox reactions. One of the non-metals is oxidised and the other is reduced. The compound formed is covalent, involving the sharing of electrons. So, how can we tell which element is oxidised, since there is no actual loss of electrons to produce ions? We use a concept called **oxidation number**.

Oxidation number in ionic substances

For bonding to take place, there must be a redistribution of electrons to create attraction between the atoms involved. The driving force for this redistribution is the formation of a stable set of outer electrons, often an octet. Each atom in a substance is assigned an oxidation number. This is the number of outer electrons of the atom which are involved in forming a stable set of electrons. The oxidation number is given a positive or a negative sign to indicate whether electrons have been added or removed from the atom to achieve the stable set.

Consider sodium chloride with the formula NaCl. It is composed of the sodium ion and the chloride ion. To form the stable octet of the sodium ion, a sodium atom loses one electron. So, in sodium chloride, sodium has an oxidation number of +1.

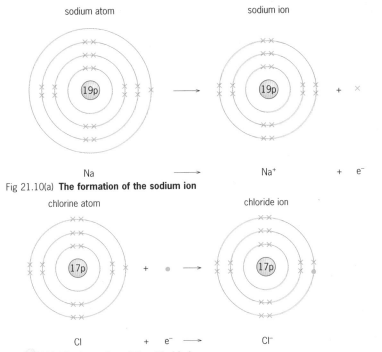

Na $\longrightarrow$ Na$^+$ + e$^-$

Fig 21.10(a) **The formation of the sodium ion**

Cl + e$^-$ $\longrightarrow$ Cl$^-$

Fig 21.10(b) **The formation of the chloride ion**

To form the stable octet of the chloride ion, a chlorine atom has to gain one electron. So, in sodium chloride, chlorine has an oxidation number of −1. Note that the oxidation number corresponds to the charge on the ion. This is not a coincidence and makes it easy to calculate the oxidation number in simple ions:

oxidation number = (number of outer electrons in the atom) − (number of outer electrons in the atom or ion)

It is assumed for this equation that a positive ion such as Mg^{2+} has 0 electrons in its outer shell.

The oxidation number is the charge on the ion.

Fig 21.9 **Sodium burning in chlorine**

The terms 'oxidation number' and 'oxidation state' are interchangeable. Both terms are used in this book.

D (a) How many outer electrons does an oxygen atom have?

(b) How many outer electrons does an oxide ion have?
(Check that the equation for working out oxidation numbers gives an answer of −2.)

E What is the oxidation number of each of the atoms in the following ionic compounds?

(a) Aluminium oxide, Al$_2$O$_3$, containing the ions Al^{3+} and O^{2-}.

(b) Calcium chloride, CaCl$_2$, containing the ions Ca^{2+} and Cl$^-$.

(c) Magnesium nitride, Mg^{2+} and N^{3-} containing the ions Mg^{2+} and N^{3-}.

(d) Copper(II) chloride, CuCl$_2$.

(e) Potassium sulphide, K$_2$S.

(f) Barium fluoride.

EXAMPLE

Q What is the oxidation number of magnesium and oxygen in magnesium oxide?

A The formula unit of magnesium oxide is MgO. It is an ionic compound composed of a magnesium ion Mg^{2+} and an oxide ion O^{2-}.

So, the oxidation number of magnesium is +2, and the oxidation number of oxygen is −2.

A magnesium atom has two outer electrons and a magnesium ion has no outer electrons. Therefore, the equation for oxidation number also gives +2 for magnesium.

Oxidation number in covalent compounds

The simple equation for oxidation number does not work with covalently bonded compounds, because the electrons are shared rather than transferred. So the equation must be modified.

Given the connection between electronegativity and polar covalent bonds, first identify the more electronegative atom in the bond. Once this is done, assume that all the electrons being shared are in the outer shell of this atom. Now it is possible to use the equation for calculating the oxidation number of the element. Another way is to pretend that the polar covalent bond is actually ionic and then work out the charge on the ions formed.

Take, for example, covalent hydrogen fluoride (Fig 21.11(a)). Since fluorine is the more electronegative element, it will form a polar covalent bond in which the fluorine end of the molecule is negative. To work out the oxidation number of the fluorine atom, assume that all the electrons being shared in the covalent bond are in the outer shell of the atom, and proceed as follows:

Number of electrons in outer shell of fluorine $= 7$

Number of electrons in outer shell of fluorine after bonding (fluorine is the more electronegative atom) $= 8$

Therefore: Oxidation number of fluorine $= 7 - 8 = -1$

Now consider the hydrogen atom. In this case, the hydrogen atom starts with one electron in its outer shell, but after bonding it has none, since it has a lower electronegativity than fluorine. Therefore, the hydrogen atom has an oxidation number of $1 - 0 = +1$.

Remember that this is a theoretical exercise in that the bond between the fluorine atom and the hydrogen atom is always *covalent*.

The more electronegative atom in a bond has a negative oxidation number that corresponds to the number of electrons it is contributing to the covalent bonds it forms. The less electronegative atom in a bond has a positive oxidation number that corresponds to the number of electrons it has contributed to the covalent bonds it forms.

Covalent bonds are covered on page 72 and electronegativity is covered on page 83.

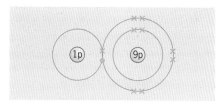

Fig 21.11(a) **Dot and cross diagram for hydrogen fluoride**

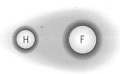

Fig 21.11(b) **Distortion of the electron cloud towards fluorine in hydrogen fluoride**

Oxidation numbers from displayed formulas

Another way to work out the oxidation number of an atom in a compound is to draw the displayed formula. First, decide which is the most electronegative atom. This atom will have a negative oxidation number. Then count the number of covalent bonds around the atom to get the oxidation number. Do the same for the least electronegative atom. This atom will have a positive oxidation number. To work out the oxidation number of any other atom, an additional rule is needed, namely:

The sum of the oxidation numbers in a compound is zero.

EXAMPLE

Q What are the oxidation numbers of each atom in sulphuric acid?

Fig 21.12 **The displayed formula of sulphuric acid**

$$H-O-\overset{\overset{O}{\|}}{\underset{\underset{O}{\|}}{S}}-O-H$$

A The most electronegative atom is oxygen. Each oxygen atom has two covalent bonds round it, so it has an oxidation number of –2.

The least electronegative atom is hydrogen. Each hydrogen atom has just one covalent bond connecting it to another atom, so it has an oxidation number of +1.

This leaves the oxidation number of sulphur to be found, as follows:

Sum of the known oxidation numbers

$$= 4 \times (-2) + (+1) = -6$$

(Note that the oxidation number of every atom is used.)

Given the sum of all the oxidation numbers of the atoms in a compound is zero, it follows that:

Oxidation number of sulphur $= 0 - (-6) = +6$

The displayed formula confirms that the sulphur atom is indeed surrounded by six covalent bonds.

Oxidation numbers and elements

So far, the discussion of oxidation numbers has concentrated on atoms in compounds. But what about the oxidation number of an atom in an element? Consider oxygen, which exists as a diatomic molecule, O_2. The bonding is covalent, but since both atoms have the same electronegativity, the molecule is non-polar. This means it is impossible to apply any of the rules used so far. In fact, the oxidation number of each atom in this case is taken as zero.

Oxidation numbers in compounds

Table 21.1

1	The oxidation number of an atom in an element is always 0.
2	The oxidation number of a simple ion is taken as its charge.
3	The oxidation number of fluorine in a compound is always –1.
4	The oxidation number of a Group 1 element in a compound is always +1.
5	The oxidation number of a Group 2 element in a compound is always +2.
6	The oxidation number of oxygen in a compound is nearly always –2.
7	The oxidation number of a Group 7 element in a compound is often –1.
8	The oxidation number of hydrogen in a compound is +1 unless the hydrogen atom is bonded to a metal ion, in which case it has an oxidation number of –1.
9	The oxidation number of a metal in a compound is always positive.
10	The sum of the oxidation numbers of all the atoms and ions in a compound is always zero.
11	The sum of the oxidation numbers of all the atoms in an ion is always the charge on the ion.

Table 21.1 shows some simple rules about oxidation numbers that should help you to calculate them in compounds.

EXAMPLE

Q What is the oxidation number of potassium, chlorine and oxygen in potassium chlorate(V), $KClO_3$?

A Being in Group 1, potassium must have an oxidation number of +1. Since oxygen almost always has an oxidation number of –2, it is assumed to be –2 in this case. This leaves the chlorine oxidation number to be found. To work this out, first add up all the known oxidation numbers and then see what the chlorine oxidation number must be in order to end up with zero as the total:

Sum of the known oxidation numbers = $(+1) + 3 \times (-2) = -5$

Sum of all the oxidation numbers = –5 + oxidation number of chlorine = 0

Therefore, the oxidation number of the chlorine must be +5.

This explains why $KClO_3$ is called potassium chlorate(V). The (V) refers to the oxidation state of the chlorine in the compound.

Oxidation numbers should be whole numbers, so why does the sulphur in question **H(f)** have an oxidation number of +2.5? The reason is that the compound has at least two different sulphur atoms with different oxidation numbers. So, what is worked out is an *average* oxidation number for all four sulphur atoms.

F (a) Draw the dot and cross diagram for tetrachloromethane (carbon tetrachloride).

(b) Which atom is more electronegative, carbon or chlorine?

(c) Work out the oxidation number for each atom.

G (a) What is the oxidation number of each atom in nitric acid (Fig 21.13)?

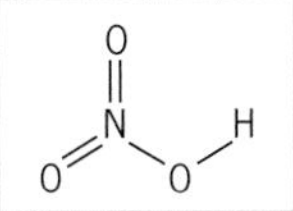

Fig 21.13 **The displayed formula of nitric acid**

(b) (i) What is the oxidation number of each atom in chloric(V) acid (Fig 21.14)?

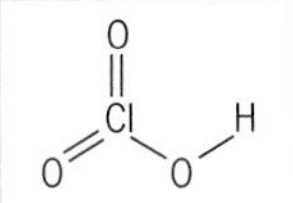

Fig 21.14 **The displayed formula of chloric(V) acid**

(ii) What is the significance of the (V) in chloric(V) acid?

■ See question 1.

When an atom can have several oxidation states in different compounds, the oxidation state is normally included in the names of the compounds, in $KClO_3$, for instance. Chlorine normally has an oxidation number of –1. So it is important to state that chlorine's oxidation number is +5, hence the name potassium chlorate(V).

■ See question 1.

H (a) What is the oxidation number of each of the elements in potassium sulphate, K_2SO_4?

(b) What is the oxidation number of each of the elements in potassium sulphite K_2SO_3?

(c) What is the oxidation number of oxygen in F_2O?

(d) What is the oxidation number of oxygen in H_2O_2?

(e) What is the oxidation number of sulphur in $Na_2S_2O_3$?

(f) What is the oxidation number of sulphur in $Na_2S_4O_6$?

Oxidation numbers of atoms in ions

Many ions have both ionic and covalent bonds present, but this poses little difficulty in determining the oxidation number of each element. What has to be remembered is that *the sum of the oxidation numbers of all the atoms is the same as the charge on the ion.*

EXAMPLE

Q What is the oxidation number of chromium in the dichromate ion $Cr_2O_7^{2-}$?

A The oxidation number of oxygen is almost always -2.

The sum of all the known oxidation numbers (due to oxygen) is
$$7 \times (-2) = -14$$

The sum overall of the oxidation numbers must be the charge on the ion $= -2$.

So, the sum of the oxidation numbers of the two chromium atoms
$$= -2 - (-14) = +12$$

This means that each chromium atom has an oxidation number of $+6$, which explains why the dichromate ion is more accurately referred to as the dichromate(VI) ion.

?

I (a) What is the oxidation number of iron in the ferrate ion FeO_4^{2-}?

(b) Suggest the systematic name for this ion.

J (a) What is the oxidation state of manganese in MnO_4^- and MnO_4^{2-}?

(b) What is the oxidation number of the following?
(i) copper in $CuCl_4^{2-}$.
(ii) nitrogen in NH_4^+.
(iii) sulphur in $S_2O_3^{2-}$.

The displayed-formula method can also be used to work out the oxidation numbers of atoms in ions. The charge on an atom also contributes to the oxidation number.

The thiosulphate ion

The thiosulphate ion has the formula $S_2O_3^{2-}$. The oxidation number of each oxygen atom is -2, which makes $+2$ the oxidation number of each sulphur atom.

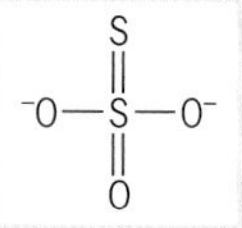

Fig 21.15 **The displayed formula of the thiosulphate ion**

The displayed formula of the thiosulphate ion (Fig 21.15) shows that the two sulphur atoms are not identical. One is bonded only to a sulphur atom, while the other is bonded to three oxygen atoms as well as a sulphur atom. Using the displayed formula to determine the oxidation numbers shows this difference between the sulphur atoms. One sulphur atom has an oxidation state of $+4$. This is the atom attached to the oxygen atoms. The other sulphur atom has an oxidation number of 0. Covalent bonds between atoms of the same element are not counted.

Naming inorganic compounds

As the rate of inorganic compounds discovered and synthesised increased all the time, it became clear that the naming of them had to be standardised. Traditional names, such as ammonia, are of no use if they do not convey information about the structures and help chemists to remember them: 'ammonia' offers no clue to the fact that the compound contains nitrogen and hydrogen.

Chemists recognised that the oxidation number should be stated in the name of a compound if there were any doubt as to its value. For example, the oxidation number of fluorine in any compound is always -1, so there is no reason to specify it. However, in different compounds chromium can have oxidation numbers ranging from $+2$ to $+6$. So, it is helpful to specify the oxidation numbers in their names. Hence, CrO, Cr_2O_3 and CrO_3 are distinguished as follows: chromium(II) oxide, chromium(III) oxide and chromium(VI) oxide.

Under the rules introduced for naming compounds, the name of a simple inorganic chemical starts with the name of the least electronegative element, (often a metal), followed by the name of the most electronegative element or the name of the anion involved. So, K_2CrO_4 becomes potassium chromate(VI). The (VI) refers to the oxidation number of chromium in the anion.

Redox reactions and oxidation number

The oxidation number is a most useful way of explaining whether a reaction is an example of a redox reaction. During oxidation, the oxidation number of an element increases; during reduction, it decreases. Do not confuse this with what happens to the oxidising agent and to the reducing agent. The oxidising agent can be identified because it contains an element whose oxidation number decreases during the reaction. The reducing agent can be identified because it contains an element whose oxidation number increases during the reaction.

During the combustion of coal at a power station, carbon reacts to form carbon dioxide. This is a redox reaction between two non-metals:

$$C(s) + O_2(g) \rightarrow CO_2(g)$$

During the reaction, the oxidation number of carbon changes from 0 in the element to +4 in carbon dioxide. This means that carbon is oxidised. At the same time, the oxidation number of oxygen has changed from 0 to –2, so oxygen has been reduced.

Consider next the reaction of two non-metals not involving oxygen, where it is less easy to spot the oxidising agent. Hydrochloric acid is made by dissolving hydrogen chloride gas in water. The hydrogen chloride is made by reacting together hydrogen and chlorine:

$$H_2(g) + Cl_2(g) \rightarrow 2HCl(g)$$

During the reaction, the oxidation number of the hydrogen atom changes from 0 to +1 (oxidation), while the oxidation number of the chlorine atom changes from 0 to –1 (reduction). That is, chlorine is the oxidising agent. The non-metal which has the higher electronegativity will be the oxidising agent in a reaction between two non-metals. (Electronegativity values are given on page 84.)

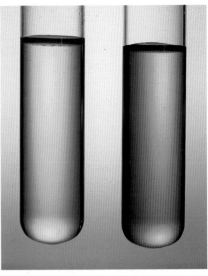

Fig 21.16 **A solution of iron(II) chloride and iron(III) chloride**

Fig 21.17 **The Ferrrybridge coal fired power station**

Disproportionation

In Self-test question **L(b)(iv)** you should find something unusual when you look at the change of oxidation number of chlorine. The numbers should go up and down. The oxidation number of chlorine in the chlorine molecule is 0, while in sodium chloride it is –1 and in sodium chlorate(I), NaOCl, it is +1. This means that chlorine is both the oxidising and the reducing agent at the same time. A reaction in which a substance can be both oxidised and reduced at the same time is called a **disproportionation reaction**.

L (a) Phosphorus(III) chloride reacts with excess chloride to form phoshorus(V) chloride:

$PCl_3(l) + Cl_2(g) \rightarrow PCl_5(s)$

(i) What are the changes in the oxidation number for each element?

(ii) Which substance is the oxidising agent?

(b) For each of the following reactions, use the change in oxidation numbers to deduce the oxidising and reducing agents.

(i) $2Cu^{2+} + 4I^- \rightarrow 2CuI + I_2$

(ii) $MnO_2 + 4HCl \rightarrow MnCl_2 + Cl_2 + 2H_2O$

(iii) $2Cu + 4HCl + O_2 \rightarrow CuCl_2 + 2H_2O$

(iv) $2NaOH + Cl_2 \rightarrow NaOCl + NaCl$

K (a) Which substance is the oxidising agent in the combustion of carbon?

(b) Which substance is the reducing agent in the combustion of carbon?

■ See questions 1 and 2.

M Work out the oxidation numbers of every chlorine atom or ion in the following equation. Use your answers to explain why the following reaction is an example of disproportionation.

$6NaOH + 3Cl_2 \rightarrow 5NaCl + NaClO_3$

4 PERIODICITY IN CHLORIDES

On page 402, the first ionisation energy is described as a periodic function of the atomic number, with each noble gas having the highest ionisation energy within a period. In this chapter, it is established that metals are reducing agents and non-metals are oxidising agents, and that as the atomic (proton) number increases across a period, the elements change from reducing agents to oxidising agents. Within a period, the best reducing agent is always in Group 1 and the best oxidising agent is in Group 7.

Periodicity is not restricted to the properties of the elements themselves. It is also reflected in the properties of compounds of the elements. By comparing the properties of a range of similar compounds, we can see that the properties are a periodic function of the atomic number of the element in the compound. The two classes of compounds most studied are the oxides and the chlorides of elements. The reason for this is that oxygen and chlorine are highly reactive non-metals which form compounds with most other elements.

Chlorides of elements in Period 3

Chlorine reacts with almost all the elements of this period. The formulas of the chlorides and the oxidation numbers of the elements in the chlorides are given in Table 21.2.

Table 21.2

Element	Formula of chloride	Oxidation number
sodium	NaCl	+1
magnesium	$MgCl_2$	+2
aluminium	Al_2Cl_6	+3
silicon	$SiCl_4$	+4
phosphorus	PCl_3	+3
	PCl_5	+5

Table 21.2 clearly shows that there is a predicable change in the oxidation number of each element as the atomic (proton) number increases. It is also evident that the highest oxidation number corresponds to the *group number* of the element involved. This is easy to explain because each successive element in a period has one more electron available in its outer shell to form a bond with chlorine.

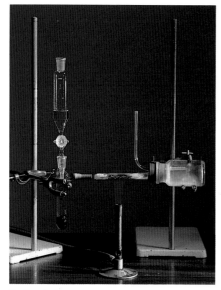

Fig 21.18 **Chlorine reacting with aluminium to form white aluminium chloride**

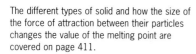

N The equation for the reaction between sodium and chlorine is:
$$2Na(s) + Cl_2(g) \rightarrow 2NaCl(s)$$
Write down the equations for the formation of all the other chlorides shown in Table 21.2.

The different types of solid and how the size of the force of attraction between their particles changes the value of the melting point are covered on page 411.

Melting points of chlorides

Fig 21.19 shows the wide range of melting points of chlorides. There is only one interpretation of this. Namely, the internal structures of the solids are notably different, and the magnitude of the force of attraction between the particles in the different crystal lattices varies widely.

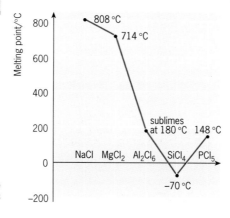

Fig 21.19 **Melting points of the chlorides of five elements in Period 3**

Giant ionic lattices

Metals react with chlorine to give ionic chlorides. Metal atoms lose electrons, and chlorine molecules accept them to become chloride ions. There is a strong electrostatic force of attraction between positive ions and negative ions. This force is not in any particular direction, as in the case of a covalent bond. The result is that positive ions attract negative ions to produce a regular pattern of ions in which each positive ion has several negative ions as its nearest neighbours, and each negative ion has several positive ions as its nearest neighbours. Eventually, a giant structure is produced which consists of the regular repetition of a unit cell in three dimensions.

The exact nature of the unit cell, and the coordination number of the positive and negative ions, depend on certain geometric considerations, the ionic radii, the formula unit of the ionic compound (the ratio of the number of positive to negative ions) and the magnitude of the forces of attraction, which is related to the charge on the ions.

For further details on ionic bonding read page 69.

■ See question 3.

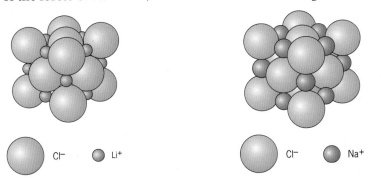
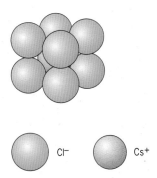

Fig 21.20 **Lithium chloride and sodium chloride are face-centred cubic structures, whereas caesium chloride is a body-centred cubic structure. The caesium ion is too large to fit in a face-centred cubic structure**

Both magnesium chloride and sodium chloride have ionic crystals.

Ionic lattice of sodium chloride

Composed of sodium ions and chloride ions, sodium chloride is a typical ionic chloride. Each sodium ion is has a coordination number of six. That is, it has six chloride ions as its nearest neighbours. Each chloride ion also has a coordination number of six. Because the force of attraction between the sodium ions and the chloride ions is very strong, separating them is difficult and therefore needs lots of energy. Hence, sodium chloride has a high melting point.

Reactions of ionic chlorides with water

Many ionic compounds dissolve in water to form solutions. The regular pattern of the cations and anions in the lattice is broken down as aqueous or hydrated ions are formed.

O What are the differences in the structure of lithium chloride, sodium chloride and caesium chloride? Suggest why you think there are differences.

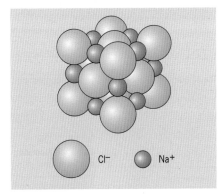

Fig 21.21(a) **The sodium chloride unit cell**

How and why ionic substances dissolve in water are explained on page 470.

The electrolysis of aqueous sodium chloride and of molten sodium chloride is covered in Chapter 24.

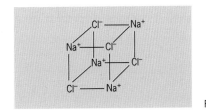

Fig 21.21(b) **Sodium chloride crystal lattice**

The pH of aqueous sodium chloride is 7.0. Magnesium chloride also dissolves in water, but it forms a solution whose pH is slightly less than 7.0. Solutions of ionic chlorides can be electrolysed because their ions are free to move and act as charge carriers. Solid ionic chlorides cannot conduct electricity because their ions are not free to move.

See question 4. ■

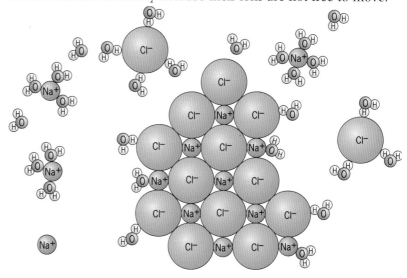

Fig 21.22 **The dissolution of a sodium chloride lattice**

Simple molecular chlorides

The melting points of all the other chlorides of Period 3 are mostly quite low. This indicates that the forces of attraction between the particles in their crystal lattices are not particularly strong. The lattices are often composed of molecules that are bonded to one another by intermolecular forces.

Aluminium chloride

As a metal, aluminium might be expected to form an ionic chloride. Indeed, a bottle of aluminium chloride picked from the chemical store cupboard will probably be ionic. This is because it is hydrated aluminium chloride rather than anhydrous aluminium chloride.

An **anhydrous** crystalline solid does not have any molecules of water as part of the structure and bonding of the crystal. A **hydrated** crystal, however, has a lattice which incorporates water molecules. It is important to realise that hydrated crystals are not wet crystals. They are completely dry, since the water is *chemically* bound into the crystal lattice.

The structure of aluminium chloride is discussed on page 75.

Anhydrous aluminium chloride is a simple molecular solid. The formula of the molecule is Al_2Cl_6 and it contains two bridging chlorine atoms (Fig 21.23). The intermolecular forces between each Al_2Cl_6 unit are quite strong, but once broken, they allow individual Al_2Cl_6 molecules to escape from the lattice. Anhydrous aluminium chloride **sublimes**. That is, when heated, it changes directly from a solid to a gas without having a liquid phase.

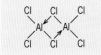

Fig 21.23 **The displayed formula of aluminium chloride**

Silicon(IV) chloride

Often referred to as silicon tetrachloride, silicon(IV) chloride is a colourless liquid with a low boiling point. Its molecules have the formula $SiCl_4$ (Fig 21.24). Each molecule has a tetrahedral shape. Solid silicon(IV) chloride is held together by weak intermolecular forces, but they are different from those found in the lattice of elements having a simple molecular structure.

?

P Draw the dot and cross diagram for silicon(IV) chloride.

The silicon–chlorine bond is polar because the two elements have different electronegativities. This means that the chlorine end of the bond is always slightly negative and the silicon end slightly positive. In the crystalline solid of silicon(IV) chloride, very weak forces of attraction exist between the negative chlorine atoms and the positive silicon atoms of different molecules. Also, repulsive forces exist between adjacent chlorine atoms in different molecules. In addition to forces of repulsion and attraction, there are induced dipole–induced dipole attractions between the $SiCl_4$ molecules. Overall, there is a net weak attractive force.

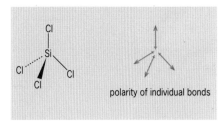

Fig 21.24 **The displayed formula of silicon(IV) chloride**

Phosphorus(III) chloride
Also known as phosphorus trichloride, phosphorus(III) chloride (Fig 21.25) is a liquid at room temperature with a low boiling point. Its molecule is polar with an overall dipole moment. That is, one end of the molecule is slightly positive and the other end is slightly negative. This happens because the molecule has polar covalent bonds and is not symmetrical, so the individual bond dipoles do not cancel out.

Since one end of the molecule is slightly positive, it can form a weak electrostatic attraction to the negative end of another phosphorus(III) chloride molecule. Thus the electrostatic force of attraction in the phosphorus(III) chloride lattice is not nearly as strong as that in an ionic lattice, since the magnitude of the positive and negative charges is quite small. The molecule has a permanent dipole and it is this that causes the intermolecular attraction. This type of intermolecular attraction is known as **permanent dipole–permanent dipole attraction**.

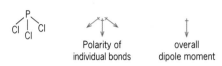

Fig 21.25 **The displayed formula of phosphorus(III) chloride**

Q Boron trichloride, BCl_3, does not have a dipole moment. Why?

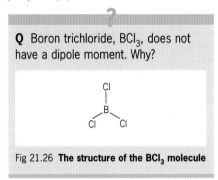

Fig 21.26 **The structure of the BCl_3 molecule**

Phosphorus(V) chloride
Also known as phosphorus pentachloride, phosphorus(V) chloride is a white crystalline solid at room temperature. This means that the forces of attraction within the crystal lattice must be stronger than those in the liquid phosphorus(III) chloride.

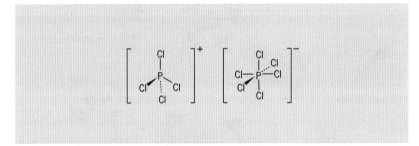

Fig 21.28 **The structure of the particles present in phosphorus(V) chloride solid**

Phosphorus(V) chloride is unusual in that the particles present in the solid and gaseous phase are different. In the gaseous phase, it is molecular phosphorus(V) chloride, PCl_5, whereas in the crystalline solid there is an interesting ionic type of interaction involving PCl_4^+ and PCl_6^- (Fig 21.28). These positive and negative ions are arranged in an ordered pattern. Because the positive and negative charges are spread over a large particle, the attraction between the PCl_4^+ and PCl_6^- is much less than that in an ionic solid such as sodium chloride whose ions have small radii.

Hydrolysis of molecular chlorides
Covalently bonded chlorides behave in a completely different way from ionic chlorides when they are added to water. Ionic chlorides

Fig 21.27(a) **The polar nature of the phosphorus(III) chloride molecule**

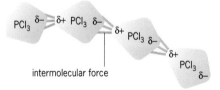

Fig 21.27(b) **Intermolecular forces in phosphorus(III) chloride**

■ See question 4.

R Why does phosphorus(V) chloride have a higher melting point than phosphorus(III) chloride?

The dot and cross diagram for phosphorus(V) chloride is given in Fig 4.17, page 75.

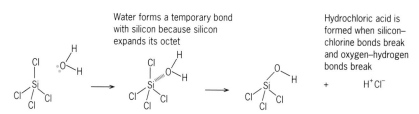

dissolve in water, but covalently bonded chlorides are hydrolysed. **Hydrolysis** involves the reaction of a compound with water which results in the decomposition or splitting up of the water.

Often an acidic solution is formed following hydrolysis of a molecular chloride. For example, when silicon(IV) chloride is dropped into water, an immediate reaction takes place with the formation of a strongly acidic solution and a white precipitate of silicon dioxide (sand):

$$SiCl_4(l) + 4H_2O(l) \rightarrow SiO_2(s) + 4HCl(aq)$$

Since carbon is the same group as silicon, you might expect tetrachloromethane (carbon tetrachloride) to behave in the same way and be hydrolysed to carbon dioxide and hydrochloric acid. This is not the case. In fact, tetrachloromethane is inert towards water or steam. What causes this difference in reactivity?

The mechanism of the hydrolysis of silicon(IV) chloride is believed to involve water molecules forming temporary bonds with the central silicon atom. Electrons from the lone pair on oxygen can be donated into vacant 3d subshells, which are sufficiently low in energy to be available. In the case of carbon, there are no energy levels of sufficiently low energy available. (Remember: Carbon has no 2d subshells.) This means that the water molecule cannot temporarily form a bond with the carbon atom and so no reaction takes place.

Fig 21.29 **The reaction of silicon(IV) chloride with water**

You may want to read about expanding the octet on page 75.

See questions 4 and 5. ■

Fig 21.30 **Possible mechanism of hydrolysis**

Water forms a temporary bond with silicon because silicon expands its octet

Hydrochloric acid is formed when silicon–chlorine bonds break and oxygen–hydrogen bonds break

TETRACHLOROMETHANE

MANY HOUSEHOLD 'SPOT' CLEANERS used to be composed of chlorinated hydrocarbons such as tetrachloromethane. Its use has recently been banned as part of the London revision of the Montreal Protocol of 1987. This international agreement was one of the first pieces of global environmental legislation that has led to the banning of chemicals believed to be responsible for environmental damage, in this case ozone depletion. In fact, in the United Kingdom, even the manufacture of tetrachloromethane has been banned.

Tetrachloromethane is a tetrahedral molecule with the same shape as silicon(IV) chloride and methane. It is non-polar, although it does contain polar covalent bonds because of the presence of the very electronegative chlorine atoms. Tetrachloromethane is capable of dissolving other non-polar materials, such as fats and greases (Fig 21.31). The tetrachloromethane molecule forms intermolecular bonds with the fat molecule of the induced dipole–induced dipole type. This helps the dissolving process.

Water-based solvents often cannot dissolve such stains. Water is a polar molecule and so forms strong intermolecular attractions with other molecules that are polar. But fat molecules are non-polar, so cannot form strong intermolecular forces of attraction with water and are therefore not dispersed throughout water.

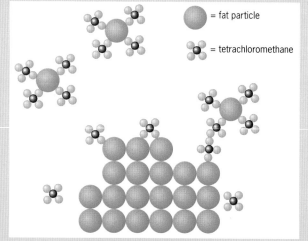

Fig 21.31 **The dissolution of fat with tetrachloromethane**

The use of tetrachloromethane or similar non-aqueous solvents to clean fat and grease off clothes is called dry cleaning since it does not involve water. The use of tetrachloromethane was widespread because it is not hydrolysed by water. However, with the realisation of its implication in ozone depletion coupled with the fact that it is a carcinogen, much research has gone into finding a safer but just as effective solvent.

Both phosphorus chlorides are hydrolysed by cold water to form highly acidic solutions, since hydrochloric acid and either phosphoric(III) acid or phosphoric(V) acid are formed:

$$PCl_3(l) + 3H_2O(l) \rightarrow H_3PO_3(aq) + 3HCl(aq)$$

$$PCl_5(s) + 5H_2O(l) \rightarrow H_3PO_4(aq) + 5HCl(aq)$$

Hydrolysis of aluminium chloride

Anhydrous aluminium chloride is described on page 440 as a simple molecular substance, so it would be expected to hydrolyse when added to water to give an acidic solution. When aluminium chloride is added to water, the molecular lattice is broken and the bonding changes to ionic, producing aqueous aluminium ions $Al^{3+}(aq)$. These ions are surrounded by water molecules, the polar negative end of the water molecule being attracted to the positive aluminium ion. So, it is more accurate to use the formula $[Al(H_2O)_6]^{3+}(aq)$ for the ions.

The aluminium ion has a high charge density which distorts the electron clouds in a water molecule, so weakening one of the O–H bonds. This distortion is called **polarisation**. The polarisation is so great that the O–H bond breaks forming an aqueous hydrogen ion:

$$[Al(H_2O)_6]^{3+}(aq) \rightleftharpoons [Al(H_2O)_5(OH)]^{2+}(aq) + H^+(aq)$$

So the solution becomes acidic. In fact, it is sufficiently acidic to fizz immediately and give off carbon dioxide when sodium carbonate is added to it.

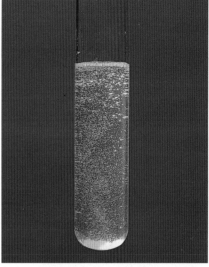

Fig 21.32 **The reaction when sodium carbonate is put into aluminium chloride solution**

An ion with a high charge density has a small ionic radius and a large positive or negative charge. You can read more about charge density on page 467.

The pH of aqueous magnesium chloride is slightly less than 7 due to a similar polarisation of water molecules by the Mg^{2+} ions. But since the Mg^{2+} ion has a much lower charge density, the position of equilibrium lies to the left: that is, a very low concentration of $H^+(aq)$.

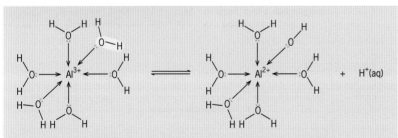

Fig 21.33 **The polarisation of water molecules by the aluminium ion. Aqueous aluminium ions are surrounded by six water molecules. The high charge density breaks one of the O–H bonds, releasing a proton**

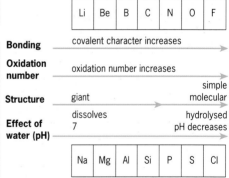

Fig 21.34 **A summary of the behaviour of chlorides across Periods 2 and 3**

5 OXIDES OF THE ELEMENTS IN PERIOD 3

Oxygen reacts with almost all the elements of Period 3. Normally, oxides have oxygen with an oxidation number of –2, but there are oxides in which oxygen has an oxidation number of –1. Such oxides are called peroxides.

Over the next few pages, the oxides are discussed in terms of the change in their properties as one goes from one element to another across the period.

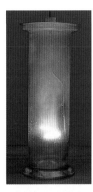

Fig 21.35(a)(i) **Sodium burning in oxygen**

Fig 21.35(a)(ii) **Sodium oxide is a white solid powder**

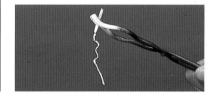

Fig 21.35(b)(i) **Magnesium ribbon burning in air**

Fig 21.35(b)(II) **Magnesium oxide is a white solid**

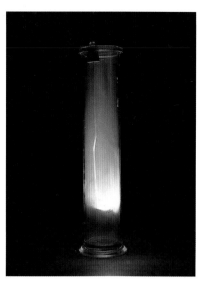

Fig 21.35(c) **Aluminium burns in oxygen to form aluminium oxide, a white solid powder**

Fig 21.35(d) **Phosphorus burns in air to give phosphorus(V) oxide, P_4O_{10}, a white solid powder**

Fig 21.35(e) **Sulphur burns in oxygen with a blue flame to give a colourless gas**

Table 21.3

Element	Formula of oxide	Oxidation number of element in oxide	Appearance of oxide
sodium	Na_2O	+1	white solid
magnesium	MgO	+2	white solid
aluminium	Al_2O_3	+3	white solid
silicon	SiO_2	+4	white solid
phosphorus	P_4O_6	+3	white solid
	P_4O_{10}	+5	white solid
sulphur	SO_2	+4	colourless gas
	SO_3	+6	colourless gas
chlorine	Cl_2O_7	+7	colourless liquid

S (a) Sodium burns in air to form sodium oxide:

$$4Na(s) + O_2(g) \rightarrow 2Na_2O(s)$$

Write down the equations for the formation of the following oxides by burning the element in oxygen: MgO, Al_2O_3, SiO_2, P_4O_{10}, and SO_2.

(b) Which of the oxides in Table 21.3 involve bonding in which an atom has had to expand its octet?

(c) Give the systematic names for each of the oxides in Table 21.3.

As in the case of the chlorides, there is a clear pattern in the maximum oxidation number of each element. Remember that elements in Period 3 can expand their octets, so that the highest oxidation state occurs when all of the outer electrons are used in bonding. Once the oxidation state of the element reaches 4 or above, the bonding between the atoms in the oxide becomes covalent. It is impossible to supply the energy during a chemical reaction for an atom to lose four or more electrons, so that sharing of electrons is the only option left.

The wide range of melting points (Fig 21.36) indicates that there are several types of structure and bonding within these oxides. In fact, they can have giant ionic structures, giant molecular structures and simple molecular structures. The structure with the highest melting point clearly has the strongest attraction between its particles.

Ionic oxides

The metals sodium, magnesium and aluminium form ionic oxides. The metal atoms lose electrons which are accepted to form oxide ions. As in the case of sodium chloride, the ions are packed in a giant lattice consisting of positive ions surrounded by negative ions, and vice versa.

Magnesium oxide has the same structure as sodium chloride. However, the magnesium ion has a smaller ionic radius than sodium's due to its increased nuclear charge. Also, it has a +2 charge rather than a +1 charge. This means that the positive charge is much more concentrated around a magnesium ion than around a sodium ion. It is said to have a higher charge density. In exactly the same way, the oxide ion has a −2 charge rather than a −1 charge, and its radius is smaller than that of the chloride ion. So, the oxide ion has a greater charge density than the chloride ion.

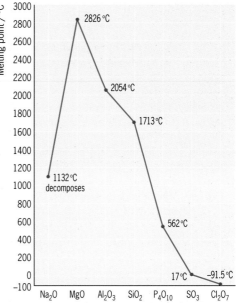

Fig 21.36 **Graph of melting points of the oxides with the highest oxidation numbers**

■ See questions 6 and 7.

Ionic radii are dealt with on page 400.

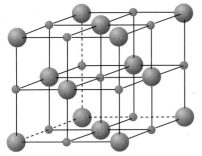

Fig 21.37 **A section of the ionic lattice of magnesium oxide**

Mg^{2+}

O^{2-}

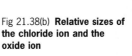

Fig 21.38(a) **Relative sizes and charges of the sodium ion and the magnesium ion**

Fig 21.38(b) **Relative sizes of the chloride ion and the oxide ion**

■ See questions 6 and 7.

With the magnesium ions and the oxide ions both having high charge densities, they have an extremely strong attraction for each other. Hence, it is difficult to separate the magnesium ions from the oxide ions in the crystal lattice of magnesium oxide. So this oxide has a very high melting point. Magnesium oxide is therefore widely used as a refractory material, such as for the linings of high temperature furnaces.

Fig 21.39 **Because of its heat resistance, magnesium oxide is used to line furnaces**

Aluminium oxide

Aluminium oxide is another ionic lattice, although there is some degree of covalent character to the bonds. This happens because the aluminium ion has a large positive charge and a very small radius. It can therefore polarise oxide ions. Nevertheless, aluminium oxide has a very high melting point.

Covalent character in ionic compounds is covered on page 85.

ALUMINIUM OXIDE AND ANODISING

OVER 3000 ARTICLES in daily use are made from aluminium. Among these are cooking utensils, kitchen appliances, kitchen foil, electrical conductors, and engineering and building components. The metal has found so many applications because of its low density coupled with a remarkable resistance to corrosion. The plaque carried on board Pioneer 10 – the first constructed object to escape from the Solar System – was made from gold and anodised aluminium because of these two properties.

by increasing the thickness of the layer of aluminium oxide. This process is called anodising, in which the aluminium is the anode during the electrolytic decomposition of sulphuric acid.

Another advantage of anodising is that the layer of aluminium oxide formed can act as a mordant and adsorb (bond to) coloured dyes. In this way, the aluminium surface can be given a more attractive, coloured finish.

Fig 21.41 **Eros, at Piccadilly Circus, London, is made of aluminium**

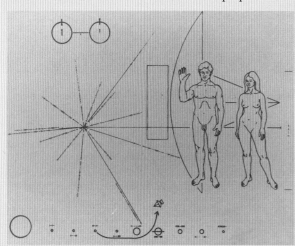

Fig 21.40 **The plaque carried on board Pioneer 10**

Aluminium normally has a dull lustre because it is coated in a thin, transparent surface film of aluminium oxide that forms on exposure to air. This layer of oxide protects the underlying metal from further reaction and oxidation. It is in complete contrast with the formation of rust on iron, which leads to further rusting. Aluminium can be made even more corrosion-resistant

Fig 21.42 **Doors and window frames are often made of aluminium**

See questions 2, 6 and 7. ■

See questions 6 and 7. ■

T (a) Given that magnesium oxide and sodium oxides are basic, what types of substance do they react with?

(b) What is the name of the salt formed when sodium oxide reacts with nitric acid?

(c) What is the name of the salt formed when sodium oxide reacts with hydrochloric acid?

Basic character of ionic oxides

Ionic oxides behave as bases. That is, they are able to accept a proton. This is because they contain the oxide ion which reacts with two protons to give water:

$$O^{2-} + 2H^+ \rightarrow H_2O$$

Metals tend to form ionic oxides, which explains why metal oxides are basic.

If a metal oxide dissolves in water, it forms an alkaline solution. Most metal oxides are insoluble in water, or at the most are sparingly soluble. Sodium oxide, however, not only dissolves in water, but reacts with it to form sodium hydroxide:

$$Na_2O(s) + H_2O(l) \rightarrow 2NaOH(aq)$$

Amphoteric nature of aluminium oxide

Aluminium oxide does not dissolve in or react with water, but it does show basic properties in its reactions with acids. Aluminium oxide also shows acidic properties, since it reacts with alkalis.

An oxide which shows both basic and acidic properties is called an **amphoteric oxide**. Often, there is some degree of covalent character in the bonding in amphoteric oxides. When aluminium oxide is heated with aqueous sodium hydroxide, it forms a salt called sodium aluminate:

$$2NaOH(aq) + Al_2O_3(s) \rightarrow 2NaAlO_2(aq) + H_2O(l)$$

The formula of sodium aluminate is open to speculation. A common formula used is $Na_3Al(OH)_6$ as well as $NaAlO_2$. Note that in this compound, aluminium is found in the *anion*.

■ See question 6.

Silicon dioxide: a giant molecular oxide

Silicon dioxide is also known as sand and quartz. Quartz is a hard, brittle, clear, colourless solid. Among its many applications are architectural decorations, semi-precious jewels, optical components and frequency controllers in radio transmitters. It melts to form a viscous liquid. When this liquid is cooled, the particles have difficulty in taking up a regular pattern, and it supercools to form a glass called silica. Silica glass is also a useful substance, being inert towards most acids. A mixture of boron oxide and silicon dioxide, heated into a liquid and then cooled, forms borosilicate glass, which is heat resistant.

Fig 21.43 **A quartz crystal in electronic watches ensures accurate time**

Fig 21.44 **The displayed formula of the unit cell of silicon dioxide**

U What are the differences between the structure of diamond and the structure of silicon dioxide?
Hint: You will need to read about diamond on page 418.

Fig 21.45 **The geometric shape of quartz crystals indicates the regular pattern of their particles**

The high melting point of quartz is attributed to its giant molecular structure. Each silicon atom is covalently bonded to four oxygen atoms in a structure like that of diamond (Fig 21.44).

The structure of silicon dioxide is in complete contrast to that of carbon dioxide, which is a simple molecular lattice held together by weak intermolecular forces. Theoretically, carbon could form four C–O bonds or two C=O bonds.

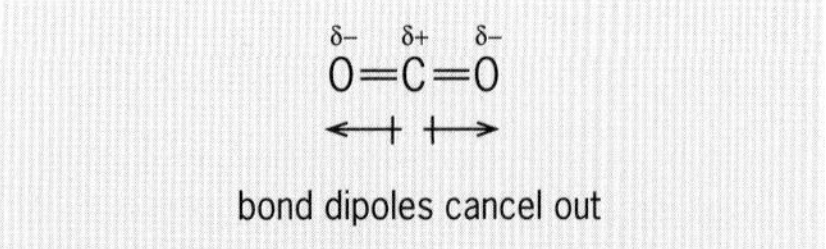

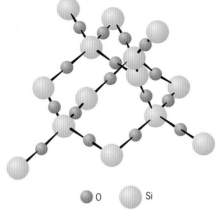

Fig 21.47 **The structure of silicon dioxide**

$$\delta- \quad \delta+ \quad \delta-$$
$$O=C=O$$
$$\leftarrow + \quad + \rightarrow$$
bond dipoles cancel out

Fig 21.46 **The displayed formula of carbon dioxide showing the bond dipoles**

More energy is released in making two C=O bonds than four C–O bonds, so carbon dioxide has the displayed formula shown in Fig 21.46.

More energy is released in making four Si–O bonds than two Si=O bonds, so silicon(IV) oxide has the structure shown in Fig 21.47.

Sulphur dioxide, SO_2 (Fig 21.48), sulphur trioxide, SO_3, phosphorus(III) oxide, P_4O_6, and phosphorus(V) oxide, P_4O_{10} (Fig 21.49), and the oxides of chlorine, are all simple molecules and so form simple molecular lattices in the solid state.

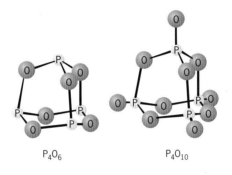

P_4O_6 $\qquad$ P_4O_{10} $\qquad$ Fig 21.48 **The structures of phosphorus oxides**

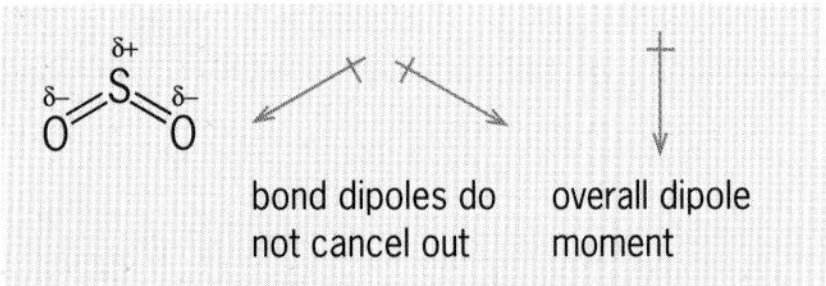

$$\delta- \quad \overset{\delta+}{\underset{}{S}} \quad \delta-$$
$$O \qquad O$$

bond dipoles do not cancel out $\qquad$ overall dipole moment

Fig 21.49 **The structure of sulphur dioxide and its dipole moments**

All these molecules have a positive end and a negative end (permanent dipole). The negative end of one molecule can attract the positive end of another, resulting in the formation of a weak intermolecular force. This force is a permanent dipole–permanent dipole attraction.

Since only weak intermolecular forces exist in all of these oxides, they almost all have relatively low melting points. P_4O_{10} has quite a high melting point because it is a large molecule. Therefore, in addition to the permanent dipole–permanent dipole attraction, there are significant forces of attraction due to the induced dipole–induced dipole interaction.

Acidic behaviour of covalent oxides

Some non-metals form covalent oxides which are normally acidic. But some metal oxides are neutral, as in the case of carbon monoxide. Acidic oxides react with bases to form salts.

Many of the oxides of elements in Period 3 react with water to form an acid. For example, sulphur trioxide reacts with water to make sulphuric acid:

$$SO_3(g) + H_2O(l) \rightarrow H_2SO_4(aq)$$

Chlorine(VII) oxide reacts with water to form chloric(VII) acid:

$$Cl_2O_7 + H_2O \rightarrow 2HClO_4$$

This is the strongest acid that has so far been discovered.

When an oxide does not dissolve in or react with water, its acidic properties are less obvious. For example, silicon dioxide does not react with water – if it did, there would be no sandy beaches. But it does react when heated with a basic oxide.

V What acid do you get when the following oxides are reacted with water?

(a) Sulphur dioxide

(b) Phosphorus(III) oxide

(c) Phosphorus(V) oxide.

Write equations for the reactions.

So, when sodium oxide and silicon dioxide are heated together, sodium silicate is formed:

$$Na_2O(s) + SiO_2(s) \rightarrow Na_2SiO_3(s)$$

Strong alkalis should not be left for a long time in glass burettes and in bottles with glass stoppers, because the stoppers and stopcocks get fused. This happens because of the slow reaction of the alkali with the silica in the glass, making a silicate.

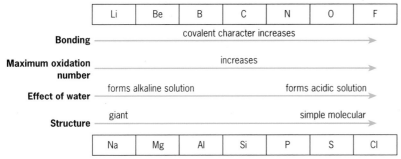

On page 12, there is a description of the reaction of calcium oxide with sand (silicon dioxide) to make calcium silicate or slag.

■ See question 7.

Fig 21.50 **A summary of the properties of the oxides of the elements of Periods 2 and 3**

SUMMARY

After studying this chapter, you should know the following.

■ Reduction is the gain of electrons by a species. Reduction can be recognised by an decrease in the oxidation number of an atom.

■ Oxidation is the loss of electrons from a species. Oxidation can be recognised by an increase in the oxidation number of an atom.

■ Non-metals often react by electron gain and are oxidising agents, whereas metals often react by electron loss and are reducing agents.

■ When any element reacts in a chemical reaction or is formed in a chemical reaction, a redox or electron transfer reaction has taken place.

■ The maximum oxidation number attained by elements when combined with chlorine increases across Period 3. To obtain an oxidation number above +4, the atom has to expand its stable set beyond an octet.

■ When a metal and a non-metal react together, the compound formed is normally ionic. When two non-metals react the compound formed is normally covalent.

■ Ionic compounds are composed of a giant lattice of positive and negative ions held in place by strong electrostatic attraction. This results in ionic crystals which have high melting points.

■ Ionic solids do not conduct electricity, since they have no mobile charge carriers. But when molten or in solution, they can be electrolysed because the ions are free to move.

■ Ionic chlorides usually dissolve in water to form neutral solutions, whereas molecular chlorides are hydrolysed in water to form hydrogen chloride or hydrochloric acid.

■ Metal oxides are basic or amphoteric in nature, non-metal oxides are acidic or neutral.

QUESTIONS

1

a) Define oxidation and reduction in terms of:
   (i) electron transfer,
   (ii) change in oxidation number.

b) Sulphur can be oxidised by concentrated nitric acid as shown in the equation:

$$S(s) + 4HNO_3(l) \rightarrow SO_2(g) + 4NO_2(g) + 2H_2O(l)$$

   (i) What is the oxidation state of nitrogen in nitric acid?

   (ii) What is the oxidation number of nitrogen in nitrogen dioxide?

   (iii) What is the change in oxidation number of the sulphur atom during the reaction ?

c) The two half equations for a redox reaction are:

$$MnO_4^-(aq) + 8H^+(aq) + 5e^- \rightarrow Mn^{2+}(aq) + 4H_2O$$
$$2Cl^-(aq) \quad Cl_2(g) + 2e^-$$

Write down the balanced equation for the whole redox reaction.

2 The rusting of iron is a redox reaction.
The two half equations for rusting are:

$$Fe(s) \rightarrow Fe^{2+}(aq) + 2e^-$$
$$O_2(g) + 2H_2O(l) + 4e^- \rightarrow 4OH^-(aq)$$

When these two processes occur the product is iron(II) hydroxide, $Fe(OH)_2(s)$. The iron(II) hydroxide then reacts with oxygen and water to form hydrated iron(III) oxide or rust. Hydrated iron(III) hydroxide has the formula $Fe_2O_3.xH_2O$.

a) Write down the equation for the redox reaction to form iron(II) hydroxide.

b) Construct the equation to show the oxidation of iron(II) hydroxide to form rust.

c) Aluminium does not corrode in the presence of oxygen and water even though it forms a surface layer of aluminium oxide. Explain why aluminium does not corrode.

d) Aluminium can be used to make iron from iron(III) oxide in the thermite process.
Construct an equation for this reaction and use the change of oxidation numbers to demonstrate that this is a redox reaction.

3 Look at the two diagrams in Fig 21.Q3. They show the unit cell of lithium chloride and caesium chloride.

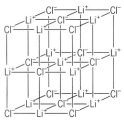
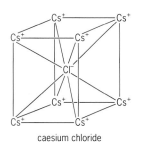

lithium chloride, LiCl   caesium chloride

Fig 21.Q3

a) Describe the differences between the two unit cells

b) Suggest factors that could account for the difference in the unit cells?

c) Explain why caesium chloride cannot conduct electricity when it is a solid but can when it is molten.

d) Which of the two chlorides will have the highest melting point? Give reasons for your answer.

4 How are the physical properties of ionic and simple molecular chlorides related to their structures?
Include in your answer references to the change of state, electrical conductivity and solubility in polar and non-polar solvents.

5
a) Copy out the table below. Write the formula or formulae of the chlorides that each element forms.

Na	Mg	Al	Si	P

b) Write equations for the changes which occur when sodium chloride and phosphorus(III) chloride are added to water.

c) When an aqueous solution of magnesium chloride was evaporated to dryness, a product of composition Mg 35.5%, Cl 52.6 %, O 11.9% by mass was obtained.
   (i) Calculate the empirical formula of the product.
   (ii) Suggest why anhydrous magnesium chloride was not formed.

d) **(i)** Draw the dot-and-cross diagram for phosphorus(V) chloride in the gaseous state.
   (ii) Sketch this molecule to show its shape, indicating the values of the bond angles.

[Adapted from ULEAC 1996 Specimen paper 9081, CH1, q.1]

6 This question refers to the oxides of elements in Period 3.

a) State the formulae of the oxides of all the elements of Period 3.

b) How does the maximum oxidation number of the element in its oxide change across the period?

Account for this change in terms of the electronic structure of the elements involved.

c) Magnesium oxide is a basic oxide. What does this indicate about the bonding in magnesium oxide ?

d) What does the term amphoteric mean ? Illustrate your answer with reference to aluminium oxide.

e) Explain why an oxide with a giant molecular structure will have a much higher melting point than with a simple molecular structure. Illustrate your answer by using examples containing an element from Period 3.

7 The oxides Na_2O, Al_2O_3 and SO_3 have the melting points 1275 °C, 2072 °C and 17 °C respectively.

a) Relate their melting points to their structure and bonding.

b) Describe their solubilities in, and reactions with, water. Give the approximate pH of any solution formed and write equations where appropriate.

[UCLES November 1995, 9250/1, q.5]

Assignment

PATTERNS ACROSS PERIOD 2

The patterns in the properties of the oxides and chlorides of the elements in Period 3 are evident in Period 2. Lithium is the only true metal in this period, so it is the only element to form an ionic oxide and an ionic chloride.

1

a) Lithium chloride has a giant ionic lattice that has the same structure as sodium chloride. Predict the pH of an aqueous solution of lithium chloride.

b) Lithium oxide, Li_2O, has a giant ionic lattice. Write down an equation to show what happens when lithium oxide reacts with water.

The next element in the period is beryllium. Although it is in Group 2, it cannot really be described as a metal. Beryllium atoms do not easily lose electrons and do not form the beryllium ion, Be^{2+}, in compounds. Any ionic beryllium compounds contain hydrated beryllium ions, $[Be(H_2O)_4]^{2+}$. The outer electrons are very tightly held to the nucleus since there is only one shielding inner shell of electrons. If it were formed, the beryllium ion, Be^{2+}, would have such a small ionic radius that its charge density would be extremely large, and so it would polarise negative ions.

So, how does a beryllium atom achieve the stability of a noble-gas electron configuration? If it cannot lose electrons, then it has to share them and share sufficient to achieve the desired electron configuration. Solid beryllium chloride forms a layered lattice (Fig 21.A1) reminiscent of aluminium chloride in that it has bridging chlorine atoms, but different in that the structure is continuous.

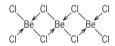

Fig 21.A1 **The layered lattice of beryllium chloride**

Beryllium oxide has a very high melting point. It is an amphoteric oxide and reacts with both acids and alkalis:

$$BeO(s) + 2H^+(aq) \rightarrow Be^{2+}(aq) + H_2O(l)$$
$$BeO(s) + 2OH^-(aq) + H_2O(l) \rightarrow Be(OH)_4^{2-}(aq)$$

2

a) The hydrated beryllium ion has very similar bonding to that of the hydrated aluminium ion shown on page 479. Describe the bonding in the hydrated beryllium ion and suggest a shape for the ion.

b) By counting up the number of electrons round the beryllium atom in the hydrated beryllium ion, suggest why this ion is stable.

c) What evidence is there in this assignment that beryllium oxide has a giant structure?

d) Explain, in terms of its electronic structure, why a simple molecule of beryllium chloride is electron deficient.

e) How does the formation of the layered lattice help a beryllium atom obtain a noble-gas electron configuration?

f) Predict, with reasons, what would happen when beryllium chloride is added to water.

Boron, the third element in the period, forms boron trichloride, which is a colourless gas at room temperature. Boron trichloride is a Lewis acid, which means that it can accept a pair of electrons. This makes boron trichloride a very useful catalyst in, for example, certain electrophilic substitution reactions of arenes. Boron oxide, on the other hand, is a white solid that has a giant structure.

3

a) Explain, in terms of its electronic structure, why boron trichloride can accept a pair of electrons.

b) Write down the equation to show the hydrolysis of boron trichloride.

c) Describe the intermolecular forces involved in a lattice of boron trichloride.

Carbon is the fourth element in Period 2. Its more useful oxide is carbon dioxide, which is a colourless gas at room temperature, and dissolves in water to form a weakly acidic solution. Carbon also forms a neutral oxide called carbon monoxide, which is poisonous due to its ability to bind with the iron(II) ion in haemoglobin, the red pigment in blood. Tetrachloromethane is something of an anomaly, because it is a simple covalent chloride which is not hydrolysed by water.

4
Compare and contrast the oxides and chlorides of silicon and carbon.

Nitrogen is the fifth element in Period 2. It forms a chloride, NCl_3, that is a very explosive yellow oil. This chloride is slowly hydrolysed by water to form ammonia:

$$NCl_3(l) + 3H_2O(l) \rightarrow NH_3(aq) + 3HClO(aq)$$

5
What is unusual about the hydrolysis of NCl_3?

Nitrogen forms not just two oxides like its fellow group member phosphorus, but several simple molecular oxides, ranging from N_2O to N_2O_5. The acidity of these oxides increases as the oxidation number of the nitrogen increases, so that dinitrogen(I) oxide, N_2O, is neutral and N_2O_5 is acidic.

6

a) Table 21.A1 shows the formula of some nitrogen oxides. Copy out and complete the table by working out the oxidation number of nitrogen for each oxide.

Table 21.A1

Formula of oxide	N_2O NO N_2O_3 NO_2 N_2O_4 N_2O_5
Oxidation no. of nitrogen	

b) Dinitrogen(V) oxide, N_2O_5, reacts with water to form an acid. Write an equation for this reaction and hence deduce the name of the acid formed.

c) Nitrogen dioxide, NO_2, reacts with water to give two acids, one of which is nitrous acid, HNO_2. Write an equation for this reaction and hence deduce the name of the other acid.

Although oxygen is the next element in the period, we normally refer to oxides of chlorine rather than chlorides of oxygen. There are several chlorine oxides, all of which are simple molecules. Lastly, there is the noble gas neon, which forms neither a chloride nor an oxide.

7 One of the oxides of chlorine has the formula Cl_2O_7.

a) What is the oxidation state of chlorine in this oxide?

b) Suggest a name for this oxide.

c) This oxide is a simple molecule that contain a bridging oxygen atom between the two chlorine atoms. Suggest a possible displayed formula for the oxide.

d) Write down the formula for the acid formed when Cl_2O_7 reacts with water.

PATTERNS ACROSS THE PERIODIC TABLE

The chapter uses the oxides and chlorides of the elements in Period 3 to explain how the variations in properties across the period relates to their structure and bonding. Use the map to clarify the connection between the many important concepts in this chapter, including the writing of equations for reactions.

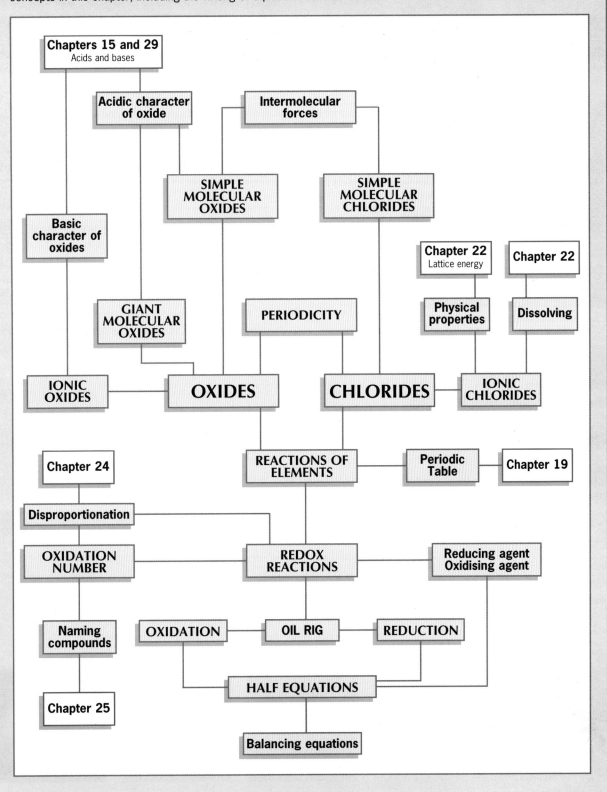

Coral reefs are composed mainly of the insoluble compound calcium carbonate

Chalk cliffs are composed of calcium carbonate

SOME PEOPLE THINK OF carbon dioxide as just the greenhouse gas that causes global warming problems, though of course carbon dioxide is essential for life as well. From earliest times on Earth and continuously since then, vast amounts of carbon dioxide from the atmosphere have been locked up in rocks of the Earth's crust as carbonates.

There are several different carbonates in rocks, but by far the most abundant is of the highly reactive metal calcium, giving calcium carbonate, which we see in the enormous chalk cliffs and widespread chalklands in the UK; also in limestone deposits and coral reefs around the world.

Chalk, limestone and coral reefs exist only because calcium carbonate is an insoluble material, while other calcium salts are soluble. The explanation is that calcium carbonate comes from the activity of marine animals and microscopic organisms that synthesise the carbonate as part of their life processes, but they can only do this by using calcium salts that are soluble in the waters around them. The calcium carbonate forms their shells, bones or coral protective structures, and as the organisms die and reach the ocean floor, these deposits feed into the rock-forming cycle.

Calcium carbonate formed at the bottom of seas and oceans is therefore a 'sink' for carbon dioxide. It has been suggested that as atmospheric carbon dioxide increases, this will to some extent be offset by an increase in the carbon dioxide content of the oceans and, in turn, by an increase in the conversion to calcium carbonate by marine creatures.

1 REACTIVE METALS

The classification of elements into metals and non-metals is based upon the physical and chemical properties of the elements and their compounds. To most people, metals are hard, strong and shiny and are good thermal and electrical conductors. These properties describe the metals we are familiar with outside the chemistry laboratory, such as iron, lead, silver, gold, zinc, copper and nickel.

These elements show the typical properties of metals. They are hard, shiny, strong and have high melting points

Fig 22.1(a) **Iron**

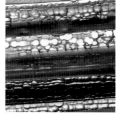

Fig 22.1(b) **Nickel**

Fig 22.2(a) **Native copper**

Fig 22.2(b) **Native silver**

Fig 22.2(c) **Native gold**

Other elements are also classified as metals but they are less recognisable as metals, in that they are soft and have a low melting point. It is only when their chemical properties are described that they are clearly seen to be metals. They include lithium, sodium, potassium, calcium and barium. These metals are found in the s block of the Periodic Table and are often collectively called the **reactive metals**.

Aluminium, in Group 3, is sometimes also referred to as a reactive metal. So aluminium is included in this chapter (see page 477).

2 CHEMICAL PROPERTIES OF METALS

The main chemical property of a metal atom is its ability to lose one, two or sometimes three electrons to form a positive ion. When an atom loses electrons, it attains a stable, noble-gas electron configuration. It is this single property that can be used to explain the reactivity of metals. Atoms of reactive metals easily lose electrons; atoms of unreactive metals lose them with difficulty.

The ability of a metal atom to lose electrons to form a positive ion explains why:

● metals are reducing agents,

● metals form ionic compounds with non-metals,

● metals do not normally form compounds with other metals.

The most reactive of all metals are those in the s block of the Periodic Table, since they have an electron configuration that contains only 1 or 2 electrons more than the nearest noble gas. This means that atoms of these elements lose electrons easily to form cations.

> ✔
> Remember OIL RIG: oxidation involves the loss of electrons and reduction the gain of electrons. So metals are reducing agents because they give away electrons easily to an oxidising agent.

3 GROUP 1: THE ALKALI METALS

The metals in Group 1 are collectively known as the **alkali metals**. There are six of them: lithium, sodium, potassium, rubidium, caesium and francium. They are the most reactive of all the s-block metals.

These six elements are all remarkably similar in terms of both their chemical and physical properties. Being in the same group, we would expect them to have similar chemical properties (see page 395). But also having some of their physical properties similar and with, in some cases, an observable and predictable trend is unusual. For example, the melting and boiling points decrease with increasing atomic (proton) number.

> **?**
> **A (a)** Francium, atomic (proton) number 87, is an alkali metal. Predict values for francium for its **(i)** melting point, **(ii)** boiling point, **(iii)** atomic radius and **(iv)** ionic radius.
>
> **(b)** In alkali metals, what does the change in the melting point suggest about the change in the strength of the metallic bonding?
> (Hint: Read page 414.)
>
> **(c)** Water has a density of $1000 \, kg \, m^{-3}$. Which of the alkali metals sinks when placed in water?

Table 22.1 **Some properties of the first five alkali metals**

Metal	Atomic (proton) number	Common oxidation state	Atomic radius/pm	Ionic radius (M^+)/pm	Density/kg m^{-3}	Melting point/°C	Boiling point/°C	Electron configuration
lithium	3	+1	152	60	534	180	1.326	$1s^2 2s^1$
sodium	11	+1	186	95	968	98	889	$1s^2 2s^2 2p^6 3s^1$
potassium	19	+1	231	133	856	63.4	757	$1s^2 2s^2 2p^6 3s^2 3p^6 4s^1$
rubidium	37	+1	244	148	1532	39	679	$[Kr]5s^1$
caesium	55	+1	262	169	1870	29	690	$[Xe]6s^1$

It is interesting that the melting points of these elements are very low for metals, which makes them easy to melt. Advantage is taken of this property in some nuclear reactors, where liquid sodium is used as the primary coolant because it also has a relatively high specific heat capacity and can be pumped easily through the pipes of the cooling system.

> ✔
> Specific heat capacity measures the energy needed to raise the temperature of 1 kg of a substance by 1 °C.

Occurrence and extraction

The physical properties of the alkali metals, coupled with their high reactivity, limit the number of large-scale applications. Nevertheless, there is significant demand for lithium, sodium and potassium.

Table 22.2 **The natural abundances of the alkali metals in the Earth's crust**

Element	Abundance (% by mass)	Common mineral
lithium	1.8×10^{-3}	lepidolite
sodium	2.63	rock salt and Chile saltpetre
potassium	2.40	sylvite and carnallite
rubidium	7.8×10^{-3}	lepidolite
caesium	3×10^{-4}	pollucite

The alkali metals are so reactive that they occur naturally only as compounds. It is impossible to reduce alkali metal compounds using a chemical process such as heating with carbon. The only successful method of reduction involves electrolytic decomposition. Francium, the last of the alkali metals to be discovered, is highly radioactive and, although its chemistry is easily predicted, it has not been fully determined experimentally. This is hardly surprising, since it is estimated that there is only 15 grams of francium in the whole of the Earth's crust.

Manufacture of sodium

Sodium is manufactured by the electrolysis of molten sodium chloride. The melting point of sodium chloride is 801 °C and so calcium chloride is added to lower the melting point to about 600 °C. The overall reaction is represented by the equation:

$$2NaCl(l) \rightarrow 2Na(l) + Cl_2(g)$$

Electrolysis is the only practical way to achieve this decomposition. Sodium ions are reduced at the cathode and chloride ions are oxidised at the anode:

$$\text{Cathode: } Na^+ + e^- \rightarrow Na$$
$$\text{Anode: } 2Cl^- \rightarrow Cl_2 + 2e^-$$

Since sodium as a highly reactive metal, it is important to ensure that the sodium and chlorine formed are not allowed to recombine. They must be produced in different parts of the electrolytic cell. Fig 22.4 shows the Down's cell used to electrolyse molten sodium chloride. A fine screen prevents the chlorine from diffusing to the cathode.

Fig 22.3 **Sodium chloride is the principal source of the reactive metal sodium. Most sodium chloride is mined**

?

B (a) What would happen in the Down's cell if sodium and chlorine are allowed to come into contact with each other? Write an equation for the reaction.

(b) Chlorine does not react with the graphite anode in the Downs cell. Suggest why the anode cannot be made from a metal such as iron.

Fig 22.4 **A Down's cell is used to manufacture sodium. An electrolyte of molten sodium chloride and calcium chloride is electrolysed using a graphite anode and an iron cathode. Molten sodium is collected as it floats on top of the molten electrolyte. A fine screen or gauze prevents chlorine and sodium from recombining. The chlorine produced is collected and stored**

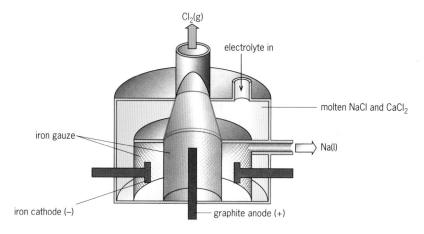

?

C Suggest how lithium can be extracted from lithium chloride.

All the alkali metals are costly to make because of the amount of the electrical energy needed.

4 REACTIONS OF THE ALKALI METALS

The alkali metals are good reducing agents because their atoms can easily transfer the outer electrons to non-metal atoms. Once electrons are lost, the resulting positive ions have noble gas electron configurations.

For example, the sodium atom ($1s^2 2s^2 2p^6 3s^1$) loses an electron to form the sodium ion ($1s^2 2s^2 2p^6$) with the same electron configuration as argon. This means that in all compounds the elements of Group 1 have an oxidation state of +1.

First ionisation energy and electrode potentials

Lithium has the highest of the first ionisation energy values, so it is the least reactive of the alkali metals. As the atomic (proton) number increases down the group, the number of inner-shell shielding electrons increases and the atomic radius increases. The outer electron is therefore attracted less strongly to the nucleus and so less energy is needed to remove it from the atom. This means that the first ionisation energy decreases within a group as the atomic (proton) number increases.

The first ionisation energy refers to the loss of an electron from a gaseous atom, which does not represent the situation for most reactions. A more appropriate way of describing the ease of electron loss from an alkali metal atom is to refer to its oxidation potential, $E^{\ominus}_{oxid}$, since this refers to the reaction of a metal atom to form an aqueous metal ion. For example, the oxidation potential for lithium refers to the following half-equation:

$$Li(s) \rightarrow Li^+(aq) + e^-$$

Table 22.4 **Oxidation potentials**

Half-equation	Oxidation potential, $E^{\ominus}_{oxid}$/volts
$Li(s) \rightarrow Li^+(aq) + e^-$	+ 3.05
$Na(s) \rightarrow Na^+(aq) + e^-$	+ 2.71
$K(s) \rightarrow K^+(aq) + e^-$	+ 2.93
$Rb(s) \rightarrow Rb^+(aq) + e^-$	+ 2.92
$Cs(s) \rightarrow Cs^+(aq) + e^-$	+ 2.92

This is precisely the reaction that occurs when lithium metal reacts with water or dilute acid.

The values of the oxidation potentials show that all the elements in Group 1 are highly reactive in that they can lose electrons easily.

Reaction with water

The alkali metals get their name from their reaction with water. All the metals react vigorously with water to form hydrogen and an alkaline solution.

Take lithium as an example (Fig 22.5). During the reaction, the metal reduces the water by losing electrons to form lithium cations and hydrogen. Lithium reacts with water to form aqueous lithium hydroxide and hydrogen:

$$2Li(s) + 2H_2O(l) \rightarrow LiOH(aq) + H_2(g)$$

Fig 22.5 **Lithium reacts with water to form aqueous lithium hydroxide and hydrogen. The water has turned pink because it contains phenolphthalein indicator**

?

D **(a)** Write down the electron configuration for each of the following: Li^+, K^+ and Rb^+.

(b) Why is sodium is more reactive than lithium? Use Table 22.3 to help you.

You can read about first ionisation energy and electron configuration on page 57 and page 401.

Table 22.3 **First ionisation energies of the Group 1 elements**

Element	First ionisation energy/kJ mol^{-1}
lithium	519
sodium	494
potassium	418
rubidium	400
caesium	380

?

E Predict the first ionisation energy for francium.

✔

The more positive an oxidation potential, the more feasible the reaction. More information on oxidation potentials is given on page 548.

■ See question 1.

The reactivity of the alkali metals increases with increasing atomic (proton) number, so that the reaction of potassium with water is often accompanied by a lilac flame as the hydrogen produced burns (Fig 22.7).

F **(a)** Write down the balanced equations for the reaction of sodium and of potassium with water.

(b) Predict what would happen if a piece of francium were added to cold water.

Fig 22.6 **Sodium reacts with water to form aqueous sodium hydroxide and hydrogen.** The yellow flame occurs when the hydrogen produced burns. Notice that sufficient energy is transferred to the surroundings to melt the sodium into a sphere

Fig 22.7 **Potassium is more reactive than sodium or lithium.** It reacts violently with water, producing hydrogen and aqueous potassium hydroxide. The reaction is exothermic and the energy transferred is sufficient to melt the potassium and to ignite the hydrogen formed

Reactions with acids

The alkali metals react explosively with dilute acids, such as hydrochloric acid and sulphuric acid:

$$2Li(s) + 2HCl(aq) \rightarrow 2LiCl(aq) + H_2(g)$$

They will even displace hydrogen from very weak acids such as alcohols, forming compounds called alkoxides. (The reactions of alkali metals with alcohols are covered on page 239.)

Reaction with air

Unlike most metals, the alkali metals are very soft and easy to cut with a knife. The surface obtained after cutting is shiny but almost immediately tarnishes by reaction with moisture and/or oxygen from the air (Fig 22.8).

Fig 22.8 **Sodium, potassium or lithium can be easily cut by a knife to reveal a shiny, silver metal.** This surface tarnishes quickly, with the formation of oxide, hydroxide and eventually carbonate

All the alkali metals react with air to form a complex mixture of compounds, including the corresponding carbonate. The following reaction scheme shows one way in which sodium may react with air:

$$4Na(s) + O_2(g) \rightarrow 2Na_2O(s)$$
$$2Na_2O(s) + H_2O(g) \rightarrow 2NaOH(s)$$
$$2NaOH(s) + CO_2(s) \rightarrow Na_2CO_3.H_2O(s)$$

The colour of a flame is a result of electron excitation and the consequent release of energy as the electron falls back to a lower energy level. You can read more about electron excitation on pages 52 and 611.

Reaction of alkali metals with oxygen

All alkali metals burn when heated in oxygen, producing oxides. The combustion is always accompanied by a coloured flame characteristic of the element. Lithium burns with a red flame, sodium with a yellow flame, and potassium with a lilac flame.

The oxides formed are not always the predicted M_2O, containing the M^+ and O^{2-} ions. Peroxides containing the O_2^{2-} ion and superoxides containing the ion O_2^- are formed with the more reactive alkali metals. The stability of the peroxides and the superoxides increases with the size of the cation. So, caesium oxide forms CsO_2 when burnt in excess oxygen, whereas lithium forms Li_2O:

$$4Li(s) + O_2(g) \rightarrow 2Li_2O(s)$$
$$Cs(s) + O_2(g) \rightarrow CsO_2(s)$$

G Write down equations to show the reaction of:

(a) sodium to form sodium peroxide, Na_2O_2,

(b) potassium to form potassium peroxide,

(c) rubidium to form rubidium superoxide.

POTASSIUM SUPEROXIDE

SUPEROXIDES ARE SOLIDS. They are very powerful oxidising agents, and can oxidise water to form oxygen. This is the reaction in some types of breathing mask used in mine rescue, where potassium superoxide can is the source of the emergency oxygen supply to the wearer. Moisture reacts with the superoxide to provide this oxygen:

$$4KO_2(s) + 2H_2O(l) \rightarrow 4KOH(s) + 3O_2(g)$$

Note that 4 moles of potassium superoxide provide 3 moles of oxygen. This means that one gram of potassium superoxide can provide approximately 250 cm^3 of oxygen at room temperature and atmospheric pressure.

The attraction of this reaction is that as the superoxide is used up, it makes potassium hydroxide, which removes carbon dioxide. This prevents the wearer from breathing in large quantities of carbon dioxide.

$$2KOH(s) + CO_2(g) \rightarrow K_2CO_3(s) + H_2O(l)$$

Fig 22.9 **Gas masks protect miners and potholers from excess carbon dioxide in the air**

The overall effect is the removal of carbon dioxide and formation of oxygen. Potassium superoxide can also be used in submarines to provide oxygen, while at the same time preventing the build-up of dangerous levels of carbon dioxide.

■ See question 1.

Basic properties of alkali metal oxides

The normal oxides of the alkali metals, are basic and react with water to give aqueous hydroxides – alkalis. Bases are protons acceptors and the oxide ion accepts a proton from water to form the hydroxide ion. Take sodium oxide, Na_2O, as an example:

$$Na_2O(s) + H_2O(l) \rightarrow 2NaOH(aq)$$

?

H Write an equation to show the reaction of rubidium oxide with cold water. Include state symbols in your answer.

✔

A soluble base forms an alkaline solution.

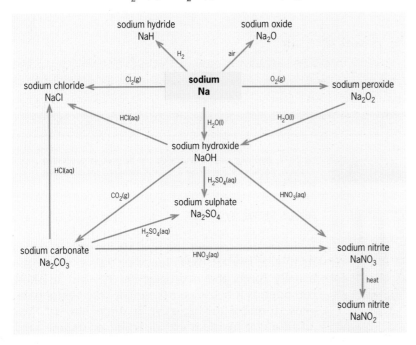

Fig 22.10 **Some important reactions of sodium and its compounds**

5 COMPOUNDS OF THE ALKALI METALS

The common feature of almost all compounds of the alkali metals is their high solubility in water. The compounds have a giant ionic lattice. So they have high melting points and can be electrolysed both in aqueous solution and as molten liquids.

The manufacture of sodium hydroxide in the chlor-alkali industry is covered on page 509.

Sodium hydroxide

Sodium hydroxide – commonly called caustic soda – is a strong alkali. In water, it is fully dissociated into aqueous sodium ions and aqueous hydroxide ions. In the laboratory, it is used as a reagent to test for metal ions in solutions. Aqueous sodium hydroxide precipitates metal ions as their insoluble hydroxides. Very often, the hydroxides have characteristic colours that aid identification of the metal ion. Table 22.5 shows the reactions of aqueous hydroxide ions with various aqueous metal ions.

Table 22.5 Reactions of aqueous sodium hydroxide with metal ions in solutions

Metal ion in solution	Reaction with aqueous sodium hydroxide	Equation
calcium	white precipitate	$Ca^{2+}(aq) + 2OH^-(aq) \rightarrow Ca(OH)_2(s)$
magnesium	white precipitate	$Mg^{2+}(aq) + 2OH^-(aq) \rightarrow Mg(OH)_2(s)$
copper(II)	pale blue precipitate	$Cu^{2+}(aq) + 2OH^-(aq) \rightarrow Cu(OH)_2(s)$
iron(II)	green precipitate that slowly darkens	$Fe^{2+}(aq) + 2OH^-(aq) \rightarrow Fe(OH)_2(s)$
iron(III)	rust-red precipitate	$Fe^{3+}(aq) + 3OH^-(aq) \rightarrow Fe(OH)_3(s)$
cobalt(II)	blue precipitate that will turn pink in excess aqueous sodium hydroxide with warming.	$Co^{2+}(aq) + 2OH^-(aq) \rightarrow Co(OH)_2(s)$
nickel(II)	apple-green precipitate	$Ni^{2+}(aq) + 2OH^-(aq) \rightarrow Ni(OH)_2(s)$
manganese(II)	white precipitate that rapidly darkens in air	$Mn^{2+}(aq) + 2OH^-(aq) \rightarrow Mn(OH)_2(s)$ followed by $2Mn(OH)_2(s) + O_2(g) \rightarrow 2MnO_2.H_2O(s)$
chromium(III)	green precipitate that redissolves in excess to give a green solution of aqueous chromate(III) ion	$Cr^{3+}(aq) + 2OH^-(aq) \rightarrow Cr(OH)_3(s)$ followed by $Cr(OH)_3(aq) + 3OH^-(aq) \rightarrow [Cr(OH)_6]^{3-}(aq)$
silver(I)	dark-brown precipitate	$2Ag^+(aq) + 2OH^-(aq) \rightarrow Ag_2O(s) + H_2O(l)$
zinc	white precipitate that redissolves into a colourless solution in excess aqueous sodium hydroxide	$Zn^{2+}(aq) + 2OH^-(aq) \rightarrow Zn(OH)_2(s)$
	and with excess aqueous sodium hydroxide the soluble zincate ion is formed	$Zn(OH)_2(s) + 2OH^-(aq) \rightarrow [Zn(OH)_4]^{2-}(aq)$
lead(II)	white precipitate that redissolves into a colourless solution in excess sodium hydroxide	$Pb^{2+}(aq) + 2OH^-(aq) \rightarrow PbO(s) + H_2O(l)$
	and with excess aqueous sodium hydroxide the soluble plumbate(II) ion is formed	$PbO(s) + 2OH^-(aq) \rightarrow PbO_2^{2-}(aq) + H_2O(l)$
aluminium	white precipitate that redissolves into a colourless solution in excess sodium hydroxide	$Al^{3+}(aq) + 3OH^-(aq) \rightarrow Al(OH)_3(s)$
	and with excess aqueous sodium hydroxide the soluble aluminate ion is formed	$Al(OH)_3(s) + OH^-(aq) \rightarrow [Al(OH)_4]^-(aq)$

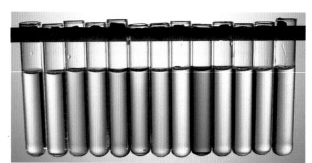

$Ca^{2+} \quad Mg^{2+} \quad Cu^{2+} \quad Fe^{2+} \quad Fe^{3+} \quad Co^{2+} \quad Ni^{2+} \quad Mn^{2+} \quad Cr^{3+} \quad Ag^+ \quad Zn^{2+} \quad Pb^{2+} \quad Al^{3+}$

Fig 22.11 **Aqueous sodium hydroxide can be used in qualitative analysis, because it gives characteristic coloured solutions and precipitates with aqueous metal ions**

Alkali metal hydrides

Alkali metals react with hydrogen to form ionic hydrides that contain the hydride ion and in which hydrogen has an oxidation state of −1. Hydrogen usually forms the hydrogen ion H^+, but in these compounds it behaves in a similar way to the halogens, forming the negative hydride ion, H^-. The alkali metal hydrides are all white crystalline salts, but are hydrolysed by water to form hydrogen and a highly alkaline solution:

$$NaH(s) + H_2O(l) \rightarrow NaOH(aq) + H_2(g)$$

Oxy-salts

The nitrates, sulphate and carbonates are much more thermally stable than those of other metals. The sulphates and carbonates are thermally stable at Bunsen-burner temperatures with the exception of lithium carbonate. Even the nitrates decompose to form nitrites and oxygen rather than the oxide and oxygen. This contrasts with most other metal nitrates, which thermally decompose to give the oxides or the metal itself. Again, the exception is provided by a lithium compound, since lithium nitrate forms lithium oxide. Potassium nitrate thermally decomposes to form potassium nitrite:

$$2KNO_3(s) \rightarrow 2KNO_2(s) + O_2(g)$$

The alkali metals are the only group of metals that form stable, solid hydrogencarbonates. Sodium hydrogencarbonate is an important constituent in baking powder. It decomposes when heated to form sodium carbonate, carbon dioxide and water:

$$2NaHCO_3(s) \rightarrow Na_2CO_3(s) + H_2O(l) + CO_2(g)$$

The thermal stability of some of carbonates and nitrates are described in more detail later on page 469.

6 ALKALINE EARTH METALS

The elements in Group 2 are collectively called the **alkaline earth metals**. With the exception of beryllium, these elements are all closely similar. The metallic character (ease of loss of electrons) of the elements increases with increasing atomic (proton) number and, with the exception of beryllium, their compounds are almost all ionic.

Occurrence and extraction

Their compounds, particularly those of calcium and magnesium, are found extensively in the Earth's crust. They are mostly insoluble in water.

Electrolysis of the molten chloride of the element is the normal method of manufacture. The process is similar to that used to manufacture sodium. Magnesium is produced from molten magnesium chloride, much of it obtained from sea-water. It is estimated that 800 tonnes of sea-water are processed to obtain just 1 tonne of magnesium.

I Write balanced equations for the thermal decomposition of:

(a) lithium carbonate, Li_2CO_3, to form lithium oxide, Li_2O,

(b) lithium nitrate, $LiNO_3$, to form lithium oxide,

(c) francium nitrate, $FrNO_3$, to form francium nitrite, $FrNO_2$.

Fig 22.12 **Baking powder contains sodium hydrogencarbonate. When heated in an oven, sodium hydrogencarbonate decomposes to form carbon dioxide, which helps the sponge cake to rise**

Table 22.6 **Occurrence of four Group 2 elements in the Earth's crust**

Element	Abundance (% by mass)	Mineral
magnesium	1.93	magnesite ($MgCO_3$) dolomite ($CaCO_3.MgCO_3$) sea-water and brines
calcium	3.39	dolomite ($CaCO_3.MgCO_3$) marble and limestone ($CaCO_3$)
strontium	0.02	celestite ($SrSO_4$)
barium	0.04	barite ($BaSO_4$)

Table 22.7 **Properties of Group 2 elements**

Metal	Atomic number	Oxidation number	Atomic radius/pm	Ionic radius (M^{2+})/pm	Density /kg/m³	Melting point/°C	Boiling point/°C	Electron configuration
beryllium	4	+2	111	31	1 850	1 278	2 970	$1s^2 2s^2$
magnesium	12	+2	160	65	1 740	651	1 107	$1s^2 2s^2 2p^6 3s^2$
calcium	20	+2	197	99	1 550	850	1 490	$1s^2 2s^2 2p^6 3s^2 3p^6 4s^2$
strontium	38	+2	215	113	2 540	770	1,384	$[Kr]5s^2$
barium	56	+2	217	135	3 500	704	1 638	$[Xe]6s^2$
radium	88	+2	220	152	See J	See J	See J	$[Rn]7s^2$

J Use the trends in the physical properties of the Group 2 elements to predict the density, the melting point and the boiling point of radium.

■ See question 2.

TEETH AND BONES

'CALCIUM IS GOOD for your bones and teeth.' Is this popular saying correct?

Teeth and bone are composed of two main constituents. One is a protein called collagen, and the other is a complex calcium phosphate compound with the approximate formula $Ca_{10}(PO_4)_6.(OH)_2$. This complex calcium phosphate is called hydroxyapatite. Bone acts as the body's calcium store but calcium can be removed from it. For unless bones are kept under load, they begin to lose their calcium, which happens to astronauts who stay in space stations for a long time.

In teeth, the complex calcium phosphate undergoes changes in the presence of fluoride ions, since there is a partial replacement of the hydroxide ion in hydroxyapatite with fluoride ions to form fluoroapatite. The fluoroapatite is much more resistant to acids in the mouth and so its presence in teeth reduces decay. This is the reason why fluoride ions are added to toothpastes and some water supplies. It is also known that fluoride ions promote bone growth, but the mechanism is not yet fully understood.

Fig 22.13 **Prolonged space travel can lead to a drastic reduction in bone mass, because the calcium ions within the bone are reabsorbed**

Fig 22.14 **The fluoride ions in the toothpaste strengthen teeth and slow down tooth decay**

7 REACTIONS OF THE ALKALINE EARTH METALS

Be²⁺ is a very small, high charge ion. It will strongly polarise negative ions, see page 85.

Atoms of Group 2 elements lose two electrons to form a stable electron configuration. Their reactivity increases with increasing atomic (proton) number. This is explained by the increasing ease with which electrons can be lost from the atoms. Beryllium is unusual in that it does not easily lose two electrons to form Be^{2+}, and many compounds of beryllium are covalent. So, with the exception of beryllium, Group 2 elements are reactive metals because they can very easily lose two electrons per atom. This means that the oxidation number of Group 2 elements in their compounds is always +2.

The data in Table 22.8 demonstrates the increasing ease with which electrons can be lost. The reactivity of the Group 2 elements is less than that of the Group 1 elements in the same period because two electrons are lost per atom rather than one, which requires more energy. For example, potassium is considerably more reactive than calcium.

Table 22.8 **Ionisation energy and oxidation potential of five alkaline earth metals. The sum of the first and second ionisation energies represents the energy transferred when two electrons are lost from an atom:**
$M(g) \rightarrow M^{2+}(aq) + 2e^-$.
The oxidation potential is a measure of electron loss in the reaction:
$M(s) \rightarrow M^{2+}(aq) + 2e^-$

Metal	First ionisation energy/kJ mol⁻¹	Second ionisation energy/kJ mol⁻¹	Sum of first and second mol⁻¹ ionisation energy/kJ	Oxidation potential, $E^{\ominus}_{oxid}$/V
beryllium	900	1760	2 660	+1.85
magnesium	736	1450	2 186	+2.37
calcium	590	1150	1 740	+2.87
strontium	548	1060	1 608	+2.89
barium	502	966	1 468	+2.91

See question 2. ■

You can read about ionisation energy and electron loss on page 57, and about oxidation potentials on page 548.

Since Group 2 elements lose two electrons per atom in reactions, it is the sum of the first and second ionisation energies that must be considered when comparing reactivities. The ionisation energy data and the electrode potential data both indicate that the reactivity of the Group 2 elements increases with atomic number.

Reaction with water

As already noted, the reactivity of Group 2 metals is lower than that of Group 1 metals in the same period. This is exemplified by the reaction of the metals with water. There is virtually no reaction between magnesium and cold water, but with hot water it forms magnesium hydroxide and hydrogen. When hot steam is passed over heated magnesium (Fig 22.15), an exothermic reaction occurs with the formation of hydrogen:

$$Mg(s) + H_2O(g) \rightarrow MgO(s) + H_2(g)$$

Note that magnesium oxide is produced rather than magnesium hydroxide.

Calcium, the next metal in Group 2, is more reactive than magnesium. It reduces cold water to form an alkaline solution, aqueous calcium hydroxide, commonly known as lime-water:

$$Ca(s) + 2H_2O(l) \rightarrow Ca(OH)_2(aq) + H_2(g)$$

Reaction with air and oxygen

All the Group 2 elements tarnish in air to form a coating of the oxide. This reaction is rapid with the elements having a high atomic number. When these metals are heated in air or oxygen, they burn vigorously to produce the white ionic oxide. Magnesium burns in air and produces a brilliant white light (Fig 22.16):

$$2Mg(s) + O_2(g) \rightarrow 2MgO(s)$$

Fig 22.15 **The reaction of magnesium with steam**

K Write down equations to show the reaction of barium and strontium with water.

Fig 22.16 **Magnesium burns with a brilliant white flame**

Fig 22.17 **Calcium oxide emits white light when it is heated strongly. Blocks of calcium oxide heated by gas burners were used as stage lights in theatres before electricity was available. It was from this that the phrase 'being in the limelight' originated**

Oxides and hydroxides

The oxides and hydroxides of Group 2 elements are basic and will neutralise acids. The oxide ion or the hydroxide ion reacts with aqueous protons to form water:

$$O^{2-} + 2H^+ \rightarrow H_2O$$
$$OH^- + H^+ \rightarrow H_2O$$

The solubility of the hydroxides in water increases with increasing atomic (proton) number. Magnesium hydroxide is insoluble in water, whereas barium hydroxide is soluble. The reason for this change in solubility is explained on page 470. When water is added to the oxides, a comparable difference in solubility is observed, but this is because a chemical reaction takes place. For example, calcium oxide (quicklime) reacts with water to form aqueous calcium hydroxide or lime-water, which is sparingly soluble in water:

$$CaO(s) + H_2O(l) \rightarrow Ca(OH)_2(aq)$$

When water is dropped slowly onto the oxide, slaked lime (solid calcium hydroxide) is formed.

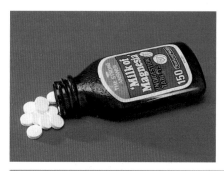

?

L (a) Stomach acid is dilute hydrochloric acid. Write an equation to show the neutralisation of stomach acid by milk of magnesia.

(b) Acid rain contains acids including dilute sulphuric acid and nitric acid. Write equations to show the neutralisation of acid rain with calcium carbonate.

The basic properties of the oxides and hydroxides are used extensively to neutralise acids in a variety of applications. Slaked lime is used to neutralise acid soils and lakes.

Fig 22.18 **Milk of magnesia can be in tablet form or a suspension of magnesium hydroxide in water. It is used to neutralise excess acid in the stomach**

Fig 22.19(a) **Farmers use slaked lime to neutralise acid soils**

Fig 22.19(b) **Most lakes in Scandinavia are highly acidic due to acid rain. The acid can be neutralised by spreading slaked lime**

Aqueous calcium hydroxide (lime-water) is used to test for carbon dioxide. It gives a characteristic white precipitate often described as 'milky'. This is a further example of the basic behaviour of the hydroxides, since carbon dioxide is an acidic gas and reacts to form insoluble calcium carbonate:

$$Ca(OH)_2(aq) + CO_2(g) \rightarrow CaCO_3(s) + H_2O(l)$$

When more carbon dioxide is bubbled into the white precipitate, it redissolves due to the formation of aqueous calcium hydrogencarbonate:

$$CaCO_3(s) + CO_2(g) + H_2O(l) \rightarrow Ca(HCO_3)_2(aq)$$

This reaction also features in relation to the hardness of water later in this chapter, on page 466.

See question 1 and 3. ◼

Oxy-salts

The oxy-salts (such as the nitrates and sulphates) of the Group 2 elements are white ionic substances. They show distinct trends in their solubility and thermal decomposition, which are explained on pages 469 to 470 in terms of the bonding between ions.

Sulphates

The solubility of the sulphates of the Group 2 elements decreases as the atomic (proton) number of the element increases. The reason for this trend is described on page 472.

Table 22.9 **Solubility of the Group 2 sulphates**

Compound	Solubility at 298 K/mol dm^{-3}
magnesium sulphate	2.8
calcium sulphate	1.4×10^{-3}
strontium sulphate	7.6×10^{-5}
barium sulphate	1.1×10^{-6}

?

M Calculate the solubility of each of the Group 2 sulphates in grams per dm^3.

✔ The solubility of a substance gives the maximum amount of the substance that will dissolve in a known volume. The solubility of a substance varies with temperature, so it is important to compare solubilities at the same temperature.

The aqueous barium chloride or barium nitrate test for sulphate ions rests on the insolubility of barium sulphate. A solution of the test chemical is mixed with aqueous barium ions and dilute nitric acid. The sulphate ion is present in the test solution if a white precipitate is formed:

$$Ba^{2+}(aq) + SO_4^{2-}(aq) \rightarrow BaSO_4(s)$$

Carbonates

The carbonates of the Group 2 elements are all considered to be insoluble in water. Therefore, each can be prepared by precipitation, by reacting a soluble carbonate, such as aqueous sodium carbonate, with a soluble salt of the element:

$$CO_3^{2-}(aq) + M^{2+}(aq) \rightarrow MCO_3(s)$$

The thermal stability of the carbonates increases with increasing atomic number of the Group 2 elements. Beryllium carbonate decomposes so easily that it cannot be isolated at room temperature. Magnesium carbonate decomposes at 540 °C and barium carbonate at about 1360 °C. The reason for this variation in thermal stability is described on page 469.

$$MCO_3(s) \rightarrow MO(s) + CO_2(g) \text{ where M = Be, Mg, Ca, Sr, Ba, and Ra}$$

Calcium oxide (quicklime) is made in large quantities by the thermal decomposition of calcium carbonate (limestone). A temperature of between 900 and 1200 °C is needed and it is important to remove the carbon dioxide produced, since the decomposition is reversible:

$$CaCO_3(s) \rightleftharpoons CaO(s) + CO_2(g)$$

Fig 22.20 **Plaster of Paris is a hydrate of calcium sulphate ($CaSO_4)_2.H_2O$. When water is added to this hydrate, it forms gypsum – a different hydrate of calcium sulphate. $CaSO_4.2H_2O$ – which sets solid. Plaster of Paris is used to make moulds**

■ See question 4.

Fig 22.21 **Cement is made from calcium carbonate. Calcium carbonate and clay are heated strongly together to form a mixture of calcium silicate and aluminium silicate. When cement is mixed first with a ballast of sand and gravel and then with water, it makes concrete**

CALCIUM CARBONATE, ACID RAIN AND FGD PLANTS

ACID RAIN is due to the presence in the air of sulphur dioxide and oxides of nitrogen. These gases react with the water and the oxygen in the air to produce a mixture of acids, including dilute sulphuric acid and dilute nitric acid. A major source of these gases is the power station that uses fossil fuels contaminated with sulphur.

Coal and orimulsion (a mixture of a tar and water imported from South America) are particularly rich in sulphur and cause the most problems at power stations. Oxides of nitrogen are formed in the very high temperatures reached when the fossil fuels burn. They are sufficiently high to allow nitrogen from the air to react directly with oxygen from the air to form nitrogen monoxide. When cool, the nitrogen monoxide reacts with more oxygen to give acidic nitrogen dioxide.

It has now become a high priority to remove these acidic gases from the waste or flue gases before they are emitted. A process called flue-gas desulphurisation (FGD) is being introduced, in which cold waste gases are treated with powdered calcium carbonate. The acidic gases react with the calcium carbonate to give calcium nitrate, calcium nitrite, $Ca(NO_2)_2$, and, mostly, calcium sulphite, $CaSO_3$:

$$SO_2(g) + CaCO_3(s) \rightarrow CaSO_3(s) + CO_2(g)$$

$$4NO_2(g) + 2CaCO_3(s)$$
$$\rightarrow \quad Ca(NO_2)_2(s) + Ca(NO_3)_2(s) + 2CO_2(g)$$

Almost 90 per cent of the sulphur dioxide and nitrogen dioxide produced by a power station can be removed by this process. The calcium sulphite produced is converted into calcium sulphate by reaction with oxygen, which is sold as gypsum and used in the building industry. The downside of the process is that large quantities of limestone have to be quarried to provide with calcium carbonate.

Fig 22.22 **Power stations remove acidic gases, such as sulphur dioxide, by reacting them with powdered calcium carbonate**

HARDNESS OF WATER

HARD WATER does not readily form a lather with soaps because it contains dissolved calcium or magnesium salts. These salts enter the water when rain percolates through rocks that contain them. For example, rain-water passing through limestone dissolves calcium salts as the soluble hydrogencarbonate:

$$CO_2(aq) + H_2O(l) + CaCO_3(s) \rightarrow Ca(HCO_3)_2(aq)$$

Other calcium salts may also enter the water because rain-water contains sulphuric and nitric acids (from acid rain), which react with limestone faster than aqueous carbon dioxide. Water purification does not remove aqueous calcium and magnesium salts. Therefore, domestic water usually contains these ions.

There are two types of hard water: permanent and temporary. Temporary hardness, which is removed by boiling, is caused by the presence of aqueous calcium hydrogencarbonate and/or magnesium hydrogencarbonate. When water is boiled, the hydrogencarbonates decompose, precipitating calcium carbonate:

$$Ca(HCO_3)_2(aq) \rightarrow CaCO_3(s) + H_2O(l) + CO_2(g)$$

This precipitate known as lime scale, is responsible for the furring of hot-water pipes, boilers and kettles (Fig 22.23). The furring of heating elements results in increased electricity bills, since the scale is a poor conductor of heat.

Permanent hardness, which cannot be removed by boiling, is caused by the presence of such salts as calcium sulphate and magnesium sulphate.

Soaps are the sodium salts of long chain carboxylic acids called fatty acids. Both forms of hardness react with soaps to form an insoluble substance called scum, which is really a precipitate of the calcium or magnesium salt of the fatty acids:

$$2C_{17}H_{35}COO^-(aq) + Ca^{2+}(aq) \rightarrow (C_{17}H_{35}COO)_2Ca(s)$$

The formation of scum wastes soap, because enough soap must be added to remove the calcium or magnesium ions before it can start its cleaning action.

Water can be softened by removing the aqueous calcium and magnesium salts. Either the aqueous calcium and magnesium ions are replaced with other positive ions, or they are precipitated in the form of insoluble calcium and magnesium salts. The boiling of temporary hard water is an example of water softening, since the aqueous calcium ions are converted into insoluble calcium carbonate.

The most efficient way to soften large quantities of water involves ion-exchange resins, which swap calcium and magnesium ions for sodium ions. Commercial dishwashers use such ion-exchange resins. This is why the water softener compartment of a dishwasher must be regularly topped up with salt (sodium chloride). There is more about ion-exchange resins on page 362.

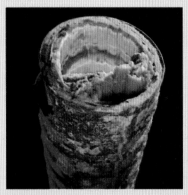

Fig 22.23 **Calcium carbonate scale is deposited on the inside of a water pipe, restricting the flow of water. Eventually, the pipe may become completely blocked**

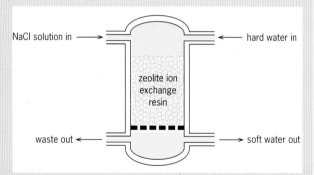

Fig 22.24 **In commercial and industrial water softeners, the magnesium and calcium ions in hard water are replaced with sodium ions. When the ion-exchange resin has exhausted its supply of sodium ions, the hard-water supply is turned off and a concentrated salt solution is run through the resin. This replenishes the stock of sodium ions in the resin**

See question 4. ■

Nitrates

The nitrates of the elements of Group 2 are all white soluble solids that thermally decompose to produce the metal oxide, oxygen and nitrogen dioxide:

$$2M(NO_3)_2(s) \rightarrow 2MO(s) + 4NO_2(g) + O_2(g)$$

where M = Mg, Ca, Sr, Ba and Ra

The thermal stability of the nitrates increase as the atomic number of the Group 2 elements increases. This trend can be explained by reference to the lattice energies of the nitrates and the oxides. This is explained later on page 470.

✔
The more thermally stable a compound, the higher the temperature required to decompose it.

8 LATTICE ENERGY

In order to explain the thermal decomposition and solubility of an ionic substance, the forces that exist between positive and negative ions in its ionic lattice must be understood. Chemists estimate the strength of attraction between a positive ion and a negative ion in an ionic lattice from the enthalpy change called **lattice energy** or **lattice enthalpy**. Lattice energy is the energy released into the surroundings when one mole of an ionic lattice is made from its constituent gaseous ions. Therefore, the lattice energy is always negative. The higher the magnitude of the lattice enthalpy, the greater the attraction between the positive and the negative ions.

For sodium chloride, the lattice enthalpy corresponds to the following reaction:

$$Na^+(g) + Cl^-(g) \rightarrow NaCl(s) \qquad \Delta H_{le}^{\ominus} = \text{lattice energy}$$

Factors affecting the lattice energy

The lattice energy of each ionic compound is different and depends on the degree of attraction between the negative and the positive ions. This attraction depends on and two factors: the ionic radius and the charge on the ion.

The smaller the ionic radius, the greater the density of the positive or negative charge. This gives a greater numerical value for the lattice energy.

The greater the charge on the ion the greater the attraction for a ion of the opposite charge. This also gives a greater numerical value for the lattice energy.

Charge density

The ionic radius and the charge on the ion can be brought together and treated as a single property of the ion called the **charge density**. The charge density is based on the assumption that the charge is spread over the outer surface of the ion, and defined as the charge per unit surface area. Although ions are not solid, we can still think of ions as having a boundary surface.

The surface area is proportional to the square of the ionic radius, and so the charge density of an ion is given by:

$$\text{charge density} = \frac{\text{charge on ion}}{(\text{ionic radius})^2}$$

Table 22.10 **Charge density of fifteen ions**

Ion	Charge	Ionic radius/nm	Charge density
lithium	+1	0.60	2.8
sodium	+1	0.95	1.1
potassium	+1	1.33	0.57
rubidium	+1	1.48	0.46
beryllium	+2	0.31	21
magnesium	+2	0.65	4.7
calcium	+2	0.99	2.0
strontium	+2	1.13	0.78
aluminium	+3	0.50	6.0
oxide	−2	1.40	1.0
sulphide	−2	1.84	0.59
fluoride	−1	1.36	0.54
chloride	−1	1.81	0.31
bromide	−1	1.95	0.26
iodide	−1	2.16	0.21

The enthalpy change for the breakdown of an ionic lattice into gaseous ions is numerically the same as the lattice energy but positive. It is endothermic.

?

N Write down the reaction that corresponds to the lattice energy for each of the following ionic solids:

(a) MgO,

(b) $MgSO_4$,

(c) $Fe_2(SO_4)_3$ and

(d) Mg_3N_2.

A third factor that affects the magnitude of the lattice energy is the type of ionic lattice formed. A discussion of this factor lies beyond the scope of this book.

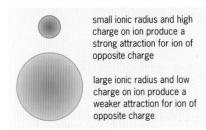

small ionic radius and high charge on ion produce a strong attraction for ion of opposite charge

large ionic radius and low charge on ion produce a weaker attraction for ion of opposite charge

Fig 22.25 **The magnitude of the attractive force between ions in a crystal lattice depends on both the ionic radius and the charge on the ion**

■ See questions 1, 3, 5, 6, 7 and 8.

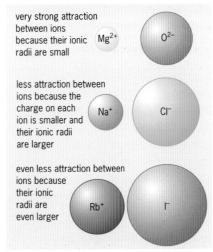

very strong attraction between ions because their ionic radii are small Mg^{2+} O^{2-}

less attraction between ions because the charge on each ion is smaller and their ionic radii are larger Na^+ Cl^-

even less attraction between ions because their ionic radii are even larger Rb^+ I^-

Fig 22.26 **Relative sizes of, and attractions between, three pairs of ions. MgO has a greater lattice energy than NaCl, which has a greater lattice energy than RbI (scale: 1 mm to 20 nm)**

Born–Haber cycles

Experimentally, it is impossible to use a direct method to determine the lattice energy of an ionic solid. So an indirect method involving Hess's law has to be used. Hess's law states that if a change can be brought about by more than one route, then the enthalpy change for each route must be the same, provided that the starting and finishing conditions are the same for each route. (There is more about Hess's law on page 128.)

Applying Hess's law to the determination of lattice energy, there is more than one route from the gaseous ions to the ionic lattice. The direct route and the indirect route shown in Fig 22.27 is known as a Born–Haber cycle. All the enthalpy changes in the indirect route can be measured experimentally.

There are many ways of drawing Born–Haber cycles, and two are shown in Figs 22.27 and 22.28. Others appear elsewhere in this book.

One way to draw a Born–Haber cycle for sodium chloride is first to put down the equation for the formation of the lattice from its gaseous ions, and then to construct an alternative pathway. The pathway will always involve the energy changes shown for sodium chloride.

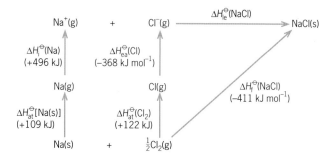

Key

$\Delta H_{le}^{\ominus}$ (NaCl) = lattice energy of sodium chloride

$\Delta H_{i}^{\ominus}$(Na) = first ionisation energy for sodium

$\Delta H_{at}^{\ominus}$(Na) = enthalpy change of atomisation for sodium. This is the energy needed to make 1 mole of gaseous atoms from the element in its standard state

$\Delta H_{at}^{\ominus}$(Cl$_2$) = enthalpy change of atomisation of chlorine

$\Delta H_{ea}^{\ominus}$(Cl) = first electron affinity for chlorine. This is the energy required to make 1 mole of gaseous negative ions X$^-$(g) from 1 mole of gaseous atoms X(g)

$\Delta H_{f}^{\ominus}$(NaCl) = enthalpy change of formation of sodium chloride

By Hess's Law:

$\Delta H_{le}^{\ominus}$ (NaCl) $= -\Delta H_{i}^{\ominus}$(Na) $- \Delta H_{at}^{\ominus}$(Na) $- \Delta H_{ea}^{\ominus}$(Cl) $- \Delta H_{at}^{\ominus}$(Cl$_2$) $+ \Delta H_{f}^{\ominus}$ (NaCl)

$= -496 - 109 - 122 + 368 - 411$

$= -770$ kJ mol^{-1}

?

O Calculate the lattice energy for calcium oxide given the following data:

Standard enthalpy change of formation of calcium oxide
$= -635$ kJ mol^{-1}

Standard enthalpy change of atomisation of calcium
$= +178$ kJ mol^{-1}

First ionisation energy and the second ionisation energy of calcium
$= +1735$ kJ mol^{-1}

Standard enthalpy change of atomisation of oxygen
$= +249$ kJ mol^{-1} of oxygen atoms

First electron affinity and second electron affinity of oxygen
$= +657$ kJ mol^{-1}

An alternative way to draw a Born–Haber cycle for sodium chloride is to use a vertical energy axis.

The elements sodium and chlorine in their standard states have an enthalpy of formation of 0 kJ mol^{-1}. All endothermic reactions are shown by an arrow pointing upwards, and all exothermic reactions are shown by an arrow pointing downwards. Notice that the lattice energy is exothermic.

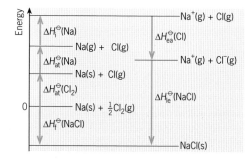

Fig 22.27 **Born–Haber cycle for working out the lattice energy of the ionic solid NaCl**

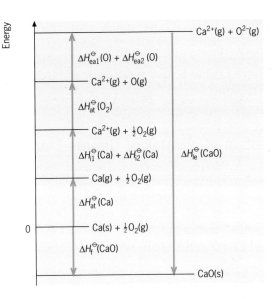

Fig 22.28 **Born–Haber cycle for the formation of calcium oxide.** Notice that the ionisation energy term for calcium involves both the first and second ionisation energies. In the same way, the electron affinity term involves both the first and second electron affinities:

$$O(g) + e^- \rightarrow O^-(g) \qquad \Delta H^{\ominus}_{ea1}(O)$$
$$O^-(g) + e^- \rightarrow O^{2-}(g) \qquad \Delta H^{\ominus}_{ea2}(O)$$

■ See questions 1, 3, 5, 6, 7, 8 and 9.

9 THERMAL DECOMPOSITION OF IONIC SALTS

The thermal decomposition of an ionic salt must necessarily involve the breakdown of one ionic lattice and the formation of another. For example, when magnesium carbonate is decomposed, it forms magnesium oxide and carbon dioxide. This requires that the lattice of magnesium carbonate is completely broken and the lattice of magnesium oxide is completely formed. It therefore follows that the enthalpy change that occurs during this decomposition must be related to the lattice energies of the two ionic substances involved.

Decomposition of the carbonates of Group 2 elements

The carbonates of Group 2 elements decompose as follows:

$$MCO_3(s) \rightarrow MO(s) + CO_2(g)$$

where M = Be, Mg, Ca, Sr, Ba and Ra.

As already stated, the thermal stability of the carbonates increases as the atomic (proton) numbers of the Group 2 elements increase. This trend is best explained in terms of the ability of the metal ion to polarise the carbonate ion and of the magnitude of the lattice energy for the oxide formed.

Small, highly charged, positive ions can polarise negative ions. That is, they are able to distort the electron density of the negative ion. Negative ions having a large ionic radius, such as the carbonate ion, are much more easily polarised than ions having a small ionic radius, such as an oxide ion. Since the cations M^{2+} (where M is one of the Group 2 elements) all have the same charge, it is the ion with the smallest ionic radius that polarises the carbonate ion the most. Be^{2+} has the smallest ionic radius and so it causes most polarisation of the carbonate ion. Once the carbonate ion is highly polarised, it forms an oxide ion and carbon dioxide. This means that $BeCO_3$ is the least thermally stable and $RaCO_3$ the most thermally stable, since Ra^{2+} has the largest ionic radius. An additional factor is the magnitude of the lattice energy of the oxide produced. This lattice energy is more exothermic with a small cation than with a large cation. So, in the decomposition of magnesium carbonate, the formation of magnesium oxide with a highly exothermic lattice energy can be considered as the driving force for the thermal decomposition.

Fig 22.29 **Magnesium oxide is often used to line furnaces. The exceptionally high lattice energy of magnesium oxide explains why it has a very high melting point**

There is more information on polarisation on page 85.

See questions 10 and 11. ■

The carbonates of Group 1 metals are much more thermally stable than those of Group 2 metals, because the cation has only a single rather than a double positive charge. Lithium carbonate is the least thermally stable, since Li^+ has a very small ionic radius and so can polarise the carbonate ion:

$$Li_2CO_3(s) \rightarrow Li_2O(s) + CO_2(g)$$

Thermal decomposition of nitrates of Groups 1 and 2

The thermal stability of the nitrates of Group 2 elements shows the same trend as the carbonates: namely, the stability increases with increasing atomic (proton) number. The reason for this trend in thermal stability is again that the polarising power of the M^{2+} decreases as the ionic radius increases.

$$2M(NO_3)_2(s) \rightarrow 2MO(s) + 4NO_2(g) + O_2(g)$$

where M = Mg, Ca, Sr, Ba and Ra.

Lithium nitrate thermally decomposes to form lithium oxide, nitrogen dioxide and oxygen.

Because the Group 1 nitrates have ions that normally are much less polarising, the decomposition products are the nitrites rather than the oxides.

$$2MNO_3(s) \rightarrow 2MNO_2(s) + O_2(g)$$

See question 10. ■

where M = Na, K, Rb and Cs.

10 SOLUBILITY OF IONIC SALTS

Most ionic salts dissolve in polar solvents such as water. A **solvent** is a liquid that can dissolve other substances. The most common solvent is water. A **solute** is the substance that is dissolved in the solvent. A **solution** is the name given to the mixture of the solute and the solvent. For example, a sodium chloride solution is simply a mixture of water, the solvent, and sodium chloride, the solute.

?

P What is the solvent and the solute in

(a) a mixture of alcohol and excess water and

(b) a solution of excess alcohol and water?

Solubility

The solubility of a substance is defined as the maximum concentration that can be obtained when the substance (the solute) is dissolved in a solvent. This concentration is usually measured either in grams of solute per 100 grams of solvent or in $mol\,dm^{-3}$. Throughout this section of the book, the chosen unit of solubility is $mol\,dm^{-3}$.

Solubility changes with temperature, so it should always be quoted

See question 12. ■

at a particular temperature, usually 298 K.

The dissolving process

This section considers what happens when an ionic salt dissolves in water.

In the regular arrangement of an ionic lattice, the cations are electrostatically attracted to the anions (see page 439). When an ionic salt dissolves, these electrostatic forces of attraction are broken and the anions and cations are free to move throughout the solution. In a polar solvent, such as water, the ions are surrounded by water molecules. Because the electronegativity of oxygen is much higher than that of hydrogen, the oxygen atom of a water molecule carries a small negative charge and so is weakly attracted to the cations. The hydrogen atoms of a water molecule carry a small positive charge and so they are weakly attracted to the anions. As a result, both cations and anions are surrounded by many water molecules.

When sodium chloride dissolves, aqueous sodium ions and aqueous chloride ions are formed:

$$NaCl(s) \rightarrow Na^+(aq) + Cl^-(aq)$$

The symbols $Na^+(aq)$ and $Cl^-(aq)$ represent the respective ion surrounded by many water molecules.

Overall, the dissolving process can be considered to be two processes:

- the breaking of the electrostatic attraction between ions in the ionic lattice, and
- the formation of aqueous ions with attractive forces being established between the water molecules and these ions.

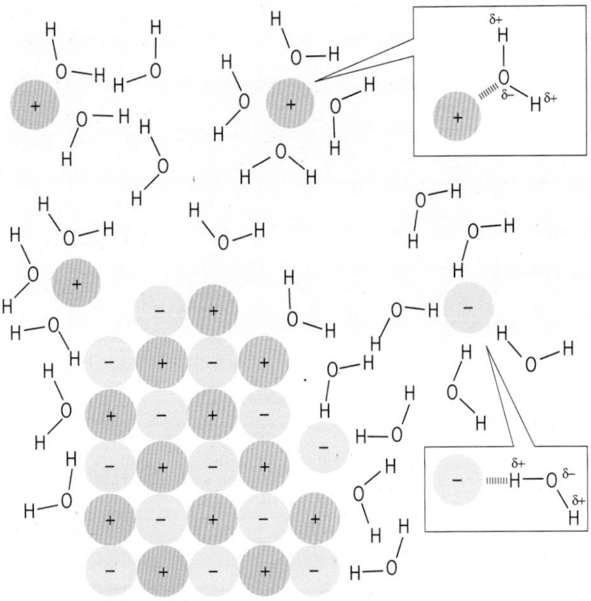

Energy transfers during dissolving

When an ionic compounds dissolves in water, there is always an energy transfer. Normally, the energy transfer process is modest and therefore there is only a small change in the temperature of the water. Occasionally, there is a dramatic change in water temperature, which is nearly always because a chemical reaction is taking place in the formation of the solution.

The **enthalpy change of solution,** ΔH_{soln}, is defined as the enthalpy change when one mole of solute is dissolved in a solvent and extra dilution causes no further change in enthalpy.

Fig 22.30 **The dissolving process**

Entropy and dissolving

On page 133, entropy is described as a measure of the disorder of a system. When an ionic solid dissolves to make a solution, the system becomes more disordered (increases in entropy), because all the particles in the solution are free to move, whereas in the solid the particles were in fixed positions (lower entropy). Processes in which the entropy – the amount of disorder – increases are favoured over those in which the entropy does not increase. This means that all substances should dissolve in a solvent. But this is not the case because entropy changes in the surroundings must also be taken into account. The energy transfer processes offer a simpler explanation.

Born–Haber cycles for dissolving

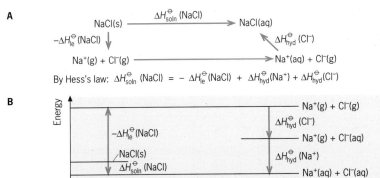

A

$$NaCl(s) \xrightarrow{\Delta H^{\ominus}_{soln} (NaCl)} NaCl(aq)$$

$-\Delta H^{\ominus}_{le} (NaCl) \downarrow \qquad \qquad \nwarrow \Delta H^{\ominus}_{hyd} (Cl^-)$

$$Na^+(g) + Cl^-(g) \longrightarrow Na^+(aq) + Cl^-(g)$$

By Hess's law: $\Delta H^{\ominus}_{soln} (NaCl) = -\Delta H^{\ominus}_{le} (NaCl) + \Delta H^{\ominus}_{hyd}(Na^+) + \Delta H^{\ominus}_{hyd}(Cl^-)$

B

Energy

$Na^+(g) + Cl^-(g)$

$-\Delta H^{\ominus}_{le} (NaCl)$

$\Delta H^{\ominus}_{hyd} (Cl^-)$

$Na^+(g) + Cl^-(aq)$

$NaCl(s)$

$\Delta H^{\ominus}_{hyd} (Na^+)$

$\Delta H^{\ominus}_{soln} (NaCl)$

$Na^+(aq) + Cl^-(aq)$

Fig 22.31 **Two ways of showing energy cycles for dissolving. The overall enthalpy change of solution is often small, since the exothermic contributions of the enthalpy changes of hydration are often cancelled out by the endothermic contribution of the lattice energy**

Fig 22.31 shows that the enthalpy change of solution is equal to the sum of three different energy transfer processes. The first of these processes is the lattice energy, the second is the enthalpy change of hydration of the cation, and the third the enthalpy change of hydration of the anion. The **enthalpy change of hydration** $\Delta H^{\ominus}_{hyd}$ is

?

Q Write down the equation for the reaction that corresponds to the enthalpy change of hydration of:

(a) a magnesium ion and

(b) a sulphate ion.

Remember to include the state symbols in your equation.

R Calculate the enthalpy change of solution for LiCl and for NaCl, given the following enthalpy changes in $kJ\,mol^{-1}$:

$\Delta H^{\ominus}_{latt}(LiCl) = -848$
$\Delta H^{\ominus}_{hyd}(Li^+) = -499$
$\Delta H^{\ominus}_{hyd}(Cl^-) = -381$
$\Delta H^{\ominus}_{latt}(NaCl) = -776$
$\Delta H^{\ominus}_{hyd}(Na^+) = -390$

the enthalpy change that occurs when 1 mole of a gaseous ions is dissolved in excess water to make one mole of aqueous ion.

Although the enthalpy change of hydration is very much a theoretical energy change, it does give a clear indication of the strength of the interaction of the water molecules with the ions. The enthalpy change of hydration is always exothermic, since it necessarily involves bond making between water molecules and the ions. The lattice energy contribution to the enthalpy change of solution is always endothermic, since it involves the breaking of the strong electrostatic interactions between the positive and the negative ions. The lattice energy and the sum of two enthalpy changes of hydration have roughly the same magnitude (but are of opposite sign), so that the enthalpy change of solution is always very small.

Enthalpy change of hydration and charge density

The magnitude of the enthalpy change of hydration depends on the ionic radius and the charge on the ion. The smaller the ionic radius and the higher the charge on the ion, the more exothermic the enthalpy change of hydration. This is because an ion with a small radius and a high charge has a high charge density, and therefore is strongly attracted towards water molecules; whereas an ion with a large radius and with a small charge has a low charge density, and is therefore only weakly attracted towards water molecules.

Within Group 2, the enthalpy change of hydration of M^{2+} becomes less exothermic as the atomic (proton) number increases:

$$M^{2+}(g) \xrightarrow{H_2O(l)} M^{2+}(aq) \quad \Delta H^{\ominus}_{hyd} = \text{enthalpy change of hydration}$$

Solubility trends of the Group 2 sulphates

On page 464, it states that the solubility of the sulphates decreases as the atomic (proton) number of the Group 2 elements increases. This trend can be explained in terms of the energy transfer processes that take place during dissolving.

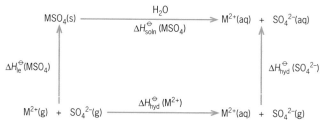

Fig 22.32 **Born–Haber cycle for the determination of the enthalpy of solution, $\Delta H^{\ominus}_{soln}$, for the sulphates of Group 2. Note that the enthalpy change of hydration of $SO_4^{2-}(g)$ is common to all the sulphates of Group 2**

As Fig 22.32 shows, the enthalpy change of hydration of the $SO_4^{2-}(g)$ is common to all Born–Haber cycles for all of the Group 2 sulphates, so it cannot be responsible for the solubility trend. The lattice energy of the Group 2 sulphates, $MSO_4(s)$, becomes less exothermic as the atomic number of M increases, but the change in lattice energy from $MgSO_4$ to $BaSO_4$ is quite small due to the large size of the sulphate ion.

However, the difference in the enthalpy change of hydration of $M^{2+}(g)$ from Mg^{2+} to Ba^{2+} is large because of the big difference in ionic radii between the very small ion Mg^{2+} and the large ion Ba^{2+}. Referring to Fig 22.32, it is the enthalpy change of hydration of $M^{2+}(g)$ that determines the solubility trend. The more exothermic this process, the more likely $MSO_4(s)$ is to dissolve.

To sum up: The enthalpy change of solution of $MSO_4(s)$ becomes less exothermic as the atomic number increases, hence the solubility decreases.

For the same reason, all salts of Group 2 elements that have an anion with a large ionic radius show the same solubility trend as the sulphates.

■ See questions 2 and 11.

Solubility trend of the Group 2 hydroxides

The solubility of hydroxides, $M(OH)_2(s)$, shows the opposite trend to that of the sulphates. Namely, as the atomic (proton) number increases, the solubility increases. This time, the key factor determining solubility is the lattice energy of the $M(OH)_2(s)$ rather than the enthalpy change of hydration. Since the hydroxide ion is small, there is a considerable difference between the very high lattice energy of magnesium hydroxide and the relatively low lattice energy of barium hydroxide.

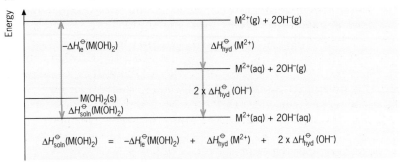

Fig 22.33 **The key factor in determining the solubility of the hydroxides of Group 2 is the change in the lattice energy from $Mg(OH)_2$ to $Ba(OH)_2$. $Mg(OH)_2$ has a much larger lattice energy than $Ba(OH)_2$, so the enthalpy change of solution of $Mg(OH)_2$ is less exothermic than that of $Ba(OH)_2$**

As Fig 22.33 shows, a large lattice energy makes a large endothermic contribution to the enthalpy change of solution and so reduces solubility. Other salts of Group 2 elements with small anions, such as the fluorides, display a solubility trend similar to that of the hydroxides.

■ See question 11.

Table 22.11 **Summary of solubility trends**

Anion	Magnesium salt	Barium salt
large, eg carbonate and sulphate	high solubility	very low solubility
small, eg hydroxide and fluoride	low solubility	high solubility

11 SOLUBILITY PRODUCT

The term 'insoluble' is not very suitable, since no ionic substance is completely insoluble in water. The dissociation process takes place even with substances referred to as insoluble, such as barium sulphate and calcium carbonate. Sometimes, the term 'sparingly soluble' is used to express the fact that the solubility of a substance is low. The term 'insoluble' should be taken to mean that the solubility of a substance is extremely low.

Solubility product

When calcium carbonate is shaken up with distilled water and left to settle, the water contains calcium ions and carbonate ions in very

See page 336 for an explanation of the equilibrium constant.

small concentrations. A dynamic equilibrium is set up that is best represented by the following equation:

$$CaCO_3(s) \rightleftharpoons Ca^{2+}(aq) + CO_3^{2-}(aq)$$

An expression can be written for the equilibrium constant for this process:

$$K_c = \frac{[Ca^{2+}(aq)][CO_3^{2-}]}{[CaCO_3(s)]}$$

The concentration of a solid is a constant and therefore can be included in a modified equilibrium constant known as the **solubility product, K_{sp}**:

$$K_{sp} = K_c[CaCO_3(s)]$$
$$= [Ca^{2+}(aq)][CO_3^{2-}(aq)]$$

The **solubility product** is the product of the concentrations of the aqueous ions formed when an insoluble or sparingly soluble ionic substance dissolves in water. Each concentration is raised to the power shown in the dissociation equation. For example, the dissociation equation for barium chromate(VI) is:

$$BaCrO_4(s) \rightleftharpoons Ba^{2+}(aq) + CrO_4^{2-}(aq)$$

Therefore: $K_{sp}(BaCrO_4) = [Ba^{2+}(aq)][CrO_4^{-}(aq)]$

For lead(II) iodide, the dissociation equation is:

$$PbI_2(s) \rightleftharpoons Pb^{2+}(aq) + 2I^-(aq)$$

Therefore: $K_{sp}(PbI_2) = [Pb^{2+}(aq)][I^-(aq)]^2$

?

S Write down expressions for the solubility product of the following sparingly soluble salts:

(a) calcium sulphate, $CaSO_4$,

(b) barium sulphate, $BaSO_4$,

(c) silver chromate(VI), Ag_2CrO_4,

(d) lead(II) chloride, $PbCl_2$.

Calculating solubility products

The solubility product of a salt can be calculated by substituting the appropriate concentrations into the expression for the solubility product.

?

T (a) The solubility of barium chromate(VI), $BaCrO_4$, at 298 K is 1.4×10^{-5} mol dm^{-3}. Calculate the solubility product for barium chromate(VI) at this temperature.

(b) The solubility of calcium hydroxide at 298 K is 1.25×10^{-2} mol dm^{-3}. Show that the solubility product for calcium hydroxide at this temperature is 7.81×10^{-6} mol^3 dm^{-9}

See questions 12 and 13. ■

EXAMPLE

Q What is the solubility product for calcium carbonate, given that the solubility of calcium carbonate at 298 K is 6.9×10^{-5} mol dm^{-3}?

A Assume that excess calcium carbonate is shaken with distilled water until equilibrium is attained. The solubility of calcium carbonate corresponds to the concentration of the aqueous calcium ions (or the aqueous carbonate ions) in the equilibrium solution:

	$CaCO_3(s) \rightleftharpoons$	$Ca^{2+}(aq)$	$+ CO_3^{2-}(aq)$
At start (before shaking)/mol dm^{-3}		0	0
At equilibrium/mol dm^{-3}		6.9×10^{-5}	6.9×10^{-5}

$$K_{sp}(CaCO_3) = [Ca^{2+}(aq)][CO_3^{2-}(aq)]$$
$$= (6.9 \times 10^{-5})(6.9 \times 10^{-5})$$
$$= 4.8 \times 10^{-9} \text{ mol}^2 \text{ dm}^{-6}$$

Notice in the Example that the solubility product has a unit that depends on the expression for the solubility product. In this case, it is concentration squared. The unit can be worked out by substituting the initial units into the expression for the solubility product:

$$K_{sp}(CaCO_3) = [Ca^{2+}(aq)][CO_3^{2-}(aq)]$$
$$= (\text{mol dm}^{-3})(\text{mol dm}^{-3}) = \text{mol}^2 \text{ dm}^{-6}$$

Calculating solubility

When the solubility product is known, it is possible to work out the solubility of the solvent.

■ See question 12 and 13.

EXAMPLE

Q The solubility product of magnesium fluoride at 298 K is $6.4 \times 10^{-9} \, mol^3 \, dm^{-9}$.
What is the solubility of magnesium fluoride at 298 K?

A Let s be the solubility of magnesium fluoride.

$$MgF_2(s) \rightleftharpoons Mg^{2+}(aq) + 2F^-(aq)$$

At equilibrium: $\qquad\qquad\qquad\quad s \qquad\quad 2s$

$$K_{sp}(MgF_2) = [Mg^{2+}(aq)][F^-(aq)]^2$$

Therefore: $6.4 \times 10^{-9} = s(2s)^2 = 4s^3$

Therefore: $s = 1.2 \times 10^{-3} \, mol \, dm^{-3}$ (to 2 sig. fig.).

U Calculate the solubility at 298 K of each of the following:

(a) barium fluoride, BaF_2
$K_{sp} = 1.7 \times 10^{-6} \, mol^3 \, dm^{-9}$

(b) calcium fluoride, CaF_2
$K_{sp} = 3.9 \times 10^{-11} \, mol^3 \, dm^{-9}$

(c) strontium sulphate, $SrSO_4$
$K_{sp} = 2.8 \times 10^{-7} \, mol^2 \, dm^{-6}$

Common ion effect

Since the process involved in the solubility product is a dynamic equilibrium, it is possible to change the position of equilibrium according to Le Chatelier's principle (see page 338).

Consider the solubility of barium carbonate. Aqueous barium ions and aqueous carbonate ions are in equilibrium with solid barium carbonate:

$$BaCO_3(s) \rightleftharpoons Ba^{2+}(aq) + CO_3^{2-}(aq)$$

When extra carbonate ions are added to the equilibrium mixture, the equilibrium shifts to the left to remove the extra carbonate ions. This causes a reduction in the solubility of barium carbonate, the concentration of aqueous barium ions having decreased. This is an example of the **common ion effect**. The solubility of barium carbonate is also reduced by the addition of extra aqueous barium ions.

The common ion effect can be demonstrated quantitatively by means of the solubility product.

V Calculate the solubility of barium chromate in $0.1 \, mol \, dm^{-3}$ barium chloride.

EXAMPLE

Q Calculate the solubility of barium chromate(VI) in **(a)** water and **(b)** $1.0 \, mol \, dm^{-3}$ potassium chromate(VI), given that the solubility product of barium chromate is $2 \times 10^{-10} \, mol^2 \, dm^{-6}$ at 298 K.

A

a) Let s be the solubility of barium chromate(VI).

$$BaCrO_4(s) \rightleftharpoons Ba^{2+}(aq) + CrO_4^{2-}(aq)$$

At equilibrium: $\qquad\qquad\qquad s \qquad\qquad\quad s$

Therefore: $K_{sp} = [Ba^{2+}(aq)][CrO_4^{2-}(aq)]$
$\qquad\qquad = s^2$

This gives: $s = 1.4 \times 10^{-5} \, mol \, dm^{-3}$.

b) In this calculation, it is necessary to consider dissolving barium chromate(VI) in aqueous potassium chromate(VI):

	$BaCrO_4(s) \rightleftharpoons$	$Ba^{2+}(aq) +$	$CrO_4^{2-}(aq)$
At start/mol dm^{-3}:		0	1.0
At equilibrium/mol dm^{-3}:		s	$(1.0 + s)$

Barium chromate(VI) is sparingly soluble in water. Therefore s is small compared with 1.0, and so $(s + 1.0)$ is approximately equal to 1.0.

Now: $\qquad\qquad K_{sp} = [Ba^{2+}(aq)][CrO_4^{2-}(aq)]$

$\qquad\qquad 2 \times 10^{-10} = s(1.0)$

This gives $s = 2 \times 10^{-10} \, mol \, dm^{-3}$.

Note that the solubility of barium chromate(VI) is very much smaller in potassium chromate(VI) than in water alone. This is the common ion effect in operation.

THE BARIUM MEAL

DOCTORS OFTEN NEED to use X-rays to look inside the intestine and the stomach for cancers, ulcers and blockages. But using X-rays to diagnose such conditions does pose a problem, because the stomach and the intestine are transparent to X-rays (they pass through), so no image is detected – unlike bone, which is opaque to X-rays.

To overcome this, doctors give their patients a barium meal containing insoluble barium sulphate and water. The stomach and intestine get coated with the barium sulphate which is opaque to X-rays, and so a shadow of these organs is cast on an X-ray photographic film.

Using barium sulphate has one drawback: aqueous barium ions are highly toxic. Even though barium sulphate is said to be insoluble, there is still a small concentration of aqueous barium ions in the stomach, which could lead to poisoning. The equilibrium equation shows the barium ions:

$$BaSO_4(s) \rightleftharpoons Ba^{2+}(aq) + SO_4^{2-}(aq)$$

The concentration of the aqueous barium ions is reduced by the common ion effect, brought about by magnesium sulphate also in the barium meal. The aqueous sulphate ions from the soluble magnesium sulphate shift the equilibrium to the left to lower the concentration of aqueous **barium** ions.

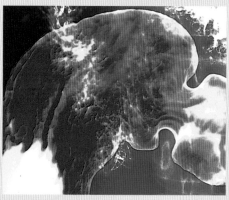

Fig 22.34 **The image of someone who has had a barium meal shows the stomach on the right and intestine on the left**

Precipitation

Precipitation is the formation of an insoluble solid when two solutions react together. For example, when a solution containing aqueous barium ions is mixed with a solution containing aqueous carbonate ions, a white precipitate of insoluble barium carbonate is formed:

$$Ba^{2+}(aq) + CO_3^{2-}(aq) \rightarrow BaCO_3(s)$$

Note that this is the opposite process to the dissolving of sparingly soluble barium carbonate in water. This means that the solubility product predicts the conditions for a precipitation reaction. In fact, precipitation occurs when the ionic product for the compound exceeds its solubility product. The ionic product of barium carbonate is the product of the concentration of the aqueous barium ion and of the aqueous carbonate ion.

See question 13.■

EXAMPLE

Q Will a precipitate of barium carbonate [$K_{sp}(BaCO_3) = 8.1 \times 10^{-9}$ mol^2 dm^{-6}] be formed from a solution that is both 0.1 mol dm^{-3} in aqueous barium ion and 1.0 mol dm^{-3} in aqueous carbonate ion?

A Ionic product (BaCO$_3$) = [Ba^{2+}(aq)][CO$_3^{2-}$(aq)]
                = 0.1 × 1.0 = 0.1 mol^2 dm^{-6}

$K_{sp}(BaCO_3) = 8.1 \times 10^{-9}$ mol^2 dm^{-6}

Since the ionic product is larger, a precipitate will be formed.

?

W Will a precipitate of magnesium fluoride,
$K_{sp}(MgF_2) = 6.4 \times 10^{-9}$ mol^3 dm^{-9}, be formed from a solution initially containing 1.0×10^{-3} mol dm^{-3} aqueous magnesium ions and 1.0×10^{-3} mol dm^{-3} aqueous fluoride ions? Explain your answer fully.

12 ALUMINIUM

So far, this chapter has concentrated on the behaviour of the Group 1 and 2 elements and their compounds. But there is one other metal that can reasonably be called reactive and that is aluminium. The surface of aluminium is covered by an impermeable layer of aluminium oxide that masks the true reactivity of the metal. Once this layer has been removed, the metal resembles magnesium in its reactivity.

Occurrence and manufacture of aluminium

Aluminium is estimated to make up 7.5 per cent of the Earth's crust, most of it as complex aluminates and aluminosilicates in clays, and also as bauxite, which is a form of aluminium oxide and hydroxide. It is not possible commercially to extract aluminium from clays and so bauxite is the major source of all aluminium metal used today.

Electrolytic manufacture of aluminium

The process dates back to 1886, when Charles Hall and Paul Heroult independently discovered a way to extract aluminium from bauxite using electrolysis. The bauxite mineral is mined and then purified to form pure aluminium hydroxide, which is in turn converted to pure aluminium oxide. This is the substance that is electrolysed to form aluminium.

The aluminium oxide is first dissolved in molten sodium aluminium fluoride (cryolite) and some calcium fluoride, and is then electrolysed. Electrolysis of pure aluminium oxide would be too expensive because of the very high temperature needed to melt it. The introduction of the two fluorides allows a much lower temperature to be employed. Because of shortages of sodium aluminium fluoride, some plants use sodium fluoride and aluminium fluoride instead.

Fig 22.35 **The thermite process involves the reaction of aluminium powder and iron(III) oxide. Aluminium is sufficiently reactive to displace iron from its oxide**

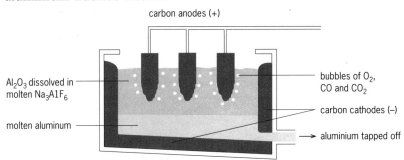

Fig 22.36 **The arrangement for the manufacture of aluminium by electrolysis**

A carbon (graphite) anode is used. Oxygen is by the discharge of oxide ions:

$$2O^{2-} \rightarrow O_2 + 4e^-$$

The high temperature of production is a nuisance, because the oxygen reacts with the carbon anode to form carbon dioxide. So the carbon anode is continually being replaced.

The carbon lining of the cell acts as the cathode, and aluminium is formed by the discharge of aluminium ions. The temperature in the cell is above the melting point of aluminium and so molten aluminium is formed. This sinks to the bottom of the cell, where it is run off and allowed to cool. The aluminium obtained is exceptionally pure, being at least 99.9 per cent aluminium.

■ See question 14.

?

X (a) Write down the equation to show the discharge of aluminium ions, Al^{3+}.

(b) Explain why the gaseous emissions from an aluminium smelter contain traces of hydrogen fluoride and fluorine.

Applications of aluminium

As soon as it was discovered, aluminium found many applications associated with its low density and its resistance to corrosion. More recent applications include foil (often incorrectly called tin foil) for use in the home and in packaging, double-glazed window frames, and now car engines and bodies.

Fig 22.37 **A car with aluminium bodywork**

Fig 22.38 **Aluminium and its alloys are used in the aviation industry because of their high strength and low density**

Chemical properties of aluminium

Table 22.12 **Some properties of aluminium**

Electron configuration	$1s^2 2s^2 2p^6 3s^2 3p^1$
Melting point	660 °C
Boiling point	2300 °C
Oxidation potential $E^{\ominus}_{\text{oxid}}$	+1.67 V
Density	2.70 g cm^{-3}

Information on anhydrous aluminium chloride is on page 440, and on polarisation on page 85.

Table 22.12 suggests that an aluminium atom should lose three electrons from an atom to form an aluminium ion. The loss of three electrons is always energetically more difficult than the loss of one or two electrons, and the cation formed will always be small and have a large charge density. This means that the small and highly charged cation is capable of attracting back the electrons it has lost in forming an ionic bond. An aluminium ion is said to polarise the anions, which leads to many aluminium compounds having covalent character.

In aqueous solution, six water molecules surround an aluminium ion to form a hydrated ion, $[\text{Al}(\text{H}_2\text{O})_6]^{3+}$(aq). For simplicity, this is often written as Al^{3+}(aq).

Reaction with air and oxygen

As already noted, aluminium forms an oxide layer on its surface which protects the rest of the metal from further corrosion. When heated in air or oxygen, aluminium powder burns to form aluminium oxide, a white ionic solid:

$$4\text{Al}(s) + 3\text{O}_2(g) \rightarrow 2\text{Al}_2\text{O}_3(s)$$

See question 14. ■ If the oxide layer is removed, for example by wiping the surface with mercury, then aluminium will react with water to form hydrogen.

Reaction with acids

Aluminium powder reacts with dilute sulphuric acid and dilute hydrochloric acid to give the corresponding aqueous aluminium salts. These reactions are initially very slow and need heat to speed up the reaction rate. But, once started, they become quite violent. The initial slow rate of reaction is due to the time it takes for the acid to react with the protective oxide layer before exposing the active metal:

$$2\text{Al}(s) + 6\text{H}^+(aq) \rightarrow 2\text{Al}^{3+}(aq) + 3\text{H}_2(g)$$

Surprisingly, aluminium does not react with pure nitric acid. It is therefore used as the lining of vessels to transport this acid.

Reaction with alkalis

Aluminium is unusual in that it reacts with both acids and alkalis. This property makes aluminium an **amphoteric** metal. Aluminium powder reacts vigorously – after a slow start – with warm aqueous sodium hydroxide to form hydrogen and aqueous sodium aluminate:

$$OH^-(aq) + 3H_2O(l) + Al(s) \rightarrow [Al(OH)_4]^-(aq) + H_2(g)$$

The formula for the aluminate ion is sometimes written as $[Al(OH)_6]^{3-}$ or $[Al(H_2O)_2(OH)_4]^-$.

Reaction with halogens

When one of the halogens is passed over heated aluminium, the corresponding halide is formed by direct combination. The halides formed have a large degree of covalent character:

$$2Al(s) + 3X_2(g) \rightarrow Al_2X_6(s) \text{ where X = a halogen atom.}$$

Compounds of aluminium

Most aluminium compounds have some covalent character, but when dissolved in water or as hydrated crystals, the compounds are ionic, containing the hydrated aluminium ion.

Aluminium oxide and aluminium hydroxide

Both these are white ionic amphoteric solids. With acids, they form the hydrated aluminium ion $[Al(H_2O)_6]^{3+}$; with alkalis they form the aluminate ion $[Al(OH)_4]^-$ in which the aluminium atom forms part of the anion.

Aluminium oxide is used as an abrasive and as a dehydrating agent, particularly in the formation of alkenes from alcohols. Aluminium hydroxide is used in the dyeing industry, since it can absorb coloured materials onto its surface. This property is also used to remove particulate matter from water during its purification. In this application, a solution of aluminium sulphate is added to the water where it forms aluminium hydroxide, which, as it settles, collects particulate matter and removes it from the water. The amount of aluminium sulphate used in this process has to be carefully controlled to prevent excess aluminium ions reaching domestic water supplies, since aluminium ions may be linked to Alzheimer's disease.

Fig 22.39 **Aluminium sulphate is used in water purification plants to remove solid particles, and its level has to be carefully monitored so as not to reach toxic levels**

Solutions of aluminium salts

Aqueous solutions of aluminium salts are highly acidic. So much so, that they can release carbon dioxide from sodium hydrogen carbonate. This acidity is due to hydrolysis and involves one of the water molecules in the aqueous aluminium cation being polarised to form an aqueous proton:

$$[Al(H_2O)_6]^{3+}(aq) \rightleftharpoons [Al(H_2O)_5OH]^{2+}(aq) + H^+(aq)$$

All aqueous solutions of aluminium salts react with aqueous hydroxide ions to give first a white precipitate of hydrated aluminium hydroxide and then, with excess hydroxide ions, a colourless solution of the aluminate ion. This reaction involves the progressive substitution of the water molecules bonded to the aluminium ion until four have been replaced by hydroxide ion:

$$[Al(H_2O)_6]^{3+}(aq) + OH^-(aq) \rightleftharpoons [Al(H_2O)_5OH]^{2+}(aq) + H_2O(l)$$

$$[Al(H_2O)_5OH]^{2+}(aq) + OH^-(aq) \rightleftharpoons [Al(H_2O)_4(OH)_2]^+(aq) + H_2O(l)$$

$$[Al(H_2O)_4(OH)_2]^+(aq) + OH^-(aq) \rightleftharpoons [Al(H_2O)_3(OH)_3](s) + H_2O(l)$$

$$[Al(H_2O)_3(OH)_3](s) + OH^-(aq) \rightleftharpoons [Al(H_2O)_2(OH)_4]^-(aq) + H_2O(l)$$

Y Would you expect aluminium carbonate to exist? Explain your answer.

Remember that the H^+ ion is really hydrated and could be written as $H_3O^+(aq)$. It is this ion that makes an aqueous solution acidic. This can be a severe problem in the environment when aluminium ions are released from the soil. This makes the very acidic and can lead to toxic metal ions being released into the soil followed by the destruction of plants and trees.

■ See question 14.

SUMMARY

■ Group 1 metals are highly reactive metals. Each atom loses one electron when it reacts. In compounds, the oxidation state of Group 1 metals is always +1.

■ Group 2 elements are less reactive than the Group 1 element in the same period. In compounds, the Group 2 elements always have an oxidation number of +2.

■ The ease with which an atom loses electrons increases with increasing atomic (proton) number in both Group 1 and Group 2.

■ The oxides and hydroxides of Group 1 and Group 2 elements are basic and when they dissolve in water, they form strongly alkaline solutions.

■ The nitrates of Group 1 (except lithium nitrate) thermally decompose to form the corresponding nitrites and oxygen, whereas the nitrates of Group 2 thermally decompose to give nitrogen dioxide, oxygen and the corresponding metal oxides. The thermal stability of the nitrates increases with increasing atomic (proton) number of the metal.

■ The carbonates of Group 1 (other than lithium carbonate) do not decompose at Bunsen temperatures but the carbonates of Group 2 do to give carbon dioxide and the metal oxides. The thermal stability of the carbonates increases with increasing atomic (proton) number of the metal.

■ Lattice energy is the enthalpy change when 1 mole of an ionic lattice is formed from its constituent ions in the gas phase. Lattice energy depends on the charge densities of the ions involved.

■ The solubility of the Group 2 sulphates, MSO_4, and the Group 2 carbonates, MCO_3, decreases with increasing atomic (proton) number of M. This trend is explained by the decrease in the magnitude of the enthalpy change of hydration of M^{2+}.

■ The solubility of the Group 2 hydroxides, $M(OH)_2$, increases with increasing atomic (proton) number of M. This trend is explained by the decrease in magnitude of the lattice energy of $M(OH)_2$.

■ The thermal decomposition of nitrates and carbonates is determined by the ability of the cation present to polarise the large carbonate and nitrate ions

■ Aluminium is manufactured by the electrolytic decomposition of molten aluminium oxide dissolved in sodium aluminium fluoride.

■ Aqueous aluminium salts are acidic due to the polarisation of water molecules by the very small and highly charged aluminium ion.

■ The solubility product can be used to explain the common ion effect.

QUESTIONS

1

a) State the electronic configurations of a sodium atom and of a magnesium atom and explain why these metals are regarded as s block elements.

b) State and explain the relative magnitudes of (i) the first ionisation energies and (ii) the second ionisation energies of sodium and magnesium.

c) The lattice energy of an ionic compound, MX, can be defined as the enthalpy change associated with the following endothermic process.

$$MX(s) \rightarrow M^+(g) + X^-(g)$$

(i) Use the date below to calculate the lattice energy of sodium chloride.

$$Na(s) + \tfrac{1}{2}Cl_2(g) \rightarrow NaCl(s) \quad \Delta H = -411\,kJ\,mol^{-1}$$

$$Na(s) \rightarrow Na(g) \quad \Delta H = +109\,kJ\,mol^{-1}$$

$$\tfrac{1}{2}Cl_2(g) \rightarrow Cl(g) \quad \Delta H = +121\,kJ\,mol^{-1}$$

$$Na(g) \rightarrow Na^+(g) + e^- \quad \Delta H = +494\,kJ\,mol^{-1}$$

$$Cl(g) + e^- \rightarrow Cl^-(g) \quad \Delta H = -364\,kJ\,mol^{-1}$$

(ii) Use the values below to discuss the factors which determine the relative magnitude of lattice energies.

	NaF	MgO
Lattice energy/kJ mol^{-1}	+918	+3791

d) Describe the reactions of the oxides of sodium and magnesium with water. Give an equation for each reaction and give the approximate pH of any solution formed.

[NEAB June 1994 6075/2, q.4]

2 This question concerns the elements from beryllium to barium in Group 2 of the Periodic Table.

a) What do the electron configurations of these elements have in common?

b) Give the electron configurations of a calcium atom and a strontium ion.

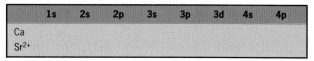

	1s	2s	2p	3s	3p	3d	4s	4p
Ca								
Sr^{2+}								

c) Sketch in the form of a graph the trends in
   (i) first ionisation energy, and
   (ii) second ionisation energy.
Of these elements, distinguishing clearly between the two.
Briefly explain the trend in first ionisation energy

d) Beryllium chloride is covalent but barium chloride is ionic.
How do you account for this?

e) Suggest why the solubilities of the sulphates of Group 2 decrease with increase in atomic number of the elements.
[ULEAC 1996 Module test 3 Specimen paper CH3, q.1]

3 Magnesium oxide is an ionic compound. It has a sodium chloride type of lattice structure in the solid state.

a) **(i)** Draw a Born–Haber cycle illustrating the formation of magnesium oxide from its elements.
   (ii) Define *lattice enthalpy*, ΔH.
   (iii) The lattice enthalpies, derived from a Born–Haber cycle, for MgO and NaCl are:

Compound	$\Delta H/kJ\,mol^{-1}$
magnesium oxide	−3889
sodium chloride	−771

   Explain why the value for magnesium oxide is so much larger than that for sodium chloride.

b) **(i)** Draw a diagram showing the lattice of solid magnesium oxide.
   (ii) Describe briefly how X-ray analysis may be used to investigate the structure of crystals.
   (iii) Explain why the structural properties of magnesium oxide make it a suitable material for the manufacture of fire bricks, which are used for lining furnaces.
[Oxford June 1994 9855/1, q.B6]

4

a) Tap water in many parts of the UK is 'hard' because of dissolved minerals. In limestone areas of the country, the water has temporary hardness because of dissolved calcium hydrogencarbonate.
   (i) Explain, with the aid of an equation, how limestone causes temporary hardness.
   (ii) Temporary hardness is removed by boiling the water. Explain why boiling removes this hardness.

b) Limestone is one of the raw materials used in the blast furnace for manufacturing iron.
   (i) What is the function of the limestone?
   (ii) Give an equation to show how it reacts.

c) A further use of limestone is to treat the waste gases from coal-fired power stations.
[Oxford June 1995 9955/52, q.3]

5 The major natural source of fluorine is the mineral fluorspar, which is mainly calcium fluoride, CaF_2.

a) **(i)** Construct a Born–Haber cycle for the formation of CaF_2 from its elements.

(ii) Use the cycle to calculate the lattice energy of $CaF_2(s)$. Incorporate the following data:
$\Delta H_{at}^{\ominus}(Ca) = +178\,kJ\,mol^{-1}$ $F(g) \rightarrow F^-(g)$
$\Delta H^{\ominus} = -328\,kJ\,mol^{-1}$
(this is the electron affinity of fluorine)
$\Delta H_f^{\ominus}(CaF_2) = -1220\,kJ\,mol^{-1}$
Bond energy for F–F = $158\,kJ\,mol^{-1}$
$Ca(g) \rightarrow Ca^{2+}(g)$ $\Delta H^{\ominus} = +1740\,kJ\,mol^{-1}$
[UCLES November 1994 Linear Chemistry 9250/1, q.2]

6
a) Draw and label carefully a Born–Haber cycle for the formation of calcium oxide.

b) Use the data below to calculate the value of the lattice energies of calcium oxide and iron(II) oxide.

Standard enthalpy change of formation of calcium oxide	$-635\,kJ\,mol^{-1}$
Standard enthalpy change of formation of iron(II) oxide	$-278\,kJ\,mol^{-1}$
Standard enthalpy change of atomisation of calcium	$+178\,kJ\,mol^{-1}$
Standard enthalpy change of atomisation of iron	$+416\,kJ\,mol^{-1}$
Standard molar first ionisation energy of calcium and the standard second ionisation energy of calcium	$+1735\,kJ\,mol^{-1}$
Standard molar first ionisation energy of iron and the standard molar second ionisation energy of iron	$+2320\,kJ\,mol^{-1}$
Standard enthalpy change of atomisation of oxygen	$+249\,kJ\,mol^{-1}$ of oxygen atoms
Standard molar enthalpy first electron affinity and second electron affinity of oxygen	$+657\,kJ\,mol^{-1}$

c) Suggest why the order of lattice energies is as given by your calculation.

d) Calcium(III) oxide has never been formed, and its enthalpy change of formation is thought to be positive.
   (i) Which terms in the Born-Haber cycle for calcium(III) oxide would be most different from those in the cycle for calcium(II) oxide, and how would they differ ?
   (ii) What is the largest factor causing the enthalpy change of formation of calcium(III) oxide to be endothermic?
[AEB 1996 Specimen paper 0654/3, q.5]

7 The formation of potassium chloride, KCl, from its elements in their standard states can be illustrated by a Born–Haber cycle. The processes which take place in the cycle are shown in the table.

Process	Name
$K(s) \rightarrow K(g)$	
$K(g) \rightarrow K^+(g) + e^-$	
$\frac{1}{2}Cl_2(g) \rightarrow Cl(g)$	
$Cl(g) + e^- \rightarrow Cl^-(g)$	
$K^+(g) + Cl^-(g) \rightarrow KCl(s)$	
$K(s) + \frac{1}{2}Cl_2(g) \rightarrow KCl(s)$	

a) (i) Copy out and complete the table.
(ii) Construct a Born–Haber cycle to show the formation of potassium chloride from its elements.

b) The lattice energy of KCl is −718 kJ mol⁻¹ but that of NaCl is −788 kJ mol⁻¹.
(i) Explain clearly what you understand by the term lattice energy.
(ii) Suggest an explanation for the difference in these values.

[UCLES Summer 1995 4826.1]

8

a) The diagram below shows an outline, *not to scale*, of the Born–Haber cycle used for the calculation of the lattice energy of strontium chloride from experimental data.

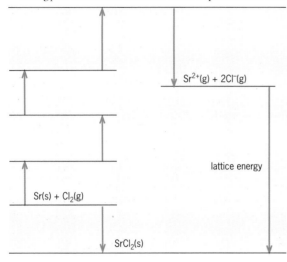

Sr²⁺(g) + 2Cl⁻(g)

lattice energy

Sr(s) + Cl₂(g)

SrCl₂(s)

Fig 22.Q8

(i) On each of the four empty lines in the Born–Haber cycle diagram above, write in the formulae for the species present at that stage in the cycle. The diagram is based on the ionization of strontium being a two-stage process.
(ii) From the table below, select the data required for the calculation of the lattice energy of strontium chloride, and write these in the correct spaces on the Born–Haber cycle diagram above.

$\Delta H^{\ominus}_{at,298}[Sr(s)]$	$= +164.4\,kJ\,mol^{-1}$
$\Delta H^{\ominus}_{at,298}[\frac{1}{2}Cl_2(g)]$	$= +121.7\,kJ\,mol^{-1}$
First ionization energy of strontium	$= +550.0\,kJ\,mol^{-1}$
Second ionization energy of strontium	$= +1064\,kJ\,mol^{-1}$
Electron affinity of chlorine	$= -348.8\,kJ\,mol^{-1}$
$\Delta H^{\ominus}_{f,298}[SrCl_2(s)]$	$= -828.9\,kJ\,mol^{-1}$

(iii) Using your completed Born–Haber cycle, calculate a value for the lattice energy of strontium chloride.

b) Theoretical values have been obtained for the standard enthalpy changes of formation of the two hypothetical compounds SrCl(s) and SrCl₃(s):

$\Delta H^{\ominus}_{f,298}[SrCl(s)] = -198\,kJ\,mol^{-1}$
$\Delta H^{\ominus}_{f,298}[SrCl_3(s)] = +571\,kJ\,mol^{-1}$

(i) Comment on the likely energetic stability of these compounds in relation to:
1. the elements strontium and chlorine,
2. SrCl₂(s).

(ii) Theoretical values for the lattice energies for these two compounds have been calculated:
Lattice energy for SrCl(s) $= -632\,kJ\,mol^{-1}$
Lattice energy for SrCl₃(s) $= -4560\,kJ\,mol^{-1}$
Suggest reasons for:
1. the large difference in the values of the lattice energies between SrCl₂(s) and SrCl(s).
2. the large difference in the values of the standard enthalpy changes of formation between SrCl₂(s) and SrCl₃(s).

[ULEAC June 1991 Nuffield 089/1, q.6]

9 The Born–Haber cycle below represents the energy changes occurring at 298 K when potassium hydride, KH, is formed from its elements.

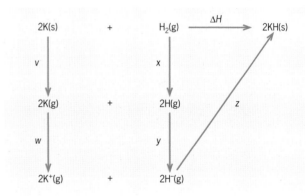

Fig 22.Q9

Enthalpy of atomisation of potassium $= +90\,kJ\,mol^{-1}$
First ionisation energy of potassium $= +418\,kJ\,mol^{-1}$
Bond enthalpy of hydrogen $= +436\,kJ\,mol^{-1}$
First electron affinity of hydrogen $= -78\,kJ\,mol^{-1}$
Lattice enthalpy of potassium hydride $= -710\,kJ\,mol^{-1}$

a) In terms of the letters v to z write down expressions for:
(i) ΔH for the reaction $2K(s) + H_2(g)$ 2KH(s);
(ii) the first ionisation energy of potassium;
(iii) the first electron affinity of hydrogen;
(iv) the lattice enthalpy of KH. (The lattice enthalpy is the enthalpy charge which accompanies the formation of 1 mol of KH(s) from its gaseous ions.)

b) Which of v to y is:
(i) the most exothermic;
(ii) the most endothermic?

c) **(i)** Calculate the value of ΔH, showing all your working.
(ii) Calculate the standard enthalpy of formation of KH.

d) **(i)** Write a balanced equation for the reaction of potassium hydride with water.
(ii) On complete reaction with water, 0.10 g of potassium hydride yielded a solution requiring 25 cm^3 of 0.10 mol dm^{-3} hydrochloric acid for neutralization. Calculate the relative atomic mass of potassium from this information.

[ULEAC June 1992 9080/1 q.4]

10 Nitrates and carbonates of the Group 2 elements thermally decompose.

a) What is meant by thermal decomposition?

b) Write down an equation with state symbols for the decomposition of magnesium nitrate

c) **(i)** Write an equation for the thermal decomposition of magnesium carbonate.
(ii) Explain why barium carbonate needs to be heated to a much higher than magnesium carbonate temperature before it will thermally decompose.

[UCLES Summer 1995 9250/3 q.5]

11 Explain the following:

a) Magnesium fluoride is much less soluble in water than barium fluoride but magnesium sulphate is much more soluble than barium sulphate.

b) Lithium carbonate will decompose when heated in a bunsen flame but sodium carbonate is not.

12 The diagram below illustrates an example of a *dynamic equilibrium*.

saturated solution of silver chloride

silver chloride solid, AgCl(s)

Fig 22.Q12

a) Explain what you understand by the terms:
(i) saturated solution,
(ii) dynamic equilibrium.
(iii) Write an equation, including state symbols, to illustrate the dynamic equilibrium.

The solubility product K_{sp} for silver chloride has the numerical value of 2.0×10^{-10} at 298 K.

b) **(i)** Write an expression, stating units for the solubility product of silver chloride.
(ii) Calculate the concentration of silver chloride in solution.
(iii) Calculate the maximum mass of silver chloride that can be dissolved in 1 dm^3 of water under these conditions.

[UCLES March 1995, Modular Chemistry 4826, q.2]

13 Chrome yellow, the pigment used for yellow road markings, is lead(II) chromate(VI), $PbCrO_4$.

a) Write an equation, with state symbols, for the formation by precipitation of $PbCrO_4$.

b) The solubility product of $PbCrO_4$ at 15 °C is 1.69×10^{-14}
(i) Write an expression for the solubility product, K_{sp}, of $PbCrO_4$.
(ii) What is the solubility, in mol dm^{-3}, of $PbCrO_4$?
(iii) Concentrated aqueous lead(II) nitrate is added dropwise to 0.010 mol dm^{-3} potassium chromate(VI).

What appears is the concentration, in mol dm^{-3} of lead(II) ions when the first trace of precipitate appears?

UCLES March 1995, Modular Chemistry 4826 q.2]

14 Aluminium is used to make drink cans.

a) Describe giving essential details how aluminium is manufactured from alumina.

b) Explain why aluminium does not corrode easily in moist air.

c) Describe the effect of adding aqueous sodium hydroxide drop by drop until it is in excess to aqueous aluminium sulphate. Write equations to describe the reactions that take place.

THERMAL STABILITY OF SALTS OF GROUP 1 AND 2 ELEMENTS

The anhydrous carbonates, chlorides, nitrates and sulphates of lithium, sodium, potassium, magnesium, calcium, strontium and barium were separately heated in a thick-walled Pyrex test-tube, under similar conditions, by using the hottest flame of a Bunsen burner. The apparatus used is shown in Fig 22.A1.

No gas was produced when the chlorides and the sulphates were heated.

1 Suggest a reason why no gases were produced when the chlorides and the sulphates were heated.

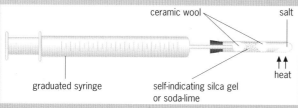

Fig 22.A1

The soda–lime (a mixture of solid sodium hydroxide and calcium hydroxide) was present to remove any acidic gases produced when the nitrates were heated, so that only neutral gases were collected in the gas syringe. The volume of gas obtained was measured every 10 seconds and results are shown in Tables 22.A1 and 22.A2.

2

a) Write down equations, including state symbols, to show the thermal decomposition of all the nitrates used in the experiments.

b) Write down the equation to show the decomposition of magnesium carbonate.

Table 22.A1 Volumes of gas from heated carbonates

Name of salt	Volume of gas collected in syringe after times/cm³										
	0s	10s	20s	30s	40s	50s	60s	70s	80s	90s	100s
lithium carbonate	0	1	4	20	47	76					
sodium carbonate	0	0	0	0	0	1	4	7	10	13	16
potassium carbonate	0	0	0	0	0	0	0	0	1	2	3
magnesium carbonate	0	4	15	35	61	91					
calcium carbonate	0	0	0	0	0	0	1	2	3	4	5
strontium carbonate	0	0	0	0	0	0	0	0	0	0	0
barium carbonate	0	0	0	0	0	0	0	0	0	0	0

Table 22.A2 Volumes of gas from heated nitrates

Name of salt	Volume of gas collected in syringe after times/cm³										
	0s	10s	20s	30s	40s	50s	60s	70s	80s	90s	100s
lithium nitrate	0	0	2.5	11	24	38	52	65	79		
sodium nitrate	0	0	1	4	13	22	31	40	49	58	67
potassium nitrate	0	0	0	1.5	4	8	12	16	20	24	28
magnesium nitrate	0	3	8	29	72						
calcium nitrate	0	0	3.5	10	25	47	79				
strontium nitrate	0	0	0	2	7	16	32	52	72	92	
barium nitrate	0	0	0	1	2.5	6.5	18	30	42	54	66

3 A gas syringe was used to collect the gases produced. Look at the results for calcium nitrate. Suggest why there are no readings taken after 60 seconds.

4

a) Plot the results shown in Table 22.A1 on graph paper. Draw a line of best fit between the points for each salt. For each line, calculate the gradient of the straight line portion. This is the rate of thermal decomposition of the carbonate.

b) Plot the results shown in Table 22.A2 on graph paper. Draw a curve of best fit between the points for each salt. This is the rate of thermal decomposition of the nitrate.

5 By referring to your graphs or the tables:

a) deduce which salts, the carbonates or the nitrates, are less stable towards heat;

b) arrange the nitrates in decreasing order of thermal stability, starting with the most stable nitrate;

c) arrange the carbonates in decreasing order of thermal stability, starting with the most stable nitrate.

6

a) Copy out and complete the following table. You will need to refer to Table 22.10 on page 467.

Table 22.A3

Ion	Charge density	Rate of thermal decomposition of nitrate
lithium		
sodium		
potassium		
magnesium		
calcium		
strontium		
barium		

b) Plot charge density against the rate of thermal decomposition of each nitrate. Comment on the curve that you get.

REACTIVE METALS AND LATTICE ENERGY

The chapter concentrates on the chemical and physical properties of the reactive metals of Groups 1 and 2. It discusses lattice energy and introduces enthalpy changes in relation to chemical reactions of these metals and their compounds. Use the Chapter Map to identify the important concepts in this chapter, and review them again if there are any you feel unsure about.

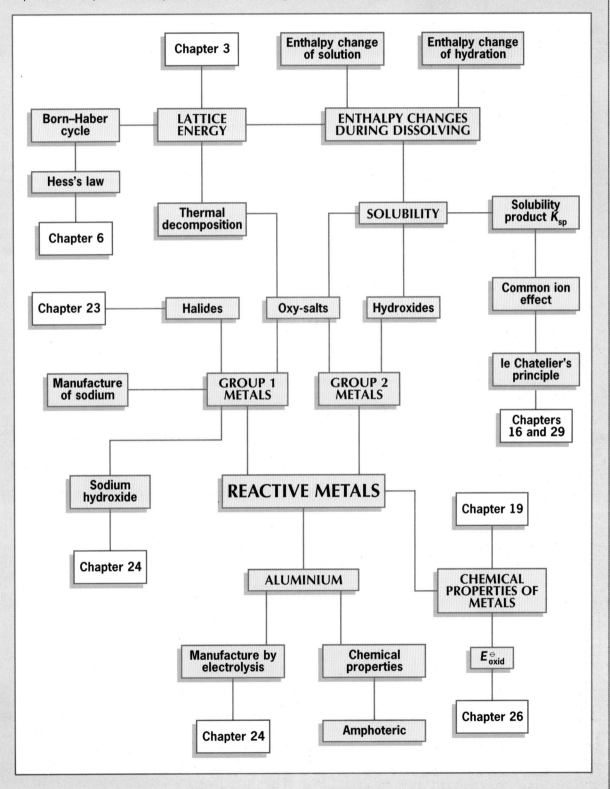

Photochromic spectacles are easy on the eyes

WE FIND IT QUITE UNCOMFORTABLE on the eyes to move rapidly in and out of brilliant sunlight and shadow, even if we are wearing sunglasses. Our eyes cannot adjust quickly enough to sudden changes of light intensity – that is, unless the sunglasses are made from photochromic glass which compensates for changes in brightness.

Lens glass is usually made photochromic by adding tiny amounts of silver chloride and copper(I) chloride to the molten glass as it cools trapping the crystals within the structure of the glass. When bright sunlight strikes the glass, the silver chloride decomposes to form metallic silver, which darkens the glass. This reduces the intensity of the light reaching the eyes. At the same time, chlorine atoms are formed and they react with copper(I) ions to form copper(II) ions and chloride ions. As soon as the exposure to bright light ends, the copper(II) ions are oxidised by silver atoms to reform silver chloride and copper(I) chloride. This lightens the glass and allows all the available light to reach the eyes.

In this way, spectacle lenses can be made which darken or lighten according to the intensity of the light, making it comfortable for people to keep their sunglasses on, whether they are in bright light or shadow.

1 WHAT ARE THE HALOGENS?

Halogens is the collective name given to the non-metal elements in Group 7 of the Periodic Table. The name is derived from *hals* (the Greek for salt) and the suffix *gen* (meaning producer). It was first used by the Swedish scientist Jöns Berzelius (1779–1884) to indicate that chlorine, bromine and iodine occurred in sea water. Chlorine was first prepared in 1774 by the Swedish chemist Carl Wilhelm Scheele, but he did not recognise it as an element. It was Humphry Davy who, in 1810, recognised chlorine as an element and named it after the Greek word for green, *chloros*. In the same way, iodine was derived from *ioides* (the Greed word for violet-like) and bromine from *bromos* (the Greek word for stench). It was not until 1940 that the last member of the halogens, astatine, a radioactive element, was prepared artificially.

The halogens are commercially of great importance although the use of many chlorine-containing compounds is controversial for environmental reasons. Chlorine and fluorine are both used in the production of polymers, such as PVC and PTFE. Many insecticides contain chlorine, but there is concern over the use of these compounds despite their obvious advantage in killing disease-carrying and crop-eating insects. Bromine has a variety of applications, including the manufacture of fuel additives, and of soil fumigators such as 1,2-dibromoethane and bromomethane, which kill pests found in the soil. Silver bromide and silver iodide both have applications in photography.

Fig 23.1 **Bromomethane is used as a soil fumigator for high value crops such as strawberries**

Fig 23.2 **We take it for granted that the water we drink is sterile. Chlorine is used to remove bacteria from our water supply**

The environmental issues concerned with chlorine and its compounds are covered on pages 219 and 512

2 PROPERTIES OF THE HALOGENS

The halogens are typical non-metals in terms of their chemical properties. Their physical properties are typical for non-metals with a simple molecular structure.

Physical properties

The halogens have relatively low melting and boiling points and are very poor conductors of heat and electricity.

All the halogens have diatomic molecules, which in the solid state are arranged in a simple molecular lattice. Halogen molecules are held in place by weak intermolecular forces known as induced dipole–induced dipole attraction. These forces result from asymmetric distribution of electrons within each halogen molecule. This produces an instantaneous dipole, which induces dipoles in neighbouring molecules. Such a weak attractive force between molecules is easily overcome, so the elements have low melting points and boiling points. The simple molecular structure has no free electrons, so the halogens cannot conduct electricity either as a solid or as a liquid.

Fig 23.3 **At room temperature and atmospheric pressure, chlorine is a pale green gas, bromine an orange liquid and iodine a dark purple solid**

?

A The appearance of the halogens has an observable trend at room temperature and atmospheric pressure. Predict the colour and physical state for fluorine and for astatine under these conditions.

Fig 23.4 **A temporary dipole is set up in an iodine molecule when its electrons move to become distributed asymmetrically, with the electron density at one end of the molecule greater than that at the other end. The top diagram shows how the electron density is temporarily distorted. The temporary dipole induces dipoles in neighbouring molecules and an intermolecular force is set up (bottom diagram). This force is quite weak. All the halogens form solids with this type of intermolecular force. The larger the halogen molecule (and the more electrons), the easier it is to distort the electron density and increase the intermolecular forces. Hence, the melting point of the halogens increases with increasing atomic number**

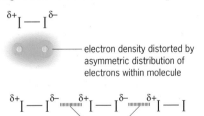

$\overset{\delta+}{I} \text{—} \overset{\delta-}{I}$

— electron density distorted by asymmetric distribution of electrons within molecule

$\overset{\delta+}{I} \text{—} \overset{\delta-}{I} \cdots \overset{\delta+}{I} \text{—} \overset{\delta-}{I} \cdots \overset{\delta+}{I} \text{—} I$

induced dipole–induced dipole attraction

■ See question 1.

Weak intermolecular forces in elements are discussed on page 422.

Fig 23.5 **Solid iodine has a cubic structure. The lines of short strokes represent the weak intermolecular forces that hold the iodine molecules in place within the lattice. The other solid halogens have a similar simple molecular lattice**

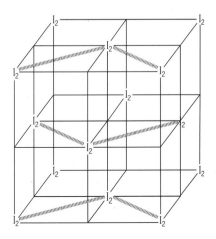

B Astatine is the last member of the halogens.

(a)(i) What is the atomic (proton) number for astatine?

(ii) How many electrons does astatine have in the outer shell of its atom?

(iii) Predict the melting point, boiling point, covalent radius and electronegativity of astatine.

(b) What is meant by the term electronegativity? Why does the electronegativity of the halogens decrease with increasing atomic (proton) number?

Check your answers on page 83.

Some anhydrous metal halides, such as aluminium chloride and iron(III) chloride, have a simple molecular structure.

C Write down the electron configurations for

(a) chloride ion, Cl⁻, and

(b) bromide ion, Br⁻.

See question 1. ■

Table 23.1 **Properties of four halogens**

Halogen	Melting point/°C	Boiling point/°C	Atomic (covalent) radius/pm	Electronegativity	Electron configuration
fluorine	−223	−188	64	4	$1s^22s^22p^5$
chlorine	−101	−34	99	3	$1s^22s^22p^63s^23p^5$
bromine	−7	59	114	2.8	$[Ar]3d^{10}4s^24p^5$
iodine	114	187	133	2.4	$[Kr]4d^{10}5s^25p^5$

Chemical properties

Halogens react by gaining electrons to form an anion in ionic halides, or by sharing electrons to form a covalent bond in molecular halides. In both cases the halogen atom attains a noble gas electron configuration. Most metals form ionic halides and most non-metals form molecular halides. The ability to gain an electron is typical of a non-metal atom.

The halogens as oxidising agents

Since their atoms accept electrons, the halogens are oxidising agents and in a reaction they are reduced. Of the halogens, fluorine is the most powerful oxidising agent and astatine the least. This can be explained by the relative size of their atoms. The fluorine atom is the smallest with fewer inner-shell shielding electrons, so its nucleus can have a greater attraction for an extra electron. The reduction potentials, $E^{\ominus}_{red}$, also illustrate this trend, with the reaction of a fluorine molecule to give a fluoride ion having a very positive reduction potential. (Electrode potentials are covered in Chapter 26.)

Table 23.2 **Reduction potentials ($E^{\ominus}_{red}$) for reaction $X_2 + 2e^- \rightarrow 2X^-$**

Half reaction	Reduction potential $E^{\ominus}_{red}$/V
$F_2 + 2e^- \rightarrow F^-$	+2.87
$Cl_2 + 2e^- \rightarrow 2Cl^-$	+1.36
$Br_2 + 2e^- \rightarrow 2Br^-$	+1.07
$I_2 + 2e^- \rightarrow 2I^-$	+0.54

Fluorine always has an oxidation number of −1 in its compounds. It can oxidise other substances by gaining an electron from them.

Displacement reactions

Since fluorine is the most reactive halogen, it can react with the halide ion of any of the other halogens. Fluorine becomes the fluoride ion and the free halogen (chlorine, bromine or iodine) is formed from the halide ion. This is called a **displacement reaction**. Experiments are not normally carried out with fluorine because its extraordinary reactivity makes it extremely dangerous. For example, if inhaled, flourine can seriously damage the respiratory tract.

In aqueous solution, chlorine displaces bromide ions and iodide ions to form bromine and iodine respectively:

$$Cl_2(aq) + 2Br^-(aq) \rightarrow 2Cl^-(aq) + Br_2(aq)$$

During this reaction, the colour of the mixture becomes orange, indicating that the element bromine has been produced. In the same way, aqueous bromine displaces aqueous iodide ion to form iodine.

The displacement reaction is an example of a redox reaction. This is because the halogen that reacts is reduced by gaining an electron to form the halide ion, and the halide ion is oxidised by loss of an electron to form the halogen.

See question 2. ■

MANUFACTURE OF BROMINE

THE CONCENTRATION of bromide ion in normal sea-water is between 65 and 70 ppm. Therefore, a large quantity of sea-water has to be processed to make significant quantities of bromine. Inland seas, such as the Dead Sea, have considerably higher concentrations of bromide ion and provide a much better feedstock (Fig 23.6).

Chlorine is used to liberate bromine by a displacement reaction. It is bubbled through the acidified sea-water and the bromine formed is removed as a gas from the water by blowing air through it:

$$Cl_2(g) + 2Br^-(aq) \rightarrow Br_2(aq) + 2Cl^-(aq)$$

The bromine vapour formed is difficult to handle and so is converted back into bromide ion by reaction with sulphur dioxide and water:

$$Br_2(g) + SO_2(g) + H_2O(l) \rightarrow H_2SO_4(aq) + 2HBr(aq)$$

This makes a much more concentrated solution of bromide ion, from which it is easier to produce high-purity bromine. A second displacement reaction with chlorine yields bromine vapour, which can be condensed and then purified by distillation.

Fig 23.6 **The Dead Sea is rich in dissolved minerals. It is about 60 times more concentrated in bromide ion than normal sea-water**

?

D State whether a reaction takes place when the following substances are mixed. If a reaction takes place, write a balanced ionic equation for the reaction:

(a) aqueous iodine and aqueous potassium bromide,

(b) aqueous chlorine and aqueous sodium iodide,

(c) aqueous chlorine and aqueous calcium fluoride,

(d) aqueous iodine and aqueous sodium astatide.

3 IONIC HALIDES

Most metals react with the halogens to form ionic halides. This reaction is necessarily a redox reaction, in which the metal is oxidised and the non-metal is reduced. Electrons are transferred to halogen atoms from metal atoms. The reaction of a metal with the halogens varies with the halogen. For instance, the reaction between a metal and fluorine is faster, more exothermic and more violent than that between the same metal and iodine.

Since halogens are good oxidising agents, the halide formed often has the metal in one of its higher oxidation states if the metal has more than one oxidation state. So, when chlorine is passed over hot iron wire it forms iron(III) chloride, $FeCl_3$, rather than iron(II) chloride. Similarly, copper and chlorine forms copper(II) chloride, $CuCl_2$, rather than copper (I) chloride.

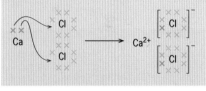

Fig 23.7 **Calcium chloride is an ionic compound. Two electrons are lost by the calcium atom, one to each chlorine atom. This transfer of electrons means that both chlorine atoms and the calcium atom have a stable octet of electrons. The Ca^{2+} and two Cl^- are held together by strong electrostatic attractions, called ionic bonds. Most metal halides are ionic compounds and have metal atoms transferring electrons to halogen atoms. Note: only the outer electrons are shown in the dot and cross diagram**

?

E (a) Write equations for the reaction between **(i)** iron and chlorine, **(ii)** copper and chlorine and **(iii)** iron and fluorine.

(b) What is the name of the product formed in the reaction between **(i)** chromium and chlorine, **(ii)** zinc and chlorine and **(iii)** barium and iodine?

■ See question 3.

Action of water on ionic chlorides

Ionic chlorides, such as sodium chloride, dissolve in water to form a neutral solution. However, ionic chlorides with covalent character dissolve to form an acidic solution due to hydrolysis. Metal halides in which the metal has an oxidation state of +3 have a high degree of covalent character. These halides have a metal cation with a charge of 3+, which is highly polarising because it has a small ionic radius and a high charge. That is, it has a high charge density (see page 467).

When metal chlorides with covalent character are added to water, the ionic lattice breaks up and the chloride ion and the metal ion are surrounded by water molecules. The highly charged metal ion polarises one of the water molecules to form a proton, so the solution becomes acidic. Chromium(III) chloride, iron(III) chloride and aluminium chloride all form acidic solutions when they are added to water, due to the polarisation of a water molecule by an M^{3+} ion:

$$[Cr(H_2O)_6]^{3+}(aq) \rightleftharpoons [Cr(H_2O)_5OH]^{2+}(aq) + H^+(aq)$$

The action of water on aluminium chloride is discussed on page 443.

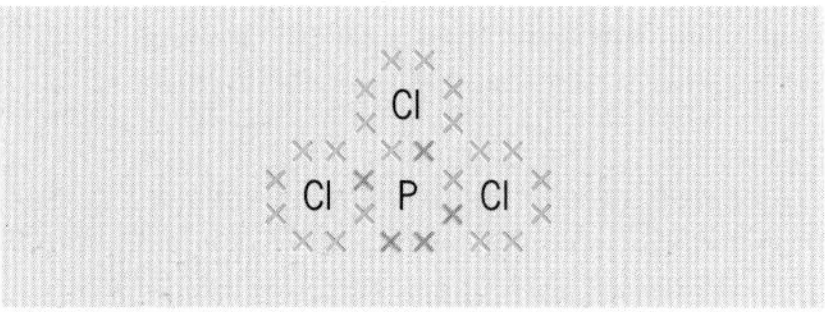

Fig 23.8 **Phosphorus(III) chloride is a covalent compound that forms a simple molecule, PCl$_3$. Electrons are shared so that all the atoms attain a stable octet of electrons. All non-metal halides form covalent compounds, with the halogen atom attaining a stable octet. Sometimes, the other atom involved expands its octet. Note: only the outer electrons are shown in the dot and cross diagram**

4 COVALENT HALIDES

Almost all non-metals react with fluorine and chlorine to form covalent halides. The halogen atom shares electrons to make a single covalent bond (Fig 23.8). Very often, the halide contains the element in its highest possible oxidation state. In the reaction between phosphorus and chlorine, the reaction can be controlled to make either phosphorus(III) chloride or phosphorus(V) chloride:

$$2P(s) + 3Cl_2(s) \rightarrow 2PCl_3(l)$$

$$2P(s) + 5Cl_2(g) \rightarrow 2PCl_5(s)$$

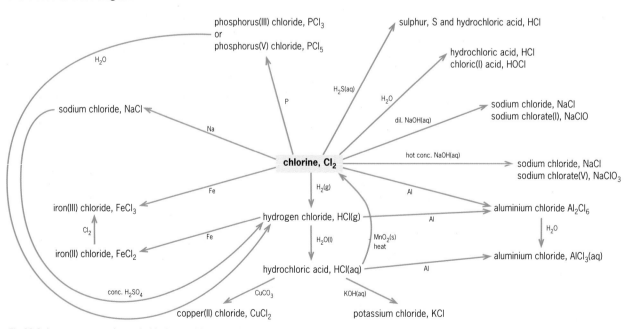

Fig 23.9 **Important reactions of chlorine and its compounds**

NOBLE GAS COMPOUNDS

UNTIL 1962, chemists believed that the noble gases, such as xenon, did not react. Since then, several compounds containing xenon and fluorine have been prepared. Xenon difluoride, for example, is formed when excess xenon is heated with fluorine gas at 400 °C:

$$Xe(g) + F_2(g) \rightarrow XeF_2(g)$$

Xenon difluoride forms colourless crystals, which are stable at room temperature in a dry atmosphere. It is quite surprising that this compound should be so stable. Xenon has a stable octet of electrons, and so by reacting with fluorine and attaining an oxidation number of +2 in the difluoride, it should lose its stability.

By changing the mole ratios of xenon to fluorine, it is also possible to prepare xenon tetrafluoride, XeF_4, and xenon hexafluoride, XeF_6. XeF_4 crystals are shown on page 75.

All the xenon fluorides are very powerful oxidising agents, since xenon in a positive oxidation state is less stable than elemental xenon with an oxidation number of 0. Xenon difluoride oxidises water to form xenon, hydrofluoric acid and oxygen:

$$2XeF_2(s) + 2H_2O(l) \rightarrow 2Xe(g) + 4HF(aq) + O_2(g)$$

Read more about compounds of noble gases on page 68.

F (a) What is the oxidation number of xenon in xenon tetrafluoride and in xenon hexafluoride?

(b) Write equations to show the reaction of fluorine with xenon to make xenon tetrafluoride and in xenon hexafluoride?

Hydrolysis of covalent halides

Almost all covalent chlorides are hydrolysed to give an acidic solution. It is a typical property of covalently bonded chlorides that they can be hydrolysed to form hydrochloric acid. One exception to this rule is tetrachloromethane, which does not react with water at all.

The hydrolysis of covalent halides, such as phosphorus(III) bromide and phosphorus(III) iodide, provides a suitable way of preparing hydrogen bromide and hydrogen iodide.

You can read about the hydrolysis of covalent chlorides of Period 2 and Period 3 and the resistance to hydrolysis of tetrachloromethane on pages 462.

■ See question 3 and 4.

G Construct the equation to show the hydrolysis of phosphorus(III) bromide, PBr_3, to make phosphoric(III) acid, H_3PO_3, and hydrogen bromide.

5 REACTIONS OF CHLORINE WITH COMPOUNDS

Chlorine and the other halogens have an affinity for hydrogen. Chlorine reacts with compounds containing hydrogen to form hydrogen chloride, or hydrochloric acid when the reaction is carried out in aqueous solution. Chlorine behaves as an oxidising agent.

The reaction of the halogens with hydrocarbons to form halogenoalkanes and hydrogen halide is described on page 207.

Reaction of chlorine with water

Chlorine reacts with water to form an acidic solution that is a mixture of two acids, hydrochloric acid and chloric(I) acid. This is an example of a *disproportionation* reaction, in which chlorine is both oxidised and reduced during the reaction:

$$Cl_2(aq) + H_2O(l) \rightleftharpoons HCl(aq) + HOCl(aq)$$

This reaction is the basis of one of the chemical tests for chlorine: namely, it turns moist blue litmus paper first red and then white. Chlorine reacts with the moisture to form the acidic solution which turns the litmus paper red. The chloric(I) acid acts as a bleach and turns the paper white.

For some more examples of disproportionation, read pages 437 and 512.

Reaction of chlorine with hydrogen sulphide and sulphur dioxide

Chlorine oxidises hydrogen sulphide to sulphur. When the reaction is carried out with aqueous solutions of both reagents, a yellow precipitate of sulphur is produced:

$$H_2S(aq) + Cl_2(aq) \rightarrow 2HCl(aq) + S(s)$$

Chlorine also oxidises aqueous sulphur dioxide (sulphurous acid) to form a mixture of hydrochloric and sulphuric acid:

$$SO_2(aq) + 2H_2O(l) + Cl_2(g) \rightarrow H_2SO_4(aq) + 2HCl(aq)$$

Oxidation of iron(II) ions

Chlorine oxidises aqueous iron(II) chloride to form aqueous iron(III) chloride:

$$Cl_2(g) + 2Fe^{2+}(aq) \rightarrow 2Fe^{3+}(aq) + 2Cl^-(aq)$$

Reaction of halogens with aqueous sodium thiosulphate

Aqueous chlorine and aqueous bromine oxidise aqueous thiosulphate ions into sulphate ions:

$$4Cl_2(aq) + S_2O_3^{2-}(aq) + 5H_2O(l) \rightarrow 10H^+(aq) + 8Cl^-(aq) + 2SO_4^{2-}(aq)$$

Iodine is a less powerful oxidising agent than either chlorine or bromine, and so the reaction does not give sulphate ions. Instead it gives $S_4O_6^{2-}(aq)$:

$$I_2(aq) + 2S_2O_3^{2-}(aq) \rightarrow 2I^-(aq) + S_4O_6^{2-}(aq)$$

One chemical test for an oxidising agent uses aqueous potassium iodide. An oxidising agent will liberate iodine from aqueous potassium iodide and the amount of iodine can be determined using volumetric analysis with a titration against aqueous sodium thiosulphate. The presence of iodine is shown by a blue-black coloration with starch solution. This is a chemical test for iodine.

? **H (a)** Write down the ionic equation for the reaction between aqueous chlorine and aqueous sulphur dioxide to form chloride ion and sulphate ion.

(b) Suggest why astatine does not oxidise aqueous iron(II) ions into iron(III) ions.

? **I** Show, by using change of oxidation numbers, that the reaction between iodine and sodium thiosulphate is an example of a redox reaction.

J In a determination to find the amount of iodine liberated by an oxidising agent, it was found that the number of moles of sodium thiosulphate needed to react with the iodine in a titration was 2.1×10^{-3}. What was the number of moles of iodine liberated by the oxidising agent?

? **K** Explain why all the hydrogen halides are polar molecules.
Hint: Look at the electronegativities of the atoms involved on page 84.

6 HYDROGEN HALIDES

All the hydrogen halides have the formula HX, where X is F, Cl, Br, I or At. They all are colourless acidic gases that are highly soluble in water to form an acidic solution. The bonding in a hydrogen halide is covalent, but the molecule is polar with its halogen end being slightly negative and its hydrogen end slightly positive.

Reaction of halogens with hydrogen

The halogens react with hydrogen to give hydrogen halides, but the rate of reaction decreases with increasing atomic (proton) number of the halogen. The reaction between hydrogen and fluorine takes place very rapidly even at low temperatures, whereas the reaction between hydrogen and iodine is reversible and needs elevated temperatures:

$$H_2(g) + F_2(g) \rightarrow 2HF(g)$$

When heated, hydrogen reacts with chlorine, and when a mixture of the two gases is subjected to ultraviolet light the reaction can be explosive.

See question 1. ■

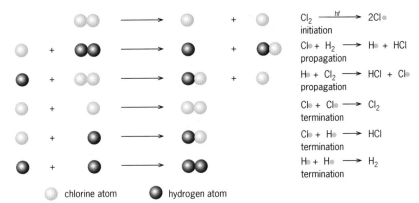

$$Cl_2 \xrightarrow{hf} 2Cl\bullet$$
initiation

$$Cl\bullet + H_2 \longrightarrow H\bullet + HCl$$
propagation

$$H\bullet + Cl_2 \longrightarrow HCl + Cl\bullet$$
propagation

$$Cl\bullet + Cl\bullet \longrightarrow Cl_2$$
termination

$$Cl\bullet + H\bullet \longrightarrow HCl$$
termination

$$H\bullet + H\bullet \longrightarrow H_2$$
termination

○ chlorine atom   ● hydrogen atom

Fig 23.10 The reaction between hydrogen and chlorine in the presence of sunlight has a free-radical mechanism. The initiation reaction involves the homolytic fission of a chlorine–chlorine single bond to form highly reactive chlorine atoms. The chlorine atoms collide with hydrogen molecules to form hydrogen chloride and hydrogen atoms. The hydrogen atoms collide with chlorine molecules to form hydrogen chloride molecules and regenerate chlorine atoms. These two stages are propagation steps, since there is no net loss of chlorine atoms. In the termination steps, pairs of atoms collide to form molecules. (Initiation, propagation and termination are covered on page 208.)

Thermal decomposition of hydrogen halides

The thermal stability of the hydrogen halides decreases with increasing relative molecular mass, which is due to the decrease in the bond energy from H–F to H–I. In the decomposition of hydrogen iodide, it is better to describe the reaction as an equilibrium process:

$$2HI(g) \rightleftharpoons H_2(g) + I_2(g) \quad \Delta H \text{ is positive}$$

Le Chatelier's principle states that the position of equilibrium of a system shifts to minimise the effect of any change in the external conditions, such as increasing the temperature or the pressure. In the equilibrium process above, pressure has no effect whatsoever, because there is no volume change during the reaction – the number of moles of gas is the same on both sides of the equation. Since the decomposition is endothermic, an increase in temperature favours the formation of the two elements, because the reaction from left to right absorbs energy.

Chemical test for hydrogen halides

Hydrogen halides are colourless acidic gases which are able to react with bases such as ammonia gas. This reaction is interesting in that two gases react together to make a white solid dispersed in a gas, correctly described as a smoke (Fig 23.11). This can be used as a chemical test for the hydrogen halides:

$$NH_3(g) + HCl(g) \rightarrow NH_4Cl(s)$$

Aqueous solutions of the hydrogen halides

All the hydrogen halides dissolve in water to form acidic solutions. Hydrogen chloride forms hydrochloric acid, hydrogen bromide forms hydrobromic acid and hydrogen iodide forms hydroiodic acid:

$$HX(g) + H_2O(l) \rightarrow H_3O^+(aq) + X^-(aq) \quad \text{where X is Cl, Br or I}$$

The acid strength increases from hydrochloric acid to hydroiodic acid. This is because the H–I bond is weaker than the H–Cl bond (see Table 23.3). The bonding changes from covalent in the hydrogen halide to ionic in the corresponding acid.

Table 23.3 Bond energies of the hydrogen halides

Hydrogen halide	Bond energy (H–X)/kJ mol⁻¹
HF	562
HCl	431
HBr	366
HI	299

■ See question 1.

Le Chatelier's principle is covered on pages 388 and 637

?

L (a) Write down an expression for the equilibrium constant for the thermal decomposition of hydrogen iodide.

(b) At 600 K, hydrogen iodide is 19.1 per cent dissociated. Calculate the mole ratios of hydrogen, iodine and hydrogen iodide when a sample of hydrogen iodide is allowed to reach equilibrium at 600 K.

■ See question 5.

Fig 23.11 Ammonia gas and hydrogen chloride gas react to form a white smoke of ammonium chloride. This can be used as a test either for ammonia or for hydrogen chloride

?

M Predict the products of the reaction of:

(a) hydrochloric acid with sodium carbonate,

(b) hydroiodic acid with magnesium oxide,

(c) hydrobromic acid with sodium hydroxide.

All three acids are strong and display the typical reactions of strong acids (see page 319):

- They form hydrogen with metals above hydrogen in the electro-chemical series.
- They form carbon dioxide with carbonates and hydrogencarbonates.
- They form salts with bases, such as metal oxides and hydroxides.
- They fully dissociate to form aqueous hydrogen ions.

Concentrated hydrochloric, hydrobromic and hydroiodic acids contain a large percentage of water, since if an attempt is made to concentrate them further, the gaseous hydrogen halide is evolved.

HYDROFLUORIC ACID AND HYDROGEN FLUORIDE

HYDROFLUORIC ACID is unique among acids in that it reacts with glass. Fortunately, it does not react with plastics, otherwise it would be difficult to find a suitable container in which to store it. During the reaction with glass, a volatile silicon compound, SiF_4, is produced:

$$SiO_2 + 4HF \rightarrow SiF_4 + 2H_2O$$

$$CaSiO_3 + 6HF \rightarrow CaF_2 + SiF_4 + 3H_2O$$

Hydrofluoric acid is extremely dangerous to handle, because it acts as a local anaesthetic while burning into the skin and flesh. So you are not aware of the severity of the damage until it is too late. You are left with acutely painful and slow-healing burns.

Dilute hydrofluoric acid is a weak acid. Only about 10 per cent of the HF molecules are dissociated in a $0.1\,mol\,dm^{-3}$ solution. This is because the H–F bond is very strong and the presence of strong intermolecular hydrogen bonds hinders dissociation.

Hydrogen fluoride is used mainly to produce fluorocarbons and the sodium aluminium fluoride required for the manufacture of aluminium. It is also used to prepare a variety of important synthetic chemicals and catalysts.

Hydrogen fluoride also attacks glass, and so it is used to etch glassware.

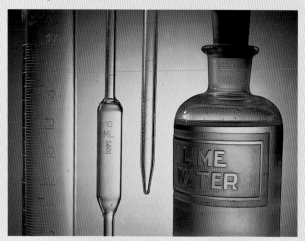

Fig 23.12 **Hydrogen fluoride is used to etch the markings on thermometers and burettes**

Oxidation

Hydrochloric acid, hydrobromic acid and hydroiodic acid can all be oxidised to form the elemental halogen. The reaction involves the removal of hydrogen, and an increase in the oxidation number of the halogen atom. For example:

$$MnO_2(s) + 4HCl(aq) \rightarrow MnCl_2(aq) + 2H_2O(l) + Cl_2(g)$$

The ease of oxidation increases as the atomic (proton) number of the halogen increases. So it is quite easy to reduce hydroiodic acid but much more difficult to reduce hydrochloric acid.

?

N Construct the equations to show the reaction of potassium manganate(VII) with concentrated hydrochloric acid. The products are manganese(II) chloride, potassium chloride, water and chlorine.

Hydrochloric acid can be reduced with lead(IV) oxide, manganese(IV) oxide or potassium manganate(VII) to make chlorine, but less powerful oxidising agents can be used to convert hydrobromic acid and hydroiodic acid into bromine and iodine respectively. In other words, the reducing power decreases from hydroiodic to hydrochloric acid.

7 CHEMISTRY OF IONIC HALIDES

On page 439 is a description of the giant ionic lattices formed by certain ionic halides, such as lithium chloride and sodium chloride. It is this particular form of lattice which gives these halides their high melting points. However, as mentioned on page 490, some metals can form ionic halides with covalent character. These have much lower melting points than those of the other ionic halides, and often sublime instead of melting.

Reaction of solid halides with concentrated sulphuric acid

Concentrated sulphuric acid reacts with solid halides to form the corresponding hydrogen halide. Since concentrated sulphuric acid is an oxidising agent, the reaction is often complicated by oxidation of the hydrogen halide.

Solid sodium chloride reacts to form hydrogen chloride. This reaction is often used to prepare hydrogen chloride in the laboratory:

$$NaCl(s) + H_2SO_4(l) \rightarrow NaHSO_4(l) + HCl(g)$$

The same reaction with sodium bromide yields a collection of products including sulphur dioxide, hydrogen bromide and bromine. This is a result of the oxidation of hydrogen bromide formed initially in the reaction by concentrated sulphuric acid:

$$NaBr(s) + H_2SO_4(l) \rightarrow NaHSO_4(l) + HBr(g)$$

$$2HBr(g) + H_2SO_4(l) \rightarrow 2H_2O(l) + SO_2(g) + Br_2(g)$$

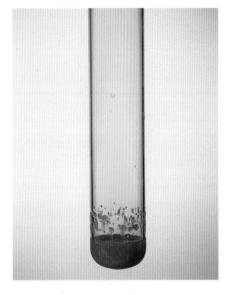

Fig 23.13 **Fumes of bromine are produced when concentrated sulphuric acid is added to sodium bromide**

When the reaction with concentrated sulphuric acid is repeated with sodium iodide, an even more complicated set of reactions takes place, with the formation of hydrogen iodide, sulphur dioxide, iodine and hydrogen sulphide. This time, violet fumes of iodine are produced (Fig 23.14):

$$8HI(g) + H_2SO_4(l) \rightarrow H_2S(g) + 4H_2O(l) + 4I_2(g)$$

Fig 23.14 **Fumes of iodine are produced when concentrated sulphuric acid is added to sodium iodide**

?

O (a) Write an equation to show the reaction between concentrated sulphuric acid and sodium iodide to form hydrogen iodide.

(b) Write an equation to show the reaction of hydrogen iodide to form iodine and sulphur dioxide.

(c) Predict the reaction products for the reaction between sodium astatide and concentrated sulphuric acid.

(d) Predict the reaction products for the reaction between sodium fluoride and concentrated sulphuric acid.

These three reactions provide a way of distinguishing solid ionic chlorides, bromides and iodides.

The reactions of solid ionic halides with concentrated sulphuric acid illustrate the relative ease with which hydrogen halides and halide ions can be oxidised. Hydrogen iodide and iodide ions are the easiest to oxidise, hydrogen fluoride and fluoride ions the most difficult.

■ See question 5.

Reactions of the aqueous halide ions

In addition to the displacement reactions described on page 488, the aqueous halide ions also take place in precipitation reactions. Most halides are soluble, but silver halides are insoluble. Therefore, silver halides can be precipitated by mixing together solutions of the appropriate aqueous solutions:

$$Ag^+(aq) + X^-(aq) \rightarrow AgX(s) \quad \text{where X is Cl, Br or I}$$

These precipitation reactions are very useful in qualitative analysis. They are summarised in Table 23.4.

Fig 23.15 **In order to avoid drought, rain is made to fall in Australia by seeding clouds with silver iodide crystals**

See question 4 and 5. ■

Table 23.4 **Action of dilute nitric acid followed by aqueous silver nitrate and aqueous ammonia on aqueous halide ions**

	Fluoride	Chloride	Bromide	Iodide
Action of dilute nitric acid followed by aqueous silver nitrate followed by addition of aqueous ammonia	No precipitate	White precipitate of silver chloride that turns violet in sunlight redissolves in dilute aqueous ammonia to form a colourless solution due to formation of diamminesilver(I) ion, $[Ag(NH_3)_2]^+(aq)$	Cream precipitate of silver bromide redissolves in concentrated aqueous ammonia to form a colourless solution due to formation of $[Ag(NH_3)_2]^+(aq)$	Yellow precipitate of silver iodide does not redissolve in concentrated aqueous ammonia, but it turns white

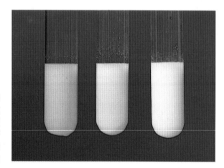

Fig 23.16 **Aqueous silver nitrate forms characteristic coloured precipitates with aqueous chlorides, bromides and iodides. Silver chloride is white, silver bromide is cream and silver iodide is pale yellow**

BLACK AND WHITE PHOTOGRAPHY

SILVER HALIDES are sensitive to light. For example, in the precipitation reaction given in Table 23.4, the silver chloride formed turns violet in the presence of light. This is due to the decomposition of silver chloride to give silver and chlorine:

$$2AgCl(s) \rightarrow 2Ag(s) + Cl_2(g)$$

The longer the exposure to light, the greater is the amount of silver produced.

Black and white photography works on a similar principle. The film consists of a very thin layer of gelatine and silver bromide crystals deposited on clear plastic. As light shines on the film, an image is captured by the silver bromide crystals. This image is developed by by immersing the film in a developer which reacts only with those silver bromide crystals that have been exposed to the light. The developer reduces the silver bromide to metallic silver:

$$2AgBr(s) + C_6H_4(OH)_2(aq) \rightarrow$$
$$2Ag(s) + C_6H_4O_2(aq) + 2HBr(aq)$$

Next, the film is placed in a fixer, where the silver bromide crystals not exposed to light, and hence unaffected by the developer, are removed from the film. This leaves the film as a negative with black areas of silver where the film was exposed to light.

The negative is then converted to a permanent picture on photographic paper. Light is shone through the negative onto the photographic paper which is coated with silver bromide. The action of light on the silver bromide produces a true image which has to be developed to give a permanent photograph.

Fig 23.17(a) **The negative image**

Fig 23.17(b) **The positive image**

8 COMPOUNDS WITH HALOGENS HAVING A POSITIVE OXIDATION NUMBER

All the halogens show an oxidation state of −1 in compounds where a halogen atom has gained an electron through ionic bonding, or has shared an electron through covalent bonding. Fluorine always has this oxidation number because it is the most electronegative element. But the other halogens can also form compounds in which the halogen has a positive oxidation number. When the halogen has a positive oxidation state, it is covalently bonded either to other halogens or to oxygen. The oxy anions of chlorine, such as chlorate(I) and chlorate(V), are described on page 512 and are products of the chlor-alkali industry.

> **?**
>
> **P** Show that the reaction of iodine with aqueous sodium hydroxide is a redox reaction by calculating the oxidation state of every iodine species in the reaction.

Iodate(V)

Iodine can be oxidised to produce the iodate(V) ion. This is in complete contrast to the normal reaction of iodine, in which the element is reduced on reaction. A number of oxidising agents can be used, such as concentrated nitric acid or potassium chlorate, but the most interesting reaction involves iodine and concentrated sodium hydroxide. This is an example of disproportionation, since the iodine is both the reducing agent and the oxidising agent:

$$3I_2(aq) + 6KOH(aq) \rightarrow KIO_3(aq) + 3H_2O(l) + 5KI(aq)$$

The reverse reaction, in which iodide ions are oxidised by iodate(V) ions, forms the basis of several iodine-based volumetric analyses.

■ See question 6.

SUMMARY

After studying this chapter, you should know that:

◼ The reactivity of the halogens decreases with increasing atomic (proton) number.

◼ The oxidising power of the halogens decreases with increasing atomic (proton) number.

◼ The oxidation state of a halogen in a compound is normally −1.

◼ A halogen atom can gain an electron through ionic bonding or share electrons through covalent bonding to attain a noble-gas electron configuration.

◼ Metals react with halogens to form ionic halides and non-metals react with them to form covalent halides.

◼ The hydrogen halides are colourless acidic gases that dissolve in water to form acid solutions. Hydrogen chloride forms hydrochloric acid, hydrogen fluoride forms hydrofluoric acid, hydrogen bromide forms hydrobromic acid, and hydrogen iodide forms hydroiodic acid.

◼ Covalent halides or ionic halides with covalent character are hydrolysed to form acidic solutions.

◼ The thermal stability of the hydrogen halides decreases with increasing atomic (proton) number of the halogen.

◼ The ease of oxidation of the hydrogen halides increases with increasing atomic (proton) number of the halogen.

◼ In aqueous solution, the halogen with the lower atomic (proton) number can displace the halide ion with the higher atomic number.

◼ Acidified silver nitrate can be used to distinguish between aqueous halide ions. The silver halides formed can be distingushed by their differing solubilities in aqueous ammonia.

QUESTIONS

1

a) State and explain the trend in volatility in the halogens chlorine, bromine and iodine.

b) Describe and explain the thermal stability of the hydrogen halides.

c) Explain why hydroiodic acid is stronger than hydrochloric acid.

d) Astatine is a member of the halogen family.
  (i) Predict two physical properties of astatine.
  (ii) Predict three chemical properties of astatine and explain your reasoning by reference to the properties of the other halogens.
  (iii) Suggest why astatine is not normally studied in schools or college laboratories.

2

a) Sea-water contains bromide ions and iodide ions.
  (i) State how the bromine is extracted from sea-water.
  (ii) Suggest how iodine may be extracted from sea-water.

b) Explain why fluorine cannot be prepared by a displacement reaction.

3

a) Explain in terms of their electron configurations why metals tend to form ionic chlorides and non-metals tend to form molecular (covalent) chlorides.

b) Draw a dot and cross diagram to show the bonding in
  (i) magnesium chloride,
  (ii) aluminium chloride.

c) Metal chlorides can be prepared by the reaction between chlorine and the metal. Name the products of the following reactions:
  (i) iron with chlorine,
  (ii) aluminium with chlorine.

d) One of the characteristic properties of molecular (covalent) chlorides is that the are hydrolysed rapidly by water to form hydrogen chloride or hydrochloric acid.
  (i) Write an equation to show the hydrolysis of phosphorus (III) chloride.
  (ii) One mole of boron trichloride reacts with 3 moles of water during its hydrolysis. Construct the equation to show the hydrolysis of boron trichloride.
  (iii) Aluminium chloride and iron(III) chloride are both hydrolysed by water to form hydrochloric acid. What does this suggest about the bonding in these two compounds?

4

Phosphorus(III) chloride is hydrolysed in cold water to form hydrochloric acid and phosphoric acid.

a) Write an equation, including state symbols, for this reaction.

b) Describe how you could confirm the presence of chloride ions in the reaction mixture.

5

Hydrogen chloride can be prepared by the reaction of concentrated sulphuric acid on solid sodium chloride.

a) Write an equation for the reaction.

b) Describe a chemical test for hydrogen chloride.

c) Explain why hydrogen iodide cannot be prepared by the reaction of sodium iodide with concentrated sulphuric acid.

6

Iodine reacts with concentrated nitric acid to make iodic(V) acid, HIO_3. Iodic(V) acid is a stable white solid.

$$I_2(s) + 10HNO_3(aq) \rightarrow 2HIO_3(s) + 1ONO_2(g) + 4H_2O(l)$$

a) This is a redox reaction. Identify
  (i) the reducing agent,
  (ii) the oxidising agent.

b) Calculate the maximum mass of iodic(V) acid that can be prepared from 5.08 grams of iodine and excess concentrated nitric acid.

c) Iodic(V) acid is mixed with dilute sulphuric acid and aqueous iodide ions are added. A reaction occurs to form iodine. Explain the reaction taking place including an ionic equation.

d) Chlorine forms oxy salts with the anions ClO^- and ClO_3^-. Identify the oxidation state of the chlorine in each of the anions and use this to name the anions.

Assignment

THE INTERHALOGENS

Compounds formed between two different halogens are called interhalogens. All interhalogens consist of an atom of the halogen with the higher atomic number bonded to a number of atoms of the halogen with the smaller atomic number. All of the interhalogens are covalently bonded. The interhalogens of the formula XY, where X and Y are two different halogens, closely resemble the halogens X_2 and Y_2.

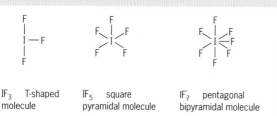

IF_3 T-shaped molecule IF_5 square pyramidal molecule IF_7 pentagonal bipyramidal molecule

Fig 23.A1 **Structures of some interhalogen molecules**

Table 23.A1 **The interhalogens. The state symbols refer to the state at room temperature and atmospheric pressure**

$ClF(g)$	$ClF_3(g)$	$ClF_5(g)$	
$BrF(g)$	$BrF_3(l)$	$BrF_5(l)$	
$BrCl(g)$			
$IF(g)$	$IF_3(s)$	$IF_5(l)$	$IF_7(g)$
$ICl(l)$	$ICl_3(s)$		

1 Predict the shape of the following interhalogen molecules:
a) ClF_3, **b)** ClF_5 and **c)** BF_3.

Hint: You may want to read about the shape of molecules on page 77.

2 Draw a dot and cross diagram to show the bonding in IF, IF_3, IF_5 and IF_7.

3
a) What type of intermolecular force is present in solid ICl?
b) Predict the structure of solid ICl based upon your knowledge of the structures of solid chlorine and solid iodine.

4 Predict the physical state of the interhalogen IBr. Give reasons for your answer.

If the molecule has a central halogen atom, it always has a positive oxidation number, because it is bonded to a more electronegative halogen. So the naming of the interhalogens is quite easy.

Start with the central halogen and its oxidation number, and then follow that with the appropriate halide. So, ICl_3 is iodine(III) chloride and IF_7 is iodine(VII) fluoride.

5 Name each of the following interhalogens:
a) BrF_3, **b)** BrF and **c)** ICl.

An interhalogen can be prepared by direct combination of the two halogens.

6
a) Write an equation to show the preparation of iodine(VII) fluoride.
b) Suggest the mole ratio of fluorine to bromine that you would need to make bromine(III) fluoride.
c) Write an equation to show the preparation of bromine(V) fluoride. Calculate the mass of fluorine needed to make 10 grams of bromine(V) fluoride.
Hint: You may want to read about reacting masses on page 7.

The interhalogens react in the same way as their constituent halogens. The halogen fluorides are more reactive than halogen chlorides.

7 Burning sodium is placed in a gas jar of bromine chloride. Suggest the names of the products formed in this reaction.

8 Chlorine and bromine will add to a molecule of ethene, C_2H_4, to give dichloroethane and dibromomethane. Suggest the product of the reaction between bromine chloride and ethene. Write an equation for the reaction.

Hint: You may want to read about addition reactions of ethene on page 256.

9 A mixture of chlorine fluoride and hydrogen is placed in sunlight.
a) Write an equation for the reaction that occurs.
b) Suggest a mechanism for the reaction.

10 Chlorine reacts with benzene, C_6H_6, in the presence of aluminium chloride to give chlorobenzene, C_6H_5Cl. The reaction is electrophilic substitution and the aluminium chloride is used to make a chlorine electrophile, Cl^+. The reaction is repeated using bromine chloride.
a) Draw the dipole in bromine chloride.
b) Suggest a product of the reaction between bromine chloride and benzene.
Hint: You may want to read about electrophilic substitution on page 278.

THE HALOGENS

The halogens are interesting in their distinctive physical properties and high reactivity. The chapter links their atomic and molecular structure with their reactions and the properties of their compounds. Review the Chapter Map for the connections between ideas and for further information in other chapters.

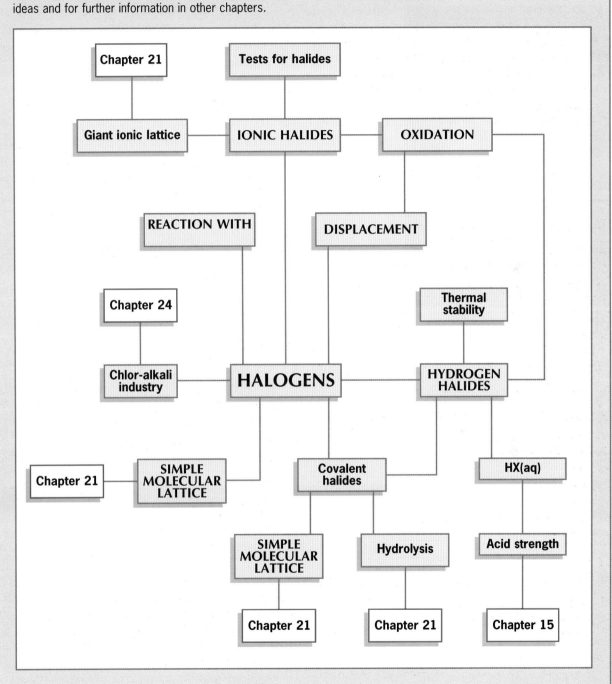

24 Electrolysis and the chlor-alkali industry

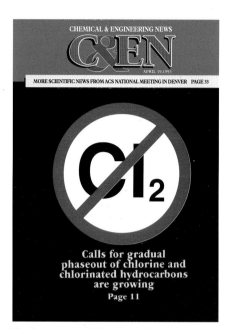

CHEMICAL & ENGINEERING NEWS

C&EN
APRIL 19,1993

MORE SCIENTIFIC NEWS FROM ACS NATIONAL MEETING IN DENVER PAGE 33

Calls for gradual phaseout of chlorine and chlorinated hydrocarbons are growing
Page 11

The front cover of *Chemical & Engineering News*, April 1993, demonstrates that the chemical industry is taking very seriously the threat to ban chlorine and its compounds

PCBs are covered on page 81, CFCs on page 205 and dioxins on page 512.

Should chlorine and chlorine-containing compounds be banned? Greenpeace have labelled chlorine 'the Devil's element' and with some justification. But chlorine and many of its compounds continue to be valued as beneficial.

So effective were the pesticide DDT and similar highly chlorinated compounds at combating insect-borne diseases such as malaria that shortages of the compounds were regarded as a threat to public health. However, their stability meant that they persisted in the environment and built up in the food chain, rising to toxic levels in birds and mammals. The danger to the environment was noticed in the 1960s, and the use of these chemicals was then severely controlled.

The same combination of toxicity and persistence in the environment emerged with PCBs (polychlorinated biphenyls) and by the late 1970s most production had ceased. Also in the 1970s, the link between CFCs and ozone layer depletion was established, and there was evidence that the deadly chemicals dioxins were accumulating in the environment.

To be set against a ghastly catalogue of mishaps, in which people died or were disabled, are the tremendous benefits derived from the use of many thousands of chlorine compounds. So, to ban the element's use completely is not feasible at present, and the necessity of a ban is questionable. The way forward is to assess the risks of each compound and where necessary to look for safer alternatives.

1 ELECTROLYSIS

In 1800 the Italian physicist Alessandro Volta (Fig 24.1) made the world's first battery from which an electric current could be drawn off continuously. The unit called the **volt** honours his achievement. Seven weeks after his work was published, an English chemist, William Nicholson, built a similar battery and passed an electric current through slightly acidified water using two platinum wires. Bubbles of hydrogen and oxygen were produced. Later in that same year a German chemist, Johann Ritter, discovered that the ratio of the volume of hydrogen to oxygen was constant at 2:1. Although the significance of Ritter's experimental result was not fully understood, it was an early indication that the water molecule contained twice as many hydrogen atoms as oxygen atoms.

What Nicholson and Ritter had done was to split water molecules using the energy of an electric current. The process of decomposing a compound using electricity is called **electrolysis**:

$$2H_2O(l) \xrightarrow{\text{electrolysis}} 2H_2(g) + O_2(g)$$

?

A Why did Nicholson acidify the water before he passed an electric current through it?

Fig 24.1 **The world's first battery was called a voltaic pile because it consisted of a stack of silver and zinc discs separated by cardboard soaked in salt solution. The reason why this produces an electric current is explained on page 545**

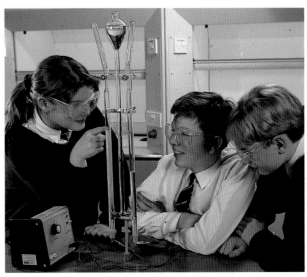

Fig 24.2 **This apparatus is called a Hofmann voltameter. At the bottom of the tube on the right is a platinum cathode which produces hydrogen. The anode in the tube on the left produces oxygen. The amount of hydrogen produced is twice that of oxygen**

Hydrogen and oxygen react **spontaneously** to produce water. It does not matter that energy is needed to start this reaction. Once started, it is spontaneous (takes place of its own accord). The decomposition of water to hydrogen and oxygen is a **non-spontaneous reaction** and must be forced using the energy from electricity.

Electrolysis is a most important process, used industrially to manufacture reactive metals such as sodium and aluminium (see pages 456 and 477), to deposit one metal on another (a process known as electroplating), and to purify metals such as copper (see page 509).

This chapter is concerned particularly with the largest and widest application of electrolysis – the manufacture of chlorine and sodium hydroxide from concentrated aqueous sodium chloride in the chlor-alkali industry.

B The suffix *lysis* in electrolysis comes from *lyo*, the Greek word meaning to loosen or break down. What do the words hydrolysis and photolysis mean?

C Why do you think the industry producing chlorine and sodium hydroxide is called the chlor-alkali industry?

Electrolysis cell

Much of the early work on electrolysis was done by Michael Faraday in the 1830s. He coined the word **electrolytes** to describe those compounds which, when molten or in solution, conduct electricity and are decomposed by it. The conducting rods dipping into the electrolyte he called **electrodes** (from two Greek words meaning 'the path of electricity'). Electrolysis works only with **direct current (d.c.)**. This means that the charge flows in one direction only, whereas the current in the mains in your house is **alternating current (a.c.)**, where the flow of electrons (charge) reverses, or alternates, fifty times every second. Direct current gives a positive charge to one electrode, which Faraday called the **anode,** and a negative charge to the other electrode, which he called the **cathode**. These terms are still in use today.

Oxidation always occurs at the anode and reduction always occurs at the cathode.

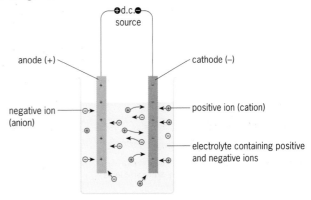

Fig 24.3 **An electrolysis cell. The positive ions (cations) are attracted to the cathode and the negative ions (anions) are attracted to the anode**

D (a) Why are positive ions called cations?

(b) Why is solid sodium chloride not called an electrolyte?

Note from Fig 24.3 that it is the anions (negative ions) and the cations (positive ions) which move in the electrolyte. They carry the charge between the electrodes and cause the electrolyte to conduct. **Anions** are so called because during electrolysis they are attracted to the anode. Electrons are the charge carriers bringing the current to and from the battery.

MICHAEL FARADAY (1791–1867)

MICHAEL FARADAY was the son of a blacksmith. As a young man, he left his home in Yorkshire to seek work in London. He became apprenticed to a bookbinder. Through reading the books he bound, he began to develop his interest in chemistry and electricity. He built himself a voltaic pile from halfpennies and was soon experimenting with the electricity he produced.

Faraday was given tickets to attend a series of lectures delivered by the famous chemist Humphry Davy, at the Royal Institution. He made detailed notes, added some excellent illustrations and bound them into a book which he presented to Davy. Davy, recognising Faraday's talents, installed him as a laboratory assistant at the Royal Institution. He was then 21. Faraday's research work was so fruitful that within 12 years he was appointed Professor of Chemistry at the Institution.

The achievements of Faraday are staggering in their range. Apart from discovering the laws of electrolysis, he studied chlorine and inadvertently liquefied it, he made the first chloroalkanes, and he invented and built the first electrical motor, the first transformer and the

first dynamo. Add to this his discovery of benzene and research into steel alloys and it is no wonder that he is regarded as one of the world's greatest scientists.

Fig 24.4 **In 1825, Faraday started the Royal Institution's Christmas lectures for young people. They are still popular today, drawing large audiences through the medium of television. In this famous painting of one of Faraday's Christmas lectures in 1855, Faraday is facing Prince Albert with his sons. Prince Edward, later to become King Edward VII, is on his left**

2 HALF EQUATIONS AND REDOX IN ELECTROLYSIS

Remember: **OIL RIG** – **O**xidation **I**s **L**oss (of electrons). **R**eduction **I**s **G**ain (of electrons). This and redox reactions are covered on page 430 and in Chapter 26.

On page 456 is a description of the extraction of sodium from molten sodium chloride by electrolysis. This provides a suitable starting point to explaining what happens during electrolysis. Sodium ions are attracted to the negatively charged cathode, where they each pick up an electron to become sodium atoms.

At the cathode: $Na^+(l) + e^- \rightarrow Na(l)$

Because each sodium ion is gaining an electron, **reduction** is occurring at the cathode. Simultaneously, electrons are drawn off from the anode by the d.c. source (a battery or power pack), giving the anode a positive charge. Chloride ions are attracted to the positively charged anode, where they give up electrons.

At the anode: $2Cl^-(l) \rightarrow Cl_2(g) + 2e^-$

So **oxidation** of the chloride ions occurs at the cathode. The electrons released by the chloride ions travel back to the d.c. source. The equations given below for the reactions at the anode are called **half equations**, because they represent **half reactions**. These combine to give the complete reaction occurring during electrolysis:

2 × cathode reaction to cancel out electrons:

$$2Na^+(l) + 2e^- \rightarrow 2Na(l)$$
$$2Cl^-(l) \rightarrow Cl_2(g) + 2e^-$$
$$2Na^+(l) + 2Cl^-(l) \rightarrow 2Na(l) + Cl_2(g)$$

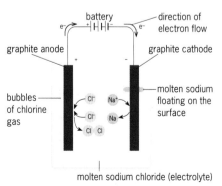

Fig 24.5 **The overall process of electrolysis using molten sodium chloride as an example. Note the direction of electron flow**

So, electrolysis involves **red**uction and **ox**idation reactions, usually abbreviated to **redox** reactions.

Predicting the products of electrolysis of aqueous solutions

In the case of molten sodium chloride, there is one cation (Na^+) and one anion (Cl^-), so the products of electrolysis are easy to predict. But what happens when sodium chloride is dissolved in water? As well as Na^+ and Cl^- ions, there are also $H^+(aq)$ and OH^- ions from the water:

$$H_2O(l) \rightleftharpoons H^+(aq) + OH^-(aq)$$

Even though the concentration of $H^+(aq)$ is extremely low at 10^{-7} mol dm^{-3}, it is enough to cause hydrogen to be discharged (released) at the cathode in preference to sodium. Why is this?

To answer this question, we must look at which of Na^+ or $H^+(aq)$ is most easily reduced to form atoms. Sodium is a very reactive metal, because it readily forms Na^+ ions by losing electrons. Thus, Na^+ ions do not accept electrons easily. Hydrogen ions are much more readily reduced than sodium ions, so hydrogen ions are discharged in preference to sodium ions:

$$2H^+(aq) + 2e^- \rightarrow H_2(g)$$

A list of cations can be drawn up in order of increasing ease of discharge at the cathode. A shortened version is given in Table 24.1. This table is sometimes referred to as the **electrochemical series, redox series** or **reactivity series**. It is discussed further on pages 551, in connection with electrode potentials.

Table 24.1 **Increasing ease of discharge of cations**

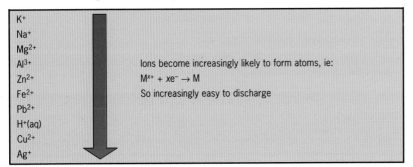

As a rule, the ion nearer the bottom of the electrochemical series is the more easily discharged. However, like all rules, there are exceptions and if the concentration of a particular ion is very high, it may affect which ion is discharged at the cathode.

A similar list can be drawn up for the anions discharging at the anode, but this time the interest is in the ease of oxidation of ions.

Table 24.2 **Increasing ease of discharge of anions. In practice, SO_4^{2-} and NO_3^- are never discharged from aqueous solutions**

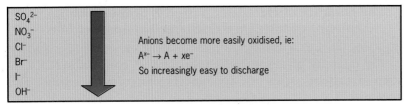

As with cations, when two anions are present in equal amounts, usually the lower one in the table is discharged. But, once again, the relative concentrations of different anions can have an effect. This is

E Molten lead(II) bromide consists of Pb^{2+} ions and Br^- ions. Write the half equations for the reactions occurring at the anode and cathode during electrolysis and state which is oxidation or reduction.

Remember: $H^+(aq)$ is more correctly written as $H_3O^+(aq)$. The $H^+(aq)$ ion is the only ion referred to in this chapter, where the state symbol (aq) is consistently included to remind you that we are dealing with the $H_3O^+(aq)$ ion.

F In the electrolysis of aqueous copper(II) sulphate, use Table 24.1 to predict which cation will be discharged.

particularly true of halide solutions, such as aqueous sodium chloride, where the two anions present are OH^- and Cl^-. If a very dilute aqueous solution of sodium chloride is electrolysed, OH^- ions are discharged as predicted by Table 24.2 and oxygen gas bubbles off at the anode.

At the anode: $4OH^-(aq) \rightarrow 2H_2O(l) + O_2(g) + 4e^-$

However, when the sodium chloride solution is concentrated, the Cl^- concentration is much greater than the OH^- concentration. So, Cl^- ions are discharged, producing chlorine instead of oxygen at the anode:

At the anode: $2Cl^-(aq) \rightarrow Cl_2(g) + 2e^-$

In the case of concentrated nitrate and sulphate solutions, even though the concentration of the hydroxide ion is extremely low, it is still discharged preferentially as predicted by Table 24.2.

G What is the concentration of OH^- ions in water or aqueous sodium chloride.
Hint: If you are not sure of your answer, look again at the equation for the dissociation for water and the concentration of the $H^+(aq)$ on page 505.

See questions 1, 2 and 4. ■

EXAMPLE

Q What products are formed at the anode and cathode from the electrolysis of aqueous sodium sulphate? Include in your answer the relevant half equations.

A Ions present in aqueous sodium sulphate:

from Na_2SO_4: $Na^+(aq)$ and $SO_4^{2-}(aq)$
from water: $H^+(aq)$ and $OH^-(aq)$

Ions attracted to the cathode (cations):
$Na^+(aq)$ and $H^+(aq)$

Ions discharged at the cathode:
$H^+(aq)$ is discharged because it is lower in the electrochemical series than Na^+

Half equation: $2H^+(aq) + 2e^- \rightarrow H_2(g)$

Ions attracted to the anode (anions):
$SO_4^{2-}(aq)$ and $OH^-(aq)$

Ions discharged at the anode:
$OH^-(aq)$ is discharged in preference to $SO_4^{2-}(aq)$

Half equation: $4OH^-(aq) \rightarrow 2H_2O(l) + O_2(g) + 4e^-$

So, the products are hydrogen at the cathode and oxygen at the anode.

H What products are formed at the anode and cathode during the electrolysis of dilute sulphuric acid? Include in your answer the reasons and relevant half equations.

3 WORKING OUT AMOUNTS PRODUCED DURING ELECTROLYSIS

It was Faraday who again led the way in calculating how much of a substance is produced from a given current in a given time during electrolysis. His work was done in 1832, before the electron had been identified. Faraday deduced that:

The quantity of electricity passed is proportional to the amount of substance discharged at an electrode.

This relationship is sometimes referred to as Faraday's first law.

The quantity of electricity is measured in **coulombs (C)**. One amp of current passes one coulomb of charge every second. This means that:

quantity of electricity (charge) = current × time

coulombs = amps × seconds

Remember: The number of particles (atoms, molecules, ions or electrons) in 1 mole is called the **Avogadro constant** (see page 6).

One mole of electrons has a charge of 96 500 C, and this quantity of charge is called the **Faraday constant, F**, in honour of Michael Faraday's pioneering work. Thus, the Faraday constant is related to the Avogadro constant, L, and the charge on an electron, e:

$$F = L \times e$$

Consider the amount of sodium produced by 1 mole of electrons in the electrolysis of molten sodium chloride. From the half equation:

$$Na^+(l) \quad + \quad e^- \quad \rightarrow \quad Na(l)$$
$$\text{1 mol} \qquad \text{1 mol} \qquad \text{1 mol}$$

it follows that 1 mole of electrons produces 1 mole of sodium atoms. At the same time, 1 mole of electrons is released from $\frac{1}{2}$ mole of chlorine molecules, since:

$$Cl^-(l) \quad \rightarrow \quad \tfrac{1}{2}Cl_2(g) \quad + \quad e^-$$
$$\text{1 mol} \qquad \tfrac{1}{2}\text{mol} \quad + \quad \text{1 mol}$$

Now consider ions with a double charge, such as Cu^{2+}. It follows that it takes 2 moles of electrons to deposit 1 mole of copper:

$$Cu^{2+} \quad + \quad 2e^- \quad \rightarrow \quad Cu$$
$$\text{1 mol} \qquad \text{2 mol} \qquad \text{1 mol}$$

Thus:

> **The number of moles of electrons required to discharge 1 mole of ions is equal to the charge on the ion.**

This is sometimes called Faraday's second law. We can use the relationships first discovered by Faraday to calculate amounts of substances produced during electrolysis.

?

I (a) How many electrons will there be in one mole of electrons? (See page 6 if you are not sure.)

(b) What is the charge, in coulombs, on 1 electron if 1 mole of electrons has a charge of 96 500 C?

?

J (a) How many moles of electrons and how many Faradays are required to produce:
(i) 1 mole of aluminium (the aluminium ion is Al^{3+}),
(ii) 1 mole of potassium?

(b) Write down the half equation for the production of oxygen from OH^- ions. How many Faradays are required to produce 1 mole of oxygen molecules?

EXAMPLE

Q An aqueous solution of sulphuric acid is electrolysed in a laboratory using platinum electrodes. The current is kept constant at 2 A for 1 hour. Write the electrode reactions and calculate the mass and volume of the products formed at the electrodes, assuming room conditions.

A The mention of platinum electrodes in the question simply tells you that the electrodes are inert (unreactive).

Ions present: from H_2SO_4:	$H^+(aq)$ and $SO_4^{2-}(aq)$
from water:	$H^+(aq)$ and $OH^-(aq)$
Ions attracted to the cathode:	$H^+(aq)$
Ions discharged:	$H^+(aq)$
Half equation:	$2H^+(aq) + 2e^- \rightarrow H_2(g)$
Ions attracted to the anode:	$SO_4^{2-}(aq)$ and $OH^-(aq)$
Ions discharged at the anode:	$OH^-(aq)$ is discharged in preference to $SO_4^{2-}(aq)$ (See Table 24.2)
Half equation:	$4OH^-(aq) \rightarrow 2H_2O(l) + O_2(g) + 4e^-$

The amount of hydrogen and oxygen formed can now be calculated by working out how many moles of electrons have passed though the electrolysis cell.

Step 1   Calculate the quantity of charge passed:

Current = 2 A   Time = 1 hour = 60 min = $1 \times 60 \times 60$ s = 3600 s
$$\text{Quantity of charge (C)} = \text{current (A)} \times \text{time (seconds)}$$
$$= 2.00 \times 3600$$
$$= 7200\,C$$

Step 2   Work out moles of electrons passing through the electrolysis cell:

1 mole of electrons carries 1 Faraday of charge = 96 500 C

$$\text{Moles of electrons carrying 7 200 C} = 1 \times \frac{7200}{96\,500} = 0.0746\,mol$$

For hydrogen production at the cathode, follow steps 3–5.

Step 3   Convert the half equation to amounts:

$$2H^+(aq) + 2e^- \rightarrow H_2(g)$$
$$2\,\text{mol} + 2\,\text{mol} \rightarrow 1\,\text{mol}$$

Step 4   Scale the amounts in the half equation:

$$2\,\text{mol e}^- \text{ produce } 1\,\text{mol } H_2(g)$$

Therefore: $0.0746\,\text{mol e}^-$ produces $\dfrac{0.0746}{2} = 0.0373\,\text{mol } H_2(g)$

Step 5   Convert amounts (moles) to masses and volumes:

$$\text{mass in grams} = \text{amount in moles} \times \text{mass of 1 mole}$$
$$= 0.0373 \times 2 = 0.0746\,\text{g } H_2$$

Remember: 1 mole of any gas occupies $24\,\text{dm}^3$ under room conditions.

$$\text{volume of } H_2 = 0.0373 \times 24 = 0.895\,\text{dm}^3 = 895\,\text{cm}^3$$

For oxygen production at the anode, repeat Steps 3–5:

Step 3   Convert the half equation to amounts:

$$4OH^-(aq) \rightarrow 2H_2O(l) + O_2(g) + 4e^-$$
$$4\,\text{mol} \quad\quad 2\,\text{mol} + 1\,\text{mol} + 4\,\text{mol}$$

Step 4   Scale the amounts in the half equation. Since $4\,\text{mol e}^-$ is produced when $1\,\text{mol } O_2(g)$ is formed, then:

$$0.0746\,\text{mol e}^- \text{ is produced when } \dfrac{0.0746}{4} = 0.0187\,\text{mol } O_2(g) \text{ is formed}$$

Step 5   Convert amounts (moles) to masses and volumes:

$$\text{mass in grams} = \text{amount in moles} \times \text{mass of 1 mole}$$
$$= 0.0187 \times 32 = 0.0598\,\text{g } O_2$$

Since 1 mol of any gas occupies $24\,\text{dm}^3$ under room conditions:

$$\text{volume of } O_2 = 0.0187 \times 24 = 0.449\,\text{dm}^3 = 449\,\text{cm}^3$$

See questions 2, 3 and 4. ■

?

K Aqueous copper(II) sulphate is electrolysed using graphite electrodes under room conditions. What mass of copper is produced at the cathode and what volume of oxygen at the anode if a constant current of 2.68 A flows for 2 hours?

(A_r of Cu = 64, A_r of O = 16)

Note: Graphite electrodes are regarded as inert because they do not take part in cell electrolysis reactions.

Determining the Avogadro constant by electrolysis

From page 507, we have:

$$F = L \times e$$

where F is the Faraday constant, L is the Avogadro constant and e is the charge on an electron.

If you have tried question **I(b)**, you should have calculated a value for e of 1.60×10^{-19} C. Using this value and the above formula, an experiment can be devised to find a value for the Avogadro constant.

The electrolysis of aqueous copper(II) sulphate using copper electrodes is fairly straightforward to carry out in the laboratory (Fig 24.6).

The electrode reaction at the copper cathode is as would be predicted from the electrochemical series. There are two cations in the electrolyte: Cu^{2+} and $H^+(aq)$. Cu^{2+} is lower in the electrochemical series, so copper is deposited. However, at the anode, neither of the anions (OH^- and SO_4^{2-}) is discharged. Instead, copper from the anode is oxidised and goes into solution as Cu^{2+} ions. This is because, of all the oxidation processes, this one is the most energetically favourable. So the copper electrode is not inert.

At the cathode: $Cu^{2+}(aq) + 2e^- \rightarrow Cu(s)$

At the anode: $Cu(s) \rightarrow Cu^{2+}(aq) + 2e^-$

The anode and cathode are washed, dried and weighed before the experiment starts. A small, constant current of about 0.2 A is passed

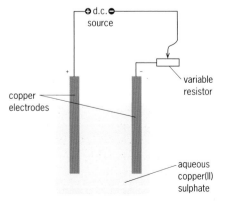

d.c. source

variable resistor

copper electrodes

aqueous copper(II) sulphate

Fig 24.6 **Apparatus used to find the Avogadro constant. The variable resistor is used to keep the current constant, while the ammeter measures the current flowing** through the electrolysis cell for at least 30 minutes. If the current is too large, the copper depositing at the cathode flakes off, reducing the accuracy of the result. After electrolysis, the anode and cathode are again cleaned, dried and weighed. The mass gained by the cathode should be the same as the mass lost by the anode, which provides a way of checking the accuracy of the experiment.

The calculation of the Avogadro constant starts by following a similar pattern to the one used in the Example on page 507.

Step 1 Calculate the quantity of charge passed.

Step 2 Calculate the mass of copper deposited at the cathode.

Step 3 Work out how much charge is required to deposit 1 mole of copper (64 g).

Step 4 Since the charge on the electron is 1.60×10^{-19} C, calculate how many electrons are required to deposit 1 mole (64 g) of copper ions.

Step 5 From the half equation, two electrons are required to deposit one copper atom. So, work out how many copper atoms are deposited in the 64 g of copper.

This is: number of copper atoms in 1 mole = Avogadro constant

?

L An experiment to determine the Avogadro constant is carried out using copper electrodes dipping into a copper(II) sulphate solution. The following measurements are taken:
Mass of copper before electrolysis
= 10.94 g
Mass of copper after electrolysis
= 11.58 g
Current = 0.21 A
Time = 2 h 30 min
Use the steps outlined to calculate a value for the Avogadro constant. Note that the value calculated falls short of the expected value of 6.02×10^{23} due to experimental error. How might the experiment be made more accurate?

REFINING COPPER

PURE COPPER IS OBTAINED industrially using electrolysis. After treatment, molten copper ore is converted to blister copper which is impure. It is purified using electrolysis. The blister copper is made the anode in an electrolysis cell. The cathode is pure copper and the electrolyte is aqueous copper (II) sulphate. The copper in the anode is oxidised to Cu^{2+} ions and dissolves into the copper (II) sulphate solution, while at the cathode Cu^{2+} is deposited (Fig 24.7). The impurities from the anode collect in the bottom of the cell as slime. The slime contains other valuable contaminating metals which are above copper in the electrochemical series.

Fig 24.7 **Copper plated sheets for electronic circuit-making being lifted from an electroplating bath**

■ See question 2.

?

M Write down the half equations for the reaction occurring at the anode and cathode during the purification of copper.

4 MANUFACTURE OF CHLORINE AND SODIUM HYDROXIDE

The chlor-alkali industry is so called because it produces chlorine and the alkali sodium hydroxide from the electrolysis of concentrated, aqueous sodium chloride (brine). The industry is more than 100 years old and is amongst the largest in the world, consuming vast quantities of electricity and producing more than 80 million tonnes of chlorine every day. The UK alone produces 1.5 million tonnes a year.

There are three types of electrolysis cell: the mercury cell, the diaphragm cell and, more recently, the membrane cell. All three are in use today. This section concentrates on the diaphragm cell. The membrane cell is the subject of the Assignment (page 516).

Diaphragm cell

In concentrated aqueous sodium chloride, four ions are present: Na^+, Cl^-, $H^+(aq)$ and OH^-.

At the cathode: $2H^+(aq) + 2e^- \rightarrow H_2(g)$

At the anode: $2Cl^-(aq) \rightarrow Cl_2(g) + 2e^-$

?

N Why are hydrogen and chlorine produced during the electrolysis of aqueous concentrated sodium chloride rather than sodium and oxygen? Hint: If you are not sure, see page 506.

> ✓
> This is an example of le Chatelier's principle. As H+(aq) ions are discharged, the equilibrium is shifted to the right. See pages 338 and 637.

$H^+(aq)$ ions are discharged at the cathode, which causes more water molecules to dissociate to produce more $H^+(aq)$ ions. At the same time, more OH^- ions are produced:

$$H_2O(l) \rightleftharpoons H^+(aq) + OH^-(aq)$$

Combining the two reactions gives:

$$2H^+(aq) + 2e^- \rightarrow H_2(g)$$
$$[H_2O(l) \rightarrow H^+(aq) + OH^-(aq)] \times 2$$
$$2H_2O(l) + 2e^- \rightarrow H_2(g) + 2OH^-(aq)$$

The ions remaining in solution are Na^+ and OH^- which tend to concentrate near the cathode to produce sodium hydroxide. In the commercial electrolysis of brine, the hydroxide ions forming must be kept away from the chlorine produced at the anode. This is because chlorine reacts with OH^- to produce chlorate(I) ions, ClO^-:

$$Cl_2(g) + 2OH^-(aq) \rightarrow Cl^-(aq) + ClO^-(aq) + H_2O(l)$$

In the diaphragm cell (Fig 24.8), a porous asbestos partition (the diaphragm), placed between the electrodes, keeps the sodium hydroxide forming at the cathode away from the chlorine at the anode. Purified fresh brine solution is fed continuously into the anode compartment and the level is kept above that of the cathode compartment. This allows the sodium chloride solution to seep into the cathode compartment and also prevents OH^- ions migrating to the anode. The brine used is purified to remove Ca^{2+} and Mg^{2+} ions. They would react with OH^- ions to form insoluble hydroxides which would block the pores of the diaphragm.

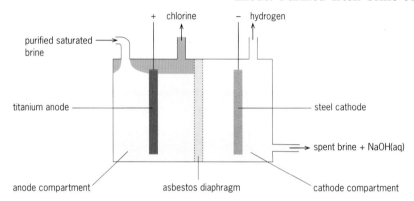

Fig 24.8 **The diaphragm cell**

The solution produced in the cathode compartment contains about 10 per cent sodium hydroxide and 15 per cent sodium chloride. The sodium chloride is separated from the sodium hydroxide by evaporating the solution to one fifth of its original volume. This causes sodium chloride to crystallise out, leaving a 50 per cent sodium hydroxide solution contaminated by 1 per cent sodium chloride.

See questions 1, 4 and 5. ■

THE MERCURY CELL AND THE MINAMATA TRAGEDY

MUCH OF THE CHLORINE and sodium hydroxide manufactured in Britain is produced using a flowing mercury cathode (Fig 24.9).

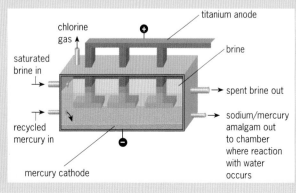

Fig 24.9 **The mercury cell**

A saturated brine solution is still the electrolyte, but sodium ions are discharged at the cathode rather than the hydrogen ions which would be expected from the electrochemical series. The sodium produced dissolves in the mercury as it passes through the cell, forming an amalgam:

$$Na^+(aq) + e^- \xrightarrow{\text{Hg}} Na/Hg(l)$$
$$\text{sodium amalgam}$$

Therefore, hydroxide ions do not build up in the cell and react with the chlorine produced. The sodium amalgam flows out of the cell before the sodium has a chance to react with the water in the brine solution. It is piped to a chamber where it is allowed to react with pure water to form sodium hydroxide and hydrogen:

$$2Na/Hg(l) + 2H_2O(l) \rightarrow 2NaOH(aq) + H_2(g) + 2Hg(l)$$

Once all the sodium has reacted the mercury is recirculated into the electrolysis cell. Fifty per cent sodium hydroxide solution of high purity is produced.

It was because of the purity of the products that the mercury cell once dominated world-wide production of sodium hydroxide. However, mercury and its compounds are highly toxic. In theory, no mercury should escape during this process, but it does through waste solutions, which pollute the environment. One of the most tragic incidents occurred in the 1950s at Minamata Bay in Japan. Mercury entered the food chain after reacting with organic compounds which were ingested by fish and shell-fish. The first to suffer from what came to be known as Minamata disease were fishermen's cats, which became paralysed and eventually died. A month or so later, the first human case was diagnosed and over the next decade 43 people died and another 60 were brain damaged.

Much work has been done to reduce mercury leakage, and it may be that as little as 0.25 g now escapes for every tonne of chlorine produced. However, such is the concern that this process is in sharp decline. For example, manufacturers around the North Sea have pledged to phase out its use by the year 2010. It is being supplanted by the membrane process, which is featured in the Assignment, page 517.

5 USING THE PRODUCTS OF THE CHLOR-ALKALI INDUSTRY

For every tonne of chlorine manufactured, 1.1 tonnes of sodium hydroxide are produced. There is no viable alternative to electrolysis for the manufacture of these chemicals. If the market were to decline for either chemical, there would be a surplus of that chemical. This would be more of a problem if it were chlorine, since its disposal presents significant problems.

In 1993, demand for sodium hydroxide slumped in the USA and some manufacturers were almost paying customers to take it away. A year later, as Fig 24.10 shows, there was an upsurge in demand and an increase in price. Forecasting demand is a difficult balancing act, requiring a knowledge of how and where these two products are used.

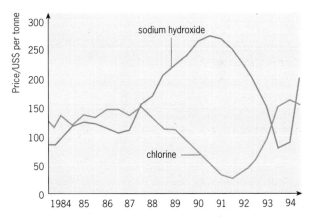

Fig 24.10 **Fluctuating prices of chlorine and sodium hydroxide**

Uses of chlorine

One of its applications as an element is to bleach the wood pulp used to make paper products and textiles. Highly toxic dioxins are by-products of this process, most of which are carried away in the wastewater. So, there is growing concern that this process is helping to increase dioxin levels in the environment. There is also evidence that dioxins do enter the paper products themselves – another cause for concern. This application of chlorine is being gradually reduced and could eventually be phased out altogether. There is also a move to find an alternative to chlorine for destroying harmful microbes in the water supply. But any alternative must be proved to be as effective as chlorine before the switch can be made. Ozone is a possibility, but it breaks down rapidly and loses its disinfectant properties. Therefore, it offers no protection against reinfection of the water.

Almost 30 per cent of all chlorine produced is used to make the monomer chloroethene ($CH_2=CHCl$), from which PVC – the world's most versatile plastic – is manufactured. Demand for PVC is likely to continue to grow. There are some fears over the safety of the plasticisers in this polymer, particularly in its use as food wrapping. Another issue is how it should be disposed of. Incineration can produce minute quantities of dioxins. However, there would seem to be no case for banning this chlorine compound, since virtually all of its uses are safe and its disposal could be made as safe.

PVC manufacture and its uses are covered on page 379.

DIOXINS

DIOXINS ARE PRESENT naturally in minute quantities and form whenever wood and certain other substances burn. However, the chemical industry has added a great deal more to the environment, much of it before the danger posed by this group of chemicals was recognised.

For seven years during the Vietnam war in the 1960s, US aircraft sprayed the jungle with a mixture of herbicides known as Agent Orange. The plan was to destroy the foliage under which the Viet Cong could hide. In all, some 50 000 tonnes of Agent Orange were used. However, Agent Orange was contaminated with dioxins, in concentrations of about 2 parts per million. So, about 100 kg of dioxins entered the Vietnamese jungles. The subsequent births of babies with abnormalities (Fig 24.11) provided the very first indication that dioxins cause genetic defects. Also much in evidence was a terrible skin complaint called chloracne, which was caused by exposure to dioxins.

In 1976 an accident at a chemical plant in Seveso, Italy, released dioxins into the air. There was an immediate outbreak of chloracne and 600 people were evacuated from the area. This brought dioxins to public attention.

Most dioxins are harmless, but one of the most deadly is TCDD (Fig 24.12).

Bleaching wood pulp with chlorine to produce paper products, such as newsprint and disposable babies' nappies, is now known to produces minute quantities of dioxins, including TCDD. This has led to a phasing out of chlorine as a bleaching agent. Chlorine dioxide provides a safer alternative.

Should we continue to be alarmed about dioxins? Now everyone is aware of the dangers of TCDD and the other deadly dioxins, the means of their production are being reduced, which is bringing levels down significantly. For example, dioxins are produced by leaded petrol, so the switch to unleaded petrol has led to a notable reduction in air pollution by dioxins. Attention is now focusing on improving the incineration of waste – another source of dioxins in the environment.

Fig 24.11 **The birth of babies with abnormalities is one of the visible signs of the dangers of dioxin**

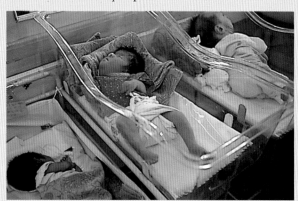

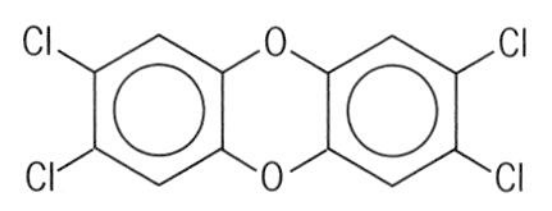

Fig 24.12 **TCDD (2,3,7,8-tetrachlorodibenzodioxin)**

Solvents are among the organic products made using chlorine. The production is being phased out of those known to cause depletion of the ozone layer in the upper atmosphere. All chlorinated organic solvents are bound to come under increasing scrutiny.

While the dangers of chlorine and its compounds must never be denied, blanket condemnation of them is not realistic. Each of the 15 000 chlorine-based compounds now produced deserves to be assessed individually according to its advantageous properties, its toxicity and its environmental effects. Many of the most effective medicines and pesticides are chlorine-based compounds, and without them, disease would be more widespread and crop production would fall.

Reaction of chlorine with alkali

The two major products of the chlor-alkali industry, sodium hydroxide solution and chlorine, can react together in the cold to produce chlorate(I) ions, ClO^-, and chlorine ions, Cl^-. This solution is the liquid bleach found in most homes:

$$Cl_2(g) + 2OH^-(aq) \rightarrow ClO^-(aq) + Cl^-(aq) + H_2O(l)$$

That is:

$$Cl_2(g) + 2NaOH(aq) \rightarrow NaClO(aq) + NaCl(aq) + H_2O(l)$$
$$\text{sodium chlorate(I)}$$

?

O (a) Disproportionation occurs when a species is both oxidised and reduced simultaneously.
What are the oxidation numbers of Cl_2, ClO^- and Cl^-?

(b) Which of the products is formed as a result of oxidation of chlorine and which as a result of reduction?
Hint: If you are not sure, look at page 437.

ClO^- ions themselves disproportionate on heating to give chlorate(V) ions, ClO_3^-, and chloride ions, Cl^-:

$$3ClO^-(aq) \rightarrow ClO_3^-(aq) + 2Cl^-(aq)$$

So, if the alkali is hot and concentrated when the chlorine is added, the overall reaction is:

$$3Cl_2(g) + 6OH^-(aq) \rightarrow ClO_3^-(aq) + 5Cl^-(aq) + H_2O(l)$$

Sodium chlorate(V), $NaClO_3$, is used as a weedkiller. It is also reduced to form ClO_2, which is safer, if less efficient, to use than elemental chlorine for bleaching paper and textiles.

?

P The reactions with cold and hot alkali are both reversed if acid is added. Explain why.

Q The halogens bromine and iodine react similarly to chlorine with aqueous alkali. Write equations for bromine and iodine reactions with $OH^-(aq)$ in both cold and hot conditions.

■ See questions 4, 5 and 6.

CHLORINATING WATER SUPPLIES AND SWIMMING POOLS

CHLORINE IS PUMPED into water as the final stage in its treatment before it enters the domestic supply. Chlorine reacts with water to form chloric(I) acid, which is the chemical which kills bacteria:

(1) $Cl_2(g) + H_2O(l) \rightleftharpoons HOCl(aq) + H^+(aq) + Cl^-(aq)$

HOCl is a weak acid and dissociates slightly:

(2) $HOCl(aq) \rightleftharpoons H^+(aq) + ClO^-(aq)$
    chlorate(I) ion

$HOCl(aq)$ is the bactericide rather than $ClO^-(aq)$, as it is 80 times more effective. It is thought that the negative charge on ClO^- hinders its penetration into the bacterial cell wall. A decrease in $H^+(aq)$ ions causes equilibrium (2) to shift to the right, according to Le Chatelier's principle. So, more $HOCl(aq)$ ionises, thereby reducing the $HOCl(aq)$ concentration.

chlorine will escape and be a health hazard. So health and safety regulations ban the use of cylinders in public pools. Instead, solid compounds of chlorine, such as Trichlor, are used to produce the chloric(I) acid.

SHALLO'

Fig 24.14 **With many people using this swimming pool, sterilisation of the water with chlorine keep it bacteria free**

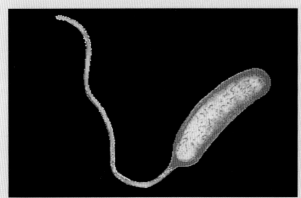

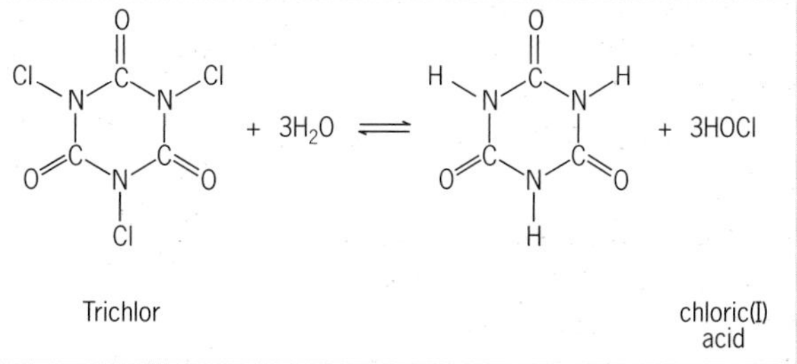

Fig 24.13 *Vibrio cholerae*, **the bacterium which causes cholera. It is found in many untreated water supplies. Cholera is spread by infected food and water**

In a water treatment works, the pH is adjusted to about 7.3. This produces a fairly high concentration of $HOCl(aq)$. A lower, more acidic pH would start to dissolve harmful substances from the water pipes.

A public swimming pool makes an ideal breeding ground for microorganisms, so it must be sterilised (Fig 24.14). The water used to be sterilised using chlorine gas from cylinders. However slight, there is a risk that

Trichlor + $3H_2O$ $\rightleftharpoons$ + $3HOCl$ chloric(I) acid

Fig 24.15 **The reaction of Trichlor with water to produce chloric(I) acid**

When a system is in equilibrium, altering the concentration of one of the species present causes the equilibrium to shift to counteract the alteration. This is Le Chatelier's principle, see pages 338 and 633.

R Solid NaOCl is another compound which can react to form chloric(I) acid. The ionic equation is:

$OCl^-(aq) + H_2O(l) \rightleftharpoons OH^-(aq) + HOCl(aq)$

Why is concentrated hydrochloric acid added to the solution that is formed in the swimming pool at the same time?
Hint: Think about the pH of the water when NaOCl is added.

Hydrogen chloride

Hydrogen chloride is in the top 30 industrial chemicals with an annual world production of over 50 million tonnes. To produce hydrogen chloride, a stream of hydrogen is burnt in chlorine:

$$H_2(g) + Cl_2(g) \rightarrow 2HCl(g)$$

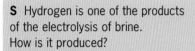

S Hydrogen is one of the products of the electrolysis of brine. How is it produced?

The hydrogen chloride, HCl, is added to water to produce hydrochloric acid. This has many surprising uses. For example, it is used in sugar refining and brewing. Its largest use is in removing oxide scale from steel and other metals.

SUMMARY

After studying this chapter, you should know that:

■ Electrolysis is the process of decomposing a compound using electricity.

■ The products of electrolysis depend on whether the electrolyte is molten or in aqueous solution, on the position of the ions in the electrochemical (redox) series, and on the concentration of the ions.

■ The quantity of electricity in coulombs
= amps × seconds.

■ The quantity of electricity passed is proportional to the amount of substance discharged at the electrode.

■ 96 500 C = the Faraday constant, F

■ $F = Le$, where L is the Avogadro constant and e the charge on an electron.

■ The number of moles of electrons required to discharge 1 mole of ions is equal to the charge on the ion.

■ The chlor-alkali industry is based on the electrolysis of concentrated aqueous sodium chloride (also called brine).

■ Chlorine and its products have tremendous industrial importance but the use of some chlorine compounds is becoming controversial due to their environmental significance.

■ The production of PVC is one of the major uses of chlorine. Others include bleaches, hydrochloric acid and organic solvents.

■ Chlorine is used in water purification.

■ Chlorine disproportionates in cold, aqueous sodium hydroxide to give Cl^- and ClO^-, and in hot, aqueous NaOH to give Cl^- and ClO_3^-.

QUESTIONS

1 Sodium and sodium hydroxide are both manufactured by electrolytic processes.

a) Name the electrolyte used in the manufacture of:
   (i) sodium,
   (ii) sodium hydroxide.

b) **(i)** What is produced at the anode during the manufacture of sodium hydroxide? Write an equation for its formation.

(ii) What other gaseous product might be given off at the anode under other conditions? Write an equation for its formation.

c) Suggest a reason why the product in **b)(i)** is formed in the industrial process rather than that in **b)(ii)**.
[ULEAC June 1996 Chemistry Module Test 3, q.2]

2 A current of 0.60 A was passed through the circuit in Fig 24.Q2 for 15 minutes.

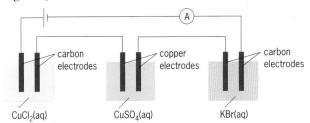

Fig 24.Q2

a) **(i)** State the electrolysis products at each of the electrodes in the table below.

	Electrolyte		
	$CuCl_2$(aq)	$CuSO_4$(aq)	KBr(aq)
product at the anode			
product at the cathode			

(ii) Which solution shows an increase in pH?

b) Calculate the change in mass of the copper anode in the aqueous copper(II) sulphate.

c) State what would happen during electrolysis to the concentration of: $CuCl_2$(aq) $CuSO_4$(aq)

d) Suggest how the appearance of the electrolyte would change if inert electrodes were used in the aqueous copper(II) sulphate.

e) State an industrial application of one of these electrolytic processes.
[UCLES March 1996 Modular: Trends and Patterns, q.4]

3 Using inert electrodes, a current was passed through two beakers containing aqueous silver nitrate and aqueous copper(II) sulphate, connected in series. After 30 min, 0.100 g of silver was deposited from the first solution. Calculate:

a) how many moles of silver were deposited,

b) the current passed,

c) the mass of copper deposited from the aqueous copper(II) sulphate.
[UCLES June 1996 Chemistry Paper 1 9254/1, q.3]

4 Chlorine is produced by the electrolysis of saturated brine (concentrated aqueous sodium chloride) in a diaphragm cell with steel cathodes and titanium anodes.

a) Write down the equation for the reaction
(i) at the anode (positive electrode),
(ii) at the cathode (negative electrode).

b) What is formed in solution?

c) What is the purpose of the diaphragm in this cell?

d) Chlorine is both oxidised and reduced in the following reaction:

$$3Cl_2(g) + 6NaOH(aq) \rightarrow 5NaCl(aq) + NaClO_3(aq) + 3H_2O(l)$$

(i) State the oxidation number of chlorine in each of the following: Cl_2, NaCl and $NaClO_3$.
(ii) To which compound has chlorine been oxidised?
(iii) State the conditions necessary for this reaction to take place.

e) When a current of 1.34 A was passed through aqueous gold chloride for 12.0 minutes, 0.650 g of gold was deposited at the cathode.
(i) Calculate the quantity of electricity (in coulombs, C) passed through the aqueous gold chloride.
(ii) Calculate the number of moles of electrons which discharged 0.650 g of gold. ($F = 96\,500\,C\,mol^{-1}$)
(iii) Calculate the charge on the aqueous gold ion. [A_r: Au, 197]
(iv) When a current is passed through aqueous potassium chloride, hydrogen is given off at the cathode.
(v) Suggest why hydrogen is not given off at the cathode when aqueous gold chloride undergoes electrolysis.
[UCLES June 1996 Modular: Trends and Patterns, q.3]

5 Sodium hydroxide and chlorine may be made simultaneously from brine in a diaphragm cell.

a) **Briefly** indicate the conditions required and sketch the plant used, outlining the principles of its operation. (A long account is not required.)

b) Give the equation and the conditions for the reaction of sodium hydroxide with ethyl ethanoate. Which industrial process uses this **type** of reaction?

c) Give the equation for the reaction of chlorine with cold, dilute sodium hydroxide solution, and use this reaction to illustrate the meaning of the term 'disproportionation'.
[ULEAC January 1996 Synoptic Paper CH6, q.5]
Note: You may need to refer to page 342 to answer **b)**.

6
a) Write an equation for the reaction which occurs at room temperature between dilute aqueous sodium hydroxide and chlorine gas and state the commercial importance of this reaction.

b) When chlorine is bubbled into water an equilibrium is established.
(i) Write an equation for this equilibrium.
(ii) State and explain what would be observed if a strip of universal indicator paper was added to this solution.

[NEAB February 1995 Equilibria and Inorganic Chemistry CH2, q.3]
Note: you may need to refer to page 491 to answer part **b)**.

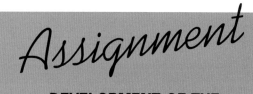

DEVELOPMENT OF THE MEMBRANE CELL

The membrane cell is the latest development in chlor-alkali electrolysis cells. It has many advantages over the older technologies of the diaphragm cell and the mercury cell. In the membrane cell, the anode and cathode compartments are kept separate by a polymer membrane which allows only sodium ions to pass through, and prevents the passage of anions. The polymer is based on PTFE, poly(tetrafluoroethene), and is very resistant to chemical attack. (The properties and use of PTFE are described on page 380.)

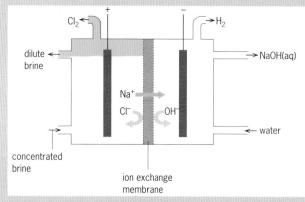

Fig 24.A1 **Simplified version of a membrane cell**

1 What is meant by the term *anions*?

2

a) In the diaphragm cell and the membrane cell, why must the OH⁻ ions be kept away from the anode?

b) What material is used to make the diaphragm in a diaphragm cell, and what are the environmental problems of using this material?

3 The electrode products of the diaphragm cell and the membrane cell are the same. Write the half-equation for the reaction occurring at the anode. Explain why sodium hydroxide solution is produced at the cathode.

Although ion-exchange materials had been known for many years, a membrane suitable for use in the chlor-alkali cell was not developed until the 1970s, by Du Pont in the USA.

Chlorine is a very strong oxidising agent and concentrated sodium hydroxide extremely corrosive. The ion-exchange membrane has to withstand this chemically hostile environment. It also has to have a long life, low maintenance, a low electrical resistance, and must not allow the passage of water molecules into the cathode compartment.

The PTFE polymer chain that Du Pont developed had negatively charged side chains ending in SO_3^-. This is shown in Fig 24.A2. The problem with this membrane was that when the concentration of the sodium hydroxide reached 12 per cent, OH⁻ ions started to migrate through the membrane towards the anode. Later developments in Japan refined this membrane to allow concentrations of 30–35 per cent sodium hydroxide to be produced. There are high hopes that further development may boost this to 40 per cent.

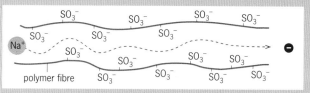

Fig 24.A2 **The sodium ion passes through the ion exchange membrane, drawn by the negative charge on the cathode. But anions OH⁻ and Cl⁻ are repelled by the negatively charged side chains in the modified polymer membrane**

4 The membrane is made as thin as possible (a thickness of 0.15–0.30 mm). Why is it important to have a very thin membrane?

5 In the membrane cell the sodium chloride solution which enters the anode compartment must be purified to remove Mg^{2+} and Ca^{2+} ions. Why is this essential?

6 The sodium hydroxide produced by the membrane cell has a high degree of purity.

a) What is the main contaminant of sodium hydroxide produced from the diaphragm cell and how is it removed?

b) Why does this not happen in the membrane cell?

c) The diaphragm cell produces a 10 per cent solution of sodium hydroxide. How does this compare with the membrane cell and why does it encourage manufacturers to install membrane cells?

d) The mercury cell produces the highest purity of sodium hydroxide at 50 per cent concentration, yet mercury cells are being phased out. Why is this?

7 A current of 30 000 amps is passed through a membrane cell in a 24-hour period.

a) Calculate the quantity of electricity passed in this time.

b) Work out the mass and volume of chlorine gas produced. Assume room conditions.

8 Hydrogen is produced during the electrolysis of brine. Research some of the major uses of this product.

ELECTROLYSIS AND THE CHLOR-ALKALI INDUSTRY

The chemical industry relies very heavily on chlorine, sodium chloride and related compounds, and so their chemistry is very important. The chapter covers aspects of industrial processes and their environmental impact as well as the reactions and concepts behind them. Study the Chapter Map and check that you understand the ideas and links between them.

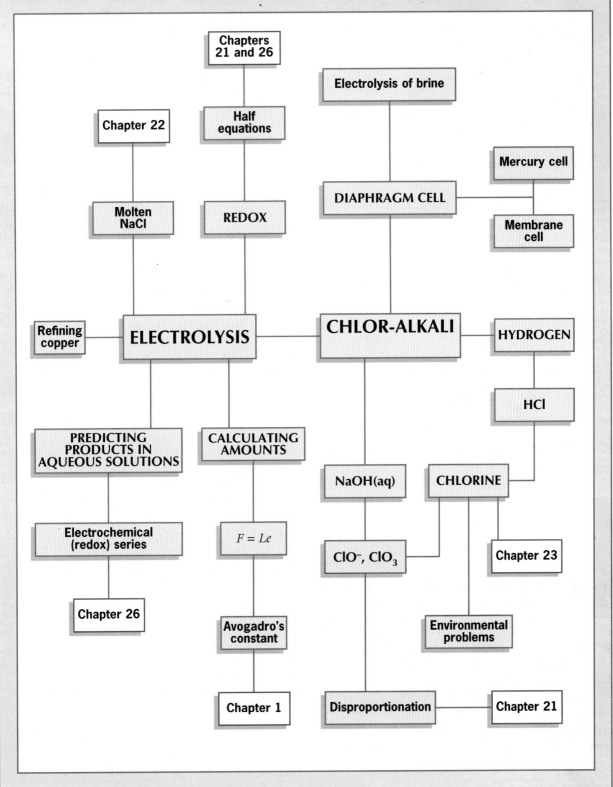

NITINOL IS A REMARKABLE ALLOY that can remember shapes. Deform a piece of the alloy and it will return to its original shape after being heated.

Nitinol is an alloy of nickel and titanium, both transition elements. It was discovered in the USA in 1962 quite by chance, when researchers in the defence industry were seeking ways to make titanium less brittle by adding nickel to it. They found that the temperature at which Nitinol returns to its original shape can be set anywhere between −100 °C and 100 °C by altering the amounts of nickel.

Nitinol wire can be used to repair damaged or blocked arteries. The wire is wound round a tube of the same diameter as the inside of an artery. It is heated so that this coiled shape is remembered. The wire is then cooled and straightened. It is passed into the artery to be repaired. The temperature of the blood warms up the wire, which returns to its coiled shape. So an artery with a weak wall can be reinforced and a constriction in an artery can be unblocked. Nitinol does not react with body chemicals, and the arterial wall soon grows round it.

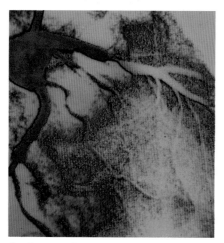

Arteries can collapse or become constricted. This image shows a severe constriction in a coronary artery, restricting blood flow from the red to the orange part of the artery. To overcome this, a coil of Nitinol wire can be inserted to hold it open and allow the blood to flow

More information on iron and steel can be found on pages 11 and 13.

1 WHAT IS A TRANSITION ELEMENT?

Ask someone to name the first metal that comes to mind, and the chances are that a transition element will be named. It may be iron, essential to the construction of many buildings, most vehicles and almost all machinery. It may be gold, a precious metal used in jewelry and other forms of ornamentation, and as a protective coating. It may be copper, used in electric wiring and for indoor water pipes, or it may be silver or platinum. It could be nickel or chromium. Everyone is familiar with the transition elements through their use, not in compounds, but on their own or in alloys, such as brass, bronze and steel.

The transition metal compound with the largest annual production (2 600 000 tonnes) is titanium(IV) oxide, TiO_2. This compound is bright white when pure, and so is used as the pigment of white paint, white paper and white plastics, as well as being used in sunscreens.

Transition metals are essential to life. Cobalt is found in vitamin B1, where it acts as a catalyst. The iron in haemoglobin is involved in transporting oxygen round the body. And nickel and copper are essential components of several enzymes.

Fig 25.1 **The pigment in white paint is TiO_2**

So what is a transition element? The central block of the Periodic Table is the **d block**. This chapter deals with the ten d block elements in Period 4, sometimes called the 'first row transition elements' as they are the top row of the d block. These elements have a closely similar set of properties, so it is tempting to call them all transition elements. However, on closer examination, scandium at one end of the first row and zinc at the other are obviously different from the rest. This has led chemists to define transition elements as **elements which form one or more ions with a partially filled d subshell**. This definition excludes zinc and scandium.

Electron configuration

Table 25.1 shows the electron configurations of the first-row transition elements. Notice that the 4s subshell has already been filled because this is at a lower energy than the 3d subshell. The full electron configuration of titanium (atomic number 22) is $1s^2 2s^2 2p^6 3s^2 3p^6 3d^2 4s^2$.

Element	Symbol	Atomic (proton) number	Electron configuration 3d		4s
scandium	Sc	21	[Ar] ↑ ▢ ▢ ▢ ▢		↑↓
titanium	Ti	22	[Ar] ↑ ↑ ▢ ▢ ▢		↑↓
vanadium	V	23	[Ar] ↑ ↑ ↑ ▢ ▢		↑↓
chromium	Cr	24	[Ar] ↑ ↑ ↑ ↑ ↑		↑
manganese	Mn	25	[Ar] ↑ ↑ ↑ ↑ ↑		↑↓
iron	Fe	26	[Ar] ↑↓ ↑ ↑ ↑ ↑		↑↓
cobalt	Co	27	[Ar] ↑↓ ↑↓ ↑ ↑ ↑		↑↓
nickel	Ni	28	[Ar] ↑↓ ↑↓ ↑↓ ↑ ↑		↑↓
copper	Cu	29	[Ar] ↑↓ ↑↓ ↑↓ ↑↓ ↑↓		↑
zinc	Zn	30	[Ar] ↑↓ ↑↓ ↑↓ ↑↓ ↑↓		↑↓

Since the noble gas core is argon ($1s^2 2s^2 2p^6 3s^2 3p^6$), titanium can be abbreviated to $[Ar]3d^2 4s^2$.

For each element from scandium to zinc, the number of protons increases by one. This increases the positive charge on the nucleus. However, because the electrons are being added to the inner 3d subshell, this tends to shield the outer 4s electrons from the increasing charge. This partly explains the similarity in physical and chemical properties. Also, because the 3d and 4s subshells have similar energies, the electrons from both can take part in bonding, which gives rise to some characteristic transition metal properties.

Electrons occupy first the orbitals of lowest energy. The orbitals in a subshell are first occupied singly by electrons spinning in the same direction, which helps to minimise the inter-electron repulsion. Only when all the d orbitals in the d subshell are singly occupied do electrons start pairing up. For the build-up of electron configurations, see page 62.

Electron configurations of Cr and Cu

Look at Table 25.1. The chromium atom and the copper atom each have only one electron in the 4s subshell. As the number of protons increases, the number of electrons in the d subshell also increases by one each time, until chromium is reached. At chromium, there is a jump of two electrons, one coming from the 4s subshell. Why is this? The half-filled subshell has five singly occupied orbitals. So, it is a lower energy arrangement to have $3d^5$ and only one 4s electron, as this removes the paired electron in the 4s orbital and thereby reduces interelectron repulsion. At copper, the most stable arrangement is to have $3d^{10}4s^1$, since a full 3d subshell is a more stable arrangement.

A Why is the central block of elements called the d block? Hint: If you are not sure, look at page 399.

B (a) Write down the full electron configuration for manganese and nickel.

(b) Look at Table 25.1. Why are atomic orbitals in the d subshell occupied by single, unpaired electrons first? Hint: See page 62 if you are not sure.

■ See question 1.

To review electron configurations, see page 62.

Table 25.1 **Arrangement of electrons in the outer 4s and inner 3d subshells of the first row of the d block. Each atomic orbital is represented by a box, and each electron by an arrow**

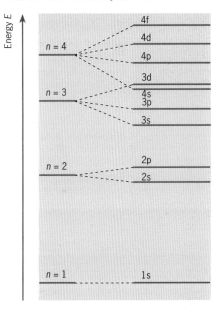

Fig 25.2 **Energy levels of the various subshells in a many-electron atom**

Fig 25.3 **Shapes of d orbitals. Four of the five d orbitals have the shape shown left and one has the shape shown right. Remember that an orbital's shape represents the boundary surface and that there is a 90 per cent probability of finding an electron within it**

✔

The more stable an arrangement, the lower its energy.

■ See question 4.

Formation of transition metal ions

Metal ions are always formed by the loss of electrons and this requires energy. In the case of transition metal ions, the **first electrons to be lost are in the 4s subshell**. This is because, once the 3d subshell starts filling, the 4s electrons are repelled further from the positive nucleus. This can be seen with Mn^{2+}:

C What is the electron configuration of:

(a) Co^{2+} and Co^{3+},

(b) Cu^+ and Cu^{2+}, and

(c) Zn^{2+}?

Hint: See Table 25.1.

$$\text{Mn [Ar]} \quad \boxed{\uparrow}\boxed{\uparrow}\boxed{\uparrow}\boxed{\uparrow}\boxed{\uparrow} \quad \boxed{\uparrow\downarrow} \xrightarrow{-2e} \text{Mn}^{2+} \text{[Ar]} \quad \boxed{\uparrow}\boxed{\uparrow}\boxed{\uparrow}\boxed{\uparrow}\boxed{\uparrow} \quad \boxed{}$$

3d 4s 3d 4s

Thus the electron configuration of Mn^{2+} is $[Ar]3d^5$.

Fe loses its 4s electrons to form Fe^{2+}:

$$\text{Fe [Ar]} \quad \boxed{\uparrow\downarrow}\boxed{\uparrow}\boxed{\uparrow}\boxed{\uparrow}\boxed{\uparrow} \quad \boxed{\uparrow\downarrow} \xrightarrow{-2e} \text{Fe}^{2+} \text{[Ar]} \quad \boxed{\uparrow\downarrow}\boxed{\uparrow}\boxed{\uparrow}\boxed{\uparrow}\boxed{\uparrow} \quad \boxed{}$$

3d 4s 3d 4s

which has an electron configuration of $[Ar]3d^6$.

Because the energies of the 4s and 3d subshells are still fairly close together, 3d electrons may also be lost to form ions with charges of 3+. In forming Fe^{3+} a 3d electron is lost together with the two 4s electrons to give an electron configuration of $[Ar]3d^5$

D Scandium forms only 3+ ions. What is the electron configuration of Sc^{3+} and why is scandium not considered to be a transition element?

$$\text{Fe [Ar]} \quad \boxed{\uparrow\downarrow}\boxed{\uparrow}\boxed{\uparrow}\boxed{\uparrow}\boxed{\uparrow} \quad \boxed{\uparrow\downarrow} \xrightarrow{-3e} \text{Fe}^{3+} \text{[Ar]} \quad \boxed{\uparrow}\boxed{\uparrow}\boxed{\uparrow}\boxed{\uparrow}\boxed{\uparrow} \quad \boxed{}$$

3d 4s 3d 4s

As already noted, scandium and zinc do not show typical transition metal properties. Zinc has an electron configuration $[Ar]3d^{10}4s^2$. The stable full d subshell means that zinc forms only Zn^{2+} ions $[Ar]3d^{10}$. Recalling the definition of transition metals as those which form one or more ions with a partially filled d subshell, zinc does not qualify as a transition element.

See question 2, 4, 5 and 10. ■

2 PHYSICAL PROPERTIES OF TRANSITION ELEMENTS

In terms of their physical properties, transition elements are typical metals. They are hard and dense, have high melting points and are good conductors of heat and electricity. They tend to be strong and durable, and have high tensile strengths, as well as other useful mechanical properties. So they find many applications, from bridges (see the Humber bridge, page 2) to cooking utensils. Contrast this with the s block metals considered on page 455, some of which are soft and have low melting points.

A more detailed examination of the physical properties reveals their close similarity. This is again explained by the electron configurations.

E What other typical properties of metals are there?
To check your answer, look at page 403.

F Fig 25.5 shows that the melting point drops at manganese. Why do you think this is? Hint: Look at the electron configuration of manganese and remember that half-filled subshells are particularly stable.

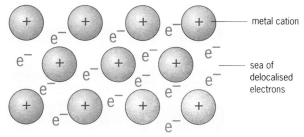

Fig 25.4 **Metallic bonding in transition metals involves 3d as well as 4s electrons**

Melting points and hardness

The high melting points and the hardness of transition metals are caused by their strong metallic bonds. As described on pages 414 and 416, metallic bonding is caused by the delocalisation of outer electrons, leaving positive metal ions surrounded by a sea of electrons. The more electrons that are delocalised, the stronger the metallic bond. In the case of transition metals, some 3d electrons can be delocalised as well as the 4s. This explains why they have higher melting points compared with the s block elements, such as potassium and calcium.

Fig 25.5 **Melting points and boiling points of the first transition series. For comparison, potassium and calcium are included. Note that all the transition elements have melting points above 1000 °C**

Remember: Electrons in metallic bonding are delocalised. They are free to move throughout the metal and so do not 'belong' to any particular ion.

Density, atomic radii and ionic radii

From Fig 25.6, it follows that the first-row transition elements are more dense than the s block elements potassium and calcium. This is partly because the atoms in the metallic lattice are packed more closely together and held more tightly by the stronger metallic bonds. Also, the atomic radii are smaller as Fig 25.7 shows.

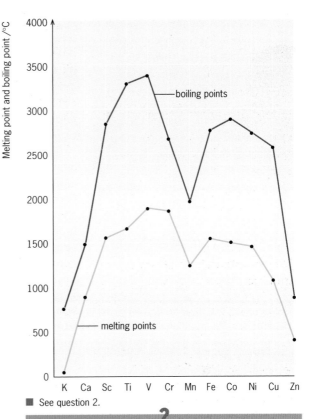

■ See question 2.

G No ionic radii are shown for K^{2+}, K^{3+}, Ca^{3+} and Sc^{2+} in Fig 25.7 as these ions do not occur in chemical reactions. Explain, using electron configurations, why these ions do not form.

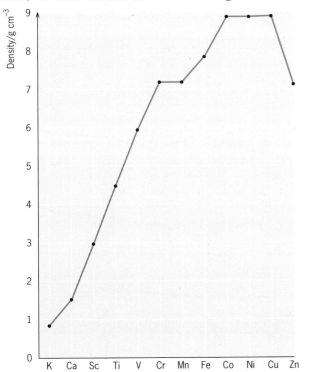

Fig 25.6 **Densities of the first transition series. For comparison, potassium and calcium are included**

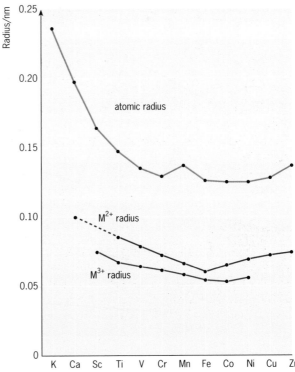

Fig 25.7 **Atomic radii and ionic radii (M^{2+} and M^{3+} ions) of the first transition series, with K and Ca included for comparison**

There can be some confusion between the term *atom* and *positive ion* when referring to metal lattices. To avoid this confusion, the radius of the atoms in metals is sometimes called the **metallic radius**. It is important to remember that when we describe atoms in metals, we are referring to positive ions surrounded by a delocalised electron sea.

The density increases across the first-row transition elements largely because the atomic mass increases, with only a minor variation in the radius of the metal atoms.

Going across a period, the atomic radius would be expected to decrease as the effective nuclear charge increases. This is seen to a certain extent at the beginning of the first transition series, but because electrons are being added to the inner 3d subshell, there is some screening of the outer shell electrons which balances the increase in nuclear charge. This tends to keep the atomic radius approximately constant.

In compounds, the ionic radius of the M^{2+} ion (where M stands for any transition metal) is much less than the atomic radius. This is because two electrons have been transferred in an ionic bond, making the effective nuclear charge on the remaining electrons greater. The radius of the M^{3+} ion is even smaller because yet another electron has been lost, increasing still further the effective nuclear charge.

Ionisation energies

Ionisation energy is discussed in several chapters of this book. Although it is a physical property, it is fundamental in determining the chemical properties of elements.

Fig 25.8 shows the first four successive ionisation energies of the elements of the first transition series. Note how similar all the first ionisation energies are across this series. The same similarity is seen with the second ionisation energies. This is because the first to be

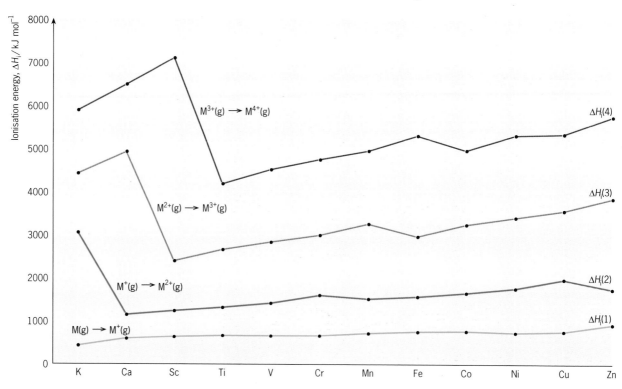

Fig 25.8 **First four successive ionisation energies of the elements of the first transition series, with K and Ca included for comparison**

removed are the 4s electrons, even though it is the 3d subshell which is being filled along the series. As with the atomic and ionic radii, this shows that the inner 3d electrons are shielding the 4s electrons from the increasing nuclear charge. In the case of the third and fourth ionisation energies, the 3d electrons are being removed from the same subshell. So, the effective nuclear charge is increasing significantly along the period.

Conduction of electricity

As explained on pages 415, the conductivity of metals is due to the delocalisation of the outer electrons in the metallic bond, making the electrons free to move under the influence of a potential difference. Transition metal atoms also have the 3d electrons as part of their metallic bond, which makes them better conductors than calcium, which can only use its 4s electrons. In fact, copper and silver are the best metallic conductors at room temperature.

?

H (a) Why is the second ionisation energy of chromium higher than expected?
Hint: Think about the electron configuration of Cr^+.

(b) The third ionisation energy of manganese is also higher than expected. Why is this?

Hint: Consider the electron configuration of Mn^{2+}.

(c) Why is there a big jump between the second and third ionisation energies of calcium?

3 CHEMICAL PROPERTIES

Having established that close similarity of physical properties tends to mark out the transition elements, what about their chemical properties? There are four that characterise transition elements:

● variable oxidation states in their compounds,
● the formation of complexes,
● the formation of coloured ions,
● catalysis of reactions both as elements and compounds.

Each of these will now be examined.

■ See question 2.

Variable oxidation states

The terms oxidation state and oxidation number tend to be used interchangeably (see pages 432 and 437). However, when considering the transition elements, the term oxidation state is usually preferred.

Lower oxidation states in ionic compounds

There is a wide variety of oxidation states in the transition metals. Contrast this with Group 1 and Group 2 elements, which have only one oxidation state of +1 and +2 respectively. The difference is explained by the closeness of the 4s and 3d energy levels. In calcium, the two 4s electrons are easily removed, but to remove another electron means breaking into the 3p subshell, which requires much more energy. This is not the case with the transition metals. Remember that the first to be lost in forming a transition metal ion are the 4s electrons, making the +2 oxidation state common, as in Fe^{2+} and Co^{2+}. But the 3d electrons may also be lost, which means that ions such as V^{3+}, Fe^{3+} and Cr^{3+} are also common. Table 25.2 shows this.

Table 25.2 **Comparison of the first four ionisation energies of calcium and iron**

Electron configuration of element		$\Delta H_i(1)$	$\Delta H_i(2)$	$\Delta H_i(3)$	$\Delta H_i(4)$
Ca	$1s^22s^22p^63s^23p^64s^2$	590	1145	4912	6474
Fe	$1s^22s^22p^63s^23p^63d^64s^2$	759	1561	2958	5290

Notice the big jump in the third ionisation energy of calcium as the 3p electron is removed. In the case of iron, the increase is more gradual and the simple ions Fe^{2+} and Fe^{3+} are both formed. The electron configurations of Fe^{2+} and Fe^{3+} are:

$$Fe^{2+} \; [Ar] \quad \underset{3d}{\boxed{\uparrow\downarrow}\,\boxed{\uparrow}\,\boxed{\uparrow}\,\boxed{\uparrow}\,\boxed{\uparrow}} \quad \underset{4s}{\boxed{\;}} \qquad Fe^{3+} \; [Ar] \quad \underset{3d}{\boxed{\uparrow}\,\boxed{\uparrow}\,\boxed{\uparrow}\,\boxed{\uparrow}\,\boxed{\uparrow}} \quad \underset{4s}{\boxed{\;}}$$

The electron configurations of manganese in the +2 and +3 oxidation states are:

$$Mn^{2+} \; [Ar] \quad \underset{3d}{\boxed{\uparrow}\,\boxed{\uparrow}\,\boxed{\uparrow}\,\boxed{\uparrow}\,\boxed{\uparrow}} \quad \underset{4s}{\boxed{\;}} \qquad Mn^{3+} \; [Ar] \quad \underset{3d}{\boxed{\uparrow}\,\boxed{\uparrow}\,\boxed{\uparrow}\,\boxed{\uparrow}\,\boxed{\;}} \quad \underset{4s}{\boxed{\;}}$$

✔

Remember: Half filled d subshells have singly occupied orbitals. This avoids electron–electron repulsion within an orbital. See page 519.

?

I (a) Solutions of $Fe^{3+}(aq)$ are more stable than $Fe^{2+}(aq)$. Suggest why?

(b) Why is Mn^{2+} more stable than Mn^{3+}?

(c) Using box diagrams, write down the electrons for Cu^+ and Cu^{2+}. Although you might predict Cu^+ to be the more stable, in fact the +2 oxidation state of copper is the more stable. The reasons for the stability of copper(II) are explained on pages 570 and 571.

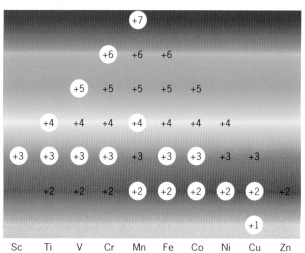

?

J All the oxidation states in Fig 25.9 are positive. Why is this? If you are not sure, see page 435.

Fig 25.9 **Oxidation states of the first transition series. The most common oxidation states are ringed**

Fig 25.9 shows all the common oxidation states of the first transition series. Note that both scandium and zinc have only one oxidation state, which is yet another reason for not classifying them as transition metals. From titanium to copper, both the +2 and +3 oxidation states exist. At first, the +3 oxidation state is common, showing the greater stability of the M^{3+} ion. But from manganese onwards the +2 oxidation state becomes more common. The removal of a third electron from the d subshell is energetically more difficult after manganese, because the effective nuclear charge becomes so much greater than it is up to manganese. The reason for the relative stabilities of the +2 and +3 oxidation states is explored further when electrode potentials are considered (see Chapter 26).

A table of typical oxidation states/oxidation numbers is given on page 435.

Higher oxidation states

From Fig 25.9, the maximum oxidation state increases across the first transition series, reaching +7 at manganese. Note that this corresponds to the total number of electrons in the 4s and 3d subshells. However, a Mn^{7+} ion or a Cr^{6+} ion would be too polarising to exist. Also, too much energy would be needed to remove so many electrons. The higher oxidation states are found covalently bonded either in simple compounds, such as TiO_2, V_2O_5, CrO_3 and Mn_2O_7, or as ions, such as VO_2^+, $Cr_2O_7^{2-}$ and MnO_4^-. The availability of partially filled or empty orbitals, particularly in the 4s and 3d subshells, allows the higher oxidation states to be reached.

?

K Many of the higher oxidation states are reached by covalently bonding to oxygen, which is highly electronegative.

(a) What does the term electronegative mean?

(b) What other element is most likely to produce these higher oxidation states? Hint: To remind yourself about electronegativity see pages 83 and 84.

After manganese, the maximum oxidation state of each element decreases because of the increasing energy needed to involve 3d electrons in bonding, and because singly filled orbitals are required in order to form a covalent bond.

Naming the transition metal compounds and ions

Ionic NaCl is easy to name. Sodium has only one oxidation state, so the compound can be called sodium chloride, and Na^+ can be called the sodium ion. However, in the case of, for example, $FeCl_3$ and $FeCl_2$ the name iron chloride does not distinguish the two compounds, so they have to be given systematic names that include the oxidation state of the transition element:

$FeCl_3$ iron(III) chloride which contains the ion Fe^{3+} iron(III) ion
$FeCl_2$ iron(II) chloride which contains the ion Fe^{2+} iron(II) ion

Note that the oxidation state is shown by a roman numeral in brackets and that there is no space between the metal name and the oxidation number.

Here are two more examples of compounds with systematic names:

CuO copper(II) oxide MnO_2 manganese(IV) oxide

Ions such as MnO_4^- and $Cr_2O_7^{2-}$ are called **oxyanions**, because they are negative ions which contain oxygen. MnO_4^- is called the manganate(VII) ion. The (VII) signifies that the oxidation state of manganese in this oxyanion is +7. $Cr_2O_7^{2-}$ is the dichromate(VI) ion, so the oxidation state of chromium in this oxyanion is +6. Thus, $KMnO_4$ is called potassium manganate(VII) and $Na_2Cr_2O_7$ is called sodium dichromate(VI).

Redox reactions and the stability of oxidation states

Since the transition elements have variable oxidation states in their compounds, they can undergo **redox** reactions. Compounds which contain transition elements in high oxidation states, such as potassium manganate(VII), tend to be oxidising agents. This is because they are usually less stable than compounds with lower oxidation states. In acid solution, the MnO_4^- ion is reduced to Mn^{2+} by gaining electrons, as can be seen in this **half equation**:

$$MnO_4^-(aq) + 8H^+(aq) + 5e^- \rightarrow Mn^{2+}(aq) + 4H_2O(l)$$

Look again at Fig 25.9 on page 524, where it is noted that, across the first transition series, that the +3 oxidation state is more stable than the +2 state until manganese is reached. This means that Ti^{2+}, V^{2+} and Cr^{2+} are highly reducing, because they are easily oxidised to the +3 state. For example:

$$Cr^{2+}(aq) \rightarrow Cr^{3+}(aq) + e^-$$

Traces of oxygen can be removed from other gases by bubbling the gases through a solution of $Cr^{2+}(aq)$.

From manganese to copper, the +2 state becomes more stable. So, compounds with oxidation states of +3 are highly oxidising. For example:

$$Co^{3+}(aq) + e^- \rightarrow Co^{2+}(aq)$$

The relative stabilities of the different oxidation states are predicted from **standard electrode potentials, $E^{\ominus}$** (see Chapter 26).

Complexes

A **complex** is formed when a central metal atom or ion is surrounded by species which donate lone pairs of electrons. The actual bonding in complexes is complicated and beyond the scope of this book. However, it is assumed that the lone pairs from the ligands form dative covalent (coordinate) bonds. A species which donates a

■ See questions 2, 4, 8, 9, 10 and 12.

L **(a)** Use oxidation states to name the following transition metal compounds: **(i)** TiO_2, **(ii)** Fe_2O_3, **(iii)** $Mn(OH)_3$, **(iv)** CrO_3, and **(v)** V_2O_5.

(b) Write down the formulas of the following compounds: **(i)** copper(II) hydroxide, **(ii)** manganese(II) carbonate, **(iii)** titanium(IV) chloride, **(iv)** copper(II) nitrate, and **(v)** iron(II) bromide.

Remember: In MnO_4^-, since O has an oxidation number of –2, the total oxidation number due to O is $-2 \times 4 = -8$. Therefore, the oxidation state of manganese is +7, because this leaves –1 as the charge on the anion.

M **(a)** What is the formula of sodium ferrate(VI)?

(b) What is the name of the oxyanion CrO_4^{2-}?

Remember: Redox means oxidation (oxidation number increases) and reduction (oxidation number decreases). To find out more about redox reactions and half equations, read Chapter 26.

Remember: A dative covalent bond is a covalent bond whose shared pair of electrons come from the same atom. It is also called a coordinate bond. See page 74

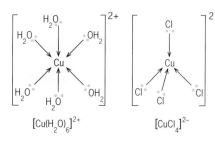

$[Cu(H_2O)_6]^{2+}$ $[CuCl_4]^{2-}$

Fig 25.10 **Two complex ions**

?

N What is the charge on the central metal ion in the following complexes?
(a) $[Ag(NH_3)_2]^+$ **(b)** $[NiCl_4]^{2-}$
(c) $[Fe(H_2O)_6]^{3+}$ **(d)** $[Ni(CN)_4]^{2-}$
(e) $[Fe(CN)_6]^{3-}$
Hint: The cyanide ligand is CN^-.

See questions 1, 2, 6, 7, and 9–11. ■

lone pair of electrons is called a **ligand**. Ligands are usually molecules such as water or negative ions such as Cl⁻. Fig 25.10 shows two complex ions.

Many complexes are positively or negatively charged, but some are neutral. In the formula, the central metal atom or ion is written first followed by the ligands. The charge on a complex is the charge of the central metal ion and the charges on the surrounding ligands added together. The overall charge of $[Cu(H_2O)_6]^{2+}$ results from the 2+ charge of Cu^{2+}, since the water molecules carry no charge. In the case of $[CuCl_4]^{2-}$, there are four Cl⁻ ions, giving a charge of 4– which when added to the 2+ charge of Cu^{2+} gives an overall charge of 2– [4(1–) + (2+) = 2–]. The charge on a complex ion is delocalised over the whole ion and is usually shown outside square brackets. However, complex ions are sometimes drawn with a charged central metal ion.

Coordination number and shape

The number of dative covalent (coordinate) bonds from ligands to the central metal ion is called the **coordination number**. The coordination number determines the shape of the complex. The most common coordination numbers are 4 and 6. Table 25.3 shows the shapes which are often associated with these two numbers, together with the shape of coordination number 2. Note that a coordination number of 4 gives two possible shapes. The more common is the tetrahedral structure. On page 77, there is a discussion of the electron pair repulsion theory, which predicts the tetrahedral, octahedral and linear shapes in Table 25.3. However, d orbital electrons affect the shape in a different way than s and p orbital electrons, and many shapes are not as predicted by this theory. For example, the shape of $[Cu(H_2O)_6]^{2+}$ is not a regular octahedron because four of the copper–oxygen bonds are short and the other two are longer, giving a distorted octahedron.

Table 25.3 **Shapes of four complexes**

Coordination number	Shape	Example	Structure
2	linear	$[Ag(NH_3)_2]^+$	$[H_3N \longrightarrow Ag \longleftarrow NH_3]^+$
4	tetrahedral	$[CuCl_4]^{2-}$	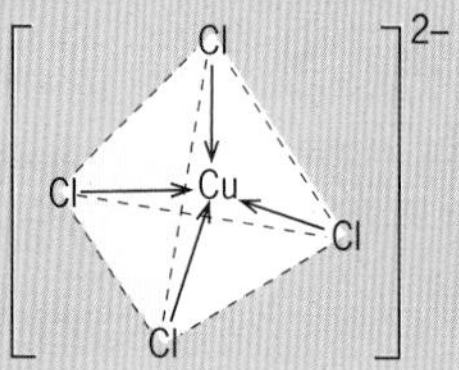
4	square planar	$[Ni(CN)_4]^{2-}$	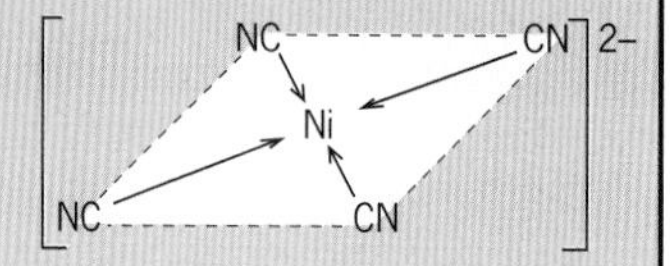
6	octahedral	$[Co(NH_3)_6]^{2+}$	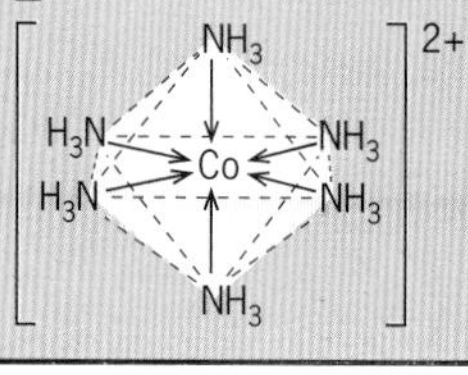

Ligands

All four ligands discussed so far – H_2O, NH_3, Cl⁻ and CN⁻ – donate one lone pair of electrons to the central metal atom, and so are called **monodentate**. This means 'single toothed' and is derived from *monos*, the Greek for one, and *dens*, the Latin for tooth. **Bidentate** ligands can form two dative covalent bonds to the metal ion, so they are 'two toothed', as shown in Fig 25.11. The lone pairs come from the nitrogen and oxygen respectively. When these ligands attach to the central metal ion, they form five-membered rings and the complexes are called **chelates** (from *chele*, the Greek for claw).

1,2-diaminoethane called en for short

ethanedioate traditional name: oxalate

Fig 25.11 **Two examples of bidentate ligands**

See questions 6, 11 and 12. ■

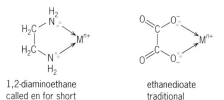

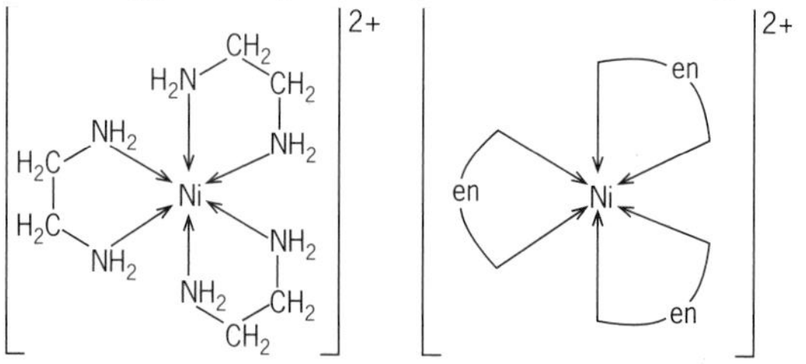

Fig 25.12 **An example of chelation with 1,2-diaminoethane. Shown on the right is the simplified version of this bidentate ligand, 'en'. The complex is written using 'en': $[Ni(en)_3]^{2+}$**

EDTA – A MOST IMPORTANT LIGAND

ETHYLENEDIAMINETETRAACETATE ION (edta) is the traditional name for a very important chelating agent. As Fig 25.13 shows, there are six lone pairs of electrons available to bond with a metal ion, so it is called a **hexadentate** ligand. This ligand surrounds and encloses metal ions to form a very stable complex ion, which explains why it is so useful.

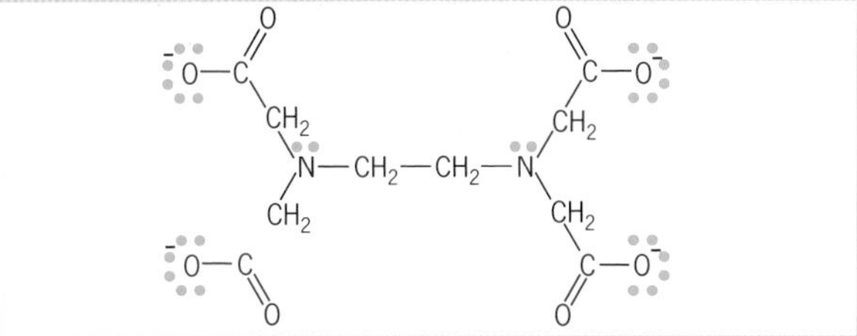

Fig 25.13 **Edta⁴⁻ ion**

Lead(II) ions (Pb^{2+}) are toxic in the human body and if they are not removed quickly they can affect the enzymes which catalyse the formation of haemoglobin. Lead(II) ions can cause permanent brain damage in children and young people. Edta is administered to remove lead(II) ions from the blood and tissue as a stable lead–edta complex ion (Fig 25.14), which is excreted in urine. It is equally effective in treating mercury poisoning. Edta is so effective at trapping and removing metal ions that it will also remove calcium and important trace metal ions which are essential to normal body function-

ing. These must be replaced during the treatment.

Edta is added to human blood when it is stored for transfusions because it keeps the calcium ions trapped in the edta complex and so prevents the blood from clotting. It is also used during operations to prevent clotting.

However, edta's applications extend far beyond the medical. It is added to some foods to remove traces of metal ions which catalyse air oxidation. In salad dressings, for example, edta prevents rancidity by removing the ions which catalyse the oxidation of oil. (There is more about this in the Assignment on page 351.) Etda is even used in liquid fertilisers, where it forms a chelate complex with the Fe^{3+} ions. Thus, OH^- ions are prevented from reacting with the Fe^{3+} to form insoluble $Fe(OH)_3$. This allows the soluble iron complex to reach and enter the plant. Edta is also added to bathroom products – particularly shampoos – to remove calcium ions from the water, thereby preventing the formation of scum.

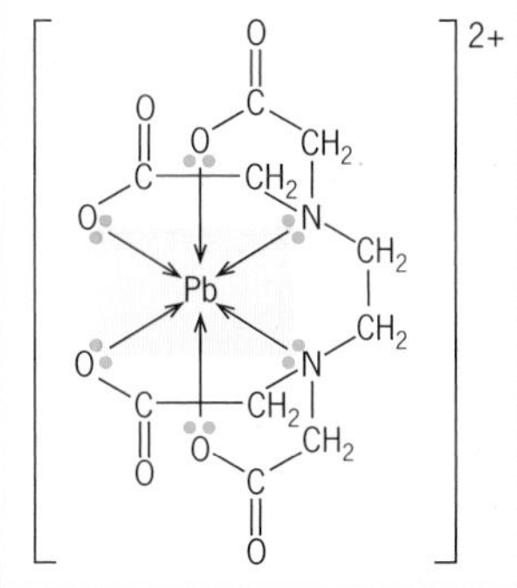

Fig 25.14 **Lead–edta complex ion. Since the charge on the lead ion is 2+ and edta has a charge of 4–, the overall charge of the complex ion is 2–**

Naming complex ions

To name a complex ion, proceed as follows.

- First, understand how the ligands are named (Table 25.4). Note: ligands that are anions are named by adding *o* to the stem of the anion names.
- The prefixes *mono, di, tri, tetra, penta* and *hexa* are used to indicate how many of a particular type of ligand are present.
- When more than one type of ligand is present, they are written in alphabetical order.
- The central metal ion is named with its oxidation state. When the complex is negatively charged, *ate* is added, shown in Table 25.5. Also included are two common non-transition metals. Note: Latinised names are used for iron and copper – ferrate and cuprate respectively.

Table 25.4 **The names of monodentate ligands**

	Ligand	Name
neutral molecules	H_2O	aqua
	NH_3	ammine
	CO	carbonyl
anions	Cl^-	chloro
	CN^-	cyano
	F^-	fluoro
	OH^-	hydroxo

Table 25.5 **The names of nine metals in complex anions**

Metal	Name of metal in complex anion
aluminium	aluminate
chromium	chromate
cobalt	cobaltate
copper	cuprate
iron	ferrate
lead	plumbate
manganese	manganate
nickel	nickelate
vanadium	vanadate

EXAMPLE

Q Name the following complex ions: **(a)** $Cu(H_2O)_6]^{2+}$, **(b)** $[Fe(CN)_6]^{4-}$ and **(c)** $[CrCl_2(H_2O)_4]^+$.

A **(a) $[Cu(H_2O)_6]^{2+}$**

Step 1 Consider the ligands and their number.

Since there are six water molecules, *hexaaqua* is used.

Step 2 Work out the oxidation state of the central metal ion.

Water is a neutral molecule, so the overall charge of the complex ion must be due to copper, which has a charge of 2+. That is, its oxidation state is +2.

Step 3 Write the name of the complex ion.

$[Cu(H_2O)_6]^{2+}$ is called hexaaquacopper(II).

(b) $[Fe(CN)_6]^{4-}$

Step 1 Consider the ligands and their number.

The ligands are cyanide ions, hence *cyano*, and there are six, hence *hexa*. So, the name starts with *hexacyano*.

Step 2 Work out the oxidation state of the central metal ion.

Six CN^- ions have a total charge of 6−. Since the overall charge on the complex is 2−, iron must have a charge of 2+, so its oxidation number is +2.

Step 3 Write the name of the complex ion.

In this Example, we are dealing with an anion (negatively charge ion), which means the Latinised name *ferrate* must be used. So, $[Fe(CN)_6]^{4-}$ is called hexacyanoferrate(II).

(c) $[CrCl_2(H_2O)_4]^+$

Step 1 Consider the ligands and their number.

In this case, there are two types of ligand: anions and neutral molecules.

Two chloride ions are *dichloro* and four water molecules are *tetraaqua*.

Anions are always named before neutral molecules, hence *dichlorotetraaqua*.

Step 2 Work out the oxidation state of the central metal ion.

Two Cl^- ions contribute a charge of 2−, while water is neutral and so contributes no charge. Therefore, the charge on Cr is 3+, giving it an oxidation number of +3.

Step 3 Write the name of the complex ion.

$[CrCl_2(H_2O)_4]^+$ is called dichlorotetraaquachromium(III).

?

O **(a)** Name the following complex ions: **(i)** $[Co(NH_3)_6]^{3+}$, **(ii)** $[Fe(CN)_6]^{3-}$, **(iii)** $[CuCl_4]^{2-}$ and **(iv)** $[Ag(NH_3)_2]^+$.

(b) Write the formula of each of the following ions: **(i)** hexaaquairon(III), **(ii)** tetraamminedichlorocobalt(III) and **(iii)** tetrachlorocobaltate(II).

Naming neutral complexes

Neutral complexes are named in exactly the same way as positively charged complexes. For example, $Ni(CO)_4$ is called tetracarbonylnickel(0). Note that the oxidation state of nickel in this complex is zero.

HAEMOGLOBIN

HAEMOGLOBIN, a protein molecule, is a vital component of blood. It transports molecular oxygen from the lungs around the body via the arteries. At the centre of this giant of a molecule is the ion Fe^{2+} bound in a complex. Four sites of attachment around the Fe^{2+} are occupied by a planar ring structure, called a porphyrin (Fig 25.15). The iron–porphyrin part of the complex is called the haem group (Fig 25.16). The fifth ligand site is occupied by a dative covalent bond to the protein globin, while molecular oxygen loosely attaches to the sixth site.

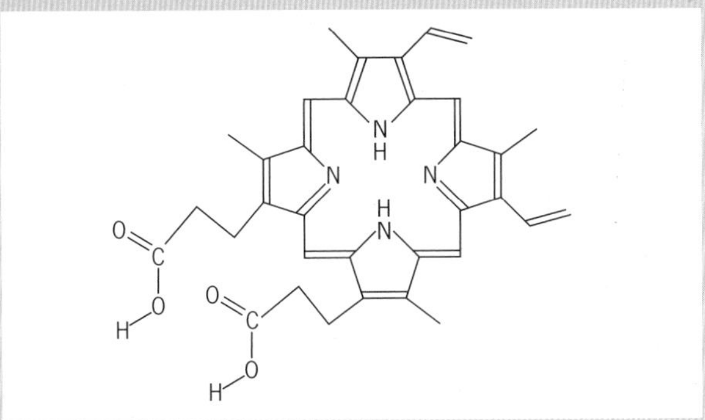

Fig 25.15 **Porphyrin ring**

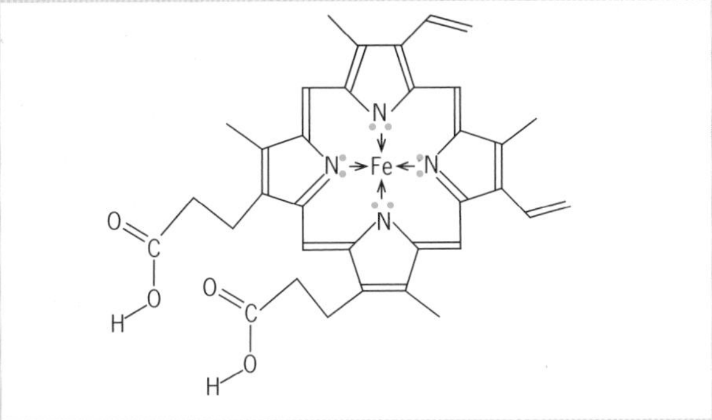

Fig 25.16 **Haem group**

When oxygen is bonded to the Fe^{2+}, the whole complex, called oxyhaemoglobin, takes on a red colour. Once the oxygen is removed, it is replaced by a water ligand, which changes the colour of the complex to blue. The complex is now called deoxyhaemoglobin. It is deoxyhaemoglobin which gives the blood in our veins its blue colour as it returns to the lungs to pick up more oxygen.

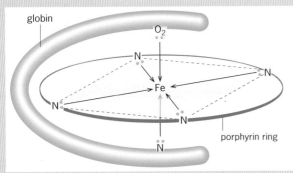

Fig 25.17 **Schematic drawing of haemoglobin**

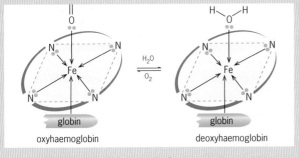

oxyhaemoglobin   deoxyhaemoglobin

Fig 25.18 **When oxygen is needed, it is replaced by water**

?

P (a) What is the coordination number of iron in the complex shown in Fig 25.17?

(b) What type of ligand is the porphyrin ring?
Hint: How many points of attachment does it have?

(c) Explain why blood in most arteries is red.

■●See questions 6 and 12.

Isomerism in complexes

Isomerism occurs when molecules have the same molecular formula but different ways of arranging their atoms. As explained on pages 144, 248 and 355, there are two principal types of isomerism: **structural isomerism** and **stereoisomerism**. The discussion on those pages is confined to organic molecules, but transition metal complexes can also exhibit isomerism. Both types of stereoisomerism – **geometric isomerism** and **optical isomerism** – occur in transition metal complexes, as the next two sections show.

Fig 25.19 **The different types of isomerism**

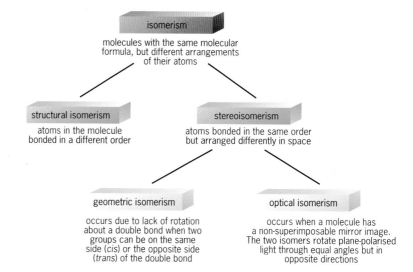

In organic chemistry, the double carbon–carbon bond prevents rotation and gives rise to geometric isomers. See page 248.

Geometric isomerism

Stereoisomers have their atoms bonded in the same order but they are arranged differently in space. Geometric isomers (or *cis–trans* isomers) occur when two different kinds of ligand are bonded in different positions around the central metal cation. The octahedral complex ion $[Co(NH_3)_4Cl_2]^+$ shows geometric isomerism. In the *cis* form, the chloride ligands are on the same side, while in the *trans* form they lie on opposite sides. (*Trans* is the Latin word for 'across'.) The *cis* and *trans* isomers shown in Fig 25.20 have different colours.

Optical isomerism

When a stereoisomer has a non-superimposable mirror image, it exhibits optical isomerism. Optical isomers have identical physical and chemical properties, but they rotate plane-polarised light in opposite directions (see page 355). Bidentate ligands, such as 1,2-diaminoethane, can give rise to optical isomerism in octahedral complexes, such as tri-1,2-diaminoethanecobalt(III) shown in Fig 25.21.

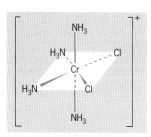

Fig 25.20(a) **The *cis* isomer of $[Cr(NH_3)_4Cl_2]^+$ is violet**

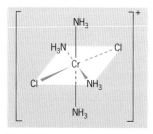

Fig 25.20(b) **The *trans* isomer of $[Cr(NH_3)_4Cl_2]^+$ is green**

?

R What is the name of the complex ion represented in Fig 25.20(a) and (b)? Hint: Look at page 527 if you are not sure how to name this.

See questions 9 and 13. ◾

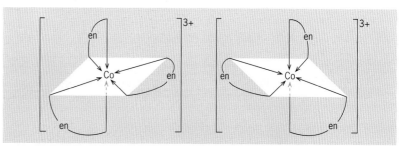

Fig 25.21 **$[Co(en)_3]^{3+}$ exists as two mirror image forms or enantiomers**

Ligand exchange and stability constants

In aqueous solutions, transition metal ions exist as aqua-complexes. The water around the central metal ion can be replaced by other ligands, and this is called **ligand exchange**. Fig 25.22(a) shows copper(II) sulphate dissolved in water, so the complex ion present is $[Cu(H_2O)_6]^{2+}$. When concentrated hydrochloric acid is added to this solution, it turns green (Fig 25.22(b)). This occurs because the water ligands of the copper(II) complex have been exchanged for chloride ions. $[CuCl_4]^{2-}$ is a more stable complex because chloride ligands have replaced the water ligands:

$$[Cu(H_2O)_6]^{2+}(aq) + 4Cl^-(aq) \rightleftharpoons [CuCl_4]^{2-}(aq) + 6H_2O(l)$$
$$\text{blue} \qquad\qquad\qquad\qquad \text{yellow}$$

However, the reaction has not gone to completion, since the solution is green – a combination of the blue and yellow complexes. As this is an equilibrium reaction, the equilibrium constant, K_c, can be calculated:

$$K_c = \frac{[CuCl_4^{2-}(aq)]}{[Cu(H_2O)_6^{2+}(aq)]\,[Cl^-(aq)]^{4-}}$$

Note that water is not included in the K_c equation because, as the solvent, its concentration is considered to be constant. (For more information on K_c, see page 336.)

The equilibrium constant is a measure of how far the position of the equilibrium is over to the right. The further the position of the equilibrium is to the right, the higher the value of K_c and the more stable the complex ion compared with the aqua-complex. K_c is called the **stability constant**. Because the numbers are often very large, they are made more manageable by using a logarithm scale. Five values of log K_c are shown in Table 25.6.

From Table 25.6, $[Cu(NH_3)_4(H_2O)_2]^{2+}$ is more stable than the chloro-complex. So, when concentrated ammonia solution is added, ammonia ligands replace chloride ligands to produce a deep blue solution. This can be seen in Fig 25.22(c). Fig 25.22(d) shows the lightening of the solution which occurs when edta is added to the solution of ammine-complex, which is again as predicted from Table 25.6.

✔ Notice in the expression for K_c that the complex ions are shown without square brackets to avoid confusion with the square brackets indicating concentration.

Table 25.6

Complex ion	Colour	Stability constant, log K_c
$[Cu(Cl_4)]^{2-}$	yellow	5.6
$[Cu(NH_3)_4(H_2O)_2]^{2+}$	deep blue	13.1
$[Cu(edta)(H_2O)_2]^{2-}$	pale blue	18.8
$[Ni(NH_3)_6]^{2+}$	purple	8.0
$[Fe(CN)_6]^{3-}$	yellow	31.0

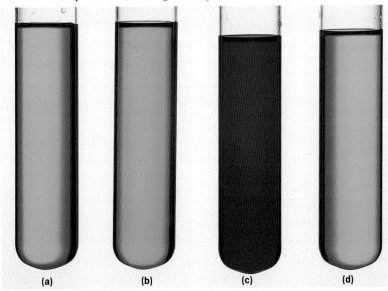

(a)   (b)   (c)   (d)

Fig 25.22 (a) **Aqueous solution of copper(II) sulphate containing** $[Cu(H_2O)_6]^{2+}(aq)$ **ions.** (b) **Cu²⁺ ions in concentrated HCl, giving the complex ion** $[CuCl_4]^{2-}(aq)$. (c) **An excess of ammonia has now been added, producing** $[Cu(NH_3)_4(H_2O)_2]^{2+}$. (d) **Edta produces a much more stable complex,** $[Cu(edta)(H_2O)_2]^{2-}$

■ See questions 7 and 10.

Aqueous complexes and acidity

As already stated, in aqueous solution, transition metal ions form aqua-complexes. When the pH of various aqueous solutions of transition metal salts are measured, a pattern emerges. There is an increase in acidity as the charge of the transition metal ion increases. So, for example, $[Fe(H_2O)_6]^{3+}(aq)$ is more acidic than $[Fe(H_2O)_6]^{2+}(aq)$. Why is this?

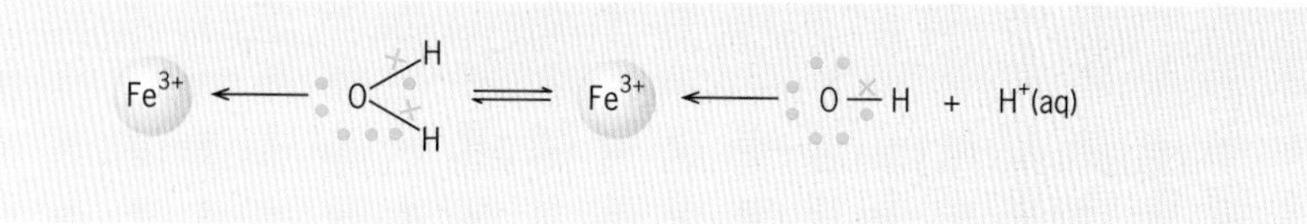

$$Fe^{3+} \longleftarrow \ddot{O}\overset{H}{\underset{H}{<}} \rightleftharpoons Fe^{3+} \longleftarrow \ddot{O} - H \; + \; H^+(aq)$$

Fig 25.23 **The highly charged cation pulls electrons from the water molecule, weakening the O–H bond. A proton is thereby released, producing H_3O^+ with water. The H_3O^+ causes acidity**

The more highly charged the central ion, the more highly polarising it is (see page 85). This attracts the electrons of the surrounding water molecules, allowing the release of protons and thus making the solution acidic. This process is called **deprotonation** of the cation. A number of equilibria exist in solution, two of which are:

Equilibrium 1:
$$[Fe(H_2O)_6]^{3+}(aq) \rightleftharpoons [Fe(OH)(H_2O)_5]^{2+}(aq) + H^+(aq)$$

Equilibrium 2:
$$[Fe(OH)(H_2O)_5]^{2+}(aq) \rightleftharpoons [Fe(OH)_2(H_2O)_4]^+(aq) + H^+(aq)$$

The polarising power of ions having charges greater than 3+ explains why oxyanions are formed. For example, $[Cr(H_2O)_6]^{6+}$ and $[Mn(H_2O)_6]^{7+}$ are theoretically possible, but the central ions are too polarising. This causes the loss of both protons from some of the surrounding water molecules to form O^{2-} ions, which dative covalently bond to give CrO_4^{2-} and MnO_4^-.

Addition of aqueous solutions of sodium hydroxide or ammonia

Aqueous sodium hydroxide contains hydroxide ions, which remove $H^+(aq)$ ions by forming water:

$$H^+(aq) + OH^-(aq) \rightarrow H_2O(l)$$

This shifts equilibria 1 and 2 to the right and causes the formation of the neutral complex $[Fe(OH)_3(H_2O)_3]$ from a third equilibrium. This complex comes down as a rusty brown, gelatinous precipitate:

Equilibrium 3:
$$[Fe(OH)_2(H_2O)_4]^+(aq) \rightleftharpoons [Fe(OH)_3(H_2O)_3](s) + H^+(aq)$$
rusty brown precipitate

Similar reactions occur between hydroxide ions and other aqueous transition metal ions, producing coloured, gelatinous precipitates. In the equations below, the aqua-complexes are represented by (aq) and the aquahydroxo-complexes by the simple metal hydroxide formulas:

$$Cr^{3+}(aq) + 3OH^-(aq) \rightarrow Cr(OH)_3(s)$$
grey-green

$$Mn^{2+}(aq) + 2OH^-(aq) \rightarrow Mn(OH)_2(s)$$
cream

$$Fe^{2+}(aq) + 2OH^-(aq) \rightarrow Fe(OH)_2(s)$$
green

?

R Name the three different complexes shown in equilibria 1 and 2. Remember: Because water is a neutral ligand, the charge on the aqua-complex is the same as the charge on the central metal cation. For example, Fe has a charge of 3+ in $[Fe(H_2O)_6]^{3+}(aq)$.

S Non-transition metal ions in solution can also be acidic. For example, $[Al(H_2O)_6]^{3+}(aq)$ releases protons into an aqueous solution. Write an equation showing the equilibrium that exists when one proton is released. You can check your answer on page 479.

See question 11. ■

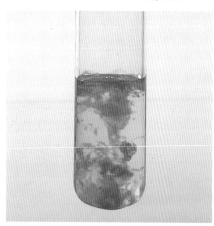

Fig 25.24 **The rusty brown precipitate produced when aqueous sodium hydroxide is added to $Fe^{3+}(aq)$ ions**

This is an example of le Chatelier's principle. See pages 338 and 637.

There are more examples of metal hydroxide precipitates on pages 460 and 645.

Fig 25.25 **Cr(OH)$_3$(s) is produced when Cr^{3+}(aq) reacts with NaOH(aq)**

Fig 25.26 **Mn(OH)$_2$(s) is precipitated when OH$^-$(aq) ions react with Mn^{2+}(aq) ions**

Fig 25.27 **The addition of OH$^-$(aq) to Fe^{3+}(aq) precipitates Fe(OH)$_3$(s)**

When excess OH$^-$(aq) is added to chromium hydroxide, the precipitate redissolves because further deprotonation takes place, as shown in equilibrium 4 to form a soluble complex:

Equilibrium 4:
$$[Cr(OH)_3(H_2O)_3](s) \rightleftharpoons [Cr(OH)_4(H_2O)_2]^-(aq) + H^+(aq)$$

Aqueous ammonia also produces coloured gelatinous precipitates because hydroxide ions are present:

$$NH_3(aq) + H_2O(l) \rightleftharpoons NH_4^+(aq) + OH^-(aq)$$

However, ammonia is also a ligand and in some cases the precipitates dissolves because a soluble ammine-complex is formed. This is seen when aqueous ammonia is added to Cu^{2+}(aq):

$$[Cu(H_2O)_6]^{2+}(aq) + 2OH^-(aq) \rightarrow [Cu(OH)_2(H_2O)_4](s)$$
blue solution   pale blue precipitate

On addition of excess ammonia solution, the precipitate dissolves to form the deep blue [Cu(NH$_3$)$_4$(H$_2$O)$_2$]$^{2+}$(aq):

$$[Cu(OH)_2(H_2O)_4]^{2+}(s) + 4NH_3(aq) \rightarrow [Cu(NH_3)_4(H_2O)_2]^{2+}(aq) + 2H_2O(l) + 2OH^-(aq)$$

For more examples of reactions with aqueous ammonia, see Chapter 29.

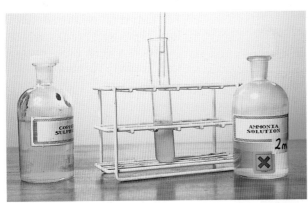

Fig 25.28(a) **When concentrated ammonia solution is added dropwise to aqueous copper(II) ions, a precipitate of copper(II) hydroxide forms**

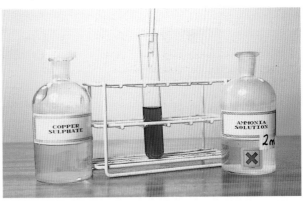

Fig 25.28(b) **On the further addition of excess ammonia solution, the precipitate dissolves as the soluble ammine complex [Cu(NH$_3$)$_4$(H$_2$O)$_2$]$^{2+}$(aq) is formed**

Table 25.7 **Colours of some common aqueous ions in the first transition series**

Ion	Colour	Outer 3d electrons
$Sc^{3+}(aq)$	colourless	$3d^0$
$Ti^{3+}(aq)$	purple	$3d^1$
$V^{3+}(aq)$	green	$3d^2$
$Cr^{3+}(aq)$	violet	$3d^3$
$Mn^{2+}(aq)$	pink	$3d^5$
$Fe^{3+}(aq)$	yellow*	$3d^5$
$Fe^{2+}(aq)$	green	$3d^6$
$Co^{2+}(aq)$	pink	$3d^7$
$Ni^{2+}(aq)$	green	$3d^8$
$Cu^{2+}(aq)$	blue	$3d^9$
$Zn^{2+}(aq)$	colourless	$3d^{10}$

* $[Fe(H_2O)_6]^{3+}(aq)$ is violet, but because of the deprotonation (see page 532) the yellow ion $[Fe(OH)(H_2O)_5]^{2+}(aq)$ predominates.

Fig 25.29 **Cobalt chloride paper before and after the addition of water**

Even the way the ligands are arranged around the central cation can affect the colour. Turn to page 530 to see the different colours of the *cis* and *trans* isomers of $[Cr(NH_3)_4Cl_2]^+$.

See questions 2, 6 and 10. ■

Fig 25.30 **The blood-red colour of $[Fe(H_2O)_5SCN]^{2+}(aq)$ is a very sensitive test for the presence of $Fe^{3+}(aq)$ ions**

4 THE FORMATION OF COLOURED IONS

The formation of coloured ions is another characteristic property of transition metals. Most of their compounds are coloured and they form coloured solutions. The colours of nine transition metal ions in aqueous solution are given in Table 25.7. Scandium and zinc ions are also included.

Being colourless is another reason why $Sc^{3+}(aq)$ and $Zn^{2+}(aq)$ are not usually regarded as transition metal ions. A coloured ion results from an incomplete d subshell which neither of these ions has.

The type of ligand also affects the colour, as already noted in the case of $[Cu(H_2O)_6]^{2+}(aq)$, which is a paler blue than the ammine complex, $[Cu(NH_3)_4(H_2O)_2]^{2+}(aq)$, which is deep blue. The cobalt chloride test for water is probably a test you have done yourself in the laboratory. Cobalt chloride paper is blue because it contains the complex ion $[CoCl_4]^{2-}$. When water is added, $[Co(H_2O)_6]^{2+}$ is formed, which is pink.

?

T (a) Write the equation for the formation of $[Co(H_2O)_6]^{2+}(aq)$ from $[CoCl_4]^{2-}(aq)$. It is an equilibrium, so remember to include the equilibrium sign.

(b) Heating moist cobalt chloride paper turns it blue again. Why does this happen? Hint: You will need to have understood Le Chatelier's principle on page 338.

The colours of ions are affected too by the number of different types of ligand, as shown by these chromium(III) complexes:

$[Cr(H_2O)_6]^{3+}(aq)$ $[CrCl(H_2O)_5]^{2+}(aq)$ $[CrCl_2(H_2O)_4]^+(aq)$
violet   green   dark green

Many transition metal complexes have characteristic colours which are so distinctive that they can be used to test for these particular ions. For example, $Fe^{3+}(aq)$ forms a blood-red complex with thiocyanate ions (SCN^-). The addition of aqueous potassium thiocyanate, KSCN, to a solution of $Fe^{3+}(aq)$ is a very sensitive test, since tiny amounts give the typical blood-red coloration:

$$[Fe(H_2O)_6]^{3+}(aq) + SCN^-(aq) \rightarrow [Fe(H_2O)_5SCN]^{2+}(aq)$$
blood-red

$Fe^{2+}(aq)$ ions, however, do not give a coloured complex.

Another way of distinguishing between $Fe^{2+}(aq)$ and $Fe^{3+}(aq)$ is to use the complex ion $[Fe(CN)_6]^{3-}(aq)$, which produces a deep blue precipitate, called Turnbull's blue, with $Fe^{2+}(aq)$.

We discuss the origin of colour in more detail in Chapter 28.

Fig 25.31 **Turnbull's blue precipitate**

5 CATALYSIS

Catalysis is the final characteristic property of transition elements to be considered here. A catalyst is a substances which alters the rate of a chemical reaction without becoming permanently involved in the reaction. A catalyst works by providing an alternative reaction pathway with a lower energy of activation. (See pages 126 and 594 for more information.)

Platinum, for example, plays a crucial role in reducing emissions from car exhausts through its use in catalytic converters. One reaction which is catalysed by platinum is the oxidation of carbon monoxide:

$$2CO(g) + O_2(g) \xrightarrow{\text{Pt catalyst}} 2CO_2(g)$$

The Assignment on page 265 shows how nickel catalyses the hydrogenation of carbon–carbon double bonds, an important reaction in the production of fats from oils.

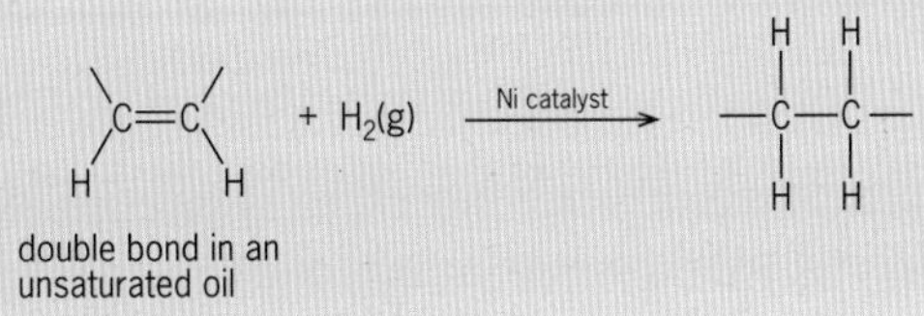

double bond in an
unsaturated oil

Fig 25.32 **Hydrogenation of carbon–carbon double bonds**

The Haber process for the production of ammonia (featured on page 652) uses finely divided iron to catalyse the reaction between nitrogen and ammonia:

$$N_2(g) + 3H_2(g) \underset{\text{Fe catalyst}}{\rightleftharpoons} 2NH_3(g)$$

It ranks among the most important industrial reactions because ammonia is used to produce nitrogenous fertilisers.

The contact process, which leads to the production of sulphuric acid (see page 672) is another important catalysed reaction:

$$2SO_2(g) + O_2(g) \underset{\text{V}_2\text{O}_5 \text{ catalyst}}{\rightleftharpoons} 2SO_3(g)$$

Fig 25.33 **Gauze of platinum and rhodium provides a huge surface area on which to catalyse the oxidation of ammonia in the production of nitric acid**

All of the processes mentioned so far are examples of **heterogeneous catalysis**, where the catalyst is in a different physical state to the reactant. The catalyst works by providing a surface on which the reactants can bond It is the availability of the 3d and 4s electrons, coupled with the ability to use variable oxidation states, which make transition metals and their compounds such good catalysts.

Transition metal compounds also make excellent **homogeneous catalysts.** Homogeneous catalysts are in the same physical state as the reactants, which usually means in solution. While these reactions are not as commercially significant as heterogeneous catalysis, they are fundamental to many biological reactions. It is the ability of transition metals to exist in more than one oxidation state that is the key to these reactions, since transition metal ions can take part in electron transfer reactions which provide an alternative pathway of lower activation energy.

See questions 8 and 11. ■

SUMMARY

After studying this chapter, you should know that:

■ A transition element is an element which forms one or more ions with a partially filled d subshell.

■ When a transition metal atom forms an ion, the first electrons to be lost are in the 4s subshell.

■ The 3d and 4s subshells have closely similar energies, leading to ions with 3+ charges.

■ Transition elements are typical metals. They are hard and dense, have high melting points and are good conductors of heat and electricity.

■ The atomic radii, ionic radii and first ionisation energies of the first-row transition metals are approximately constant.

■ The chemical properties that characterise transition elements are: variable oxidation states in their compounds, the formation of complexes, the formation of coloured ions, and the catalysis of reactions both as elements and compounds.

■ A complex is formed when a central metal atom or ion is surrounded by species which donate lone pairs of electrons.

■ A ligand is a species which donates a lone pair of electrons to a central metal atom or ion.

■ The coordination number is the number of dative covalent (coordinate) bonds from ligands to the central metal ion. It determines the shape of the ligands.

■ A monodentate ligand forms a single dative covalent bond with the central metal cation.

■ A bidentate ligand can form two dative covalent bonds with the central metal ion. When the ligands form five-membered rings with the metal ion, they are called chelates.

■ There is a system for naming complex ions.

■ Some complex ions show isomerism.

■ Ligand exchange may occur if the complex ion produced is more stable.

■ The stability of complex ions is measured using the stability constant.

■ Hydrated cations (aqua-complexes) may become deprotonated, causing acidity.

■ The addition of aqueous solutions of sodium hydroxide or ammonia may cause the production of coloured hydroxide precipitates. Some of these precipitates dissolve in excess alkali, while others dissolve in excess ammonia.

■ Many transition metal complexes have characteristic colours which are so distinctive that they can be used to test for these particular ions.

QUESTIONS

1

a) Explain the following terms, and give an example in each case.

    (i) transition element,

    (ii) ligand,

    (iii) complex ion.

2

a) State three characteristic properties shown by transition metals and their compounds.

b) Give the full electronic configuration for each of the following ions: **(i)** Sc^{3+}, **(ii)** Fe^{3+} and **(iii)** Cu^{2+}.

c) Explain why Sc^{3+} does not show the characteristic properties of a transition metal ion.

d)   **(i)** Give the colour, formula and shape of the cobalt species present in an aqueous solution of cobalt(II) sulphate.

    (ii) Give the colour, formula and shape of the cobalt species formed when an excess of concentrated hydrochloric acid is added to the aqueous solution of cobalt(II) sulphate.

[NEAB February 1996 Equilibria and Inorganic Chemistry CH2, q.4]

3

The transition metals have a tendency to vary in their oxidation states, whereas s block elements such as calcium do not.

a) Suggest an explanation for this difference

b) For the elements chromium and iron, choose two common oxidation states and, for each one, write the formula of a compound that contains the element in that oxidation state.

[UCLES November 1996 Chemistry Paper 9250, q.6]

4

a)   **(i)** Enter the electron structures required in the boxes below.

Table 25.Q4

		3d	**4s**
Cr	[Ar]	□□□□□	□
Cr^{2+}	[Ar]	□□□□□	□
Cr^{3+}	[Ar]	□□□□□	□

    (ii) How is the electron structure of Cr unusual, and why?

b)   **(i)** Calculate the oxidation number of Mn in MnO_4^{2-}.

    (ii) Why does Sc form only Sc^{3+} ions?

    (iii) Why are transition metals able to show a variety of oxidation states?

[ULEAC January 1996 Synoptic Paper CH6, q.1]

5

Write a complete equation to represent the second ionisation energy of iron, and state the electron configuration of the resulting ion.

6

a)   **(i)** State what is meant by the term *ligand*.

    (ii) Describe briefly how the bond is formed between a metal ion and a ligand in a complex ion.

b) Explain what is meant by the term *bidentate* as applied to a ligand.

c) The bidentate ligand 1,2-diaminoethane, $NH_2CH_2CH_2NH_2$, reacts with an aqueous solution of copper(II) sulphate to give a deep blue solution containing the ion $[Cu(NH_2CH_2CH_2NH_2)_2(H_2O)_2]^{2+}$.

    (i) What is the oxidation state of copper in this ion?

    (ii) What is the coordination number of copper in this ion?

    (iii) What causes the colour to change in this reaction?

    (iv) Write an equation for this reaction. (You may use 'en' for $NH_2CH_2CH_2NH_2$).

d) Give the name of a transition metal complex found in the human body, state the transition metal it contains and give its oxidation state.

[NEAB February 1996 Further Inorganic Chemistry CH05 q.4]

7

a)   **(i)** What do you understand by the term *ligand*? State the type of bonding that occurs between a ligand and a transition metal ion.

    (ii) State, giving a reason, whether or not each of the following molecules or ions can act as a ligand: NH_3, BH_3, Zn^{2+}, Cl^-.

b) The following table lists some stability constants for the following reaction:

$$[M(H_2O)_6]^{m+} + nL^- \rightleftharpoons [M(H_2O)_{6-n}L_n]^{(m-n)+} + nH_2O$$

(where m and n are whole numbers).

Table 25.Q7

M^{m+}	L^-	n	K_{stab}
Fe^{3+}	SCN^-	1	9×10^2
Fe^{3+}	CN^-	6	1×10^{31}
Co^{3+}	CN^-	6	1×10^{64}

    (i) Rewrite the above equation for the case of $M^{m+} = Fe^{3+}$ and $L^- = CN^-$. Write the expression for the equilibrium constant K_{stab}, and state its units.

    (ii) Use the data given in the table to predict what would be the predominant complex formed when:

1: a solution containing equal concentrations of both SCN^- and CN^- ions was added to a solution containing Fe^{3+}(aq) ions;

2: a solution containing equal concentrations of Fe^{3+}(aq) and Co^{3+} (aq) ions was added to a solution containing CN^- ions.

[UCLES June 1996 Paper 4 Option Topics 9254 q.22]

8

a) Deduce the oxidation state of the transition metal in each of the following species.
  (i) Cu in $[CuCl_4]^{2-}$
  (ii) Cr in $[Cr_2O_7]^{2-}$
  (iii) V in $[VO(H_2O)_5]^{2+}$

b) Give two examples of the use of transition elements as catalysts in industrial processes.

[NEAB June1995 Equilibria and Inorganic Chemistry CH2, q.5]

9

a) State what shapes are possible for transition metal complexes with 4 or 6 ligands bonded to the central metal ion.

b) Draw displayed formulae showing the possible shapes of, and suggest the isomerism present in, the following complex ions:
  (i) $[CuCl_4]^{3-}$
  (ii) $[FeF_5(H_2O)]^{2-}$
  (iii) $[Co(NH_2CH_2CH_2NH_2)_2F_2]^+$

c) Calculate the oxidation number of the metal in each of the above complexes.

[UCLES November 1995 Paper 2 Option Topics 9252, q.1]

10

a) Copper(II) chloride dissolves in water to form the blue copper-containing species $[Cu(H_2O_6]^{2+}$ and in concentrated hydrochloric acid to form the copper-containing species $[CuCl_4]^{2-}$.
  (i) What general name is given to this type of species?
  (ii) What is the coordination number of copper in the species $[Cu(H_2O_6]^{2+}$?
  (iii) Give the name used to describe the role of water in the formation of the copper-containing species $[Cu(H_2O_6]^{2+}$ and explain why water is able to behave in this way.

b) When an excess of sulphur dioxide is bubbled through a solution containing $[CuCl_4]^{2-}$ the following reaction occurs.

$$2[CuCl_4]^{2-} + SO_2 + 2H_2O \rightarrow SO_4^{2-} + 4Cl^- + 4H^+ + 2[CuCl_2]^-$$

  (i) State the colour and shape of the species $[CuCl_4]^{2-}$.
  (ii) Complete the electronic configurations of the following ions: $Cu^{2+}[Ar]$ and $Cu^+[Ar]$.
  (iii) Deduce the oxidation state of copper in the species $[CuCl_2]^-$.
  (iv) Explain, in terms of the electronic configurations of the copper ions present, why the species $[CuCl_4]^{2-}$ is coloured but the species $[CuCl_2]^-$ is not.
  (v) State the role of sulphur dioxide in the conversion of $[CuCl_4]^{2-}$ into $[CuCl_2]^-$.

[NEAB June 1996 Equilibria and Inorganic Chemistry CH02, q.4]

11

a) Draw a diagram to show the shape of the $[Fe(H_2O)_6]^{3+}$ complex ion.

b) **(i)** Solutions containing iron(III) ions are acidic (pH 2 approximately). Explain why this is so.
  (ii) Suggest why solutions containing iron(II) ions, of the same molarity (concentration) with respect to the metal ion, have a higher pH.

c) Draw a diagram to show the bonding between the ligands and the iron ion in the ion $[Fe(H_2NCH_2CH_2NH_2)_3]^{3+}$.

[ULEAC June 1995 AS Chemistry Synoptic Paper CH05, q.3]

12

a) The ethanedioate ion, $C_2O_4^{2-}$, acts as a bidentate ligand.
  (i) Explain what is meant by *bidentate*.
  (ii) Iron(III) ions form an octahedral complex with ethanedioate ions. Deduce the formula of this complex and draw its structure.
  (iii) Iron occurs in the body as an iron(II) complex of a multidentate ligand. Explain the meaning of *multidentate* and give the name of this ligand.

b) When aqueous cobalt(II) solutions are treated with an excess of potassium cyanide, a green solution of $[Co(CN)_5]^{3-}$ is formed which acts as an homogeneous catalyst for the hydrogenation of alkenes. The green solution reacts with molecular hydrogen to form the cobalt(III) hydrido complex according to the equation:

$$2[Co(CN)_5]^{3-} + H_2 \rightarrow 2[Co(CN)_5H]^{3-}$$

  (i) What is meant by homogeneous and by catalyst?
  (ii) What property of cobalt enables it to act as a catalyst in this reaction?
  (iii) What is the oxidation state and coordination number of cobalt in $[CoCl_4]^{2-}$?
  (iv) What is the chemical role of molecular hydrogen in the formation of the cobalt(III) hydrido complex? Explain your answer.

[NEAB June 1996 Further Inorganic Chemistry Module test CH05, q.4]

13

a) Compounds can exhibit structural, geometrical and optical isomerism. Explain what is meant by *geometrical isomerism*.

b) The following formula represents a compound which exists as a geometrical isomer. Draw the formula to show both isomers for the compound $[Cr(H_2O)_4Cl_2]^+$.

[AEB June 1996 Module Paper , q.1]

Assignment

PLATINUM COMPLEXES FIGHT CANCER

Barnett Rosenberg's first degree and his PhD were in physics, and he earned his living as a physicist. So, why is he being featured in a chemistry textbook? The answer is that he and a group of colleagues set up a biophysics department at Michigan State University, and it was in that department that a momentous discovery in chemistry was made in 1964. Like so many discoveries in science, it was made by accident. But, as Louis Pasteur said, 'Chance favours the prepared mind.'

Rosenberg was investigating the effect of alternating current on mammalian cell division. To test the apparatus, he first passed a current through a culture of bacterial cells growing and dividing in a nutrient medium. To his amazement, the cells stopped dividing and started growing into long filaments.

Upon further investigation, Rosenberg and his team discovered that the platinum electrodes inserted in the nutrient medium – chosen because they were believed to be unreactive – were forming a product by electrolysis. It was this product which was inhibiting cell division, but not cell growth. After much research, it appeared that platinum was forming complex ions with ammonia and chloride ions. Two likely candidates were $[PtCl_2(NH_3)_2]$ and $[PtCl_4(NH_3)_2]$.

1 Platinum is a transition element.
a) What is meant by *transition element*?
b) What are the characteristic chemical properties of transition elements?

2
a) Explain what is meant by **(i)** complex ion and **(ii)** ligand.
b) Ammonia molecules and chloride ions are ligands in the two platinum complexes mentioned. Draw diagrams to help explain how these species act as ligands.

3 The platinum complexes formed in the nutrient medium are both neutral.
a) What is the oxidation state of platinum in:
   (i) $[PtCl_2(NH_3)_2]$ and **(ii)** $[PtCl_4(NH_3)_2]$?
b) Predict the shape of $[PtCl_4(NH_3)_2]$.

An English chemist, Andy Thompson, working with the Rosenberg team, synthesised *trans*-$[Pt(NH_3)_2Cl_2]$ and dissolved some into the bacterial solution. To everyone's intense disappointment, nothing happened and the bacterial cells continued to divide. He subsequently made the *cis*-isomer and this did inhibit cell division. The active chemical had been identified.

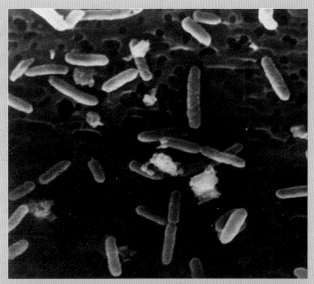

Fig 25.A1 **Bacterial cells before the passage of an electric current**

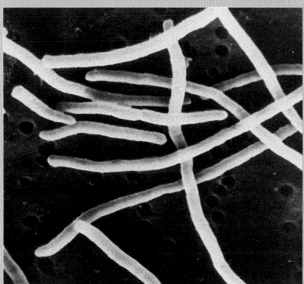

Fig 25.A2 **Long filaments seen after the electric current had passed**

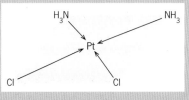

Fig 25.A3 *cis*-$[Pt(NH_3)_2Cl_2]$, now commonly known as cisplatin

4
a) Geometric isomerism is a form of stereoisomerism. What is meant by stereoisomerism?
b) Draw the *trans* isomer of $[Pt(NH_3)_2Cl_2]$.
c) $[PtCl_4(NH_3)_2]$ can also exist as *cis* and *trans* isomers. Draw these two isomers and label them.

Cancer cells divide in an uncontrolled way, often giving rise to tumours. Rosenberg approached the USA National Cancer Institute and suggested that *cis*-$[Pt(NH_3)_2Cl_2]$, now called cisplatin, might have the same effect on cancer cells as it had on bacterial cell division. At first they were sceptical. After all, many platinum compounds were known to be toxic to the liver. However, Rosenberg demonstrated that cisplatin could destroy tumours in mice, and so cisplatin began the long journey to becoming accepted as an anti-cancer drug. One of the biggest problems to overcome was the predicted toxicity to the kidneys. By giving the patient large amounts of water before and after the injection of cisplatin, it was diluted in the kidneys and the toxic effects were reduced. It is now amongst the most widely used anti-cancer drugs, being particularly effective in the treatment of tumours on the ovaries and testes.

However, the toxicity and its side effects remain. This has stimulated the search for other complexes which may be equally effective but safer. The way cisplatin works has recently been determined by X-ray crystallography. The chloride ligands are exchanged for dative covalent bonds with nitrogen atoms of DNA. This bends the DNA, causing a loss of function and cell death. However, the ease with which chloride ligands can be exchanged causes the toxicity of cisplatin and some of the unpleasant side effects. Carboplatin replaces the chloride ligands with a bidentate ligand called 1,1-cyclobutanedicarboxylic acid. It, too, is licensed for use in Britain.

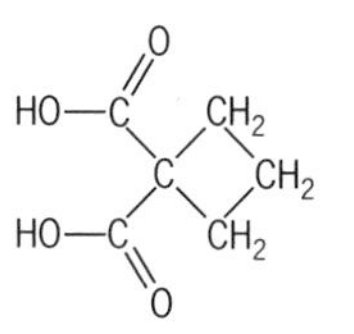

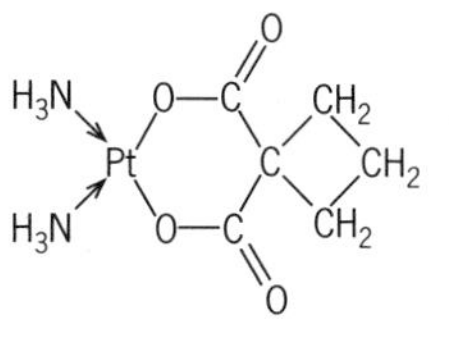

5

a) Why is 1,1-cyclobutanedicarboxylic acid called a bidentate ligand?

b) The complex formed is called a chelate. What is meant by this term?

6 Another platinum complex which shows anti-tumour activity replaces the two NH_3 ligands with 1,2-diaminoethane ($NH_2CH_2CH_2NH_2$).

a) Draw this square planar complex

b) Why do you think this complex is likely to be as toxic as cisplatin?

7 Before a drug is licensed, extensive clinical trials must take place.

a) Why do you think this is important?

b) Is there ever a justification for speeding up the process?

c) Clinical trials use placebos. Find out what this word means and why the use of placebos is considered essential.

Fig 25.A4 (left) **1,1-cyclobutanedicarboxylic acid**

Fig 25.A5 (right) **Carboplatin**

THE TRANSITION ELEMENTS

The different oxidation states of the transition elements allows them to form a very wide range of compounds (including complexes) that leads in this chapter to a review of electron configurations. Use the Chapter Map to identify the main aspects covered by the chapter, and to plan your revision.

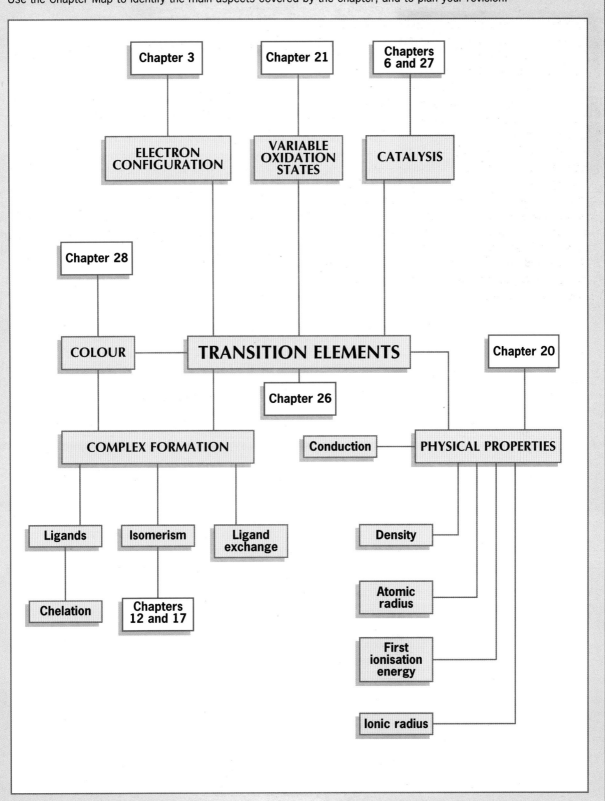

26 Electrode potentials and transition elements

An electrically powered bus in Sweden

Electric cars and vans would dramatically reduce atmospheric pollution. So, why haven't they yet supplanted petrol and diesel-driven vehicles?

Their widespread adoption has been stunted by the absence of a battery capable of providing sufficient motive power for a sufficient length of time.

Much is being done to rectify this with the development of lightweight batteries capable of running a vehicle for at least 500 km between charges. It is hoped that these batteries can be recharged many times using cheap-rate electricity.

There has also been progress with the development of fuel cells that use hydrogen or petrol in a reaction with oxygen. No burning occurs and electric current is generated directly. Appropriate technology does exist, but it is largely exotic and costly.

1 REDOX REACTIONS

Redox is a type of chemical reaction that involves electron transfer. At its simplest, one atom loses electrons and another atom gains electrons. Atoms of metals lose electrons usually to attain a stable electron configuration, and atoms of non-metals gain electrons usually to attain a stable electron configuration.

For example, a typical reaction of the metal magnesium is with dilute hydrochloric acid to form magnesium chloride (Fig 26.1):

$$Mg(s) + 2HCl(aq) \rightarrow MgCl_2(aq) + H_2(g)$$

This reaction is a redox reaction because an electron transfer occurs. An atom of magnesium loses two electrons during the reaction, but is not immediately obvious where these electrons go. Hydrochloric acid is a strong acid and it is completely dissociated into aqueous chloride ions and aqueous hydrogen ions. It is the hydrogen ions that gain electrons: two hydrogen ions gain one electron each eventually to form a hydrogen molecule. The hydrogen ions are said to be **reduced** to hydrogen. The chloride ions do not take part in the reaction at all. They are sometimes called **spectator ions**, to indicate that they are present in the solution during the reaction but take no part in it.

Strong acids and dissociation are covered on pages 309 to 313.

Fig 26.1 **The redox reaction between magnesium and hydrochloric acid forms hydrogen and aqueous magnesium chloride**

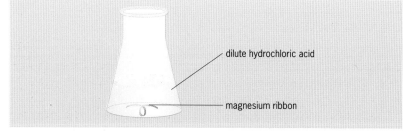

dilute hydrochloric acid

magnesium ribbon

The overall redox reaction can be represented by two half equations, one to show the reduction and the other to show the oxidation:

Oxidation half equation: $\qquad Mg(s) \rightarrow Mg^{2+}(aq) + 2e^-$

Reduction half equation: $\qquad 2H^+(aq) + 2e^- \rightarrow H_2(g)$

By combining these two half equations, an ionic equation can be written which does not show the spectator ions:

$$Mg(s) + 2H^+(aq) \rightarrow Mg^{2+}(aq) + H_2(g)$$

However complicated a redox reaction, may be, it is always possible to write two half equations, one for the oxidation and the other for the reduction.

Working out the half equations

Before writing down the two half equations, the species being oxidised and the species being reduced must be established. This is best done using oxidation numbers (see pages 432 to 436). During oxidation, the oxidation number of an atom increases. During reduction, it decreases. The change in oxidation number also gives the number of electrons lost (oxidation) or gained (reduction).

Consider the reaction of aqueous iron(II) ions with acidified manganate(VII) ions. The overall ionic equation is:

$$5Fe^{2+}(aq) + MnO_4^-(aq) + 8H^+(aq) \rightarrow 5Fe^{3+}(aq) + Mn^{2+}(aq) + 4H_2O(l)$$

The oxidation state of Fe changes from +2 to +3 (Fig 26.2). This is oxidation and involves the loss of one electron. The oxidation state of Mn changes from +7 to +2. This is reduction and involves the gain of five electrons. We are now in a position to write the half equations.

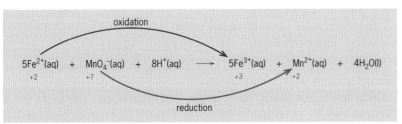

Fig 26.2 **The reaction of acidified manganate(VII) ions, MnO$_4^-$(aq), with aqueous iron(II) ions, Fe^{2-}(aq). The oxidation numbers that change during the reaction are shown in red**

The oxidation involves the conversion of Fe^{2+} to Fe^{3+} and is written as:

$$Fe^{2+}(aq) \rightarrow Fe^{3+}(aq) + e^-$$

The reduction involves the conversion of the manganate(VII) ion to the manganese(II) ion. This involves the gain of five electrons per manganate(VII) ion:

$$5e^- + MnO_4^-(aq) + 8H^+(aq) \rightarrow Mn^{2+}(aq) + 4H_2O(l)$$

Note that the half equations are balanced both in terms of their symbols and in terms of the charge. Note also that the aqueous hydrogen ions are not spectator ions but are needed for the reduction to occur, and that the hydrogen ion is not itself reduced.

Electron transfer

The two half equations clearly demonstrate the electron transfer processes that occur during the redox reaction. The processes shown by the half equations cannot take place independently, because reduction cannot occur without the simultaneous occurrence of oxidation. It is best to think of the half equations as a 'book-keeping' exercise which shows where electrons are lost and where they are gained.

?

A Write down the half equations that correspond to the following overall reactions:

(a) $Cu(s) + 2Ag^+(aq) \rightarrow 2Ag(s) + Cu^{2+}(aq)$

(b) $6Fe^{2+}(aq) + 14H^+(aq) + Cr_2O_7^{2-}(aq) \rightarrow 6Fe^{3+}(aq) + 2Cr^{3+}(aq) + 7H_2O(l)$

Electrolysis reactions

As described on pages 502 to 504, electrolysis is the decomposition of a liquid by the passage of an electric current, which enters and leaves the compound through electrodes. Electrolysis is necessarily a redox reaction, since it involves electron transfer. The reactions represented by the two half equations occur in different parts of an electrolytic cell. Reduction always occurs at the cathode (negative electrode) and oxidation always occurs at the anode (positive electrode).

Consider the electrolysis of molten lead(II) iodide. The two half equations are:

Oxidation half equation: $\quad 2I^- \rightarrow I_2 + 2e^-$ occurs at the anode

Reduction half equation: $\quad Pb^{2+} + 2e^- \rightarrow Pb$ occurs at the cathode

In electrolysis, these half equations are referred to as **electrode reactions**.

?

B Write down the two half reactions (electrode reactions) that occur during the electrolysis of

(a) molten sodium chloride and

(b) molten lead(II) bromide

Oxidising agents

An **oxidising agent** or **oxidant** is the name given to the substance or species that gains electrons during a redox reaction. In effect, it oxidises another substance by gaining electrons from it. So an oxidising agent is reduced during a redox reaction.

Typically, oxidising agents are non-metal elements or compounds that have an element in a high positive oxidation state. For example, fluorine is an oxidising agent, as is potassium dichromate(VI), in which chromium has an oxidation state of +6. In every reaction, the oxidising agent gains electrons. Fluorine molecules gain electrons to form fluoride ions, and a dichromate(VI) ion gains six electrons to form two chromium(III) ions:

$$F_2 + 2e^- \rightarrow 2F^-$$
$$Cr_2O_7{}^{2-} + 14H^+ + 6e^- \rightarrow 2Cr^{3+} + 7H_2O$$

Note that these two half equations are written to show that the oxidising agent is gaining electrons.

Sometimes, we want to compare the oxidising power of substances. That is, we want to compare the ability of oxidising agents to gain electrons. For example, fluorine is the better oxidising agent of the two shown above, but it is impossible to tell just from the half equation. This is dealt with on page 551.

Reducing agents

A **reducing agent** or **reductant** is the name given to the substance or species that loses electrons during a redox reaction. In effect, it reduces another substance by losing electrons to it. So a reducing agent is oxidised during a redox reaction.

Typically, reducing agents are metal elements or compounds that have an element in a low, positive oxidation state or a negative oxidation state. For example, potassium is a reducing agent, as is the sulphide ion in which sulphur has an oxidation state of −2. In every reaction, the reducing agent loses electrons. A potassium atom loses an electron to form a potassium ion, and a sulphide ion loses two electrons to form a sulphur atom.

$$K \rightarrow K^+ + e^-$$
$$S^{2-} \rightarrow S + 2e^-$$

Note that the two half equations are written to show that the reducing agent is losing electrons.

Sometimes, we want to compare the reducing power of substances. That is, we want to compare the ability of reducing agents to lose electrons. For example, potassium is the better reducing agent of the two cited above, but it is impossible to tell this just from the half equations. This also is discussed on page 551.

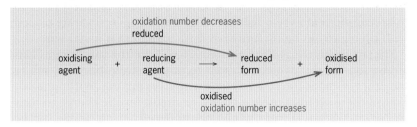

Fig 26.3 **A summary of the action of oxidising agents and reducing agents**

2 SIMPLE CELLS

It has been known for two centuries that a potential difference is generated when two dissimilar metal electrodes are put into an electrolyte. What takes place in this so-called electrochemical cell is a redox reaction, in which oxidation occurs at one electrode and reduction at the other.

This poses a problem, since in a redox reaction there must be an electron transfer. Given that the two half reactions (oxidation and reduction) are at different places, the transfer of electrons cannot take place during collision between the oxidising and the reducing agents. Instead, the electrons are transferred via an external circuit (a metal wire). This may be regarded as electrolysis in reverse. Instead of a reaction occurring because of the passage of an electric current, an electric current (electron transfer) is produced because a redox reaction is occurring.

Daniell cell

In 1836, the English chemist John Fredrick Daniell constructed a simple battery that employed this idea. He used zinc and copper plates as the electrodes and two different electrolytes – aqueous copper(II) sulphate and aqueous zinc(II) sulphate (Fig 26.4). (It is now known that in the Daniell cell zinc is in equilibrium with aqueous zinc ions and copper is in equilibrium with copper(II) ions.) When the two metal plates are connected by a metal wire, a current flows through the wire. The current is a result of the gain and loss of electrons that occur in the cell.

During the operation of the cell, the zinc plate forms zinc ions and loses electrons. This corresponds to the oxidation half reaction:

$$Zn(s) \rightarrow Zn^{2+}(aq) + 2e^-$$

Meanwhile, at the copper plate, copper(II) ions gain electrons to form copper. This corresponds to the reduction half equation:

$$Cu^{2+}(aq) + 2e^- \rightarrow Cu(s)$$

Now, a redox reaction can occur only if electrons can be transferred. Only when the two plates are connected by a metal wire can this happen. The zinc plate, at which oxidation takes place, is the anode; the copper, at which reduction takes place, is the cathode.

The overall reaction occurring in the cell is a combination of the two half reactions:

$$Zn(s) + Cu^{2+}(aq) \rightarrow Zn^{2+}(aq) + Cu(s)$$

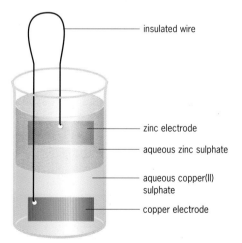

Fig 26.4 **A Daniell cell consists of a copper plate surrounded by saturated aqueous copper(II) sulphate solution and a zinc plate surrounded by saturated aqueous zinc sulphate. The aqueous zinc sulphate must be carefully added so that it floats on top of the more dense aqueous copper(II) sulphate solution but does not mix with it. When the two different metals are connected by a wire, a current flows. Eventually, the cell stops producing a potential difference when the solutions mix through diffusion**

Fig 26.5 **When zinc is dipped into aqueous copper(II) sulphate, a spontaneous redox reaction occurs to form copper and aqueous zinc sulphate**

See question 2. ◼

When zinc is placed directly into aqueous copper(II) sulphate, the same reaction takes place, but the electron transfer occurs during a collision between a zinc atom and a copper(II) ion (Fig 26.5).

Another simple cell

It is possible to arrange the reaction between magnesium and hydrochloric acid as two half reactions occurring in separate places, with the electrons being transferred via an external metal wire.

The arrangement is shown in Fig 26.6. Note the salt bridge. This allows ions in the two electrolytes to migrate from one half-cell to the other without the electrolytes themselves mixing. Without a salt bridge, there would not be a complete circuit for the charge to flow round, and so no current would be produced. A salt bridge can be

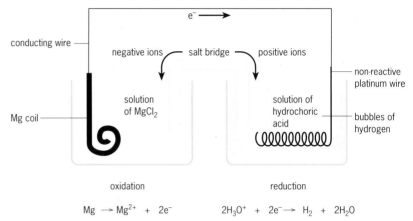

Fig 26.6 **The oxidation of magnesium ions and reduction of hydrogen ions occur in separate parts of the cell. There is no reaction unless both the salt bridge and the external wire are in place**

$$Mg \longrightarrow Mg^{2+} + 2e^-$$

$$2H_3O^+ + 2e^- \longrightarrow H_2 + 2H_2O$$

as simple as a piece of filter paper dipped in saturated aqueous potassium nitrate. Potassium nitrate is usually used because it does not react with most of the electrolytes used in electrochemical cells.

See question 1. ◼

Cell potential

For a current to flow, there must be a potential difference between the two halves of the cell. This is known as the **cell potential** or the **electromotive force (e.m.f.)**. It is given the symbol $E^{\ominus}_{cell}$ and is measured in volts. The cell potential is independent of the amount of each substance present in the cell but is dependent on each of their concentrations. The effect of concentration on cell potentials and electrode potentials is described on pages 553 and 554.

Measuring the cell potential with a voltmeter

The potential of a cell can be measured using a high-resistance voltmeter, as shown in Fig 26.7. This simple set-up does not quite measure the true maximum cell potential. As the current flows from one electrode to the other the circuit heats up due to the resistance of the wire. So, the cell transfers some of its energy as heat rather than as electric current. To measure the true maximum cell potential possible, no energy should be transferred as heat. That is, the potential difference should be measured when there is no current flowing. This is why a high resistance voltmeter must be used, in order to draw almost no current from the cell.

Fig 26.7 **A cell consisting of a zinc electrode dipped into aqueous zinc ions, and a copper electrode dipped into aqueous copper(II) ions, should have a cell potential of 1.10 V (measured on a high-resistance voltmeter) when solutions of 1.0 mol dm^{-3} are used a temperature of 298 K**

Electrode potentials

Generally, the term 'electrode' is used to describe the conductor that allows the passage of electric current in and out of the cell. In some applications, the electrode is inert, as in the use of graphite or platinum for the electrolysis of acidified water. In other applications, it actually takes part in a reaction. In work on electrochemical cells, however, the term 'electrode' is extended to include what is known as a half-cell. So it refers not only to the conductor but also to the conducting solution in which it is placed.

As explained earlier, a cell consists of an oxidation and a reduction reaction. Therefore, the overall cell potential should be the sum of the potential of the oxidation process and the potential of the reduction process. The potential for the oxidation process is called the oxidation potential of the anode, which for convenience is shortened to $E^{\ominus}_{oxid}$ or **oxidation potential**. Likewise, the potential for the reduction process which is called the reduction potential of the cathode, is shortened to $E^{\ominus}_{red}$ or the **reduction potential**. So, in an electrochemical cell:

$$E^{\ominus}_{cell} = E^{\ominus}_{oxid} + E^{\ominus}_{red}$$

■ See question 2.

Standard electrode potentials

The word 'standard' in the term **standard electrode potential $E^{\ominus}_i$** signifies that the electrode potential has been measured (or calculated) under standard conditions, which are defined as 298 K, 101 kPa (1 atmosphere), with all aqueous solutions at a concentration of $1.0\,mol\,dm^{-3}$. (Standard conditions in thermochemistry are discussed on page 117.)

■ See question 3.

Standard reduction potential

This is the potential difference between a cathode and the solution into which it is dipped, measured under standard conditions. Its symbol is $E^{\ominus}_{red}$. It is impossible to measure an absolute value for $E^{\ominus}_{red}$, so data books give a value of the potential of the cathode with reference to the standard hydrogen electrode whose cell potential has been assigned a value of 0.00 V. (The standard hydrogen electrode is discussed in more detail on page 548.) In a Daniell cell, the copper(II) ions electrode are in equilibrium with the copper electrode:

$$Cu^{2+}(aq) + 2e^- \rightleftharpoons Cu(s)$$

The value of $E^{\ominus}_{red}$ gives an indication of the position of this equilibrium. The greater its positive value, the more the equilibrium lies to the right.

Standard oxidation potential

This is the potential difference between an anode and the solution into which it is dipped, measured under standard conditions. Again, it is impossible to measure absolute values for $E^{\ominus}_{oxid}$, so a value is used that is the potential of the anode with reference to the standard hydrogen electrode whose cell potential has been assigned a value of 0.00 V. In a Daniell cell, the zinc ions are in equilibrium with the zinc anode:

$$Zn^{2+}(aq) + 2e^- \rightleftharpoons Zn(s)$$

The value $E^{\ominus}_{oxid}$ gives an indication of the position of this equilibrium. The greater its positive value, the more the equilibrium lies to the left.

Measuring electrode potentials

As already stated, it is not possible to measure absolute values for the oxidation and reduction potentials. However, if the potential for one of the processes is assigned a value, then it is possible to determine a value for any other electrode potential. The chosen process is the redox reaction involving aqueous hydrogen ions and gaseous hydrogen under standard conditions (temperature 298 K, pressure of the hydrogen gas 101 kPa, concentration of the aqueous hydrogen ion 1.00 mol dm⁻³). Both $E^{\ominus}_{oxid}$ and the $E^{\ominus}_{red}$ are arbitrarily given a value of zero. Therefore:

Oxidation: $\frac{1}{2}H_2(g) \rightarrow H^+(aq) + e^-$ $E^{\ominus}_{oxid} = 0.00\,V$

Reduction: $H^+(aq) + e^- \rightarrow \frac{1}{2}H_2(g)$ $E^{\ominus}_{red} = 0.00\,V$

Hence, all other electrode potentials are compared with either the oxidation potential of gaseous hydrogen or the reduction potential of aqueous hydrogen ions. Remember that the oxidation and reduction reactions are part of the reference equilibrium reaction:

$$2H^+(aq) + 2e^- \rightleftharpoons H_2(g)$$

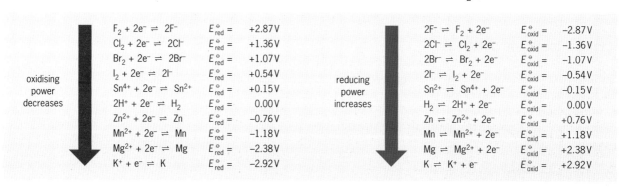

C You want to measure the standard reduction potential for the following reaction:

$$Cl_2(g) + 2e^- \rightarrow 2Cl^-(aq)$$

Write down the conditions that you must have to measure the standard reduction potential.

Fig 26.8 **A summary of the values of electrode potentials**

Standard hydrogen electrode

The standard hydrogen electrode is a half-cell that allows $H_2(g)$ to be in equilibrium with $H^+(aq)$. As an electrode the half-cell must also allow electric current to flow in and out. This poses a problem, because gaseous hydrogen is not an electrical conductor. It is overcome by using platinum foil (which is inert) as the conducting part of the electrode (Fig 26.9).

Using the standard hydrogen potential to measure other standard electrode potentials

Since the reference equilibrium reaction involved $H_2(g)$ and $H^+(aq)$, it is possible to determine the standard electrode potential of other half-cells just by combining them with a standard hydrogen electrode, as shown in Fig 26.10.

D What concentration of dilute sulphuric acid would be appropriate for use in a standard hydrogen electrode?

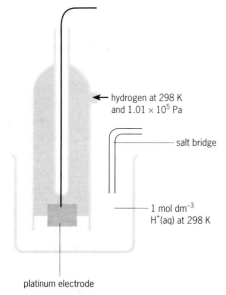

hydrogen at 298 K and 1.01×10^5 Pa

salt bridge

1 mol dm⁻³ $H^+(aq)$ at 298 K

platinum electrode

Fig 26.9 **In the standard hydrogen electrode, hydrogen gas under a pressure of 101 kPa is in contact with aqueous hydrogen ions at a concentration of 1.00 mol dm⁻³. The platinum electrode allows electrical current to enter and leave the electrode. The platinum does not react with the hydrogen or the aqueous hydrogen ions. The aqueous hydrogen ions are normally provided by dilute sulphuric acid of the appropriate concentration**

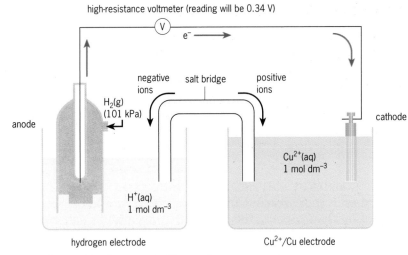

high-resistance voltmeter (reading will be 0.34 V)

Fig 26.10 **A hydrogen electrode is connected to a copper/copper(II) ion electrode using a salt bridge. A high-resistance voltmeter measures the electrode potential of the cell. The arrows show the electron flow from the hydrogen electrode to the copper electrode via the external wire**

In Fig 26.10, the two half reactions are:

At the anode: $H_2(g) \rightarrow 2H^+(aq) + 2e^-$
At the cathode: $Cu^{2+}(aq) + 2e^- \rightarrow Cu(s)$

Remember: Oxidation occurs at the anode and reduction at the cathode. The value of $E^\ominus_{cell}$ is +0.34 V, and:

$$E^\ominus_{cell} = E^\ominus_{oxid} + E^\ominus_{red}$$

Therefore:

$$+0.34 = 0.00 + E^\ominus_{red}$$

The $E^\ominus_{red}$ for the copper electrode is +0.34 V. So $E^\ominus_{oxid} = -0.34$ V. It is a general rule that, for the same electrode, the values of $E^\ominus_{red}$ and $E^\ominus_{oxid}$ have the same magnitude but are of opposite sign.

It is also worth stressing that the electrode potentials do not depend on the amounts of reactants and products involved in redox equations. So, for instance, the reduction potential for:

$$Cu^{2+}(aq) + 2e^- \rightarrow Cu(s)$$

is the same as that for:

$$2Cu^{2+}(aq) + 4e^- \rightarrow 2Cu(s)$$

■ See question 2.

Cell convention

It is cumbersome to keep drawing the electrodes used in electrochemical cells. Therefore, a system of notation has been devised whereby a whole cell can be described on a single line. The anode is written on the left and the cathode on the right. A single vertical bar distinguishes components that are in different phases: for example, a solid electrode and the aqueous ions with which it is in contact. The salt bridge is shown by two dashed vertical bars. Thus, the cell of Fig 26.10 can be represented by:

$$Pt(s) \mid H_2(g) \mid H^+(aq) \,\lvert\lvert\, Cu^{2+}(aq) \mid Cu(s)$$

Note that the half-cell with the greater positive value of $E^\ominus_{red}$ is put on the right.

For the Daniell cell, the notation is:

$$Zn(s) \mid Zn^{2+}(aq) \,\lvert\lvert\, Cu^{2+}(aq) \mid Cu(s)$$

✔ Sometimes a comma is used to separate components that are in the same phase.

Other ways of measuring standard electrode potentials

The standard hydrogen electrode does not always have to be used to measure the standard electrode potential of another half-cell. When it is known for certain that a copper electrode has a standard reduction potential of 0.34 V, then it can be used to determine the standard electrode potential of another half-cell.

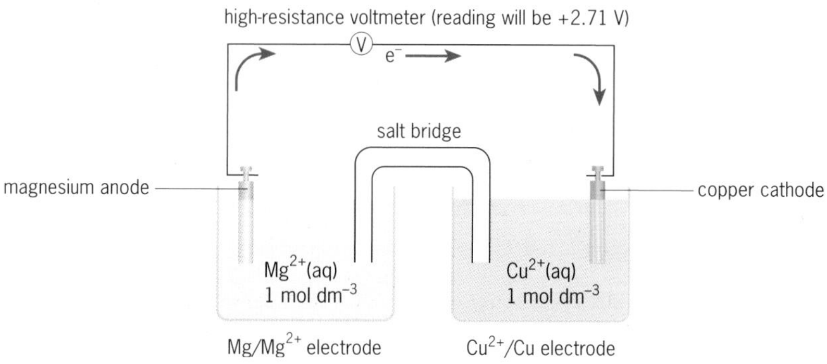

Fig 26.11 **To determine the standard electrode potential for magnesium, two half-cells are required. One cell contains a copper strip and 1.0 mol dm^{-3} copper(II) ions, and the other a magnesium strip and 1.0 mol dm^{-3} magnesium ions. A high-resistance voltmeter records the cell potential, from which the electrode potential of magnesium can be determined:**

$$E^{\ominus}_{cell} = E^{\ominus}_{oxid} + E^{\ominus}_{red}$$
$$+ 2.71 \quad\quad E^{\ominus}_{oxid} + 0.34$$
So: $\quad E^{\ominus}_{oxid} = +2.37 \text{ V}$

It is possible to experimentally determine any electrode potential providing a suitable cell is set up

high-resistance voltmeter (reading will be +2.71 V)

magnesium anode — — copper cathode

salt bridge

Mg^{2+}(aq) 1 mol dm^{-3} Cu^{2+}(aq) 1 mol dm^{-3}

Mg/Mg^{2+} electrode   Cu^{2+}/Cu electrode

See question 1. ■

An example of this method is illustrated in Fig 26.11. Magnesium is more reactive than copper. That is, it loses electrons more easily than copper. This makes the magnesium half-cell the anode, since this is where oxidation occurs. So, the notation for the cell in Fig 26.11 is:

$$Mg(s) \mid Mg^{2+}(aq) \parallel Cu^{2+}(aq) \mid Cu(s)$$

Electrodes involving gases or solutions

Many redox half reactions do not involve a metal, but it is still possible to construct a half-cell using the reagents shown in the half equation. For example, with the aid of gas electrodes, gases can be involved in redox half equations. Since gases do not conduct electricity, an inert metal (usually platinum) has to be used as the conducting part of the gas electrode. Platinum does not react with dilute acids or most aqueous solutions. For example, the chlorine electrode shown in Fig 26.12 allows Cl$_2$(g) and Cl$^-$(aq) to be in equilibrium:

$$Cl_2(g) + 2e^- \rightleftharpoons 2Cl^-(aq)$$

Some half-cells involve only solutions. Take, for example, a half-cell involving the acidified manganate(VII) ions. It must allow the following equilibrium to be set up:

$$MnO_4^-(aq) + 8H^+(aq) + 5e^- \rightleftharpoons Mn^{2+}(aq) + 4H_2O(l)$$

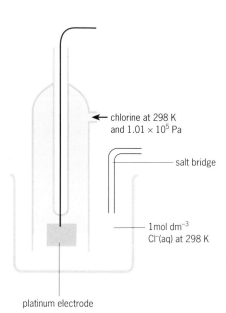

chlorine at 298 K and 1.01 × 10^5 Pa

salt bridge

1 mol dm^{-3} Cl$^-$(aq) at 298 K

platinum electrode

Fig 26.12 **A chlorine electrode consists of chlorine gas at 101 kPa, aqueous chloride ions at a concentration of 1.0 mol dm^{-3} and an inert platinum electrode to conduct current into or out of the solution**

None of the species given in the equation can act as the electrode. Therefore, a platinum electrode is again needed. Despite the stoichiometry of the equation, all the concentrations of the aqueous species should be 1.0 mol dm^{-3}, the temperature 298 K and the pressure 101 kPa, for the half-cell to be at standard conditions.

See question 1. ■

3 USING STANDARD ELECTRODE POTENTIALS

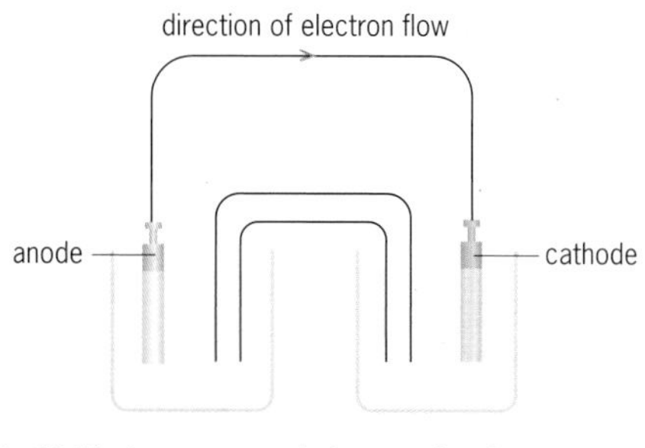

Knowledge of electrode potentials allows predictions to be made about oxidising and reducing agents, and about electrolysis products. It also allows speculation on the feasibility of redox reactions.

When the external circuit in an electrochemical cell is closed, electrons flow from the anode to the cathode. This is always the direction of flow of electrons. The reason is that oxidation, accompanied by the release of electrons, always takes place at the anode. The electrons then travel along the external circuit until, at the cathode, they are used in the reduction process.

direction of electron flow

anode — — cathode

Fig 26.13 **A summary of electron flow in an electrochemical cell**

Predicting the flow of electrons

The cell convention includes all the components of the cell with the anode placed on the far left and the cathode on the far right. In this convention, the external flow of electrons always goes from left to right. That is, from the anode to the cathode.

Comparing oxidising agents

To compare oxidising agents, it is necessary to look at the $E_{red}^{\ominus}$ of the species involved. This is because an oxidising agent must accept electrons in order to be reduced. Since the figures are all comparative, the most powerful oxidising agent is the species with the highest positive (or lowest negative) $E_{red}^{\ominus}$. (The significance of the sign and size of electrode potentials is summarised in Fig 26.8, page 548.)

EXAMPLE

Q Which is the more powerful oxidising agent, F_2 or Cl_2?

A The relevant reduction half reactions and electrode potentials (given on page 679) are:

$$F_2 + 2e^- \rightleftharpoons 2F^- \qquad E_{red}^{\ominus} = +2.87 \text{ V}$$
$$Cl_2 + 2e^- \rightleftharpoons 2Cl^- \qquad E_{red}^{\ominus} = +1.36 \text{ V}$$

So fluorine is the more powerful oxidising agent.

Comparing reducing agents

To compare reducing agents, it is necessary to look at the $E_{oxid}^{\ominus}$ of the species involved. This is because a reducing agent must give away electrons in order to be oxidised. Since the figures are all comparative, then the most powerful reducing agent is the species with the highest positive (or lowest negative) value of $E_{oxid}^{\ominus}$.

EXAMPLE

Q Which is the better reducing agent, I^- or Cl^-?

A The relevant oxidation half reactions and electrode potentials (given on page 679) are:

$$I_2 + 2e^- \rightleftharpoons 2I^- \quad E_{red}^{\ominus} = +0.54 \text{ V} \quad \text{so} \quad E_{oxid}^{\ominus} = -0.54 \text{ V}$$
$$Cl_2 + 2e^- \rightleftharpoons 2Cl^- \quad E_{red}^{\ominus} = +1.36 \text{ V} \quad \text{so} \quad E_{oxid}^{\ominus} = -1.36 \text{ V}$$

So the iodide ion is the better reducing agent, since its $E_{oxid}^{\ominus}$ has a lower negative value than that of the chloride ion.

■ See questions 6 and 8.

?

E Write the following electrochemical cells using the cell convention. In each case predict the direction of the flow of electrons in the external circuit.

(a) A cell made of a copper electrode and a silver electrode.

(b) A cell made up of a hydrogen electrode and a zinc electrode.

?

F In each of the following pairs, which is the better oxidising agent:

(a) Cu^{2+} or Cr^{2+},

(b) Acidified MnO_4^- or acidified $Cr_2O_7^{2-}(aq)$.

?

G In each of the following pairs, decide which is the better reducing agent:

(a) Ni or Sn^{2+}, **(b)** F^- or Au.

Electrochemical series and electrode potentials

Metals are reducing agents because they lose electrons. The most reactive metals lose electrons easily, whereas the least reactive metals lose electrons with difficulty. The electrochemical series ranks metals in order of their reactivities with the most reactive metal at the top. Since the most reactive metals are also the best reducing

Table 26.1 **Electrochemical series**

Metal		Reduction potential $E^{\ominus}_{red}/V$	Oxidation potential $E^{\ominus}_{oxid}/V$
potassium	$K^+ + e^- \rightleftharpoons K$	-2.92	$+2.92$
calcium	$Ca^{2+} + 2e^- \rightleftharpoons Ca$	-2.87	$+2.87$
magnesium	$Mg^{2+} + 2e^- \rightleftharpoons Mg$	-2.38	$+2.38$
aluminium	$Al^{3+} + 3e^- \rightleftharpoons Al$	-1.66	$+1.66$
zinc	$Zn^{2+} + 2e^- \rightleftharpoons Zn$	-0.76	$+0.76$
iron	$Fe^{2+} + 2e^- \rightleftharpoons Fe$	-0.44	$+0.44$
lead	$Pb^{2+} + 2e^- \rightleftharpoons Pb$	-0.13	$+0.13$
hydrogen	$2H^+ + 2e^- \rightleftharpoons H_2$	0.00	0.00
copper	$Cu^{2+} + 2e^- \rightleftharpoons Cu$	$+0.34$	-0.34
silver	$Ag^+ + e^- \rightleftharpoons Ag$	$+0.8$	-0.8

agents, electrode potentials can be used to deduce the electrochemical series, as Table 26.1 shows.

Note that there is a good correlation between the position of the metal in the electrochemical series and its $E^{\ominus}_{oxid}$.

Predicting the products of electrolysis

As mentioned on page 544, electrolysis involves two half reactions, which are known as electrode reactions. In solutions that contain several ions, it can be difficult to predict which ion will react at the anode and which at the cathode. Since oxidation always occurs at the anode, it is possible to compare the relevant $E^{\ominus}_{oxid}$ to predict which ion is most likely to react there. In the same way, it is possible to predict which ion will react at the cathode by comparing the relevant $E^{\ominus}_{red}$. There is, however, one major drawback with this approach, which is that the electrode potentials are quoted for standard conditions, involving concentrations of $1.0\,mol\,dm^{-3}$ of aqueous ionic species. Therefore, unless these are the conditions of electrolysis, there will always be some doubt about accuracy of the prediction. On page 553, the effect of concentration on electrode potential is considered, and the same approach can be used to make better predictions about the electrolysis products of an aqueous solution.

?

H (a) Predict the products of the electrolysis of aqueous zinc nitrate solution using inert electrodes of graphite.

(b) The electrolysis of concentrated aqueous sodium chloride with inert electrodes gives chlorine and hydrogen. Is this what you would expect from inspection of the relevant electrode potentials? If it is not, suggest possible reasons for the discrepancy.

EXAMPLE

Q Predict the products of the electrolysis of aqueous copper(II) nitrate using carbon electrodes.

A Ions present: $Cu^{2+}(aq)$ and $NO_3^-(aq)$, and from water $H^+(aq)$ and $OH^-(aq)$
Ions attracted to cathode: $Cu^{2+}(aq)$ and $H^+(aq)$
Possible cathode reactions: $Cu^{2+}(aq) + 2e^- \rightarrow Cu(s)$ $E^{\ominus}_{red} = +0.34\,V$
                                                    $2H^+(aq) + 2e^- \rightarrow H_2(g)$ $E^{\ominus}_{red} = 0.00\,V$
By inspection, the more favourable reduction is that involving copper(II) ions, since its electrode potential has the higher positive value.
Ions attracted to anode: $OH^-(aq)$ and $NO_3^-(aq)$
Anode reaction: $4OH^-(aq) \rightarrow O_2(g) + 2H_2O(l) + 4e^-$ $E^{\ominus}_{oxid} = -0.40\,V$

The nitrate ion is attracted to the anode, but is not oxidised.

Calculating cell potentials

When any simple cell is set up its e.m.f., $E^{\ominus}_{cell}$, can be calculated from the electrode potentials of the two half reactions taking place. $E^{\ominus}_{cell}$ is given by:

$$E^{\ominus}_{cell} = E^{\ominus}_{oxid} + E^{\ominus}_{red}$$

(For the rest of the chapter, $E^{\ominus}_{cell}$ is used rather than e.m.f.)

The values of some electrode potentials are given on page 679. The values and those quoted in most data books are standard electrode potentials. Therefore, any cell potential calculated from them will be a standard cell potential. Most data books list only the reduction half equations together with their $E_{red}^{\ominus}$ values. The corresponding $E_{oxid}^{\ominus}$ values are obtained by changing the sign of the $E_{red}^{\ominus}$ values.

■ See questions 2–5.

EXAMPLES

Q Work out the cell potential for the following cell:

$$Co(s) \mid Co^{2+}(aq) \;\vdots\; Cr^{3+}(aq) \mid Cr(s)$$

A By the cell convention, the anode is on the left side of the cell, so this is where the oxidation occurs:

$$Co(s) \rightarrow Co^{2+}(aq) + 2e^-$$

From the table of electrode potentials, $E_{oxid}^{\ominus} = +0.28\,V$ (since $E_{red}^{\ominus} = -0.28\,V$ for $Co^{2+}(aq) + 2e^- \rightleftharpoons Co(s)$).

At the cathode, reduction takes place, so the half reaction must involve the gain of electrons:

$$Cr^{3+}(aq) + 3e^- \rightarrow Cr(s)$$

From the table of electrode potentials, $E_{red}^{\ominus} = -0.74\,V$. Since $E_{cell}^{\ominus} = E_{oxid}^{\ominus} + E_{red}^{\ominus}$, then:

$$E_{cell}^{\ominus} = +0.28 + (-0.78) = -0.50\,V$$

Q Calculate the cell potential of the cell that has the following overall reaction:

$$Zn + I_2 \rightarrow Zn^{2+} + 2I^-$$

A The oxidation half reaction is:

$$Zn \rightarrow Zn^{2+} + 2e^-$$

for which $E_{oxid}^{\ominus} = +0.76\,V$

The reduction half reaction is:

$$I_2 + 2e^- \rightarrow 2I^-$$

for which $E_{red}^{\ominus} = +0.54\,V$

Using $E_{cell}^{\ominus} = E_{oxid}^{\ominus} + E_{red}^{\ominus}$ gives:

$$E_{cell}^{\ominus} = +0.76 + 0.54 = +1.30\,V$$

Electrode potentials under non-standard conditions

So far, the assumption has been that the reactions have occurred under standard conditions. That is, all solutions are $1\,mol\,dm^{-3}$ in concentration, the temperature is $298\,K$ and the pressure is $101\,kPa$. This is not the case for most reactions. Even if standard temperature and pressure could be maintained, as soon as the cell reaction had started, the concentrations of the reactants and products would necessarily change. The effect of changing conditions can be predicted qualitatively by assuming that the reaction taking place is an equilibrium and applying Le Chatelier's principle.

If you wish to read more about the quantitative effects of changing temperature, pressure and concentration on electrode potentials, then you should look up the Nernst equation in a more advanced textbook.

Temperature and cell potential

If the cell reaction as written is exothermic, then as the temperature increases the equilibrium shifts to the left. This means that the cell potential assumes a lower positive (or larger negative) value.

Concentration and cell potential

If the concentrations of the reactants are increased, then the equilibrium shifts to the right and the cell potential assumes a higher positive (or lower negative) value. If the concentration of one of the products increases, then the opposite effect is observed and the cell potential assumes a lower positive (or larger negative) value.

Le Chatelier's principle can also be applied to half-cells, affecting E_{red} or E_{oxid} values. Consider the equilibrium between hydrogen ions and hydrogen:

$$2H^+(aq) + 2e^- \rightleftharpoons H_2(g) \qquad E_{red}^{\ominus} = E_{oxid}^{\ominus} = 0.00\,V$$

I Consider the following cell reaction:
$Zn(s) + 2H^+(aq) \rightarrow Zn^{2+}(aq) + H_2(g)$

(a) Calculate the standard cell potential for this reaction.

(b) Predict qualitatively the effect on E_{cell} of a cell with:
(i) $[Zn^{2+}(aq)] = 2.0\,mol\,dm^{-3}$
$[H^+(aq)] = 1.0\,mol\,dm^{-3}$ and pressure of $H_2 = 101\,kPa$
(ii) $[Zn^{2+}(aq)] = 1.0\,mol\,dm^{-3}$
$[H^+(aq)] = 2.0\,mol\,dm^{-3}$ and pressure of $H_2 = 101\,kPa$
(iii) $[Zn^{2+}(aq)] = 1.0\,mol\,dm^{-3}$
$[H^+(aq)] = 1.0\,mol\,dm^{-3}$ and pressure of $H_2 = 202\,kPa$

There is more information on spontaneous reactions on pages 131 and 581.

See questions 1, 2 and 3. ■

J (a) Explain whether each one of the following reactions will occur spontaneously:
(i) $Zn^{2+} + Mg \rightarrow Mg^{2+} + Zn$
(ii) $2Fe^{3+} + 2F^- \rightarrow 2Fe^{2+} + F_2$

(b) Work out the cell potential for the following cell:
$Mn(s) \mid Mn^{2+}(aq) \vdots Fe^{2+}(aq) \mid Fe(s)$
Hence write down the overall cell reaction for the spontaneous reaction that occurs.

K Predict the direction of the electron flow in each of the following electrochemical cells, given the overall cell reaction:

(a) $Cu + Br_2 \rightarrow Cu^{2+} + Br^-$
(b) $Cu^{2+} + Cr \rightarrow Cu + Cr^{2+}$

If the concentration of the aqueous hydrogen ion is increased, the position of the equilibrium shifts to the right and the reduction potential becomes positive. At the same time, the oxidation potential for the reaction becomes negative.

Pressure and cell potential

A change in pressure affects only those cell reactions that involve a gas. Essentially, increasing the pressure of a gas increases its concentration. Therefore, the effect of increasing pressure on cell potential is the same as that with increasing concentration.

Consider the hydrogen half cell equilibrium again:

$$2H^+(aq) + 2e^- \rightleftharpoons H_2(g) \qquad E_{oxid}^{\ominus} = E_{red}^{\ominus} = 0.00\,V$$

If the pressure of the hydrogen is increased, the position of the equilibrium shifts to the left. Therefore, the oxidation potential becomes positive and the reduction potential negative.

4 FEASIBILITY OF REACTIONS

The absolute value of the cell potential determines the feasibility of the reaction. When the cell potential is positive, the reaction is spontaneous. When it is negative, the reaction is not spontaneous. The description 'spontaneous' refers to the tendency of a reaction to occur. It says nothing about the rate of reaction. So it is possible for a spontaneous reaction to be so slow as not to occur. In an electrochemical cell, if $E_{cell}^{\ominus}$ is positive, the reaction is spontaneous; if $E_{cell}^{\ominus}$ is negative, the reaction is not spontaneous.

Electron flow in the external circuit

As already stated, the external flow of electrons is from the anode to the cathode. The cell potential can be used to identify the anode. Provided the cell potential is positive, the cell works spontaneously and the anode is the electrode at which the oxidation occurs.

One battery being developed uses liquid sulphur and sodium (Fig 26.14). The overall cell reaction is:

$$2Na + S \rightarrow 2Na^+ + S^{2-}$$

The two half equations are:

$$Na \rightarrow Na^+ + 2e^- \qquad\qquad E_{oxid}^{\ominus} = +2.71\,V$$

$$S + 2e^- \rightarrow S^{2-} \qquad\qquad E_{red}^{\ominus} = +0.14\,V$$

So, the cell potential is +2.85 V. This suggests that the cell reaction is proceeding in the correct direction. Therefore, electrons flow from the sodium electrode to the sulphur electrode.

Now consider a cell that has a theoretical overall cell reaction of:

$$2Ag + Cu^{2+} \rightarrow 2Ag^+ + Cu$$

The half equations are:

$$Ag \rightarrow Ag^+ + e^- \qquad\qquad E_{oxid}^{\ominus} = -0.80\,V$$

$$Cu^{2+} + 2e^- \rightarrow Cu \qquad\qquad E_{red}^{\ominus} = +0.34\,V$$

So $E_{cell}^{\ominus} = -0.46\,V$, indicating that, as written, the reaction will not proceed spontaneously. If the equation is reversed, then the cell potential becomes positive, indicating that electrons will flow from the copper electrode to the silver electrode:

$$Cu(s) + 2Ag^+(aq) \rightarrow Cu^{2+}(aq) + 2Ag(s) \qquad E_{cell}^{\ominus} = +0.46\,V$$

Cell potential and free energy

Cells are a source of electrical energy that can be used to do work. A potential of 1 volt imparts 1 joule of energy to a charge of 1 coulomb. If the energy is used to do work, such as running an electric motor, then:

work = charge × potential difference

In this case, the potential difference is the cell potential. Since the cell potential is necessarily positive in order to produce a current, then the work done is negative. This means that work is done on the surroundings.

Consider now the amount of work done when the molar quantities as shown in the overall cell reaction are used:

work = (charge on number of electrons transferred during cell reaction) × $E^{\ominus}_{cell}$

The charge on the number of electrons transferred is the charge on n moles of electrons, where n is the number of moles transferred in the cell reaction. Therefore:

$$\text{work} = -nFE^{\ominus}_{cell}$$

n is the number of electrons transferred in the cell reaction, and F is the Faraday constant, which is the charge on 1 mole of electrons.

The work done according to this equation is the maximum amount of work that can be done. In reality, some electrical energy is transferred by the heating of the wires. The maximum amount of work available from a process carried out under standard conditions is known as the **free energy change**, $\Delta G^{\ominus}$ (G was chosen to celebrate the American Willard Gibbs.) So, in an electrochemical cell:

$$\Delta G^{\ominus} = -nFE^{\ominus}_{cell}$$

The unit of $\Delta G^{\ominus}$ is $J\,mol^{-1}$.

> ✔ Remember: Electrons have a negative charge.

> ✔ The Faraday constant F is 96 500 coulombs. For more information, read page 507.

■ See questions 1 and 2.

EXAMPLE

Q Calculate the free energy change for an electrochemical cell based on the following cell reaction:

$$Mn(s) + Cd^{2+}(aq) \rightarrow Mn^{2+}(aq) + Cd(s)$$

A From the overall reaction, the two half reactions are:

Oxidation half reaction: $Mn(s) \rightarrow Mn^{2+}(aq) + 2e^-$ $E^{\ominus}_{oxid} = +1.18\,V$

Reduction half reaction $Cd^{2+}(aq) + 2e^- \rightarrow Cd(s)$ $E^{\ominus}_{red} = -0.40\,V$

Since: $E^{\ominus}_{cell} = E^{\ominus}_{oxid} + E^{\ominus}_{red}$

then: $E^{\ominus}_{cell} = +1.18 - 0.40 = +0.78\,V$

From the two half reactions, it can be seen that 2 moles of electrons are transferred during the reaction.

So: $\Delta G^{\ominus} = -nFE^{\ominus}_{cell}$

$$\Delta G^{\ominus} = -2 \times 96500 \times 0.78\,J\,mol^{-1}$$

$$= -150.5\,kJ\,mol^{-1}$$

> **?**
> **L** Calculate the free energy changes, $\Delta G^{\ominus}$, for each of the following reactions:
> **(a)** $Cd(s) + Pb^{2+}(aq) \rightarrow Cd^{2+}(aq) + Pb(s)$
> **(b)** $2Fe^{3+}(aq) + Cu(s)$
> $\rightarrow 2Fe^{2+}(aq) + Cu^{2+}(aq)$
> **(c)** $Cl_2(g) + 2Br^-(aq) \rightarrow Br_2(l) + 2Cl^-(aq)$

Feasibility of reactions

Just as the cell potential must be positive for a reaction to occur spontaneously, so the value of $\Delta G^{\ominus}$ must be negative. The free energy change of a reaction can be used in non- electrochemical cells to predict the feasibility of reactions. (On page 573 is a description of the application of free energy changes in predicting the feasibility of the reduction of some metal oxides.) Any discussion of the feasibility of reactions must be taken with caution, since the $E_{cell}^{\ominus}$ or $\Delta G^{\ominus}$ values do not contain any information about the rate of reaction. Therefore, a reaction may have a high negative $\Delta G^{\ominus}$ but still not take place because its activation energy is too large. (Activation energy is covered on pages 127 and 594.)

See questions 1, 2, and 3. ■

EXAMPLE

Q Predict whether the following cell reaction should proceed spontaneously:

$$Cr^{3+}(aq) + Fe^{2+}(aq) \rightarrow Cr^{2+}(aq) + Fe^{3+}(aq)$$

A From the overall cell reaction, the two half equations are:

Oxidation half reaction:

$$Fe^{2+}(aq) \rightarrow Fe^{3+}(aq) + e^{-} \qquad E_{oxid}^{\ominus} = -0.77\,V$$

Reduction half equation:

$$Cr^{3+}(aq) + e^{-} \rightarrow Cr^{2+}(aq) \qquad E_{red}^{\ominus} = -0.41\,V$$

Since the cell potential is given by $E_{cell}^{\ominus} = E_{oxid}^{\ominus} + E_{red}^{\ominus}$, then:

$$E_{cell}^{\ominus} = -0.77 - 0.41 = -1.18\,V$$

A negative cell potential predicts that the reaction should not take place spontaneously.

The free energy change for this reaction can also be calculated to show that the free energy change is positive:

$$\begin{aligned} \Delta G &= -nFE_{cell}^{\ominus} \\ &= -1 \times 96500 \times (-1.18)\,J\,mol^{-1} \\ &= +114\,kJ\,mol^{-1} \end{aligned}$$

The positive value of the free energy change is another indicator that the reaction will not take place spontaneously.

?

M Predict whether the following reactions will take place spontaneously. In each case, work out the cell potential and the free energy change for the reaction.

(a) $Cl_2(g) + 2F^-(aq) \rightarrow F_2(g) + 2Cl^-(aq)$

(b) $MnO_4^- + 5Cr^{2+}(aq) + 8H^+(aq)$
$\rightarrow Mn^{2+}(aq) + 5Cr^{3+}(aq) + 4H_2O(l)$

---

5 BATTERIES AND FUEL CELLS

A battery is an electrochemical cell that is used as an energy source. Some kinds of battery have several electrochemical cells in series, thereby combining the individual cell potentials to give a large potential at the output terminals. Batteries are normally designed to deliver a reasonably large current and to be able to withstand fairly rough handling.

Batteries are of two types: **primary cells** and **secondary cells**.

Primary cells

Primary cells cannot be recharged. They are the most familiar type of battery on sale today.

Leclanché or dry cell

The dry cell (Fig 26.15) consists of a zinc anode (also the cell's casing) and a graphite cathode. A paste of ammonium chloride, manganese(IV)

Fig 26.14 **This Walkman is powered by batteries of the primary-cell type. Typically, they have to be replaced every two or three months**

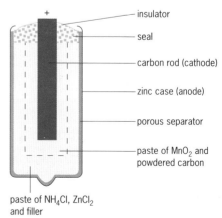

paste of NH_4Cl, $ZnCl_2$ and filler

Fig 26.15 **A cross-section through a dry-cell battery**

insulator
seal
carbon rod (cathode)
zinc case (anode)
porous separator
paste of MnO_2 and powdered carbon

oxide and zinc chloride surrounds the graphite electrode. The porous separator acts as a salt bridge. When the cell is connected into an external circuit, electrons flow from the zinc anode to the graphite cathode:

Oxidation half reaction: $Zn \rightarrow Zn^{2+} + 2e^-$

Reduction half reaction: $MnO_2 + NH_4^+ + e^- \rightarrow MnO(OH) + NH_3$

The cell potential is about 1.5 V, which is impossible to verify using standard electrode potentials because the cell reaction occurs under non-standard conditions. The zinc ions present in the paste prevent ammonia being given off by forming an ammine complex, $[Zn(NH_3)_4]^{2+}$. In addition to the nuisance of having to replace this type of battery at frequent intervals, there is the disadvantage that the acidic ammonium chloride corrodes the zinc casing, even when the battery is not being used.

■ See questions 2 and 4.

Secondary cells

These are batteries that can be recharged and therefore have a much longer life than primary cells. A typical rechargeable battery is the lead–acid battery used in most motor vehicles (Figs 26.16 and 26.17).

Fig 26.16 **Topping up a lead–acid car battery with distilled water**

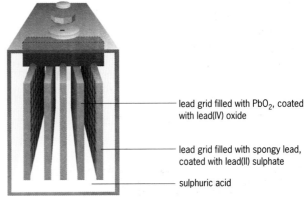

lead grid filled with PbO$_2$, coated with lead(IV) oxide

lead grid filled with spongy lead, coated with lead(II) sulphate

sulphuric acid

Fig 26.17 **A lead–acid storage battery**

The lead–acid battery consists of an aqueous electrolyte (30 per cent by volume sulphuric acid) and two sets of plates which form the electrodes. The positive plates are lead grids filled with a paste of spongy lead. The negative plates are lead grids filled with a paste of lead(IV) oxide. At first, the lead reacts with the dilute sulphuric acid to form an insoluble coating of lead(II) sulphate, on both sets of plates:

$$Pb(s) + H_2SO_4(aq) \rightarrow PbSO_4(s) + H_2(g)$$

The battery is initially charged by direct current. During the charging process, the plates become chemically different. A layer of lead(IV) oxide is deposited on each negative plate, but the positive plates retain their layer of lead(II) sulphate. The charging half reactions are:

Oxidation half reaction:
$$PbSO_4(s) + 2e^- \rightarrow Pb(s) + SO_4^{2-}(aq)$$

Reduction half reaction:
$$PbSO_4(s) + 2H_2O(l) \rightarrow PbO_2(s)(s) + 4H^+(aq) + SO_4^{2-}(aq) + 2e^-$$

The overall reaction during charging is:
$$2PbSO_4(s) + 2H_2O(l) \rightarrow Pb(s) + PbO_2(s) + 4H^+(aq) + 2SO_4^{2-}(aq)$$

Electrolysis takes place during charging.

N Car batteries are normally described as 12 V batteries. They contain six individual cells, each connected in series.

(a) Estimate the cell potential of one lead–acid electrochemical cell.

(b) Use the electrode potentials on page 679 to estimate the cell potential of a lead–acid electrochemical cell.

(c) Comment on your answers to parts **(a)** and **(b)**.

See question 6. ■

Once the battery is charged, the half reactions can be reversed to provide an external current or flow of electrons. The discharging half reactions are:

Reduction half reaction:

$$Pb(s) + SO_4^{2-}(aq) \rightarrow PbSO_4(s) + 2e^-$$

Oxidation half reaction:

$$PbO_2(s) + 4H^+(aq) + SO_4^{2-}(aq) + 2e^- \rightarrow PbSO_4(s) + 2H_2O(l)$$

The overall discharging reaction is:

$$Pb(s) + PbO_2(s) + 4H^+(aq) + 2SO_4^{2-}(aq) \rightarrow 2PbSO_4(s) + 2H_2O(l)$$

Note that sulphuric acid is used up during the discharging process and so its concentration decreases. This provides a convenient test for a lead–acid battery. Being proportional to concentration, the density of the sulphuric acid in the battery is simply measured with a hydrometer.

Fuel cells

A fuel cell is an electrochemical cell designed so that the reactants, often gases, are replenished continuously. This enables the cell continuously to supply electric current. Because its reactants are kept topped up, a fuel cell does not need recharging.

Hydrogen–oxygen fuel cell

A spacecraft needs a continuous supply of electrical energy. This cannot be achieved using conventional batteries, so much of it is provided by a hydrogen–oxygen fuel cell. Essentially, the overall cell reaction is that of oxygen and hydrogen to form water:

$$2H_2(g) + O_2(g) \rightarrow 2H_2O(l)$$

This is a redox reaction, in which electrons are transferred from hydrogen to oxygen. In a fuel cell, this transfer takes place via an external circuit rather than directly during a collision between particles.

The electrolyte is aqueous sodium hydroxide, which is contained within the cell using porous electrodes. These electrodes allow the passage of water, hydrogen and oxygen.

During their passage through the cathode, oxygen molecules are reduced to hydroxide ions which enter the electrolyte.

Reduction half equation:

$$O_2(g) + 2H_2O(l) + 4e^- \rightarrow 4OH^-(aq)$$

During their passage through the anode, hydrogen molecules are oxidised to water mole-

cules, thereby removing hydroxide ions from the electrolyte:

Oxidation half–equation:

$$H_2(g) + 2OH^-(aq) \rightarrow 2H_2O(l) + 2e^-$$

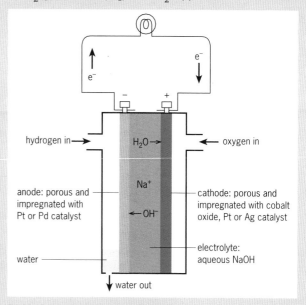

Fig 26.18 **A hydrogen–oxygen fuel cell**

O Construct the overall cell reaction that takes place within the oxygen–hydrogen fuel cell to convince yourself that all that is happening is the reaction of hydrogen and oxygen to make water.

6 ELECTRODE POTENTIALS AND TRANSITION ELEMENTS

The first-row transition elements are a series of metals that share several key characteristics. One of these is that they can have more than one oxidation state in their compounds. This is related to the electron configurations of these element. The existence of several oxidation states of the transition elements is described fully on pages 523 to 525.

Redox reactions and transition elements

Since transition elements can have several different oxidation states, it is possible for their compounds, and the elements themselves, to take part in redox reactions. That is, the lower oxidation states of a transition element can be converted into one of the higher states by oxidation, and its higher oxidation states can be converted into one of the lower states by reduction. These changes necessarily involve the loss and gain of electrons, so they must be redox reactions.

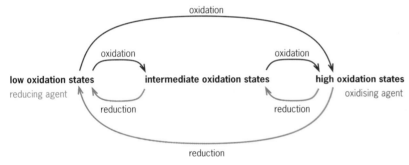

Fig 26.19 **A summary of redox reactions of the transition elements**

It is shown on page 547 how $E^{\ominus}_{red}$ and $E^{\ominus}_{oxid}$ can be used to explain redox reactions. So, it follows that the chemistry of transition elements and their compounds involve electrode potentials.

7 CHEMISTRY OF SEVEN FIRST-ROW TRANSITION ELEMENTS

The first-row transition elements starts with scandium and finishes with zinc. (See page 519 for the definition of a transition element.) The important redox reactions of six of these elements are the subject of this section, particular attention being paid to the electrode potentials involved.

Titanium and its compounds

Titanium exhibits three oxidation states: +2, +3 and +4. The first two are principally ionic oxidation states, involving Ti^{2+} and Ti^{3+}, while the +4 state involves covalent bonding to the titanium atom.

Despite its negative reduction potential, titanium does not react with dilute acids or hot aqueous alkalis. This lack of reactivity combined with its low density favours the use of titanium in the aerospace industry. The former Soviet Union developed many military aircraft that were made from titanium alloys despite the prohibitive cost of the metal.

Table 26.2 **Electrode potentials of three titanium species**

Reduction half equation	$E^{\ominus}_{red}/V$
$Ti^{2+}(aq) + 2e^- \rightleftharpoons Ti(s)$	−1.63
$Ti^{3+}(aq) + e^- \rightleftharpoons Ti^{2+}(aq)$	−0.37
$TiO^{2+}(aq) + 2H^+(aq) + e^- \rightleftharpoons Ti^{3+}(aq) + H_2O(l)$	+0.10

Fig 26.20 **Low density and high tensile strength are among the physical properties that make titanium and its alloys the ideal materials for this Mig 29**

Fig 26.21 **Military equipment which is taken across rough ground and is subject to stress in use, like this Howitzer, needs to be as light and as strong as possible**

?

P (a) Write an equation to show the reduction of titanium(IV) chloride using sodium.

(b) Suggest why titanium is so costly.

(c) Show that acidified Ti^{3+}(aq) can be oxidised by atmospheric oxygen to give TiO^{2+}(aq). Use the following electrode potential:

$\frac{1}{2}O_2$(g) $+ 2H^+$(aq) $+ e^- \rightleftharpoons 2H_2O$(l)

$E^{\ominus}_{red} = +1.23\,V$

Titanium is prepared by the reduction of titanium(IV) chloride, using sodium or magnesium. This is a batch process. The reduction is done and the titanium isolated to meet a particular requirement. When more titanium is wanted, the reaction is carried out again:

$$Mg + TiCl_4 \rightarrow 2MgCl_2 + Ti$$

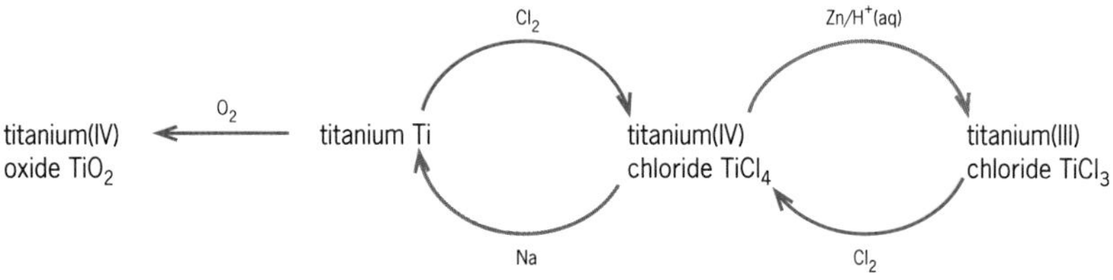

titanium(IV) oxide TiO_2 $\xleftarrow{O_2}$ titanium Ti $\xrightarrow{Cl_2}$ titanium(IV) chloride $TiCl_4$ $\xrightarrow{Zn/H^+(aq)}$ titanium(III) chloride $TiCl_3$

Na $\qquad$ Cl_2

Fig 26.22 **Some reactions of titanium and its compounds. Oxidation is represented by red arrows, and reduction by blue arrows**

Vanadium and its compounds

Table 26.3 **Electrode potentials of five vanadium species**

Reduction half equation	$E^{\ominus}_{red}/V$
V^{2+}(aq) $+ 2e^- \rightleftharpoons V$(s)	−1.18
V^{3+}(aq) $+ e^- \rightleftharpoons V^{2+}$(aq)	−0.26
VO^{2+}(aq) $+ 2H^+$(aq) $+ e^- \rightleftharpoons V^{3+}$(aq) $+ H_2O$(l)	+0.34
VO_2^+(aq) $+ 2H^+$(aq) $+ e^- \rightleftharpoons VO^{2+}$(aq) $+ H_2O$(l)	+1.00
VO_3^-(aq) $+ 4H^+$(aq) $+ e^- \rightleftharpoons VO^{2+}$(aq) $+ 2H_2O$(l)	+1.00

✓

The electrode potentials suggest that the most stable aqueous oxidation state of titanium is the +4 state, and that it involves the titanyl(IV) ion, TiO^{2+}(aq), rather than Ti^{4+}(aq), which would be too polarising since it has a high charge density.

Vanadium exhibits four common oxidation states: +2, +3, +4 and +5. Under ordinary conditions, vanadium(IV) is considered to be the most stable oxidation state. The lower oxidation states are reducing agents and the highest oxidation state is an oxidising agent. Therefore the chemistry of vanadium compounds typically involves a conversion from one oxidation state to another.

Vanadium in the +5 oxidation state

In the +5 oxidation state, the bonding to the vanadium atom is covalent in character, since it is impossible for a vanadium atom to lose five electrons to form V^{5+}. Probably, the most important compound in this oxidation state is vanadium(V) oxide, which is used as a catalyst in the manufacture of sulphuric acid in the contact process.

The aqueous chemistry of vanadium(V) is centred around $VO_2^+(aq)$ and $VO_3^-(aq)$.

Since vanadium(V) is the highest oxidation state of vanadium, one would expect it to be highly oxidising, being reduced to one of the lower oxidation states. For example, zinc can reduce $VO_2^+(aq)$ to $V^{2+}(aq)$ in a series of steps that involves the formation of different coloured solutions as the oxidation state of vanadium changes. Each of these steps can be explained by use of the appropriate electrode potential.

The first step is the reduction of $VO_2^+(aq)$:

$$Zn(s) \rightarrow Zn^{2+}(aq) + 2e^- \qquad E^{\ominus}_{oxid} = +0.76\,V$$

$$VO_2^+(aq) + 4H^+(aq) + e^- \rightarrow VO^{2+}(aq) + H_2O(l) \qquad E^{\ominus}_{red} = +1.00\,V$$

Therefore: $E^{\ominus}_{cell} = +1.76\,V$

The overall equation can be obtained by combining the two half equations:

$$Zn(s) + 2VO_2^+(aq) + 4H^+(aq) + \rightarrow 2VO^{2+}(aq) + 2H_2O(l) + Zn^{2+}(aq)$$

The second step is the reduction of $VO^{2+}(aq)$:

$$VO^{2+}(aq) + 2H^+(aq) + e^- \rightarrow V^{3+}(aq) + H_2O(l) \;\; +0.34\; E^{\ominus}_{red} = +0.34\,V$$

Therefore: $E^{\ominus}_{cell} = +1.10\,V$

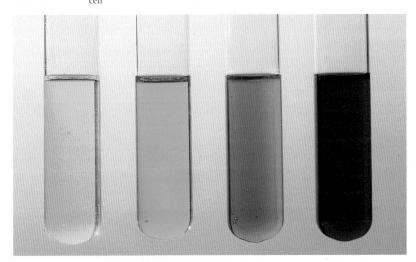

Fig 26.23 **When the yellow vanadyl(V) ion, $VO_2^+(aq)$, is reduced by zinc, the vanadium is reduced through the +4 and +3 oxidation states, and finally forms the +2 oxidation state. The reduction can be followed by the changes in colour of the solution: +5 yellow, +4 blue, +3 green and +2 purple**

Q **(a)** Construct the overall equation for the reaction between acidified $VO^{2+}(aq)$ and zinc to give $V^{3+}(aq)$.

(b) By use of the appropriate electrode potentials, show that zinc can reduce acidified $V^{3+}(aq)$ to form $V^{2+}(aq)$.

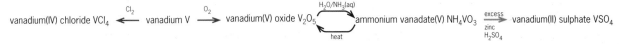

Fig 26.24 **A summary of the reactions of vanadium and its compounds. Reactions involving oxidation are represented by red arrows, and the reaction involving reduction by a blue arrow**

Chromium and its compounds

Chromium exhibits three common oxidation states: +2, +3 and +6, of which chromium(III) is the most stable. Chromium is manufactured by the reduction of chromium(III) oxide by a reactive metal (which must be above chromium in the reactivity series). Chromium reacts with dilute acids, such as hydrochloric or sulphuric acid, to give a sky-blue solution that contains the aqueous chromium(II) ion, as indicated by the electrode potential data. The reaction must be carried out in an inert atmosphere to avoid atmospheric oxidation, which would give chromium(III).

Oxidation of aqueous chromium(III) ions

Aqueous chromium(III) ions can be oxidised to form chromate(VI). First, they are reacted with aqueous sodium hydroxide to form chromium(III) hydroxide, and then the mixture obtained is boiled with hydrogen peroxide:

$$Cr^{3+}(aq) + 3OH^-(aq) \rightarrow Cr(OH)_3(s)$$

$$2Cr(OH)_3(s) + 3H_2O_2(aq) + 4OH^-(aq) \rightarrow 2CrO_4^{2-}(aq) + 8H_2O(l)$$

Chromium in the +6 oxidation state

The highest oxidation number of a transition element often involves covalent bonding to the transition metal atom. Such is the case with compounds of chromium(VI). These compounds are also very powerful oxidising agents.

See question 7. ■

Table 26.4 **Electrode potentials of seven chromium species**

Reduction half equation	$E^{\ominus}_{red}$/V
$Cr^{2+}(aq) + 2e^- \rightleftharpoons Cr(s)$	−0.91
$Cr^{3+}(aq) + 3e^- \rightleftharpoons Cr(s)$	−0.74
$Cr^{3+}(aq) + e^- \rightleftharpoons Cr^{2+}(aq)$	−0.41
$Cr(OH)_3(s) + 3e^- \rightleftharpoons Cr(s) + 3OH^-(aq)$	−1.30
$[Cr(OH)_4]^-(aq) + 3e^- \rightleftharpoons Cr(s) + 4OH^-(aq)$	−1.20
$CrO_4^{2-}(aq) + 4H_2O(l) + 3e^- \rightleftharpoons Cr(OH)_3(s) + 5OH^-(aq)$	−0.13
$Cr_2O_7^{2-}(aq) + 14H^+(aq) + 6e^- \rightleftharpoons 2Cr^{3+}(aq) + 7H_2O(l)$	+1.33

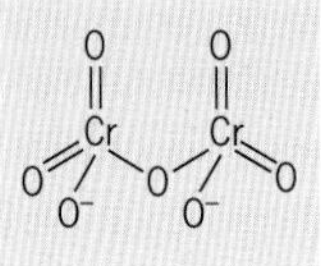

Fig 26.25 **The dichromate(VI) ion has one bridging oxygen atom**

As Table 26.4 shows, $E^{\ominus}_{red}$ for dichromate(VI) has a fairly large positive value, which indicates the ability of dichromate(VI) to oxidise other substances. The equation shows that the product of this reduction is normally the aqueous chromium(III) ion. The use of aqueous dichromate(VI) ion as an oxidising agent is always associated with the presence of aqueous hydrogen ions (dilute sulphuric acid).

In an alkaline solution, the oxidising ability is greatly reduced, since dichromate(VI) is converted into chromate(VI). As Table 26.4 shows, $E^{\ominus}_{red}$ for the reduction of the CrO_4^{2-} ion has a low negative value:

$$2OH^-(aq) + Cr_2O_7^{2-}(aq) \rightleftharpoons 2CrO_4^{2-}(aq) + H_2O(l)$$

The conversion of dichromate(VII) to chromate(VI) is pH dependent. In acid, the equilibrium shifts to the left to form orange dichromate(VI). In alkali, the equilibrium shifts to the right to form yellow chromate(VI) ion.

Iron(II) ions are oxidised by acidified $Cr_2O_7^{2-}(aq)$ to form $Fe^{3+}(aq)$, and $Cr_2O_7^{2-}(aq)$ is reduced to $Cr^{3+}(aq)$. The colour changes in this reaction are complicated, since green $Fe^{2+}(aq)$ react with orange $Cr_2O_7^{2-}(aq)$ to form orange-rust $Fe^{3+}(aq)$ and blue-green $Cr^{3+}(aq)$:

$$6Fe^{2+}(aq) + Cr_2O_7^{2-}(aq) + 14H^+(aq) \rightarrow 6Fe^{3+}(aq) + 2Cr^{3+}(aq) + 7H_2O(l)$$

R **(a)** Write down an equation to show the reaction between chromium metal and dilute sulphuric acid in an inert atmosphere.

(b) Use the electrode potential to work out $E^{\ominus}_{cell}$ for the following electrochemical cell:

Cr(s) I Cr²⁺(aq) ┊┊ H⁺(aq) I H₂(g) I Pt

(c) Suggest why the oxidation of chromium(III) into chromium(VI) is usually carried out in alkaline conditions. Use the electrode potentials in Table 26.4 to help you to explain your answer.

Information about acidified dichromate(VI) in the oxidation of alcohols and aldehydes is on pages 236 and 300.

Acidified potassium dichromate(VI) can be reduced by zinc in an inert atmosphere to give chromium(II). The reaction must be carried out in an inert atmosphere to prevent oxidation of $Cr^{2+}(aq)$ to $Cr^{3+}(aq)$:

■ See question 7.

$$4Zn(s) + Cr_2O_7^{2-}(aq) + 14H^+(aq) \rightarrow 4Zn^{2+}(aq) + 2Cr^{2+}(aq) + 7H_2O(l)$$

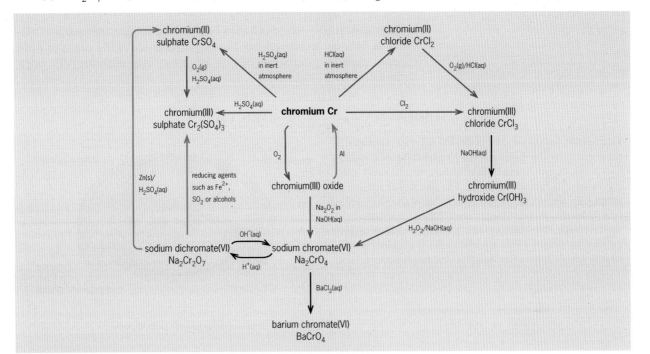

Fig 26.26 **A summary of the reactions of chromium and its compounds. Reactions involving oxidation are represented by red arrows, and those involving reduction by blue arrows**

Manganese and its compounds

Table 26.5 **Electrode potentials of eight manganese species**

Reduction half equation	$E^{\ominus}_{red}$/V
$Mn^{2+}(aq) + 2e^- = Mn(s)$	−1.18
$Mn^{3+}(aq) + e^- = Mn^{2+}(aq)$	+1.49
$MnO_2(s) + 2H_2O(l) + 2e^- = Mn(OH)_2(s) + 2OH^-(aq)$	+0.05
$MnO_2(s) + 4H^+(aq) + 2e^- = Mn^{2+}(aq) + 2H_2O(l)$	+1.23
$MnO_4^-(aq) + e^- = MnO_4^{2-}(aq)$	+0.56
$MnO_4^-(aq) + 2H_2O(l) + 3e^- = MnO_2(s) + 4OH^-(aq)$	+0.59
$MnO_4^-(aq) + 4H^+(aq) + 3e^- = MnO_2(s) + 2H_2O(l)$	+1.67
$MnO_4^-(aq) + 8H^+(aq) + 5e^- = Mn^{2+}(aq) + 4H_2O(l)$	+1.54

S (a) Use the electrode potentials to suggest why manganese(III) is considered to be a very unstable oxidation state with respect to the +2 oxidation state

(b) Predict whether you would expect manganese to react with dilute hydrochloric acid? Explain your answer using electrode potentials.

Manganese exhibits several common oxidation states, including +2, +4, +6 and +7. The +2 oxidation state is generally considered to be the most stable under normal conditions.

■ See question 7.

MANGANESE(IV) OXIDE

MANGANESE(IV) OXIDE is generally given the formula MnO_2, but its empirical formula is much closer to $MnO_{1.85}$. Although the structure has a highly covalent character, it can be considered to be an ionic lattice of Mn^{4+} and O^{2-}, in which some of the oxide ions are missing. That is, the structure has a number of holes. The best interpretation of this is that Mn^{3+} ions are in place of some Mn^{4+} ions, thereby ensuring that the absent oxide ions do not leave the lattice with an overall charge.

Manganese(IV) oxide is an electrical conductor since the oxide ions can move through the structure from one hole to another. Therefore it contains a mobile charge carrier. This is an important property that is used in the dry cell described on page 556.

Manganese(IV) oxide as an oxidising and a reducing agent

Manganese(IV) oxide has an intermediate oxidation number. Therefore, it can act both as a reducing agent and as an oxidising agent. Manganese(IV) oxide can reduce hydrochloric acid to form chlorine:

$$MnO_2(s) + 4HCl(aq) \rightarrow MnCl_2(aq) + 2H_2O(l) + Cl_2(g)$$

Manganese(IV) oxide can also be oxidised to give manganate(VI). This is usually achieved by heating the oxide with an oxidising agent, such as potassium nitrate or potassium chlorate(VI), with potassium hydroxide.

LITHIUM–MANGANESE(IV) OXIDE CELL

THE LITHIUM–MANGANESE(IV) OXIDE cell – popularly referred to as the lithium cell – cannot have a water-based electrolyte because the lithium would react with the water to form hydrogen. The great advantage of using lithium as one of the electrodes is that its oxidation potential is very large, which gives the battery a high voltage. The battery can therefore deliver a low current for a long time, which makes it an ideal power supply for such items as watches and heart pacemakers.

Oxidation half reaction at the anode:

$$Li \rightarrow Li^+ + e^-$$

Reduction half reaction at the cathode:

$$Li^+ + MnO_2 + e^- \rightarrow LiMnO_2$$

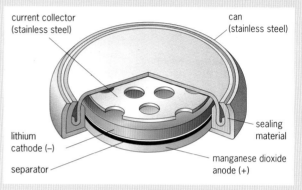

Fig 26.27 **A lithium-manganese(IV) oxide battery**

Higher oxidation states of manganese

Both the +6 and the +7 oxidation states are highly oxidising, since the manganese can be reduced to manganese(IV) or manganese(II). Aqueous manganate(VI) is a green solution, which is easily oxidised to give the familiar purple colour of the manganate(VII) ion. The manganate(VII) ion can be prepared directly by oxidising manganese(II) ions with oxidising agents such as sodium bismuthate, $NaBiO_3$, or lead(IV) oxide. This reaction is used in the estimation of the percentage of manganese in a sample of steel. The steel is reacted with dilute acid and the resultant aqueous manganese(II) ions oxidised to give purple manganate(VII). The concentration of the manganate(VII) can be determined using ultraviolet–visible spectroscopy (see page 618).

Volumetric analysis using potassium manganate(VII)

Aqueous potassium manganate(VII) is used in laboratories as an oxidising agent for organic preparations, volumetric analysis and qualitative analysis.

Acidified potassium manganate(VII) is used to test for reducing agents: it reacts to form manganese(II) ions and the distinct colour of the manganate(VII) ions disappears. For example, iodide ions reduce acidified manganate(VII) ions to form manganese(II) ions and iodine.

In volumetric analysis, acidified potassium manganate(VII) is used to determine the concentration of reducing agents. Since it changes colour during the titration, there is no need to have an indicator. The end-point is the first appearance of a purple-pink colour. A typical example (Fig 26.28) would be the reaction of aqueous iron(II) ions with acidified potassium manganate(VII):

$$5Fe^{2+}(aq) + MnO_4^-(aq) + 8H^+(aq) \rightarrow 5Fe^{3+}(aq) + Mn^{2+}(aq) + 4H_2O(l)$$

T (a) Write down:
(i) the half equation to show the reduction of acidified manganate(VII) ions to give manganese(II) ions,
(ii) the oxidation of aqueous iodine ions to form aqueous iodine.

(b) Hence construct the ionic equation for the reaction between acidified manganate(VII) ions and aqueous iodide ions.

EXAMPLE

Q A solution of a moss-killer contained aqueous iron(II) ions. 25.0 cm³ of this solution was acidified with dilute sulphuric acid and titrated with 0.0200 mol dm⁻³ potassium manganate(VII). It was found that 21.0 cm³ of the $KMnO_4$(aq) was needed to fully react with the Fe^{2+}(aq) in the solution of the moss-killer. Calculate the concentration of Fe^{2+}(aq) in the solution of the moss-killer.

A $5Fe^{2+}(aq) + MnO_4^-(aq) + 8H^+(aq)$
$\rightarrow 5Fe^{3+}(aq) + Mn^{2+}(aq) + 4H_2O(l)$

moles of MnO_4^- = volume in dm³ × conc
$= 0.0210 \times 0.0200 = 4.20 \times 10^{-4}$

From the equation:
moles of $Fe^{2+} = 5 \times$ moles of $MnO_4^- = 2.10 \times 10^{-5}$

Therefore:
$$[MnO_4^-(aq)] = \frac{\text{moles of } MnO_4^-}{\text{volume of } MnO_4^- \text{ (in dm}^3)}$$

$$= \frac{2.10 \times 10^{-3}}{0.0250} = 0.0840 \, \text{mol dm}^{-3}$$

?

U Potassium manganate(VII) was titrated with acidified iron(II) sulphate solution. 25.0 cm³ of $KMnO_4$(aq) required 35.9 cm³ of 0.100 mol dm⁻³ $FeSO_4$(aq) to fully react. Calculate the concentration of MnO_4^-(aq).

Fig 26.28 **A titration involving potassium manganate(VII) and iron(II) ions**

For more information about the concentration of aqueous solutions, read page 111.

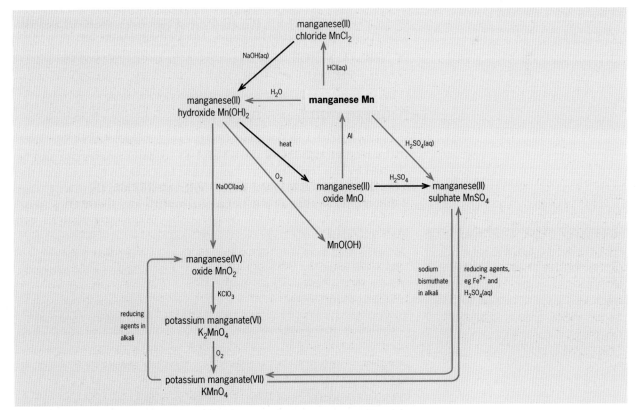

Fig 26.29 **A summary of the reactions of manganese and its compounds. Reactions involving oxidation are represented by red arrows, and those involving reduction by blue arrows**

In this description of the oxidising abilities of manganate(VII), there have been references to acidified conditions. This is important, because the pH at which the reaction is carried out affects the nature of the reduction product. If the pH is reduced so that the reaction is carried out in neutral or alkaline conditions, then manganese(IV) oxide is produced instead of manganese(II) ions. As Table 26.5 shows, in alkaline conditions there is a different half reaction.

See question 7. ■

Iron and its compounds

Table 26.6 **Electrode potentials of six iron species**

Reduction half equation	$E_{red}^{\ominus}/V$
$Fe^{2+}(aq) + 2e^- \rightleftharpoons Fe(s)$	−0.44
$Fe^{3+}(aq) + 3e^- \rightleftharpoons Fe(s)$	−0.04
$Fe^{3+}(aq) + e^- \rightleftharpoons Fe^{2+}(aq)$	+ 0.77
$[Fe(CN)_6]^{3-}(aq) + e^- \rightleftharpoons [Fe(CN)_6]^{4-}(aq)$	+ 0.36
$Fe(OH)_3(s) + e^- \rightleftharpoons Fe(OH)_2(s) + OH^-(aq)$	−0.56
$Fe(OH)_2(s) + 2e^- \rightleftharpoons Fe(s) + 2OH^-(aq)$	−0.88

Iron exhibits two common oxidation states, +2 and +3, both of which are ionic. Iron does form another oxidation state, the +6, but there are only a few compounds in which it occurs.

Stability of the +2 and +3 oxidation states

As the electrode potentials in Table 26.6 suggest, iron reacts with dilute acids, such as sulphuric acid, to form iron(II) salts:

$$Fe(s) + 2H^+(aq) \rightarrow Fe^{2+}(aq) + H_2(g) \qquad E_{cell}^{\ominus} = +0.44\,V$$

The iron(II) ions are very susceptible to aerial oxidation to form iron(III) ions. The stability of these two oxidation states is very much dependent on the pH. In acidic conditions, aqueous iron(II) ions are oxidised to iron(III) ions. The half equations are:

$$Fe^{2+}(aq) \rightarrow Fe^{3+}(aq) + e^- \qquad\qquad E_{oxid}^{\ominus} = -0.77\,V$$
$$\tfrac{1}{2}O_2(g) + 2H^+(aq) + e^- \rightarrow 2H_2O(l) \qquad E_{red}^{\ominus} = +1.23\,V$$

In alkaline conditions, the oxidation is even more favourable:

$$Fe(OH)_2(s) + OH^-(aq) \rightarrow Fe(OH)_3(s) + e^- \qquad E_{oxid}^{\ominus} = +0.56\,V$$
$$O_2(g) + 2H_2O(l) + 2e^- \rightarrow 4OH^-(aq) \qquad E_{red}^{\ominus} = + 0.40\,V$$

The relative stability of the +2 and +3 oxidation states can also be affected by the formation of complexes. In Table 26.6, note that the reduction potential for the hexacyanoferrate(III) ion, $[Fe(CN)_6]^{3-}(aq)$ is different from that for the hexaaquairon(III) ion, $[Fe(H_2O)_6]^{3+}(aq)$.

For convenience, aqueous metal ions such as $[M(H_2O)_6]^{Z+}(aq)$ are written as $M^{Z+}(aq)$.

V (a) (i) Write down the overall equation for the aerial oxidation of acidified iron(II) ions.

(ii) What is the $E_{cell}^{\ominus}$ value for this reaction?

(b) What is the $E_{cell}^{\ominus}$ value for the oxidation of iron(II) hydroxide, into iron(III) hydroxide in alkaline conditions?

W Compare the $E_{cell}^{\ominus}$ values for the oxidation of the hexaaquairon(II) ion, $[Fe(H_2O)_6]^{2+}(aq)$, by chlorine with those for the oxidation of aqueous hexacyanoferrate(II), $[Fe(CN)_6]^{4-}(aq)$, by chlorine.

Rusting of iron

Any unpainted iron object shows evidence of rusting. The surface of iron forms a flaky orange solid whose composition is best described as hydrated iron(III) oxide. Rusting is, in fact, a complicated electrochemical process occurring on the surface of iron.

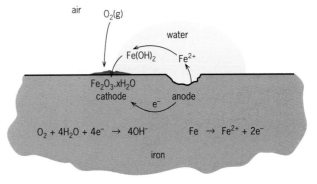

Fig 26.30 **How rusting occurs**

Fig 26.31 **The railway bridge over the Tyne at Newcastle is an iron structure which has to be painted to prevent rust damage**

Fig 26.30 summarises some of the complex electrochemical processes that take place when iron rusts. When iron is in contact with a drop of water, a redox reaction occurs:

Oxidation half equation: $Fe \rightarrow Fe^{2+} + 2e^-$

Reduction half equation: $O_2 + 2H_2O + 4e^- \rightarrow 4OH^-$

These two reactions take place in different areas of the iron, resulting in the formation of an anodic region and a cathodic region. The electrons move through the metal from the anodic region to the cathodic region. The circuit is completed by ions moving through the water. Without the water, the circuit is not complete and rusting cannot take place. If the water contains electrolytes, such as sodium chloride, then the concentration of ions in the droplet is higher and so the rate of rusting increases. The iron(II) ions and the hydroxide in the water droplet are precipitated as iron(II) hydroxide, which is further oxidised to form hydrated iron(III) oxide or rust:

$$Fe^{2+}(aq) + 2OH^-(aq) \rightarrow Fe(OH)_2(s)$$
$$4Fe(OH)_2(s) + O_2(g) + 2H_2O(l) \rightarrow 4Fe(OH)_3(s)$$

Rust protection

Any layer that is impervious to water protects iron from rusting. However, the protection provided by paints and other widely used materials is of limited duration, because of such factors as physical damage, chemical deterioration and weathering. So, alternative methods of rust protection use electrochemical principles instead. One of the best known involves giving the iron a protective layer of zinc by a process called galvanisation, which is described on page 568.

Iron pipes and tanks in the ground are often protected by a block of magnesium or zinc (Fig 26.32). The block of magnesium (or zinc) is attached to the iron object and, since magnesium (or zinc) has a higher positive electrode potential than iron, it oxidises in preference (sacrificially) to the iron. The iron object acts as the cathode in this method.

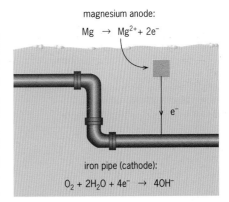

magnesium anode:

$Mg \rightarrow Mg^{2+} + 2e^-$

iron pipe (cathode):

$O_2 + 2H_2O + 4e^- \rightarrow 4OH^-$

Fig 26.32 **Sacrificial protection**

The tin-plated cans used in the food industry provide another example of electrochemical protection. The oxidation potential for tin has a lower positive value than that for iron. Therefore, tin is less likely to react with moist oxygen and so protects the surface of the iron. There is one drawback with tin plating. It is easily scratched to reveal the iron, in which case the can rusts very rapidly. What happens is that once the iron is in contact with moist air, it gives sacrificial protection to the less reactive tin.

See question 5. ■

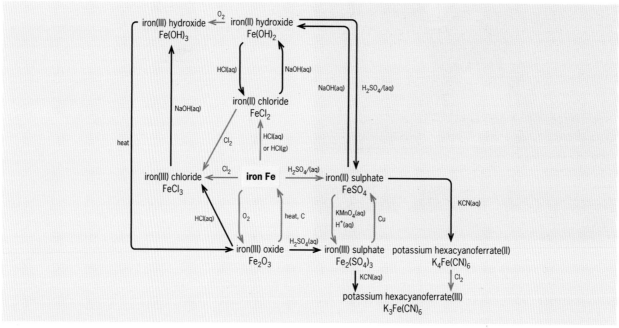

Fig 26.33 **A summary of the reactions of iron and its compounds. Reactions involving oxidation are represented by red arrows, and those involving reduction by blue arrows**

Galvanising iron

As already stated, a coating of zinc protects iron from rusting. Zinc-coated iron is known as galvanised iron.

Galvanised iron is protected mainly because, in the electrochemical cell formed by galvanisation, the zinc is preferentially oxidised. (The oxidation potential for zinc has a larger positive value than that for iron.) However, were it not for another reaction taking place at the same time, all the zinc would eventually be oxidised and rusting could start. The zinc hydroxide produced reacts with carbon dioxide in the air to form a layer of a zinc hydroxide–zinc carbonate compound that adheres firmly to the iron to give further protection.

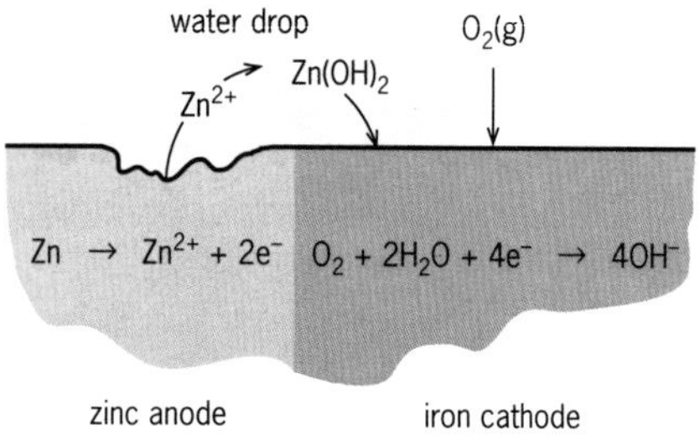

Fig 26.34 **Galvanised iron. The protective layer of zinc forms an electrochemical cell with the iron. The overall cell reaction is:**

$$2Zn + O_2 + 2H_2O \rightarrow 2Zn(OH)_2$$

Fig 26.35 **Galvanised iron does not rust as fast as iron on its own. The coating of zinc corrodes in preference to the iron, in the course of which it forms a further protective layer over the iron**

Cobalt

Table 26.7 **Electrode potentials of four cobalt species**

Reduction half equation	$E^{\ominus}_{red}$/V
$Co^{2+}(aq) + 2e^- \rightleftharpoons Co(s)$	−0.28
$Co^{3+}(aq) + e^- \rightleftharpoons Co^{2+}(aq)$	+1.82
$[Co(NH_3)_6]^{3+}(aq) + e^- \rightleftharpoons [Co(NH_3)_6]^{2+}(aq)$	+0.10
$Co(OH)_3(s) + e^- \rightleftharpoons Co(OH)_2(s) + OH^-(aq)$	+0.17

Cobalt exhibits only two common oxidation states, +2 and +3, both of which are ionic in nature. As expected from the reduction potential of $Co^{2+}(aq)$, cobalt reacts slowly with dilute acids to form aqueous cobalt(II) ion:

■ See question 8.

$$Co(s) + 2H^+(aq) \rightarrow Co^{2+}(aq) + H_2(g) \qquad E^{\ominus}_{cell} = +0.28 \text{ V}$$

Redox reactions involving cobalt(III)

The absence of a higher oxidation state would suggest that redox reactions are not particularly significant, but this would be some way from the truth. Just a glance at the electrode potential for $Co^{3+}(aq)$ in Table 26.7 indicates that it should be easy to reduce aqueous cobalt(III) ions to aqueous cobalt(II) ions. In aqueous solution, water reduces cobalt(III) ions to give cobalt(II) ions and oxygen:

$$Co^{3+}(aq) + e^- \rightarrow Co^{2+}(aq) \qquad E^{\ominus}_{red} = +1.82 \text{ V}$$

$$H_2O(l) \rightarrow 2H^+(aq) + \tfrac{1}{2}O_2(g) + 2e^- \qquad E^{\ominus}_{oxid} = -1.23 \text{ V}$$

The overall equation is:

$$4Co^{3+}(aq) + 2H_2O(l) \rightarrow 4Co^{2+}(aq) + 4H^+(aq) + O_2(g) \quad E^{\ominus}_{cell} = +0.59 \text{ V}$$

As already mentioned, pH can affect the relative stabilities of oxidation states, an example of which is provided by cobalt. $Co^{3+}(aq)$ is much more stable in basic conditions than in acidic conditions. This means that the oxidation of $Co^{2+}(aq)$ to form $Co^{3+}(aq)$ must be carried out in the presence of aqueous sodium hydroxide. The oxidising agent of choice is hydrogen peroxide.

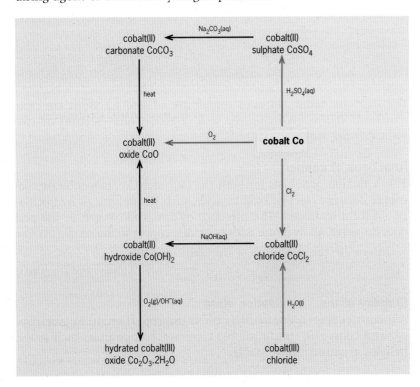

Fig 26.36 **A summary of the reactions of cobalt and its compounds. Reactions involving oxidation are represented by red arrows, and those involving reduction by blue arrows**

The formation of complex ions can also affect the stability of an oxidation state. this is exemplified by the stability of aqueous hexaamminecobalt(III), $[Co(NH_3)_6]^{3+}(aq)$, when compared with the aqueous hexaaquacobalt(III) ion, $[Co(H_2O)_6]^{3+}(aq)$. As Table 26.7 shows, the redox potential for the hexammine complex is only just above zero, therefore it is much more difficult to reduce than $Co^{3+}(aq)$.

NICKEL–CADMIUM RECHARGEABLE BATTERIES

A NICKEL–CADMIUM BATTERY employs the reaction between cadmium and nickel(IV) oxide to produce a current. It can be recharged, so it is a secondary cell. Cadmium forms one electrode, where it is oxidised to cadmium(II) hydroxide. The electrolyte is a concentrated solution of hydroxide ions:

$$Cd + 2OH^-(aq) \rightarrow Cd(OH)_2(s) + 2e^- \quad E^\ominus_{oxid} = +0.81 \text{ V}$$

At the other electrode, nickel(IV) oxide is reduced to nickel(II) hydroxide:

$$NiO_2(s) + 2H_2O(l) + 2e^- \rightarrow Ni(OH)_2(s) + 2OH^-(aq)$$
$$E^\ominus_{red} = +0.49 \text{ V}$$

When the battery is being charged, the reactions are reversed. The overall reaction is:

$$Cd(OH)_2(s) + Ni(OH)_2(s) \rightarrow Cd(s) + NiO_2(s) + 2H_2O(l)$$
$$E^\ominus_{cell} = -1.30 \text{ V}$$

The voltage of a nickel–cadmium battery is about 1.35 V. Because the reactants and the products are solids, their concentrations do not change while the battery is discharging. Therefore the voltage remains almost constant until the battery is fully discharged.

Fig 26.37 **Nickel–cadmium batteries which can be recharged are used in some calculators, and power the pH meter that this electronic circuit comes from**

X (a) Calculate the $E^\ominus_{cell}$ values for the reactions that take place in a nickel–cadmium battery when it delivers a current.

(b) Write down the overall cell reaction that occurs when a nickel–cadmium battery is discharging.

(c) The voltage of a nickel–cadmium battery is about 1.35 V. Suggest why your answer to part **(a)** differs from this value.

Copper

Table 26.8 **Six important reduction potentials involving copper species**

Reduction half equation	$E^\ominus_{red}$/V
$Cu^{2+}(aq) + 2e^- \rightleftharpoons Cu(s)$	+ 0.34
$Cu^+(aq) + e^- \rightleftharpoons Cu(s)$	+ 0.52
$Cu^{2+}(aq) + e^- \rightleftharpoons Cu^+(aq)$	+ 0.15
$[Cu(CN)_2]^-(aq) + e^- \rightleftharpoons Cu(s) + 2CN^-(aq)$	+ 0.43
$[Cu(NH_3)_2]^+(aq) + e^- \rightleftharpoons Cu(s) + 2NH_3(aq)$	–0.12
$[Cu(NH_3)_4]^{2+}(aq) + 2e^- \rightleftharpoons Cu(s) + 4NH_3(aq)$	–0.05

The main oxidation states of copper are +1 and +2. Both are ionic oxidation states, involving the loss of either one electron or two electrons per atom.

Reactions of copper

The reduction potentials for both $Cu^+(aq)$ and $Cu^{2+}(aq)$ indicate that copper does not react with dilute acids, such as sulphuric or hydrochloric, to form hydrogen. The presence of dissolved oxygen in the acid does however, allow dilute acids to oxidise copper to the copper(II) ion:

$$Cu(s) + 2H^+(aq) + \tfrac{1}{2}O_2(g) \rightarrow Cu^{2+}(aq) + H_2O(l)$$
$$E^\ominus_{cell} = E^\ominus_{oxid} + E^\ominus_{red} = -0.34 + (+1.23) = +0.89 \text{ V}$$

Stability of the +1 oxidation state

Aqueous copper(I) compounds often disproportionate to give copper and copper(II), but insoluble copper(I) compounds, such as the halides, are much more stable:

$$Cu_2SO_4(aq) \rightarrow Cu(s) + CuSO_4(aq)$$

Stability of copper(II) compounds

Copper(II) compounds are not really considered to be oxidising agents, but there a few examples of their reduction to copper(I) compounds. Aldehydes reduce complexed copper(II) ions into copper(I) oxide, which forms a red-brown precipitate. This is the basis of Benedict's or Fehlings test for aldehydes and reducing sugars.

Read more about the Benedict's or Fehling's test on page 301.

Iodide ion reduces aqueous copper(II) ions to give a white precipitate of copper(I) iodide, and so copper(II) iodide does not exist:

$$2Cu^{2+}(aq) + 4I^-(aq) \rightarrow 2CuI(s) + I_2(s)$$

Fig 26.38 **A summary of the reactions of copper and its compounds. Reactions involving oxidation are represented by red arrows, and those involving reduction by blue arrows**

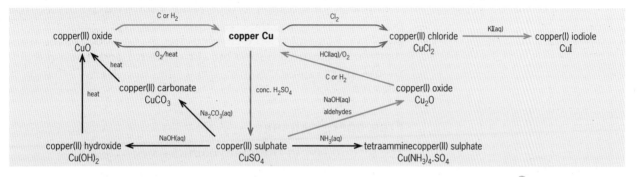

THE ALKALINE AND MERCURY CELLS

THE ALKALINE CELL is much used in calculators, cameras and clocks. One of its electrodes is zinc, the other is manganese(IV) oxide. The electrolyte is potassium hydroxide in a gel, hence the name alkaline cell.

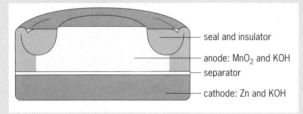

Fig 26.39 **The cross-section of an alkaline cell**

The electrode reactions are:

$$Zn(s) + 2OH^-(aq) \rightarrow Zn(OH)_2(s) + 2e^-$$

and:

$$MnO_2(s) + 2H_2O(l) + 2e^- \rightarrow Mn(OH)_2(s) + 2OH^-(aq)$$

Another battery that contains zinc is the so-called **mercury cell**, which is used mainly in hearing aids. One electrode consists of a zinc–mercury amalgam, the other consists of a paste of carbon and mercury oxide. The electrolyte is a paste of potassium hydroxide. The electrode potentials quoted earlier for the half reactions cannot be used, because they were measured in the presence of mercury rather than under standard conditions. The two half reactions are:

Oxidation: $Zn + 2OH^- \rightarrow ZnO + H_2O + 2e^-$
Reduction: $HgO + H_2O + 2e^- \rightarrow Hg + 2OH^-$

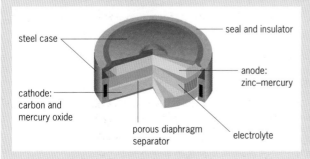

Fig 26.40 **A mercury cell in section**

Y Write an overall equation for the reactions taking place within an alkaline cell when it is delivering a current.

Z Write the overall reaction that occurs within a mercury cell when it delivers a current.

8 EXTRACTION OF METALS

Several different methods of extracting metals have already been covered. On page 11 is a description of the reduction of iron(III) oxide with carbon in the blast furnace, and Chapter 22 contains a description of the electrolytic extraction of the alkali metals and of aluminium. In this section, some of the free energy changes associated with the extraction of metals, such as aluminium and iron, are going to be reviewed.

Although this section is not really connected with electrode potentials, it does use the idea of free energy, $\Delta G^{\ominus}$, introduced on page 555. Remember: free energy is the maximum available work that could be carried out on the surroundings, and that a reaction should occur spontaneously when the free energy change is negative.

Free energy change

The **second law of thermodynamics** states:

Any spontaneous change that occurs in the universe must be accompanied by an increase in the entropy of the universe.

On pages 111 and 133, entropy is described as a measure of the disorder of a system.

Reactions proceed spontaneously if they are energetically downhill (ΔH is negative) and if the process leads to more disorder (ΔS is positive). These two ideas of entropy change and enthalpy change can be combined to give the free energy change of a reaction, ΔG, expressed as:

$$\Delta G = \Delta H - T\Delta S$$

As already stated, reactions in which ΔG is negative are spontaneous. Therefore, provided the enthalpy change, the entropy change and the temperature of a reaction are known, it can be predicted whether the reaction is spontaneous.

Remember: The description of a reaction as 'spontaneous' does not mean that the rate of reaction has to be fast. In fact, the rate of reaction may be so slow that the reaction does not actually take place. In this case, one of the reactants is said to be kinetically stable but energetically unstable.

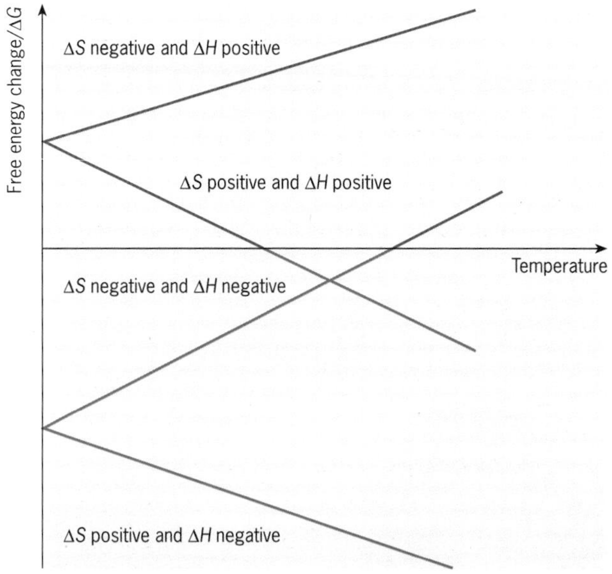

Fig 26.41 **The four graphs show how the free energy change, ΔG, depends on temperature. They refer to every combination of ΔH and ΔS. The blue sections indicate that the reaction should be spontaneous, since ΔG is negative. Note that when ΔS is negative and ΔH is positive, the reaction cannot be spontaneous**

EXAMPLES

Q Predict whether the reaction between hydrogen and chlorine is spontaneous at 298 K:

$$H_2(g) + Cl_2(g) \rightarrow 2HCl(g) \qquad \Delta H^{\ominus} = -185\,kJ\,mol^{-1}$$
$$\Delta S^{\ominus} = 141\,J\,K^{-1}\,mol^{-1}$$

A For these figures, there is no need to do a calculation.

Since $\Delta H^{\ominus}$ is negative and $-T\Delta S^{\ominus}$ is negative (absolute temperature cannot be negative),

then $\Delta G^{\ominus} = \Delta H^{\ominus} - T\Delta S^{\ominus}$ must also be negative. Therefore, the reaction is spontaneous.

Q Predict whether the thermal dissociation of ammonium chloride will proceed spontaneously at 298 K:

$$NH_4Cl(s) \rightarrow NH_3(g) + HCl(g) \qquad \Delta H^{\ominus} = +176\,kJ\,mol^{-1}$$
$$\Delta S^{\ominus} = +284\,J\,K^{-1}\,mol^{-1}$$

A $\Delta G^{\ominus} = \Delta H^{\ominus} - T\Delta S^{\ominus}$
$= +176 - 298\,(+284 \times 10^{-3})$
[Remember: kJ must be used throughout.]
$= +91\,kJ\,mol^{-1}$

Since the free energy change is positive, the reaction cannot be spontaneous at 298 K.

Entropy and spontaneous reactions

The **third law of thermodynamics** states:

At absolute zero the entropy of a pure substance is zero.

As the temperature increases, so does the entropy of the substance. That is, the more the particles move, the greater the entropy becomes. Therefore, gases have a much greater entropy than liquids, and liquids have a much greater entropy than solids. This allows the entropy change of a reaction to be predicted just by looking at the number of moles of gas shown in the equation. No matter what the enthalpy change of a reaction is, if the entropy change is positive, the reaction will be spontaneous for some temperature range.

Free energy change and temperature

Fig 26.41 shows that the free energy change for a reaction, ΔG, alters with the temperature. Assuming that the enthalpy change is a constant, then the change in the value of ΔG is due to the effect of entropy. This means that a reaction involving a positive entropy change will always have a range of temperatures in which the reaction is spontaneous.

A' Predict whether the following reactions are spontaneous at 298 K:

(a) $3O_2(g) \rightarrow 2O_3(g)$
$\Delta H^{\ominus} = +286\,kJ\,mol^{-1}$ and
$\Delta S^{\ominus} = -137\,J\,K^{-1}\,mol^{-1}$

(b) $2SO_2(g) + O_2(g) \rightarrow 2SO_3(g)$
$\Delta H^{\ominus} = -198\,kJ\,mol^{-1}$ and
$\Delta S^{\ominus} = -187\,J\,K^{-1}\,mol^{-1}$

Read more about entropy and spontaneous reactions on page 131.

EXAMPLE

Q Predict the temperature range over which the reaction between nitrogen and oxygen becomes spontaneous:

$$N_2(g) + O_2(g) \rightarrow 2NO(g) \qquad \Delta H = +180\,kJ\,mol^{-1} \qquad \Delta S = +25\,J\,K^{-1}\,mol^{-1}$$

A Assuming that both ΔH and ΔS are constants, the reaction becomes spontaneous when $\Delta G = 0$.

That is: $\qquad 0 = \Delta H - T\Delta S$
$\qquad\qquad 0 = +184 - (T \times 25 \times 10^{-3})$

[Note: energy is measured in kJ throughout.]

Therefore: $\quad T = \dfrac{184}{25 \times 10^{-3}} = 7360\,K$

The temperature range is therefore any temperature above 7360 K.

In the Example, in reality, both the enthalpy change and the entropy change are not constants. So the actual temperature calculated in not reliable. However, the calculation does demonstrate that this reaction only becomes spontaneous at high temperatures.

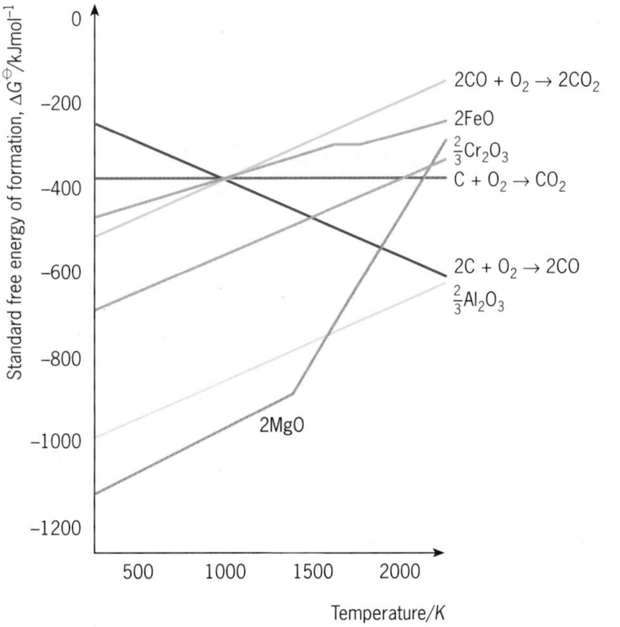

Fig 26.42 **An Ellingham diagram for the formation of some oxides**

See question 9. ■

?

B' **(a)** Which metals in the Ellingham diagram in Fig 26.42 could be obtained by reduction by carbon at 1500 °C?

(b) The free energy changes at various temperatures for the following reaction are shown in the first table:

$$Ti(s) + O_2(g) \rightarrow TiO_2(s)$$

Temperature/K	Free energy change, ΔG/kJ mol^{-1}
300	−856
600	−801
1200	−690
2000	−542

The free energy changes at various temperatures for the following reaction are shown in the second table:

$$2C(s) + O_2(g) \rightarrow 2CO(g)$$

Temperature/K	Free energy change, ΔG/kJ mol^{-1}
300	−276
600	−330
1200	−440
2000	−582

(i) Plot both sets of data on graph paper.
(ii) Use your results to predict the likelihood of obtaining titanium by the reduction of titanium(IV) oxide with carbon.

Ellingham diagrams

Since the free energy change is a function of temperature, one way of describing the change is to draw an Ellingham diagram. An Ellingham diagram shows how the free energy change for the oxidation of an element depends on temperature. Note that in each case the free energy change refers to the equation with 1 mole of oxygen. Consider, for example, the oxidation of carbon to carbon monoxide:

$$2C(s) + O_2(g) \rightarrow 2CO(g)$$

The entropy change for this reaction is positive, since the 2 moles of gas are made from 1 mole of gaseous reactant. It follows that, as the temperature increases, the free energy change for this reaction has increasing negative values, as shown in Fig 26.42.

The oxidation of carbon to carbon dioxide is much more difficult to assess, since there is 1 mole of gaseous reactant and 1 mole of gaseous product:

$$C(s) + O_2(g) \rightarrow CO_2(g)$$

The entropy change for this reaction has a very small negative value. Therefore, the free energy change for the oxidation of carbon dioxide remains fairly constant.

In the case of the oxidation of metals by gaseous oxygen to form metal oxides, it is much easier to assess the entropy change because there are no gaseous products. So, the entropy change must be negative. It follows from this that the free energy change for such reactions assumes lower and lower negative values as the temperature increases.

Free energy changes during the extraction of metals

The extraction of a metal by reduction of its oxide with carbon can be considered to be the sum of two reactions. The first reaction is the oxidation of carbon, and the second is the decomposition of the oxide to give the metal and oxygen.

For example, the reduction of iron(II) oxide to give iron has an overall reaction of:

$$2FeO + 2C \rightarrow 2Fe + 2CO$$

This can be written as the combination of two reactions:

$2C + O_2 \rightarrow 2CO$	ΔG is negative
$2FeO \rightarrow 2Fe + O_2$	ΔG is positive because it is the opposite of that shown in the Ellingham diagram.

Note that the overall equation is written so that it involves 1 mole of oxygen in each of the reactions.

A reaction is spontaneous when the free energy change is negative. The minimum temperature at which this happens is given by the point of intersection of the two appropriate lines on the Ellingham diagram. Beyond that temperature, the magnitude of the negative free energy of oxidation of carbon is greater than the magnitude of the positive free energy change of decomposition.

SUMMARY

After studying this chapter, you should know that:

■ A redox reaction involves the transfer of electrons from a reducing agent to an oxidising agent.

■ All redox reactions can be written as a sum of two half equations, one for oxidation and the other for reduction.

■ An electrochemical cell, is a way of carrying out a redox reaction such that the two half reactions take place separately and the electrons are transferred via an external circuit.

■ In an electrochemical cell, oxidation always takes place at the anode and reduction always takes place at the cathode.

■ An electrode potential is the potential difference between an electrode and the ion-containing solution into which the electrode dips. All electrode potentials are compared to the standard hydrogen electrode, which has been assigned a standard electrode potential of 0.00 V

■ The standard hydrogen electrode involves the reversible half reaction of aqueous hydrogen ions and electrons to form hydrogen gas.

■ The chemistry of transition elements can be explained by using electrode potentials.

■ The cell potential of an electrochemical cell is the sum of the oxidation potential and the reduction potential. A process whose cell potential is positive takes place spontaneously.

■ A primary cell is a battery that cannot be recharged. A secondary cell can be recharged.

■ The higher oxidation states of the transition elements are oxidising agents, and the lower oxidation states are reducing agents.

■ Electrode potentials and cell potentials are affected by changes in concentration of the aqueous species, temperature, pressure of gases, pH and the complexing of ions.

■ Free energy change is a measure of the maximum available work that can be done on the surroundings. When a process has a negative free energy change, it should take place spontaneously.

■ The standard free energy change, $\Delta G^{\ominus}$, is related to the standard cell potential, $E^{\ominus}_{cell}$, by the equation $\Delta G^{\ominus} = nFE^{\ominus}_{cell}$.

■ The free energy change, ΔG, is related to the enthalpy change, ΔH, entropy change, ΔS and the absolute temperature, T, by the following equation $\Delta G = \Delta H - T\Delta S$.

QUESTIONS

1 An arrangement to measure the potential difference of an electrochemical cell is shown, incompletely, in Fig 26.Q1.

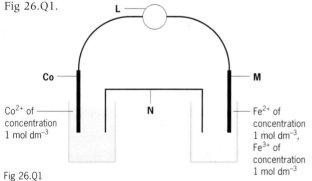

Fig 26.Q1

a) (i) What is **N**, and what is its function?
(ii) What is **L**?
(iii) What could the electrode **M** be made of?

b) In this cell, the right hand electrode has a more positive potential than the left hand electrode. Give an ionic equation for the reaction which would occur if the two electrodes were connected by a wire.

c) This apparatus is to be used to measure the standard electrode potential of the Co(s)/Co²⁺(aq) system. What further piece of information would need to be known, when the potential difference (p.d.) of this cell has been measured?

d) Would the p.d. of the cell become larger, smaller or remain unchanged if the left hand half cell were replaced by a Cd/Cd²⁺ half cell, given that Cd is a more reactive metal than Co? Explain your reasoning.

e) Calculate the free energy change ΔG for the reaction given in (b), if the p.d. of the cell is 1.05 V ($\Delta G^{\ominus} = zFE^{\ominus}$, F = 96 500 C mol⁻¹).

[AEB 1996 Specimen Paper CH3, q.1]

2
a) (i) What is meant by the term *standard electrode potential*?
(ii) Draw a detailed labelled diagram of the apparatus used to measure the standard electrode potential of zinc metal. Explain how the value of the standard electrode potential is determined

b) Excess dilute sulphuric acid is added to a freshly prepared solution containing equimolar amounts of Fe²⁺(aq), Fe³⁺(aq), Cr³⁺(aq) and Cr₂O₇²⁻aq). By reference to the following data, deduce what happens and explain the role of each reactant. Write a balanced ionic equation for the reaction.

$$Fe^{3+}(aq) + e^- \rightarrow Fe^{2+}(aq) \qquad E^{\ominus} = +0.77\,V$$

$$Cr_2O_7^{2-}(aq) + 14H^+(aq) + 6e^- \rightarrow 2Cr^{3+}(aq) + 7H_2O(l)$$
$$E^{\ominus} = +1.33\,V$$

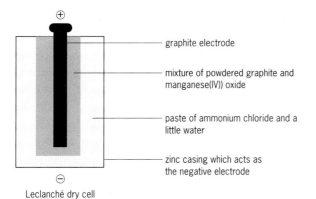

Leclanché dry cell

Fig 26.Q2

c) Fig 26.Q2 shows a cross-section of a common type of torch battery (a Leclanché dry cell). The half cell reaction for the negative electrode is shown in equation (1) and one possibility for the other half cell reaction is shown in equation (2).

(1) $[Zn(NH_3)_4]^{2+}(aq) + 2e \rightarrow Zn(s) + 4NH_3(aq)$
$E^{\ominus} = -1.03\,V$

(2) $NH_4^{+}(aq) + MnO_2(s) + H_2O(l) + e$
$\rightarrow Mn(OH)_3(s) + NH_3(aq)$
$E^{\ominus} = +1.00\,V$

   (i) Calculate what the e.m.f. of this cell would be under standard conditions.

  (ii) Suggest a reason why such cells tend to leak when nearing exhaustion.

 (iii) The actual e.m.f. of this cell is + 1.50 V. Suggest why this value is different from the one calculated in (c)(i).

 (iv) Calculate the value of the free energy change, ΔG, for the actual cell.

(Faraday constant = $9.65 \times 10^4\,C\,mol^{-1}$)

[AEB June 1994 0654/1, q.3]

3 Some standard electrode potentials are given below.

$I_2(aq) + 2e^- \rightleftharpoons 2I^-(aq)$ $E^{\ominus} = +0.54\,V$
$Br^2(aq) + 2e^- \rightleftharpoons 2Br^-(aq)$ $E^{\ominus} = +1.07\,V$
$Cl_2(aq) + 2e^- \rightleftharpoons 2Cl^-(aq)$ $E^{\ominus} = +1.36\,V$
$Fe^{3+}(aq) + e^- \rightleftharpoons Fe^{2+}(aq)$ $E^{\ominus} = +0.77\,V$

a) Explain what is meant by *standard conditions* for electrode potential measurements.

b) Suggest a value of $E^{\ominus}$ for fluorine $(F_2(aq) + 2e^- \rightarrow 2F^-(aq))$.

c) Which species listed above is the strongest reducing agent?

d) Write down the ionic equation for the reaction between bromine and iron(II) sulphate.

e) Explain, using the $E^{\ominus}$ values, why you would not expect iodine to react with iron(II) sulphate solution.

f) Calculate the e.m.f. of the following cell under standard conditions.

   $Pt(s) \mid Fe^{2+}(aq), Fe^{3+}(aq) \vdots Cl_2(g), Cl^-(aq) \mid Pt(s)$

[Oxford June 1995 9955/53, q.3]

4

a) A nickel-cadmium cell contains electrodes made from thin strips of perforated nickel separated by a very thin sheet of porous polymeric material. The electrolyte is concentrated aqueous potassium hydroxide. The simplified overall cell reaction is shown below.

   $Cd + 2Ni(OH)_3 \rightleftharpoons Cd(OH)_2 + 2Ni(OH)_2$

   (i) Write equations for the electrode half reactions and state which half reaction occurs at the positive electrode.

  (ii) Why is the cell designed to have electrodes with a large surface area?

 (iii) Why is the cell designed so that the separation between the positive and the negative electrodes is small?

 (iv) Why does the cell contain a thin sheet of polymeric material?

  (v) State a major advantage of a nickel-cadmium cell over a Leclanché cell.

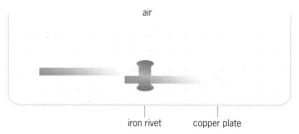

Fig 26.Q4

b) Fig 26.Q4 shows an experiment set up to investigate the corrosion of an iron rivet which has been used to hold together two small copper plates.

   (i) Write an equation for the anodic site half reaction occurring at the iron rivet.

  (ii) Write an equation for the cathodic site half reaction.

 (iii) Indicate, on the diagram, the most likely place for the cathodic site reaction.

 (iv) State why the rate of corrosion of the rivet is influenced by the surface area of the copper plates

  (v) Explain why the rate of corrosion of the rivet is influenced by the surface area of the copper plates.

 (vi) State the effect of increasing the pH of the water on the rate of corrosion of the rivet and explain your answer.

[NEAB June 1994 6070/3, q.2]

5 The generation and storage of electric power in electric cells, including batteries, fuel cells and biological cells, is a feature of everyday life. The transport of electrons from one substance to another in the course of a chemical reaction can be harnessed to do work.

Fig 26.Q5 illustrates a simple electrochemical cell.

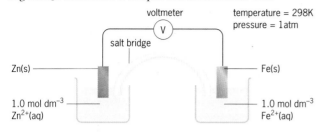

Fig 26.Q5

a) **(i)** Explain the function of the salt bridge.
  (ii) State the materials from which the salt bridge could be made in the laboratory.
  (iii) Suggest a reason why the salt bridge could not be made from a metallic strip.

b) **(i)** Use the data below to calculate the standard electrode potential for the electrochemical cell illustrated in Fig 26.Q5. Show your working

Standard electrode potential	$E^{\ominus}$/V (at 298 K)
$Zn^{2+}(aq) + 2e^- \rightleftharpoons Zn(s)$	-0.76
$Fe^{2+}(aq) + 2e^- \rightleftharpoons Fe(s)$	-0.44

  (ii) Identify which half of the cell undergoes reduction. Justify your answer.

c) Galvanised steel consists essentially of iron plated with zinc.
Suggest a reason why galvanised steel does not rust even if the zinc plating is scratched and the iron is left exposed to both water and to oxygen.
[UCLES Spring 1996, 4826 S95, q.2]

6 A simplified diagram of the lead accumulator car battery is shown in Fig 26.Q6

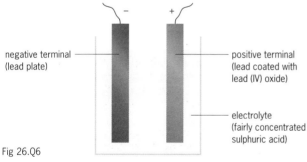

Fig 26.Q6

a) The reaction at the positive terminal when the battery is supplying current can be represented by the following unbalanced ionic half equation.

$$PbO_2 + H^+ + e^- \rightarrow Pb^{2+} + H_2O$$

Copy and balance the equation.

b) Pb^{2+} ions are also formed at the negative terminal when the battery is supplying current. Construct the ionic half equation for this reaction.

c) Why does a white precipitate form when the battery is working?

d) The lead accumulator can be recharged. What can you deduce about the reaction in **(a)** and **(b)**?

e) Suggest why some hydrogen gas is produced by the recharging process.
[Oxford June 1993, 8755/2, q.B5]

7 Acidified potassium dichromate(VI) and acidified potassium manganate(VII) can be used in redox titrations.
a) A 0.0200 mol dm^{-3} potassium dichromate(VI) solution was added using a burette to 25.0 cm^3 of an impure sample of acidified iron(III) sulphate. The titre was 23.6 cm^3.
  (i) Use half equations to write down the equation for the reaction between dichromate(VI) ions and acidified iron(II) ions.
  (ii) Calculate the concentration of iron(II) sulphate used in the titration.
  (iii) Give the colour changes to each of the ions containing transition elements during this redox reaction.

b) Construct the equation for the reaction between acidified manganate(VII) ions and aqueous iodide ions.

c) Describe and explain the colour changes that occur when aqueous sodium hydroxide is added to an aqueous solution of potassium dichromate(VI).
[AEB June 1994 0654/1, q.3]

8 The stability of an oxidation state can be affected by:

a) changes in the ligand in a complex,

b) changes in pH.
Illustrate this statement taking examples from the chemistry of cobalt and iron.
[Oxford June 1993 8755/2, q.B2]

9
a) Explain why the plots of change of free energy, ΔG, with temperature T, (Fig 26.Q9) for the reactions
$2C(s) + O_2(g) \rightarrow 2CO(g)$ $\Delta G = (-224 - 0.18T)$ kJ mol^{-1}
$C(s) + O_2(g) \rightarrow CO_2(g)$ $\Delta G = (-394 - 0.00008T)$ kJ mol^{-1}
have such different gradients.

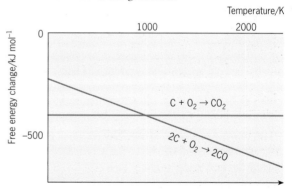

Fig 26.Q9

b) For the reaction
$\frac{4}{3}Al(s) + O_2(g) \rightarrow \frac{2}{3}Al_2O_3(s)$ $\Delta G = (-1115 - 0.21T)$ kJ mol^{-1}
predict, graphically, using the grid in **(a)** above, the minimum temperature required for the reduction of alumina with graphite.

c) Calculate the free energy change, ΔG, for the overall reaction that occurs at 1300 K for the extraction of aluminium in the Hall–Héroult cell.

$$\tfrac{1}{2}Al_2O_3 + \tfrac{3}{4}C \rightarrow Al + \tfrac{3}{4}CO_2$$

[NEAB 1996 Chemistry Specimen questions, CH7 q.]

Assignment

MOLYBDENUM AND ITS COMPOUNDS

Molybdenum is a member of the second series of transition elements. It is in the same group of the Periodic Table as chromium, and has the electron configuration of $[Kr]4d^5 5s^1$.

1

a) Suggest why molybdenum has the electron configuration $[Kr]4d^5 5s^1$ rather than $[Kr]4d^4 4s^2$.
Hint: Read page 519.

b) What oxidation states would you expect to be shown by molybdenum in its compounds?

c) For each oxidation state, write down whether it is reducing, oxidising or both.

Molybdenum can be manufactured from molybdenum(VI) oxide. This oxide is obtained by roasting the sulphide ore, MoS_2, in air to give molybdenum(VI) oxide.

2
Construct an equation to show the reaction of the sulphide ore with oxygen from the air.

Pure molybdenum is obtained by reducing molybdenum(VI) oxide with hydrogen at high temperature. Reduction using carbon cannot be used, since the molybdenum formed in the reduction then reacts with excess carbon to form an unwanted carbide of molybdenum.

3
Construct an equation to show the reduction of molybdenum(VI) oxide with hydrogen.

A major use of molybdenum is as an alloy, ferromolybdenum, with iron. Extremely hard and strong even at high temperatures, this alloy is used in filament supports, in heating elements for furnaces, and for drill bits. Ferromolybdenum can be made from molybdenum(VI) oxide without having to make pure molybdenum. A mixture of iron(III) oxide and molybdenum(VI) oxide is reduced using aluminium powder to give a ferromolybdenum that is at least 60 per cent molybdenum by mass. The process is carried out in batches, and at the height of the reduction the temperature inside the reaction vessel reaches 2000 °C.

4

a) Suggest why it is cheaper to make ferromolybdenum directly from molybdenum(VI) oxide and iron(III) oxide rather than making it from pure iron and pure molybdenum.

b) Write balanced equations to show the reduction of
(i) iron(III) oxide with aluminium, and
(ii) molybdenum(VI) oxide with aluminium.

c) Why is such a high temperature needed for the manufacture of ferromolybdenum? Use ideas about free energy.

Most of the ferromolybdenum made in the United Kingdom comes from a factory in Stowmarket, Suffolk, which is near to the major seaport at Felixstowe. This plant imports all of its molybdenum(VI) oxide from the United States. Almost half of the ferromolybdenum made in Stowmarket is exported back to the United States.

5
It is usual to site a chemical factory as near as possible to the sources of its raw materials and to its major customers. Suggest possible reasons why a major ferromolybdenum factory is sited in the United Kingdom rather than the United States.

Molybdenum is a relatively unreactive metal, but it does react with halogens to form halides, with oxygen to form oxides, and with sulphur to form molybdenum(IV) sulphide. Molybdenum(IV) sulphide is used as a solid lubricant and as an additive in greases and oils. It has a layered structure with very weak forces between the layers, so its properties resemble those of graphite.

6
Write an equation to show the formation of molybdenum(IV) sulphide and hence calculate the maximum mass of molybdenum(IV) sulphide that can be made from 1.00 kg of molybdenum.

Table 26.A1 shows six reduction potentials for molybdenum-containing species.

Table 26.9 **Six standard electrode potentials for molybdenum containing species**

Half reaction	Reduction potential ($E^{\ominus}_{red}$)/V
$Mo^{3+} + 3e^- \rightleftharpoons Mo$	−0.20
$MoO_2^+ + 4H^+ + 2e^- \rightleftharpoons Mo^{3+}$	0.00
$MoO_4^{2-} + 4H^+ + 2e^- \rightleftharpoons MoO_2 + 2H_2O$	−1.40
$MoO_3 + 6H^+ + 6e^- \rightleftharpoons Mo + 3H_2O$	+0.10
$MoO_4^{2-} + 4H_2O + 6e^- \rightleftharpoons Mo + 8OH^-$	−0.97
$H_2MoO_4 + 2H^+ + e^- \rightleftharpoons MoO_2^+ + 2H_2O$	+0.40

7
Consider the following reaction:
$$Mo(s) + 3H^+(aq) \rightarrow Mo^{3+}(aq) + \tfrac{3}{2}H_2$$

a) Calculate the cell potential for this process and hence deduce whether the reaction is feasible.

b) Calculate the free energy change for this reaction.

8
Suggest a reducing agent that could reduce aqueous molybdate(VI) ion, $MoO_4^{2-}(aq)$, **(a)** to molybdenum(IV) oxide, and **(b)** to molybdenum. Explain your answers.

9

a) An aqueous solution of molybdenum(III) sulphate is electrolysed using inert electrodes.
Predict, with reasons, the products of this electrolysis.

b) $H_2MoO_4(aq)$ is reacted with excess zinc and dilute sulphuric acid.
Predict the products of this reaction. Explain your answer.

ELECTRODE POTENTIALS AND TRANSITION ELEMENTS

This chapter covers the chemistry of the main transition elements. Through their compounds, electrolysis and standard electrode potentials are discussed, introducing energy changes. When you have studied the chapter, review the Chapter Map to check that you have understood the important concepts in it.

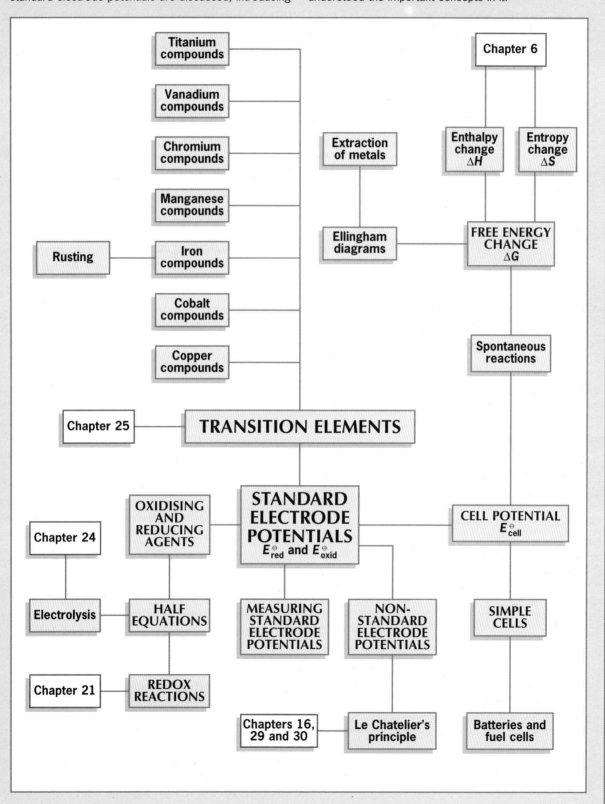

27 Reaction kinetics

The long-term effect of hydrogen ions on paper

UNLIKE INDUSTRIAL CHEMISTS, who mostly want to speed up chemical reactions, curators of the world's great libraries are desperate to stop reactions. If they fail, they will be the keepers of a growing collection of crumbling paper. Millions of books, documents, drawings and photographs are already falling to pieces. Many rare and valuable publications are close to total disintegration as their paper gets brittle and starts crumbling. This applies not just to publications of many centuries ago, but those as recent as the mid-1800s. What is the cause, and is it preventable?

Untreated paper is too porous to print on. Ink would seep into the pores to produce fuzzy print. So it has to be sized, a process that fills in the pores with a compound which leaves the paper with a smooth surface. Since 1850, the majority of book paper has been sized with aluminium sulphate – and this is the culprit.

Aluminium ions in the paper react with moisture to produce hydrogen ions. These hydrogen ions break down the cellulose molecules that the paper is composed of, and so it becomes brittle and eventually crumbles.

Neutralising the acidity due to hydrogen ions will halt this slow decomposition, and there are ways of doing this without damaging the books. But the cost can be prohibitive – sometimes over £1000 per book.

Paper manufacturers are helping to prevent this problem in future by producing more acid-free paper treated with sizing agents that do not produce hydrogen ions. Papers treated with them should have a life expectancy of well over 200 years – nearly ten times that of the crumbling paper.

The rate of the reaction destroying these millions of publications is certainly slow, but already too many important and irreplaceable books have been damaged. Understanding reaction kinetics will have helped to save some of the world's most treasured volumes, but for others it is too late.

1 WHY BOTHER WITH REACTION KINETICS?

Reaction kinetics is the study of **rates of reaction**. The rate at which a reaction is going to occur and how it can be slowed down, or speeded up, are crucial information. For example, unwanted chemical reactions leading to food deterioration are slowed down by putting food in a refrigerator or freezer; desired chemical reactions in the cooking of food are speeded up by the energy from an oven.

Billions of chemical reactions are happening all round us all the time – from those occurring inside our bodies to those involved in rusting and rotting, and in the life processes of plants and animals. The factors which affect their reaction rates are all part of the study of reaction kinetics.

Fig 27.1 **The gas explosion that caused this fire took only a fraction of a second**

Fig 27.2 **Divers find that wrecks do not alter much over decades. The rusting of the *Titanic*, which sank in the North Atlantic in 1912, is such a slow reaction that it has been possible to salvage many iron artefacts from the ship more than 90 years later**

We describe a reaction as **spontaneous** if it tends to occur. You met this concept first on page 131. A very important spontaneous reaction is that between petrol and air in a car engine (see page 161). Petrol and air do not react in a petrol tank at 25 °C because the reaction rate is so slow that it cannot be measured. But petrol explodes in air when the energy from a spark is added, as in the internal combustion engine. Being spontaneous does not mean that a reaction is necessarily fast.

The reaction between nitrogen and hydrogen is another which is spontaneous, yet nothing seems to happen at room temperature. But under the conditions of the Haber process, ammonia is produced – one of the world's most important industrial chemical reactions. Industrial chemists need to know just how fast they can make a reaction go. A reaction which is too slow is unlikely to be a commercial proposition.

With a knowledge of the kinetics of a reaction, you can also understand how the reaction takes place and which species are involved in each step. The series of steps involved in a reaction is called the **reaction mechanism**. When the reaction mechanism is known, then ways to alter the rate of reaction by changing the conditions can be determined. This information is, of course, essential to industrial chemists looking for cheaper ways to bring about higher yields. But information about the reaction mechanism of a drug in the body can tell doctors how long the drug will remain effective before another dose is required. This often helps pharmaceutical companies to produce drugs with fewer side effects from unwanted reactions.

✔

Remember: For a reaction to occur spontaneously, there must be an overall increase in entropy. This is the Second Law of Thermodynamics. This information can be used to predict whether a reaction is spontaneous. But it cannot predict how fast a reaction will be.

The Haber process is covered on page 632.

Rates of reaction and their measurement

This is a definition for the rate of a reaction:

> **The rate of a reaction is either the change in the concentration of product formed per unit of time, or the change in the concentration of reactant used per unit of time.**

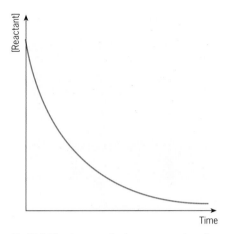

Fig 27.3 **The decrease in the concentration of a reactant, [reactant], during the course of a typical chemical reaction**

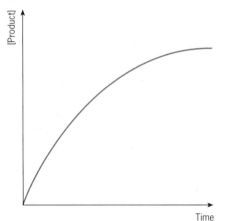

Fig 27.4 **The increase in the concentration of a product, [product], during the course of a typical chemical reaction**

?

A What do Figs 27.3 and 27.4 tell you about how the rate of reaction changes during the course of a reaction?

?

B What is the initial rate of the reaction shown in Fig 27.5?
Hint: The tangent at time zero has been drawn for you.

See question 1. ■

The reaction rate for a reactant which is used up is negative.

Fig 27.3 shows how the concentration of a reactant changes during the course of a typical chemical reaction. Note that concentration is denoted by the use of square brackets. So, the concentration of a reactant is shown as [reactant]. The similar graph Fig 27.4 shows the increase in concentration of a product of a chemical reaction. However, in any given reaction, the decrease in the concentration of the reactant is not necessarily the same as the increase in concentration of the product. For example, if 2 moles of reactant produces 1 mole of product, then the initial concentration of the reactant in Fig 27.3 would be twice that of the final concentration of the product in Fig 27.4.

Finding the rate of reaction at a particular time

Look again at Fig 27.4. If the rate of reaction were constant, the graph would be a straight line. Clearly, it is changing with time and will eventually fall to zero when the reaction is finished. The graph shows the change of concentration during the course of the reaction and is therefore known as a **rate curve.** The rate of reaction at any instant in time is given by the gradient of the curve at that instant.

The gradient at any point on a curve is found by drawing the tangent to the curve at that point and taking its gradient. Fig 27.5 includes two tangents. The tangent at time zero is called the **initial rate**, which occurs when the reactants are first mixed. The gradient of this tangent is the steepest of any taken along the rate curve, which means that the reaction is fastest at the start. The reaction rate at 50 seconds is calculated as follows:

$$\text{rate at 50 s} = \text{gradient of tangent at 50 s} = \frac{3.0\,\text{mol}}{40\,\text{s}} = 0.75\,\text{mol s}^{-1}$$

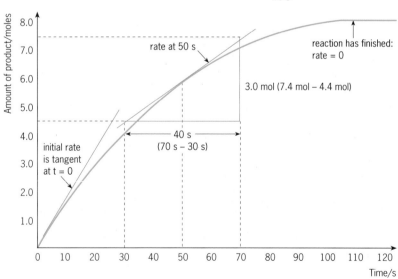

Fig 27.5 **The rate curve for a reaction. The method for calculating the rate at 50 s is shown**

Measuring reaction rates

When the rate of a reaction is being studied, it is crucial to know what the reactants are, what the products are and what state these substances are in. This is conveniently found in the **stoichiometric equation**. This is the balanced chemical equation which states the amount of each reactant which reacts and the amount of each product formed (see page 7). For example, the stoichiometric equation for the formation of nitrogen dioxide, an atmospheric pollutant, from nitrogen monoxide and oxygen in a car exhaust is:

$$2NO(g) + O_2(g) \rightarrow 2NO_2(g)$$

Although this does not detail the steps by which the reaction occurs, it clearly states that only one product is formed and that only two reactant are involved. It also states that three volumes of reactants produce two volumes of product.

Provided we know the stoichiometric equation, we can decide on how to measure the concentration changes occurring as the reaction proceeds. In the above case, there is a reduction in volume which we could use to measure changes in the rate of reaction with time. If the reaction is carried out at a constant volume in a pressure vessel, then change in pressure could be measured.

Anything that changes during a reaction, which can be measured, may be used to determine a reaction rate, provided that it is proportional in some way to the concentration of a particular reactant or product.

Fig 27.6 **The reaction between nitrogen monoxide and oxygen could be followed by measuring the variation of pressure with time**

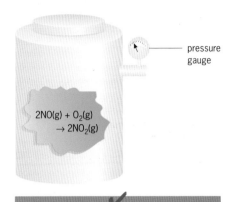

pressure gauge

$2NO(g) + O_2(g)$
$\rightarrow 2NO_2(g)$

C What is the name given to the steps by which a chemical reaction takes place?
If you want to check your answer, see page 581.

Remember: The rate of a reaction may be defined as the change in concentration of product or the change in concentration of reactant used per unit of time.

Measuring change in volume of gas produced

The reaction between dilute hydrochloric acid and magnesium ribbon produces hydrogen according to this stoichiometric equation:

$$Mg(s) + 2HCl(aq) \rightarrow MgCl_2(aq) + H_2(g)$$

The volume of hydrogen produced could be used to follow (monitor) changes in the rate of this reaction. Apparatus for doing this is shown in Fig 27.7.

Changes in colour

A colorimeter can be used to measure the change in colour of a reaction. This instrument (see page 620) measures the amount of electromagnetic radiation absorbed by substances in the visible part of the spectrum. In the reaction between zinc and aqueous copper(II) sulphate, for example, the blue coloration of the copper(II) sulphate disappears as the colourless zinc sulphate solution is formed:

$$Zn(s) + CuSO_4(aq) \rightarrow ZnSO_4(aq) + Cu(s)$$

blue solution   colourless solution

Fig 27.8 **When one of the reactants or products is coloured, the reaction can be followed by measuring the change in absorbance with a colorimeter**

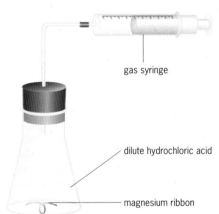

gas syringe

dilute hydrochloric acid

magnesium ribbon

Fig 27.7 **The change in volume of this reaction due to the evolution of hydrogen gas can be used to measure the reaction rate**

D As hydrogen is being lost in the Mg/HCl(aq) reaction, what other properties are changing during the course of the reaction and how can they be measured?

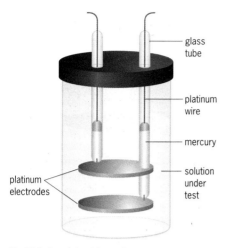

Fig 27.9 **A conductivity cell**

Esters are covered on page **342**.

?

E A 10.0 cm³ sample of the reaction solution of methyl methanoate and aqueous sodium hydroxide was withdrawn after 2.00 minutes and titrated with 1.0×10^{-3} mol dm⁻³ dilute hydrochloric acid. 15.0 cm³ of HCl(aq) was required to neutralise the OH⁻ ions remaining.

(a) How many moles of H⁺(aq) ions would be present in 15 cm³ HCl(aq)?

(b) Write down the ionic equation for the neutralisation of H⁺(aq) ions by OH⁻(aq).

(c) How many moles of OH⁻(aq) ions were present in the 10.0 cm³ sample?

(d) What was the concentration of OH⁻(aq) ions after 2.00 minutes?

Hint: If you are not sure how to do these calculations, look at page 111.

F Suggest a method by which you could follow the rates of the following reactions:

(a) $SO_2Cl_2(g) \rightarrow SO_2(g) + Cl_2(g)$

(b) $2H_2O_2(aq) \rightarrow 2H_2O(l) + O_2(g)$

(c) $BrO_3^-(aq) + 5Br^-(aq) + 6H^+(aq) \rightarrow 3Br_2(aq) + 3H_2O(l)$

(d) $CH_3Br + OH^- \rightarrow CH_3OH + Br^-$

(e) $CH_3COCH_3 + I_2(aq) \rightarrow CH_3COCH_2I(aq) + H^+(aq) + I^-(aq)$

Use a different method for each reaction, if you can.

Changes in electrical conductivity

Many reactions involve a change of conductivity because the number of ions in the reaction mixture changes during the reaction. In the following reaction, the number of ions decreases as the products are formed and the conductivity of the reaction can be followed using a conductivity cell (Fig 27.9):

$$BrO_3^-(aq) + 6I^-(aq) + 6H^+(aq) \rightarrow 3I_2(s) + 3H_2O(l) + Br^-(aq)$$

Chemical analysis

All the techniques so far described have followed a reaction continuously and have not interfered with the progress of the reaction. Chemical analysis, however, involves taking samples of the reaction mixture at regular intervals of time. The reaction in the sample is stopped as soon as it is withdrawn. This can be accomplished by rapid cooling, by removing one of the reactants or the catalyst, or by diluting the reaction mixture. The process of stopping a reaction (or slowing it down to a rate of almost zero) is called **quenching**.

Methyl methanoate, $CH_3CO_2CH_3$, an ester, is an important industrial solvent. It can be hydrolysed using aqueous sodium hydroxide:

$$CH_3CO_2CH_3(l) + NaOH(aq) \rightarrow CH_3CO_2^-Na^+(aq) + CH_3OH(aq)$$

The rate of reaction can be followed by monitoring the concentration of sodium hydroxide as it is used up during the course of the reaction. Several identical reaction solutions are set to react. The temperature is kept constant, since changes in temperature affect the reaction rate. They are quenched by dilution with ice-cold water, at different time intervals from the start of the reaction. The concentration of sodium hydroxide remaining in each reaction solution is determined by titrating it with an acid, such as dilute hydrochloric acid.

SONOCHEMISTRY

IN THE 1920s it was first discovered that ultrasound – sound with a frequency above 18 kHz – produces chemical effects. The study of sonochemistry, as it is called, did not really take off until the 1980s when reliable and inexpensive ultrasound generators became readily available. Now, there is a host of interesting and important applications of ultrasound in chemistry.

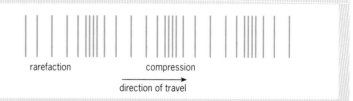

rarefaction   compression

direction of travel

Fig 27.10 **The propagation of a sound wave through a liquid. As the wave travels through the liquid, it creates alternate regions of high pressure (compression) and low pressure (rarefaction). These travelling pressure changes are exceptionally rapid when the liquid is excited by ultrasound.**

When a liquid is excited by ultrasound, the rapid changes in pressure (see Fig 27.10) produce an effect known as cavitation. As the rarefactions travel through the liquid, they pull its molecules apart to produce tiny cavities or bubbles. The compressions cause the bubbles to collapse, releasing tremendous amounts of energy. It has been estimated that the temperature near the collapse may be about 7000 K, which is the temperature at the surface of the Sun. Even higher temperatures –

up to $2 \times 10^6 \, K$ – may be generated as cavitation bubbles implode. The pressure created could make a gas as dense as a metal. However, the rate of cooling is astonishing at $10^{10} \, K$ per second, so overall the liquid does not become hot.

These localised energy hot spots are used to increase the rates of chemical reactions. They also produce highly reactive radicals. For example, the water molecule can be torn apart to produce H• and OH• radicals. Radicals have unpaired electrons, making them highly reactive. So these radicals can combine to produce hydrogen gas and hydrogen peroxide. The OH• radical is also a potent oxidising agent, which can react with other chemicals placed in the water. (For more about radicals – often called free radicals – see page 206.)

Early on, sonochemistry led to the production of catalysts which have particles so minute that they are called nanostructured catalysts. (A nanometre is 10^{-9} metres.) The surface area of these catalyst particles is huge. Nowadays, special combinations of metals in catalysts produced with the aid of ultrasound are making chemical processes more efficient, and it is likely that alternatives to platinum-based catalysts will be found.

Tailoring polymer molecules with ultrasound to enhance particular properties is another exciting prospect. The polymer chains are dissolved in a solvent where they are subjected to the awesome energy of cavitation bubbles. The chains break into smaller structures which, under the action of the bubbles, recombine to form different monomers in blocks along the chains.

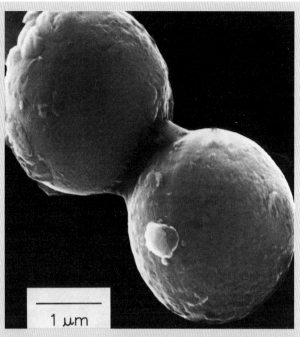

Fig 27.11 **Cavitation bubbles produced by ultrasonic waves**

There is so much unexplored potential in sonochemistry. Another possibility is that some organochlorine pollutants in water supplies could be broken down by ultrasound into harmless products. In a contrasting application, tiny haemoglobin spheres have been synthesised which may make it possible to produce artificial blood.

2 RATE EQUATIONS

Figs 27.3 and 27.4 show that the rate of reaction is fastest at the beginning of a reaction. This is because the concentrations of the reactants are at their highest value. As the concentrations of the reactants fall so does the rate of reaction. The **rate equation** states the relationship between the rate of reaction and the concentration of each reactant. It is also known as the **rate law**. As shown later, the rate equation helps chemists to work out how a reaction takes place. The dependence of the rate of reaction on the concentration of a reactant can be expressed mathematically in the form:

$$\text{rate} \propto [\text{reactant}]^n$$

which gives the rate equation as:

$$\text{rate} = k \times [\text{reactant}]^n \qquad \text{or} \qquad \text{rate} = k[\text{reactant}]^n$$

where:

k is a constant called the **rate constant:** the larger the rate constant, the faster the reaction,

n is called the **order of the reaction** with respect to the given reactant:

The order of the reaction is the power to which the concentration of the reactant is raised in the experimentally determined rate equation.

The definition of order of reaction states that the rate equation must be determined by experiment. It has nothing to do with the

?

G For a reaction $A + B \rightarrow C + D$ the rate equation is:

$$\text{rate} = k[A]^m[B]^n$$

What are the orders of reaction with respect to the reactants A and B?

Table 27.1 **The effect of changing the concentration on the rate of reaction between calcium carbonate and hydrochloric acid**

Mixture	[HCl(aq)] / mol dm^{-3}	Relative rate
A	2.0	8
B	1.0	4
C	0.5	2
D	0.25	1

?

H Explain how the calcium carbonate/hydrochloric acid reaction can be followed.

stoichiometric equation. For example, the equation for the reaction of dilute hydrochloric acid with marble chips is:

$$CaCO_3(s) + 2HCl(aq) \rightarrow CaCl_2(aq) + CO_2(g) + H_2O(l)$$

Yet when experiments are done to find how the rate of reaction varies with the concentration of each reactant, it is discovered that the rate is directly proportional to the concentration of hydrochloric acid. So, when the concentration doubles, so does the reaction rate. In this case:

$$rate \propto [HCl(aq)]^1$$

Therefore, the rate equation is:

$$rate = k[HCl(aq)]^1 = k[HCl(aq)]$$

(since power 1 is conventionally omitted)

This reaction is **first order** with respect to hydrochloric acid, because the concentration is raised to the power 1 in the experimentally determined rate equation.

EXAMPLE

Q An experiment is carried out to determine the reaction kinetics of this reaction:

$$BrO_3^-(aq) + 6I^-(aq) + 6H^+(aq) \rightarrow 3I_2(s) + 3H_2O(l) + Br^-(aq)$$

The results obtained are given in Table 27.2.

Table 27.2 **Results of a study of the kinetics of the reaction between bromate(V) ions and iodide ions in acid solution**

Mixture	[BrO$_3^-$(aq)] /mol dm^{-3}	[I$^-$(aq)] /mol dm^{-3}	[H$^+$(aq)] /mol dm^{-3}	Relative initial rate
A	0.10	0.60	0.60	1
B	0.20	0.60	0.60	2
C	0.20	1.20	0.60	4
D	0.20	0.60	1.20	8

Work out the orders of reaction with respect to each reactant, and hence write the overall rate equation.

A Comparing the relative rates for A and B shows that the rate in B doubles when [BrO$_3^-$(aq)] doubles. Note that the other concentrations remain the same. Therefore:

$$rate \propto [BrO_3^-(aq)]$$

Comparing the relative rates for B and C shows that [BrO$_3^-$(aq)] and [H$^+$(aq)] are the same in both experiments, while [I$^-$(aq)] doubles in C. This doubles the rate in C. Therefore:

$$rate \propto [I^-(aq)]$$

Comparing the relative rates of B and D shows that, while the other two concentrations stay the same, doubling [H$^+$(aq)] quadruples the rate in D. Therefore:

$$rate \propto [H^+(aq)]^2$$

Combining the three reaction rates gives:

$$rate \propto [BrO_3^-(aq)] \times [I^-(aq)] \times [H^+(aq)]^2$$

So, the rate equation is:

$$rate = k[BrO_3^-(aq)][I^-(aq)][H^+(aq)]^2$$

The reaction is **first order** with respect to [BrO$_3^-$(aq)], because in the rate equation the power to which this concentration is raised is 1.

It is also **first order** with respect to [I$^-$(aq)], because the power to which this concentration is raised is also 1.

The reaction is **second order** with respect to [H$^+$(aq)], because in the rate equation the power to which this concentration is raised is 2.

The overall order of the reaction is the sum of the individual orders, which gives 1+1+2 = 4.

Hence, the reaction is **fourth order.**

Determining the rate equation by the initial-rate method

In the previous worked example, the reaction rates quoted are initial reaction rates. These are the rates at the start of the reaction. They were found by doing four separate experiments and plotting rate curves for each experiment. The tangent at time zero is drawn for each experiment and the gradient of each tangent is determined. This was the procedure followed to find the initial rate in Fig 27.5, page 582.

In the next Example, the initial-rate method is used to find the rate equation and the rate constant of a reaction which is believed to occur in the exhaust gases of car engines to produce the atmospheric pollutant nitrogen dioxide. In each experiment, the concentration of only one reactant is varied

?

I When using the initial-rate method, chemists often stop the experiment long before the reaction is complete. Why is this?

■ See questions 1, 2, 3, 4, 5, 6 and 7.

EXAMPLE

Q The reaction between nitrogen monoxide and oxygen was investigated using the initial rate method. The stoichiometric equation is:

$$2NO(g) + O_2(g) \rightarrow 2NO_2(g)$$

The results obtained at a particular temperature are given in Table 27.3 below.

a) Deduce the orders of the reaction with respect to $NO(g)$ and $O_2(g)$.
b) Write the expression for the rate equation.
c) Determine the overall order of the reaction.
d) Work out the value of the rate constant, showing its units.

Table 27.3

Experiment	$[NO(g)]$/mol dm^{-3}	$[O_2(g)]$/mol dm^{-3}	Initial rate of production of $NO_2(g)$/mol dm^{-3} s^{-1}
1	1.00×10^{-3}	3.00×10^{-3}	4.00×10^{-4}
2	1.00×10^{-3}	6.00×10^{-3}	8.00×10^{-4}
3	2.00×10^{-3}	3.00×10^{-3}	1.60×10^{-3}

A

a) Comparing experiments 1 and 3, the concentration of $NO(g)$ doubles, which quadruples the rate of reaction.

The concentration of $O_2(g)$ is constant.

Therefore: rate $\propto [NO(g)]^2$

So, the reaction is **second order** with respect to $NO(g)$.

Comparing experiments 1 and 2 the concentration of $O_2(g)$ is doubled, which doubles the rate of reaction.

The concentration of $NO(g)$ is the same in both experiments.

Therefore: rate $\propto [O_2(g)]$

So, the reaction is **first order** with respect to $O_2(g)$.

b) Since rate $\propto [NO(g)]^2[O_2(g)]$, the rate equation is:

rate $= k[NO(g)]^2[O_2(g)]$

Note that on this occasion the stoichiometric coefficients (the numbers of moles of each substance

in the balanced equation) match those of the orders of the reaction. But do remember that the rate equation can only be determined by experiment.

c) The overall order of the reaction is the sum of the powers in the experimentally determined rate equation. This is 2+1 = 3. ($[O_2(g)]$ is to the power 1.) So, the overall order is third.

d) The rate equation is: rate $= k[NO(g)]^2[O_2(g)]$ which gives:

$k = \dfrac{\text{rate}}{[NO(g)]^2[O_2(g)]}$ and units of $k = \dfrac{\text{mol dm}^{-3}\text{ s}^{-1}}{(\text{mol dm}^{-3})^2(\text{mol dm}^{-3})}$

Now substitute one of the sets of values into the equation to determine k. For example, take those for experiment 1:

$k = \dfrac{4.00 \times 10^{-4}}{(1.00 \times 10^{-3})^2 \times 3.00 \times 10^{-3}}$ and units of $k = \text{dm}^6\text{ mol}^{-2}\text{s}^{-1}$

Therefore: $k = 1.33 \times 10^5 \text{ dm}^5\text{ mol}^{-2}\text{ s}^{-1}$

Note that dm^6 is placed first when quoting the units. This follows the convention whereby a unit raised to a positive power is placed first.

?

J The antiseptic chlorophenol is made using $SO_2Cl_2(g)$. The latter breaks down according to the equation:

$$SO_2Cl_2(g) \rightarrow SO_2(g) + Cl_2(g)$$

Three experiments were performed to determine the rate equation at a particular temperature. The results obtained are given in Table 27.4.

Table 27.4 **Kinetic data used to determine the rate equation for the decomposition of $SO_2Cl_2(g)$**

$[SO_2Cl_2(g)]$ /mol dm^{-3}	Initial rate of formation of $Cl_2(g)$/mol $dm^{-3}\,s^{-1}$
0.02	4.4×10^{-7}
0.04	8.8×10^{-7}
0.06	1.32×10^{-6}

Deduce the rate equation for this reaction and calculate the rate constant, stating the units of k.

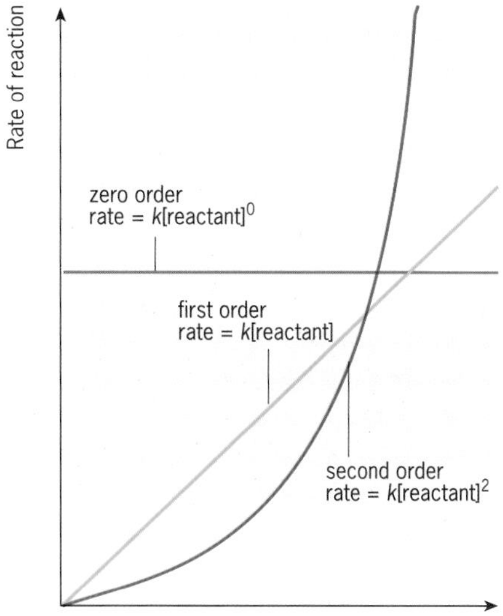

Fig 27.12 **The effect of reactant concentration on the rate of zero, first- and second-order reactions**

Zero order and other orders

In the Examples so far, reactions have been first or second order with respect to each reactant. Another common order of reaction is **zero order** (sometimes called **zeroth order**):

A zero-order reaction is one in which the concentration of a reactant has no effect on the rate of reaction.

For example, the decomposition of ammonia on a tungsten wire takes place according to the equation:

$$2NH_3(g) \xrightarrow{W} N_2(g) + 3H_2(g)$$

The rate equation for this reaction is:

$$\text{rate} = k[NH_3(g)]^0 = k \quad (\text{since } [\text{reactant}]^0 = 1)$$

It does not matter what the concentration of ammonia is, the rate is always the same at a particular temperature.

Fig 27.12 illustrates the effect of reactant concentration on the rate of reaction for zero, first and second orders. For a zero-order reaction, the concentration has no effect on the rate, hence the graph is a horizontal line. For a first-order reaction, the rate is directly proportional to the reactant concentration, giving a straight-line graph. Since rate = k[reactant], the gradient is equal to the rate constant, k. For a second-order reaction, where:

$$\text{rate} \propto [\text{reactant}]^2$$

the graph is a curve.

The reaction of propanone (CH_3COCH_3) with iodine is interesting. Although in the stoichiometric equation hydrogen ions are not involved as reactants, they catalyse the reaction. Because the reaction itself produces these ions, the reaction is said to be **auto-catalysed** (self-catalysed):

$$CH_3COCH_3(aq) + I_2(aq) \rightarrow CH_3COCH_2I(aq) + H^+(aq) + I^-(aq)$$

The rate equation for this reaction can be written:

$$\text{rate} = k[CH_3COCH_3(aq)]^1[H^+(aq)]^1[I_2(aq)]^0$$
$$= k[CH_3COCH_3(aq)]\,[H^+(aq)] \quad (\text{since } [\ ]^0 = 1$$

Because the concentration of iodine has no effect on the rate, the reaction is zero order with respect to iodine. But it is first order with respect to both propanone and hydrogen ions.

?

K What is the overall order for the reaction of iodine with propanone?

See question 4. ■

?

L The rate equations are given for the following reactions. Give the order with respect to each reactant and the overall order for the reaction.

(a) $BrO_3^-(aq) + 3SO_3^{2-}(aq) \rightarrow Br^-(aq) + 3SO_4^{2-}(aq)$
rate $= k[BrO_3^-(aq)][SO_3^{2-}(aq)]$

(b) $2H_2(g) + 2NO(g) \rightarrow 2H_2O(g) + N_2(g)$
rate $= k[NO(g)]^2[H_2(g)]$

(c) $NO_2(g) + CO(g) \rightarrow NO(g) + CO_2(g)$
rate $= k[NO_2(g)]^2$

Work out the units of the rate constant for each reaction. In all cases, concentration is measured in $mol\,dm^{-3}$, and rate in $mol\,dm^{-3}\,s^{-1}$.

An order of reaction need not be zero, first or second order. An order of reaction may be a fraction, but this lies outside the scope of this book.

Half-lives and first-order reactions

The half-life of a chemical reaction is the time taken for the concentration of a reactant to decrease to half of its initial value.

In the case of first-order reactions, the half life is constant. This means that, whatever the starting concentration of a reactant, it will always takes the same time for this concentration to be halved. The decomposition of hydrogen peroxide using manganese(IV) oxide catalyst is a first-order reaction (Fig 27.13):

$$H_2O_2(aq) \rightarrow H_2O(l) + O_2(g)$$
$$\text{rate} = k[H_2O_2(aq)]$$

The concept of half-life in relation to radioactive decay is discussed on page 35.

?

M How can the decomposition of hydrogen peroxide reaction be followed?
Hint: One of the products is a gas.

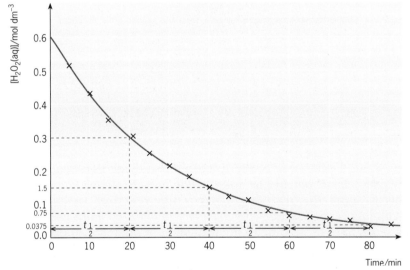

Fig 27.13 **Graph showing the change in concentration of hydrogen peroxide with time in the catalytic decomposition of hydrogen peroxide, using MnO_2 as the catalyst at 20 °C**

Four successive half-lives from the graph in Fig 27.13 are given in Table 27.5. Note that the four half-lives are all constant. This is a characteristic of first-order reactions.

Using successive half-lives may involve very small concentrations, which can lead to inaccuracies. In Fig 27.13, the time taken for other concentrations of $H_2O_2(aq)$ to decrease by half (e.g. $0.5\,mol\,dm^{-3}$ falling to $0.25\,mol\,dm^{-3}$) could have been used.

Table 27.5 **Four successive half-lives from the decomposition of hydrogen peroxide**

Initial concentration $H_2O_2(aq)$ /$mol\,dm^{-3}$	Half-life $t_{1/2}$/min
0.60	20
0.30	20
0.15	20
0.075	20

?

N The determination of the catalytic decomposition of hydrogen peroxide as a first-order reaction can be made with a single experiment (as shown on page 589). Another method for studying the kinetics of this reaction involves initial rates. Explain how you would study this reaction using the initial-rates method. How would you show that the reaction is first order?

O Radioactive decay is another first-order reaction, because successive half-lives are constant. The half-life of sodium-24 is 15 hours.

(a) Starting with 1 kg of a radioactive sample of sodium-24, how much of it will be left after 30 hours?
Hint: If you are not sure about how to answer this question, turn to page 85.

(b) What is the rate constant for this decay?

See question 6. ■

Therefore, half-lives can be used to identify a first-order reaction from a single kinetics experiment. If the half-life of a reactant is known, the rate constant of a first-order reaction can be calculated using the following relationship between the half-life and the rate constant:

$$k = \frac{0.693}{t_{\frac{1}{2}}}$$

You do not have to know how to derive this equation. But you should note its usefulness in calculating rate constants.

Concentration–time graphs

When a reaction is zero order with respect to a reactant, the reactant concentration has no effect on the rate of reaction:

$$\text{rate} = k[\text{reactant}]^0 = k \qquad \text{(since } [\text{reactant}]^0 \text{ is 1)}$$

In Fig 27.14, the concentration–time graph for a zero-order reaction shows a constant decline in concentration as the reaction proceeds.

For a first-order reaction:

$$\text{rate} = k[\text{reactant}]^1 = k[\text{reactant}] \qquad \text{(since } [\text{reactant}]^1 \equiv [\text{reactant}])$$

As already stated, irrespective of the starting concentration, the half-life has a fixed value, so the concentration–time graph has the characteristic shape shown in Fig 27.14.

For a second-order reaction:

$$\text{rate} = k[\text{reactant}]^2$$

When the starting rate is the same as that of a first-order reaction, the concentration–time graph approaches zero much more slowly, as Fig 27.14 shows. This is because in a second-order reaction the half-life increases as the concentration diminishes, unlike in a first-order reaction where the half-life is independent of the concentration.

Fig 27.14 **Concentration–time graphs for zero, first- and second-order reactions**

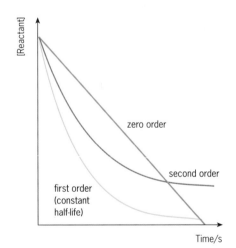

There is more about the reaction mechanism of ozone depletion by CFCs in the Assignment on page 606.

3 RATE EQUATIONS IN THE DETERMINATION OF REACTION MECHANISMS

As stated earlier, one of the reasons for studying the kinetics of a reaction is to obtain the information which allows chemists to decide how the reaction occurs – the **reaction mechanism**. Although some reactions do take place in one step, most proceed in a series of steps, leading to the formation of products. In each step, bonds are broken or made.

Rate equations provide evidence of what the reaction mechanism might be. For example, knowledge of the likely reaction mechanism of ozone depletion in the upper atmosphere by CFCs proved to be crucial in helping governments to agree to ban their manufacture.

For a sequence of bond-breaking and bond-making steps to occur, the reactants must collide with sufficient energy. This is the **collision theory** of chemical reactions, which is discussed in more detail in the next section. Each step in a reaction mechanism usually involves one or two molecules. Such steps are sometimes called **elementary steps.**

Consider a proposed single-step reaction mechanism: the high-temperature conversion of cyclopropane to propene (Fig 27.15). The experimentally derived rate equation (or rate law) for this reaction is:

$$rate = k[cyclopropane]$$

The reaction is first order. So, given the single-step mechanism, only one molecule of cyclopropane can be involved. Hence, the energy given to this molecule must cause it to shake itself apart. This is called a **unimolecular step**. The **molecularity** of a step is the number of species (atoms, molecules or ions) involved.

It is unusual to find reactions which have just one elementary step. Most involve at least two, even when they are first-order reactions. For example, the stoichiometric equation for the hydrolysis of 2-bromo-2-methylpropane is:

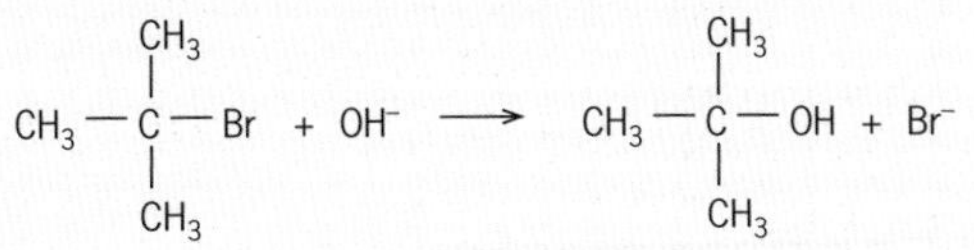

$$CH_3 - \underset{\underset{CH_3}{|}}{\overset{\overset{CH_3}{|}}{C}} - Br\ +\ OH^- \longrightarrow CH_3 - \underset{\underset{CH_3}{|}}{\overset{\overset{CH_3}{|}}{C}} - OH\ +\ Br^-$$

and its rate equation is:

$$rate = k[(CH_3)_3CBr]$$

The stoichiometric equation gives no clue as to the rate equation, which always has to be determined by experiment. A proposed mechanism which fits this rate equation is:

$$(CH_3)_3CBr \xrightarrow{\text{slow}} (CH_3)_3C^+ + Br^-$$

$$(CH_3)_3C^+ + OH^- \xrightarrow{\text{fast}} (CH_3)_3COH$$

It is the slower step which governs the rate of reaction. This is called the **rate-determining step**. Suppose you are throwing a party and send out invitations. You have three people helping you. You write the invitations, which is the slow step. One friend folds them, which does not take long, while another friend puts them in envelopes. The last person addresses the envelopes and sticks on the stamps. It is your step which takes the longest. It does not matter how fast your friends work, the rate is determined by the slowest step. Writing the invitations is the rate-determining step. It is the same with chemical reactions: the slowest elementary step determines the rate of the entire reaction.

The rate-determining step for this hydrolysis reaction is unimolecular because it involves only one molecule. The fast step is referred to as **bimolecular** because it involves two reacting species. Although the stoichiometry of the overall reaction does not give the rate equation, the stoichiometry of each elementary reaction can.

In the rate-determining step:

$$(CH_3)_3CBr \xrightarrow{\text{slow}} (CH_3)_3C^+ + Br^-$$

the rate of reaction is governed by the breaking of a chemical bond in the reactant molecule. As only this molecule is involved, the rate is proportional to the concentration. The higher the concentration, the faster the reaction. So, the rate equation for this elementary step is:

$$rate = k[(CH_3)_3CBr]$$

which is also the rate of the overall reaction. The overall order is zero for OH^- ions, since these react after the rate-determining step, their concentration therefore having no effect on the reaction rate.

Fig 27.15 **The conversion of cyclopropane to propene**

?

P The conversion of cyclopropane to propene is sometimes called an isomerisation reaction. Can you explain why?
Hint: If you are not sure, refer to page 144.

$$(CH_3)_3CBr \xrightarrow{\text{slow}} (CH_3)_3C^+ + Br^-$$

$$(CH_3)_3C^+ + OH^- \xrightarrow{\text{fast}} (CH_3)_3COH$$

$$(CH_3)_3CBr + OH^- \longrightarrow (CH_3)_3COH + Br^-$$

Fig 27.16 **Hydrolysis of 2-bromo-2-methylpropane**

?

Q NO_2F is an explosive compound. The mechanism for its production is thought to be:

$$NO_2 + F_2 \xrightarrow{\text{slow}} NO_2F + F$$

$$NO_2 + F \xrightarrow{\text{fast}} NO_2F$$

What is the overall stoichiometric equation for this reaction?

R 2-bromo-2-methylpropane is called a tertiary halogenoalkane. Primary halogenoalkanes, such as 1-bromobutane, $CH_3CH_2CH_2CH_2Br$, are believed to react by the mechanism displayed in Fig 27.17. The rate equation is:

$$\text{rate} = k[CH_3CH_2CH_2CH_2Br][OH^-]$$

Why do you think this is called an S_N2 reaction?

Read more about S_N2 reactions on page 215.

Reacting species which occur before the slow step may feature in the overall rate equation.

This reaction is sometimes called an S_N1 reaction. S signifies that it is a substitution reaction, N that it is nucleophilic, and 1 that it is first order with one molecule involved in the rate-determining step. For more information on this reaction, turn to page 215.

Whatever reaction mechanism is proposed, the sum of its steps must equal the overall stoichiometric equation. In the case of the hydrolysis of 2-bromo-2-methylpropane, it does (Fig 27.16).

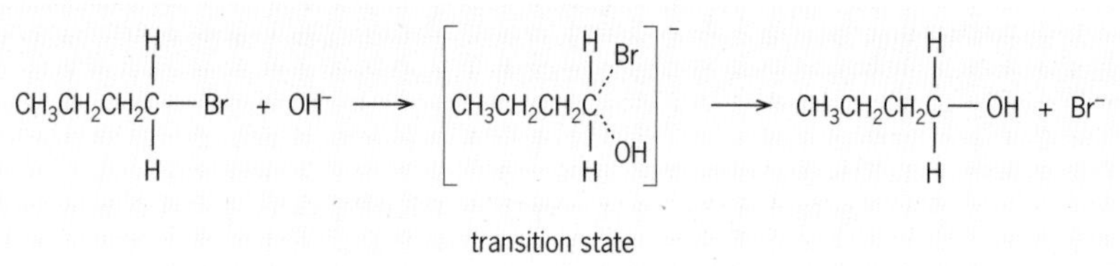

transition state

Fig 27.17 **The S_N2 reaction mechanism for the hydrolysis of 1-bromobutane**

Working out another mechanism

The reaction of carbon monoxide with nitrogen dioxide is believed to take place in the exhaust gases of car engines. To determine the mechanism, first write down the stoichiometric equation:

$$NO_2(g) + CO(g) \rightarrow NO(g) + CO_2(g)$$

Note that this equation gives no information about how the reaction occurs. At first sight, the reaction might appear to be a **termolecular** reaction, in which three molecules come together and collide at the same time. This is highly unlikely.

The next stage is to do experiments to determine the overall rate equation. This has been found to be:

$$\text{rate} = k[NO_2]^2$$

The reaction is zero order with respect to carbon monoxide, which means it does not take part in the rate-determining step.

Now a mechanism has to be proposed which is consistent with the rate equation and which, when the steps are added together, gives the overall stoichiometric equation. This is really an educated guess:

$$NO_2 + NO_2 \xrightarrow{\text{slow}} N_2O_4$$
$$N_2O_4 + CO \xrightarrow{\text{fast}} NO + CO_2 + NO_2$$

$$NO_2(g) + CO(g) \rightarrow NO(g) + CO_2(g)$$

The slower step is the rate-determining step. This involves a bimolecular collision between two nitrogen dioxide molecules, so the rate equation for this step is rate = $k[NO_2]^2$, and the overall rate equation is also rate = $k[NO_2]^2$. Carbon monoxide appears in the fast step, so its concentration does not affect the rate. Therefore, the proposed mechanism is consistent with the rate equation and the steps when added together give the overall equation.

However, when this reaction is analysed, a short-lived intermediate NO_3, is discovered. Also, no N_2O_4 is found. This means that the educated guess was incorrect and another mechanism must be proposed, which is:

$$NO_2 + NO_2 \xrightarrow{\text{slow}} NO_3 + NO$$
$$NO_3 + CO \xrightarrow{\text{fast}} NO_2 + CO_2$$

$$NO_2(g) + CO(g) \rightarrow NO(g) + CO_2(g)$$

This still gives a bimolecular rate-determining step and the rate equation is consistent with this. Also, the overall stoichiometric equation is obtained when the two steps are added together. This is a good example of a mechanism being proposed which is consistent with the rate equation but is not consistent with other experimental evidence and therefore has to be amended accordingly. No-one can prove that this mechanism *is* correct. What can be said is that, based on current evidence, it is thought to be likely.

Sometime mechanisms are proposed which have a fast step followed by a slow step. In this case, a reaction intermediate builds up and could be sufficiently long-lived to be detected. This would give another clue to the mechanism.

Predicting rate equations from elementary steps

Table 27.6 shows three possible elementary steps in reaction mechanisms, together with the rate equations which can be derived from them. The molecularity of each step and the order are the same. So when the elementary step is unimolecular, it is a first-order reaction. Similarly, a bimolecular reaction gives a second-order reaction. On very rare occasions, a termolecular elementary step is thought to be involved, but this requires three particles to collide simultaneously, which is improbable. When these are the slow steps, they govern the overall rate of the reaction. Therefore, the overall rate equation can be predicted to be the same as this rate determining step.

Table 27.6

Elementary step	Molecularity	Rate equation
A → products	unimolecular	rate = $k[A]$
A + A → products	bimolecular	rate = $k[A]^2$
A + B → products	bimolecular	rate = $k[A][B]$

4 COLLISION THEORY

The collision theory is a model which chemists use to explain how reactions occur. When two molecules react, bonds are broken or made, and there is usually a rearrangement of the atoms. According to the collision theory, for this to happen the molecules first have to collide. The collision model was developed from the kinetic-molecular model of gases discussed on pages 99 to 101.

In 1 cm^3 of gas at atmospheric pressure and room temperature, it has been calculated that there are about 10^{27} collisions between two molecules every second. If all these collisions were to lead to reactions, then all reactions involving gases would be over in microseconds. For example, nitrogen and oxygen molecules, which under normal conditions coexist without reacting, would have long ago reacted to fill the atmosphere with polluting nitrogen oxides. This means that only a certain number of collisions result in reactions. These are called **effective collisions**.

Explaining the effect of concentration and pressure on reaction rate

As shown earlier in connection with rate equations, increasing the concentrations of certain reacting species speeds up reactions in which they are involved. Can the collision theory explain this observation?

✔

Remember: The rate equation can be predicted from an elementary step but not from the overall stoichiometric equation.

?

S The decomposition of hydrogen peroxide can be catalysed by bromide ions:

$$2H_2O_2(aq) \xrightarrow{Br^-(aq)} 2H_2O(l) + O_2(g)$$

The rate equation is:

$$rate = k[H_2O_2][Br^-(aq)]$$

Which of the following mechanisms is consistent with this rate equation? Give reasons for your choice.

Mechanism 1

$$H_2O_2 \xrightarrow{slow} 2HO$$

$$2HO + Br^- \xrightarrow{fast} BrO^- + H_2O$$

$$H_2O_2 + BrO^- \xrightarrow{fast} H_2O + O_2 + Br^-$$

Mechanism 2

$$H_2O_2 + Br^- \xrightarrow{slow} H_2O + BrO^-$$

$$BrO^- + H_2O_2 \xrightarrow{fast} H_2O + O_2 + Br^-$$

✔

Remember: Although the order of an elementary step in a mechanism can be obtained from the number of reactant species in the equation, for the elementary step the overall order cannot be predicted from the overall stoichiometric equation.

■ See questions 5 and 7.

?

T The stoichiometric equation for a reaction is:

$$NO(g) + N_2O_5(g) \rightarrow 3NO_2(g)$$

A proposed mechanism is:

$$N_2O_5 \xrightarrow{slow} NO_2 + NO_3$$

$$NO + NO_3 \xrightarrow{fast} 2NO_2$$

(a) What is the rate equation for each elementary step?

(b) Which is the rate-determining step?

(c) Predict the overall rate equation.

(d) Why is the overall reaction zero order with respect to NO?

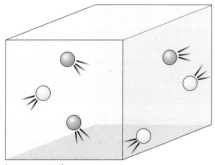

low concentration:
few particles in a given volume

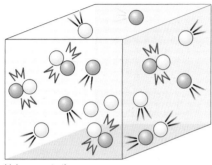

high concentration:
many particles in the same volume

Fig 27.18 **Effect of increasing the concentration of reacting species**

low pressure:
molecules are
spread out

high pressure:
volume has been decreased
(at constant temperature),
forcing the molecules
closer together

Fig 27.19 **The effect of increasing the pressure of reacting gases, held at a constant temperature**

The term activation energy is introduced
on page 126.
Urban pollution from nitrogen oxides is
covered on pages 169 to 171.

To react, particles must first collide. So, increasing the number of particles in a given volume must increase the number of collisions and therefore, it would be reasonable to assume, increase the number of effective collisions (Fig 27.18).

The collision theory also explains why increasing the pressure under which gaseous reactions take place, increases their rate of reaction. This is illustrated in Fig 27.19. Note that, at a given temperature, increasing the pressure in gases increases the concentration of molecules.

Explaining the effect of increasing the surface area of solid reactants on the rate of reaction

If solid particles are large, they have a small surface area compared to the amount of reactant molecules they contain, and only the reactant molecules at the surface can take part in collisions with other molecules. If a solid particle is ground into a fine powder, then many more molecules are available for effective collisions. Miners have long known about the hazards of dust explosions, but dust explosions are not confined to underground mines. Fig 27.20 shows the effect of a dust explosion in a grain silo. Milling flour also has the same risks.

Fig 27.20 **In 1977, in New Orleans, an explosion of dust killed 37 people. A spark ignited very fine dust in grain silos and the terrifyingly fast rate of combustion with the oxygen in the air caused the explosion**

Activation energy

Molecules must collide with sufficient energy to break bonds or make them. The minimum energy with which they must collide is called the **activation energy, E_a**. The reason that nitrogen and oxygen molecules in the room you are sitting in do not suddenly start reacting is they are not colliding with sufficient energy to break the very strong triple bond of the nitrogen molecule. However, in the much higher temperatures of a car engine, some of the molecules do collide with this minimum energy to produce the nitrogen oxides of urban pollution.

The activation energy is sometimes referred to as the energy barrier. Fig 27.21 is an energy profile diagram for an exothermic reaction, showing the activation energy. The higher this activation energy is, the fewer molecules are going to have sufficient energy to react at any particular temperature, so the rate of reaction will be

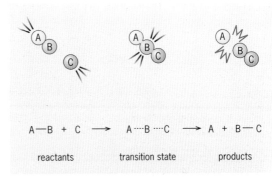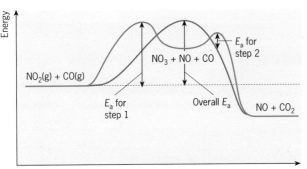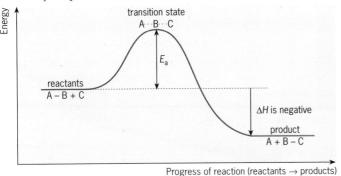

slow. At the very top of the energy barrier, bonds are forming and being broken, and the molecules are in a **transition state** between reactants and products (Fig 27.22). The idea of a transition state comes from another model of reaction kinetics called the **transition state theory**. This model looks at the collision in detail. While the collision theory is a good model for simple gaseous reactions, the transition state theory is more generally applicable. However, all subsequent discussions in this chapter are based on the collision theory.

Many of the reactions discussed so far have more than one elementary step in their reaction mechanisms. Each of these steps has

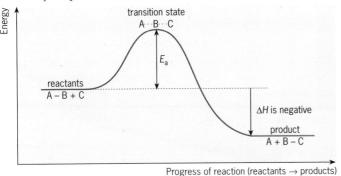

Fig 27.21 **An energy profile diagram for an exothermic reaction**

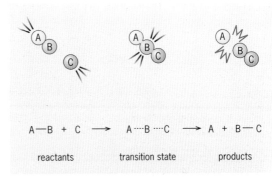

$A—B + C \longrightarrow A \cdots B \cdots C \longrightarrow A + B—C$

reactants   transition state   products

Fig 27.22 **Effective collision between two particles, both with the required activation energy. The transition state shows bonds breaking and forming as a result of the collision**

an activation energy. The mechanism for the reaction of carbon monoxide with nitrogen dioxide (discussed on page 592) has the energy profile shown in Fig 27.23. It has two steps, with the slower step having the larger activation energy.

This much fuller energy profile diagram, is given to illustrate the point that each elementary step has its own individual activation

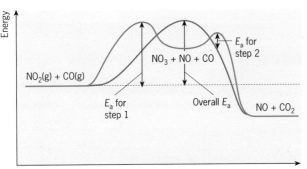

Fig 27.23 **An energy profile diagram. Note the two elementary steps. The orange line represents the energy profile without showing the individual steps**

energy. However, it is more usual to show the activation energy for the entire reaction, hence the dashed line in Fig 27.33. The species in the middle of the two activation energies is called the **reactive intermediate**, which in this case is NO_3.

?

U The reaction between nitrogen and oxygen to produce nitrogen monoxide is endothermic.

(a) Draw the energy profile diagram for this reaction. To check your answer, see Fig 6.11 on page 126. Hint: This reaction has a very high energy of activation.

(b) In the rate equation for this reaction, would the value for the rate constant be small or large?

■ See question 3.

A scientist puts forward a model to explain observations, and so long as this model explains all known observations, it is accepted by the scientific community (see page 24). However, even if a model does not fully explain the observations, it can still be useful in helping understanding.

EXPLOSIVE REACTIONS AND NOBEL PRIZES

FOR CENTURIES, gunpowder was the only high explosive. Then, in 1846, the compounds nitrocellulose (gun cotton) and nitroglycerine were made. Both compounds have very low activation energies for their decomposition and so are highly unstable.

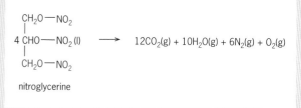

$$4 \begin{array}{l} CH_2O-NO_2 \\ | \\ CHO-NO_2 \ (l) \\ | \\ CH_2O-NO_2 \end{array} \longrightarrow 12CO_2(g) + 10H_2O(g) + 6N_2(g) + O_2(g)$$

nitroglycerine

Fig 27.25(a) **Four moles of liquid gives 29 moles of gases. So it is the expansion of the hot gases from a small volume of liquid which produces the explosion**

Fig 27.25(b) **An engraving from *The Illustrated London News* in 1884 publicising dynamite made at the Nobel Explosives Company in Ardeer, Ayrshire**

Fig 27.24 **Alfred Nobel (1833–96) in his laboratory**

The Swedish Nobel family were manufacturers of explosives. In 1863, Alfred Nobel invented a detonator which would set off liquid nitroglycerine. However, in 1864, a nitroglycerine explosion at the Nobel factory killed Alfred's younger brother, Emil, and four other people. Alfred set about making nitroglycerine safe, and within four years he had produced dynamite. (The name is derived from *dynamis*, the Greek for 'power'.)

In dynamite, the nitroglycerine is absorbed by an inert solid called kieselguhr, which renders it stable until it is set off by a detonator. In 1875, Nobel produced gelignite – an even more powerful explosive. This, too, contained nitroglycerine. This time it was mixed with nitrocellulose in a gel. These explosives were soon put to use in civil engineering projects, such as blasting routes for new roads and excavating the ground for canals and the foundations of buildings.

Alfred Nobel was convinced that the only way to stop wars was to produce an explosive so powerful that no one would dare use it. In this he did not succeed, but in

Fig 27.25(c) **Dynamite is sometimes used to demolish unwanted buildings and other structures such as these cooling towers. The explosive has to be correctly positioned to ensure that the building will collapse in on itself and not be scattered over the surrounding area**

his will he left most of the vast fortune he had amassed from selling explosives to the establishment of five prizes to be awarded annually for outstanding achievements in chemistry, physics, physiology or medicine, literature and peace. In 1969, a sixth prize was added for economics. These Nobel prizes are now acknowledged to be the world's most prestigious accolade. They cannot be awarded posthumously, and no more than three people can share each prize.

Energy distribution amongst molecules in a gas

Molecules have energy due to their motion. It is called **kinetic energy**. At any instant in time, some molecules have very high energies relative to the rest, because they are moving very fast, while other molecules have very low energies relative to the rest, because they are moving very slowly. Most molecules, however, have a range of energies between these extremes. The distribution of energies amongst molecules was calculated statistically by the Scots physicist James Clerk Maxwell in 1859, and more generally applied by the Austrian physicist Ludwig Eduard Boltzmann in 1871. The result is the **Maxwell–Boltzmann distribution of molecular energies**, shown in Fig 27.26.

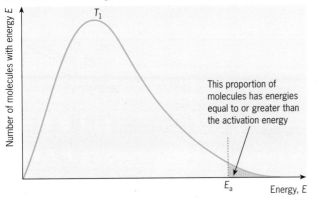

Fig 27.26 **Maxwell–Boltzmann distribution curve at a particular temperature**

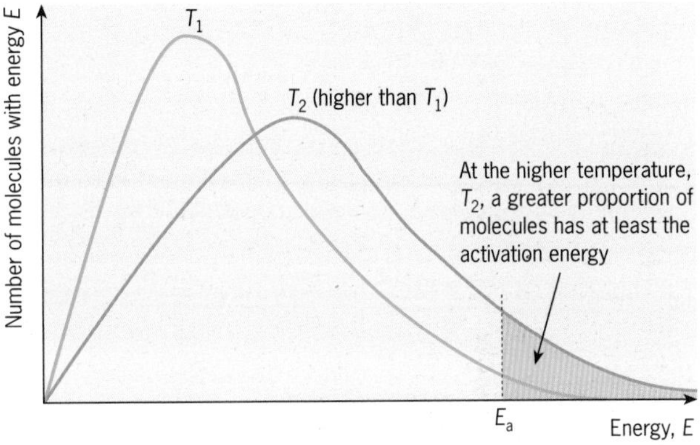

Fig 27.27 **Maxwell–Boltzmann distribution curve at temperatures T_1 and T_2**

The Maxwell–Boltzmann distribution explains why, at a particular temperature, only a certain number of collisions are effective ones. Fig 27.27 shows the effect of increasing temperature. At the higher temperatures, a greater proportion of molecules have higher energies and so a greater proportion possess energies equal to, or above, the activation energy, giving more effective collisions.

Effect of temperature on the reaction rate and the rate constant

As Fig 27.27 shows, increasing the temperature increases the proportion of molecules which have the minimum activation energy needed for them to react when they collide. This means that the rate of reaction increases with temperature. For every 10 °C rise, the rate of most reactions approximately doubles.

Consider the reaction:

$$A + B \rightarrow C + D$$

for which the rate equation is:

$$\text{rate} = k[A]^m[B]^n$$

If the concentrations of A and B are kept constant, then the rate constant must increase with increasing temperature.

> ✔ Remember: The rate equation can only be determined by doing experiments.

> ❓
>
> **V** If a 10 °C rise in temperature doubles the rate of a chemical reaction at constant concentrations, what is the effect on the rate constant, k?

■ See question 8.

5 CATALYSIS: LOWERING THE ENERGY BARRIER

Catalysts play a crucial role in the lives of everybody. Protein catalysts called enzymes dramatically increase the rates of thousands of different chemical reactions that take place in our bodies every second. And catalysts are involved in the manufacture of most of the chemicals on which people rely.

Enzymes are covered on page 368.

The Arrhenius equation

The Swedish chemist Svante Arrhenius was the first to discover a mathematical relationship between temperature and the rate constant. The **Arrhenius equation** is:

$$k = Ae^{-E_a/RT}$$

where k is the rate constant.

A, also a constant, is the collision frequency. However, when molecules collide, they must have the correct orientation in order to react, and this factor includes the collision frequency. A is sometimes called the Arrhenius constant.

The term $e^{-E_a/RT}$ gives the fraction of collisions which have the minimum activation energy at a particular temperature, where E_a is the activation energy in joules, R is the gas constant $8.31\,\text{J K}^{-1}\,\text{mol}^{-1}$ (see page 97), T is the absolute temperature in K, and e means it is an exponential relationship. It expresses the condition that increasing the temperature increases the reaction rate exponentially.

Another way of expressing the Arrhenius equation is to take natural logarithms of both sides:

$$\ln k = \ln A - \frac{E_a}{RT}$$

A straight-line graph of $\ln k$ against $1/T$ can be plotted, as in Fig 27.28. Its gradient is $-E_a/R$, so E_a can be determined.

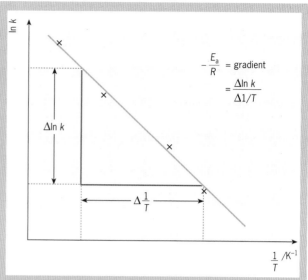

Fig 27.28 **The activation energy can be determined from the gradient of this graph**

Fig 27.29 **Svante Arrhenius (1859–1927). As well as for his equation, he is famous for formulating the idea that electrolytes dissociate in solution to give charged particles**

SIR GEORGE PORTER AND VERY FAST REACTIONS

SIR GEORGE PORTER was born in 1920, in Stainforth, Yorkshire. He was studying for his chemistry degree at Leeds University when World War 2 broke out. Along with other undergraduates, he was asked to take up radio physics during the last year or so of his course. At the time, he was told only that it had 'very high priority'. On graduating in 1941, he became a radar officer in the Royal Navy when radar was in its infancy.

Sir George has said that his time in the Navy convinced him that he wanted to do scientific research, and in 1945 he began a research career at Cambridge University. He was research student to Professor Ronald Norrish who did much to establish the study of reaction kinetics.

Sir George was given the task of investigating short-lived free radicals (highly reactive species with at least one unpaired electron). In this research, Norrish had been using an old army searchlight. During a visit to a factory to collect a new bulb for the searchlight, Sir George saw flash-bulbs being made. This was the turning point in his research, when he realised that the pulse techniques he had used in radar could be applied to the problem he had been set.

Together with Norrish, he used rapid flashes of light to investigate species which were very short-lived. Another pulse of light fired shortly after the first was used to identify the reactive intermediates by absorption spectroscopy.

By 1950, Sir George could identify reactive intermediates which lasted for a microsecond. In 1967 he observed intermediates which lasted for only nanoseconds ($10^{-9}\,\text{s}$) through using laser beam flashes. By 1975, he had reduced this to picoseconds ($10^{-12}\,\text{s}$). In 1966 he received the Nobel Prize together with Norrish and another chemist, Max Eigen, for his work on extremely fast chemical reactions.

Sir George became Director of the Royal Institution in 1967, where he has done much to continue the work of Michael Faraday (see page 504) in making science accessible to young people through the Christmas Lectures and other promotional work. He was knighted in 1972.

As a definition of catalysts:

Catalysts are substances which alter the rate of a chemical reaction without becoming permanently involved in it.

They do, however, become involved in the reaction temporarily, but are chemically unchanged at the end of it. It is for this reason that a small amount of catalyst can catalyse the reaction of a large amount of reactant. Catalysts work by lowering the activation energy of a reaction. To do this, they must change the mechanism of the reaction.

Catalysis is discussed briefly on page 9 and taken further on page 127.

Catalytic converters in vehicle exhaust systems and the catalysis of some atmospheric pollution reactions are covered on pages 167 to 171.

The manufacture of ammonia by the Haber process is described on page 632, and the manufacture of sulphuric acid by the contact process is described on page 668.

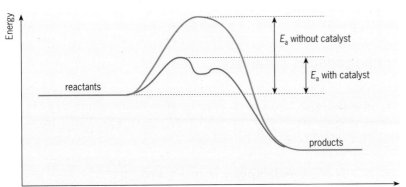

Fig 27.30 **Energy profiles of an uncatalysed reaction and the same reaction using a catalyst. The effect of the catalyst is to reduce the activation energy by providing an alternative reaction pathway**

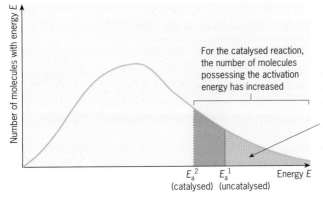

Fig 27.31 **Maxwell–Boltzmann distribution of molecular energies, showing the effect of adding a catalyst. Note that, by lowering the activation energy, there is a large increase in the number of molecules possessing at least the activation energy**

So, although a catalyst does not become permanently involved in the reaction it is catalysing it does get involved in some of the elementary steps of the mechanism. By having its energy of activation lowered, a reaction occurs at a faster rate. To explain this in terms of the collision theory, consider again the Maxwell–Boltzmann distribution of molecular energies (see page 597). If the activation energy is lowered a greater proportion of molecules have sufficient energy to make effective collisions. This is illustrated in Fig 27.31.

■ See question 8.

Inhibitors

There is debate amongst chemists as to whether some catalysts can actually slow down the rate of a reaction. These negative catalysts are often called **inhibitors** and they do play an essential role in slowing down the deterioration of certain foodstuffs.

Anti-oxidants, for instance, slow down the rate at which fats become oxidised by oxygen in the air and turn rancid. It is tempting to think that they must raise the activation energy of the reaction. This is not the case. They usually remove molecules from one of the elementary steps in a reaction mechanism by reacting with them.

6 HOMOGENEOUS AND HETEROGENEOUS CATALYSTS

There are two types of catalyst. **Homogenous catalysts** are in the same phase as the reactants they catalyse, while **heterogeneous catalysts** are in a different phase from the reactants they catalyse.

Homogeneous catalysts

Until the 1850s, sulphuric acid was manufactured by the lead chamber process, which had been developed in Birmingham in 1746. Its name was derived from the lead reacting vessels. Right from the outset, it was realised that nitrogen monoxide speeded up the rate of this reaction:

$$2SO_2(g) + O_2(g) \rightarrow 2SO_3(g)$$

The sulphur trioxide produced is used to make sulphuric acid (see page 668). The activation energy for the production of sulphur trioxide is high and nitrogen monoxide provides an alternative route of lower activation energy:

$$2NO(g) + O_2(g) \rightarrow 2NO_2(g)$$
$$\underline{2SO_2(g) + 2NO_2(g) \rightarrow 2SO_3(g) + 2NO(g)}$$
$$2SO_2(g) + O_2(g) \rightarrow 2SO_3(g)$$

Since the nitrogen monoxide is unchanged chemically at the end of the reaction and the same amount is present at the end of the reaction, nitrogen monoxide can be called a catalyst. It is a homogeneous catalyst because it is a gas and the reactants are gases.

Another example of homogeneous catalysis is the addition of carbon monoxide to methanol, using a rhodium/iodine-based catalyst:

$$CH_3OH + CO \rightarrow CH_3CO_2H$$

The reaction and the catalyst are all in the liquid phase and there is more than a 99 per cent yield of ethanoic acid. This process was introduced in 1970 and now accounts for a large slice of the world's production of this important chemical. A major use of ethanoic acid is the production of ethenyl ethanoate (vinyl acetate), which is the monomer of poly(vinyl acetate), or PVA, found in adhesives and certain paints.

Many homogeneous catalysts are found in aqueous solution. Transition metal ions, with their ability to exist in more than one oxidation state, act as very effective homogeneous catalysts. The reaction between iodide ions, $I^-(aq)$, and peroxodisulphate(VI) ions, $S_2O_8^{2-}(aq)$, is catalysed by $Fe^{2+}(aq)$ ions:

$$S_2O_8^{2-}(aq) + 2I^-(aq) \rightarrow 2SO_4^{2-}(aq) + I_2(aq)$$

$Fe^{2+}(aq)$ is first oxidised to $Fe^{3+}(aq)$:
$$S_2O_8^{2-}(aq) + 2Fe^{2+}(aq) \rightarrow 2SO_4^{2-}(aq) + 2Fe^{3+}(aq)$$

$Fe^{3+}(aq)$ is then reduced back to $Fe^{2+}(aq)$ by $I^-(aq)$:
$$2I^-(aq) + 2Fe^{3+}(aq) \rightarrow 2Fe^{2+}(aq) + I_2(aq)$$

A phase is defined on page 104 as a homogeneous (uniform) portion of matter separated from other portions of matter by a boundary surface.

?

W The contact process for the production of sulphuric acid uses a solid vanadium pentoxide catalyst to convert sulphur dioxide to sulphur trioxide. Why is vanadium pentoxide called a heterogeneous catalyst?

Enzymes are homogeneous catalysts. You can read about them on page 368.

Fig 27.32 **The reaction between $S_2O_8^{2-}(aq)$ and $2I^-(aq)$ is slow without the addition of $Fe^{2+}(aq)$ catalyst, which provides an alternative route of lower activation energy**

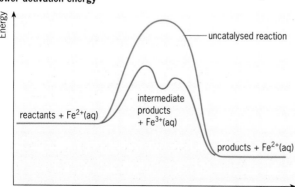

Exciting research is continuing to discover new homogeneous catalysts. One promising area involves organometallic catalysts, which could build up complex organic molecules from carbon monoxide or carbon dioxide. Compared with heterogeneous catalysts, which often involve the use of precious metals such as platinum, homogeneous catalysts generally cost less and their catalytic action often takes place at lower temperatures and pressures.

Heterogeneous catalysts

Having sung the praises of homogeneous catalysts, it is only fair to say that heterogeneous catalysts are more important in industrial chemistry at the moment and are likely to remain so for the foreseeable future. Usually, the heterogeneous catalyst is in the solid phase and the reactants are either gases or liquids.

One of the most famous and important examples of heterogeneous catalysis is the use of iron in the Haber process. This process was developed by the German chemist Fritz Haber in the early 1900s to produce ammonia from nitrogen and hydrogen:

$$N_2(g) + 3H_2(g) \xrightleftharpoons{\text{Fe catalyst}} 2NH_3(g)$$

The stimulus for this research was almost certainly its use in the manufacture of explosives. However, its use in the production of fertilisers has helped to sustain much of the growth in the world's population.

Heterogeneous catalysts work by **adsorbing** (weakly bonding) the reactant molecules on the catalyst surface. In the case of iron, it is believed that this adsorption weakens the bonds between the nitrogen and hydrogen atoms in the N_2 and H_2 molecules, to leave separate nitrogen and hydrogen atoms bonded to the metal surface. The reaction between these atoms produces ammonia. Fig 27.33 represents the process.

The use of the heterogeneous catalysts platinum and rhodium in the catalytic converters is described on pages 167 to 169. One of the reactions catalysed by platinum is:

$$2CO(g) + O_2(g) \xrightarrow{\text{Pt catalyst}} 2CO_2(g)$$

Most transition metals make good catalysts because of the availability of 3d and 4s electrons at their surfaces. However, the strength of the weak bonds formed with the reactants and the products is critical. Too strong and the product molecules cannot leave the catalyst surface; too weak and the reactant molecules are not held in place. In many reactions, silver cannot be used as a catalyst because the bonds it forms with reactant molecules are too weak, while tungsten often adsorbs too strongly. The reason why platinum and nickel often make good heterogeneous catalysts relates to the appropriate strength of bond formed during adsorption.

Autocatalysis

Sometimes, catalysts are produced by the reaction itself. This is known as **autocatalysis**. One example is on page 588. Another is the reaction of $MnO_4^-(aq)$ with $C_2O_4^{2-}(aq)$:

$$2MnO_4^-(aq) + 5C_2O_4^{2-}(aq) + 16H^+(aq) \rightarrow$$
$$2Mn^{2+}(aq) + 10CO_2(g) + 8H_2O(l)$$

The reaction is slow to begin with, but speeds up once $Mn^{2+}(aq)$ ions are formed (see Fig 27.34). The $Mn^{2+}(aq)$ is acting as a homogeneous catalyst.

Apart from the iron catalyst, a temperature of 450 °C and a pressure of 250 atmospheres is required for the Haber process. For more details about this reaction, see page 632.

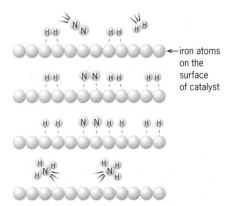

Fig 27.33 **Proposed mechanism for the functioning of the iron catalyst in the Haber process. The nitrogen and hydrogen molecules are adsorbed on the surface of the catalyst. The bonds within the molecules break, leaving separate nitrogen and hydrogen atoms. The atoms then rearrange and form new bonds. The ammonia molecules fly off. This mechanism offers an alternative reaction pathway of lower activation energy**

?

X Why is platinum called a heterogeneous catalyst?

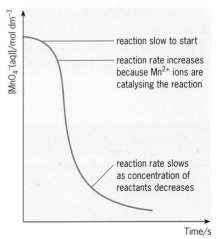

Fig 27.34 **The change of concentration of $MnO_4^-(aq)$ when reacted with $C_2O_4^{2-}(aq)$. This graph is typical of autocatalysed reactions**

?

Y Sketch a graph of the volume of CO_2 produced against time for the reaction of $MnO_4^-(aq)$ with $C_2O_4^{2-}(aq)$.

SUMMARY

After studying this chapter, you should know that:

■ Reaction kinetics is the study of rates of reactions.

■ The rate of a reaction is the change in concentration of a product, or the change in concentration of a reactant, per unit of time.

■ Concentration is indicated by square brackets as in [reactant].

■ The gradient of a graph of reactant (or product) concentration against time gives the rate of the reaction at any particular instant in time. It is usually worked out using tangents. The initial rate is the gradient at time zero.

■ Anything that changes during a reaction, which can be measured, may be used to determine a reaction rate provided that it is proportional in some way to the concentration of a particular reactant or product.

$$\text{Rate of reaction} = k[\text{A}]^m[\text{B}]^n$$

is the rate equation for the reaction:
$$\text{A} + \text{B} \rightarrow \text{C} + \text{D}$$

where m and n are the orders of the reaction with respect to A and B, and k is the rate constant.

■ The overall rate equation must be experimentally determined. It cannot be worked out from the stoichiometric equation.

■ When a reaction is zero order with respect to a reactant, its concentration has no effect on the rate of the reaction.

■ The half-life of a chemical reaction is the time taken for the concentration of a reactant to fall to half of its initial value. First-order reactions have constant half-lives.

■ The series of steps (sometimes called elementary steps) involved in a reaction is called the reaction mechanisms.

■ Rate equations provide evidence for proposed reaction mechanisms.

■ The rate-determining step is the slowest step in a reaction.

■ A unimolecular rate-determining step produces a first-order reaction, while a bimolecular rate-determining step produces a second-order reaction.

■ The collision theory states that reactions can occur only when collisions take place between particles having sufficient energy. This minimum energy is called the activation energy, E_a.

■ The Maxwell–Boltzmann distribution of molecular energies shows that increasing the temperature increases the proportion of molecules which have the activation energy. So, small changes in temperature can cause a large increase in reaction rate.

■ Increasing the temperature increases the rate constant. The relationship between the rate constant and temperature is given by the Arrhenius equation, $k = Ae^{-E_a/RT}$.

■ Increasing the pressure of gases increases the rate of reaction but has no effect on the rate constant.

■ A catalyst provides an alternative reaction mechanism of lower activation energy.

■ There are two types of catalyst: a homogeneous catalyst, which is in the same phase as the reactants, and a heterogeneous catalyst, which is in a different phase.

■ Some reactions are autocatalysed.

QUESTIONS

1 The oxidation of nitrogen monoxide to nitrogen dioxide in car exhausts may involve carbon monoxide and oxygen:

$$\text{NO(g)} + \text{CO(g)} + \text{O}_2\text{(g)} \rightarrow \text{NO}_2\text{(g)} + \text{CO}_2\text{(g)}$$

The rate of this reaction can be followed colorimetrically because $\text{NO}_2\text{(g)}$ is coloured.

a)   **(i)** Use the axes on Fig 27.Q1 to show how the concentration of $\text{NO}_2\text{(g)}$ produced varies with time.

     (ii) Show, with reference to your sketch, how the initial rate of reaction could be deduced.

Fig 27.Q1

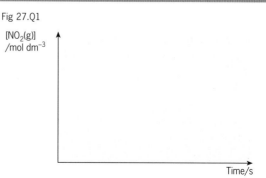

b) The results from a series of experiments are given in Table 27.Q1

Table 27.Q1

Experiment	[NO(g)] /mol dm⁻³	[CO(g)] /mol dm⁻³	[O₂(g)] /mol dm⁻³	Initial rate/mol dm⁻³ s⁻¹
1	1.00×10^{-3}	1.00×10^{-3}	1.00×10^{-1}	4.40×10^{-4}
2	2.00×10^{-3}	1.00×10^{-3}	1.00×10^{-1}	1.76×10^{-3}
3	2.00×10^{-3}	2.00×10^{-3}	1.00×10^{-1}	1.76×10^{-3}
4	4.00×10^{-3}	1.00×10^{-3}	2.00×10^{-1}	7.04×10^{-3}

(i) Deduce the order of reaction with respect to NO(g). Show your reasoning.
(ii) State the order of reaction with respect to CO(g) and O_2(g).
(iii) Write an expression for the rate equation.
(iv) Calculate a value for the rate constant, k. State the units of k.

[UCLES June 1996 Modular Sciences How Far, How Fast?, 4826, q.1]

2 The initial rate of the reaction between substances **A** and **B** was measured in a series of experiments and the following rate equation was deduced.

$$\text{rate} = k[A]^2[B]$$

a) Copy and complete the table of data below for the reaction between **A** and **B**.

Experiment	Initial [A] /mol dm⁻³	Initial [B] /mol dm⁻³	Initial rate of reaction /mol dm⁻³ s⁻¹
1	3.0×10^{-2}	4.0×10^{-2}	1.6×10^{-5}
2	6.0×10^{-2}	4.0×10^{-2}	
3	3.0×10^{-2}		6.4×10^{-5}
4		16.0×10^{-2}	1.6×10^{-5}

(b) Using the data for experiment 1, calculate a value for the rate constant, k, and state its units.

(c) State the effect on the rate constant, k, of increasing the temperature.

(d) State the effect on the rate constant, k, of increasing the concentration of **B** at a fixed temperature.

[NEAB June 1996 Kinetics and Organic Chemistry Module Test, CH03, q.1]

3

a) Copy Fig 27.Q3 and sketch on the axes the reaction profiles (enthalpy level diagrams) for
(i) a single stage exothermic reaction,
(ii) a two-stage reaction in which an intermediate compound is formed, the first stage being endothermic and the overall reaction being exothermic.

Fig 27.Q3   Energy

Progress of reaction (reactants → products)

b) Bromide, bromate(V) and hydrogen ions react according to the following equation:

$$6H^+(aq) + 5Br^-(aq) + BrO_3^-(aq) \rightarrow 3Br_2(aq) + 3H_2O(l)$$

The reaction may be carried out in the presence of small amounts of phenol and methyl orange. When sufficient bromine is formed to use up all the phenol, the methyl orange is decolorised by the bromine. The time taken for this decolorisation may be used to calculate the initial rate of reaction. Results obtained in such an experiment were:

Experiment number	Initial concentration of Br⁻/mol dm⁻³	Initial concentration of H⁺/mol dm⁻³	Initial concentration of BrO₃⁻/mol dm⁻³	Relative initial rate
1	0.00278	0.0333	0.00139	4
2	0.00139	0.0333	0.00139	2
3	0.00278	0.0333	0.00069	2
4	0.00278	0.0167	0.00139	1

(i) Find the order of the reaction with respect to each of the following, giving your reasoning: Br^-, H^+ and BrO_3^-.
(ii) Write a rate equation for the reaction.
(iii) What is the overall order of the reaction?

[ULEAC January 1996 Module Test 2, q.3]

4

a) The rate of reaction between propanone, CH_3COCH_3, and iodine to give iodopropanone, CH_3COCH_2I, is found to be independent of $[I_2]$, but directly proportional to $[H^+]$ and directly proportional to [propanone].
(i) Construct the balanced stoichiometric equation for the overall reaction.
(ii) Write the *rate equation* for this reaction, and state the overall order and the units of the rate constant.
(iii) Suggest with reasons which of the following two possible mechanisms, **A** or **B**, fits the observed kinetic data (**X** and **Y** are intermediates):

$$
\begin{aligned}
CH_3COCH_3 + H^+ &\rightarrow X & \text{(slow)} \\
X + I_2 &\rightarrow \text{products} & \text{(fast)}
\end{aligned}
\Bigg]\ \mathbf{A}
$$

$$
\begin{aligned}
CH_3COCH_3 + I_2 &\rightarrow Y & \text{(slow)} \\
Y + H^+ &\rightarrow \text{products} & \text{(fast)}
\end{aligned}
\Bigg]\ \mathbf{B}
$$

(iv) Describe the roles of I_2 and H^+ in this reaction.
(v) The reaction between propanone and bromine proceeds by a similar mechanism. How would you expect the rate of this reaction to compare with that of the above reaction? Explain your answer.

b) Oxides of nitrogen in the atmosphere contribute to the formation of acid rain by catalysing the oxidation of SO_2 to SO_3. Describe the type of catalysis observed here.
[UCLES June 1997 Paper 1 9254/1, q.2]

5 One reaction which occurs in air polluted with nitrogen oxides is shown below.
$$2NO(g) + O_2(g) \rightarrow 2NO_2(g)$$
Five experiments were carried out to find the relationship between the initial concentration of NO and of O_2, and the initial rate of formation of NO_2.

Experiment	Initial concentrations /mol dm^{-3}		Initial rate of formation of NO_2/mol dm^{-3} s^{-1}
	[NO]	[O_2]	
1	0.001	0.001	7×10^{-6}
2	0.001	0.002	14×10^{-6}
3	0.001	0.003	21×10^{-6}
4	0.002	0.003	84×10^{-6}
5	0.003	0.003	189×10^{-6}

a) What is the order of the reaction with respect to each of the reactants?

b) What equation for the rate-determining step does this suggest?

c) Comment on why this rate-determining step is unusual.
[UCLES June 1996 Paper 2 9254/1, q.4]

6
a) Explain what is meant by the following terms:
  (i) half-life;
  (ii) first order reaction;
  (iii) rate constant as applied to a first-order reaction.

b) The rate of removal of the pain-killing drug paracetamol from the body is a first-order reaction with a rate constant, k, of $0.26 h^{-1}$ [h = hour].
  (i) Calculate the half-life $t_{\frac{1}{2}}$, of the removal of paracetamol from the body using the equation $0.693 = kt_{\frac{1}{2}}$.
  (ii) How long will it take for four half-lives to pass?
  (iii) What percentage of the original dose of paracetamol remains at this time?
  (iv) Suggest a reason why this sort of calculation is important in medicine.
[UCLES December 1995 Paper 3, 9253/3, q.6]

7
a) Aqueous sodium hydroxide can be used to hydrolyse the two isomers. This was investigated experimentally and the following results were obtained.

Table 27.Q7(a) **Data for the hydrolysis of 1-bromobutane**

Experiment	[1-bromobutane] /mol dm^{-3}	[OH$^-$]/mol dm^{-3}	Rate/mol dm^{-3} s^{-1}
A	0.010	0.0050	0.17
B	0.010	0.020	0.68
C	0.020	0.020	1.36

  (i) Use the data in the table above to deduce the order of reaction with respect to each reactant. Justify your deduction in each case.
  (ii) Write the rate equation for the hydrolysis of 1-bromobutane.
  (iii) Calculate a value for the rate constant, k.
  (iv) Suggest, with reasons, the number of particles involved in the rate determining step.

Table 27.Q7(b) **Data for the hydrolysis of 2-bromo-2-methylpropane**

Experiment	[2-bromo-2-methyl-propane]/mol dm^{-3}	[OH$^-$]/mol dm^{-3}	Rate/mol dm^{-3} s^{-1}
D	0.010	0.0050	20.20
E	0.010	0.020	20.19
F	0.020	0.020	40.40

b) **(i)** Use the data in the table above to deduce the order with respect to each reactant and hence write the rate equation for the hydrolysis of 2-bromo-2-methylpropane.
  (ii) Suggest the number of particles involved in the rate determining step.

c) The two isomers, 1-bromobutane and 2-bromo-2-methylpropane, can both be represented by the general formula, R-Br. It is thought that the hydrolysis can proceed by one of two mechanisms.

Mechanism 1
slow step $R-Br + OH^- \rightarrow \left(R \begin{smallmatrix} /Br \\ \backslash OH \end{smallmatrix} \right)^-$

fast step $\left(R \begin{smallmatrix} /OH \\ \backslash Br \end{smallmatrix} \right)^- \rightarrow R-OH + Br^-$

Mechanism 2
slow step $R-Br \rightarrow R^+ + Br^-$
fast step $R^+ + OH^- \rightarrow R-OH$

Suggest and explain whether mechanism 1 or 2 is more likely to represent the hydrolysis of 2-bromo-2-methylpropane.
[UCLES March 1996 Sciences: How Far, How Fast? 4826, q.4]

8
a) With the aid of a sketch of the Boltzmann distribution, explain how both an increase in temperature and the presence of a catalyst increase the rate of a chemical reaction.

b) The reaction below has an activation energy of $+173.2 kJ mol^{-1}$.
    A $H_2(g) + I_2(g) \rightarrow 2HI(g)$; $\Delta H = -9.6 kJ mol^{-1}$
  (i) Calculate the activation energy of the reverse reaction.
    B $2HI(g) \rightarrow H_2(g) + I_2(g)$
  (ii) Predict, with a reason, which reaction, **A** or **B**, will increase more in rate as the temperature is increased.
[UCLES November 1996 Paper 1 9250/1, q.2]

Assignment

REACTION KINETICS AND THE BANNING OF CFCS

In the early 1970s, there was concern that high-flying jet aircraft such as Concorde would damage the stratospheric ozone layer. The ozone layer shields the lower atmosphere and all terrestrial life from harmful ultraviolet radiation. The source of this concern was an understanding of the reaction kinetics of ozone and nitrogen monoxide. One of the mechanisms proposed was:

Step 1 $NO(g) + O_3(g) \xrightarrow{slow} NO_2(g) + O_2(g)$

Step 2 $NO_2(g) + O(g) \xrightarrow{fast} NO(g) + O_2(g)$

The rate equation for this reaction was found to be:

Rate of reaction = $k[NO(g)][O_3(g)]$

Oxygen atoms can form in the stratosphere from molecular oxygen. The energy to break the bonds in the oxygen molecule is provided by ultraviolet radiation:

$$O_2(g) \xrightarrow{hf} O(g) + O(g)$$

1

a) What is meant by the terms *mechanism* and *reaction kinetics*?

b) Explain which of the above steps is the rate-determining step in the reaction between NO and O_3.

c) Explain what is meant by the term *homogeneous catalyst* and decide which species in the mechanism is a homogenous catalyst.

2

a) Work out the stoichiometric equation for the reaction involving NO and O_3.

b) Why is the proposed mechanism consistent with the rate equation?

c) What is the overall order for the reaction and what is the order with respect to each of the following: ozone, atomic oxygen and nitrogen monoxide?

The effect of jet aircraft on the ozone layer was found to be insignificant – there were not enough aircraft to inflict lasting harm. However, in 1973 Professor Sherry Rowland and his colleague Dr Mario Molina began investigating chlorofluorocarbons, or CFCs as they are now known.

Because they were such stable compounds, CFCs were used extensively as aerosol propellants, refrigerants and in insulation foam. So Rowland and Molina decided to find out how long CFC molecules, such as CFC-11 and CFC-12, the two commonest gases (Fig 27.A1), could remain unreacted in the lower atmosphere, and what could happen when they were subjected to the high-energy ultraviolet radiation of the stratosphere. The answer to the first part of their investigation was that, due to their stability, CFCs could remain unreacted for many centuries. It was the answer to the second part which began to excite their interest.

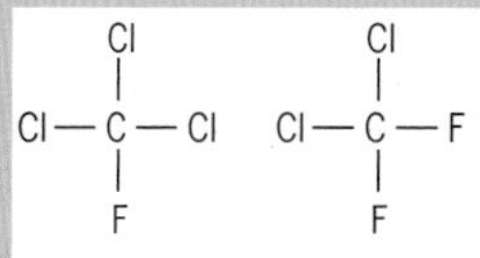

Fig 27.A1

The breakdown of CFCs by ultraviolet radiation produces chlorine atoms:

$$CCl_2F_2 \xrightarrow{hf} CF_2Cl + Cl$$

Rowland and Molina then began to wonder what could happen to the chlorine atoms and concluded that they would react with the ozone, according to the following mechanism:

Step 1 $Cl(g) + O_3(g) \xrightarrow{slow} ClO(g) + O_2(g)$

Step 2 $ClO(g) + O(g) \xrightarrow{fast} Cl(g) + O_2(g)$

3

a) Predict a rate equation from the mechanism involving chlorine atoms.

b) Work out the stoichiometric equation.

4

Ozone can react with NO or with Cl. The activation energy for step 1 involving chlorine atoms is $2\,kJ\,mol^{-1}$, and the activation energy for step 1 involving nitrogen monoxide is $12\,kJ\,mol^{-1}$.

a) What is meant by the term activation energy?

b) Which is the more effective catalyst, NO or Cl?

c) Which reaction has the greater rate constant - the reaction with NO or that with Cl?

d) Explain how Cl acts as a catalyst.

5

Predict a rate equation for the chlorine-atom-catalysed destruction of ozone.

On average, one chlorine atom can destroy 100 000 ozone molecules. Such destructive power is awesome when related to the millions of tonnes of CFCs that had been produced up to the time of Rowland and Molina's research.

When they calculated the likely effect on the ozone layer, they could not believe their figures. They consulted Hal Johnson, who had done many calculations of the effect on the ozone layer of nitrogen monoxide from high-flying aircraft. He too knew that chlorine atoms could react with ozone, but did not realise what the source of chlorine atoms might be. This confirmed Molina and Rowland's results and in 1974 they published their predictions in the scientific journal *Nature*.

The United States were quick to ban the production of CFCs, but many countries, amongst them Britain, France and Japan, did not, and continued with production.

However, in 1985 the British scientist Joe Farman and his team, who were working in the Antarctic, discovered huge losses in the ozone layer. This led to concerted international action to ban the production of CFCs world-wide.

Fig 27.A2 **Sherwood Rowland receives his Nobel Prize from Sweden's King Carl Gustaf in 1995**

In 1995, Sherwood Rowland and his colleague Mario Molina were awarded the Nobel Prize for Chemistry. They shared it with Paul Crutzen, a Dutch chemist, who had demonstrated a link between soil bacteria and the production of dinitrogen oxide gas, N_2O. This gas also reacts in the stratosphere to form nitrogen monoxide (NO):

$$N_2O(g) + O \rightarrow 2NO(g)$$

6 Why do scientists publish their findings in journals? The research of Rowland and Molina can be classed as pure research, as there was no apparent commercial benefit. Much of the funding for science is for targeted research. This type of research is designed to yield commercial benefit and to find useful applications.

7 Choose another scientific discovery or invention and decide whether it was the product of pure or targeted research. If you were in charge of Britain's scientific budget, what proportion would you devote to pure research? Explain your reasoning.

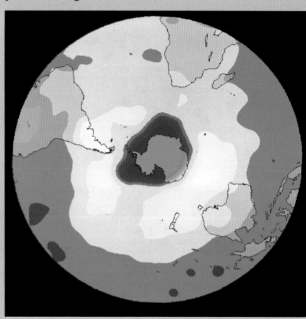

Fig 27.A3 **The hole in the ozone layer over Antarctica**

There is more information on ozone and CFCs on page 223.

REACTION KINETICS

Experimental studies on the rate of chemical reactions allow reaction mechanisms to be predicted. This chapter describes the effect of concentration, temperature, surface area and catalysts on the rate of a reaction, and uses collision theory to explain these factors. Use the Chapter Map to identify the main concepts and how these concepts have been developed in other chapters.

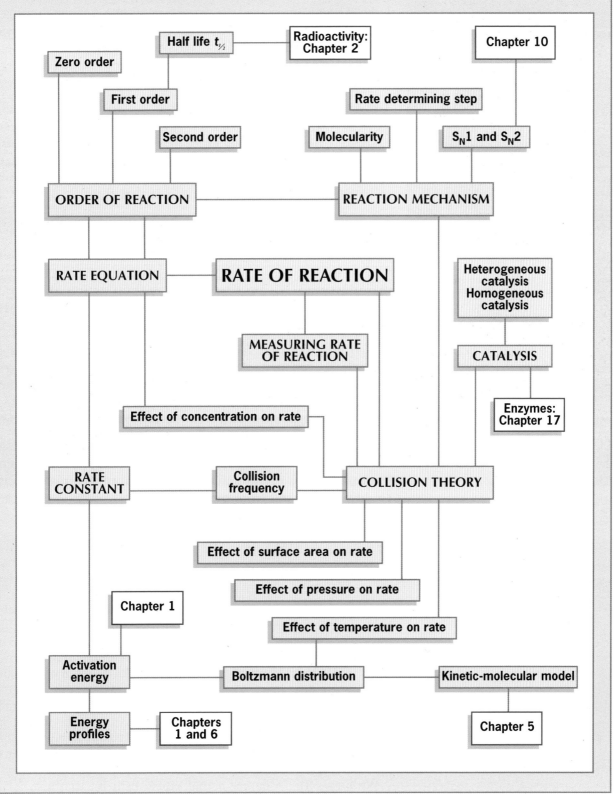

28 Colour in organic and inorganic compounds

Denim jeans seem to be here to stay

THE BLUE OF DENIM JEANS has a long and colourful history. Levi Strauss emigrated to America in 1850 during the gold rush, taking with him some heavy cotton canvas called *serge de Nîmes*. Instead of making tents with the canvas, he used the hard-wearing cloth to make trousers for the gold miners. This was the start of a multi-million pound industry.

The blue dye Levi Strauss used was indigo, which has been used as a dye for at least 3000 years. In 1850, all dyes were extracted from plants or animals, and indigo came almost exclusively from indigo-bearing plants grown in huge plantations in India. The indigo market brought in a revenue of £4 000 000 per annum, a fortune at that time.

Six years after Strauss dyed his first pairs of denim jeans, a chance discovery in England by William Perkin led to the world's first synthetic dye. In 1880, Adolph von Baeyer synthesised indigo, and by 1897 synthetic indigo was being manufactured. Within a few years the cultivation of natural indigo had ceased, wiping out one of India's major export industries.

Indigo is a dye that fades, and during the first half of the twentieth century, its popularity waned as chemists synthesised new dyes which did not fade. However, in the 1960s blue denim jeans came back into fashion. The fact that synthetic indigo fades with wear became part of its attraction.

The synthesis of indigo is a chemical success story, with chemists first determining indigo's structure, and then finding ways to manufacture it much more cheaply than it could be extracted from plants.

1 WHY ARE THINGS COLOURED?

Colours play an enormous part in your life. Your eyes detect the colours of objects and send messages to your brain, providing you with a constant stream of information. The colour of traffic lights helps to control traffic flow and the blue flashing light of the emergency services alerts you to their presence. The colour of a food determines how appetising it appears and may indicate how fresh it is. The colours of your clothes make a statement about your personality.

Advertisers are well aware of how we are influenced by colours. They use warm colours such as orange and red to make us feel at home with a product, whereas blue is a colder colour giving the hint of sophistication. Whether we realise it or not we are very influenced every waking moment by colour. So just what is colour?

We know from Chapter 3 that visible light is electromagnetic radiation with wavelengths between approximately 400 nm and 700 nm. Visible light forms a very small part of the electromagnetic spectrum. Isaac Newton, in 1666, was the first to realise that what we perceive as white light (such as sunlight) is in fact made up of seven colours – red, orange, yellow, green, blue, indigo and violet. These seven colours form the visible spectrum shown in Fig 28.1.

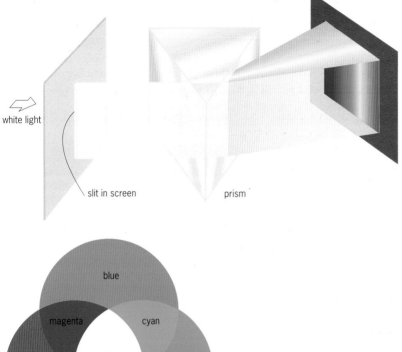

white light

slit in screen   prism

Fig 28.1 **The visible part of the electromagnetic spectrum is formed by passing light through a prism**

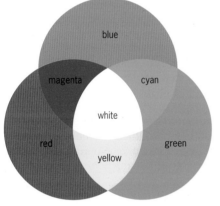

Fig 28.2 **Mixing coloured light produces secondary colours and white light**

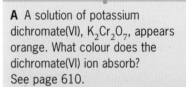

A A solution of potassium dichromate(VI), $K_2Cr_2O_7$, appears orange. What colour does the dichromate(VI) ion absorb? See page 610.

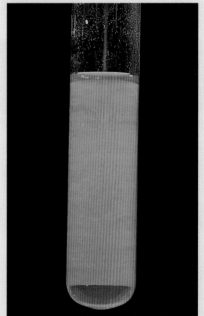

Fig 28.4 **Potassium dichromate(VI) solution**

Newton passed sunlight through a prism to obtain the visible spectrum. He also demonstrated that when this spectrum of colours passed through a second prism it produced white light once more. One hundred and fifty years later, Thomas Young and George Palmer independently suggested that receptors in our eyes were sensitive to blue, green or red light and that different stimulation of these three colour receptors (now called cones) enabled us to perceive all the different colours. In 1861, James Clerk Maxwell, a scots physicist, combined beams of these three coloured lights to produce white light.

The three colours – blue, green and red – are called **additive primary colours** because they cannot be produced by the combination of other coloured lights. However yellow can be made from the addition of green and red lights, cyan from green and blue lights and magenta from red and blue (Fig 28.2). Yellow, cyan and magenta are called **secondary colours**. Colour televisions make use of the three additive primary colours. The inside of the screen is coated with about a million phosphor dots which glow either blue, red or green when they are struck by an electron beam. These dots combine to form coloured images.

You can read about receptors in the eye on page 250.

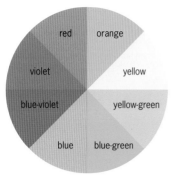

Fig 28.3 **A colour wheel. Complementary colours are opposite one another on this colour wheel**

See question 1. ■

The reason why the world appears so colourful is that the multitude of chemical compounds around us absorb and reflect different wavelengths from the light that falls onto them. For example, a leaf appears green because it absorbs red light and reflects light of other wavelengths. A substance that is white reflects all visible wavelengths of electromagnetic radiation. However, a substance that appears black absorbs all visible wavelengths. A substance appears coloured if it absorbs some of the electromagnetic radiation from white light, but not all of it.

When a compound absorbs wavelengths of one particular colour, a **complementary** colour appears. Pairs of complementary colours are represented on the colour wheel in Fig 28.3. The coloured wavelengths that are absorbed lie opposite their complementary colours. For example, crystals of hydrated copper(II) sulphate appear blue because they absorb light in the orange region of the spectrum.

DYES AND PIGMENTS

DYES AND PIGMENTS DIFFER in one important way: dyes are soluble in the medium in which they are applied and pigments are insoluble. Dyes and pigments have been used by humans since early times. Some cave paintings discovered in southern France and northern Spain are up to 30 000 years old. The artists of these paintings used mineral pigments to colour them. Iron(III) oxide provided the red colour; iron(II) carbonate provided the yellow colour; either soot or manganese(IV) oxide were used for black. The pigments were applied to surfaces by first mixing them into a paste using mud or oil. Neanderthal tribes painted the bodies of their dead using iron(III) oxide, also known as red ochre. The Ancient Egyptians used some chemical reactions to extend the range of pigments available. For example red lead, Pb_3O_4, was produced by heating together lead and white lead, $PbCO_3.Pb(OH)_2$.

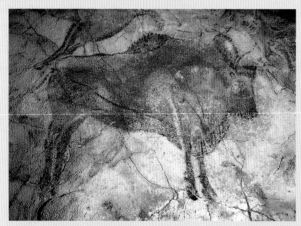

Fig 28.5 **The prehistoric painting of a bison in the caves at Altamira, northern Spain**

Pigments are spread as a surface layer in paints and in coloured plastic articles. Pigments are dispersed throughout the plastic. Until the nineteenth century, nearly all pigments were inorganic. Artists' paints used to contain lead and chromium compounds but they are now known to pose a health hazard. They have been replaced by safer red and yellow organic pigments that can been synthesised.

In contrast to pigments, dyes are soluble. Dye molecules attach themselves to the molecules of the substance they are colouring. In some cases, dye molecules use ionic or covalent bonds, but more usually they attach themselves by hydrogen bonds or induced dipole–induced dipole forces (van der Waals forces or non-polar forces). Sometimes a fabric is first treated with a mordant, an intermediate substance which bonds to the fabric and to the dye. The mordant most commonly used in ancient times was potassium aluminium sulphate (also called potash alum) but other metal salts were also used. The metal ions bonded to the fabric and – through the formation of complexes – to the dye molecules. Potassium aluminium sulphate may have been the first chemical to be purified to avoid contaminants, such as iron(III) salts, which introduced other colours into the dyeing process.

The dyeing of fabrics has a very long history and until the end of the nineteenth century dyes came from animals or plants. This meant that colouring clothes could be an expensive business. One of the most highly prized dyes in the days of the Roman Empire was Tyrian purple. A quarter of a million Mediterranean molluscs were required to produce just 30 g of the dye. Only members of the Emperor's family could wear togas dyed with Tyrian purple, so it became known as royal purple.

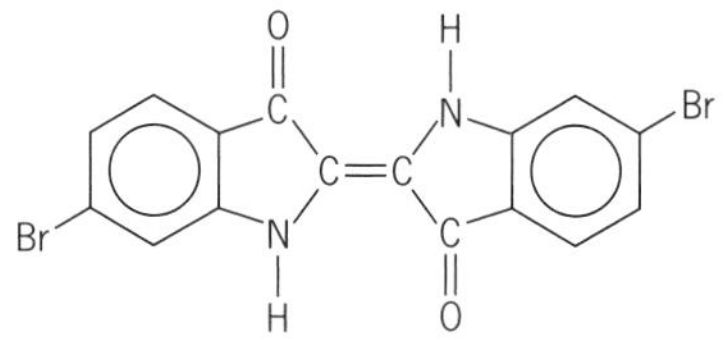

Fig 28.6(a) **The structural formula of Tyrian purple**

Early Britons used the woad plant to dye their clothes blue. This contained the chemical indigo. Three thousand years ago, Mexicans started using a red dye, cochineal, produced from crushing the Coccus insect. It was not until the sixteenth century that the Spanish brought cochineal to Europe. The production of this dye was a painstaking process which involved collecting about 150 000 insects by hand for every kilogram of dye produced.

Another red dye, alizarin, came from the roots of the madder plant. This red dye was used by the Ancient Egyptians and was very widely cultivated. One of the reasons why many military uniforms were red was the availability of this dye and the fact that it did not fade very quickly in sunlight.

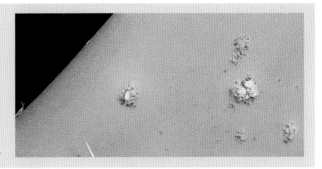

Fig 28.6(b) **The insects that provide cochineal dye are tiny**

Flame tests and atomic emission spectroscopy

You have probably done some flame tests on inorganic compounds yourself. The presence of certain metal ions gives rise to characteristic colours. In Fig 28.7 you can see the characteristic flame colour due to the potassium cation, showing that the substance being tested must contain a potassium compound. Table 28.1 gives the characteristic flame colours of some other cations.

Fig 28.7 **The lilac colour indicates that the compound in the flame contains potassium**

Table 28.1 **Characteristic flame colours of metal ions in Groups 1 and 2**

Group 1:

Metal ion	Flame colour
Li^+	deep red
Na^+	yellow
K^+	lilac
Rb^+	red
Cs^+	blue

Group 2:

Metal ion	Flame colour
Be^{2+}	no colour
Mg^{2+}	no colour
Ca^{2+}	brick red
Sr^{2+}	deep red
Ba^{2+}	apple green

In Chapter 3, we said that flame colours were due to electron transitions. The energy from the Bunsen flame causes electrons in the cation to jump up to higher energy levels by absorbing amounts of energy. As they fall back down to their original energy levels they each release a certain amount of energy. If the energy corresponds to a frequency (and wavelength) in the visible spectrum, then a colour is observed. You will notice from Table 28.1 that some Group 2 cations do not produce a coloured flame. Many ions do not emit light with frequencies in the visible part of the spectrum so these do not colour the flame.

When viewed through a spectroscope, the flame colour produced by a particular cation gives rise to a series of coloured lines. This series of lines is called a **line emission spectrum**. Other emission lines are found in other parts of the spectrum such as the ultraviolet and infrared. A line emission spectrum is characteristic of a particular cation and it can be used to identify elements in compounds rather like fingerprints can be used to identify individuals. It is possible to determine the amount of an element present in a sample by measuring the intensities of the different emission lines in its spectrum.

If bright white light shining onto a coloured flame is observed through a spectroscope, a series of black lines result, forming a **line absorption spectrum**. The metal ions in the flame remove the frequencies from the white light which they would normally emit when excited.

Remember that $E = h \times f$, where E is energy, h is Planck's constant and f is the frequency. Light is electromagnetic radiation; you can read more about the nature of electromagnetic radiation in Chapter 3

■ See question 2.

You can see some line emission spectra on page 50.

Emission spectrum

Increasing wavelength/λ ⟶

Absorption spectrum

Increasing wavelength/λ ⟶

Fig 28.8 **Emission and absorption spectra for sodium. Notice that the frequencies are the same in the emission and absorption spectra because electrons absorb photons of a particular frequency when they get excited and release photons of the same frequency when they return to their ground state**

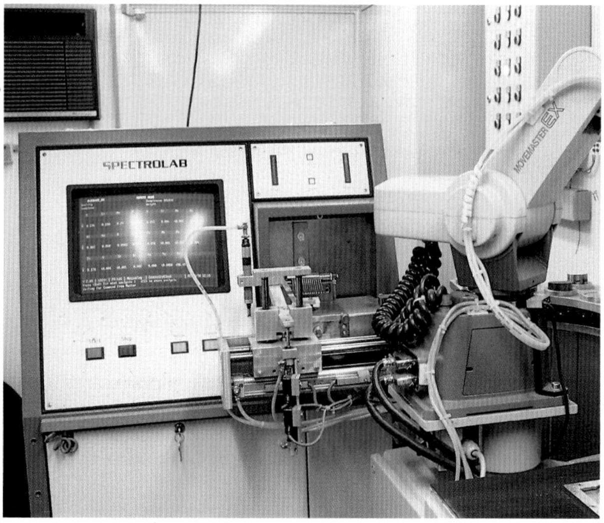

Atomic emission spectroscopy is used in the steel manufacturing process to determine the composition of different steels. Up to 20 elements are used in steels; the amount and presence of these elements has a profound effect on the properties of a particular steel. Atomic emission spectroscopy is also used to monitor the levels of potassium and sodium in blood.

Fig 28.9 **Atomic emission spectrometers are used in the steel industry to determine the presence and percentage content of certain elements in steel**

You can read more about steel manufacture on page 13.

You can read more about Perkin's discovery of mauve in the Feature box on page 606.

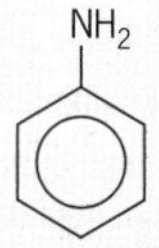

Fig 28.10 **The structural formula of phenylamine**

?

B What is meant by the term functional group?

For more information on functional groups see page 151.

You can find out more about delocalisation on page 272.

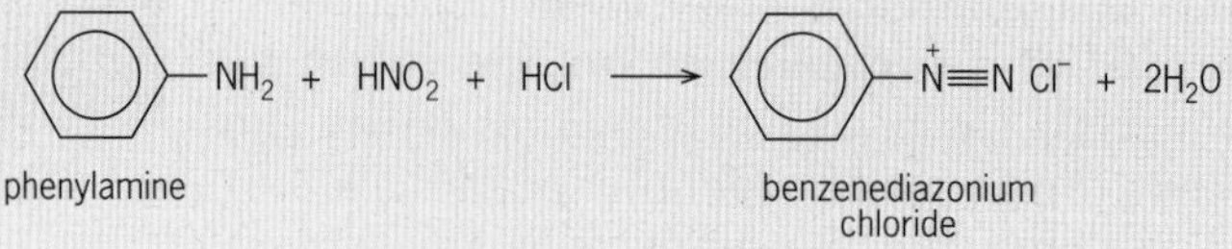

?

C Write the equations for the production of nitrous acid and the diazonium salt using sulphuric acid.

---

2 DIAZONIUM COMPOUNDS AND AZO DYES

The first synthetic dye, **mauve**, was accidentally discovered in 1856 by an eighteen-year-old Englishman, William Perkin. Perkin's discovery led to a search for new dyes and prompted the start of the organic chemical industry. One of the chemicals Perkin used in the production of mauve was phenylamine (Fig 28.10).

Phenylamine is an aromatic amine (arylamine). It has a benzene ring with an NH_2 amino functional group.

Diazotisation

Six years after the discovery of mauve, Johann Peter Griess used aromatic amines to produce **diazonium compounds** (also known as **diazonium salts**). Diazonium compounds are produced when nitrous acid, HNO_2, reacts with an aromatic amine. The reaction mixture must be kept below 5 °C because the diazonium salt is unstable. Nitrous acid is also unstable and it has to be made in situ by reacting sodium nitrite with concentrated hydrochloric acid:

$$NaNO_2(aq) + HCl(aq) \rightarrow HNO_2(aq) + NaCl(aq)$$

The nitrous acid reacts with the aryl amine and more of the concentrated hydrochloric acid to give the diazonium salt:

phenylamine + HNO_2 + HCl → benzenediazonium chloride + $2H_2O$

This reaction is called a **diazotisation**. The usual way to carry out this reaction in the laboratory is to add a cold aqueous solution of sodium nitrite to a solution of phenylamine dissolved in concentrated hydrochloric acid. The reaction mixture is kept below 5 °C by using ice.

The benzene ring stabilises the diazonium ion by **delocalisation** of its electrons. Alkylamines, such as ethylamine ($C_2H_5NH_2$), produce diazonium salts which decompose immediately even below 5 °C.

Above 5 °C, the solution of benzenediazonium compound rapidly decomposes, giving off nitrogen gas according to the equation:

$$C_6H_5N_2^+Cl^- + H_2O \rightarrow C_6H_5OH + N_2 + HCl$$

The production of azo dyes using coupling reactions

A diazonium ion may act as an **electrophile** and attack the benzene ring of another compound. This reaction is called a **coupling reaction**. The first coupling reaction was observed by Griess: an aromatic amine coupled with a diazonium salt to produce a stable **azo compound**.

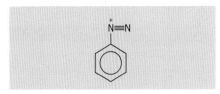

Fig 28.11 **The benzenediazonium ion**

D Why are solid benzenediazonium compounds explosive?
Hint: think about the relative volumes of solid and gas produced on decomposition.

phenylamine

yellow azo dye

In the 1870s, coupling reactions involving alkaline solutions of phenols were first observed (Fig 28.12).

Remember that an **electrophile** is a species which accepts a lone pair of electrons to form a covalent bond. It is attracted to an electron rich centre. See pages 253 and 277.

phenol

orange azo dye

Fig 28.12(a) **The coupling reaction of a diazonium salt with an alkaline solution of phenol**

?

E (a) Why must a diazo coupling reaction be carried out below 5 °C?

(b) What happens to phenol molecules when they react with aqueous sodium hydroxide? Draw the structure of the species produced. Hint: Look back to page 239 to help you answer this question.

(c) Why is the species you have drawn in (b) more reactive with electrophiles than benzene?

Fig 28.12(b) **The orange azo dye produced when benzenediazonium chloride couples with phenol**

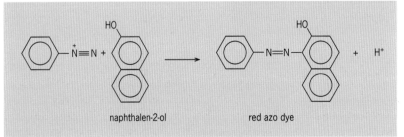

naphthalen-2-ol

red azo dye

Fig 28.12(c) **The coupling reaction of a diazonium salt with alkaline naphthalen-2-ol**

The functional group of an azo compound is the azo group, –N=N–. In a compound R–N=N–R′, if the R groups are aromatic (aryl) groups, the azo group becomes part of the delocalised systems of the adjoining benzene rings. This gives extra stability to the molecule and is also responsible for the bright colours of azo dyes.

■ See questions 3 and 4.

PERKIN AND THE START OF THE DYESTUFFS INDUSTRY

WILLIAM PERKIN WAS the son of a carpenter in East London. Having some artistic talent, his father hoped William would train as an architect. However, a fascination with chemistry led to him to become a student at the Royal College of Chemistry. At the age of eighteen he made an accidental discovery that was to prove to be the start of not only of the dyestuffs industry but also the whole organic chemicals industry.

Fig 28.13 **William Henry Perkin (1838–1907) and the original bottle of dye that he produced**

At the Royal College of Chemistry, Perkin became an assistant of Professor August von Hofmann, a German chemist. Hofmann suggested that he might like to try synthesising the important, naturally occurring drug quinine which was used to treat malaria. The starting material was coal tar because it was known to contain arylamines.

At this time, the structures of organic chemicals had not been deduced. However, the molecular formula of quinine was known, as was the empirical formula of the arylamine he intended to use. Perkin thought that if he oxidised the arylamine he would produce the reaction:

$$2C_{10}H_{13}N + 3[O] \rightarrow \underset{\text{quinine}}{C_{20}H_{24}N_2O_2} + H_2O$$

All Perkin managed to produce was a dirty brown precipitate. Undeterred, he set about oxidising a simpler compound, phenylamine. This time he produced a black precipitate which, when dried and dissolved in ethanol, produced a brilliant purple solution. The product's structure was nothing like that of quinine, but Perkin was quick to see its potential as a dye. He dyed some silk with the purple dye and sent it to a firm of dyers.

The reply came back, 'If your discovery does not make the goods too expensive, it is decidedly one of the most valuable that has come out for a very long time.'

One of the most important properties of the dye was that it was 'fast' – it didn't fade or change colour even when exposed to light and air. Perkin named the dye mauve after a French flower.

He left the Royal College of Chemistry and with the help of his father and brother set about building a factory for the large-scale production of mauve. Perkin used coal tar as the starting material because it was a cheap, plentiful by-product of the coal gas industry. Fig 28.14 shows the steps involved in his synthesis of mauve.

He produced benzene by fractionally distilling coal tar. He then nitrated the benzene to produce nitrobenzene. The nitrobenzene was reduced using a mixture of iron filings and ethanoic acid to form phenylamine. This phenylamine he then oxidised using acidified potassium dichromate(VI).

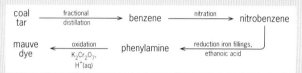

Fig 28.14 **A flow chart showing Perkin's synthesis of mauve**

Queen Victoria wore a dress dyed with mauve to the International Exhibition of 1862. *Punch*, the satirical magazine proclaimed that policeman could be heard telling people to 'get a mauve on!'

It was not long before other dyes of different colours were made using phenylamine. Although the synthesis of dyes began in England, Germany soon became the centre of the dyestuffs industry. Perkin's

mauve was superseded because it cost too much to produce. One of its last applications was in the production of the stamp shown in Fig 28.15(a).

Fig 28.15(a) **The 1d stamp printed in 1881 was dyed with Perkin's mauve**

At the age of 36 Perkin sold his factory and returned to his first love, chemistry research. He made many important contributions to organic chemistry including the production of a perfume from coal tar. However, the synthesis of the quinine molecule was not finally achieved until 1944, almost 90 years after Perkin's attempt.

Fig 28.15(b) **A sketch by William Perkin of his first synthetic dye factory which made Perkin's mauve**

F (a) What reagents are used to nitrate benzene?

(b) Perkin use ethanoic acid and iron filings to produce phenylamine from nitrobenzene. What reagents are used to produce phenylamine from nitrobenzene in the laboratory?

G (a) If a substance reflects all light with frequencies in the visible range of the spectrum, what colour will it be?

(b) If a substance absorbs all the radiation in the visible spectrum, what colour will it be?

If you have trouble answering these questions, see page 280.

Colour in organic molecules

What gives rise to the bright colours of azo dyes? We have already seen on page 610 that colour is due to electron transitions. If a substance absorbs electromagnetic radiation with frequencies in the visible spectrum then it will be coloured. This is because the substance reflects or transmits only part of the visible spectrum.

The absorption of a photon (a quantum of electromagnetic radiation) causes an electron to jump from its **ground state** (the lowest possible energy level) to an **excited state** (a higher energy level). If the difference in energy between the ground state and the excited state is equivalent to a photon with a frequency (or wavelength) in the visible part of the spectrum, the substance will absorb at that frequency when white light falls on it. Only outer-shell electrons are excited by visible and ultraviolet radiation. Electrons from inner shells are held much more firmly by the nucleus, so they require much more energy to become excited.

Remember that $E = h \times f$, where E is the energy of the photon, h is Planck's constant and f is the frequency of radiation. A photon with a particular energy has a corresponding frequency. You can read more about photons and the excitation of electrons in Chapter 3.

Different types of energy levels in organic molecules

On page 81, we discussed how atoms bond together by the overlap of atomic orbitals to form covalent bonds. A **σ bond** (sigma bond) forms when two atomic orbitals overlap at one point. There is always a σ bond between two covalently bonded atoms.

Double and triple bonds consist of not only a σ bond, but also π bonds (pi bonds). π bonds form by the sideways overlap of p orbitals. A π bond is usually at a higher energy level than a σ bond.

Scientists have taken the concept of overlapping atomic orbitals a bit further in the **molecular orbital model**. This is based on advanced mathematics and involves treating electrons as waves.

When two atomic orbitals overlap they form two molecular orbitals and each of these is capable of holding two electrons just as atomic orbitals do. One is called a **bonding molecular orbital** and the other is called an **antibonding molecular orbital**. The bonding orbital is at a lower energy than the individual atomic orbitals, so it is energetically favourable to bonding. The antibonding orbital draws electrons away from between the two positive nuclei of the covalent

bond, and this is energetically unfavourable to bonding. An antibonding orbital is therefore at a higher energy level than both the bonding orbital and the atomic orbitals that formed it.

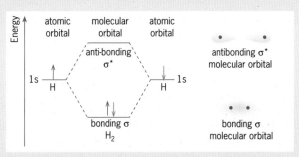

Fig 28.16 **When two 1s atomic orbitals combine in the H₂ molecule, two molecular orbitals form. One increases the electron density between the two nuclei and is called a bonding σ orbital. The high electron density attracts the two positive nuclei and holds them together.**
The antibonding σ* orbital tends to remove electrons from between the nuclei and is at a higher energy level.

You can see this in Fig 28.16, where we consider the formation of two σ molecular orbitals. An anti-bonding molecular orbital is always denoted with an asterisk, in this case σ*.

Notice that the Pauli exclusion principle still applies and a maximum of two electrons, of opposite spin, can occupy a molecular orbital. See Chapter 3 if you need to remind yourself of the Pauli exclusion principle.

When two p orbitals overlap sideways to form a π bond, a π (bonding) molecular orbital and a π* (antibonding) molecular orbital result. The electrons which are not involved in bonding are the non-bonding pairs (the lone pairs). These are in **n (non-bonding) orbitals**. Fig 28.17 is an energy level diagram of the various bonding, non-bonding, and antibonding orbitals.

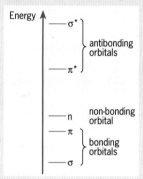

Fig 28.17 **The energy levels of σ, π, n, σ* and π* orbitals**

Electron transitions in organic molecules

When electrons are excited, a number of transitions are possible. The compound's colour or lack of colour depends on which transitions are taking place. For example, a transition from σ to σ* in ethane gas absorbs in the ultraviolet part of the electromagnetic spectrum and not in the visible range. Therefore, ethane is colourless. Halogenomethanes, such as CH_3Cl, also appear colourless. Electrons may be excited from n to σ* orbitals so the compounds absorb in the ultraviolet part of the spectrum. However azo dyes absorb within the visible region of the spectrum with n to π* electron transitions. π to π* transitions may take place in the visible or ultraviolet regions and they often occur in aromatic compounds.

Conjugated systems of bonds

Ethene has a double bond which comprises one σ bond and one π bond. The π bond is restricted to the two carbon atoms (Fig 28.18).

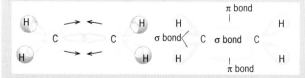

Fig 28.18 **Bonding in ethene. A π bond is formed by the sideways overlap of the p orbitals**

However, in buta-1,3-diene, $CH_2=CH-CH=CH_2$, there are two double bonds. The p orbitals can

overlap so that the two π bonds interact with one another forming a delocalised system. We say that the system is **conjugated**. Conjugated systems have alternating double and single bonds and the delocalisation that occurs lowers the energy of the π to π* transitions.

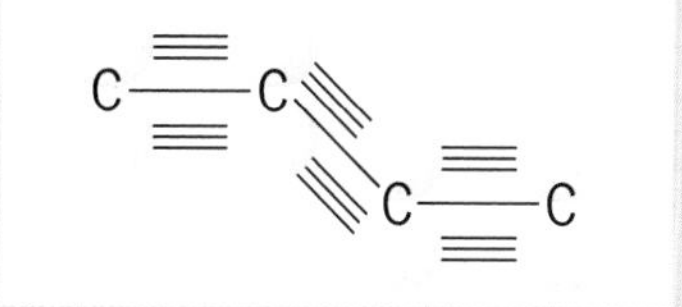

Fig 28.19 **Conjugation in buta-1,3-diene**

Although buta-1,3-diene absorbs in the ultraviolet region, its maximum absorption wavelength, λ_{max}, is 220 nm (compared with 185 nm in ethene) and the **intensity** of absorption also increases. The intensity depends on how many photons are absorbed from the radiation falling on the substance.

Carotene (Fig 28.20) is a vitamin found in carrots and it is used as a food colorant. Its conjugated system involves 11 double bonds and this shifts its maximum absorption into the blue part of the visible spectrum. Because blue light is removed from the white light falling on carotene it appears orange. The part of a molecule responsible for absorbing coloured radiation is called the **chromophore**. It is usually an extended delocalised electron system.

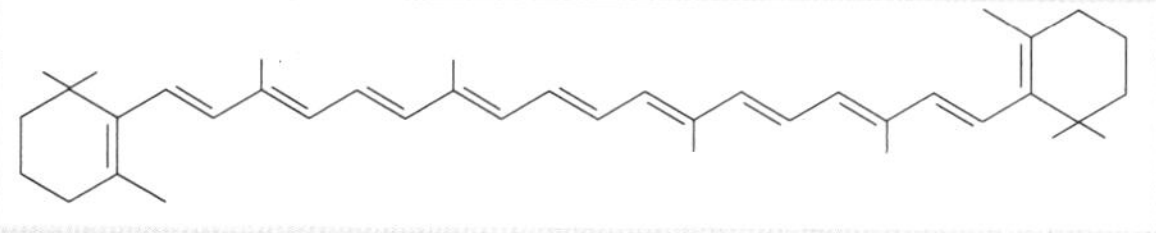

Fig 28.20 **The skeletal formula of carotene showing its extended conjugated system which forms the chromophore**

Orange is the complementary colour to blue. Refer back to the colour wheel on page 610 to remind yourself about complementary colours.

Colour in azo compounds

The first commercially successful azo dye was Chrysoidine (Fig 28.21). The azo group, –N=N–, acts as a 'delocalisation bridge' between the two benzene rings, forming an extended delocalised system which is the chromophore.

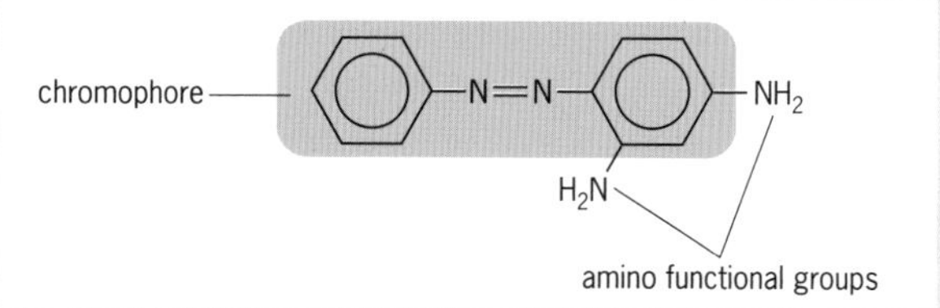

Fig 28.21 **Chrysoidine, an orange azo dye**

The two amine functional groups of Chrysoidine have lone pairs of electrons on the nitrogen atoms.

These lone pairs interact with the delocalised system. The nature of the functional groups which interact with the chromophore can dramatically alter the colour of the azo dye molecule by causing a shift in the electrons of the chromophore. This electron shift alters the energy required to promote them into an excited state and so shifts the wavelength of light absorbed. A group attached to the chromophore that alters the wavelength of colour is called an **auxochrome**. A shift towards longer wavelengths (towards the red end of the visible spectrum) is called a **bathochromic shift**, while a shift towards shorter wavelengths (towards blue) is called a **hipsochromic shift**.

?

H In which region of the electromagnetic spectrum does Chrysoidine absorb?

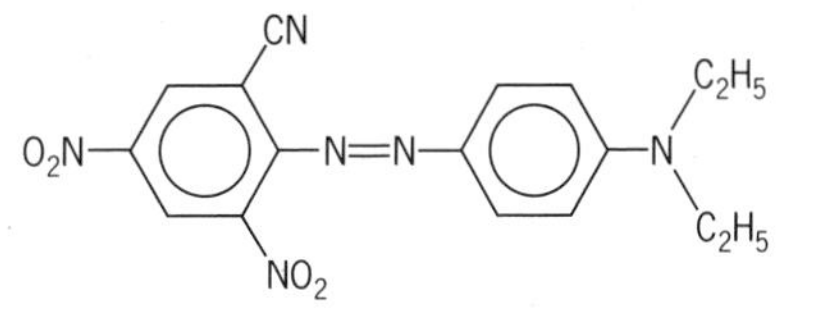

Fig 28.22 **Blue azo dye. The substituent groups on the left of the molecule tend to accept electrons while those on the right are electron-donating groups. This shifts the electrons of the chromophore considerably, making the molecule appear blue.**

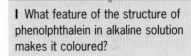

pH indicators

Methyl orange is an azo compound that has different colours depending on the pH of the solution it is in. This property means that it is used as an indicator in acid–base reactions. Adding or removing an H$^+$ ion causes an electron shift in the molecule, altering the wavelength at which methyl orange absorbs.

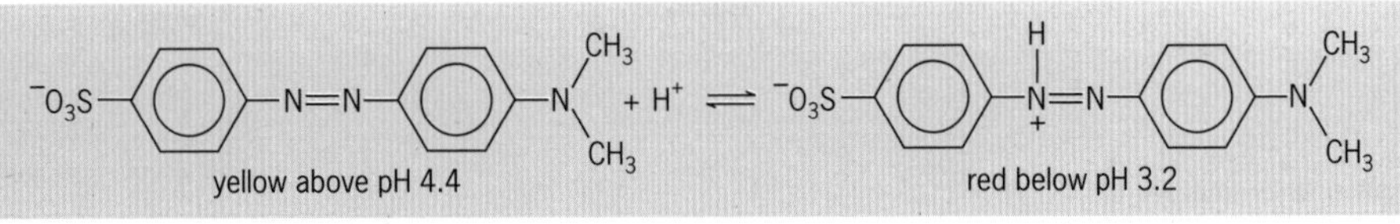

yellow above pH 4.4   red below pH 3.2

Fig 28.23 **Methyl orange is used as an acid–base indicator. Its colour depends on the pH of the solution it is in.**

On page 321, we saw that indicators change colour depending on the concentration of H$^+$(aq) ions in the solution. Each indicator changes colour at a specific pH; using the correct indicator, any neutralisation reaction can be monitored to its end point. Methyl orange changes colour between pH 3.2 and pH 4.4. It can be used to determine the neutralisation point of a strong acid and a weak base.

Phenolphthalein is colourless below pH 8.2, but above this value it changes to. purple. This indicator can be used in titrations with strong alkalis and weak acids.

?

I What feature of the structure of phenolphthalein in alkaline solution makes it coloured?

■ See questions 1 and 6.

Fig 28.24 **The ultraviolet–visible spectra of phenolphthalein at pH 1 and pH 13. You can read about how to interpret these spectra in the next section**

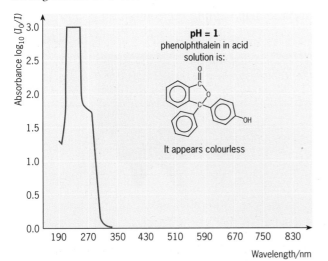

pH = 1
phenolphthalein in acid solution is:

It appears colourless

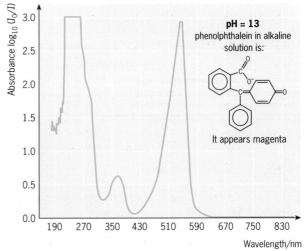

pH = 13
phenolphthalein in alkaline solution is:

It appears magenta

Ultraviolet and visible spectroscopy

In Chapter 9, we discussed two types of spectroscopy which involve absorption of electromagnetic radiation by a substance under investigation. In infrared spectroscopy, light is absorbed in the infrared part of the spectrum, due to the increased vibration of different bonds within a molecule. In nuclear magnetic resonance spectroscopy, radio waves are absorbed due to the excitation of nuclei within molecules.

Ultraviolet and visible spectroscopy is possible because outer electrons of atoms or ions in compounds absorb in the ultraviolet or visible part of the spectrum when they are excited. Compounds which absorb *only* in the ultraviolet part of the spectrum are colourless. In the spectrometer, a beam of electromagnetic radiation passes through a monochromator which selects varying wavelengths. The beam is then split and one beam passes through a solution of the substance under investigation, while the other passes through the pure solvent.

J (a) Why is the ideal solvent in an ultraviolet/visible spectrometer one which does not absorb in the ultraviolet/visible range?

(b) Why is it rare to find a solvent which is ideal?

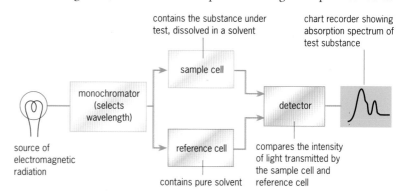

Fig 28.25 **A simplified schematic diagram of how an ultraviolet/visible spectrometer works**

The spectra produced usually have broad absorption bands, in contrast to atomic absorption spectra where gaseous atoms and ions have definite sharp lines. The broad absorption bands occur because in solution a number of vibrational and rotational energy levels are possible for each energy level of the electrons. You can read more about vibrational and rotational energy levels on page 187.

Interpreting ultraviolet/visible absorption spectra

The horizontal axis of an ultraviolet/visible absorption spectrum gives the wavelength in nanometres (nm). The wavelength at which maximum absorption occurs is λ_{max}. The shape of the absorption peak is usually characteristic of a particular compound and so the spectrum can be used to help identify the compound.

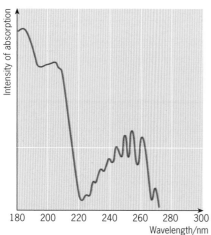

Fig 28.26 **The ultraviolet/visible absorption spectrum of benzene. Notice that all the absorption appears in the UV part of the spectrum so the compound appears colourless**

Atomic absorption spectra are described on pages 55 and 612.

Fig 28.27 **The absorption spectrum of a blue dye. Red, orange and yellow light is absorbed by the dye, so blue light is transmitted. (See the colour wheel on page 610)**

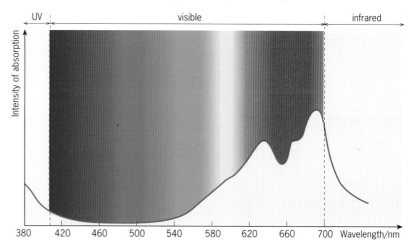

However, a more common use of this type of spectroscopy is to measure concentrations accurately from the intensity of absorption on the *y*-axis. For example, the uptake of a drug at different sites around the body can be monitored using ultraviolet/visible spectroscopy by taking samples from these sites and analysing their solutions.

In the steel industry, the amount of trace metal, such as manganese, can be analysed by reacting the metal to form an identifiable coloured ion and measuring the absorption of its solution. In this case, the manganese may be oxidised to form the purple MnO_4^- ion.

The food industry also uses ultraviolet/visible spectroscopy to determine how much nitrite has been added to meat.

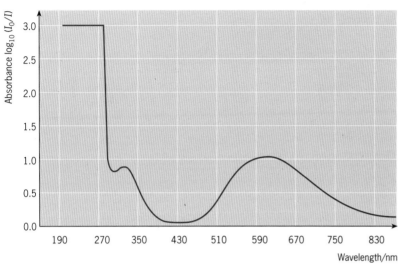

Fig 28.28 **The ultraviolet/visible spectrum of $[Cu(NH_3)_4(H_2O)_2]^{2+}$. The solution of this complex appears blue-violet**

K Look at Fig 28.28. What is λ_{max} for a solution of $[Cu(NH_3)_4(H_2O)_2]^{2+}$ and which colour(s) is/are being absorbed?

L Sketch the absorption spectrum of β-carotene, the orange pigment found in carrots.

The Beer–Lambert law

The Beer–Lambert law states that the absorption of light is proportional to the concentration of the solution and the length of the cell through which the light travels (known as **path length**).

$$\log_{10} \frac{I_0}{I} = \varepsilon \times l \times c$$

where:

I_0 = the intensity of incident radiation
(the radiation that falls on the solution in the cell);

I = the intensity of transmitted radiation
(the radiation that emerges from the solution in the cell);

ε = a constant that is characteristic of the substance concerned
(sometimes called the molar absorption coefficient);

l = the path length of the solution in cm
(the length of the cell through which the light travels);

c = the concentration of the absorbing solution in $mol\,dm^{-3}$.

$\log_{10} \frac{I_0}{I}$ is called the **absorbance (A)** of the solution.

It is a measure of the ability of a material to absorb radiation.

The Beer–Lambert law is used to calculate the concentration of a particular species in a solution if ε and λ_{max} are known. This is a common application for UV/visible spectrometers.

See question 1. ■

THE COLORIMETER

A COLORIMETER IS A SIMPLE FORM of visible spectrometer. A fixed wavelength of visible light is selected using a filter. This is then passed through the solution under test. The light that has not been absorbed by the solution is transmitted to a photocell. The light generates an electric current which is measured by a meter. The more light that is transmitted by the solution, the greater the electric current produced. However, most colorimeter meters are calibrated so that they record the light absorbed by the solution rather than the light transmitted. The absorbance of a solution is proportional to the concentration of the coloured compound in the solution. Rates of reaction can be determined if one of the species in the reaction is coloured.

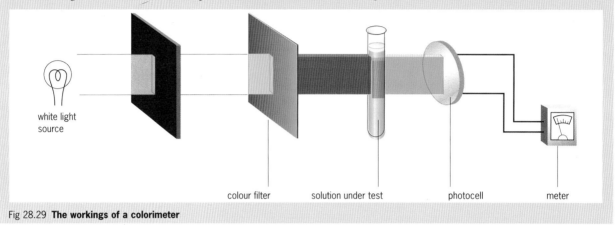

white light source

colour filter　　solution under test　　photocell　　meter

Fig 28.29 **The workings of a colorimeter**

3 TRANSITION METAL IONS AND COLOUR

M Which photons have the lowest energy: photons of red light or photons of blue light?
Remember the equations $E = h \times f$ and $c = f \times \lambda$.

Remember: A **complex** is formed when a central metal atom or ion is surrounded by species which donate lone pairs of electrons. A species which donates a lone pair of electrons is called a **ligand**. You can read more about this on page 526.

N The difference in energy of the two sets of d orbitals in $[Cu(H_2O)_6]^{2+}$ causes absorption at the red end of the spectrum. What colour is the $[Cu(H_2O)_6]^{2+}$ ion? Hint: Look at the colour wheel on page 610.

A characteristic of transition metals is that many of their compounds are coloured (see Chapter 25). Transition metal compounds are responsible for the colours in gemstones, stained glass windows and pottery glazes. From reading this chapter, you will realise that transition metal ions appear coloured because they absorb some wavelengths in the visible spectrum, while transmitting or reflecting the rest. The electrons absorb photons of a specific wavelength, become excited and jump up to higher energy levels. In compounds of transition elements, colour is due to a difference in energies between d orbitals.

d–d transitions

You are probably wondering how d orbitals can be at different energy levels. When we discussed d orbitals in Chapter 25, they were drawn at the same energy level (**degenerate**) on energy level diagrams. (See Fig 25.3, page 519.)

However, this is only true for gaseous transition metal ions. When ligands bond to transition metal ions they cause a splitting of the energy level of the d orbitals. The energy difference between the two sets of d orbitals is often such that the wavelength of photons absorbed is in the coloured part of the spectrum.

Copper(I) compounds are white because the Cu^+ ion has a $3d^{10}$ outer electron configuration. Since the 3d subshell is full, there can be no transition of electrons between d orbitals. You would expect the same to be true of scandium(III) compounds which have no electrons in the 3d subshell ($3d^0$). But not all colour is due to d–d transitions;

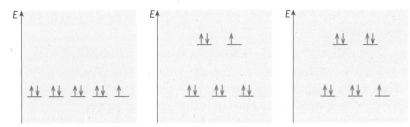

Fig 28.30(a) (left) **d orbitals are all at the same energy level in a gaseous Cu^{2+} ion. We say they are degenerate**

Fig 28.30(b) (centre) **In $[Cu(H_2O)_6]^{2+}$, the water ligands cause the d orbitals to split so they are now non-degenerate**

Fig 28.30(c) (right) **An electron is excited from a lower energy level d orbital to a higher energy level d orbital**

sometimes electrons can jump from the ligand to the metal. This is called **charge transfer** or **electron transfer** and it is responsible for the bright colours of Prussian blue and chrome yellow.

Factors affecting d–d splitting and colour

The colour of a transition metal complex depends chiefly on the central metal cation. The oxidation state of the metal affects the splitting of the d orbitals and, as a result, the colour. This is well illustrated by vanadium complexes in aqueous solution.

Ion	Oxidation state	Colour of aqueous solution
VO_2^+	+5	yellow
VO^{2+}	+4	blue
V^{3+}	+3	green
V^{2+}	+2	violet

The nature of the ligand also has an effect. Different ligands cause different separation of energy between d orbitals. This is called d–d splitting. The **spectrochemical series** is a list of ligands arranged in order of their ability to cause the d–d splitting.

$$I^- < Br^- < Cl^- < F^- < OH^- < H_2O < (CO_2)^{2-} < NH_3 < en < CN^-$$

longest wavelength (λ_{max}) ⟶ shortest wavelength (λ_{max})
smallest splitting ⟶ greatest splitting
smallest energy gap ⟶ greatest energy gap

$[Cu(H_2O)_6]^{2+}$ absorbs at the red end of the spectrum making an aqueous solution of copper(II) ions appear pale blue.

However, by substituting H_2O with NH_3 ligands to form the ion $[Cu(NH_3)_4(H_2O)_2]^{2+}$, the difference in energy of the d orbital split increases. This shifts the absorption into the yellow part of the spectrum, making the solution deep blue.

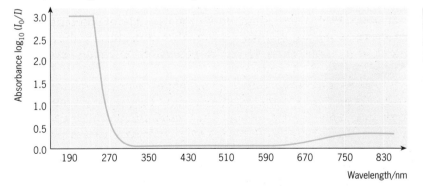

Fig 28.31 **The ultraviolet/visible spectrum of $[Cu(H_2O)_6]^{2+}$. Compare this with the ultraviolet/visible spectrum of $[Cu(NH_3)_4(H_2O)_2]^{2+}$ in Fig 28.28**

Fig 28.32 **Left: An aqueous solution of copper(II) sulphate contains the $[Cu(H_2O)_6]^{2+}$ ion. Right: In this solution, concentrated ammonia has been added, replacing some water ligands to form the ammine complex $[Cu(NH_3)_4(H_2O)_2]^{2+}$. The ammonia ligand increases the energy gap between the split d orbitals. This affects the energy of the electron transition and therefore the colour of the complex solution.**

?

O (a) What is the full electron configuration of Zn^{2+}?

(b) Explain why zinc compounds are white.

■ See question 1.

Table 28.1 **The relationship between the oxidation state of vanadium and the colour of its complexes**

?

P Using the colour wheel on page 610, work out which colour is being absorbed by each of the vanadium ions in Table 28.1.

You can see some of these colours in Fig 26.23, page 561.

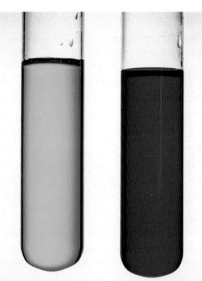

Fig 25.20 on page 530 is another example of *cis-trans* isomerism affecting the colour of a complex.

Another factor which has an effect on d–d splitting is the number of each type of ligand in the complex:

$$[Cr(H_2O)_6]^{3+} \quad [Cr(H_2O)_5Cl]^{2+} \quad [Cr(H_2O)_4Cl_2]^+$$
$$\text{violet} \qquad\qquad \text{green} \qquad\qquad \text{dark green}$$

The arrangement of ligands around the central metal cation can also have an effect the colour of a complex (Fig 28.33).

Q $[CuCl_4]^{2-}$(aq) is a yellow colour. Predict where λ_{max} will be and sketch its ultraviolet/visible spectrum.

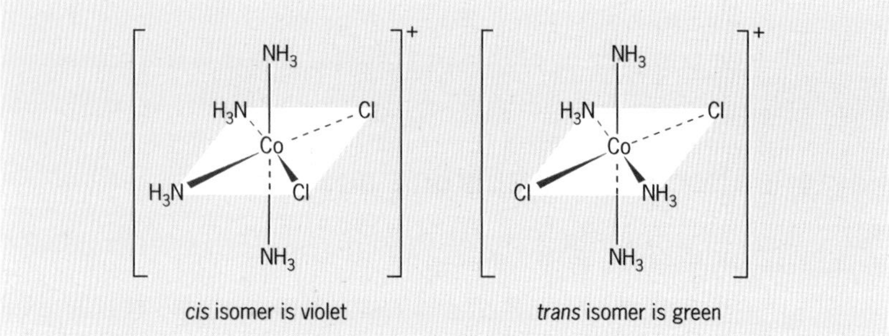

Fig 28.33 **The *cis* and *trans* isomers of [Co(NH₃)₄Cl₂]⁺**

THE COLOURS OF GEMSTONES

SOME OF THE MOST BEAUTIFUL and highly prized examples of the colours that transition metal ions can impart are found in gemstones. In many cases, the transition metal ions are actually impurities. For example, the deep red of rubies comes from traces of Cr^{3+} ions embedded in a lattice of aluminium oxide. Because Cr^{3+} ions have the same charge as Al^{3+} ions and are about the same size they occupy about 5% of the Al^{3+} positions.

Fig 28.34 **The deep red of these rubies is due to the presence of Cr^{3+} ions**

Fig 28.35 **The green colour of the emeralds in this specimen is caused by Cr^{3+} ions present as an impurity in $Be_3Al_2Si_6O_{18}$**

Emeralds are coloured green because Cr^{3+} ions are present. This time Cr^{3+} ions are embedded in a lattice containing large silicate anions $Si_6O_{18}^{12-}$ together with the cations Be^{2+} and Al^{3+}.

So how can Cr^{3+} impart different colours? The answer lies in the splitting of the d orbitals. There are three 3d electrons in Cr^{3+} (Fig 28.36). One of these d electrons becomes excited by absorbing a photon of light with a wavelength in the visible spectrum. The wavelengths that are transmitted through the gemstone are predominantly red which is why a ruby is red. In the case of emerald, the different environment of the Cr^{3+} ion lead to a different energy gap between the two sets of d orbitals, allowing the transmission of blue-green light while absorbing violet, yellow and red wavelengths.

Other precious gemstones are coloured by different transition metal ions. The blue of sapphire is due to Ti^{4+}, V^{3+} or Co^{3+} ions. Aquamarine, named after the colour of a tropical sea, owes its pale blue colour to Fe^{3+} ions. The Fe^{3+} ion also gives a yellow colour to topaz and a red colour to garnet. The purple of amethyst is due to Mn^{3+} ions.

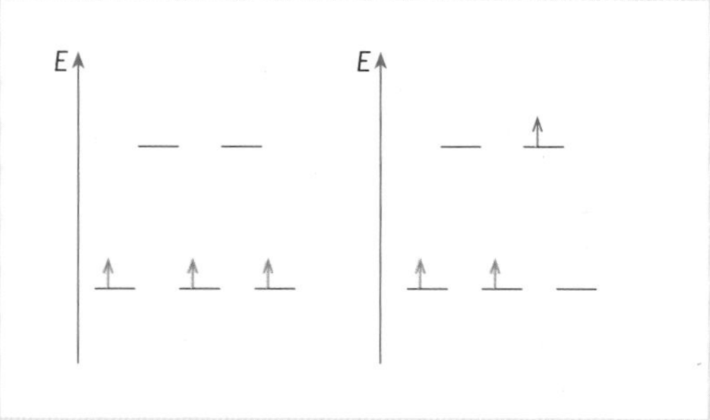

Fig 28.36 **Excitation of electrons in Cr^{3+}. Cr^{3+} has three d electrons. The energy difference between the two sets of d orbitals in emerald or ruby causes the absorption of some of the visible spectrum wavelengths as photons excite the electrons to the higher energy d orbitals.**

Chemiluminescence

Chemiluminescence is the emission of photons of light in the visible spectrum brought about by a chemical reaction. Such reactions occur at around room temperature, and their energy excites electrons in fluorescer molecules which absorb photons at one wavelength – usually outside the visible spectrum – and give out light with a wavelength in the visible spectrum. The fluorescer molecules emit visible light when the electrons fall back to a lower energy level.

Fireflies use chemiluminescent reactions to produce light and attract a mate. The reaction occurs inside a living organism and is called **bioluminescence**. The substance involved, luciferin, reacts with oxygen in the presence of the enzyme luciferase to produce light.

Light sticks use chemiluminescence. They contain an ethanedioate ester and hydrogen peroxide. When a stick is 'broken', the reactants mix together. The energy from the reaction excites electrons in fluorescer molecules and light is released. The type of fluorescer molecule determines the colour of the light.

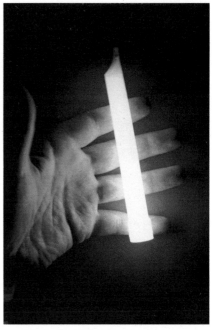

Fig 28.37 **A light stick releases its energy as light**

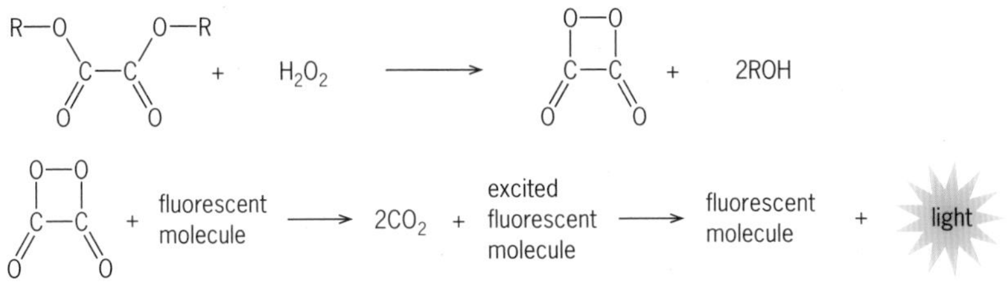

Fig 28.38 **Energy to excite electrons in the fluorescer comes from the reaction of a diester and hydrogen peroxide. As the electrons fall back to their ground states light is released**

SUMMARY

■ Electron energy levels exist in atoms and molecules. Electron transitions between these levels emit or absorb radiation.

■ Colour arises when a substance absorbs or emits electromagnetic radiation partly in the visible spectrum.

■ Absorption spectra record the wavelengths of photons that excite electrons, causing them to jump to higher energy levels. Emission spectra record the wavelengths of photons emitted when excited electrons return to lower energy levels.

■ Dyes are soluble in the medium in which they are applied; pigments are insoluble.

■ Azo dyes are produced by coupling reactions such as that between benzenediazonium chloride and phenol.

■ The functional group of an azo compound is the azo group, $-N=N-$.

■ Electron transitions occur between σ bonding molecular orbitals, σ^* antibonding molecular orbitals, π bonding molecular orbitals, π^* anti-bonding molecular orbitals and lone pairs (n orbitals).

■ Conjugated systems have alternating double and single bonds; the delocalisation that occurs lowers the energy of π to π^* electron transitions so conjugated compounds may appear coloured.

■ The part of a molecule responsible for absorbing coloured radiation is called the chromophore. It is usually an extended delocalised electron system.

■ The colour changes of acid–base indicators is due to a change in the delocalisation of the chromophore when an H^+ ion is added or removed.

■ Ultraviolet/visible spectroscopy is possible because when outer electrons of atoms or ions in compounds are excited they absorb in the ultraviolet or visible part of the spectrum.

■ The Beer–Lambert law is represented by the expression:

$$\log_{10} \frac{I_0}{I} = \varepsilon \times l \times c$$

■ The colour of transition elements ions is due to a difference in energies between d orbitals caused by the ligands around the metal cation. This splitting allows d–d electron transitions.

■ Factors which affect d–d splitting include: the oxidation state of the metal; the nature and number of the ligands; and the arrangement of the ligands around the metal cation.

■ Complexes of Zn^{2+} and Cu^+ are white because the 3d subshell is full.

QUESTIONS

1

a) Use the information given in the colour circle below to help you to answer the questions which follow.

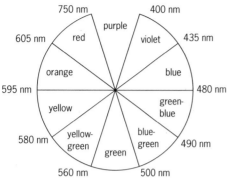

Fig 28.Q1

  (i) What is the complementary colour of blue?
  (ii) What is the colour of a dye solution which absorbs light maximally at 485 nm?
  (iii) What would be the colour of the dye solution in **(ii)** if a change of solvent caused a bathochromic shift of 50 nm? Give the wavelength of the absorption maximum of this solution.

b) Calculate the molar absorption coefficient (ε) of a dye which has a maximum absorbance value of 1.60 in a cell of pathlength 1 cm at a concentration of 4.0×10^{-5} mol dm^{-3}.
[NEAB 1996: Chemistry of Colour Module Test, q.3]

2

a) What colour, if any, is produced in flame tests on the following compounds:
  (i) sodium nitrate;
  (ii) barium carbonate;
  (iii) magnesium sulphate?

b) Explain how flame colours are produced.

3

(a) Write an equation for the reaction of phenol with benzenediazonium chloride.

(b) Give the conditions for this reaction.

(c) What can the product be used for?

4

Azo dyes are used to colour many synthetic materials. Describe how an azo dye can be produced in the laboratory, giving essential conditions and reagents. Write equations for any reactions described.

5

Electronic transitions occur when energy is absorbed from the visible or ultraviolet region of the electromagnetic spectrum.

a) For each of the following compounds state one type of electronic transition that may occur.
  (i) $(CH_3)_2C=O$
  (ii) $CH_2=CH-CH=CH_2$

b) Why does $CH_2=CH_2$ show an absorption band at a shorter wavelength than $CH_2=CH-CH=CH_2$?

c) The hexa-aquatitanium(III) ion, $[Ti(H_2O)_6]^{3+}$, is coloured.
  (i) How does the presence of the ligand affect the d orbitals of the uncomplexed titanium ion?
  (ii) How does the absorption of light affect the unpaired electron in $[Ti(H_2O)_6]^{3+}$ and hence give this hydrated ion a purple colour?
[UCLES Modular Sciences March 1995: Methods of Analysis and Detection, q.4]

6

The structures of octa-2,4,6-triene and β-carotene are shown below.

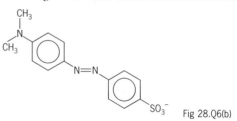

β-carotene

Fig 28.Q6(a)

a) Suggest why octa-2,4,6-triene absorbs in the ultraviolet whereas β-carotene absorbs in the visible region of the spectrum.

b) The diagram below shows the indicator methyl orange as it exists under alkaline conditions.

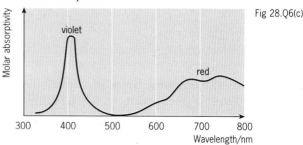

Fig 28.Q6(b)

This form is yellow, whereas methyl orange has a red form under acidic conditions. Suggest how this change in colour might result from a change in structure of the indicator.

c) The absorption spectrum below is that of a transition metal complex.

Fig 28.Q6(c)

Predict the colour of the complex, indicating how you arrive at your answer.
[UCLES Modular Sciences March 1996: Methods of Analysis and Detection, q.3]

Assignment

HOW ARE DYES STUCK ONTO TEXTILES?

The dye of blue denim jeans is indigo and it is called a **vat dye**. A vat dye is usually soluble in its reduced form but when oxidised becomes insoluble, precipitating in the pores of the denim cotton fibres. This property means that vat dyes do not wash out of clothes.

(To learn a little more about the history of blue denim and indigo, read the Opener of this chapter.)

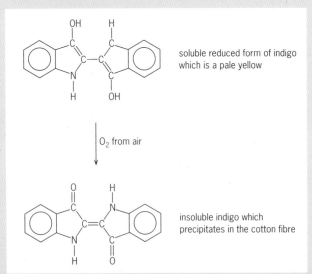

soluble reduced form of indigo which is a pale yellow

O₂ from air

insoluble indigo which precipitates in the cotton fibre

Fig 28.A1 **The soluble and insoluble forms of indigo**

Vat dyes are particularly effective for cotton fibres and other fabrics containing cellulose. The large number of hydroxyl groups on the cellulose molecules mean that the fabric readily absorbs water and hence the water soluble dye.

1
a) The reduced form of indigo is pale yellow, while indigo is blue. Both molecules have conjugated systems. What is meant by the term *conjugated system*?

b) Which form of indigo absorbs the longest wavelength of light?

c) What happens to the p electrons in an indigo molecule when light falls upon them? Hint: See page 6.

2
a) Cellulose is a polymer made up of glucose units. Draw the repeat unit of cellulose.

b) What type of bonding occurs between water molecules and the hydroxyl group? (See page 231.)

Another type of cotton dye is called a **direct dye**. Direct dyes are long planar molecules that can lie alongside the cellulose polymer chains, forming intermolecular hydrogen bonds and induced dipole–induced dipole forces. Such large dye molecules are made water-soluble using SO_3^- Na^+ groups. Direct dyes are usually diazo or triazo dyes (Fig 28.A2).

Fig 28.A2 **C.I. Direct Brown 138, a direct dye. C.I. are the initials for the Colour Index, an internationally recognised publication that lists and categorises almost 40 000 commercial pigments and dyes**

3
Why is Direct Brown called a triazo dye?

4
What is meant by the term chromophore?

5
A much simpler azo compound is produced starting with phenylamine to produce the benzenediazonium ion. This undergoes a coupling reaction with phenol to produce a bright orange azo compound. Explain how you would synthesise this orange azo compound in the laboratory stating the conditions required. Write balanced equations for the reactions you describe.

The intermolecular forces between direct dyes and cotton are relatively weak, so the water-fastness of the dye is poor and some of the dye comes out when the material is washed. However, in 1956 chemists at ICI produced a dye which would form covalent bonds with the cellulose fibres of cotton. The covalent bonds are formed by reactive groups which first bond to the dye molecules (Fig 28.A3). These groups then react with the hydroxyl groups on the cellulose fibres (Fig 28.A4). The dye is water-fast and the colour does not run when the textile is washed because covalent bonds have formed with the cellulosic fibres. Such a dye is called **fibre-reactive**.

trichlorotriazine

Fig 28.A3 **Trichlorotriazine reacts with a dye molecule**

cellulose fibre

Fig 28.A4 **The reactive chlorotriazine group forms a covalent bond with cotton**

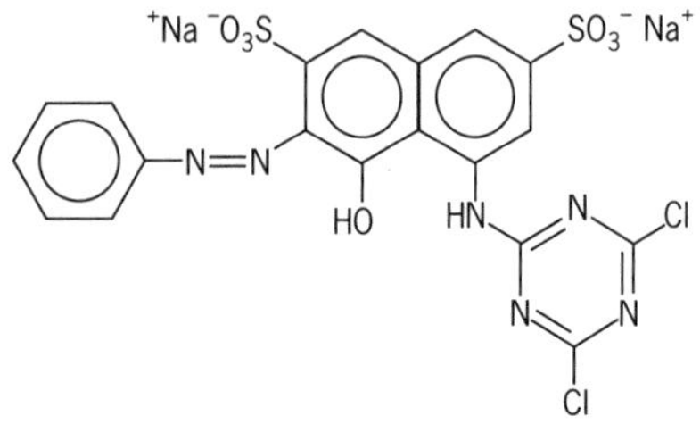

Fig 28.A5 **Reactive Red 2**

6

a) Draw the dye molecule shown in Fig 28.A5 before the reactive group has bonded to it.

b) Which functional groups make the dye water-soluble?

7

Why does the covalent bond between the dye and cotton make it water-fast?

Wool and silk contain many amino functional groups (NH_2). These groups are basic and react with acid dyes which contain sulphonic acid groups (SO_3H) to form ionic bonds (Fig 28.A6).

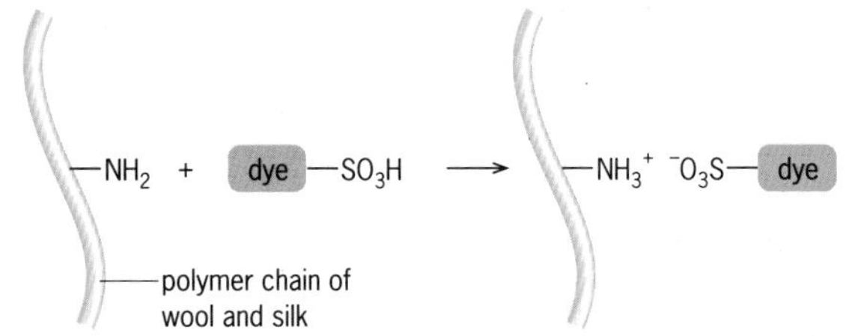

Fig 28.A6 **Acidic dyes bond to fibres containing basic NH_2 groups, so this type of dye is used for wool and silk.**

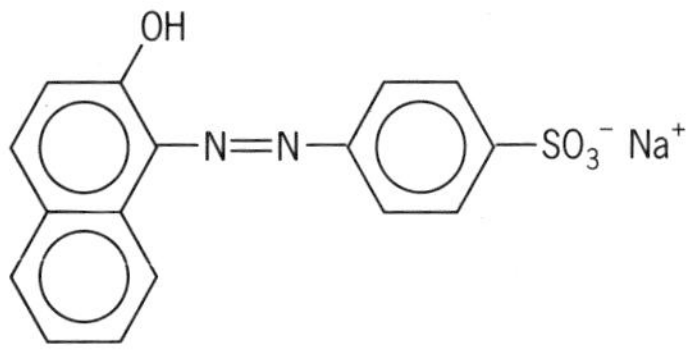

Fig 28.A7 **C.I. Acid Orange 7 is a salt of the sulphonic acid, which makes it more soluble.**

Poly(propenenitrile) fibres (acrylics) contain CO_2H and SO_3H groups which are acidic. These can form ionic bonds with basic dyes.

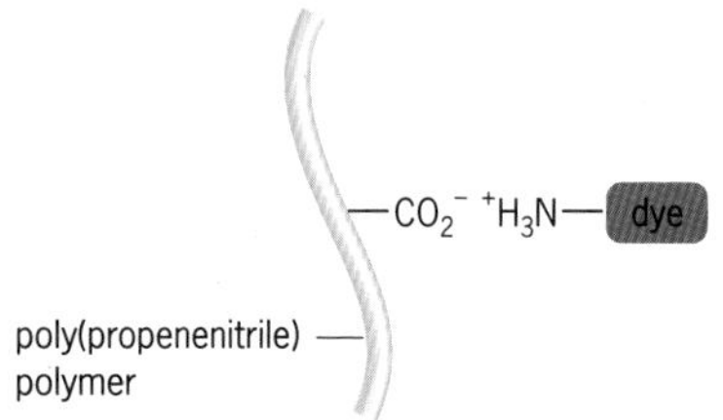

Fig 28.A8 **Basic dyes form ionic bonds with acid functional groups on poly(propenenitrile) fibres**

The last group of dyes we will consider are **disperse dyes**. All the other dye groups are water-soluble when applied, but polyester fibres do not form hydrogen bonds with water and are known as **hydrophobic** (water-hating). They do not allow water molecules to penetrate them. Disperse dyes are a fine suspension of dye particles which get absorbed by the fibres and are held there by induced dipole–induced dipole forces and some hydrogen bonding. Because the dye is only sparingly soluble it tends to stay in the fibres, so it is water-fast.

8

Draw the structures of the monomers which make up the polymer fibre chains of nylon, wool, polyester and poly(propenenitrile). Chapter 12 and Chapter 18 will help you.

COLOUR IN ORGANIC AND INORGANIC COMPOUNDS

This chapter describes the characteristic properties of coloured substances such as dyes, pH indicators and transition metal compounds. The Chapter Map links ideas about electronic transitions in substances to colour and UV–visible spectroscopy. See the syllabus you are following for the items you need to study.

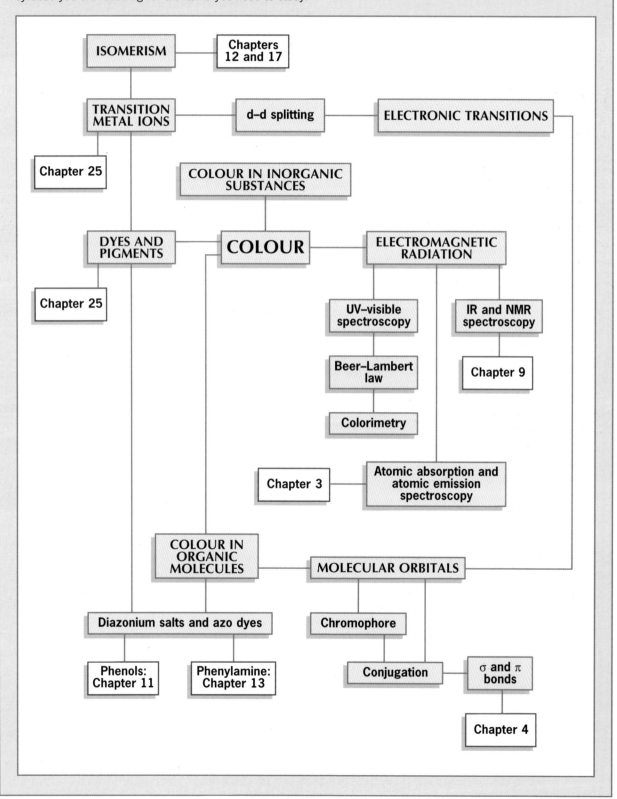

29 Ammonia, bases and food production

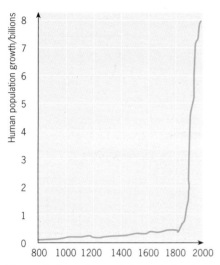

The graph shows the population explosion that has taken place in recent years

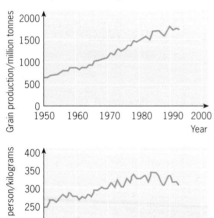

Grains are the world's leading food crops, but the increase in production has not kept up with the increase in demand

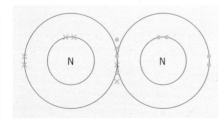

Fig 29.1 **Dot and cross diagram for a nitrogen molecule**

You can read about amino acids, polypeptides and proteins in Chapter 17.

WITH THE WORLD'S POPULATION increasing at more than 250 000 people per day, the question arises: How will enough food for these extra mouths be produced? The overall output of staple foods such as grain has risen significantly since 1950 through better farming methods and the use of fertilisers. But in many African and Latin American countries food production is actually falling.

As crops grow, they take essential elements such as nitrogen and phosphorus from the soil. Farmers in poorer countries cannot afford fertilisers to restore these elements to the soil. As a result, crop yields fall and in time the soil becomes unable to sustain useful growth.

In richer countries, there is pressure to build homes, factories and roads on good agricultural land, so farmers have worked to get higher crop yields from smaller amounts of land by using pesticides and fertilisers. But the use of these agrochemicals has its problems: the over-use of fertilisers has polluted groundwater, and hence rivers which feed into reservoirs.

There are moves to develop fertilisers that are needed in smaller amounts to maintain maximum crop yields. These would also reduce the harmful effects on the environment. If the manufacturers do manage to hit on the right formula, and can convince farmers everywhere that these new fertilisers are effective, then there could be a better chance of meeting the needs of the world's ever-swelling population.

1 THE NITROGEN CYCLE

For nearly all manufactured fertilisers, the starting substance is ammonia – a compound of hydrogen and nitrogen. Nitrogen is readily available since it forms about 80 per cent by volume of the lower atmosphere. But it is a very unreactive gas due to the strong triple covalent bond in each nitrogen molecule (Fig 29.1). The bond energy for this triple bond is 994 kJ mol^{-1}.

All plants and animals contain nitrogen in amino acids, polypeptides, proteins and nucleic acids. Plants cannot obtain nitrogen directly from the air. Instead, they take up nitrogen-containing compounds from the soil. The **nitrogen cycle** (Fig 29.2) describes the way that nitrogen and its compounds circulate within the environment and living organisms.

Fig 29.2 shows the processes that remove nitrogen-containing compounds from the soil. There must be a constant supply of nitrates to the soil for plants to grow healthily. Much of the nitrogen cycle has taken place naturally for many millions of years. In

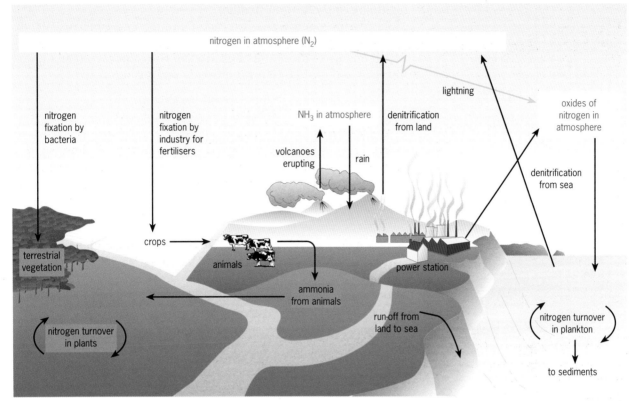

nitrogen in atmosphere (N$_2$)

nitrogen
fixation by
bacteria

nitrogen
fixation by
industry for
fertilisers

NH$_3$ in atmosphere

denitrification
from land

lightning

oxides of
nitrogen in
atmosphere

volcanoes
erupting

rain

denitrification
from sea

crops

terrestrial
vegetation

animals

power station

ammonia
from animals

run-off from
land to sea

nitrogen turnover
in plants

nitrogen turnover
in plankton

to sediments

Fig 29.2 **The nitrogen cycle**

recent times, however, human activity has added some extra stages to the cycle. The advent of intensive farming has affected the delicate balance of the nitrogen cycle. Intensive farming removes more nitrogen-containing compounds than are naturally put back into the soil, so it has become necessary to supplement the supply of nitrogen by adding synthetic fertilisers such as ammonium nitrate.

■ See question 5.

Nitrogen fixation

Processes that convert atmospheric nitrogen to nitrogen-containing substances are a very important part of the nitrogen cycle. They are known as **nitrogen fixation** processes. Nitrogen fixation occurs by natural processes and as a result of human activity. The most important synthetic nitrogen fixation process is the manufacture of ammonia. This chapter will show how the synthesis of such a simple molecule has had a profound effect on agriculture and the chemical industry.

?

A The oxidation state of nitrogen in the ammonium ion is −3. Is atmospheric nitrogen oxidised or reduced within root nodules to make ammonium ions? Explain your answer.

LEGUMINOUS PLANTS AND NITROGEN FIXATION

Fig 29.3 **The bacteria in root nodules of peas, clover and beans convert atmospheric nitrogen to ammonium ions and nitrates**

SOME PLANTS such as peas and clover are able to convert atmospheric nitrogen to ammonium ions, NH$_4^+$, by the action of bacteria found in root nodules. The ammonium ions may be directly absorbed into the roots and metabolised by plants to form plant protein. Alternatively, the ammonium ions may be oxidised by nitrifying bacteria to nitrate ions:

$$NH_4^+(aq) + \tfrac{3}{2}O_2(g) \rightarrow NO_2^-(aq) + 2H^+(aq) + H_2O(l)$$

$$NO_2^-(aq) + \tfrac{1}{2}O_2(g) \rightarrow NO_3^-(aq)$$

The aqueous nitrate ions can then be absorbed through the roots by osmosis and later assimilated into plant protein.

B The compounds or ions listed below form part of the nitrogen cycle. Write down the oxidation state of nitrogen in each case:
(a) NO_2^- (b) NO_3^- (c) KNO_3 (d) NO
(e) NO_2

For determining oxidation numbers, see page 435.

Nitrogen monoxide, NO, is also known as nitric oxide or nitrogen(II) oxide.

See question 2. ■

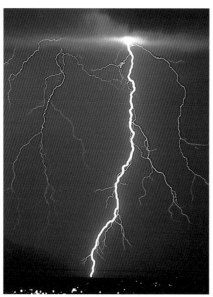

Table 29.4 **The enormous quantity of electrical energy available within a lightning bolt is sufficient to allow nitrogen to react with oxygen. This is one of the most important natural nitrogen fixation processes.**

See question 6. ■

We have already described some equilibria in Chapters 15 and 16. You may want to read pages 309 and 336 before continuing.

Table 29.1 **K_c at different temperatures for the equilibrium $N_2(g) + 3H_2(g) \rightleftharpoons 2NH_3(g)$**

Temperature/K	K_c/dm^6 mol^{-2}
298	4.05×10^8
400	4.39×10^3
500	59.8
600	4.03
700	0.256
800	2.98×10^{-2}
900	5.45×10^{-3}

Lightning and nitrogen fixation

Molecular nitrogen will only react if enough energy is available to break the very strong triple covalent bond. Lightning provides sufficient energy to break the bond, allowing the direct combination of nitrogen and oxygen to form nitrogen monoxide:

$$N_2(g) + O_2(g) \rightarrow 2NO(g)$$

Nitrogen monoxide oxidises to nitrogen dioxide even at low temperatures. Nitrogen dioxide may be further oxidised in the presence of water and oxygen to give dilute nitric acid, a solution containing nitrate ions. These processes are represented by the equations below.

$$NO(g) + \tfrac{1}{2}O_2(g) \rightarrow NO_2(g)$$

$$2NO_2(g) + H_2O(l) + \tfrac{1}{2}O_2(g) \rightarrow 2HNO_3(aq)$$

2 THE HABER PROCESS AND NITROGEN FIXATION

Ammonia is a starting material in the production of many fertilisers. The **Haber process** is the industrial process used to manufacture ammonia by reacting nitrogen with hydrogen:

$$N_2(g) + 3H_2(g) \rightleftharpoons 2NH_3(g)$$

The presence of the triple bond in each nitrogen molecule means that nitrogen and hydrogen react very slowly under normal conditions. You will also notice that the reaction is reversible. The choice of conditions used in the manufacture of ammonia determine the rate of reaction and the equilibrium position of the reaction mixture.

The position of equilibrium for the reaction between nitrogen and hydrogen can be estimated by looking at the numerical value of the equilibrium constant. The equilibrium constant, K_c, for this reaction is represented by the equation:

$$K_c = \frac{[NH_3(g)]^2}{[H_2(g)]^3[N_2(g)]}$$

The concentrations refer to the concentrations at equilibrium.

Table 29.1 illustrates that at low temperatures the numerical value of K_c is higher – the equilibrium position lies well to the right. At higher temperatures the equilibrium position lies to the left, the side of the reactants nitrogen and hydrogen. In contrast, the rate of reaction is very slow at low temperatures but speeds up at higher temperatures. This conflict between rate of reaction and position of equilibrium will be explored later on in this chapter.

Partial pressure

For a mixture of gases it is convenient to express the composition in terms of **partial pressures** rather than concentrations.

The partial pressure of a gas in a container of several gases is the pressure that particular gas would have if it were the only gas present in the container.

Consider a mixture of neon and helium gases. The partial pressure of neon, $p\text{Ne}$, is proportional to the **mole fraction** of neon, $x\text{Ne}$, in the mixture, and:

$$p\text{Ne} = x\text{Ne} \times P$$

where P is the total pressure of the mixture of gases.

The mole fraction of neon is the number of moles of neon gas in the mixture divided by the sum of the number of moles of each gas present:

$$x\text{Ne} = \frac{n\text{Ne}}{n\text{He} + n\text{Ne}}$$

where $n\text{Ne}$ = number of moles of neon and $n\text{He}$ = number of moles of helium.

EXAMPLE

Q A mixture of gases at a total pressure of 1.0×10^5 Pa contains 3.4 mol of carbon dioxide, 4.5 mol of oxygen and 1.1 mol of nitrogen. What is the partial pressure of each gas in the mixture?

A The mole fraction of $CO_2 = \dfrac{3.4}{3.4 + 4.5 + 1.1} = 0.38$

So: $\quad p CO_2 = 0.38 \times 1.0 \times 10^5 = 3.8 \times 10^4$ Pa

The mole fraction of $O_2 = \dfrac{4.5}{3.4 + 4.5 + 1.1} = 0.50$

So: $\quad p O_2 = 0.50 \times 1.0 \times 10^5 = 5.0 \times 10^4$ Pa

The mole fraction of $N_2 = \dfrac{1.1}{3.5 + 4.5 + 1.1} = 0.12$

So: $\quad p N_2 = 0.12 \times 1.0 \times 10^5$ Pa $= 1.2 \times 10^4$ Pa

---

The equilibrium constant, K_p

In reactions that involve gaseous reactants or products, the equilibrium constant is often stated in terms of the partial pressures of the gases present. The expression for this equilibrium constant resembles that for K_c except that the partial pressures of the gases in the equilibrium mixture are used instead of the concentrations of the components in the mixture. The expression for the equilibrium constant, K_p, for the Haber process is:

$$K_p = \frac{(p\text{NH}_3)^2}{(p\text{H}_2)^3(p\text{N}_2)}$$

where $p\text{NH}_3$ is the partial pressure of ammonia gas.

Notice that the partial pressures are raised to same powers as the concentrations in the expression for K_c. The equilibrium constant K_p will have both a numerical value and a unit. The higher the numerical value, the greater the proportion of ammonia in the equilibrium mixture. If the partial pressures are measured in pascal, the units of K_p for this equilibrium will be Pa^{-2}.

If an equilibrium involves solids, liquids and solutions then only the gases in the process are used in the K_p expression. For the reaction:

$$\text{NH}_4\text{Cl(s)} \rightleftharpoons \text{NH}_3\text{(g)} + \text{HCl(g)} \quad K_p = (p\text{NH}_3)(p\text{HCl})$$

The unit for this equilibrium constant is Pa $\times$ Pa = Pa^2.

We introduced the concept of the mole fraction on page 106.

C A cylinder contains 2.0 mol of oxygen gas, and 5.6 mol of gaseous dinitrogen oxide. The pressure inside the cylinder is 450 kPa. What is the partial pressure of oxygen in the cylinder?

Later in this chapter, we discuss the factors affecting the position the equilibrium reaches and the numerical value of the equilibrium constant.

D Write down expressions for the equilibrium constant, K_p, for each of the following equilibria.

(a) $H_2(g) + I_2(g) \rightleftharpoons 2HI(g)$

(b) $2NO(g) + O_2(g) \rightleftharpoons 2NO_2(g)$

(c) $CaCO_3(s) \rightleftharpoons CaO(s) + CO_2(g)$

E For each of the equilibria in question **D** state the units of the equilibrium constant K_p. Assume that the partial pressures are all measured in Pa.

F A mixture of nitrogen and hydrogen were heated at a constant temperature in a reaction vessel until equilibrium was reached. The partial pressures of each gaseous component in the reaction mixture at equilibrium were:

$$pNH_3 = 8.3 \times 10^5 \text{ Pa}$$
$$pN_2 = 3.5 \times 10^4 \text{ Pa}$$
$$pH_2 = 1.1 \times 10^5 \text{ Pa}$$

Calculate the numerical value for the equilibrium constant, K_p.

✔

In a gaseous mixture, the mole ratio of each gas equals the ratio of the partial pressures of the gases.

See question 1, 3, 4 and 6. ■

?

G Sulphur dioxide and oxygen were mixed in a mole ratio of 2:1 at a total initial pressure of 300 kPa. The mixture was held at a temperature of 430 °C in the presence of a suitable catalyst until it reached equilibrium:

$$2SO_2(g) + O_2(g) \rightleftharpoons 2SO_3(g)$$

At equilibrium, the partial pressure of sulphur trioxide was 190 kPa.

(a) Calculate the initial partial pressures of SO_2 and O_2.

(b) Calculate the partial pressures of SO_2 and O_2 at equilibrium.

(c) Calculate the value for K_p for this equilibrium.

EXAMPLE

Q Fritz Haber studied the reaction between hydrogen and ammonia. He mixed nitrogen and hydrogen in a mole ratio of 1:3, at 300 °C and in the presence of a catalyst. The reaction was allowed to reach equilibrium. At equilibrium, the total pressure of the equilibrium mixture was 800 kPa and the partial pressure of the ammonia was 75 kPa. Calculate the numerical value for K_p under these conditions.

A As in other equilibrium questions, we need to start with a balanced equation. Under each term we write the partial pressure at equilibrium.

$$N_2(g) + 3H_2(g) \rightleftharpoons 2NH_3(g)$$

Partial pressures at equilibrium: x $3x$ 75 kPa

If the partial pressure of nitrogen is x kPa, then the partial pressure of hydrogen must be $3x$. This follows because the initial mole ratio was 1:3 and this remains unchanged througout the reaction, since the stoichiometry of the reaction indicates that for every mole of nitrogen that reacts, three moles of hydrogen react.

The total pressure is the sum of the partial pressures:

$$x + 3x + 75 = 800 \text{ kPa}$$

So: $x = 181 \text{ kPa}$

Therefore: $pN_2 = 181 \text{ kPa}$ and $pH_2 = 544 \text{ kPa}$.

Substituting these values into the expression for the equilibrium constant gives:

$$K_p = 1.93 \times 10^{-7} \text{ kPa}^{-2}.$$

Manufacturing ammonia

The manufacture of any chemical involves:
- obtaining a cheap and plentiful supply of the raw materials needed for the process;
- purification of the reactants from the raw materials;
- conversion of the reactants to the product;
- isolation of the product from the reaction mixture.

Obtaining the reactants for the Haber process

Air is an abundant source of nitrogen. One way to obtain nitrogen is to liquefy air and then to use fractional distillation to isolate the nitrogen. However, this method is quite expensive and is rarely used commercially.

The nitrogen and hydrogen for the Haber process are normally made simultaneously by a complex series of reactions in which methane, water and air are converted to nitrogen, hydrogen, carbon dioxide and carbon monoxide. When carbon dioxide and carbon monoxide are removed, a mixture remains that is almost entirely nitrogen and hydrogen in the mole ratio of 1:3.

Synthesis of ammonia

The conditions used for the direct reaction between hydrogen and nitrogen vary from one factory to another. Most manufacturers use:
- a temperature of about 450 °C;
- a pressure of between 200 and 400 atmospheres;
- an iron catalyst with potassium hydroxide promoter.

The conditions are chosen for economic reasons. A typical factory produces up to 1500 tonnes of ammonia per day. Some manufacturers use pressures as high as 1000 atmospheres but this presents technological difficulties in the construction of the plant. The use of better catalysts has allowed some modern plants to reduce the operating pressures to as low as 80 atmospheres.

The Haber process is a continuous process (Fig 29.5). As nitrogen and hydrogen continually enter the reaction vessel, manufacturers isolate ammonia from unreacted hydrogen and nitrogen by liquefaction. Only about 15 per cent of the nitrogen reacts as it passes through the reaction vessel for the first time – the rest is recycled. Being a continuous process it is vital that all traces of carbon monoxide are removed from the nitrogen and hydrogen to avoid poisoning and reducing the efficiency of the catalyst.

To understand the chemical basis of the conditions chosen for the Haber process, we need to apply **Le Chatelier's principle**.

Le Chatelier's principle and the Haber process

Le Chatelier's principle predicts how changes in temperature, pressure and concentration will affect a system at equilibrium. The principle states:

> **When an equilibrium reaction mixture is subjected to a change in conditions, the composition of the mixture alters to counteract that change.**

Fig 29.6 summarises the effects on the equilibrium position when the conditions of a system change. We can apply Le Chatelier's principle to the Haber process and predict how changes of temperature, pressure and concentration affect ammonia production.

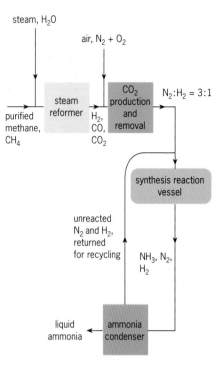

Fig 29.5 **A flow diagram of the ammonia manufacturing process**

■ See questions 1, 3, 4 and 6.

reactants ⇌ products

Change	Type or part of system	Effect on equilibrium
pressure increasing	If ΔV is positive, ie there are more moles of gaseous products than gaseous reactants	shift to left
	If ΔV is negative, ie there are more moles of gaseous reactants than gaseous products	shift to right
temperature increasing	If $\Delta H^{\ominus}_{\text{forward reaction}}$ is positive, ie the forward reaction is endothermic	shift to right
	If $\Delta H^{\ominus}_{\text{forward reaction}}$ is negative, ie the forward reaction is exothermic	shift to left
concentration increasing	of reactants	shift to right
	of products	shift to left
catalyst added		no effect

Fig 29.6 **A summary of Le Chatelier's principle**

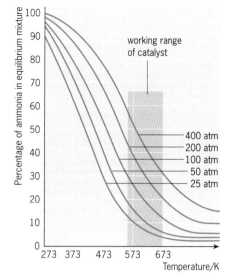

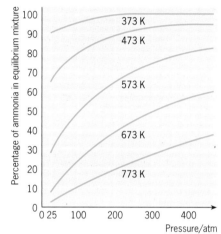

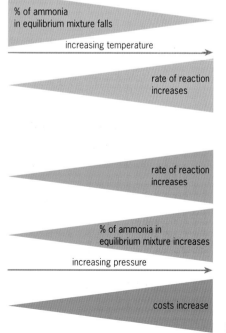

Changes in temperature

The forward reaction for the production of ammonia is exothermic and the reverse reaction is endothermic:

$$N_2(g) + 3H_2(g) \xrightleftharpoons[\Delta H^\ominus = +92 \text{ kJ mol}^{-1}]{\Delta H^\ominus = -92 \text{ kJ mol}^{-1}} 2NH_3(g)$$

If the temperature of the equilibrium mixture increases, the position of equilibrium will shift to counteract this change of conditions. The only way that this can happen is for the position of equilibrium to move in the direction of the endothermic reaction. As a result, the equilibrium concentration of ammonia decreases with increasing temperature. Fig 29.7 shows how the equilibrium concentration decreases as temperature rises. Le Chatelier's principle suggests that a lower temperature would favour ammonia production.

Fig 29.7 **The effect of temperature on the percentage of ammonia in the equilibrium mixture**

Changes in pressure

If the pressure of the reaction mixture increases, the position of equilibrium will change to counteract the increase in pressure. This is achieved by a reduction in the overall volume of the equilibrium mixture. Since 1 volume of nitrogen and 3 volumes of hydrogen (total 4 volumes) react to form two volumes of ammonia, the increase in pressure causes a shift in the equilibrium position to the right. This means that as the pressure increases, the percentage of ammonia in the equilibrium mixture will increase (Fig 29.8). The chemical prediction based on Le Chatelier's principle would be to use as high a pressure as possible.

Fig 29.8 **The percentage of ammonia in the equilibrium mixture as pressure changes**

Changes in concentration

If the concentration of ammonia in the equilibrium mixture suddenly decreases, the equilibrium position will alter to counteract the change in concentration. This change in conditions favours the forward reaction to produce more ammonia. Removing ammonia from the reaction mixture before the mixture of gases is recycled promotes ammonia production the next time the mixture enters the reaction vessel.

Using a catalyst

A catalyst has no effect on the position of equilibrium. However, by increasing both the forward and the backward rates of reaction, a catalyst can reduce the time it takes to reach equilibrium.

Obtaining an economic yield

Le Chatelier's principle suggests that low temperature and high pressure conditions would maximise ammonia production. However, the chemical industry does not use these conditions for economic reasons. In choosing the right temperature, manufacturers must consider:

● the yield, that is, the percentage of ammonia in the equilibrium mixture;
● the rate of reaction.

Fig 29.9 **The effects of changing conditions on the Haber process**

The rate of reaction is related to temperature. If the temperature is too low the reaction proceeds too slowly. Therefore, manufacturers use a combination of a moderate temperature and a catalyst to ensure that the rate of ammonia production is high.

High pressure gives a fast rate of reaction for a gas-phase reaction, but using higher pressures drastically increases the cost of building and running the plant.

▦ See question 2.

In economic terms, the best conditions for the Haber process are a compromise between achieving a high rate of reaction and a high percentage of ammonia in the equilibrium mixture.

Not all ammonia produced by the Haber process is used to make fertilisers; nitric acid and polyamides such as nylon are other important derivatives.

3 MANUFACTURING NITRIC ACID

Some of the ammonia that is produced in the Haber process is used to manufacture nitric acid. The **Ostwald process** uses cheap materials – ammonia, air and water – to manufacture nitric acid (Fig 29.11).

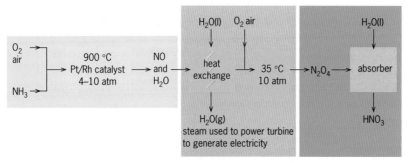

Fig 29.11 **A flow diagram showing the Otswald process for manufacturing nitric acid**

The flow diagram illustrates the three key steps in the manufacture of nitric acid:

- oxidation of ammonia to give nitrogen monoxide (NO);
- oxidation of nitrogen monoxide to nitrogen dioxide;
- disproportionation of dinitrogen tetroxide to form nitric acid.

Each of these reactions is an equilibrium process, so the compromise between rate and yield is an important economic consideration.

During the manufacturing process, the oxidation state of nitrogen changes from –3 in ammonia to +5 in nitric acid. This change also occurs in the bacterial oxidation of ammonium ions to nitrate ions in the soil.

AMMONIUM NITRATE FERTILISER

Conc NITRIC ACID

Fig 29.10 **Some uses of ammonia**

Oxidation of ammonia

Ammonia can be oxidised to nitrogen monoxide by reacting excess air and ammonia at 900 °C and about 10 atmospheres, using a platinum–rhodium catalyst (page 535).

$$4NH_3(g) + 5O_2(g) \rightleftharpoons 4NO(g) + 6H_2O(g) \quad \Delta H^\ominus = -909\,\text{kJ}\,\text{mol}^{-1}$$

The ammonia must be purified to remove any catalytic poisons because, although the starting materials are cheap, the catalyst itself is very expensive. Although the conditions are a compromise between rate and yield, they are able to give 96 per cent conversion.

Oxidation of nitrogen monoxide

The gases from the oxidation of ammonia are extremely hot and they must be cooled down to about 25 °C. At this temperature, extra air is added to the nitrogen monoxide. Two exothermic reactions take place to finally form dinitrogen tetroxide, N_2O_4.

H (a) Using Le Chatelier's principle, predict the conditions which would give the maximum conversion of ammonia to nitrogen monoxide.

(b) Predict conditions that would give the maximum rate of reaction.

(c) Comment on the conditions actually used for the catalytic oxidation.

(d) Write down an expression for the equilibrium constant, K_p, for the oxidation of ammonia.

I At 25 °C and 100 kPa the partial pressures in an equilibrium mixture of N_2O_4 and NO_2 are $pN_2O_4 = 70\,kPa$ and $pNO_2 = 30\,kPa$.

(a) Calculate the numerical value for the equilibrium constant K_p and state the units for the constant.

(b) Describe the effect on the numerical value of K_p if the temperature of the equilibrium mixture increases, assuming the total pressure remains at 100 kPa.

(c) Describe the effect on the numerical value of the K_p if the total pressure of the equilibrium mixture increases, assuming the temperature remains at 25 °C.

J Le Chatelier's principle suggests that the conversion of NO to N_2O_4 should be carried out at high pressure. Suggest advantages of this reaction at low pressures.

K Write down the oxidation state of nitrogen in: **(a)** N_2O_4 **(b)** HNO_3 **(c)** NO

L (a) Confirm that the reaction of dinitrogen tetroxide, N_2O_4, with water is a disproportionation by using the change in oxidation state.

(b) Explain why the reaction of N_2O_4 with water is carried out at low temperature.

Table 29.2 **Some chemical fertilisers and their NPK ratios. All the figures in this table can be worked out from the percentage composition by mass of the compounds**

Fertiliser	Formula	%N	%P	%K
ammonium nitrate	NH_4NO_3	35	0	0
ammonium phosphate	$(NH_4)_3PO_4$	28	21	0
potassium nitrate	KNO_3	39	0	14
ammonium sulphate	$(NH_4)_2SO_4$	21	0	0
urea	$(NH_2)_2CO$	47	0	0

M A 1 kg bag of fertiliser is made up of 500 g of potassium nitrate and 500 g of ammonium phosphate. Calculate the NPK ratio for this bag of fertiliser.

See question 5. ■

$$2NO(g) + O_2(g) \rightleftharpoons 2NO_2(g) \qquad \Delta H^\ominus = -115\,kJ\,mol^{-1}$$
$$2NO_2(g) \rightleftharpoons N_2O_4(g) \qquad \Delta H^\ominus = -58\,kJ\,mol^{-1}$$

Low temperatures are used for both of these reactions. According to Le Chatelier's principle, lower temperatures favour a shift in the equilibrium position to the right. Le Chatelier's principle also predicts that high pressures promote product formation. In practice, a pressure of only 4 to 10 atmospheres is sufficient to obtain a reasonable yield and to move the gases around the pipes within the plant.

Formation of nitric acid

In the final stage of the manufacture of nitric acid, dinitrogen tetroxide (N_2O_4) reacts with water to form nitric acid (HNO_3) and nitrogen monoxide (NO).

$$3N_2O_4(g) + 2H_2O(l) \rightleftharpoons 4HNO_3(aq) + 2NO(g) \quad \Delta H^\ominus = -103\,kJ\,mol^{-1}$$

This is an example of disproportionation since nitrogen in N_2O_4 is both oxidised and reduced during the reaction. The nitrogen monoxide produced can be recycled so that it is not wasted.

The nitric acid formed by the reaction still contains some water. This water can be removed by treatment with concentrated sulphuric acid.

Fig 29.12 **Nitric acid is used to make explosives such as TNT and nitroglycerine**

4 FERTILISERS AND THE NITROGEN CYCLE

All plants require essential elements for healthy growth. The three most important elements required are nitrogen, phosphorus and potassium. When fertilisers are sold they often quote an NPK value which gives the percentage by mass of each of these three elements in the fertiliser.

As you can see from Table 29.2, no single compound gives all three of the essential elements. Commercial fertilisers are normally a mixture of at least two chemicals in order to provide all three essential elements.

Fertilisers need to be soluble in water so that they can be absorbed through the roots of plants. It is also preferred if they can be manufactured in pellet form so that they can be easily applied to farm land.

Manufacture of fertilisers

Most fertilisers are manufactured by reacting either ammonia or nitric acid with another compound (Fig 29.13). Ammonia is a **base**. It reacts with acids to give ammonium salts, some of which are listed in Table 29.2. For example, ammonia and phosphoric acid react to form ammonium phosphate which contains two of the essential elements needed by plants.

Problems arise when fertilisers such as ammonium nitrate are applied to alkaline soils. Under these conditions, ammonia can be formed either as a gas or as aqueous ammonia:

$$(NH_4)_2SO_4(s) + 2OH^-(aq) \rightleftharpoons 2NH_3(g) + SO_4^{2-}(aq) + 2H_2O(l)$$

Ammonia gas can be identified by:

- its reaction with hydrogen chloride with which it forms a white smoke of ammonium chloride;
- its effect on moist red litmus which turns blue.

We discuss the basic characteristics of ammonia in more detail later on in the chapter.

N Write down the equation to show the formation of the fertiliser ammonium nitrate from nitric acid and aqueous ammonia.

■ See question 2.

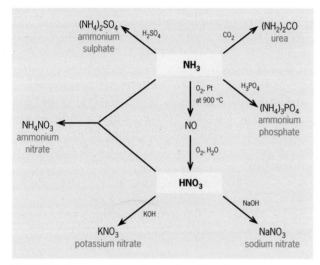

Fig 29.13(a) **Some reactions of ammonia, giving rise to many fertilisers**

Fig 29.13(b) **Ammonium nitrate fertiliser being sprayed on to a field. In some parts of the world, liquid ammonia is pumped directly into the ground as a fertiliser. This can be quite dangerous – liquid ammonia can cause chemical burns and irritate the respiratory tract**

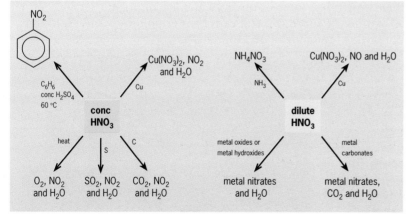

Fig 29.13(c) **Some reactions of nitric acid. Concentrated nitric acid acts as an oxidising agent, whereas dilute nitric acid acts as a strong acid. Notice that dilute nitric acid reacts with copper to form nitrogen monoxide rather than hydrogen**

Fig 29.13(d) **Concentrated nitric acid oxidises the non-reactive metal copper to form a blue solution of aqueous copper(II) nitrate. The brown gas in the photograph is nitrogen dioxide**

Over-use of fertilisers

Although fertilisers can increase crop yields it is important to use the correct amount of fertiliser so that most of it is absorbed by the plants. If too much fertiliser is applied then it is leached from the ground by water and eventually it can reach rivers and even domestic water supplies. This is a particular problem with nitrate fertilisers which are more likely to dissolve into the soil solution. In East Anglia there is some concern because the nitrate level in domestic water supplies exceeds the acceptable concentration of 50 mg dm^{-3} recommended by the European Union.

There is still much research to be done about the level of fertiliser run-off and leaching. It is not only the amount and type of fertiliser used that affect nitrate levels – the time of year, type of crop, soil type and underlying bedrock are all factors that must be considered.

Eutrophication

Leaching of fertilisers from the ground by water causes aqueous nitrate and phosphate ions to enter rivers. Nitrate ions and, to a greater extent, phosphate ions help the growth of all plants in a river. Green algae reproduce in huge numbers using the nitrate and phosphate nutrients and form an algal bloom that covers the surface and clogs up the river.

The algal bloom prevents sunlight from reaching plants growing beneath the surface of the water. These underwater plants cannot photosynthesise and they die. Colonies of bacteria feed on the decaying plant material. The bacteria respire using up most of the dissolved oxygen. As a result, other aerobic forms of life, such as fish, die. The whole process – resulting in the death of a river – is known as **eutrophication**.

Organic fertilisers

The process of bacterial decay provides a route by which animal and plant material may be recycled into ammonium ions and nitrate ions. Many farmers now use organic fertilisers such as manure, fish blood and bone. These fertilisers derive from living organisms rather than the synthetic fixation of nitrogen via the Haber process. Organic farming uses no pesticides or herbicides so it produces crops that contain less toxins. However, the use of organic fertilisers such as manure or silage can still cause water pollution and eutrophication if they are allowed to enter a river.

Fig 29.14 **Excess phosphate and nitrate nutrients in river water cause the accelerated growth of green algae. The algae form a thick surface layer causing underwater plants and fish to die. There is also concern over increased algal growth in the sea near river estuaries**

See question 2 and 5. ■

THE NITRATE–NITRITE DEBATE

EXCESSIVE LEVELS OF NITRATES in tap water can cause methaemoglobinaemia (blue-baby syndrome) in bottle-fed babies. In this syndrome, fetal haemoglobin stays in the baby's blood after birth instead of being replaced at the usual rate by normal haemoglobin.

Fetal haemoglobin has a greater affinity for nitrogen monoxide (NO) than normal haemoglobin, reducing the oxygen-carrying efficiency of the blood. Breast-fed babies are at a much lower risk of this happening. The NO that enters a bottle-fed baby's blood is thought to come from nitrite and nitrate ions in the water that the milk powder is mixed with.

It is believed that the nitrate and nitrite ions in tap

Fig 29.15 **Sodium nitrite is responsible for the pink colour of ham. It inhibits the growth of dangerous bacteria**

water are probably from fertiliser run-off that enters the water supply, but this is by no means the whole story. There are nitrates in many vegetables, particularly leaf and root crops, and other products such as beer. Nitrite ions are also in the body as a result of the biochemical reduction of nitrate ions.

Nitrates are added to cured meats to prevent bacterial spoilage and food poisoning, as the labelling on packaging indicates. An average sized ham may contain several grams of potassium nitrate or sodium nitrate. Most cured meats also contain sodium nitrite or potassium nitrite to inhibit the growth of the toxin-producing bacterium *Clostridium botulinum*.

Some scientists also think that nitrates in our diet are responsible for some stomach cancers. When nitrite ions reach the stomach, the acidic conditions are sufficient to produce nitrous acid and this in turn can be protonated to form $[H_2ONO]^+$.

$$NO_2^-(aq) + H^+(aq) \rightleftharpoons HNO_2(aq)$$
$$HNO_2(aq) + H^+(aq) \rightleftharpoons [H_2ONO]^+(aq)$$

The protonated form of nitrous acid reacts with nitrogen-containing compounds in food to produce suspected carcinogens (chemicals that cause cancer).

There will continue to be scrutiny of nitrate and nitrite ions in food preservation and tap-water until we fully understand the implications to our health.

5 AMMONIA AS A BASE

Ammonia is one of the most important bases. In aqueous conditions, an ammonia molecule can accept a proton from a water molecule to form an ammonium ion and a hydroxide ion.

$$NH_3(aq) + H_2O(l) \rightleftharpoons = NH_4^+(aq) + OH^-(aq)$$

The presence of OH^- ions means that the solution is alkaline.

Base dissociation constant

In Chapter 15, we defined Brønsted–Lowry acids as proton donors and Brønsted–Lowry bases as proton acceptors. We also described Lewis acids as electron pair acceptors and Lewis bases as electron pair donors. Fig 29.16 shows that when ammonia dissolves in water, ammonia behaves as both a Brønsted–Lowry base and as a Lewis base. Look at the equation:

$$NH_3(aq) + H_2O(l) \rightleftharpoons NH_4^+(aq) + OH^-(aq)$$

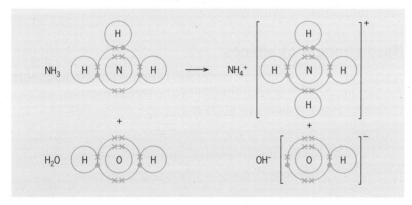

Fig 29.16 **A dot and cross diagram for ammonia, water, the ammonium ion and the hydroxide ion**

NH_3 accepts a proton from NH_4^+, which explains why NH_3 is considered a base. In this case, H_2O is the conjugate acid and donates a proton to the NH_3 base. Ammonia is considered a Lewis base because it donates an electron pair to a proton to form NH_4^+.

Although one of the four bonds in NH_4^+ is a dative covalent bond (see Fig 29.16), the four bonds are indistinguishable.

The reaction of ammonia with water is an equilibrium process, so it is possible to write an expression for the equilibrium constant:

$$K_c = \frac{[NH_4^+(aq)][OH^-(aq)]}{[NH_3(aq)][H_2O(l)]}$$

You can read more about conjugate acids on page 311.

We have included water in the expression because it is a reactant, not just a solvent. However, because water is a solvent to all components of the equilibrium, its concentration is almost constant and can be ignored. By removing the water term from the expression, we can write down a new equilibrium constant called the **base dissociation constant**, K_b.

$$K_b = \frac{[NH_4^+(aq)][OH^-(aq)]}{[NH_3(aq)]}$$

The numerical value for K_b is often very small so pK_b, the negative logarithm to base 10 of the base dissociation constant, is sometimes used instead:

See question 7. ■

$$pK_b = -\log_{10} K_b$$

Strong and weak bases

We have already described the reaction of ammonia with water to form aqueous hydroxide ions. In aqueous solutions, a **base** is a substance that will increase the concentration $OH^-(aq)$ either by reacting with water or by adding extra OH^- ions. Sodium hydroxide is a base since it fully dissociates in water to form aqueous sodium ions and aqueous hydroxide ions:

$$NaOH(s) + \xrightarrow{H_2O(l)} Na^+(aq) + OH^-(aq)$$

Bases, such as sodium hydroxide, that dissolve in water are called **alkalis**.

Sodium hydroxide and ammonia show an important difference in their behaviour with water. Sodium hydroxide fully dissociates in water, so it is known as a **strong base**; ammonia only partially dissociates, so it is known as a **weak base**.

$$NH_3(aq) + H_2O(l) \rightleftharpoons NH_4^+(aq) + OH^-(aq)$$

The position of equilibrium lies almost completely on the side of the undissociated NH_3, so a solution of a weak base will contain only a small proportion of hydroxide ions.

Base strength of amines

Amines are a class of organic molecules closely related to ammonia. Amines are derived from ammonia by the replacement of one, two or three hydrogen atoms by alkyl and or aryl groups (Fig 29.17).

> ✔ Do not confuse the idea of *strong* and *weak* bases with *concentrated* and *dilute* bases. Strong and weak in this context refer to the extent of dissociation of the base in water.

> ✔ Amines are called primary, secondary or tertiary depending on how many alkyl or aryl groups are bonded to the nitrogen atom, for example, diethylamine is a secondary amine.

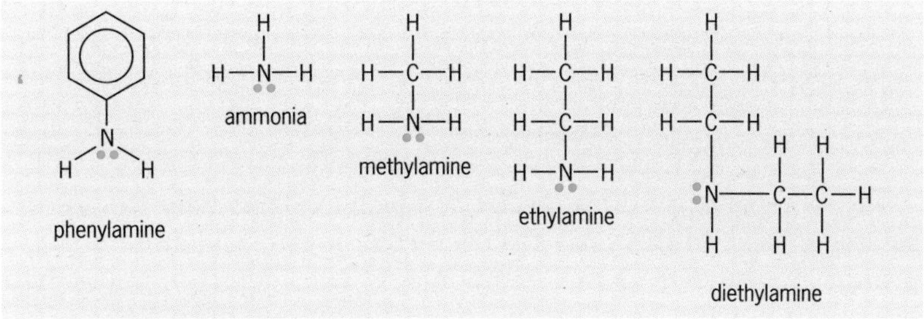

Fig 29.17 **The structure of some amines**

Amines are bases because they have a lone pair of electrons on the nitrogen atom that can be donated to $H^+(aq)$. This means they are proton acceptors.

$$R^1R^2R^3N(l) + H_2O(l) \rightleftharpoons R^1R^2R^3NH^+(aq) + OH^-(aq)$$

R^1, R^2 and R^3 can be H, an aryl or an alkyl group.

The strength of amines are compared by looking at their base dissociation constants. More dissociation occurs in a strong base, so it has a higher dissociation constant.

Table 29.3 **The base dissociation constant of some amines**

Amine	Formula	Base dissociation constant, K_b/mol dm^{-3}	pK_b
ammonia	NH_3	1.8×10^{-5}	4.7
methylamine	CH_3NH_2	4.38×10^{-4}	3.4
ethylamine	$C_2H_5NH_2$	5.6×10^{-4}	3.3
diethylamine	$(C_2H_5)_2NH$	1.3×10^{-3}	2.9
phenylamine	$C_6H_5NH_2$	3.8×10^{-10}	9.4

The base strengths of the amines in Table 29.3 can be explained in terms of the availability of the lone pair on nitrogen; the more available the lone-pair, the stronger the base. In methylamine and ethylamine, the alkyl groups are electron-releasing groups, making the lone pair on the nitrogen atom more available for donation, and therefore for accepting protons. Substituting another hydrogen atom with an alkyl group further increases the availability of the lone pair. Therefore, diethylamine is a stronger base than ethylamine. Phenylamine is a much weaker base than ammonia because the lone pair is delocalised into the π system of the benzene ring. This makes the lone pair less available for donating to a H$^+$(aq).

All amines react with dilute acids, such as hydrochloric acid, to give a salt that is soluble in water. Phenylamine reacts with dilute hydrochloric acid to give a solution of phenylammonium chloride.

$$C_6H_5NH_2(l) + HCl(aq) \rightarrow C_6H_5NH_3^+(aq) + Cl^-(aq)$$

pH of an alkaline solution

In Chapter 15, we defined the pH of an aqueous solution as the negative logarithm to base 10 of the hydrogen ion concentration.

$$pH = -\log_{10}[H^+(aq)]$$

We can determine the pH of a solution by knowing the hydrogen ion concentration. When bases dissolve in water they increase the aqueous hydroxide ion concentration. In order to find out what effect this has on the aqueous hydrogen ion concentration we must study the acid–base behaviour of water.

Ionisation of water

Water is considered to be a covalent substance, but even in the most pure sample of water there is a very small concentration of H$^+$(aq) and OH$^-$(aq). These ions are a result of **self-ionisation**:

$$H_2O(l) + H_2O(l) \rightleftharpoons H_3O^+(aq) + OH^-(aq)$$
$$\text{acid} \quad + \quad \text{base} \quad \quad \text{conjugate acid} + \text{conjugate base}$$

Look at the equation. Two molecules of water react with one another; one behaves as a base and the other as an acid. In this way, a proton is transferred from one water molecule to the other one. The self-ionisation is an equilibrium process and is often written in a simpler form:

$$H_2O(l) \rightleftharpoons H^+(aq) + OH^-(aq)$$

The position of this equilibrium lies very much to the left. The concentration of H$^+$(aq) and of OH$^-$(aq) is extremely small.

O (a) Write an equation to show the dissociation of methylamine in water.

(b) Write an expression for the base dissociation constant for methylamine.

P (a) Write an equation for the reaction of aqueous ammonia with sulphuric acid.

(b) Write an equation to show the reaction between ethylamine and dilute hydrochloric acid.

Remember: H$^+$(aq) is used to represent H$_3$O$^+$(aq).

Q The ionisation of water is an endothermic process.

(a) Using Le Chatelier's principle, predict what will happen to the position of equilibrium as the temperature of the water increases.

(b) What will happen to the numerical value of the ionic product of water as the temperature of the water increases?

(c) The electrical conductivity of water increases with increasing temperature. Suggest a reason why.

R A sample of stomach acid has an aqueous hydrogen concentration of 5.78×10^{-3} mol dm^{-3}. Calculate the OH$^-$(aq) concentration in the sample.

S The pH of an aqueous solution at 298 K is 7.6.

(a) Calculate the value of [H$^+$(aq)]?

(b) Hence calculate the value of [OH$^-$(aq)]

T The pH of pure water at 298 K is 7.0. Calculate the concentrations of the H$^+$(aq) and of the OH$^-$(aq) in pure water.

See question 8. ■

Table 29.4 **pH and pOH values for aqueous solutions**

[H$^+$(aq)]	[OH$^-$(aq)]	pH	pOH
10	1×10^{-15}	−1	15
1	1×10^{-14}	0	14
1×10^{-1}	1×10^{-13}	1	13
1×10^{-2}	1×10^{-12}	2	12
1×10^{-3}	1×10^{-11}	3	11
1×10^{-4}	1×10^{-10}	4	10
1×10^{-5}	1×10^{-9}	5	9
1×10^{-6}	1×10^{-8}	6	8
1×10^{-7}	1×10^{-7}	7	7
1×10^{-8}	1×10^{-6}	8	6
1×10^{-9}	1×10^{-5}	9	5
1×10^{-10}	1×10^{-4}	10	4
1×10^{-11}	1×10^{-3}	11	3
1×10^{-12}	1×10^{-2}	12	2
1×10^{-13}	1×10^{-1}	13	1
1×10^{-14}	1	14	0

Ionic product of water

The equilibrium constant for the ionisation of water is:

$$K_c = \frac{[H^+(aq)][OH^-(aq)]}{[H_2O(l)]}$$

Since the concentration of water is so large, it is considered to be constant. The expression simplifies to:

$$K_w = [H^+(aq)][OH^-(aq)]$$

where K_w is the **ionic product of water**. The ionic product is defined as the product of the concentrations in mol dm^{-3} of aqueous hydrogen ions and of aqueous hydroxide ions in water. Its unit is mol^2 dm^{-6}.

K_w is a constant at a particular temperature, so it will not change even if the concentration of H$^+$(aq) changes. At 298 K, the ionic product of water is 1.0×10^{-14} mol^2 dm^{-6}. This means that the concentrations of aqueous hydroxide ions and aqueous hydrogen ions are mathematically linked. In any aqueous solution, provided that one of the two concentrations is known the other one can be calculated.

EXAMPLE

Q The concentration of hydrogen ions in a sample of tap water at a temperature of 298 K is 2.5×10^{-8} mol dm^{-3}. Calculate the concentration of aqueous hydroxide ions in the water sample.

A Use the ionic product of water:

$$K_w = [H^+(aq)][OH^-(aq)]$$

Substitute into this equation the hydrogen ion concentration and the numerical value for the ionic product:

$$1.0 \times 10^{-14} = 2.5 \times 10^{-8} \times [OH^-(aq)]$$

Rearranging this equation gives:

$$[OH^-(aq)] = \frac{1.0 \times 10^{-14}}{2.5 \times 10^{-8}}$$
$$= 4.0 \times 10^{-7} \, \text{mol dm}^{-3}$$

pOH

The concentration of OH$^-$(aq) in pure water is 1.0×10^{-7} mol dm^{-3}. In most aqueous solutions, [OH$^-$(aq)] has a small value, so it is convenient to use a logarithmic scale like the one used to measure the aqueous hydrogen ion concentration. The scale that is used is called the **pOH scale**. pOH is the negative logarithm to base 10 of the hydroxide ion concentration in mol dm^{-3}.

$$\textbf{pOH} = \mathbf{-log_{10}[OH^-(aq)]}$$

There is a simple connection between the pH and the pOH of an aqueous solution. The sum of the pH and the pOH values is 14.

$$\textbf{pOH + pH = 14}$$

This equation is very useful in calculating the pH of alkaline solutions.

Determining the pH of aqueous solutions of strong bases

The pH of a strong base such as aqueous sodium hydroxide can be determined simply if the overall concentration of the base is known. We have described two ways which link the H$^+$(aq) and the OH$^-$(aq) concentration and either can be used to calculate the pH of a basic solution.

EXAMPLE

Q What is the pH of $0.150 \, mol \, dm^{-3}$ aqueous potassium hydroxide?

A Potassium hydroxide is a strong base that fully dissociates into its constituent aqueous ions.

$$KOH(aq) \rightarrow K^+(aq) + OH^-(aq)$$

The stoichiometry of the equation shows that in $0.150 \, mol \, dm^{-3}$ aqueous potassium hydroxide, $[OH^-(aq)] = 0.150 \, mol \, dm^{-3}$. Using the ionic product of water gives:

$$[H^+(aq)] = \frac{K_w}{[OH^-(aq)]} = \frac{1.00 \times 10^{-14}}{0.150} = 6.67 \times 10^{-14} \, mol \, dm^{-3}$$

So:
$$pH = -\log_{10}(6.67 \times 10^{-14}) = 13.2$$

The next Example shows another way of working out the pH of an alkaline solution. This time it uses the idea of the pOH value of a solution. You must decide for yourself which of the two methods for calculating the pH of an alkaline solution you find easier to use.

EXAMPLE

Q What is the pH of $0.200 \, mol \, dm^{-3}$ aqueous barium hydroxide?

A Aqueous barium hydroxide is a strong base. It fully dissociates in water to give $Ba^{2+}(aq)$ and $OH^-(aq)$.

$$Ba(OH)_2(aq) \rightarrow Ba^{2+}(aq) + 2OH^-(aq)$$

1 mol of barium hydroxide contains 2 mol of hydroxide ions, so:

$$[OH^-(aq)] = 2 \times [Ba(OH)_2(aq)] = 0.400 \, mol \, dm^{-3}$$

$$pOH = -\log_{10}(0.400) = 0.40$$

Using the relationship between pOH and pH gives:

$$pH = 14 - pOH = 13.60$$

Determining the pH of weak bases

Provided that you know the pK_b or K_b value of a weak base, it is easy to calculate the pH of an aqueous solution.

EXAMPLE

Q Calculate the pH of $0.10 \, mol \, dm^{-3}$ aqueous ammonia ($K_b = 1.8 \times 10^{-5} \, mol \, dm^{-3}$).

A
$$NH_3(aq) + H_2O(l) \rightleftharpoons NH_4^+(aq) + OH^-(aq)$$

At start: $\quad$ $0.10 \, mol \, dm^{-3}$ $\qquad$ $0 \, mol \, dm^{-3}$ $\quad$ $0 \, mol \, dm^{-3}$

At equilibrium: $\quad$ $0.10 - x \, mol \, dm^{-3}$ $\qquad$ $x \, mol \, dm^{-3}$ $\quad$ $x \, mol \, dm^{-3}$

Using the expression for K_b: $\quad$ $1.8 \times 10^{-5} = \frac{x \times x}{0.10 - x}$

Ammonia is a weak base, so the equilibrium lies to the left. Therefore, x is small compared to 0.10, so:

$$1.8 \times 10^{-5} = \frac{x \times x}{0.10}$$

Solving this equation gives: $\quad$ $x = 1.34 \times 10^{-3} \, mol \, dm^{-3}$

Since x is $[OH^-(aq)]$, using the expression $pOH + pH = 14$ gives the pH = 11.1.

?

U Calculate the pH of each of the following aqueous solutions at 298 K:

(a) a solution with a pOH of −0.34,

(b) a solution with $[OH^-(aq)] = 3.67 \times 10^{-4} \, mol \, dm^{-3}$,

(c) $0.100 \, mol \, dm^{-3}$ aqueous caesium hydroxide, CsOH,

(d) $2.00 \times 10^{-3} \, mol \, dm^{-3}$ aqueous calcium hydroxide, $Ca(OH)_2$.

V The pH of an aqueous solution of calcium hydroxide is 12.1. Calculate the concentrations in $mol \, dm^{-3}$ of each of the following ions in the solution:

(a) $H^+(aq)$ **(b)** $OH^-(aq)$ **(c)** $Ca^{2+}(aq)$

?

W Use the K_b value in table 29.3 to calculate the pH of $0.020 \, mol \, dm^{-3}$ methylamine.

■ See questions 7 and 8.

The titration of carbonate ion with dilute hydrochloric acid

In Chapter 15, various titration curves involving strong and weak acids are described. Titrating sodium carbonate with aqueous hydrochloric acid shows two rapid changes in pH in the titration curve (Fig 29.18)

When sodium carbonate reacts with hydrochloric acid, first hydrogencarbonate ion is formed and then carbonic acid, which decomposes to give carbon dioxide.

$$Na_2CO_3(aq) + HCl(aq) \rightarrow NaCl(aq) + NaHCO_3(aq)$$
$$NaHCO_3(aq) + HCl(aq) \rightarrow NaCl(aq) + H_2CO_3(aq)$$
$$H_2CO_3(aq) \rightleftharpoons CO_2(g) + H_2O(l)$$

In the first reaction, $CO_3^{2-}(aq)$ acts as a base and accepts an aqueous proton, $H^+(aq)$. In the second reaction $HCO_3^-(aq)$ acts a base. The two-step reaction means that the carbonate ion will have two K_b values. With the use of appropriate indicators it is possible to titrate sodium carbonate to form sodium hydrogencarbonate (using phenolphthalein) or sodium carbonate (methyl orange).

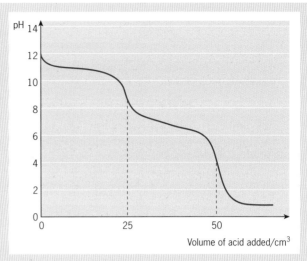

Fig 29.18 **Titration curve for the titration of 25 cm³ of 0.100 mol dm⁻³ Na₂CO₃ with 0.100 mol dm⁻³ HCl**

Buffers

On page 323, there is a description of how buffer solutions can resist a change of pH when small volumes of acid or alkali are added to them. Many buffers are made from a mixture of a weak acid and its conjugate base. Another form of buffer can be made from a mixture of a weak base and its conjugate acid. Ammonia is a weak base and its conjugate acid is the ammonium ion, so a mixture of $NH_3(aq)$ and $NH_4Cl(aq)$ is a buffer solution.

When $H^+(aq)$ is added to this buffer solution it reacts with $NH_3(aq)$, so the pH of the solution hardly changes:

$$NH_3(aq) + H^+(aq) \rightarrow NH_4^+(aq)$$

If hydroxide ions are added, the equilibrium below shifts to the right so as to minimise the increase.

$$OH^-(aq) + NH_4^+(aq) \rightleftharpoons NH_3(aq) + H_2O(l)$$

There is a vast excess of $NH_4^+(aq)$ to react with the extra $OH^-(aq)$. The $NH_4^+(aq)$ is provided by the complete dissociation of the ionic salt NH_4Cl.

EXAMPLE

Calculating the pH of a buffer solution

Q Calculate the pH of a buffer solution that contains 0.10 mol dm⁻³ ammonia and 0.20 mol dm⁻³ ammonium chloride.

A The $NH_3(aq)$ will be in equilibrium with its conjugate acid:

	$NH_3(aq)$	+	$H_2O(l) \rightleftharpoons NH_4^+(aq)$	+	$OH^-(aq)$
At start:	0.10 mol dm⁻³		0.20 mol dm⁻³		0 mol dm⁻³
			(from the dissociation of NH_4Cl)		
At equilibrium:	0.10 − x mol dm⁻³		0.20 + x mol dm⁻³	x mol dm⁻³	

Since $NH_3(aq)$ is a weak base, the equilibrium lies almost completely on the left.

Therefore, x is very small compared to 0.10 and 0.20.

At equilibrium: $[NH_3(aq)] = 0.10\,mol\,dm^{-3}$

$[NH_4^+(aq)] = 0.20\,mol\,dm^{-3}$

$[OH^-(aq)] = x\,mol\,dm^{-3}$

Substituting these values into the expression for the base dissociation constant gives:

$$K_b = 1.8 \times 10^{-5} = \frac{0.20 \times x}{0.10}$$

Solving for x gives: $x = 9 \times 10^{-6}\,mol\,dm^{-3}$

So $pOH = 5.0$ and $pH = 9.0$.

X Using the value for K_b in Table 29.3 calculate the pH of a buffer solution that is 0.200 mol dm^{-3} methylamine and 0.100 mol dm^{-3} methylammonium chloride.

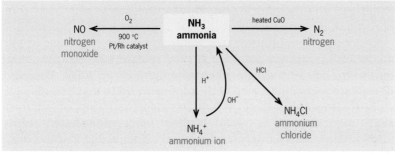

Fig 29.19 **Some important reactions of ammonia**

THE USE OF AQUEOUS AMMONIA IN IDENTIFYING METAL IONS

AQUEOUS AMMONIA is in equilibrium with aqueous ammonium ions and aqueous hydroxide ions. The aqueous hydroxide ions react with any aqueous metal ions present to form insoluble precipitates of the metal hydroxides.

These hydroxides have characteristic colours, as shown in Table 29.5, and they help chemists to identify metal ions in solution. The hydroxides formed sometimes redissolve in excess ammonia due to the formation of ammine complexes with the central metal ions. You can read more about complex ions on page 526.

Table 29.5

Metal ion	Effect of adding aqueous ammonia	Effect of adding excess ammonia	Chemical equations
aluminium	white ppt	white ppt	$Al^{3+}(aq) + 3OH^-(aq) \rightarrow Al(OH)_3(s)$
calcium	none	none	
chromium(III)	green ppt	green ppt	$Cr^{3+}(aq) + 3OH^-(aq) \rightarrow Cr(OH)_3(s)$
cobalt(II)	blue ppt	redissolves giving a brownish-yellow solution	$Co^{2+}(aq) + 2OH^-(aq) \rightarrow Co(OH)_2(s)$ The ppt redissolves because of the formation of $[Co(NH_3)_6]^{2+}(aq)$
copper(II)	light-blue ppt	redissolves giving a dark blue solution	$Cu^{2+}(aq) + 2OH^-(aq) \rightarrow Cu(OH)_2(s)$ $Cu(OH)_2(s) + 4NH_3(aq) \rightarrow [Cu(NH_3)_4]^{2+}(aq) + 2OH^-(aq)$
iron(II)	green ppt	green ppt	$Fe^{2+}(aq) + 2OH^-(aq) \rightarrow Fe(OH)_2(s)$
iron(III)	red-brown ppt	red-brown ppt	$Fe^{3+}(aq) + 3OH^-(aq) \rightarrow Fe(OH)_3(s)$
lead(II)	white ppt	white ppt	$Pb^{2+}(aq) + 2OH^-(aq) \rightarrow Pb(OH)_2(s)$
lithium	none	none	
magnesium	white ppt	white ppt	$Mg^{2+}(aq) + 2OH^-(aq) \rightarrow Mg(OH)_2(s)$
manganese	white ppt	white ppt	$Mn^{2+}(aq) + 2OH^-(aq) \rightarrow Mn(OH)_2(s)$
nickel(II)	green ppt	redissolves giving a blue solution	$Ni^{2+}(aq) + 2OH^-(aq) \rightarrow Ni(OH)_2(s)$ $Ni(OH)_2(s) + 6NH_3(aq) \rightarrow [Ni(NH_3)_6]^{2+}(aq) + 2OH^-(aq)$
potassium	none	none	
silver	brown ppt	redissolves to give a colourless solution	$2Ag^+(aq) + 2OH^-(aq) \rightarrow Ag_2O(s) + H_2O(l)$ $Ag_2O(s) + H_2O(l) + 4NH_3(aq) \rightarrow 2[Ag(NH_3)_2]^+(aq) + 2OH^-(aq)$
sodium	none	none	
zinc	white ppt	redissolves giving a colourless solution	$Zn^{2+}(aq) + 2OH^-(aq) \rightarrow Zn(OH)_2(s)$ $Zn(OH)_2(s) + 6NH_3(aq) \rightarrow [Zn(NH_3)_6]^{2+}(aq) + 2OH^-(aq)$

6 USE OF PHOSPHORUS COMPOUNDS IN AGRICULTURE

In this chapter, we have concentrated on the chemistry of nitrogen, but phosphorus compounds also have an important role to play in increasing food production. Unlike nitrogen, which is available from the unreactive reservoir of atmospheric nitrogen, phosphorus occurs naturally in a combined form as phosphate rocks. Elemental phosphorus does not appear in the phosphorus cycle. Nitrogen exists in protein, DNA and RNA, whereas phosphorus is principally found in cell membranes as phospholipids.

Phosphate fertilisers

? **Y** Calculate the percentage by mass of phosphorus in superphosphate, $Ca(H_2PO_4)_2.2CaSO_4.5H_2O(s)$.

Some fertilisers contain phosphorus(V) oxide as a source of phosphorus. When it is applied to soil, phosphorus(V) oxide reacts with water to form phosphoric acid. This in turn reacts with basic components of the soil, such as carbonate ions, to form phosphate ions.

Rocks containing phosphates are plentiful. But many are insoluble or only sparingly soluble, so they release aqueous phosphate ions to the soil very slowly, even when ground up small. Therefore phosphate rocks are treated with sulphuric acid to make soluble calcium hydrogenphosphate. When controlled amounts of sulphuric acid are added, a solid called superphosphate forms. Superphosphate is a mixture of calcium sulphate and calcium dihydrogenphosphate. this fertiliser is rich in soluble phosphate:

$$Ca_3(PO_4)_2(s) + 2H_2SO_4(aq) + 5H_2O(l) \rightarrow$$
$$Ca(H_2PO_4)_2.H_2O(s) + 2CaSO_4.2H_2O(s)$$

Herbicides

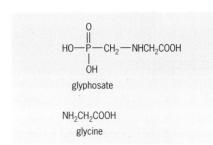

glyphosate

NH_2CH_2COOH

glycine

Fig 29.20 **The herbicide glyphosate is a derivative of the amino acid glycine**

Agrochemicals not only increase crop yields by supplying the essential elements, they can also kill off unwanted plants or weeds, reducing the competition for the essential nutrients. Such agrochemicals are known as herbicides. Herbicides are often polychlorinated compounds but there are examples of herbicides that contain phosphorus.

Insecticides

Insecticides are used to kill insects that reduce crop yields by feeding on the crops before they are harvested. It is estimated that over £2500 million is spent world-wide each year on insecticides; more than 15 per cent of crops planted are lost to feeding insects.

Reducing the amount of crop lost to insect feeding causes a dramatic increase in crop yield without the need for extra fertilisers or extra agricultural land. Insecticides are often toxic – not only to insects, but also to mammals and birds – so there are concerns about their continued use. A good insecticide must have the following characteristics:

Fig 29.21 **Insecticides help farmers to reduce the number of insects that feed on crops**

● it must act against all the insects that infest the particular crop;
● it must not damage the crop;
● it must persist for a sufficient time to avoid the need for repeat spraying or application;
● it must not react with herbicides that may be used on the crop;
● it must be safe to use and must leave no harmful residues.

These characteristics are difficult to achieve, so a compromise is often reached. Future development of new insecticides will try to achieve all five characteristics.

Organophosphorus compounds are often used as insecticides (Fig 29.22). These organophosphorus insecticides are less persistent in nature the polychlorinated compounds, discussed in page 512, since they can be broken down by bacterial enzymes in the soil.

Future developments in insecticides include the development of insect antifeedants, which do not kill the insect directly, but inhibit feeding so that the insect dies through starvation. Another possibility is to develop an insecticide that uses an aggregation pheromone to bring all the insects to a particular location where they are treated with another insecticide. Using this method, most of the crop remains unaffected by the application of the insecticide.

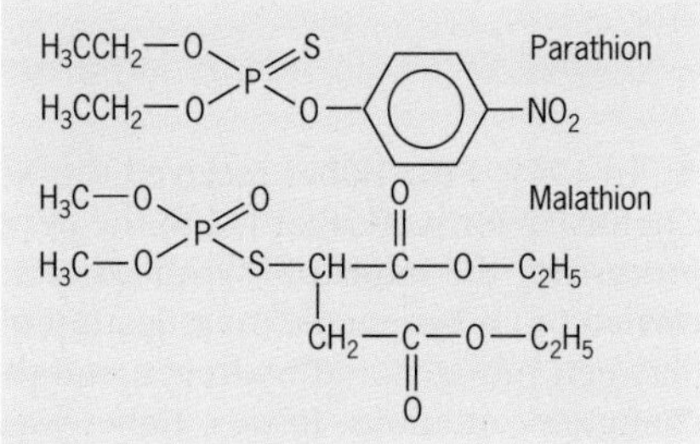

Fig 29.22 **Two organophosphorus insecticides**

■ See question 5.

You can find out more about pheromones in the Assignment on page 88.

SUMMARY

After studying this chapter, you should know the following:

■ Nitrogen is a very unreactive element because of the presence of a triple covalent bond in its molecule.

■ Nitrogen, phosphorus and potassium are essential elements for plant growth.

■ The nitrogen cycle describes the processes involved in the passage of nitrogen and its compounds through both the living and the non-living environment.

■ The Haber process is the only viable synthetic way of converting atmospheric nitrogen to nitrogen-containing compounds. In the Haber process, nitrogen and hydrogen react to form ammonia. The synthesis typically takes place at 450 °C and 200 atmospheres, in the presence of an iron catalyst.

■ In an industrial process, there is always a compromise between the position of equilibrium and the rate of reaction to ensure that the chemical is produced using the most economic conditions.

■ Le Chatelier's principle predicts the effects of external changes, such as increasing temperature and pressure, on the concentrations of reactants and products in an equilibrium reaction.

■ An increase of temperature shifts the position of equilibrium to the left-hand side in an exothermic reaction.

■ An increase in pressure shifts the position of equilibrium to the side of the stoichiometric equation that has the lesser number of moles of gaseous substances.

■ For equilibria that involve at least one gaseous component, you can write an equilibrium constant, K_p, based upon partial pressures.

■ The partial pressure of a gas in a mixture of gas is equal to the product of its mole fraction and the total pressure.

■ Ammonia is a weak base and reacts with acids, such as sulphuric acid, phosphoric acid and nitric acid, to form salts that are used as fertilisers.

■ Ammonia is converted to nitric acid by its catalytic oxidation to nitrogen monoxide and subsequent reaction of nitrogen monoxide with oxygen and water.

■ Strong bases fully dissociate when dissolved in water, whereas weak bases form an equilibrium mixture. The equilibrium constant for reaction between a weak base and water is called the base dissociation constant, K_b.

■ The larger the value of K_b, the stronger the base. Phenylamine is a weaker base than ammonia, which is a weaker base than methylamine.

■ Herbicides and insecticides are used to increase crop yields; they are often organophosphorus compounds.

QUESTIONS

1 In 1919, Fritz Haber received the Nobel Prize for Chemistry for work that led to the development of a process for the industrial synthesis of ammonia. He carried out a systematic investigation of the reaction between nitrogen and hydrogen and the effect of changing conditions. In this, Haber was able to draw on the recent advances made by Le Chatelier.

a) State Le Chatelier's principle and explain how a system under equilibrium responds to changes in (i) concentration, (ii) pressure, (iii) temperature.

b) The equilibrium

$$N_2(g) + 3H_2(g) \rightleftharpoons 2NH_3(g)$$

was studied by Haber and his team by passing a mixture of nitrogen and hydrogen in a fixed molar ratio over an appropriate catalyst and analysing the issuing gas mixture for ammonia. The following data was obtained when the total pressure was 8.00 atm and the molar ratio of nitrogen to hydrogen was 1:3.

Temperature/°C	Partial pressure of $NH_3(g)$/atm
300	0.75
500	0.20

(i) Write an expression for K_p and, by first calculating the partial pressures of nitrogen and hydrogen at each temperature, calculate K_p at each of the two temperatures. Deduce the sign of ΔH for the formation of ammonia.

(ii) At 300 °C when the total pressure is 40.0 atm, the partial pressure of ammonia is 15.0 atm. Calculate K_p under these conditions and comment on the result.

[UCLES March 1995 Modular: How Far How Fast, q.6]

2 Fig 29.Q2 shows the nitrogen cycle.

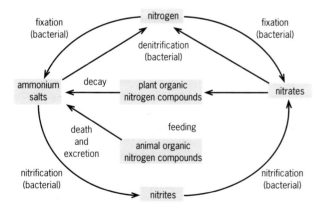

Fig 29.Q2

a) Which processes lead to an increase in the concentration of nitrogen compounds which can be utilised by plants?

b) The process of bacterial nitrification may be represented by the following equations.

$$NH_4^+(aq) + 1\tfrac{1}{2}O_2(g) \rightarrow NO_2^-(aq) + 2H^+(aq) + H_2O(l)$$

$$NO_2^-(aq) + \tfrac{1}{2}O_2(g) \rightarrow NO_3^-(aq)$$

Give the oxidation state of nitrogen in each of the three nitrogen-containing species involved.

c) With reference to the diagram of the nitrogen cycle, explain why it has become necessary to supplement naturally formed nutrients with manufactured fertilisers.

d) The basis of fertiliser production is the Haber process which is shown in the following equation.

$$N_2(g) + 3H_2(g) = 2NH_3(g) \qquad \Delta H^\ominus = -92\,kJ\,mol^{-1}$$

(i) Which part of the nitrogen cycle does it mimic?

(ii) The percentage of ammonia in the equilibrium mixture under different conditions of temperature and pressure is tabulated below.

Pressure/10^5 Pa	Temperature/K			
	473	573	673	773
10	51	15	4	1
100	32	53	25	11
300	93	71	47	24
500	95	84	65	42

Describe and explain the effects of both temperature and pressure on the equilibrium mixture.

e) Briefly state the main causes of eutrophication.

[OCSEB June 1996 Environmental Chemistry, 127/27 q.4]

3 Part of the process by which coal can be converted into a combustible mixture of gases involves passing steam over white hot coke:

$$H_2O(g) + C(s) = H_2(g) + CO(g) \qquad \Delta H = +131\ kJ\,mol^{-1}$$

a) For this reaction, write an expression for K_p, the equilibrium constant, in terms of partial pressures. State the units of K_p.

b) State and explain how the composition of the equilibrium mixture would change if there were an increase in: (i) the pressure, (ii) the temperature.

c) When steam was passed over coke at 730 °C, the following partial pressures were measured at equilibrium:

$$p(H_2O) = 90\,kPa,$$

$$p(H_2) = 183\,kPa.$$

(i) State what the equilibrium partial pressure of carbon monoxide is and hence calculate the equilibrium constant.

(ii) What will be the new equilibrium partial pressure of hydrogen if the partial pressure of steam is increased to 150 kPa?

[UCLES November 1994 Modular: How Far How Fast, q.4]

4 Ethanol, C_2H_5OH, is an important industrial chemical. Around 200 000 tonnes are manufactured in Britain each year. The usual method of manufacture is by the hydration of ethene with steam in the presence of a phosphoric acid catalyst.

$$C_2H_4(g) + H_2O(g) \rightleftharpoons C_2H_5OH(g)$$

Table 29.Q4 below gives details of various experiments carried out under different conditions in order to measure the percentage of ethene converted into ethanol at equilibrium.

Experiment	Mole ratio of reactants ethene:steam	Temperature /°C	Pressure /atm	% ethene converted
A	1:1	300	50	32
B	1:2	300	50	40
C	1:3	300	50	50
D	1:2	300	60	46
E	1:2	300	70	55
F	1:2	250	50	42
G	1:2	350	50	38

Table 29.Q4

a)   **(i)** State Le Chatelier's principle.

  (ii) Use the data in the table above to explain how the position of the equilibrium varies with changes in concentration, temperature and pressure. Show clearly your reasoning and identify which experiments you use to assist in each of your deductions.

  (iii) Predict, with justification, whether the forward reaction is exothermic or endothermic.

b) Write an expression for the equilibrium constant, K_p, for this reaction. Calculate a value for K_p under the conditions used in experiment **B** in the table above.

c) Phosphoric acid, suspended on silica, is used as a catalyst in this reaction. State the effect of the catalyst on the percentage of ethene converted to ethanol at equilibrium.

[UCLES March 1996: Modular: How Far How Fast, 4826, q.6]

5 Discuss critically the use of fertilisers, herbicides and insecticides.

6 When heated, gaseous phosphorus(V) chloride, PCl_5, dissociates to form gaseous phosphorus(III) chloride, PCl_3, and chlorine. This is an equilibrium process.

a) Write down the symbol equation, including state symbols, for the dissociation of phosphorus(V) chloride.

b) Write down an expression, and state the units, for the equilibrium constant K_c for the dissociation of phosphorus(V) chloride.

c) State and explain the effect of an increase in the external pressure, at constant temperature, on the position of equilibrium

d) At a certain temperature the partial pressures at equilibrium are shown in Table 29.Q6.

Gas	Partial pressure/Pa
$PCl_5(g)$	1.13×10^6
$PCl_3(g)$	1.66×10^6
$Cl_2(g)$	1.66×10^6

Table 29.Q6

Calculate the numerical value, and state the units, for the equilibrium constant, K_p.

7 Hydrazine is a derivative of ammonia. It has the formula N_2H_4. It is made by the reaction of chloramine, NH_2Cl, ammonia and aqueous hydroxide ions.

a) Construct an equation to show the reaction between chloramine, ammonia and hydroxide ions.

b)   **(i)** Draw a dot and cross diagram for hydrazine.

  (ii) Use the dot and cross diagram to explain why one mole of hydrazine can accept two moles of aqueous hydrogen ions.

c) Aqueous hydrazine is a weak base and reacts with water according to the equation below.

$$N_2H_4(aq) + H_2O(l) \rightleftharpoons N_2H_5^+(aq) + OH^-(aq)$$

The base dissociation constant, K_b is $3 \times 10^{-6}\,mol\,dm^{-3}$.

  (i) Write an expression for the base dissociation constant, K_b.

  (ii) Calculate the pH of $0.300\,mol\,dm^{-3}$ aqueous hydrazine.

8 The ionic product for water at 50 °C is $5.5 \times 10^{-14}\,mol^2\,dm^{-6}$.

a) What is meant by the term *ionic product* of water?

b) At 25 °C the numerical value for the ionic product of water is 1.0×10^{-14}. Use Le Chatelier's principle to account for the different values for the ionic product of water.

c) The numerical value for the base dissociation constant, K_b, of ammonia at 50 °C is 1.89×10^{-5}.

  (i) What is the pH of $0.100\,mol\,dm^{-3}$ aqueous ammonia at 50 °C?

  (ii) Would you expect the pH of $0.100\,mol\,dm^{-3}$ ammonia to be greater or less than its pH at 50 °C? Explain your answer.

Assignment

THE MANUFACTURE AND PURIFICATION OF SYNTHESIS GAS

Ammonia is made from nitrogen and hydrogen.
$$N_2(g) + 3H_2(g) \rightleftharpoons 2NH_3(g)$$
Typical conditions for the reaction are a temperature of 450 °C and a pressure of 200 to 1000 atmospheres. An iron catalyst is also used to speed up the reaction. To ensure that there is little wastage of nitrogen and hydrogen it is important that the mole ratio (hence volume ratio) of hydrogen to nitrogen is 3:1.

1 Suggest why it is important to have a 3:1 mole ratio of hydrogen to nitrogen in the Haber process.
Synthesis gas is a mixture of hydrogen and nitrogen used in the Haber process. In the United Kingdom most synthesis gas is obtained from methane, water and air. A complex series of reactions converts these materials to carbon monoxide, carbon dioxide, hydrogen and nitrogen. Synthesis gas is made once the carbon dioxide and carbon monoxide are removed. Fig 29.A1 shows the processes involved.

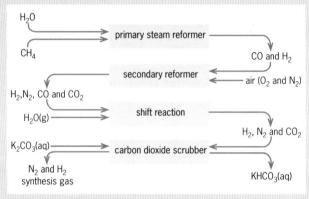

Fig 29.A1 **The production of synthesis gas for the Haber process**

2 Give advantages in using raw materials (eg air and water) in an industrial process such as the Haber process.

The first reaction in the process is called primary steam reforming. In this reaction, methane and steam are heated in the presence of a nickel catalyst at a temperature of about 1100 K and 30 atmospheres pressure:
$$CH_4(g) + H_2O(g) = CO(g) + 3H_2(g)$$

3
a) Write down an expression for the equilibrium constant K_p for the primary steam reforming.
b) The partial pressures at equilibrium are as follows:
$pCH_4 = 80\,kPa$ atm, $pH_2O = 80\,kPa$, $pCO = 710\,kPa$ and $pH_2 = 2130\,kPa$. Calculate a numerical value, and state the units for K_p.

c) Primary steam reforming is endothermic. Use Le Chatelier's principle to predict the conditions that make the position of equilibrium lie to the right-hand side.
d) Comment on the actual conditions used for the primary steam reforming step.

The next stage is the secondary steam reforming. At the end of this stage, a mixture of nitrogen, hydrogen, carbon dioxide and carbon monoxide is produced. Most of the unconverted methane from the primary reforming stage is converted to hydrogen and carbon dioxide while at the same time oxygen is removed as oxides:
$$2H_2(g) + O_2(g) \rightarrow 2H_2O(g)$$
$$CH_4(g) + H_2O(g) \rightleftharpoons CO(g) + 3H_2(g) \quad \Delta H^\ominus = +210\,kJ\,mol^{-1}$$

4 Predict the reaction conditions needed to obtain a high yield from the reaction of methane and steam.
Carbon dioxide and carbon monoxide must be then be removed so that only hydrogen and nitrogen remain. The shift reaction converts carbon monoxide to carbon dioxide by reaction with steam at 670 K using an iron oxide catalyst.

5
a) Construct the equation for the reaction between carbon monoxide and steam.
b) Suggest why it is important to remove all the carbon monoxide before the gases enter the Haber process.
Finally carbon dioxide is removed in a scrubber which involves reaction with aqueous potassium carbonate:
$$K_2CO_3(aq) + H_2O(l) + CO_2(g) \rightarrow 2KHCO_3(aq)$$
It is possible to regenerate the aqueous potassium carbonate by heating the aqueous potassium carbonate with steam.

6 Suggest why it is useful to be able to regenerate the aqueous potassium carbonate.

After scrubbing, the gases present are nitrogen and hydrogen. Any small traces of carbon monoxide or carbon dioxide are removed by reaction with hydrogen using a nickel catalyst. This results in the formation of a trace of methane, CH_4.

7 Construct equations to show the reaction of:
a) carbon monoxide with hydrogen;
b) carbon dioxide with hydrogen.

8 Nitrogen is also obtained by the fractional distillation of liquid air; hydrogen is obtained from the cracking of hydrocarbons. Suggest advantages of making nitrogen and hydrogen in the process described earlier in the passage rather than from the fractional distillation and cracking routes.

9 A company wants to build a plant to make ammonia starting from methane and air. Discuss the geographical location that the company should choose to build the plant.

AMMONIA, BASES AND FOOD PRODUCTION

The main use of ammonia is in the production of artificial fertilisers to supply crops for the world's population. Through a review of the production of ammonia and its reactions, the chapter covers the properties and behaviour of bases and calculation of the pH of basic solutions. Study the Chapter Map to see how the ideas in the chapter interlink.

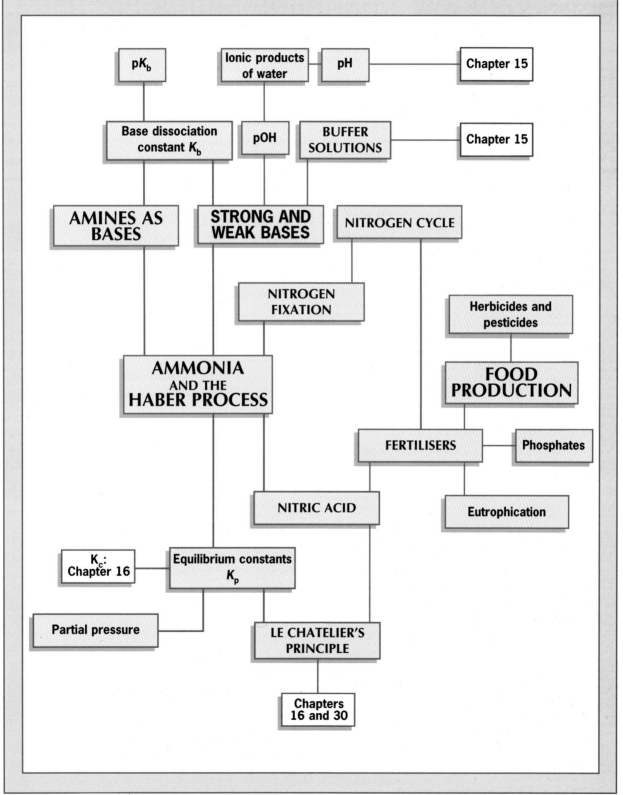

30 Group 4 and Group 6 elements

SILICON COMPOUNDS are at the centre of materials science and vital to the glass, cement and quartz industries. The element silicon is now being used on a smaller scale in the manufacture of semiconductors, solar cells and microchips. The impact of silicon in computing has been enormous. The introduction of micromachines involving silicon technology means that the applications of silicon-based materials will continue to expand.

Specialised silicon compounds are being developed to withstand harsh conditions. For example, materials in spacecraft have to perform over a wide temperature range and while bombarded by high levels of cosmic radiation.

Amongst the materials that involve silicon that chemists have been developing are:

ceramics, such as silicon carbide, that can withstand extremely high temperatures;

glasses, some of them used to store radioactive waste;

silicones that can be used as oils or water resistant sealants;

aerogels that are solids with a density only 4 times that of air.

Almost all of these materials contain silicon–oxygen single bonds in their structure. This bond is fundamental to large areas of materials science.

1 GROUP 4 AND GROUP 6 ELEMENTS

This chapter describes the chemistry of some non-metals, a semi-metal and some metals. We consider the elements in Group 4, one of the most diverse groups of elements in the Periodic Table. At the top of Group 4 is carbon, a non-metal; at the bottom of the group is lead, a metal. We identify some of the trends and patterns within the group, and concentrate on the chemistry of silicon and its manufacturing applications.

In addition, we describe some aspects of the chemistry of sulphur, one of the non-metals in Group 6. (The chemistry of oxygen and oxides has been covered in detail in earlier chapters, so this aspect of Group 6 chemistry is not covered in depth in this chapter.)

2 GROUP 4 ELEMENTS

When we described the properties of the halogens in Chapter 23 and the elements of Groups 1 and 2 in Chapter 22, we were able to emphasise the similarity in chemical properties and the predictable variation of physical properties with increasing atomic number. This is not really possible with the elements of Group 4 because the elements vary from non-metal to metal within the group.

Occurrence of the elements

Carbon occurs naturally in the Earth's crust as carbonate minerals, crude oil, natural gases and coals. Furthermore, all living organisms contain compounds of carbon. Elemental carbon occurs in small quantities as graphite or diamond deposits.

Silicon comprises almost a quarter of the Earth's crust and is almost always found combined with oxygen. Clays, sands and most of the components of soils contain compounds of silicon and oxygen.

Table 30.1 **Group 4 elements**

Element	Symbol
carbon	C
silicon	Si
germanium	Ge
tin	Sn
lead	Pb

Some of the minerals that contain silicon and oxygen are described later in the chapter.

Fig 30.1 **Clays are complex silicates and aluminosilicates. Silicates contain strong silicon–oxygen bonds**

The manufacture of silicon

The extraction process for each of the Group 4 elements is quite similar. The favoured method is to reduce the oxide of the Group 4 element using carbon or a reducing agent of similar reactivity.

Silicon is manufactured by the high temperature reduction of silica (silicon dioxide) with either magnesium or carbon:

$$SiO_2 + 2C \rightarrow 2CO + Si$$

The silicon obtained by the reduction of silica is not pure enough for use in making semiconductors, microchips and solar cells. It is purified by converting silicon to silicon(IV) chloride, then reducing it back to silicon:

$$Si + 2Cl_2 \rightarrow SiCl_4$$

$$SiCl_4 + 2Mg \rightarrow Si + 2MgCl_2$$

It is easy to remove the soluble magnesium chloride from the silicon by washing with hot water. A further process called zone refining yields very pure silicon (Fig 30.2).

Fig 30.2 **The zone refining process. Zone refining is used to make ultra-pure silicon. A rod of silicon is heated at one end by a moving heat source. The heat source produces a thin cross section of molten silicon. As the heat source moves downwards so does the cross section of molten silicon, taking dissolved impurities with it. Eventually the impurities are concentrated at the bottom of the rod while the rest of the silicon is ultra-pure**

?

A Write down the equation for the reaction of magnesium with silicon dioxide.

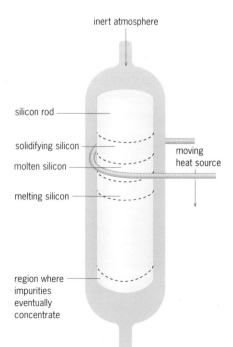

inert atmosphere

silicon rod

solidifying silicon

molten silicon

melting silicon

moving heat source

region where impurities eventually concentrate

?

B Suggest reasons why silicon is very expensive to make, even though the raw material silicon dioxide is both cheap and plentiful.

C (a) Why must zone refining take place in an inert atmosphere rather than in air?

(b) Suggest a gas that could be used to provide the inert atmosphere.

Read about the blast furnace on page 11.

?

D Write balanced equations for the reduction by carbon of: **(a)** lead(II) oxide, PbO, **(b)** tin(IV) oxide, SnO_2.

E Lead(II) oxide is obtained from galena, PbS. Galena is roasted in air and forms lead(II) oxide and sulphur dioxide.

(a) Suggest one environmental problem with this roasting process.

(b) Write down the balanced chemical equation for the roasting process.

Read about the structure and properties of diamond, graphite and silicon on page 417.

Extraction of tin and lead

Both tin and lead are extracted by reduction of an oxide (lead(II) oxide or tin(IV) oxide) with carbon. In both cases, the chemistry of the reduction is similar to that taking place in the blast furnace during the extraction of iron.

Physical properties of Group 4 elements

We described in Chapter 20 how the physical properties of an element are related to its structure. Giant molecular structures have high melting points and simple molecular structures have low melting points. Giant metallic structures conduct heat and electricity very well but molecular structures in general do not.

SILICON CARBIDE

SILICON CARBIDE is a very useful ceramic material. It has an extremely high melting point and it is extremely hard. These two properties explain its use as an abrasive.

The structure of silicon carbide is similar to that of diamond (Fig 30.3) and as a result the two substances share many physical properties.

Research is under way to produce silicon carbide fibres that could be incorporated into a composite material. Such a fibre would have an extremely high tensile fracture strength.

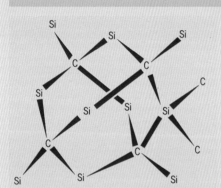

Fig 30.3 **The structure of silicon carbide. Silicon carbide has a diamond-like structure; each silicon atom is surrounded by four carbon atoms and each carbon atom is surrounded by four silicon atoms**

Table 30.2 **Physical properties of the Group 4 elements**

	Carbon	Silicon	Germanium	Tin	Lead
Atomic number	6	14	32	50	82
Electron configuration	$1s^22s^22p^2$	$1s^22s^22p^63s^23p^2$	$[Ar]3d^{10}4s^24p^2$	$[Kr]4d^{10}5s^25p^2$	$[Xe]4f^{14}5d^{10}6s^26p^2$
Covalent atomic radius/pm	77	117	122	140	146
Electronegativity	2.5	1.7	2.0	1.7	1.6
First ionisation energy/kJ mol^{-1}	1090	786	762	707	716
Melting point/°C	3570 (diamond)	1414	959	232	328
Boiling point/°C	sublimes above 3700	3309	2837	2687	1755
Density/kg m^{-3}	3510 (diamond); 2220 (graphite)	2330	5360	5750 (grey tin); 5750 (white tin)	1130
Electrical conductivity	good (graphite); poor (diamond)	semiconductor	semiconductor	good	good
Structure of solid	giant molecular	giant molecular	giant molecular	giant metallic	giant metallic

?

F List the similarities and the differences between the structures of diamond and silicon carbide.

The metallic character of the elements increases as the atomic (proton) number increases. With a larger atomic radius, the outer electrons are farther from the nucleus and are better shielded by inner shells of electrons.

Read more about metallic bonding and the properties of metals on page 413.

Tin and lead have the typical physical properties of metals. They are:

- dense;
- lustrous;
- good conductors of heat and electricity;
- malleable;
- ductile.

Tin and lead have relatively low melting points, indicating that the metallic bonding is not as strong as in the transition elements. Transition elements are able to use d electrons in the sea of delocalised electrons, but tin and lead use only p electrons from the 5p and 6p subshells respectively.

■ See questions 1 and 7.

Fig 30.4 **An alloy of tin and lead can be used to mend broken electrical connections**

G What properties of tin and lead make them suitable for producing an alloy to be used in soldering?

3 CHEMICAL PROPERTIES OF THE ELEMENTS OF GROUP 4

You can see from Table 30.2 that all the elements in Group 4 have four electrons in the outer shell. So one atom of the element could either gain or lose four electrons to attain a stable electron configuration. It is virtually impossible for any atom to lose four electrons to form an X^{4+} ion. Firstly, the ion's high charge density would polarise any anion in its vicinity and so would form a covalent bond. Secondly, the energy required to remove four electrons is extremely large.

This means that an atom of a Group 4 element must gain four electrons, which give the X^{4+} ion. But the ion is not very stable. Four electrons are more likely to be gained by covalent bonding, giving all the elements an oxidation state of +4 in some of their compounds. In fact, almost all the compounds of silicon are covalent with an oxidation state of +4.

Read more about charge density and polarisation of anions on pages 85 and 467.

The inert pair effect

Germanium, tin and lead form ionic compounds as well as covalent compounds. In ionic compounds, an atom of these elements loses two electrons to form Ge^{2+}, Sn^{2+} or Pb^{2+} ions. For example, if a lead atom loses two electrons it attains an electron configuration involving a filled outer sub-shell, $6s^2$. The two electrons in the 6s orbital are known as the **inert pair** because they are in the outer shell of electrons but are not used in bonding. This effect means that lead, germanium and tin can show two oxidation states:

- the ionic, +2 oxidation state;
- the covalent, +4 oxidation state.

It is impossible for carbon and silicon atoms to behave in the same way, because the loss of two electrons does not give a sufficiently stable electron configuration.

H Write down the electronic configuration for:

(a) Sn and Sn^{2+},

(b) Ge and Ge^{2+},

(c) Si and Si^{2+}.

(d) Use electron configurations to show the existence of an inert pair of electrons in tin and germanium but not in silicon.

I (a) Copy out and complete Table 30.3.

(b) Explain why the second ionisation energy is always bigger than the corresponding first ionisation energy.

(c) Explain why the first ionisation energy of carbon is larger than the first ionisation energy of germanium.

(d) Comment on any unexpected pattern in the first and second ionisation energies.

Table 30.3 **The ionisation energies of Group 4 elements**

Element	First ionisation energy/kJ mol⁻¹, $X(g) \rightarrow X^+(g) + e^-$	Second ionisation energy/kJ mol⁻¹, $X^+(g) \rightarrow X^{2+}(g) + e^-$	Energy needed to make one mole of $X^{2+}(g)$ ions from X atoms/kJ mol⁻¹, $X(g) \rightarrow X^{2+}(g) + 2e^-$
carbon	799	2420	
silicon	786	1580	
germanium	762	1540	
tin	707	1410	
lead	716	1450	

Metallic character in Group 4

We have seen how the loss of electrons from an atom to form a cation is characteristic of a metal atom and the gain of electrons to form either an anion or a covalent bond is characteristic of a non-metal atom. The loss of electrons resulting in a +2 oxidation state shows the metallic character of germanium, tin and lead. The metallic character of the elements increases with increasing atomic number, so that lead has the most metallic character of all the Group 4 elements.

Elements with higher atomic (proton) numbers have more shielding electrons between the outer electrons and the nucleus. This means that the outer electrons experience a reduced effective nuclear charge. In addition, the outer electrons are further away from the nucleus so the two 6p electrons can be lost easily by an atom of lead.

Carbon and silicon show no evidence whatsoever of metallic character; in fact, the +2 oxidation state is virtually absent from the chemistry of both elements.

See question 7. ■

Non-metallic character in Group 4

See question 1. ■

J Draw a dot and cross diagram to show the covalent bonding in lead(IV) chloride. You need only draw the electrons in the outermost shell.

The non-metallic character of the elements decreases as atomic (proton) number increases. However, there is evidence of some non-metallic character as far down the group as lead. Lead(IV) compounds and, in particular, the lead(IV) halides are covalent in nature; they involve a lead atom gaining four electrons through covalent bonding to achieve a stable electron configuration.

Whether metallic or non-metallic character is considered, the elements in Group 4 are members of a relatively unreactive group.

Reactions of Group 4 elements with oxygen

Most Group 4 elements react with air or oxygen when heated to form a dioxide in which the element has a +4 oxidation state. Carbon forms a gaseous dioxide, whereas the other elements form solid dioxides.

$$C(s) + O_2(g) \rightarrow CO_2(g)$$
$$X(s) + O_2(g) \rightarrow XO_2(g)$$

where X is Si, Ge and Sn.

Lead forms lead(II) oxide when it is heated in air:

$$Pb(s) + \tfrac{1}{2}O_2(g) \rightarrow PbO(s)$$

Even if lead(IV) oxide were to form, it would thermally decompose at Bunsen flame temperatures to give lead(II) oxide.

Fig 30.5 **Charcoal is mainly carbon. It burns to give carbon dioxide in a highly exothermic**

LEAD POLLUTION IN WATER

LEAD REACTS SLOWLY with soft water if the water contains dissolved air. Hydrogen is not produced in this reaction. The lead hydroxide that forms is insoluble in water but, as we mentioned in Chapter 22, even substances that we call insoluble do actually dissolve a little. Therefore, a small proportion of aqueous lead(II) ions exist, commonly referred to as 'dissolved lead.'

$$Pb(s) + H_2O(l) + \tfrac{1}{2}O_2(g) \rightarrow Pb(OH)_2(s)$$

$$Pb(OH)_2(s) \rightleftharpoons Pb^{2+}(aq) + 2OH^-(aq)$$

Lead has been extensively used in water pipes. In fact, the name plumber comes from the Latin name for lead, *plumbum*. Lead water pipes pose a health hazard because some water supplies dissolve the lead to form lead(II) hydroxide faster than other supplies.

Soft water dissolves lead pipes but acidic moorland water is the worst culprit. Hydrogen ions in the water increase the rate of dissolving and produce a higher concentration of dissolved lead(II) ions.

$$Pb(s) + 2H^+(aq) + \tfrac{1}{2}O_2(g) \rightarrow Pb^{2+}(aq) + H_2O(l)$$

Hard water areas are relatively immune from the problem because insoluble calcium carbonate lines the pipes, preventing any contact between the water supply and the lead pipe.

Lead in tap water is known to retard the mental development of small children. It is also known to be a cumulative poison. In some areas, small flakes of lead have been reported in drinking water but the effect of these flakes is not yet clear. Accidental ingestion of a lead flake may have no effect at all or it may remain in the gut for sufficient time to change into dissolved lead.

Water companies are under pressure from environmental legislation to reduce the concentration of dissolved lead in domestic water to the permitted level. One way they try to do this is to add phosphates to the water. The phosphates precipitate lead(II) phosphate and also line the pipes with insoluble calcium phosphate. However, the only real way to prevent the source of lead poisoning is for water companies to completely replace lead water pipes with plastic ones.

Fig 30.6 **This scale or fur is formed from hard water; it lines the inside of the pipes and prevents the lead from reacting with water**

Reactions with halogens

All the elements except carbon react when heated with halogens to give a halide:

$$X(s) + 2Cl_2(g) \rightarrow XCl_4(l)$$

where X = Si, Ge and Sn. Lead forms the chloride $PbCl_2$ rather than the tetrachloride due to the thermal instability of lead(IV) chloride.

$$Pb(s) + Cl_2 \rightarrow PbCl_2(s)$$

■ See question 2.

?

K Write down equations for the reactions between each pair of elements:

(a) lead and iodine,

(b) tin and fluorine,

(c) germanium and bromine.

4 OXIDES OF GROUP 4 ELEMENTS

Most of the Group 4 elements form two oxides. These are an oxide of formula XO with the element in the +2 oxidation state and an oxide of formula XO_2 with the element in the +4 oxidation state.

XO_2 Oxides (the dioxides)

Table 30.4 **The dioxides of Group 4 elements**

Oxide	Formula	Structure and bonding	Acid–base behaviour	Thermal stability	Oxidising power
carbon dioxide	CO_2	simple molecular	acidic	does not decompose on heating	very weak oxidising agent
silicon(IV) oxide	SiO_2	giant molecular	acidic	does not decompose on heating	increasing oxidising power
germanium(IV) oxide	GeO_2	giant molecular	amphoteric	does not decompose on heating	
tin(IV) oxide	SnO_2	giant molecular with ionic character	amphoteric	does not decompose at Bunsen burner temperatures	
lead(IV) oxide	PbO_2	giant molecular with ionic character	amphoteric	decomposes on heating	powerful oxidising agent

All Group 4 elements form a dioxide with the empirical formula XO_2, where X is C, Si, Ge, Sn or Pb. These dioxides are often referred to as the element(IV) oxide, such as silicon(IV) oxide. There is a distinct change in the chemical properties of these oxides as the atomic (proton) number of the Group 4 element increases. This reflects a change in the stability of the +4 oxidation state.

Thermal stability of the dioxides

The thermal stability of the dioxides decreases as the atomic (proton) number of the Group 4 element increases. Strong heating of lead(IV) oxide will give oxygen and lead(II) oxide.

$$PbO_2(s) \rightarrow PbO(s) + \tfrac{1}{2}O_2(g)$$

Silicon(IV) oxide is very thermally stable; silicon dioxide is often a component of ceramics. One crystalline form of silicon dioxide is quartz. Quartz is a hard, brittle, clear and colourless solid. It is used for architectural decorations, semi-precious jewels, optical instruments and as a frequency controller in radio transmitters. When quartz is eroded it forms almost pure sand.

Quartz melts at 1600 °C to form a viscous liquid. When this liquid cools, it does not crystallise and the internal structure remains random. A substance with this type of structure is known as a glass.

Oxidising power of the dioxides

Group 4 elements form two sets of oxides, XO_2 (oxidation state of X +4) and XO (oxidation state of X +2). It is possible to covert XO_2 to

Read about why carbon dioxide forms a simple molecule and silicon dioxide forms a giant molecule on page 447.

Fig 30.7 **Radioactive material is easily stored in glass which is enclosed in steel. As long as it remains dry, radiation is confined by this process called vitrification**

See question 9. ■

Read more about quartz and silicon dioxide on page 447.

L Write down the equation for the reaction of aqueous sodium silicate, Na_2SiO_3, with dilute hydrochloric acid. Hint: in this reaction the sodium silicate behaves in a similar way to sodium carbonate.

AEROGELS

AEROGELS ARE an exciting new class of synthetic materials that have an extremely low density. They consist of 10 per cent silica or silicon(IV) oxide, the same material found in sand, and 90 per cent gas. They have such a low density that they can float on whisked egg white. In addition, they have unusual optical, thermal, electrical and acoustic properties.

It has been known for some time that an aqueous solution of sodium silicate and hydrochloric acid react to form a gelatinous solid. Heating this mixture eventually gives a solid called silica gel which has a large surface area and readily adsorbs water. Aerogels are similar in nature, but are solids with gas, rather than a liquid, trapped within a cage of atoms.

Fig 30.8 **Silica gel absorbs water from the air to make a dry atmosphere**

When aerogels were first discovered, preparing them was a long and difficult process which involved using potentially dangerous methanol to make the gel. Later on, a method was developed to make an aerogel filled with carbon dioxide. Such aerogels could be made into dry pellets containing strings of silica tetrahedra encircling the gas spaces.

Aerogels are excellent insulators because there are fewer solid atoms to conduct heat than in conventional insulators and the gas pores are too small for the gas inside to conduct heat effectively. Some aerogels have

XO. This is reduction. This means that the dioxides, XO_2, are oxidising agents. Lead(IV) oxide and tin(IV) oxide are the most powerful oxidation agents. Lead(IV) oxide and tin(IV) oxide can both oxidise hydrochloric acid to form chlorine:

$$PbO_2(s) + 4HCl(aq) \rightarrow PbCl_2(aq) + 2H_2O(l) + Cl_2(g)$$

Acid–base reactions of the dioxides

Chapter 21 covered the acid–base reactions of oxides: covalent oxides are often acidic and ionic oxides are basic. Most metal oxides are ionic and most non-metal oxides are covalent, so we can say that metal oxides are often basic and non-metal oxides are often acidic.

On this basis, we would expect most Group 4 oxides to show some acidic behaviour because bonding in carbon dioxide and silicon dioxide is covalent, and even in lead(IV) oxide there will be a high degree of covalent bonding. This acidic behaviour is shown by the reactions of the dioxides. The test for carbon dioxide, in which limewater (aqueous calcium hydroxide) turns milky, is an example of an acidic reaction of carbon dioxide. The precipitate formed is calcium carbonate. In the same way, sodium hydroxide pellets react with carbon dioxide to form sodium carbonate:

$$2NaOH(s) + CO_2(g) \rightarrow Na_2CO_3(s) + H_2O(l)$$

Limestone is added to blast furnaces. This is decomposed to calcium oxide which reacts with SiO_2 (sand) impurity to remove it as calcium silicate, $CaSiO_3$. This is an example of silicon dioxide behaving as an acidic oxide.

M Explain why lead(IV) oxide is a better oxidising agent than silicon dioxide.
Hint: think about the relative stabilities of the +2 oxidation states.

If carbon dioxide is bubbled through lime-water for several minutes, a white precipitate, $CaCO_3(s)$, is formed first. This reacts with further carbon dioxide to form a colourless solution of calcium hydrogencarbonate.

N Write down the equation for the reaction of carbon dioxide with limewater to form insoluble calcium carbonate.

For more information about blast furnaces, see Chapter 1

one fifth of the thermal conductivity of poly(phenylethene) and others have a density that is only four times that of air.

One application of aerogels is in windows. A layer of aerogel can be sandwiched between two layers of glass to improve the insulation properties of the glass. The aerogel also scatters light and produces a frosted glass effect.

Research is underway to improve the thermal insulation properties of aerogels still further by removing all the gas from the pores, leaving a vacuum. There is also scope to make aerogel catalysts where the reaction between gases takes place within the gel itself.

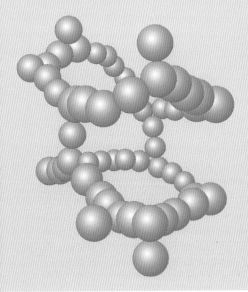

Fig 30.9 **An aerogel is made of silica chains that encircle air-filled pores. The circles in the diagram represent SiO_4 tetrahedra**

Even lead(IV) oxide shows some acidic character when it reacts with concentrated aqueous sodium hydroxide to form the plumbate(VI) ion.

$$PbO_2(s) + 2NaOH(aq) \rightarrow Na_2PbO_3(aq) + H_2O(l)$$

Basic properties of the dioxides are shown by tin and lead, but the reactions with acids are often complicated by subsequent redox reactions.

See questions 1 and 9. ■

XO oxides (the monoxides)

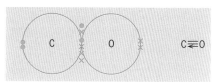

Carbon monoxide is a simple molecule that is iso-electronic with a nitrogen molecule. It has two covalent bonds and one dative covalent bond.

Table 30.5 **The oxides of Group 4 elements (SiO is omitted from the table because it does not exist under standard conditions)**

Oxide	Formula	Structure and bonding		Acid–base behaviour	
carbon monoxide	CO	simple molecular	Increasing ionic character	neutral	Increasing basic character
germanium(II) oxide	GeO	giant ionic		amphoteric	
tin(II) oxide	SnO	giant ionic		amphoteric	
lead(II) oxide	PbO	giant ionic		amphoteric	

METAL CARBONYLS

CARBON MONOXIDE FORMS A RANGE of compounds with transition metals. They are known as carbonyls. Carbon monoxide acts as a **ligand** and donates a pair of electrons to an empty orbital of an atom of the transition element. An interesting feature of many of these carbonyls is that the oxidation state of the transition element is often 0.

Fig 30.10 **The structure of tetracarbonylnickel(0). Tetracarbonylnickel(0) is a tetrahedral neutral complex. Carbon monoxide ligands form dative bonds with the central nickel atom**

The first metal carbonyl was discovered by Ludwig Mond in 1889. It was tetracarbonylnickel(0), $Ni(CO)_4$, a colourless, volatile liquid. The discovery of $Ni(CO)_4$ opened up the way for large scale production of pure nickel.

Carbon monoxide reacts with nickel at 50 °C to give volatile $Ni(CO)_4$ which evaporates, leaving behind impurities.

$$Ni(s) + 4CO(g) \rightarrow Ni(CO)_4(l)$$

The $Ni(CO)_4$ decomposes at 200 °C to yield pure nickel and CO. Fortunately for Mond, the discovery of stainless steel at that time created a demand for large quantities of nickel, so he was able to develop a large manufacturing plant producing pure nickel for a ready made market.

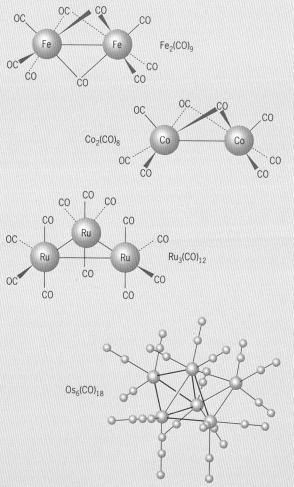

Fig 30.11 **Some other metal carbonyls. Some metal carbonyls contain bridging carbon monoxide ligands**

Fig 30.12 **Nickel prepared via $Ni(CO)_4$ is used as an alloy with tungsten and other metals to make the engines for this airliner**

Oxidation of the monoxides

Since lead(IV) oxide is the least thermally stable of the dioxides it forms the most stable monoxide.

CO, GeO and SnO all readily react with oxygen to give the respective dioxides. For example, carbon monoxide combusts to give carbon dioxide and anhydrous tin(II) oxide reacts with oxygen in the air to give SnO_2:

$$2SnO(s) + O_2(g) \rightarrow 2SnO_2(s)$$

Lead(II) oxide will not form lead(IV) oxide when heated in air, but at 400 °C with prolonged heating it will form red lead (see Self-test question **P**).

Acid–base reactions of the monoxides

The oxides become more basic as the atomic (proton) number of the Group 4 element increases. This is because bonding in the oxide becomes more ionic in character and ionic oxides show basic properties. Even though the basic character increases, lead(II) oxide is not a basic oxide; it is amphoteric because it reacts with acids and bases. In acids, lead(II) oxide forms lead(II) salts and with aqueous alkalis it forms plumbate(II), PbO_2^{2-}:

$$PbO(s) + 2HNO_3(aq) \rightarrow Pb(NO_3)_2(aq) + H_2O(l)$$

$$PbO(s) + 2NaOH(aq) \rightarrow Na_2PbO_2(aq) + H_2O(l)$$

Fig 30.13 **A summary of the properties of Group 4 oxides**

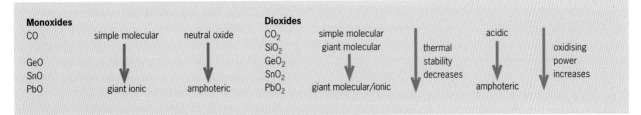

5 THE CHLORIDES OF GROUP 4 ELEMENTS

Earlier in the chapter we described how the stability of Group 4 dioxides (with the element in the +4 oxidation state) decreases as the atomic (proton) number of the element increases whereas the stability of the monoxide (element in the +2 oxidation state) increases. Exactly the same trend in stability is observed with the two sets of chlorides, XCl_4 (with the element in the +4 oxidation state) and XCl_2 (with the element in the +2 oxidation state). The +4 oxidation state involves covalent bonding and the +2 oxidation state involves ionic bonding.

The tetrachlorides

Table 30.6

Formula	Structure and bonding	Bond length of X–Cl /nm	Thermal stability	Action of cold water
CCl_4	simple molecular	0.177	thermally stable	none
$SiCl_4$	simple molecular		thermal	rapidly hydrolysed to form SiO_2 and HCl
$GeCl_4$	simple molecular	increases	stability	rapidly hydrolysed to form GeO_2 and HCl
$SnCl_4$	simple molecular		decreases	rapidly hydrolysed to form SnO_2 and HCl
$PbCl_4$	simple molecular		thermally decomposes at room temperature to form $PbCl_2$ and Cl_2	rapidly hydrolysed to form PbO_2 and HCl

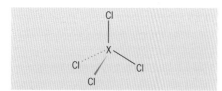

Fig 30.14 **The shape of the covalent tetrachlorides. The tetrachlorides of Group 4 elements are all simple, tetrahedral molecules**

?

Q Write an equation to show the thermal decomposition of lead(IV) chloride.

Read why tetrachloromethane cannot be hydrolysed on page 442.

See questions 1 and 8. ■

With the exception of carbon, the tetrachlorides (XCl_4) are named element(IV) chloride. In the case of carbon, the name tetrachloromethane is preferred to show its relationship to the hydrocarbon methane. All of the tetrachlorides have a simple molecular structure and so have low boiling points and melting points.

Thermal stability of the tetrachlorides
The thermal stability of the tetrachlorides decreases with increasing atomic (proton) number of the Group 4 element. This trend in thermal stability is explained in terms of the bond strengths of the X–Cl bond. We have described that a covalent bond is formed by the overlap of atomic orbitals; in the case of the Pb–Cl bond, there is very little overlap because of the difference in energy between the orbitals involved. With very little overlap, the covalent bond is extremely weak and is therefore easy to break.

Hydrolysis of the tetrachlorides
In Chapters 21 and 23 we described the hydrolysis of covalent chlorides. With the exception of tetrachloromethane all the tetrachlorides are readily hydrolysed to form the dioxide as a precipitate and either hydrogen chloride or hydrochloric acid, depending on the amount of water available during the hydrolysis:

$$XCl_4(l) + 2H_2O(l) \rightarrow XO_2(s) + 4HCl \quad X = Si, Ge, Sn \text{ and } Pb$$

Chlorides with the element in the +2 oxidation state
We have already described the inert pair effect to explain why germanium, tin and lead can have an oxidation state of +2. The three elements form chlorides of the general formula XCl_2 in this oxidation state. Germanium(II) chloride is not really ionic and anhydrous tin(II) chloride has a great deal of covalent character. The only chloride where the term ionic is really appropriate is lead(II) chloride.

?

R Construct an ionic equation to show the reaction of $Fe^{3+}(aq)$ with $Sn^{2+}(aq)$ to form $Fe^{2+}(aq)$.

S Write an ionic equation for the reaction that occurs when chlorine bubbles through a solution of acidified aqueous tin(II) chloride. Suggest the name(s) of the product(s).
Hint: you can read about the reactions of chlorine in Chapter 23.

Reducing properties
Germanium(II) chloride and tin(II) chloride are both reducing agents. Aqueous solutions of tin(II) chloride are best stored with a little tin metal to prevent aerial oxidation. Aqueous acidified tin(II) chloride reduces iron(III) ions and dichromate(VI) ions:

$$3Sn^{2+}(aq) + 14H^+(aq) + Cr_2O_7^{2-}(aq) \rightarrow 2Cr^{3+}(aq) + 3Sn^{4+}(aq) + 7H_2O(l)$$

The aqueous Sn^{4+} ions have too high a charge density to exist on their own and so they form complex hydrated ions.

Lead(II) chloride is not a reducing agent, as shown by the following electrode potentials:

$$Pb^{4+}(aq) + 2e^- \rightleftharpoons Pb^{2+}(aq) \qquad\qquad E_{red}^{\ominus} = +1.69\,V$$
$$Sn^{4+}(aq) + 2e^- \rightleftharpoons Sn^{2+}(aq) \qquad\qquad E_{red}^{\ominus} = +0.15\,V$$

The highly positive $E_{red}^{\ominus}$ for the reduction of $Pb^{4+}(aq)$ indicates that lead(IV) is very easily reduced to Pb^{2+} and so the reverse reaction, Pb^{2+} to Pb^{4+}, will be much more difficult than the corresponding reaction of Sn^{2+} to Sn^{4+}.

The silanes

Carbon forms an almost infinite number of compounds that contain the carbon–hydrogen single bonds. Among these compounds are the alkanes which have the general formula C_nH_{2n+2}. Silicon forms a range of compounds similar in terms of general formula to the alkanes and these are collectively called the silanes. The chain length of carbon–carbon bonds is not limited. However, the longest chain silane that has been isolated at present has six silicon atoms.

All silanes are simple molecular compounds and the single bonds are arranged tetrahedrally about the central silicon atoms.

The vacant 3d orbitals in silicon atoms makes the properties of the silanes different from those of the corresponding alkanes. The enthalpy changes of formation of silane (SiH_4) and methane indicate that silane is considerably less stable with respect to the elements silicon and hydrogen than methane is to carbon and hydrogen. In fact, the enthalpy change of formation of silane is positive.

$$Si(s) + 2H_2(g) \rightarrow SiH_4(g) \qquad \Delta H_f = +34 \, kJ \, mol^{-1}$$

$$C(s) + 2H_2(g) \rightarrow CH_4(g) \qquad \Delta H_f = -75 \, kJ \, mol^{-1}$$

Silane spontaneously ignites in air forming silicon dioxide and water:

$$SiH_4(g) + 2O_2(g) \rightarrow SiO_2(s) + 2H_2O(g) \qquad \Delta H_f = -1429 \, kJ \, mol^{-1}$$

The enthalpy change of combustion of silane is much higher than that of methane ($-802 \, kJ \, mol^{-1}$), explained in terms of the weakness of the Si–H single bonds broken and the strength of the Si–O bonds formed in silicon dioxide. Silane reacts with aqueous sodium hydroxide forming hydrogen and the silicate ion.

$$SiH_4(g) + 2OH^-(aq) + H_2O(l) \rightarrow SiO_3^{2-}(aq) + 4H_2(g)$$

Again, the formation of the very strong silicon–oxygen single bond acts as a driving force for this reaction. In contrast, methane is inert to aqueous sodium hydroxide.

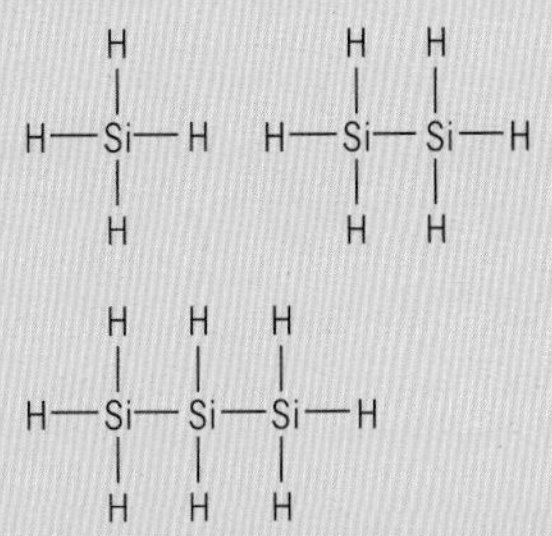

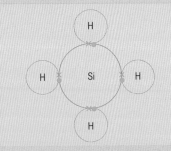

Fig 30.15 **The structures of some silanes. Notice the similarity to the homologous series called the alkanes**

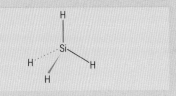

Fig 30.16 **The dot and cross diagram for silane**

Fig 30.17 **The tetrahedral arrangement of the silane molecule**

T (a) What is the molecular formula of the silane that contains six silicon atoms per molecule?

(b) Draw a possible structural formula for this silane.

SILICONES

SILICONES ARE POLYMERS that have a backbone of alternating silicon and oxygen atoms with carbon-based side chains. They are characteristically non-toxic and are stable over a wide range of temperatures.

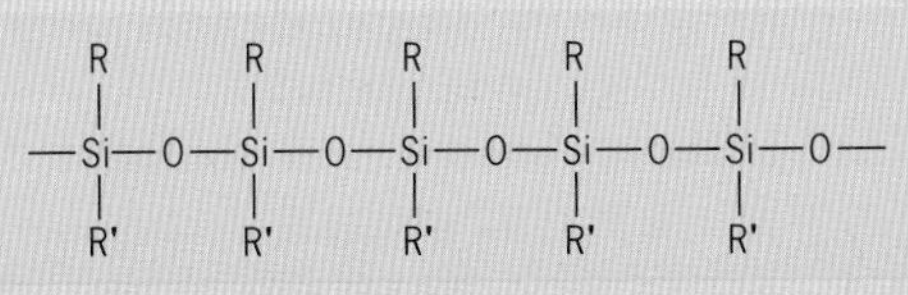

Fig 30.18 **Silicones have a polymer chain of alternate oxygen and silicon atoms joined by a single bond. The side chains R and R^1 are alkyl groups or aryl groups**

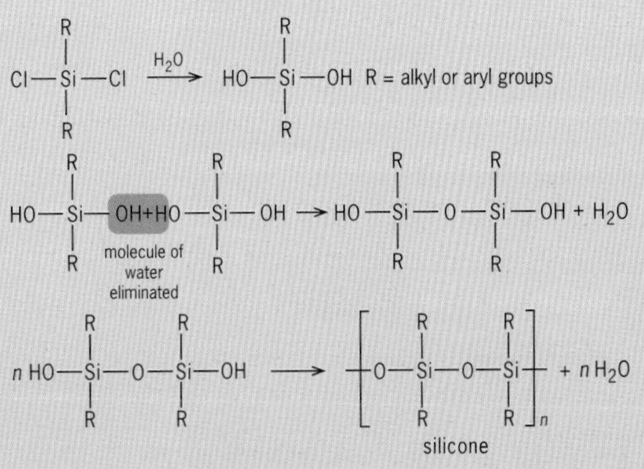

Fig 30.19 **Silicones are manufactured by the hydrolysis of dichlorosilanes, followed by condensation of the resulting dihydroxysilanes. A molecule of water is eliminated during each condensation step**

The side chain shown in Fig 30.18 can be varied to develop a wide range of silicones with different properties.

If the side chain of the silicone is a methyl group then the resulting polymer is a liquid. These polymers are linear with no cross-linking between polymer chains.

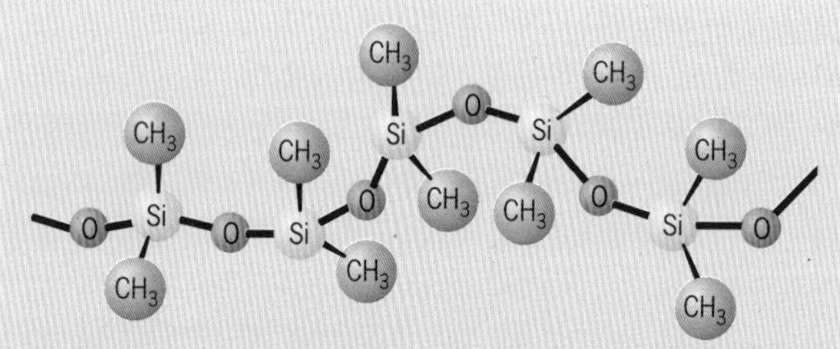

Fig 30.20 **The structure of silicone fluid. A silicone fluid has an R group such as a methyl or ethyl group. There are no cross-links with other polymer chains and only weak intermolecular forces exist between the polymer chains**

Fig 30.21 **Many bathroom sealants used to seal the sides of baths and showers are made from silicone rubber**

This means that the polymer chains only have weak intermolecular forces between them, so the silicone has a relatively low melting point.

Fig 30.20 shows that there are no double bonds in the polymer chain, so all the bonds in the polymer molecule can freely rotate. Such a feature gives this type of silicone the physical properties required to make the non-stick coating on pans.

Another use of silicone fluids is to protect masonry from rain damage. Silicone bonds to masonry and the hydrophobic (water-hating) methyl groups repel water molecules from the surface of the building.

An advantage of silicones is the way that the side chain can be manipulated to change the property of the material. If the side chains contain more reactive groups – such as alkenes or hydroxyl groups – then some degree of cross linking between the polymer chain can occur. Providing the cross-linking is not extensive, the silicone will be solid at room temperature but still retain a great deal of flexibility and resistance to water.

Silicones are electrical insulators and they can be used to insulate electric cables so long as an inert filler is added to increase the rigidity of the material.

Fig 30.22 **An extensive network of cross-links are present in more rigid and less flexible silicone resins. Some racing helmets are made of silicone resin mixed with glass fibre**

?

U The relative molecular mass of a silicone fluid with the structure shown in Fig 30.20 having an R group of CH_3. Estimate is approximately 1500. Calculate how many silicon atoms there are in the polymer chain.

Fig 30.23 **Lead(II) chromate(VI) is used to make the yellow lines on roads**

6 OXY-SALTS OF LEAD

The metal elements of Group 4 form oxy-salts but the non-metal elements do not. Lead is the most metallic of the Group 4 elements and forms many oxy-salts containing the cation Pb^{2+}.

Most lead(II) salts are insoluble but two of the oxy-salts – lead(II) ethanoate, $Pb(CH_3COO)_2$, and lead(II) nitrate, $Pb(NO_3)_2$ – are soluble in water. They are often used in qualitative analysis to precipitate anions as insoluble lead(II) compounds.

When aqueous lead(II) nitrate is added to any soluble sulphate, white lead(II) sulphate forms as a precipitate:

$$Pb^{2+}(aq) + SO_4^{2-}(aq) \rightarrow PbSO_4(s)$$

Lead(II) chromate(VI) forms as a yellow precipitate when aqueous lead(II) nitrate is added to aqueous sodium chromate(VI):

$$Pb^{2+}(aq) + CrO_4^{2-}(aq) \rightarrow PbCrO_4(s)$$

Solutions containing aqueous iodide ions and lead(II) ions react to form yellow lead(II) iodide precipitate.

Carbonates

Carbonates are derived from the weak acid carbonic acid, formed when carbon dioxide dissolves in water.

$$CO_2(aq) + H_2O(l) \rightleftharpoons H_2CO_3(aq)$$

Carbonates are salts that contain the CO_3^{2-} ion and hydrogencarbonates contain the HCO_3^- ion. Only carbonates of the Group 1 elements and ammonium carbonate are soluble in water. Therefore, most carbonates are prepared by precipitation:

$$M^{2+}(aq) + CO_3^{2-}(aq) \rightarrow MCO_3(s)$$

where M is a metal in the +2 oxidation state.

Metals that form a positive ion with a high charge density, such as Fe^{3+}, Al^{3+} and Cr^{3+}, do not form carbonates. In solution, these ions polarise water molecules to form sufficient aqueous hydrogen ions to react with the carbonate ion to form carbon dioxide.

$$CO_3^{2-}(s) + 2H^+(aq) \rightarrow CO_2(g) + H_2O(l)$$

With the exception of the Group 1 carbonates, all carbonates thermally decompose to give carbon dioxide. The energy changes that accompany this decomposition are discussed in detail in Chapter 22.

Treating any carbonate with acid evolves carbon dioxide and produces a salt. Lead(II) carbonate reacts with dilute nitric acid to form lead(II) nitrate, water and carbon dioxide:

$$PbCO_3(s) + 2HNO_3(aq) \rightarrow Pb(NO_3)_2(aq) + CO_2(g) + H_2O(l)$$

?

V Write an equation to show the decomposition of lead(II) carbonate.

Read about hydrogencarbonates on page 466.

■ See question 3.

Silicates

We have just stated that carbonates contain the anion CO_3^{2-}; the corresponding silicon compounds, called the silicates, have a very different structure and contain more complex negative ions. The simplest silicate structure contains the tetrahedral SiO_4^{4-} ion.

The structure of the anion in silicates is based on an SiO_4 tetrahedron which contains covalent silicon–oxygen single bonds. If two SiO_4 tetrahedral units share an oxygen atom, the silicate contains the $Si_2O_7^{6-}$ ion.

Fig 30.24 **Minerals such as olivine, Mg_2SiO_4, and zircon, $ZrSiO_4$, contain the tetrahedral silicate ion, SiO_4^{4-}**

THE ASBESTOS PROBLEM

ASBESTOS IS A SILICATE MINERAL which is fibrous. It has long been used for fireproofing and insulating buildings. Since it has been known that exposure to asbestos fibres can cause serious respiratory disorders such as asbestosis, asbestos has been removed from many buildings.

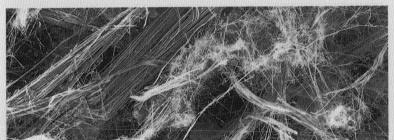

Fig 30.25 **A scanning electron micrograph of the fibres of blue asbestos. The lung disease asbestosis is caused by breathing in these fibres**

Fig 30.26 **Removing asbestos has become a priority to avoid exposure to asbestos fibres. Many buildings, including schools, have been temporarily closed during the controlled removal of asbestos. This sack of asbestos will be buried in a landfill site**

7 GROUP 6 – OXYGEN AND SULPHUR

Table 30.7 **The elements of Group 6**

Element	Symbol	Electron configuration
oxygen	O	$1s^22s^22p^4$
sulphur	S	$1s^22s^22p^63s^23p^4$
selenium	Se	$[Ar]3d^{10}4s^24p^4$
tellurium	Te	$[Kr]4d^{10}5s^25p^4$
polonium	Po	$[Xe]4f^{14}5d^{10}6s^26p^4$

Group 6 contains two well known elements – oxygen and sulphur – together with three less well known elements – selenium, tellurium and polonium. (We do not discuss selenium, tellurium and polonium because their chemistry is well beyond the scope of this book.)

The chemistry of oxygen and oxides has been described in earlier chapters so the discussion in this chapter will centre around the element sulphur. Figs 30.27 and 30.28 show some general information about oxygen and oxides.

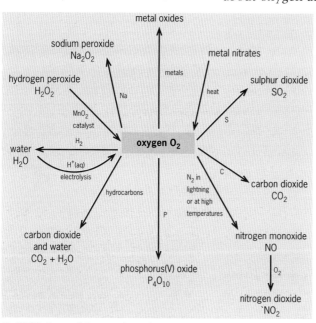

Fig 30.28 **Some of the reactions of oxygen**

Basic oxides	Ionic oxides, contain O^{2-}. React with acids to give salt and water eg Na_2O, CuO
Amphoteric oxides	Contain O^{2-}. React with both acids and alkalis to give salts, eg Al_2O_3, PbO, ZnO
Acidic oxides	Covalent oxides. Often react with bases to give salts eg CO_2, SO_2, SO_3
Neutral oxides	Covalent oxides, often having a non-metal in a low oxidation state eg CO, NO

Fig 30.27 **A summary of the oxides**

Detailes on the chemistry of oxygen can be found on the following pages:
Reactions of oxygen with elements on page 443.
Basic oxides on page 446.
Acidic oxides on page 448.

See question 9. ■

Occurrence of sulphur

Sulphur is an element that has been known to humans since the earliest times. It was once known as brimstone. Sulphur deposits are widespread, as are sulphur's compounds with metals and non-metals. Many of the ores of metals are sulphides, a combination of a metal and sulphur. A few sulphate ores also exist.

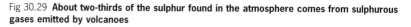

Fig 30.29 **About two-thirds of the sulphur found in the atmosphere comes from sulphurous gases emitted by volcanoes**

Chemical properties of sulphur

Sulphur has the electron configuration $1s^22s^22p^63s^23p^4$; it has six electrons in its outermost shell. To obtain a stable octet of electrons, the sulphur atom gains two electrons either by sharing electrons with the atoms of a non-metal to form covalent bonds or by gaining electrons lost by metal atoms to form ionic bonds. The ionic compounds contain S^{2-} ions and are sulphur's equivalent to oxides. The oxidation number of sulphur in a sulphide is –2.

A sulphur atom can also expand its octet by accepting electrons into its vacant 3d orbitals to form compounds in which sulphur has an oxidation state of +4 or +6.

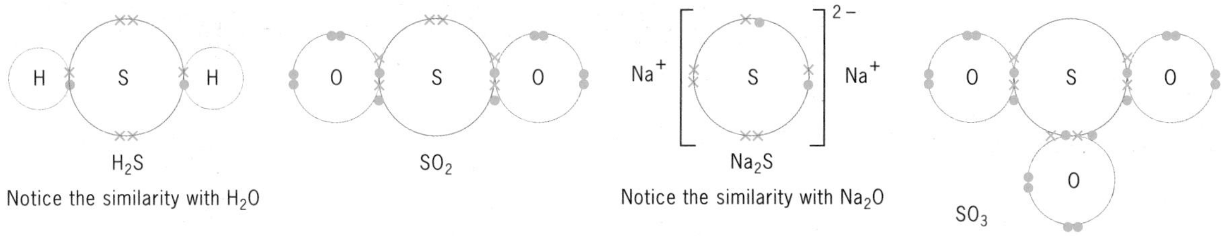

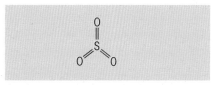

H_2S
Notice the similarity with H_2O

SO_2

Na_2S
Notice the similarity with Na_2O

SO_3

Fig 30.30 **Some dot and cross diagrams of sulphur compounds. In H_2S and Na_2S, sulphur has a stable octet and an oxidation number of –2. In SO_2 and SO_3, the sulphur atom has expanded its octet and as a result the oxidation numbers of sulphur are +4 in SO_2 and +6 in SO_3**

Sulphur dioxide and sulphurous acid

Sulphur dioxide is produced when almost any compound containing sulphur burns in air. In Chapter 8 we discussed the formation of sulphur dioxide in power stations and indicated how it is implicated in the formation of acid rain.

Acidic properties of sulphur dioxide

Sulphur dioxide dissolves in water to form sulphurous acid, $H_2SO_3(aq)$, a moderately strong acid. An aqueous solution of sulphurous acid normally has about 25 per cent of the acid molecules dissociated to form HSO_3^- ions. Only a small proportion of these ions dissociate further to form SO_3^{2-} ions:

$$SO_2(aq) + H_2O(l) \rightleftharpoons H_2SO_3(aq)$$
$$H_2SO_3(aq) \rightleftharpoons HSO_3^-(aq) + H^+(aq)$$
$$HSO_3^-(aq) \rightleftharpoons SO_3^{2-}(aq) + H^+(aq)$$

Alkalis such as aqueous potassium hydroxide neutralise sulphurous acid to give the metal sulphite:

$$2KOH(aq) + H_2SO_3(aq) \rightarrow K_2SO_3(aq) + 2H_2O(l)$$

It is also possible to obtain potassium hydrogensulphite by controlling the mole ratios of acid and alkali that react.

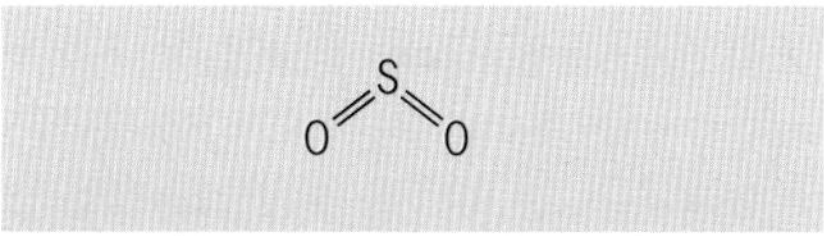

Reducing properties of sulphur dioxide

Sulphurous acid and sulphur dioxide are both reducing agents. Sulphur dioxide is used as an antioxidant to preserve food: it is oxidised easily, removing oxygen in the air that could have oxidised the food. Aqueous chlorine, aqueous dichromate(VI), aqueous iron(III) and air are all reduced by sulphurous acid. The reaction of moist sulphur dioxide and potassium dichromate(VI) is a test for sulphur dioxide.

$$Cr_2O_7^{2-}(aq) + 3SO_2(aq) + 2H^+(aq) \rightarrow 2Cr^{3+}(aq) + 3SO_4^{2-}(aq) + H_2O(l):$$
changing from orange to blue-green.

Sulphites

Salts of sulphurous acid are known as sulphites. These salts react with dilute acid to release sulphur dioxide.

$$K_2SO_3(s) + 2HNO_3(aq) \rightarrow KNO_3(aq) + SO_2(g) + H_2O(l)$$

Many solid sulphites thermally decompose when heated.

$$ZnSO_3(s) \rightarrow ZnO(s) + SO_2(g)$$

Sulphur trioxide

Sulphur trioxide is a typical acidic oxide and it dissolves in water to form the strong acid sulphuric acid:

$$H_2O(l) + SO_3(g) \rightarrow H_2SO_4(aq)$$

It also reacts directly with solid bases to form sulphates; barium oxide reacts to form barium sulphate:

$$BaO(s) + SO_3(g) \rightarrow BaSO_4(s)$$

Fig 30.31 **Sulphur dioxide is a bent or V-shaped molecule**

?

W What is the mole ratio of potassium hydroxide to sulphurous acid needed to make:

(a) potassium sulphite,

(b) potassium hydrogensulphite.

?

X Write down the equations for the reduction by sulphur dioxide of:

(a) aqueous chlorine,

(b) aqueous iron(III) ions.

Hint: Use the half equations in Appendix 4, page 679 to help.

■ See question 5.

Fig 30.32 **Gaseous sulphur trioxide is a trigonal planar molecule**

9 SULPHURIC ACID

Sulphuric acid is one of the world's key industrial chemicals. Justus von Liebig wrote in 1843 that the consumption of sulphuric acid is a barometer of a nation's commercial prosperity. Sulphuric acid's wide range of uses means that Liebig's statement still holds today. Sulphuric acid is widely used in the oil and petroleum industry. It is also involved in making:

● fertilisers, such as ammonium phosphate and superphosphate,
● paints, pigments and dyes,
● soaps and detergents,
● plastics and fibres.
● general chemicals, such as salts and battery acid.

The contact process

Sulphuric acid is manufactured using the contact process. It was patented in 1831 by Peregrine Phillips and later improved by Rudolf Messel. The contact process is an efficient and economical way of converting relatively cheap raw materials to sulphuric acid.

Raw materials

The raw materials chosen in the United Kingdom are sulphur, air and water. Water and air are very cheap raw materials, but most sulphur needs to be imported.

About 10 per cent of the sulphur comes from the petroleum industry; sulphur is an impurity that must be removed from crude oil before the oil can be processed.

The three stages of the contact process

The contact process involves three stages:

● the oxidation of molten sulphur to give sulphur dioxide:

$$S + O_2 \rightarrow SO_2 \qquad\qquad \Delta H = -297\,\text{kJ}\,\text{mol}^{-1}$$

● the reaction of sulphur dioxide with oxygen to give sulphur trioxide:

$$SO_2(g) + \tfrac{1}{2}O_2(g) \rightleftharpoons SO_3(g) \qquad \Delta H = -98\,\text{kJ}\,\text{mol}^{-1}$$

● the reaction of sulphur trioxide with water:

$$SO_3(g) + H_2O(l) \rightarrow H_2SO_4(l) \qquad \Delta H = -130\,\text{kJ}\,\text{mol}^{-1}$$

In theory, it is a simple process. However, there are a number of problems to overcome before the yield of sulphuric acid is economically viable.

Oxidation of sulphur

In the combustion of molten sulphur the enthalpy change of reaction is negative. The temperature used ensures that the rate of reaction is sufficient to provide an economic rate of production of sulphur dioxide.

Catalytic conversion of sulphur dioxide into sulphur trioxide

The second stage is the oxidation of sulphur dioxide to give sulphur trioxide. The reaction is very slow and needs a catalyst.

Originally, the precious metal platinum was used but now manufacturers use vanadium(V) oxide. The reaction is exothermic, so Le Chatelier's principle suggests that the forward reaction is favoured by low temperatures. The volume of products is smaller than reactants so high pressure also favours the forward reaction. Maintaining an excess of reactants and continually removing the product from the reaction mixture is another way of shifting the equilibrium position to the right.

A low temperature slows down the rate of reaction and high pressures are expensive to maintain so a compromise set of conditions are chosen that give an economic yield of sulphur trioxide. Manufacturers use a temperature of between 450 °C and 600 °C. A pressure of around 10 atmospheres is sufficient to push the gases around the plant. There is no need to use a high pressure in this reaction despite Le Chatelier's prediction because even at low pressure the position of equilibrium lies well to the right.

At least three catalyst chambers or beds are used to ensure maximum conversion of sulphur dioxide (Fig 30.33). The conversion yield can exceed 98 per cent. As well as being economically viable, this high yield has environmental benefits because very little sulphur dioxide waste enters the atmosphere.

The hydration of sulphur trioxide

The reaction of sulphur trioxide with water does not work with large quantities of sulphur trioxide. The normal way of dissolving a gas industrially is to use a counter flow system where water is sprayed downwards and gas flows upwards. In the case of sulphur trioxide, this technique causes clouds of sulphuric acid droplets to form. These droplets are difficult to condense, so a different method is used.

The sulphur trioxide is dissolved in concentrated sulphuric acid to form oleum, $H_2S_2O_7$. The oleum is diluted with measured amounts of water to give concentrated sulphuric acid.

$$SO_3(g) + H_2SO_4(l) \rightarrow H_2S_2O_7(l)$$
$$H_2S_2O_7(l) \rightarrow 2H_2SO_4(l)$$

Both of the processes are exothermic and are carried out at low temperature.

Throughout the plant, the flow of energy is vital. The reactions are exothermic and the conditions needed vary from high to low temperatures. Complex heat exchangers ensure that little heat is wasted.

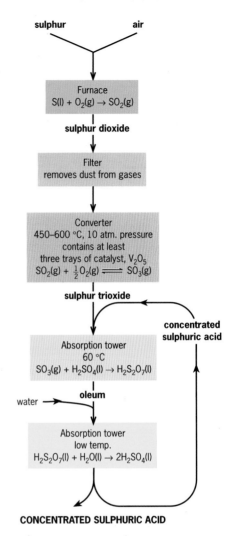

Fig 30.33 **Flow chart to show the manufacture of sulphuric acid**

?

Y Look at Fig 30.33. In which reactions does sulphuric acid act as:

(a) an acid,

(b) an oxidising agent?

■ See question 4.

Reactions of sulphuric acid

Sulphuric acid has a wide range of reactions in addition to those expected of a strong acid. They include:

- redox reactions with both dilute and concentrated sulphuric acid,
- dehydration reactions,
- sulphonation reactions,
- reactions as a non-volatile acid.

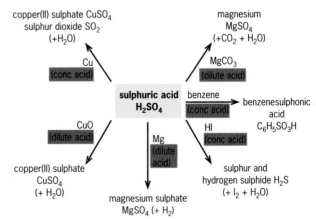

Fig 30.34 **Some of the reactions of sulphuric acid**

?

Z What is the name of the acid formed when concentrated sulphuric acid reacts with:

(a) potassium benzoate,

(b) magnesium ethanoate?

See question 6. ■

Reactions as a non-volatile acid

Sulphuric acid reacts with the salts of many other acids to liberate the acid. We have already described the reaction of concentrated sulphuric acid with sodium chloride where it forms hydrogen chloride. In the same way, concentrated sulphuric acid reacts when heated with sodium nitrate to form nitric acid:

$$NaNO_3 + H_2SO_4 \rightarrow NaHSO_4 + HNO_3$$

Sulphates

Sulphuric acid forms a class of oxy-salts called sulphates. Sulphates are generally soluble in water and are relatively resistant to thermal decomposition. Many sulphates do not change when heated at Bunsen burner temperatures, but at higher temperatures they decompose to form the corresponding oxide.

We described the trend of solubility of the sulphates of the Group 2 elements in Chapter 22. The lack of solubility of barium sulphate in water is the basis of the test for aqueous sulphate ions.

See question 3. ■

Table 30.8 **The tests for sulphate, carbonate, sulphite and thiosulphate ions**

	Add aqueous barium nitrate followed by excess dilute nitric acid
sulphate	white precipitate of barium sulphate that does not redissolve in the acid
carbonate	white precipitate of barium carbonate that redissolves in acid with the formation of carbon dioxide
sulphite	white precipitate of barium sulphite that redissolves slowly and forms sulphur dioxide
thiosulphate	white precipitate of barium thiosulphate that changes to a yellow precipitate on addition of acid, with the formation of sulphur dioxide

For more information on thiosulphates, see page 436.

Thiosulphates

Thiosulphates contain the $S_2O_3^{2-}$ ion. This ion is really a sulphate ion in which one oxygen atom has been replaced by a sulphur atom. On reaction with dilute acids, thiosulphates form yellow sulphur as a precipitate:

$$S_2O_3^{2-}(aq) + 2H^+(aq) \rightarrow S(s) + H_2O(l) + SO_2(g)$$

SUMMARY

After studying this chapter, you should know that:

■ The metallic character of the elements in Group 4 increases with atomic number and the non-metallic character decreases with atomic number.

■ The stability of the +4 oxidation state in Group 4 decreases with increasing atomic number and the stability of the +2 oxidation state increases with increasing atomic number.

■ All the tetrachlorides of Group 4 elements except carbon are readily hydrolysed by cold water to form the corresponding dioxide and HCl.

■ The thermal stability of the Group 4 tetrachlorides decreases with increasing atomic number of the Group 4 element.

■ The tetrachlorides of Group 4 are all simple molecular covalent molecules.

■ The thermal stability of the Group 4 dioxides decreases with increasing atomic number of the Group 4 element.

■ The acidic character of Group 4 oxides decreases with increasing atomic number of the Group 4 element.

■ The oxidising power of the dioxides of Group 4 elements increases with increasing atomic number of the element.

■ Sulphuric acid is manufactured by the catalysed oxidation of sulphur dioxide by oxygen followed by a controlled two-step hydration with water.

■ The presence of sulphates in solution can be tested by using aqueous barium chloride or aqueous barium nitrate solution.

QUESTIONS

1 This question relates to the elements in Group 4 and their compounds.

a) Explain the differences in the melting points and electrical conductivities of the Group 4 elements in terms of structure and bonding.

b) Carbon dioxide is a gas that dissolves in water and reacts slightly with it.
Silicon(IV) oxide is a solid that is insoluble in water and does not react with it.
The tetrachlorides of carbon and silicon are both liquids, one of which reacts with water and the other does not.
Explain the differences in the physical and chemical properties of the four compounds described by these statements. Write balanced equations for all reactions that occur.

c) Describe and explain the variation in the stable oxidation states of the Group 4 elements as the group is descended.

d) The element germanium was once an important component of transistors. It can be made by heating the ore germanite with hydrogen chloride, distilling off the germanium chloride formed, hydrolysing the chloride to the oxide and reducing the oxide to the metal.
When 1.00 g of germanite was treated in this way, the germanium present was completely converted into 0.177 g of a chloride containing 33.9% by mass of germanium.
Calculate, showing all your working:
  (i) the empirical formula of the chloride;
  (ii) the oxidation number of germanium in the chloride;
  (iii) the percentage by mass of germanium in germanite.

[UCLES Spring 1996 Modular: Trends and Patterns, q.7]

2 Domestic water sometimes contains aqueous lead(II) ions.

a) Explain how the aqueous lead(II) ions could have entered the water supply.

b) Describe how you could confirm the presence of aqueous lead(II) ions in tap water.

3 Samples of lead(II) salts were heated strongly in a Bunsen flame. State the name of the solid product formed and the name of the gas formed in each case when each of the following salts were heated:

a) Lead(II) nitrate;

b) Lead(II) carbonate;

c) Lead(II) sulphate.

4 **(i)** Describe the large scale production of sulphuric acid from sulphur, giving essential conditions and equations where relevant.
   (ii) State two large scale uses of sulphuric acid.
   (iii) Sulphuric acid reacts with hydrogen bromide and hydrogen iodide as shown below.

$$H_2SO_4 + 2HBr \rightarrow 2H_2O + SO_2 + Br_2$$

$$H_2SO_4 + 8HI \rightarrow 4H_2O + H_2S + 4I_2$$

What is the oxidation state of sulphur in each of H_2SO_4, SO_2 and H_2S.
[UCLES Spring 1996 Modular: Trends and Patterns, q.6]

5 Ethanol in wine is oxidised by air. To prevent this, sulphur dioxide is added to wines, as the air oxidises this instead. It also kills unwanted bacteria.
If too little sulphur dioxide is used, the wine may become oxidised, or affected by unwanted bacteria, while too much may affect the flavour. It is important to be able to determine the concentration of sulphur dioxide in wine with reasonable accuracy. This can be done by titration with a solution of iodine of known concentration.

Iodine, I_2, is reduced by sulphur dioxide.

a) To what is the iodine reduced by the sulphur dioxide?

b) Write down the change in oxidation number for iodine in this reaction.
In this reaction, one mole of sulphur dioxide is oxidised by one mole of iodine molecules.

c) Deduce the change in oxidation number that must occur for sulphur in this reaction.

d) Suggest what the sulphur dioxide is oxidised to in this reaction.

e) Write a balanced equation, with state symbols, for the reaction of iodine solution with sulphur dioxide.
[ULEAC 1996 CN2 Specimen paper, q.1]

6 **a)** Describe the reaction of sulphuric acid with each of the following. In each case write an equation for the reaction.
  (i) the reaction of dilute sulphuric acid with magnesium;
  (ii) the reaction of concentrated sulphuric acid with sucrose, $C_{12}H_{22}O_{11}$;
  (iii) the reaction of concentrated sulphuric acid with sodium bromide.

b) Concentrated sulphuric acid reacts when heated with carbon to form carbon dioxide and sulphur dioxide.
  (i) Write an equation for the reaction.
  (ii) The reaction is an example of a redox reaction. By using oxidation numbers identify the reducing agent and the oxidising agent in the reaction.

7 a) Describe and explain the following variation of physical properties within Group 4:
  (i) electrical conductivity of the elements;
  (ii) melting points of the elements.

b) Explain why the metallic character of the elements in Group 4 increases with increasing atomic (proton) number.

c) Explain why the principal oxidation state of lead in its compounds is +2 but that of silicon in its compounds is +4.

8 Explain each of the following observations.

a) Both lead(II) oxide and lead(IV) oxide react with warm concentrated hydrochloric acid to form lead(II) chloride.

b) Lead(II) oxide reacts with both aqueous sodium hydroxide and dilute nitric acid whereas carbon monoxide does not react with aqueous sodium hydroxide or dilute nitric acid.

c) Tetrachloromethane does not react with water but silicon(IV) chloride immediately forms a white precipitate and an acidic solution.

In each case, write balanced equations to illustrate your answers.

9 Oxides may be classified as acidic, amphoteric, basic or neutral.

a) Give an example of each type of oxide and describe the reaction, if any, of your chosen oxides with dilute sodium hydroxide.

b) Group 4 elements form two series of oxides, one with formula XO and the other with formula XO_2.
  (i) Explain why the basic character of the oxides XO increases with increasing atomic number of X.
  (ii) Suggest why tin(II) oxide is more basic in character than tin(IV) oxide.

c) Describe and explain the variation in thermal stability of the Group 4 oxide, XO_2.

Assignment

SILICATES AND ALUMINOSILICATES

Soil is a mixture of water, organic materials, air and inorganic materials. The inorganic materials can be classified as sand, silt and clay.

Sand is composed almost entirely of silica or silicon(IV) oxide and consists of particles with a diameter of between 0.05 mm and 2 mm. Silt has much the same chemical composition as sand but contains some silicate and aluminosilicates. The particle size of silt is between 0.002 mm and 0.05 mm in diameter. Clay is almost entirely silicates and aluminosilicates and has the smallest particle size, being less than 0.002 mm diameter.

1 Draw the structure of silicon(IV) oxide.

The silicates are based on a tetrahedral SiO_4 unit. Fig 30.A1 shows part of the structure of a silicate. Cations bind together the silicate chains.

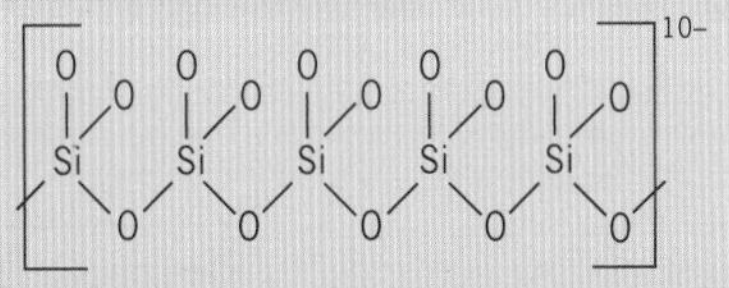

Fig 30.A1 **The structure of a silicate chain. Silicate chains are bound together by cations occupying the space between the chains. The empirical formula of this silicate is SiO_3^{2-}, so a five silicon unit will carry a net charge of 10–.**

2 If the cation present in the silicate drawn in Fig 30.A1 is a magnesium ion, what is the empirical formula of the silicate?

Aluminosilicates are also based on a SiO_4 tetrahedral unit but sometimes the silicon atom is replaced by an aluminium atom.

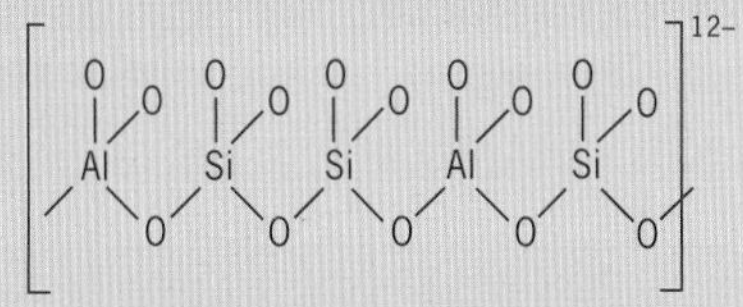

Fig 30.A2 **The chain structure of an aluminosilicate. In this chain some silicon atoms are replaced by aluminium atoms. The net charge on this five silicon/aluminium unit is 12–.**

3 List the similarities and the differences between the silicate drawn in Fig 30.A1 and the aluminosilicate in Fig 30.A2.

Aluminosilicates can facilitate ion exchange in soils. This is a surface action and involves cations binding at the surface of the clay. Other cations such as protons can replace the cations at the surface of the clay, often releasing cations that are toxic to plants.

4 Give two reasons why sand cannot facilitate ion-exchange in soils.

5 The oxidation number of aluminium in an aluminosilicate is +3 and that of silicon is +4. Explain why having some aluminium atoms replacing silicon atoms increases the number of cations that can bind with the silicate.

6 Suggest why acid rain can increase the amounts of toxic aqueous metal ions within the soil.

7 Suggest why acid rain will have little effect on soils with a high sand content.

Clays should be a potential source of both elemental aluminium and elemental silicon. However, aluminium is manufactured by the electrolytic decomposition of aluminium oxide derived from Bauxite (impure aluminium oxide) and silicon is made from the reduction of silica or silicon(IV) oxide by carbon or magnesium.

8 Clays are far more widespread than silica or Bauxite. Suggest why clay is not used as a raw material in the manufacture of either silicon or aluminium.

9 Give the names of two materials that are manufactured from clay.

GROUP 4 AND GROUP 6

These two groups in the Periodic Table contain elements with very diverse properties. The chapter covers a range of these elements, looking at the trends in their properties and chemistry, and the concepts underlying their reactions. In particular, the chapter focuses on carbon, oxygen and oxides, silicon and sulphur. Study the Chapter Map to see the links between the topics and to check that you have covered your syllabus requirements.

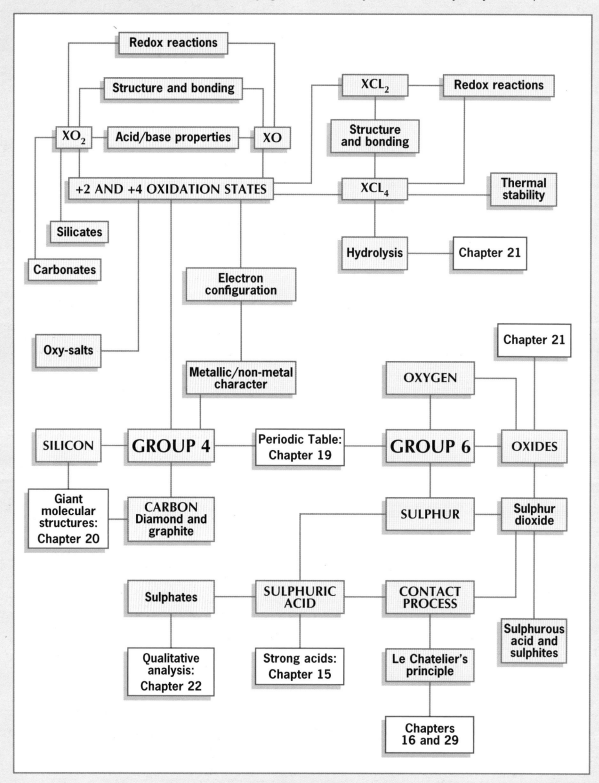

Photograph credits

Every effort has been made to contact the holders of copyright material, but if any have been inadvertently overlooked the publishers will be pleased to make the necessary arrangements at the first opportunity.

The publishers would like to thank the following for permission to reproduce photographs:

Andrew Lambert, p iv top left, bottom left and centre; John Birdsall Photography, p iv bottom right; Tony Waltham/Geophotos, p 2 top; British Steel - Sections, Plates & Commercial Steels, p 2 bottom; C & S Thompson, 1.1; J King-Holmes/SPL, 1.2; M Edwards/Still Pictures, 1.3; British Steel - Sections, Plates & Commercial Steels, 1.4, 1.5; Tony Waltham/Geophotos, 1.9, 1.10, 1.13A, 1.13B, 1.13C; Getty Images, 1.13D; Tony Waltham/Geophotos, 1.13E; Dept. of Clinical Radiology, Salisbury District Hospital/SPL, 1.15A; British Steel - Sections, Plates & Commercial Steels, 1.15B; Blackpool Pleasure Beach Ltd, 1.15C; British Steel, 1.15D; British Steel - Sections, Plates & Commercial Steels, 1.15E, 1.17; AP Photo, 1.17; SPL, p 20; Ann Ronan/Image Select, 2.1; Science Museum/Science & Society Picture Library, 2.2; Vivien Fifield, 2.3 top; Science Museum/Science & Society Picture Library, 2.3 bottom; AIP Emilio Segre Visual Archives/William G Myers Collection H1, 2.5; Popperfoto, 2.6; Vivien Fifield, 2.11(a); Image Select, 2.13; SPL, 2.15; Princeton University, 2.16; SPL, 2.17; Will & Deni McIntyre/SPL, 2.21; UK AEA, 2.23; G Tortoli/Ancient Art & Architecture Collection, 2.24; P Plailly/SPL, 2.25; J Dielenschneider/Holt Studios International, p 42; NRPB, 2.A3 & 2.A4; ROE/SPL, p 46 top; P Freytag/ACE Photo Agency, 3.1; Ann Ronan/Image Select, 3.2(b) & 3.3; Vivien Fifield, 3.7; C & S Thompson, 3.8; R Megna/Fundamental Photos/SPL, 3.9(a); Vivien Fifield, 3.11(a); D Kerwin/ACE Photo Agency, 3.12; SPL, 3.14; S Camazine/SPL, 3.16(a); IBM UK, 3.16(b); ACE Photo Agency, 3.A1; G Tompkinson/SPL, p 68; GSF Picture Library, 4.2(b); Argonne National Laboratory, managed and operated by the University of Chicago for the U.S. Department of Energy under Contract No. W-31-109-ENG-38, 4.16(a); P Plailly/Eurelios/SPL, 4.20(c); R Crane/Camera Press, p 77 centre; Andrew Lambert, 4.21(c), 4.22(c), 4.23(d), 4.24(c), 4.25(c), 4.26(b), 4.27(b), 4.28(b), 4.29(b), 4.30(b); C Priest/SPL, p 81; SPL, p 83; H Rogers/OSF, 4.A1; Kairos/Latin Stock/SPL, p 90; SPL, 5.2, 5.3, 5.8; Peter Gould, 5.17(a); Andrew Lambert, 5.17(b), 5.17(d); C D Winters/SPL, 5.19; G Tompkinson/SPL, 5.20; Andrew Lambert, 5.21; Dr A Clifford & Professor K D Bartle, School of Chemistry, University of Leeds, 5.A1, 5.A2; Getty Images, p 116 top; NASA, p 116 centre; Daimler-Benz, p 116 bottom; M Hamblin/Woodfall Wild Images, 6.2(a); South American Pictures, 6.2(b); Volvo, 6.3; SuperStock Ltd, 6.8; Southeastern Technology Center, Augusta, Georgia, 6.10; NASA, 6.16; Getty Images, 6.Q8; Thomas Eisner & Daniel Aneshansley, Cornell University, 6.Q10; South American Pictures, 6.A1; D Garcia/Still Pictures, p 138 centre left; Rosenfeld Images Ltd/SPL, p 138 centre; Andrew Lambert, p 138 centre right; D Drain/Still Pictures, p 138 bottom left; Rex Features Ltd, p 138 bottom right; Shell Photographic Services, 7.1, 7.2, p 140; B Barbey/Magnum Photos, 7.22; Shout Pictures, 7.24; ICI Chemicals & Polymers, 7.A1; Rex Features Ltd, p 156; Getty Images, 8.8; SPL, 8.13, 8.14, 8.15; Mitchell-UNEP/Still Pictures, 8.17(a); AP photo/NOAA, 8.17(b); Ford Motor Company Ltd, 8.18; A & H-F Michler/SPL, 8.19; Tony Waltham/Geophotos, 8.21; M Edwards/Still Pictures, 8.25; Broadleaf Design & Marketing Ltd, 8.26; K Rushby/Bruce Coleman Ltd, p 176 top; N Myers/Bruce Coleman Ltd, 9.1; E Young/SPL, 9.3; Sassoferratto - The Virgin and Child Embracing, © National Gallery, London, 9.6; Andrew Lambert, 9.8, 9.11, 9.23, 9.24; Shout Pictures, 9.28; S Fraser/SPL, 9.41; G Tompkinson/SPL, 9.42; by permission of the President and Council of the Royal Society, 9.A1; Shout Pictures, p 202; Andrew Lambert, 10.1; John Birdsall Photography, 10.2; Andrew Lambert, 10.7; Chubb Fire Ltd, 10.8; Sally & Richard Greenhill, 10.18; Andrew Lambert, 10.19(a), 10.19(b), 10.22, 10.32; SPL, 10.43; Popperfoto/Reuter, 10.44; M Edwards/Still Pictures, p 226; H Lange/Bruce Coleman Ltd, 11.3; Roger Scruton, 11.21; Andrew Lambert, 11.26, 11.33, 11.36, 11.37; SPL, 11.43; D Drain/Still Pictures, 12.1; Getty Images, 12.2; SPL, 12.10; Andrew Lambert, 12.13; Rosenfeld Images Ltd/SPL, 12.28; Andrew Lambert, 12.34 left; Getty Images, 12.34 right; M Plage/Bruce Coleman Ltd, 12.42; Tony Waltham/Geophotos, 12.44; J Allan Cash Ltd, 12.45; KOS Picture Source Ltd, 12.49; Woodfall Wild Images, p 268 top; J Durham/SPL, 13.3; IBM Almaden Research Center, 13.8(a); Andrew Lambert, 13.11, 13.18; Getty Images, 13.26; J Hester & P Scowen/SPL, 13.27; Andrew Lambert, 13.41(a); Getty Images, 13.41(b); Tony Waltham/Geophotos, 13.58; Woodfall Wild Images, 13.66; Saturn Stills/SPL, p 294; Andrew Lambert, 14.6; K G Preston-Mafham/Premaphotos Wildlife, 14.12; Andrew Lambert, 14.16; Barnaby's Picture Library, 14.17; Andrew Lambert, 14.23, 14.25, 14.27; J C Revy/SPL, p 308; John Birdsall Photography, 15.1; Andrew Lambert, 15.3, 15.10, 15.11, N Cattlin/Holt Studios International, 15.12; S Dalton/NHPA, 15.13; K Taylor/Bruce Coleman Ltd, 15.14; N Cattlin/Holt Studios International, 15.15; Andrew Lambert, 15.23; A Ackerley/NHPA, 15.28; John Birdsall Photography, 15.32; M Hewitt/Allsport, 15.36; John Birdsall Photography, p 334; P Fryer/Panos Pictures, 16.2; Andrew Lambert, 16.3; J King-Holmes/SPL, 16.4; Andrew Lambert, 16.11 & 16.12; H Pincis/SPL, 16.14; 'PA' News Photo Library, 16.17; Andrew Lambert, 16.18 & 16.19; Getty Images, 16.24; Reading Buses, 16.25; Chris Bonington Picture Library, 16.34; Tony Waltham/Geophotos, p 354; SPL, 17.11; Charlotte Roberts, Calvin Wells Laboratory, Department of Archeological Sciences, University of Bradford, 17.19; SPL, 17.25; Andrew Lambert, 17.A2; BIOPOL: Trademark and Property of Monsanto plc, p 374; Bob Masini/Phototake, NYC, 18.7; Andrew Lambert, 18.10(b); Sally & Richard Greenhill, 18.15; Andrew Lambert, 18.17; DuPont, 18.19 & 18.21(a); Andrew Lambert, 18.23; Gavin Rowe, 18.30; Woodfall Wild Images, 18.35; M Thompson/Allsport, 18.A3; DuPont, 18.A6 & 18.A7; Kristin Lehman/yachtShots, 18.A8; D Parker/SPL, p 392 top; P Plailly/Eurelios/SPL, p 392 top; D Medeleeff/SPL, 19.1; J-L Charmet/SPL, 19.2; Ann Ronan/Image Select, 19.3 & 19.5; GSF Picture Library, 19.6 centre right; A Pasieka/SPL, 19.6 bottom right; GSF Picture Library, 19.6 centre & 19.6 left; John Birdsall Photography, 19.6 far left; Andrew Lambert, 19.17 & 19.18; Robin Whymer, p 410 top; Andrew Lambert, p 410 centre; G Tompkinson/SPL, p 410 bottom; Natural History Museum, London, 20.3; Andrew Lambert, 20.7; G Muller, Struers GmbH/SPL, 20.8; Andrew Lambert, 20.9; D Parker/SPL, 20.14; Getty Images, 20.18; Rex Features Ltd, 20.21; G M Prior/Allsport, 20.23; Natural History Museum, London, 20.24 left; Andrew Lambert, 20.24 right; P Menzel/SPL, 20.28; NASA, 20.29; M Schroder/Still Pictures, 20.30; SPL, p 428; SPL, 21.1; Andrew Lambert, 21.2, 21.5, 21.6, 21.9, 21.16, 21.17, 21.18, 21.29, 21.32, 21.35(a)(i), 21.35(a)(ii), 21.35(b)(i), 21.35(b)(ii), 21.35(c), 21.35(d), 21.35(e); Rosenfeld Images Ltd/SPL, 21.39; NASA, 21.40; Getty Images, 21.41; Andrew Lambert, 21.42 & 21.43; Tony Waltham/Geophotos, 21.45; Getty Images, p 454 top; Tony Waltham/Geophotos, p 454 centre; R Lappa/SPL, 22.1 left; S Stammers, 22.1 left centre; Tony Waltham/Geophotos, 22.1 centre; Natural History Museum, London, 22.1 right centre; K Guldbrandsen/SPL, 22.1 right; Tony Waltham/Geophotos, 22.3; Andrew Lambert, 22.5, 22.6, 22.7, 22.8; Shout Pictures, 22.9; Andrew Lambert, 22.11 & 22.12; NASA, 22.13; Andrew Lambert, 22.14, 22.15, 22.16, 22.17, 22.18; Woodfall Wild Images, 22.19(a); M Edwards/Still Pictures, 22.19(b); J Selby/SPL, 22.20; Leslie Garland Picture Library, 22.21; Andrew Lambert, 22.22; Waterking JGB, 22.23; Rosenfeld Images Ltd/SPL, 22.29; A Pasieka/SPL, 22.34; Andrew Lambert, 22.35; C & S Thompson, 22.37; British Aerospace Airbus, 22.38; Getty Images, 22.39; John Birdsall Photography, p 486; N Cattlin/Holt Studios International, 23.1; Andrew Lambert, 23.2, 23.3; Getty Images, 23.6; Andrew Lambert, 23.11, 23.12, 23.13, 23.14; Getty Images, 23.15; Andrew Lambert, 23.16; C & S Thompson, 23.17; Science Museum/Science & Society Picture Library, 24.1; Andrew Lambert, 24.2; Science Museum/Science & Society Picture Library, 24.4; S Fraser/SPL, 24.7; N Dunlop/Panos Pictures, 24.11; Moredun Animal Health Ltd/SPL, 24.13; Sally & Richard Greenhill, 24.14; S Fraser/SPL, p 518; Leslie Garland Picture Library, 25.1; Andrew Lambert, 25.22, 25.24, 25.25, 25.26, 25.27, 25.28(a) & (b), 25.29, 25.30, 25.31; M Fielding/SPL, 25.33; Doris J Beck, Dept of Biological Sciences, Bowling Green State University, 25.A1 & A2; Leslie Garland Picture Library, 542; Andrew Lambert, 26.5, 26.7; John Birdsall Photography, 26.14; Andrew Lambert, 26.16; R Adshead/Military Picture Library, 26.20; P Russell/Military Picture Library, 26.21; Andrew Lambert, 26.23, 26.28; Leslie Garland Picture Library, 26.31, 26.35; Andrew Lambert, 26.37; Kristen Brochmann/Fundamental Photographs, NYC, p 580; 'PA' News Photo Library, 27.1; Getty Images, 27.2; Andrew Lambert, 27.8; Kenneth Suslick, Dept of Chemistry, University of Illinois, 27.11; Science VU/Visuals Unlimited, 27.20; The Nobel Foundation, 27.24; Image Select/Ann Ronan Picture Library, 27.25(b); Popperfoto/Reuter, 27.25(c); SPL, 27.29; J Henriksson/FLT-PICA Bild AB, 27.A1; NOAA/SPL, 27.A2; Sally & Richard Greenhill, p 608; Andrew Lambert, 28.4; Michael Holford, 28.5; Heather Angel, 28.6(b); Andrew Lambert, 28.7; British Steel/PPL, 28.9; Rex Features Ltd, 28.12(b) left; Andrew Lambert, 28.12(b) right; SPL, 28.13 left; Science Museum/Science & Society Picture Library, 28.13 right; Stanley Gibbons Ltd, 28.15(a); Science Museum/Science & Society Picture Library, 28.15(b); Andrew Lambert, 28.32; J C Revy/SPL, 28.34; R de Gugliemo/SPL, 28.35; Dr John Sleigh, 28.37; N Cattlin/Holt Studios International, 29.3; K Wood/SPL, 29.4; 'PA' News Photo Library, 29.12; Complete Weed Control Ltd, 29.13(b); Andrew Lambert, 29.13(d); Woodfall Wild Images, 29.14; Andrew Lambert, 29.15; Woodfall Wild Images, 29.21; M Davidson/SPL, p 652; B Boswell/Collections, 30.1; Leslie Garland Picture Library, 30.4; Getty Images, 30.5; Waterking JGB, 30.6; UK AEA, 30.7; Andrew Lambert, 30.8; Rolls-Royce plc, 30.12; Andrew Lambert, 30.21; M Cooper/Allsport, 30.22; Andrew Lambert, 30.23; J Burgess/SPL, 30.25; A Hart-Davis/SPL, 30.26; S Summerhays/SPL, 30.29.

Cover photograph: C Kocher/SPL.

APPENDIX 1: SIGNIFICANT FIGURES AND DECIMAL PLACES

Students and teachers alike have difficulty with the use of significant figures and decimal places in calculations. This appendix contains simple rules that will enable you to give answers to calculations to the appropriate number of decimal places or significant figures.

Significant figures

Whenever you make a measurement of a physical quantity in the laboratory, such as the temperature of a liquid or the mass of a test-tube, there will be an uncertainty in the measurement. When you use an electronic balance to measure the mass of a test-tube, the last figure on the balance reading almost always fluctuates. One moment it may be 16.41 g and the next it is 16.40 g. This shows that the last figure in the mass must be uncertain. We say that 16.40 g has four significant figures and the last figure, in this case the zero, is uncertain.

Whenever you measure a physical quantity, always quote the figure to include the first one which is uncertain. Sometimes this will be a zero but it must be quoted.

Determining the number of significant figures in a measurement

In this book you must assume that the measurements have been determined correctly and that they have the correct number of significant figures. To determine the number of significant figures, use the following rules.

- Find the first non-zero digit on the left and count the total number of digits, eg 0.00234 has 3 significant figures and 234.12 has 5 significant figures.
- If the number has a decimal point, count all the digits to the right even if they are zero eg 0.120 has 3 significant figures.
- If the number is written in standard form, do not count the exponential part of the number. eg 1.23×10^{-3} has 3 significant figures and 9.560×10^6 has 4 significant figures.

These rules do not apply to quantities such as 100 m. Does this have 1, 2 or 3 significant figures? Also, if you cannot tell, for instance, if you did not make the measurement yourself, then the number of significant figures is uncertain.

Other numbers are exact, for example there are

1000 cm^3 in 1 dm^3. There is no uncertainty with the 1000; it cannot be anything else.

Table A1.1

Measurement	Number of significant figures
24.0 °C	3
$5.67 \times 10{-5}$ m^3	3
0.00560 moles	3
2500 cm^3	uncertain

Decimal places

To determine the number of decimal places in a number, simply count the number of digits to the right of the decimal place. Even zeros will be counted if they are significant. So if the mass of a sample of copper(II) oxide is measured as 0.300 g (we assume that the mass was determined to the nearest milligram), then this number has 3 decimal places. Remember, the number of significant figures is normally different from the number of decimal places.

Calculations

You must be very careful during a calculation not to quote too many or too few decimal places or significant figures. Do not just copy the answer from your calculator. Think about how many significant figures or decimal places should be used. These are some simple rules.

- When adding or subtracting numbers, it is the number of decimal places that is important. Decide which number in the calculation has the least number of decimal places. This tells you the number of decimal places in the answer.
  For example the M_r of NO is 14.0 + 16.0 = 30.0.
- When multiplying or dividing numbers, it is the number of significant figures that is important. Decide which number in the calculation has the least number of significant figures. This tells you how many significant figures in the answer. For example, the number of moles of carbon in 14.20 g = $\frac{14.2}{12.0}$ = 1.183333
  but the answer should be quoted only to three significant figures: 1.18.
- Remember that exact numbers are just that, and so do not affect the number of significant figures.

APPENDIX 2: THE PERIODIC TABLE

Relative atomic masses given in brackets refer to the isotopic mass of the most abundant isotope of the elements concerned.

Key:

atomic no
symbol
name
relative atomic mass

metal | non-metal

Group	1	2			3	4	5	6	7	0
Period 1	1 **H** hydrogen 1.0									2 **He** helium 4.0
Period 2	3 **Li** lithium 6.9	4 **Be** beryllium 9.0			5 **B** boron 10.8	6 **C** carbon 12.0	7 **N** nitrogen 14.0	8 **O** oxygen 16.0	9 **F** fluorine 19.0	10 **Ne** neon 20.2
Period 3	11 **Na** sodium 23.0	12 **Mg** magnesium 24.3			13 **Al** aluminium 6.9	14 **Si** silicon 28.1	15 **P** phosphorus 31.0	16 **S** sulphur 32.1	17 **Cl** chlorine 35.5	18 **Ar** argon 39.9
Period 4	19 **K** potassium 39.1	20 **Ca** calcium 40.1			31 **Ga** gallium 69.7	32 **Ge** germanium 72.6	33 **As** arsenic 74.9	34 **Se** selenium 79.0	35 **Br** bromine 79.9	36 **Kr** krypton 83.8
Period 5	37 **Rb** rubidium 85.5	38 **Sr** strontium 87.6			49 **In** indium 114.8	50 **Sn** tin 118.7	51 **Sb** antimony 121.8	52 **Te** tellurium 127.6	53 **I** iodine 126.9	54 **Xe** xenon 131.3
Period 6	55 **Cs** caesium 132.9	56 **Ba** barium 137.3			81 **Tl** thallium 204.4	82 **Pb** lead 207.2	83 **Bi** bismuth 209.0	84 **Po** polonium (209)	85 **At** astatine (210)	86 **Rn** radon (222)
Period 7	87 **Fr** francium (223)	88 **Ra** radium (226)								

Transition elements:

21 **Sc** scandium 45.0	22 **Ti** titanium 47.8	23 **V** vanadium 50.9	24 **Cr** chromium 52.0	25 **Mn** manganese 54.9	26 **Fe** iron 55.9	27 **Co** cobalt 58.9	28 **Ni** nickel 58.7	29 **Cu** copper 63.5	30 **Zn** zinc 65.4
39 **Y** yttrium 88.9	40 **Zr** zirconium 91.2	41 **Nb** niobium 92.9	42 **Mo** molybdenum 95.9	43 **Tc** technetium (98)	44 **Ru** ruthenium 101.1	45 **Rh** rhodium 102.9	46 **Pd** palladium 106.4	47 **Ag** silver 107.9	48 **Cd** cadmium 112.4
57 **La** lanthanum 138.9	72 **Hf** hafnium 178.5	73 **Ta** tantalum 181.0	74 **W** tungsten 183.9	75 **Re** rhenium 186.2	76 **Os** osmium 190.2	77 **Ir** iridium 192.2	78 **Pt** platinum 195.1	79 **Au** gold 197.0	80 **Hg** mercury 200.6
89 **Ac** actinium (227)	104 **Unq** unnilquadium (261)	105 **Unp** unnilpentium (262)	106 **Unh** unnilhexium (263)	107 **Uns** unnilseptium (262)	108 **Uno** unniloctium (265)	109 **Une** unnilennium (266)			

Lanthanides

58 **Ce** cerium 140.1	59 **Pr** praseodymium 140.9	60 **Nd** neodymium 144.2	61 **Pm** promethium (145)	62 **Sm** samarium 150.4	63 **Eu** europium 152.0	64 **Gd** gadolinium 157.3	65 **Tb** terbium 158.9	66 **Dy** dysprosium 162.5	67 **Ho** holmium 164.9	68 **Er** erbium 167.3	69 **Tm** thulium 168.9	70 **Yb** ytterbium 173.0	71 **Lu** lutetium 175.5

Actinides

90 **Th** thorium 232.0	91 **Pa** protactinium (231)	92 **U** uranium 238.1	93 **Np** neptunium (237)	94 **Pu** plutonium (244)	95 **Am** americium (243)	96 **Cm** curium (247)	97 **Bk** berkelium (247)	98 **Cf** californium (251)	99 **Es** einsteinium (254)	100 **Fm** fermium (253)	101 **Md** mendelevium (256)	102 **No** nobelium (254)	103 **Lr** lawrencium (257)

APPENDIX 3: IONISATION ENERGIES

First ionisation energies of the elements

These values are in kJ mol^{-1}.

H 1310																	**He** 2370
Li 519	**Be** 900											**B** 799	**C** 1090	**N** 1400	**O** 1310	**F** 1680	**Ne** 2080
Na 494	**Mg** 736											**Al** 577	**Si** 786	**P** 1060	**S** 1000	**Cl** 1260	**Ar** 1520
K 418	**Ca** 590	**Sc** 632	**Ti** 661	**V** 648	**Cr** 653	**Mn** 716	**Fe** 762	**Co** 757	**Ni** 736	**Cu** 745	**Zn** 908	**Ga** 577	**Ge** 762	**As** 966	**Se** 941	**Br** 1140	**Kr** 1350
Rb 402	**Sr** 548	**Y** 636	**Zr** 669	**Nb** 653	**Mo** 694	**Tc** 699	**Ru** 724	**Rh** 745	**Pd** 803	**Ag** 732	**Cd** 866	**In** 556	**Sn** 707	**Sb** 833	**Te** 870	**I** 1010	**Xe** 1170
Cs 376	**Ba** 502	**La** 540	**Hf** 531	**Ta** 577	**W** 770	**Re** 762	**Os** 841	**Ir** 887	**Pt** 866	**Au** 891	**Hg** 1010	**Tl** 590	**Pb** 716	**Bi** 774	**Po** 812	**At**	**Rn** 1040
Fr 381	**Ra** 510	**Ac** 669															

Ce 665	**Pr** 556	**Nd** 607	**Pm** 556	**Sm** 540	**Eu** 548	**Gd** 594	**Tb** 648	**Dy** 657	**Ho**	**Er**	**Tm**	**Yb** 598	**Lu** 481
Th 674	**Pa**	**U** 385	**Np**	**Pu**	**Am**	**Cm**	**Bk**	**Cf**	**Es**	**Fm**	**Md**	**No**	**Lr**

Ionisation energies of selected elements

Element	Atomic (proton) energy/kJ mol^{-1}	First ionisation energy/kJ mol^{-1}	Second ionisation energy/kJ mol^{-1}	Third ionisation energy/kJ mol^{-1}	Fourth ionisation energy/kJ mol^{-1}
K	19	420	3070	4600	5860
Ca	20	590	1150	4940	6480
Sc	21	630	1240	2390	7110
Ti	22	660	1310	2720	4170
V	23	650	1370	2870	4600
Cr	24	650	1590	2990	4770
Mn	25	720	1510	3250	5190
Fe	26	760	1560	2960	5400
Co	27	760	1640	3230	5100
Ni	28	740	1750	3390	5400
Cu	29	750	1960	3350	5690
Zn	30	910	1730	3830	6190

APPENDIX 4: STANDARD ELECTRODE POTENTIALS

Electrode reaction	$E^{\ominus}$/V	Electrode reaction	$E^{\ominus}$/V
$Ag^+ + e^- \rightleftharpoons Ag$	+ 0.80	$Hg^{2+} + 2e^- \rightleftharpoons Hg$	+0.85
$Ag^{2+} + e^- \rightleftharpoons Ag^+$	+1.98	$2Hg^{2+} + 2e^- \rightleftharpoons Hg_2^{2+}$	+0.91
$AgBr + e^- \rightleftharpoons Ag + Br^-$	+0.07	$Hg_2Cl_2 + 2e^- \rightleftharpoons 2Hg + 2Cl^-$	+0.27
$AgCN + e^- \rightleftharpoons Ag + CN^-$	−0.04	$I_2 + 2e^- \rightleftharpoons 2I^-$	+0.54
$Ag(CN)_2^- + e^- \rightleftharpoons Ag + 2CN^-$	−0.38	$2HOI + 2H^+ + 2e^- \rightleftharpoons I_2 + 2H_2O$	+1.45
$AgCl + e^- \rightleftharpoons Ag + Cl^-$	+0.22	$2IO_3^- + 12H^+ + 10e^- \rightleftharpoons I_2 + 6H_2O$	+1.19
$AgI + e^- \rightleftharpoons Ag + I^-$	−0.15	$K^+ + e^- \rightleftharpoons K$	−2.92
$Ag(NH_3)_2^+ + e^- \rightleftharpoons Ag + 2NH_3$	+0.37	$Li^+ + e^- \rightleftharpoons Li$	−3.04
$Ag_2O + H_2O + 2e^- \rightleftharpoons 2Ag + 2OH^-$	+0.34	$Mg^{2+} + 2e^- \rightleftharpoons Mg$	−2.38
$Al^{3+} + 3e^- \rightleftharpoons Al$	−1.66	$Mn^{2+} + 2e^- \rightleftharpoons Mn$	−1.18
$Al(OH)_4^- + 3e^- \rightleftharpoons Al + 4OH^-$	−2.35	$MnO_2 + 4H^+ + 2e^- \rightleftharpoons Mn^{2+} + 2H_2O$	+1.23
$As + 3H^+ + 3e^- \rightleftharpoons AsH_3$	−0.38	$MnO_4^- + e^- \rightleftharpoons MnO_4^{2-}$	+0.56
$H_3AsO_4 + 2H^+ + 2e^- \rightleftharpoons H_3AsO_3 + H_2O$	+0.56	$MnO_4^- + 4H^+ + 3e^- \rightleftharpoons MnO_2 + 2H_2O$	+1.67
$Au^+ + e^- \rightleftharpoons Au$	+1.68	$MnO_4^- + 8H^+ + 5e^- \rightleftharpoons Mn^{2+} + 4H_2O$	+1.52
$Au^{3+} + 3e^- \rightleftharpoons Au$	+1.50	$N_2 + 8H^+ + 6e^- \rightleftharpoons 2NH_4^+$	+0.27
$H_3BO_3 + 3H^+ + 3e^- \rightleftharpoons B + 3H_2O$	−0.73	$HNO_2 + H^+ + e^- \rightleftharpoons NO + H_2O$	+0.99
$Ba^{2+} + 2e^- \rightleftharpoons Ba$	−2.90	$NO_3^- + 2H^+ + e^- \rightleftharpoons NO_2 + H_2O$	+0.81
$Ba^{2+} + 2e^- \rightleftharpoons Be$	−1.85	$NO_3^- + 3H^+ + 2e^- \rightleftharpoons HNO_2 + H_2O$	+0.94
$BiO^+ + 2H^+ + 3e^- \rightleftharpoons Bi + H_2O$	+0.28	$NO_3^- + 4H^+ + 3e^- \rightleftharpoons NO + 2H_2O$	+0.96
$Br_2 + 2e^- \rightleftharpoons 2Br^-$	+1.07	$2NO_3^- + 10H^+ + 8e^- \rightleftharpoons N_2O + 5H_2O$	+1.11
$2HOBr + 2H^+ + 2e^- \rightleftharpoons Br_2 + 2H_2O$	+1.59	$2NO_3^- + 12H^+ + 10e^- \rightleftharpoons N_2 + 6H_2O$	+1.24
$2BrO_3^- + 12H^+ + 10e^- \rightleftharpoons Br_2 + 6H_2O$	+1.52	$NO_3^- + 10H^+ + 8e^- \rightleftharpoons NH_4^+ + 3H_2O$	+0.87
$CO_2 + H^+ + e^- \rightleftharpoons {}^*H_2C_2O_4$	−0.49	$Na^+ + e^- \rightleftharpoons Na$	−2.71
$Ca^{2+} + 2e^- \rightleftharpoons Ca$	−2.87	$Ni^{2+} + 2e^- \rightleftharpoons Ni$	⁻0.25
$Cd^{2+} + 2e^- \rightleftharpoons Cd$	−0.40	$Ni(NH_3)_6^{2+} + 2e^- \rightleftharpoons Ni + 6NH_3$	⁻0.51
$Ce^{4+} + e^- \rightleftharpoons Ce^{3+}$	+1.45	$H_2O_2 + 2H^+ + 2e^- \rightleftharpoons 2H_2O$	+1.77
$Cl_2 + 2e^- \rightleftharpoons 2Cl^-$	+1.36	$O_2 + 4H^+ + 4e^- \rightleftharpoons 2H_2O$	+1.23
$2HOCl + 2H^+ + 2e^- \rightleftharpoons Cl_2 + 2H_2O$	+1.64	$O_2 + 2H^+ + 2e^- \rightleftharpoons H_2O_2$	+0.68
$2ClO_3^- + 12H + 10e^- \rightleftharpoons Cl_2 + 6H_2O$	+1.47	$O_2 + 2H_2O + 4e^- \rightleftharpoons 4OH^-$	+0.40
$CO^{2+} + 2e^- \rightleftharpoons CO$	−0.28	$O_3 + 2H^+ + 2e^- \rightleftharpoons O2 + H_2O$	+2.07
$CO^{3+} + e^- \rightleftharpoons Co^{2+}$	+1.82	$P + 3H^+ + 3e^- \rightleftharpoons PH_3$	⁻0.04
$Co(NH_3)_6^{2+} + 2e^- \rightleftharpoons Co + 6NH_3$	−0.43	$H_3PO_4 + 2H^+ + 2e^- \rightleftharpoons H_3PO_3 + H_2O$	⁻0.28
$Cr^{2+} + 2e^- \rightleftharpoons Cr$	−0.91	$Pb^{2+} + 2e^- \rightleftharpoons Pb$	⁻0.13
$Cr^{3+} + 3e^- \rightleftharpoons Cr$	−0.74	$PB^{4+} + 2e^- \rightleftharpoons PB^{2+}$	+1.69
$Cr^{3+} + e^- \rightleftharpoons Cr^{2+}$	−0.41	$PbO_2 + 4H^+ + 2e^- \rightleftharpoons Pb^{2+} + 2H_2O$	+1.47
$Cr_2O_7^{2-} + 14H^+ + 6e^- \rightleftharpoons 2Cr^{3+} + 7H_2O$	+1.33	$PbO_2 + H_2O + 2e^- \rightleftharpoons PBO + 2OH^-$	+0.28
$Cs^+ + e^- \rightleftharpoons Cs$	−2.92	$Ra^{2+} + 2e^- \rightleftharpoons Ra$	⁻2.92
$Cu^+ + e^- \rightleftharpoons Cu$	+0.52	$Rb^+ + e^- \rightleftharpoons Rb$	⁻2.92
$Cu^{2+} + 2e^- \rightleftharpoons Cu$	+0.34	$S + 2e^- \rightleftharpoons S^{2-}$	⁻0.51
$Cu^{2+} + e^- \rightleftharpoons Cu^+$	+0.15	$S + 2H^+ + 2e^- \rightleftharpoons H_2S$	+0.14
$Cu^{2+} + I^- + e^- \rightleftharpoons CuI$	+0.86	$SO_4^{2-} + 4H^+ + 2e^- \rightleftharpoons H_2SO_3 + H_2O$	+0.17
$Cu(NH_3)_4^{2+} + 2e^- \rightleftharpoons Cu + 4NH_3$	−0.05	$S_2O_8^{2-} + 2e^- \rightleftharpoons 2SO_4^{2-}$	+2.01
$2D^+ + 2e^- \rightleftharpoons D_2$	−0.003	$S_4O_6^{2-} + 2e^- \rightleftharpoons 2S_2O_3^{2-}$	+0.09
$F_2 + 2e^- \rightleftharpoons 2F^-$	+2.87	$Sb + 3H^+ + 3e^- \rightleftharpoons SbH_3$	⁻0.51
$Fe^{2+} + 2e^- \rightleftharpoons Fe$	−0.44	$SbO^+ + 2H^+ + 3e^- \rightleftharpoons Sb + H_2O$	+0.21
$Fe^{3+} + 3e^- \rightleftharpoons Fe$	−0.04	$Sn^{2+} + 2e^- \rightleftharpoons Sn$	⁻0.14
$Fe^{3+} + e^- \rightleftharpoons Fe^{2+}$	+0.77	$Sn^{4+} + 2e^- \rightleftharpoons Sn^{2+}$	+0.15
$Fe(CN)_6^{3-} + e^- \rightleftharpoons Fe(CN)_6^{4-}$	+0.36	$V^{2+} + 2e^- \rightleftharpoons V$	⁻1.2
$FeO_4^{2-} + 8H^+ + 3e^- \rightleftharpoons Fe^{3+} + 4H_2O$	+2.20	$V^{3+} + e^- \rightleftharpoons V^{2+}$	⁻0.26
$2H^+ + 2e^- \rightleftharpoons H_2$	0.00	$VO^{2+} + 2H^+ + e^- \rightleftharpoons V^{3+} + H_2O$	+0.34
$H2 + 2e^- \rightleftharpoons 2H^-$	−2.25	$VO^{2+} + 2H^+ + e^- \rightleftharpoons VO^{2+} + H_2O$	+1.00
$Hg_2^{2+} + 2e^- \rightleftharpoons 2Hg$	+0.79	$VO^{3-} + 4H^+ + e^- \rightleftharpoons VO^{2+} + 2H_2O$	+1.00
		$Zn^{2+} + 2e^- \rightleftharpoons Zn$	⁻0.76

ANSWERS TO QUESTIONS

The following are the answers to marginal Self-test questions that are in word, equation or numerical form.

CHAPTER 1
A (a) $CaCO_3 \rightarrow CaO + CO_2$ (b)$2Mn + O_2 \rightarrow 2MnO$
(c) $4P + 5O_2 \rightarrow P_4O_{10}$
B (a) 56 (b) 2 (c) 3.5
C (a) 1.0 mol of iron, 0.50 mol of calcium, 2.0 mol of copper, 0.125 (0.1 to 1 sig. fig) mol of sulphur
(b) 120 g of calcium (c) 6 g of neon
D (a) P_4O_{10} 284, O_2 32, $CaSiO_3$ 116 **E** (a) 90 (b) 342 (c) 102
F (a) $Fe_2O_3 + 3C \rightarrow 3CO + 2Fe$ (b) 0.75 tonnes **G** 96%
H (a) $Fe_3O_4 + 4CO \rightarrow 3Fe + 4CO_2$ (b) 0.724 tonnes (c) 3%
I (a) exothermic (b) endothermic (c) exothermic
J Continuous processes need less labour, no need to close and reset reactor vessel, product formed has more consistent quality.
K (a) To ensure thorough mixing of reactants.
(b) Allows easy passage of gases.
L Melting point in excess of 2000 ºC. Does not react with substances present in blast furnace.
M Saving on cost of raw materials and energy for the blast furnace.
Environmental reasons eg less mining or quarrying for raw materials, less slag produced.

CHAPTER 2
A Crystals not exposed to sunlight
B (a) α positive, β negative, γ neutral (b) β has smaller mass than γ particles
C 3 km **D** Number of protons = number of electrons = $Z = 11$
E $^{56}_{26}Fe$ $A = 56$, $Z = 26$, 26 protons, 26 electrons, 30 neutrons
$^{200}_{80}Ag$ $A = 200$, $Z = 80$, 80 protons, 80 electrons, 120 neutrons
F $^{13}_{6}C$ $A = 13$, $Z = 6$, 6 protons, 6 electrons, 7 neutrons
$^{14}_{6}C$ $A = 14$, $Z = 6$, 6 protons, 6 electrons, 8 neutrons
G Br = 80.0 and Mg = 24.3 **H** $^4_2He + ^4_2He \rightarrow ^8_4Be + energy$
I $^{226}_{88}Ra \rightarrow ^4_2He + ^{222}_{86}Rn$
J (a) Since α particles can only penetrate a few cm in air, they will not escape from detector. (b) Americium oxide in detector will still be radioactive.
K $^{90}_{38}Sr \rightarrow ^0_{-1}e + ^{90}_{39}Y$ Y = yttrium
L $^{235}_{92}U \rightarrow ^{231}_{90}Th + ^4_2He$
$^{131}_{53}I \rightarrow ^{131}_{54}Xe + ^0_{-1}e$
$^{32}_{14}Si \rightarrow ^{32}_{15}P + ^0_{-1}e$
M $^{234}_{92}U \rightarrow ^{230}_{90}Th + ^4_2He$
$^{230}_{90}Th \rightarrow ^{226}_{88}Ra + ^4_2He$
$^{226}_{88}Ra \rightarrow ^{222}_{86}Rn + ^4_2He$
N (a) So that the amount of radioactive isotope in the body decreases very quickly. (b) 0.098 g
O 6.6 half lives, ie about 38000 years **P** 1.0×10^{-15} g
Q Place radioactive source on one side of container and detector on the other side. Monitor the level of radioactivity that is detected. Level of radioactivity will suddenly increase once source and detector are above level of liquid.
Nature of source will depend on dimensions and nature of container. Could use β or γ radiation.

CHAPTER 3
A 5.50×10^{-7} m. Green.
B (a) 3.0×10^{-2} m (b) 2.0×10^{-35} J (c) 1.2×10^{-11} J
C Since frequency of gamma radiation is greater than that of UV, a photon of gamma radiation will have more energy than that of UV.
D Higher energy end of spectrum.
E (b) $n = 4 \rightarrow n = 3$
F Yellow **G** $2n^2$ **I** (a) $Mg^{10+}(g) \rightarrow Mg^{11+}(g) + e^-$
(b) Mg^{10+} has noble gas configuration $1s^2$ which has no inner shell shielding electrons, so the two electrons are very strongly attracted to nucleus. In Mg^{9+}, electron configuration is $1s^22s^1$ which has an inner shell of shielding electrons, so the outer electron is much less firmly attracted to the nucleus than outer electrons in Mg^{10+}.
K (a) The enthalpy change when one mole of gaseous atoms, M, lose one mole of electrons to form one mole of gaseous positive ions, $M^+(g)$.
(b) Lithium has a core charge of +1 and an inner shielding electron shell of two electrons, whereas neon has a core charge of +8 and an inner shielding shell of two electrons containing two electrons. So outer electrons in a neon atom are attracted much more strongly to nucleus than those in lithium.
L (a) Same number of inner shell shielding electrons but core charge of magnesium is +2, whereas in sodium it is +1, so outer electrons in magnesium much more firmly attracted to nucleus.
(b) (i) In magnesium the electron is removed from the 3s orbital, whereas in aluminium the electron is removed from the 3p energy level which is higher in energy (and further away from the nucleus) than the 3s energy level, so requires less energy.
(ii) In phosphorus, each 3p orbitals contains just one electron, so no electron-electron repulsion in these orbitals. But in sulphur one 3p orbital contains two electrons so there is some electron-electron repulsion, making it easier to remove one electron from a sulphur atom than from a phosphorus atom.
M Be ($1s^22s^2$) has a full 2s subshell, whereas B ($1s^22s^22p^1$) has an extra electron in the 2s subshell. The 2p subshell has a higher energy level and the electron in this subshell is further away from the nucleus, so it requires less energy to be removed from the atom.
N Na $1s^22s^22p^63s^1$ Cl $1s^22s^22p^63s^23p^5$ Al $1s^22s^22p^63s^23p^1$

CHAPTER 4
A ns^2np^6
B Na^+ has electron configuration of Ne atom. Cl^- has electron configuration of Ar.
D (a) 7 (b) 1 (c) 2
E Na^+ is isoelectronic with Ne. Cl^- is isoelectronic with Ar.
F (a) K ($1s^22s^22p^63s^23p^64s^1$) $\rightarrow K^+$ ($1s^22s^22p^63s^23p^6$)
F ($1s^22s^22p^5$) $\rightarrow F^-$ ($1s^22s^22p^6$)
(b) Mg ($1s^22s^22p^63s^2$) $\rightarrow Mg^{2+}$ ($1s^22s^22p^6$)
$2 \times Cl$ ($1s^22s^22p^63s^23p^5$) $\rightarrow 2 \times Cl^-$ ($1s^22s^22p^63s^23p^6$)
(c) $2 \times Al$ ($1s^22s^22p^63s^23p^1$) $\rightarrow 2 \times Al^{3+}$ ($1s^22s^22p^6$)
$3 \times O$ ($1s^22s^22p^4$) $\rightarrow 3 \times O^{2-}$ ($1s^22s^22p^6$)
G It is exothermic, energy is released into surroundings when a gaseous fluorine atom gains an electron.
M Outer shell of carbon atom is surrounded by 1 single bond (a bonding pair of electrons), a triple bond (which acts as one bonding pair of electrons) and no lone pairs. To minimise repulsion of the bonding pairs of electrons, the electron pairs are arranged as far away from each other as possible, ie at angle of 180º.
O Tetrahedral (outer shell of aluminium surrounded by four bonding pairs).
R H-F, O-H, N-H, C-Cl, P-H, C-I, F-F
S +6. Core charge remains constant but as atomic number decreases so does the atomic radius and number of inner shielding electron shells, so nucleus has a greater attraction for electron pair within a covalent bond.
T (a) covalent (b) ionic (c) polar covalent **U** Aluminium chloride.

CHAPTER 5
A 2:1:2 ($H_2:O_2:H_2O(g)$)
B Using Avogadro's hypothesis, 1 molecule of hydrogen reacts with ½ molecule of oxygen to make 1 molecule of water. Assuming both water and hydrogen are diatomic, formula of water must be H_2O.
C 25 ºC **I** 100 cm³
D 0.25 mole **J** (a) 298 K (b) 373 K (c) 223 K
E 1.7×10^3 dm³ (to 2 sig. fig) **K** 63.7 cm³
F 29 dm³ **L** (a) 4.9×10^4 cm³
G 25 ºC (298 K) and 101 kPa (b) 3.1×10^4 dm³
H 2 dm³ **M** 146
N So that it can be subtracted from volume of gaseous compound under test, otherwise this volume will include the small volume of air.
O 46
P (a) Pressure decreases because fewer particles will collide with unit area of container wall per second. (b) 2.41×10^{22}
(c) If amount of gas increases, so will number of particles. So to keep number of particles that collide with container wall per second constant the volume, eg gas will have to increase. If amount doubles, then volume will need to double to keep number of collisions per second the same.
Q (a) Steam is a gas, so particles are very spread out with lots of space between them; when the gas condenses the particles are close together with only a very little space between them.
(b) Lots of space between particles in a gas but little space between particles in a liquid.
(c) More particles per unit volume in a liquid since the particles are much closer together than in a gas.
(d) Particles in a liquid free to move and are not in fixed positions.
(e) Particles in a solid not free to move but particles in gases and liquids are free to move.
R ΔH_m is much smaller than ΔH_b. **S** (a) 2, (b) 1
T Suggestions could include: Much less liquid water present in the oceans, so less ocean currents such as Gulf Stream. Weather may be drier since less water available to be evaporated. May not be polar ice-cap at North Pole since it will sink under the surface of the water once formed. Possibly warmer weather as a result. Sea-water may become saltier and so less likely that marine life could survive.
U -240 ºC (b) helium **W** 0.2
V $X_{ethanol} = 0.80$ and $X_{water} = 0.20$. **X** Increases.
Y (a) (i) 0.2 mole (ii) 0.125 mole (iii) 1 mole (iv) 5×10^{-3} mole
(v) 2.5×10^{-3} mole (b) (i) 1.6 mol dm⁻³ (ii) 1.0 mol dm⁻³
Z (a) Increase (b) decrease (c) decrease (d) increase (e) increase (f) decrease

CHAPTER 6
A Energy released cannot be used to do useful work.
B Enthalpy change of combustion will be different if gaseous water is produced. Also under standard conditions water must be a liquid.
D (a) 4.2 kJ (b) 80.4 kJ
E (a) Metal is a much better conductor of heat than glass.
(b) The temperature rise is a difference in temperature and since absolute temperature is temperature in ºC + 273, the difference in temperature on both scales is identical.
(c) Use a lid. Calculate the energy absorbed by the metal calorimeter using the specific heat capacity of the metal. Have the calorimeter at the optimum height above the burner.
F Incomplete combustion. Loss of energy to the surroundings. No account taken of the energy absorbed by the calorimeter itself. Experiment not carried out under standard conditions. Possible loss of liquid fuel through evaporation.
G (a) (i) Lower value. (ii) Weigh inside the bomb calorimeter so that no vapour can escape.
(b) (i) Insulated container which prevents energy loss by conduction from the water into the surroundings. Water in the calorimeter completely surrounds the chamber where the fuel is burnt, so almost all the energy will be transferred into the water. (ii) To ensure that the temperature of the water is constant all through the calorimeter.
H 2758 + (mass of crisps/100) × energy value of crisps in kJ.
I N_2 has an extremely high bond energy since it has a triple covalent bond.
J (a) H-H and O=O since they are the bonds in the molecules H_2 and O_2. C=O figure refers to the C=O bond in carbon dioxide.
(b) +2061 kJ mol⁻¹

(c) Bond energies are quoted for one mole of gaseous bonds, so all reactants and products must be gases. If methanol is not a gas in the calculation, then the enthalpy change for $CH_3OH(l)$ to $CH_3OH(g)$ must be accounted for.

K (a) By experiment, $\Delta H = -286$ kJ mol^{-1} and by calculation using bond energies it is -243 kJ mol^{-1}. The calculation uses average O-H bond energy, not the bond energy for O-H in H_2O.
(b) The energy or enthalpy of the products is higher than the energy or enthalpy of the reactants.

L -658 kJ mol^{-1}

M (a) The fire will not be put out. Often it will become worse because more gaseous petrol is produced.
(b) Methanol has a low energy density value.

N (a) $C_8H_{18}(l) + 12\frac{1}{2}O_2(g)$ ($8CO_2(g) + 9H_2O(l)$
(b) Per mole of C_8H_{18}: 16 moles of C=O and 18 moles of O-H

O (a) 50432 kJ kg^{-1} (b) 12000 dm^3 (c) 1.35 litres

P (c) Not exothermic, does not involve the reaction of 1 mole of N_2.

Q (a) $C(s) + O_2(g) \rightarrow CO_2(g)$ (b) $C(s) + 2H_2(g) \rightarrow CH_4(g)$
(c) Both transfer energy to the surroundings and are more stable than the elements that make them up.

R The standard state of carbon is graphite since it is energetically more stable than diamond.

S (a) -104 kJ mol^{-1} (b) -110 kJ mol^{-1}
(c) It is impossible to react carbon with oxygen without at least making some carbon dioxide.

T (a) ΔH_f for N_2 is 0 since it is an element. (b) -129 kJ mol^{-1}

U To provide the energy to overcome the activation energy.

V Because the number of moles of N_2 reacting is different. With $\frac{1}{2}$ mole of N_2, $\Delta H = +90$ kJ mol^{-1}, but with 1 mole of N_2 it is +180 kJ mol^{-1}.

W (a) decrease (b) decrease (c) increase (d) no significant change

X Infrared **Y** 19020 J mol^{-1} K^{-1}

CHAPTER 7

A Methane, CH_4.

B Loss of 4 electrons from a carbon atom to form C^{4+} requires too much energy. Gain of 4 electrons to form C^{4-} also requires too much energy.

C Methane. Water.

D Dative covalent bond.

E C_8H_{18}

F Ethane. Pentane.

G (a) C_7H_{14} and C_9H_{18} unsaturated. (b) Both have same molecular formula.

H (b) Same molecular formula.

K They all have a 4-carbon atom chain with no branches.

L $CH_3CH_2CH_2CH_2CH_2CH_3$
$(CH_3)_2CHCH_2CH_2CH_3$
$CH_3CH_2CH(CH_3)CH_2CH_3$
$CH_3CH(CH_3)CH_2CH_2CH_3$
$CH_3C(CH_3)_2CH_2CH_3$

M (a) C_4H_8 (b) Molecular formula C_4H_6 not C_4H_8.

O Isomers. **P** C_9H_{20}

Q (a) sulphur dioxide (b) Acid rain.

R (a) kerosene.
(b) (i) $C_{12}H_{26} \rightarrow C_{10}H_{22}$ (decane) + C_2H_4
(ii) $C_{12}H_{26} \rightarrow C_9H_{18}$ (2-methyloctane) + C_3H_6

S (a) Because sometimes reforming converts a hydrocarbon into a branched chain isomer.
(b) Unbranched hydrocarbons fit into zeolite pore but branched hydrocarbons do not.

T (a) hexane → cyclohexane → benzene (b) hydrogen

CHAPTER 8

A C_7H_{16} $CH_3CH_2CH_2CH_2CH_2CH_2CH_3$
C_8H_{18} $CH_3CH_2CH_2CH_2CH_2CH_2CH_2CH_3$

B (a) $CH_3CH_2CH_2CH_2CH_2CH_2CH_2CH_2CH_2CH_3$
(b) decane

C (a) pentyl (b) C_nH_{2n+1}

D $CH_3CH_2CH_2CH_3$

E (a) It is another way of drawing methylbutane. (b) Methyl group can only be on carbon 2. If it was on carbon 1, the molecule would be butane.

F $CH_3C(CH_3)_2CH(C_2H_5)CH_2CH_2CH_3$
$CH_3CH_2CH(C_3H_7)CH_2CH_2CH_2CH_3$

G 2

H (a) Methane, ethane, propane, butane.
(b) (i) Boiling point is 216 ºC, density is 0.748 g cm^{-3} (ii) 18

I The δ+ and the δ- are quite large, so there is a fairly strong intermolecular attraction.

J As atomic number increases a noble gas atom has more electrons and a greater atomic radius, hence the formation of an instantaneous dipole is easier so that the induced dipole-induced dipole intermolecular attractive force increases.

K (a) Hotter in Spain, so petrol more volatile. (b) Use branched chain alkanes.

L (a) Exothermic (b) Spontaneous reactions are ones that have a tendency to occur and the entropy change is positive. Activation energy is the minimum energy per mole of particles needed in order for collision between particles to lead to a reaction.
(c) Reaction of alkanes and oxygen is exothermic, so alkanes and oxygen have more enthalpy than carbon dioxide and water (energetically unstable). But at room temperature, activation energy sufficiently high for rate of reaction between petrol and oxygen to be very slow (kinetically stable).
(d) Reacts with oxygen to release lots of energy (large value of energy released per gram of fuel). Easily stored. Easily transported. Non-toxic. Readily available.

M (a) $C_nH_{2n+1}OH$ (b) Same chemical properties. Physical properties vary with increasing M_r (boiling point, melting point and density all increase with increasing M_r).

N $C_{10}H_{22} + 15\frac{1}{2}O_2 \rightarrow 10CO_2 + 11H_2O$

O (a) Visible light.
(b) Absorbed by coloured substances and gases in atmosphere.

P Plants that can photosynthesise, using up carbon dioxide, are not present on Mars and Venus.

Q (a) Summer months: green plants growing very fast, so high rate of photosynthesis, using up carbon dioxide.
(b) Winter months: an increase in mass of fuel burnt and rate of growth by green plants is low, so not much photosynthesis.

R (a) EU nations agreed in Kyoto December 1997 to reduce emissions of greenhouse gases to that of 1990 by the year 2012. This about an 8% reduction per year.
(b) (i) 700g (ii) $C_{18}H_{18} + 12\frac{1}{2}O_2 \rightarrow 8CO_2 + 9H_2O$
(iii) 2160g (iv) 8.6×10^{11}g

S Catalyst is a solid but the reactants are gases, so large surface area required to maximise number of collisions between reactant and catalyst. The catalyst will also work by adsorption (surface action), so it needs a large surface area.

T At the start of a journey when the engine is cold or when the car is stationary.

U (a) $C_6H_6 + 7\frac{1}{2}O_2 \rightarrow 6CO_2 + 3H_2O$ (b) Greenhouse effect.

V $N_2 + O_2 \rightarrow 2NO$ **W** Greenhouse effect.

X NO_2 is regenerated at end of reaction steps, it speeds up rate of reaction and mechanism of oxidation of SO_2 has been changed.

Y $1s^2 2s^2 2p^4$. When occupying the three 2p atomic orbitals the electrons are arranged so as to minimise the electron-electron repulsion that occurs if two electrons are in the same orbital, so only one orbital, the $2p_x$, is occupied by two electrons. The other two, $2p_y$ and $2p_z$ have one electron in each.

CHAPTER 9

A Compound Y.

B (a) Pencil will not dissolve in any solvent used. (b) So that as the solvent will move up the chromatography paper and will not evaporate. (c) 0.15, 0.50
(d) It is not soluble in the mobile phase.

C Adsorption.

D (a) The liquid must not boil when the GLC column is in a hot oven.
(b) GLC works by the difference in solubility between the liquid and the carrier gas.

E Since retention time is dependent on flow-rate, temperature, packing of column, length of column, any data-base used must have same GLC characteristics as used in chromatographic separation.

F Adsorption.

G Organic compounds that contains mostly carbon and hydrogen are more likely to be completely combusted, and the products of the combustion, and the mass of H_2O and CO_2, can be easily determined since they are easily absorbed.

H Ethane CH_3 **I** (a) C_5H_{11} (b) $C_2H_5O_2N$
Ethanedioic acid CH_2O CH_2O

K (a) C_6H_6 (b) CH_2O_2 (c) $C_8H_{10}N_4O_2$

L Prevents collisions between positive ions and other particles. Avoids undue contamination of the sample with air since the molecules in air will also be ionised be electron bombardment.

M 72.8 **N** CH_2O_2

O (a) Since all the particles have a charge of +1, $m/e = m$, since $e = 1$.
(b) $C_2H_4^+$ (c) $m/e = 43$, $C_3H_7^+$

P (a) It has an unpaired electron in the outer shell of carbon, and free radicals have an unpaired electron in their outer shell.
(b) Only positive particles are detected by the mass spectrometer and $CH_3\bullet$ is neutral

Q (a) CO or C_2H_4 (b) $CH_3CH_2O\bullet$ (c) $C_6H_5\bullet$

R (a) OH$\bullet$ (b) $m/e = 45$: CH_2O^+, $m/e = 29$: CHO$^+$, $m/e = 28$: CO$^+$

S (a) 10
(b) (i) $m/e = 49$: $CH_2{}^{35}Cl^+$, $m/e = 51$: $CH_2{}^{37}Cl^+$
(ii) $m/e = 64$: $CH_3CH_2{}^{35}Cl^+$, $m/e = 66$: $CH_3CH_2{}^{37}Cl^+$
(iii) $CH_3\bullet$
(d) (i) $m/e = 74$: $({}^{35}Cl_2)^+$, $m/e = 72$: $({}^{35}Cl{}^{37}Cl)^+$: $m/e = 70$: $({}^{35}Cl_2)^+$
(ii) ratio ^{35}Cl:^{37}Cl = 3:1, so ratio $({}^{35}Cl_2)^+:({}^{35}Cl{}^{37}Cl)^+:({}^{37}Cl_2)^+ = 9:6:1$

T (a) H_2 does not have a dipole moment.
(b) Only one vibration is possible with a diatomic molecule.
(c) Bond energy of HCl is greater than that of HI.

U A Hydrogen bonded O-H stretch.
B C-O stretch.

V (a) O-H stretch.
(b) Confusion between the stretching frequency for O-H in water and in ethanol
(c) Propanone also contains C-H bonds, so the C-H stretching frequency at 3000 cm^{-1} can be due to ethanol or propanone.

W Mass number is odd. **X** Proton magnetic resonance. **Y** (a) 1 (b) 1 (c) 2

Z Signal at δ = 2.1 (a doublet) integrated trace 3 protons.
Signal at δ = 9.7 (a quartet) integrated trace 1 proton.

A´ CHO protons 4, CH_3 protons 2

CHAPTER 10

A 5 atoms (4 Cl and 1 I)

B (a) C 1,1-dibromo-1,2-dichloroethane, D 1,1-dibromo-1,2-dichloroethane

C (a) perflurobutane or decafluorobutane
(b) 2-chlorobutane (c) perchlorohexane

D (a) (i) CF_3Cl (ii) $C_2F_2Cl_4$ (b) tetrachloro-difluoroethane

E So that it can smother and prevent oxygen from reaching the flame.

F (a) 52 ºC (b) Stronger intermolecular bonds in 1-chlorobutane.
(c) Isomers with branched chains are less able to pack efficiently with one another, so overall a weaker intermolecular attraction than in an unbranched isomer.

H $CH_3\bullet$ is the only free radical.

I (a) 79 kJ mol^{-1} (b) fluorine.

J (a) There is no net change when an ethyl free radical collides with an ethane molecule.
$C_2H_5\bullet + C_2H_6 \rightarrow C_2H_6 + C_2H_5\bullet$

K (a) Have a small mole ratio of Cl_2:C_2H_6 and carry out chlorination over a short time period.
(b) Have a high mole ratio Cl_2:C_2H_6 and carry out reaction over a long time period.

L Any two reactions that involve two free radicals present in the reaction mixture, for example:
$Cl\bullet + C_2H_3Cl_2\bullet \rightarrow C_2H_3Cl_3$
$Cl\bullet + C_2H_5\bullet \rightarrow C_2H_5Cl$

M Initiation step: $Cl_2 \rightarrow 2Cl\bullet$
Propagation steps:
$Cl\bullet + CH_4 \rightarrow CH_3\bullet + HCl$
$CH_3\bullet + Cl_2 \rightarrow CH_3Cl + Cl\bullet$
$Cl\bullet + CH_3Cl \rightarrow CH_2Cl\bullet + HCl$
$CH_2Cl\bullet + Cl_2 \rightarrow CH_2Cl_2 + Cl\bullet$
$Cl\bullet + CH_2Cl_2 \rightarrow CHCl_2\bullet + HCl$
$CHCl_2\bullet + Cl_2 \rightarrow CHCl_3 + Cl\bullet$
$Cl\bullet + CHCl_3 \rightarrow CCl_3\bullet + HCl$
$CCl_3\bullet + Cl_2 \rightarrow CCl_4 + Cl\bullet$
Termination steps:
$Cl\bullet + CH_3\bullet \rightarrow CH_3Cl$
$CH_3\bullet + CH_3\bullet \rightarrow C_2H_6$

N Initiation step: $F_2 \rightarrow 2F\bullet$
Propagation steps:
$F\bullet + CH_4 \rightarrow CH_3\bullet + HF$
$CH_3\bullet + F_2 \rightarrow CH_3F + F\bullet$
$F\bullet + CH_3F \rightarrow CH_2F\bullet + HF$
$CH_2F\bullet + F_2 \rightarrow CH_2F_2 + F\bullet$
$F\bullet + CH_2F_2 \rightarrow CHF_2\bullet + HF$
$CHF_2\bullet + F_2 \rightarrow CHF_3 + F\bullet$
$F\bullet + CHF_3 \rightarrow CF_3\bullet + HF$
$CF_3\bullet + F_2 \rightarrow CF_4 + F\bullet$
Termination steps:
$F\bullet + CH_3\bullet \rightarrow CH_3F$
$CH_3\bullet + CH_3\bullet \rightarrow C_2H_6$

P Bubble chlorine into refluxing methylbenzene in the presence of UV light over a long period of time.
$C_6H_5CH_3 + 3Cl_2 \rightarrow C_6H_5CCl_3 + 3HCl$

Q (a) 2-iodo-3-methylhexane
(b) Ethanol, red phosphorus and iodine or ethanol and PI_3.

R fluoromethane

S (a) NH_2 nucleophile (b) CN^- nucleophile (c) $Bcl3$ not a nucleophile

T (a) +90 kJ mol^{-1} (b) -80 kJ mol^{-1}

U pentan-2-ol

Y (a) Substitution: $CH_3CH_2CH_2I + NaOH \rightarrow CH_3CH_2CH_2OH + NaI$
Elimination: $CH_3CH_2CH_2I + NaOH \rightarrow CH_3CH=CH_2 + NaI + H_2O$
(b) pent-1-ene

Z Catalyst.

CHAPTER 11

C (b) Geraniol primary, nerol primary, linalool tertiary.
D (a) Dihydric.
(c) Geraniol monohydric, nerol monohydric, linalool monohydric, maltose polyhydric.
E 97 ºC
F (a) Stronger intermolecular forces in butan-1-ol (both hydrogen bonds and induced dipole-induced dipole).
(b) Decane and decan-1-ol are structurally similar since both contain a very long non-polar alkyl group, so intermolecular force in both compounds is primarily and induced dipole-induced dipole (van der Waals). Methanol is polar and methane is non-polar so strong hydrogen bonding in methanol and weaker and induced dipole-induced dipole (van der Waals) forces in methane.
G Nonan-1-ol molecules have long non-polar alkyl group which forms van der Waals attractions with the non polar nonane molecules. Methanol is a polar molecule and cannot form intermolecular attractions with nonane molecules.
H Chain form has a free aldehyde group but ring form does not. Ring form has a C-O-C bond that is not present in the chain form.
I (a) Glucose molecule has an aldehyde group at carbon 1 but sorbitol has a primary alcohol functional group at carbon 1.
(b) Can form many intermolecular hydrogen bonds with water molecules due to the presence of the polar OH bonds.
J Quite strong intermolecular force comprised of hydrogen bonds and and induced dipole (van der Waals) attractions.
K (a) $C_3H_6 + H_2SO_4 \rightarrow C_3H_7OSO_3H$
(b) $C_3H_7OSO_3H + H_2O \rightarrow C_3H_7OH + H_2O$
(c) cyclopentanol
L $CO_2 + 4H_2 \rightarrow CH_3OH + 2H_2O$
M (a) 2-bromopentane (b) iodocyclohexane (c) 1-chloropropane
N (a) Reflux with heating C_2H_5OH with HI(aq) or react with reflux C_2H_5OH and PI_3.
(b) Reflux with heating H_2SO_4(l), NaCl(s) and pentan-2-ol, or heat together PCl_5 or $SOCl_2$ with pentan-2-ol.
(c) Reflux with heating 3-methylhexan-2-ol with HI(aq), or heat together PI_3 and 3-methylhexan-2-ol.
O Lack of HCl(g) with PCl_5 indicates no OH group present. So compound is methoxymethane, CH_3OCH_3.
T (a) $CH_3CH_2CH_2CH_2OH + 2[O] \rightarrow CH_3CH_2CH_2COOH + H_2O$
U (a) cyclohexanone (b) $CH_3CH_2CHOHCH_3 + [O] \rightarrow CH_3CH_2COCH_3 + H_2O$
W (a) butanal (b) butanone (c) no reaction.
Y (a) Highly electronegative chlorine atom withdraws electrons from the OH bond, making it weaker. Weaker OH bond will give a stronger acid.
(b) $2Na + 2CH_3OH \rightarrow 2CH_3O^-Na^+ + H_2$. Sodium methoxide.
Z (a) Secondary alcohol.

CHAPTER 12

A $C_2H_4 + 3O_2 \rightarrow 2CO_2 + 2H_2O$ $C_3H_6 + 4\frac{1}{2}O_2 \rightarrow 3CO_2 + 3H_2O$
B (a) $CH_4 + 2O_2 \rightarrow CO_2 + 2H_2O$
(b) Keep mole ratio of O_2:CH_4 to 1:2 since combustion requires ratio of 2:1.
C Carbon atom is surrounded by 1 double bond (counts as one bonding pair) and 2 single bonds (2 bonding pairs). These electron pairs repel each other and move apart as far as possible, ie about 120 º from each other.
D (b) (i) oct-1-ene (ii) 3-ethyl-2-methylpent-2-ene (iii) cyclohexene.
E (b) (i) *trans*-hep-3-ene (ii) *cis*-1,2-dichloroethene
(c) hex-2-ene and hex-3-ene.
F 265 kJ mol^{-1}
G (a) Increase in molecular size and number of electrons per molecule so that the induced dipole-induced dipole (van der Waals) intermolecular attraction increases, so it requires more energy to overcome the intermolecular bonding.
(b) Approximately 60 ºC
H (a) (i) ethanol (ii) propan-1-ol or propan-2-ol (iii) cycloheptanol
(b) (i) pent-1-ene, *cis*- and *trans*-pent-2-ene (ii) pent-2-ene
J Lower bond energy than the σ bond.   **K** Br^+ and CH_3^+
N (a) 2-bromobutane (b) bromocyclohexane (c) 2-bromopentane
O Primary carbocations are the least stable so product of electrophilic addition will come from the secondary carbocation which means the OH group cannot be on the number 1 carbon atom.
R Both form same carbocation after the electrophilic attack, $CH_3CHCHBrCH_3$. This carbocation can react with either Br^- or H_2O to form $CH_3CHBrCHBrCH_3$ or $CH_3CHOHCHBrCH_3$.
S 5

T (a) propane-1,2-diol (b) butane-2,3-diol (c) cyclopentane-1,2-diol
U (a) ethanoic acid (b) ethanoic acid, propanoic acid (c) pentane-1,5-dioic acid
V (a) ethene with Br_2, HCl, C_6H_6, Cl_2 and H_2O (b) chloroethene to poly(chloroethene), ethene to poly(ethene), phenylethene to poly(phenylethene).

CHAPTER 13

B (a) and (b)
(i) $C_6H_{10} + H_2 \rightarrow C_6H_{12}$ $\Delta H = -120$ kJ mol^{-1}
(ii) $C_6H_8 + 2H_2 \rightarrow C_6H_{12}$ $\Delta H = -240$ kJ mol^{-1}
(iii) $C_6H_6 + 3H_2 \rightarrow C_6H_{12}$ $\Delta H = -360$ kJ mol^{-1}
C (a) $C_6H_6 + 7\frac{1}{2}O_2 \rightarrow 6CO_2 + 3H_2O$ (b) Expect it to be less than that predicted using the Kekulé structure. Since benzene. it requires more energy to break the bonds in a benzene ring than in three separate double bonds.
D (a) $C_{10}H_8$ (b) $C_{13}H_9$
F (b) 4,5-dichlorobenzene would mean two chlorine atoms on carbon atoms joined to each other. since there are no other substituents, the numbers of the carbons must be as low as possible, ie on carbon atoms number 1 and 2.
H (ii) $C_6H_5CH=CH_2$ (b)1-phenylpropan-1-one, 1-phenylpropan-2-one, 3-phenylpropan-1-ol, 3-phenylpropanal
I Naphthalene $C_{10}H_8$, pyrene $C_{13}H_9$, anthracene $C_{14}H_{10}$ **J** (a) methylbenzene
K (a) $C_6H_6 + Cl^+ \rightarrow C_6H_5Cl + H^+$ **L** $H^+ + AlCl_4^- \rightarrow HCl + AlCl_3$
O (a) $C_6H_5COCH_3$ (b)CH_3CH_2COCl
P $C_6H_5SO_3H + 3NaOH \rightarrow C_6H_5O^-Na^+ + Na_2SO_3 + 2H_2O$ **Q** $C_{10}H_{18}$
R $C_6H_6 + 3Cl_2 \rightarrow C_6H_6Cl_6$
U (a) 1,2-dimethylbenzene (b) (i) C_6H_5COOH (ii) C_6H_5COOH
V (b) $C_6H_5CH_2Cl$, $C_6H_5CHCl_2$ and $C_6H_5CCl_3$
X Cheaper since no need to separate oxygen from air.

CHAPTER 14

A (a) Aldehydes, citral, $CH_3(CH_2)_9CHO$. Ketones, menthone, oestrone. (b) phenol
B (a) (i) Both have same molecular formula, C_3H_6O. (ii) Structural isomers.
(b) CH_3CH_2CHO and CH_3COCH_3.
C (a) Hydrogen bonding (c) The benzene ring part of molecule is non-polar, so cannot form intermolecular hydrogen bonds with water molecules.
E (a) Ethanal gives ethanol, CH_3CH_2OH.
Propanone gives propan-2-ol, $CH_3CHOHCH_3$.
(b) Ethanol is a primary alcohol, propan-2-ol is a secondary alcohol.
(c) $CH_3COCH_3 + 2[H] \rightarrow CH_3CHOHCH_3$
G R and R′ are alkyl or aryl groups.
H (a) H^-
(b) $CH_3CHO + 2[H] \rightarrow CH_3CH_2OH$ $CH_3COCH_3 + 2[H]$ ($CH_3CHOHCH_3$
I (a) $RCHO + H_2 \rightarrow RCH_2OH$ (b) $C_6H_5COCH_3 + H_2 \rightarrow C_6H_5CHOHCH_3$
J Methanal and ethanal.   **K** CH_3CHO, $C_6H_5COCH_3$, $C_2H_5COCH_3$ and C_2H_5OH

CHAPTER 15

A (a) $HCl(g) + H_2O(l) \rightarrow H_3O^+(aq) + Cl^-(aq)$
(b) $HI(g) + H_2O(l) \rightarrow H_3O^+(aq) + I^-(aq)$
B (a) $HBr(aq) \rightarrow H^+(aq) + Br^-(aq)$ (b) $HI(aq) \rightarrow H^+(aq) + I^-(aq)$
C (a) F^- (b) OH^- (c) SO_4^{2-} **D** (a) H_3O^+ (b) OH^- (c) H_2SO_4
E (a) $HNO_2(aq) \rightleftharpoons H^+(aq) + NO_2^-(aq)$
(b) $K_a = \dfrac{[H^+(aq)][NO_2^-(aq)]}{[HNO_2(aq)]}$
(c) Ethanoic acid.
F (a) (i) 9.9 (ii) 4.8 (b) Acid is dibasic and the protons are lost sequentially, so the first proton is transferred before the second is transferred to a water molecule.
G (a) Stronger the acid the weaker the conjugate base.
(b) Acid strength HI > HBr > HCl > HF as bond strength HF > HCl > HBr > HI
H (a) 0.0 (ii) 4.0 (iii) 0.98 (b) 2.2
I $[H^+(aq)] = [OH^-(aq)] = 6.6 \times 10^{-7}$ mol dm^{-3} **J** 2.37
K (a) (i) pentanoic acid (ii) butanoic acid (iii) pentanedioic acid
(b) (i) $ClCH_2COOH$
L (a) $C_nH_{2n+1}COOH$ (b) (i) 185 ºC, (ii) No observable trend.
M (a) Fluoroethanoic acid. Fluorine is the most electronegative halogen so that it withdraw the most electron density from the O-H bond and forms the most stable carboxylate ion.
(b) CF_3COOH. Fluorine is the most electronegative halogen so that it withdraws the most electron density from the O-H bond and forms the most stable carboxylate ion.
N $K_a(HIn) = \dfrac{[H^+(aq)][In^-(aq)]}{[HIn(aq)]}$
O (a) Methyl orange/bromocresol green/methyl red
(b) phenolphthalein $pK_a = 9.15$ (c) thymolphthalein $pK_a = 9.9$
P $K_{a1} = \dfrac{[H^+(aq)][COOH.COO^-(aq)]}{[(COOH)_2(aq)]}$
$K_{a2} = \dfrac{[H^+(aq)][COO^-)_2(aq)]}{[COOH.COO^-(aq)]}$
Q $H_2PO_4^-(aq)$
R $[C_2H_5COOH] = 0.750$ mol dm^{-3}
$[C_2H_5COO^-] = 0.350$ mol dm^{-3}
S Decreases.
T (a) Sodium benzoate is ionic and the negative carboxylate group can form strong electrostatic attractions with the polar water molecules, so it dissolves in water. Benzoic acid does not have an ionic structure, so the carboxyl group can only form hydrogen bonds with water molecules which are weaker.
(b) Many foods are contain lots of water and if the additive is to control acidity it needs to dissolve in water.
U (a) $CH_3COOH + PCl_5 \rightarrow CH_3COCl + HCl + POCl_3$
(b) $C_6H_5COOH + SOCl_2 \rightarrow C_6H_5COCl + SO_2 + HCl$
V (a) $C_6H_5COOC_2H_5$ (b) C_6H_5COOH (c) $C_6H_5CONH_2$

CHAPTER 16

A Electronegativity is the capacity of an atom in a covalent bond to attract the bonding pair of electrons towards itself.

C (a) (i) $K_c = \dfrac{[(COOC_2H_5)_2][H_2O]}{[(COOH_2)][C_2H_5OH]^2}$

Units $= \dfrac{(mol\ dm^{-3})(mol\ dm^{-3})^2}{(mol\ dm^{-3})(mol\ dm^{-3})^2}$

The units cancel out.

(ii) $K_c = \dfrac{[N_2O_4]}{[NO_2]^2}$

Units $= \dfrac{(mol\ dm^{-3})}{(mol\ dm^{-3})^2} = \dfrac{1}{(mol\ dm^{-3})} = mol^{-1}\ dm^3$

(b) (i) $CH_3COOH + C_5H_{11}OH \rightleftharpoons CH_3COOC_5H_{11} + H_2O$

(ii) $K_c = \dfrac{[CH_3CPPC_5H_{11}][H_2O]}{[CH_3COOH][C_5H_{11}OH]}$

(iii) 4.15

D (a) 0.67 (b) 0.67 (c) 0.33 (d) 0.33

E Reflux under heating excess ethanol with carboxylic acid in the presence of a little concentrated sulphuric acid as a catalyst, and remove the water as it is formed.

F Increase temperature: position of equilibrium shifts towards left.
Increase catalyst concentration: has no effect on equilibrium position.
Increase ammonia concentration: equilibrium position shifts to right.

G (a) ethanol and ethanoic acid (b) ethanol and butanoic acid
(c) prop-2-en-1-ol and ethanoic acid

H To minimise increase of $[C_2H_5OH]$, position of equilibrium shifts to right to try to use up C_2H_5OH.

I (a) ethanol and sodium ethanoate (b) propan-1-ol, sodium propanoate
(c) ethanol and sodium benzoate

J (a) $CH_3CH_2CH_2CH_3$ (b) CH_3COOH (c) CH_3CH_2OH, $(COOH)_2$

K To shift the equilibrium to the product side.

M (a) $C_6H_5COCl + H_2O \rightarrow C_6H_5COOH + HCl$
(b) $CH_3CH_2COCl + H_2O \rightarrow CH_3CH_2COOH + HCl$

N (a) $C_6H_5COCl + 2NaOH \rightarrow C_6H_5COO^-Na^+ + 2NaCl + H_2O$
(b) C-Cl in chlorobenzene is much stronger than the C-Cl in benzoyl chloride due to the (delocalised system of the benzene ring being extended over the C-Cl. Carbonyl carbon is much more electron deficient than the carbon atom in the C-Cl bond in chlorobenzene.

CHAPTER 17

B (a) Lysine, serine, aspartic acid and glutamic acid.
(b) Leucine and isoleucine are structural isomers.
(c) (ii) Secondary alcohol. (iii) The R group in serine has one less carbon atom and is a primary alcohol.

C 2-hydroxypropanoic acid

D (a) An enantiomer is one of a pair of optical isomers. Its mirror image is not superimposable.

F $NH_2CHRCOOH + NaOH \rightarrow NH_2CHRCOO^-Na^+ + H_2O$
or $^+NH_3CHRCOO^- + NaOH \rightarrow NH_2CHRCOO^-Na^+ + H_2O$
(a) R = H (b) R = $(CH_3)_2CHCH_2$

G Aspartic acid and glutamic acid. **H** Aspartic acid or glutamic acid.

J 4527.6 **L** Tyr-Gly-Gly-Phe-Met

M (a) Lysine, serine, aspartic acid and glutamic acid.
(b) Alanine, valine, leucine, isoleucine, proline and phenylalanine.

CHAPTER 18

A Two substances, one with a double bond (or triple bond), react together to form one product in which the double bond has changed to a single bond (or the triple bond has changed to a double bond or a single bond).

B (b) Polymer is a hydrocarbon which is fully saturated with no carbon-carbon double bonds.

C Breaking a covalent bond so that one electron from the bonding shared pair goes to each atom.

D Linear polymers can lie closer to one another, allowing more contact between molecules so that induced dipole-induced dipole forces of attraction can operate over a larger surface, hence intermolecular force is stronger than in a branched chain where the molecules cannot lie as close to one another.

E (b) Syndiotactic poly(propene) will have a higher melting point, will be more dense, will be harder than atactic poly(propene).

F $C_6H_5CH=CH_2$

G $nCF_2=CF_2 \rightarrow +CF_2CF_2\frac{}{\ }_n$

H $CH_3COOH(l) + CH_3CH_2OH(l) \rightleftharpoons CH_3COOCH_2CH_3(l) + H_2O(l)$

J Perspiration is absorbed when the fabric is blended with cotton fibres. This makes it more comfortable to wear.

K $nCH_3CHOHCOOH \rightarrow +OCH(CH_3)CO\frac{}{\ }_n + nH_2O$

L $H_2NCH_2CH_2CH_2CH_2CH_2NH_2$, $COOHCH_2CH_2CH_2CH_2CH_2CH_2CH_2COOH$

M NaOH(aq)/reflux under heating.
$H_2NCH_2CH_2CH_2CH_2CH_2NH_2$, Na^+ $^-OOCCH_2CH_2CH_2CH_2COO^-$ Na^+
6 mol dm^{-3} HCl(aq)/reflux under heating.
$Cl^-H_3NCH_2CH_2CH_2CH_2CH_2NH_3Cl^-$, $HOOCCH_2CH_2CH_2CH_2COOH$

N (a) (i) condensation, (ii) thermosetting. (b) High melting point, strong and rigid, relatively low density and a good thermal conductor.

P Intermolecular hydrogen bonds.

Q Thermoplastics have weak intermolecular forces such as induced dipole-induced dipole interactions which are easily broken and overcome so that the melting point is low. Once melted, the polymer chains can take up new positions. On cooling, the intermolecular forces are easily reformed.

R You cannot remould the plastic, so it cannot be recycled.

S Collection of bottles, eg fuel. Cleaning of bottles. Relabelling of bottles.

T Issues include: toxic gases such as hydrogen chloride and hydrogen cyanide will be produced; high temperatures are often required for the incineration process to prevent the formation of toxic materials; incineration means that less landfill sites are needed for plastic waste; need to sort out household waste; less crude oil needed for fuels; energy locked in the bonds of plastics is not wasted.

CHAPTER 19

A Unreactive, so found as elements in the Earth's crust rather than compounds or ores. Easy to reduce use of carbon.

B Discovery of radioactivity.

C Difference in A_r between first two elements is the same or nearly the same as the difference between A_r of second two elements. Difference in atomic number between first two elements is the same as between second two elements.

D (a) They are in atomic number order.
(b) Argon ($A_r = 40.0$) and potassium ($A_r = 39.1$).
Tellurium ($A_r = 127.6$) and iodine ($A_r = 126.9$).

E Selenium.

F N $1s^22s^22p^3$
Cl $1s^22s^22p^63s^23p^5$
Ca $1s^22s^22p^63s^23p^64s^2$
Ti $1s^22s^22p^63s^23p^63d^24s^2$

G (a) 7 (b) 3 (c) 4 **H** (a) p (b) p (c) d (d) d

I Effective nuclear charge decreases since more inner shell shielding electrons, so outermost electrons less firmly attracted to nucleus.

J (a) (i) OH = 96 pm (ii) NH = 100 pm (b) Atomic radii determined from single bonds.
(c) Does not form He_2.

K (a) Greater nuclear charge.
(b) Cl has equal numbers of electrons and protons. Cl$^-$ has one more electron than protons, so outer electron less firmly attracted to nucleus.
(c) As atomic number increases, atoms have same number of inner shell shielding electrons but increased nuclear charge.

L Greatest effective nuclear charge, no shielding electrons, smallest atomic radii.

M Increase in nuclear charge but no extra shielding electrons.

N Has a full 3d subshell.

O $Ca \rightarrow Ca^{2+} + 2e^-$ $Cl_2 + 2e^- \rightarrow 2Cl^-$

P Na loses electrons (oxidation) and H_2 gains electrons (reduction).

Q Least effective nuclear charge since largest number of inner shell shielding electrons so outermost electrons held less firmly and the most easily lost.

R Selenium: is a non-metal; forms Se^{2-}; forms an acidic oxide; is a solid at s.t.p.; reacts with metals to form ionic compounds; is less reactive than sulphur; is a poor oxidising agent; is a poor conductor of heat and electricity; hydride has formula H_2Se.

CHAPTER 20

A Liquid particles: are in random motion, collide with one another and with the container wall, are not in an ordered pattern, are attracted to one another but less so than in a solid, are moving faster than in a solid and slower than in a gas; the distance between particles is very small.
Gas particles: are in random motion, collide with one another and with the container wall, are not in an ordered pattern, are only weakly attracted towards each other, are moving faster than in a liquid; the distance between particles is large.

B $Zn(s) + 2Ag^+(aq) \rightarrow Zn^{2+}(aq) + 2Ag(s)$
(b) $Zn(s) + Pb^{2+}(aq) \rightarrow Zn^{2+}(aq) + Pb(s)$

C (a) 12 (b) 12 (c) 8

D Stronger metallic bonding because of electrostatic attraction between two moles of delocalised electrons with one mole of Mg^{2+}, ie larger charge of cation and more delocalised electrons.

E Aluminium. 2 moles of electrons per mole of metal compared to 2 moles for Mg and 1 mole for Na.

F Under extreme conditions get closely packed H^+ by loss of electrons to form a sea of delocalised electrons.

G Carbon dioxide.

H (a) The layers of carbon atoms easily slide over each other because of the weak induced dipole-induced dipole (van der Waals) forces between each layer.
(b) Has a very high melting point. (c) Diamond, since each carbon atom is bonded covalently to four other carbon atoms, but in graphite a carbon atom is only covalently bonded to three others.

I (a) Silicon is a giant molecule, each silicon atom bonded covalently to four other silicon atoms. Covalent bonds are much stronger than intermolecular attractions, so it takes a large amount of energy to break the covalent bonds.
(b) (i) Giant molecular structure.

J As temperature is increased, more thermal energy available so that a greater fraction of the electrons can be promoted to an excited energy level.

K (a) Si has 4 electrons in its outer shell and As has 5 electrons.
(b) Each As atom will provide one extra electron. These extra electrons are easier to excite.

L (a) $1s^22s^22p^1$ (b) Each B atom will provide one electron hole since it has one less electron in its outer shell than Si.

M Radon.

N Astatine since it has more electrons than the other halogens, so there is more of a chance to have asymmetric distribution of electrons hence there are stronger induced dipole-induced dipole attractions between molecules.

O Both have weak intermolecular forces that are induced dipole-induced dipole attractions. P_4 and S_8 have more electrons than N_2 and O_2 so that it is easier to have asymmetric distribution of electrons in P_4 and S_8. So the intermolecular forces in P_4 and S_8 are stronger and they have much higher melting points and boiling points than N_2 and O_2.

CHAPTER 21

A (a) oxidation (b) oxidation (c) reduction (d) neither (e) oxidation (f) oxidation (g) reduction

B (a) $Ca \rightarrow Ca^{2+} + 2e^-$ (c) $Mg \rightarrow Mg^{2+} + 2e^-$
  $Cl_2 + 2e^- \rightarrow 2Cl^-$ $O_2 + 4e^- \rightarrow 2O^{2-}$
(b) $Mg \rightarrow Mg^{2+} + 2e^-$ (d) $Na \rightarrow Na^+ + e^-$
  $F_2 + 2e^- \rightarrow 2F^-$ $N_2 + 6e^- \rightarrow 2N^{3-}$

C (a) $Al \rightarrow (Al^{3+} + 3e^-$
  $O_2 + 4e^- \rightarrow 2O^{2-}$
  $4Al + 3O_2 \rightarrow 2Al_2O_3$
(b) $Zn + 2Fe^{3+} \rightarrow Zn^{2+} + 2Fe^{2+}$
  (ii) $5Fe^{2+} + MnO_4^- + 8H^+ \rightarrow 5Fe^{3+} + Mn^{2+} + 4H_2O$
  (iii) $6Fe^{2+} + Cr_2O_7^{2-} + 14H^+ \rightarrow 6Fe^{3+} + 2Cr^{3+} + 7H_2O$

D (a) 6 (b) 8

E (a) Al is +3 (Al) and O is -2
(b) Ca is +2 and Cl is -1
(c) Mg is +2 and N is -3
(d) Cu is +2 and Cl is -1

(e) K is +1 and S is -2
(f) Ba is +2 and F is -1

F (b) Chlorine
(c) +4 (C) and -1 (Cl)

G (a) H is +1, O is -2 and N is +5
(b) (i) H is +1, O is -2, Cl is +5
(ii) Is the oxidation number of the chlorine.

H (a) K is +1, S is +6, O is -2
(b) K is +1, S is +4, O is -2
(c) +2 (d) -1 (e) +2 (f) +2.5

I (a) +6 (b) ferrate(VI)

J (a) Mn is +7 in MnO_4^- and Mn is +6 in MnO_4^{2-}
(b) (i) +2 (ii) -3 (iii) +2

L (a) (i) Cl in Cl_2 changes from 0 to -1. Cl in PCl_3 no change. P changes from +3 to +5. (ii) Cl_2.
(b) (i) Oxidising agent is Cu^{2+}, reducing agent is I^-. (ii) Oxidising agent is MnO_2, reducing agent is HCl. (iii) Oxidising agent is O_2, reducing agent is Cu. (iv) Oxidising agent is Cl_2, reducing agent is Cl_2.

K (a) oxygen (b) carbon

M Oxidation state of Cl in Cl_2 is 0, in NaCl is -1, in $NaClO_3$ is +5. Chlorine, Cl_2, is oxidised to $NaClO_3$ and is reduced to NaCl.

N $Mg(s) + Cl_2(g) \rightarrow MgCl_2(s)$
$2Al(s) + 3Cl_2(g) \rightarrow Al_2Cl_6(s)$
$Si(s) + 2Cl_2(g) \rightarrow SiCl_4(l)$
$P_4(s) + 6Cl_2(g) \rightarrow 4PCl_3(l)$
$P_4(s) + 10Cl_2(g) \rightarrow 4PCl_5(s)$

O LiCl and NaCl face centred cubic structure, but CsCl body centred cubic structure. Coordination number of Li^+ and Na^+ = 6 but of Cs^+ = 8. Change in structure due to the increase in the ratio of the cation radius to the anion radius from LiCl to CsCl.

Q BCl_3 has a trigonal planar shape: all individual bond dipoles cancel out.

R Ionic attraction between PCl_4^+ and PCl_6^- in PCl_5 is stronger than the permanent dipole-permanent dipole intermolecular attraction in PCl_3.

S (a) $Mg(s) + \frac{1}{2}O_2(g) \rightarrow MgO(s)$
$2Al(s) + \frac{3}{2}O_2(g) \rightarrow Al_2O_3(s)$
$Si(s) + O_2(g) \rightarrow SiO_2(s)$
$P_4(s) + 5O_2(g) \rightarrow P_4O_{10}(s)$
(b) P_4O_{10}, SO_3 and Cl_2O_7.
(c) Na_2O sodium oxide, MgO magnesium oxide, Al_2O_3 aluminium oxide, SiO_2 silicon(IV) oxide or silicon dioxide, SO_2 sulphur(IV) oxide or sulphur dioxide, SO_3 sulphur(VI) oxide or sulphur trioxide, Cl_2O_7 chlorine(VII) oxide.

T (a) acids (b) sodium nitrate (c) sodium chloride

U

	Diamond	SiO_2
atoms present	all carbon	silicon and oxygen
coordination number	4	4 around Si 2 around O
bond length	shorter than in SiO_2	longer than in diamond

V (a) $SO_2(g) + H_2O(l) \rightleftharpoons H_2SO_3(aq)$ sulphurous acid
(b) $P_4O_6(s) + 6H_2O(l) \rightarrow 4H_3PO_3(aq)$ phosphoric(III) acid
(c) $P_4O_{10}(s) + 6H_2O(l) \rightarrow 4H_3PO_4(aq)$ phosphoric(V) acid

CHAPTER 22

A (a) (i) ~23 °C (ii) ~680 °C (iii) ~275 nm (iv) ~187 nm
(b) Strength of metallic bonding decreases as atomic (proton) number increases.
(c) Rubidium, caesium and francium.

B (a) Reacts (recombines) to give sodium chloride. $2Na + Cl_2 \rightarrow 2NaCl$
(b) Chlorine will react with iron to give iron(III) chloride.

C Electrolysis of molten lithium chloride.

D (a) Li^+ $1s^2$
K^+ $1s^2 2s^2 2p^6 3s^2 3p^6$
Rb^+ $1s^2 2s^2 2p^6 3s^2 3p^6 3d^{10} 4s^2 4p^6$
(b) Na atoms require less energy to lose an electron than Li atoms, since the outer electrons are less strongly attracted to the nucleus because of the increased atomic radius and the increased number of inner shell shielding electrons.

E ~360 kJ mol^{-1}

F (a) $2Na(s) + 2H_2O(l) \rightarrow 2NaOH(aq) + H_2(g)$
$2K(s) + 2H_2O(l) \rightarrow 2KOH(aq) + H_2(g)$
(b) Francium sinks in water, and there is an extremely rapid (possibly explosive) exothermic reaction to form hydrogen and an alkaline solution.
$2Fr(s) + 2H_2O(l) \rightarrow 2FrOH(aq) + H_2(g)$

G (a) $2Na(s) + O_2(g) \rightarrow Na_2O_2(s)$
(b) $2K(s) + O_2(g) \rightarrow K_2O_2(s)$
(c) $Rb(s) + O_2(g) \rightarrow RbO_2(s)$

H $Rb_2O_2(s) + H_2O(l) \rightarrow 2RbOH(aq)$

I (a) $Li_2CO_3(s) \rightarrow Li_2O(s) + CO_2(g)$
(b) $2LiNO_3(s) \rightarrow Li_2O(s) + 2NO_2(g) + \_O_2(g)$
(c) $FrNO_3(s) \rightarrow FrNO_2(s) + \frac{1}{2}O_2(g)$

J Density ~4500 kg m^{-3}
Melting point ~640 °C
Boiling point ~1500 °C
(difficult to estimate since no obvious trend)

K $Ba(s) + 2H_2O(l) \rightarrow Ba(OH)_2(aq) + H_2(g)$
$Sr(s) + 2H_2O(l) \rightarrow Sr(OH)_2(aq) + H_2(g)$

L (a) $Mg(OH)_2(s) + 2HCl(aq) \rightarrow MgCl_2(aq) + 2H_2O(l)$
(b) $CaCO_3 + H_2SO_4 \rightarrow CaSO_4 + CO_2 + H_2O$
$CaCO_3 + 2HNO_3 \rightarrow Ca(NO_3)_2 + CO_2 + H_2O$

M $MgSO_4$ 337 g dm^{-3}
$CaSO_4$ 1.9 (10^{-1} g dm^{-3})
$SrSO_4$ 1.4 (10^{-3} g dm^{-3})
$BaSO_4$ 2.6 (10^{-4} g dm^{-3})

N (a) $Mg^{2+}(g) + O^{2-}(g) \rightarrow MgO(s)$
(b) $Mg^{2+}(g) + SO_4^{2-}(g) \rightarrow MgSO_4(s)$
(c) $2Fe^{3+}(g) + 3SO_4^{2-}(g) \rightarrow Fe_2(SO_4)_3(s)$
(d) $3Mg^{2+}(g) + 2N^{3-}(g) \rightarrow Mg_3N_2(s)$

O -3454 kJ mol^{-1}

P (a) Solvent is water and solute is alcohol.
(b) Solvent is alcohol and solute is water.

Q (a) $Mg^{2+}(g) \xrightarrow{H_2O} Mg^{2+}(aq)$
(b) $SO_4^{2-}(g) \xrightarrow{H_2O} SO_4^{2-}(aq)$

R $\Delta H^\theta_{soln}(NaCl) = +5$ kJ mol^{-1}
$\Delta H^\theta_{soln}(LiCl) = -32$ kJ mol^{-1}

S (a) $K_{sp}(CaSO_4) = [Ca^{2+}(aq)][SO_4^{2-}(aq)]$
(b) $K_{sp}(BaSO_4) = [Ba^{2+}(aq)][SO_4^{2-}(aq)]$
(c) $K_{sp}(Ag_2CrO_4) = [Ag^+(aq)]^2[CrO_4^{2-}(aq)]$
(d) $K_{sp}(PbCl_2) = [Pb^{2+}(aq)][Cl^-(aq)]^2$

T (a) 2.0 (10^{-10} mol^2 dm^{-6})
(b) $[Ca^{2+}(aq)] = 1.25 \times 10^{-2}$ mol dm^{-3}
$[OH^-(aq)] = 2 \times 1.25 \times 10^{-2} = 2.50$ mol dm^{-3}
$K_{sp}(Ca(OH)_2) = [Ca^{2+}(aq)][OH^-(aq)]^2$
$= (1.25 \times 10^{-2})(2.50 \times 10^{-2})^2$
$= 7.81 \times 10^{-6}$ mol^3 dm^{-9}

U (a) 7.5×10^{-3} mol dm^{-3}
(b) 2.1×10^{-4} mol dm^{-3}
(c) 5.3×10^{-4} mol dm^{-3}

V 2×10^{-9} mol dm^{-3}

W No: the ionic product 1.0×10^{-9} is less than K_{sp}.

X (a) $Al^{3+} + 3e^- \rightarrow Al$
(b) Some F^- will be oxidised at the anode to form F_2 and some of the fluorine will react with moisture in the atmosphere to give HF.

Y No, since aluminium carbonate would have to be formed in aqueous conditions and in aqueous solution $Al^{3+}(aq)$ is highly acidic because Al^{3+} polarises water molecules to form $H^+(aq)$ and so the solution will react with carbonate ions to give carbon dioxide and water.

CHAPTER 23

A Fluorine, a pale yellow gas. Astatine, a black solid.

B (a) (i) 85 (ii) 7
(iii) Melting point ~210 °C boiling point ~280 °C covalent radius ~150 pm electronegativity ~2.2
(b) Electronegativity is the ability of an atom in a covalent bond to attract the bonding pair of electrons. Increased number of inner shielding shells and same core charge of +7. This means the effective nuclear charge decreases as atomic number increases so the nucleus has a less powerful attraction for electrons in the shared bonding pair.

C (a) $1s^2 2s^2 2p^6 3s^2 3p^6$
(b) $[Ar]3d^{10}4s^24p^6$

D (a) No reaction. (b) $Cl_2(aq) + 2I^-(aq) \rightarrow I_2(aq) + 2Cl^-(aq)$
(c) No reaction (d) $Cl_2(aq) + 2At^-(aq) \rightarrow At_2(s) + 2I^-(aq)$

E (a) (i) $2Fe(s) + 3Cl_2(g) \rightarrow 2FeCl_3(s)$
(ii) $Cu(s) + Cl_2(g) \rightarrow CuCl_2(s)$
(iii) $2Fe(s) + 3F_2(g) \rightarrow 2FeF_3(s)$
(b) (i) chromium(III) chloride (ii) zinc chloride (iii) barium iodide

F (a) +4 in XeF_4, +6 in XeF_6 (b) $Xe + 2F_2 \rightarrow XeF_4$ $Xe + 3F_2 \rightarrow XeF_6$

G $PBr_3(l) + 3H_2O(l) \rightarrow H_3PO_3(aq) + 3HBr(aq)$

H (a) $Cl_2(aq) + SO_2(aq) + 2H_2O(l) \rightarrow 2Cl^-(aq) + SO_4^{2-}(aq) + 4H^+(aq)$
(b) Astatine is the least powerful oxidising agent of the halogens, and iodine also cannot oxidise $Fe^{2+}(aq)$.

I The iodine changes oxidation state from 0 (I_2) to -1 (I^-), whereas the oxidation state of sulphur changes from +2 ($S_2O_3^{2-}$) to +2.5 ($S_4O_6^{2-}$). So I_2 is reduced and $S_2O_3^{2-}$ is oxidised.

J 1.05×10^{-3} mol dm^{-3}

K Halogens have high electronegativities so that the halogen end of the H-X (where X is F, Cl, Br and I) will be δ- and the hydrogen δ+.

L (a) $K_c = \dfrac{[H_2(g)][I_2(g)]}{[HI(g)]^2}$
(b) Mole ratio $HI:H_2:I_2$ is 8.47:1:1

M (a) Sodium chloride or sodium hydrogencarbonate, water and carbon dioxide.
(b) Magnesium iodide and water. (c) Sodium bromide and water.

N $KMnO_4(s) + 8HCl(aq) \rightarrow KCl(aq) + MnCl_2(aq) + 4H_2O(l) + 2\frac{1}{2}Cl_2(g)$

O (a) $NaI(s) + H_2SO_4(l) \rightarrow NaHSO_4(s) + HI(g)$
(b) $2HI(g) + H_2SO_4(l) \rightarrow SO_2(g) + I_2(s) + 2H_2O(l)$
(c) Initially hydrogen astatide and sodium hydrogensulphate. Then hydrogen astatide reduces sulphuric acid to form astatine, hydrogen sulphide, sulphur dioxide, sulphur and water.
(d) Hydrogen fluoride and sodium hydrogensulphate.

P Oxidation number of iodine changes from 0 (I_2) to +5 (KIO_3) which is oxidation, and from 0 (I_2) to -1 (KI) which is reduction.

CHAPTER 24

A To make the water conduct electricity, acid provides ions that act as mobile charge carriers.

B Hydrolysis is literally the decomposition of water, and the reaction is normally associated with the reaction of water with compounds in which water molecules are broken up. Photolysis is the decomposition of a compound by ultraviolet light.

C Makes chlorine (chlor) and sodium hydroxide (alkali).

D (a) They are attracted towards the cathode.
(b) It cannot conduct electricity since the ions are fixed in position in a crystal lattice.

E At anode oxidation $2Br^- \rightarrow Br_2 + 2e^-$
At cathode reduction $Pb^{2+} + 2e^- \rightarrow Pb$

F Cu^{2+}

G 1.0×10^{-7} mol dm^{-3}

H At anode: oxygen $4OH^-(aq) \rightarrow O_2(g) + 2H_2O(l) + 4e^-$
OH^- discharged in preference to SO_4^{2-}
At cathode: hydrogen $2H^+(aq) + 2e^- \rightarrow H_2(g)$
H^+ is only cation present in the solution.

I (a) Avogadro's number, 6.02×10^{23}.
(b) 1.60×10^{-19} C

J (a) (i) 3 moles of electrons (3 F)
(ii) 1 mole of electrons (1 F)
(b) $4OH^- \rightarrow O_2 + 2H_2O + 4e^-$
4 F

K 6.4 g of copper, 1.2 dm^3 of oxygen.

L Step 1 Q = 1890 C
Step 2 mass of Cu = 0.64 g
Step 3 charge = 18900 C mol^{-1}
Step 4 number of electrons = 1.2×10^{24}
Step 5 number of copper atoms in one mole = 5.9×10^{23}
Use more accurate balance to measure mass to mg. Measure both mass of copper gained and mass of copper lost to see if there is a discrepancy. Pass the current through the solution for a longer time. Use a smaller current. Collect any copper that has not been plated on the cathode.

M At anode $Cu(s) \rightarrow Cu^{2+}(aq) + 2e^-$
At cathode $Cu^{2+}(aq) + 2e^- \rightarrow Cu(s)$

N H^+ is lower in the electrochemical series than Na^+.
OH^- should be discharged preferentially but Cl^- is discharged since the concentration of Cl^- is so much higher than that of OH^-.

O (a) Oxidation number of Cl in Cl_2 is 0, in ClO^- is +1 and in Cl^- is -1.
(b) ClO^- from oxidation of Cl_2.
Cl^- from reduction of Cl_2.

P When acid is added, the reactions are reversed and Cl_2 is produced. Assuming that the reactions are equilibria, addition of acid ($H^+(aq)$) will shift the position of equilibrium left, since any $OH^-(aq)$ will be removed by reaction with $H^+(aq)$ to form water.

Q Cold $Br_2 + 2OH^- Br^- + BrO^- + H_2O$
$I_2 + 2OH^- \rightarrow I^- + IO^- + H_2O$
Hot $3Br_2 + 6OH^- \rightarrow 5Br^- + BrO_3^- + 3H_2O$
$3I_2 + 6OH^- \rightarrow 6I^- + IO_3^- + 3H_2O$

R pH of water will increase as NaOCl is added as $[OH^-(aq)]$ increases. Addition of acid, $H^+(aq)$ will react with $OH^-(aq)$ to form water. The position of equilibrium will shift to the right to compensate for the loss of $OH^-(aq)$ so making more HOCl.

S In membrane or diaphragm cells:
$2H_2O(l) + 2e^- \rightarrow H_2(g) + 2OH^-(aq)$
In mercury cathode cell:
$2Na/Hg(l) + 2H_2O(l) \rightarrow 2Na^+(aq) + 2OH^-(aq) + 2Hg(l) + H_2(g)$

CHAPTER 25

A As the atomic number of each element in the period increases, electrons fill the 3d subshell rather than the outer sub shells.

B (a) Mn $1s^22s^22p^63s^23p^63d^54s^2$ Ni $1s^22s^22p^63s^23p^63d^84s^2$
(b) It minimises electron-electron repulsion within the 3d orbitals.

C (a) Co^{2+} $[Ar]3d^7$ Co^{3+} $[Ar]3d^6$
(b) Cu^+ $[Ar]3d^{10}$ Cu^{2+} $[Ar]3d^9$ (c) Zn^{2+} $[Ar]3d^{10}$

D Sc^{3+} [Ar]
Sc^{3+} does not have any 3d electrons and a transition element needs a partially filled d subshell in the electron configuration of one of its oxidation states.

E Metals: form cations; normally form basic oxides; are reducing agents; normally react with non-metals to form ionic compounds; are malleable and ductile.

F Less strong metallic bonding in manganese, since manganese does not use 3d electrons in the sea of delocalised electrons. Manganese has Mn^{2+} in a sea of delocalised electrons. The positive ion is Mn^{2+} because it has a stable $3d^5$ half-filled subshell which minimises electron-electron repulsion within orbitals.

G To form K^{2+}, K^{3+} and Ca^{3+}, electrons have to be removed from a stable octet of outer electrons, ie from an inner subshell. This needs too much energy to happen during a chemical reaction. Sc will form Sc^{3+} since it will has a stable octet of outer electrons whereas Sc^{2+} is $[Ar]3d^1$ which is not a stable octet of outer electrons.

H (a) Cr^+ is $[Ar]3d^5$ and this is a stable electron configuration since it minimises electron-electron repulsion within the d orbitals. To remove an electron from this stable electron configuration needs more energy than from a less stable electron configuration.
(b) Mn^{2+} is $[Ar]3d^5$ and this is a stable electron configuration since it minimises electron-electron repulsion within the d orbitals. To remove an electron from this stable electron configuration needs more energy than from a less stable electron configuration.
(c) Ca^{2+} is [Ar] so that next electron to be removed must be from a new shell of electrons that has a much lower energy level so much more energy is needed.

I (a) Fe^{3+} is $[Ar]3d^5$ which has a stable half-filled subshell, whereas Fe^{2+} is $[Ar]3d^6$.
(b) Mn^{2+} is $[Ar]3d^5$ which has a stable half-filled subshell, whereas Mn^{3+} is $[Ar]3d^4$.

J Transition metal atoms always lose electrons in reaction since they often have only 2 electrons in their outer shell, and metals have a low electronegativity.

K (a) The ability of an atom in a covalent bond to attract the bonding pair of electrons.
(b) Fluorine

L (a) (i) titanium(IV) oxide (ii) iron(III) oxide (iii) manganese(III) hydroxide (iv) vhromium(VI) oxide (v) vanadium(V) oxide
(b) (i) $Cu(OH)_2$ (ii) $MnCO_3$ (iii) $TiCl_4$ (iv) $Cu(NO_3)_2$ (v) $FeBr_2$

M (a) Na_2FeO_4 (b) chromate(VI)

N (a) +1 (b) +2 (c) +3 (d) +2 (e) +3

O (a) (i) hexaamminecobalt(III) (ii) hexacyanoferrate(III) (iii) tetrachlorocuprate(II) (iv) diamminesilver(I)
(b) (i) $[Fe(H_2O)_6]^{3+}$ (ii) $[Co(NH_3)_4Cl_2]^+$ (iii) $[CoCl_4]^{2+}$

P (a) 6 (b) Tetradentate
(c) Most arteries contain a high concentration of oxyhaemoglobin in which an oxygen molecule is complexed with the Fe^{2+} and this is red in colour.

Q *cis* or *trans* tetraamminedichlorochromium(III)

R $[Fe(H_2O)_6]^{3+}$ is hexaaquairon(III)
$[Fe(OH)(H_2O)_5]^{2+}$ is pentaaquamonohydroxoiron(III)
$[Fe(OH)_2(H_2O)_4]^+$ is tetraaquadihydroxoiron(III)

S $[Al(H_2O)_6]^{3+}(aq) \rightleftharpoons [Al(H_2O)_5(OH)]^{2+}(aq) + H^+(aq)$

T (a) $[Co(H_2O)_6]^{2+}(aq) + 4Cl^-(aq) \rightleftharpoons [CoCl_4]^{2-}(aq) + 6H_2O(l)$
(b) On heating, water evaporates and so the position of equilibrium will shift to the right to try to minimise this loss, this results in an increase in $[CoCl_4]^{2-}$(aq) and so the solution takes on the colour of this complex: blue.

CHAPTER 26

A (a) $Cu(s) \rightarrow Cu(aq) + 2e^-$ $Ag^+(aq) + e^- \rightarrow Ag(s)$
(b) $Fe^{2+}(aq) \rightarrow Fe^{3+}(aq) + e^-$
$Cr_2O_7^{2-}(aq) + 14H^+(aq) + 6e^- \rightarrow 2Cr^{3+}(aq) + 7H_2O(l)$

B (a) $Na^+ + e^- \rightarrow Na$ $2Cl^- \rightarrow Cl_2 + 2e^-$
(b) $Pb^{2+} + 2e^- \rightarrow Pb$ $2Br^- \rightarrow Br_2 + 2e^-$

C 298 K, $[Cl^-(aq)] = 1.0$ mol dm^{-3}, and pressure of $Cl_2(g) = 101$ kPa.

D 0.5 mol dm^{-3}

E (a) $Cu(s) \mid Cu^{2+}(aq) \parallel Ag^+(aq) \mid Ag(s)$
Electrons flow from copper to silver.
(b) $Zn(s) \mid Zn^{2+}(aq) \parallel H^+(aq) \mid H_2(g) \mid Pt(s)$
Electrons flow from zinc to platinum (hydrogen).

F (a) Cu^{2+} (b) Acidified MnO_4^-

G (a) Ni (b) Au

H (a) Hydrogen at cathode and oxygen at anode.
(b) Expect hydrogen at cathode and oxygen at anode. Prediction based on $[OH^-(aq)] = [Cl^-(aq)] = 1.0$ mol dm^{-3}, but in concentrated NaCl(aq), $[Cl^-(aq)]$ (1.0 mol dm^{-3} and $[OH^-(aq)] << 1.0$ mol dm^{-3}.

I (a) +0.76 V
(b) (i) Less positive (ii) More positive (iii) Less positive

J (a) (i) $E^\theta_{cell} = +1.62$ V, so spontaneous. (ii) $E^\theta_{cell} = -2.10$ V, so not spontaneous.
(b) +0.74 V $Mn(s) + Fe^{2+}(aq) \rightarrow Mn^{2+}(aq) + Fe(s)$

K (a) From Cu to Br_2 (b) From Cr to Cu^{2+}

L (a) -52 kJ mol^{-1} (b) -83 kJ mol^{-1} (c) -56 kJ mol^{-1}

M (a) $E^\theta_{cell} = -1.51$ V. $\Delta G^\theta = +291$ kJ mol^{-1}. Not spontaneous.
(b) $E^\theta_{cell} = +1.93$ V. $\Delta G^\theta = -931$ kJ mol^{-1}. Spontaneous.

N (a) 2 V
(b) +1.60 V
(c) The lead-acid battery does not operate under standard conditions, eg $[H_2SO_4(aq)] > 1.0$ mol dm^{-3} and the temperature will not be 298 K.

O $O_2(g) + 2H_2O(l) + 4e^- \rightarrow 4OH^-(aq)$
+ $2H_2(g) + 4OH^-(aq) \rightarrow 4H_2O(l) + 4e^-$
$= O_2(g) + 2H_2(g) + 2H_2O(l) + 4e^- + 4OH^-(aq) \rightarrow 4OH^-(aq) + 4e^- + 4H_2O(l)$
Cancelling gives $O_2(g) + 2H_2(g) \rightarrow 2H_2O(l)$

P (a) $TiCl_4 + 4Na \rightarrow Ti + 4NaCl$
(b) Needs to use expensive metals magnesium and sodium in its extraction. The ores of titanium are not very common and many processes are needed to make pure titanium(IV) chloride.
(c) The electrode potential for the aerial oxidation of $Ti^{3+}(aq)$ is +1.13 V which shows it is feasible.
$2Ti^{3+}(aq) + \frac{1}{2}O_2(g) + H_2O(l) \rightarrow 2TiO^{2+}(aq) + 2H^+(aq)$

Q (a) $2VO^{2+}(aq) + 4H^+(aq) + Zn(s) \rightarrow Zn^{2+}(aq) + 2V^{3+}(aq) + 2H_2O(l)$
(b) $2V^{3+}(aq) + Zn(s) \rightarrow Zn^{2+}(aq) + 2V^{2+}(aq)$
$E^\theta_{cell} = +0.50$ V, ie the process should be spontaneous.

R (a) $Cr(s) + H_2SO_4(aq) \rightarrow CrSO_4(aq) + H_2(g)$ (b) +0.91 V
(c) In acidic conditions $2Cr^{3+}(aq) + 7H_2O(l) \rightarrow Cr_2O_7^{2-}(aq) + 14H^+(aq) + 6e^-$
$E^\theta_{cell} = -1.33$ V
In alkaline conditions $Cr(OH)_3(s) + 5OH^-(aq) \rightarrow CrO_4^{2-}(aq) + 4H_2O(l) + 3e^-$
$E^\theta_{cell} = +0.13$V
So using the same oxidising agent, the E^θ_{cell} for the alkaline conditions will be more positive (so it is more feasible) than for the acidic conditions.

S (a) The reduction potential for $Mn^{3+}(aq) + e^- \rightleftharpoons Mn^{2+}(aq)$ is +1.49 V. The highly positive nature of the reduction potential indicates that manganese(III) it is a powerful oxidising agent and so is easily reduced to manganese(II), ie manganese(II) is more stable than manganese(III).
(b) Manganese should react with HCl(aq) to give hydrogen since the standard electrode potential for the following reaction is positive (+1.18 V).
$Mn(s) + 2H^+(aq) \rightarrow Mn^{2+}(aq) + H_2(g)$

T (a) (i) $MnO_4^-(aq) + 8H^+(aq) + 5e^- \rightarrow Mn^{2+}(aq) + 4H_2O(l)$
(ii) $2I^-(aq)$ ($I_2(aq) + 2e^-$
(b) $2MnO_4^-(aq) + 16H^+(aq) + 10I^-(aq) \rightarrow 5I_2(aq) + 2Mn^{2+}(aq) + 8H_2O(l)$

U 0.0287 mol dm^{-3}

V (a) (i) $Fe^{2+}(aq) + O_2(g) + 2H^+(aq) \rightarrow Fe^{3+}(aq) + 2H_2O(l)$
(ii) +0.46 V
(b) +0.96 V

W $E^\theta_{cell} = +0.59$V for oxidation of $[Fe(H_2O)_6]^{2+}$
$E^\theta_{cell} = +1.00$ V for oxidation of $[Fe(CN)_6]^{4-}$

X (a) +1.30 V
(b) $Cd(s) + NiO_2(s) + 2H_2O(l) \rightarrow Cd(OH)_2(s) + Ni(OH)_2(s)$
(c) The calculation assumes standard conditions which will not be true for the battery.

Y $Zn(s) + MnO_2(s) + 2H_2O(l) \rightarrow Zn(OH)_2(s) + Mn(OH)_2(s)$

Z Zn + HgO (ZnO + Hg

A´ (a) Not spontaneous since ΔH is positive and ΔS is negative.
(b) Spontaneous since $\Delta G = -142$ kJ mol^{-1}

B´ (a) Iron and possibly chromium.
(b) (ii) Should be feasible above approximately 1770 K.

CHAPTER 27

A Rate of reaction decreases during the course of a reaction.

B 0.17 mol s^{-1}

C Reaction mechanism.

D Mass of reaction mixture: place reaction container on a balance.
Concentration of $H^+(aq)$: measure with a pH meter since pH will change during reaction.

E (a) 1.50×10^{-5}
(b) $H^+(aq) + OH^-(aq) \rightarrow H_2O(l)$
(c) 1.50×10^{-5}
(d) 1.50×10^{-3} mol dm^{-3}

F (a) Monitor the increase in pressure if reaction carried out in a sealed container.
(b) Measure the volume of oxygen produced using a gas syringe.
(c) Monitor the change in conductivity of the reaction mixture. Use colorimetry to monitor the appearance of bromine.
(d) Take aliquots out of reaction mixture and titrate against acid of known concentration. Take aliquots out of reaction mixture and acidify with

HNO$_3$(aq), then add AgNO$_3$(aq). Measure the mass of AgBr precipitate formed.
(e) Monitor the change in conductivity of the solution. Monitor the change in I$_2$(aq) concentration using colorimetry or taking out aliquots and titrating with Na$_2$S$_2$O$_3$(aq).

G *m* with respect to A, *n* with respect to B.

H Change in total mass of the reaction mixture.
Change in the total volume of carbon dioxide collected.

I Rate at time zero is all that is required once there are sufficient results to construct the gradient at time zero, so no more are needed.

J Rate = k[SO$_2$Cl$_2$], $k = 4.5 \times 10^4$ s^{-1}

K second

L (a) First order w.r.t. BrO$_3^-$ and first order w.r.t. SO$_3^{2-}$ giving a total order of 2. Units: dm^3 mol^{-1} s^{-1}
(b) Second order w.r.t. NO$_2$ and first order w.r.t. H$_2$, giving a total order of 3. Units dm^6 mol^{-2} s^{-2}
(c) Second order w.r.t. NO$_2$, giving a total order of 2. Units dm^3 mol^{-1} s^{-1}

M Loss of mass from the reaction mixture. Volume of oxygen formed.

N Record the change in either the mass lost by reaction mixture or volume of oxygen formed at regular time intervals over a set time period. Use same mass of catalyst, volume of H$_2$O$_2$(aq) and same temperature. Do experiment five times using different concentrations of H$_2$O$_2$(aq). Plot graph of time against either the mass loss or volume of oxygen for each concentration. Determine the initial rate of reaction by drawing a tangent to the curve at time zero. Plot the initial rates obtained against the concentration of H$_2$O$_2$(aq). First order kinetics will give a straight line through the origin.

O (a) 0.25 kg (b) $k = 4.62 \times 10^{-2}$ h^{-1}

P Cyclopropane and propene are structural isomers since they have the same molecular formula but different structural formulae.

Q 2NO$_2$ + F$_2 \rightarrow$ 2NO$_2$F

R It is a substitution reaction involving a nucleophile and it has second order kinetics.

S Mechanism 2, since the slowest step involves a collision between H$_2$O$_2$ and Br$^-$.

T (a) Slow step rate = k[N$_2$O$_5$]
Fast step rate = k[NO][NO$_3$]
(b) N$_2$O$_5 \rightarrow$ NO$_2$ + NO$_3$
(c) Rate = k[N$_2$O$_5$]
(d) Because NO is not involved in the slowest step of the reaction.

U (b) Small.

V It doubles.

W V$_2$O$_5$ is a solid the reactants SO$_2$ and O$_2$ are gases.

X Pt is a solid and it normally catalyses the reactions between gases.

CHAPTER 28

A Blue

B A group of atoms in a molecule that gives the molecule a characteristic set of reactions.

C 2NaNO$_2$(aq) + H$_2$SO$_4$(aq) $\rightarrow$ Na$_2$SO$_4$(aq) + 2HNO$_2$(aq)
C$_6$H$_5$NH$_2$(l) + H$_2$SO$_4$(aq) + HNO$_2$(aq) $\rightarrow$ C$_6$H$_5$N$_2^+$(aq) + HSO$_4^-$(aq) + 2H$_2$O(l)
or 2C$_6$H$_5$NH$_2$(l) + H$_2$SO$_4$(aq) + 2HNO$_2$(aq) $\rightarrow$ 2C$_6$H$_5$N$_2^+$(aq) + SO$_4^{2-}$(aq) + 4H$_2$O(l)

D They decompose very easily to produce nitrogen gas so that a small volume of solid will produce a large volume of gas.

E (a) At a higher temperature the diazonium salt will react with water to give phenol and nitrogen.
(b) Phenol reacts in an acid-base reaction to give sodium phenoxide.
C$_6$H$_5$OH + OH$^- \rightarrow$ C$_6$H$_5$O$^-$ + H$_2$O
(c) A lone pair on the oxygen atom is donated into the π system of the benzene ring to extend the π system over seven atoms. This increases the electron density in the benzene ring so that the species is more reactive towards electrophiles than benzene.

F (a) Concentrated sulphuric acid and concentrated nitric acid.
(b) Tin and concentrated hydrochloric acid.

G (a) White. (b) Black.

H Blue

I Extended π system over the whole of the molecule.

J (a) So that the only absorbance is due to the substance under test.
(b) Many solvent molecules will contain chromophores which absorb UV/visible light, eg carbonyl groups, carbon-carbon double bonds or benzene rings.

K ~620 nm

M Red light.

N Blue.

O (a) 1s^{2}2s^{2}2p^{6}3s^{2}3p^{6}3d^{10}
(b) Even though the energy of the 3d orbitals can be split in Zn^{2+}. There is no possibility of a d → d transition since all the 3d orbitals are full.

P VO$_2^+$ blue-violet VO^{2+} orange V^{3+} red-violet V^{2+} yellow-green

Q ~430 nm

CHAPTER 29

A Reduced since the oxidation number of nitrogen changes from 0 to -3, ie nitrogen gains electrons.

B (a) +3 (b) +5 (c) +5 (d) +2 (e) +4

C 118 kPa

D (a) $K_p = \dfrac{(p\text{HI})^2}{(p\text{H}_2)(p\text{I}_2)}$
(b) $K_p = \dfrac{(p\text{NO}_2)^2}{(p\text{NO})^2(p\text{O}_2)}$
(c) $K_p = p\text{CO}_2$

E (a) None. (b) Pa^{-1} (c) Pa

F 1.5×10^{-8}

G (a) pSO$_2$ = 200 kPa and pO$_2$ = 100 kPa
(b) pSO$_2$ = 10 kPa and pO$_2$ = 5 kPa
(c) 72.2 kPa^{-1}

H Low temperature since it is an exothermic reaction. Low pressure since the volume of the products is more than the volume of the reactants. Increase concentration of oxygen.
(b) High pressure, high temperature and the addition of a catalyst.
(c) Very high temperature used to ensure a rapid rate of reaction. A low pressure is used. This also reduces the operating costs as expensive high pressure apparatus need not be used. A catalyst is used which increases the rate of reaction. Excess air used ensures that concentration of oxygen is higher than mole ratio predicted from equation.
(d) $K_p = \dfrac{(p\text{NO})^4(p\text{H}_2\text{O})^6}{(p\text{NH}_3)^4(p\text{O}_2)^5}$

I (a) For 2NO$_2$(g) $\rightleftharpoons$ N$_2$O$_4$(g) $K_p = 7.7 \times 10^{-2}$ kPa^{-1}
(b) K_p decreases. (c) K_p increases.

J Less maintenance costs, no need for expensive apparatus that can withstand high pressure.

K (a) +4 (b) +5 (c) +2

L (a) N$_2$O$_4$ (N +4 oxidation state) is oxidised to HNO$_3$ (N +5) and reduced to NO (N is +2).
(b) Shifts the position of equilibrium to the right and ensure that the water remains liquid.

M NPK ratio is 33.5:10.5:7

N HNO$_3$(aq) + NH$_3$(aq) $\rightarrow$ NH$_4$NO$_3$(aq)

O (a) CH$_3$NH$_2$(aq) + H$_2$O(l) $\rightleftharpoons$ CH$_3$NH$_3^+$(aq) + OH$^-$(aq)
(b) $K_p = \dfrac{[\text{CH}_3\text{NH}_3^+][\text{OH}^-]}{[\text{CH}_3\text{NH}_2]}$

P (a) NH$_3$(aq) + H$_2$SO$_4$(aq) $\rightarrow$ NH$_4$HSO$_4$(aq) or 2NH$_3$(aq) + H$_2$SO$_4$(aq) $\rightarrow$ (NH$_4$)$_2$SO$_4$(aq)
(b) C$_2$H$_5$NH$_2$(aq) + HCl(aq) $\rightarrow$ C$_2$H$_5$NH$_3^+$(aq) + Cl$^-$(aq)

Q (a) Position of equilibrium shifts right.
(b) Increases.
(c) The position of equilibrium moves right, so there is a greater [H$^+$(aq)] and [OH$^-$(aq)]. These are the mobile charge carriers so the electrical conductivity increases.

R 1.73×10^{-12} mol dm^{-3}

S (a) 2.5×10^{-8} mol dm^{-3}
(b) 4.0×10^{-7} mol dm^{-3}

T [H$^+$(aq)] = [OH$^-$(aq)] = 1.0×10^{-7} mol dm^{-3}

U (a) 14.34 (b) 10.56 (c) 13.0 (d) 11.60

V (a) 7.94×10^{-13} mol dm^{-3}
(b) 1.26×10^{-2} mol dm^{-3}
(c) 6.3×10^{-3} mol dm^{-3}

W 11.5 **X** 10.9

Y 12.4%

CHAPTER 30

A SiO$_2$ + 2Mg $\rightarrow$ Si + 2MgO

B High temperatures needed (high energy costs). Magnesium is a very expensive metal. Silicon produced must be ultra-pure, so further expensive processing.

C (a) To stop silicon oxidising to form SiO$_2$.
(b) Neon, argon or nitrogen.

D (a) PbO + C $\rightarrow$ Pb + CO or 2PbO + C $\rightarrow$ 2Pb + CO$_2$
(b) SnO$_2$ + 2C $\rightarrow$ Sn + 2CO or SnO$_2$ + C $\rightarrow$ Sn + CO$_2$

E (a) Acid rain.
(b) 2PbS + 3O$_2 \rightarrow$ 2PbO + 2SO$_2$

F Both have a giant molecular structure held together by strong covalent bonds, both have atoms with a coordination number of 4, both have a tetrahedral arrangement about each atom in the lattice. The bond angles in both are 109°. C-C bond length is shorter than the Si-C. In diamond, each carbon atom is surrounded by 4 carbon atoms. In SiC a carbon atom is surrounded by 4 silicon atoms.

G Low melting points and high electrical conductivity.

H (a) Sn [Kr]4d^{10}5s^{2}5p^2 Sn^{2+} [Kr]4d^{10}5s^2
(b) Ge [Ar]3d^{10}4s^{2}4p^2 Ge^{2+} [Ar]3d^{10}4s^2
(c) Si 1s^{2}2s^{2}2p^{6}3s^{2}3p^2 Si^{2+} 1s^{2}2s^{2}2p^{6}3s^2
(d) The inert pair of electrons are the 5s^2 and 4s^2 electrons in Sn^{2+} and Ge^{2+} respectively: in the outer shell of electrons but not used in bonding.

I (a)

Element	Energy needed to make one mole of X^{2+}(g) from X(g)/kJ mol^{-1}
carbon	3219
silicon	2366
germanium	2302
tin	2117
lead	2166

(b) X$^+$(g) has more protons than electrons so the electrons are held more strongly to the nucleus and so are more difficult to remove than in X(g) in which the number of electrons and protons are equal.
(c) Both have the same core charge of +4 but in Ge there are more inner-shell shielding electrons than in C. Since the atomic radius of Ge is greater than that of C, outer electrons are at a greater distance from nucleus.
(d) 1st and 2nd ionisation energies of tin are lower than expected, or those for Pb are greater than expected. Accounted by presence of inner shell 4f electrons in Pb.

K (a) Pb + I$_2 \rightarrow$ PbI$_2$ (b) Sn + 2F$_2 \rightarrow$ SnF$_4$ (c) Ge + 2Br$_2 \rightarrow$ GeBr$_4$

L Na$_2$SiO$_3$(aq) + 2HCl(aq) $\rightarrow$ 2NaCl(aq) + SiO$_2$(s) + H$_2$O(l)

M PbO$_2$ is less stable than SiO$_2$, but PbO is much more stable SiO, so that PbO$_2$ can accept electrons (act as an oxidising agent) to form Pb^{2+}, whereas SiO$_2$ will not accept electrons to form Si^{2+}.

N CO$_2$(g) + Ca(OH)$_2$(aq) $\rightarrow$ CaCO$_3$(s) + H$_2$O(l)

O (a) Pb(CH$_3$COO)$_2$(aq) and H$_2$O(l)
(b) Na$_2$SnO$_2$(aq) and H$_2$O(l)

P (a) Pb$_3$O$_4$(s) $\rightarrow$ 3PbO(s) + ½O$_2$(g)
lead(II) oxide and oxygen
(b) Pb$_3$O$_4$(s) + 8HCl(aq) $\rightarrow$ 3PbCl$_2$(aq) + Cl$_2$(g) + 4H$_2$O(l)
lead(II) chloride, chlorine and water
(c) Pb$_3$O$_4$(s) + 6NaOH(aq) $\rightarrow$ 2Na$_2$PbO$_2$(aq) + Na$_2$PbO$_3$(aq) + 3H$_2$O(l)
sodium plumbate(IV), sodium plumbate(VI) and water

Q PbCl$_4 \rightarrow$ PbCl$_2$ + Cl$_2$ **R** 2Fe^{3+}(aq) + Sn^{2+}(aq) $\rightarrow$ 2Fe^{2+}(aq) + Sn^{4+}(aq)

S Cl$_2$(g) + Sn^{2+}(aq) $\rightarrow$ Sn^{4+}(aq) + 2Cl$^-$(aq) tin(IV) chloride

T (a) Si$_6$H$_{14}$ (b) SiH$_3$SiH$_2$SiH$_2$SiH$_2$SiH$_2$SiH$_3$ or any other structural isomer.

U 20 **V** PbCO$_3$(s) $\rightarrow$ PbO(s) + CO$_2$(g)

W (a) 2 mole KOH to 1 mole H$_2$SO$_3$
(b) 1 mole KOH to 1 mole H$_2$SO$_3$

X (a) Cl$_2$(aq) + SO$_2$(aq) + 2H$_2$O(l) $\rightarrow$ 2HCl(aq) + H$_2$SO$_4$(aq)
(b) 2Fe^{3+}(aq) + SO$_2$(aq) + 2H$_2$O(l) $\rightarrow$ 2Fe^{2+}(aq) + SO$_4^{2-}$(aq) + 4H$^+$(aq)

Y CuO, MgCO$_3$ and Mg. (b) Cu and HI.

Z (a) Benzoic acid (b) Ethanoic acid

INDEX